Western Civilization

Western Civilization
IDEAS, POLITICS & SOCIETY / THIRD EDITION

From the 1400s

Marvin Perry
Baruch College, City University of New York

Myrna Chase
Baruch College, City University of New York

James R. Jacob
John Jay College of Criminal Justice, City University of New York

Margaret C. Jacob
Lang College, New School for Social Research

Theodore H. Von Laue
Clark University

George W. Bock, Editorial Associate

HOUGHTON MIFFLIN COMPANY   BOSTON
Dallas   Geneva, Illinois   Palo Alto   Princeton, New Jersey

The following authors are members of The Institute for Research in History: Marvin Perry, Myrna Chase, James R. Jacob, and Margaret C. Jacob.

Printed in the U.S.A.

Library of Congress Catalog Card Number: 88-81370

ISBN: 0-395-48647-5

CREDITS

Cover: Pietro Longhi, *The Geography Lesson,* mid-eighteenth century. Galleria Querini-Stampalia, Venice. Scala/Art Resource.

Text Credits

Page 279: From *Hamlet, Prince of Denmark,* in *The Complete Plays and Poems of William Shakespeare,* ed. by William Allan Neilson and Charles Jarvis Hill (Boston: Houghton Mifflin, 1942), p. 1067. Copyright 1942 by Houghton Mifflin Company, © renewed 1969 by Caroline Steiner and Margaret N. Helburn. Used by permission of Houghton Mifflin Company.
Page 732: Poem from *The Nazi Persecution of Churches* by J. S. Conway, copyright © 1968 Basic Books, Inc., publisher.
Page 746: Excerpted from "Second Coming." Reprinted with permission of Macmillan Publishing Company from *The Collected Poems of W. B. Yeats,* edited by Richard J. Finneran. Copyright 1924 by Macmillan Publishing Co., Inc., renewed 1952 by Bertha Georgie Yeats. With the permission of Michael B. Yeats and Macmillan London Ltd.

CDEFGHIJ-D-9543210-89

Contents

22
Ferment of Ideas: Romanticism, Conservatism, Liberalism, Radicalism, Early Socialism, Nationalism 480

23
Europe, 1815–1848: Revolution and Counterrevolution 500

V
AN AGE OF CONTRADICTION: PROGRESS AND BREAKDOWN 1848–1914

24
Thought and Culture in the Mid-Nineteenth Century: Realism and Social Criticism   526

25
The Surge of Nationalism: From Liberal to Extreme Nationalism   545

26
The Industrial West: Responses to Modernization   569

27
Western Imperialism:
Global Dominance 601

28
Modern Consciousness: New Views
of Nature, Human Nature,
and the Arts 632

32

The Rise of Fascism:
The Attack on Democracy   *716*

33

Thought and Culture in an Era of
World Wars: Disorientation,
Doubt, and Commitment   *744*

List of Maps

Preface

Western civilization is a grand but tragic drama. The West has forged the instruments of reason that make possible a rational comprehension of physical nature and human culture, conceived the idea of political liberty, and recognized the intrinsic worth of the individual. But the modern West, though it has unravelled nature's mysteries, has been less successful at finding rational solutions to social ills and conflicts between nations. Science, the great achievement of the Western intellect, while improving conditions of life, has also produced weapons of mass destruction. Though the West has pioneered in the protection of human rights, it has also produced totalitarian regimes that have trampled on individual freedom and human dignity. And although the West has demonstrated a commitment to human equality, it has also practiced brutal racism.

Despite the value that Westerners have given to reason and freedom, they have shown a frightening capacity for irrational behavior and a fascination for violence and irrational ideologies, and they have willingly sacrificed liberty for security or national grandeur. The world wars and totalitarian movements of the twentieth century have demonstrated that Western civilization, despite its extraordinary achievements, is fragile and perishable.

Western Civilization: Ideas, Politics, and Society examines the Western tradition—those unique patterns of thought and systems of values that constitute the Western heritage. While focusing on key ideas and broad themes, the text also provides a balanced treatment of economic, political, and social history for students in Western civilization courses.

The text is written with the conviction that history is not a meaningless tale. Without a knowledge of history, men and women cannot fully know themselves, for all human beings have been shaped by institutions and values inherited from the past. Without an awareness of the historical evolution of reason and freedom, the dominant ideals of Western civilization, commitment to these ideals will diminish. Without a knowledge of history, the West cannot fully comprehend or adequately cope with the problems that burden its civilization and the world.

In attempting to make sense out of the past, the authors have been careful to avoid superficial generalizations that oversimplify historical events and forces and arrange history into too neat a structure. But we have striven to interpret and to synthesize in order to provide students with a frame of reference with which to comprehend the principal events and eras in Western history.

Changes in the Third Edition

For the third edition, every chapter has been reworked to some extent. In particular, the final part, "The Contemporary World: The Global Age Since 1945," has been restructured and rewritten. Chapter 35, "Europe After 1945: Recovery, Realignment, Division," examines domestic developments in both Western and Eastern Europe. Chapter 36, "International Relations in an Age of Superpowers," discusses postwar international politics, focusing on superpower rivalries and their global ramifications. The last chapter, "The New Globalism," reviews postwar decolonization and the problems of modernization, and concludes with reflections on the world condition today—cause for optimism, cause for concern, and coping with the future.

Further changes include the addition of a section on art to Chapter 4, "Greek Thought." The discussion of culture in Chapter 7, "The Roman Empire," has been restructured and the material on philosophy and law enlarged. In Chapter 9, which has been retitled "The Heirs of Rome: Byzantium, Islam, and Latin Christendom," greater coverage is given to Islam. The treatment of women in Greece, Rome, and the Middle Ages has been enlarged. A discussion of popular culture in early modern times—including the witch craze—has been added to Chapter 15, "European Expansion." Chapter 16, "The Rise of Sovereignty," has been reorganized to give greater coherence to the rise and decline of Hapsburg Spain. The section on the social context of the Scientific Revolution in Chapter 18 has been completely recast and given a different focus. Interpretations of recent scholarship have been incorporated in Chapter 19, "The French Revolution." The discussion of Romanticism in Chapter 22, "Ferment of Ideas," has been expanded. So too has the treatment of the Holocaust in Chapter 32, "The Rise of Fascism." In several chapters, the concluding essays have been enlarged and improved.

A second color has been added to the design. It not only makes the book more attractive, but draws the reader's attention to pedagogical aids, such as the heading structure. The additional color is most effective in enhancing the detail and readability of the maps. Four color inserts contain essays, along with color reproductions of paintings and architecture, that link crucial periods in the history of art and architecture to their wider cultural settings.

overviews of key themes and give a sense of direction and coherence to the flow of history. Many chapters contain concluding essays that treat the larger meaning of the material. Facts have been carefully selected to illustrate key relationships and concepts and to avoid overwhelming students with unrelated and disconnected data. Appropriate quotations, many not commonly found in texts, have been integrated into the discussion.

Each chapter contains notes, an annotated bibliography, and review questions that refer students to principal points. The questions have an emphasis on eliciting thoughtful answers, rather than memorized facts.

Western Civilization: Ideas, Politics, and Society is available in both one- and two-volume editions, and in a third edition, *From the 1400s*. *From the 1400s* (25 chapters) has been prepared for those instructors whose courses begin with the Renaissance or the Reformation; it includes the entire section on early modern Europe including "European Expansion: Economic and Social Transformations."

Volume I of the two-volume edition treats the period from the first civilizations in the Near East through the Age of Enlightenment in the eighteenth century (18 chapters). Volume II covers the period from the growth of national states in the seventeenth century to the contemporary age (22 chapters). Because some instructors start the second half of their course with the period prior to the French Revolution, Volume II incorporates the last three chapters of Volume I: "The Rise of Sovereignty," "The Scientific Revolution," and "The Age of Enlightenment." Volume II also contains a comprehensive introduction that surveys the ancient world, the Middle Ages, and the opening centuries of the modern era; the introduction is designed particularly for students who did not take the first half of the course. *From the 1400s* also contains an introduction that covers the ancient world and the Middle Ages.

Distinctive Features

The text contains several pedagogical features. Chapter introductions provide comprehensive

Ancillaries

Learning and teaching ancillaries, including a *Study Guide, MicroStudy Plus, Instructor's*

Manual, Test Bank, MicroTest, and *Map Transparencies,* also contribute to the text's usefulness. The new *Study Guide,* available in two volumes, has been prepared by Professor Lyle E. Linville of Prince George's Community College. For each text chapter, the *Study Guide* contains an introduction, learning objectives, words to know, identifications, a map study exercise, chronological/relational exercises, multiple-choice and essay questions, and a "transition," which reflects back on the chapter and looks forward to the next chapter's topic. In the map study, two copies of one or two different outline maps are provided and the student is asked to locate geographical features on one set of the maps. The second set is available for use by instructors in giving quizzes. In the chronological/relational exercises, students are asked to put a list of items in their chronological order; then in an exercise that brings to bear a deeper understanding of the material, students are asked to write a paragraph indicating the relationship of the items to one another, along with their historical significance. The *Study Guide*'s two volumes are designed so that Volume I covers all the chapters in Volume I of the text and Volume II covers all the chapters of Volume II and those of *From the 1400s.* So Volume II of the *Study Guide* can be used with either Volume II of the text or *From the 1400s.* The multiple-choice sections of the *Study Guide* are also available in a computerized version, *MicroStudy Plus.* This interactive tutorial instruction program allows the student to answer the question, then explains why the answer is right or wrong, and refers the student to the pages in the text where the question is discussed.

The *Instructor's Manual* has been extensively revised for this third edition by Professors George Shriver of Georgia Southern College (Chapters 1–18) and Dorothy Vogel of Indiana University of Pennsylvania (Chapters 19–37). The *Manual* contains chapter outlines, learning objectives, lecture topics, and a film bibliography. The accompanying *Test Bank,* also by Professors Shriver and Vogel, offers multiple-choice and essay questions, and identification terms. *MicroTest* offers the test items to adopters on computer tape and disk (IBM and Apple). In addition, a set of 40 map transparencies is available on adoption, as is GPA, a computer-based class management system.

The text represents the efforts of several authors. Marvin Perry, general editor of the project, wrote Chapters 1–12, 19, 20, 22–25, 28–30, and 32–34, and the section on the American Revolution in Chapter 18. James R. Jacob is the author of Chapters 13 and 15. Margaret C. Jacob provided Chapters 14 and 16–18. Myrna Chase wrote Chapters 21, 26–27, and contributed to the section on reform in Britain in Chapter 23. Theodore H. Von Laue is the author of Chapters 31, 35–37, and the section on Russia in Chapter 26. The four art essays were written by Katherine Crum, and some of the material on Gothic cathedrals and modern art that she wrote for the first edition has been incorporated into the text. Marvin Perry and George W. Bock edited the manuscript for clarity and continuity.

Acknowledgments

The authors would like to thank the following instructors for their critical reading of sections of the manuscript:

Martin Arbagi, *Wright State University*

Peter Barty, *University of North Alabama*

John Bohstedt, *University of Tennessee, Knoxville*

Ronald G. Brown, *Charles County Community College*

Helen Callahan, *Augusta College*

Cecil Culpepper, *Mississippi Delta Junior College*

Mark Fissel, *Ball State University*

William E. Farr, *University of Montana*

Larry E. Holmes, *University of South Alabama*

Carlton Jackson, *Western Kentucky University*

Douglas Legg, *Southern Oregon State College*

James E. McGoldrick, *Cedarville College*

Robert Michael, *Southeastern Massachusetts University*

John Moore, *Hofstra University*

James E. Parry, *Seattle University*

Anne T. Quartararo, *United States Naval Academy*

C. John Sommerville, *University of Florida*

Richard Wires, *Ball State University*

Many of their suggestions were incorporated into the final version. We are also grateful to the staff of Houghton Mifflin Company who lent their considerable talents to the project. I would like to express my personal gratitude to George Bock who assisted in the planning of the text from its inception and who read the manuscript with an eye for major concepts and essential relationships.

M.P.

Introduction

The Foundations of Western Civilization

Western civilization is a blending of two traditions that emerged in the ancient world: the Judeo-Christian and the Greco-Roman. Before these traditions took shape, the drama of civilization was well advanced, having arisen some five thousand years ago in Mesopotamia and Egypt.

Religion was the central force in these first civilizations in the Near East. Religion provided explanations for the operations of nature, justified traditional rules of morality, and helped people to deal with their fear of death. Law was considered sacred, a commandment of the gods. Religion united people in the common enterprises needed for survival, such as the construction of irrigation works. Religion also promoted creative achievements in art, literature, and science. In addition, the power of rulers, who were regarded as gods or as agents of the gods, derived from the religious outlook. The many achievements of the Egyptians and the Mesopotamians were inherited and assimilated by both the Greeks and the Hebrews, the spiritual ancestors of Western civilization. But Greeks and Hebrews also rejected and transformed elements of the older Near Eastern traditions and conceived a new view of God, nature, and the individual.

awareness of the individual. In confronting God, the Hebrews developed an awareness of *self,* or *I.* The individual became conscious of his or her moral autonomy and personal worth. The Hebrews believed that God had bestowed on his people the capacity for moral freedom—they could choose between good and evil. Fundamental to Hebrew belief was the insistence that God had created human beings to be free moral agents. God did not want people to grovel before him, but to fulfill their moral potential by freely making the choice to follow, or not to follow, God's law. Thus, the Hebrews conceived the idea of moral freedom—that each individual is responsible for his or her own actions. Inherited by Christianity, this idea of moral autonomy is central to the Western tradition.

The Hebrew conception of ethical monotheism, with its stress on human dignity, is one source of the Western tradition. The other source derives from the ancient Greeks; they originated scientific and philosophic thought and conceived both the idea and the practice of political freedom.

The Greeks

In the Near East, religion dominated political activity, and following the mandates of the gods was a ruler's first responsibility. What made Greek political life different from that of earlier civilizations—and gives it enduring significance—was the Greeks' gradual realization that community problems were caused by human beings and required human solutions. The Greeks came to un-

The Hebrews

By asserting that God was one, sovereign, transcendent, and good, the Hebrews effected a religious revolution that separated them forever from the world-views of the Mesopotamians and Egyptians. This new conception of God led to a new

derstand law as an achievement of the rational mind, rather than as an edict imposed by the gods. In the process, they also originated the idea of political freedom and created democratic institutions.

Greece comprised small, independent city-states. In the fifth century B.C., the city-state (*polis*) was in its maturity. A self-governing community, it expressed the will of free citizens, not the desires of gods, hereditary kings, or priests. The democratic orientation of the city-states was best exemplified by Athens, which was also the leading cultural center of Greece. In the Assembly, which was open to all adult male citizens, Athenians debated and voted on key issues of state.

In addition to the idea of political freedom, the Greeks conceived a new way of viewing nature and human society. The first speculative philosophers emerged during the sixth century B.C. in Greek cities located in Ionia in Asia Minor. Curious about the basic composition of nature and dissatisfied with earlier legends about creation, the Ionians sought physical, rather than mythico-religious, explanations for natural occurrences.

During this search, these philosophers arrived at a new concept of nature and a new method of inquiry. They maintained that nature was not manipulated by arbitrary and willful gods and that it was not governed by blind chance. The Ionians said that underlying the seeming chaos of nature were principles of order, that is, general rules that could be ascertained by human minds. This discovery marks the beginning of scientific thought. It made possible theoretical thinking and the systematization of knowledge. This is distinct from the mere observation and collection of data. Greek mathematicians, for example, organized the Egyptians' practical experience with land measurements into the logical and coherent science of geometry. In another instance, the Greeks used the data collected by Babylonian priests, who observed the heavens because they believed that the stars revealed their gods' wishes. The Greeks' purpose was not religious—they sought to discover the geometrical laws underlying the motion of heavenly bodies. At the same time, Greek physicians drew a distinction between medicine and magic, and began to examine human illness in an empirical and rational way. By the fifth century the Greek mind had applied reason to the physical world and to all human activities. This empha-

sis on reason marks a turning point for human civilization.

In their effort to understand the external world, early Greek thinkers had created the tools of reason. Greek thinkers now began a rational investigation of the human being and the human community. The key figure in this development was Socrates.

Socrates' central concern was the perfection of individual human character, the achievement of moral excellence. Excellence of character was achieved, said Socrates, when individuals regulated their lives according to objective standards arrived at through rational reflection, that is, when reason became the formative, guiding, and ruling agency of the soul. Socrates wanted to subject all human beliefs and behavior to the clear light of reason and in this way to remove ethics from the realm of authority, tradition, dogma, superstition, and myth. He believed that reason was the only proper guide to the most crucial problem of human existence—the question of good and evil.

Plato, Socrates' most important disciple, used his master's teachings to create a comprehensive system of philosophy that embraced the world of nature and the social world. Socrates had taught that there were universal standards of right and justice and that these were arrived at through thought. Building on the insights of his teacher, Plato insisted on the existence of a higher world of reality, independent of the world of things experienced every day. This higher reality, he said, is the realm of Ideas or Forms—unchanging, eternal, absolute, and universal standards of beauty, goodness, justice, and so forth. Truth resides in this world of Forms and not in the world revealed through the human senses.

Aristotle, Plato's student, was the leading expert of his time in every field of knowledge, with the possible exception of mathematics. Aristotle objected to Plato's devaluing of the material world. Possessing a scientist's curiosity to understand the facts of nature, Aristotle appreciated the world of phenomena, of concrete things, and respected knowledge obtained through the senses. Like Plato, Aristotle believed that understanding universal principles is the ultimate aim of knowledge. But unlike Plato, Aristotle held that to obtain such knowledge, the individual must study the world of facts and objects revealed through sight, hearing, and touch. Aristotle adapted Plato's stress on universal principles to the requirements of natural science.

By discovering theoretical reason, by defining political freedom, and by affirming the worth and potential of human personality, the Greeks broke with the past and founded the rational and humanist tradition of the West. "Had Greek civilization never existed," said poet W. H. Auden, "we would never have become fully conscious, which is to say that we would never have become, for better or worse, fully human."[1]

The Hellenistic Age

By 338 B.C., Philip of Macedonia (a kingdom to the north of Greece) had extended his dominion over the Greek city-states. After the assassination of Philip in 336 B.C., his twenty-year-old son Alexander succeeded to the throne. Fiery, proud, and ambitious, Alexander sought to conquer the vast Persian Empire. Winning every battle, Alexander's army carved an empire that stretched from Greece to India. In 323 B.C., Alexander not yet thirty-three years of age, died of a fever. His generals engaged in a long and bitter struggle to succeed him. As none of the generals or their heirs could predominate, Alexander's empire was fractured into separate states.

The period from the early city-states that emerged in 800 B.C. until the death of Alexander the Great in 323 B.C. is called the *Hellenic Age.* The next stage in the evolution of Greek civilization (*Hellenism*) is called the *Hellenistic Age.* It ended in 30 B.C. when Egypt, the last major Hellenistic state, fell to Rome.

Although the Hellenistic Age had absorbed the heritage of classical (Hellenic) Greece, its style of civilization changed. During the first phase of Hellenism, the polis had been the center of political life. The polis had given the individual identity, and it was believed that only within the polis could a Greek live a good and civilized life. During the Hellenistic Age, this situation changed. The city-state was eclipsed in power and importance by kingdoms. While cities retained a large measure of autonomy in domestic affairs, they had lost their freedom of action in foreign affairs. No longer were they the self-sufficient and independent communities of the Hellenic period.

Hellenistic society was characterized by a mingling of peoples and an interchange of cultures. As a result of Alexander's conquests, tens of thousands of Greek soldiers, merchants, and administrators settled in eastern lands. Greek traditions spread to the Near East, and Mesopotamian, Hebrew, and Persian traditions—particularly religious beliefs—moved westward. Cities were founded in the east patterned after the city-states of Greece. The ruling class in each Hellenistic city was united by a common Hellenism that overcame national, linguistic, and racial distinctions.

During the Hellenistic Age, Greek scientific achievement reached its height. Hellenistic scientists attempted a rational analysis of nature, engaged in research, organized knowledge in logical fashion, devised procedures for mathematical proof, separated medicine from magic, grasped the theory of experiment, and applied scientific principles to mechanical devices. Hellenistic science, says historian Benjamin Farrington, stood "on the threshold of the modern world. When modern science began in the sixteenth century, it took up where the Greeks left off."[2]

Hellenistic philosophers preserved the rational tradition of Greek philosophy. Like their Hellenic predecessors, they regarded the cosmos as governed by universal principles intelligible to the rational mind. The most important philosophy in the Hellenistic world was Stoicism. By teaching that the world constituted a single society, Stoicism gave theoretical expression to the world-mindedness of the age. Stoicism with its concept of a world-state offered an answer to the problems of the loss of community and the alienation caused by the decline of the city-state. By stressing inner strength in dealing with life's misfortunes, Stoicism offered an avenue to individual happiness in a world fraught with uncertainty.

At the core of Stoicism was the belief that the universe contained a principle of order: the *logos* (reason). This ruling principle permeated all things; it accounted for the orderliness of nature. Because people were part of the universe, said the Stoics, they also shared in the logos that operated throughout the cosmos. Since reason was common to all, human beings were essentially brothers and fundamentally equal.

Stoicism had an enduring impact on the Western mind. To some Roman political theorists, their Empire fulfilled the Stoic ideal of a world community in which people of different nationalities held citizenship and were governed by a worldwide law that accorded with the law of reason and by natural law that operated throughout the universe. Stoic beliefs—such as all human beings are members of one family; each person is significant; distinctions of rank are of no account; and human law should not conflict with natural law—were incorporated into Roman jurisprudence, Christian thought, and modern liberalism. There is continuity between Stoic thought and the principle of inalienable rights stated in the American Declaration of Independence.

Rome

Rome, conqueror of the Mediterranean world and transmitter of Hellenism, inherited the universalist tendencies of the Hellenistic Age and embodied them in its law and institutions. Roman history falls into two periods: the Republic, which began in 509 B.C. with the overthrow of the Etruscan monarchy; and the Empire, which started in 27 B.C. when Octavian became, in effect, the first Roman emperor.

The Roman Republic

The history of the Roman Republic was marked by three principal developments: the struggle between patricians and plebeians, the conquest of Italy and the Mediterranean world, and the civil wars. At the beginning of the fifth century B.C., Rome was dominated by *patricians* (the landowning aristocrats). The *plebeians* (commoners) had many grievances; these included enslavement for debt, discrimination in the courts, prevention of intermarriage with patricians, lack of political representation, and the absence of a written code of laws.

Resentful of their inferior status, the plebeians organized and waged a struggle for political, legal, and social equality. They were resisted every step of the way by the patricians, who wanted to pre-serve their dominance. The plebeians had one decisive weapon: their threat to secede from Rome, that is, not to pay taxes, work, nor serve in the army. Realizing that Rome, which was constantly involved in warfare on the Italian peninsula, could not endure without plebeian help, the pragmatic patricians begrudgingly made concessions. Thus the plebeians slowly gained legal equality.

Although many plebeian grievances were resolved and the plebeians gained the right to sit in the Senate, the principal organ of government, Rome was still ruled by an upper class. Power was concentrated in a ruling oligarchy consisting of patricians and influential plebeians who had joined forces with the old nobility.

By 146 B.C., Rome had become the dominant power in the Mediterranean world. Roman expansion occurred in three main stages: the uniting of the Italian peninsula, which gave Rome the manpower that transformed it from a city-state into a great power; the struggle with Carthage, from which Rome emerged as ruler of the western Mediterranean; and the subjugation of the Hellenistic states of the eastern Mediterranean, which brought Romans into close contact with Greek civilization.

A crucial consequence of expansion was Roman contact with the legal experience of other peoples. Roman jurists, demonstrating the Roman virtues of pragmatism and common sense, selectively incorporated elements of the legal codes and traditions of these nations into Roman law. Thus Roman jurists gradually and empirically fashioned the *jus gentium,* the law of nations or peoples.

Roman jurists then identified the jus gentium with the natural law (*jus naturale*) of the Stoics. The jurists said that law should accord with rational principles inherent in nature—universal norms capable of being discerned by rational people. The law of nations—Roman civil law (the law of the Roman state) combined with principles drawn from Greek and other sources—eventually replaced much of the local law in the Empire. This evolution of a universal code of law that gave expression to the Stoic principles of common rationality and humanity was the great achievement of Roman rule.

Another consequence of expansion was increased contact with Greek culture. Gradually the Romans acquired knowledge about scientific thought, philosophy, medicine, and geography from Greece. Adopting the humanist outlook of the Greeks, the Romans came to value human intelligence and eloquent and graceful prose and oratory. Rome creatively assimilated the Greek achievement and transmitted it to others, thereby extending the orbit of Hellenism.

During Rome's march to empire, all its classes had demonstrated a magnificent spirit in fighting foreign wars. With Carthage and Macedonia no longer threats to Rome, this cooperation deteriorated. Rome became torn apart by internal dissension during the first century B.C.

Julius Caesar, a popular military commander, gained control of the government. Caesar believed that only strong and enlightened leadership could permanently end the civil warfare destroying Rome. Rome's ruling class feared that Caesar would destroy the Republic and turn Rome into a monarchy. Regarding themselves as defenders of republican liberties and senatorial leadership, aristocratic conspirators assassinated Caesar in 44 B.C. The murder of Caesar plunged Rome into renewed civil war. Finally, in 31 B.C., Octavian, Caesar's adopted son, defeated his rivals and emerged as master of Rome. Four years later, Octavian, now called Augustus, became in effect the first Roman emperor.

The Roman Empire

The rule of Augustus signified the end of the Roman Republic and the beginning of the Roman Empire, the termination of aristocratic politics and the emergence of one-man rule. Under Augustus the power of the ruler was disguised; in ensuing generations, however, emperors would wield absolute power openly.

Augustus was by no means a self-seeking tyrant, but a creative statesman. His reforms rescued a dying Roman world and inaugurated Rome's greatest age. For the next two hundred years the Mediterranean world enjoyed the blessings of the *pax Romana,* the Roman peace.

The ancient world had never experienced such a long period of peace, order, efficient administration, and prosperity. The Romans called the pax Romana a "Time of Happiness." It was the fulfillment of Rome's mission—the creation of a world-state that provided peace, security, ordered civilization, and the rule of law. The cities of the Roman Empire served as centers of Greco-Roman civilization, which spread to the furthest reaches of the Mediterranean. Roman citizenship, gradually granted, was finally extended to virtually all free men by an edict in A.D. 212.

In the third century, the ordered civilization of the pax Romana ended. The Roman Empire was plunged into military anarchy, as generals supported by their soldiers fought for the throne. Germanic tribesmen broke through the deteriorating border defenses to raid, loot, and destroy. Economic problems caused cities, the centers of civilization, to decay. Increasingly people turned away from the humanist values of Greco-Roman civilization and embraced Near Eastern religions that offered a sense of belonging, a promise of immortality, and relief from earthly misery.

The emperors Diocletian (285–305) and Constantine (306–337) tried to contain the forces of disintegration by tightening the reins of government and squeezing more taxes out of the citizens. In the process they divided the Empire into eastern and western halves, and transformed Rome into a bureaucratic, regimented, and militarized state.

Diocletian and Constantine had given Rome a reprieve, but in the last part of the fourth century, the problem of guarding the frontier grew more acute. At the end of 406, the borders finally collapsed; numerous German tribes overran the Empire's western provinces. In 410 and again in 455, Rome was sacked by Germanic invaders. German soldiers in the pay of Rome gained control of the government and dictated the choice of emperor. In 476, German officers overthrew the Roman Emperor Romulus and placed a fellow German on the throne. This act is traditionally regarded as the end of the Roman Empire in the West.

Early Christianity

When the Roman Empire was in decline, a new religion, Christianity, was sweeping across the Mediterranean world. Christianity was based on the life, death, and teachings of Jesus, a Palestinian Jew who was executed by the Roman authorities. Jesus was heir to the ethical monotheism of the Hebrew prophets. He also taught the imminent coming of the reign of God and the need for people to repent their sins—to transform themselves morally in order to enter God's kingdom. People must love God and their fellow human beings.

In the time immediately following the crucifixion of Jesus, his followers were almost exclusively Jews, who could more appropriately be called Jewish-Christians. To the first members of the Christian movement, Jesus was both a prophet who proclaimed God's power and purpose and the Messiah whose coming heralded a new age. To Paul, another Jewish-Christian, Jesus was the redeemer who held out the promise of salvation to the entire world and the savior-god who took on human flesh and atoned for the sins of humanity by suffering death upon the cross. And Saint Paul carried this message to Jews and especially to non-Jews (Gentiles).

The Christian message of a divine Savior, a concerned Father, and brotherly love inspired men and women who were dissatisfied with the world of here-and-now, who felt no attachment to city or Empire, who derived no inspiration from philosophy, and who suffered from a profound sense of loneliness. Christianity offered the individual what the city and the Roman world-state could not: a personal relationship with God, a promise of eternal life, and membership in a community of the faithful (the church) who cared for each other.

Unable to crush Christianity by persecution, Roman emperors decided to gain the support of the growing number of Christians within the Empire. By A.D. 392, Theodosius I had made Christianity the state religion of the Empire and declared the worship of pagan gods illegal.

The Judeo-Christian and Greco-Roman traditions are the two principal components of Western civilization. Both traditions valued the individual. For classical humanism, individual worth derived from the human capacity to reason, to shape character and life according to rational standards. Christianity also places great stress on the individual. It teaches that God cares for each person and wants people to behave righteously, and that He made them morally autonomous.

Despite their common emphasis on the individual, the Judeo-Christian and Greco-Roman traditions essentially have different world-views. With the victory of Christianity, the ultimate goal of life shifted away from achieving excellence in this world through the full and creative development of human talent, toward attaining salvation in a heavenly city. For Christians, a person's worldly accomplishments counted very little if he or she did not accept God and his revelation. Greek classicism held that there was no authority higher than reason; Christianity taught that without God as the starting point, knowledge is formless, purposeless, and error-prone.

But Christian thinkers did not seek to eradicate the rational tradition of Greece. Rather, they sought to fit Greek philosophy into a Christian framework. In doing so, Christians performed a task of immense historical significance—the preservation of Greek philosophy.

The Middle Ages

The triumph of Christianity and the establishment of Germanic kingdoms on once-Roman lands constituted a new phase in Western history: the end of the ancient world and the beginning of the Middle Ages. In the ancient world the locus of Greco-Roman civilization was the Mediterranean Sea. The heartland of medieval civilization shifted to the north, to regions of Europe that Greco-Roman civilization had barely penetrated.

The Early Middle Ages

During the Early Middle Ages (500–1050), a common civilization evolved with Christianity at the center, Rome as the spiritual capital, and Latin as the language of intellectual life. The opening centuries of the Middle Ages were marked by a decline in trade, town life, central authority, and learning. The Germans were culturally unprepared to breathe new life into classical civilization. A new civilization with its own distinctive style was taking root, however. It consisted of Greco-Roman survivals, the native traditions of the Germans, and the Christian outlook.

Christianity was the integrating principle of the Middle Ages, and the church its dominant institution. People came to see themselves as participants in a great drama of salvation. There was only one truth—God's revelation to humanity. There was only one avenue to heaven—the church. To the medieval mind, society without the church was as inconceivable as life without the Christian view of God. By teaching a higher morality, the church tamed the warrior habits of the Germanic peoples. By copying and preserving ancient texts, monks kept alive elements of the high civilization of Greece and Rome.

One German people, the Franks, built a viable kingdom with major centers in France and the Rhine Valley of Germany. Under Charlemagne, who ruled from 768 to 814, the Frankish empire reached its height. On Christmas day in the year 800, Pope Leo crowned Charlemagne as "Emperor of the Romans." The title signified that the tradition of a world empire still survived, despite the demise of the Roman Empire three hundred years earlier. Because the pope crowned Charlemagne, this act meant that the emperor had a spiritual responsibility to spread and defend the faith.

The crowning of a German ruler as emperor of the Romans by the head of the church represented the merging of German, Christian, and Roman elements—the essential characteristic of medieval civilization. This blending of traditions was also evident on a cultural plane, for Charlemagne, a German warrior-king, showed respect for classical learning and Christianity, both non-Germanic traditions. During his reign, a distinct European civilization took root, but it was centuries away from fruition.

Charlemagne's successors could not hold the empire together, and it disintegrated. As central authority waned, large landowners began to exercise authority over their own regions. Furthering this movement toward localism and decentralization were simultaneous invasions by Muslims, Vikings from Scandinavia, and Magyars originally from Western Asia. They devastated villages, destroyed ports, and killed many people. Trade was at a standstill, coins no longer circulated, and untended farms became wastelands. The European economy collapsed, the political authority of kings disappeared, and cultural life and learning withered.

During these times, large landowners, or lords, wielded power formerly held by kings over their subjects, an arrangement called *feudalism*. Arising during a period of collapsing central authority, invasion, scanty public revenues, and declining commerce and town life, feudalism attempted to provide some order and security. A principal feature of feudalism was the practice of *vassalage,* in which a man in a solemn ceremony pledged loyalty to a lord. The lord received military service from his vassal, and the vassal obtained land, called a *fief,* from his lord.

Feudalism was built on an economic foundation known as *manorialism*. A village community (manor), consisting of serfs bound to the land, became the essential agricultural arrangement in medieval society. In return for protection and the right to cultivate fields, serfs owed obligations to their lords, and their personal freedom was restricted in a variety of ways.

Manorialism and feudalism presupposed an unchanging social order with a rigid system of estates, or orders—clergy who prayed, lords who fought, and peasants who toiled. The revival of an urban economy and the re-emergence of the king's authority in the High Middle Ages (about 1050 to 1270) would undermine feudal and manorial relationships.

The High Middle Ages

By the end of the eleventh century, Europe showed many signs of recovery and vitality. The invasions of Magyars and Vikings had ended, and kings and powerful lords imposed greater order in their territories. Improvements in technology and the clearing of new lands increased agricultural production. More food, the fortunate absence of plagues, and the limited nature of feudal warfare contributed to a population increase.

Expanding agricultural production, the end of Viking attacks, greater political stability, and a larger population revived commerce. In the twelfth and thirteenth centuries, local, regional, and long-distance trade gained such a momentum that some historians describe the period as a commercial revolution that surpassed commerce in the Roman Empire during the pax Romana.

In the eleventh century, towns re-emerged throughout Europe, and in the next century became active centers of commerce and intellectual life. Socially, economically, and culturally, towns were a new and revolutionary force. Towns contributed to the decline of manorialism because they provided new opportunities for commoners, apart from food-producing.

A new class (the middle class) of merchants and artisans appeared; unlike the lords and serfs, the members of this class were not affiliated with the land. Townspeople possessed a value system different from that of lords, serfs, or clerics. Whereas the clergy prepared people for heaven, the feudal lords fought and hunted, and the serfs toiled in small villages, townspeople engaged in business and had money and freedom. Townspeople were freeing themselves from the prejudices of both feudal aristocrats, who considered trade and manual work degrading, and the clergy, who cursed the pursuit of riches as an obstacle to salvation. Townspeople were critical, dynamic, and progressive—a force for change.

Other signs of growing vitality in Latin Christendom (western and central Europe) were the greater order and security provided by the emergence of states. While feudalism fostered a Europe that was split into many local regions, each ruled by a lord, the church envisioned a vast Christian commonwealth, *Republica Christiana*, guided by the pope. During the High Middle Ages, the ideal of a universal Christian community seemed close to fruition. Never again would Europe possess such spiritual unity.

But forces were propelling Europe into a different direction. Aided by educated and trained officials who enforced royal law, tried people in royal courts, and collected royal taxes, kings enlarged their territories and slowly fashioned strong central governments. Gradually, subjects began to transfer their prime loyalty away from the church and their lords to the person of the king. In the process the foundations of European states were laid. Not all areas followed the same pattern. England and France achieved a large measure of unity during the Middle Ages; Germany and Italy remained divided into numerous independent territories.

Accompanying economic recovery and political stability in the High Middle Ages was a growing spiritual vitality. This vigor was marked by several developments. The common people showed greater devotion to the church. Within the church, reform movements attacked clerical abuses, and the papacy grew more powerful. Holy wars against the Muslims drew the Christian community closer together. During this period, the church with great determination tried to make society follow divine standards, that is, to shape all institutions according to a comprehensive Christian outlook.

European economic and religious vitality was paralleled by a cultural flowering in philosophy, literature, and the visual arts. Creative intellects achieved on a cultural level what the papacy accomplished on an institutional level—the integration of society around a Christian viewpoint. The High Middle Ages saw the restoration of some learning of the ancient world, the rise of universities, the emergence of an original form of architecture (the Gothic), and the creation of an imposing system of thought (scholasticism).

Medieval theologian-philosophers called *scholastics* fashioned Christian teachings into an all-embracing philosophy that represented the spiritual essence of medieval civilization. They achieved what Christian thinkers in the Roman Empire had initiated and what learned men of the Early Middle Ages were groping for: a synthesis of Greek philosophy and Christian revelation.

The Late Middle Ages

By the opening of the fourteenth century, Latin Christendom had experienced more than 250 years of growth, but during the Late Middle Ages, roughly the fourteenth and early fifteenth centuries, medieval civilization declined. The fourteenth century, an age of adversity, was marked by crop failures, famine, population decline, plagues, stagnating production, unemployment, inflation, devastating warfare, abandoned villages, and violent rebellions by the poor and weak of towns and countryside, who were ruthlessly suppressed by the upper classes. This century witnessed flights into mysticism, outbreaks of mass hysteria, and massacres of Jews; it was an age of pessimism and general insecurity. The papacy declined in power, heresy proliferated, and the synthesis of faith and reason erected by the Christian thinkers during the High Middle Ages began to disintegrate. All these developments were signs that the stable and coherent civilization of the thirteenth century was drawing to a close.

But the decline of medieval civilization in the fourteenth century brought no new dark age to Europe. Its economic and political institutions and technological skills had grown too strong. Instead, the waning of the Middle Ages opened up possibilities for another stage in Western civilization—the modern age.

In innumerable ways the modern world is linked to the Middle Ages. European cities, the middle class, the state system, English common law, universities—all had their origins in the Middle Ages. During the Middle Ages, important advances were made in business practices, such as double-entry bookkeeping and the growth of credit and banking facilities. By translating and commenting on the writings of Greek philosophers and scientists, medieval scholars preserved a priceless intellectual heritage without which the modern mind could never have evolved. During the Middle Ages, Europeans began to lead the rest of the world in the development of technology.

Medieval philosophers, believing that God's law was superior to the decrees of states, provided a theoretical basis for opposing tyrannical kings who violated Christian principles. The idea that both the ruler and the ruled are bound by a higher law would become a principal element of modern liberal thought. The Christian stress on the sacred worth of the individual and on the higher law of God has never ceased to influence Western civilization. The Christian commandment to "love thy neighbor" has permeated modern reform movements.

Feudalism contributed to the history of liberty. The idea evolved that law should not be imposed by an absolute monarch, but requires the collaboration of king and subjects; that a king too should be bound by the law; and that lords should have the right to resist a monarch who violates agreements. Related to this development was the emergence of representative institutions, notably the English Parliament. The king was expected to consult its members on matters concerning the realm's affairs.

Despite these concrete elements of continuity, the characteristic outlook of the Middle Ages is much different from that of the modern world. Religion was the integrating feature of the Middle Ages, whereas science and secularism determine the modern outlook. Medieval thought began with the existence of God and the truth of his revelation as interpreted by the church, which set the standards and defined the purposes for human endeavor.

The medieval mind rejected the fundamental principle of Greek philosophy and modern thought—the autonomy of reason. Without the guidance of revealed truth, reason was seen as feeble. Unlike either ancient or modern thinkers, medieval scholars believed ultimately that reason alone could not provide a unified view of nature or society. To understand nature, law, morality, or the state, it was necessary to know its relationship to a supernatural order, a higher world.

In the modern view, both nature and the human intellect are self-sufficient. Nature is a mathematical system that operates without miracles or any other form of divine intervention. To comprehend nature and society, the mind needs no divine assistance; it accepts no authority above reason. The modern mind finds it unacceptable to reject conclusions of science on the basis of clerical authority and revelation, or to base politics, law, and economics on religion; it rejects the medieval division of the universe into a heavenly realm of perfection and a lower earthly realm. Almost ruthlessly, scientific and secular attitudes have driven Christianity and faith from their central position to the periphery of human concerns.

The transformation of the medieval worldview based on religion into the modern view based on science and reason occurred over a span of four centuries. We shall now examine the movements that helped shape the modern world: the Renaissance, the Reformation, the Commercial Revolution, the growth of national states, the Scientific Revolution, the Enlightenment, and the Industrial Revolution.

Notes

1. W. H. Auden, ed., *The Portable Greek Reader* (New York: Viking, 1952), p. 38.

2. Benjamin Farrington, *Greek Science* (Baltimore: Penguin Books, 1961), p. 301.

III

Early Modern Europe: From Renaissance to Enlightenment

1350–1789

13

The Renaissance: Transition to the Modern Age

From the Italian Renaissance of the fifteenth century through the Age of Enlightenment of the eighteenth century, the outlook and institutions of the Middle Ages disintegrated and distinctly modern forms emerged. The radical change in European civilization could be seen on every level of society. On the economic level, commerce and industry expanded greatly, and capitalism largely replaced medieval forms of economic organization. On the political level, central government grew stronger at the expense of feudalism. On the religious level, the rise of Protestantism fragmented the unity of Christendom. On the social level, middle-class townspeople, increasing in number and wealth, were playing a more important role in economic and cultural life. On the cultural level, the clergy lost its monopoly over learning, and the otherworldly orientation of the Middle Ages gave way to a secular outlook in literature and the arts. Theology, the queen of knowledge in the Middle Ages, surrendered its crown to science. Reason, which in the Middle Ages had been subordinate to revelation, asserted its independence.

Many of these tendencies manifested themselves dramatically during the Renaissance. The word *renaissance* means "rebirth," and it is used to refer to the attempt by artists and thinkers to recover and apply the ancient learning and standards of Greece and Rome. In historical terms, the Renaissance is both a cultural movement and a period. As a movement it was born in the city-states of northern Italy and spread to the rest of Europe. As a period it runs from about 1350 to 1600. Until the late fifteenth century the Renaissance was restricted to Italy. What happened there in the fourteenth and fifteenth centuries sharply contrasts with civilization in the rest of Europe, which until the end of the fifteenth century still belonged to the Late Middle Ages.

Andrea Palladio (1508–1580): The Villa Rotonda in Vicenza. (*Alinari/Art Resource*)

The nineteenth-century historian Jacob Burckhardt in his classic study, *The Civilization of the Renaissance in Italy* (1860), held that the Renaissance is the point of departure for the modern world. During the Renaissance, said Burckhardt, individuals showed an increasing concern for worldly life and self-consciously aspired to shape their destinies, an attitude that is the key to modernity.

Burckhardt's thesis has been challenged, particularly by medievalists who view the Renaissance as an extension of the Middle Ages, not as a sudden break with the past. These critics argue that Burckhardt neglected important links between medieval and Renaissance culture. A distinguishing feature of the Renaissance, the revival of classical learning, had already emerged in the High Middle Ages to such an extent that historians speak of "the renaissance of the twelfth century." The Renaissance owes much to the legal and scholastic studies that flourished in the Italian universities of Padua and Bologna before 1300. Town life and trade, hallmarks of Renaissance society, were also a heritage from the Middle Ages.

To be sure, the Renaissance was not a complete and sudden break with the Middle Ages. Many medieval ways and attitudes persisted. Nevertheless, Burckhardt's thesis that the Renaissance represents the birth of modernity has much to recommend it. Renaissance writers and artists themselves were aware of their age's novelty. They looked back on the medieval centuries as a "Dark Age" that followed the grandeur of ancient Greece and Rome, and they believed that they were experiencing a rebirth of cultural greatness. Renaissance artists and writers were fascinated with the cultural forms of Greece and Rome; they sought to imitate classical style and to capture the secular spirit of antiquity. In the process they broke with medieval artistic and literary forms. They valued the full development of human talent and expressed a new excitement about the possibilities of life in this world. This outlook represents a new trend in European civilization.

The Renaissance, then, was an age of transition that saw the rejection of certain elements of the medieval outlook, the revival of classical cultural forms, and the emergence of distinctly modern attitudes. This rebirth began in Italy during the fourteenth century and gradually spread north and west to Germany, France, England, and Spain during the late fifteenth and the sixteenth centuries.

Italy: Birthplace of the Renaissance

The city-states of northern Italy that spawned the Renaissance were developed urban centers where people had the wealth, freedom, and inclination to cultivate the arts and to enjoy the fruits of worldly life. In Italy, moreover, reminders of ancient Rome's grandeur were visible everywhere. Roman roads, monuments, and manuscripts intensified the Italians' links to their Roman past.

Political Evolution of the City-States

During the Middle Ages the feudal states of northern Italy had been absorbed into the Holy Roman Empire. They continued to owe nominal allegiance to the German emperor during the early Renaissance. But its protracted wars with the papacy had sapped the empire of vitality. Its subsequent weakness meant that the states of northern Italy were able to develop as autonomous political entities. Also promoting this development was the weakening of the papacy in the fourteenth century (see pages 247–250).

The city-states that developed in northern Italy were similar in their size and their varied types of governments to those of ancient Greece. Among the more important city-states were Rome, Milan, Florence, Venice, Mantua, Ferrara, Padua, Bologna, and Genoa. These city-states differed markedly from most of Europe in two fundamental respects. First, by the late eleventh and twelfth centuries the city-states had developed as flourishing commercial and banking centers and had monopolized the trade in Mediterranean areas, which included trade between the Orient and the West. So the merchant fleets, especially those of

Map 13.1 Italian City-States, c. 1494 ▶

DUCHY OF SAVOY

DUCHY OF MILAN

Milan
Pavia
Lodi
Turin

SALUZZO

REP. OF GENOA
Genoa

M. OF MANTUA
Mantua
Po R.

Padua
Venice

REPUBLIC OF VENICE

OTTOMAN EMPIRE

DALMATIA

Ferrara
D. OF FERRARA

D. OF MODENA

Bologna
Ravenna

REP. OF LUCCA
Arno R.
Pisa

REP. OF FLORENCE
Florence

FLORENCE

Siena

REP. OF SIENA

Urbino

Assisi

Tiber R.

PAPAL STATES

ADRIATIC SEA

CORSICA

Rome

KINGDOM OF NAPLES

Bari

Naples
Salerno

SARDINIA

MEDITERRANEAN SEA

Palermo

KINGDOM OF SICILY

0   100 Mi.
0   100 Km.

Venice and Genoa, carried goods from ports in the eastern Mediterranean westward into the Atlantic and from there north to the Baltic Sea. Unlike that of the rest of Europe, the wealth of these cities lay not in land but in commerce and industry. When popes, monarchs, and feudal magnates of Europe needed money, they borrowed it from Italian, especially Florentine, merchant-bankers.

Second, the predominance of business and commerce within these city-states meant that the feudal nobility, who held the land beyond the city walls, played a much less important part in government than they did elsewhere in Europe. By the end of the twelfth century the city-states had ceased to be dominated by the feudal nobility, or landed aristocracy. The aristocracy and the rich merchants had to share power, and when their alliances broke down, as they often did, the two groups struggled for power based on their opposing interests and outlooks. The interests of the smaller merchants and the artisans in the towns also had to be catered to. When they were not, these groups rioted and rebelled, as they did, for instance, in 1378 during the revolt of the *Ciompi* (the wool-workers) in Florence.

Politically these city-states were inherently unstable. This instability arose from two sources—the internal conflict between merchants and nobles and the external rivalry between the city-states themselves. The city-states managed to keep both papacy and empire at bay, sometimes by playing one giant against the other in the manner of Third World nations today. But the price of this continued independence was that the city-states, without any externally imposed power structure, had to seek their own solutions to their instability. Out of this situation came experiments in the form and technique of government. The origins of modern political thought and practice can be discerned in this experimentation, thus forging an important connection between the Renaissance and the modern age.

The political experimentation that went on in the northern Italian city-states can usefully, if only roughly, be divided into two periods—the first (1300–1450) marked by the defense of republicanism and the second (1450–1550) by the triumph of despotism. By the end of the twelfth century the city-states had adopted a fairly uniform pattern of republican self-government built around the office of a chief magistrate. He was elected by the citizens on the basis of a broad franchise, and he ruled with the advice of two councils—a large public one and a small secret one. His powers were tightly circumscribed by the constitution; with his term of office restricted ordinarily to six months, he could be removed from government or punished at the end of his tenure.

The city-states not only developed republican institutions, they devised important theories to defend and justify their liberty and self-government in the face of their external enemies, the papacy and the empire. To the emperor they argued that their customary feudal subjection to his authority must be radically adjusted to fit the changed reality that they were in fact self-governing. To the papacy they argued that Christ had denied all political jurisdiction to the clergy, including the pope, and so undercut the papal claim to political control in Italy and elsewhere.

However, the republicanism of the city-states, with their internal instability and their rivalry, proved precarious. During the fourteenth and early fifteenth centuries the republican institutions in one city after another toppled in favor of rule by despots. Three conditions were responsible for this development. First, class war between rich merchants and nobles caused one group or the other, or both, to seek a resolution of the crisis by turning to one-man rule. Second, the economic disasters, famine, and disease of the period from 1350 to 1450 encouraged the drift toward despotism. Northern Italy was particularly hard hit by the bubonic plague. The citizenry lost faith in the ability of short-term republican governments to cope with such emergencies and put their trust in long-term, one-man rule. Third, and perhaps most important, the city-states had come to rely on mercenary troops, whose leaders, the notorious *condottieri*—unschooled in and owing no loyalty to the republican tradition—simply seized power during emergencies.

Some city-states held out against the trend toward despotism for a long time; among those that did, Florence was by far the most successful. In the process, the Florentines developed new arguments and theories for the maintenance of republicanism and liberty (see pages 269–270). But by the mid-fifteenth century, even Florentine republicanism was giving way before the intrigues of a rich bank-

Giotto (c. 1276–1337): The Epiphany. Whether or not Giotto is classified as a Late Gothic or Early Renaissance painter, he was a revolutionary innovator. His choice of eye-level perspective and his habit of capturing dramatic gesture brought viewers directly into his pictorial space. (*The Metropolitan Museum of Art, John Stewart Kennedy Fund, 1911. 11.126.1*)

ing family—the Medici. They had installed themselves in power in the 1430s with the return of Cosimo de' Medici from exile. Cosimo's grandson, Lorenzo the Magnificent, completed the destruction of the republican constitution in 1480, when he managed to set up a government staffed by his own supporters.

The one city-state where republicanism survived until the advent of Napoleon was Venice. Protected from the rest of Italy by lagoons, Venice during the Middle Ages controlled a far-flung and exceptionally lucrative seagoing trade and a maritime empire stretching along the Adriatic and the eastern Mediterranean seas. Venice's maritime commercial successes were matched by political ones at home. For centuries, Venice managed to govern itself without major upheaval; its republican constitution made this stability possible. Its chief executive offices, the Council of Ten, were elective, but after 1297, both these offices and the electorate were narrowly restricted by law to old patrician families. Venice was an aristocratic republic. The government proved remarkably effective because the ruling elite was able to engender a sense of public duty in its young that passed on from one generation—and one century—to the next. Venetian government, because it was at once stable and republican, served as a powerful model to republican theorists in seventeenth- and eighteenth-century Europe.

The city-states, excepting Venice, were not only internally unstable, but they were also constantly at war with one another. By the middle of the fifteenth century, however, five major powers had emerged from the fighting: the kingdom of Naples and Sicily in the south; the Papal States, where the popes had built up, bit by bit, a territory running across the center of the Italian peninsula; and in the north the city-states of Florence, Venice, and Milan. In 1454 these five powers, largely through the efforts of Cosimo de' Medici, concluded the Peace of Lodi. For the next forty years they were relatively peaceful, until the French king Charles VIII invaded northern Italy in 1494.

The Peace of Lodi endured so long because of diplomacy. The essential techniques of modern diplomacy were worked out and applied in the second half of the fifteenth century in Italy. The practices of establishing embassies with ambassadors, sending and analyzing intelligence reports, consulting and negotiating during emergencies, and forming alliances all developed during this period. Some historians also see this time in Italian history as the seedbed for the notion of balance of power—a pattern that eventually became fundamental to the diplomacy of all Europe. Later, in the early modern period, European governments formed alliances so that no single state or group of allied states could dominate the Continent. Some elements of this balance of power were anticipated in the struggles among the Italian city-states.

Renaissance Society

Paralleling the new developments in relations among city-states was the new way of life emerging within the city-states. Prosperous merchants played a leading role in the political and cultural life of the city. With the expansion of commerce and industry, the feudal values of birth, military prowess, and a fixed hierarchy of lords and vassals decayed in favor of ambition and individual achievement, whether at court, in the counting house, or inside the artist's studio. Not that the old feudal chivalric code was destroyed—rather, it was transformed to serve different purposes.

The new urban, commercial oligarchies could not justify their power in the old way, through heredity. Moreover, they had to function within the inherently unstable political climate of the city-states. Faced with this dual problem, the oligarchs fell back on the feudal idea of honor and developed elaborate codes. These codes differed in significant ways from their medieval antecedents. First came a depreciation (although never a complete elimination) of birth as a basis of merit, with a corresponding emphasis on effort, talent, and (in the case of the artist) creative genius. Second, honor was no longer defined in narrow, largely military terms, but was expanded to include both the civic and courtly virtues of the worthy citizen and courtier and the artistic achievement of the painter, sculptor, architect, and poet.

The new code did, however, remain elitist and even aristocratic. Indeed, because of their very newness and insecurity, the new oligarchs of the

Renaissance were all the more anxious to adopt the aristocratic outlook of the old nobility. The *nouveaux riches* (new rich) aped the feudal aristocracy in dress and manners, even as they accommodated the code of knightly chivalry to the demands of a new urban and commercial culture. Renaissance society was a highly unstable compound of old and new.

Marriage and Family Life   City life profoundly altered family structure, marriage patterns, and relations between the sexes. Elsewhere in Europe most people still lived on the land and tended to marry early in order to produce large families to work the fields. But in cities, early marriage could be a liability for a man who was attempting to make his fortune. The results were that older men married young brides, which meant that wives usually outlived their husbands. Because a widow inherited her husband's property, she was not pressed to remarry, and she brought up her children in a single-parent household.

The large number of single, relatively prosperous, and leisured adults probably explains why Renaissance cities were notorious for sodomy, prostitution, and triangles involving an older husband, a young wife, and a young lover. Such sexual behavior was encouraged by the relative anonymity of the large cities and by the constant influx of young men of talent from the country districts.

Single-parent households might also account for the high incidence of homosexuality during the Renaissance. Historian David Herlihy maintains that sons became attached to their mothers in the absence of their fathers and their heterosexual development was stifled. Whether one accepts this Freudian interpretation or not, Herlihy's other conclusion has much to recommend it: that so many women were responsible for nurturing their children may have encouraged the development of the Renaissance idea of a gentleman, which emphasized civility, courtliness, and an appreciation of art, literature, and the feminine graces.

Whatever the effect on their sons, upper-class women enjoyed greater freedom in greater numbers than they had since the Fall of Rome. If they were married, they had the income to pursue pleasure in the form of clothes, conversation, and ro-

Michelangelo (1475–1564): Study for the Battle of Cascina. Although a Neo-Platonist who believed that the soul was trapped within the human body, Michelangelo found the human form to be the measure of all things. His cosmic ceiling fresco in the Sistine Chapel at the Vatican Palace and his floor plan for St. Peter's Church in Rome can be called organic; they are as articulated as a perfect human form. (*Reproduced by Courtesy of the Trustees of the British Museum*)

mance. If a well-to-do husband died while his wife was still young, she had no financial reasons to remarry. She was then free, to a degree previously unknown, to go her own way.

Patronage of the Arts   Members of the urban upper class became patrons of the arts, providing funds to support promising artists and writers. Urban patricians whose wealth was based on commerce and banking, not land, had become dominant in both republican Florence and despotic Milan. Unable to claim power by birth or to rely on traditional loyalties, they looked to culture to provide the trappings and justification of power.

For the newly rich, art could serve a political function. In its sheer magnificence, art could manifest power and cast that spell over subjects or citizens that all governments must depend on to some extent. Art could also serve as a focus of civic pride and patriotism, just as literature could (see page 267). Just as they contended on the battlefield, insecure rulers competed for art and artists to bolster their egos. Art became a desirable political investment, especially when, in the fifteenth century, economic investments were not offering as much return as they had a century or two before. The popes, too, invested in art. Having lost the battle for temporal dominion in Europe, the papacy concentrated on increasing its direct dominion in Italy by consolidating and expanding the Papal States. As an adjunct to this policy, the popes heaped wealth on artists to enhance their own papal prestige and perhaps to recover some of their shattered self-esteem. So the popes became the most lavish patrons of all, as the works of Michelangelo, Botticelli, and Raphael testify.

The result of this new patronage by popes and patricians was an explosion of artistic creativity. The amount and especially the nature of this patronage also helped to shape both art and the artist. Portraiture became a separate genre for the first time since antiquity and was developed much further than ever before. Patrician rivalry and insecurity of status, fed by the Renaissance ethic of achievement and reward, produced a scramble for honor and reputation. This pursuit fostered the desire to be memorialized in a painting, if not in a sculpture. A painter like Titian was in great demand.

The great artists emerged as famous men by virtue of their exercise of brush and chisel. In the Middle Ages, artists had been regarded as craftsmen who did lowly (manual) labor and who, as a result, were to be accorded little if any status. Indeed, they remained anonymous for the most part. But the unparalleled Renaissance demand for art brought artists public recognition for the first time. They enjoyed this status until the Industrial Revolution of the eighteenth century, when art once more depreciated in value. Artistic fame did not come without effort, and the drive for it, stimulated again by the Renaissance ethos of competition and by the humanist ethic, may have spurred artists to greater creative achievements than might otherwise have developed.

Secularism Renaissance society was marked by a growing secular outlook. Intrigued by the active life of the city and eager to enjoy the worldly pleasures that their money could obtain, wealthy merchants and bankers moved away from the medieval preoccupation with salvation. To be sure, they were neither nonbelievers nor atheists, but increasingly religion had to compete with worldly concerns. Consequently, members of the urban upper class paid religion less heed, or at least did not allow it to interfere with their quest for the full life. The challenge and pleasure of living well in this world seemed more exciting than the promise of heaven. This outlook found concrete expression in Renaissance art and literature.

Individualism Individualism was another hallmark of Renaissance society. Urban life released people of wealth and talent from the old constraints of manor and church. The urban elite sought to assert their own personalities, to discover and to express their own peculiar feelings, to demonstrate their unique talents, to win fame and glory, and to fulfill their ambitions. This Renaissance ideal was explicitly elitist. It applied only to the few, entirely disregarding the masses; it valued what was distinctive and superior in an individual, not what was common to all; it was concerned with the distinctions of the few, not the needs or rights of the many. Individualism became deeply embedded in the Western soul and was expressed by artists who sought to capture individual character, by explorers who ventured into uncharted seas, by conquerors who carved out empires in the New World, and by merchant-capitalists who amassed fortunes.

The Renaissance Outlook: Humanism and Secular Politics

Humanism

The most characteristic intellectual movement of the Renaissance was *humanism,* an educational and cultural program based on the study of ancient Greek and Roman literature. The humanist attitude toward antiquity differed from that of medieval scholars. Medieval scholars sought to fit classical learning into a Christian world-view. Renaissance humanists, in contrast, did not subordinate the classics to the requirements of Christian doctrines; rather, they valued ancient literature for its own sake—for its clear and graceful style, for its insights into human nature. From the ancient classics, humanists expected to learn much that could not be provided by medieval writings—how to live well in this world and how to perform one's civic duties, for example. For the humanists the classics were a guide to the good life, the active life. To achieve self-cultivation, to write well, to speak well, and to live well, it was necessary to know the classics. In contrast to scholastic philosophers who used Greek philosophy to prove the truth of Christian doctrines, Italian humanists used classical learning to nourish their new interest in a worldly life.

Whereas medieval scholars were familiar with only some ancient Latin writers, Renaissance humanists restored to circulation every Roman work that could be found. Similarly, whereas knowledge of Greek was very rare in Latin Christendom during the Middle Ages, Renaissance humanists increasingly cultivated the study of Greek in order to read Homer, Demosthenes, Plato, and other ancients in the original.

Although predominantly a secular movement, Italian humanism was not un-Christian. True, humanists often treated moral problems in a purely secular manner, but when they did deal with religious and theological questions, they did not challenge Christian belief or question the validity of the Bible. They did, however, attack scholasticism for its hairsplitting arguments and preoccupation with trivial questions. They stressed instead a purer form of Christianity based on the direct study of the Bible and writings by the church fathers.

A principal source of humanism was the study of law that flourished in the thirteenth and fourteenth centuries in Bologna, Padua, and Ravenna. Not only did students learn the law, they also learned rhetoric—how to argue and how to speak. In these adjuncts to legal study lie some origins of humanism. Using classical Roman models for their arguments, teachers and students went beyond their textbook exercises to make comments on contemporary political issues. Here was the earliest regular use of classical sources to make a judgment or to point to a moral for the present. The Roman classics in the hands of the legists and rhetoricians became source books for the defense of liberty and independence, first against emperors and popes and later against the threat of homegrown despots. So well developed did this tradition become that it eventually outgrew the bounds of the legal studies where it was first nurtured and took the form of a separate enterprise. Men of letters wrote chronicles of their cities, glorifying the historical struggle against tyranny.

One of the earliest examples of this development is Boncompagno da Signa's account of *The Siege of Ancona,* probably written between 1201 and 1202. A speech in praise of liberty forms the centerpiece of the story. An elderly patriot addresses the assembled people of the city of Ancona at a difficult moment during the siege. Food is running short, and the citizens have begun to despair. The old man persuades them that they must never give up fighting for the preservation of liberty.

An early humanist, sometimes called the father of humanism, was Petrarch (1304–1374). Petrarch and his followers carried the recovery of the classics further by making a systematic attempt to discover the classical roots of medieval Italian rhetoric. Petrarch's own efforts to learn Greek were largely unsuccessful, but by encouraging his students to master the ancient tongue, he advanced humanist learning. Petrarch was particularly drawn to Cicero, the ancient Roman orator. Following the example of Cicero, Petrarch insisted that education should consist not only of learning and knowing things, but also of learning how to communicate one's knowledge and how to use it for the public good. Therefore, the emphasis in education should be on rhetoric and moral philosophy, wisdom combined with eloquence. This was the key to virtue in the ruler, the citizen, and the republic. Petrarch helped to make Ciceronian values dominant among the humanists. His followers set up schools to inculcate the new Ciceronian educational ideal.

Implicit in the humanist educational ideal was a radical transformation of the Christian idea of men and women. According to the medieval (Augustinian) view, men and women were not only incapable of attaining excellence through their own efforts and talents, but it was wrong and sinful for them even to try. Human beings were completely subject to divine will. In contrast, the humanists, recalling the classical Greek concept of *areté*, made the achievement of excellence through individual striving the end not only of education but of life itself. Because individuals were capable of this goal, moreover, it was their duty to pursue it as the end of life. The pursuit was not effortless; indeed, it took extraordinary energy and skill.

People, then, were capable of excellence in every sphere and duty-bound to make the effort. This emphasis on human creative powers was one of the most characteristic and influential doctrines of the Renaissance. A classic expression of it is found in the *Oration on the Dignity of Man* (1486) by Giovanni Pico della Mirandola (1463–1494). Man, said Pico, has the freedom to shape his own life. Pico has God say to man: "We have made you a creature" such that "you may, as the free and proud shaper of your own being, fashion yourself in the form you may prefer."[1]

Pico also spelled out another implication of man's duty to realize his potential: through his own exertions, man can come to understand and control nature. One of the new and powerful Renaissance images of man was as the *magus,* the magician. The vision of the mastery of nature continued to inspire experimentalists, like Francis Bacon, and natural philosophers, like Robert Boyle and Isaac Newton, until at least the early eighteenth century. A major psychological driving force of the Scientific Revolution, this vision

stemmed in large part from the philosophy of Italian humanists like Pico.

The attack on the medieval scholastics was implicit in the humanist educational ideal. From the humanist perspective, scholasticism failed not only because its terms and Latin usage were barbarous but also because it did not provide useful knowledge. This humanist emphasis on the uses of knowledge also offered a stimulus to science and art.

So hostile were the humanists to all things scholastic and medieval that they reversed the prevailing view of history. The Christian view saw history as a simple unfolding of God's will and providence. The humanists stressed the importance of human actions and human wills in history—of people as active participants in the shaping of events. The humanists rejected the providentialist scheme in favor of a cyclical view deriving from the ancients, particularly Aristotle, Polybius, and Cicero. History alternated between times of darkness and times of light, of ignorance and illumination, of decline and rebirth.

This cyclical view allowed the humanists to characterize the epoch preceding their own as a period of declension from classical heights. Equally, it allowed them to see themselves and their own time as representing a period of rebirth, the recovery of classical wisdom and ideals. On the basis of this cyclical view, the humanists invented the notion of the Middle Ages as that period separating the ancient world from their own by a gulf of darkness. To the humanists, then, we owe the current periodization of history into ancient, medieval, and modern. There was also an element in the humanist view of today's idea of progress: they dared to think that they, "the moderns," might even surpass the ancient glories of Greece and Rome.

The humanist emphasis on historical scholarship yielded a method of critical inquiry that in the right hands could help to undermine traditional loyalties and institutions. The work of Lorenzo Valla (c. 1407–1457) provides the clearest example of this trend. Educated as a classicist, Valla trained the guns of critical scholarship on the papacy in his most famous work, *Declamation Concerning the False Decretals of Constantine.* The papal claim to temporal authority rested on a document that purported to verify the so-called Donation of Constantine, whereby when Emperor Constantine moved the capital of the Roman Empire to Constantinople in the fourth century, he bestowed on the pope dominion over the entire western Empire. But Valla proved that the document was based on an eighth-century forgery because the language at certain points was unknown in Constantine's own time and did not come into use until much later.

Also embedded in the humanist re-evaluation of individual potential was a new appreciation of the moral significance of work. For the humanist the honor, fame, and even glory bestowed by one's city or patron for meritorious deeds was the ultimate reward for effort. The humanist pursuit of praise and reputation became something of a Renaissance cult.

In fourteenth- and fifteenth-century republican Florence, at least until the Medicis took control, Petrarchan humanism was not meant for a court elite. Humanism was meant rather as a civic idea—to educate and inform citizens so that they could contribute to the common good to the greatest possible extent. In this sense, humanism was put in the service of republican values and the republican cause, and the mixture of the two is what has come to be called *civic humanism* by recent historians. This civic ideal developed furthest in the Florentine republic.

By the second half of the fifteenth century, as the Medici gained increasing control, the civic ideal was being replaced by another that was more fitting to the times, the ideal of princely rule. This princely ideal borrowed much from civic humanism, even though it was directed toward princes and courtiers and not toward citizens. The emphasis on the pursuit of virtue and honor was still there, however. Like the ideal gentleman, the ideal prince evolved through a humanistic education that would prepare him for the struggle between virtue and fortune so that virtue would prove victorious.

But the similarities between the civic and princely ideals were not as important as the differences. The aim of princely rule was no longer liberty but peace and security. The best means to this end was no longer a republic but hereditary monarchy. This new princely ideal was reflected in

Lorenzo de' Medici. The Medici preferred to wield power behind the scenes through secret alliances and intrigue. Lorenzo, who became head of the family in his teens, fostered the notion of the good citizen; this portrait of him is by Agnolo Bronzino. *(Scala/Art Resource)*

a new spate of advice books, the most influential of which was *The Book of the Courtier*, written between 1513 and 1518 by Baldassare Castiglione (1478–1529). These books promoted the notion that the ideal ruler should be universally talented and skillful, equally commanding on the battlefield, at court, and in the state, and virtuous throughout. These advice books, especially Castiglione's, were to serve as indispensable handbooks for courtiers and would-be gentlemen not only in Renaissance Italy, but throughout Europe. This ideal held sway until well into the seventeenth century, when the type finally began to give way before a new idea of virtue and virtuosity.

A Revolution in Political Thought

One advice book transcended the class of these works: *The Prince,* written in 1513 by the Florentine Niccolò Machiavelli (1469–1527). Machiavelli's book offered a critique of the humanist ideal of princely rule and in so doing made some fundamental contributions to political theory. Indeed, Machiavelli may be called the first major modern political thinker. To Machiavelli the humanist ideal was naive in its insistence on the prince's virtues and eloquence to the exclusion of all other considerations. He attacked the medieval and humanist tradition of theoretical politics:

> *Since my intention is to say something that will prove of practical use to the inquirer, I have thought it proper to represent things as they are in real truth, rather than as they are imagined. Many have dreamed up republics and principalities which have never in truth been known to exist; the gulf between how one should live and how one does live is so wide that a man who neglects what is actually done for what should be done learns the way to self-destruction.*[2]

Politics, Machiavelli argued, requires the rational deployment of force as well as, and even prior to, the exercise of virtue.

On this point, Machiavelli's advice is quite specific. He wrote *The Prince* in part as a plea. Since 1494, Italy had fallen prey to France and Spain. Their great royal armies overpowered the mercenary armies of the city-states and went on to lay waste to Italy in their struggle for domination of the peninsula. To prevent this, Machiavelli said, the Italians should unite behind a leader—the prince—whose first act would be to disband the mercenaries and forge a new citizen army, worthy of the glorious Roman past and capable of repelling the "barbarian" invasion. "Mercenaries," Machiavelli claimed, "are useless and dangerous."

They are useless because "there is no . . . inducement to keep them on the field apart from the little they are paid, and this is not enough to make them want to die for you." And they are dangerous because their leaders, the infamous *condottieri,* "are anxious to advance their own greatness" at the expense of the city-state. Reliance on mercenaries was the sole cause of "the present ruin of Italy,"[3] and the cure lay in the creation of a national militia, led by a prince.

This prince had to be both wily and virtuous—not (as humanists had said) virtuous alone: "The fact is that a man who wants to act virtuously in every way necessarily comes to grief among so many who are not virtuous." So Machiavelli scandalized Christian Europe by asserting that "if a prince wants to maintain his rule he must learn how not to be virtuous, and to make use of this or not according to his need."[4] Even more shocking, the prince must know how to dissemble, that is, to make all his actions appear virtuous, whether they are so or not. In ironic parody of conventional advice-book wisdom, Machiavelli argued that a ruler must cultivate a *reputation* for virtue rather than virtue itself. In this connection Machiavelli arrived at a fundamental political truth—that politics (and especially the relationship between ruler and ruled) being what it is, the road to success for the prince lies in dissimulation. "Everyone sees what you appear to be, few experience what you really are. And those few dare not [contradict] the many who are backed by the majesty of the state."[5] Here again the Renaissance arrived at modernity.

Machiavelli broke with both the medieval and the humanist traditions of political thought. He was a secularist who tried to understand and explain the state without recourse to Christian teachings. Influenced by classical thought, especially the works of Livy, he rejected the prevailing view that the state is God's creation and that the ruler should base his policies on Christian moral principles. For Machiavelli, religion was not the foundation for politics but merely a useful tool in the prince's struggle for success. The prince might even dissemble, if he thought he had to, in matters of the faith, by appearing pious, whether or not he was, and by playing on and exploiting the piety of his subjects.

Early Modern Europe: From Renaissance to Enlightenment

Brunelleschi (1377–1446): Dome of the Florence Cathedral. Brunelleschi spent years drawing the ruins of classical Rome. In the process, he rediscovered the art of drawing in true perspective. The dome of the Florence Cathedral was designed to recapture the splendor of classical domed structures, such as the Pantheon. (*Management James Sawders, Nutley, N.J.*)

Renaissance Art

The most graphic image of the Renaissance is conveyed through its art, particularly architecture, sculpture, and painting. Renaissance examples of all three art forms reflect a style that stressed proportion, balance, and harmony. These artistic values were achieved through a new, revolutionary conceptualization of space and spatial relations. Renaissance art also reflects to a considerable extent the values of Renaissance humanism, a return to classical models in architecture, to the rendering of the nude human figure, and to a heroic vision of human beings.

Medieval art sought to represent spiritual aspiration; the world was a veil merely hinting at the other perfect and eternal world. Renaissance art did not stop expressing spiritual aspiration, but its setting and character differ altogether. This world is no longer a veil, but becomes the *place* where people live, act, and worship. The reference is less to the other world and more to this world, and people are treated as creatures who find their spiritual destiny as they fulfill their human one.

The Middle Ages had produced a distinctive art known as the Gothic. By the fourteenth and fifteenth centuries, Gothic art had evolved into what is known as the International Style, characterized by careful drawing, flowing and delicate lines, harmonious composition, and delightful naturalistic detail.

Renaissance art at its most distinctive represents a conscious revolt against this late Gothic trend. This revolt produced revolutionary discoveries that served as the foundation of Western art up to this century. In art, as in philosophy, the Florentines played a leading role in this esthetic transformation. They, more than anyone else, were responsible for the way artists saw and drew for centuries and for the way most Western people still see or want to see.

Early Renaissance Art

The first major contributor to Renaissance painting was the Florentine painter Giotto (c. 1276–1337). Borrowing from Byzantine painting, he created figures modeled by alterations in light and shade. He also developed several techniques of perspective, representing three-dimensional figures and objects in two-dimensional surfaces so that they appear to stand in space. Giotto's figures look remarkably alive (see page 263). They are drawn and arranged in space to tell a story, and the expressions they wear and the illusion of movement they convey heighten the dramatic effect. Giotto's best works were *frescoes,* wall paintings painted while the plaster was still wet, or *fresh.* Lionized in his own day, Giotto had no immediate successors, and his ideas were not taken up and developed further for almost a century.

By the early fifteenth century the revival of classical learning had begun in earnest. In Florence it had its artistic counterpart among a circle of architects, painters, and sculptors who sought to revive classical art. The leader of this group was an architect, Filippo Brunelleschi (1377–1446). He abandoned Gothic prescriptions altogether and designed churches (Florence Cathedral, page 271, for instance) reflecting classical models. To him, we also owe a scientific discovery of the first importance in the history of art: the rules of perspective. Giotto had revived the ancient technique of foreshortening; Brunelleschi completed the discovery by rendering perspective in mathematical terms. Brunelleschi's devotion to ancient models and his new tool of mathematical perspective set the stage for the further development of Renaissance painting.

Brunelleschi's young Florentine friend Masaccio (1401–1428) took up the challenge. Faithful to the new rules of perspective, Masaccio was also concerned with painting statuesque figures and endowing his paintings with a grandeur and simplicity whose inspiration is classical. Perspective came with all the force of religious revelation.

Early Renaissance artists were dedicated to representing things as they are, or at least as they are seen to be. Part of the inspiration for this was also classical. The ancient ideal of beauty was the beautiful nude. Renaissance admiration for ancient art meant that artists for the first time since the Fall of Rome studied anatomy; they learned to draw the human form by having models pose for them, a practice fundamental to artistic training to this day. Another member of Brunelleschi's circle, the Florentine sculptor Donatello (1386–1466), also showed renewed interest in the human form and conscious rejection of Gothic taste.

Another approach to the observation of nature—besides the imitation of the ancients—developed in northern Europe, principally in the Netherlands. Its original exponent was Jan van Eyck (c. 1390—1441), who worked mostly in what is now Belgium. Van Eyck's art developed out of the International Style. Within that style there was an interest in the faithful depiction of objects and creatures in the natural world. Van Eyck carried this tendency so far that it became the principal aim of his art: his pictures are like photographs in their infinitely scrupulous attention to the way things look. Unlike his contemporaries in Florence, van Eyck subordinated

Botticelli (1444–1510): The Birth of Venus. Botticelli was a member of the Florentine group of Neo-Platonists. They tried to harmonize Greco-Roman ideals with those of Christianity. The nude goddess is Venus, but the modest tilt of the head is the traditional pose of the Virgin Mary. To Botticelli the beauty of Venus and the purity of Mary were identical. (*Alinari/Art Resource*)

accuracy and perspective to appearance—the way things look—and showed no interest in classical models. In his concern to paint what he saw, he also developed oil painting. At that time, most paints were egg-based, but oil-based paints allowed him to obtain more lifelike and virtuoso effects. The technique spread quickly to Italy, with astonishing results.

Late Renaissance Art

The use of perspective posed a fundamental problem for Renaissance painters: how to reconcile perspective with composition—dramatic arrangement—and the search for harmony. A chief interest of later fifteenth-century Italian painting lay in how artists tackled this problem.

Among the Florentine artists of the second half of the fifteenth century who strove for a solution of this question was the painter Sandro Botticelli (c. 1444–1510). One of his most famous pictures depicts not a Christian legend but a classical myth—*The Birth of Venus*. Representing, as it does, the way that beauty came into the world, this painting is another expression of the Renaissance desire to recover the lost wisdom of the ancients. Botticelli succeeded in rendering a perfectly harmonious pattern—but at the cost of sacrificing solidity and anatomical correctness. In *The Birth of Venus*, what the viewer notices are the graceful, flowing lines that unify and vivify the painting. Even the liberties that Botticelli took with nature—for example, the unnatural proportions of Venus's neck and shoulders—enhance the esthetic outcome.

Leonardo da Vinci (1452–1519): Mona Lisa.
Leonardo da Vinci's paintings are few in number and difficult to interpret. Psychological mystery characterizes the *Mona Lisa*. Poets, essayists, and art historians have not fully explained her smile. Like most of his paintings, it is in an unfinished state. (*Louvre/Cliché des Musées Nationaux*)

New approaches to this problem of perspective and composition were developed by the three greatest artists of the Renaissance—Leonardo da Vinci (1452–1519), Michelangelo Buonarroti (1475–1564), and Raphael Santi (1483–1520). All of them were closely associated with Florence, and all of them were contemporaries.

Leonardo was a scientist and engineer as well as a great artist. He was an expert at fortifications and gunnery, an inventor, an anatomist, and a naturalist. He brought this close observation of nature to his paintings and combined it with powerful psychological insight to produce works that although few in number are of unsurpassed genius. Among the most important of these are *The Last Supper, St. John,* and *La Gioconda* (the Mona Lisa). The Mona Lisa is an example of an artistic invention of Leonardo's—what the Italians call *sfumato.* Leonardo left the outlines of the face a little vague and shadowy; this freed it of any wooden quality, which more exact drawing would impart, and thus made it more lifelike and mysterious. Here was a major breakthrough in solving the problem of perspective. The artist must not be too exact and rigid in adhering to the rules; he must introduce a correcting softness and atmosphere to achieve a reconciliation between perspective and the demands of design.

Michelangelo's creation of artistic harmony derived from a mastery of anatomy and drawing. His model in painting came from sculpture; his paintings are sculpted drawings (see page 265). He was of course a sculptor of the highest genius whose approach to his art was poetic and visionary. Instead of trying to impose form on marble, he thought of sculpting as releasing the form from the rock. Among his greatest sculptures are *David, Moses,* and *The Dying Slave.* Michelangelo was also an architect and, patronized by the pope, he designed the dome of the new St. Peter's basilica in Rome. But perhaps his most stupendous work was the ceiling of the Sistine Chapel in the Vatican, commissioned by Pope Julius II. In four years, working with little assistance, Michelangelo covered the empty space with the most monumental sculpted pictures ever painted, pictures that summarize the Old Testament story. The Creation of Adam is the most famous of these superlative frescoes.

Raphael, the last of these three artistic giants, was the complete master of design in painting. His balanced compositions sacrifice nothing to perspective. Rather, perspective becomes just another tool, along with *sfumato* and mathematical proportion, for achieving harmony. Raphael is especially famous for the sweetness of his Madonnas.

But he was capable of painting other subjects and of conveying other moods as well, as his portrait of his patron, *Pope Leo X with Two Cardinals*, reveals.

Renaissance painting came late to Venice, but when it arrived in the late fifteenth and early sixteenth centuries, it produced a tradition of sustained inventiveness whose keynote was the handling of color. Giovanni Bellini (c. 1431–1516) may be said to have discovered color as a tool of composition. He borrowed perspective from Florentine painting, but he used color too as a principal means of achieving unity and harmony.

This use of color was extended in a revolutionary direction by another Venetian, Giorgione (c. 1478–1510), to whom only five paintings can be ascribed with absolute certainty. Until Giorgione, landscape had functioned primarily as decorative and sometimes imaginative background, as in the Mona Lisa. But Giorgione made landscape a part of the subject of his paintings and, through his handling of light and color, used it to unify and integrate his canvases. According to art historian E. H. Gombrich, "This was almost as big a step forward . . . as the invention of perspective had been."[6] Perhaps Giorgione's greatest experiment in this respect was *The Tempest*.

The bewitching effects of color were carried to their fullest development by Titian (c. 1477–1576), a leading Venetian painter. He was a complete professional for whom the brushstroke was all. His portraits are magical in their ability to capture both features and personality. Titian also defied artistic convention by deliberately using unbalanced groups of figures and by achieving harmony not through positioning but by means of light and color.

Raphael (1483–1520): Pope Leo X and Two Cardinals. Raphael is often called the great synthesizer because he emulated Michelangelo in *The School of Athens* and Leonardo da Vinci in many paintings of the Madonna and the Christ child. His portraits of individual statesmen, like this one of Pope Leo X with Cardinals Giulio de' Medici and Luigi de' Rossi, are among his most perceptive works psychologically. (*Alinari/Art Resource*)

The Spread of the Renaissance

The Renaissance spread to Germany, France, England, and Spain in the late fifteenth and the sixteenth centuries. In its migration northward, Renaissance culture adapted itself to conditions unknown in Italy, such as the growth of the monarchical state and the strength of lay piety. In England, France, and Spain, Renaissance culture tended to be court-centered and hence antirepublican, as it was, for instance, under Francis I in France and Elizabeth I in England. In Germany and the Rhineland, no monarchical state existed, but a vital tradition of lay piety was present in the Low Countries. For example, the Brethren of the Common Life was a lay movement emphasizing education and practical piety. Intensely Christian and at the same time anticlerical, the people in such lay movements found in Renaissance culture tools for sharpening their wits against the clergy— not to undermine the faith but rather to restore it to its apostolic purity.

Thus, northern humanists were profoundly devoted to ancient learning, just as the humanists in Italy had been. But nothing in northern humanism compares to the paganizing trend associated with the Italian Renaissance. The northerners were chiefly interested in the problem of the ancient church and, in particular, the question of what constituted original Christianity. They sought a model in light of which they might reform the corrupted church of their own time.

Everywhere, two factors operated to accelerate the spread of Renaissance culture after 1450: growing prosperity and the printing press. Prosperity, brought on by peace and the decline of famine and plague, led to the founding of schools and colleges. The sons (women were excluded) of gentlemen and merchants were sent to school to receive a humanistic education imported from Italy. The purpose of such education was to prepare men for a career in the church or the civil service of the expanding state and for acceptance into higher social spheres.

Printing with movable type, which was invented in the middle of the fifteenth century, quickened the spread of Renaissance ideas. Back in the Late Middle Ages the West had learned, through the Muslims from the Chinese, of printing, paper, and ink. However, in this block printing process, a new block had to be carved from wood for each new impression, and the block was discarded as unusable as soon as a slightly different impression was needed. About 1445, Johann Gutenberg (c. 1398–1468) and other printers in Mainz in the Rhineland invented movable metal type to replace the cumbersome blocks. It was possible to use and reuse the separate pieces of type, as long as the metal in which they were cast did not wear down, simply by arranging them in the desired order. This invention made books, and hence ideas, more quickly available, cheaper, and

more numerous than ever before; it also made literacy easier to achieve. Printing provided a surer basis for scholarship and prevented the further corruption of texts through hand copying. By giving all scholars the same text to work from, it made progress in critical scholarship and science faster and more reliable.

Humanism outside Italy was less concerned with the revival of classical values than with the reform of Christianity and society through a program of Christian humanism that stressed the human capacity for knowledge and goodness. The Christian humanists cultivated the new arts of rhetoric and history, as well as the classical languages—Latin, Greek, and Hebrew. But the ultimate purpose of these pursuits was more religious than it had been in Italy, where secular interests predominated.

Erasmian Humanism

To Erasmus (c. 1466–1536) belongs the credit for making Renaissance humanism an international movement. He was educated in the Netherlands by the Brethren of the Common Life, which was one of the most advanced religious movements of the age, combining mystical piety with rigorous humanist pedagogy. Erasmus traveled throughout Europe as a humanist educator and biblical scholar. Like other Christian humanists, Erasmus trusted the power of words and used his pen to attack scholastic theology and clerical abuses and to promote his philosophy of Christ. His weapon was satire, and his *Praise of Folly* and *Colloquies* won him a reputation for acid wit vented at the expense of conventional religion.

True religion, Erasmus argued, does not depend on dogma, ritual, or clerical power. Rather it is revealed clearly and simply in the Bible and therefore is directly accessible to all people, from the wise and great to the poor and humble. Nor is true religion opposed to nature. Rather, people are naturally capable of both apprehending and living according to the good as set out in the Scriptures. A perfect harmony between human nature and true religion allows humanity to attain, if not perfection, at least the next best thing, peace and happiness in this life.

This clear but quiet voice was drowned out by the storms of the Reformation (see Chapter 14), and the Erasmian emphasis on the individual's natural capacities could not hold its own before a renewed emphasis on human sinfulness and dogmatic theology. Erasmus was caught in the middle and condemned on all sides; for him, the Reformation was both a personal and historical tragedy. He had worked for peace and unity and was treated to a spectacle of war and fragmentation. Erasmian humanism, however, survived these horrors as an ideal, and during the next two centuries, whenever thinkers sought toleration and rational religion (Rabelais and Montaigne, for instance), they looked back to Erasmus for inspiration.

Germany and France

German and French humanists pursued Christian humanist aims. They used humanist scholarship and language to satirize and vilify medieval scholastic Christianity and to build a purer, more Scriptural Christianity. These northern humanists had great faith in the power of words. The discovery of accurate biblical texts, it was hoped, would lead to a great religious awakening. Protestant reformers, including Martin Luther, relied on humanist scholarship.

French thinkers of the next generation exploited and carried the humanist legacy in more radical directions. Among them, two were outstanding: Michel de Montaigne (1533–1592) and François Rabelais (c. 1494–1553). Both thought and wrote in reaction to the religious wars resulting from the Reformation. In the face of competing religious dogmatisms—Catholic, Protestant, and sectarian—Montaigne advanced a skepticism in which he maintained that one can know little or nothing with certainty. He therefore advocated political quietism and acceptance of Christianity on faith. This skepticism also entailed tolerance. An individual was not fully responsible for his or her beliefs, since they were the product of frail reason and force of circumstance. Thus, people should not be punished for their beliefs. The only ones who deserved to be severely dealt with were the dogmatists in religion, because their certainty

Erasmus by Hans Holbein the Younger (c. 1497–1543). The brilliance and honesty of Erasmus's philosophical treatises endeared him to both conservative Catholic and Protestant reformers. As a humanist and in his pursuit of truth, he travelled freely throughout Europe. (*Louvre/Cliché des Musées Nationaux*)

and self-righteousness flew in the face of a fundamental epistemological fact—that "reason does nothing but go astray in everything, and especially when it meddles with divine things."

Montaigne was not a systematic philosopher but devoted himself to what he could learn by Socratic self-examination, the results of which he set down in his *Essays*. In their urbane and caustic wit and their intense self-absorption, the *Essays* betray a crucial shift in humanist thought that became more pronounced in the next century. Gone is the optimism and emphasis on civic virtue of the High Renaissance. In their place come skepticism and introspection, the attempt to base morality on the self rather than on public values. This shift represented a retreat from the idealism of Renaissance humanism, no doubt produced by the increasing scale and violence of religious war.

Rabelais took a different route from Montaigne's. In response to religious dogmatism, Rabelais asserted the essential goodness of the individual and the right to be free to enjoy the world rather than being bound down, as Calvin later would have it, by fear of a vengeful God. Rabelais's folk-epic, *Gargantua and Pantagruel,* in which he celebrates earthly and earthy life, is the greatest French work of its kind and perhaps the greatest in any literature. Rabelais said that once freed from dogmatic religion, people could, by virtue of their native goodness, build a paradise on earth and disregard the one dreamed up by theologians. In *Gargantua and Pantagruel,* Rabelais imagined a monastery where men and women spend their lives "not in laws, statutes, or rules, but according to their own free will and pleasure." They slept and ate when they desired and learned to "read, write, sing, play upon several musical instruments, and speak five or six . . . languages and compose in them all very quaintly." They observed one rule: "DO WHAT THOU WILT."[7]

Spanish Humanism

Spanish humanism represents a special case. The church hierarchy gained such a tight grip in Spain during the late fifteenth and early sixteenth centuries that it monopolized humanist learning and exploited it for its own repressive purposes. There was little or no room for a dissenting humanist voice such as there was in Germany, France, or England. The mastermind behind this authoritarian Spanish humanism was Cardinal Francisco Jiménez de Cisneros (1436–1517). Jiménez founded the University of Alcalá not far from Madrid for the instruction of the clergy. He also sponsored and published the Complutensian Polyglot Bible with Hebrew, Latin, and Greek texts in parallel columns. Jiménez, like Christian humanists elsewhere, sought the enlightenment of the clergy through a return to the pure sources of religion, and he saw his Polyglot Bible as furnishing a principal means of realizing that goal.

A century after Jiménez, Miguel de Cervantes Saavedra (1547–1616) produced his great novel, *Don Quixote,* in which he satirized the ideals of knighthood and chivalry. Don Quixote, the victim of his own illusions, roams the countryside looking for romance and the chance to prove his knightly worth. To Quixote's servant Sancho Panza, Cervantes assigned the role of pointing up the inanity of his master's quest by always acting prudently and judging according to common sense. Despite his earthy realism, however, Panza must share his master's misfortunes—so much for realism in a world run by men full of illusions. Cervantes's satire is very gentle. That knightly valor was still a valid subject for satire indicates how wedded Spain was even in the early seventeenth century to the conservative values of its crusading past.

English Humanism

Christian humanism in England sharply contrasted to that in Spain. It was developed by secular men in government as much as by clerics, and its objectives were often opposed to authority and tradition. Various Italian humanists came to England during the fifteenth century as bishops, merchants, court physicians, or artists. Englishmen also studied in Italy, especially in Florence, and introduced the serious humanistic study of the classics at Oxford University toward the end of the century.

The most influential humanist of the early English Renaissance was Sir Thomas More (1478–1535), who studied at Oxford. His impact arose from both his writing and his career. Trained as a lawyer, he became a successful civil servant and member of Parliament. His most famous book is *Utopia,* the major utopian treatise to be written in the West since Plato's *Republic* and one of the most original works of the entire Renaissance.

Many humanists had attacked private wealth as the principal source of pride, greed, and human cruelty. But More was the only one to carry this insight to its logical conclusion: in *Utopia,* he called for the elimination of private property. He had too keen a sense of human weakness to think that people could become perfect, but he used *Utopia* to call attention to contemporary abuses and to suggest radical reforms. He exploited the satirical and ironical potential of recent overseas discoveries by setting *Utopia* among a non-Christian people, which made his criticism more caustic and pointed. More succeeded Cardinal Wolsey as lord chancellor under Henry VIII. But when the king broke with the Roman Catholic church, More resigned, unable to reconcile his conscience with the king's rejection of papal supremacy. Three years later, in July 1535, More was executed for treason for refusing to swear an oath acknowledging the king's ecclesiastical supremacy.

William Shakespeare (1564–1616), widely considered the greatest playwright the world has ever produced, gave expression to conventional Renaissance values—honor, heroism, and the struggle against fate and fortune. But there is nothing conventional about Shakespeare's treatment of characters possessed of these virtues. His greatest plays, the tragedies (*King Lear, Julius Caesar,* and others), explore a common theme: men, even heroic men, despite virtue, are able only with the greatest difficulty, if at all, to overcome their human weaknesses. What fascinated Shakespeare was the contradiction between the Renaissance image of nobility, which is often the self-image of Shakespeare's heroes, and man's capacity for evil and self-destruction. Thus Ophelia says of Hamlet, her lover, in the play of the same name:

> O, *what a noble mind is here o'erthrown!*
> *The courtier's, soldier's, scholar's, eye, tongue, sword;*
> *The expectancy and rose of the fair state,*
> *The glass of fashion and the mould of form,*
> *The observ'd of all observers, quite, quite down!*
> [*And*] *I, of ladies most deject and wretched,*
> *That suck'd the honey of his music vows,*
> *Now see that noble and most sovereign reason,*
> *Like sweet bells jangled, out of tune and harsh;*
> *That unmatch'd form and feature of blown youth*
> *Blasted with ecstasy. O, woe is me,*
> *T' have seen what I have seen, see what I see!*[8]

The plays are thus intensely human, so much so that humanism fades into the background. Thus, art transcends doctrine to represent life itself.

The Renaissance and the Modern Age

The Renaissance, then, marks the birth of modernity—in art, in the idea of the individual's role in history and in nature, and in society, politics, war, and diplomacy. Central to this birth is a bold new view of human nature: individuals in all endeavors are free of a given destiny imposed by God from the outside—free to make their own destiny guided only by the example of the past, the force of present circumstances, and the drives of their own inner nature. Individuals, set free from theology, are seen to be the products, and in turn the shapers, of history. Their future is not wholly determined by providence but is partly the work of their own free will.

Within the Italian city-states where the Renaissance was born, rich merchants were at least as important as the church hierarchy and the old nobility. The city-states were almost completely independent because of the weakness of church and empire. So the northern Italians were left free to invent new forms of government in which merchant-oligarchs, humanists, and condottieri played a more important part than the priests and nobles who dominated politics in the rest of Europe. Of course this newness and lack of tradition produced, along with the inventiveness, disorder and violence. Condottieri grabbed power from hapless citizens, and republics gave way to despotism.

But the problems created by novelty and instability demanded solutions, and the wealth of the cities called forth the talent to find them. Commercial wealth and a new politics produced a new culture: Renaissance art and humanism. Talented individuals—scholars, poets, artists, and government officials—returned to classical antiquity, which in any case lay near to hand in Italy and Greece. Ancient models in art, architecture, literature, and philosophy provided the answers to their

Chronology 13.1 The Renaissance

1200–1300	Bologna, Padua, and Ravenna become centers of legal studies
1300–1450	Republicanism reigns in northern Italian city-states
1304–1374	Petrarch, "father of humanism"
1378	The Ciompi revolt in Florence
c. 1407–1457	Lorenzo Valla, author of the *Declamation Concerning the False Decretals of Constantine*
c. 1445	Johann Gutenberg invents movable metal type
1454	The Peace of Lodi is signed
1494	Charles VIII of France invades northern Italy; Pope Julius II commissions frescoes by Michelangelo in the Vatican's Sistine Chapel
1513	Machiavelli writes *The Prince*
1528	*The Courtier,* by Baldassare Castiglione, is published
1535	Sir Thomas More, English humanist and author of *Utopia,* is executed for treason

questions. This return to antiquity also entailed a rejection of the Middle Ages as dark, barbarous, and rude. The humanists clearly preferred the secular learning of ancient Greece and Rome to the clerical learning of the more recent past. The reason for this was obvious: the ancients had the same worldly concerns as the humanists; the scholastics did not.

The revival of antiquity by the humanists did not mean, however, that they identified completely with it. The revival itself was done too self-consciously for that. In the very act of looking back, the humanists differentiated themselves from the past and recognized that they were different. They were in this sense the first modern historians, because they could study and appreciate the past for its own sake and to some degree on its own terms.

In the works of Renaissance artists and thinkers the world was, to a large extent, depicted and explained without reference to a higher supernatural realm of meaning and authority. This is clearly seen in Machiavelli's analysis of politics. Closely associated with this secular element in Renaissance culture was a new realism that beckoned toward the modern outlook. What else is Machiavelli's new politics but a politics of realism, dealing with the world as he finds it rather than as it ought to be? This realism also manifests itself in the realm of art, where mathematical perspective renders the world in its spatial dimension and gives it a solidity and drama that constitute a modern visual and esthetic realism. The sources for both the esthetic and the political realism were the cultural forms of ancient Greece and Rome.

Renaissance humanism exuded a deep confidence in the capacities of able people, instructed in the wisdom of the ancients, to understand and change the world. Renaissance realism, then, was mixed with idealism, and this potent combination departed sharply from the medieval outlook. In place of Christian resignation there grew a willingness to confront life directly and a belief that able humans can succeed even against great odds.

This new confidence is closely related to another distinctive feature of the Renaissance—the cult of the individual. Both prince and painter were motivated in part by the desire to display their talents and to satisfy their ambitions. This individual striving was rewarded and encouraged by the larger society of rich patrons and calculating princes who valued ability. Gone was the medieval Christian emphasis on the virtue of self-denial and the sin of vainglory. Instead, the Renaissance placed the highest value on self-expression and self-fulfillment, on the realization of individual potential, especially of the gifted few. The Renaissance fostered an atmosphere in which talent, even genius, was allowed to flourish. The ideal, at least, was meritocracy.

To be sure, the Renaissance image of the individual and the world, bold and novel, was the exclusive prerogative of a small, well-educated urban elite and did not reach down to include the masses. Nevertheless, the Renaissance set an example of what people might achieve in art and architecture, taste and refinement, education and urban culture. In many fields the Renaissance set the cultural standards of the modern age.

Notes

1. Giovanni Pico della Mirandola, *Oration on the Dignity of Man,* trans. by A. Robert Caponigri (Chicago: Henry Regnery, 1956), p. 7.

2. Niccolò Machiavelli, *The Prince,* trans. by George Bull (Harmondsworth, England: Penguin Books, 1961), pp. 90–91.

3. Ibid., pp. 77–78.

4. Ibid., p. 91.

5. Ibid., p. 101.

6. E. H. Gombrich, *The Story of Art,* 12th ed. (London: Phaidon, 1972), p. 250.

7. François Rabelais, *Gargantua and Pantagruel,* trans. by Sir Thomas Urquhart (1883), bk. I, ch. 57.

8. From *Hamlet, Prince of Denmark,* in *The Complete Plays and Poems of William Shakespeare,* ed. by William Allan Neilson and Charles Jarvis Hill (Boston: Houghton Mifflin, 1942), p. 1067.

Suggested Reading

Baron, Hans, *The Crisis of the Early Italian Renaissance* (1966). An influential interpretation of the origins of civic humanism.

Bouwsma, William J., *Venice and the Defense of Republican Liberty* (1968). The Venetian origins of Western republicanism.

Brucker, Gene A., *Renaissance Florence* (rev. ed., 1983). An excellent analysis of the city's physical character, its economic and social structure, its political and religious life, and its cultural achievements.

Burckhardt, Jacob, *The Civilization of the Renaissance in Italy* (1860). 2 vols. (1958). The first major interpretative synthesis of the Renaissance; still an essential resource.

Burke, Peter, *Popular Culture in Early Modern Europe* (1978). A fascinating account of the social underside from the Renaissance to the French Revolution.

Caspari, Fritz, *Humanism and the Social Order in Tudor England* (1968). Relations between thought and society.

Eisenstein, Elizabeth, *The Printing Press as an Agent of Change,* 2 vols. (1978). The definitive treatment—informative, argumentative, and suggestive.

Gilbert, Felix, *Machiavelli and Guicciardini* (1965). Florentine political and historical writing in the fifteenth and early sixteenth centuries.

Ginzburg, Carlo, *The Cheese and the Worms* (1982). A lively, penetrating account of the cosmos as seen from the point of view of a sixteenth-century Italian miller.

Harbison, E. Harris, *The Christian Scholar in the Age of Reformation* (1956). Relations between humanism and Protestantism.

Huizinga, Johan, *Erasmus and the Age of Reformation* (1957). A readable study of the greatest northern European humanist.

Maclean, Ian, *The Renaissance Notion of Woman* (1980). The birth of modern ideas and attitudes regarding women.

Pocock, J. G. A., *The Machiavellian Moment* (1975). A heady adventure in the history of ideas, tracing republicanism from its Italian Renaissance origins through the English and American revolutions.

Pullan, Brian S., *A History of Early Renaissance Italy* (1973). A solid, brief account.

Skinner, Quentin, *The Foundations of Modern Political Thought*, 2 vols. (1978). The first volume covers the Renaissance; highly informed.

Wittkower, R., *Architectural Principles in the Age of Humanism* (1952). Architecture as the expression of Renaissance values and ideas.

Review Questions

1. What does the word *renaissance* mean, and where and when did the Renaissance first occur?

2. What is the connection between the Renaissance and the Middle Ages? What special conditions gave rise to the Italian Renaissance?

3. Which forms of government predominated among the Italian city-states? In the end, which was the most successful? Why?

4. In what ways did the social patterns of Renaissance Italy depart from those of the rest of Europe?

5. What are some connections between Renaissance society and Renaissance art and culture?

6. What is humanism and how did it begin? What did the humanists contribute to education and history?

7. What is the difference between civic humanism and the princely ideal of government, and from what does this difference come?

8. How can it be said that Machiavelli invented a new politics by standing the ideal of princely rule on its head?

9. What is perspective? To whom do we owe the discovery of its rules?

10. What is the basic difference between Early and Late Renaissance painting?

11. What factors encouraged the spread of the Renaissance into the western European monarchies and the Rhineland?

12. To what key invention do we owe the rise of the printing press? What were the effects of the printing press on European civilization?

13. Why is the Renaissance considered the departure from the Middle Ages and the beginning of modernity?

14

The Reformation: Shattering of Christendom

By the early sixteenth century the one European institution that transcended geographic, ethnic, linguistic, and national boundaries had come under severe attack from reformers. For centuries the Catholic church, with its center in Rome, had extended its influence into every aspect of European society and culture. As a result, however, the church's massive wealth and power appeared to take predominance over its commitment to the search for holiness in this world and salvation in the next. Encumbered by wealth, addicted to international power, and protective of their own interests, the clergy, from the pope on down, became the center of a storm of criticism. Humanists, made self-confident by the new learning of the Renaissance, called for the reform and renewal of the church, setting the stage for the Protestant Reformation. Eventually, though, that movement came to deviate quite significantly from what the Renaissance humanists had in mind.

Schooled in the techniques of criticism developed during the Renaissance, humanists first used those techniques on the documents that supposedly justified papal authority. Thus did they refute the Donation of Constantine (see page 269). But the fraud that especially vexed the humanists lay not on parchments but in the very practices by which the church governed the faithful.

However, the Protestant Reformation did not originate in elite circles of humanistic scholars. Rather, it began in the mind of Martin Luther (1483–1546), an obscure German monk and a brilliant theologian. Luther rejected the church's claim to be the only vehicle for human salvation and defied the pope's right to silence, reprimand, and excommunicate any Christian who rejected papal authority or denied the truth of certain of

Martin Luther (left) and the Wittenberg Reformers (Frederick of Saxony and Zwingli in center) by Lucas Cranach the Younger. (*The Toledo Museum of Art, Gift of Edward Drummond Libbey*)

the church's teachings. In a public defiance, undertaken after much soul-searching, Luther instituted a rebellion against the church's authority that in less than one decade shattered irrevocably the religious unity of Christendom. The Reformation, begun in 1517, dominated European history throughout much of the sixteenth century.

The Renaissance breathed new energy into European intellectual life and in the process discarded the medieval preoccupation with theology. Similarly, the Reformation marked the beginning of a new religious outlook. Personal faith, rather than adherence to the practices of the church, became central to the religious life of European Protestants. Local congregations and national churches came to replace the international church, which survived the Reformation but lost large amounts of its wealth and power. Like the Renaissance humanists, most Protestant leaders were trained in ancient learning, but they gave humanism a religious cast. Renaissance humanists had sought to reinstitute the wisdom of ancient times; Protestant reformers wanted to restore the spirit of early Christianity, in which faith seemed purer, believers more sincere, and clergy uncorrupted by luxury and power. By the 1540s, the Roman Catholic church had initiated its own internal reformation, but it came too late to stop the movement toward Protestantism in some parts of northern and western Europe.

During the Late Middle Ages various attempts had been made to reform the church from within. These movements were generated by bishops, monks, and scholars who assumed that the church's difficulties stemmed from the inefficiency and corruption of the papacy. Some reformers sought to wrest power from the popes and to place it in the hands of a general council of the church's hierarchy. This was indeed one of the aims, in addition to ending the Great Schism and combating heresy, of the conciliar movement in the first half of the fifteenth century. However, the councils of Constance and of Basel (see page 249) failed to leave a meaningful inheritance to the church, largely because the special interests of kings and nations undercut their authority. The defeat of the conciliar movement prevented the church from reforming itself from within and made possible a more general reformation.

Background to the Reformation: The Medieval Church in Crisis

During the Early Middle Ages the church had served as the great unifying and civilizing force in Latin Christendom. Culturally, and even administratively, it performed functions formerly carried out by the Roman Empire. By the fourteenth century, however, the usefulness and authority of its popes and bishops, as well as the vitality of its teachings, were being doubted. As kings increased their power and as urban centers with their sophisticated laity grew in size and numbers, people began to question the authority and independence of the international church and its clergy.

Several areas of the church's power came under close scrutiny. In theory, both popes and kings derived their authority from God. But where did one authority begin and the other leave off? According to Christian teachings, popes could instruct monarchs in the proper use of their authority; lay kings must serve and not challenge the church. Yet increasingly, monarchs did challenge the church's supremacy in worldly matters. The church also taught that new ideas must bend to the primacy of theology. But new learning in the hands of laymen endangered the supremacy of the monasteries and clergy-dominated universities as centers of learning. Lay scholarship also threatened the church's teachings on matters of authority. As national economies and local elites grew stronger, trouble brewed over the issue of paying taxes to a distant spiritual ruler in Rome whose wealth seemed more than sufficient. The manner in which church officials were appointed, with greater emphasis on their social place than their piety, also led to widespread attacks on the church's leadership. Not least, the church in every country controlled vast tracts of land that it used to its benefit, not necessarily to increase the wealth of a region or the coffers of the tax-collecting authorities.

By the Late Middle Ages the church had entered a time of crisis. During this period, political theorists rejected the pope's claim to supremacy over kings. The central idea of medieval Christen-

The Sacred Heart of Jesus, Hand-colored Woodcut Sold as an Indulgence, Nuremberg, 1480s. The practice of selling indulgences to erase purgatory time disgusted Martin Luther. The veneration of relics—objects associated with the life of Christ or his saints, even bones or hair—was also condemned. Rival churches would often claim to have the "only authentic" head of a certain saint. (*The Metropolitan Museum of Art, Bequest of James Clarck McGuire, 1931. 31.54.142*)

dom—a Christian commonwealth led by the papacy—increasingly fell into disrepute. Theorists were arguing that the church was only a spiritual body, and therefore its power did not extend to the political realm. They said that the pope had no authority over kings, that the state needed no guidance from the papacy, and that the clergy were not above secular law.

Political theories were aimed at the educated elite, but the common people of town and coun-

tryside also expressed dissatisfaction with the church. By the Late Middle Ages, new material forces were affecting large segments of European society. Towns and cities contributed to the growth of an indigenous culture that focused on vernacular languages and regional dialects rather than on the Latin of the clergy and their schools. The townspeople had achieved a new wealth and a new self-confidence that made them resent any interference by bishops in their economic affairs. Urban centers also challenged the role of monasteries as economic innovators and centers of commercial life. By the early fourteenth century the church no longer held the initiative in worldly matters. When economic and social crises enveloped Europe in the second half of the fourteenth century, new reformers, despairing of the church's traditional privilege and even of its teachings, cast doubt on its authority.

For all these social and economic reasons, Latin Christendom during the late fourteenth century witnessed the first systematic attacks ever launched against the church. Church corruption—such as the selling of indulgences, nepotism (the practice of appointing one's relatives to offices), the holding of many bishoprics, and the sexual indulgence of the clergy—was nothing new. What was new and startling was the willingness of educated and uneducated Christians to attack these practices publicly. In *The Canterbury Tales*, Chaucer singles out two of his characters, who held clerical offices, for special scorn: the pardoner, who sold indulgences, that is, the remission of time spent in purgatory for one's sins; and the summoner, who served writs to appear in church courts. Chaucer paints a black picture of their arrogance and corruption. Less corrupt figures, such as his prioress, are let off with only mild caricatures. But in this first major English poem, Chaucer made the point that the church was corrupt.

Millenarianism

The peasant revolts during the Late Middle Ages frequently assumed a heretical cast. These movements foreshadowed the popular unrest so characteristic of the German Reformation. In many instances, they combined heretical beliefs with hatred for church officials and protest against social and economic inequities and injustices. These popular heretical protest movements often took a doctrine accepted by the official church and reinterpreted it to express their vision of a society where religion ensures justice for the poor and oppressed. For instance, the church preached that at some time in the future the world would end and Christ would come again to finally judge all men. Those whom Christ chose to be with him would be called saints, and they would reign with him in heaven. Medieval reformers, many drawn from, and followed by, the poorer segments of European society, interpreted that doctrine to mean that Christ would condemn the rich and propertied and would establish a new society where the poor would inherit the earth. For a thousand years, a millennium, the poor would rule in Christ's kingdom.

Millenarianism, as this radical interpretation of the Last Judgment is called, gave its believers religious justification for attacking established institutions and institutional corruption. That Christ would rule with the poor in a future paradise meant that the society of their own day must be ruled by Antichrist. For many later medieval reformers, the concept of Antichrist, or the image of the "whore of Babylon" taken from the Bible, became a shorthand for the corruption of the church. When in the early sixteenth century Luther and other reformers called the pope himself the Antichrist, or the whore of Babylon, they were appealing to a tradition of reform and protest that had existed in the West for centuries.

Wycliffe and Huss

The two most serious attempts to reform the church, prior to Luther, occurred in the late fourteenth century in England and Bohemia. In both cases the leaders of these movements, John Wycliffe in England and John Huss in Bohemia, were learned theologians who attacked some church doctrines and practices (see Chapter 12). By expressing their ideas in learned and precise language, Wycliffe and Huss made heresy intellec-

tually respectable. By incorporating popularly held beliefs, they also appealed to the common people and found mass support.

John Wycliffe (c. 1320–1384), a master at Oxford University, attacked the church's authority at its root by arguing simply that the church did not control the individual's eternal destiny. He said that salvation came only to those who possess faith, a gift freely given by God and not contingent on participating in the church's rituals or on receiving its sacraments. From this position, which in effect made the clergy far less important, Wycliffe attacked the church's wealth and argued that all true believers in Christ were equal and were, in effect, Christ's priests. To make faith accessible to them, Wycliffe translated portions of the Bible into English.

Wycliffe received powerful support from members of the English nobility, who hated the church's economic and secular power. However, when his ideas were taken up by articulate peasants during the abortive Peasants' Revolt of 1381 (see page 245), Wycliffe lost many powerful backers. In the end his attempt to reform the church by bringing it under secular control failed. Partly because he retained strong supporters and because he was more interested in scholarship than leadership, Wycliffe survived the failure of his movement and died a natural death. His ideas remained alive in popular religious beliefs, and his followers, called the Lollards, helped foster Protestantism during the sixteenth-century English Reformation.

A harsher fate awaited the Bohemian (Czech) reformer John Huss (b. 1374) who was burned at the stake in 1415. Partly under the influence of Wycliffe's writings, Huss, in his native Prague, attacked the church for its wealth and power. He also preached for Bohemian independence at a time when the Holy Roman emperor sought to increase his control over that territory. After Huss's execution, his followers broke with the Roman Catholic Church and for a brief time nationalized the Bohemian church. This movement, like the Lollards in England, prepared the ground for the success of the Protestant Reformation. Until well into the seventeenth century, Bohemia remained a battleground of popular Protestantism against the official church.

Mysticism and Humanism

Wycliffe's and Huss's attempts to initiate reform coincided with the appearance of a powerful new religiosity. Late medieval mystics sought an immediate and personal communication with God; such experiences inspired them to advocate concrete reforms for the purpose of renewing the church's spirituality. Many late medieval mystics were women who, by virtue of their sex, had been deprived of an active role in governing the church. First mysticism and then Protestantism offered women a way of expressing their independence from ecclesiastical authority in religious matters. The church hierarchy inevitably regarded mysticism with some suspicion. For if individuals can experience God directly, they would seemingly have little need for the church and its rituals. In the fourteenth century, these mystical movements seldom became heretical. But in the sixteenth and seventeenth centuries, radical reformers often found in Christian mysticism a powerful alternative to institutional control and even to the necessity of a priesthood.

The Brethren of the Common Life, in the Low Countries, propounded a religious movement known as the *devotio moderna*, which was inspired by mysticism. A semimonastic order of laity and clergy, the Brethren expressed their practical piety by dedicating their lives to the service of the entire community. With their teaching, they trained a new generation of scholars and humanists who became, during the late fifteenth century, some of the church's severest critics. Significantly, the Brethren's new schools flourished in the most heavily urbanized part of western Europe.

Both mysticism and humanistic Christianity seemed for a time to offer sufficient alternatives to the scholasticism of the clergy. Certainly Erasmus thought that the critical gaze of the humanist would be sufficient to show the clergy the folly of their ways, which he ridiculed in *The Praise of Folly* (1510). Yet mysticism, with its emphasis on inner spirituality, and humanism, with its emphasis on classical learning, could not in themselves capture the attention of thousands of ordinary Europeans. A successful reform movement required leaders of an active and aggressive temperament who could do battle with political realities and win lay support against the local and international power of the church.

The Lutheran Revolt

Only an attack on papal and clerical authority could alter the power and practices of the church. Such an attack would have to involve winning over the multitudes, appealing to princes, and making heresy respectable. This feat required someone who had experienced the personal agony of doubting the church's power to give salvation and who could translate that agony into language understandable to all Christians. Martin Luther had experienced just such a personal crisis, and he possessed the will and the talent to offer it as an example for other Christians. Luther wrote voluminously and talked freely to his friends and students. Using this mass of recorded material, historians have been able to reconstruct the life and personality of this Augustinian monk who began the Reformation.

Luther's father, born a peasant, apparently was unusually ambitious. Hans Luther left the land, became a miner, and finally a manager and lessee of several mines, in an industry that was booming in late-fifteenth century Germany. Like many newly successful individuals, Hans Luther had ambitious plans for his son; he wanted Martin to study law at the university in order to attain the status of an educated man. Luther's mother came from a burgher family and displayed an intense piety, thus putting him in closer touch with German popular religion than was common among contemporary scholars.

At the prestigious University of Erfurt, Luther embarked on an intellectual career that was to make him one of the foremost theologians and biblical scholars of his day. As a young student, Luther fulfilled his father's wish and studied law. His earlier education gave him a fine grounding in classical learning, which served him throughout his life. At the university, Luther developed an interest in theology and philosophy, particularly the teachings of the fourteenth-century philosopher William of Ockham (see Chapter 12). Ockham had stressed the difference between faith and reason; he had insisted that truth learned through revelation was a matter of faith that might not be capable of demonstration by human reason; thus church teachings, and consequently salvation, rested entirely on faith. Since the church supported the synthesis of faith and reason achieved by the scholastics, notably Thomas Aquinas, it regarded Ockham's notions with suspicion.

At the age of twenty-one, Luther suddenly abandoned his legal studies to enter the Augustinian monastery at Erfurt. Not all of the steps that led to this rebellion against parental authority are known, but the actual decision was made swiftly. In later life, Luther recounted that the decision had been made in fear, as a vow to Saint Anne in the midst of a fierce lightning storm, by a young man convinced that his death at that moment would bring him eternal damnation. Why Luther thought he was damned is also not known, but his guilt conspired with his vivid imagination to kindle what must have been a growing resentment against his father's domination. Luther began his search for spiritual and personal identity, and therefore for salvation, within the strict confinement and discipline of the monastery. He pursued his theological studies there and prepared for ordination into the priesthood.

The Break with Catholicism

As he studied and prayed, Luther grew increasingly terrified about the possibility of his damnation. As a monk he sought union with God, and he understood the church's teaching that salvation depended on faith, works (meaning acts of charity, prayer, fasting, and so on), and grace. He participated in the sacraments of the church, which according to its teaching were intended to give grace. Indeed, after his ordination, Luther administered the sacraments. Yet he still felt the weight of his sins, and nothing the church could offer seemed to relieve that burden. Seeking solace and salvation, Luther increasingly turned to reading the Bible. Two passages seemed to speak directly to him: "For in it the righteousness of God is revealed through faith for faith: as it is written,

Portrait of Martin Luther by Lucas Cranach the Elder (1472–1553). Martin Luther's personal struggle to attain spiritual peace through faith led to the Protestant Reformation. The time was right for reform. The church was worldly and corrupt, and a nationalistic temper made many European monarchs and aristocrats hostile toward Roman authority. (*Herzog Anton Ulrich-Museum, Braunschweig*)

'He who through faith is righteous shall live' " (Romans 1:17); and "They are justified by his grace as a gift, through the redemption which is in Christ Jesus" (Romans 3:24). In these two passages, Luther found, for the first time in his adult life, some hope for his own salvation. Faith, freely given by God through Christ, enables the recipient to receive salvation.

The concept of salvation by faith alone provided an answer to Luther's spiritual quest. Practicing such good works as prayer, fasting, pilgrimages, participation in the Mass and the other sacraments had never brought Luther peace of mind. He concluded that no amount of good works, however necessary for maintaining the Christian community, would bring salvation. Through reading the Bible and through faith alone, the Christian could find the meaning of earthly existence. For Luther, the true Christian was a courageous figure who faced the terrifying quest for salvation armed only with the hope that God had granted the gift of faith. The new Christian served others not to trade good works for salvation but solely to fulfill the demands of Christian love.

Pursuing his theological studies, Luther became a professor at the nearby university at Wittenberg and a preacher in that city's church. From approximately 1513 onward, Luther shared his personal and intellectual struggle with his students and his congregations. At the University of Wittenberg and in the province of Saxony in general, Luther found an audience receptive to his views, and his popularity and reputation grew as a result. Before 1517, he was considered a dynamic and controversial preacher whose passionate interest lay in turning Christians away from their worldly interests and from reliance on good works, while focusing their attention on Christ and the truth contained within Scripture. After 1517, he became a figure of international reputation and eventually a publicly condemned heretic in the eyes of the church.

The starting point for the Reformation was Luther's attack in 1517 on the church's practice of selling indulgences. The church taught that some individuals go directly to heaven or hell, while others go to heaven only after spending time in purgatory; this waiting period is necessary for those who have sinned excessively in this life but who have had the good fortune to repent before death. To die in a state of mortal sin meant to suffer in hell eternally. Naturally people worried about how long they might have to spend in purgatory. Indulgences were intended to remit por-

tions of that time and were granted to individuals by the church for their prayers, attendance at Mass, and almost any acts of charity—including monetary offerings to the church. This last was the most controversial—it could easily appear that people were buying their way into heaven.

In the autumn of 1517 a monk named Tetzel was selling indulgences in the area near Wittenberg. Some of the money he obtained was for rebuilding St. Peter's Basilica in Rome, but the rest was for paying off debts incurred by a local archbishop in purchasing his office from the pope. Although Luther did not know about this second purpose, he was incensed both by Tetzel's crude manner and by his flagrant exploitation of the people's ignorance and money. Luther launched his attack on Tetzel and the selling of indulgences by tacking on the door of the Wittenberg castle church his ninety-five theses.* Luther's theses (propositions) challenged the entire notion of selling indulgences, not only as a corrupt practice but also as a theologically unsound assumption—namely, that salvation can be earned by good works. In the ninety-five theses the outline of Luther's later theology is already evident, and his reliance on faith as the only means to salvation is implicitly stated.

At the heart of Luther's argument in the ninety-five theses and in his later writings was the belief that the individual achieves salvation through personal religiosity, a sense of contrition for sins, and trust in God's mercy. He also believed that church attendance, fasting, pilgrimages, charity, and other good works did not earn salvation. The church, on the other hand, held that *both* faith and good works were necessary for salvation. Luther further insisted that every individual could discover the meaning of the Bible unaided by the clergy; the church, however, maintained that only the clergy could read and interpret the Bible properly. Luther argued that in matters of faith there was no difference between the clergy and the laity. Each person could receive faith directly and freely from God. But the church held that the clergy were intermediaries between

*Some scholars debate whether this public display ever occurred. If it did not, the document was nevertheless widely circulated almost immediately.

individuals and God and that in effect Christians reached eternal salvation through the clergy. For Luther, no priest, no ceremony, no sacrament could bridge the gulf between the Creator and his creatures, and the possibility of personal damnation remained a distinct reality. Hope lay only in a personal relationship between the individual and God, as expressed through faith in God's mercy and grace. No church could mediate that faith for the individual, and to that extent Luther's theology destroyed the foundations of the church's spiritual power. By holding that clergy and church rituals do not hold the key to salvation, Luther rejected the church's claim that it alone offered men and women the way to eternal life.

If faith alone, freely given by God, brings salvation to the believer, how can a person know if he or she has faith? Luther seemed content to assert that the search itself was a sign that God had favored a pious and penitent supplicant. Yet in Luther's doctrine of faith the notion of predestination is barely beneath the surface. The discussion about predestination continues today; it is one of the most difficult theological issues. Predestination begins with the assumption that God is all-knowing and eternal and his will is absolute. Not only does he give faith to whomever he chooses, but he does so for his own inscrutable reasons. Since God's existence, and therefore his will, is timeless, he knows the fate of each individual even as he or she is searching for salvation. In that sense every person is predestined either for heaven or for hell. But the problem remains, how can one know if one has been chosen? Luther said simply that one could hope and trust in salvation but never really know. Subsequent reformers would make much of the doctrine of predestination in their struggle to systematize Protestant doctrine and to create an identifying experience for all true Christians.

Although Luther did not realize it in 1517, the Reformation had begun. Quickly translating the theses from Latin into German, his students printed and distributed them, first in Saxony and eventually throughout Germany. Local church authorities recognized in Luther a serious threat and prepared to silence him. But Luther was tenacious; he began to write and preach his theology with increasing vigor.

At this point, politics intervened. Recognizing that his life might be in danger if he continued to preach without a protector, Luther appealed for support to the prince of his district, Frederick, the elector of Saxony. The elector was a powerful man in international politics—one of seven lay and ecclesiastical princes who chose the Holy Roman emperor. Frederick's support convinced church officials, including the pope, that this monk would have to be dealt with cautiously.

The years 1518 and 1519 were momentous ones for the Holy Roman Empire. Before his death in 1519, Holy Roman Emperor Maximilian I wanted to see his grandson, Charles, king of Spain, elected to succeed him. The papacy at first opposed Charles's candidacy, even looking to Frederick of Saxony as a possible alternative. Frederick wisely declined to be a candidate; as one of the seven electors, however, his vote was courted by the contenders—Charles, Francis I of France, and Henry VIII of England. Charles bribed the electors, and the throne became his own. Therefore during this crucial election period and for some years afterward, he had to proceed cautiously on issues that might offend powerful German princes.

These political considerations explain the delay in Luther's official condemnation and excommunication by the pope. When in 1520 the pope finally acted against him, it was too late; Luther had been given the needed time to promote his views. He proclaimed that the pope was Antichrist and that the church was the "most lawless den of robbers, the most shameless of all brothels, the very kingdom of sin, death and Hell."[1] When the papal bull excommunicating him was delivered, Luther burned it.

No longer members of the church, Luther and his followers established congregations for the purpose of Christian worship. Christians without the church needed protection, and in 1520 Luther published the *Address to the Christian Nobility of the German Nation*. In it, he appealed to the emperor and the German princes to reform the church and to cast off their allegiance to the pope who, he argued, had used taxes and political power to exploit them for centuries. His appeal produced some success; the Reformation flourished on the resentment against foreign papal in-

Print Shop, Sixteenth-Century Print. Neither the Renaissance nor the Reformation would have been so widespread without printing, which was invented in Nuremberg in the 1450s. The printed word was the medium for the rapid transmission of Luther's and Calvin's revolutionary treatises, first in Germany and Switzerland and then elsewhere in Europe. (*The Bettmann Archive/BBC Hulton*)

tervention that had long festered in Germany. Luther also wrote to the German people and conveyed the meaning of his personal experience as a Christian. In *The Freedom of the Christian Man* (1520), Luther called on his followers to strive for true spiritual freedom through faith in Christ, to discipline themselves to live as law-abiding members of society, to obey legitimate political authority, and to perform good works according to the dictates of Christian love. In these treatises Luther made it clear that he wanted to present no threat to legitimate political authority, that is, to the power of the German princes.

In 1521, Charles V, the Holy Roman emperor, who was a devout Catholic, summoned Luther to Worms, giving him a pass of safe conduct. There Luther was to answer to the charge of heresy, both an ecclesiastical and a civil offense. On his journey, Luther received a warm public response from great crowds of people, but the emperor and his officials coldly demanded that he recant. Luther's reply, delivered after some deliberation, is undoubtedly his most famous statement: "Unless I am convinced of error by the testimony of Scripture or by clear reason . . . I cannot and will not recant anything, for it is neither safe nor honest to act against one's conscience. God help me. Amen." Shortly after this confrontation with the emperor, Luther went into hiding to escape arrest. During that one-year period he translated the New Testament into German. With this work he offered his compatriots the opportunity to take the same arduous spiritual odyssey that he had and to join him as a new type of Christian. These followers, or Lutherans, were eventually called *Protestants*, those who protested against the established church, and the term became generic for all followers of the Reformation.

The Appeal and Spread of Lutheranism

Once Luther recognized the need for followers, he appealed to every level of German society for support. And he was successful. His brilliance as a theologian was matched by his ability to bridge the gap between his scholarly version of Christianity and the beliefs and aspirations of all Christians. Spread rapidly by the new printing press, the tenets of Protestantism offered the hope of revitalization and renewal not only for true religion but for society and government.

Lutheranism appealed to the devout, who resented the worldliness and lack of piety of many clergy. But the movement found its greatest following among German townspeople who objected to money flowing from their country to Rome in the form of church taxes and payment for church offices. In addition, the Reformation provided the nobility with the unprecedented opportunity to confiscate church lands, to eliminate church taxes, and to gain the support of their subjects by serving as leaders of a popular and dynamic religious movement. The Reformation also gave the nobles a way of resisting the Catholic Holy Roman emperor, Charles V, who wanted to extend his authority over the German princes. Resenting the Italian domination of the church, many other Germans who supported Martin Luther believed that they were freeing German Christians from foreign control.

Lutheranism also drew support from the peasants, who saw Luther as their champion against their oppressors—both lay and ecclesiastical lords and the townspeople. Indeed, in his writings and sermons, Luther often attacked the greed of the princes and bemoaned the plight of the poor. Nevertheless, Luther was a political conservative who hesitated to challenge secular authority. To him, the good Christian was an obedient citizen.

Although Luther had spoken forcefully about the discontent of Christians with their church, he never understood that in the minds of the poor and socially oppressed, the church's abuses were visible signs of the exploitation encountered in their daily lives. Wealthy and powerful feudal lords who dominated every aspect of their lives and prosperous townspeople who bought their labor for the lowest possible wages were no different from the venal clergy; indeed, in some cases the lord was a local bishop.

In the early sixteenth century, a rapid population explosion throughout Europe had produced severe inflation coupled with high unemployment and low wages. These conditions seriously affected the poor. The peasantry in Germany was probably worse off than the peasantry in England and the Low Countries; and in the German states, the feudal power of lords over every feature of peasant life remained unbroken. In 1524, the long-suffering peasants openly rebelled against their lords. The Peasants' Revolt spread to over one-third of Germany; some 300,000 people took up arms against their masters.

Undoubtedly, Luther's successful confrontation with the authorities had served to inspire the peasants, and he had at one time chastised the nobles for failing to care for the poor as commanded in the Gospel. But he had no intention of associating his movement with a peasant uprising at the risk of alienating the nobility who supported him. Luther virulently attacked the rebellious peasants, urging the nobility to become "both judge and executioner" and to "knock down, strangle, and stab . . . and think nothing so venomous, pernicious, Satanic as an insurgent. . . . Such wonderful times are these that a prince can merit heaven better with bloodshed than another with prayer."[2] By 1525, the peasants had been put down by the sword. Thousands died or were left homeless, and many were permanently alienated from Lutheranism. In addition the failure of the Peasants' Revolt meant that the German peasantry remained among the most backward and oppressed until well into the nineteenth century.

The Peasants' Revolt was not the last violent confrontation for the German Reformation. Catholic power also threatened. Initially, the Holy Roman emperor hesitated to intervene militarily, a delay that proved crucial. His involvement in international power politics at first precluded him from acting in Germany: he was at war with France over control of portions of Italy, and the Ottoman Empire threatened his territories in the east, particularly Austria. Soon, however, Catholic and Protestant princes in various territories of the empire were waging intermittent warfare over its religious fate.

Religious strife was settled, and then only in a piecemeal fashion, by the Peace of Augsburg (1555). It decreed by the famous dictum *cuius regio, eius religio* ("Whoever rules, his religion") that each territorial prince should determine the religion of his subjects. Broadly speaking, northern Germany became largely Protestant, while Bavaria and other southern territories remained in the Roman Catholic church. The victors were the local princes. Toward the end of his life, Charles V expressed his bitter regret for not having intervened more forcefully in those early years. The decentralization of the empire and its division into Catholic and Protestant areas would block German unity until the last part of the nineteenth century.

The Spread of the Reformation

Nothing better illustrates people's dissatisfaction with the church in the early sixteenth century than the rapid spread of Protestantism. There was a pattern to this phenomenon. Protestantism grew strong in northern Europe—northern Germany, Scandinavia, the Netherlands, and England; it failed in the Romance countries, although not without a struggle in France. In general, Protestantism was an urban phenomenon, and it prospered where local magistrates supported it and where the distance from Rome was greatest.

Protestantism also appeared simultaneously in different places—a sure indication of its popular roots. For example, in the Swiss city of Zurich, the priest and reformer Ulrich Zwingli (1484–1531) preached a form of Christianity very close to that of Luther and claimed that he developed his ideas independently of Luther. Zwingli and Luther both sought a ceremonial alternative to the doctrine of transubstantiation—the priest's transformation of communion bread and wine into the substance of Christ's body and blood—and the enormous power it gave to the priesthood. But the two reformers came to differ bitterly over the exact form of the ceremony. Luther retained the traditional Catholic form whereas Zwingli radically altered the communion service. Their quarrel enacts the fate that awaited many reformers. Once free to read and interpret the Bible for themselves, they could not agree on its meaning or on the ritual expressions they would give their new versions of Christianity.

Zwingli died on the battlefield defending the Reformation. His teachings laid the foundation for a strong reformation in Switzerland, and the major reform movement of the next generation, Calvinism, benefited from Zwingli's reforms.

Calvinism

The success of the Reformation outside Germany and Scandinavia derived largely from the work of John Calvin (1509–1564), a French scholar and theologian. For decades, French humanists had attacked the corruption of the church. Their views found sympathy at the court of Francis I, the French king. His sister Margaret of Navarre had helped foster this critical humanism, and her intellectual circle looked favorably on Luther's writings. By the 1530s, Lutheran treatises circulated widely in Paris. Some university students, including the young John Calvin, were impressed by the reformer's ideas.

Calvin had been born into a French family of recent and substantial bourgeois status; his father, somewhat like Luther's, was self-made and ambitious. A lawyer and administrator, the elder

Map 14.1 The Protestant and the Catholic Reformations ▶

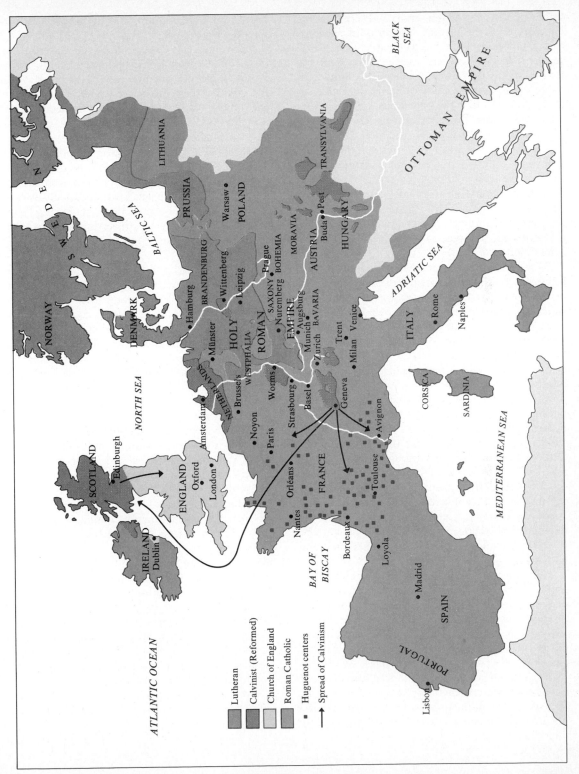

BLACK SEA

OTTOMAN EMPIRE

LITHUANIA

PRUSSIA

Warsaw •

POLAND

BRANDENBURG

Wittenberg •
Leipzig •

Prague •

BOHEMIA

MORAVIA

TRANSYLVANIA

Pest •
Buda •

HUNGARY

AUSTRIA

ADRIATIC SEA

BALTIC SEA

SWEDEN

NORWAY

DENMARK

Hamburg •

HOLY

ROMAN

EMPIRE

SAXONY

Nuremberg •

Augsburg •

BAVARIA

Munich •

Trent •

Venice •

Milan •

ITALY

Rome •

Naples •

Münster •

WESTPHALIA

NETHERLANDS

Brussels •

Amsterdam •

NORTH SEA

Noyon •

Paris •

Worms •

Strasbourg •

Basel •

Zurich •

Geneva •

Avignon •

CORSICA

SARDINIA

MEDITERRANEAN SEA

SCOTLAND

Edinburgh •

ENGLAND

Oxford •

London •

IRELAND

Dublin •

Orléans •

FRANCE

Toulouse •

Nantes •

Bordeaux •

Loyola •

BAY OF
BISCAY

Madrid •

SPAIN

ATLANTIC OCEAN

PORTUGAL

Lisbon •

Lutheran
Calvinist (Reformed)
Church of England
Roman Catholic
Huguenot centers
Spread of Calvinism

Calvin had served the civil and ecclesiastical authorities of the city of Noyon until a dispute over finances led to his excommunication. He desired prosperous careers for his sons. John first studied to be a priest and then, at his father's insistence, took up the study of law at the University of Orléans. Unlike the rebellious Luther, Calvin waited until his father's death to return to Paris and resume his theological studies.

Sometime in 1533 or 1534, Calvin met French followers of Luther and became convinced of the truth of the new theology. He began to spread its beliefs immediately after his conversion, and within a year he and his friends were in trouble with the civil and ecclesiastical authorities. Calvin was arrested, but was released because of insufficient evidence.

King Francis I, a bitter rival of the Holy Roman emperor, could countenance Protestantism in Germany, but he had no intention of permitting disruptive religious divisions in his own France. Riots had already broken out in Paris between Catholics and supporters of the Reformation. In 1534, the French church, supported by royal decree, declared the Protestants heretics and subjected them to arrest and execution.

Within a year, young Calvin had abandoned his humanistic and literary studies to become a preacher of the Reformation. Calvin explained his sudden conversion as an act of God—"He subdued and reduced my heart to docility, which, for my age, was over-much hardened in such matters."[3] From early in his religious experience, Calvin emphasized the power of God over sinful and corrupt humanity. Calvin's God thundered and demanded obedience, and the terrible distance between God and the individual was mediated only by Christ.

Calvin's understanding of God's relationship to the individual stressed its legal, rather than its personal nature. Calvin said that God's laws must be rigorously obeyed, that social and moral righteousness must be earnestly pursued, that political life must be carefully regulated, and that human emotions must be strictly controlled. What psychological and social forces induced Calvin to embrace such a stern theology are not known, but they were not unique to him. The compelling force of Calvinist belief is an extraordinary aspect of the

Protestant Reformation, and its historical consequences were great.

Like Luther, Calvin explained salvation in terms of uncertain predestination. He argued that although people are predestined to salvation or damnation, they can never know with certainty their fate in advance. This terrible decree could and did lead some people to despair. For others—in a paradox difficult for the modern mind to comprehend—Calvinism gave a sense of self-assurance and righteousness that made the saint, that is, the truly predestined man or woman, into a new kind of European. Most of Calvin's followers seemed to believe that in having comprehended the fact of predestination, they had received a bold insight into their unique relationship with God.

The social and political implications of that insight were immediate: Calvinists became militant Protestants capable of ruling their town or city with the same iron will used to control their unruly passions. Again like Luther, Calvin always stressed that Christians should obey legitimate political authority. But Calvinists were individuals who assumed that only unfailing dedication to God's law could be seen as a sign of salvation; their obedience to human laws would always be contingent on their inner sense of righteousness. Thus, Calvinism made for stern men and women, active in their congregations and willing to suppress vice in themselves and others. Calvinism could also produce revolutionaries willing to defy any temporal authorities that were perceived to be in violation of God's laws. For Calvin, obedience to Christian law became the dominating principle of his life. Rigorous enforcement of the law ensured obedience to God's law; it also served as an alternative to the decrees and obligations formerly imposed by the Catholic church.

The political situation in France forced Calvin to leave. After his flight from Paris, he finally sought safety in Geneva, a small, prosperous Swiss city near the French border. There Calvin eventually established a Protestant church that did not hesitate to dominate the lives of many others less committed to the Reformation.

Switzerland was a logical choice; its cities had long been in the vanguard of the Reformation. Before Calvin's arrival, Geneva's citizens were in revolt against their Catholic bishops. The French-born reformer Guillaume (William) Farel led a small Protestant congregation there and implored Calvin to stay with him to continue the work of the Reformation. Together they became the leaders of the Protestant movement in Geneva. After many setbacks, Calvin emerged as the most dynamic agent of reform in the city. Until his death in 1564, his beliefs and actions dominated Geneva's religious and social life.

Calvin established a kind of theocracy—a society where the Calvinist elders regulated the personal social lives of the citizens and did so independently of the governing authority of the state. The older and more pious male members of the community governed the city. These elders of the Calvinist church imposed strict discipline in dress, sexual mores, church attendance, and business affairs; they severely punished irreligious and sinful behavior. This rigid discipline contributed to Geneva's prosperity; indeed, Calvin instituted the kind of social discipline that some of the ruling merchants had always wanted. At every turn, prosperous merchants, as well as small shopkeepers, saw in Calvinism a series of doctrines that justified the self-discipline they already exercised in their own lives and wished to impose on the unruly masses. They particularly approved of his economic views, for Calvin saw nothing sinful about commercial activities and even gave his assent to the practice of charging interest.

Geneva became the center of international Protestantism. Calvin trained a new generation of Protestant reformers of many nationalities, who carried his message back to their homelands. Calvin's *Institutes of the Christian Religion* (1536), in its many editions, became (after the Bible) the leading textbook of the new theology. In the second half of the sixteenth century, Calvin's theology of predestination spread into France, England, the Netherlands, and parts of the Holy Roman Empire.

Calvin always opposed any recourse to violence and supported the authority of magistrates. Yet when monarchy became their persecutor, his followers felt compelled to respond. Calvinist theologians became the first political theoreticians of modern times to publish cogent arguments for opposition to monarchy, and eventually for

political revolution. In France and later in the Netherlands, Calvinism became a revolutionary ideology, complete with an underground organization composed of dedicated followers who challenged monarchical authority. (In the seventeenth century, the English version of Calvinism—Puritanism—performed the same function.) In certain circumstances, Calvinism possessed the moral force to undermine the claims of the monarchical state over the individual.

France

Although Protestantism was illegal in France after 1534, its persecution was halfhearted and never systematic. The Protestant minority in France, the Huguenots, grew and became a well-organized underground movement that attracted nobles, urban dwellers, some peasants, and women especially. Huguenot churches, often under the protection of powerful nobles, assumed an increasingly political character in response to the monarchy-sponsored persecution. By 1559, French Protestants were sufficiently organized and militant to challenge their persecutors, King Henry II and the Guise—one of the foremost Catholic families in Europe, tied by marriage and conviction to the Spanish monarchy and its rigorous form of Catholicism. Guise power in the French court meant that all Protestant appeals for more lenient treatment went unheeded, and in 1562 civil war erupted between Catholics and Protestants. What followed was one of the most brutal religious wars in the history of Europe. In 1572, an effort at conciliation through the marriage of a Protestant leader into the royal family failed when the Catholics, urged on by the queen mother, Catherine de' Medici, murdered the assembled Protestant wedding guests. Over the next week, a popular uprising against Protestants left thousands of them dead; the streets, according to eyewitness accounts, were stained red with blood. These murders and the ensuing slaughter, known as the Saint Bartholomew's Day Massacre, inspired the pope to have a mass said in thanksgiving for a Catholic "victory." Such was the extent of religious hatred in Europe by the late sixteenth century.

Henry VIII. Henry initiated the English break with Rome. Ironically, as a youthful monarch, he received from a grateful papacy the title "Defender of the Faith" for a published treatise against Martin Luther. (*National Portrait Gallery, London*)

toleration, as well as its practice, remained tenuous in early modern Europe.

England

The Reformation was initiated in England not by religious reformers but by the king himself. Henry VIII (1509–1547) removed the English church from the jurisdiction of the papacy because the pope refused to grant him an annulment of his marriage to his first wife. The English Reformation thus began as a political act on the part of a self-confident Renaissance king. But its origins stretched back into the Middle Ages, and its character, once it got under way, became intensely religious and increasingly Protestant. There was a long tradition of heresy as well as anticlericalism in England, which also laid the foundations for a successful state-inspired Reformation.

Unlike the French and Spanish kings, the English Tudors had never frightened the papacy. The Tudors had enjoyed a good measure of control over the English church, but they had never played a major role in European and papal politics. When Henry VIII decided that he wanted a divorce from the Spanish princess Catherine of Aragon, in 1527–28, the pope in effect ignored his request. Henry had a shaky case from a theological point of view and not enough international political power to force his will on the papacy. As the pope stalled, Henry grew more desperate—he needed a male heir and presumed that the failure to produce one lay with his wife. At the same time, he desired the shrewd and tempting Anne Boleyn. But Spain's power over the papacy, symbolized by the Spanish army that had sacked Rome in 1525, ensured that Henry's pleas for an annulment would go unheeded.

Although anticlericalism and resentment toward the papacy were rife throughout Europe at this time, the English also possessed a tradition of popular opposition to the church that stretched back to Wycliffe in the fourteenth century. Aware of that tradition, Henry VIII arranged to grant himself a divorce by severing England from the church. To do so, he had to call Parliament, which in turn passed a series of statutes drawn up at his initiative and guided through Parliament by his

After nearly thirty years of brutal fighting throughout France, victory went to the Catholic side—but only barely. Henry of Navarre, the Protestant bridegroom who in 1572 had managed to escape the fate of his supporters, became king, but only after he had reconverted to Catholicism. He established a tentative peace by granting Protestants limited toleration. In 1598, he issued the Edict of Nantes, the first document in any nation-state that attempted to institutionalize a degree of religious toleration. In the seventeenth century the successors of Henry IV (who was assassinated in 1610) gradually weakened and then in 1685 revoked the edict. The theoretical foundations of

minister, Thomas Cromwell. Beginning in 1529, Henry convinced both houses of Parliament to accept his Reformation, and so began an administrative and religious revolution. In 1534, he had himself declared supreme head of the Church of England. In 1536, he dissolved the monasteries and seized their property, which was distributed or sold to his loyal supporters. In most cases, it went to the lesser nobility and landed gentry. By involving Parliament and the gentry, Henry VIII turned the Reformation into a national movement.

In the eleven years following Henry's death in 1547, there were three monarchs. Henry VIII was succeeded by his son, Edward VI, a Protestant, who reigned from 1547 to 1553. On his death, he was succeeded by Mary (1553–1558), the daughter of Henry VIII and Catherine of Aragon. With the remaining Catholic minority in England, Mary, a devout Catholic, persecuted Protestants more severely than any of her predecessors had done. By the 1558 succession of Elizabeth I, Henry's second daughter (by Anne Boleyn), England was a Protestant country again.

The English, or Anglican, church as it developed in the sixteenth century differed only to a limited degree in its customs and ceremonies from the Roman Catholicism it replaced. Large sections of the English population, including aristocratic families, remained Catholic and even used their homes as centers for Catholic rituals performed by clandestine priests. Thus, the exact nature of England's Protestantism became a subject of growing dispute. Was the Anglican church to be truly Protestant? Was its hierarchy to be responsive to, and possibly even appointed by, the laity? Were its services and churches to be simple, lacking in "popish" rites and rituals and centered only around Scripture and sermon? Was Anglicanism to conform to Protestantism as practiced in Switzerland, either in Calvinist Geneva or Zwinglian Zurich? Obviously the clergy, especially the English bishops, would accept no form of Protestantism that might limit their ancient privileges, ceremonial functions, and power.

Despite these religious issues, raised in large measure by the growing number of English Calvinists, or Puritans as they were called, Elizabeth's reign was characterized by a heightened sense of national identity and by the persecution of Catho-

Elizabeth I. The genius of Elizabeth I confounded her countrymen and the Roman Catholic Church alike. Parliament wanted her to marry and give power over to her husband. The church long held hopes for the English monarchy to reconcile with Rome. Elizabeth capitulated to no one and carefully charted a course that consolidated her personal power and allowed England to gain strength as a Protestant nation. Her portrait is by Nicholas Hilliard. (*National Museums and Galleries on Merseyside/Walker Art Gallery*)

lics, who were seen to threaten national security. The English Reformation enhanced that sense, as did the increasing fear of invasion by Spain, a Catholic power with twice England's population and a vast colonial empire, which was intent on returning England to the papacy.

Spain and Italy

In Spain, Protestantism met with no success. In the Middle Ages, church and state had successfully allied in a religious and nationalist crusade to drive out the Muslims, forging strong links between the Spanish monarchy and the church. The church augmented and justified the power and authority of the monarchy and at the same time retained its economic and political power. About one-quarter of the Spanish population held clerical office of one kind or another, and the church owned one-half of Spain's land. Furthermore, the church possessed judicial authority sanctioned by the state; its judicial arm, the Inquisition, enforced public and private morality.

Luther's works circulated in Spain for a brief time, but the Spanish authorities quickly and thoroughly stamped out Protestantism. After 1560, even the Inquisition was hard-pressed to find Protestants. The Spanish church was efficient, self-confident, and undoubtedly the most repressive in Europe. The absence of civil liberty and freedom of thought until very recently in modern Spain has historical roots in the Inquisition of the sixteenth century. Late in that century, Spain became the main defender of Catholicism in Europe, and that mission gradually sapped its vast military power.

A similar pattern developed in Italy, where Luther's ideas were discussed in Italian humanist circles but gained no popular audience. The Italian humanists distrusted Luther's emphasis on human sinfulness, and church authorities persecuted the few converts. Attempts to reform the Italian church were largely unsuccessful, and even reform-minded popes in the 1520s and 1530s had little support among the Vatican's Italian bureaucracy.

The Radical Reformation

The mainstream of the Protestant Reformation can be described as *magisterial;* that is, the leading reformers generally supported established political authorities, whether they were territorial princes or urban magistrates. For the reformers, human freedom was a spiritual, not a social, concept. Yet the Reformation did help trigger revolts among the artisan and peasant classes of central and then western Europe. Indications are that church doctrine had not made great inroads into the folk beliefs of large segments of the European masses. Late medieval records of church interrogations, usually in towns and villages where heresy or witchcraft was suspected, show the people to have deviated to an extraordinary degree from official doctrines and beliefs. For example, some peasants held the very unchristian beliefs that Nature was God or that witches had as much spiritual power as priests did. By the 1520s, several radical reformers arose, often from the lower classes of European society, and attempted to channel popular religion and folk beliefs into a new version of reformed Christianity that spoke directly to the temporal and spiritual needs of the oppressed.

The proliferation of many radical groups throughout the Continent makes them difficult to classify. Nevertheless, some beliefs were common to the Radical Reformation. Like Lutherans and Calvinists, the radicals struggled with the problem of salvation. Luther argued that faith alone, freely given by God, provides salvation for the believer. Radical reformers proclaimed that God's will was known by his saints—those predestined for salvation. In a world where survival itself was often precarious for the poor and oppressed, the radicals argued that even ordinary men and women have certain knowledge of their salvation through the *inner light*—a direct and immediate communication from God to his chosen saints. That knowledge makes the saint free. For the radicals, such spiritual freedom justified their demands for social and economic freedom and equality. Protestantism, radically interpreted, proclaimed the righteousness and the priesthood of all believers. It said that all people can have faith if God wills it, and that God would not abandon the wretched and humble of the earth.

The radicals said that the poor shall inherit an earth that at present is ruled by Antichrist, and that the end of the world has been proclaimed by Scripture. The saint's task is to purge this earth of evil to make it ready for Christ's Second Coming. For the radicals the faith-alone doctrine came to mean certain salvation for the poor and lowly, and the Scriptures became an inspiration for social revolution. The doctrine could also inspire a quietism or retreat from this world in anticipation of a better world to come. Luther, Calvin, and the other reformers vigorously condemned the social doctrines that were preached by the radical reformers.

The largest group in the Radical Reformation prior to 1550 has the general name of Anabaptists. Having received the inner light—the message of salvation—the Anabaptist felt born anew and yearned to be rebaptized. This notion had a revolutionary implication: the first baptism—one's first Christian allegiance to an established church (Protestant or Catholic)—does not count. The Anabaptist is a new Christian, a new person led by the light of conscience to seek reform and renewal of all institutions in preparation for the Second Coming of Christ. Millenarian doctrines about the end of the world provided a sense of time and of the urgency of the moment.

In 1534, the Anabaptists captured the city of Münster in Westphalia near the western border of Germany. They seized the property of nonbelievers, burned all books except the Bible, and in a mood of jubilation and sexual excess, openly practiced a repressive (as far as women were concerned) polygamy. All the while the Anabaptists proclaimed that the Day of Judgment was close at hand. The leaders at Münster were men totally unprepared for power, and their actions led to a universal condemnation of the radicals. Their defeat was achieved by an army led by the Lutheran prince, Philip of Hesse.

In early modern Europe, *Münster* became a byword for dangerous revolution. Determined to prevent these wild enthusiasts from gaining strength in their own territories, princes attacked them with ferocity. In Münster today, the cages still hang from the church steeple where the Anabaptist leaders were tortured and left to die as a warning to all would-be imitators.

By the late sixteenth century, many radical movements had either gone underground or grown quiet. But a century later, during the English Revolution (1640–1660), the beliefs and political goals of the Radical Reformation again surfaced, threatening to push the revolution in a direction that its gentry leaders desperately feared. Although the radicals failed in England too, they left a tradition of democratic and antihierarchical thought. The radical assertion that saints, who have received the inner light, *are the equal of anyone*, regardless of social status, helped shape modern democratic thought.

The Catholic Response

The church could never have predicted the force of the Protestant Reformation, especially the number of powerful noblemen attracted to it. When it developed, the papacy seemed incapable of responding with needed reforms of its own, perhaps because it feared the forces that would be unleashed within the church and might challenge its own power. In the first instance, the energy for reform came from ordinary clergy as well as lay people, such as Ignatius Loyola (1491–1556), rather than from the hierarchy or the established religious orders. Trained as a soldier, this pious Spanish reformer sought to create a new religious order fusing the intellectual excellence of humanism with a reformed Catholicism that would appeal to powerful economic and political groups. Founded in 1534, the Society of Jesus, more commonly known as the Jesuits, became the backbone of the Catholic Reformation (also called the Counter Reformation) in southern and western Europe. The Jesuits combined traditional monastic discipline with a dedication to teaching and an emphasis on the power of preaching, and they sought to use both to win converts back to the church.

The Jesuits sought to bypass local corruption and appealed to the papacy to lead a truly international movement to revive Christian universalism. The Jesuits saw most clearly the power of the bitter fragmentation produced by the Reformation, and they also saw one of the central flaws in Protestant theology. Predestination offered salvation especially to the literate and prosperous laity and also, at least in theory, to the poor. It also, however, included the possibility of despair for the individual and a life tormented by a fear of damnation. In response, the Jesuits offered hope—a religious revival based on ceremony, tradition,

El Greco (1541–1614): Portrait of a Cardinal (probably Don Fernando Niño de Guevara). The Spanish church fiercely opposed the Reformation. The Inquisition persecuted Protestants relentlessly. The tenseness of the sitter captures the wary militancy of Spanish Catholicism. The cardinal's cool glance is belied by his claw-like hand. (*The Metropolitan Museum of Art, Bequest of Mrs. H. O. Havemeyer, 1929. The H. O. Havemeyer Collection. 29.100.5*)

and the power of the priest to offer forgiveness. In addition, they opened some of the finest schools in Europe. Just as the Lutherans in Germany sought to bring literacy to the masses so that they might read the Bible, the Jesuits sought to bring intellec-

tual enhancement to the laity, especially to the rich and powerful. The Jesuits pursued positions as confessors to princes and urged them to press their efforts to strengthen the church in their territories. They even sought to develop a theology that permitted "small sins" in the service of an ultimately just cause. In this way the Jesuits, by the seventeenth century, became the greatest teachers in Europe, and also the most controversial religious group within the church—were they the true voice of a reformed church, or did they use religion simply as a disguise to seek political power of their own, to make themselves the Machiavellian servants of princes? It was a controversy that neither their contemporaries nor historians have been able to solve.

The Jesuits built schools and universities throughout Europe, designed churches, and even fostered a distinct style of art and architecture: cherubic angles grace the ornate decor of Jesuit churches; heaven-bound virgins beckon the penitent. This baroque style, so lavish and emotive, was intended to move the heart, just as the skilled preacher sought to move the intellect. The Protestant message had been heard: religion is ultimately a private, psychological matter that is not always satisfied by scholastic argumentation.

By the 1540s the Counter Reformation was well under way. This attempt to reform the church from within combined several elements that had always stood for renewal within traditional Catholicism. For example, the Jesuits were imitating such preaching orders of the Middle Ages as the Dominicans and the Franciscans, and some Catholic reformers looked to Renaissance humanism like that of Erasmus as the key to the church's total reformation. The leaders of this Catholic movement attacked many of the same abuses that had impelled Luther to speak out, but they avoided a break with the doctrinal and spiritual authority of the clergy.

The Counter Reformation also took aggressive and hostile measures against Protestantism. The church tried to counter the popular appeal of Protestantism by offering dramatic, emotional, even sentimental piety to the faithful. For individuals who were unmoved by this appeal to sentiment or by the church's more traditional spirituality and who allied with Protestant heresy,

The Council of Trent. This drawing shows the prelates who gathered in council from time to time during 1545–1563 at Trent. The site, north of Italy, did not draw the hoped-for attendance of Protestants, but bishops did come from as far away as Ireland and Portugal. Despite problems of travel and attendance, the council achieved reforms in the Roman Catholic Church and a basis for its spiritual renewal. (*John Freeman*)

the church resorted to sterner measures. The Inquisition expanded its activities, and wherever Catholic jurisdiction prevailed, unrepentant heretics were subject to death or imprisonment. Catholics did not hold a monopoly on persecution: wherever Protestantism obtained official status—in England, Scotland, and Geneva, for instance—Catholics or religious radicals also sometimes faced persecution. Calvin, for example, approved the execution in 1563 of the naturalist and skeptic Michael Servetus, who opposed the doctrine of the Trinity. (In 1600, the church burned Giordano Bruno for similar reasons.)

One of the Catholic church's main tools was censorship. By the 1520s the impulse to censor and burn dangerous books intensified dramatically as the church tried to prevent the spread of Protestant ideas. In the rush to eliminate heretical literature, the church condemned the works of reforming Catholic humanists as well as those by Protestants. The Index of Prohibited Books became an institutional part of the church's life. Over the centuries, the works of many leading European thinkers were placed on the Index, which was not abolished until 1966.

These Counter Reformation policies of enlightened education, vigorous preaching, church building, persecution, and censorship did succeed in bringing thousands of people, Germans and Bohemians in particular, back into the church. In addition, the church implemented some concrete changes in policy and doctrine. In 1545, the Council of Trent met to reform the church and to strengthen it to face the Protestant challenge. Over the many years that it was convened (until 1563), the council modified and unified church doctrine; abolished many corrupt practices, such as the selling of indulgences; and vested final authority in the papacy, thereby ending the long and bitter struggle within the church over papal authority. The Council of Trent purged the church and gave it doctrinal clarity on such matters as the roles of faith and good works in attaining salvation. It passed a decree that the church shall be the final arbiter of the Bible and demanded that texts be taken literally wherever possible. Galileo was to experience great difficulties in the next century because that decree made the motion of the earth into a contradiction of Scripture (see pages 378–379). But the intention of the decree was to offer the church as a clear voice amid the babble of Protestant tongues. All compromise with Protestantism was rejected (not that Protestants were anxious for it). The Reformation had split western Christendom irrevocably.

The Reformation and the Modern Age

At first glance, the Reformation would seem to have renewed the medieval stress on other-worldliness and reversed the direction toward a secularized humanism taken by the Renaissance. Yet a careful analysis shows decisively modern elements in Reformation thought, as well as antifeudal tendencies in its political history. The Reformation shattered the religious unity of Europe, the chief characteristic of the Middle Ages, and further weakened the church, the principal institution of medieval society, whose moral authority and political power waned considerably. To this day Europe remains a continent of Catholic and Protestant. Although doctrinal rigidity (and in some places church attendance) has largely disappeared, the split between the southern Catholic countries and the Protestant north is still alive in various customs and traditions.

By strengthening the power of monarchs and magistrates at the expense of religious bodies, the Reformation furthered the growth of the modern state. Protestant rulers totally repudiated the pope's claim to temporal power and extended their authority over Protestant churches in their lands. In Catholic lands, the church reacted to the onslaught of Protestantism by supporting the monarchies, but at the same time it preserved a significant degree of political independence. Protestantism did not create the modern secular state; it did, however, help to free the state from subordination to religious authority; such autonomy is an essential feature of modern political life. From the Reformation onward, religious rivalries had to be calculated into foreign and domestic policies, and religious minorities were suspect everywhere.

Very indirectly, Protestantism contributed to the growth of political liberty—another ideal, although not always a reality, in the modern West. To be sure, neither Luther nor Calvin championed political freedom. Luther said that subjects should obey the commands of their rulers, and Calvinists created a theocracy in Geneva that closely regulated its citizens. Nevertheless, the Reformation provided a basis for challenging monarchical authority. During the religious wars, some Protestant theorists supported resistance to monarchs whose edicts, they believed, defied God's law. Moreover, the Protestant view that all believers—laity, clergy, lords, kings—were masters of their own spiritual destiny eroded hierarchical authority and accorded with emerging constitutional government.

Chronology 14.1 The Reformation

1381	English peasants revolt; support John Wycliffe, an early reformer
1414–1418	The Council of Constance
1431–1449	The Council of Basel
1517	Martin Luther writes his ninety-five theses and the Reformation begins
1520	Pope Leo X excommunicates Luther
1524–1526	The German peasants revolt
1529	The English Parliament accepts Henry VIII's Reformation
1534	Henry VIII is declared head of the Church of England; King Francis I of France declares Protestants heretics; Ignatius Loyola founds the Society of Jesus; Anabaptists, radical reformers, capture Münster in Westphalia
1536	Henry VIII dissolves monasteries and seizes their properties; Calvin publishes *Institutes of the Christian Religion*
1536–1564	Calvin leads the Reformation in Geneva with Guillaume (William) Farel
1545–1563	The Council of Trent
1553–1558	Mary, Catholic Queen of England, persecutes Protestants
1555	The Peace of Augsburg
1562–1598	French wars of religion between Catholics and Protestants are settled by the Edict of Nantes in 1598
1640–1660	The English Revolution

The Reformation also contributed to the creation of an individualistic ethic. Protestants sought a direct and personal relationship with God and interpreted the Bible for themselves. Facing the prospect of salvation or damnation entirely on their own, without the church to provide aid and security, and believing that God had chosen them to be saved, Protestants developed an inner confidence and assertiveness. This religious individualism was the counterpart of the intellectual individualism of the Renaissance humanists.

The Protestant ethic of the Reformation developed concurrently with a new economic system. Theorists have argued ever since about whether the new individualism of the Protestants brought on the growth of capitalism or whether the capitalistic values of the middle class gave rise to the Protestant ethic. In the middle of the nineteenth century, Karl Marx theorized that Protestantism gave expression to the new capitalistic values of the bourgeois: thrift, hard work, self-reliance, and rationality. Hence, Marx argued, the success of

Protestantism can be explained by reference to the emergence of Western capitalism. In 1904, the German sociologist Max Weber argued that Marx had got it backwards, that Protestantism encouraged the growth of capitalism, not vice versa.[4] Weber began with the assumption that religious beliefs do in fact have relevance to the way individuals act in the world. Religion is not primarily a series of doctrines, said Weber, but an ethic that possesses a spirit. Weber saw in the Protestant ethic of the Reformation, as it evolved through the life experiences of its followers, the spirit of a nascent capitalism.

Weber acknowledged that capitalism existed in Europe before the Reformation—for example, the merchant-bankers in Italian and German towns. But, argued Weber, not all capitalism is the same, and in the West it has been a particular type of capitalism that has proved most dynamic. Weber saw the spirit of capitalism embodied in the entrepreneur, the *parvenu*, the self-made man. He strives for business success and brings to his enterprise self-discipline and self-restraint. He makes profit not for pleasure, but for more profit. He brings to his enterprise moral virtues of frugality and honesty. And he strives to render work and business efficient and planned, with profits carefully accumulated over time.

For Weber, Protestants made the best capitalists because predestination made them *worldly ascetics*—Christians forced to find salvation without assistance and through activity in this world. The reformers had condemned the monastery as an unnatural life, and their concomitant emphasis on human sinfulness established a psychology of striving that could only be channeled into worldly activity. So Protestants fulfilled their vocation, or calling, by service to the community or state and by dedication to this daily work. Commerce could become, if Weber is right, sanctified. But this ethic did little to alleviate the condition of the poor, which had worsened by the end of the sixteenth century.

By the late seventeenth century in Europe, the center of economic growth was shifting away from Mediterranean and Catholic countries toward northern Atlantic areas: England, the Netherlands, and parts of northern France. Protestant cities, with their freer printing presses, were also becoming centers of intellectual creativity. The characteristics of the modern world—individual expression, economic exploitation, and scientific learning—were to become most visibly present in western European Protestant cities like London, Amsterdam, and Geneva. Both the Protestant entrepreneur and the Protestant intellectual began to symbolize the most advanced forms of economic and creative life.

The tradition of individual striving for material gain, so much a part of Western culture today, developed out of what had once been a religious quest for salvation, made urgent in this world by the theology of the Protestant Reformation. Sixteenth-century Protestantism created a new, highly individual spirituality. Survival in this world and salvation in the next came to depend on inner faith and self-discipline; for the prosperous, both eventually became useful in a highly competitive world where individuals rule their own lives and the labor of others and represent themselves and others in government.

Notes

1. John Dillenberger, ed., *Martin Luther: Selections from His Writings* (New York: Doubleday, 1961), p. 46, taken from *The Freedom of a Christian* (1520).

2. Martin Luther, *Luther's Works,* ed. by Robert Schultz (Philadelphia: Fortress Press, 1967), 46: 50–52.

3. François Wendel, *Calvin* (Paris: Presses Universitaires de France, 1950), p. 20.

4. See Max Weber, *Protestant Ethic and the Spirit of Capitalism*, trans. by Talcott Parsons (New York: Scribners, 1958).

Suggested Reading

Davidson, N. S., *The Counter-Reformation* (1987). A short, readable account.

Erikson, Erik H., *Young Man Luther* (1958). A psychological interpretation of Luther.

Grimm, Harold J., *The Reformation Era*, 1500–1650, 2nd ed. (1973). The best and most complete narrative available.

Hoffman, Philip T., *Church and Community in Lyon, 1500–1789* (1984). A good case study of one French city as it experienced the Reformation and the changes that came in its wake.

Huizinga, Johan, *Erasmus and the Age of Reformation* (1957). The best available survey.

R. T. Kendall, *Calvin and English Calvinism to 1649* (1979). An excellent treatment of the complexities of English Protestantism.

Koenigsberger, H. G., and George L. Mosse, *Europe in the Sixteenth Century* (1968). Some very good chapters on the Reformation.

Neale, J. E., *The Age of Catherine de Medici* (1960). This book manages to make sense out of a complex period.

O'Day, Rosemary, *The Debate on the English Reformation* (1986). A good account of what historians of all persuasions have said about the Reformation.

Ozment, Steven E., *The Reformation in the Cities* (1975). A good survey of the Reformation in Germany.

Scarisbrick, J. J., *Henry VIII* (1968). A very fair and balanced account of a most complex and willful monarch.

Tawney, R. H., *Religion and the Rise of Capitalism* (1962; reprint of 1926 ed.). Should be read by all students of Protestantism.

Weber, Max, *The Protestant Ethic and the Spirit of Capitalism*, trans. by Talcott Parsons (rev. ed. 1977). This classic essay argues the case for Protestantism as a force encouraging the development of capitalism. Written before World War I, it has never been surpassed.

Wendel, François, *Calvin* (1950). This is the standard biography.

Review Questions

1. Why did the Reformation begin in the early sixteenth century rather than in the fourteenth century at the time of Huss and Wycliffe? Describe the conditions and personalities responsible for starting the Reformation.

2. What personality traits did Martin Luther possess? Which traits seemed responsible for his role and actions in the Reformation? How did Luther's theology mark a break with the church? Why did many Germans become followers of Luther?

3. What role did the printing press play in the Reformation?

4. What were Calvin's major achievements?

5. In what ways did the radical reformers differ from the other Protestants?

6. What did *Münster* symbolize in early modern Europe?

7. How did the Reformation in England differ from that in Germany?

8. Why did France not become a Protestant country? Give the reasons and describe the circumstances.

9. What role did the Jesuits and the Inquisition play in the Counter Reformation? What did the Counter Reformation accomplish?

10. Which features of Protestantism were likely to have made its followers more successful capitalists than their Catholic contemporaries?

11. How did the Reformation weaken medieval institutions and traditions?

15

European Expansion: Economic and Social Transformations

During the period from 1450 to 1750, western Europe entered an era of overseas exploration and economic expansion that transformed society. By 1450, Europe had recovered from the severe contraction of the fourteenth century, produced by plague and marginal agriculture, and was resuming the economic growth that had been the pattern in the twelfth and early thirteenth centuries. This new period of growth, however, was no mere extension of the earlier one, but a radical departure from medieval economic forms.

Overseas exploration changed the patterns of economic growth and society. European adventurers discovered a new way to reach the rich trading centers of India by sailing around Africa. They also conquered, colonized, and exploited a new world across the Atlantic. These discoveries and conquests brought about an extraordinary increase in business activity and the supply of money, which stimulated the growth of capitalism. People's values changed in ways that were alien and hostile to the medieval outlook. By 1750, the model Christian in northwestern Europe was no longer the selfless saint but the enterprising businessman. The era of secluded manors and walled towns was drawing to a close. A world economy was emerging in which European economic life depended on the market in Eastern spices, African slaves, and American silver. During this age of exploration and commercial expansion, Europe generated a peculiar dynamism unmatched by any other civilization. A process was initiated that, by 1900, would give Europe mastery over most of the globe and wide-ranging influence over other civilizations.

The economic expansion from 1450 to 1650 or 1700 did not, however, raise the living standards of the masses. The vast majority of the people, 80 to 90 percent, lived on the land, and their main

Dutch Man-of-War Saluting (detail) by Van de Velde. (*Reproduced by Permission of the Trustees of the Wallace Collection*)

business was the production of primary goods—food, especially cereals, and wool. For most of these people, life hovered around the subsistence level, sometimes falling below subsistence during times of famine and disease. Whenever the standard of living improved, any surplus resources would soon be taken up by the survival of more children and hence more mouths to feed. The beneficiaries of the commercial expansion, those whose income rose, were the rich, especially the *nouveaux riches* (new rich).

In these respects, then, early modern Europe was comparable to an underdeveloped country today whose society consists of two main economic groups—a small, wealthy elite and a large and growing population that exists on the margin of subsistence and is wracked by recurrent hunger and disease. Developments during overseas exploration and economic expansion should be viewed in the context of these social conditions.

European Expansion

During the Middle Ages the frontiers of Europe had expanded, even if only temporarily in some instances. The Crusaders carved out feudal kingdoms in the Near East. Christian knights pushed back the Muslims on the Iberian Peninsula and drove them from Mediterranean islands. Germans expanded in the Baltic region at the expense of non-Christian Balts, Prussians, and Slavs. Genoa and Venice established commercial ports in the Adriatic Sea, the Black Sea, and the eastern Mediterranean. In the fifteenth and sixteenth centuries, western Europeans embarked on a second and more lasting movement of expansion that led them into the uncharted waters of the Atlantic, Indian, and Pacific oceans. Combined forces propelled Europeans outward and enabled them to dominate Asians, Africans, and American Indians.

Forces Behind Expansion

The population of western Europe increased rapidly between 1450 and 1600. This increase occurred at all levels of society, and among the gentry (hereditary landlords) it was translated into land hunger. As the numbers of the landed classes exceeded the supply of available land, the sons of the aristocracy looked beyond Europe for the lands and fortunes denied them at home. Nor was it unnatural for them to do so by plunder and conquest—their ancestors had done the same thing for centuries. Exploits undertaken and accomplished in the name of family, church, and king were legitimate, perhaps the most legitimate, ways of earning merit and fame, as well as fortune. So the gentry provided the leadership—Cortés is an example—for the expeditions to the New World.

Merchants and shippers, as well as the sons of the aristocracy, also had reason to look abroad. Trade between Europe, Africa, and the Orient had gone on for centuries, but always through intermediaries who increased the costs and decreased the profits on the European end. Gold had been transported by Arab nomads across the Sahara from the riverbeds of West Africa. Spices had been shipped from India and the East Indies by way of Muslim and Venetian merchants. Western European merchants now sought to break those monopolies by going directly to the source—to West Africa for gold, slaves, and pepper, and to India for pepper, spices, and silks. Moreover, incentive grew for such commercial enterprise because between 1450 and 1600 the wealth of prosperous Europeans increased dramatically. This wealth was translated into new purchasing power and the capacity to invest in foreign ventures that would meet the rising demand among the prosperous for luxury goods.

The centralizing monarchical state also played its part in expansion. Monarchs, like Ferdinand and Isabella of Spain, who had successfully established royal hegemony at home looked for opportunities to extend their control overseas. The Spanish rulers looked over their shoulders at their neighbors, the Portuguese, and this competition spurred the efforts of both countries in their drive to the East. Later the Dutch, English, and French engaged in a century-long rivalry. From overseas empires came gold, silver, and commerce that paid for ever-more-expensive royal government at home and for war against rival dynasties abroad.

Map of the New World. The development of the sailing ship and the gunship allowed Spain and Portugal to roam the seas with impunity. Spain had hoped that the New World would provide an abundance of costly spices. However, the land and precious metals there more than made up for the lack of spices. (*Fotomas Index, London*)

Finally, religion helped in expansion. The crusading tradition was well established, especially on the Iberian Peninsula, where a five-hundred-year struggle known as the Reconquest had taken place to drive out the Muslims. Cortés, for example, saw himself as following in the footsteps of Paladin Roland, the great medieval military hero who had fought to drive back Muslim and pagan. The Portuguese too were imbued with the crusading mission. Prince Henry the Navigator hoped that the Portuguese expansion into Africa would serve two purposes: the discovery of gold and the extension of Christianity at the expense of Islam. In this second aim, his imagination was fired by the legend of Prester John, which told of an ancient Christian kingdom of fabled wealth in the heart of Africa. If the Portuguese could reach that land, Prince Henry reckoned, the two kingdoms would join in a crusade against Islam.

Thus, expansion involved a mixture of economic, political, and religious forces and motives. The West possessed a crusading faith; divided into a handful of competing, warlike states, it expanded by virtue of forces built into its structure and culture. Not only did the West have the will to expand, it also possessed the technology needed for successful expansion. This factor also distinguished the West from China and the lands of Islam and helps to explain why the West, not the oriental civilizations, launched an age of conquest resulting in global mastery.

Not since the Early Middle Ages had there

been such a rapid technological revolution as that which began in the fifteenth century. Europeans learned about gunpowder from the Chinese as early as the late thirteenth century, and by the fifteenth century its military application had become widespread. The earliest guns were big cannons meant to knock holes in the walled defenses characteristic of the Middle Ages. In the sixteenth and seventeenth centuries, hand-held firearms (particularly the musket) and smaller, more mobile field artillery were perfected. Dynastic and religious wars and overseas expansion kept demand for armaments high, and the armament industry was, as a result, important to the growth of trade and manufacturing.

Another technological development during the period from 1400 to 1650 was the sailing ship. The vessels of the ancient world had been driven principally by oars and human energy. Such vessels, called galleys, were suitable for the shorter distances, calmer waters, and less variable conditions of the Mediterranean and the Black and Red seas. But galleys were unsuitable for the Atlantic and other great oceans that Europeans began to ply in the early sixteenth century. In western Europe by the fifteenth century, moreover, labor was in short supply, making it difficult to recruit or condemn men to the galleys. For these reasons the Portuguese, the Dutch, and the English abandoned the galley in favor of the sailing ship.

The sail and the gun were crucially important in allowing Europeans to overcome non-Europeans and penetrate and exploit their worlds. Western Europeans combined these devices in the form of the gunned ship. Not only was the sailing vessel more maneuverable and faster in the open seas than the galley, but the addition of guns gave it another tactical advantage over its rivals. The galleys of the Arabs in the Indian Ocean and the junks of the Chinese were not armed with guns below deck for firing at a distance to cripple or sink the enemy. In battle they relied instead on the ancient tactic of coming up alongside the enemy vessel, shearing off its oars, and boarding to fight on deck.

The gunned ship gave the West naval superiority from the beginning. The Portuguese, for example, made short work of the Muslim fleet sent to drive them out of the Indian Ocean in 1509. That victory at Diu, off the western coast of India, indicated that the West not only had found an all-water route to the Orient but was there to stay. Material and religious motives led Europeans to explore and conquer; superior technology ensured the success of their enterprises.

The Portuguese Empire

Several reasons account for Portugal's overseas success. Portugal's long Atlantic coastline ensured that its people would look to the sea—initially for fishing and trade and then for exploration. A sunny climate also spurred seafaring and commercial expansion. Portugal was northern Europe's closest supplier of subtropical products—olive oil, cork, wine, and fruit. The feudal nobility, typically antagonistic to trade and industry, was not as powerful in Portugal as elsewhere in Europe. Although feudal warriors had carved Portugal out of Moorish Iberia in the twelfth century, their descendants were blocked from further interior expansion by the presence of the strong Christian kingdom of Castile in the east. The only other outlet for expansion was the sea.

Royal policy also favored expansion. The central government promoted trading interests, especially after 1385, when the merchants of Lisbon and the lesser ports helped establish a new dynasty in opposition to the feudal aristocracy. In the first half of the fifteenth century a younger son of the king, named Prince Henry the Navigator (1394–1460) by English writers, sponsored voyages of exploration and the nautical studies needed to undertake them. In these endeavors he spent his own fortune and the wealth of the church's crusading order that he headed. Prince Henry sought to revive the anti-Muslim crusade to which Portugal owed its existence as a Christian state. This connection between the medieval crusades and the early modern expansion of Europe ran through Portuguese and Spanish history.

As early as the fifteenth century the Portuguese expanded into islands in the Atlantic Ocean. In 1420 they began to settle Madeira and raise corn there, and in the 1430s they pushed into the Canaries and the Azores in search of new farmlands and slaves for their colonies. In the middle decades of the century they moved down the

Map 15.1 Overseas Exploration and Conquest, c. 1400–1600 ▶

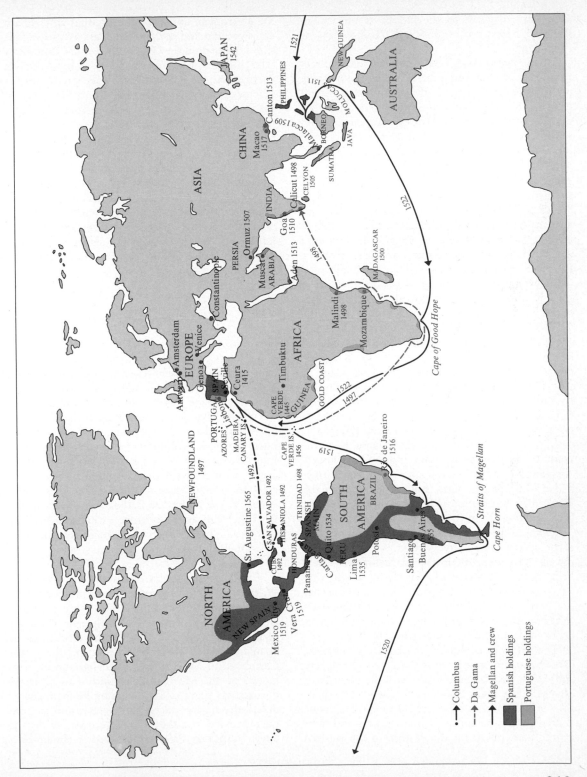

NORTH AMERICA

NEW SPAIN

Mexico City 1519
Vera Cruz 1519
HONDURAS
CUBA 1492
SAN SALVADOR 1492
HISPANIOLA 1492
TRINIDAD 1498
St. Augustine 1565

NEWFOUNDLAND 1497

SPANISH MAIN
Cartagena
Panama 1519
PERU
Lima 1535
Quito 1534
Potosí
SOUTH AMERICA
BRAZIL
Rio de Janeiro 1516
Santiago
Buenos Aires 1535

Straits of Magellan
Cape Horn

1519
1520

EUROPE
Amsterdam
Antwerp
Genoa Venice
Constantinople
SPAIN
Seville
PORTUGAL
Lisbon
AZORES
MADEIRA
CANARY IS.
CAPE VERDE IS. 1456

AFRICA
Ceuta 1415
Timbuktu
CAPE VERDE 1445
GUINEA
GOLD COAST
Malindi 1498
Mozambique
MADAGASCAR 1500
Cape of Good Hope

PERSIA
ARABIA
Muscat
Ormuz 1507
Aden 1513
1498

ASIA

INDIA
Goa 1510
Calicut 1498
CEYLON 1505

CHINA
Macao 1517
Canton 1513
MALACCA 1509
JAPAN 1542

PHILIPPINES
BORNEO 1511
SUMATRA
JAVA
MOLUCCAS
NEW GUINEA
AUSTRALIA

1497
1522
1519
1521
1522

• Columbus
- - - Da Gama
→ Magellan and crew
Spanish holdings
Portuguese holdings

west African coast to the mouth of the Congo River and beyond, establishing trading posts as they went.

By the last quarter of the century they had developed a viable imperial economy among the ports of West Africa, their Atlantic islands, and western Europe—an economy based on sugar, black slaves, and gold. Africans panned the gold in the riverbeds of central and western Africa, and the Portuguese purchased it at its source. They paid in cloth and slaves at a profit of at least 500 percent. Then the Portuguese transported the gold to Europe, where they sold it for even more profit. Slaves figured not only in the purchase of gold but also in the production of sugar. In their Atlantic islands the Portuguese grew sugar cane, and little else by the end of the century, as a cash crop for European consumption, and slaves were imported from West Africa to do the work. There was also a lively trade in slaves to Portugal itself and elsewhere in southern Europe.

The Portuguese did not stop in western Africa. By 1488, Bartholomeu Dias had reached the southern tip of the African continent; a decade later Vasco da Gama sailed around the Cape of Good Hope and across the Indian Ocean to India. By discovering an all-water route to the Orient, Portugal broke the commercial monopoly of Eastern goods that Genoa and Venice had enjoyed.

In search of spices, the Portuguese went directly to the source, to India and the East Indies. As along the African coast, they established fortified trading posts—most notably at Goa on the western coast of India (Malabar) and at Malacca (now Singapore) in the Malay Peninsula.

Demand for spices was insatiable. Pepper and other spices are relatively unimportant items in the modern diet, but in the era before refrigeration, fresh meat was available only at slaughtering time, customarily twice a year. The rest of the year the only meat available, for those who could afford it at all, was dried, stringy, and tough; spices made meat and other foods palatable.

The infusion of Italian, particularly Genoese, investment and talent contributed to Portuguese expansion. As Genoese trade with the Near East, especially the Black Sea, shrank due to the expansion of the Ottoman Empire, Genoese merchants shifted more and more of their capital and mercantile activities from the eastern to the western Mediterranean and the Atlantic, that is, to Spain and Portugal and their possessions overseas. This shift is evident in the life of Christopher Columbus (1451–1506), a Genoese sailor, who worked in Portugal before finally winning acceptance for his scheme to find a westward route to the spices of the East at the court of Castile in Spain. Initially, much of the Genoese investment was in the sugar plantations in Portuguese colonies in the Atlantic. The Portuguese gained not only Genoese capital but also the expertise to put it to use. The Genoese had established their own sugar colonies in Cyprus and Crete two centuries before, and they knew from long experience that would work. The plantation system based on slave labor was an Italian import; only now the slaves were black Africans instead of Slavs, as they had often been in the eastern Mediterranean.

The Spanish Empire

Spain stumbled onto its overseas empire, which nonetheless proved to be the biggest and richest of any until the eighteenth century. Columbus won the support of Isabella, queen of Castile. But on his first voyage (1492) he landed on the large Caribbean island that he named Española (Little Spain). To the end of his life, even after subsequent voyages, Columbus believed that the West Indies were part of the East. Two forthcoming events would reveal that Columbus had discovered not a new route to the East but new continents: Vasco Nuñez de Balboa's discovery of the Pacific Ocean at the Isthmus of Panama in 1513 and Ferdinand Magellan's circumnavigation of the globe (1520–21) through the strait at the tip of South America bearing his name.

The Spanish found no spices in the New World, but they were more than compensated by the abundant land and the large quantities of precious metals. Stories of the existence of larger quantities of gold and silver to the west lured the Spaniards from their initial settlements in the Caribbean to Mexico. In 1519, Hernando Cortés landed on the Mexican coast with a small army; during two years of campaigning he managed to defeat the native rulers, the Aztecs, and to conquer Mexico for the Spanish crown. A decade later, Francisco Pizarro achieved a similar vic-

Isabella and Ferdinand. With the marriage of Ferdinand of Aragon to Isabella of Castile, Spain came into being as a nation. At the battle of Granada, they defeated the last of the Islamic forces on the Spanish mainland. Columbus courted and won the patronage of Isabella. Monies that had previously been used to fight Islam were diverted to exploration. The wealth of the New World would repay her patronage beyond all expectation. (*Copyright reserved to H.M. The Queen*)

tory over the mountain empire of the Incas in Peru. Both Cortés and Pizarro exploited the hostility that the subject tribes of Mexico and Peru felt toward their Aztec and Incan overlords, a strategy that accounts in large part for the Spaniards' success.

For good reasons, the Mexican and Peruvian conquests became the centers of the Spanish overseas empire. First, there were the gold hoards accumulated over the centuries by the rulers for religious and ceremonial purposes. And when these supplies were exhausted, the Spanish discovered silver at Potosí in Upper Peru in 1545 and at Zacatecas in Mexico a few years later. From the middle of the century, the annual treasure fleets sailing to Spain became the financial bedrock of Philip II's war against the Muslim Turks and the Protestant Dutch and English.

Not only gold and silver lured Spaniards to the New World. The crusading tradition also acted as a spur. Cortés, Pizarro, and many of their followers were *hidalgos*—lesser gentry whose status depended on the possession of landed estates and whose training and experience taught that holy war was a legitimate avenue to wealth and power. Their fathers had conquered Granada, the last Muslim kingdom in Spain, in 1492; they had expelled the Jews the same year and had carried the Christian crusade across to North Africa. The conquest and conversion of the pagan peoples of

Indian Workers Mining for Gold, Overseen by Their Spanish Conquerors. The Spanish conquest of the Indians in Latin America filled the coffers of Spain with gold and silver. The native population was decimated, largely by disease, and most native artifacts were destroyed, regarded by the Europeans as heathen work and beneath their consideration. (*Historical Pictures Service, Chicago*)

the New World was an extension of the crusading spirit that marked the five previous centuries of Spanish history. The rewards were what they had always been: the propagation of the true faith, service to the Crown, handsome land grants, and control over the inhabitants, who would work the fields. The land was especially attractive in the sixteenth century because the number of hidalgos was increasing with the general rise in population, and the amount of land available to them at home was as a result shrinking.

The conquerors initially obtained two kinds of grants from the Crown, *encomiendas* and *estancias*. The latter were land grants, either of land formerly belonging to the native priestly and noble castes or of land in remoter and less fertile regions. Encomiendas were royal grants of authority over the natives. Those who received such authority, the *encomenderos,* promised to give protection and instruction in the Christian religion to their charges. In return they gained the power to extract labor and tribute from the peasant masses, who were worked beyond their capacity.

The royal grants of encomiendas during the first generation of Spanish settlement were partially responsible for the decimation within a century of European occupation of the native population in the New World. Between 1500 and 1600, the number of natives shrank from about 20 million to little more than 2 million. The major cause of this catastrophe, however, was not forced labor but the diseases introduced from Europe—dysentery, malaria, hookworm, smallpox—against which the natives had little or no natural resistance. Beginning in the 1540s, the position of the natives gradually improved as the Crown withdrew grants that gave authority over the natives and took increasing responsibility for controlling the Indians.

Power and wealth gradually concentrated in fewer and fewer hands. As the Spanish landholders lost authority over the native population to royal officials and their associates, the latter gained substantially in power and privilege. As recurrent depressions ruined smaller landowners, they were forced to sell out to their bigger neighbors. On their conversion to Christianity, the Indians were persuaded to give more and more land to the church. Thus, Spanish America became permanently divided between the privileged elite and the impoverished masses.

One group suffered even more than the Indians: the blacks. The natives at least escaped the degradation of slavery. But blacks were imported from Africa in increasing numbers, especially as the Indian population declined, to work as slaves in the fields and the mines. The Portuguese and, in the eighteenth century, the British were the most important slave traders. Africans were captured by rival black tribes in western Africa, then enslaved and sold to Europeans in ports along the west African coast. The Africans were then herded onto ships for passage to the New World under such brutal conditions that only about half of them survived. Those who did were sold at auction in the ports of the Caribbean and North America; sellers and buyers considered the age and physical condition of the slaves, with little or no regard for any other aspects of their wellbeing—family ties for instance.

The Price Revolution

Linked to overseas expansion was another phenomenon—an unprecedented inflation during the sixteenth century, known as the *price revolution*. Evidence is insufficient on the general rise in prices. However, cereal prices multiplied by as much as eight times or more in certain regions in the course of the sixteenth century, and they continued to rise, although more slowly, during the first half of the next century. After 1650, prices leveled off or fell in most places; this pattern continued throughout the eighteenth century in England and off and on in France up to the Revolution. Economic historians have generally assumed that the prices of goods other than cereals increased by half as much as grain prices. Since people at that time did not understand why prices rose so rapidly, inflation was not subject to control. On the contrary, the remedies governments applied, like currency debasement, often worsened the problem.

Like colonization, the price revolution played an enormous role in the commercial revolution and did, in fact, partially result from the silver mining conducted in New Spain. The main cause of the price revolution, however, was the population growth during the late fifteenth and sixteenth centuries.

The population of Europe almost doubled between 1460 and 1620, and then it leveled off and decreased in some places. The patterns of population growth and of cereal prices thus match in the sixteenth and seventeenth centuries. Until the middle of the seventeenth century the number of mouths to feed outran the capacity of agriculture to supply basic foodstuffs, causing the vast majority of people to live close to subsistence. Until food production could catch up with the increasing population, prices, especially those of the staple food, bread, would continue to rise.

Why population grew so rapidly in the fifteenth and sixteenth centuries is not known, but the reasons why the population declined in the seventeenth century are. By then, the population had so outgrown the food supply that scarcity began to take its toll. Malnourishment, starvation, and disease pushed the death rate higher than the birthrate. With time, of course, prices lowered as population and hence demand declined in the 1600s.

The other principal cause of the price revolution was *probably* the silver that, beginning in 1552, flowed into Europe from the New World via Spain. But as a cause, the influx of silver lies on shakier ground than the inflationary effects of an expanding population. The increases in production and consumption following the growth in population would, to some degree, have necessitated an increase in the money supply to accommodate the greater number of commercial transactions. At some point it is assumed that the influx of silver exceeded the necessary expansion of the money supply and itself began contributing to the inflation. The most that can now be said is that the price revolution was caused by *too many people with too much money chasing too few goods*. The effects of the price revolution were momentous.

The Expansion of Agriculture

The greatest effects of the price revolution were on the land. Food prices, rising roughly twice as much as the prices of other goods, spurred ambitious farmers to take advantage of the situation and to produce for the expanding market. The opportunity for profit drove some farmers to work harder and manage their land better. The impact of the price revolution follows from that incentive.

The Old Pattern of Farming

The effects of the price revolution on farming were governed by the general social and political conditions operating in any given region or country. The effects in England were one sort; among the Dutch, another; in France, Spain, and the Mediterranean, still another; and in the Holy Ro-

man Empire east of the Elbe River, in Poland, and in Russia, yet a fourth type. These differences must be compared against a background of European agriculture as it was practiced before the price revolution.

All over Europe, landlords held their properties in the form of manors. A particular type of rural society and economy had evolved on these manors in the Late Middle Ages. By the fifteenth century, much manor land was held by peasant-tenants according to the terms of a tenure known in England as *copyhold*. The tenants had certain hereditary rights to the land in return for the performance of certain services and the payment of certain fees to the landlord. Principal among these rights was the use of the commons—the pasture, woods, and pond. For the copyholder, access to the commons often made the difference between subsistence and real want, because the land tilled on the manor might not produce enough to keep a family.

Arable land was worked according to ancient custom. The land was divided into strips, and each peasant of the manor was assigned a certain number of strips. This whole pattern of peasant tillage and rights in the commons was known as the *open-field system*. After changing little for centuries, it was met head-on by the incentives generated by the price revolution.

Enclosure

In England, landlords aggressively pursued the possibilities for profit resulting from the inflation of farm prices. This pursuit required far-reaching changes in ancient manorial agriculture, changes that are called *enclosure*. The open-field system was geared to providing subsistence for the local village and, as such, prevented large-scale farming for a distant market. In the open-field system, the commons could not be diverted to the production of crops for sale. Moreover, the division of the arable land into strips made it difficult to engage in profitable commercial agriculture.

English landlords in the sixteenth century fought a two-pronged attack against the open-field system in their attempt to transform their holdings into market-oriented, commercial ven-

Harvesting Scene by Peter Brueghel the Younger (1564–1637). England and the Netherlands underwent major agricultural changes in the sixteenth and seventeenth centuries. The enclosure system in England intensified land use and led to commercialization of agriculture. Convertible husbandry in the Netherlands ensured that the land was engaged for diversified agriculture, with no plots of land remaining unused. (*Nelson-Atkins Museum of Art, Kansas City, Mo.; Nelson Fund*)

tures. First they deprived their tenant peasantry of the use of the commons; then they changed the conditions of tenure from copyhold to leasehold. Whereas copyhold was heritable and fixed, leasehold was not. When a lease came up for renewal, the landlord could raise the rent beyond the tenant's capacity to pay. Restriction of rights to the commons deprived the poor tenant of critically needed produce. Both acts of the landlord forced peasants off the manor or into the landlord's employ as farm laborers.

With tenants gone, fields could be incorporated into larger, more productive units. Subsistence farming gave way to commercial agriculture—the growing of a surplus for the marketplace. Landlords would either hire laborers to work recently enclosed fields or rent these fields to prosperous farmers in the neighborhood. Either way, landlords stood to gain. They could hire labor at bargain prices because of the swelling population and the large supply of peasants forced off the land by enclosure. If the landlords chose to rent out their fields, they also profited. Prosperous farmers who themselves grew for the market could afford to pay higher rents than the previous tenants, the subsistence farmers; and they were willing to pay more because farm prices tended to rise even faster than rents.

The Yeomanry in England

The existence of prosperous farmers, sometimes called *yeomen*, in English rural society was crucial to the commercialization of farming. Yeomen were men who may not have owned much land themselves, but who rented enough to produce a marketable surplus, sometimes a substantial one. They emerged as a discernible rural group in the High Middle Ages and were a product of the unique English inheritance custom, observed by peasantry and gentry alike, of *primogeniture*. The eldest son inherited the land, and the younger sons had to fend for themselves. Thus the land remained undivided, and the heirs among the peasantry often had enough land to produce a surplus for market. Many a gentleman landowner enclosed his fields not to work them himself but to rent them to neighboring yeomen at rates allowing him to keep abreast of spiraling prices. Yeomen were better suited to work the land than the landlord, depending on it as they did for their livelihood.

One other process growing out of the price revolution promoted the commercialization of farming. Rising prices forced less businesslike landlords, who did not take advantage of the profit to be made from farming, to sell property in order to meet current expenses. The conditions of the price revolution thus tended to put an increasing amount of land into more productive hands. But rural poverty and violence increased because of the mass evictions of tenant farmers.

Convertible Husbandry

The effects of the price revolution on agriculture in the Netherlands were as dramatic and important as those in England. The Dutch population had soared and the majority of people had moved to the cities by the seventeenth century. As a result, a situation unique in all Europe—the problem of land use—became vitally important, especially as there was so little land to start with. The Dutch continued their efforts to reclaim land from the sea, which began in the Middle Ages. More significant, however, was their development in the fifteenth and sixteenth centuries, of a new kind of farming, known as *convertible husbandry*. This farming system employed a series of innovations that replaced the old three-field system of crop rotation, which had left one-third of the land unused at any given time. The new techniques used all the land every year and provided a more diversified agriculture.

The techniques combined soil-depleting cereals with soil-restoring legumes and grazing. For a couple of years, a field would be planted in cereals; in the third year, peas or beans would be sown to return essential nitrogen to the soil; for the next four or five years, the field became pasture for grazing animals, whose manure would further restore the soil for replanting cereals to restart the cycle. Land thus returned to grain would produce much more than land used in the three-field system. These devices for increasing productivity, when exported from the Netherlands and applied in England and France between 1650 and 1750, were essential in the complicated process by which these countries eventually became industrialized. For industrialization requires an agriculture productive enough to feed large, nonfarming urban populations.

Agricultural Change in Eastern Europe

In the Europe that stretches from the Elbe River across the Baltic plain to Russia, the effects of the price revolution were as dramatic as they were in England. The Baltic plain played an essential role in the European economy in the fifteenth, sixteenth, and early seventeenth centuries. Because western Europeans continued to outrun their food supply (in some places until the middle of the seventeenth century), they turned to the Baltic for regular shipments of grain.

Thus the landlords in the Baltic plain became commercial farmers producing for an international market. This trade led to a reorganization in the region south and east of the Baltic. There, as in England, enclosure to produce an agricultural surplus took place on a vast scale. But in contrast to the English experience, the peasant-tenants who had engaged in subsistence farming

Departure of East Indiamen from England. Both England and the Netherlands formed East India Companies—joint stock companies. Distant ports around the globe found Dutch and British traders selling goods and buying raw materials, and in the process establishing colonies for their countries. (*National Maritime Museum Greenwich*)

on these lands for generations were not evicted; nor did they become farm laborers working for low wages. Instead they remained on the land, and the terms of their tenure gradually shifted toward serfdom. As in Spain, a two-caste society emerged, a world of noble landlords and serfs. But unlike Spain's, this society produced for the marketplace.

The Expansion of Trade and Industry

The conditions of the price revolution also caused trade and industry to expand. Population growth exceeding the capacity of local food supplies stimulated commerce in basic foodstuffs, for example the Baltic trade with western Europe. Equally important as a stimulus to trade and industry was the growing income of landlords, merchants, and in some instances, peasants. This income created a rising demand for consumer goods, which helps explain several activities already mentioned. For example, the Portuguese spice trade with the East and the sugar industry in the Portuguese islands developed because prosperous people wanted such products. Rising income also created a demand for farm products other than cereals—meat, cheese, fruit, wine, and vegetables. The resulting land use reduced the area available for grain production and contributed to the rise in bread prices, which meant even larger profits.

Another factor in the commercial and industrial expansion was the growth of the state. With increasing amounts of tax revenue to spend, the expanding monarchies of the sixteenth and seventeenth centuries bought more and more supplies—ships, weapons, uniforms, paper—and so spurred economic expansion.

The Putting-Out System

Along with commercial and industrial expansion came a change in the nature of the productive enterprise. Just as the price revolution produced, in the enclosure movement, a reorganization of agriculture and agrarian society, it similarly affected trade and manufacturing. The reorganization there took place especially in the faster-growing industries—woolen and linen textiles—where an increasingly large mass market outpaced supply and thus made prices rise. This basic condition of the price revolution operated, just as it did in food production, to produce expansion. In the textile industries, increasing demand promoted specialization. For example, eastern and southwestern England made woolens, and northwestern France and the Netherlands produced linen.

Markets tended to shift from local to regional or even to international, a condition that gave rise to the merchant-capitalist. Unlike local producers, the merchant-capitalists' operations extended across local and national boundaries. This mobility allowed these capitalists to buy or produce

goods where costs were lowest and to sell where prices and volume were highest. Because of the size and range of a business, an individual capitalist could control the traditional local producers, who increasingly depended on him for the widespread marketing of their expanded production.

This procedure, which was well developed by the seventeeth century, gave rise to what is known as the *putting-out system* of production. The manufacture of woolen textiles is a good example of how the system worked. The merchant-capitalist would buy the raw wool from English landlords who had enclosed their manors to take advantage of the rising price of wool. The merchant's agents collected the wool and took it (put it out) to nearby villages for spinning, dyeing, and weaving. The work was done in the cottages of peasants, many of whom had been evicted from the surrounding manors as a result of enclosure and therefore had to take what work they could get at the lowest possible wages. When the wool was processed into cloth, it was picked up and shipped to market.

The putting-out system represents an important step in the evolution of capitalism. It was not industrial capitalism, because there were no factories and the work was done by hand rather than by power machinery; nevertheless, the putting-out system significantly broke with the medieval guild system (see page 203). The new merchant-capitalists saw that the work was performed in the countryside, rather than in the cities and towns, to avoid guild restrictions (on output, quality, pay, and working conditions). The distinction between a master and an apprentice who will someday replace the master, which is assumed in the guild framework, gave way to the distinction between the merchant-owner (the person who provided the capital) and the worker (the one who provided the labor in return for wages and would probably never be an owner).

Enclosure also served to capitalize industry. Mass evictions lowered the wages of cottage workers because labor was plentiful. This condition provided additional incentive on the part of the merchant-capitalist to invest in cottage industry. But the changes in farming were much more important in the economic development of Europe than the changes in industry, because agriculture represented a much larger share of total wealth.

The Syndics of the Cloth Guild by Rembrandt van Rijn (1606–1669). Power and wealth came into the hands of merchants and tradesmen. Collecting art, commissioning a portrait, and sitting for a group portrait—once the privileges of royalty—became bourgeois preoccupations. (*Rijksmuseum, Amsterdam*)

Innovations in Business

Accompanying the emergence of the merchant-capitalist and the putting-out system was a cluster of other innovations in business life, some of them having roots in the Middle Ages (see page 200). Banking operations grew more sophisticated, making it possible for depositors to pay their debts by issuing written orders to their banks to make transfers to their creditors' accounts—the origins of the modern check. Accounting methods also improved. The widespread use of double-entry bookkeeping made errors immediately evident and gave a clear picture of the financial position of a commercial enterprise. Although known in the ancient world, double-entry bookkeeping was not widely practiced in the West until the fourteenth century. In this and other business practices the lands of southern Europe, especially Italy, were the forerunners; their accounting techniques spread to the rest of Europe in the sixteenth century.

The fourteenth century also saw the development of business practices related to shipping. A system of maritime insurance, without which investors would have been highly reluctant to risk their money on expensive vessels, evolved in Florence. By 1400, maritime insurance had become a regular item of the shipping business, and it was destined to play a major role in the opening of

Atlantic trade. At least equally important to overseas expansion was the form of business enterprise known as the joint-stock company, which allowed small investors to buy shares in a venture. These companies made possible the accumulation of the large amounts of capital needed for large-scale operations, like the building and deployment of merchant fleets, which were quite beyond the resources of one person.

Different Patterns of Commercial Development

The response to the price revolution in trade and industry differed in various parts of Europe—and the different responses hinged again on social and political conditions. In both the United Provinces (the Netherlands) and England there were far fewer strictures on trade and industry than in France and Spain. Thus, in the sixteenth and seventeenth centuries, England and the United Provinces were better placed than France and Spain to take advantage of the favorable conditions for business expansion. In the United Provinces, this favorable position resulted from the weakness of feudal culture and values in comparison to commercial ones; other factors were its small land area and a far larger percentage of urban population than elsewhere in western Europe.

England's advantage derived from a different source: not the weakness of the landed gentry but its habits. Primogeniture operated among those who owned large estates just as it did among the yeomanry, with much the same effect. Younger sons were forced to make their fortunes elsewhere. Those who did so by going into business would often benefit from an infusion of venture capital that came from their elder brothers' landed estates. And of course capital was forthcoming from such quarters because of the profitable nature of English farming. In a reverse process, those who made fortunes in trade would typically invest money in land and rise gradually into landed society. Those skills that had brought wealth in commerce would then be applied to new estates, usually with equal success.

England and the Netherlands In both England and the United Provinces the favorable conditions led to large-scale commercial expansion. In the

1590s the Dutch devised a new ship, the *fluit,* or flyboat, to handle bulky grain shipments at the lowest possible cost. This innovation allowed them to capture the Baltic trade, which became a principal source of their phenomenal commercial expansion between 1560 and 1660. Equally dramatic was their commercial penetration of the Orient. Profits from the European carrying trade built ships that allowed them first to challenge and then to displace the Portuguese in the spice trade with the East Indies during the early seventeenth century. The Dutch chartered the United East India Company in 1602 and established trading posts in the islands, which were the beginnings of a Dutch empire that lasted until World War II.

The English traded throughout Europe in the sixteenth and seventeenth centuries, especially with Spain and the Netherlands. The staples of this trade were raw wool and woolens, but increasingly they included such items as ships and guns. The seventeenth century saw the foundation of a British colonial empire along the Atlantic seaboard in North America from Maine to the Carolinas and in the West Indies, where the English managed to dislodge the Spanish in some places.

In both England and the United Provinces, government promoted the interests of business. In the late sixteenth and early seventeenth centuries the northern provinces of the Spanish Netherlands, centered around Holland, won their independence from Spain in a protracted struggle. Political power in these so-called United Provinces passed increasingly into the hands of an urban patriciate of merchants and manufacturers based in cities like Delft, Haarlem, and especially Amsterdam. These urban interests pursued public policies that served their pocketbooks. Flanders (the southern provinces of the Netherlands) and Antwerp, their commercial capital, remained under Spanish domination. From the 1590s the Dutch, as the inhabitants of the United Provinces were called, sent ships to close the Scheldt (the river linking Antwerp to the North Sea) to commercial traffic. This act dealt a fatal blow to the economic fortunes of the city that had dominated trade between northern and southern Europe and between England

Map 15.2 Industrial Centers in the Sixteenth Century ▶

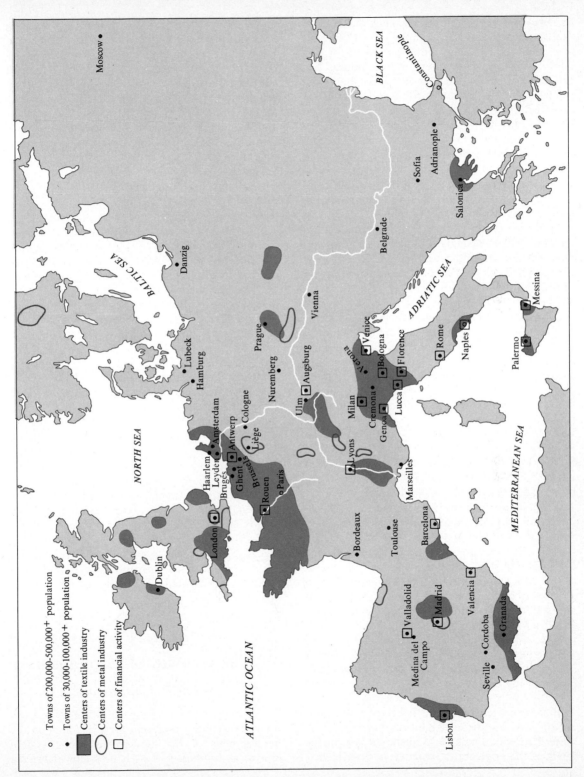

Towns of 200,000-500,000+ population ○

Towns of 30,000-100,000+ population •

Centers of textile industry

Centers of metal industry

Centers of financial activity

BLACK SEA

Constantinople

Moscow

Sofia · Adrianople

Salonica

Danzig

Belgrade

ADRIATIC SEA

BALTIC SEA

Vienna

Messina

Lübeck

Hamburg

Prague

Venice

Verona · Bologna · Rome · Naples

Palermo

Nuremberg

Augsburg

Florence

Ulm

Milan · Cremona · Lucca

Genoa

Cologne

Amsterdam

Antwerp · Liège

Haarlem

Leyden · Brussels

Bruges · Ghent

Lyons

Marseilles

MEDITERRANEAN SEA

London

Rouen · Paris

NORTH SEA

Bordeaux

Toulouse

Barcelona

Dublin

ATLANTIC OCEAN

Valladolid · Madrid

Valencia

Medina del Campo

Granada

Seville · Cordoba

Lisbon

and the Continent in the late fifteenth and much of the sixteenth centuries. Antwerp's position of leadership as a trading center passed to Amsterdam, and later to London and Hamburg. The founding of the Dutch East India Company and the Bank of Amsterdam in the first decade of the seventeenth century also stemmed from an alliance between business and government for their mutual interests. The Bank of Amsterdam expanded credit, lowered interest rates, and increased confidence. The Dutch East India Company regulated trade, reduced wasteful competition between formerly independent traders, and hence consolidated investment.

In seventeenth-century England the central government increasingly took the side of the capitalist producer. At the beginning of the century the king had imposed feudal fees on landed property, acted against enclosures, and granted monopolies in trade and manufacture to court favorites, which restricted opportunities for investment. The king also spent revenues on maintaining an unproductive aristocracy. But by the end of the century, due to the revolutionary transfer of power from the king to Parliament, economic policy more closely reflected the interests of big business, whether agricultural or commercial. Landowners no longer paid feudal dues to the king. Enclosure went on unimpeded, in fact abetted, by parliamentary enactment. The Bank of England, founded in 1694, brought the same benefits to English investors that the Bank of Amsterdam had been offering the Dutch for almost a century.

The Navigation Act, first passed in 1651, allowed all English shippers to carry goods anywhere, replacing the old system that had restricted trade with certain areas to specific traders. The act also required that all goods be carried in English ships, allowing merchants, as Christopher Hill writes, "to buy English and colonial exports cheap and sell them dear abroad, to buy foreign goods cheap and sell them dear in England."[1] English shippers also gained the profits of the carrying trade, one factor leading to the displacement of the Dutch by the English as the leading power in international commerce after 1660.

France and Spain   France benefited from commercial and industrial expansion, but not to the same degree as England. A principal reason for this was the aristocratic structure of French society. Family ties and social intercourse between aristocracy and merchants, such as existed in England, were largely absent in France. Consequently, the French aristocracy remained contemptuous of commerce. Also inhibiting economic expansion were the guilds—remnants of the Middle Ages that restricted competition and production. In France there was relatively less room than in England for the merchant-capitalist operating outside the guild structures.

Spain presents an even clearer example of failure to grasp the opportunities afforded by the price revolution. By the third quarter of the sixteenth century, Spain possessed the makings of economic expansion: unrivaled amounts of capital in the form of silver, a large and growing population, rising consumer demand, and a vast overseas empire. These factors did not bear fruit because the Spanish value system regarded business as a form of social heresy. The Spanish held in high esteem those gentlemen who possessed land gained through military service and crusading ardor, which enabled them to live on rents and privileges. So commerce and industry remained contemptible pursuits.

Numerous wars in the sixteenth century (with France, the Lutheran princes, the Ottoman Turks, the Dutch, and the English) put an increasing strain on the Spanish treasury, even with the annual shipments of silver from the New World. Spain spent its resources on maintaining and extending its imperial power and Catholicism, rather than on investing in economic expansion. In the end, the wars cost even more than Spain could handle. The Dutch, for a time, and the English and the French, more permanently, displaced Spain as the great power. The English and the Dutch had taken advantage of the opportunities presented by the price revolution; the Spanish had not.

The Growth of Capitalism

What Is Capitalism?

The changes described—especially in England and the Netherlands—represent a crucial stage in the development of the modern economic system known as *capitalism*. This is a system of *private enterprise:* the main economic decisions (what, how much, where, and at what price to produce, buy, and sell) are made by private individuals in their capacity as either owners, workers, or consumers. Capitalism is also said to be a system of *free enterprise:* the basic decisions are not left to individuals only; these decisions are also made in response to market forces. People are free, in other words, to obey the law of supply and demand. When goods and labor are scarce, prices and wages rise; when they are plentiful, prices and wages fall.

In the Middle Ages, capitalistic enterprise had not been widespread because the market and therefore the operation of market forces were severely restricted. The vast majority of people lived as self-sufficient subsistence farmers (peasants or serfs) on the land. There was some trade and a few small cities, especially in Italy, where capitalistic enterprise was conducted, but this commerce accounted for only a tiny fraction of total economic activity. Even in the cities, capitalistic forms of enterprise were hampered by guild restrictions, which set limits on production, wages, and prices without regard for market forces. In addition, the economic decay of the fourteenth and early fifteenth centuries did not predispose those who had surplus money to gamble on the future.

But conditions changed in certain quarters beginning in the fifteenth and sixteenth centuries, generating the incentive to invest—to take risks for future profit rather than to consume. This process was due, more than anything else, to the economic situation prevailing in Europe between 1450 and 1600.

The Fostering of Mercantile Capitalism

Several conditions fostered a sustained incentive to invest and reinvest—a basic factor in the emergence of modern capitalism. One was the price revolution stemming from a supply of basic commodities that could not keep pace with rising demand. Prices continued to climb, creating the most powerful incentive of all to invest rather than to consume. Why spend now, those with surplus wealth must have asked, when investment in commercial farming, mining, shipping, and publishing (to name a few important outlets) is almost

certain to yield greater wealth in the future? The price revolution reduced the risk involved in investment, thus helping overcome the reluctance of the wealthy to engage in capitalistic enterprise.

Another condition that encouraged investment was that wealth was distributed in a way that promoted investment. Three distinct patterns of distribution worked to this effect. First, inflation widened the gap between rich and poor during the sixteenth century; the rich who chose to invest garnered increasing amounts of wealth, which probably added to their incentive to go on investing. Because of the growing population and the resulting shortage of jobs, employers could pay lower and lower wages; thus, again, their profits increased, encouraging reinvestment. Merchant-capitalists were an important group of investors who gained from these factors. As they grew, they were able to exercise a controlling influence in the marketplace because they operated on a large scale, from regional to international; thus they were able to dictate terms of production and employment, displacing the local guilds. This displacement represents another factor in the pattern of wealth distribution (and redistribution) favorable to investment and growth. Mercantile capitalism did not benefit all alike; in fact it produced increasing inequities between rich and poor, owners and workers, independent merchant-capitalists and local guildsmen.

The second pattern of wealth distribution that encouraged investment grew out of the practice of primogeniture. The concentration of inherited property in the hands of the eldest child (usually the oldest son) meant that he had sufficient wealth to be persuaded to invest at least part of it. Any younger sons were left to make their own way in the world and often turned their drive and ambition into profits.

Finally, a pattern of international distribution of wealth promoted investment in some lands. The classic example is that of Spain in relation, say, to England. Spain in the sixteenth century devoted its wealth and energies to religious war and empire and relied on producers elsewhere for many of its supplies. So Spanish treasure was exported to England to pay for imports, stimulating investment there rather than in Spain. Capitalism did not develop everywhere at the same pace, and as the Spanish case shows, the very conditions that

Inside the Amsterdam Stock Exchange by J. Berckheyde. Seventeenth-century Holland saw the rise of a solid bourgeosie and produced an economic system that looked toward twentieth-century capitalism. Every available commodity was sold, from spices and slaves to tulips. (*Amsterdams Historisch Museum*)

discouraged it in one place encouraged it somewhere else.

Another stimulus for investment came from government—and this occurred in two ways. First, governments acted as giant consumers whose appetites throughout the early modern period were expanding. Merchants who supplied governments with everything from guns to frescoes not only prospered but were led to reinvest because of the constancy and growth of government demand. Governments also sponsored new forms of investment, whether to supply the de-

bauched taste for new luxuries at the king's court or to meet the requirements of the military. Private investors also reaped incalculable advantages from overseas empires. Colonies supplied cheap raw materials and cheap (slave) labor and served as markets for exports. They greatly stimulated the construction of both ships and harbor facilities and the sale of insurance.

The second government stimulus was state policies meant to increase investment, which they no doubt sometimes, although not always, did. Collectively, these policies constitute what is known as *mercantilism:* the conscious pursuit by governments of those courses supposed to augment national wealth and power. One characteristic expression of mercantilism was the pursuit of a favorable balance of international payments. According to conventional wisdom, wealth from trade was measured in gold and silver, of which there was believed to be a more or less fixed quantity. The state's goal in international trade became to sell more abroad than it bought, that is, to establish a favorable balance of payments. When the amount received for sales abroad was greater than that spent for purchases, the difference would be an influx of precious metal into the state. By this logic, mercantilists were led to argue for the goal of national sufficiency: a country should try to supply most of its own needs to keep imports to a minimum. This argument, of course, ignored the fact that in international trade, the more a country buys, the more it can sell because its purchases abroad create purchasing power for its goods overseas.

Mercantilism did have a positive side. Governments increased economic activity by employing the poor, subsidizing new industries, and chartering companies to engage in overseas trade. Particularly valuable were the steps taken by states to break down local trade barriers, such as guild regulations and internal tariffs, in an attempt to create national markets and internal economic unity.

The English also saw that mercantilistic calculations of national wealth should be made over the long run. For example, Thomas Mun (1571–1641) argued that a country might import more than it exported in the short run and still come out ahead in the end, because raw materials that are imported and then reprocessed for export will eventually yield a handsome profit.

In addition, Mun was one of the first to see the virtues of *consumerism,* a phenomenon that is still extremely important for achieving sustained economic growth. Speaking of foreign trade, he maintained that the more English merchants did to advertise English goods to potential customers, the greater the overseas market for those goods would be. In other words, demand can be *created.* Just as there is an urge to invest and make profits, so there is an appetite to consume and enjoy the products of industry, and both inclinations have played their part in the growth of capitalism. Nor was the message restricted to the foreign market. Between 1660 and 1750, England became the world's first consumer society: more and more people had more and more money to spend, and they acquired a taste for conspicuous consumption (which had always before been confined to the aristocracy). Discretionary goods were available—lace, tobacco, housewares, flowers—and consumers wanted them. Concomitantly, just as today, the more stimulus there was to buy, the harder the consumer worked, which induced further growth.

The price revolution, the concentration of wealth in private hands, and government activity combined to provide the foundation for sustained investment and for the emergence of mercantile capitalism. This new force in the world should not be confused with industrial capitalism. The latter evolved with the first Industrial Revolution in eighteenth-century England, but mercantile capitalism paved the way for it.

Seventeenth-Century Decline and Renewal

Population began to decline in Spain as early as the 1590s, and by the second quarter of the seventeenth century, it was declining throughout Europe. The decline resulted because during the price revolution demand continued to outrun supply, prices rose, and real wages fell. The diet of the masses deteriorated because they could not earn enough to buy sufficient bread. Bad harvests produced massive famines, and cities became overgrown and increasingly unsanitary. When plague struck, as it continued to do periodically, it did so among a weakened populace and took more lives. Finally, there was the Thirty Years' War (1618–1648), which ravaged the Holy Roman Empire and reduced its population by at least one-third.

The economic consequences of these factors were quick to follow. Prices fell and there was general economic dislocation. The new Atlantic powers, however, responded in a way that would lead to their recovery—England by the last quarter of the century and France by the 1730s. English and French farmers turned increasingly to enclosure and the application of the Dutch technique of convertible husbandry. Initially, these efforts attempted to make up for falling prices by increasing productivity. But over the long run they had the effect of increasing production and of sustaining a growing population.

By the second quarter of the eighteenth century, the population of western Europe was once more growing—but with significant differences from the earlier increase. The food supply tended to keep pace with rising demand, so the prices of basic foodstuffs stabilized and even declined. This achievement had enormous impact on the subsequent history of France and England. At last, enough was produced to feed a growing population without a rise in prices. Less income would have to be spent on food at a time when national income was rising because of expanded production for the needs of a growing population.

Given these developments, who benefited, why, and to what effect? First of all, many peasants could for the first time produce a surplus for market. This increased production meant a rise in income. The largest farmers, curiously enough, probably did not benefit, unless they were also landlords; they had long been producing for the market, sometimes for generations, and their increased production did not make up for the falling off of farm prices.

Second, the landlords' income increased. They had land to rent to the growing number of farmers who engaged in commercial farming and whose growing profits enabled them to pay even higher rents. This tendency was especially prevalent in France. There, enclosure was not widespread, and inherited land was divided among all the children in a family, a practice called *partible inheritance*. As a result, more and more peasants, because of population growth, sought a livelihood from the soil.

Third, there was a growth in the incomes of everyone whose earnings were in excess of the price of bread. This group would have included at least a majority of the urban population because, of course, bread prices were falling.

Thus the new agronomy produced a situation in which *more and more people had more and more money to spend on, or to invest in, things other than food*—namely, industry and its products. This increasing income manifested itself in rising demand for goods and services. This demand was one of the basic preconditions for the Industrial Revolution in the eighteenth and early nineteenth centuries, particularly in England. Before large-scale industry could come into being, a market for its products was necessary.

In the process of industrialization, England gained the advantage over France largely because of the different patterns that agriculture took in the two countries. Beginning in the 1780s, French agriculture could not sustain the pattern that it had shared with England from the 1730s. By the 1780s, too many people were living on the land in France to allow adequate surpluses in years of poor harvest. At such times, peasants produced only enough to feed themselves, if that, and shortages caused bread prices to soar. Peasant incomes shrank from the lack of a marketable surplus. And higher bread prices reduced consumer spending power. The momentum for industrialization weakened or dissolved, a situation prevailing until the next century. Partible inheritance in France slowed industrial development. Primogeniture and enclosure in England speeded it up.

The Elite and the People
Traditional Popular Culture

The economic expansion of Europe was accompanied by some equally important social and cultural changes in the relations between ordinary people and their rulers, whether kings, nobles, landlords, or clergy. Throughout the Middle Ages there had always been two cultures: the elite culture of the royal court, the feudal lords, and the educated clergy, and the popular culture of largely illiterate peasants and artisans.

Over the centuries the common people had evolved a distinctive culture that their rulers patronized and to some degree participated in. This popular culture was made up of a mosaic of the customs of various groups of people—shepherds, peasants, cobblers, weavers, miners—each with its own traditions. Even a youth culture of apprentices was to be found in the towns, and in addition to the settled culture of the villages and towns, there was a vagabond culture of sailors, soldiers, beggars, thieves, and other "masterless men."[2]

The prosperous and the powerful called on the services of learned professionals—clergy, physicians, and lawyers—but the people had their own humbler and cheaper equivalents—lay preachers, folk healers, and witches, that is, sorcerers and fortunetellers. The royal courts, manor houses, monasteries, and universities were the centers of elite culture. Ordinary people, on the other hand, worked, played, and worshiped in meaner settings—the village church, the tavern, the street, and especially the marketplace or village square. In the church and churchyard they danced, feasted, and performed religious pageants; in the tavern and street they gossiped, played games, watched puppet shows, staged cockfights, listened to folk preachers, and consulted healers, astrologers, and magicians.

Certain special occasions granted people the freedom to express themselves. Beginning in the thirteenth century the most important of these occasions was Carnival, the three- to six-day festival preceding the onset of Lent—a time of revelry and ritual processions through church and streets, marked by excessive eating and drinking and a sharp increase in sexual activity. It was also a time during which ordinary people, at least in their parades and public displays, engaged in what was called "turning the world upside down." So, for instance, in a procession a horse would be made to walk backward with its rider facing its tail. Or popular illustrations of the era show a son beating his father, a pupil beating his teacher, servants giving orders to their masters, the laity preaching to the clergy, the husband minding the baby, and the wife smoking and holding a gun. What does all this mean? Was it a safety valve, allowing the people to blow off the steam generated by an otherwise oppressive and monotonous existence? Perhaps, but it sometimes led to real violence, and the elite, by the sixteenth century at any rate, looked on such behavior as subversive and fraught with danger. As a noble said on the occasion of the Carnival at Palermo in 1648: "On the pretext of these assemblies of the people for these ridiculous spectacles, factious spirits would be able . . . to encourage some new riot."[3]

Nor was Carnival the only occasion for this ritual mockery of authority. The calendar year was punctuated by the observance of religious feast days on which similar behavior took place. So, for instance, in France on the Feast of Fools (the Innocents) on December 28, an abbot or bishop of fools was elected, and a mock mass took place in which the clergy dressed in women's clothes, played cards, ate sausages, sang ribald songs, and cursed their congregations rather than blessing them.

Among the most prevalent popular traditions was the ritual mockery of marriage known as the *charivari*. Only unconventional marriages qualified for such rude treatment at the hands of one's neighbors—an old man and a young wife, a second marriage, a husband beaten or cuckolded by his wife. The charivari consisted of a ritual procession in which the victim or his effigy would be mounted backward on an ass and drawn through the streets accompanied by "rough music" (the beating of pots and pans). Charivaris were sometimes conducted at the expense of tax collectors, preachers, and landlords. Here then was a kind of popular justice, another version of the world turned upside down.

The Reform of Popular Culture

Throughout the Middle Ages and up to the early sixteenth century, elite culture and popular culture existed in more or less stable balance. Indeed the two worlds, high and low, occupied considerable common ground. Landlords and clergy took part in village games and feasts and shared with their inferiors an outlook that stressed communal values—pulling together in a subsistence world, making sure that everyone had enough for survival, and extending relief to those in need. The emphasis was on communalism, not individualism, especially in the countryside.

In the sixteenth century, however, a drastic change took place in the attitude of the elite toward the people. No longer willing to patronize and foster popular culture, they became increasingly suspicious of and hostile to it. This shift in attitude occurred because of two developments. The first was the fear the elite felt—fear of the growing numbers of the poor and fear of the growing numbers of the people, some poor and some not, who, inspired by the new religious movements and the new printed literature, began to question the old authorities and sometimes even joined in rebellion against them. Encouraged by the greater accessibility of printed books and also by the Protestant emphasis on Bible reading, more and more people became literate, and a popular literature of religious instruction, astrological almanacs, and chivalric romances poured from the presses to meet the growing demand. On this score, too, the authorities had their misgivings; books of the right sort were acceptable, even useful, but a little learning was thought to be a dangerous thing.

The second reason for this shift in attitude toward the people was not fear but hope. Not only were the elite alarmed by the growing poverty and unrest among the people, they also thought they knew how to control it and even perhaps in some measure to overcome it. Just as religion inspired the people, so the Reformation, the Counter Reformation, and the Christian humanism of the Renaissance inspired leaders to reform society and in particular to attack popular culture for being both too pagan and too disorderly. The customs of the people, it was thought, must be purified, made more decent and sober, and the people themselves disciplined to be made obedient subjects of king and church. Society came to be seen as being divided between the godly (among whom the elite included themselves) and the ungodly multitude who needed to be controlled and if possible educated for service in the Christian commonwealth.

What followed was a wide-ranging onslaught against all forms of traditional popular culture—what one historian has called "the triumph of Lent" over "the world of Carnival."[4] This reform movement included attacks on popular festivals, lay preaching, charivaris, and "the world turned upside down." The Florentine ruler Girolamo Savonarola, a few days before the Carnival of 1496, preached a sermon recommending that "boys should collect alms for the respectable poor, instead of mad pranks, throwing stones and making floats."[5] A century later, in England, Phillip Stubbe drew up a comprehensive indictment of May games, Lords of Misrule, Christmas feasting, church ales, wakes, bearbaiting, cockfighting, and dancing. Popular religious dramas disappeared in northern Italy during the third quarter of the sixteenth century and in England by the end of that century.

The new bureaucratic state joined the clergy in the reforming enterprise. In the sixteenth and seventeenth centuries, many forms of behavior that had been thought of as spiritual sins now became secular crimes as well, subject to prosecution and punishment by the state. These newly criminalized activities included adultery, blasphemy, sodomy, infanticide, and witchcraft. In this period, too, public brothels, which had existed for centuries, were gradually shut down, a process beginning in Lutheran Germany between 1530 and 1560. The state enforced what the new moral puritanism decreed.

Witchcraft and the Witch Craze

The prosecution of witches constitutes a particularly important chapter in this attack on popular culture. Although it had always been suspect, witchcraft had been a part of traditional village culture for centuries. There were two kinds of witchcraft, black and white. The white variety involved healing and fortunetelling. Black witchcraft, on the other hand, referred to the conjuring of evil powers by a curse or by the manipulation of objects, such as the entrails of animals.

The medieval church developed a more theological and sinister interpretation of the phenomenon; according to this, witches entered into a conspiracy with the Devil to work against God and human society, held secret meetings, and had carnal relations with the Devil. In the late twelfth century, Christian thinkers began to emphasize the idea of a Devil who roamed the world at the head of an army of demons, attempting to undermine the saving mission of Christ and tempting people to sin. Witches were regarded as those who had succumbed to temptation and entered a pact to worship Satan in place of God. This worship was thought to take place at secret, nocturnal meetings (the legendary witches' sabbats) during which witches and demons were supposed to engage in sexual orgies, to sacrifice infants, and to desecrate the Eucharist.

As early as the thirteenth century, bishops and popes prosecuted witches for heresy. Confessions were usually extracted by means of torture. Those found guilty were burned at the stake (on the Continent) or hanged (in England), and their property was confiscated by the authorities. The church held that a witch's "only hope of salvation was to be arrested and to recant before her execution. By such reasoning the torment and killing of witches was for their own good as well as that of God and society."[6]

The growth of printed literature on the subject of witchcraft was especially influential in the spread of the church's view that witchcraft involved a diabolical plot. In 1486 there appeared a handbook called *Malleus Maleficarum, The Hammer of Witches,* by two German Dominicans who claimed to show what witches did at the Devil's behest. These Dominicans had tried almost fifty people for witchcraft, all but two of them women.

By the sixteenth century, the linkage of women to witchcraft had been firmly established. Men could also be accused of the crime, but almost everywhere that witches were tried in the sixteenth and seventeenth centuries, more than 75 percent were women, often elderly widows and spinsters. The so-called witch craze is a phenomenon of these two centuries, when perhaps as many as 100,000 people were tried all over Europe.

In the sixteenth century, witchcraft also became a secular crime, no longer merely a village or community matter. It became a state responsibility to ferret out witches. A few thinkers attacked witchcraft on the grounds that it was pure nonsense, an invention of simple people and superstitious clergy. "It is rating our conjectures too high to roast people alive for them," the skeptic Michel de Montaigne exclaimed.[7] But most people, learned and unlearned alike, believed that witches existed, feared them, and wished to see them exterminated. Witchcraft was a despicable and dangerous heresy that had to be rooted out by the authorities if society was to be reformed and if men and women were to be put on the right path to salvation.

Why were most of those accused women? No doubt this pattern reflected an ancient prejudice that women were less rational and more lustful than men and so more susceptible to the Devil's wiles. One explanation of English witch-hunts during the period may throw light on this question. In traditional society, widows and the elderly were objects of local charity. An old woman, so the theory goes, would beg for alms and be rebuffed by a more prosperous neighbor; later some misfortune would befall the neighbor, and he would blame it on the old woman, accusing her of witchcraft as a way of assuaging his guilt for having refused her request for help. According to this interpretation, such behavior characterizes a period of rapid transition from communal subsistence to an ethic of economic individualism that demanded that each person look out for himself or herself. Just such a period in England coincided with the large number of witchcraft prosecutions brought against poor old women.

By 1700 the witch craze had ended in western Europe—first in Holland, the most tolerant country, and in Spain, the most intolerant. Sometimes it is assumed that the rise of modern science was responsible for ending the witch-hunts. But this connection is difficult to sustain because of the fact that some leading scientists were among those most interested in proving the existence of witches. For thinkers like Robert Boyle, Sir Matthew Hale, Joseph Glanvill, and Henry More, evidence of witchcraft would demonstrate that spiritual forces operated in the world and so answer materialists like Thomas Hobbes who argued that witches and spirits were nothing but figments of popular and clerical imagination. We must look elsewhere, therefore, to explain the demise of witch-hunts, and in particular to the social and economic transformations of the period—increasing prosperity, declining epidemic disease, growing political stability within the European states, and decreasing religious tensions.

Economic and Social Transformation

The transformations considered in this chapter were among the most momentous in the world's history. In an unprecedented development that may never be repeated, one small part of the world, western Europe, had become the lord of

Chronology 15.1 The Commercial Revolution

1394–1460	Henry the Navigator, prince of Portugal, encourages expansion into Africa for gold and his anti-Muslim crusade
1430	The Portuguese expand into the Canaries and the Azores
1488	Bartholomeu Dias reaches the tip of Africa
1492	Christopher Columbus reaches the Caribbean island of Española on his first voyage; the Jews are expelled from Spain; Granada, the last Muslim kingdom in Spain, is conquered, ending the Reconquest
1497	Vasco da Gama sails around Cape of Good Hope (Africa) to India
1509	The Portuguese defeat the Muslim fleet at Diu in the Indian Ocean
1513	Balboa discovers the Pacific Ocean at the Isthmus of Panama
1519–1521	Hernando Cortés conquers the Aztecs in Mexico
1520–1521	Magellan's soldiers circumnavigate the globe
1531–1533	Francisco Pizarro conquers the Incas in Peru
1545	Silver is discovered by the Spaniards at Potosí, Peru
1552	Silver from the New World flows into Europe via Spain, contributing to a price revolution
1590s	The Dutch develop shipping carriers for grain
1602–1609	The Dutch East India Company is founded; the Bank of Amsterdam is founded, expanding credit
1651	The Navigation Act is passed in England to accomplish the goals of mercantilism
1694	The Bank of England is founded

the sea-lanes, the master of many lands throughout the globe, and the banker and profit-taker in an emerging world economy. Western Europe's global hegemony was to last well into this century. In conquering and settling new lands, Europeans exported Western culture around the globe, a process that accelerated in the twentieth century.

The effects of overseas expansion were profound. The native populations of the New World were decimated. As a result of the labor shortage, millions of blacks were imported from Africa to work as slaves on plantations and in mines. Black slavery would produce large-scale effects on culture, politics, and society that have lasted to the present day.

The widespread circulation of plant and animal life also had great consequences. Horses and cattle were introduced to the New World. (So amazed were the Aztecs to see man on horseback that at first they thought horse and rider were one demonic creature.) In return the Old World was introduced to corn, the tomato, and most important, the potato, which was to become a staple of the northern European diet. Manioc, from which tapioca is made, was transplanted from the New World to Africa, where it helped sustain the population.

Western Europe was wrenched out of the subsistence economy of the Middle Ages and launched on a course of sustained economic growth. This transformation resulted from the grafting of traditional forms, like primogeniture and holy war, onto new forces, like global exploration, price revolution, and convertible husbandry. Out of this change emerged the beginnings of a new economic system, mercantile capitalism, which in large measure provided the economic thrust for European world predominance and paved the way for the Industrial Revolution of the eighteenth and nineteenth centuries.

Finally, these economic changes were accompanied by a profound shift in relations between the rulers and the ruled. For centuries the elite had tolerated and even patronized the culture of the people. But under the impact of the commercial revolution and the Reformation, the authorities became increasingly suspicious of the people and undertook to purify and reform popular culture. The degree to which they succeeded is an open question. But the gap between the elite and the people widened, as the elite found less and less in popular culture to identify with and more and more to condemn and try to undo. The elite distanced themselves from the people even as they attempted to impose their will on them. The result was the emergence of two separate cultures, divorced from and hostile to each other. Only in moments of mass hysteria such as the witch craze could the people and their rulers join forces against a common and defenseless victim.

Notes

1. Christopher Hill, *Reformation to Industrial Revolution* (Baltimore: Penguin, 1969), pp. 159–160.

2. Christopher Hill, *The World Turned Upside Down* (New York: Viking, 1972), ch. 3.

3. Quoted in Peter Burke, *Popular Culture in Early Modern Europe* (New York: Harper & Row, 1978), p. 203.

4. Ibid., chs. 7–8.

5. Quoted in ibid., p. 217.

6. Jeffrey B. Russell, *A History of Witchcraft* (London: Thames and Hudson, 1980), p. 78.

7. Ibid., p. 73.

Suggested Reading

Appleby, Joyce, *Economic Thought and Ideology in Seventeenth-Century England* (1978). The invention of a science of economics in the context of an emerging capitalist society.

Boxer, C. R., *The Portuguese Seaborne Empire, 1415–1825* (1969). A comprehensive treatment.

Cipolla, Carlo M., *Guns, Sails and Empires* (1965). Connections between technological innovation and overseas expansion, 1400 to 1700.

Davis, David Brion, *The Problem of Slavery in Western Culture* (1966). Authoritative and highly suggestive.

Davis, Ralph, *The Rise of the Atlantic Economies* (1973). A reliable recent survey of early modern economic history.

Elliott, J. H., *The Old World and the New, 1492–1650* (1972). The impact of America on early modern Europe.

Haley, K. H. D., *The Dutch in the Seventeenth Century* (1972). A very readable, informative survey.

Hanke, Lewis, *The Spanish Struggle for Justice in the Conquest of America* (1949). A treatment of the priestly view of Indian rights under Spanish rule.

Hill, Christopher, *Reformation to Industrial Revolution* (1969). A concise Marxist interpretation of English economic development.

Kamen, H., *The Iron Century* (1971). Insight into the social and class basis of economic change.

Parry, J. H., *The Age of Reconnaissance* (1963). A short survey of exploration.

Wilson, C., *England's Apprenticeship, 1600–1763* (1965). Authoritative account.

Review Questions

1. What are the links between the Middle Ages and early modern overseas expansion? What were the new forces for expansion operating in early modern Europe?

2. Compare Spanish and Portuguese overseas expansion in terms of their motives, their areas of expansion, and the character of the two empires.

3. What is the connection between the price revolution and overseas expansion? What was the principal cause of the price revolution? Why?

4. What was enclosure? How did the price revolution encourage it?

5. Compare open-field farming and enclosure in terms of who worked the land, how the land was worked, and what the results of each method were.

6. What was convertible husbandry, where did it originate, and why was it such an important innovation?

7. What was the putting-out system? What were its advantages over the guilds and its long-term effects?

8. What is mercantile capitalism? What three patterns of the distribution of wealth fostered its development?

9. How did economic decline in the seventeenth century provide conditions for the subsequent economic recovery and progress? Where was this progress greatest, and why?

10. What was the traditional relationship between the people and their rulers? How and why did this relationship begin to change in the sixteenth century, and with what result?

11. What accounts for the witch craze, and why were most of its victims women?

16

The Rise of Sovereignty:
Transition to the Modern State

From the thirteenth to the seventeenth century a new and unique form of political organization emerged in the West: the dynastic, or national, state, which harnessed the power of its nobility and the material resources of its territory. Neither capitalism nor technology could have enabled the West to dominate other lands and peoples had it not been for the power of the European states. They channeled and organized violence into the service of national power by directing the energies of the ruling elite into national service and international competition. A degree of domestic stability ensued, and the states encouraged commerce and industry, which could in turn be taxed. Although they nurtured the aristocracy, many states also required that both lord and peasant serve in national armies for the purpose of foreign conquest as well as for defense.

In some medieval lands, kings had begun to forge national states in the Middle Ages. However, medieval political forms differed considerably from those that developed in the early modern period. During the Middle Ages, feudal lords gave homage to their kings but continued to rule over their local territories, resisting the centralizing efforts of monarchs. Local and even national representative assemblies, which met frequently to give advice to kings, at times acted as a brake on the king's power. The clergy supported the monarch but governed their congregations or monasteries as separate spiritual realms. The papacy challenged the authority of monarchs who, it believed, did not fulfill their duty to rule in accordance with Christian teachings as interpreted by the church. In early modern times, powerful monarchs subdued these competing systems of political authority and established strong central governments.

At every turn the pivotal figures in the development of states were the kings. Europeans, whether landed or urban, grudgingly gave allegiance to

Versailles, painted by Pierre Patel in 1668.
(*Versailles/Cliché des Musées Nationaux*)

these ambitious, and at times ruthless, authority figures. In general, a single monarch seemed the only alternative to the even more brutal pattern of war and disorder so basic to the governing habits of the feudal aristocracy. In the process of increasing their own power, the kings of Europe not only subordinated the aristocracy to their needs and interests but also gained firm control over the Christian churches in their territories. Gradually, religious zeal was made compatible with and largely supportive of the state's goals, rather than papal dictates or even universal Christian aspirations. The demise of medieval representative assemblies—with the notable exception of the English Parliament—is a dramatic illustration of how monarchs subjected to their will all other political authorities, whether local, regional, or national.

Various components characterized the dynastic states of the early modern period. All states required a language that was dominant enough to be used for government. Moreover, states maintained standing armies as soon as the system of tax collection gave them a sufficient economic foundation to do so. If kings were to subdue local aristocrats and terrify other kings, armies were essential, and they were established by the seventeenth century in Spain, France, and finally late in the century in England. These domestic armies, often used in conjunction with foreign mercenaries, were crucial to the maintenance and extension of state power. In many early modern states a vast bureaucracy coordinated and administered the activities of the central government and its army. Another characteristic was that the creation of a strong central government required a struggle between the monarch and localized systems of power, feudal aristocrats, bishops, and even occasionally representative assemblies.

Where early modern European monarchs succeeded in subduing, destroying, or reconstituting local aristocratic and ecclesiastical power systems, strong dynastic states were formed. Where the monarchs failed, as they did in the Holy Roman Empire and Italy, no viable states evolved until well into the nineteenth century. Those failures derived from the independent authority of local princes or city-states, and in the case of Italy, from the decentralizing influence of papal authority. In the Holy Roman Empire, feudal princes found al-

lies in the newly formed Protestant communities, and in such a situation, religion worked as a decentralizing force. Successful early modern kings had to bring the churches under their authority and subordinate religion to the needs of the state. They did so not by separating church and state (as was later done in the United States) but rather by linking their subjects' religious identity with the national identity. For example, in England by the late seventeenth century, to be a true Protestant was to be a true English subject, while in Spain the same equation operated for the Catholic (as opposed to the Muslim or the Jew, who came to be regarded as non-Spanish).

The elements that made up the early modern state evolved slowly and at first haltingly. In the thirteenth century, most Europeans still identified themselves with their localities: their villages, manors, or towns. They gave political allegiance to their local lord or bishop. They knew little, and probably cared less, about the activities of the king and his court, except when the monarch called on them for taxes or military service. By the late seventeenth century, in contrast, aristocrats in many European countries defined the extent of their political power in terms of their relationship to king and court. By then the lives of very ordinary people were being affected by national systems of tax collection, by the doctrines and practices of national churches, and by conscription.

Increasingly, prosperous town dwellers, the bourgeoisie, realized also that their prosperity hinged, in part, on court-supported foreign and domestic policies. If the king assisted their commercial ventures, the bourgeoisie gave their support to the growth of a strong central state. In only two states, England and the Netherlands, did a successful bourgeoisie manage to redistribute political power so that by the late seventeenth century it could be shared by monarchy and parliament, or in the Netherlands monopolized by a social oligarchy.

The effects of state building were visible in Europe and the world by the late seventeenth century. Commercial rivalry between states and colonial expansion, two major activities of the period, were directly related to the ability of elites to protect their interests under the mantle of the state, and to the state's willingness to encourage trade in order to enrich its own treasury. The modern world, thus, was ushered in by monarchs and states just as much as by commercial expansion, capitalism, and science.

The Rise and Fall of Hapsburg Spain

The Spanish political experience of the sixteenth century stands as one of the most extraordinary in the history of modern Europe. Spanish kings built a dynastic state that burst through its frontiers and encompassed Portugal, part of Italy, the Netherlands, and enormous areas in the New World. Spain became an intercontinental empire—the first in the West since Roman times.

In the eighth and ninth centuries, the Muslims controlled all of Spain except for some tiny Christian kingdoms in the far north. In the ninth century, these Christian states began a 500-year struggle—the Reconquest—to drive the Muslims from the Iberian Peninsula. By the middle of the thirteenth century, Granada in the south was all that remained of Muslim lands in Spain.

Hispania as a concept and geographical area existed in Roman times, and citizens of Portugal, Castile, Aragon, Catalonia, and Andalusia, to name only the larger and more important areas of the peninsula, recognized a certain common identity—no more, no less. Until 1469, however, Spain did not exist as a political entity. In that year, Ferdinand, heir to the throne of Aragon, married his more powerful and prosperous cousin, Isabella, heiress of Castile. Yet even after the unification of Castile and the Crown of Aragon (Catalonia, Aragon, and Valencia), relations among the various and fiercely independent provinces of Spain were often tense.

Rich from the wool trade and more populous than other provinces, Castile became the heart of Spain. But the Crown of Aragon supplied commercial expertise to the union, as well as control over the western Mediterranean. Ferdinand's Aragon also contributed a vibrant tradition of constitutional government characterized by a concern for individual and class rights, as distinct from the rights of kings. Perhaps no territory in Europe possessed a more vital set of representative and judicial institutions. Aragonese independence is best summed up in the famous oath said to be taken by its nobility to the king: "We who are as good as you swear to you who are no better than we to accept you as our king and sovereign lord, provided you observe all our liberties and laws; but, if not, not."[1] Obviously, any monarch set on increasing royal authority in Aragon would have to proceed cautiously.

Ferdinand and Isabella

Ferdinand and Isabella displayed extraordinary statecraft in managing the various areas within their newly formed land. The success of their rule (1479–1516) laid the foundations for Spanish empire and Spanish domination of European affairs throughout the sixteenth century. They used Castile as their power base and set about ridding it of its military caste—those aristocrats who, in effect, operated from their fortified castles like private kings waging at will their private wars. In contrast, Ferdinand and Isabella rationalized and modernized the Spanish state's government.

Beginning in the late fifteenth century, Castilian dominance over government and administration was recognized and continually preserved, yet Aragonese rights were left more or less intact. Ferdinand and Isabella never established a unified state: there was no common currency and no single legal or tax system. Commonality of interests, rather than of administration and law, united Spain; and certain policies of Ferdinand and Isabella contributed decisively to this unity. They sought the reconquest of Spanish territory still held by the Muslims, and at the same time they sought to assert the uniquely Christian character of the peninsula, to bring the Spanish church into alliance with the state.

Given the territorial and legal divisions within Spain, it is understandable why the church became the only universal institution in Spain, and why its legal arm, the Inquisition, played such an important role in the intellectual and religious life of this most disparate of kingdoms. It was most impor-

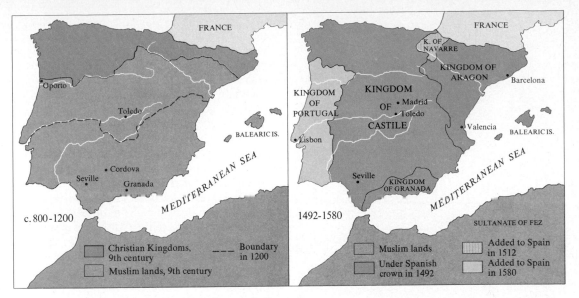

Map 16.1 Spain During the Ninth to Sixteenth Centuries

tant for the development of strong monarchy that the Spanish rulers bring the church's interests in line with their own. Ferdinand and Isabella's alliance with the church and their war against the Muslims in the southern portion of the peninsula were interrelated. A crusade against the Muslim infidel presupposed an energetic church and a deep and militant Catholicism, with the rulers committed to the aims of the church, and the church to the aims of the rulers. While other Europeans, partly under the impact of the Renaissance, questioned the church's leadership and attacked its corruption, the Catholic Kings (as Ferdinand and Isabella were called) reformed the church, making it responsive to their needs and also invulnerable to criticism. Popular piety and royal policy led in 1492 to a victory over Granada, the last Muslim-ruled territory in Spain.

The 500-year struggle for Christian hegemony in the Iberian Peninsula left the Spanish fiercely religious and strongly suspicious of foreigners. Despite centuries of intermarriage with non-Christians, by the early sixteenth century, purity of blood and orthodoxy of faith became necessary for, and synonymous with Spanish identity. In 1492, the Jews and the Muslims were physically expelled from Spain or forced to convert. This process of detection and conversion was supervised by the church, or more precisely, by the Inquisition. Run by clerics but responsive to state policies, the Inquisition existed to enforce religious uniformity and to ferret out the increasing numbers of Muslims and Jews who ostensibly converted to Catholicism but who remained secretly loyal to their own religions. The Inquisition developed extremely sophisticated systems of interrogation, used its legal right to torture as well as burn heretics, and eventually extended its authority to Christians as well. It represented the dark side of Spanish genius at conquest and administration, and its shadow stretched down through the centuries well into the twentieth.

The wars against the Muslims gave the Spanish invaluable military experience and rendered their army one of the finest in Europe. The wars also created a pattern in the growth of the Spanish empire: its victories always lay in the south—in Italy, in Latin America, and against the Turks—while its defeats and setbacks occurred in the north—in the Netherlands, in opposition to the Lutheran Reformation in the Holy Roman Empire, and against England.

Portrait of the Emperor Charles V by Titian (1477–1576). With the wealth of the New World and the Hapsburg domination of the Holy Roman Empire, Charles V was the greatest ruler of his age. Titian's portraits reveal the character of his subjects. (*Bayerischen Staatsgemäldesammlungen, Munich*)

With a superior army, with the great magnates pacified, and with the church and the Inquisition under monarchical control, the Catholic Kings expanded their interests and embarked on an imperialist foreign policy in Europe and abroad that had extraordinary consequences. Ultimately it made Spain dominant in the New World.

Ferdinand and Isabella gambled on Columbus's voyage, and they won. Then, beginning in 1519, the conquistador Cortés defeated the Aztec nation with 600 foot soldiers and 16 horses, a feat

that cannot be explained simply by citing the superior technology of the Spanish. This conquest rested primarily on the character and achievements of Spain's lesser gentry—the hidalgos. The willingness of the hidalgos to serve crown and church was equaled or surpassed only by their desire to get rich. Lured by gold and land, they made excellent soldiers and explorers in foreign lands, while at home they entered the governmental and ecclesiastical bureaucracies. They formed the core of a loyal civil service that was responsive to the needs of the monarchy and distrustful of and resentful toward the great nobles, or *grandees*. Spanish bureaucracy in the sixteenth century became a primary vehicle for social mobility, and the foreign and domestic policies initiated by Ferdinand and Isabella and continued by their successors received their greatest support from the gentry.

The Reign of Charles V: King of Spain and Holy Roman Emperor

Dynastic marriage constituted another crucial part of Ferdinand and Isabella's foreign policy. They strengthened their ties with the Austrian and Flemish (or Burgundian) kings by marrying one of their children, Juana (called "the Mad" for her insanity), to Philip the Fair, son of Maximilian of Austria, the head of the ruling Hapsburg family. Philip and Juana's son Charles (1516–1556) inherited the kingdom of Ferdinand and Isabella; through his other grandparents, he also inherited the Netherlands, Austria, Sardinia, Sicily, the kingdom of Naples, and Franche Comté. In 1519, he was also elected Charles V, Holy Roman emperor. Charles became the most powerful ruler in Europe, but his reign also saw the emergence of political, economic, and social problems that eventually led to Spain's decline.

Charles's inheritance was simply too vast to be governed effectively, but that was only dimly perceived at the time. The Lutheran Reformation proved to be the first successful challenge to Hapsburg power. It was the first phase of a religious and political struggle between Catholic Spain and Protestant Europe that would dominate the last half of the sixteenth century.

Charles established a court filled with foreigners and spent much of his time in the northern provinces, while still collecting taxes in Castile. These policies produced a full-scale revolt in the Castilian towns in 1520 and 1521. Led by artisans and merchants, the revolt took on elements of a class war against the landed nobility. The nobles, in turn, rallied around Charles's royal army, and eventually the revolt was crushed. But the event and its outcome reveals much about the nature of Spanish absolutism. It relied on its aristocracy (unlike the French kings, who tried to suppress their aristocrats), and it never encouraged the growth of a bourgeoisie.

The achievements of Charles V's reign rested on the twin instruments of army and bureaucracy. The Hapsburg Empire in the New World was vast, and, on the whole, effectively administered and policed. Out of this sprawling empire with its exploited native populations came the greatest flow of gold and silver ever witnessed by Europeans. Although constant warfare in Europe, coupled with the immensity of the Spanish administrative network, required a steady intake of capital, this easy access to income appears to have been detrimental in the long run to the Spanish economy (see Chapter 15). There was no incentive for the development of domestic industry, bourgeois entrepreneurship, or international commerce. Moreover, constant war engendered and perpetuated a social order geared to the aggrandizement of a military class rather than to the development of a commercial class. Although war expanded Spain's power in the sixteenth century, it also sowed the seeds for the financial crises of the 1590s and beyond, and for the eventual decline of Spain as a world power.

Philip II

In the reign of Philip II (1556–1598) the strengths and weaknesses of the Spanish state are fully evident. It is the pivotal period in early modern Spanish history. Philip II inherited the throne from his father, Charles V, who abdicated in 1556 and left his son with a large empire in both the Old and New Worlds that had been administered effectively enough, yet was also burdened by the specters of bankruptcy and heresy. Heresy, more than any other problem, compelled the attention of this obsessively devout monarch, whose zeal for Catholicism ruled his private conduct and infused his foreign policy. Philip bided his time with foreign infidels and heretics and waited for the moment when the Crown would possess the revenue necessary to launch an offensive against the Turks and international Protestantism.

To Philip II, being truly Spanish meant being Christian in faith and blood; the racist tendencies, already evident in the later fifteenth century, gained full expression during his reign. Increasingly, the country came to be ruled by an exclusive class of old Christians who claimed to be untainted because for centuries they had refused to marry Muslims or Jews. Traditional in their thinking and in their control over the church, the religious orders, and the Inquisition, the old Christians tried to preserve an imperial system badly in need of reform.

Melancholic and standoffish by temperament, Philip II worked arduously and declined most of life's enjoyments. He pored over his ministers' reports, editing and commenting, yet in the end he was strangely indecisive. Some problems remained unsolved for years, as frustrated advisers begged in vain for the king to take action.

In the 1560s, Philip sent the largest land army ever assembled in Europe into the Netherlands with the intention of crushing Protestant-inspired opposition to Spanish authority. The ensuing revolt of the Netherlands lasted until 1609 (see page 324), and the Spanish lost their industrial heartland as a result of it. In 1576, the Spanish in a desperate attempt to defeat the rebels were forced to flood and sack Antwerp, their leading commercial and banking city in northern Europe. Antwerp's trade gradually moved to Amsterdam, a Protestant stronghold, which replaced its southern rival as an international capital and the center of the new Dutch national state.

By the 1580s, Philip's foreign policy was overextended in every direction, and his religious zeal shaped all his decisions. He intervened in the French religious wars on the side of the Catholic family of the Guise, although his intervention gave little to Spain in the way of power or influence. By far the most dramatic of Philip's exploits in this period was the disastrous attempt to invade England, universally regarded as the inferior power.

Spain regarded an assault on England, a Protestant country, as a holy crusade against the "heretic and bastard" Queen Elizabeth. Some Spanish officials also reasoned, incorrectly, that a successful invasion would ignite an uprising of the remaining Catholic population in England. Philip II longed for the opportunity to conquer England; it was the main Protestant power in Europe, and Philip particularly resented its assistance to Dutch rebels.

Outfitted in Lisbon harbor and constantly delayed by shortages of equipment, the Armada was composed of 130 ships, only a fourth of the originally planned fleet. These main ships and numerous smaller vessels carried 22,000 seamen and soldiers. The English fleet numbered less than 75. Sailing from Lisbon in May 1588 under the command of a Spanish general, the Armada was poorly equipped. Its ships were too large and cumbersome to negotiate the treacherous English Channel, where the English sailing ships easily outmaneuvered them. The English sent fire ships against the Armada, which broke its formation; a Spanish army to be launched from Flanders failed to make its rendezvous; and perhaps most decisively, strong winds, typical for this time of year, drove the Armada out of striking position. The victory went to the English, and both sides believed it to be a sign from God.

This defeat had an enormous psychological effect on the Spanish. They openly pondered what they had done to incur divine displeasure. Protestant Europe, on the other hand, hailed the victory as a sign of its election, and the "Protestant wind" stirred by divine intervention entered the mythology of many a proud Englishman. In the rise and fall of nations, self-confidence has played a crucial, if inexplicable, role. The cultural renaissance associated with the England of Shakespeare owed its vigor and confidence in part to its pride at being Protestant and independent of Spanish influence.

The End of the Spanish Hapsburgs

After the defeat of the Armada, Spain gradually and reluctantly abandoned its imperial ambitions in northern Europe. The administrative structure built by Charles V and Philip II did remain strong throughout the seventeenth century; nevertheless, by the first quarter of the century enormous weaknesses had surfaced in Spanish economic and social life. In 1596, Philip II was bankrupt, his vast wealth overextended by the cost of foreign wars. Bankruptcy reappeared at various times in the seventeenth century, while the agricultural economy, at the heart of any early modern nation, stagnated. The Spanish in their golden age had never devoted enough attention to increasing domestic production.

Although Spain retained vast portions of its empire during the seventeenth century, important pieces broke away. First, the northern Netherlands secured its virtual independence. Then, in 1640, Portugal successfully revolted, as did Catalonia, although Catalonia was eventually brought back into the empire. And from 1606 to 1650, Spanish trade with the Americas dropped by 60 percent.

Despite these setbacks, Spain was still capable of taking a very aggressive posture during the Thirty Years' War (1618–1648). The Austrian branch of the Hapsburg family joined forces with their Spanish cousins, and neither the Swedes and Germans nor the Dutch could stop them. Only French participation in the Thirty Years' War on the Protestant side tipped the balance decisively against the Hapsburgs. Spanish aggression brought no victories, and with the Peace of Westphalia (1648), Spain officially recognized the independence of the Netherlands and severed its diplomatic ties with the Austrian branch of the family. The latter signed a separate treaty with the French. Austria itself would develop under this central European branch of the Hapsburg dynasty as a dynamic state, but not until the eighteenth century.

Spain had only one great statesman in the seventeenth century—Gaspar de Guzmán, count of Olivares (d. 1645), whose skill and efficiency matched his craving to restore Spain's imperial glory. He served Philip IV for over twenty years until his aggressive foreign and domestic policies brought ruin. One strength of the Spanish monarchy had been its ability to favor Castile while respecting the liberties and privileges of the provinces, Aragon and Catalonia in particular. Olivares attempted to bring the provincial laws into conformity with those of Castile and to force greater provincial participation in Spanish affairs. Clearly neither the provincial assemblies, the *Cortes,* nor the provincial aristocrats wished to undo the status quo, and Olivares's policies led to revolt in Catalonia.

By 1660, the imperial age of the Spanish Hapsburgs had come to an end. The rule of the Protestant princes had been secured in the Holy Roman Empire; the Protestant and Dutch Republic flourished; Portugal and its colony of Brazil were independent of Spain; and dominance over European affairs had passed to France. The quality of material life in Spain deteriorated rapidly, and the ever-present gap between rich and poor widened even more drastically. The traditional aristocracy and the church retained their land and power but failed conspicuously to produce effective leadership.

In the second half of the seventeenth century, Spanish leadership grew markedly worse. Palace intrigue replaced diplomacy and statesmanship. The reign of Charles II (1665–1700), whose Hapsburg parents were related as uncle and niece, witnessed the total administrative and economic collapse of Castile. What vitality remained in Spain could be found in its periphery, in Catalonia and Andalusia. At his death in 1700, Charles II (whose marriages had been childless) declared in favor of a French successor, Philip of Anjou, Louis XIV's grandson.

Charles's act, coupled with Louis XIV's designs on the kingdom of Spain, provoked another European war. The War of the Spanish Succession (1701–1713) pitted the Holy Roman Empire, England, and the Netherlands against France. Its outcome defeated Louis's desire to unite Spain and France under the Bourbons. Philip V, although king of Spain, was forced to renounce his claim to the French throne. Spain retained its political independence, but the Hapsburg dynasty in Spain had come to an end. From 1700 until very recently the Spanish state has been ruled by either Bourbons or dictators.

Of all the sovereign states of Europe to emerge in the early modern period, Spain presents the greatest set of paradoxes. It was the least centralized of all the states of the sixteenth and seventeenth centuries. In that lay its strength and its weakness. In the sixteenth century, Castile led the nation without crippling it. Spanish achievements in that century are nothing short of extraordinary in art, literature, navigation, exploration, administration, and even religious zeal. Then came the gradual and almost inexplicably precipitous decline in the seventeenth century, the effects of which endured into the twentieth century.

The Spanish experience leads to two observations on the history of the European state. First, the state as empire could only survive and prosper if the domestic economic base remained sound. The Spanish reliance on bullion from its colonies and its failure to cultivate industry and to reform the taxation system spelled disaster. Second, states with a vital and aggressive bourgeoisie flourished at the expense of societies where aristocracy and church dominated and controlled society and its mores—as in Spain. The latter social groups tended to despise manual labor, profit taking, and technological progress. Although kings and dynastic families originally created them, after 1700 the major dynastic states were increasingly nurtured by the economic activities of merchants and traders—the bourgeoisie. Nonetheless, the bureaucracy of the dynastic states continued to be dominated by men drawn from the lesser aristocracy. This was nowhere truer than in France where, once again, monarchs created the national state.

The Growth of French Power

Two states in the early modern period succeeded most effectively in consolidating the power of their central governments: France and England. Each became a model of a very different form of statehood. The French model emphasized, at every turn, the glory of the king and, by implication, the sovereignty of the state and its right to stand above the interests of its subjects. France's monarchy became *absolute,* although the evolution of the French state was a very gradual process, which was not completed until the late seventeenth century.

When Hugh Capet became king of France in 987 he was, in relation to France's other great feudal lords, merely first among equals. He could demand military service from his vassals (only forty days a year) and was regarded as the protector of the church, but he ruled only a small area around Paris, and the succession of his heirs to the kingship was by no means secure. Yet even at this early date, his title and his person were regarded as sacred. He was God's anointed, and his power, such as it was, rested on divine authority.

From this small power base, more symbolic than real, Hugh Capet's successors extended their territory and dominion at the expense of the power of the feudal lords. By 1328, when the Capetian family became extinct and the crown passed to the Valois family, the Capetians had made the French monarch the ruler of areas as distant from Paris as Languedoc in the south and Flanders in the north. To administer their territories, the Capetians established an efficient bureaucracy composed of townsmen and trustworthy lesser nobles who, unlike the great feudal lords, owed their wealth and status directly to the king. These royal officials, an essential element of monarchical power, collected the king's feudal dues and administered justice. At the same time, French kings emphasized that they had been selected by God to rule, a theory known as the divine right of kings. This theory gave monarchy a sanctity that various French kings used to enforce their commands over rebellious feudal lords and to defend themselves against papal claims of dominance over the French church.

Yet medieval French kings never sought absolute power. Not until the seventeenth century was the power base of the French monarchy consolidated to the extent that kings and their courts could attempt to rule without formal consultations with their subjects. In the Middle Ages the French monarchs recognized the rights of, and consulted with, local representative assemblies, which represented the three estates, or orders, in society. These assemblies (whether regional or national) were composed of deputies drawn from the various elites: the clergy, the nobility, and significantly, the leadership of cities and towns in a given region. The Estates met as circumstance—wars, taxes, local disputes—warranted, and the nationally representative assembly, the *Estates*

General, was always summoned by the king. In general, medieval French kings consulted these assemblies to give legitimacy to their demands and credibility to their administration. They also recognized that the courts—especially the highest court, the Parlement of Paris—had the right to administer the king's justice with a minimum of royal interference. Medieval kings did not see themselves as originators of law; they were its guarantors and administrators.

War came to serve the interests of a monarchy bent on consolidating its power and authority. As a result of the Hundred Years' War (1338–1453), the English were eventually driven from France and their claims to the French throne dashed. In the process of war, the French monarchy grew richer. The necessities of war enabled the French kings to levy new taxes, often enacted without the consent of the Estates General, and to maintain a large standing army under royal command. The Hundred Years' War also inspired allegiance to the king as the visible symbol of France. The war heightened the French sense of national identity; the English were a common enemy, discernibly different in manners, language, dress, and appearance.

With revenue and an army at their disposal, the French kings subsequently embarked on territorial aggrandizement. Charles VIII (1483–1498) invaded Italy in 1494. Machiavelli, a shrewd assessor of the implications of power, observed that while Italy's weakness derived from its lack of unity, the power of this new cohesive state of France derived in large measure from the strength of its prince and his huge and mostly native-born army. Although the French gained little territory from the Italian campaign, they did effectively challenge Spanish power in Italy and intimidate an already weakened papacy.

Religion and the French State

In every emergent state, tension existed between the monarch and the papacy. At issue was control over the church within that territory—over its personnel, its wealth, and, of course, its pulpits, from which an illiterate majority learned what their leaders believed they should know, not only in matters of religious belief but also about questions of obedience to civil authority. The monarch's power to make church appointments could ensure a complacent church. A church that was willing to preach about the king's divine right and was compliant on matters of taxes was especially important in France because legally the church had to pay no taxes and had only to give donations to the Crown. Centuries of tough bargaining with the papacy paid off when, in 1516, Francis I concluded the Concordat of Bologna, by which Pope Leo X permitted the French king to nominate, and therefore effectively to appoint, men of his choice to all the highest offices in the French church.

The Concordat of Bologna laid the foundation for what became known as the *Gallican church*— a term signifying the immense power and authority of the Catholic church in France—which was sanctioned and overseen by the French kings. By the early sixteenth century, religious homogeneity had strengthened the central government at the expense of papal authority and the traditional privileges enjoyed by local aristocracy. This ecclesiastical and religious settlement lay at the heart of monarchical authority. Consequently, the Protestant Reformation threatened the very survival of France as a unified state. Throughout the early modern period the French kings had assumed that their states must be governed by one king, one faith, and one set of laws. Any alternative to that unity offered local power elites, whether aristocratic or cleric, the opportunity to channel religious dissent into their service at the expense of royal authority. Once linked, religious and political opposition to any central government could be extremely dangerous.

Francis I (1515–1547) perceived that Protestantism in France would undermine the sacredness of his office, challenge his authority, and diminish his control over church officials. In 1534, the king, in conjunction with the court of Paris (the Parlement), declared Protestant beliefs and practices illegal and punishable by fine, imprisonment, and even execution. The Protestant reformer Calvin and his friends fled from Paris and eventually to Geneva (see Chapter 14), but they never abandoned the hope of converting Francis and France to the Protestant cause.

During the decades that followed, partly through the efforts of the Huguenot underground

Francis I of France by Jean Clouet (1486–1541). Francis I was a true Renaissance prince, power hungry and a patron of the arts. The aged Leonardo da Vinci ended his days at Francis's court at Amboise as guest of the French king. Francis was also a brilliant politician; through his concordat of Bologna with Pope Leo X, French monarchs could appoint men of their choice to high church offices in France. (*Louvre/Cliché des Musées Nationaux*)

and partly because the French king and his ministers vacillated in their efforts at persecution, the Protestant minority grew in strength and dedication. By challenging the authority of the Catholic church, Protestants were also inadvertently challenging royal authority, for the French church and the French monarchy supported each other. Protestantism became the basis for a political movement of an increasingly revolutionary nature.

From 1562 to 1598, France experienced waves of religious wars that cost the king control over vast areas of the kingdom. Protestantism became for some adherents a vehicle for expressing their rage against both the French church and the increasing power of the Valois kings. The great aristocratic families, the Guise for the Catholics and the Bourbons for the Protestants, drew up armies that scourged the land, killing and maiming their religious opponents. When entwined with religion, local grievances for a time proved capable of dismantling the authority of the central government. In Protestant urban centers, townsmen asserted their right to control local government, as well as to worship publicly in the Protestant manner. They allied with those aristocrats who would convert to the Reformation, for whatever reasons. The French Catholics, on the other hand, turned to the House of Guise for protection—a vivid reminder of the strength of feudal elites centuries after feudalism as an institution had ceased to be the main expression of political authority.

In 1579, extreme Huguenot theorists published the *Vindiciae contra Tyrannos*. This theoretical statement combined with a call to action was the first of its kind in early modern times. It justified rebellion against, and even the execution of, an unjust king. European monarchs might claim power and divinely sanctioned authority, but by the late sixteenth century, their subjects had available the moral justification to oppose by force, if necessary, their monarch's will, and this justification rested on Scripture and religious conviction. Significantly, this same treatise was translated into English in 1648, a year before Parliament publicly executed Charles I, king of England.

The Valois kings floundered in the face of this kind of political and religious opposition. The era of royal supremacy instituted by Francis I came to an abrupt end during the reign of his successor, Henry II (1547–1559). Wed to Catherine de' Medici, a member of the powerful Italian banking family, Henry occupied himself not with the concerns of government but with the pleasures of the hunt. The sons who succeeded Henry—Francis II (1559–1560), Charles IX (1560–1574), and Henry III (1574–1589)—were uniformly weak. In this power vacuum, their mother Catherine emerged as virtual ruler—a queen despised for her foreign and nonaristocratic lineage, for the fact that she was a woman, and for her propensity for

dangerous intrigue. One of the most hated figures of her day, Catherine de' Medici defies dispassionate assessment. She ordered the execution of Protestants by royal troops in Paris—the beginning of the infamous St. Bartholomew's Day Massacre (1572) which, with the blood bath that followed, became both a symbol and a legend in subsequent European history: a symbol of the excesses of religious zeal and a legend of Protestant martyrdom that gave renewed energy to the cause of international Protestantism.

The civil wars begun in 1562 were renewed in the massacre's aftermath. They dragged on until the death of the last Valois king in 1589. The Valois failure to produce a male heir to the throne placed Henry, duke of Bourbon and a Protestant, in line to succeed to the French throne. Realizing that the overwhelmingly Catholic population would not accept a Protestant king, Henry (apparently without much regret) renounced his adopted religion and embraced the church. His private religious beliefs may never be known, but outward conformity to the religion of the Catholic majority was the only means to effect peace and reestablish political stability. Under the reign of Henry IV (1589–1610) the French throne acquired its central position in national politics. Henry granted to his Protestant subjects and former followers a degree of religious toleration through the Edict of Nantes (1598), but they were never welcomed in significant numbers into the royal bureaucracy. Throughout the seventeenth century, every French king attempted to undermine the Protestants' regional power bases and ultimately to destroy their religious liberties.

The Consolidation of French Monarchical Power

The defeat of Protestantism as a national force set the stage for the final consolidation of the French state in the seventeenth century under the great Bourbon kings, Louis XIII and Louis XIV. Louis XIII (1610–1643) realized that his rule depended on an efficient and trustworthy bureaucracy, an ever-replenishable treasury, and constant vigilance against the localized claims to power made

Map 16.2 Europe, 1648 ▶

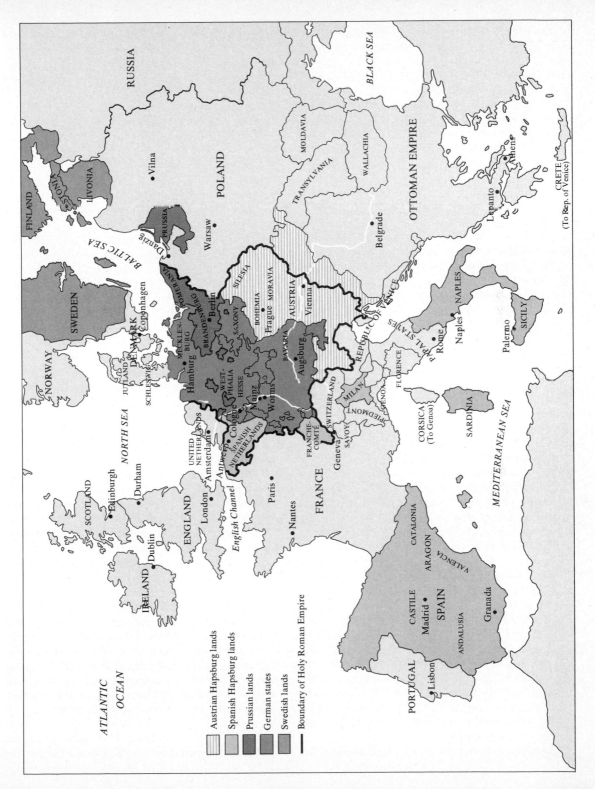

RUSSIA

BLACK SEA

SWEDEN

FINLAND

ESTONIA

LIVONIA

• Vilna

POLAND

MOLDAVIA

TRANSYLVANIA

WALLACHIA

OTTOMAN EMPIRE

CRETE
(To Rep. of Venice)

Lepanto

Athens

NORWAY

BALTIC SEA

PRUSSIA

Danzig

Warsaw

POMERANIA

• Belgrade

DENMARK

Copenhagen

JUTLAND

SCHLESWIG

MECKLEN-BURG

BRANDENBURG

Berlin

SILESIA

SAXONY

BOHEMIA

Prague

MORAVIA

AUSTRIA

Vienna

NAPLES

NAPLES

SICILY

Palermo

Hamburg

WEST-PHALIA

HESSE

BAVARIA

Augsburg

PAPAL STATES

Rome

Naples

REPUBLIC OF VENICE

FLORENCE

GENOA

Cologne

Mainz

Worms

FRANCHE-COMTÉ

SWITZERLAND

MILAN

PIEDMONT

SAVOY

CORSICA
(To Genoa)

SARDINIA

MEDITERRANEAN SEA

UNITED NETHERLANDS

Amsterdam

Antwerp

SPANISH NETHERLANDS

Geneva

SCOTLAND

Edinburgh

• Durham

NORTH SEA

ENGLAND

London •

English Channel

• Paris

FRANCE

• Nantes

IRELAND

Dublin

ATLANTIC
OCEAN

PORTUGAL

Lisbon •

CATALONIA

ARAGON

VALENCIA

CASTILE

Madrid •

SPAIN

ANDALUSIA

Granada

Austrian Hapsburg lands
Spanish Hapsburg lands
Prussian lands
German states
Swedish lands
Boundary of Holy Roman Empire

by the great aristocracy and the Protestant cities and towns. Many of the latter were capable of taking military action against the central government or even of forming alliances with foreign princes. To weaken the power of local elites, Louis XIII called their representative assembly, the Estates General, only once, in 1614. It did not meet again until 1789. Cardinal Richelieu, who served as Louis XIII's chief minister from 1624 to 1642, became the great architect of French absolutism.

Richelieu was the king's loyal servant; in this way he served the state. His morality rested on one sacred principle embodied in the phrase he invented: *raison d'état,* "reason of state." For Richelieu the state's necessities and the king's absolute authority were synonymous; one was inconceivable without the other. In accordance with his political philosophy, Richelieu brought under control the disruptive and antimonarchical elements within French society. He increased the power of the central bureaucracy, attacked the power of independent, and often Protestant, towns and cities, and persecuted the Huguenots. Above all, he humbled the great nobles by limiting their effectiveness as councilors to the king and by prohibiting their traditional privileges, such as using a duel rather than court action to settle grievances.

Reason of state also guided Richelieu's foreign policy. Since the treaty of Cateau-Cambrésis (1559), which ended nearly a century of French-Spanish rivalry, both countries had ceased their armed hostilities and concentrated on the threat posed to internal order by the Protestant Reformation. This relative peace had enhanced Spanish power at the expense of the French, yet both countries were Catholic powers, interrelated by aristocratic marriages. When Richelieu came to power at the French court in 1624, the king and his mother were pursuing a policy of appeasement toward the Spanish. But reason of state, as Richelieu saw it, necessitated that France turn against Spain and enter on the Protestant and anti-Spanish side of the war that was raging at the time in the Holy Roman Empire. The outcome of France's entry into the Thirty Years' War (1618–1648) produced a decided victory for French power on the Continent.

By the time of his death in 1642, Richelieu had established certain practices and policies that were continued by his successors to great effect. First, the avaricious and unprincipled Cardinal Mazarin, who took charge during the minority of Louis XIV (who was five years old when Louis XIII died), continued Richelieu's policies. Then Louis XIV (1643–1715) himself continued the work of his father's minister. The growth of royal absolutism produced a severe reaction among its victims: peasants, who paid the burden of the state's taxes; aristocrats, who bitterly resented their loss of power; and judges in the royal courts, the parlements, who resented attempts by the king and his ministers to bypass their authority.

Richelieu's policies, as administered by his corrupt successor Mazarin, produced a rebellious reaction, the *Fronde*—a series of street riots that lasted from 1648 to 1653 and eventually cost the government control over Paris. Centered in Paris and supported by the great aristocracy, the courts, and the city's poorer classes, the Fronde threatened to develop into a full-scale uprising. It did not because of one crucial factor: its leadership was fundamentally divided. Court judges (lesser nobility who had often just risen from the ranks of the bourgeoisie) deeply distrusted the great nobility and refused in the end to make common cause with them. And both groups feared disorder among the urban masses. The discontented elites could not unite, and as a result they could offer no viable alternative except disorder to the rule of absolute kings and their ministers.

When Louis XIV finally assumed responsibility for governing in 1661, he vowed that the events he witnessed as a child during the Fronde would never be repeated. In the course of his reign, he achieved the greatest degree of monarchical power ever witnessed during the early modern period. No absolute monarch in western Europe had ever before held so much personal authority or commanded such a vast and effective military and administrative machine. Louis XIV's reign represents the culmination of a process of increasing monarchical authority that had been under way for centuries. Intelligent, cunning, and possessing a unique understanding of the requirements of his office, Louis XIV became the envy of his age.

Louis XIV's education had been practical, rather than theoretical. He knew that a hardworking monarch could dispense with chief ministers while still maintaining the effectiveness of his administration. Louis XIV worked long hours at being king, and he never undertook a venture without an eye to his personal grandeur. The sumptuous royal palace at Versailles was built for that reason; similarly, etiquette and style were cultivated there on a scale never before seen in any European court. A lengthy visit to Versailles, a necessity for any aristocrat who wanted his views and needs attended to, could bankrupt the less well-to-do.

Perhaps the most brilliant of Louis XIV's many policies was his treatment of the aristocracy. He simply dispensed with their services as influential advisers; indeed, Louis XIV would not have any minister assume the power that his father had accorded to Richelieu. He treated the aristocrats to elaborate rituals, feasts, processions, displays, and banquets; but amid all the clamor, their political power dwindled. The wiser members of the aristocracy stayed home and managed their estates; others made their way at court as minor functionaries and basked in the glory of the Sun King.

Louis XIV's domestic policies centered around his incessant search for new revenues. Not only the building of Versailles, but also wars cost money, and Louis XIV waged them to excess. To raise capital, he used the services of Jean Baptiste Colbert, a brilliant administrator who improved methods of tax collecting, promoted new industries, and encouraged international trade. Such ambitious national policies were possible because Louis XIV had inherited an efficient system of administration introduced by Richelieu. Instead of relying on the local aristocracy to collect royal taxes and to administer royal policies, Richelieu had appointed the king's own men as *intendants,* functionaries dispatched with wide powers into the provinces. At first, their missions had been temporary and their success minimal, but gradually they became a permanent feature of royal administration. During the reign of Louis XIV, the country was divided into thirty-two districts controlled by intendants. Operating with a total bureaucracy of about a thousand officials and no longer bothering even to consult the parlements or Estates, Louis XIV ruled absolutely.

Why did such a system of absolute authority work? Did the peasants not revolt? Why did the

Portrait of Louis XIV by Hyacinthe Rigaud (1659–1743). Rigaud has captured the authority of his monarch as well as the dazzling splendor and pomp of his court. Louis unabashedly saw himself as the "Sun King." He turned every moment of his waking day into a quasi-religious ritual. *(Louvre/ Cliché des Musées Nationaux)*

old aristocracy not rise in rebellion? For the aristocrats, the loss of political authority was not accompanied by a comparable loss in wealth and social position; indeed, quite the contrary was true. During the seventeenth century, the French nobility—2 percent of the population—controlled approximately 20 to 30 percent of the total national income. The church, too, fared well under Louis, receiving good tax arrangements provided it preached about the king's divinely given rights. While there were peasant upheavals throughout the century, the sheer size of the royal army and police—over 300,000 by the end of Louis's reign—made successful revolt nearly impossible. When in the early 1700s a popular religious rebellion led by Protestant visionaries broke out in the south, royal troops crushed it. Thus, absolutism rested on the complicity of the old aristocracy, the self-aggrandizement of government officials, the church's doctrines, the revenues squeezed out of the peasantry, and the power of a huge military machine.

Yet Louis XIV's system was fatally flawed. Without any effective check on his power and dreams of international conquest, there was no limit imposed on the state's capacity to make war or on the ensuing national debt. Louis XIV coveted vast sections of the Holy Roman Empire; he also sought to check Dutch commercial prosperity and had designs on the Spanish Netherlands. By the 1680s, his domestic and foreign policies took on a violently aggressive posture. In 1685, he revoked the Edict of Nantes, forcing many of the country's remaining Protestants to flee. In 1689, he embarked on a military campaign to secure territory from the Holy Roman Empire. And in 1701, he tried to bring Spain under the control of the Bourbon dynasty. Louis XIV, however, underestimated the power of his northern rivals, England and the Netherlands. The combined power of England and the Netherlands in alliance with the Holy Roman Empire and the Austrians brought defeat to Louis XIV's ambitions.

The ensuing War of the Spanish Succession was essentially a land war fought on the battlefields of northern Europe. Out of it the Austrians secured the southern Netherlands (Belgium) and thereby gained a buffer against the possibility of a French overrun of the Low Countries. Most dramatically, however, the war created a balance of power in Europe with Britain emerging as a major force in European affairs, the counterweight against the French colossus. The relative peace of the eighteenth century has often been attributed to the creation of this real, but fragile, balance among the major European powers.

Louis XIV's participation in these long wars emptied the royal treasury. By the late seventeenth century taxes had risen intolerably, and they were essentially levied on those least able to pay—the peasants. In the 1690s, the combination of taxes, bad harvests, and plague led to widespread poverty, misery, and starvation in large areas of France. Thus, for the great majority of French people, absolutism meant a decline in living standards and a significant increase in mortality rates. Absolutism also meant increased surveillance over the population: royal authorities censored books; spied on heretics, Protestants, and freethinkers; and even tortured and executed opponents of state policy.

By 1715, France was a tightly governed society whose treasury was bankrupt. Protestants had been driven into exile or forced to convert. Strict censorship laws closely governed publishing, causing a brisk trade in clandestine books and manuscripts. Direct taxes burdened the poor and were legally evaded by the aristocracy. Critics of state policy within the church had been effectively silenced. And over the long run, foreign wars had brought no significant gains.

In the France of Louis XIV, the dynastic state had reached maturity and had begun to display some of its classic characteristics: centralized bureaucracy; royal patronage to enforce allegiance; a system of taxation universally but inequitably applied; and suppression of political opposition either through the use of patronage or, if necessary, through force. Another important feature was the state's cultivation of the arts and sciences as a means of increasing national power and prestige. Together, these policies enabled France and its monarchs to achieve political stability, to enforce a uniform system of law, and to channel the country's wealth and resources into the service of the state as a whole.

Yet at his death in 1715, Louis XIV left his successors a system of bureaucracy and taxation that was vastly in need of overhaul but was still locked into the traditional social privileges of the church and nobility to an extent that made reform virtually impossible. The pattern of war, excessive taxation of the lower classes, and expenditure in excess of revenues had severely damaged French finances. Failure to reform the system led to the French Revolution of 1789.

The Growth of Limited Monarchy and Constitutionalism in England

England achieved national unity earlier than any other major European state. Its fortunate geography freed it from the border disputes that plagued emerging states on the Continent. By an accident of fate, its administrative structure also developed in such a way as to encourage centralization. In 1066, William, duke of Normandy and vassal to the French king, had invaded and conquered England, acquiring at a stroke the entire kingdom. In contrast, the French kings took centuries to bring the territory of France under their domain.

The conquering Norman kings and their followers represented a distinct minority in England. Eventually they intermarried and merged with the larger population. In the first century of their rule, the Norman kings frequently lived in France for long periods and thus depended on an efficient bureaucracy and on their own knowledge of the English kingdom to maintain their power.

Out of necessity, therefore, these medieval Norman kings consulted with their powerful subjects—archbishops, bishops, earls, and barons. By the middle of the thirteenth century, these consultations, or *parlays*, came to be called *parliaments*. Increasingly, the practice grew of inviting to these parliaments representatives from the counties—knights and burgesses. Gradually, these lesser-than-noble but often wealthy and prominent representatives grew to see Parliament as a means of self-expression for redressing their grievances. In turn, the later medieval kings saw Parliament as an effective means of exercising control and of raising taxes. By 1297, the Lords and Commons (as the lower house was called) had obtained the king's agreement that no direct taxes could be levied without their consent. By the fourteenth century, Parliament had become a permanent institution of government. Its power was entirely subservient to the Crown, but its right to question royal decisions had been established.

The medieval Parliament possessed two characteristics that distinguished it from its many Continental counterparts, such as the various French Estates. The English Parliament was national and not provincial, and more important, its representatives were elected across caste lines, with voting rights dependent on property, not on noble birth or status. These representatives voted as individuals, not collectively as clergy, nobles, or commoners, that is, as Estates. In the Middle Ages, Parliament and monarchy were interdependent; they were seen not as rivals but as complementary forms of centralized government. That very interdependence, however, would ultimately lead to conflict.

Also emerging during the Middle Ages in England was the constitution—a set of precedents, laws, and royal acts that came to embody the basic principles of government. And in contrast to the French model, England grew to be a *constitutional* monarchy. This theoretical foundation—up to this time not written as a single constitution—grew out of legal practices and customs described under the generic title *common law*. As opposed to feudal law, which applied only to a local region, the common law extended throughout the realm and served as a force for unity.

The strength of the monarchy during the later Middle Ages received dramatic expression in English victories against France during the Hundred Years' War. The power of the English kings enabled them to rally the nobility, who in turn benefited enormously from pillaging France. Only after the revitalization of the French monarchy and its subsequent victories were the English aristocrats forced to take their skills and taste for war back home. The consequences of their return were devastating. Civil war ensued—the Wars of the Roses (1455–1485)—and the medieval war machine turned inward. Gangs of noblemen with retainers roamed the English countryside, and lawlessness prevailed for a generation. Only in 1485 did the Tudor family emerge triumphant.

The Tudor Achievement

Victory in the civil wars allowed Henry VII (1485–1509) to begin the Tudor dynasty. Henry and his successors strove to secure their power by remaking and revitalizing the institutions of government. Henry VII's goal was to bring an unruly nobility into check. Toward this end, he brought commoners into the government; these commoners, unlike the great magnates, could be channeled into royal service because they craved what the king offered—financial rewards and elevated social status. Although they did not fully displace the aristocracy, commoners were brought into Henry VII's inner circle, into the Privy Council, into the courts, and eventually into all the highest offices of the government. The strength and efficiency of Tudor government were shown during the Reformation, when Henry VIII (1509–1547) made himself head of the English church (see Chapter 14). He was able to take this giant step toward increasing royal power because his father had restored order and stability.

The Protestant Reformation in England was a revolution in royal, as well as ecclesiastical, government. It attacked and defeated a main obstacle to monarchical authority—the power of the papacy. At the same time, the Reformation greatly enhanced the power of Parliament. Henry used Parliament to make the Reformation because he knew that he needed the support of the lords, the country gentry, and the merchants. No change in religious practice could be instituted by the monarchy alone. Parliament's participation in the Reformation gave it a greater role and sense of importance than it had ever possessed in the past. Nonetheless, the final outcome of this administrative revolution enhanced monarchical power. By the end of his reign, Henry VIII easily possessed as much power as his French rival, Francis I. Indeed, up to the early seventeenth century the history of monarchical power in England, with its absolutist tendencies, was remarkably similar to the Continental pattern.

At Henry's death, the Tudor bureaucracy and centralized government was strained to its utmost, yet it survived. The government weathered the reign of Henry's sickly son Edward VI (1547–1553) and the extreme Protestantism of some of his advisers, and it survived the brief and deeply troubled reign of Henry's first daughter Mary (1553–1558), who attempted to return England to Catholicism. At Mary's death, England had come dangerously close to the religious instability and sectarian tension that undermined the French kings during the final decades of the sixteenth century.

Henry's second daughter, Elizabeth I became queen in 1558. The Elizabethan period was characterized by a heightened sense of national identity. The English Reformation enhanced that sense, as did the increasing fear of foreign invasion by Spain. The fear was real enough and was abated only by the defeat—more psychologically than militarily crippling—of the Spanish Armada in 1588. In the seventeenth century, the English would look back on Elizabeth's reign as a golden age. It was the calm before the storm, a time when a new commercial class was formed that, in the seventeenth century, would demand a greater say in government operations.

The social and economic changes of the Elizabethan age can be seen, in microcosm, by looking at the Durham region in northern England. From 1580 to 1640, a new coal-mining industry developed there through the efforts of entrepreneurs—gentlemen with minor lands whose industry and skill enabled them to exploit their mineral resources. The wool trade also prospered in Durham. By 1600, social and political tensions had developed. The wool merchants and the entrepreneurial gentry were demanding a greater say in governing the region. They were opposed by the traditional leaders of Durham society—the bishops and the dozen or so aristocratic families with major lands and access to the court in London.

This split can be described as one between court and country. *Court* refers to the traditional aristocratic magnates, the hierarchy of the church, and royal officialdom. *Country* denotes a loose coalition of merchants and rising agricultural and industrial entrepreneurs from the prosperous gentry class, whose economic worth far exceeded their political power. The pattern found in Durham was repeated in other parts of the country, generally where industry and commerce grew and prospered. The agricultural and industrial gentry grew in social status and wealth. In the seventeenth century, these social and economic tensions would help foster revolution.

By the early seventeenth century in England the descendants of the old feudal aristocracy differed markedly from their Continental counterparts.

Their isolation from the great wars of the Reformation had produced an aristocracy less military and more commercial in orientation. Furthermore, the lesser ranks of the landowning aristocracy, gentlemen without titles (the gentry), had prospered significantly in Tudor times. In commercial matters they were often no shrewder than the great landed magnates, but they had in Parliament, as well as in their counties, an effective and institutionalized means of expressing their political interests. The great nobles, on the other hand, had largely abandoned the sword as the primary expression of their political authority without putting anything comparable in its place. Gradually, political initiative was slipping away from the great lords into the hands of a gentry that was commercially and agriculturally innovative, as well as fiercely protective of its local base of political power.

Religion played a vital role in this realignment of political interests and forces. Many of the old aristocracy clung to the Anglicanism of the Henrican Reformation, and in some cases to Catholicism. The newly risen gentry found in the Protestant Reformation of Switzerland and Germany a form of religious worship more suited to their independent and entrepreneurial spirit. They felt that it was their right to appoint their own preachers and that the church should reflect local tastes and beliefs rather than a series of doctrines and ceremonies inherited from a discredited Catholicism. In late Tudor times, gentry and merchant interests fused with Puritanism—the English variety of Calvinism—to produce a political-religious vision with ominous potential.

The English Revolution, 1640–1689

The forces threatening established authority were dealt with ineffectively by the first two Stuart kings—James I (1603–1625) and Charles I (1625–1649). Both believed, as did their Continental counterparts, in royal absolutism. Essentially, these Stuart kings tried to do in England what Louis XIII and later Louis XIV were to do in France: to establish court and crown as the sole governing bodies within the state. What the Stuarts lacked, however, was an adequate social and institutional base for absolutism, not least of all a standing army. They did not possess the vast independent wealth of their French counterparts.

These kings preached, through the established church, the doctrine of the divine right of kings. James I, an effective and shrewd administrator, conducted foreign policy without consulting Parliament. Both kings tried to revitalize the old aristocracy and to create new peers to re-establish the feudal base of monarchical authority. After 1629, Charles brought his hand-picked advisers into government in the hope that they would purge the church of Puritans and the nation of his opponents. Charles also disbanded Parliament and attempted to collect taxes without its consent. These policies ended in disaster.

The English Revolution broke out in 1640 because Charles I needed new taxes to defend the realm against a Scottish invasion. Parliament, finally called after an eleven-year absence, refused his request unless he granted certain basic rights: Parliament to be consulted in matters of taxation, trial by jury, *habeas corpus*, and a truly Protestant church responsive to the beliefs and interests of its laity. Charles refused, for he saw these demands as an assault on royal authority. The ensuing civil war was directed by Parliament, financed by taxes and the merchants, and fought by the New Model Army led by Oliver Cromwell (1599–1658), a Puritan squire who gradually realized his potential for leadership.

The New Model Army was unmatched by any ever seen before in Europe. Parliament's rich supporters financed it, gentleman farmers led it, and religious zealots filled its ranks, along with the usual cross-section of poor artisans and day laborers. This army brought defeat to the king, his aristocratic followers, and the Anglican church's hierarchy.

In January 1649, Charles I was publicly executed by order of Parliament. During the interregnum (time between kings) of the next eleven years, one Parliament after another joined with the army to govern the country as a republic. In the distribution of power between the army and the Parliament, Cromwell proved to be a key element. He had the support of the army's officers and some of its rank and file, and he had been a member of Parliament for many years. His control over the army was secured, however, only after its rank and file was purged of radical groups. Some of these radicals wanted to level society, that is, to redistribute property by ending monopolies and to give the vote to all male citizens. In the context of the 1650s, Cromwell was a moderate republican who also believed in limited religious toleration, yet history has painted him, somewhat unjustly, as a military dictator.

The English Revolution was begun by urban merchants as well as landed gentry, who were imbued with the strict Protestantism of the Continental Reformation. In the 1650s, however, the success of their revolution was jeopardized by growing discontent from the poor, who made up the rank and file of the army and who demanded that their economic and social grievances be rectified. Also vast areas of the country were administered inefficiently, and this increased popular discontent. The radicals of the English Revolution—men like Gerrard Winstanley, the first theoretician of social democracy in modern times, and John Lilburne, the Leveller—demanded redistribution of property, voting rights for the majority of the male population, and abolition of religious and intellectual elites whose power and ideology supported the interests of the ruling classes. The radicals rejected Anglicanism, moderate Puritanism, and even, in a few cases, the lifestyle of the middle class; they opted instead for libertine and communistic beliefs and practices. The radicals terrified even devoted Puritans like Cromwell. By 1660, the country was adrift, without effective leadership.

Parliament, having secured the economic interests of its constituency (gentry, merchants, and some small landowners), chose to restore court and crown, and invited the exiled son of the executed king to return to the kingship. Having learned the lesson his father had spurned, Charles II (1660–1685) never instituted royal absolutism, although he did try to minimize Parliament's role in the government. His court was a far more open institution than his father's had been, for Charles II feared a similar death.

But Charles's brother James II (1685–1688) was a foolishly fearless Catholic and admirer of French absolutism. James gathered at his court a coterie of Catholic advisers and supporters of royal prerogative and attempted to bend Parliament and local government to the royal will. James's Catholicism was the crucial element in his failure. The Anglican church would not back him, and political forces similar to those that had gathered against his father, Charles I, in 1640 descended on him. The ruling elites, however, had learned their lesson back in the 1650s: civil war would produce social discontent among the masses. The upper classes wanted to avoid open warfare and preserve the monarchy as a constitutional authority, but not as an absolute one. Puritanism, with its sectarian fervor and its dangerous association with republicanism, was allowed to play no part in this second and last phase of the English Revolution.

In early 1688, Anglicans, some aristocrats, and opponents of royal prerogative (Whigs and a few Tories) formed a conspiracy against James II. Their purpose was to invite his son-in-law, William of Orange, *stadholder* (head) of the Netherlands and husband of James's Protestant daughter Mary, to invade England and rescue its government from James's control. It was hoped that the final outcome of this invasion would be determined by William and his conspirators, in conjunction with a freely elected Parliament. This dangerous plan succeeded for three main reasons: William and the Dutch desperately needed English support against the threat of a French invasion; James had lost the loyalty of key men in the army, powerful gentlemen in the counties, and the Anglican church; and the political elite was committed and united in its intentions. James II fled the country, and William and Mary were declared king and queen by act of Parliament.

This bloodless revolution—sometimes called the Glorious Revolution—created a new political and constitutional reality. Parliament secured its rights to assemble regularly and to vote on all matters of taxation; the rights of *habeas corpus* and trial by jury (for men of property and social status) were also secured. These rights were in turn legitimated in a constitutionally binding document, the Bill of Rights (1689). All Protestants, regardless of their sectarian bias, were granted toleration. The Revolution Settlement of 1688–89 resolved the profound constitutional and social tensions of the seventeenth century and laid the foundations of English government until well into

Sir Christopher Wren (1632–1723): The Royal Hospital at Greenwich. The classical design of the Royal Hospital derives ultimately from Palladio and Michelangelo, but its blend of grave monumentality and simplicity reflects the taste of late-seventeenth-century England. The buildings are now part of the Royal Naval College: left, the Chapel; right, the Painted Hall. In the middle distance is the Queen's House, designed by Inigo Jones. (*A. F. Kersting*)

the nineteenth century. The revolution, says historian J. H. Plumb, established "the authority of certain men of property, particularly those of high social standing, either aristocrats or linked with aristocracy, whose tap root was in land but whose side roots reached out to commerce, industry and finance."[2] Throughout the eighteenth century, England was ruled by kings and Parliaments that represented the interests of an oligarchy whose cohesiveness and prosperity ensured social and political stability.

The English Revolution, in both its 1640 and its 1688 phases, secured English parliamentary government and the rule of law, and it also provided a degree of freedom for the propertied. In retrospect, we can see that absolutism according to the French model probably never had a chance in England. There were simply too many gentlemen there who possessed enough land to be independent of the Crown, and yet not so much that they could control whole sections of the kingdom. In addition, monarchs possessed no effective standing army. But to contemporaries, the issues seemed different: the English opponents of absolutism spoke of their rights as granted by their ancient constitution and the feudal law, of the

William and Mary in Triumph. This detail of the ceiling painting by Sir James Thornhill in the Painted Hall of the Royal Hospital (see page 357) shows William III and Mary being received trium- phantly after the ouster of James II in the Glorious Revolution of 1688–89. (*By Permission of the Admiral President RN College Greenwich and the Director of the Greenwich Hospital*)

need to make the English church truly Protestant, and, among the radicals, of the right of lesser men to secure their property. These opponents possessed an institution—Parliament—by which they could express their grievances; eventually, they also acquired an army that waged war to secure the demands of the propertied classes. The result was limited monarchy as established in 1689 and a constitutional system based on the laws made by Parliament and sanctioned by the king. Very gradually the monarchical element in that system would yield to the power and authority of parliamentary ministers and state officials.

The Revolution of 1688–89 was England's last revolution. In the nineteenth and twentieth centuries, parliamentary institutions would be gradually and peacefully reformed to express a more democratic social reality. The events of 1688–89 have rightly been described as "the year one," in that they fashioned a system of government that operated effectively in Britain and was also capable of being adopted with modification elsewhere.

The British system became a model for other forms of bourgeois representative government adopted in France and former British colonies, beginning with the United States.

The Netherlands: A Bourgeois Republic

One other area in Europe developed a system of representative government that also survived for centuries. The Netherlands, or Low Countries (Holland and Belgium), had been part of Hapsburg territory since the fifteenth century. When Charles V ascended to the Spanish throne in 1516, the Netherlands grew into an economic linchpin of the Spanish empire. Spain exported wool and bullion to the Low Countries in return for manufactured textiles, hardware, grain, and naval stores. Flanders, with Antwerp as its capital, was the manufacturing and banking center of the Spanish empire.

The Spanish monarchy exploited its colonies in both the old and new worlds to finance wars against the Turks and the Italian city-states, and by the 1540s, its crusade against Protestant Germany. In the northern Low Countries especially, this tax burden joined with administrative inefficiency, unemployment, and religious repression to create the conditions that sparked the first successful bourgeois revolution in history.

During the reign of Charles V's successor, Philip II, a tightly organized Calvinist minority, with its popular base in the cities and its military strategy founded on sea raids, at first harassed and then aggressively challenged Spanish power. In the 1560s the Spanish responded by trying to export the Inquisition into the Netherlands and by sending an enormous standing army there under the duke of Alva. It was a classic example of overkill; thousands of once-loyal Flemish and Dutch subjects turned against the Spanish Crown. The people either converted secretly to Calvinism or aided the revolutionaries. Led by William the Silent (1533–1584), head of the Orange dynasty, the seven northern provinces (Holland, Zeeland,

Utrecht, Gelderland, Overijssel, Friesland, and Groningen) joined in the Union of Utrecht (1579) to protect themselves against Spanish aggression. Their determined resistance, coupled with the serious economic weaknesses of the overextended Spanish empire, eventually produced unexpected success for the northern colonies.

By 1609, the seven northern provinces were effectively free of Spanish control and loosely tied together under a republican form of government. Seventeenth-century Netherlands became a prosperous bourgeois state. Rich from the fruits of manufacture and trade in everything from tulip bulbs to ships, and not least, slaves, the Dutch merchants ruled their cities and provinces with a fierce pride. By the early seventeenth century, this new nation of only 1.5 million practiced the most innovative commercial and financial techniques in Europe.

In this fascinating instance, capitalism and Protestantism fused to do the work of princes; the Dutch state emerged without absolute monarchy, and indeed in opposition to it. From that experience, the ruling Dutch oligarchy retained a deep distrust of hereditary monarchy. The exact position of the House of Orange remained a vexing constitutional question until well into the eighteenth century. The oligarchs and their party, the Patriots, favored a republic without a single head, ruled by them through the Estates General. The Calvinist clergy, old aristocrats, and a vast section of the populace—all for very different reasons— wanted the head of the House of Orange to govern as stadholder of the provinces, in effect as a limited monarch in a republican state. These unresolved political tensions prevented the Netherlands from developing a form of republican government that might have rivaled the stability of the British system of limited monarchy. The Dutch achievement came in other areas.

Calvinism had provided the ideology of revolution and national identity. Capital, in turn, created a unique cultural milieu in the Dutch urban centers of Amsterdam, Rotterdam, Utrecht, and The Hague. Wide toleration without a centralized system of censorship made the Dutch book trade, which often disseminated works by refugees from the Spanish Inquisition and later by French Protestants, the most vital in Europe right up to the French Revolution. And the sights and sounds of an active and prosperous population, coupled with a politically engaged and rich bourgeoisie, fed the imagination as well as the purses of various artistic schools. Rembrandt van Rijn, Jan Steen, Frans Hals, Jan Vermeer, and Jan van del Velde are at the top of a long list of great Dutch artists—many of them also refugees. They left timeless images portraying the people of the only republican national state to endure throughout the seventeenth century.

The Holy Roman Empire: The Failure to Unify Germany

In contrast to the French, English, Spanish, and Dutch experiences in the early modern period, the Germans failed to achieve national unity, which produced a legacy of frustration and antagonism toward the other powerful European states. The German failure to unify is tied to the history of the Holy Roman Empire. That union of various distinct central European territories was created in the tenth century when Otto I, in a deliberate attempt to revive Charlemagne's empire, was crowned emperor of the Romans. Later the title was changed to Holy Roman emperor, with the kingdom consisting of mostly German-speaking principalities.

Most medieval emperors busied themselves not with administering their territories but with attempting to secure control over the rich Italian peninsula and with challenging the rival authority of various popes. In the meantime, the German nobility extended and consolidated their rule over their peasants and over various towns and cities. Their aristocratic power remained a constant obstacle to German unity. Only by incorporating the nobility into the fabric of the state's power, into the court and the army, and by sanctioning their oppressive control over the peasants, would German rulers manage to create a unified German state. But that process of assimila-

tion only commenced (first in Prussia) during the eighteenth century.

In the medieval and early modern periods the Holy Roman emperors were dependent on their most powerful noble lords—including an archbishop or two—because the office of emperor was an elected one, not the result of hereditary succession. German noble princes—some of whom were electors—such as the archbishops of Cologne and Mainz, the Hohenzollern elector of Brandenburg, the landgrave of Hesse, and the duke of Saxony—were fiercely independent. All belonged to the empire, yet all regarded themselves as autonomous powers. These decentralizing tendencies were highly developed by the fifteenth century, when the emperors gradually realized that the outer frontiers of their empire were slipping away. The French had conducted a successful military incursion into northern Italy and on the western frontier of the empire. Hungary had fallen to the Turks, while the Swiss were hard to govern and, given their terrain, impossible to beat into submission. At the same time, the Hapsburgs maneuvered themselves into a position from which they could monopolize the imperial elections. The empire became increasingly German and Hapsburg, with Worms as the seat of imperial power.

The Holy Roman Empire in the reigns of the Hapsburg emperors Maximilian I (1493–1519) and Charles V (1519–1556) might have achieved a degree of cohesion comparable to that in France and Spain. Certainly the impetus of war—against France and against the Turks—required the creation of a large standing army and the taxation to maintain it. Both additions could have worked to the benefit of a centralized, imperial power. But the Protestant Reformation, begun in 1517, meshed with the already well-developed tendencies toward local independence. As a result, it destroyed the last hope of Hapsburg domination and German unity. The German nobility were all too ready to use the Reformation as a vindication of their local power, and indeed Luther made just such an appeal to their interests.

At precisely the moment, in the 1520s, when Charles V had to act with great determination to stop the spread of Lutheranism, he was at war with France over its claims to Italian territory. Charles had no sooner won his Italian territories, in particular the rich city-state of Milan, when he had to make war against the Turks, who in 1529 besieged Vienna. Not until the 1540s was Charles V in a position to attack the Lutheran princes. By then they had had considerable time to solidify their position and had united for mutual protection in the Schmalkaldic League.

War raged in Germany between the Protestant princes and the imperial army led by Charles V. In 1551, Catholic France entered the war on the Protestant side, and Charles V had to flee for his life. Defeated and exhausted, Charles abdicated and retired to a Spanish monastery. The Treaty of Augsburg (1555) conferred on every German prince the right to determine the religion of his subjects. The princes had won their territories, and a unified German state was never constructed by the Hapsburgs.

When Emperor Charles V abdicated in 1556, he gave his kingdom to his son Philip and his brother Ferdinand. Philip inherited Spain and its colonies, as well as the Netherlands, and Ferdinand acquired the Austrian territories. Two branches of the Hapsburg family were thus created, and well into the late seventeenth century they defined their interests in common and often waged war accordingly. The enormous international power of the Hapsburgs was checked only by their uncertain authority over the Holy Roman Empire. Throughout the sixteenth century the Austrian Hapsburgs barely managed to control these sprawling and deeply divided German territories. Protestantism, as protected by the Treaty of Augsburg, and the particularism and provinciality of the German nobility continued to prevent the creation of a German state.

The Austrian Hapsburg emperors, however, never missed an opportunity to further the cause of the Counter Reformation and to court the favor of local interests opposed to the nobility. No Hapsburg was ever more fervid in that regard than the Jesuit-trained Archduke Ferdinand II, who ascended to the throne in Vienna in 1619. He immediately embarked on a policy of religious intolerance and used Spanish officials as his administrators. His policies provoked a war within the empire that engulfed the whole of Europe.

The Thirty Years' War (1618–1648) began when the Bohemians, whose anti-Catholic tenden-

Jan Vermeer (1632–1675): The Music Lesson.
Vermeer's views of the interiors of Dutch homes are marked by the presence of fine oriental rugs, landscape paintings, rich clothing, and superbly crafted musical instruments—all of which attest to the solid wealth of his patrons. (*Isabella Stewart Gardner Museum, Boston*)

cies can be traced back to the Hussite reformation, attempted to put a Protestant king on their throne. The Austrian and Spanish Hapsburgs reacted by sending an army into the kingdom of Bohemia, and suddenly the whole empire was forced to take sides along religious lines. The Bohemian nobility, after centuries of enforcing serfdom, failed to rally the rural masses behind them, and victory went to the emperor. Indeed, Bohemia suffered an almost unimaginable devastation; the ravaging Catholic army sacked and burned three-fourths of the kingdom's towns and practically exterminated its aristocracy.

Until the 1630s, it looked as if the Hapsburgs would be able to use the war to enhance their

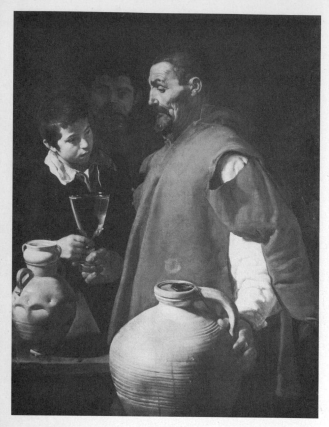

Diego Velázquez (1599–1660): The Water-Seller of Seville. The dramatic use of light makes Velázquez a Baroque artist, but his subject matter drawn from the lower classes shows the influence of Dutch genre scenes of everyday life. (*Victoria and Albert Museum*)

states of the kingdom with Vienna as their capital. Austria took shape as a dynastic state, while the German territories in the empire remained fragmented by the independent interests of their largely unreformed feudal nobility.

The Emergence of Austria and Prussia

Austria

As a result of the settlement at Westphalia, the Austrian Hapsburgs gained firm control over Hungary and Bohemia, where they installed a virtually new and foreign nobility. At the same time, they strengthened their rule in Vienna. In one of the few spectacular successes achieved by the Counter Reformation, the ruling elites in all three territories were forcibly, or in many cases willingly, converted back to Catholicism. At long last, religious predominance could be used as a force—long delayed in eastern Europe because of the Protestant Reformation—for the creation of the Austrian dynastic state.

One severe obstacle to territorial hegemony remained: the military threat posed by the Turks, who sought to control much of Hungary. During the reign of Austrian Emperor Leopold I (1658–1705), warfare against the Ottoman Empire—a recurrent theme in Hapsburg history beginning with Charles V—once again erupted, and in 1683 the Turks besieged the gates of Vienna. However, the Ottoman Empire no longer possessed its former strength and cohesiveness. A Catholic and unified Austrian army, composed of a variety of peoples from that kingdom and assisted by the Poles, managed to defeat the Turks and recapture the whole of Hungary and Transylvania and part of Croatia. Austria's right to govern these lands was firmly accepted by the Turks at the Treaty of Karlowitz (1699).

The Austrian Hapsburgs and their victorious army had now entered the larger arena of European power politics. In 1700, at the death of the last Spanish Hapsburg, Leopold I sought to place his second son, Archduke Charles, on the Spanish throne. But this brought Leopold into a violent

power and to promote centralization. But the intervention of Protestant Sweden, led by Gustavus Adolphus and encouraged by France, wrecked Hapsburg ambitions. The ensuing military conflict devastated vast areas of northern and central Europe. The civilian population suffered untold hardships: soldiers raped women and pillaged the land, and thousands of refugees took to the roads and forests. Partly because the French finally intervened directly, the Spanish Hapsburgs emerged from the Thirty Years' War with no benefits. At the Treaty of Westphalia (1648), their Austrian cousins reaffirmed their right to govern the eastern

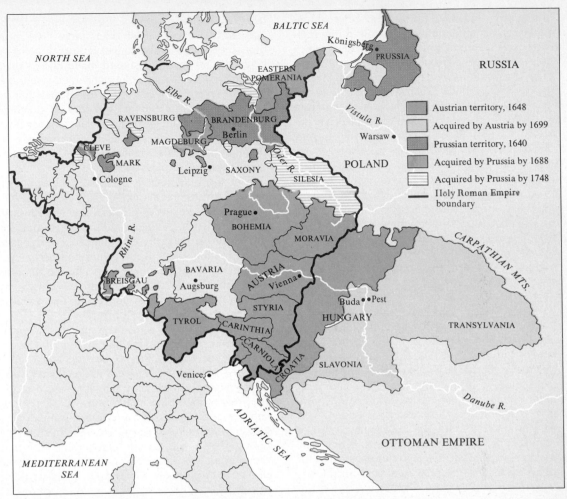

Map 16.3 The Growth of Austria and Brandenburg-Prussia, c. 1650–1750

clash with Louis XIV. Once again Bourbon and Hapsburg rivalry, a dominant theme in early modern history, provoked a major European war.

In the War of the Spanish Succession, the Austrians, with their army led by the brilliant Prince Eugene of Savoy, joined forces with the English and the Dutch. This war brought rewards in western Europe to the Austrian Hapsburgs, who acquired the Spanish Netherlands (Belgium today), as well as Milan and small holdings in Italy. But the Hapsburgs did not succeed in capturing the Spanish throne.

In the reign of Emperor Charles VI (1711–1740) Austria emerged as a major European power. Vienna became a cultural center in its own right. Austria's vast but loosely governed territories in the east, however, were not matched by territories in western and southern Europe.

Up to the early eighteenth century the Austrian Hapsburgs had struggled to achieve territorial hegemony and to subdue the dissident religious groups (Protestant and Turkish Muslim) that in very different ways threatened to undermine their authority. Warfare and the maintenance of a standing army had taken precedence over administrative reform and commercial growth. Yet military victory created the conditions within which centralization could occur.

The Austrian achievement of the eighteenth century, which made Austria a major force in European affairs, derived in large measure from the administrative reforms and cultural revival initiated by Charles VI (assisted militarily by Eugene of Savoy) and continued by his successors, Maria Theresa and Joseph II. These eighteenth-century monarchs embraced a style of government sometimes described as *enlightened* (see pages 408–410). They sought through education and liberal policies to catch up with the more established and older dynastic states of Europe.

Prussia

By the seventeenth century in northern Europe, the cohesive state governed by an absolute monarch (or by bourgeois oligarchs as in the Netherlands) had replaced feudalism as a system of government. Serfdom had largely disappeared in western Europe by the late sixteenth century, although it remained in parts of central and eastern Europe. The feudal aristocracy recouped their losses, however. No longer free to play at war or to control the lives of their peasants, progressive aristocrats improved their agricultural systems or sought offices and military commands in the service of the absolutist state. On the whole, western European aristocrats did not fare too badly under absolutism, but in the course of the early modern period, the state decisively checked their independent power.

Prussia was different. Prussia was a state, within the Holy Roman Empire, that had emerged very late in northern Europe (in the late seventeenth century). Like Austria, Prussia displayed certain unique characteristics. Although it did develop an absolute monarchy like France, its powerful aristocracy acquiesced to monarchical power only in exchange for guarantees of their feudal power over the peasantry. In 1653, the Prussian nobility granted the elector power to collect taxes for the maintenance of a powerful army, but only after he issued decrees rendering serfdom permanent.

The ruling dynasty of Prussia, the Hohenzol-

lerns, had a most inauspicious beginning in the later Middle Ages. These rulers were little more than dukes in the Holy Roman Empire until 1415, when the Emperor Sigismund made one of them an imperial elector with the right to choose imperial successors. For centuries, the Hohenzollerns had made weak claims to territory in northern Germany. They finally achieved control over Prussia and certain other smaller principalities by claiming the inheritance of one wife (1608) and by single-minded, ruthless aggression.

The most aggressive of these Hohenzollerns was the Elector Frederick William (1640–1688), who played a key role in forging the new Prussian state. Frederick William had inherited the territories of the beleaguered Hohenzollern dynasty, whose main holding, Brandenburg in Prussia, was very poor in natural resources. Indeed, Prussia had barely survived the devastation wrought by the Thirty Years' War, especially the Swedish army's occupation of the electorate.

A distaste for foreign intervention in Prussia, and for the accompanying humiliation and excessive taxes, prompted the *Junker* class (the landed Prussian nobility) to support national unity and strong central government. But they would brook no threat to their economic power over their lands and peasants. By 1672, the Prussian army, led by Junker officers, was strong enough to enter the Franco-Dutch war on the Dutch side. The war brought no territorial gains, but it allowed the elector to raise taxes. Once again the pattern of foreign war, taxes, and military conscription led to an increase in the power of the central government. But in Prussia, in contrast to western lands, the bureaucracy was entirely military. No clerics or rich bourgeois shared power with this Junker class. The pattern initiated by the Great Elector (Frederick William) would be continued in the reigns of his successors: Frederick I (d. 1713), Frederick William I, and Frederick the Great.

The alliance between aristocracy and monarchy was especially strengthened in the reign of Frederick William I (1713–1740). In the older dynastic states, absolute monarchs in every case tried to dispense with representative institutions once the monarchy's power could stand on its own. So, too, did Frederick William undercut the Prussian

Map 16.4 The Expansion of Russia, 1300–1725 ▶

BARENTS SEA

FINLAND

Arkhangelsk

U R A L   M T S.

Ob R.

L. Onega

N. Dvina R.

L. Ladoga

ESTONIA

NOVGOROD

Novgorod

Riga

Pskov

G R E A T   R U S S I A N S

Nizhni Novgorod

LITHUANIA

Dvina R.

Moscow

Vladimir

Kama R.

Smolensk

Ryazan

Samara

POLAND

Saratov

COSSACKS

Ural R.

Chernigov

Uralsk

Kiev

UKRAINIANS

Don R.

Volga R.

KIRGHIZ

CARPATHIAN MTS.

Dniester R.

Dnieper R.

Tsaritsyn

(New) Saray

ARAL
SEA

HUNGARY

BESSARABIA

COSSACKS

Saray

WALLACHIA

Astrakhan

CASPIAN SEA

BLACK SEA

OTTOMAN

Constantinople

GEORGIA

EMPIRE

ARMENIA

MEDITERRANEAN SEA

BALTIC SEA

The Principality of Moscow, c. 1300

Acquired by 1584

Acquired, 1584-1725

provincial assemblies, the *Landtage,* which still had power over taxation and army recruitment. Gradually, he rendered the Landtage superfluous. But he was able to do so only by incorporating the landowning Junker class into the machinery of government—especially into the army—and by keeping the tax-paying peasants in the status of serfs.

In a nation where representative institutions in the twentieth century have struggled, often unsuccessfully, for survival, it is interesting to note that such institutions did exercise considerable influence in Prussia up to the early eighteenth century. Like the Austrians during the eighteenth century, the Prussians also embarked on a program of modernization, which has occasionally been described as enlightened.

Russia

Although remote from developments in western Europe, Russia in the early modern period took on some characteristics remarkably similar to those of western European states. Russia, also, relied on absolute monarchy reinforced by a feudal aristocracy. As in Europe, the power of the aristocracy to wreak havoc had to be checked and its energies channeled into the state's service. But the Russian pattern of absolutism breaks with the Western model and resembles that adopted in Prussia, where serfdom increased as the power of centralized monarchy grew. The award of peasants was the bribe by which the monarchy secured the aristocrats' cooperation in the state's growth.

Russian absolutism experienced a false start under Ivan IV, "The Terrible" (1547–1584). Late in the sixteenth century Ivan sought to impose a tsarist autocracy. He waged a futile war against Sweden and created an internal police force that was entrusted with the administration of central Russia. His failure in war and an irrational policy of repression (fueled in part by Ivan's mental instability) doomed his premature attempt to impose absolutism. Much of Ivan's state-building was undone with his death, which launched a "Time of Troubles"—a period of foreign invasion and civil warfare—that endured for years.

Order was restored in the country only in 1613, when the Romanov dynasty gained the sup-port of the aristocracy. The accession of Michael Romanov as tsar marks the emergence of a unified Russian state. Of that dynasty, by far the most important ruler was Peter the Great (1689–1725). He ruthlessly suppressed the independent aristocrats, while inventing new titles and ranks for those loyal to the court. The army was reformed in accordance with the standards of western lands. The peasants were made the personal property of their lords, to be sold at will; thus, the distinction between serf and slave was obliterated. Finally, Peter brought the church under the control of the state by establishing a new office called the Holy Synod; its head was a government official.

From 1700 to 1707, taxes on the peasants multiplied five times over. Predictably, the money went toward the creation of a professional army along European lines and to making war. The preparation led this time to victory over the Swedes.

Peter succeeded in wedding the aristocracy to the absolutist state, and the union was so successful that strong Russian monarchs in the eighteenth century, like Catherine the Great, could embrace enlightened reforms without jeopardizing the stability of their regimes. Once again, repression and violence in the form of taxation, serfdom, and war led to the creation of a dynastic state—one that proved the least susceptible to reform, eventually to be dismantled in 1917 by the Russian Revolution.

The State and Modern Political Development

By the early seventeenth century, Europeans had developed the concept of a *state*—a distinctive political entity to which its subjects owed duties and obligations. That concept became the foundation of the modern science of politics. The one essential ingredient of the Western concept of the state, as it emerged in the early modern period, was the notion of *sovereignty,* that is, within its borders the state was supreme, and other institutions and organizations—by implication even the church—were allowed to exist only if they recognized the state's authority. The art of government

St. Basil's Cathedral, Moscow. The cathedral of St. Basil is a fusion of native folk art and late Byzantine architecture. Russia in the seventeenth century had strong roots in its medieval past. Peter the Great forcefully rejected many traditions and made Russia turn to the West for inspiration. (*William Brumfield*)

Chronology 16.1 The Rise of Sovereignty

1453	The Hundred Years' War ends
1455–1485	The War of Roses in England between rival nobles
1469	Ferdinand and Isabella begin their rule of Castile and Aragon
1485	Henry VII begins the reign of the Tudor dynasty in England
1517	The Protestant Reformation begins in Germany
1519	Charles V of Spain becomes Hapsburg emperor of the Holy Roman Empire
1553–1558	Queen Mary attempts to return England to Catholicism
1556–1598	Philip II of Spain persecutes Jews and Muslims
1559	The Treaty of Cateau-Cambrésis between France and Spain
1560s–1609	The Netherlands revolts against Spanish rule
1562–1598	Religious wars in France
1572	The St. Bartholomew's Day Massacre—Queen Catherine of France orders thousands of Protestants executed
1579	*Vindiciae contra Tyrannos,* published by Huguenots, justifies regicide
1588	The Spanish Armada is defeated by the English fleet
1590s	A reaction in Russia against Ivan IV, "The Terrible"
1593	Henry IV of France renounces his Protestantism to restore peace in France
1598	French Protestants granted religious toleration by the Edict of Nantes

thus entailed molding the ambitions and strength of the powerful into service to the state. The state, its power growing through war and taxation, became the basic unit of political authority in the West.

Interestingly, the concept of human liberty, now so basic to Western thought, was not articulated first in the sovereign states of Europe. Rather, the idea was largely an Italian creation, discussed with great vehemence by the Italian theorists of the later Middle Ages and the Renaissance. These humanists lived and wrote in the independent city-states, and they often aimed their treatises against the encroachments of the Holy Roman emperor—in short, against princes and

their search for absolute power. In the sixteenth and seventeenth centuries, the idea of liberty was rarely discussed and was generally found only in the writings of Calvinist opponents of absolutism. Not until the mid-seventeenth century in England did a body of political thought emerge that argued that human liberty can be ensured within the confines of a powerful national state—one governed by mere mortals and not by divinely sanctioned and absolute kings. In general, despite the English and Dutch developments, absolutism in its varied forms (Spanish, French, Prussian) dominated the political development of early modern Europe.

Although first articulated in the Italian republics and then enacted briefly in England and more

Chronology 16.1 continued

1624–1642	Cardinal Richelieu, Louis XIII's chief minister, determines royal policies
1640	The Portuguese revolt successfully against Spain
1640–1660	The English Revolution
1648	The Treaty of Westphalia ends the Thirty Years' War
1648–1653	The Fronde, a rebellious reaction centered in Paris
1649	Charles I, Stuart king of England, is executed by an act of Parliament
1649–1660	England is co-ruled by Parliament and the army under Oliver Cromwell
1660	Charles II returns from exile and becomes king of England
1683	The Turks attack Vienna and are defeated
1685	Louis XIV of France revokes the Edict of Nantes
1688–1689	Revolution in England; end of absolutism
1699	Treaty of Karlowitz—Austrians defeat Turks and recapture Hungary, Transylvania, and parts of Croatia
1701	Louis XIV tries to bring Spain under French control
1702–1713	The War of the Spanish Succession; established a balance of power between England and France
1740	Frederick the Great of Prussia invades Silesia, starting war with Austria
1789	The French Revolution begins

durably in the Netherlands, the republican ideal did not gain acceptance as a viable alternative to absolutism until the European Enlightenment of the eighteenth century. At the heart of that ideal lay the notion that the power of the state serves the interests of those who support and create it. In the democratic and republican revolutions of the late eighteenth century, western Europeans and Americans repudiated monarchical systems of government in response to the republican ideal. By then, princes and the aristocratic and military elites had outlived their usefulness in many parts of Europe. The states they had created, in large measure to further their own interests, had become larger than their creators. Eventually the na-

tional states of western Europe, as well as of the Americas, proved able to survive and prosper without kings or aristocrats, though they retained the administrative and military mechanisms so skillfully and relentlessly developed by early modern kings and their court officials.

The power of the state became the focal point of Western political life by the eighteenth century. Concomitantly, peace became the art of balancing the powers of the various European states so that no single state could imagine that it would win domination, or *hegemony*, over all the others. Whenever a European state believed that it could dominate, the result was war. In early modern times, first the Spanish under Charles V and Philip

II and then the French under Louis XIV sought, and for a brief time achieved, hegemony over European politics. In the end, however, these great states faltered because of the internal pressures that war-making created. Nonetheless, the belief persisted, until 1945, that one state could dominate Western affairs. In the twentieth century that belief produced not simply war but world war. By then the power of Western states had overtaken vast areas of the world, and the ability to impose a balance of power became a matter of world survival.

Notes

1. J. H. Elliott, *Imperial Spain, 1469–1716* (New York: St. Martin's Press, 1963), p. 18.

2. J. H. Plumb, *The Growth of Political Stability in England: 1675–1725* (London: Macmillan, 1967), p. 69.

Suggested Reading

Anderson, Perry, *Lineages of the Absolutist State* (1974). An excellent survey, written from a Marxist perspective.

Elliott, J. H., *Imperial Spain, 1469–1716* (1963). An excellent survey of the major European power of the early modern period.

Goubert, Pierre, *Louis XIV and Twenty Million Frenchmen* (1966). An important reappraisal of the Sun King, emphasizing the effects of his policies on ordinary French people.

Hill, Christopher, *God's Englishman* (1970). A biography of Oliver Cromwell.

Koenigsberger, H. G., *Early Modern Europe, 1500–1789* (1987). The best survey of the period, by a master historian.

Parker, Geoffrey, *Spain and the Netherlands, 1559–1659* (1979). A good survey of a complex relationship.

Plumb, J. H., *The Growth of Political Stability in England, 1675–1725* (1967). A basic book, clear and readable.

Shennan, J. H., *The Origins of the Modern European State* (1974). An excellent brief introduction.

Smith, Lacey Baldwin, *This Realm of England, 1399 to 1688* (revised ed. 1983). Still the best survey of England during this period.

Wedgwood, C. V., *William the Silent* (1944). A good biography of one of the founders of the Dutch republic.

Zagorin, Perez, *Rebels and Rulers, 1500–1660,* 2 vols. (1982). A good general survey of recent scholarship, with a conservative bias.

Review Questions

1. What role did the aristocracy play in the formation of the European states?

2. In what ways did early modern kings increase their power, and what relationship did they have to the commercial bourgeoisie in their countries?

3. What is meant by *raison d'état* and by the divine right of kings?

4. What role did religion and national churches play in creating the state?

5. What were the strengths and weaknesses of the Spanish state?

6. Why did England move in the direction of parliamentary government, while most countries on the Continent embraced absolutism? Describe the main factors.

7. What made the Dutch state so different from its neighbors? Describe the differences.

8. What made the Prussian, Russian, and Austrian experiences of statehood roughly comparable?

9. Discuss the differences between the treatment of the peasants in eastern and western Europe.

10. Government has sometimes been described as being, in the final analysis, organized violence. Is that an adequate description of early modern European governments?

17

The Scientific Revolution:
The Mechanical Universe

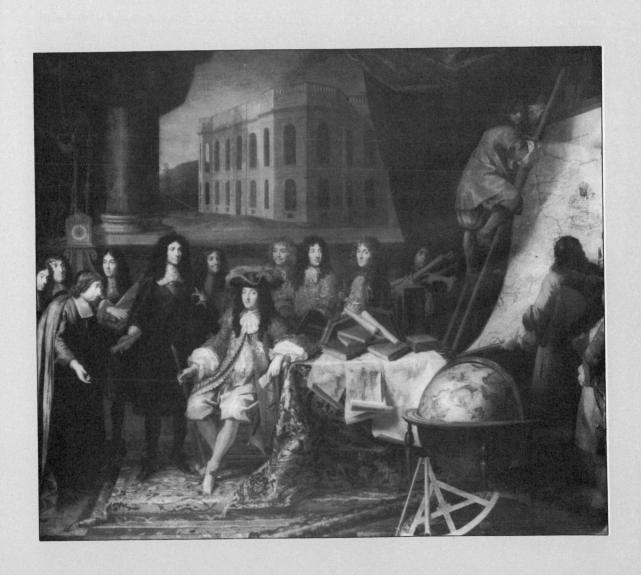

S tarting in the late fourteenth century, the cohesive medieval world began to disintegrate, a process that lasted to the late seventeenth century. Not only did basic medieval institutions like feudalism weaken but also the medieval view of the universe, or world-view, faded and was gradually replaced by the modern, scientific understanding of nature. This transformation occurred within the particular historical context created by the Renaissance and the Reformation, as well as by the growth in commercial prosperity and state power. Increasingly, literate elites in early modern Europe came to see the mastery of nature as both desirable and possible, an assumption that has remained basic to Western thought since the late seventeenth century.

The unique contribution of the Scientific Revolution to the making of the modern world-view lay in its new mechanical conception of nature, which enabled Westerners to discover and explain the laws of nature mathematically. They came to see nature as composed solely of matter whose motion, occurring in space and measurable by time, was governed by laws of force. This philosophically elegant construction renders the physical world knowable, and even possibly manageable.

The Scientific Revolution also entailed the discovery of a new, scientific methodology. Because of the successful experiments performed by scientists and natural philosophers such as Galileo Galilei, William Harvey, Robert Boyle, and Isaac Newton, Western science acquired its still-characteristic methodology of observation and experimentation. By the late seventeenth century, no one could entertain a serious interest in any aspect of the physical order without actually doing experiments or without observing, in a rigorous and systematic way, the behavior of physical phenom-

Foundation of the Academy of Sciences in 1666 by Testelin. The commemorative painting shows Louis XIV (seated) with Colbert at his side. (*Versailles/ Cliché des Musées Nationaux*)

ena. The mechanical concept of nature coupled with a rigorous methodology gave modern scientists the means to unlock and explain the secrets of nature.

Mathematics increasingly became the language of the new science. For centuries, Europeans had used algebra and geometry to explain certain physical phenomena. With the Scientific Revolution came a new mathematics, the calculus; but even more important, philosophers became increasingly convinced that all nature—physical objects as well as invisible forces—could be expressed mathematically. By the late seventeenth century, even geometry had become so complex that a gifted philosopher like John Locke (1632–1704), a friend and contemporary of Isaac Newton, could not understand the sophisticated mathematics used by Newton in the *Principia*. A new scientific culture had been born that during the eighteenth-century Enlightenment (see Chapter 18) achieved great importance as a model for progress in both the natural and human sciences.

Medieval Cosmology

The unique character of the modern scientific outlook is most understandable in contrast with what went before it—the medieval understanding of the natural world and its physical properties. That understanding rested on a blend of Christian thought with theories derived from ancient Greek writers like Aristotle and Ptolemy.

The explanations given by Aristotle (384–322 B.C.) for the motion of heavy bodies permeated medieval scientific literature. In trying to understand motion, Aristotle had argued simply that it was in the nature of things to move in certain ways. A stone falls because it is absolutely heavy; fire rises because it is absolutely light. Weight is an absolute property of a physical thing; therefore, motion results from the properties of bodies, and not from the forces or laws of motion at work in nature. It follows (logically but incorrectly) that if the medium through which a body falls is taken

as a constant, then the speed of its fall could be doubled if its weight were doubled. Only rigorous experimentation could refute this erroneous concept of motion; it was many centuries before such experimentation was undertaken.

Aristotle's physics fitted neatly into his *cosmology*, or world picture. The earth, being the heaviest object, lay stationary and suspended at the center of the universe. The sun, the planets, and the moon revolved in circles around the earth. Aristotle presumed that since the planets were round themselves, always in motion and seemingly never altered, the most "natural" motion for them should be circular.

Aristotle's physics and cosmology were unified. He could put the earth stationary at the center of the universe because he presumed its absolute heaviness; all other heavy bodies that he had observed do fall toward it. He presumed that the planets were made of a kind of a fine, luminous ether and were held in their circular orbits by luminous spheres, or "tracks." These spheres possessed a certain reality, although invisible to human beings, and hence they came to be known as the crystalline spheres.

Aristotle believed that everything in motion had been moved by another object that was itself in motion—a continuing chain of movers and moved. By inference, this belief led back to some object or being that began the motion. Christian philosophers of the Middle Ages argued that Aristotle's Unmoved Mover must be the God of Christianity. For Aristotle, who had no conception of a personal God or an afterlife, and who believed that the universe was eternal rather than created at a specific point in time, such an identification would have been meaningless.

Although Aristotle's cosmology never obtained the stature of orthodoxy among the ancient Greeks, by the second century A.D. in Alexandria, Greek astronomy became codified and then rigid. Ptolemy of Alexandria produced the *Almagest* (A.D. 150), a handbook of Greek astronomy based on the theories of Aristotle. Central to that work was the assumption that a motionless earth stood at the center of the universe (although some Greeks had disputed the notion) and that the planets move about it in a series of circular orbits interrupted by smaller, circular orbits called epicycles. By the Late Middle Ages, Ptolemy's handbook, because of the support it lent to Aristotelian cosmology, had come to embody standard astronomical wisdom. As late as the middle of the seventeenth century, over one hundred years after the Polish astronomer Nicolaus Copernicus had argued mathematically that the sun was the center of the universe, educated Europeans in most universities still believed the earth held that central position.

In the thirteenth century, mainly through the philosophical efforts of Thomas Aquinas (1225–1274), Aristotle's thought was adapted to Christian beliefs, often in tortured ways. Aquinas emphasized that order pervaded nature and that every physical effect had a physical cause. The tendency in Aquinas's thought and that of his followers in succeeding centuries, who were called scholastics by their seventeenth-century critics, was to search for these causes—again to ask why things move, rather than how they move. But Aquinas denied that these causes stretched back to infinity. Instead, he insisted that nature proves God's existence; God is the First Cause of all physical phenomena. Despite the scholastic adaptations of Aristotle, the church still regarded Christian Aristotelianism with some suspicion, and in 1277 many of Aristotle's theories were condemned. The condemnation of Aristotle helped give rise to an anti-Aristotelian physics that may have influenced the Scientific Revolution.

Medieval thinkers integrated the cosmology of Aristotle and Ptolemy into a Christian framework that drew a sharp distinction between the world beyond the moon and an earthly realm. Celestial bodies were composed of the divine ether, a substance too pure, too spiritual to be found on earth; heavenly bodies, unlike those on earth, were immune to all change and obeyed different laws of motion than earthly bodies did. The universe was not homogeneous but was divided into a higher world of the heavens and a lower world of earth. Earth could not compare with the heavens in spiritual dignity, but God had nevertheless situated it in the center of the universe. Earth deserved this position of importance, for only here was the drama of salvation performed. This vision of the universe was to be shattered by the Scientific Revolution.

A New View of Nature

Renaissance Background

With the advent of the Renaissance, which began in Italy in the late fourteenth century, a new breed of intellectuals began to challenge medieval assumptions about human beings and nature, armed with a collection of newly discovered ancient Greek and Roman texts (see Chapter 13). The philosophy of Plato was seized on as an alternative to medieval scholasticism.

The great strength of Plato's philosophy lay in his belief that one must look beyond the appearance of things to an invisible reality that is simple, rational, and given to coherent, mathematical explanation. Plato's search for this fundamental reality thus influenced thinkers of the Scientific Revolution.

Renaissance Platonists interpreted Plato from a Christian perspective, and they believed that the Platonic search for truth about nature, about God's work, was but another aspect of the search for knowledge about God. The universities of Italy, as well as the independent academies founded in Italian cities, became centers where the Platonists taught, translated, and wrote commentaries about Plato's philosophy. These humanists tried to study the invisible world of Ideas and Forms that Plato claimed to be the essence of reality. Music and mathematics, they believed, provided contact with this universal, eternal, and unchanging higher reality. The leading thinkers of the Scientific Revolution found inspiration in the Platonic tradition that nature's truths apply universally and possess the elegance and simplicity of mathematics.

With this impulse to mathematize nature also came the desire to measure and experience it. The rediscovery of nature found expression in the study of the human anatomy as well as in the study of objects in motion. Renaissance art shows the fruits of this inquiry as artists attempted to depict the human body as exactly as possible yet also as ideally formed. In this sense the revival of artistic creativity associated with the Renaissance is linked to an interest in the natural world.

The thinkers of the Scientific Revolution also

drew on a tradition of magic that reached back to the ancient world. In the first and second centuries A.D., various practitioners and writers elaborated on the mystical and magical approach to nature. Many of these anonymous students of magic were in contact with the Hermetic tradition. They believed that there had once been an ancient Egyptian priest, Hermes Trismegistus, who had possessed secret knowledge about nature's processes and the ultimate forces at work in the universe. In the second century A.D., this magical tradition was written down in a series of mystical dialogues about the universe. When Renaissance Europeans rediscovered these second-century writings, they erroneously assumed the author to be Hermes and his followers. Hence the writings seemed to be even older than the Bible.

This Hermetic literature glorified the mystical and the magical. It stated that true knowledge comes from a contemplation of the One, or the Whole—a spiritual reality higher than yet embedded in nature. Some of these ancient writings argued that the sun was the natural symbol of this Oneness, and such an argument seemed to give weight to a heliocentric picture of the universe. The Hermetic approach to nature also incorporated elements of the Pythagorean and Neo-Platonic traditions that laid emphasis on the inner mathematical harmony that pervades nature. The early modern debt to Hermeticism could therefore be expressed in ways that seem to be contradictory. A follower of Hermeticism might approach nature mathematically as well as magically. For example, Johannes Kepler was both a fine mathematician and a believer in the magical power of nature. Although not directly influenced by Hermeticism as a system of belief, Isaac Newton saw no contradiction in searching for the mathematical laws of nature while practicing alchemy during much of his life.

The Renaissance followers of Hermes, then, indulged both in what would now be called magic and what would be called science without seeing any fundamental distinction between them. The route that the searcher for nature's wisdom took did not matter as much as the quest itself did. As a result, in early modern Europe the practitioners of alchemy and astrology could also be mathematicians and astronomers, and the sharp distinction

drawn today between magic and science—between the irrational and the rational—would not have been made by many leading natural philosophers who lived in the sixteenth and seventeenth centuries.

The Renaissance revival of ancient learning contributed a new approach to nature, one that was simultaneously mathematical, experimental, and magical. Although the achievements of modern science depend on experimentation and logic, the compelling impulse to search for nature's secrets presumes a degree of self-confidence best exemplified and symbolized by the magician. Eventually, in one of the important by-products of the Scientific Revolution, the main practitioners of the new science repudiated magic, largely because of its secretive quality and because of its associations with popular culture and religion. But the demise of magic should not obscure its initial role, among many other factors, as a stimulus for scientific inquiry and enthusiasm.

The Copernican Revolution

Nicolaus Copernicus was born in Poland in 1473. As a young man, he enrolled in the University of Krakow, where he may have come under the influence of Renaissance Platonism, which was spreading outward from the Italian city-states. Copernicus also journeyed to Italy, and in Bologna and Padua he may have become aware of ancient Greek texts containing arguments for the sun being the center of the universe.

Copernicus's interest in mathematics and astronomy was stimulated by contemporary discussions of the need for calendar reform, which required a thorough understanding of Ptolemaic astronomy. The mathematical complexity of the Ptolemaic system troubled Copernicus, who believed that truth was the product of elegance and simplicity. In addition, Copernicus knew that Ptolemy had predecessors among the ancients who philosophized about a heliocentric universe or who held Aristotle in little regard. Thus, his Renaissance education gave Copernicus not a body of new scientific truth but rather the courage to break with traditional truth taught in the universities.

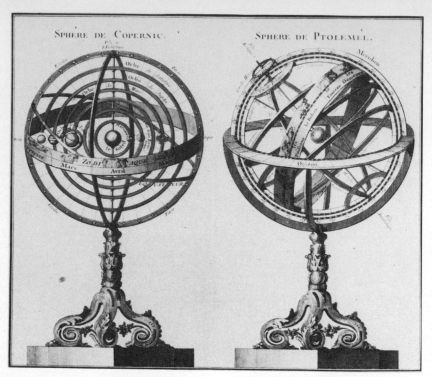

Armillary Spheres According to Copernicus and Ptolemy. Copernicus overturned thirteen hundred years of cosmology with the appearance of his treatise on heavenly motion. The idea of a heliocentric universe supported by mathematical evidence brought the medieval mind-set to an irrefutable end. (*Smithsonian Institution Photo No. 65,420*)

Toward the end of his stay in Italy, Copernicus became convinced that the sun lay at the center of the universe. So he set out on a lifelong task to work out mathematical explanations of how a heliocentric universe operated. Because he did not want to engage in controversy with the followers of Aristotle, Copernicus published his findings only in 1543 in a work entitled *On the Revolutions of the Heavenly Spheres*. Legend says his book, which in effect began the Scientific Revolution, was brought to him on his deathbed.

The treatise retained some elements of the Aristotelian-Ptolemaic system. Copernicus never doubted Aristotle's basic notion of the perfect circular motion of the planets or the existence of crystalline spheres within which the stars revolved, and he retained many of Ptolemy's epicycles. But Copernicus proposed a heliocentric model of the universe that was mathematically simpler than Ptolemy's earth-centered universe. Thus, he eliminated some of Ptolemy's epicycles and cleared up various problems that had troubled astronomers who had worked from an earth-centered universe.

Copernicus's genius was expressed in his ability to pursue an idea—a sun-centered universe—and to bring to that pursuit lifelong dedication and brilliance in mathematics. By removing the earth from its central position and by giving it motion—that is, by making the earth just another planet—Copernicus undermined the system of medieval cosmology and made the birth of modern astronomy possible.

But because they were committed to the Aristotelian-Ptolemaic system and to biblical statements that supported it, most thinkers rejected Copernicus's conclusions. They also raised specific objections. The earth, they said, is too heavy to move. How, they asked, can an object falling from a high tower land directly below the point from which it was dropped if the earth is moving so rapidly?

Tycho and Kepler: The Laws of Planetary Motion

The most gifted astronomer in the generation after Copernicus, Tycho Brahe (1546–1601), never accepted the Copernican system. He did, however, realize more fully than any contemporaries the necessity for new observations. Aided by the king of Denmark, Tycho built the finest observatory in Europe to use in his work.

In 1572, he observed a new star in the heavens—a discovery that offered a direct and serious challenge to the Aristotelian assumption that the heavens are unalterable, fixed, and perfect. To this discovery of what eventually proved to be an exploding star, Tycho added his observations on the comet of 1577. He demonstrated that it moved unimpeded through the areas between the planets, that it passed right through the crystalline spheres. This discovery raised the question of whether such spheres existed, but Tycho himself remained an Aristotelian. Although his devotion to a literal reading of the Bible led Tycho to reject the Copernican sun-centered universe, he did propose an alternative system in which the planets revolved around the sun, but the sun moved about a motionless earth.

Tycho's fame ultimately rests on his skill as a practicing astronomer. He bequeathed to future generations precise calculations about the movements of heavenly bodies, which proved invaluable. These calculations were put to greatest use by Johannes Kepler (1571–1630), a German who collaborated with Tycho during the latter's final years. Tycho bequeathed his astronomical papers to Kepler, who brought to this data a scientific vision that was both experimental and mystical.

Kepler searched persistently for harmonious laws of planetary motion. He did so because he believed profoundly in the Platonic ideal: a spiritual force infuses the physical order; beneath appearances are harmony and unity; and the human mind can begin to comprehend that unity only through *gnosis*—a direct and mystical realization of unity—and through mathematics. Kepler believed that both approaches were compatible, and he managed to combine them. He believed in and practiced astrology (as did Tycho), and throughout his lifetime, Kepler tried to contact an ancient but lost and secret wisdom.

In the course of his studies and observations of

Tycho Brahe and His Observatory's Interior. Although Tycho Brahe remained a staunch Aristotelian, his observation of a new star in 1572 and a comet in 1577 challenged these traditional views. His precise scientific approach to astronomy and careful mathematical calculations were to be his greatest legacy. (*The British Library*)

the heavens, Kepler discovered the three basic laws of planetary motion. First, the orbits of the planets are elliptical, nor circular as Aristotle and Ptolemy had assumed, and the sun is one focus of the ellipse. Unlike Tycho, Kepler accepted Copernicus's theory and provided proof for it. Kepler's second law demonstrated that the velocity of a planet is not uniform, as had been believed, but increases as its distance from the sun decreases. Kepler's third law—that the squares of the times taken by any two planets in their revolutions around the sun are in the same ratio as the cubes of their average distances from the sun—brought the planets into a unified mathematical system.

The significance of Kepler's work was immense. He gave sound mathematical proof to Copernicus's theory, eliminated forever the use of epicycles that had saved the appearance of circular motion, and demonstrated that mathematical relationships can describe the planetary system. But Kepler left a significant question unresolved: what kept the planets in their orbits? Why did they not fly out into space or crash into the sun? The answer would be supplied by Isaac Newton, who synthesized the astronomy of Copernicus and Kepler with the new physics developed by Galileo.

Galileo: Experimental Physics

At the same time that Kepler was developing a new astronomy, his contemporary, Galileo Galilei (1564–1642), was breaking with the older physics of Aristotle. A Pisan by birth, Galileo lived for many years in Padua, where he conducted some of his first experiments on the motion of bodies. Guided by the dominant philosophy of the Italian Renaissance—the revived doctrines of Plato—Galileo believed that beyond the visible world lay universal truths, subject to mathematical verification. Galileo insisted that the study of motion entails not only the use of logic (as Aristotle had believed) but also the application of mathematics. For this Late Renaissance natural philosopher, mathematics became the language of nature. Galileo also believed that only after experimenting with the operations of nature can the philosopher formulate the harmonious laws of the universe and give them mathematical expression.

In his mechanical experiments, Galileo discovered that, all other things being equal, bodies of unequal weight will experience a uniform acceleration (due to gravity). He demonstrated that bodies fall with arithmetic regularity. Motion could, therefore, be treated mathematically.

Galileo came very close to perceiving that inertia governs the motion of bodies, but his concept of inertia was flawed. He believed that inertial force was circular. He did not grasp what Newton would later proclaim, that bodies move in a straight line at a uniform velocity unless impeded. But Galileo's contribution was enormous; he had suggested that terrestrial objects could in theory stay in motion forever.

Galileo established a fundamental principle of modern science—the order and uniformity of nature. There are no distinctions in rank or quality between the heavens and earth; heavenly bodies are not perfect and changeless as Aristotle had believed. In 1609, Galileo built a telescope through which he viewed the surface of the moon. The next year, in a treatise called *The Starry Messenger,* he proclaimed to the world that the moon "is not smooth, uniform, and precisely spherical as a great number of philosophers believe it and the other heavenly bodies to be, but is uneven, rough, and full of cavities . . . being not unlike the face of the earth, relieved by chains of mountains and deep valleys."[1] In addition, Galileo observed spots on the sun, providing further evidence that heavenly objects, like earthly objects, undergo change. There are no higher and lower worlds; nature is the same throughout.

Through his telescope Galileo also saw moons around Jupiter—a discovery that served to support the Copernican hypothesis. If Jupiter had moons, then all heavenly bodies did not orbit the earth. The moons of Jupiter removed a fundamental criticism leveled against Copernicus and opened up the possibility that indeed the earth, with its own moon, might be just like the planet Jupiter, and both might in turn revolve around a central point—the sun.

With Galileo, the science of Copernicus and the assault on Aristotle entered a new phase. Priests began to attack Galileo from their pulpits in Florence, backed by teachers within the academic community who routinely taught the old astronomy. These teachers saw a threat to their own power in Galileo's public notoriety and following among the laity. A secret group of priests and academics, named the Liga, formed with the express purpose of silencing Galileo; they used Aristotle and the Bible to attack him. Galileo boldly defied this old elite and championed a new scientific learning for the laity; he proclaimed the new science as a new body of learning that required a new elite freed from the chains of tradition, knowledgeable in mathematics, and committed to experimentation. But in the early seventeenth century the Catholic church saw danger on every front: Protestants in Germany, recalcitrant people in nearly every state, laity demanding new schools offering practical education for their children. Now Galileo was supporting a view of the universe that conflicted with certain scriptural texts.

In 1632, Galileo's teachings were condemned and he was placed under house arrest. In this confrontation between the old clerical elite and the new secular elite, the old won out. But the price paid was high indeed. Science as preached by Galileo was not, as he knew perfectly well, inherently dangerous to Catholicism. But the clergy and their academic allies saw it as a challenge to their power, and they could enlist the papacy and the Inquisition in their support. As a result, students of the new science in Catholic countries looked to Protestant countries as places to live or publish their books. Censorship worked to stifle intellectual inquiry, and by the middle of the seventeenth century science had become, because of historical circumstance, an increasingly Protestant and northern European phenomenon.

The Newtonian Achievement

By the middle of the seventeenth century, largely because of the work of Copernicus, Kepler, and Galileo, Aristotle and Ptolemy had been dethroned. A new philosophy of nature and a new science had come into being whose essence lay in the mathematical expression of physical laws that describe matter in motion. Yet what was missing was an overriding law that could explain the motion observed in the heavens and on earth. This law was supplied by Isaac Newton.

Newton was born in 1642 in Lincolnshire, England, the son of a modest yeoman. He acquired a place at Trinity College, Cambridge, because of his intellectual promise, and there he devoted himself to natural philosophy and mathematics. His native talents were cultivated by tutors who gave him the latest works in philosophy to read; some of these works, in a form of Christian Platonism, emphasized the workings in the universe of spiritual forces derived from God. Newton's student notebooks survive and show him mastering these texts while also trying to understand the fundamental truths of Protestant Christianity as taught at Cambridge. Combining a

Sir Isaac Newton by Sir Godfrey Kneller (1646–1723). Newton's discovery of universal gravitation, a phenomenon that could be expressed mathematically, capped the Scientific Revolution. Pope's epitaph for him proclaimed, "Nature, and Nature's Laws lay hid in Night./ God said, 'Let Newton be!' and All was Light." (*National Portrait Gallery, London*)

Christian Platonism with a genius for mathematics, Newton produced an elegant synthesis of the science of Kepler and Galileo that eventually captured the imagination of European intellectuals.

In 1666, Newton formulated the mathematics for the universal law of gravitation, and in the same year, after rigorous experimentation, he determined the nature of light. The sciences of physics and optics were transformed. However, for many years, Newton did not publish his discoveries, partly because even he did not see the immense significance of his work. Finally, another mathematician and friend, Edmund Halley, persuaded him to publish under the sponsorship of the Royal Society. The result was the *Principia Mathematica* of 1687. In 1704, Newton published his *Opticks* and revealed his theory that light was corpuscular in nature and that it emanated from luminous bodies in a way that scientists later described as waves.

Of the two books, both monumental achievements in the history of science, the *Principia* made the greater impact on contemporaries. Newton not only formulated universal mathematical laws but offered a philosophy of nature that sought to explain the essential structure of the universe: matter is always the same; it is atomic in structure, and in its essential nature it is dead or lifeless; and it is acted upon by immaterial forces that are placed in the universe by God. Newton said that the motion of matter could be explained by three laws: inertia, that a body remains in a state of rest or continues its motion in a straight line unless impelled to change by forces impressed on it; acceleration, that the change in the motion of a body is proportional to the force acting on it; and that for every action there is an equal and opposite reaction.

Newton argued that these laws apply not only to observable matter on earth but also to the motion of planets in their orbits. He showed that planets did not remain in their orbits because circular motion was "natural" or because crystalline spheres kept them in place. Rather, said Newton, planets keep to their orbits because every body in the universe exercises a force on every other body, a force that he called *universal gravitation.* Gravity is proportional to the product of the masses of two bodies and inversely proportional to the square of the distance between them. It is operative throughout the universe, whether on earth or in the heavens, and it is capable of mathematical expression. Newton built his theory on the work of other scientific giants, notably Kepler and Galileo; yet no one before him had possessed the breadth of vision, mathematical skill, and dedication to rigorous observation to combine this knowledge into one grand synthesis.

With Newton's discovery of universal gravitation, the Scientific Revolution reached its culmination. The universe could now be described as matter in motion; it was governed by invisible forces that operated everywhere, both on earth and in the heavens, and these forces could be ex-

pressed mathematically. The medieval picture of the universe as closed, earthbound, and earth-centered was replaced by a universe seen to be infinite and governed by universal laws. The earth was now regarded as simply another planet.

But what was God's role in this new universe? Newton and his circle labored to create a mechanical world-view dependent on the will of God, and in those efforts they were largely successful. Newton retained a central place for a providential deity who operates constantly in the universe; at one time he believed that gravity was simply the will of God operating on the universe. As Newton said in the *Opticks,* the physical order "can be the effect of nothing else than the wisdom and skill of a powerful ever-living agent."[2] Because of his deeply held religious convictions, Newton allowed his science to be used in the service of the established Anglican church. Newton, a scientific genius, was also a deeply religious thinker who was committed to the maintenance of Protestantism in England.

Biology, Medicine, and Chemistry

The spectacular advances made in physics and astronomy in the sixteenth and seventeenth centuries were not matched in the biological sciences. Indeed, the day-to-day practice of medicine throughout western Europe changed little in the period from 1600 to 1700, for much of medical practice relied frequently on astrology.

Doctors clung to the teachings of the ancient practitioners Galen and Hippocrates. In general, Galenic medicine paid little attention to the discovery of specific cures for particular diseases. As a follower of Aristotle, Galen emphasized the elements that make up the body—he called their manifestations *humors.* A person with an excess of blood was sanguine; a person with too much bile was choleric. Health consisted of a restoration of balances among these various elements, so Galenic doctors often prescribed purges of one sort or another. The most famous of these was bloodletting, but sweating was also a favorite remedy.

These methods were often as dangerous as the diseases they sought to cure, but they were taught religiously in the medical schools of Europe.

Despite the tenacity of Galenic medicine, innovators and reformers attempted during the sixteenth and seventeenth centuries to challenge and overturn medical orthodoxy. With an almost missionary zeal, Paracelsus (1493–1541), a Swiss-German physician and Hermeticist, introduced the concept of diagnostic medicine. He argued that particular diseases can be differentiated and are related to chemical imbalances. His treatments relied on chemicals and not on bloodletting or the positions of the stars (although he did not discount such influences), and he proclaimed an almost ecstatic vision of human vitality and longevity. In most universities the faculties of medicine bitterly opposed his views, but by the mid-seventeenth century in England, and later in that century in France, Paracelsian ideas had many advocates. Support for Paracelsian medicine invariably accompanied an attack on the traditional medical establishment and its professional monopoly, and it often indicated support for the new science in general. The struggle between Galenists and Paracelsians quickly took on a social dimension; the innovators saw themselves pitted against a medical elite that, in their opinion, had lost its commitment to medical research and existed solely to perpetuate itself.

Victory came very slowly to the Paracelsians. In late-seventeenth-century France, the king himself intervened to allow medical students at the Sorbonne to read the writings of the medical reformers. But Paracelsian medicine was not really accepted until the eighteenth century. Universities like Leiden in the Netherlands adopted a new chemical approach to medicine and spawned a new generation of doctors who were capable of advancing daily medical practice beyond a slavish following of the ancient texts. Simultaneously, there was an upgrading in the social position of surgeons, who had been seen until then as lowly handworkers quite separate from and beneath medical practitioners. Gradually during the eighteenth century, enlightened doctors developed skill in both chemistry and surgery.

The medical reforms of the eighteenth century did not rest solely on the Paracelsian approach; they also relied heavily on the experimental breakthroughs made in the science of anatomy. A pioneer in this field was the Belgian surgeon Andreas Vesalius (1514–1564), who published *The Structure of the Human Body* in 1543. Opposing Galenic practice, Vesalius argued for observation and anatomical dissection as the keys to knowing how the human body works. By the late seventeenth century, doctors had learned a great deal about the human body, its structure, and its chemistry.

The study of anatomy yielded dramatic results. In 1628, William Harvey (1578–1657) announced that he had discovered the circulation of the blood. Harvey compared the functioning of the heart to that of a mechanical pump, and once again this tendency to mechanize nature, so basic to the Scientific Revolution in physics, led to a significant discovery. Yet the acceptance of Harvey's work was very slow, and the practical uses of his discovery were not readily apparent.

The mechanization of the world-view entailed more than the destruction of the cosmology advanced by Aristotle and Ptolemy. Also at stake were the explanations offered for everyday physical events. In the Aristotelian and medieval outlook, bodies moved because it was in their nature to do so. Aristotle had postulated "forms" at work in nature; Latin translations and scholastic commentaries identified these forms as spirits, invisible forces inherent in nature that produced changes as diverse as the growth in plants, the fall of heavy objects to the earth, or even (according to Catholic theologians) the transformation of bread and wine into the body and blood of Christ. The dethroning of Aristotelian explanations for physical phenomena assaulted whole systems of knowledge, often of a theological nature, that went to the heart of medieval belief about the nature of creation and God's relation to it.

Predictably, the final assault on the Aristotelian world-view came from Protestant England. By the seventeenth century, English scientific reformers had begun to equate Aristotle with Catholic teachings. Robert Boyle (1627–1691), the father of modern chemistry, believed that Aristotle's physics amounted to little more than magic. Boyle wanted to abolish the spirits on which Catholic theology rested; he advocated that scientists adopt the zeal of the magicians without their secretive practices and their conjuring with spirits.

As an alternative to spirits, Boyle adopted the atomic explanation that matter is made up of small, hard, indestructible particles that behave with regularity and explain changes in gases, fluids, and solids.

Boyle pioneered in the experimental method with such exciting and accurate results that by the time of his death, no serious scientist could attempt chemical experiments without following his guidelines. Thus the science of chemistry acquired its characteristic experimentalism; it was also based on an atomic theory of matter. But not until late in the eighteenth century was this new discipline applied to medical research.

Prophets and Proponents of the New Science

The spectacular scientific discoveries of the early modern period necessitated a complete rethinking of the social and intellectual role of scientific inquiry. Science needed prophets and social theorists to give it direction and to assess its implications. During the early modern period, three major reformers attempted, in disparate ways, to channel science into the service of specific social programs: Giordano Bruno (1548–1600), Francis Bacon (1561–1626), and René Descartes (1596–1650).

Bruno

Giordano Bruno's life is one of the most fascinating and tragic to be found in the turbulent world of the Reformation and Counter Reformation. Born in Italy, Bruno began his mature years as a monk, yet the same church he set out to serve ended his life by having him burned at the stake. What led him to this cruel fate was his espousal of new religious ideas, which were in fact as old as the second century A.D., but which threatened the beliefs of the church. Bruno found in Hermetic philosophy, which he believed to be confirmed by Copernicus's heliocentric theory, the foundation

of a new universal religion. He proposed that religion be based on the laws found in nature and not on supernaturally inspired doctrines taught by the clergy.

Bruno was one of those Late Renaissance reformers who believed that the Hermetic philosophy, with its mystical approach to God and nature, held the key to true wisdom. The Hermetic philosophy accords the sun a special symbolic role because it infuses life into nature. On the basis of his belief, Bruno accepted Copernicus's sun-centered concept of the universe and began to write and preach about it all over Europe. Indeed, Bruno's fertile imagination, fired by Hermetic mysticism and the new science, led him to be one of the first Europeans to proclaim that the universe is infinite, filled with innumerable worlds. He also speculated that there might be life on other planets.

All of these notions were regarded by the church as dangerous. Bruno was in effect presenting the Hermetic philosophy, coupled with the new science, as an alternative religious vision to either Protestantism or Catholicism. His sense of awe and enchantment with the natural order is similar to that found later among eighteenth-century freethinkers, who saw in the scientific study and contemplation of nature, along with a vague sense of the Creator's majesty, an alternative to organized religious worship. Bruno was a prophet of the new science to the extent that he saw its discoveries as confirming his belief in the wonders of creation. Creation was indeed so wondrous that it could be worshiped—the natural world could replace the supernatural as a fitting object for human curiosity and glorification.

Bacon

In contrast to Bruno's mysticism, the decidedly practical and empirical Francis Bacon stands as the most important English proponent of the new science, although not its most important practitioner. Unlike Bruno, Bacon became profoundly suspicious of magic and the magical arts, not because they might not work, but because he saw secrecy and arrogance as characteristic of their practitioners. Bacon was lord chancellor of England under James I, and he wrote about the usefulness of science partly in an effort to convince the Crown of its advantages.

No philosopher of modern science has surpassed Bacon in elevating the study of nature into a humanistic discipline. In the *Advancement of Learning* (1605), Bacon argued that science must be open and free and all ideas must be allowed a hearing. Science must have human goals: the improvement of humanity's material condition and the advancement of trade and industry, but not the making of war or the taking of lives. Bacon also preached the need for science to possess an inductive methodology grounded in experience; the scientist should first of all be a collector of facts.

Although Bacon was rather vague about how the scientist as a theorist actually works, he knew that preconceived ideas imposed on nature seldom yield positive results. An opponent of Aristotle, Bacon argued that university education should move away from the ancient texts and toward the new learning. As a powerful civil servant, Bacon was not afraid to attack the guardians of tradition. The Baconian vision of progress in science leading to an improvement of the human condition inspired much scientific activity in the seventeenth century, particularly in England.

Descartes

René Descartes, a French philosopher of the first half of the seventeenth century, went to the best French schools and was trained by the Jesuits in mathematics and scholastic philosophy. Yet in his early twenties, he experienced a crisis in confidence. He felt that everything he had been taught was irrelevant and meaningless.

Descartes began to search within himself for what he could be sure was clear and distinct knowledge. All he could know with certainty was the fact of his existence, and even that he knew only because he experienced not his body, but his mind: "I think, therefore I am." From this point of certitude, Descartes deduced God's existence. God exists because Descartes had in his mind an idea of a supreme, perfect being which, he reasoned, could only have been put there by such a being, not by any ordinary mortal. Therefore, God's existence means that the physical world must be

René Descartes by Frans Hals (c. 1580–1666). Descartes is both the father of modern philosophy and the prophet of modern science. He placed his faith above all in the human intellect and its ability to achieve scientific knowledge, and made significant practical contributions in algebra. (*Royal Museum of Fine Arts, Copenhagen*)

real, for no Creator would play such a cruel trick and invent a vast hoax.

Descartes thus found confidence in the fact of his own existence and in the reality of the physical world, which he thought could best be understood through reason and mathematics. Scientific thought for Descartes meant an alternative to the chaos of conflicting opinions and the tyranny of truths learned, but not experienced, for oneself. Descartes, possibly as a result of knowing Bacon's ideas, also believed that "it is possible to attain knowledge which is very useful in life, and that, instead of that speculative philosophy which is taught in the schools, we may find a practical philosophy by means of which . . . we can . . . thus render ourselves the masters and possessors of nature."[3]

Descartes has rightly been called the father of modern philosophy and one of the first prophets of modern science. He recognized the power that can come to individuals who ground knowledge not on the fact of God's existence but on a willful assertion of their own ability as thinkers and investigators. Solely by applying their minds to the world around them, human beings can achieve scientific knowledge that will make them the masters and possessors of nature. Descartes believed so fully in the power of unaided human reason that his practical science was largely deductive and not sufficiently based on rigorous experimentation. He thought that the scientist, aided by mathematics, could arrive at correct theories without necessarily testing them against experience.

The prophetic visions of Bruno, Bacon, and Descartes brought for the first time in the West the realization of the potential importance of scientific knowledge. Science could become the foundation of a new religiosity grounded on the practical study of nature—one that was eventually used by Enlightenment reformers to displace the authority of traditional religion. At the same time, science could also serve the needs of humanity. It could give to its practitioners a sense of power and self-confidence unimagined even by Renaissance proponents of individualism.

The Social Context of the Scientific Revolution

The new science played a major role in the profound change that occurred in the thinking of literate Europeans between the early seventeenth century and the middle of the eighteenth century. Historians used to view the Scientific Revolution as the legacy of a few great scientists whose mathematical and experimental genius created a profoundly new understanding of nature. Now, however, the acceptance and use by educated elites of the new science is seen as perhaps the critical factor in causing the historical phenomenon described as the Scientific Revolution. The science of Galileo, Kepler, Descartes, Boyle, and Newton would have remained the specialized knowledge of the few—or worse still, a suspect, even heretical, approach to nature—had it not been for other social and political factors that permitted its acceptance.

The great scientists and their immediate followers or propagandists were hardly naive about those factors. Galileo appealed to the literate classes for their support and argued that this new mechanical science was fit only for them and not for the larger populace. He pitted the new science against the old learning of the scholastic clergy and tied their understanding of nature to the simplistic assumptions of the masses. In so doing he aroused the wrath of the clerical authorities who eventually silenced him. Persecution and censorship meant that the new science made far less of an impact in Catholic than in Protestant Europe.

Access to the printing press was critical to the acceptance of the new mechanical understanding of nature. Descartes understood that fact when he left France, after the condemnation of Galileo, and chose to publish and live in the Netherlands, where his exposition of the new science stressed at every turn its advantages in promoting order and stability and diverting people to the search for mastery over nature rather than having them meddle in state affairs.

The other social factor that contributed to the acceptance of the new science lay in the dream of power that mechanical knowledge offered to governments as well as to the early promoters of industry. In the seventeenth century, such knowledge was no more than a dream, but it nevertheless enticed monarchs and statesmen to give their patronage to scientific academies and projects.

The new mechanical learning—not that found in Newton's *Principia*, which was far too technical for most people, but the mechanical information in handbooks and lectures—gained application first in Britain and Scotland during the second half of the eighteenth century. The applied mechanics that produced the steam engine and improved coal mining and water engineering in general had its origin in the Newtonian lectures and books that proliferated in Britain during the eighteenth century. The road from the Scientific Revolution to the Industrial Revolution is more direct than has often been realized.

Figure 1 Jan Vermeer: *View of Delft*, 1660. (*Mauritshuis, The Hague*)

European Art of the Seventeenth Century

Figure 2 Michelangelo Amerighi Caravaggio: *Madonna of Loreto,* 1604–1605, in Cavalletti Chapel, S. Agostino, Rome. (*Scala/Art Resource*)

The seventeenth century saw the rise of a centralized government, agonizing religious conflict, and vast infusions, shifts, and redistributions of wealth. All of these changes are manifest in the stylistically rich art of the era, in tiny landscape paintings as well as in palaces and piazzas.

At the Council of Trent, the Roman Catholic Church rejected the proscription of images that Protestants had advocated in taking literally the biblical commandment forbidding "graven images." Instead, Catholics put great artists to work expressing newly clarified Catholic theology in bold, vivid, human terms. This trend is perhaps best exemplified by the work of architect and sculptor Gian Lorenzo Bernini (1598–1680). In the Cornaro Chapel of Rome's Santa Maria della Vittoria, Bernini represented the moment of St. Teresa's religious ecstasy (Figure 3), in which she saw Christ and felt her heart pierced by love and longing. The saint and attending angel are carved in white marble, seemingly

Figure 3 Gian Lorenzo Bernini: *Saint Theresa in Ecstasy*, 1644–1647, in Cornaro Chapel, Santa Maria della Vittoria, Rome. (*Scala/Art Resource*)

Figure 4 Peter Paul Rubens: *The Horrors of War*, 1637–1638, in Palazzo Pitti, Florence. (*Scala/Art Resource*)

suspended on a "cloud" of cream-colored travertine. A bundle of radiating metal rods symbolize the emanation of heavenly rays and the white marble figures are bathed in an unearthly golden glow; the effect is created by the flow of sunlight shining through a concealed yellow glass window.

The seventeenth century, considered as an era in the history of art, is often called the Baroque era. It refers to an exuberant, highly decorated style filled with intense emotion, of which Bernini's art is the quintessential example.

However, some of the Baroque era's greatest artists worked in very different styles. One of the most influential was the realist Michelangelo Amerighi Caravaggio (c. 1565–1610), a very influential, yet controversial artist with passionate religious convictions and an equally passionate temperament. Works such as

the *Madonna of Loreto* (Figure 2), an altarpiece in the Cavalletti Chapel in Rome's Sant' Agostino, were produced for patrons receptive to the cutting edge in artistic styles but who were also "born again" Catholics. Caravaggio's new style included both dramatic use of intense light seemingly beamed into cavernous darkness and realism so convincing that one seems to be observing transcendent beings in the guise of contemporary Roman city dwellers.

A third style developed in Rome in the seventeenth century was the Baroque classicism of Nicolas Poussin (1594–1665), a French painter who worked in Rome throughout his career. The majesty of God is shown by Poussin not through theatrical brilliance nor through compassionate realism, but through compositions balanced so delicately that they seem to act as metaphors for the order of God's creation. In *The Holy Family on the Steps* (Figure

Figure 5 Nicolas Poussin: *Holy Family on the Steps*, 1648. (*National Gallery of Art, Washington; Samuel H. Kress Collection*)

5), the pyramidal arrangement of figures is counterbalanced by the steps, the buildings, and the urn, and a low vantage point causes the viewer to look up toward the majestic holy family. The painting bespeaks appreciation of human science and invention, as symbolized by the architectural setting and by Joseph's tools— a compass and T-square—but these are both literally and figuratively overshadowed by the transcendent strength of Christ and the Virgin.

Holland enjoyed unprecedented prosperity in the seventeenth century, and that wealth was widely dispersed among members of a fairly broad-based bourgeoisie (see Chapter 16). Such widespread prosperity made possible a booming art market, for the Old Masters of the Renaissance and for contemporary Dutch

paintings as well. One English visitor to Holland in that century described a Dutch farmer's art collection so vast that the walls of his barn, as well as of his house, were covered with pictures. The peace and prosperity of seventeenth-century Holland are beautifully conveyed in Figure 1, the *View of Delft* by Jan Vermeer (1632–1675). (See also an interior painting by Vermeer on page 361.)

The United Provinces were Protestant, which meant that no devotional images were produced for churches. Most popular subjects were secular, and religious subjects tended to draw on Old Testament stories, which Protestants knew well. Holland's greatest artist, Rembrandt van Rijn (1606–1669), produced many paintings based on the Scriptures, among

them *Joseph Accused by Potiphar's Wife* (Figure 8). In this Old Testament story, Joseph had been the trusted servant of Potiphar. Potiphar's wife, attracted by Joseph's youth and handsomeness, attempted to seduce him and was spurned. She took revenge by falsely accusing Joseph of rape. Reluctantly, Potiphar had Joseph imprisoned. In the painting through the figures' gestures and expressions, Rembrandt conveys the tragedy of the story: the wife's anger and shame, Joseph's recognition of the futility of protesting, and the husband's sadness over his apparent betrayal by one who had served him faithfully and responsibly.

Dutch patrons were especially fond of portraits, making them a mainstay of income for many successful artists, one of whom was Judith Leyster (c. 1609–1660). In this *Self-Portrait* (Figure 6), the bright, self-confident expression of the artist as she turns from her easel to look out at the viewer seems an accurate portrayal of her personality. She was the first woman admitted to the Haarlem Guild of St. Luke. *The Smokers* (Figure 7) by Adriaen Brouwer (c. 1605–1638), a Flemish artist who had worked in Haarlem and Antwerp, is a good example of such a genre painting. All of his subjects, except for a few landscapes, come from common life, and the rustic subjects contrast with the delicate style of the painting.

Spain was yet another important center of painting in the seventeenth century. Diego Velázquez (1599–1660) was the court painter for Phillip IV. The Velázquez painting traditionally known as *Las Hilanderas* ("the spinners") is a good example of the multilayered meanings found in some of the best Baroque art (Figure 9). (See also page 362.) On one level the painting depicts a scene taken from contempo-

Figure 6 *Top:* Judith Leyster: *Self-Portrait*, 1635. (*National Gallery of Art, Washington; Gift of Mr. and Mrs. Robert Woods Bliss*)

Figure 7 *Bottom:* Adriaen Brouwer: *The Smokers*, 1636. Oil on wood. H. 18¼ in. W. 14½ in. (*The Metropolitan Museum of Art, Bequest of Michael Friedsam, 1931, The Friedsam Collection. 32.100.21*)

Figure 8 Rembrandt van Rijn: *Joseph Accused by Potiphar's Wife,* 1655. Oil on canvas. (*National Gallery of Art, Washington; Andrew W. Mellon Collection*)

Figure 9 Diego Velázquez: *Las Hilanderas*, 1656–1658. (*Museo del Prado, Madrid*)

rary life: spinners are shown at work in the tapestry factory of Santa Isabel in Madrid. The finished tapestry hanging on the rear wall of the painting replicates Titian's *Rape of Europa,* which belonged to the Spanish royal family at the time. On a second level the painting recounts the Greek myth of Arachne. Finally, the painting is a meditation in the art and craft of painting, on the artist's challenge, with his own creation, to the creations of nature and of deities.

The works of art in this essay do not reflect the war, poverty, plague, and suffering of the seventeenth century. The reason for this omission lies with the art patrons, who did not commission or buy works of art with painful subject matter. Occasionally, however, artists did produce paintings and sculpture that dealt with contemporary social and political conditions. The Flemish artist Peter Paul Rubens (1577–1640), who traveled all over Europe on diplomatic missions, expressed his own— and Europe's—anguish in a brilliant allegorical painting, *The Horrors of War* (Figure 4). The grief-stricken figure at left, representing Europe, throws up her arms helplessly as the goddess of love tries, unsuccessfully, to restrain the god of war and the figure of fury, who trample art, learning, and family life in their obsessive march toward chaos.

—KATHERINE CRUM

The Meaning of the Scientific Revolution

The Scientific Revolution was decisive in shaping the modern mentality; it shattered the medieval view of the universe and replaced it with a wholly different world-view. Gone was the belief that a motionless earth lay at the center of a universe that was finite and enclosed by a ring of stars. Gone too was the belief that the universe was divided into higher and lower worlds and that different laws of motion operated in the heavens than operated on earth. The universe was now viewed as a giant machine functioning according to universal laws that could be expressed mathematically; nature could be mastered.

The methodology that produced this new view of nature—the new science—played a crucial historical role in reorienting Western thought away from medieval theology and metaphysics and toward the study of physical and human problems. In the later Middle Ages, most men of learning were Aristotelians and theologians. But by the mid-eighteenth century, knowledge of Newtonian science and the dissemination of useful learning had become the goal of the educated classes. All knowledge, it was believed, could emulate scientific knowledge; it could be based on observation, experimentation, and rational deduction; it could be systematic, verifiable, progressive, and useful. At every turn the advocates of this new approach to learning hailed the scientists of the sixteenth and seventeenth centuries as proof that no institution or dogma had a monopoly on truth—the scientific approach would yield knowledge that might, if properly applied for the good of all people, produce a new and better age. Such an outlook gave thinkers new confidence in the power of the human mind to master nature and led them to examine European institutions and traditions with an inquiring, critical, and skeptical spirit. Thus inspired, the reformers of the eighteenth century would seek to create an Age of Enlightenment.

The Scientific Revolution ultimately weakened traditional Christianity. God's role in a mechanical universe was not clear. Newton had argued that God not only set the universe in motion but still intervened in its operations, thus leaving room for miracles. Others retained a place for God as Creator but regarded miracles as limitations on nature's mechanical perfection. Soon other Christian teachings came under attack as contrary to the standards of verification postulated by the new science. Applied to religious doctrines, Descartes' reliance on methodical doubt and clarity of thought and Bacon's insistence on careful observation led thinkers to question the validity of Christian teachings. Theology came to be regarded as a separate and somewhat irrelevant area of intellectual inquiry that was not fit for the interests of practical, well-informed people. Not only Christian doctrines but also various widespread and popular beliefs came under attack. Magic, witchcraft, and astrology, still widespread among the European masses, were regarded with disdain by elite culture. The Scientific Revolution widened the gap between the elite culture of the rich and landed, and the popular culture. The masses of people remained devoted to some form of traditional Christianity, while the uncertainty of a universe governed by devils, witches, or the stars continued to make sense to peasants and laborers who remained powerless in the face of nature or the domination of the rich and landed.

In Catholic countries, where the Scientific Revolution began, there was, by the early seventeenth century, a growing hostility toward scientific ideas. The mentality of the Counter Reformation enabled lesser minds to exercise their fears and arrogance against any idea they regarded as suspicious. Galileo was caught in this hostile environment, and the Copernican system was condemned by the church in 1616.

As a result, by the second half of the seventeenth century science had become an increasingly Protestant phenomenon. The major Protestant countries, like England and the Netherlands, accorded greater intellectual freedom, and their presses were relatively free. Eventually, science also proved to be more compatible with the Protestant mind's emphasis on individual striving and the mercantile exploitation of nature for material gain.

Gradually the science of Newton became the science of western Europe: nature mechanized, analyzed, regulated, and mathematicized. As a result of the Scientific Revolution, learned Westerners came to believe more strongly than ever that nature could be mastered. Mechanical science—applied to canals, engines, pumps, and levers—became the science of industry. Thus the Scientific Revolution, operating on both intellectual and commercial levels, laid the groundwork for two major developments of the modern West—the Age of Enlightenment and the Industrial Revolution.

Notes

1. Excerpted in Stillman Drake, ed., *Discoveries and Opinions of Galileo* (New York: Doubleday, 1957), p. 28.

2. Excerpted in *Newton's Philosophy of Nature,* H. S. Thayer, ed. (New York: Hafner, 1953), p. 177.

3. Excerpted in Norman Kemp Smith, ed., *Descartes' Philosophical Writings* (New York: Modern Library, 1958), pp. 130–131.

Suggested Reading

Bernal, J. D., *Science in History* (1969). A learned classic that discusses the meaning of science in history.

Briggs, Robin, *The Scientific Revolution of the Seventeenth Century* (1969). A clearly written survey with documents.

Butterfield, Herbert, *The Origins of Modern Science* (1957). An analysis of the emergence of modern science.

Clark, G. N., *Science and Social Welfare in the Age of Newton* (1949). A standard work on the social uses of the new science.

Cohen, I. B., *The Birth of a New Physics* (1960). Authoritative, but difficult for the novice.

Drake, Stillman, ed., *Discoveries and Opinions of Galileo* (1957). A good place to start to learn Galileo's most important ideas.

Jacob, James R., *Robert Boyle and the English Revolution* (1977). Deals with the relationship between Boyle's science and the English Revolution.

Jacob, Margaret C., *The Cultural Meaning of the Scientific Revolution* (1988). Offers a general interpretation of the social context of the Scientific Revolution.

Kearney, Hugh, *Science and Social Change, 1500–1700* (1971). Includes a discussion of the social setting of the Scientific Revolution.

Koestler, Arthur, *The Watershed: A Biography of Johannes Kepler* (1960). A fascinating biography of a founder of modern science and a practitioner of magic.

Kuhn, Thomas, *The Structure of Scientific Revolutions* (1962). One of the first non-Marxist attempts to show that science has social implications.

Whitehead, Alfred North, *Science and the Modern World* (1960). An early and important meditation on the meaning of modern science.

Review Questions

1. What was the difference between the scientific understanding of the universe and the medieval understanding of it?

2. Describe the major achievements of Copernicus, Kepler, Galileo, and Newton.

3. How did the practice of medicine change during the Scientific Revolution? Describe the changes.

4. What were Bruno's differences with the church? Describe what happened.

5. Does modern science conform to Francis Bacon's ideals? List these ideals and discuss why it does/does not conform.

6. Was the Scientific Revolution essentially the achievement of a few men of genius, or was the process more complex than that?

7. How did early modern Europeans perceive the new science as it was developing?

8. What was the relationship between science and magic in this period?

9. What role did the Scientific Revolution play in shaping a modern mentality?

18

The Age of Enlightenment:
Reason and Reform

T

he eighteenth century is called the Age of Enlightenment, or Age of Reason, for during this period an educated elite, expressing supreme confidence in the power of reason, attempted a rational analysis of European institutions and beliefs. The Enlightenment was heavily indebted to the discoveries of the seventeenth-century Scientific Revolution—to the experimental method pioneered by Galileo, Boyle, and Newton, and to the mechanical picture of the universe formed by Newton. The Scientific Revolution seemed to show that order and mathematically demonstrable laws were at work in the physical universe. The thinkers of the Enlightenment, called *philosophes,* argued that it should be possible to examine *human* institutions with the intention of imposing a comparable order and rationality.

Late in the eighteenth century, Immanuel Kant (1724–1804), a German philosopher, defined the Enlightenment as the bringing of "light into the dark corners of the mind," the dispelling of ignorance and superstition. Kant went to the heart of one aspect of the Enlightenment, that is, its insistence that each individual should reason independently without recourse to the authority of the schools, churches, and universities.[1]

Kant, a moderate, believed that this call for self-education meant no revolutionary disruption of the political order. In general, modern liberal and enlightened culture aimed at a gradual evolutionary transformation of the human condition; only a few radical thinkers during the eighteenth century were prepared to envision an immediate political disruption of the traditional authority of monarchy, aristocracy, and church. The mainstream of the Enlightenment was politically moderate, worshipful of the new science, critical of the clergy and all rigid dogma, tolerant in religious matters, and even loyal to enlightened monarchs who were prepared to keep the clerical censors away from the new books.

The Winter Palace, St. Petersburg. (*William Brumfield*)

Philosophes were found most commonly in the major European cities, with Paris becoming the center of the Enlightenment during the 1770s. The philosophes developed a new style of writing philosophy, one that tried to make it understandable and even simple, sometimes entertaining. In the process they became journalists, propagandists, and in some cases brilliant literary stylists who made their various languages more readable for literate laymen and also the growing number of literate women.

Enlightenment culture relied heavily on the printing press as an agent of propaganda. Through it, the philosophes could address the increasingly large audiences found in the major European cities—London, Amsterdam, and Paris, in particular. Thanks to the power of the printed word, the philosophes were able to agitate for reform by addressing an educated and urban lay audience directly. In essays, monthly journals, works of fiction, and even mildly pornographic and anonymous tales, they attacked many of the abuses of eighteenth-century society—religious fanaticism and intolerance, corruption of the aristocracy, the use of torture, terrible prison conditions, slavery, and violations of natural rights.

Although not profoundly original, the philosophes were bold in their criticism of existing institutions, especially the churches and the clergy. In essence, the philosophes condemned all vestiges of medieval culture. Inevitably, modern liberal thought, initiated by the Enlightenment, emerged as hostile to scholastic learning, priests, and, eventually in some quarters, to Christianity itself. The philosophes expressed confidence in science and reason, espoused humanitarianism, and struggled for religious liberty and freedom of thought and person. Combining these values with a secular orientation and a belief in future progress, the philosophes helped shape, if not define, the modern outlook.

The Science of Religion

Christianity Under Attack

No single thread had united Western culture more powerfully than Christianity. Until the eighteenth century, educated people, especially rulers and servants of the state, had to give allegiance to one or another of the Christian churches—however un-Christian their actions. The Enlightenment, however, produced the first widely read and systematic assault on Christianity launched from within the ranks of the educated. The philosophes argued that many Christian dogmas defied logic—for example, the conversion of the substance of bread and wine into the body and the blood of Christ during the Eucharist—and they ridiculed theologians for arguing over obscure issues that seemed irrelevant to the human condition and a hindrance to clear thinking. "Theology amuses me," wrote Voltaire. "That's where we find the madness of the human spirit in all its plenitude." In the same spirit, the philosophes denounced the churches for inciting the fanaticism and intolerance that led to the horrors of the Crusades, the Inquisition, and the wars of the Reformation. They viewed Christianity's preoccupation with salvation and its belief in the depravity of human nature, a consequence of Adam and Eve's defiance of God, as barriers to social improvement and earthly happiness.

Skeptics, Freethinkers, Deists

An early attack on Christian dogma was made by the skeptic Pierre Bayle (1647–1706), who came to distrust Christian dogma and to see superstition as a social evil far more dangerous than atheism. Bayle was a French Protestant forced to flee to the Netherlands as a result of Louis XIV's campaign against his coreligionists. Although a Calvinist himself, Bayle also ran into opposition from the strict Calvinist clergy, who regarded him as lax on doctrinal matters. He attacked his critics and persecutors in a new and brilliant form of journalism, his *Historical and Critical Dictionary* (1697), which was more an encyclopedia than a dictionary. Under alphabetically arranged subjects and in copious footnotes, Bayle discussed the most recent learning of the day on various matters and never missed an opportunity to ridicule the dogmatic, the superstitious, or the just plain arrogant. In Bayle's hands, the ancient philosophy of skepticism, the doubting of all dogma, was revived and it became a tool; rigorous questioning of accepted ideas became a method for arriving at new truths. As Bayle noted in his *Dictionary*: "It is therefore only religion that has anything to fear from Pyrrhonism [i.e., skepticism]."[2] In this same critical spirit, Bayle, in his dictionary article entitled "David," compared Louis XIV to Goliath. The message was clear enough: great tyrants and the clergy who prop them up should beware of self-confident, independently minded citizens who are skeptical of the claims of authority made by kings and churches and are eager to use their own minds to search for truth.

Bayle's *Dictionary,* which was in effect the first encyclopedia, had an enormous impact throughout Europe. Its very format captured the imagination of the philosophes. Here was a way of simply, even scientifically, classifying and ordering knowledge. Partly through Bayle's writings, skepticism became an integral part of the Enlightenment approach to religion. It taught its readers to be skeptical of the clerical claim that God's design governs human events, that "God ordains" certain human actions. Skepticism dealt a serious blow to revealed religion and seemed to point in the direction of "natural" religion, that is, toward a system of beliefs and ethics designed by rational people on the basis of their own needs.

Also contributing to the religious outlook of the philosophes were late seventeenth- and early eighteenth-century English freethinkers. These early representatives of the Enlightenment used the term *freethinking* to signal their hostility to established church dogmas and their ability to think for themselves. They looked back to the English Revolution of midcentury for their ideas about government; many English freethinkers were republicans in the tradition established by important figures of the Interregnum (see Chapter 16). Indeed, the English freethinkers of the 1690s and beyond helped popularize English republican ideas at home and in the American colonies, where in 1776 these views would figure prominently in the thinking of American revolutionaries.

The freethinkers had little use for organized religion or even for Christianity itself. In 1696 the freethinker John Toland (1670–1722) published a tract called *Christianity Not Mysterious,* in which he argued that any religious doctrine that seemed to contradict reason or common sense—for example, the resurrection of Jesus or the miracles of the Bible—ought to be discarded. Toland also attacked the clergy's power; in his opinion the Revolution of 1688–89 had not gone far enough in undermining the power of the established church and the king. Toland and his freethinking associates Anthony Collins and Matthew Tindal wanted England to be a republic governed by "reasonable" people who worshiped, as Toland proposed, not a mysterious God but intelligible nature.

In science combined with skepticism, freethinking, and anticlericalism, thoughtful critics could find ample reason for abandoning all traditional authority. By 1700, a general crisis of confidence in established authority had been provoked by the works of Bayle, the freethinkers, and such seventeenth-century philosophers as Descartes. Once started in England and the Netherlands and broadcast via Dutch printers, the Enlightenment almost immediately became international.

The leaders of the Enlightenment sought to repudiate traditional Christianity and to put in its place a rational system of ethics and philosophy based on scientific truths. Although some philosophes were atheists, most were *deists* who tried to make religion compatible with a scientific understanding of nature. Deists believed only those Christian doctrines that could meet the test of reason. For example, they considered it reasonable to believe in God, for only with a creator, they said, could such a superbly organized universe have come into being. But after God set the universe in motion, according to the deists, he took no further part in its operations. Thus, although deists retained a belief in God the Creator, they rejected clerical authority, revelation, original sin, and miracles. They held that biblical accounts of the resurrection and of Jesus walking on water or waking the dead could not be reconciled with natural law. Deists viewed Jesus as a great moral teacher, not as the son of God, and they regarded ethics, not faith, as the essence of religion; rational people, they said, served God best by treating their fellow human beings justly.

David Hume (1711–1776), a Scottish skeptic, attacked both revealed religion and the deists' natural religion. He maintained that all religious ideas, including Christian teachings and even the idea of God, stemmed ultimately from human fears and superstitions. Hume rejected the deist argument that this seemingly orderly universe required a designing mind to create it. The universe, said Hume, might very well be eternal, and the seeming universal order simply a natural condition that requires no explanation. Hume's attack made it impossible to establish a necessary link between a mechanical universe and a creator. As a consequence of Hume's critique, more than ever before Christian belief rested on faith, not reason.

Freemasons

As the Enlightenment's search for a new foundation of religious belief went on, some seekers inevitably attempted to found new clubs or societies. These groups tried to fulfill social and intellectual needs no longer being met by the traditional churches. In 1717, a group of London gentlemen, many of them very interested in the new science and in the spread of learning in general, founded the Grand Lodge, a collection of various Masonic lodges that had met in pubs around the city. From that date can be traced the origins of European Freemasonry and its spread into almost every European country.

Freemasonry was not originally intended to rival the churches. Nevertheless, the lodges became, especially on the Continent, alternative meeting places for men interested in the Enlightenment. Some French philosophes joined lodges in Paris, as did some clergy. In Vienna at the time of Mozart, who was a Freemason, and in Berlin during the reign of Frederick the Great, Masonic membership came to denote support for enlightened and centralized government, often in opposition to the local power of the clergy and the old aristocracy. For a few extreme rationalists bent on destroying the Christian churches, the Masonic lodges also seemed to function as a commendable alternative form of religion, complete with ritual, charitable funds, and sense of community. By the middle of the eighteenth century, perhaps as many as 50,000 men belonged to Masonic lodges in just about every major European city and in many towns as well. These lodges became places where men could gather and openly discuss their beliefs and the writings of the philosophes if they cared to do so. The ideals of equality and liberty took on

Voltaire and Frederick II, King of Prussia at the Latter's Palace Called Sans Souci. The intellectual confidence of the Enlightenment brought together writers and despots. Ruthless politically, Frederick nonetheless could converse about philosophical matters with the writer-reformer Voltaire; he also wrote over a hundred flute sonatas. (*Ullstein Bilderdienst*)

meaning in these private gatherings, where the participants could reflect on the inequality they perceived in the world around them. Eventually some lodges admitted women as members.

Voltaire the Philosophe

The French possessed a vital tradition of intellectual skepticism going back to the late sixteenth century, as well as a tradition of scientific rationalism exemplified by Descartes. In the early eighteenth century, however, the French found it difficult to gain access to the new literature of the

Enlightenment because the French printing presses were among the most tightly controlled and censored in Europe. As a result, a brisk but risky traffic developed in clandestine books and manuscripts subversive of authority, and French-language journals poured from Dutch presses.

As a poet and writer struggling for recognition in Paris, the young François Marie Arouet, known to the world as Voltaire (1694–1778), encountered some of the new ideas that were being discussed in private gatherings (called *salons*) in Paris. Care had to be taken in the French capital by those educated people who wanted to read books and discuss ideas hostile to the church or to the Sorbonne, the clerically controlled university. Individuals had been imprisoned for writing, publishing, or owning books hostile to Catholic doctrine. Although Voltaire learned something of the new enlightened culture in Paris, it was in 1726, when he journeyed to London, that Voltaire the poet became Voltaire the philosophe.

In England, Voltaire became acquainted with the ideas of John Locke (1632–1704) and Isaac Newton. From Newton, Voltaire learned the mathematical laws that govern the universe; he witnessed the power of human reason to establish general rules that seemed to explain the behavior of physical objects. From Locke, Voltaire learned that people should believe only those ideas received from the senses. Locke's theory of learning, his *epistemology,* impressed many of the proponents of the Enlightenment. Again, the implications for religion were most serious: if people believe only those things that they experience, they will be unable to accept mysteries and doctrines simply because they are taught by churches and the clergy. Voltaire experienced considerable freedom of thought in England and saw a religious toleration that stood in stark contrast to the absolutism of the French kings and the power of the French clergy. He also witnessed a freer mixing of bourgeois and aristocratic social groups than was permitted in France at this time.

Throughout his life, Voltaire was a fierce supporter of the Enlightenment and a bitter critic of churches and the Inquisition. Although his books were banned in France, he probably did more there than any other philosophe to popularize the Enlightenment and to mock the authority of the clergy. In *Letters Concerning the English Nation* (1733), Voltaire wrote about his experiences in England. He offered constitutional monarchy, new science, and religious toleration as models to be followed by all of Europe. In the *Letters,* he praised English society for its encouragement of these ideals; as he put it, "This is the country of sects. An Englishman, as a free man, goes to Heaven by whatever road he pleases."[3] Voltaire never ceased to mock the purveyors of superstition and blind obedience to religious authority. In such works as *Candide* (1759) and *Micromegas* (1752), he castigated the clergy, as well as other philosophical supporters of the status quo who would have people believe that this was the best of all possible worlds.

Voltaire was also a practical reformer who campaigned for the rule of law, a freer press, religious toleration, humane treatment of criminals, and a more effective system of government administration. His writings constituted a radical attack on aspects of eighteenth-century French society. Yet, like so many philosophes, Voltaire feared the power of the people, especially if goaded by the clergy. He was happiest in the company of the rich and powerful, provided they tolerated his ideas and supported reform. Not surprisingly, Voltaire was frequently disappointed by eighteenth-century monarchs, like Frederick the Great in Prussia, who promised enlightenment but sought mainly to increase their own power and that of their armies.

Political Thought

With the exception of Machiavelli (see page 270) in the Renaissance and Thomas Hobbes and the republicans during the English Revolution, the Enlightenment produced the greatest originality in political thought witnessed in the West up to that time. Three major European thinkers and a host of minor ones wrote treatises on politics that remain relevant to this day: John Locke, *Two Treatises of Government* (1690); Baron de la Brède et de Montesquieu, *The Spirit of the Laws* (1748); and Jean Jacques Rousseau, *The Social Contract*

Map 18.1 Europe, 1715 ▶

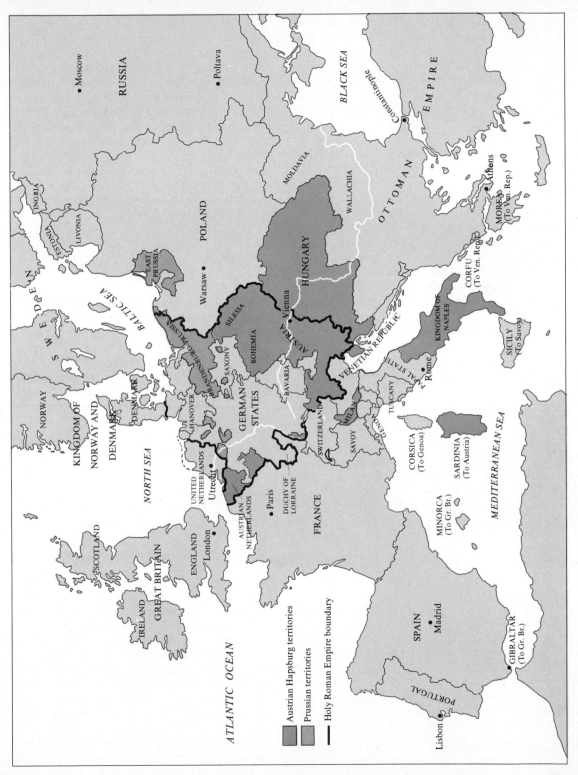

Moscow

RUSSIA

Poltava

BLACK SEA

OTTOMAN EMPIRE

Constantinople

Athens

MOREA
(To Ven. Rep.)

INGRIA

ESTONIA

LIVONIA

POLAND

MOLDAVIA

WALLACHIA

Warsaw

EAST PRUSSIA

SILESIA

HUNGARY

CORFU
(To Ven. Rep.)

S W E D E N

BALTIC SEA

BRANDENBURG-PRUSSIA

BOHEMIA

AUSTRIA

Vienna

VENETIAN REPUBLIC

KINGDOM OF NAPLES

SICILY
(To Savoy)

NORWAY

KINGDOM OF NORWAY AND DENMARK

DENMARK

HANOVER

SAXONY

BAVARIA

GERMAN STATES

SWITZERLAND

MILAN

GENOA

PAPAL STATES

Rome

TUSCANY

CORSICA
(To Genoa)

SARDINIA
(To Austria)

MEDITERRANEAN SEA

NORTH SEA

UNITED NETHERLANDS

Utrecht

AUSTRIAN NETHERLANDS

Paris

DUCHY OF LORRAINE

FRANCE

SAVOY

MINORCA
(To Gr. Br.)

SCOTLAND

ENGLAND

London

GREAT BRITAIN

IRELAND

ATLANTIC OCEAN

SPAIN

Madrid

GIBRALTAR
(To Gr. Br.)

PORTUGAL

Lisbon

Austrian Hapsburg territories

Prussian territories

Holy Roman Empire boundary

(1762). All repudiated the divine right of kings and were concerned with checking the power of monarchy; each offered different formulas for achieving that goal. These major political theorists of the Enlightenment were also aware of the writings of Machiavelli and Hobbes and, although often disagreeing with them, borrowed some of their ideas.

Machiavelli had analyzed politics in terms of power, fortune, and the ability of the individual ruler; he did not call in God to justify the power of princes or to explain their demise. Machiavelli had also preferred a republican form of government to monarchy, and his republican vision did not lose its appeal during the Enlightenment. Very late in the century, most liberal theorists recognized that the republican form of government, or at the least the virtues practiced by citizens in a republic, offered the only alternative to the corruption and repression associated with absolutist monarchy.

Enlightenment political thinkers were ambivalent toward much of the writing of Thomas Hobbes (1588–1679). All, however, liked his belief that self-interest is a valid reason for engaging in political activity and his refusal to bring God into his system to justify the power of kings. Hobbes said power did not rest on divine right but arose out of a contract made among men (women are not included in his system) who agreed to elevate the state, and hence the monarch, to a position of power over them. That contract, once made, could not be broken. As a consequence, the power of the government, whether embodied in a king or a parliament, was absolute.

Hobbes published his major work, *Leviathan*, in 1651, soon after England had been torn by civil war; thus, he was obsessed with the issue of political stability. He feared that, left to their own devices, men would kill one another; the "war of all against all"[4] would prevail without the firm hand of a sovereign to stop it. Hobbes's vision of human nature was dark and forbidding. In the state of nature, the original men had lived lives that could only have been "nasty, brutish, and short." Their only recourse was to set up a power over themselves that would restrain them. For Hobbes the state was, as he put it, a "mortal god," the only guarantee of peace and stability. He was the first political thinker to realize the extraordinary

power that had come into existence with the creation of strong centralized governments. Most Enlightenment theorists, however, beginning with John Locke, denied that governments possessed absolute power over their subjects, and to that extent they repudiated Hobbes. Many European thinkers of the eighteenth century, including Rousseau, also rejected Hobbes's gloomy view that human nature is greedy and warlike. Yet Hobbes lurks in the background of the Enlightenment. He is the first wholly secular political theorist and he sounded the death knell for theories of the divine right of kings. The Enlightenment theorists started where he left off.

Locke

Probably the most widely read political philosopher during the first half of the eighteenth century was John Locke. His *Two Treatises of Government* was seen as a justification for the Revolution of 1688–89 and the notion of government by consent of the people. (Although they were published in 1690, Locke wrote the treatises before the English Revolution; that fact, however, was not known during the Enlightenment.)

Locke's theory, in its broad outlines, stated that the right to govern derived from the consent of the governed and was a form of contract. When people gave their consent to a government, they expected it to govern justly, to protect their property, and to ensure certain liberties for the propertied. If a government attempted to rule absolutely and arbitrarily—if it violated the natural rights of the individual—it reneged on its contract and forfeited the loyalty of its subjects. Such a government could legitimately be overthrown. Locke believed that a constitutional government that limited the power of rulers was the best defense of property and individual rights. He also advocated religious toleration for those religious groups whose beliefs did not threaten the state. Locke denied toleration to Catholics because of their association with the Stuarts, and to atheists because their oaths to God could not be trusted. He also promoted the necessity for education, particularly for those who saw themselves as the natural leaders of society. And not least, he advocated commerce and trade as one of the foundations of England's national strength.

Late in the eighteenth century, Locke's ideas were used to justify liberal revolutions in both Europe and America. Indeed, the importance of Locke's political philosophy was not simply his recourse to contract theory as a justification of constitutional government; it was also his assertion that the community could take up arms against its sovereign in the name of the natural rights of liberty and property. Locke's ideas about the foundation of government had greater impact on the Continent and in America during the eighteenth century than they did in England.

Montesquieu

Baron de la Brède et de Montesquieu (1689–1755) was a French aristocrat who, like Voltaire, visited England late in the 1720s and knew the writings of Locke. Montesquieu had little sympathy for revolutions, but he did approve of constitutional monarchy. His primary concern was to check the unbridled authority of the French kings. In opposition to the Old Regime, Montesquieu proposed a balanced system of government, with an executive branch offset by a legislature whose members were drawn from the landed and educated elements in society. Montesquieu genuinely believed that the aristocracy possessed a natural and sacred obligation to rule and that their honor called them to serve the community. He also aimed to fashion a government that channeled the interests and energies of its people, a government that was not bogged down in corruption and inefficiency. In stressing the rule of law and the importance of nonmonarchical authority, Montesquieu became a source for legitimating the authority of representative institutions. Hardly an advocate of democracy, nonetheless Montesquieu was seen as a powerful critic of royal absolutism. His writings, particularly *The Spirit of the Laws,* established Montesquieu both as a major philosophe who possessed republican tendencies and as a critic of the Old Regime in France. Once again, innovative political thinking highlighted the failures of absolutist government and pointed to the need for some kind of representative assembly in every European country. In addition, Montesquieu's ideas on a balanced system of government found favor in the new American republic.

Rousseau

Not until the 1760s did democracy find its champion in Jean Jacques Rousseau (1712–1778). Rousseau based his politics on contract theory—the people choose their government and, in so doing, effectively give birth to civil society. But Rousseau further demanded that the contract be constantly renewed and that government be made immediately and directly responsible to the will of the people. *The Social Contract* opened with this stirring cry for reform: "Man is born free; and everywhere he is in chains," and went on to ask how that restriction could be changed. Freedom is in the very nature of man: "to renounce liberty is to renounce being a man, to surrender the rights of humanity and even its duties."[5]

Rousseau's political ideal was the city-state of ancient Greece, where people participated actively and directly in politics and were willing to sacrifice self-interest to the community's needs. To the ancient Greek, said Rousseau, the state was a moral association that made him a better person, and good citizenship was the highest form of excellence. In contrast, modern society was prey to many conflicting interests; the rich and powerful used the state to preserve their interests and power, and the poor and powerless viewed it as an oppressor. Consequently, the obedience to law, the devotion to the state, and the freedom that had characterized the Greek city-state had been lost.

In *The Social Contract,* Rousseau tried to resolve the conflict between individual freedom and the demands of the state. His solution was a small state, modeled after the Greek city-state. Such a state, said Rousseau, should be based on the *general will*—that which is best for the community, which expresses its common interests. Rousseau wanted laws of the state to coincide with the general will; he felt that people have the wisdom to arrive at laws that serve the common good, but to do so they have to set aside selfish interests for the good of the community. For Rousseau, freedom consisted of obeying laws prescribed by citizens inspired by the general will. Citizens themselves must constitute the law-making body; law making cannot be entrusted to a single person or a small group.

For Rousseau, those who disobey laws—who act according to their private will rather than in accordance with the general will as expressed in law—degrade themselves and undermine the community. Therefore, government has the right to force citizens to be obedient—to compel them to exercise their individual wills in the proper way. Rousseau believed that government has the right to enforce freedom, but he did leave the problem of minority rights unresolved.

No philosopher of the Enlightenment was more dangerous to the Old Regime than Rousseau. His ideas were perceived as truly revolutionary—as a direct challenge to the power of kings, churches, and aristocrats. Although Rousseau thought that many leaders of the Enlightenment had been corrupted by easy living and the life of the salons, with their attendant aristocrats and dandies, he nevertheless earned an uneasy place in the ranks of the philosophes. In the French Revolution, his name would be invoked to justify democracy, and of all the philosophes, Rousseau would probably have been the least horrified by the early phase of that revolutionary upheaval.

Social Thought

Rousseau saw society as the corrupter of human beings who, left to their own devices, were inherently virtuous and freedom-loving. A wide spectrum of thinkers in the Enlightenment also viewed society if not as corrupting, then at least as needing constant reform. Some enlightened critics were prepared to work with those in power in an effort to bring about concrete social reforms. Other philosophes believed that the key to reform lay not in social and political institutions but in a change in mentality brought about by education and propaganda.

Psychology and Education

Just as Locke's *Two Treatises of Government* was instrumental in shaping the political thought of the Enlightenment, his *Essay Concerning Human Understanding* (1689) provided the theoretical foundations for an unprecedented interest in education. Locke's view that at birth the mind is blank, a clean slate, or *tabula rasa,* held two important implications. First, if human beings were not born with innate ideas, then they were not, as Christianity taught, inherently sinful. Second, a person's environment was the decisive force in shaping that person's character and intelligence. Nine of every ten men, wrote Locke, "are good or evil, useful or not, [because of] their education." Such a theory was eagerly received by the reform-minded philosophes, who preferred attributing wickedness to faulty institutions, improper rearing, and poor education—which could be remedied—rather than to a defective human nature.

"Locke has unfolded to man the nature of human reason," Voltaire wrote in his *Letters.* For the Enlightenment, the proper study of humanity addressed the process by which people can and do know. Locke had said that individuals take the data produced by their senses and reflect on it; in that way they arrive at complex ideas. Education obviously requires, in addition to an environment that promotes learning, the active participation of students. Merely receiving knowledge not tested by their own sense experience is inadequate.

More treatises were written on education during the eighteenth century than in all previous centuries combined. On the Continent, where the clergy controlled many schools and all the universities, the educated laity began to demand state regulation and inspection of educational facilities. This insistence was one practical expression of the growing discontent with the clergy and their independent authority. By the second half of the century, new schools and universities in Prussia, Belgium, Austria, and Russia attempted to teach practical subjects suited to the interests of the laity. Predictably, science was given a special place in these new institutions.

Prussia and Scotland excelled in the field of education, but for very different reasons. In Prussia, Frederick the Great decreed universal public education for boys as part of his effort to surpass the level of technical expertise found in other countries. His educational policy was another example of his using the Enlightenment to increase the power of the central government. In Scotland, the improvements in education were largely sponsored by the established Calvinist church. The heirs of the Protestant Reformation, with its emphasis on the Bible and hence on the printed word, were fully capable of sponsoring progressive educational policies without the help of the Enlightenment.

In the teaching of medicine, the University of Leiden in the Netherlands became the most advanced institution in Europe in the eighteenth century. Indeed, its scientific faculty presented Newtonian physics and the latest chemistry to a generation of doctors and engineers assembled from all over Europe. A new medical school was also founded in Vienna. Many Scottish students, often trained in Leiden, brought their knowledge home to make Edinburgh University a major center for medical students.

Locke's doctrine that knowledge comes primarily through experience found its most extreme expression in the writings of Rousseau on education. In *Émile* (1762), Rousseau argued that individuals learn from nature, from people, or from things. Indeed, Rousseau wanted the early years of a child's education to be centered on developing the senses, not spent chained to a schoolroom desk. Later, attention would be paid to intellectual pursuits, then finally to morality. Rousseau grasped a fundamental principle of modern psychology—the child is not a small adult, and childhood is not merely preparation for adulthood but a particular stage, with its own distinguishing characteristics, in human development. Children, said Rousseau astutely, should be permitted to behave like children.

Rousseau appealed especially to women to protect their children from social convention, that is, to teach their children about life. There were problems with Rousseau's educational system. He would render the family into the major educational force and he wanted its products to be cosmopolitan and enlightened, singularly free from superstition and prejudice. In the process, women (whom Rousseau would confine to the home) would bear the burden of instilling enlightenment, although they had little experience of the world beyond the family.

Rousseau's contradictions sprang in large measure from his desperate search for an alternative to the formal educational systems that existed in his day. In the field of education, the reality of most European schools fell far below the ideal put forward by the philosophes. In 1762, one French author estimated that fewer than one-tenth of all school-age boys in France were receiving a proper education. France, however, was one of the more advanced European countries, and by 1789, probably about half of the men and about 20 percent of the women were literate.

Humanitarianism

Crime and Punishment   No society founded on the principles of the Enlightenment could condone the torture of prisoners and the inhumanity of a corrupt legal system. On that view, all the philosophes were clear, and they had plenty of evidence from their own societies on which to base their condemnation of torture and the inhumanity of the criminal justice system.

If the education of children in the eighteenth century was poor, the treatment of criminals was appalling. Whether an individual was imprisoned for unpaid debts or for banditry or murder, prison conditions differed little. Prisoners were often starved or exposed to disease, or both. In many Continental countries, where torture was still legal, prisoners could be subjected to brutal interrogation or to random punishment. In 1777, English reformer John Howard published a report on the state of prisons in England and Wales: "The want of food is to be found in many country gaols. In about half these, debtors have no bread, although it is granted to the highwayman, the housebreaker, and the murderer; and medical assistance, which is provided for the latter, is withheld from the former." Torture was illegal in England, except in cases of treason, but prison conditions were often as harmful to the physical and mental health of inmates as torture was.

Although there is something particularly reprehensible about the torturer, his skills were consciously applauded in many countries during the eighteenth century. Fittingly, the most powerful critique of the European system of punishment came from Italy, where the Inquisition and its torture chambers had reigned with little opposition for centuries. In Milan during the early 1760s, the Enlightenment had made very gradual inroads, and in a small circle of reformers the practices of the Inquisition and the relationship between church and state in the matter of criminal justice were avidly discussed.

Slaves Processing Sugar in a Colonial Plantation.
This diagram shows slaves running machinery to grind sugar cane into pulp. In the colonies of European countries in the New World and other lands, subjected peoples were used to perform hard labor in the plantations and mines. The immorality of slavery was raised initially by religious thinkers, especially the Quakers, and then taken up by Diderot in his *Encyclopedia*. (*Courtesy of the University of Minnesota Libraries*)

Out of that intellectual ferment came one of the most important books of the Enlightenment, *Of Crime and Punishment* (1764), by the Milanese reformer Cesare Beccaria (1738–1794). For centuries, sin and crime had been wedded in the eyes of the church; the function of the state was to punish crime because it was a manifestation of sin. Beccaria cut through that thicket of moralizing and argued that the church should concern itself with sin; it should abandon its prisons and courts. The state should concern itself with crimes against society, and the purpose of punishment should be to reintegrate the individual into society.

Beccaria also went further and inquired into the causes of crime. Abandoning the concept of sin, Beccaria, rather like Rousseau who saw injustice and corruption in the very fabric of society, regarded private property as the root of social injustice and hence the root of crime. Pointedly he asked: "What are these laws I must respect, that they leave such a huge gap between me and the rich? Who made these laws? Rich and powerful men. . . . Let us break these fatal connections. . . . let us attack injustice at its source."[6]

Beccaria's attackers labeled him a *socialist*—the first time (1765) that term was used—by which they meant that Beccaria paid attention only to people as social creatures and that he wanted a society of free and equal citizens. In contrast, the defenders of the use of torture and capital punishment, and of the necessity of social inequality, argued that Beccaria's teachings would lead to chaos and to the loss of all property rights and legitimate authority. These critics sensed the utopian aspect of Beccaria's thought. His humanitarianism was not directed toward the reform of the criminal justice system alone; he sought to restructure society in such a way as to render crime far less prevalent and, whenever possible, to reeducate its perpetrators.

When Beccaria's book and then the author himself turned up in Paris, the philosophes greeted them with universal acclaim. All the leaders of the period—Voltaire, Rousseau, Diderot, and the atheist d'Holbach—embraced one or another of Beccaria's views. But if the criminal justice system and the schools were subject to scrutiny by enlightened critics, what did the philosophes have to say about slavery, the most pernicious of all Western institutions?

Slavery On both sides of the Atlantic during the eighteenth century, criticism of slavery was growing. At first it came from religious thinkers like the Quakers, whose own religious version of enlightenment predated the European wide phenomenon by several decades. The Quakers were born out of the turmoil of the English Revolution, and their strong adherence to democratic ideas grew out of their conviction that the light of God's truth works in every man and woman. Many philosophes on both sides of the Atlantic knew Quaker thought, and Voltaire, who had mixed feelings about slavery, and Benjamin Franklin, who condemned it, admired the Quakers and their principles.

On the problem of slavery the Enlightenment was strangely ambivalent. In an ideal world—just about all philosophes agreed—slavery would not exist. But such was not the world, and given human wickedness, greed, and lust for power, Voltaire thought that slavery as well as exploitation might be inevitable. "The human race," Voltaire wrote in his *Philosophical Dictionary* (1764), "constituted as it is, cannot subsist unless there be an infinite number of useful individuals possessed of no property at all."[7] Denis Diderot thought that slavery was probably immoral, but given that the French empire subsisted in part on its slaves, their rights could not be discussed, he argued, in a monarchy. Indeed, not until 1794, and only after agonized debate, did the French government, no longer a monarchy, finally abolish slavery.

It must be remembered that Enlightenment political thinkers, among them Locke (who condoned slavery) and Montesquieu (whose ideas were used to condone it), rejected God-given political authority and argued for the rights of property-holders and for social utility as the foundations of good government. Those criteria, property and utility, played right into the hands of the proslavery apologists. They particularly cited Montesquieu, who had said that in tropical countries, where sloth was "natural," slavery might be useful and even necessary to force people to work. Montesquieu was ambivalent about the absolute immorality of slavery, but he had also argued that in despotisms the individual would lose little by willingly choosing enslavement. Proslavery propagandists argued, as well, that since most African tribes were despotic, the slaves in European colonies were in effect better off.

Yet the Enlightenment must also be credited with bringing the problem of slavery into the forefront of public discussion in Europe and the American colonies. The utility argument cut both ways. If the principle held, as so many philosophes argued, that human happiness was the greatest good, how could slavery be justified? In his short novel *Candide,* Voltaire has his main character, Candide, confront the spectacle of a young Negro who has had his leg and arm cut off merely because it is the custom of a country. Candide's philosophical optimism is shattered as he reflects on the human price paid by this slave who harvested the sugar that Europeans enjoyed so abundantly. Throughout the eighteenth century the emphasis placed by the Enlightenment on moral sensibility produced a literature that used shock to emphasize over and over again, and with genuine revulsion, the inhumanity of slavery.

By the second half of the century, strongly worded attacks on slavery were issued by a new generation of philosophes. With Rousseau in the vanguard, they condemned slavery as a violation of the natural rights of man. In a volume issued in 1755, the great *Encyclopedia* of the Enlightenment, edited by Denis Diderot, condemned slavery in no uncertain terms: "There is not a single one of these hapless souls . . . who does not have the right to be declared free . . . since neither his ruler nor his father nor anyone else had the right to dispose of his freedom."[8] That statement made its way into thousands of copies and various editions of an encyclopedia that was probably the most influential publication resulting from the French Enlightenment.

The *Encyclopedia*'s wide circulation (about 25,000 copies were sold before 1789), often despite the vigorous efforts of censors to stop it, probably tipped the scales to put the followers of the Enlightenment in the antislavery camp. But that victory for humanitarian principles was clouded by much ambiguous language, coming straight from the pens of some of Eu-

Mme. Geoffrin's Salon. The High Enlightenment in the 1750s had Paris as its capital. The new thinking concentrated on social inequalities, especially those that stifled talented human beings. The salons of exclusive Parisian society, such as that of Mme. Geoffrin, became the forum for the next generation of philosophers after Voltaire and Diderot. (*Giraudon/Art Resource*)

rope's supposedly most enlightened thinkers, and by downright prejudice against the Negro as a non-European.

Women The men of the Enlightenment also had some ambiguous things to say about women. Not entirely unlike slaves, women had few property rights within marriage, and their physical abuse by husbands was widely regarded as beyond the purview of the law. Women's education was slighted, and social theorists had for centuries regarded them as inferior. The origins of that sexual inequality intrigued the earliest political theorists, Hobbes and Locke. Both saw that neither nature nor Scripture gave the father dominion in the household. As Hobbes said in *Leviathan*, "In the state of nature, if a man and woman contract so, as neither is subject to the command of the other, the children are the mother's."[9] Yet this perception was never taken up by any of the major philosophes, and indeed neither Hobbes nor Locke concerned himself with correcting the legal inferiority of women.

Yet by the middle of the eighteenth century, many French philosophes had begun to think about the condition of women and, in the cases of Voltaire and Diderot, had taken up with women, outside of marriage, who were in several areas their intellectual equals. As a result, Diderot fretted about the poor education accorded to women, but he also distrusted their apparent commitment to the old religiosity. By the 1750s in Paris, rich women had become the organizers of fashionable salons where writers and enlightened reformers gathered for free and open conversation; Diderot attended such a salon. But Baron d'Holbach, who led the most famous gathering of the 1770s, specifically excluded women because he believed that they lowered the tone and seriousness of the discussion. Rousseau, who had little use for Paris and its fashionable salons, also disdained the elegant women of the drawing rooms.

Rousseau's own conception of women specifically excluded them from the social contract, in that he saw nature as having given men dominion over women and children. Outside the family, in civil society, that dominion is never absolute; it rests on the will of the majority (presumably of men, because in *The Social Contract* Rousseau never mentions women as a part of civil society). In *A Discourse on Political Economy* (1755), Rousseau insists that the patriarchal structure of the family is natural; the primary function of the family is to "preserve and increase the patrimony of the father."[10] Yet Rousseau does allot to women the education of children, and at the end of the eighteenth century, many women saw Rousseau as an ally because his views would lead to an improvement in their domestic status and conceivably in their educational benefits.

With his characteristic skepticism, Hume saw all this ambiguity about women as resulting from men's desire to preserve their power and patrimony. Since men had no guarantees that the children their wives bore were in fact fathered by them, the only recourse was to try to repress women sexually. According to Hume the necessity "to impose a due restraint on the female sex"[11] led to sexual inequality. But Hume was never troubled sufficiently by that inequality to discuss the point in any detail. And Kant, who defined the Enlightenment so eloquently, argued that the differences between men and women were simply natural. In *Observations on the Feeling of the Beautiful and Sublime* (1764), Kant argued that "women have a strong inborn feeling for all that is beautiful, elegant, and decorated . . . they love pleasantry and can be entertained by trivialities." Predictably, Kant concluded that "laborious learning or painful pondering, even if a woman should greatly succeed to it, destroys the merits that are proper to her sex." In that treatise, Kant came dangerously close to denying women any need to know the new science or to speculate: "her philosophy is not to reason, but to sense."[12] This major philosophe almost denied women a right to enlightenment.

Only late in the century, after the French Revolution had begun, did any thinker representative of the Enlightenment challenge Rousseau's views on women. Educated in enlightened circles and familiar with radical philosophes like the American revolutionary Thomas Paine, the English

Antoine Laurent Lavoisier and His Wife by Jacques Louis David (1748–1825). Although Rousseau, Hume, and Kant had excluded women from the realm of politics, later Enlightenment philosophers began to rethink traditional views of women's roles. David portrays Marie Anne Lavoisier both as her husband's muse and intellectual helpmate—she had illustrated her husband's treatise on chemistry. Seated writing a manuscript, Lavoisier is shown with instruments relating to his experiments with gunpowder and oxygen. (*The Metropolitan Museum of Art, Purchase, Mr. and Mrs. Charles Wrightsman Gift, 1977. 1977.10*)

feminist Mary Wollstonecraft (1759–1797) extended the principles of the Enlightenment to the position and status of women. With devastating logic, her *Vindication of the Rights of Woman* (1792) called for "a revolution in female manners—time to restore to them their lost dignity—and make them, as part of the human species, labor by reforming themselves, to reform the world." She mocked the notion of sexual virtues, such as the beauty and modesty of which Kant had written. She believed, somewhat in the manner of Rousseau, only without his one-sex conclusions, that society had corrupted women: "from the tyranny of man the greater part of female follies proceed." Wollstonecraft viewed this corruption as analogous to the evils stemming from property rights and the vast inequalities in privilege and opportunity between the rich and the poor. True to Enlightenment ideals, Wollstonecraft did not attack property rights as such, but she did urge a significant reduction in the gap between the wealthy and the poor. Again in keeping with enlightened prescriptions, she urged that equal public education be made available to both men and women. For Wollstonecraft, feminism brought with it a commitment to universal human values, to excellence in learning—which she had never had the opportunity to pursue—and to "the power of generalizing ideas, of drawing comprehensive conclusions from individual observations."[13] Although she explicitly wrote for middle- and upper-class women and her work had little impact during her lifetime, Wollstonecraft's *Vindication* became a text on which nineteenth-century reformers and socialists could and did build.

Economic Thought

The Enlightenment's emphasis on property as the foundation for individual rights and its search for uniform laws inspired by Newton's scientific achievement led to the development of the science of economics. Appropriately, that intellectual achievement occurred in the most advanced capitalistic nation in Europe, Great Britain. Not only were the British in the vanguard of capitalist expansion; by the third quarter of the eighteenth century, that expansion had brought on the start of the Industrial Revolution. Its new factories and markets for the manufacture and distribution of goods provided a natural laboratory where theorists, schooled in the Enlightenment's insistence on observation and experimentation, could observe the ebb and flow of capitalist production and distribution. In contrast to its harsh criticisms leveled against existing institutions and old elites, the Enlightenment on the whole approved of the independent businessman—the entrepreneur. And there was no one more approving than

Adam Smith (1732–1790), whose *Wealth of Nations* (1776) became a kind of bible for those who regarded capitalist activity as uniformly worthwhile, never to be inhibited by outside regulation.

Throughout the seventeenth century in England there had been a long tradition of economic thought. The resulting ideology stressed independent initiative and the freedom of market forces to determine the value of money and the goods it can buy. By 1700, English economic thought was already well ahead of what could be found on the Continent, with the exception of some Dutch writings. That sophistication undoubtedly reflected the complexity of market life in cities like London and Amsterdam.

One important element in seventeenth-century economic thought, as well as in the most advanced thinking on ethics, was the role of self-interest. Far from being viewed as crude or socially dangerous, it was seen as a good thing, to be accepted and even encouraged. In the mid-seventeenth century, Hobbes took the view that self-interest lay at the root of political action, and by the end of the century, Locke argued that government, rather than primarily restraining the extremes of human greed and the search for power, should first reflect the interests of its citizens. By the middle of the eighteenth century, enlightened theorists all over Europe—especially in England, Scotland, and France—had decided that self-interest was the foundation of all human actions and that at every turn government should assist people in expressing their interests and thus in finding true happiness.

Of course in the area of economic life, government had for centuries regulated most aspects of the market. The classic economic theory behind such regulation was mercantilism. Mercantilists believed that a constant shortage of riches—bullion, goods, whatever—existed, and that governments must so direct economic activity in their states as to compete successfully with other nations for a share of the world's scarce resources. There was also another assumption implicit in mercantilist theory: that money has a "real" value, which governments must protect. Its value is not to be determined solely by market forces.

It required enormous faith in the inherent usefulness of self-interest to assert that government

Map 18.2 European Expansion, 1715 ▶

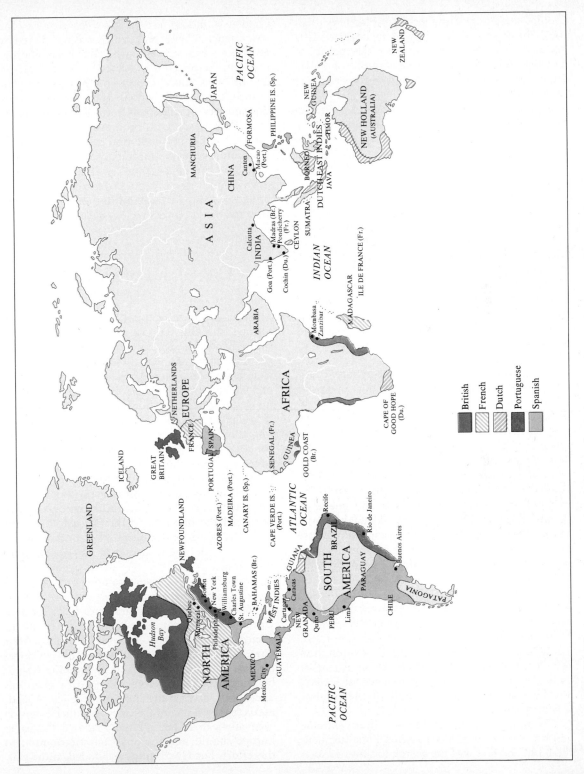

PACIFIC OCEAN

NEW ZEALAND

JAPAN

MANCHURIA

CHINA

FORMOSA

Canton

Macao (Port.)

PHILIPPINE IS. (Sp.)

NEW GUINEA

NEW HOLLAND (AUSTRALIA)

TIMOR

BORNEO

DUTCH EAST INDIES

SUMATRA

JAVA

ASIA

Calcutta

INDIA

Madras (Br.)

Pondicherry (Fr.)

CEYLON

Goa (Port.)

Cochin (Du.)

INDIAN OCEAN

ILE DE FRANCE (Fr.)

MADAGASCAR

Mombasa

Zanzibar

ARABIA

AFRICA

NETHERLANDS

EUROPE

FRANCE

SPAIN

GREAT BRITAIN

ICELAND

PORTUGAL

SENEGAL (Fr.)

GUINEA

GOLD COAST (Br.)

CAPE OF GOOD HOPE (Du.)

British

French

Dutch

Portuguese

Spanish

GREENLAND

NEWFOUNDLAND

AZORES (Port.)

MADEIRA (Port.)

CANARY IS. (Sp.)

CAPE VERDE IS. (Port.)

ATLANTIC OCEAN

Recife

BRAZIL

Rio de Janeiro

SOUTH AMERICA

PARAGUAY

Buenos Aires

PATAGONIA

Hudson Bay

NORTH AMERICA

Quebec

Montreal

Boston

New York

Philadelphia

Williamsburg

Charles Town

St. Augustine

BAHAMAS (Br.)

WEST INDIES

GUIANA

Cartagena

Caracas

NEW GRANADA

Quito

PERU

Lima

CHILE

GUATEMALA

MEXICO

Mexico City

PACIFIC OCEAN

should cease regulating economic activity, that the market should be allowed to be free. That doctrine of *laissez faire*—to leave the market to its own devices—was the centerpiece of Adam Smith's massive economic study on the origins of the wealth of nations.

As a professor in Glasgow, Scotland, Smith actually went out and observed factories at work; he was one of the first theorists to see the importance of the division of labor in making possible the manufacture of more and cheaper consumer goods. Smith viewed labor as the critical factor in a capitalist economy: the value of money, or of an individual for that matter, rested on the ability to buy labor or the by-products of labor, namely goods and services. According to *The Wealth of Nations*, "labor is the real measure of the exchangeable value of all commodities."[14] The value of labor is in turn determined by market forces, by supply and demand. Before the invention of money or capital, labor belonged to the laborer, but in the money and market society that had evolved since the Middle Ages, labor belonged to the highest bidder.

Smith was not distressed by the apparent randomness of market forces. Beneath this superficial chaos he saw order—the same order he saw in physical nature through his understanding of the new science. He used the metaphor of "the invisible hand" to explain the source of this order; by that he probably meant Newton's regulatory God, made very distant by Smith, who was a deist. That hand would invisibly reconcile self-interest to the common or public interest. With the image of the invisible hand, Smith expressed his faith in the rationality of commercial society and laid the first principle for the modern science of capitalist economics. He did not mean to license the oppression of the poor and the laborer. Statements in *The Wealth of Nations* such as: "Landlords, like all other men, love to reap where they never sowed," or "Whenever there is great property, there is great inequality"[15] reveal Smith to be a moralist. Yet he knew of no means to stop the exploitation of labor. He believed that its purchase at market value ensured the working of commercial society, and he assumed that the supply of cheap labor was inexhaustible.

The thought of Adam Smith includes extreme versions of two tendencies within Enlightenment thought. The first was the search for laws of society that would imitate the laws postulated by the new science. The second, which was not shared by all philosophes, was an unshakable belief in progress: "In the progress of society . . . each individual becomes more expert in his own peculiar branch, more work is done upon the whole, and the quantity of science is considerably increased by it."[16] Knowledge is progressive, and by implication, the human condition also yields to constant improvement. Smith ignored the appallingly low life-expectancy rates in the new factory towns, and in the process bequeathed a vision of progress wedded to capitalism that remains powerful in some quarters to this day.

The High Enlightenment

More than any other political system in western Europe, the Old Regime in France was directly threatened by the doctrines and reforming impulse of the Enlightenment. The Roman Catholic church was deeply entrenched in every aspect of life—landownership, control over universities and presses, and access to both the court and, through the pulpit, the people. For decades the church had brought its influence to bear against the philosophes, yet by 1750 the Enlightenment had penetrated learned circles and academies in Paris and the provinces. After 1750, censorship of the press was relaxed by a new censor deeply influenced by Enlightenment ideals. In fact, censorship had produced the opposite of the desired effect: the more irreligious and atheistic the book or manuscript was, the more attractive and sought-after it became.

By the 1740s, the fashion among proponents of the Enlightenment was to seek an encyclopedic format for presenting their ideas. This form of writing was the natural by-product of the Enlightenment's desire to encompass all learning. After Bayle's *Dictionary*, the first successful encyclopedia was published in England by Ephraim Chambers in 1728, and before too long, a plan was under way for its translation into French. A leading Freemason in France, the Chevalier Ramsay, even advocated that all the Masonic lodges in Europe should make a financial contribution to this effort, but few, if any, responded to the call.

Four aggressive Parisian publishers took up the task of producing the encyclopedia. One of them had had some shady dealings in clandestine literature that had acquainted him with the more irreligious and daring philosophes in Paris, which is how he knew the young Denis Diderot (1713–1784), who had spent six months in jail for his philosophical and libertine writings. Out of that consortium of publishers and philosophes came the most important book of the Enlightenment, Diderot's *Encyclopedia*. Published in 1751 and in succeeding years and editions, the *Encyclopedia* initiated a new stage in the history of Enlightenment publishing. In the process, it brought to the forefront pantheistic and materialistic ideas that, until that time, only the most radical freethinkers in England and the Netherlands had openly written about. The new era thus ushered in, called the High Enlightenment, was characterized by a violent attack on the church's privileges and the very foundations of Christian belief. From the 1750s to the 1780s, Paris became the capital of the Enlightenment. The philosophes were no longer a persecuted minority. Instead, they became cultural heroes. The *Encyclopedia* had to be read by anyone claiming to be educated.

In his preface to the *Encyclopedia*, Diderot's collaborator, Jean d'Alembert (c. 1717–1783), summed up the principles on which it had been compiled. In effect, he wrote a powerful summation of the Enlightenment's highest ideals. He also extolled Newton's science and gave a short description of its universal laws. The progress of geometry and mechanics in combination, d'Alembert wrote in his preface, "may be considered the most incontestable monument of the success to which the human mind can rise by its efforts."[17] In turn, he urged that revealed religion should be reduced to a few precepts to be practiced; religion should, he implied, be made scientific and rational. The *Encyclopedia* itself was self-consciously modeled on Bacon's admonition that the scientist should first of all be a collector of facts; in addition, it gave dozens of examples of useful new mechanical devices.

D'Alembert's preface also praised the psychology of Locke: all that is known, is known through the senses. He added that all learning should be catalogued and made easily and readily available, that the printing press should serve the needs of enlightenment, and that literary societies should be set up that would encourage men of talent. D'Alembert added that "they should banish all inequalities that might exclude or discourage men who are endowed with talents that will enlighten others."[18]

During the High Enlightenment, reformers dwelled increasingly on the Old Regime's inequalities, which seemed to stifle men of talent. The aristocracy and the clergy were not always talented and seldom were they agitators for enlightenment and reform. Their privileges seemed increasingly less rational. By the 1780s, Paris had spawned a new generation of philosophes for whom Voltaire, Diderot, and Rousseau were aged or dead heroes. But these young authors found the life of the propagandist to be poor and solitary, and they looked at society's ills as victims rather than as reformers. They gained firsthand knowledge of the injustices catalogued so brilliantly by Rousseau in *The Social Contract*.

The High Enlightenment's systematic, sustained, and occasionally violent attacks on the clergy and the irrationality of privilege link that movement with the French Revolution. The link did not lie in the comfortable heresies of the great philosophes, ensconced as they were in the fashionable Parisian salons. Rather, it lay in the way those heresies were interpreted by a new generation of reformers, Marat and Robespierre among them, who in the early days of the Revolution used the Enlightenment as a mirror against which they reflected the evils of the old order.

European Political and Diplomatic Developments

Warfare

The dreams of the philosophes, articulated in almost every area of human experience, seemed unable to forestall troublesome developments in power politics, war, and diplomacy. The century was dominated by two areas of extreme conflict: Anglo-French rivalry over control of territory in the New World and hegemony in northern Europe; and intense rivalry between Austria and Prussia over control of central Europe. These major powers, with their imperialistic ambitions, were led by cadres of aristocratic ministers or generals; the Enlightenment did little to displace the war-making role that had belonged to the aristocracy since the Middle Ages.

Yet even in international affairs there was a growing realization, not unrelated to the propaganda of the philosophes, that extreme power held by one state would threaten the order and stability of the whole of Europe. By the early eighteenth century, every European state identified France, by virtue of its sheer wealth and size, as the major threat of European stability.

By this time, France and England were the great rivals in the New World, although colonization had been well under way since the early sixteenth century. Spain had been the first sovereign state to establish an empire in America; located principally in South America and Central America, this empire was based on mining, trade, and slaves. The English and Dutch had followed, first as settlers and then also as slave traders, but their colonies lay to the north—in Virginia, New Amsterdam (later to become New York), and New England. Further north, the French explored and exploited Canada and the region now known as the midwestern United States. By the early eighteenth century, the Dutch and the Spanish had largely dropped out of the race for colonies in North America, leaving the field to the French and the English.

By the middle of the eighteenth century, the rivalry of these two powers for territory in the New World infected European rivalry in the Old World. Earlier the British had sought to contain the French colossus and to ensure their historic trading interests in the Low Countries and the Rhineland by allying with the Dutch Republic and the Austrians, who controlled what is today called Belgium. This alliance of the Maritime Powers (Britain and the Netherlands) with Austria provided the balance of power against France for the entire first half of the eighteenth century.

The English obsession with the security of the Low Countries and with the protection of the market there for English grain and wool led Britain to intervene in Dutch internal affairs. The French were given to invading the Netherlands; they actually did so during the War of the Spanish Succession (1701–1713) and during the War of the Austrian Succession (1740–1748). As a result of the constant French threats, England sought to

secure a government in The Hague that would be favorable to British interests, and in 1747 assisted in the restoration of the Dutch stadtholderate to William IV for that purpose. From that time on, the central government in the Netherlands remained cordial to British interests, although Dutch merchants were frequently hostile to that relationship.

The other major European rivalries broke out into hostilities in the 1740s. Wars between Prussia and Austria and between Austria and France were fought because these major powers wanted to secure their areas of domination in western and central Europe. The wars signaled the rise of Prussia to the status of a major power but left the control of northern Europe open to negotiation. If any power could be described as the loser in that decade, it was the French. The wars exposed weaknesses in the French military system, without resolving the larger question of hegemony in Europe and the New World.

The wars also had an unexpected result. In the 1740s it became clear to the English and their Austrian allies that the Dutch did not possess the will or the resources to guard their southern borders adequately. No longer viewed as the centerpiece in the anti-French alliance, the Dutch Republic appeared to be best suited to a weak and ineffectual neutrality.

With the weakening of this tie with the Netherlands, Austria grew discontented with its old allies, while realizing that it was mortally threatened by the growing power of Prussia. In 1740, Frederick the Great of Prussia launched an aggressive foreign policy against neighboring states—the Austrian state of Silesia, in particular. The forces of the new Austrian queen, Maria Theresa, were powerless to resist this kind of military onslaught. In two years, Prussia had acquired what was probably the largest territory captured by any Continental European state in that era. Silesia augmented the Prussian population by 50 percent, and Frederick also acquired a relatively advanced textile manufacturing area. The Austrians never forgave his transgression.

In 1756, Maria Theresa formed an alliance with France against Prussia; the ensuing Seven Years' War (1756–1763) involved every major

Map 18.3 Europe, 1789 ▶

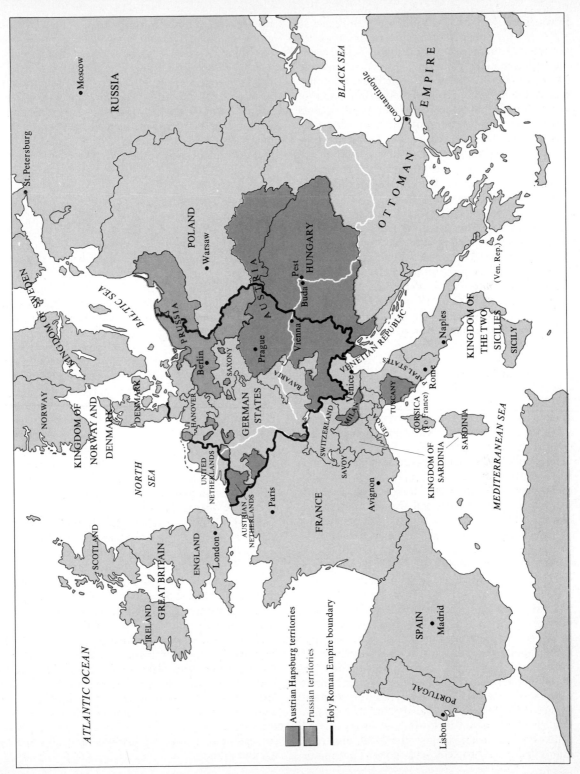

MOSCOW •

RUSSIA

St. Petersburg •

BLACK SEA

CONSTANTINOPLE •

OTTOMAN EMPIRE

POLAND

Warsaw •

KINGDOM OF SWEDEN

BALTIC SEA

PRUSSIA

HUNGARY

AUSTRIA

Pest •
Buda •

Vienna •

Prague •

Berlin •

SAXONY

GERMAN STATES

BAVARIA

VENETIAN REPUBLIC

(Ven. Rep.)

NAPLES •

KINGDOM OF THE TWO SICILIES

SICILY

NORWAY

KINGDOM OF NORWAY AND DENMARK

DENMARK

HANOVER

NORTH SEA

UNITED NETHERLANDS

AUSTRIAN NETHERLANDS

Paris •

FRANCE

Avignon •

SWITZERLAND

SAVOY

MILAN

GENOA

CORSICA
(To France)

TUSCANY

Venice •

PAPAL STATES

Rome •

SARDINIA

KINGDOM OF SARDINIA

MEDITERRANEAN SEA

SCOTLAND

IRELAND

GREAT BRITAIN

ENGLAND

London •

ATLANTIC OCEAN

SPAIN

Madrid •

PORTUGAL

Lisbon •

Austrian Hapsburg territories
Prussian territories
Holy Roman Empire boundary

European power. Austria's alliance with France in 1756, which ended the historic rivalry between France and the house of Hapsburg, is known as the "diplomatic revolution." The Austrians had grown to fear Prussia in the north more than they feared the French. From the Austrian point of view, Prussia had stolen Silesia in 1740, and its restoration was more important than preserving historic rivalries with France. On the French side, King Louis XV longed for an alliance with a Roman Catholic power and for peace in Europe so that France would be better able to wage war against Britain in the New World.

For their part, the British had long since grown disaffected with the Austrians, and they sought and won a new ally in Frederick the Great. He stood at the head of a new state that was highly belligerent yet insecure, for all the European powers had reasons to want to keep Prussia weak and small. The Seven Years' War—which seesawed back and forth, with French, Austrian, and Russian forces ranged against Frederick's Prussians—changed things little in Europe, but it did reveal the extraordinary power of the Prussian war machine. Prussia joined the ranks of the Great Powers.

Hostilities in North America tipped the balance of power there in favor of the English. From 1754 to 1763, the French and the English fought over their claims in the New World. England's victory in this conflict—known in American history as the French and Indian War—led ultimately to the American Revolution. England secured its claim to control the colonies of the eastern seaboard, a market that would enrich its industrialists of the next generation enormously—although, from the colonists' view, unjustly.

The Dutch Revolution of 1747–48—the only one to occur in western Europe outside of a city-state or colony in the period from 1689 to 1787—provided the only indication that the Great Powers or the merchant capitalists had anything to fear from their home populations (or from their slave populations), or that the ideas advanced by the philosophes might be put into practice. Inspired by the return of the House of Orange, unrest began in Amsterdam in 1747, when minor philosophes, Freemasons, journalists, and devotees of English ideas shared in leading an artisan-based democratic uprising against the local oligarchy that failed utterly to achieve its goals. That minor ripple went unnoticed by the many kings, aristocrats, and oligarchs who ruled so comfortably elsewhere. A generation later, their complacency would wither as democratic revolutions swept first through the American colonies and then through every western European state on the Continent. The wars in the mid-1700s, though destructive in many ways, seemed to confirm the internal security and stability of the ruling elites that controlled their respective states.

Enlightened Despotism

Although some of the enlightened prescriptions for the operation of modern society, such as laissez faire, remain current, one ideal commonly discussed and occasionally advocated by the philosophes has long since fallen by the wayside. It was extinguished in large measure by the democratic revolutions of the late eighteenth century.

Enlightened despotism, an apparent contradiction in terms, was used as a phrase by the French philosophe Diderot as early as the 1760s. Wherever this phrase is used by the philosophes, it refers to an ideal shared by many of them: the strong monarch who would implement rational reforms, who would remove obstacles to freedom and allow the laws of nature to work, particularly in trade, commerce, and book censorship. When historians use the term *enlightened despotism,* they generally are describing the reigns of specific European monarchs and their ministers—Frederick the Great in Prussia; Catherine the Great in Russia; Charles III of Spain; Maria Theresa and, to a greater extent, her son Joseph II in Austria; and Louis XV of France.

These eighteenth-century monarchs instituted specific reforms in education, trade, and commerce, and against the clergy. This type of enlightened government must be understood in context: these countries developed late relative to the older states of Europe. Prussia, Austria, and Russia had to move very quickly if they were to catch up to the degree of centralization achieved in England and France. And when monarchies in France and Spain also occasionally adopted techniques associated with enlightened despotism, they generally did so to compete against a more advanced rival—for example, France against England and Spain against France.

Austria   In the course of the eighteenth century, Austria became a major centralized state as a result of the reforms of Charles VI and his successors (see Chapter 16). Although Catholic and devout at home, Charles allied abroad with Protestant Europe against France. In the newly acquired Austrian Netherlands, he supported the progressive and reforming elements in the nobility that opposed the old aristocracy and clergy.

His daughter Maria Theresa (1740–1780) continued this pattern, and the Austrian administration became one of the most innovative and progressive on the Continent. Many of its leading ministers, like the Comte du Cobenzl in the Netherlands or Gerard van Swieten, Joseph II's great reforming minister, were Freemasons. This movement often attracted progressive Catholics (as well as Protestants and freethinkers) who despised what they regarded as the medieval outlook of the traditional clergy.

Dynastic consolidation and warfare did contribute decisively to the creation of the Austrian state. But in the eighteenth century, the intellectual and cultural forces of the Enlightenment enabled the state to establish an efficient system of government and a European breadth of vision. With these attributes, Austria came to rival (and in Spain's case to surpass) the older, more established states in Europe. Frustrated in their German territories, the Austrian Hapsburgs concentrated their attention increasingly on their eastern states. Vienna gave them a natural power base, while Catholic religiosity gradually united the ruling elites in Bohemia and Hungary with their Hapsburg kings. Hapsburg power created a dynastic state in Austria, yet all efforts to consolidate the western Empire and to establish effective imperial rule met with failure. The unification of Germany would proceed very slowly and come from somewhat unexpected quarters.

Prussia   Under the most famous and enlightened Hohenzollern of the eighteenth century, Prussian absolutism (see Chapter 16) acquired some unique and resilient features. Frederick II, the Great (1740–1786), pursued a policy of religious toleration and, in so doing, attracted French Protestant refugees, who had manufacturing and commercial skills. Intellectual dissidents, such as Voltaire, were also attracted to Prussia. Voltaire eventually went home disillusioned with this new Prussian

"enlightened despotism," but not before Frederick had used him and in the process acquired a reputation for learning. By inviting various refugees from French clerical oppression, Frederick gave Berlin a minor reputation as a center for Enlightenment culture. But along with Frederick's courtship of the French philosophes with their enlightened ideals, there remained the reality of Prussian militarism and the servitude of its peasants.

Yet the Hohenzollern dynasty succeeded in creating a viable state built by the labor of its serfs and the power of its Junker-controlled army. This state managed to survive as a monarchy until World War I. By the middle of the eighteenth century, this small nation of no more than 2.5 million inhabitants exercised inordinate influence in European affairs because of its military prowess.

Prussian absolutism rested on the army and the Junker class, and its economy was state directed and financed. Its court expenses were held to a minimum—most state expenditures went into maintaining an army of 200,000 troops—the largest in relation to population for all Europe.

Russia   Russia during the eighteenth century made significant strides, under various monarchs, toward joining the European state system. During the reign of Peter the Great (1682–1725), the Russians established strong diplomatic ties in almost every European capital. In addition, the Russian metal industry became vital to European development. The English, who lacked the forest lands and wood necessary to fire smelting furnaces, grew dependent on Russian-produced iron.

Catherine the Great (1762–1796) consciously pursued policies intended to reflect her understanding of the Enlightenment. These presented contradictions. She entered into respectful correspondence with philosophes, but at the same time extended serfdom to the entire Ukraine. She promulgated a new, more secular educational system and sought at every turn to improve Russian industry, but her policies rested on the aggrandizement of the agriculturally based aristocracy. The Charter of Nobility in 1785 forever guaranteed the aristocracy's right to hold the peasants in servitude. The Enlightenment, as interpreted by this shrewd monarch, completed the tendency to monarchical absolutism that had been well under way since the sixteenth century.

The Effects of Enlightened Despotism

Enlightened despotism was, in reality, the use of Enlightenment principles by enlightened monarchs to enhance the central government's power and thereby their own. These eighteenth-century monarchs knew, in ways their predecessors had not, that knowledge is power; they saw that application of learned theories to policy can produce useful results.

But did these enlightened despots try to create more humanitarian societies in which individual freedom flourished on all levels? In this area, enlightened despotism must be pronounced a shallow deployment of Enlightenment ideals. For example, Frederick the Great decreed the abolition of serfdom in Prussia, but had no means to force the aristocracy to conform because he desperately needed their support. In the 1780s, Joseph II instituted liberalized publishing laws in Austria, until artisans began reading pamphlets about the French Revolution. The state quickly retreated and reimposed censorship. In the 1750s, Frederick the Great also had loosened the censorship laws, and writers were free to attack traditional religion, but they never were allowed to criticize the army, the key to Frederick's aggressive foreign policy. Catherine the Great gave Diderot a pension, but she would hear of nothing that compromised her political power, and her ministers were expected to give her unquestioning service.

Finally, if the Enlightenment means the endorsement of reason over force, and peace and cosmopolitan unity over ruthless competition, then the foreign policies of these enlightened despots were uniformly despotic. The evidence lies in a long series of aggressions, including Frederick's invasion of Silesia in 1740, Austria's secret betrayal of its alliance with the English and Dutch and the ensuing Seven Years' War, and Austria's attempt in the 1770s to claim Bavaria. In short, the Enlightenment provided a theory around which central and eastern European states that were only recently unified could organize their policies. The theory also justified centralization over the power of local elites grown comfortable through centuries of unopposed authority. There were no major philosophes who did not grow disillusioned with enlightened monarchs on the rare occasions when their actions could be observed at close range. The Enlightenment did provide new principles for the organization of centralized monarchical power, but centralization with economic rationalization and management did not make their practitioners or beneficiaries any more enlightened. Enlightened despotism was extinguished largely by the democratic revolutions of the late eighteenth century.

The American Revolution

England's victory over France in the French and Indian War (1754–1763) set in motion a train of events that culminated in the American Revolution. The war drained the British treasury, and now Britain had the additional expense of paying for troops to guard the new North American territories that it had gained in the war. As strapped British taxpayers could not shoulder the whole burden, the members of Parliament thought it quite reasonable that American colonists help pay the bill; they reasoned that Britain had protected the colonists from the French and was still protecting them in their conflicts with Indians. New colonial taxes and import duties were thus imposed. Particularly galling to the colonists were the Stamp Act (which placed a tax on newspapers, playing cards, liquor licenses, and legal documents) and the Quartering Act (which required colonists to provide living quarters and supplies to English troops stationed in America).

Vigorous colonial protest compelled the British Parliament to repeal the Stamp Act, but new taxes were imposed that raised the price of many everyday articles, including tea. The stationing of British troops in Boston, the center of rebelliousness, worsened tensions. In March 1770, a crisis ensued after a squad of British soldiers fired into a crowd of Bostonians who had been taunting them and pelting them with rocks and snowballs. Five Bostonians died, and six were wounded. A greater crisis occurred in 1773, when Parliament granted the East India Company exclusive rights to sell tea in America. The colonists regarded this as yet another example of British tyranny. When a crowd of Bostonians dressed as Indians climbed aboard East Indian ships and dumped about 90,000

The Signing of the Declaration of Independence, July 4, 1776 (detail) by John Trumbull. The success of the American Revolution was hailed as a victory of liberty over tyranny. Jefferson and Franklin were intimately familiar with the thinking of the Enlightenment and stressed a confidence in reason, freedom of religion and thought, and the existence of natural rights. (*Copyright Yale University Art Gallery*)

pounds of tea overboard, the British responded with a series of repressive measures, including suppressing self-government in Massachusetts and closing the port of Boston.

The quarrel turned to bloodshed in April and June 1775. On July 4, 1776, delegates from the various colonies adopted the Declaration of Independence, written mainly by Thomas Jefferson. Applying Locke's theory of natural rights, this document declared that government derives its power from the consent of the governed, that it is the duty of a government to protect the rights of its citizens, and that people have the right to "alter or abolish" a government that deprives them of their "unalienable rights."

Why were the American colonists so ready to revolt? For one thing, they had brought with them a highly idealized understanding of English liberties; long before 1776, they had extended representative institutions to include small property owners who probably could not have voted in England. The colonists had come to expect representative government, trial by jury, and protection from unlawful imprisonment. Each of the thirteen colonies had an elected assembly that acted like a miniature parliament; in these assemblies, Americans gained political experience and quickly learned to be self-governing.

Familiarity with the thought of the Enlightenment and the republican writers of the English Revolution also contributed to the Americans' awareness of liberty. The ideas of the philosophes traversed the Atlantic and influenced educated Americans, particularly Thomas Jefferson and Benjamin Franklin. Like the philosophes, American thinkers expressed a growing confidence in reason, valued freedom of religion and of thought, and championed the principle of natural rights.

Another source of hostility toward established authority among the American colonists was their religious traditions, particularly that of the Puritans, who believed that the Bible was infallible and its teachings a higher law than the law of the state. Like their counterparts in England, American Puritans challenged political and religious authorities who, in their view, contravened God's law. Thus, Puritans acquired two habits that were crucial to the development of political liberty—dissent and resistance. When transferred to the realm of politics, these Puritan tendencies led Americans to resist authority that they considered unjust.

American victory came in 1783 as a result of several factors. George Washington proved a superior leader, able to organize and retain the loyalty of his troops. France, seeking to avenge its defeat in the Seven Years' War, helped the Americans with money and provisions and then in 1778 entered the conflict. Britain had difficulty shipping supplies across three thousand miles of ocean, was fighting the French in the West Indies and elsewhere at the same time, and ultimately lacked commitment to the struggle.

Reformers in other lands quickly interpreted the American victory as a successful struggle of liberty against tyranny. During the Revolution the various states drew up constitutions based on the principle of popular sovereignty and included bills of rights that protected individual liberty. They also managed, somewhat reluctantly, to forge a nation. Rejecting both monarchy and hereditary aristocracy, the Constitution of the United States created a republic in which power derived from the people. A system of separation of powers and checks and balances set safeguards against the abuse of power, and the Bill of Rights provided

for protection of individual rights. To be sure, the ideals of liberty and equality were not extended to all people—slaves knew nothing of the freedom that white Americans cherished, and women were denied the vote and equal opportunity. But to reform-minded Europeans, it seemed that Americans were fulfilling the promise of the Enlightenment; they were creating a freer and better society.

The Enlightenment and the Modern World

Enlightenment thought was the culmination of a trend instituted by Renaissance artists and humanists who attacked medieval otherworldliness and gave value to individual achievement and the worldly life. It was a direct outgrowth of the Scientific Revolution, which provided a new method of inquiry and verification and demonstrated the power and self-sufficiency of the human intellect. If nature were autonomous—that is, if it operated according to natural laws that did not require divine intervention—then the human intellect could also be autonomous. Through its own powers, it could uncover those general principles that operate in the social world as well as in nature.

The philosophes sought to analyze nature, government, religion, law, economics, and education through reason alone, without any reference to Christian teachings, and they rejected completely the claims of clerics to a special wisdom. The philosophes broke decisively with the medieval view that the individual is naturally depraved, that heaven is the true end of life, and that human values and norms derive from a higher reality and are made known through revelation. Instead, they upheld the potential goodness of the individual, regarded the good life on earth as the true end of life, and insisted that individuals could improve themselves and their society solely by the light of reason.

In addition, the political philosophies of Locke, Montesquieu, and Rousseau were based on an entirely new (and modern) concept of the relation-

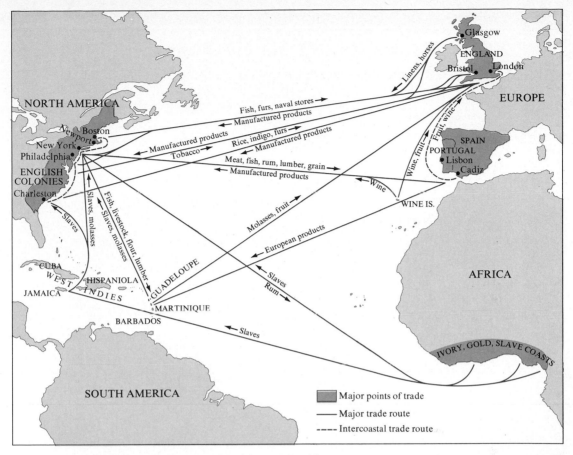

Map 18.4 Trade Routes Between the Old and New Worlds

ship between the state and the individual: states should exist not simply to accumulate power unto themselves but also to enhance human happiness. From that perspective, monarchy and even oligarchy not based upon merit began to seem increasingly less useful. And if happiness is a goal, then it must be assumed that some sort of progress is possible in history.

The French leaders of the late Enlightenment, in fact, possessed a wholehearted belief in the infinite possibility of human progress. If human knowledge is ever-increasing and dependent only on the ability to sense and experience the world, then surely, they believed, the human condition can constantly improve. Western thought has never entirely relinquished this brave dream.

The philosophes wanted a freer, more humane, and more rational society, but they feared the people and their potential for revolutionary action. As an alternative to revolution, most philosophes offered science as the universal improver of the human condition. Faith in reform without the necessity of revolution proved to be a doctrine for the elite of the salons. In that sense the French Revolution can be said to have repudiated the essential moderation of philosophes like Voltaire, d'Alembert, and Kant. Yet the Enlightenment established a vision of humanity so independent of Christianity and so focused on the needs and abuses of present society that no established institution, once grown corrupt and ineffectual, could long withstand its penetrating critique. To

Chronology 18.1 The Enlightenment

1685	Revocation of the Edict of Nantes; persecution of Protestants in France
1687	Publication of Newton's *Principia*
1688–89	Revolution in England; weakening of the clergy's power and loosening of censorship
1690	Publication of Locke's *Two Treatises of Government*
1717	Founding of the Grand Lodge, London; the beginning of organized Freemasonry
1733	Voltaire publishes *Letters Concerning the English Nation*
1740	Frederick the Great invades Silesia; the War of Austrian Succession ensues
1748	Hume publishes *An Enquiry Concerning Human Understanding;* Montesquieu publishes *The Spirit of the Laws*
1751	Publication of Diderot's *Encyclopedia* in Paris
1762	Rousseau publishes *Émile*
1775	The American Revolution
1776	Adam Smith publishes *Wealth of Nations*
1785	The Russian Charter of Nobility; the servitude of the peasants is guaranteed
1787	The Dutch Revolution begins
1789	The French Revolution

that extent the writings of the philosophes point toward the democratic revolutions of the late eighteenth century. To a lesser extent the writers of the Enlightenment also point toward ideals that remain strong in most democratic Western societies: religious toleration, a distain for prejudice and superstition, a fear of unchecked political authority, and, of course, a belief in the power of the human mind to recognize the irrational and to attempt to correct it.

Notes

1. "An Answer to the Question: 'What Is Enlightenment?' " in Hans Reiss, ed., *Kant's Political Writings* (Cambridge, England: Cambridge University Press, 1970), pp. 54–60.

2. Pierre Bayle, *Historical and Critical Dictionary*, Richard H. Popkin, ed. (New York: Bobbs-Merrill, 1965), p. 195.

3. Voltaire, *Philosophical Letters* (New York: Bobbs-Merrill, 1961), p. 22.

4. Thomas Hobbes, *Leviathan*, C. B. Macpherson, ed. (Harmondsworth, England: Penguin, 1977), p. 189.

5. Jean Jacques Rousseau, *The Social Contract and Discourses* (New York: Dutton, 1950), pp. 3, 9.

6. Quoted in Franco Venturi, *Utopia and Reform in the Enlightenment* (Cambridge, England: Cambridge University Press, 1971), p. 101.

7. Voltaire, *Philosophical Dictionary*, Theodore Besterman, ed. (Harmondsworth, England: Penguin, 1974), p. 183.

8. Quoted in David B. Davis, *The Problem of Slavery in Western Culture* (Harmondsworth, England: Penguin, 1970), p. 449.

9. Quoted in Rosemary Agonito, ed., *History of Ideas on Women: A Source Book* (New York: G. P. Putnam's Sons, 1977), p. 101.

10. Ibid., p. 118.

11. Ibid., p. 124.

12. Ibid., p. 130.

13. Ibid., pp. 154–155.

14. Adam Smith, *The Wealth of Nations*, George Stigler, ed. (New York: Appleton, 1957), p. 3.

15. Ibid., p. 98.

16. Ibid., p. 7.

17. Jean Le Rond d'Alembert, *Preliminary Discourse to the Encyclopedia of Diderot*, trans. by Richard N. Schwab (New York: Bobbs-Merrill, 1963), p. 22.

18. Ibid., pp. 101–102.

Suggested Reading

Anderson, M. S., *Europe in the Eighteenth Century, 1713–1783* (1961). A good general survey of the century with excellent chapters on cultural and intellectual life.

Becker, Carl, *The Heavenly City of the Eighteenth-Century Philosophers* (1932). Still a provocative assessment of the Enlightenment's relation to Christianity.

Cassirer, Ernst, *The Philosophy of the Enlightenment* (1951). A classic and basic account of Enlightenment philosophy; difficult reading.

Gay, Peter, *The Enlightenment, An Interpretation* (1967). A good survey.

Goldmann, Lucien, *The Philosophy of the Enlightenment: The Christian Burgess and the Enlightenment* (1968). Intended as a corrective to Cassirer, by a prominent European Marxist historian.

The Institute for Research in History, ed., *Women and the Enlightenment* (1984). A collection of essays asking the question: "Did women have an Enlightenment?"

Jacob, Margaret, *The Radical Enlightenment: Pantheists, Freemasons and Republicans* (1981). A study of the radical materialists and their contribution to the Enlightenment, especially in the first half of the century.

Porter, Roy, and Mikulas Teich, eds., *The Enlightenment in National Context* (1981). The discussion shows that there were many versions of the Enlightenment.

Porter, Roy, and G. S. Rousseau, eds., *Sexual Underworlds of the Enlightenment* (1988). A close look at the question of freedom, in this case sexual; it suggests that the Enlightenment repressed as much as it liberated.

Spencer, Sarnia I., *French Women and the Age of Enlightenment* (1984). A good general survey.

Venturi, Franco, *Utopia and Reform in the Enlightenment* (1971). A difficult but rewarding book, focused on the more extreme reformers of the age.

Wangermann, Ernst, *The Austrian Achievement, 1700–1800* (1973). An excellent case study of the strengths and weaknesses of the most enlightened of European monarchies.

Woloch, Isser, *Eighteenth-Century Europe: Tradition and Progress, 1715–1789* (1982). An interesting general survey.

Review Questions

1. What is meant by the Age of Enlightenment? Where did the Enlightenment begin, and what contributed to its spread?

2. How did Christianity come under attack by deists, skeptics, and freethinkers?

3. In what ways does Voltaire exemplify the philosophes?

4. Why was Freemasonry important in the eighteenth century?

5. What were the essential characteristics of the political thought of each of the following: Hobbes, Locke, Montesquieu, and Rousseau? Make relevant comparisons and contrasts.

6. Describe Locke's theory of learning. What was its significance for the Enlightenment?

7. How did the philosophes come to terms with the status of slaves and criminals?

8. What were the views of Rousseau and Wollstonecraft on the position of women in society?

9. Did the philosophes approve of capitalism? Explain why or why not.

10. What made the High Enlightenment different from what went before it? Describe how it differed. How did the *Encyclopedia* exemplify the High Enlightenment?

11. List the major military conflicts of the eighteenth century. Discuss the significance of each.

12. Enlightened despotism was in reality the use of Enlightenment principles by monarchs to enhance the central government's power and thereby their own. Discuss this statement.

13. In what ways was the American Revolution based on Enlightenment principles?

14. The Enlightenment was a pivotal period in the shaping of the modern mentality. Discuss this statement.

IV

An Age of Revolution: Liberal, National, Industrial

1789–1848

19

The French Revolution: Affirmation of Liberty and Equality

The outbreak of the French Revolution in 1789 stirred the imagination of Europeans. Both participants and observers sensed that they were living in a pivotal age. On the ruins of the Old Order founded on privilege and despotism, a new era was forming that promised to realize the ideals of the Enlightenment. These ideals included the emancipation of the human personality from superstition and tradition, the triumph of liberty over tyranny, the refashioning of institutions in accordance with reason and justice, and the tearing down of barriers to equality. It seemed that the natural rights of the individual, hitherto a distant ideal, would now become reality, and centuries of oppression and misery would end. Never before had people shown such confidence in the power of human intelligence to shape the conditions of existence. Never before had the future seemed so full of hope.

This lofty vision kindled emotions akin to religious enthusiasm and attracted converts throughout the Western world. "If we succeed," wrote the French poet André Chénier, "the destiny of Europe will be changed. Men will regain their rights and the people their sovereignty."[1] The editor of the Viennese publication *Wiener Zeitung* wrote to a friend: "In France a light is beginning to shine which will benefit the whole of humanity."[2] British reformer John Cartwright expressed the hopes of reformers everywhere: "Degenerate must be that heart which expands not with sentiments of delight at what is now transacting in . . . France. The French . . . are not only asserting their own rights, but they are asserting and advancing the general liberties of mankind."[3]

The Storming of the Bastille. (*Brown Brothers*)

The Old Regime

The causes of the French Revolution reach back into the aristocratic structure of society in the Old Regime. Eighteenth-century French society was divided into three orders, or Estates: the clergy constituted the First Estate, the nobility the Second Estate, and everyone else (about 96 percent of the population) belonged to the Third Estate. The clergy and nobility, totaling about 400,000 out of a population of 26 million, enjoyed special privileges. The semifeudal social structure of the Old Regime, based on inequalities sanctioned by law, produced the tensions that precipitated the Revolution.

The First Estate

The powers and privileges of the French Catholic church made it a state within a state. As it had done for centuries, the church registered births, marriages, and deaths; collected tithes (a tax on products from the soil); censored books considered dangerous to religion and morals; operated schools; and distributed relief to the poor. Since it was illegal for Protestants to assemble together for prayer, the Catholic church enjoyed a monopoly on public worship. Although it owned an estimated 10 percent of the land, which brought in an immense revenue, the church paid no taxes. Instead it made a "free gift" to the state—the church determined the amount—which was always smaller than direct taxes would have been. Critics denounced the church for promoting superstition and obscurantism, for impeding reforms, and for being more concerned with wealth and power than with the spiritual message of Jesus.

The clergy reflected the social divisions in France. The upper clergy shared the attitudes and way of life of the nobility from which they sprang. The parish priests, commoners by birth, resented the haughtiness and luxurious living of the upper clergy. In 1789, when the Revolution began, many priests sympathized with the reform-minded people of the Third Estate.

The Second Estate

Like the clergy, the nobility was a privileged order. Nobles held the highest positions in the church, army, and government. They were exempt from most taxes (or used their influence to evade taxes), collected manorial dues from peasants, and owned between one-quarter and one-third of the land. In addition to the income they drew from their estates, nobles were becoming increasingly involved in such nonaristocratic enterprises as banking and finance. Many key philosophes—Montesquieu, Condorcet, d'Holbach—were nobles, and nobles were the leading patrons of the arts. Most nobles, however, were suspicious and intolerant of the liberal ideas advanced by the philosophes.

All nobles were not equal; there were gradations of dignity among the 200,000 to 250,000 members of the nobility. Enjoying the most prestige were *nobles of the race*—families who could trace their aristocratic status back to time immemorial. (Of these, many were officers in the king's army and were called *nobles of the sword.*) The highest of the ancient nobles were engaged in the social whirl at Versailles and Paris, receiving pensions and sinecures from the king but performing few useful services for the state. Most nobles of the race, unable to afford the gilded life at court, remained on their provincial estates, the poorest of them barely distinguishable from prosperous peasants.

Alongside this ancient nobility, a new nobility had arisen, created by the monarchy. To obtain money, reward favorites, and weaken the old nobility, French kings had sold titles of nobility to members of the bourgeoisie and had conferred noble status on certain government offices bought by wealthy members of the bourgeoisie. Particularly significant were the *nobles of the robe,* whose ranks included many former bourgeois who had purchased judicial offices in the parlements, the high law courts. In the late eighteenth century the nobles of the robe vigorously championed the cause of aristocratic privilege.

In the seventeenth century, Louis XIII's minister Richelieu had humbled the great nobles. Determined not to share his power and fearful of threats to the throne, Louis XIV (1643–1715) had allowed the nobility social prestige but denied it a voice in formulating high policy. In the eighteenth century, nobles sought to regain the power that they had lost under Louis XIV. This resurgence of the nobility was led not by a revitalized ancient aristocracy but by the new nobility, the nobles of the robe. The parlements became obstreperous critics of royal policy and opponents of any reform that threatened aristocratic and provincial privileges. This "feudal reaction" triggered the Revolution.

However, all nobles did not think alike. A minority, influenced by the liberal ideals of the philosophes, sought to reform France; they wanted to end royal despotism and establish a constitutional government. To this extent, the liberal nobility had a great deal in common with the bourgeoisie. These liberal nobles saw the king's difficulties in 1788 as an opportunity to regenerate the nation under enlightened leadership. But the majority of nobles, hostile to liberal ideals, resisted enlightened reforms. In doing so, they contributed to the destruction of the aristocracy in 1789.

The Third Estate

The Third Estate was composed of the bourgeoisie, peasants, and urban laborers. Although the bourgeoisie provided the leadership for the Revolution, its success depended on the support given by the rest of the Third Estate.

The Bourgeoisie The bourgeoisie consisted of merchant-manufacturers, wholesale merchants, bankers, master craftsmen, doctors, lawyers, intellectuals, and government officials below the top ranks. Although the bourgeoisie had wealth, they lacked social prestige. A merchant, despite his worldly success, felt that his occupation denied him the esteem enjoyed by the nobility. "There are few rich people who at times do not feel humiliated at being nothing but wealthy," observed an eighteenth-century Frenchman.[4]

Influenced by the aristocratic values of the day, the bourgeoisie sought to erase the stigma of common birth by obtaining the most esteemed positions in the nation and by entering the ranks of the nobility, whose style of life they envied. Traditionally, some bourgeoisie had risen socially either by purchasing a judicial or political office that carried with it a title of nobility or by gaining admission to the upper clergy and the officer ranks of the army. As long as these avenues of upward social mobility remained open, the bourgeoisie did not challenge the existing social structure, including the special privileges of the nobility.

But in the last part of the eighteenth century it became increasingly difficult for the bourgeois to gain the most honored offices in the land. Finding the path to upward mobility and social dignity blocked, the bourgeois came to resent a social system that valued birth more than talent. Increasingly, members of the bourgeoisie, imbued with the rational outlook of the Enlightenment, sought to abolish the privileges of birth and to open careers to talent.

Practical considerations of social prestige and economic gain, however, do not alone explain the revolutionary mentality of the bourgeoisie. When they challenged the Old Regime, the bourgeois felt that they were fulfilling the ideals of the philosophes and serving all humanity. This idealism would inspire sacrifice and heroism.

By 1789, the bourgeois had many grievances. They wanted all positions in church, army, and state open to men of talent regardless of birth. They sought a parliament; a constitution that would limit the king's power and guarantee freedom of thought, a fair trial, and religious toleration; and administrative reforms that would eliminate waste, inefficiency, and interference with business. Because the bourgeois were the principal leaders and chief beneficiaries of the French Revolution, many historians view it, along with the English revolutions of the seventeenth century and the growth of capitalism, as "an episode in the general rise of the bourgeoisie."[5]

The Peasantry The condition of the more than 21 million French peasants was a paradox. On the one hand, they were better off than peasants in Austria, Prussia, Poland, and Russia, where serfdom still predominated. In France, serfdom had largely disappeared; many peasants owned their own land, and some were even prosperous. On the other hand, most French peasants lived in poverty,

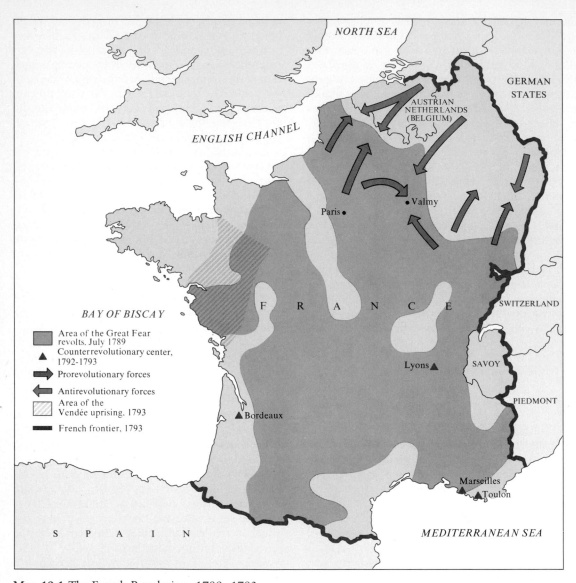

Map 19.1 The French Revolution, 1789–1793

which worsened in the closing years of the Old Regime.

Peasants owned between 30 and 40 percent of the land, but the typical holding was barely large enough to eke out a living. The rising birthrate (between 1715 and 1789 the population may have increased from 18 million to 26 million) led to the continual subdivision of farms among heirs. Moreover, many peasants did not own their own

land but rented it from a nobleman or a prosperous neighbor. Others worked as sharecroppers, turning over to their creditors a considerable share of the harvest.

Unable to survive on their small holdings, many peasants tried to supplement their incomes. They hired themselves out for whatever employment was available in their region—as agricultural day laborers, charcoal burners, transporters of wine, or textile workers in their own homes. Landless peasants tried to earn a living in such ways. The increasing birthrate resulted in an overabundance of rural wage earners. This worsened the plight of small landowners and reduced the landless to beggary. "The number of our children reduces us to desperation,"[6] was a common complaint of the peasants by 1789.

An unjust and corrupt system of taxation weighed heavily on the peasantry. Louis XIV had maintained his grandeur and financed his wars by milking ever more taxes from the peasants, a practice that continued throughout the eighteenth century. An army of tax collectors victimized the peasantry. In addition to royal taxes, peasants paid the tithe to the church and manorial dues to lords.

Although serfdom had ended in most parts of France, lords continued to demand obligations from peasants as they had done in the Middle Ages. In addition to performing labor services on the lord's estate, peasants still had to grind their corn in the lord's mill, bake their bread in his oven, press their grapes in his winepress, and give him part of their produce in payment. In addition, the lord collected a land rent from peasant proprietors, levied dues on goods at markets and fairs, and exercised exclusive hunting rights on lands tilled by peasants. The last was a particularly onerous right, for the lord's hunting parties damaged crops. Lords were determined to hold on to these privileges not only because of the income they brought but because they were symbols of authority and social esteem. The peasants, on the other hand, regarded these obligations as hateful legacies of the past from which they derived no benefit.

In the last part of the eighteenth century, lords sought to exact more income from their lands by reviving manorial dues that had not been collected for generations, by increasing the rates on existing dues, and by contracting businessmen to collect payments from the peasants. These capitalists naturally tried to squeeze as much income as possible from the peasants, making them hate the whole system of manorial obligations even more.

Inefficient farming methods also contributed to the poverty of the French peasants. In the eighteenth century, France did not experience a series of agricultural improvements comparable to those in England. Failure to invest capital in modernizing agricultural methods meant low yields per acre and a shortage of farm animals.

A rise in the price of necessities during the closing years of the Old Regime worked hardship on those peasants who depended on wages for survival. With prices rising faster than wages, only the more prosperous peasants with produce to sell benefited. The great majority of peasants were driven deeper into poverty, and the number of beggars roaming the countryside increased.

A poor harvest in 1788–89 aggravated peasant misery and produced an atmosphere of crisis. The granaries were empty; the price of bread, the staple food of the French, soared; and starvation threatened. Hatred of the manorial order and worsening poverty sparked a spontaneous and autonomous peasant revolution in 1789.

Urban Laborers The urban laboring class in this preindustrial age consisted of journeymen working for master craftsmen, factory workers in small-scale industries, and wage earners such as day laborers, gardeners, handymen, and deliverymen, who were paid by those they served. The poverty of the urban poor, like that of the peasant wage earners, worsened in the late eighteenth century. From 1785 to 1789, the cost of living increased by 62 percent, while wages rose only 22 percent. For virtually the entire decade of the Revolution, urban workers struggled to keep body and soul together in the face of food shortages and rising prices, particularly that of their staple food, bread. Material want drove the urban poor to acts of violence that affected the course of the Revolution.

Inefficient Administration and Financial Disorder

The administration of France was complex, confusing, and ineffective. The practice of buying state offices from the king, introduced as a means of raising money, resulted in many incompetent officeholders. "When his Majesty created an office," stated one administrator, "Providence called into being an imbecile to buy it."[7] Tariffs on goods shipped from one province to another and differing systems of weights and measures hampered trade. No single law code applied to all the provinces; instead, there were overlapping and conflicting law systems based on old Roman law or customary feudal law, which made the administration of justice slow, arbitrary, and unjust. To admirers of the philosophes, the administrative system was an insult to reason. The Revolution would sweep the system away.

Financial disorders also contributed to the weakness of the Old Regime. In the last years of the Old Regime the government could not raise sufficient funds to cover expenses. By 1787, it still had not paid off the enormous debt incurred during the wars of Louis XIV, let alone the costs of succeeding wars during the eighteenth century, particularly France's aid to the colonists in the American Revolution. The king's gifts and pensions to court nobles and the extravagant court life further drained the treasury.

Finances were in a shambles not because France was impoverished but because it had an inefficient and unjust tax system. Few wealthy Frenchmen, including the bourgeois, paid their fair share of taxes. Because tax revenue came chiefly from the peasants, it was bound to be inadequate. Excise duties and indirect taxes on consumer goods yielded much-needed revenue in the last decades of the Old Regime. However, instead of replenishing the royal treasury, these additional funds were pocketed by rich tax collectors who, for a fixed payment to the state, had obtained the right to collect these indirect taxes. The financial crisis, although serious, was solvable if the clergy, nobility, and bourgeoisie would pay their fair share of taxes. Some progressive ministers recognized the need for comprehensive reforms, but they were resisted by nobles and clergy who clung tenaciously to their ancient privileges. The irresolution of the king and the intrigues and rivalries of his ministers were also barriers to reform.

The nobles were able to thwart royal will mainly through the parlements. Many parlementaires were originally wealthy bourgeois who had purchased their offices from the state (nobles of the robe). Both the office and status of nobility remained within the family. The Paris parlement and twelve provincial parlements reviewed the judgments of lower courts and registered royal edicts. The parlements had the right to *remonstrate*, that is, to pass judgment on the legality of royal edicts before registering them. If the courts considered the king's new laws at variance with previous legislation or ancient traditions, they would refuse to register them. The king could revise the edicts in accordance with the parlements' instructions, or force their registration by means of a *lit de justice*—a solemn ceremony in which the monarch appeared before the court. If the parlementaires persisted in their resistance, the king might order the arrest of their leaders. Although the king could force his will on the parlements, their bold opposition damaged royal prestige.

With France on the brink of bankruptcy, the king's ministers proposed that the nobility and church surrender some of their tax privileges. The parlements, steadfast defenders of noble prerogative, protested and remonstrated, and the church insisted on the immunity of its property from taxation. Throughout the nation, members of the privileged orders united in their determination to preserve their social exclusiveness.

The resistance of the nobility forced the government, in July 1788, to call for a meeting of the Estates General—a medieval representative assembly that had last met in 1614—to deal with the financial crisis. The body was to convene in May 1789. Certain that they would dominate the Estates General, the nobles intended to weaken the power of the throne and to regain power that they had lost under Louis XIV. Once in control of the government, they would introduce financial reforms. But the revolt of the nobility against the Crown had unexpected consequences; it opened the way for revolutions by the Third Estate that destroyed the Old Regime and with it the aristocracy and its privileges.

The Moderate Stage, 1789–1791

The Clash Between the Nobility and the Third Estate

Frenchmen in great numbers met in electoral assemblies to elect deputies to the Estates General. Churchmen and nobles voted directly for their representatives. Most deputies of the clergy were parish priests, many of them sympathetic to reform. Although the majority of deputies of the Second Estate were conservative country nobles, there was a sizable liberal minority, including some who had fought in the American Revolution, that favored reform; political liberalism was not a monopoly of the bourgeoisie. The representatives from the Third Estate were elected indirectly, with virtually all taxpaying males over age twenty-five eligible to vote. The delegates of the Third Estate consisted predominantly of bourgeois drawn from government service and the professions, including many articulate lawyers.

Each Estate drew up lists of grievances and suggestions (cahiers de doléances). The cahiers from all three orders expressed loyalty to monarchy and church, recognized the sanctity of property rights, and called for a written constitution and an elected assembly. The cahiers drawn up by the bourgeoisie stressed guarantees of personal liberty; the cahiers of the nobility predictably insisted on the preservation of manorial rights and honorific privileges.

As the Estates General prepared to meet, reform-minded Frenchmen held great hopes for the regeneration of France and the advancement of liberty. There was general agreement that a constitutional government, with an assembly that met regularly to pass laws (including the levying of taxes), was preferable to absolute monarchy. At this stage, with a significant number of nobles sympathetic to reform, there was no insuperable gulf between the bourgeoisie and the nobility. It soon became clear, however, that the hopes of reformers clashed with the intentions of many aristocrats. What had started as a struggle between the Crown and the aristocracy was turning into something far more significant—a conflict between the two privileged orders on one side and the Third Estate on the other. One pamphleteer, Abbé Sieyès (1748–1836), expressed the hatred the bourgeoisie held for the aristocracy. "The privileged order has said to the Third Estate: 'Whatever be your services, whatever be your talents, you shall go thus far and no farther. It is not fitting that you be honored.'" The higher positions in the land, said Sieyès, should be the "reward for talents," not the prerogative of birth. Without the Third Estate, "nothing can progress"; without the nobility, "everything would proceed infinitely better."[8]

Formation of the National Assembly

The Estates General convened at Versailles on May 5, 1789, but was stalemated by the question of procedure. Seeking to control the assembly, the nobility insisted that the three Estates follow the traditional practice of meeting separately and voting as individual bodies. Since the two privileged orders were likely to stand together, the Third Estate would always be outvoted, two to one. But the delegates from the Third Estate, unwilling to allow the nobility and the higher clergy to dominate the Estates General, proposed instead that the three Estates meet as one body and vote by head. There were some 610 delegates from the Third Estate; the nobility and clergy together had an equivalent number. Since the Third Estate could rely on the support of sympathetic parish priests and liberal nobles, it would be assured a majority if all orders met together.

On June 10, the Third Estate broke the stalemate. It invited the clergy and nobility to join with it in a common assembly; if they refused, the Third Estate would go ahead without them. A handful of priests answered the roll call, but not one noble. On June 17, the Third Estate made a revolutionary move. It declared itself the National Assembly. On June 20, locked out of their customary meeting hall (apparently by accident), the Third Estate delegates moved to a nearby tennis court and took a solemn oath not to disband until a constitution had been drawn up for France. By these acts the bourgeois delegates demonstrated their desire and determination to reform the state.

Louis XVI commanded the National Assembly to separate into orders, but the Third Estate held firm. The steadfastness of the delegates and the menacing actions of Parisians who supported the National Assembly forced Louis XVI to yield. On June 27, he ordered the nobility (some had already done so) and the clergy (a majority had already done so) to join with the Third Estate in the National Assembly. The Third Estate had successfully challenged the nobility and defied the king. It would use the National Assembly to institute reforms, including the drawing up of a constitution that limited the king's power.

But the victory of the bourgeoisie was not yet secure, for most nobles had not resigned them-

Approval of the Tennis Court Oath (detail). On June 17, 1789, the Third Estate declared itself the National Assembly. On June 20, they met on a nearby tennis court when they found their customary meeting hall locked. They vowed not to dis-band until a constitution had been drawn up for the entire nation. In this painting by Jacques Louis David, aristocrat, clergyman, and commoner embrace before a cheering National Assembly. (*Versailles/Cliché des Musées Nationaux*)

selves to a bourgeois-dominated National Assembly. Recognizing that France was on the threshold of a social revolution that threatened their status, the nobles reversed their position of previous years; they joined with the king in an effort to crush the National Assembly. Louis XVI, influenced by his wife Queen Marie Antoinette, his brother Comte d'Artois, and court aristocrats, ordered special foreign regiments to the outskirts of Paris and Versailles. He also replaced Jacques Necker, a reform-minded minister, with a nominee of the queen. It appeared that Louis XVI, overcoming his usual hesitancy and vacillation, had resolved to use force against the National Assembly and to stop the incipient revolution. At this point, uprisings by the common people of Paris and peasants in the countryside saved the National Assembly and ensured the victory of the forces of reform.

Storming of the Bastille

In July 1789, the level of tension in Paris was high for three reasons. First, the calling of the Estates General had aroused hopes for reform. Second, the price of bread was soaring: in August 1788, a Parisian laborer had spent 50 percent of his income on bread; by July 1789, he was spending 80 percent. A third element in the tension was the fear of an aristocratic plot to crush the National Assembly. Fearful that royal troops would bombard and pillage the city, Parisians searched for weapons.

On July 14, eight hundred to nine hundred Parisians gathered in front of the Bastille, a fortress used as a prison and a despised symbol of royal despotism. They gathered primarily to obtain gunpowder and to remove the cannon that threatened a heavily populated working-class district. Fearing an attack, the governor of the Bastille, de Launay, ordered his men to fire into the crowd; they killed ninety-eight and wounded seventy-three of the people. When the tables were turned and five cannons were aimed on the main gate of the Bastille, de Launay surrendered. Although promised that no harm would come to him, de Launay and five of his men were killed, and their heads were paraded on pikes through the city.

Historians hostile to the French Revolution have long depicted the besiegers of the Bastille as a destructive mob composed of the dregs of society—smugglers, beggars, bandits, degenerates. However, more contemporary scholarship[9] reveals that the Bastille crowd was not drawn from the criminal elements but consisted almost entirely of small tradesmen, artisans, and wage earners—concerned citizens driven by hunger, fear of an aristocratic conspiracy, and hopes for reform.

The fall of the Bastille had far-reaching consequences: a symbol of the Old Regime had fallen; some court nobles hostile to the Revolution decided to flee the country; the frightened king told the National Assembly that he would withdraw the troops ringing Paris. The revolutionary act of the Parisians had indirectly saved the National Assembly and with it the bourgeois revolution.

The Great Fear

The uprising of the Parisians strengthened the hand of the National Assembly. Revolution in the countryside also served the interests of the reformers. The economic crisis of 1788–89 had worsened conditions for the peasantry; the price of bread soared, and the number of hungry beggars wandering the roads spreading terror multiplied. Also contributing to this revolutionary mentality were the great expectations unleashed by the summoning of the Estates General, for like the urban poor, the peasants hoped that their grievances would be remedied. In the spring of 1789, peasants were attacking food convoys and refusing to pay royal taxes, tithes, and manorial dues. These revolutionary outbreaks intensified at the end of July. Inflamed by economic misery and stirred by the uprisings of the Parisians, peasants began to burn manor houses and to destroy the registers on which their obligations to the lords were inscribed.

The flames of the peasants' insurrection were fanned by rumors that aristocrats were organizing bands of brigands to attack the peasants. The large number of vagrants roaming the countryside helped trigger irrational fears among the peasantry. The mythical army of brigands never materialized, but the Great Fear, as this episode is called, led more peasants to take up arms. Suspicious of an aristocratic plot to thwart efforts at reform, the peasants attacked the lords' chateaux with greater fury, letting loose centuries of stored-up hatred against the nobles.

The peasant upheavals in late July and early August, like the insurrection in Paris, worked to the advantage of the reformers. The attacks provided the National Assembly with an opportunity to strike at noble privileges by putting into law what the peasants had accomplished with the torch—the destruction of feudal remnants. On the night of August 4, 1789, aristocrats, seeking to restore calm in the countryside, surrendered their special privileges—exclusive hunting rights, tax exemptions, monopoly of highest offices, manorial courts, and the right to demand labor services from peasants. The Assembly maintained that "the feudal regime had been utterly destroyed."*

In the decrees of August 5 and 11, the National Assembly implemented the resolutions of August 4. The Assembly also declared that the planned constitution should be prefaced by a declaration of rights. On August 26, it adopted the Declaration of the Rights of Man and of the Citizen. The

---

* This was not entirely true. Some peasant obligations were abolished outright. However, for being released from other specified obligations, peasants were required to compensate their former lords. The peasants simply refused to pay, and in 1793 the Jacobins, recognizing reality, declared the remaining debt null and void.

Women's March to Versailles. A bread shortage and high prices sparked the protest march of thousands of women to Versailles in October 1789. The king was compelled to return to Paris, a sign of his diminishing power, and many aristocrats hostile to the Revolution fled the country. (*Bibliothèque Nationale, Paris*)

August Decrees and the Declaration of Rights marked the death of the Old Regime.

October Days

Louis XVI, cool to these reforms, postponed his approval of the August Decrees and the Declaration of Rights. It would require a second uprising by the Parisians to force the king to agree to the reforms and to nail down the victory of the reformers.

On October 5, 1789, Parisian housewives (and men) marched twelve miles to Versailles to protest the lack of bread to the National Assembly and the king. A few hours later, 20,000 Paris Guards, a citizen militia sympathetic to the Revolution, also set out for Versailles in support of the protesters. The king had no choice but to promise bread and to return with the demonstrators to Paris. Two weeks later the National Assembly abandoned Versailles for Paris.

Once again the "little people" had aided the bourgeoisie. Louis XVI, aware that he had no con-

trol over the Parisians and fearful of further violence, approved the August Decrees and the Declaration of the Rights of Man and of the Citizen. Nobles who had urged the king to use force against the Assembly and had tried to block reforms fled the country in large numbers.

Reforms of the National Assembly

With resistance enfeebled, the National Assembly continued the work of reform begun in the summer of 1789. By abolishing both special privileges of the nobility and the clergy and absolutism based on the divine right of kings, the National Assembly completed the destruction of the Old Regime:

1. *Abolition of special privileges.* By ending the special privileges of the nobility and the clergy in the August Decrees, the National Assembly legalized the equality that the bourgeoisie had de-

manded. The aristocratic structure of the Old Regime, a remnant of the Middle Ages that had hindered the progressive bourgeoisie, was eliminated.

2. *Statement of human rights.* The Declaration of the Rights of Man and of the Citizen expressed liberal and universal goals of the philosophes and the particular interests of the bourgeoisie. To contemporaries it was a refutation of the Old Regime, a statement of ideals that, if realized, would end longstanding abuses and usher in a new society. In proclaiming the inalienable right to liberty of person and thought and to equal treatment under the law, the declaration affirmed the dignity of human personality; it asserted that government belonged not to any ruler but to the people as a whole, and that its aim was the preservation of the natural rights of the individual. Because the declaration stood in sharp contrast to the principles espoused by an intolerant clergy, a privileged aristocracy, and a despotic monarch, it has been called the death warrant of the Old Regime.

The declaration expressed the view of the philosophes that people need not resign themselves to the abuses and misfortunes of human existence: through reason, they could improve society. But in 1789, the declaration was only a statement of intent; it remained to be seen whether its principles would be achieved.

3. *Subordination of church to state.* The National Assembly also struck at the privileges of the Roman Catholic church. The August Decrees declared the end of tithes. To obtain badly needed funds, the Assembly in November 1789 confiscated church lands and put them up for sale. In 1790, the Assembly passed the Civil Constitution of the Clergy, which altered the boundaries of the dioceses, reducing the number of bishops and priests, and transformed the clergy into government officials elected by the people and paid by the state.

Almost all bishops and many priests opposed the Civil Constitution. One reason was that reorganization deprived a sizable number of clergymen of their positions. Moreover, Protestants and nonbelievers could, in theory, participate in the election of Catholic clergy. In addition, the Assembly had issued the decree without consulting the pope or the French clergy as a body. When the Assembly required the clergy to take an oath that they would uphold the Civil Constitution, only about one-half would do so, and many believing Catholics supported the dissenting clergy. The Civil Constitution divided the French and gave opponents of the Revolution an emotional issue around which to rally supporters.

4. *Constitution for France.* In September 1791, the National Assembly achieved the goal at which it had been aiming since June 1789: a constitution limiting the power of the king and guaranteeing all French citizens equal treatment under the law. Citizens paying less than a specified amount in taxes could not vote. Probably about 30 percent of the males over age twenty-five were excluded by this stipulation, and only the more well-to-do citizens qualified to sit in the Legislative Assembly, a unicameral parliament created to succeed the National Assembly. Despite this restriction, suffrage requirements under the constitution of 1791 were far more generous than in Britain.

5. *Administrative and judicial reforms.* The National Assembly aimed to reform the chaotic administrative system of France. It replaced the patchwork of provincial units with eighty-three new administrative units, or departments, approximately equal in size. The departments and their subdivisions were allowed a large measure of self-government.

Judicial reforms complemented the administrative changes. A standardized system of courts replaced the innumerable juridictions of the Old Regime, and the sale of judicial offices was ended. All judges were selected from graduate lawyers, and citizen juries were introduced in criminal cases. In the penal code completed by the National Assembly, torture and barbarous punishments were abolished.

6. *Aid for business.* The National Assembly abolished all tolls and duties on goods transported within the country, maintained a tariff to protect French manufacturers, and insisted that French colonies trade only with the mother country. The Assembly also established a uniform system of weights and measures, eliminated the guilds (medieval survivals that blocked business expansion), and forbade workingmen to form unions or to strike.

By ending absolutism, striking at the privileges of the nobility, and preventing the mass of people from gaining control over the government, the National Assembly consolidated the rule of the bourgeoisie. With one arm, it broke the power of aristocracy and throne; with the other, it held back the common people. Although the reforms benefited the bourgeoisie, it would be a mistake to view them merely as a selfish expression of bourgeois interests. The Declaration of the Rights of Man and of the Citizen was addressed to all; it proclaimed liberty and equality as the right of all and called for citizens to treat one another with respect. Both French and foreign intellectuals believed that the Revolution would lead ultimately to the emancipation of humanity. "The men of 1789," says Lefebvre, "thought of liberty and equality as the common birthright of mankind."[10] These ideals became the core of the liberal-democratic credo that spread throughout much of the West in the nineteenth century.

The Radical Stage, 1792–1794

The Sans-Culottes

Pleased with their accomplishments—equality before the law, careers open to talent, a written constitution, parliamentary government—the men of 1789 wished the Revolution to go no further. But revolutionary times are unpredictable. Soon the Revolution moved in a direction neither anticipated nor desired by the reformers. A counter-revolution was led by irreconcilable nobles and alienated churchmen; supported by socially unprogressive and strongly Catholic peasants, it began to threaten the changes made by the Revolution, forcing the revolutionary leadership to resort to extreme measures.

Also propelling the Revolution in the direction of radicalism was the discontent of the *sans-culottes**—small shopkeepers, artisans, and wage

*Literally, *sans-culottes* means without culottes—and refers to the people who did not wear the knee breeches that aristocrats wore before the Revolution.

earners. Although they had played a significant role in the Revolution, particularly in the storming of the Bastille and the October Days, they had gained little. The sans-culottes, says French historian Albert Soboul, "began to realize that a privilege of wealth was taking the place of a privilege of birth. They foresaw that the bourgeoisie would succeed the fallen aristocracy as the ruling class."[11] Inflamed by poverty and their hatred of the rich, the sans-culottes insisted that it was the government's duty to guarantee them the "right of existence," a policy that ran counter to the economic individualism of the bourgeoisie. They demanded that the government increase wages, set price controls on food supplies, end food shortages, punish food speculators and profiteers, and deal severely with counterrevolutionaries.

Although most sans-culottes upheld the principle of private property, they wanted laws to prevent extremes of wealth and poverty. Socially, their ideal was a nation of small shopkeepers and small farmers. "No one should own more than one workshop or one store," read a sans-culotte petition.[12] Whereas the men of 1789 sought equality of rights, liberties, and opportunities, the sans-culottes expanded the principle of equality to include narrowing the gap between the rich and poor. To reduce economic inequality, the sans-culottes called for higher taxes for the wealthy and the redistribution of land. Politically, they favored a democratic republic in which the common man had a voice.

In 1789, the bourgeoisie had demanded equality with the aristocrats—the right to hold the most honored position in the nation and an end to the special privileges of the nobility. By the end of 1792, the sans-culottes were demanding equality with the bourgeois—political reforms that would give the poor a voice in the government and social reforms that would improve their lot.

Foreign Invasion

Despite the pressures exerted by reactionary nobles and clergy on the one hand and discontented sans-culottes on the other, the Revolution might not have taken a radical turn had France remained at peace. The war that broke out with Austria and Prussia in April 1792 exacerbated internal dissensions, worsened economic conditions, and threatened to undo the reforms of the Revolution. It was under these circumstances that the Revolution moved from its moderate stage into a radical one that historians refer to as the Second French Revolution.

In June 1791, Louis XVI and the royal family, traveling in disguise, fled Paris for the northeast of France to join with *émigrés* (nobles who had left revolutionary France and were organizing a counterrevolutionary army) and to rally foreign support against the Revolution. Discovered at Varennes by a village postmaster, they were brought back to Paris as virtual prisoners. The flight of the king turned many French people against the monarchy, strengthening the position of radicals who wanted to do away with kingship altogether and establish a republic. But it was foreign invasion that led ultimately to the destruction of the monarchy.

In the Legislative Assembly, the lawmaking body that had succeeded the National Assembly in October 1791, one group, called the Girondins, urged an immediate war against Austria, which was harboring and supporting the émigrés. The Girondins believed that a successful war would unite France under their leadership, and they were convinced that Austria was already preparing to invade France and destroy the Revolution. Moreover, regarding themselves as crusaders in the struggle of liberty against tyranny, the Girondins hoped to spread revolutionary reforms to other lands to provoke a war of the people against kings.

On April 20, 1792, the Legislative Assembly declared war on Austria. Commanded by the duke of Brunswick, a combined Austrian and Prussian army crossed into France. French forces, short of arms and poorly led (about 6,000 of some 9,000 officers had abandoned their command), could not halt the enemy's advance. Food shortages and a counterrevolution in the west increased the unrest. Into an atmosphere already charged with tension, the duke of Brunswick issued a manifesto declaring that if the royal family were harmed he would exact a terrible vengeance on the Parisians. On August 10, 1792, enraged Parisians and militia from other cities attacked the king's palace, killing several hundred Swiss guards.

In early September, as foreign troops advanced deeper into France, there occurred an event analogous to the Great Fear of 1789. As rumors spread that jailed priests and aristocrats were planning to break out of their cells to support the duke of Brunswick, the Parisians panicked. Driven by fear, patriotism, and murderous impulses, they raided the prisons and massacred 1,100 to 1,200 prisoners. Most of the victims were not political prisoners but ordinary criminals.

On September 21–22, 1792, the National Convention (the successor to the Legislative Assembly) abolished the monarchy and established a republic. In December 1792, Louis XVI was placed on trial, and in January 1793, he was executed for conspiring against the liberty of the French people. The execution of Louis XVI intensified tensions between the revolutionaries and the crowned heads of Europe. The uprising of August 10, the September Massacres, the creation of a republic, and the execution of Louis XVI all confirmed that the Revolution was falling into radicalism.

Meanwhile, the war continued. Short of supplies, hampered by bad weather, and possessing insufficient manpower, the duke of Brunswick never did reach Paris. Outmaneuvered at Valmy on September 20, 1792, the foreign forces retreated to the frontier, and the armies of the republic took the offensive. By the beginning of 1793, French forces had overrun Belgium (then a part of the Austrian Empire), the German Rhineland, and the Sardinian provinces of Nice and Savoy. To the peoples of Europe the National Convention solemnly announced that it was waging a popular crusade against privilege and tyranny, against aristocrats and princes.

Frightened by these revolutionary social ideas, by the execution of Louis XVI, and most importantly by French expansion that threatened the balance of power, the rulers of Europe, urged on by Britain, formed an anti-French alliance by the spring of 1793. The allies' forces pressed toward the French borders. The republic was endangered.

Counterrevolutionary insurrections further undermined the fledgling republic. In the Vendée in western France, peasants who were protesting against taxation and conscription and were still loyal to their priests took up arms against the republic. Led by local nobles, the peasants of the

Vendée waged a guerrilla war for religion, royalism, and their traditional way of life. In other quarters, federalists revolted in the provinces, objecting to the power wielded by the centralized government in Paris. The republic was unable to exercise control over much of the country.

The Jacobins

As the republic tottered under the weight of foreign invasion, internal insurrection, and economic crisis, the revolutionary leadership grew still more radical. In June 1793, the Jacobins replaced the Girondins as the dominant group in the National Convention. Whereas the Girondins favored a government in which the departments would exercise control over their own affairs, the Jacobins wanted a strong central government with Paris as the center of power. Whereas the Girondins opposed government interference with business, the Jacobins supported temporary governmental controls to deal with the needs of war and economic crisis. This last point was crucial; it won the Jacobins the support of the sans-culottes.

Both Girondins and Jacobins came from the bourgeoisie, but some Jacobin leaders were more willing to listen to the economic and political demands of the hard-pressed sans-culottes. The Jacobins also sought an alliance with the sans-culottes in order to defend the Revolution against foreign and domestic enemies. The Jacobins had a further advantage in the power struggle: they were tightly organized, well-disciplined, and convinced that only they could save the republic. On June 2, 1793, some 80,000 armed sans-culottes surrounded the Convention and demanded the arrest of Girondin delegates—an act that enabled the Jacobins to gain control of the government.

The problems confronting the Jacobins were staggering. They had to cope with civil war, particularly in the Vendée, economic distress, blockaded ports, and foreign invasion. They lived with the terrible dread that if they failed, the Revolution for liberty and equality would perish. Only strong leadership could save the republic; it was provided by the Committee of Public Safety. Serving as a cabinet for the Convention, the Committee of Public Safety organized the nation's defenses, formulated foreign policy, supervised

Jacobin Poster. When the Jacobins assumed power in 1793, they saved the foundering Republic and continued the work of reform. However, as this poster not so subtly suggests ("Liberty, Equality, Fraternity or Death"), they also made terror a government policy. (*The Mansell Collection*)

ministers, ordered arrests, and imposed the central government's authority throughout the nation. The twelve members of the committee, all ardent patriots and veterans of revolutionary politics, constituted "a government of perhaps the ablest and most determined men who have ever held power in France."[13]

Jacobin Achievements

The Jacobins continued the work of reform. A new constitution, in 1793, expressed Jacobin enthusiasm for political democracy. It contained a new Declaration of Rights that affirmed and amplified the principles of 1789. By giving all adult males the right to vote, it overcame sans-culotte objections to the constitution of 1791. However, due to the threat of invasion and the revolts, implementation of the constitution of 1793 was postponed, and it never was put into effect. By abolishing both slavery in the French colonies and imprisonment for debt and by making plans for free public education, the Jacobins revealed their humanitarianism and their debt to the philosophes.

Jacobin economic policies derived from the exigencies of war. To halt inflation and gain the support of the poor—both necessary for the war effort—the Jacobins decreed the *law of the maximum*, which fixed prices on bread and other essential goods and raised wages. To win over the peasants, the Jacobins made it easier for them to buy the property of émigré nobles. To equip the Army of the Republic, the Committee of Public Safety requisitioned grain, wool, arms, shoes, and other items from individual citizens, required factories and mines to produce at full capacity, and established state-operated armament and munitions plants.

The Nation in Arms

To fight the war against foreign invaders, the Jacobins, in an act that anticipated modern conscription, drafted unmarried men between eighteen and twenty-five years of age. They mobilized all the resources of the nation, infused the army with a love for *la patrie* (the nation), and in a remarkable demonstration of administrative skill, equipped an army of more than 800,000 men. In creating the nation in arms, the Jacobins heralded the emergence of modern warfare. The citizen-soldiers of the republic, commanded by officers who had proved their skill on the battlefield and inspired by the ideals of liberty, equality, and fraternity, won decisive victories. In May and June of 1794, the French routed the allied forces on the vital northern frontier, and by the end of July, France had become the triumphant master of Belgium.

In demanding complete devotion to the nation,

the Jacobin phase of the Revolution also heralded the rise of modern nationalism. In the schools; in newspapers, speeches, and poems; on the stage; and at rallies and meetings of patriotic societies, the French people were told of the glory won by republican soldiers on the battlefield and were reminded of their duties to la patrie. "The citizen is born, lives and dies for the fatherland."[14] These words were written in public places for all citizens to read and ponder. The soldiers of the Revolution fought not for money or for a king, but for the nation. "When *la patrie* calls us for her defense," wrote a young soldier to his mother, "we should rush to her. . . . Our life, our goods, and our talents do not belong to us. It is to the nation, to *la patrie,* to which everything belongs."[15] Could this heightened sense of nationality that concentrated on the special interests of the French people be reconciled with the Declaration of the Rights of Man, whose principles were addressed to all humanity? The revolutionaries themselves did not understand the implications of the new force that they had unleashed.

The Republic of Virtue and the Reign of Terror

Robespierre At the same time that the Committee of Public Safety was forging a revolutionary army to deal with external enemies, it was also waging war against internal opposition. The pivotal personality in this struggle was Maximilien Robespierre (1758–1794). Robespierre had served in the National Assembly and was an active Jacobin. Although neither a brilliant orator nor a hero in appearance, he was distinguished by a fervent faith in the rightness of his beliefs, a total commitment to republican democracy, and a pure integrity that earned him the name "the Incorruptible."

Robespierre wanted to create a better society founded on reason, good citizenship, and patriotism. In his Republic of Virtue, there would be no kings or nobles; men would be free, equal, and educated; reason would be glorified and superstition ridiculed; there would be no extremes of wealth or poverty; man's natural goodness would prevail over vice and greed; laws would preserve,

LÉGISLATEUR INCORRUPTIBLE

M. M. J. ROBERSPIERRE

Député de Paris à la Convention Nationale en 1792.
Été Président le 22 Août 1793.

À Paris chez Villeneuve Graveur Rue Zacharie ... Maison du Passage. N° 72.

Robespierre, an Engraving by Fiésinger After a Drawing by Pierre-Narcisse Guérin. To create a Republic of Virtue where men would be free and equal, Maximilien Robespierre considered terror necessary. Robespierre lost favor with his own party and was himself guillotined. (*Bibliothèque Nationale, Paris*)

not violate, inalienable rights. In this utopian vision, an individual's duties would be "to detest bad faith and despotism, to punish tyrants and traitors, to assist the unfortunate, to respect the weak, to defend the oppressed, to do all the good one can to one's neighbor, and to behave with justice towards all men."[16]

A disciple of Rousseau, Robespierre conceived the national general will as ultimate and infallible. Its realization meant the establishment of a Republic of Virtue; its denial meant the death of an ideal and a return to despotism. Robespierre felt certain that he and his colleagues in the Committee of Public Safety had correctly ascertained the needs of the French people. He was sure the committee members were the genuine interpreters of the general will, and he felt duty-bound to ensure its realization. He pursued his ideal society with religious zeal. Knowing that the Republic of Virtue could not be established while France was threatened by foreign and civil war, Robespierre urged harsh treatment for enemies of the republic, who "must be prosecuted by all not as ordinary enemies, but as rebels, brigands, and assassins."[17]

The Jacobin leadership, with Robespierre playing a key role, attacked those they considered enemies of the republic: Girondins who challenged Jacobin authority, federalists who opposed a strong central government emanating from Paris, counterrevolutionary priests and nobles and their peasant supporters, and profiteers who hoarded food. The Robespierrists also executed Danton, a hero of the Revolution, who wished to end the terror and negotiate peace with the enemy. The Jacobins even sought to discipline the ardor of the sans-culottes who had given them power. Fearful that sans-culotte spontaneity would undermine central authority and promote anarchy, Robespierrists brought about the dissolution of sans-culotte societies. Robespierrists also executed radical revolutionaries known as the *enragés* (madmen), who had considerable influence on the Paris sans-culottes. The leaders of the enragés threatened insurrection against Jacobin rule and pushed for more social reforms than the Jacobins would allow, including setting limits on incomes and on the size of farms and businesses.

To preserve republican liberty, the Jacobins made terror a deliberate government policy. Said Robespierre:

> *Does not liberty, that inestimable blessing . . . have the . . . right to sacrifice lives, fortunes, and even, for a time, individual liberties? . . . Is not the French Revolution . . . a war to the death between those who want to be free and those content to be slaves? . . . There is no middle ground; France must be entirely free or perish in the attempt, and any means are justifiable in fighting for so fine a cause.*[18]

Perhaps as many as 40,000 people perished during the Reign of Terror.

Robespierre and his fellow Jacobins did not resort to the guillotine because they were bloodthirsty or power mad. Instead, they sought to establish a temporary dictatorship in a desperate attempt to save the republic and the Revolution. Deeply devoted to republican democracy, the Jacobins viewed themselves as bearers of a higher faith. Like all visionaries, Robespierre was convinced that he knew the right way, that the new society he envisaged would benefit all humanity, and that those who impeded its implementation were not just opponents but sinners who had to be liquidated for the good of humanity.

The Jacobins did save the republic. Their regime expelled foreign armies, crushed the federalist uprisings, contained the counterrevolutionaries in the Vendée, and prevented anarchy. Without the discipline, order, and unity imposed on France by the Robespierrists, it is likely that the republic would have collapsed under the twin blows of foreign invasion and domestic anarchy.

The Significance of the Terror. The Reign of Terror poses fundamental questions about the meaning of the French Revolution and the validity of the Enlightenment conception of man. To what extent was the Terror a reversal of the ideals of the Revolution as formulated in the Declaration of the Rights of Man? To what extent did the feverish passions and fascination for violence demonstrated in the mass executions in the provinces and in the public spectacles in Paris indicate a darker side of human nature beyond control of reason? Did Robespierre's religion of humanity revive the fanaticism and cruelty of the wars of religion that had so disgusted the philosophes? Did the Robespierrists, who considered themselves the staunchest defenders of the Revolution's ideals, soil and subvert these ideals by their zeal? By mobilizing the might of the nation, by creating the mystique of la patrie, by imposing temporary dictatorial rule in defense of liberty and equality, and by legalizing and justifying terror committed in the people's name, were the Jacobins unwittingly unleashing new forces that, in later years, would be harnessed by totalitarian ideologies consciously resolved to stamp out the liberal heritage of the Revolution? Did 1793 mark a change in the direction of Western civilization: a movement away from the ideals of the philosophes, and the opening of an age of violence and irrationalism that would culminate in the cataclysms of the twentieth century?

The Fall of Robespierre

The Terror had been instituted during a time of crisis and keyed-up emotions. By the summer of 1794, with the victory of the republic seemingly assured, the fear of an aristocratic conspiracy had subsided, the will to punish "traitors" had slackened, and popular fervor for the Terror had diminished. As the need and enthusiasm for the Terror abated, Robespierre's political position weakened.

Opponents of Robespierre in the Convention, feeling the chill of the guillotine blade on their own necks, ordered the arrest of Robespierre and some of his supporters. On July 27, 1794, the ninth of Thermidor according to the new republican calendar, Robespierre was guillotined. Parisian sans-culottes might have saved him, but they made no attempt. With their political clubs dissolved, the organization needed for an armed uprising was lacking. Moreover, the sans-culottes' ardor for Jacobinism had waned. They resented Robespierre for having executed their leaders, and apparently the social legislation instituted by the Robespierrist leadership had not been sufficient to soothe sans-culotte discontent.

After the fall of Robespierre, the machinery of the Jacobin republic was dismantled. Leadership passed to the property-owning bourgeois who had endorsed the constitutional ideas of 1789–1791, the moderate stage of the Revolution. The new leadership, known as Thermidoreans until the end of 1795, wanted no more of the Jacobins or of Robespierre's society. They had considered Robespierre a threat to their political power because he would have allowed the common people a considerable voice in the government, and a threat to their property because he would have introduced some state regulation of the economy to aid the poor.

The Thermidorean reaction was a counterrevolution. The new government purged the army of officers who were suspected of Jacobin leanings, abolished the law of the maximum, and declared void the constitution of 1793. A new constitution, approved in 1795, re-established property requirements for voting. The counterrevolution also produced a counterterror, as royalists and Catholics massacred Jacobins in the provinces.

At the end of 1795, the new republican government, called the Directory, was burdened by war, a sagging economy, and internal unrest. The Directory crushed insurrections by Parisian sansculottes maddened by hunger and hatred of the rich (1795, 1796) and by royalists seeking to restore the monarchy (1797). As military and domestic pressures worsened, power began to pass into the hands of generals. One of them, Napoleon Bonaparte, seized control of the government in November 1799, pushing the Revolution into yet another stage.

The Meaning of the French Revolution

The French Revolution has been described as a series of concurrent revolutions. In addition to the revolution of the bourgeoisie, there occurred an autonomous peasant revolution precipitated by increasing poverty, hatred of the manorial order, and rising hopes aroused by the calling of the Estates General. There also occurred a third uprising, that of urban journeymen, wage earners, and lesser bourgeois shopkeepers and craftsmen hard hit by food shortages and rising prices.

But bad economic conditions alone need not lead to revolution. "No great event in history," states Henri Peyre, a twentieth-century student of French culture, "has been due to causes chiefly economic in nature, and certainly not the French Revolution."[19] For centuries, Indian untouchables and Egyptian fellahin lived under the most wretched of conditions, bearing their misery without raising a voice in protest. In the eighteenth century, the peoples of eastern and central Europe were far worse off than the average French citizen. Yet it was in France that the great revolution broke out.

Revolutions are born in the realm of the spirit. Revolutionary movements, says George Rudé, a historian of the French Revolution, require "some unifying body of ideas, a common vocabulary of hope and protest, something, in short, like a common 'revolutionary psychology.' "[20] The philosophes were not revolutionaries themselves, but their attacks on the pillars of the established order helped to create revolutionary psychology, as Peyre observes:

> *Eighteenth-century philosophy taught the Frenchman to find his condition wretched, or in any case, unjust and illogical and made him disinclined to the patient resignation to his troubles that had long characterized his ancestors. . . . The propaganda of the "Philosophes" perhaps more than any other factor accounted for the fulfillment of the preliminary condition of the French Revolution, namely discontent with the existing state of things.[21]*

The American Revolution, which gave practical expression to the liberal philosophy of the philosophes, helped to pave the way for the French Revolution. The Declaration of Independence proclaimed the natural rights of man and sanctioned resistance against a government that deprived men of these rights. The United States showed that a nation could be established on the principle that sovereign power derived from the people. The Americans set an example of social equality unparalleled in Europe. In the United States there was no hereditary aristocracy, no serfdom, and no state church. Liberal French aristocrats, such as the Marquis de Lafayette, who had fought in the American Revolution returned to France more optimistic about the possibilities of reforming French society.

The French Revolution was a decisive period in the shaping of the modern West. It implemented the thought of the philosophes, destroyed the hierarchic and corporate society of the Old Regime, promoted the interests of the bourgeoisie, and speeded the growth of the modern state.

The French Revolution weakened the aristocracy. With their feudal rights and privileges eliminated, the nobles became simply ordinary citizens. Throughout the nineteenth century, France would be governed by both the aristocracy and the bourgeoisie; property, not noble birth, determined the composition of the new ruling elite.

The principle of careers open to talent gave the bourgeoisie access to the highest positions in the state. Possessing wealth, talent, ambition, and now opportunity, the bourgeoisie would play an ever more important role in French political life. Throughout the Continent, the reforms of the

French Revolution served as a model for progressive bourgeois who, sooner or later, would challenge the Old Regime in their own lands.

The French Revolution transformed the dynastic state of the Old Regime into the modern state: national, liberal, secular, and rational. When the Declaration of the Rights of Man and of the Citizen stated that "the source of all sovereignty resides essentially in the nation," the concept of the state took on a new meaning. The state was no longer merely a territory or a federation of provinces; it was not the private possession of the king claiming to be God's lieutenant on earth. In the new conception, the state belonged to the people as a whole, and the individual, formerly a subject, was now a citizen with both rights and duties and was governed by laws that drew no distinction on the basis of birth.

The liberal thought of the Enlightenment found practical expression in the reforms of the Revolution. Absolutism and divine right of monarchy, repudiated in theory by the philosophes, were invalidated by constitutions that set limits to the powers of government and by elected parliaments that represented the governed. By providing for equality before the law and the protection of human rights—habeas corpus, trial by jury, freedom of religion, speech, and the press—the Revolution struck at the abuses of the Old Regime. These gains seemed at times more theoretical than actual, because of violations and interruptions; nevertheless, these liberal ideals reverberated throughout the Continent. During the nineteenth century the pace of reform would quicken. And with the demands of the sans-culottes for equality with the bourgeois, for political democracy and social reform, the voice of the common people in politics began to be heard. This phenomenon would intensify increasingly with growing industrialization.

By disavowing any divine justification for the monarch's power and by depriving the church of its special position, the Revolution accelerated the secularization of European political life. Sweeping aside the administrative chaos of the Old Regime, the Revolution attempted to impose rational norms on the state. The sale of public offices that produced ineffective and corrupt administrators was eliminated, and the highest positions in the land were opened to men of talent, regardless of birth. The Revolution abolished the peasantry's manorial obligations that hampered agriculture and swept away barriers to economic expansion. It based taxes on income and streamlined their collection. The destruction of feudal remnants, internal tolls, and guilds speeded up the expansion of a competitive market economy. In the nineteenth century, reformers in the rest of Europe would follow the lead set by France.

The French Revolution also unleashed two potentially destructive forces identified with the modern state: total war and nationalism. These contradicted the rational and universal aims of the reformers as stated in the Declaration of the Rights of Man. Whereas eighteenth-century wars were fought by professional soldiers for limited aims, the French Revolution, says British historian Herbert Butterfield,

> brings conscription, the nation in arms, the mobilization of all the resources of the state for unrelenting conflict. It heralds the age when peoples, woefully ignorant of one another, bitterly uncomprehending, lie in uneasy juxtaposition watching one another's sins with hysteria and indignation. It heralds Armageddon, the giant conflict for justice and right between angered populations each of which thinks it is the righteous one. So a new kind of warfare is born—the modern counterpart to the old conflicts of religions.[22]

The world wars of the twentieth century are the terrible fulfillment of this new development in warfare.

The French Revolution also gave birth to modern nationalism. During the Revolution, loyalty was directed to the entire nation, not to a village or province or to the person of the king. The whole of France became the fatherland. Under the Jacobins, the French became converts to a secular faith preaching total reverence for the nation. "In 1794 we believed in no supernatural religion; our serious interior sentiments were all summed up in the one idea, how to be useful to the fatherland. Everything else . . . . was, in our eyes, only trivial. . . . It was our only religion."[23] Few suspected that the new religion of nationalism was fraught with danger. Saint-Just, a young, ardent Robespierrist, was gazing into our own century when he declared: "There is something terrible in the sacred love of the fatherland. This love is so exclusive

Chronology 19.1 The French Revolution

July 1788	Calling of the Estates General
May 5, 1789	Convening of the Estates General
June 17, 1789	The Third Estate declares itself the National Assembly
July 14, 1789	The storming of the Bastille
Late July 1789	The Great Fear
August 4, 1789	Nobles surrender their special privileges
June 1791	Flight of Louis XVI
October 1791	The Legislative Assembly succeeds the National Assembly
April 20, 1792	The Legislative Assembly declares war on Austria
August 10, 1792	Parisians attack the king's palace
September 1792	The September Massacres
September 20, 1792	The battle of Valmy
September 21–22, 1792	Abolition of the monarchy
June 1793	Jacobins replace the Girondins as the dominant group in the National Convention
July 27, 1794	Robespierre is guillotined
1795 and 1796	Failed insurrections by the poor of Paris
September 1797	A royalist coup d'état against the Directory is crushed
November 1799	Napoleon seizes power

that it sacrifices everything to the public interest, without pity, without fear, with no respect for the human individual."[24]

The Revolution attempted to reconstruct society on the basis of Enlightenment thought. The Declaration of the Rights of Man and of the Citizen, whose spirit permeated the reforms of the Revolution, upheld the dignity of the individual, demanded respect for the individual, attributed to each person natural rights, and barred the state from denying these rights. It insisted that society and state have no higher duty than to promote the freedom and autonomy of the individual. "It is not enough to have overturned the throne," said Robespierre; "our concern is to erect upon its remains holy Equality and the sacred Rights of Man."[25] The tragedy of the Western experience is that this humanist vision, brilliantly expressed by the Enlightenment and given recognition in the reforms of the French Revolution, would be undermined in later generations. And, ironically, by spawning total war, nationalism, terror as government policy, and a revolutionary mentality that sought to change the world through violence, the French Revolution itself contributed to the shattering of this vision.

An Age of Revolution: Liberal, National, Industrial

Notes

1. Quoted in G. P. Gooch, *Germany and the French Revolution* (New York: Russell & Russell, 1966), p. 39.

2. Quoted in Ernst Wangermann, *From Joseph II to the Jacobin Trials* (New York: Oxford University Press, 1959), p. 24.

3. Excerpted in Alfred Cobban, ed., *The Debate on the French Revolution* (London: Adam & Charles Black, 1960), p. 41.

4. Quoted in Elinor G. Barber, *The Bourgeoisie in Eighteenth-Century France* (Princeton, N.J.: Princeton University Press, 1967), p. 57.

5. Georges Lefebvre, *The French Revolution from 1793 to 1799* (New York: Columbia University Press, 1964), 2: 360.

6. Quoted in C. B. A. Behrens, *The Ancien Régime* (New York: Harcourt, Brace and World, 1967), p. 43.

7. Quoted in Leo Gershoy, *The French Revolution and Napoleon* (New York: Appleton-Century-Crofts, 1933), p. 18.

8. Excerpted in John Hall Stewart, ed., *A Documentary Survey of the French Revolution* (New York: Macmillan, 1951), pp. 43–44.

9. See George Rudé, *The Crowd in the French Revolution* (New York: Oxford University Press, 1959).

10. Georges Lefebvre, *The Coming of the French Revolution* (Princeton, N.J.: Princeton University Press, 1967), p. 210.

11. Albert Soboul, *The Parisian Sans-Culottes and the French Revolution, 1793–94*, trans. by Gwynne Lewis (London: Oxford University Press, 1964), pp. 28–29.

12. Quoted in ibid., p. 64.

13. Alfred Cobban, *A History of Modern France* (Baltimore: Penguin, 1961), 1: 213.

14. Quoted in Hans Kohn, *Nationalism: Its Meaning and History* (Princeton, N.J.: D. Van Nostrand, 1965), p. 25.

15. Quoted in Carlton J. H. Hayes, *The Historical Evolution of Modern Nationalism* (New York: Richard R. Smith, 1931), p. 55.

16. Excerpted in George Rudé, ed., *Robespierre* (Englewood Cliffs, N.J.: Prentice-Hall, 1976), p. 72.

17. Ibid., p. 57.

18. Excerpted in E. L. Higgins, ed., *The French Revolution* (Boston: Houghton Mifflin, 1938), pp. 306–307.

19. Henri Peyre, "The Influence of Eighteenth-Century Ideas on the French Revolution," *Journal of the History of Ideas,* 10(1949): 72.

20. George Rudé, *Revolutionary Europe, 1783–1815* (New York: Harper Torchbooks, 1966), p. 74.

21. Peyre, "The Influence of Eighteenth-Century Ideas," p. 73.

22. Herbert Butterfield, *Napoleon* (New York: Collier Books, 1962), p. 18.

23. Quoted in Carlton J. H. Hayes, *The Historical Evolution of Modern Nationalism* (New York: Richard R. Smith, 1931), p. 55.

24. Quoted in Hans Kohn, *Making of the Modern French Mind* (New York: D. Van Nostrand, 1955), p. 17.

25. Quoted in Christopher Dawson, *The Gods of Revolution* (New York: New York University Press, 1972), p. 83.

Suggested Reading

Carr, John L., *Robespierre* (1972). A biography of the revolutionary leader.

Doyle, William, *Origins of the French Revolution* (1980). In recent decades, several historians have challenged the traditional view that the French Revolution was an attempt by the bourgeoisie to overthrow the remnants of aristocratic power and privilege, that it was a victory of a capitalist bourgeois order over feudalism. This book summarizes the new scholarship and argues that the nobility and bourgeoisie had much in common prior to the Revolution.

Ford, Franklin L., *Robe and Sword* (1953). A still useful discussion of the French aristocracy.

Gershoy, Leo, *The Era of the French Revolution* (1957). A brief survey with useful documents.

Gottschalk, Louis, and Donald Lach, *Toward the*

French Revolution (1973). A survey of the eighteenth-century background to the French Revolution.

Gourbet, Pierre, *The Ancien Régime* (1973). A survey of French society from 1600 to 1750.

Higgins, E. L., ed. *The French Revolution* (1938). Excerpts from contemporaries.

Kafker, F. A., and J. M. Laux, *The French Revolution: Conflicting Interpretations* (1976). Excerpts from leading historians.

Lefebvre, Georges, *The French Revolution*, 2 vols. (1962, 1964). A detailed analysis by a master historian.

———, *The Coming of the French Revolution* (1967). A brilliant analysis of the social structure of the Old Regime and the opening phase of the Revolution.

Palmer, R. R., *The Age of the Democratic Revolution*, 2 vols. (1959, 1964). The French Revolution as part of a revolutionary movement that spread on both sides of the Atlantic.

———, *Twelve Who Ruled* (1965). An admirable treatment of the Terror.

Rudé, George, *The Crowd in the French Revolution* (1959). An analysis of the composition of the crowds that stormed the Bastille, marched to Versailles, and attacked the king's palace.

———, *Robespierre: Portrait of a Revolutionary Democrat* (1976). A biography of the revolutionary leader.

Soboul, Albert, *The Sans-Culottes* (1972). An abridgment of the classic study of the popular movement of 1793–94.

Stewart, J. H., *A Documentary Survey of the French Revolution* (1951). A valuable collection of documents.

Review Questions

1. What privileges were enjoyed by clergy and nobility in the Old Regime?

2. What were the grievances of the bourgeoisie, the peasantry and the urban laborers?

3. Why was France in financial difficulty?

4. Analyze the causes of the French Revolution.

5. Identify and explain the significance of the following: formation of the National Assembly, storming of the Bastille, the Great Fear, and the October Days.

6. Analyze the nature and significance of the reforms of the National Assembly.

7. What were the grievances of the sans-culottes?

8. Identify and explain the significance of the following: flight of the King, the Brunswick manifesto, and the September Massacres.

9. What were the principal differences between the Jacobins and the Girondins?

10. What were the accomplishments of the Jacobins?

11. Describe Robespierre's basic philosophy.

12. Why was the French Revolution a decisive period in the shaping of the West?

20

Napoleon: Destroyer and Preserver of the Revolution

The loosening of the bonds of authority in a revolutionary age offers opportunities for popular and ambitious military commanders to seize power. History affords numerous examples of revolutions culminating in military dictatorships. The upheavals of the French Revolution made possible the extraordinary career of Napoleon Bonaparte. This popular general combined a passion for power with a genius for leadership. Under Napoleon's military dictatorship, the constitutional government for which the people of 1789 had fought and the republican democracy for which the Jacobins had rallied the nation seemed lost. Nevertheless, during the Napoleonic era, many achievements of the Revolution were preserved, strengthened, and carried to other lands.

Rise to Power

Napoleon was born on August 15, 1769, on the island of Corsica, the son of a petty noble. After finishing military school in France, he became an artillery officer; the wars of the French Revolution afforded him an opportunity to advance his career. In December 1793, Napoleon's brilliant handling of artillery forced the British to lift their siege of the city of Toulon. Two years later he saved the Thermidorean Convention from a royalist insurrection by ordering his troops to fire into the riotous mob—the famous "whiff of grapeshot." In 1796, he was given command of the French Army of Italy. His star was rising.

In Italy, against the Austrians, Napoleon demonstrated a dazzling talent for military planning and leadership that earned him an instant reputation. Having tasted glory, he could never do with-

Napoleon Crossing the Great St. Bernard Pass. (*Bulloz, Paris*)

out it; having experienced only success, nothing seemed impossible. He sensed that he was headed for greatness. Years later he recalled: "[In Italy] I realized I was a superior being and conceived the ambition of performing great things, which hitherto had filled my thoughts only as a fantastic dream."[1]

In November 1797, Napoleon was ordered to plan an invasion of England. Aware of the weakness of the French navy, he recommended postponement of the invasion, urging instead an expedition to the Near East to strike at British power in the Mediterranean and British commerce with India, and perhaps to carve out a French empire in the Near East. With more than 35,000 troops, Napoleon set out for Egypt, then a part of the Turkish empire. Although he captured Cairo, the Egyptian campaign was far from a success. At the battle of the Nile (1798), the British, commanded by Admiral Horatio Nelson, annihilated Napoleon's fleet. Deprived of reinforcements and supplies, with his manpower reduced by battle and plague, Napoleon was compelled to abandon whatever dreams he might have had of threatening India. Although the Egyptian expedition was a failure, Napoleon, always seeking to improve his image, sent home glowing bulletins about French victories. To people in France, he was seen as the conqueror of Egypt as well as of Italy.

Meanwhile, political unrest, financial disorder, and military reversals produced an atmosphere of crisis in France. Napoleon knew that in such times people seek out a savior. A man of destiny must act. Without informing his men, he slipped out of Egypt, avoided British cruisers, and landed in France in October 1799.

Coup d'État

When Napoleon arrived in France, a conspiracy was already under way against the government of the Directory. Convinced that only firm leadership could solve France's problems, some politicians plotted to seize power and establish a strong executive. Needing the assistance of a popular general, they turned to Napoleon, whom they thought they could control. Although the hastily prepared coup d'état was almost bungled, the government of the Directory was overthrown. The French Revolution entered a new stage, that of military dictatorship.

Demoralized by a decade of political instability, economic distress, domestic violence, and war, most of the French welcomed the leadership of a strong man. The bourgeois, in particular, expected Napoleon to protect their wealth and the influence they had gained during the Revolution.

The new constitution (1799) created a strong executive. Although three consuls shared the executive, the first consul, Napoleon, monopolized power. Whereas Napoleon's fellow conspirators, who were political moderates, sought only to strengthen the executive, Napoleon aspired to personal rule. He captured the reins of power after the coup, and his authority continued to expand. In 1802, he was made first consul for life with the right to name his successor. And on December 2, 1804, in a magnificent ceremony at the Cathedral of Notre Dame in Paris, Napoleon crowned himself emperor of the French. General, first consul, and then emperor—it was a breathless climb to the heights of power. And Napoleon, who once said he loved "power as a musician loves his violin,"[2] was determined never to lose it.

The Character of Napoleon

What sort of man was it on whom the fate of France and Europe depended? Napoleon's personality, complex and mysterious, continues to baffle biographers. However, certain distinctive characteristics are evident. Napoleon's intellectual ability was impressive. His mind swiftly absorbed details that his photographic memory classified and stored. With surgical precision he could probe his way to the heart of a problem while still retaining a grasp of peripheral considerations. Ideas forever danced in his head, and his imagination was illuminated by sudden flashes of insight. He could work for eighteen or twenty hours at a stretch, deep in concentration, ruling out boredom or tiredness by an act of will. Napoleon, man of action, warrior par excellence, was in many ways, says Georges Lefebvre, "a typical man of the eighteenth century, a rationalist, a *philosophe* . . . [who] placed his trust in reason, in knowledge, and in methodical effort."[3]

Rationalism was only one part of his personality. There was also that elemental, irresistible urge for action, "the romantic Napoleon, a force seeking to expand and for which the world was no more than an occasion for acting dangerously."[4] This love of action fused with his boundless ambition. Continues Lefebvre:

> His greatest ambition was glory. "I live only for posterity," he exclaimed, "death is nothing, but to live defeated and without glory is to die every day." His eyes were fixed on the world's great leaders: Alexander who conquered the East and dreamed of conquering the world; Caesar, Augustus, Charlemagne. . . . They were for him examples, which stimulated his imagination and lent an unalterable charm to action. He was an artist, a poet of action, for whom France and mankind were but instruments.[5]

He also exuded an indefinable quality of personality, a charismatic force that made people feel they were in the presence of a superior man. Contemporaries remarked that his large gray eyes, penetrating, knowing, yet strangely expressionless, seemed to possess a hypnotic power. He was capable of moving men to obedience, to loyalty, to heroism.

The rationalist's clarity of mind and the romantic's impassioned soul, the adventurer's love of glory and the hero's personal magnetism—these were the components of Napoleon's personality. There was also an aloofness, some would say callousness, that led him to regard people as pawns to be manipulated in the pursuit of his destiny. "A man like me," he once said, "troubles himself little about the lives of a million men."[6]

Napoleon's genius might have gone unheralded, his destiny unfulfilled, had it not been for the opportunities created by the French Revolution. By opening careers to talent, the Revolution enabled a young Corsican of undistinguished birth to achieve fame and popularity. By creating a national army and embroiling France in war, it provided a military commander with enormous sources of power. By plunging France into one crisis after another, it opened up extraordinary possibilities for a man with a gift of leadership and an ambition "so intimately linked with my very being that it is like the blood that circulates in my

veins."[7] It was the Revolution that made Napoleon conscious of his genius and certain of his destiny.

Napoleon and France

Living in a revolutionary age, Napoleon had observed firsthand the precariousness of power and the fleetingness of popularity. A superb realist, he knew that his past reputation would not sustain him. If he could not solve the problems caused by a decade of revolution and war and bind together the different classes of French people, his prestige would diminish and his power collapse. The general must become a statesman, and when necessary, a tyrant. His domestic policies, showing the influence of both eighteenth-century enlightened despotism and the Revolution, affected every aspect of society and had an enduring impact on French history. They continued the work of the Revolution in destroying the institutions of the Old Regime.

Government: Centralization and Repression

In providing France with a strong central government, Napoleon continued a policy initiated centuries earlier by Bourbon monarchs. Although the Bourbons had not been able completely to overcome the barriers presented by provinces, local traditions, feudal remnants, and corporate institutions, Napoleon succeeded in giving France administrative uniformity. An army of officials, subject to the emperor's will, reached into every village, linking together the entire nation. This centralized state suited Napoleon's desire for orderly government and rational administration, enabled him to concentrate power in his own hands, and provided him with the taxes and soldiers needed to fight his wars. To suppress irreconcilable opponents, primarily die-hard royalists and republicans, Napoleon used the instruments of the police state—secret agents, arbitrary arrest, summary trials, executions.

Napoleon also shaped public opinion to prevent hostile criticism of his rule and to promote popular support for his policies and person. In these actions, he was a precursor of twentieth-century dictators. Liberty of the press came to an end. Printers swore an oath of obedience to the emperor, and newspapers were converted into government mouthpieces. Printers were forbidden to print, and booksellers to sell or circulate, "anything which may involve injury to the duties of subjects toward the sovereign or the interests of the state."[8] When Napoleon's secretary read him the morning newspapers, Napoleon would interrupt: "Skip it, skip it. I know what is in them. They only say what I tell them to."[9] These efforts at indoctrination even reached schoolchildren, who were required to memorize a catechism glorifying the ruler, which ran, in part,

> Q. *What are the duties of Christians with respect to the princes who govern them, and what in particular are our duties toward Napoleon I, our Emperor?*
> A. *Christians owe to the princes who govern them, and we owe in particular to Napoleon I, our Emperor, love, respect, obedience, fidelity, military service; . . . we also owe him . . . prayers for his safety. . . .*
> Q. *Why are we bound to all these duties towards our Emperor?*
> A. *First of all, because God, who creates emperors and distributes them according to his will, in loading our Emperor with gifts, both in peace and war, has established him as our sovereign. . . . To honor and to serve our Emperor is then to honor and to serve God himself.*
> Q. *What . . . of those who may be lacking in their duty towards our Emperor?*
> A. *. . . they would be resisting the order established by God himself and would make themselves worthy of eternal damnation.*[10]

By repressing liberty, subverting republicanism, and restoring absolutism, Napoleon reversed some of the liberal gains of the Revolution. Although favoring equality before the law and equality of opportunity as necessary for a well-run state, Napoleon believed that political liberty impeded efficiency and threatened the state with anarchy. He would govern in the interest of the people as an enlightened but absolute ruler.

Religion: Reconciliation with the Church

For Napoleon, who was a deist if not an atheist, the value of religion was not salvation but social and political cohesion. It promoted national unity and prevented class war. He stated:

> *Society cannot exist without inequality of fortunes, and inequality of fortunes cannot exist without religion. When a man is dying of hunger alongside another who stuffs himself, it is impossible to make him accede to the difference unless there is an authority which says to him God wishes it thus; there must be some poor and some rich in the world, but hereafter and for all eternity the division will be made differently.*[11]

This is what Napoleon probably had in mind when he said: "Men who do not believe in God—one does not govern them, one shoots them."[12]

Napoleon attempted to close the breach between the state and the Catholic church, which had emerged during the Revolution. Such a reconciliation would gain the approval of the mass of the French people, who still remained devoted to their faith, and would reassure those peasants and bourgeois who had bought confiscated church lands. For these reasons, Napoleon negotiated an agreement with the pope. The Concordat of 1801 recognized Catholicism as the religion of the great majority of the French, rather than as the official state religion (the proposal that the pope desired). The clergy were to be paid and nominated by the state but consecrated by the pope.

In effect, the Concordat guaranteed the reforms of the Revolution. The church did not regain its confiscated lands nor its right to collect the tithe. The French clergy remained largely subject to state control. And by not establishing Catholicism as the state religion, the Concordat did not jeopardize the newly won toleration of Jews and Protestants. Napoleon had achieved his aim. The Concordat made his regime acceptable to Catholics and to owners of former church lands.

Napoleon at Arcole by Antoine-Jean Gros. Gros idealized Napoleon in this ultra-Romantic portrait. Here he is a conqueror of nations and a political visionary. In his reminiscences written at St. Helena, the exiled emperor depicted himself as a defeated unifier of Europe who had sought peace and a restoration of order. (*Louvre/Cliché des Musées Nationaux*)

Law: The Code Napoléon

Under the Old Regime, France was plagued with numerous and conflicting law codes. Reflecting local interests and feudal traditions, these codes obstructed national unity and administrative efficiency. Efforts by the revolutionaries to draw up a unified code of laws bogged down. Recognizing the value of such a code in promoting effective administration throughout France, Napoleon pressed for the completion of the project. The Code Napoléon incorporated many principles of the Revolution: equality before the law, the right to choose one's profession, freedom of conscience, protection of property rights, the abolition of serfdom, and the secular character of the state.

The code also had its less liberal side, denying equal treatment to workers in their dealings with employers, to women in their relations with their husbands, to children in their relations with their fathers. In making wives inferior to their husbands in matters of property, adultery, and divorce, the code reflected both Napoleon's personal attitude and the general view of the times toward women and family stability. Of women, he once said that "the husband must possess the absolute power and right to say to his wife: 'Madam, you shall not go out, you shall not go to the theater, you shall not receive such and such a person: for the children you shall bear shall be mine!' "[13]

Adopted in lands conquered by France, the Code Napoléon helped to weaken feudal privileges and institutions and clerical interference with the secular state. With justice, Napoleon could say: "My true glory is not to have won forty battles. . . . Waterloo will erase the memory of so many victories. . . . But what nothing will destroy, what will live forever, is my Civil Code."[14]

Education: The Imperial University

Napoleon's educational policy was in many ways an elaboration of the school reforms initiated during the Revolution. Like the revolutionaries, Napoleon favored a system of public education with a secular curriculum and a minimum of church involvement. For Napoleon, education served a dual purpose: it would provide him with capable officials to administer his laws and trained officers to lead his armies; and it would indoctrinate the young in obedience and loyalty. He established the University of France, a giant board of education that placed education under state control. To this day the French school system, unlike that in the United States, is strictly centralized, with curriculum and standards set for the entire state.

The emperor did not consider education for girls important, holding that "marriage is their whole destination."[15] Whatever education girls did receive, he believed, should stress religion.

"What we ask of education is not that girls should think but that they should believe. The weakness of women's brains, the instability of their ideas, the place they fill in society, their need for perpetual resignation . . . all this can only be met by religion."[16]

Economy: Strengthening the State

Napoleon's financial and economic policies were designed to strengthen France and enhance his popularity. To stimulate the economy and to retain the favor of the bourgeois who supported his seizure of power, Napoleon aided industry through tariffs and loans and fostered commerce (while also speeding up troop movements) by building or repairing roads, bridges, and canals. To protect the currency from inflation, he established the Bank of France, which was controlled by the nation's leading financiers. By keeping careers open to talent, he endorsed one of the key demands of the bourgeoisie during the Revolution. Fearing a revolution based on lack of bread, he provided food at low prices and stimulated employment for the laboring poor. He endeared himself to the peasants by not restoring feudal privileges and by allowing them to keep the land they had obtained during the Revolution.

Napoleon did not identify with the republicanism and democracy of the Jacobins, but rather he belonged to the tradition of eighteenth-century enlightened despotism. Like the reforming despots, Napoleon admired administrative uniformity and efficiency, hated feudalism, religious persecution, and civil inequality, and favored government regulation of trade and industry. He saw in enlightened despotism a means of ensuring political stability, overcoming the confusion presented by feudal and corporative institutions, avoiding the dangers of democracy, which he equated with mob rule, and strengthening the state militarily. By preserving many social gains of the Revolution while suppressing political liberty, Napoleon showed himself to be an heir of the enlightened despots.

Although Napoleon's domestic policies gained him wide support, it was his victories on the battlefield that mesmerized the French people and gratified their national vanity. Ultimately his popularity and his power rested on the sword.

Napoleon and Europe

Napoleon, the Corsican adventurer, realized Louis XIV's dream of French mastery of Europe. Between 1805 and 1807, Napoleon inflicted decisive defeats on Austria, Prussia, and Russia, to become the virtual ruler of Europe. In these campaigns, as in his earlier successes in Italy, Napoleon demonstrated his greatness as a military commander.

Napoleon's Art of War

Although forgoing a set battle plan in favor of flexibility, Napoleon was guided by certain general principles that comprised his art of war. He stressed the advantage of "a rapid and audacious attack" in preference to waging defensive war from a fixed position. "Make war offensively; it is the sole means to become a great captain and to fathom the secrets of the art."[17] Warfare could not be left to chance, but required mastering every detail and anticipating every contingency. "I am accustomed to thinking out what I shall do three or four months in advance, and I base my calculations on the worst of conceivable circumstances."[18] Every master plan contained numerous alternatives to cover all contingencies.

Surprise and speed were essential ingredients of Napoleonic warfare. Relying heavily on surprise, Napoleon employed various stratagems to confuse and deceive his opponents: providing newspapers with misleading information, launching secondary offensives, and placing a dense screen of cavalry ahead of marching columns to prevent penetration by enemy patrols. Determined to surprise and consequently demoralize the enemy by arriving at a battlefield ahead of schedule, he carefully selected the best routes to the chosen destination, eliminated slow-moving supply convoys by living off the countryside, and inspired his men to incredible feats of marching as they drew closer to the opposing army. In the first Italian campaign, his men drove 50 miles in thirty-six hours; in 1805, against Austria, they marched 275 miles in twenty-three days.

His campaigns anticipated the blitzkrieg, or lightning warfare, of the twentieth century. As the moment of battle neared, Napoleon would disperse his troops over a wide area; the enemy would counter by dividing its forces. Then, by rapid marches, Napoleon would concentrate a superior force against a segment of the enemy's strung-out forces. Here the hammer blow would fall. Employing some troops to pin down the opposing force, he would move his main army to the enemy's rear or flank, cutting off the enemy supply line. Conducted with speed and deception, these moves broke the spirit of the opposing troops. Heavy barrages by concentrated artillery opened a hole in the enemy lines that was penetrated first by heavy columns of infantry and then by shock waves of cavalry. Unlike the typical eighteenth-century commander, who maneuvered for position and was satisfied with his opponent's retreat, Napoleon sought to annihilate the enemy army, thereby destroying its source of power.

The emperor thoroughly understood the importance of morale in warfare. "Moral force rather than numbers decides victory," he once said.[19] He deliberately sought to shatter his opponent's confidence by surprise moves and lightning thrusts. Similarly, he recognized that he must maintain a high level of morale among his own troops. By sharing danger with his men, he gained their affection and admiration. He inspired his men by appealing to their honor, vanity, credulity, and love of France. "A man does not have himself killed for a few halfpence a day or for a petty distinction," he declared. "You must speak to the soul in order to electrify the man."[20] This Napoleon could do. It was Napoleon's charisma that led the duke of Wellington to remark: "I used to say of him that his presence on the field made a difference of 40,000 men."[21]

Despite his reputation, Napoleon was not essentially an original military thinker. His greatness lay rather in his ability to implement and coordinate the theories of earlier strategists. Eighteenth-century military planners had stressed the importance of massed artillery, rapid movement, deception, living off the countryside, and the an-

nihilation of the enemy army. Napoleon alone had the will and ingenuity to convert these theories into battlefield victories.

Similarly, Napoleon harnessed the military energies generated during a decade of revolutionary war. The Revolution had created a mass army, had instilled in the republican soldier a love for la patrie, and had enabled promising young soldiers to gain promotions on the basis of talent rather than birth. Napoleon took this inheritance and perfected it.

The Grand Empire: Diffusion of Revolutionary Institutions

In 1802, Napoleon made peace with Austria and Great Britain. But when the French ruler expanded his interests in Italy and the Rhineland, Britain organized another coalition against France. In 1805, Britain signed an alliance with both Austria and Russia, and in the summer, Austrian and Russian armies advanced westward.

Napoleon acted swiftly. He outmaneuvered an Austrian army at Ulm in Bavaria (October 1805), forcing its surrender, and occupied Vienna. At Austerlitz (December 1805), he decimated a Russo-Austrian force. In the peace of Pressburg, Austria surrendered its Italian possessions to the Kingdom of Italy, a French satellite in northern Italy.

In October 1806, Napoleon decisively defeated the Prussians at Jena and entered Berlin. Another French victory at Friedland (June 1807) compelled the Russian Tsar Alexander I to request an armistice. In 1807, peace treaties were concluded at Tilsit with Prussia and with Russia. Prussia's Polish territories became the Grand Duchy of Warsaw, a French protectorate ruled by the king of Saxony. Prussian territories west of the Elbe River became the Kingdom of Westphalia, ruled by Napoleon's youngest brother Jerome. These territorial losses reduced the number of subjects controlled by Prussia from 10 to 5 million. Russia's territorial losses were slight. More important was the tsar's promise to side with France if Brit-

Map 20.1 Napoleon's Europe, 1810 ▶

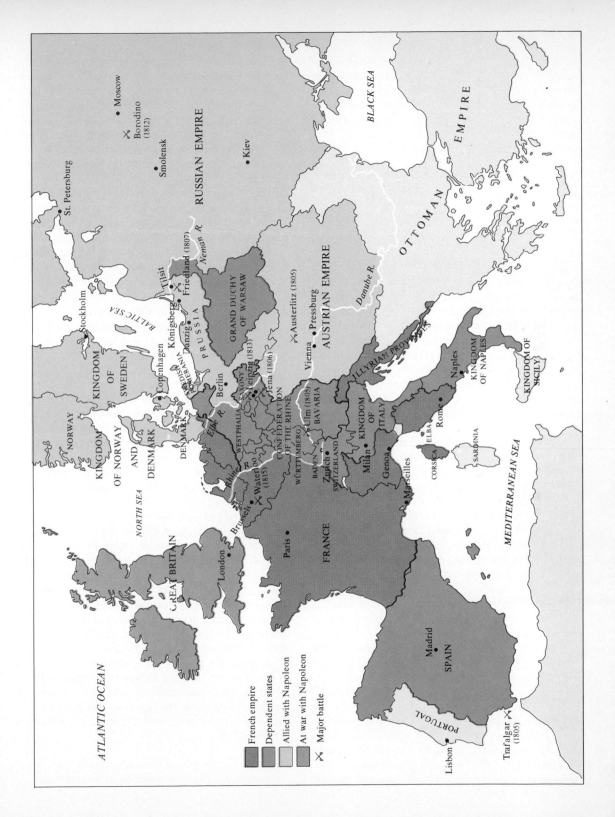

ATLANTIC OCEAN

NORTH SEA

BALTIC SEA

BLACK SEA

MEDITERRANEAN SEA

RUSSIAN EMPIRE

OTTOMAN EMPIRE

AUSTRIAN EMPIRE

GREAT BRITAIN

NORWAY

KINGDOM OF SWEDEN

KINGDOM OF NORWAY AND DENMARK

DENMARK

PRUSSIA

GRAND DUCHY OF WARSAW

SAXONY

WESTPHALIA

CONFEDERATION OF THE RHINE

WÜRTTEMBERG

BADEN

BAVARIA

SWITZERLAND

FRANCE

KINGDOM OF ITALY

ILLYRIAN PROVINCES

SARDINIA

POMERANIA

KINGDOM OF NAPLES

KINGDOM OF SICILY

CORSICA

SARDINIA

ELBA

SPAIN

PORTUGAL

Moscow
Borodino (1812)
Smolensk
Kiev
St. Petersburg
Stockholm
Copenhagen
Königsberg
Danzig
Tilsit
Friedland (1807)
Neman R.
Berlin
Leipzig (1813)
Jena (1806)
Elbe R.
Rhine R.
Waterloo (1815)
Brussels
London
Paris
Zurich
Ulm (1805)
Vienna
Austerlitz (1805)
Pressburg
Danube R.
Milan
Genoa
Marseilles
Rome
Naples
Madrid
Lisbon
Trafalgar (1805)

French empire
Dependent states
Allied with Napoleon
At war with Napoleon
✗ Major battle

ain refused to make peace with Napoleon. In an incredibly short period of time, the terrible Corsican had routed the three leading continental powers and established his hegemony over Europe.

By 1810, Napoleon dominated the Continent, except for the Balkan peninsula. The Grand Empire comprised lands annexed to France, vassal states, and cowed allies. The French republic had already annexed Belgium and the German Left Bank of the Rhine. Napoleon incorporated several other areas into France: German coastal regions as far as the western Baltic and large areas of Italy, including Rome, Geneva and its environs, Trieste, and the Dalmatian Coast.

Vassal states in the Grand Empire included five kingdoms ruled by Napoleon's relatives, two of them in Italy. In 1796, Napoleon, then a young general, had defeated the Austrians in Italy, and the following year he organized northern Italy into the Cisalpine Republic. The leaders of the republic, imbued with the reforming spirit of the Enlightenment and the French Revolution, attacked the privileges of the nobility and the church, granted Jews equal rights, did away with guilds and internal tolls, and established a free press. However, in 1799 the Austrians drove the French from northern Italy and imprisoned or executed supporters of the republic. After his successful coup d'état, Napoleon crossed into Italy, crushed the Austrians at Marengo (1800), and restored republican government to northern Italy. In 1805, he transformed the republic into the Kingdom of Italy, with himself as king and Eugène de Beauharnais as viceroy. Eugène, a twenty-three-year-old cavalry officer, was the son, by her first marriage, of Josephine, Napoleon's wife. In 1806, Napoleon seized Naples in southern Italy to deny Britain a Mediterranean port. The Bourbon rulers fled, and Napoleon installed his brother Joseph as king of Naples.

In 1794–95 the French republic had overrun the United Provinces (Holland), converting it into the Batavian Republic. In 1806, Napoleon renamed the Batavian Republic the Kingdom of Holland and placed his brother Louis on the throne. But in 1810, Louis was forced to abdicate, and Holland was annexed to France. The Kingdom of Westphalia, ruled by Jerome Bonaparte, was formed in 1807 from Prussian lands. In 1808, Napoleon turned his Spanish ally into still another satellite kingdom, giving the Spanish throne to his brother Joseph, who was transferred from Naples.

Besides the five satellite kingdoms in Italy, Holland, Westphalia, and Spain, there were several other vassal states within the Grand Empire. Napoleon formed the Confederation of the Rhine in 1806. Its members, a loose association of sixteen (later eighteen) German states, were subservient to the emperor, as were the nineteen cantons of the Swiss confederation. The Grand Duchy of Warsaw, formed in 1807 from Prussia's Polish lands, was placed under the rule of the German king of Saxony, one of Napoleon's vassals.

Finally, the Grand Empire included states compelled to be French allies—Austria, Prussia, and Russia, as well as Sweden and Denmark. Napoleon required these "allies" not to import goods from Britain, his implacable enemy.

With varying degrees of determination and success, Napoleon extended the reforms of the Revolution to other lands. His officials instituted the Code Napoléon, organized an effective civil service, opened careers to talent, and equalized the tax burden. They abolished serfdom, manorial payments, and the courts of the nobility. They did away with clerical courts, promoted freedom of religion, permitted civil marriage, pressed for civil rights for Jews, and fought clerical interference with secular authority. They abolished guilds, introduced a uniform system of weights and measures, did away with internal tolls, and built roads, bridges, and canals. They promoted secular education and improved public health. Napoleon had launched a European-wide social revolution that attacked the privileges of the aristocracy and the clergy—who regarded him as that "crowned Jacobin"—and worked to the advantage of the bourgeoisie. This diffusion of revolutionary institutions weakened the Old Regime irreparably in much of Europe and speeded up the modernization of nineteenth-century Europe.

Napoleon's purpose in implementing these reforms was twofold: he wished to promote administrative efficiency and to win the support of conquered peoples. He explained his position in a letter to his brother Jerome, ruler of the Kingdom of Westphalia.

What the people of Germany desire with impatience is that the individuals who are not nobles and who have talents have an equal right to your consideration and to positions; it is that every kind of serfdom and intermediary bonds between the sovereign and the lowest class of people be entirely abolished.[22]

Pleased by the overhaul of feudal practices and the reduction of clerical power, many Europeans, particularly the progressive bourgeoisie, welcomed Napoleon as a liberator.

But there was another side to Napoleon's rule. Napoleon, the tyrant of Europe, turned conquered lands into satellite kingdoms and exploited them for the benefit of France. The following, from a letter to Prince Eugène, viceroy of Italy, reveals Napoleon's policy:

All the raw silk from the Kingdom of Italy goes to England. I wish to divert it from this route to the advantage of my French manufacturers: otherwise my silk factories, one of the chief supports of French commerce, will suffer substantial losses. My principle is France first. You must never lose sight of the fact that . . . France should claim commercial supremacy on the continent.[23]

The satellite states and annexed territories were compelled to provide recruits for Napoleon's army and taxes for his war treasury. Opponents of Napoleon faced confiscation of property, the galleys, and execution.

These methods of exploitation and repression increased hatred against Napoleon and French rule. Subject peoples, including bourgeois liberals who felt that he had betrayed the ideals of the Revolution, came to view Napoleon as a tyrant ready for his downfall.

The Fall of Napoleon

In addition to the hostility of subject nationals, Napoleon had to cope with the determined opposition of Great Britain. Its subsidies and encouragement kept resistance to the emperor alive. But perhaps Napoleon's greatest obstacle was his own boundless ambition, which warped his judgment;

from its short-lived peak, the emperor's career slid downhill from defeat to dethronement to deportation.

Failure to Subdue England

Britain was Napoleon's most resolute opponent. It could not be otherwise, for any power that dominated the Continent could organize sufficient naval might to threaten British commerce, challenge its sea power, and invade the island kingdom. Britain would not make peace with any state that sought European hegemony, and Napoleon's ambition would settle for nothing less.

Unable to make peace with Britain, Napoleon resolved to crush it. Between 1803 and 1805, he assembled an invasion flotilla on the English Channel. But there could be no invasion of Britain while British warships commanded the channel. In 1805, the battle of Trafalgar demonstrated British naval power when Admiral Nelson devastated a combined French and Spanish fleet. Napoleon was forced to postpone his invasion scheme indefinitely.

Unable to conquer Britain by arms, Napoleon decided to bring what he called "the nation of shopkeepers" to its knees by damaging the British economy. His plan, called the Continental System, was to bar all countries under France's control from buying British goods. However, by smuggling goods onto the Continent and increasing trade with the New World, Britain, although hurt, escaped economic ruin. Moreover, the Continental System punished European lands dependent on British imports; hundreds of ships lay idle in European ports, and industries closed down. The bourgeoisie, generally supportive of Napoleon's social and administrative reforms, turned against him because of the economic distress caused by the Continental System. Furthermore, Napoleon's efforts to enforce the system enmeshed him in two catastrophic blunders: the occupation of Spain and the invasion of Russia.

The Spanish Ulcer

An ally of France since 1796, Spain proved a disappointment to Napoleon. It failed to prevent the

Death of Nelson by Daniel Maclise. Although Admiral Horatio Nelson died during the battle of Trafalgar, England was victorious. Napoleon could not destroy British seapower, and he had to abandon his plans for invasion. The dying Nelson is pictured in the traditional pose of a "Lamentation of Christ." (*National Museums and Galleries on Merseyside/Walker Art Gallery*)

Portuguese from trading with Britain and contributed little military or financial aid to France's war effort. Napoleon decided to incorporate Spain into his empire. In 1808, while a French army moved toward Madrid, Charles IV, the aged and mentally feeble Spanish ruler, was forced to abdicate by his son, who proclaimed himself Ferdinand VII. The change in rulers pleased the Spanish people, but Napoleon had other plans. Determined to control Spain, he forced both Charles and Ferdinand to surrender their rights to the throne and designated his brother Joseph as king of Spain.

Napoleon believed the Spanish would rally round the gentle Joseph and welcome his liberal reforms. This confidence was a fatal illusion and an immense blunder, for what appeared to be another French victory and the establishment of another satellite kingdom became, in Napoleon's words, "that miserable Spanish affair . . . [that]

killed me."[24] Spanish nobles and clergy feared French liberalism; the overwhelmingly peasant population, illiterate and credulous, intensely proud, fanatically religious, and easily aroused by the clergy, viewed Napoleon as the devil's agent. Loyal to the Spanish monarchy and faithful to the church, the Spanish fought a "War to the Knife" against the invaders.

The Peninsular War was fought with a special cruelty. Wrote one shocked French officer: "At La Carolina we established a hospital and left 167 of our sick and wounded men. That hospital was set afire . . . all were burned alive or horribly massacred. The barbarians believed they had done a glorious thing for God and religion!"[25] Guerrilla bands, aided and encouraged by priests preaching holy war, congregated in mountain hideouts. Striking from ambush, they raided French convoys and outposts, preventing the French from consolidating their occupation and keeping the

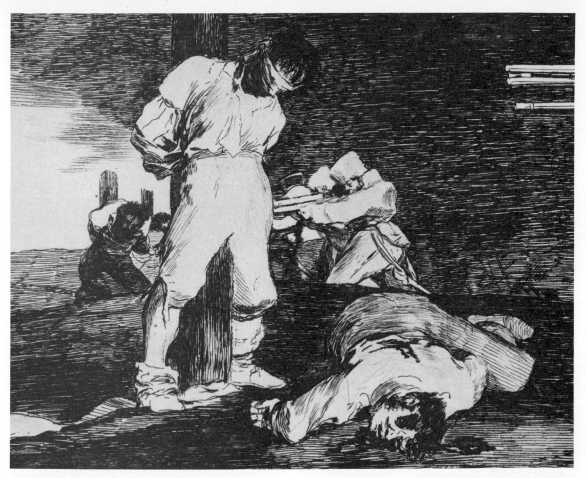

And There Is No Remedy—Etching by Francisco Goya (1746–1828). Napoleon could not understand the resistance of Spain to his grand plan. Spaniards rejected Napoleon's gentle brother as their new monarch. Their revolt was a "war to the knife." Executions and repression followed. Napoleon would state, "That miserable Spanish affair killed me." (*Philadelphia Museum of Art: SmithKline Beckman Corporation Fund*)

French forces in a permanent state of anxiety. An invisible army had spread itself over Spain. The war waged by Spanish partisans foreshadowed a twentieth-century phenomenon—the inability of a great power, using trained soldiers and modern weapons, to subdue peasant guerrillas.

Seeking to keep alive the struggle against Napoleon, Britain came to the aid of the Spanish insurgents. The intervention of British troops commanded by Sir Arthur Wellesley, the future duke of Wellington, led to the ultimate defeat of Joseph in 1813. The "Spanish ulcer" drained Napoleon's treasury, tied down hundreds of thousands of French troops, enabled Britain to gain a foothold on the Continent from which to invade southern France, and inspired patriots in other lands to resist the French emperor.

The German War of Liberation

Anti-French feeling also broke out in the German states. Hatred of the French invaders evoked a feeling of national outrage among some Germans, who up to this time had thought only in terms of their own particular state and prince.

The humiliation of defeat, combined with a flourishing national culture fashioned by talented writers using a common literary language, imbued some German intellectuals with a sense of national identity and national purpose. Using the emotional language of nationalism, these intellectuals called for a war of liberation against Napoleon and, in some instances, for the creation of a unified Germany. In urging Germans to seek vengeance against the conqueror, poet Ernst Moritz Arndt insisted that it was "the highest religion to love the Fatherland more dearly than lords and princes, fathers and mothers, wives and children."[26]

Other than this handful of intellectuals, however, few Germans were aroused by a desire for political unification. Nor did there occur anything like the general uprising that took place in Spain. Nevertheless, during the Napoleonic era, German nationalism took shape and would continue to grow in intensity, for students, professors, and poets had found a cause worthy of their idealism.

In addition to arousing a desire for national independence and unity, French domination of Germany stimulated a movement for reform and revitalization. The impact of revolutionary ideals, armies, and administration reached into Prussia, giving rise to a reform movement among members of the Prussian high bureaucracy and officer corps. The disastrous defeat of the Prussians at Jena (1806), the oppressive Peace of Tilsit (1807), the presence of a French army of occupation, and the weakening of the Prussian economy by Napoleon's policy of "France first" spurred the reform party to act. If Prussia were to survive in a world altered by the French Revolution, it would have to learn the principal lessons of the Revolution— that aroused citizens fighting for a cause make better soldiers than mercenaries and oppressed serfs, and that officers selected for daring and intelligence command better than nobles possessing only a gilded birthright.

To drive the French out of Prussia, it would be necessary to overcome the apathy of the Prussian people—so painfully demonstrated at Jena and in their passive responses to French occupation— and to bind the Prussians to the monarchy in a spirit of cooperation and loyalty. The heart of the Prussian nation must beat with the same national energy that spurred the armies of the Jacobin republic against foreign invaders. This strengthening of the state, it was felt, could be accomplished only through immediate and far-reaching social and political reforms.

The reforms were largely achieved by Baron Karl vom Stein, who served for a while as first minister to King Frederick William III. Stein believed that the elimination of social abuses would overcome defeatism and apathy and encourage Prussians to serve the state willingly and to fight bravely for national honor. A revitalized Prussia could then deal with the French. "The chief idea," said Stein, "was to arouse a moral, religious, and patriotic spirit in the nation, to instill into it again courage, confidence, readiness for every sacrifice in behalf of independence from foreigners and for the national honor, and to seize the first favorable opportunity to begin the bloody and hazardous struggle."[27]

Among the important reforms introduced in Prussia between 1807 and 1813 were the abolition of serfdom, the granting to towns of a large measure of self-administration, the awarding of army commissions on the basis of merit instead of birth, the elimination of cruel punishment in the ranks, and the establishment of national conscription. In 1813, the reform party forced King Frederick William III to declare war on France. The military reforms did improve the quality of the Prussian army. In the War of Liberation (1813), Prussian soldiers demonstrated far more enthusiasm and patriotism than they had at Jena in 1806, and the French were driven from Germany. The German War of Liberation came on the heels of Napoleon's disastrous Russian campaign.

Disaster in Russia

The unsuccessful invasion of Russia in 1812 diminished Napoleon's glory and hastened the collapse of his empire. Deteriorating relations between Russia and France led Napoleon to his fatal decision to attack the Eastern giant. Unwilling to permit Russia to become a Mediterranean power, the emperor resisted the tsar's attempts to acquire Constantinople. Napoleon's creation of the Grand Duchy of Warsaw irritated the tsar, who feared a revival of Polish power and resented French influence on Russia's border. Another source of friction between the tsar and Napoleon was Russia's illicit trade with Britain in violation of the Continental System. If the tsar were permitted to violate the trade regulations, Napoleon reasoned, other lands would soon follow and England would never be subdued. No doubt Napoleon's inexhaustible craving for power also compelled him to strike at Russia.

Napoleon assembled one of the largest armies in history—some 614,000 men, 200,000 animals, and 20,000 vehicles. Frenchmen comprised about half the *Grande Armée de la Russie;* the other soldiers, many serving under compulsion, were drawn from a score of nationalities. The emperor intended to deal the Russians a crushing blow, compelling Tsar Alexander I to sue for peace. But the Russians had other plans—to avoid pitched battles, retreat eastward, and refuse to make peace with the invader. Napoleon would be drawn ever deeper into Russia in pursuit of the enemy.

In June 1812, the Grand Army crossed the Neman River into Russia. Fighting only rearguard battles and retreating according to plan, the tsar's forces lured the invaders into the vastness of Russia, far from their lines of supply. In September the Russians made a stand at Borodino, some seventy miles west of Moscow. Although the French won, opening the road to Moscow, they lost 40,000 men and failed to destroy the Russian army, which withdrew in order. Napoleon still did not have the decisive victory with which he hoped to force the tsar to make peace. At midnight on September 14, the Grand Army, its numbers greatly reduced by disease, hunger, exhaustion, desertion, and battle, entered Moscow. Expecting to be greeted by a deputation of nobles, Napoleon found instead that the Muscovites had virtually evacuated their holy city. To show their contempt for the French conquerors, and to hinder their stay, the Russians set fire to the city, which burned for five days.

Taking up headquarters in Moscow, Napoleon waited for Alexander I to admit defeat and come to terms. But the tsar remained intransigent. Napoleon was in a dilemma: to penetrate deeper into Russia was certain death; to stay in Moscow with winter approaching meant possible starvation. Faced with these alternatives, Napoleon decided to retreat westward to his sources of supply. On October 19, 1812, 95,000 troops and thousands of wagons loaded with loot left Moscow for the long trek back.

In early November came the first snow and frost. Army stragglers were slaughtered by Russian Cossacks and peasant partisans. Hungry soldiers pounced on fallen horses, carving them up alive. The wounded were left to lie where they dropped. Some wretches, wrote a French officer, "dragged themselves along, shivering . . . until the snow packed under the soles of their boots, a bit of debris, a branch, or the body of a fallen comrade tripped them and threw them down. Then their moans for help went unheeded. The snow soon covered them up and only low white mounds showed where they lay. Our road was strewn with these hummocks, like a cemetery." [28]

In the middle of December, with the Russians in pursuit, the remnants of the Grand Army staggered across the Neman River into East Prussia. Napoleon had left his men earlier in the month and, traveling in disguise, reached Paris on December 18. Napoleon had lost his army; he would soon lose his throne.

Final Defeat

After the destruction of the Grand Army, the empire crumbled. Although Napoleon raised a new army, he could not replace the equipment, cavalry horses, and experienced soldiers squandered in Russia. Now he had to rely on schoolboys and overage veterans.

Most of Europe joined in a final coalition against France. In October 1813, allied forces from Austria, Prussia, Russia, and Sweden defeated Napoleon at Leipzig; in November, Anglo-Spanish forces crossed the Pyrenees into France. Finally, in the spring of 1814, the allies captured Paris. Napoleon abdicated and was exiled to the tiny island of Elba off the coast of Italy. The Bourbon dynasty was restored to the throne of France in the person of Louis XVIII, younger brother of the executed Louis XVI and the acknowledged leader of the émigrés.

Only forty-four years of age, Napoleon did not believe that it was his destiny to die on Elba. On March 1, 1815, he landed on the French coast with a thousand soldiers. Louis XVIII ordered his troops to stop Napoleon's advance. When Napoleon's small force approached the king's troops,

Napoleon walked up to the soldiers who blocked the road. "If there is one soldier among you who wishes to kill his Emperor, here I am." It was a brilliant move by a man who thoroughly understood the French soldier. The king's troops shouted, "Long live the Emperor!" and joined Napoleon. On March 20, 1815, Napoleon entered Paris to a hero's welcome. He had not lost his charisma.

Raising a new army, Napoleon moved against the allied forces in Belgium. There the Prussians, led by Field Marshal Gebhard von Blücher, and the British, led by the duke of Wellington, defeated Napoleon at Waterloo in June 1815. Napoleon's desperate gamble to regain power—the famous "hundred days"—had failed. This time the allies sent Napoleon to St. Helena, a lonely island in the South Atlantic a thousand miles off the coast of southern Africa. On this gloomy and rugged rock, Napoleon Bonaparte, emperor of France and would-be conqueror of Europe, spent the last six years of his life.

The Legend and the Achievement

"Is there anyone whose decisions have had a greater consequence for the whole of Europe?" asks Dutch historian Pieter Geyl about Napoleon.[29] It might also be asked: Is there anyone about whom there has been such a wide range of conflicting interpretations? Both Napoleon's contemporaries and later analysts have seen Napoleon in many different lights.

Napoleon himself contributed to the historical debate. Concerned as ever with his reputation, he reconstructed his career while on St. Helena. His reminiscences are the chief source of the Napoleonic legend. According to this account, Napoleon's principal aim was to defend the Revolution and consolidate its gains. He emerges as a champion of equality, a supporter of popular sovereignty, a destroyer of aristocratic privileges, a restorer of order, an opponent of religious intolerance, and a lover of peace forced to take up the sword because of the implacable hatred of Europe's reactionary rulers. According to this re-

construction, it was Napoleon's intention to spread the blessings of the Revolution to the Germans, Dutch, Spanish, Poles, and Italians, and to create a United States of Europe, a federation of free and enlightened nations living in peace. Had Napoleon realized this vision of a socially modernized, economically integrated, rationally ruled, and politically unified western Europe, which already shared a common cultural tradition, he would have performed one of the great creative acts in human history.

Undoubtedly, Napoleon did disseminate many gains of the Revolution. Nevertheless, say his critics, this account overlooks much. It ignores the repression of liberty, the subverting of republicanism, the oppression of conquered peoples, and the terrible suffering resulting from his pursuit of glory. The reminiscences were another example of Napoleonic propaganda.

Although the debate over Napoleon continues, historians agree on two points. First, his was no ordinary life. A self-made man who harnessed the revolutionary forces of the age and imposed his will on history, Napoleon was right to call his life a romance. His drive, military genius, and charisma propelled him to the peak of power; his inability to moderate his ambition bled Europe, distorted his judgment, and caused his downfall. His overweening pride, the hubris of the Greek tragedians, would have awed Sophocles; the dimensions of his mind and the intricacies of his personality would have intrigued Shakespeare; his cynicism and utter unscrupulousness would have impressed Machiavelli. Second, historians agree that by spreading revolutionary ideals and institutions, Napoleon made it impossible for the traditional rulers to restore the Old Regime intact after the emperor's downfall. The destruction of feudal remnants, the secularization of society, the transformation of the dynastic state into the modern national state, and the prominence of the bourgeoisie were assured.

The new concept of warfare and the new spirit of nationalism also became an indelible part of the European scene. In the course of succeeding generations, the methods of total warfare in the service of a belligerent nationalism would shatter Napoleon's grandiose vision of a united Europe and subvert the liberal humanism that was the essential heritage of the Enlightenment and the French Revolution.

Chronology 20.1 Napoleon's Career

1796	Napoleon gets command of French Army of Italy
1798	The battle of the Nile; the British annihilate Napoleon's fleet
November 10, 1799	He helps overthrow the Directory's rule, establishing a strong executive in France
1802	He becomes first consul for life; peace is made with Austria and Britain
March 21, 1804	The Civil Code (called Code Napoléon in 1807)
December 2, 1804	He crowns himself emperor of the French
October 1805	French forces occupy Vienna
October 21, 1805	The battle of Trafalgar—French and Spanish fleets are defeated by the British
December 1805	The battle of Austerlitz—Napoleon defeats Russo-Austrian forces
1806	War against Prussia and Russia
October 1806	He defeats the Prussians at Jena, and French forces occupy Berlin
June 1807	French victory over the Russians at Friedland
July 1807	The treaties of Tilsit
1808–1813	The Peninsular War—Spaniards, aided by the British, fight against French occupation
September 14, 1812	The Grand Army reaches Moscow
October–December 1812	The Grand Army retreats from Russia
October 1813	Allied forces defeat Napoleon at Leipzig
1814	Paris is captured and Napoleon is exiled to Elba
March 20, 1815	Escaping, he enters Paris and begins 100 days' rule
June 1815	Defeated at Waterloo, he is exiled to St. Helena

Notes

1. Quoted in Felix Markham, *Napoleon and the Awakening of Europe* (New York: Collier Books, 1965), p. 27.

2. Excerpted in J. Christopher Herold, ed., *The Mind of Napoleon* (New York: Columbia University Press, 1955), p. 260.

3. Georges Lefebvre, *Napoleon* (New York: Columbia University Press, 1969), 2:65.

4. Ibid., 2: 67.

5. Ibid., 2: 66.

6. Quoted in David Chandler, *The Campaigns of Napoleon* (New York: Macmillan, 1966), p. 157.

7. Excerpted in Maurice Hutt, ed., *Napoleon* (Englewood Cliffs, N.J.: Prentice-Hall, 1972), p. 3.

8. Excerpted in David L. Dowd, ed., *Napoleon: Was He the Heir of the Revolution?* (New York: Holt, Rinehart, and Winston, 1966), p. 42.

9. Quoted in Felix Markham, *Napoleon* (New York: Mentor Books, 1963), p. 100.

10. Excerpted in Frank Malloy Anderson, ed., *The Constitution and Other Select Documents Illustrative of the History of France* (Minneapolis: H. W. Wilson, 1908), pp. 312–313.

11. Quoted in Robert B. Holtman, *The Napoleonic Revolution* (Philadelphia: J. B. Lippincott, 1967), pp. 123–124.

12. Quoted in ibid., p. 121.

13. Quoted in Markham, *Napoleon,* p. 97.

14. Dowd, *Napoleon,* p. 27.

15. Quoted in Holtman, *The Napoleonic Revolution,* p. 143.

16. Excerpted in Hutt, *Napoleon,* pp. 49–50.

17. Quoted in Chandler, *The Campaigns of Napoleon,* p. 145.

18. Ibid.

19. Ibid., p. 155.

20. Ibid.

21. Ibid., p. 157.

22. Quoted in Jacques Godechot, Beatrice F. Hyslop, and David L. Dowd, *The Napoleonic Era in Europe* (New York: Holt, Rinehart, and Winston, 1971), pp. 170, 172.

23. Excerpted in Dowd, *Napoleon,* p. 57.

24. Quoted in Owen Connelly, *Napoleon's Satellite Kingdoms* (New York: The Free Press, 1965), p. 223.

25. Quoted in Owen Connelly, *The Gentle Bonaparte* (New York: Macmillan, 1968), pp. 110–111.

26. Quoted in Boyd C. Shafer, *Nationalism: Myth and Reality* (New York: Harcourt, Brace, 1955), p. 139.

27. Quoted in Gordon A. Craig, *The Politics of the Prussian Army, 1640–1945* (New York: Oxford University Press, 1964), p. 40.

28. Quoted in J. Christopher Herold, *The Age of Napoleon* (New York: Dell, 1963), p. 320.

29. Pieter Geyl, *Napoleon For and Against* (New Haven: Yale University Press, 1964), p. 16.

Suggested Reading

Chandler, David, *The Campaigns of Napoleon* (1966). An exhaustive analysis of Napoleon's art of war.

Connelly, Owen, *Napoleon's Satellite Kingdoms* (1965). Focuses on the kingdoms in Naples, Italy, Holland, Spain, and Westphalia that were created by Napoleon and ruled by his relatives.

———, *The Gentle Bonaparte* (1968). A biography of Napoleon's elder brother; a good treatment of Napoleon's involvement in Spain.

Cronin, Vincent, *Napoleon Bonaparte* (1972). A highly acclaimed biography.

Geyl, Pieter, *Napoleon For and Against* (1964). A critical evaluation of French writers' views of Napoleon.

Herold, J. Christopher, ed., *The Mind of Napoleon* (1955). A valuable selection from the written and spoken words of Napoleon.

———, *The Horizon Book of the Age of Napoleon* (1965). Napoleon and his times.

Holtman, Robert B., *The Napoleonic Revolution* (1967). Napoleon as revolutionary innovator who influenced every aspect of European life; particularly good on Napoleon the propagandist.

Howarth, David, *Waterloo* (1968). A re-creation of the battle as it appeared to those who fought it.

Hutt, Maurice, ed., *Napoleon* (1972). Excerpts from Napoleon's words and the views of contemporaries and later historians.

Lefebvre, Georges, *Napoleon,* 2 vols. (1969). An authoritative biography.

Markham, Felix, *Napoleon* (1963). A first-rate short biography.

——, *Napoleon and the Awakening of Europe* (1965). Napoleon's influence on other lands.

Review Questions

1. What made it possible for Napoleon to gain power?

2. What personality traits did Napoleon possess?

3. What principles underlay Napoleon's domestic reforms?

4. What was Napoleon's "art of war"? Describe his tactics.

5. Napoleon both preserved and destroyed the ideals of the French Revolution. Discuss this statement.

6. Why did England feel compelled to resist Napoleon? What were the intent and significance of the Continental System?

7. What was the significance of the Peninsular War?

8. Why did Prussian officials urge reforms? Describe the nature and significance of these reforms.

9. Account for Napoleon's defeat in Russia.

10. Identify and explain the historical significance of the battle of Leipzig and the "hundred days."

11. What were Napoleon's greatest achievements? What were his greatest failures?

12. Why do some people regret that Napoleon did not establish a "United States of Europe"?

21

The Industrial Revolution: The Transformation of Society

Forces at work in the European economy and society in the second half of the eighteenth century were destined to have an even greater significance for humanity than the French Revolution. Experimentation with crops and animals, the development of new forms of organizing labor and capital, and the beginnings of technological change had so startling an impact that French observers of the English economy in the 1820s gave these developments a name—*industrialism,* or the *Industrial Revolution.* These changes took place first in England, but within a short time the "English system" spread to Europe and the United States, and by the twentieth century it had affected the entire world.

The term *Industrial Revolution* refers to the shift from an agrarian, handicraft, labor-intensive economy to one dominated by machine manufacture, specialization of tasks, factories, a freer flow of capital, and the concentration of people in cities. For contemporaries of the Industrial Revolution, the application of machines to human tasks seemed the most significant change taking place. They thought that technology might alleviate poverty, want, and harsh labor. The early inventions are less impressive today—many being simple alterations of existing tools. Instead, what stands out are the era's new and more efficient ways of organizing tasks, the increase in agricultural productivity, the harnessing of plentiful labor, and the expanded role of financial institutions.

Industrial progress did not proceed everywhere at the same pace. The changes that began in England in the middle of the eighteenth century did not start in France until the French Revolution. From the 1780s to 1850, the social and political turmoil in France had a mixed effect on economic development: in some respects, conflict advanced it; in others, it hindered growth. Because the German states were not united politically, industry began there in the 1840s, a century after England

Pithead of a Coal Mine. (*National Museums and Galleries on Merseyside/Walker Art Gallery*)

461

began industrialization. Rapid economic expansion caused such severe hardships for artisans, craftsmen, and rural laborers that social and political revolution swept the region. After German unification in 1870, industry grew phenomenally, but many aspects of traditional economy persisted alongside the revolutionary industrial changes. Industrialization began slowly in Italy, too, where it was hampered by the sharp economic divisions between north and south, the comparative lack of natural resources, and the slow political unification of the peninsula. In eastern Europe, the beginnings of industrialization were delayed to the very last decade of the nineteenth century.

In the first half of the century, then, Britain stepped out ahead of Belgium, the United States, France, and the states in the west of Germany. By the second half of the nineteenth century, Germany, France, and the United States had moved into genuine competition with Britain as industrial powers; and Italy, Russia, and Austria-Hungary were being drawn into the Industrial Revolution. Almost inevitably, Europeans and Americans, and eventually people in countries around the globe, were driven to adopt the changes in agriculture and industry that had originated in England. Everywhere, as the economy changed, the conditions of labor and life were altered profoundly. The Industrial Revolution is truly a revolution without boundaries and, thus far, without an end in sight.

The Rise of the Industrial Age

The Roots of Industrialization

The process of industrialization began in western Europe for a number of reasons. Western Europe was wealthier than much of the world, and its wealth was spread across more classes of people. This wealth had accumulated slowly over the centuries, despite the devastations of famine, plague, and war. The widespread production of diverse rural handicrafts, such as weaving, leather tanning, jewelry making, for the preceding two centuries provided the foundation for the comparatively rapid expansion of trade, both overseas and on the Continent, during the sixteenth and seventeenth centuries (the Commercial Revolution). This expansion resulted from an aggressive search for new markets rather than from new methods of production; it built on the capitalist practices of medieval and Renaissance bankers and merchants, and tapped the wealth of a much larger area of the world than the Mediterranean lands accessible to earlier generations. Thus the resources of the New World and of Africa, both human and material, fueled Europe's accumulation of wealth.

Western agriculture, which differed from that of the Orient in many ways, also contributed greatly to the coming of the industrial age in Europe. Western agriculture was comparatively thrifty of land, capital, and human labor. Grain crops could grow on lands that varied in fertility and contour and did not require the costly irrigation ditches, dams, and canals of rice cultivation. Over the centuries, the decline of serfdom and manorial obligations and the increasing efficiency of agriculture freed people for new forms of labor; there was no development in western Europe of state power comparable to that of China or Russia, which kept labor tied to the land.

In the early modern period the states that had centralized power in the hands of a strong monarch—England, Spain, Portugal, France—competed for markets, for territory, and for prestige in ways that contributed to economic expansion. Engaged in fierce military and commercial rivalries, these states, with varying degrees of success, actively promoted industries to manufacture weaponry, uniforms, and ships, and encouraged commerce for tax revenues. Thus aided, the growth in commerce nurtured a greatly expanded economy in which many levels of society participated—great estate owners, merchant princes, innovative entrepreneurs, the sugar plantation colonials, slave traders, sailors, and peasants. (See Chapter 15.)

The Population Explosion

The enormous European population growth of the eighteenth century provided industry with both consumers and labor. Most of this growth took place after the middle of the century and continued into the nineteenth century. In the Europe of 1800, there were about 190 million people; by 1914 there were 460 million people, with about 200 million other Europeans scattered throughout the world.

The population expanded rapidly for several reasons. First, the number of births increased as women married at younger ages—on the average, as much as three years younger. Early marriage—particularly among agriculturalists, a sign of their greater prosperity—meant more children with a better chance to survive because of improved nutrition. Second, the number of deaths from war, famine, and disease declined at the same time. More efficient agriculture and better food distribution reduced malnutrition, which meant better health, more births, and fewer deaths. The signs of better nutrition and better health included greater height—the average European man was five feet six inches tall in 1900, compared to five feet a century earlier—and a lower age at which girls began to menstruate, which contributed to more births. With better nutrition, more children survived, grew stronger and taller, could work harder and longer, and were intellectually more able.

The Agricultural Revolution

Population growth might have brought famine, disease, and misery to Europe as it had so many times before, and as it continued to do in other areas of the world—but it did not. Certainly, signs of rural destitution existed in Europe in the last part of the eighteenth century, when many people actually believed that population was declining because the countryside was deserted. This rural poverty contributed to social unrest. Major changes in agriculture, which took place over a period of two centuries—a "green revolution" of new crops and new ways of utilizing land and labor—not only increased productivity enough to feed the growing population but also improved the diet of many Europeans.

By the eighteenth century, traditional patterns of farming were breaking up in western Europe. Agriculture became more and more a capitalist enterprise; production was undertaken for the market, not for family or village consumption. Land freed from traditional obligations became just another commodity to be bought, sold, and traded. Many people, aristocrats as well as peasants, may have persisted in traditional patterns and obligations, but powerful market forces gradually drew most farmers to the marketplace, first in western European lands, then in central Europe, and finally in eastern Europe. After 1750 the British and Dutch practice of selective breeding of animals became more widespread, and land use grew more efficient. Through convertible husbandry, which cycled land from grain production through soil-restoring crops of legumes and then pasturage, farmers could keep all their fields in production rather than leave some fallow as had been the practice for centuries. The improved methods gradually spread to the peasantry. However, in some areas within every country, particularly in central and eastern Europe, the old farming practices continued well into the nineteenth century.

Peasants freed from manorial obligations joined the ranks of entrepreneurs and tenants and wage laborers, all farming produce for the market. Undeveloped land was brought under cultivation. Land formerly used in common by villagers for grazing animals was claimed for private use. Usually the great landowners took advantage of their power or of the law and laid claim to these common lands. This process of *enclosure,* or fencing off formerly communal land for private use, took place over much of Europe. In England most of the enclosure took place in the sixteenth and seventeenth centuries as powerful landlords increased and consolidated their total holdings. At the end of the eighteenth century, however, the severe social disruption caused by the new agricultural trends made people believe that a relatively small number of additional enclosures caused displaced farmers to emigrate to urban areas or to the Americas and Australia.

By the middle of the nineteenth century—after two centuries of increased agricultural productivity with little change in technology—the application of technical ingenuity to farming brought improved plows, reapers, horse-drawn rakes, and threshers. (The Americans were very inventive in this area; their agricultural machinery formed a substantial part of their manufacturing exports.)

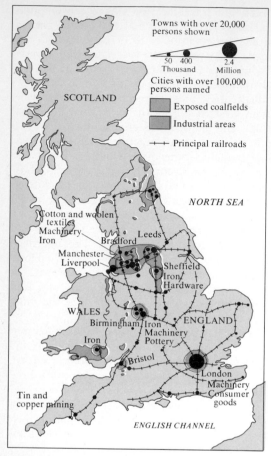

Map 21.1 Industrial Growth in England, Mid-1800s

These technological improvements greatly increased efficiency and production and meant that fewer men and women could produce more food and raw materials.

Britain First

Why was Great Britain the first country to industrialize? What advantages did it possess that other European nations lacked? France, for example, was wealthier and more populous and possessed an empire equal to England's in trading importance. The French had a skilled populace, and the government, if anything, was more responsive than Britain's to the need for transportation and communication. The French had established schools for technicians and fostered civil engineers for such public works as waterworks, canals, roads, and bridges. The French, however, seemed less willing than the British to change traditional ways—methods of agriculture or of craft production, for example. The size of the landholdings, which were smaller than in England, may have discouraged experimentation. Although the French populace generally lived less well than the English, they had enough wealth to make an effective demand for products at home. Well into the nineteenth century, the demand was for fine handmade goods for the few rather than cheap, machine-made goods for the many. As a result, French industrialization was slow. A more serious obstacle to industrialization, which German and Italian states faced later, was the existence of internal tariffs, which lasted until the French Revolution. England did not have these obstacles to the free flow of goods within the country, and after the union of Scotland with England in 1707, trade flourished throughout the British Isles.

In some ways, the French Revolution, which gave so much political freedom and opportunity, perpetuated traditional agricultural and commercial practices. Peasants who acquired land in the Revolution often gained plots so small that the new farming methods were difficult to apply; they continued the old agricultural practices. They tried to restrict the size of their families so they could feed themselves. But inefficient small farms prevented the raising of a surplus for the market. Under such conditions, it was even harder for the French to develop or maintain the optimistic, expansive mentality that contributes to economic development.

Like France, the Netherlands had sufficient wealth to support industrialization. During the seventeenth century, the Dutch had developed techniques of finance and commerce that every nation tried to imitate. They had a good transportation system, a fine navy, and technical know-how. They were skilled farmers. The Netherlands, however, lacks natural resources. In the eighteenth century, the Dutch put their best efforts into finance rather than into expanding manufacturing and trade.

Britain, thus, possessed several advantages that

enabled it to take the lead. Large and easily developed supplies of coal and iron had given the British a long tradition of metallurgy and mining. In the early stages of industrialization, Britain's river transportation system was supplemented by canals and toll roads (turnpikes) that private entrepreneurs financed and built for profit. In addition, Britain had a labor pool of farmers who could no longer earn a living for themselves and their families on the land.

The role played by private enterprise in Britain's economic development was extraordinary and unique, but the state played a part as well. Parliament created a climate favorable to economic expansion. The state aided industrialization by providing law, order, and protection of private property. The laws allowed for the enclosure of common lands, which pushed the remaining small farmers off the land and permitted large holdings to be consolidated. Parliament chartered businesses, such as toll bridge and canal builders and the East India Company, which expanded trade routes and enriched the British economy. The freedom of entry into economic activity was remarkable; entrepreneurs were much less restricted by monopolies, charters, and guilds than their countrymen of the previous century or other Europeans of the eighteenth and nineteenth centuries.

Changes in Technology

The Industrial Revolution brought a change from handicrafts to machine manufacture and from human or animal power to other forms of energy, such as steam and the internal combustion engine. The first stages of industrialization in any particular trade, however, often resulted from simple changes made by workers as they plied their craft and involved very little, if any, capital.

The Cotton Industry   Long the home of an important wool trade, Britain in the eighteenth century jumped ahead in the production of cotton, the industry that first showed the possibility of unprecedented growth rates. British cotton production expanded tenfold between 1760 and 1785, and another tenfold between 1785 and 1825. A series of inventions revolutionized the

industry and drastically altered the social conditions of the work. In 1733, long before expansion started, a simple invention—John Kay's flying shuttle—made it possible for weavers to double their output. This shuttle, which could be used in the home, was an adaptation of a device that had been used in the wool trade for generations. The flying shuttle enabled weavers to produce faster than spinners could spin until James Hargreaves' spinning jenny, perfected by 1768, allowed an operator to work several spindles at once—powered only by human energy. Within five years, Richard Arkwright's water frame spinning machine could be powered by water or animals, and Samuel Crompton's spinning mule (1779) powered many spindles first by human power, later by animal and water energy. These changes improved spinning productivity so much that bottlenecks in weaving developed until Edmund Cartwright developed a power loom in 1787.* To the end of the century there was a race to speed up the spinning part of the process and then the weaving part by applying water power to looms or new, larger devices to the jenny.

Arkwright's water frame made it more efficient to bring many workers together, rather than sending work out to individuals in their own homes. This development was the beginning of the factory system, which within a generation would revolutionize the conditions of labor. Because water power drove these early machines, mills were located near rivers and streams. Towns thus grew up where machinery could be powered by water; the factory system concentrated laborers and their families near the factories. When steam power became widely applied, laborers could be dispersed, but the other advantages of urbanized factory labor continued the trend toward greater concentrations of population.

Weavers and spinners—not technicians, engineers, or scientists—invented these simple de-

---

*Technological developments in America helped meet the growing demand for raw cotton. Eli Whitney's cotton gin (1793) removed the seeds from raw cotton quickly and cheaply, leading farmers and plantation owners to devote more land to cotton. Within a generation, more laborers were required for the fields and less to process the cotton. The increased demand for slave labor brought far-reaching changes.

Woman at Hargreaves's Spinning Jenny. The textile trade was one of the first to be mechanized. In the cottage industries, farmers and their families were weavers and spinners—sometimes even inventors. (*Mary Evans Picture Library*)

vices, modeled after machines already in use. These inventions did not cause the cotton industry's explosive expansion—that resulted from social and economic demand—but once begun, the expansion was so great, the demand so urgent, and the potential profits so great that more and more complicated technology was developed. A role emerged for the engineer, an expert in building and adapting machines.

The Steam Engine James Watt, a Scottish engineer, developed the steam engine in the 1760s, although it was too expensive to be adapted to production for some time. Women, children, and even men laborers were cheaper than a steam engine. As engines and fuel became cheaper,

however, entrepreneurs began to use them, and industrial expansion became even more rapid. Because they ran on coal or wood, not water power, steam engines allowed greater flexibility in locating textile mills. Factories were no longer restricted to the power supplied by a river or a stream or to the space available beside flowing water; they could be built anywhere.

Once steam power was applied to industries in the middle of the nineteenth century—particularly to transportation—this change produced the incredible rate of progress that most people identify with the Industrial Revolution. The two centuries of increasing productivity, which made possible the accumulation of capital and provisioning of population growth—the first steps of industrialization—were powered by people, animals, and water. With steam, the whole pattern of work changed because weaker, younger, and less-skilled workers could be taught the few simple tasks necessary to mind the machine. The shift from male to female and child labor was a major social change. Moreover, as steam took hold, human participation in the process of manufacture diminished; engines replaced people, and workers began to be referred to as "hired hands" who drove machines.

The Iron Industry   Although steam power made it possible to hire weaker people to operate machinery, it required machines made of stronger metal to withstand the forces generated by a stronger power source. The history of the search for better iron illustrates how developments in one industry led to change in related industries; it furnishes many examples of trial and error, leading to better techniques; and it shows both the narrowness of inventiveness as a trait exhibited by persons within a single family and the breadth of inventiveness as a process to which developers from much of western Europe ultimately contributed.

Before the eighteenth century, the methods of producing iron had changed little since the Middle Ages. The first step in increasing the production of high-quality iron came when Abraham Darby produced coke-smelted cast iron in 1709. His son and grandson further improved the quality of the iron by improving the quality of coke (a form of coal) and making a better bellows to heat the furnaces. Their methods worked, and by the mid-eighteenth century, the quality of cast iron was so high that it began to replace wood in construction. Another major advance came when ironmakers learned to turn cast iron into wrought iron. High-quality wrought iron was expensive because the cost of wood to fire the furnaces was so high. This led Englishmen to look for ways to use coal, which was cheap but contained impurities that made a poor, brittle metal. Henry Cort borrowed a French idea of making a furnace with two separate compartments, one for coal and one for iron, but he altered the process by puddling (stirring the molten iron) and then rolling it as it cooled. His methods reduced the impurities and made the process much faster. By the 1780s, trial and error

had perfected the production of wrought iron, which became the most widely used metal until steel began to be cheaply produced in the 1860s.

The iron industry made great demands on the coal mines to fuel its furnaces. Because steam engines enabled miners to pump water from the mines more efficiently and at a much deeper level, rich veins in existing mines became accessible for the first time. Steam engines also lifted the coal up the main shaft to the surface. Britain's production of coal kept pace with the industrial growth it powered; it rose from 16 million tons at the end of the Napoleonic wars to 30 million in 1836 and to 65 million in 1856.

The greater productivity in coal allowed the continued improvement of iron smelting. Then in 1856, Henry Bessemer developed a process for converting pig iron into steel by removing the impurities in the iron. In the 1860s, William Siemens and Pierre and Émile Martin (brothers) developed the open-hearth process, which could handle much greater amounts of metal than Bessemer's converter. Steel became so cheap to produce that it quickly replaced iron in industry because of its greater tensile strength and durability.

Transportation and Communications   Changes in mining, metallurgy, textiles, pottery, and farming speeded change in other industries, especially transportation and communications. Transportation was revolutionized, thus providing a network that could support expansion in many other areas of the economy. Major road-building took place in the eighteenth century in England and France, and later in the rest of Europe. Canals were constructed in Britain and the United States between 1760 and 1820, only to be quickly outmoded by railroads. Railroads were so successful that in mid-nineteenth-century England, roads became mere auxiliaries to the railroads—just paths leading to the station. Not until the turn of the century was a complete network of roads thought essential to public transport in Britain.

Britain was not the leader in every new mode of transportation. Because Britain's rivers were small, steamboats could not be widely used for internal navigation. But in the United States, many steamboats plied its broad rivers in the first part of the nineteenth century. For long journeys, such as transatlantic crossings, however, steamboats could not compete with the tall-masted clipper ships of the 1850s. These sailing ships were faster and did not have to carry coal for an engine, so their cargo holds could be filled entirely with profitable trade goods.

Unprecedented amounts of private British capital built Britain's system of roads, canals, and railways. Continental states were slower to adopt steam transport because they lacked capital and skilled civil engineering. Only France invested a great percentage of private capital in transportation. It took various failures of management and finance before the French government assumed control of its railroads, but in most of Europe, state construction and control was the rule. In the United States, Congress gave enormous grants of land to railroad companies to encourage the laying of tracks. Everywhere during the railroad building boom that extended throughout the nineteenth century, financiers invested heavily in railroads, and the flow of capital from western Europe, particularly Britain and France, to other lands in Europe and to America was an awesome achievement. The flow of finance across borders and oceans was matched only by the flow of labor, as Europeans and Asians built railroad networks to support the expanding agriculture and industry of the New World.

Communications changed as spectacularly as transportation. Britain inaugurated the penny post in 1840, making it possible to send a letter to any part of the kingdom for one cent. But the cost of postage was so high elsewhere that letters were rarely written; many letters of the time fill every space on a single sheet of paper because the postage rate was cheapest for one sheet. When the telegraph was invented, the rapidity of its development indicated the business demand for cheap and fast communications. The first telegraphic message was sent from Baltimore to Washington, D.C., in 1844. Within seven years, the first submarine cable was laid under the English Channel, and by 1866, transatlantic cable was operating.

Changes in Finance

The first steps of industrialization—the agricultural advances and the early spinning and weaving machines—did not require much capital. Subsequent growth, however—from the spread of factories to the extensive application of machinery to agriculture, to the expansion of mining, and to construction in cities—required the investment of enormous capital. Railroads and steamship lines were often so expensive that only governments could finance them; even in Belgium, where they were privately financed at first, the king was the major investor. Funding the steel industry also required large investments.

In the earliest stages of industrialization, the owning family was the source of a company's finance, its management, and even its technical innovation. Family firms dominated industry. But outside investment grew with the demand for capital, which rose steadily from 1760 to the end of World War I (1918). In Britain, wealthy merchants and landlords provided investment capital, and low interest rates encouraged borrowing. On the Continent, the supply of capital was limited, so the British became international investors of the first rank, furnishing much of the capital for the industrialization of other nations. French investors, who were sometimes reluctant to invest at home because they feared its political instability, financed railroads in Austria and were the major investors in the Suez Canal and in the first canal project in Panama, which failed. People of the same religion or region would often band together to gather capital for development, as the Protestant and Jewish bankers of France did. Among banking families—including the Barings of London and the Rothschilds of France, England, and Germany—kinship ties joined together large amounts of investment capital. These investor groups were very important to European industrialization.

Banking, however, was risky business in the nineteenth century; dozens of banks failed in every financial crisis. Lacking insurance for deposits and possessing only limited resources, banks could not protect their investors. They tended toward cautious investment policies because they were vulnerable. To avoid the risk of losing everything in the failure of a single industry, banks diversified their investments. Thus, in any given country the number of industries able to borrow substantial amounts of capital was limited in the early stages of industrialization. In some countries, bankers preferred the safety of investing in

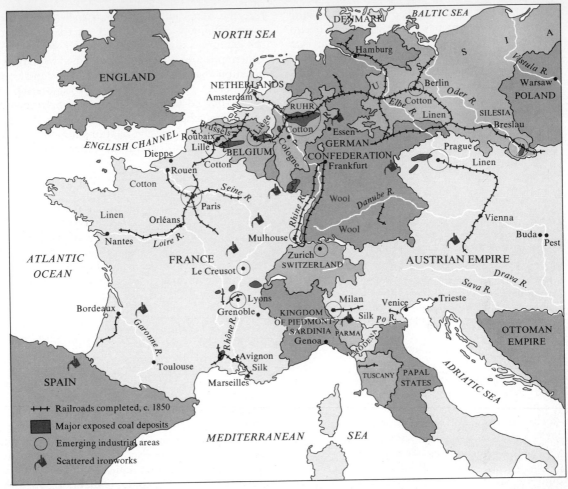

Map 21.2 Industrial Growth on the Continent, Mid-1800s

government debt, a preference that slowed down the development of industry.

One major difficulty in financing industry was the lack of a formal organization that would enable a number of people to pool their capital safely. In the existing joint-stock companies, individuals could be held responsible for all the debts of the enterprise. Although joint-stock companies were thought risky, more and more individuals joined together in this manner and retained the right to transfer their shares without the consent of other stockholders. England finally repealed the laws against this practice in 1825 and permitted incorporation in 1844. By incorporating, an organization would be treated as an individual before the law, although it was composed of a number of individuals joined together for commerce. This practice created firms that could live long after all the founders had died or sold their shares. More importantly, investors were liable for a corporation's debts only in proportion to the number of shares they owned. In 1844, after nearly a century of industrial progress, England had almost a thousand such companies, with a stock value of 345 million pounds, ready to incorporate legally, compared to only 260 similar companies in France. In the 1850s, limited liability was applied to the stock of most English businesses, and a little later it was extended to banking and insurance companies. This legal change meant that investors endangered only the amount that they paid for their stock, not all the funds that they possessed. By the 1860s, France, Germany, and the United States permitted limited liability, which released such a flow of savings that it sparked a surge of industrial growth.

Society Transformed

The changes in agricultural production, business organization, and technology had revolutionary consequences for society and politics. People were drawn from the countryside into cities and from one country to another. Traditional ways of life changed for Europeans, and eventually for non-Westerners, too. Industrialization made the world smaller; the whole world was drawn into commerce and, ultimately, manufacturing at a dizzying speed.

European society before industrialization was based on kinship. Property in the form of land formed the basis of social class and social power, which was usually exercised on a local or provincial level. Industrialization brought a new world with many forms of property and several kinds of power, and the nation ultimately became more important than the province, region, or local area. In this new world, individuals were increasingly important—before the law, in trade, and in political thought—but in trying to make their way through day-to-day adversity, they came to feel small, powerless, and isolated—cut adrift from families and villages. In a sense, the breakdown of family and town controls made individuals freer, but towns and families had offered irreplaceable support in time of need, such as unemployment or illness.

While the foundations of new socioeconomic patterns were being laid, much of the old life persisted, particularly during the first half of the nineteenth century. Landed property was still the principal form of wealth, and large landowners continued to exercise political power. From England to Russia, families of landed wealth (often the old noble families) continued to consti-

tute the social elite. European society remained overwhelmingly rural; as late as the middle of the century, only England was half urban. Still, contemporaries were so overwhelmed by industrialization that they saw it as a sudden and complete break with the past—the shattering of traditional moral and social patterns. Some people could remember the past; others idealized it as a golden age in which the relations between classes had been based on values other than wages and hours.

Historians, however, view industrialization as a process of gradual but sustained growth over 150 to 200 years and see the developments of the first half of the nineteenth century as laying the foundation for the rapid changes of the next 100 years. The fact that such a long process is still called a revolution is a sign of how great the total change was, rather than an indication of the rapidity with which it took place.

Urbanization

Cities grew in number, size, and population as a result of industrialization. No longer just seats of government and commerce, they became places of manufacture and industry as well. Before 1800, about 10 percent of the European population lived in cities (20 percent did in Great Britain and the Netherlands, the leading areas of urban living). A mere forty-five cities in the world had more than 100,000 people. Halfway through the nineteenth century, 52 percent of the British lived in cities, although only 25 percent of the French, 36 percent of the Germans, 7 percent of the Russians, and 10 percent of U.S. inhabitants did. Most of the shift from rural to urban living in Europe and the United States has taken place in the twentieth century, but the increase in Europe's urban population during the 1800s was acute in its influence. In some regions, industrial areas grew up almost overnight—the Midlands in England, the Lowlands in Scotland, the northern plains in France, the German Rhineland, the U.S. northeast, and parts of northern Italy.

Industrial cities in the nineteenth century, particularly in England, grew rapidly, without planning or much regulation by local or national governments. Government and business were often reluctant to use taxation to finance remedies

Jean François Millet (1814–1875): Harvesters
Resting, 1850–1853. The 1840s and 1850s were
decades of bitter social dislocation as machinery
was introduced to perform traditional tasks. The
most traditional of classes in Europe was the peasantry, here depicted in Millet's painting of French
men and women laboring for survival. (*Courtesy
Museum of Fine Arts, Boston*)

for poor working and living conditions. Civic
pride and private patronage were too weak to
combat the effects of unregulated private enterprise. On the European continent, where industrialization came later, states were more willing to
regulate industrial and urban development; they
also had the bureaucracy for planning and regulation, but such efforts were still inadequate. So
much growth with so little planning or control
led to cities with little sanitation, no lighting,
wretched housing, poor transportation, and little
security. Cities had grown without planning before, but they had not been home and workplace
for such large numbers of people, many of them
new arrivals. Rich and poor alike suffered in
this environment of disease, crime, and ugliness,
although the poor obviously bore the brunt of
these evils.

Major industrial cities developed similar housing patterns, due for the most part to the wide
disparity in economic and social power between
the classes. By mid-nineteenth century, the

wealthiest inhabitants circled the city's edge and
were close to the country, living in "suburbs" that
were roomier and cleaner than the city proper. As
a general rule, the farther one lived from the central city, the wealthier one was; the suburban
houses were detached (stood alone—not row
houses) and usually had gardens. The outer ring of
the city itself was the location most preferred by
the middle class, and it shared many of the characteristics of the wealthier suburbs. In the city's inner ring were the artisans' dwellings, ranging from
middle-class residences to small, attached row
houses, perhaps with small gardens. Further down
the social scale came workers' row houses, located
in the center of industrial towns. Long rows of
houses, several stories high, were jammed together
as close to the factories as possible, separated one
from the next by a courtyard. Usually this yard
comprised a strip of mud or cobblestones, with a
water pump in the middle that served all the residents adjoining the courtyard. When public transportation developed in the second half of the

century, workers' districts dispersed, sometimes to circle great governmental cities, such as London and Paris, where the wealthy monopolized the central city. In industrial cities, the earlier pattern remained, although new workers' housing might be scattered.

Almost universally, those who wrote about industrial cities—England's Manchester, Leeds, and Liverpool, and France's Lyons—described the stench, the filth, the inhumane crowding, the poverty, and the immorality. Novelists Charles Dickens, George Sand, and Émile Zola captured the horrors of urban industrial life and the plight of the poor. Parliamentary reports rivaled the novels in describing a London row:

> In the centre of this street there is a gutter into which potato parings, the refuse of vegetable and animal matter of all kinds, the dirty water from the washing of clothes and of the houses are all poured, and where they stagnate and putrefy . . . all the lanes and alleys of the neighbourhood pour their contents into the centre of the main street. . . . Families live in the cellars and kitchens of these undrained houses.

An 1842 government report from Leeds depicted

> Walls unwhitewashed for years, black with the smoke of foul chimneys, without water . . . and sacking for bedclothing, with floors unwashed from year to year, without out-offices [lavatories]. Outside there are streets, raised a foot, sometimes two above the level of the causeway, by the accumulation of years . . . stagnant puddles here and there . . . and excrementitious deposits on all sides as a consequence, undrained, unpaved, unventilated, uncared-for by any authority but the landlord, who weekly collects his miserable rents from his miserable tenants.

Changes in Social Structure

The Industrial Revolution destroyed forever the old division of society into clergy, nobility, and commoners. The development of industry and commerce caused a corresponding development of a bourgeoisie, a middle class comprised of people of common birth who engaged in trade and other capitalist ventures. The middle class (usually referred to as the middle classes) was made up of several economic layers. The wealthiest bourgeois were bankers, factory and mine owners, and merchants, but the middle class also included shopkeepers, managers, lawyers, and doctors. The virtues of work, thrift, ambition, and caution characterized the middle class as a whole, as did the perversion of these virtues into materialism, selfishness, callousness, harsh individualism, and smugness.

From the eighteenth century on, as industry and commerce developed, the middle class grew in size, first in England and then throughout western Europe. But its increased size did not automatically bring increased power. The Industrial Revolution had begun in a preindustrial, agrarian society characterized by centuries-old political organizations and social classes. Throughout the eighteenth and nineteenth centuries, the middle class struggled against this entrenched social structure to end political, economic, and social discrimination. The bourgeoisie was indeed able to force radical changes, but its members still functioned in a political and social world that had existed long before they gained power and influence.

During the nineteenth century, the social changes resulting from industrialization brought the middle class greater power and social respectability. By the end of the century, bourgeois politicians held the highest offices in much of western Europe and shared authority with aristocrats, whose birth no longer guaranteed them the only political and social power in the nation. As industrial wealth became more important, the middle class became more influential. It was common throughout Europe for wealthy bourgeois to spend fortunes buying great estates and emulating aristocratic manners and pleasures. The middle class also valued respectability. In this and many other ways, its members copied the aristocracy for most of the century.

Industrialization may have reduced some barriers between the landed elites and the middle class, but it sharpened the distinctions between middle class and the laboring class (the *pro-*

letariat). Like the middle class, it encompassed different economic levels: rural laborers, miners, and city workers. Many gradations existed among city workers, from artisans to factory workers to servants. Factory workers were the newest and most rapidly growing social group; at midcentury, however, they did not constitute the majority of laboring people in any major city. For example, as late as 1890 they comprised only one-sixth of London's population.

The artisans were the largest group of workers in the cities for the first half of the nineteenth century, and in some places for much longer than that. They worked in construction, in printing, in small tailoring or dress-making establishments, in food preparation and processing, and in crafts producing such luxury items as furniture, jewelry, lace, and velvet. Artisans were distinct from factory workers; their technical skills were difficult to learn, and traditionally their crafts were acquired in guilds, which still functioned as both social and economic organizations. Artisans were usually educated (they could read and write), lived in one city or village for generations, and maintained stable families, often securing places for their children in their craft.

As the Industrial Revolution progressed, artisans were threatened by the increase in the numbers of factory workers and the extension of machinery into their crafts. To compete with cheap, factory-produced goods, artisans began to downgrade their skills by dropping apprenticeship training or by forcing journeymen to work longer hours and use shoddy materials. By the nineteenth century in Britain and in France, the guilds had lost their special economic role in regulating the hours and conditions of labor, the ages of workers, and similar concerns. In central Europe, guilds fared better; in 1848, artisans were at the forefront of the revolutionary movement as they tried to save themselves from the effects of the Industrial Revolution. (See pages 512–515.) Artisans, rather than factory workers, seem to have been the center of political and economic protest decrying industrialization and favoring political representation. Their guild organizations were models for many early socialists, and artisans were generally in the front ranks of the supporters of utopian movements.

The third group of urban workers were the servants, who were especially numerous in capital cities. In the first half of the nineteenth century in cities like Paris and London where the number of factories was not great, there were more servants than factory workers. The great increase in domestic labor in the nineteenth century freed middle-class women from household chores, so they could spend more time with their husbands and children or pursue interests in the outside world if they chose to do so.

Working in a middle- or upper-class household, urban servants lived in a world apart from factory workers and artisans; they were often women who had come to the city from the country, where they might also have been servants. They were completely at the command of their employers; they might be treated decently, or they might be exploited, but they had little recourse when they were abused. Some worked their entire lives as servants; other women left service to marry working-class men. (Domestic help could not remain in their jobs when they married.) Servants usually had some education. If they married and had a family, they taught their children to read and write and sometimes to observe the manners and values of the household in which the parent had worked. Many historians believe that these servants passed on to their children their own deference to authority and their aspirations to bourgeois status, which may have limited social discontent and radical political activity.

Working-Class Life

Life was not easy for those whose labor contributed to the industrializing process. Usually recent arrivals from agricultural areas where they had been driven off the land, the workers of the Industrial Revolution had no special skills or traditions of working with others in a craft. Frequently, factory workers moved to the city without their families, leaving them behind until they could afford to support them in town; other workers were single men or women who could not find jobs as servants or farm laborers in their villages. These people entered rapidly growing industries where long hours—sometimes fifteen a day—were not unusual; farming had meant long hours, too, as had the various forms of labor for piecework rates

Gustave Doré (1833–1883): Engraving of a London Slum. A population explosion took place between 1700 and 1850, as well as a population shift that peopled the new industrial cities. Rapid industrialization and inadequate city planning gave rise to urban slums with their disease, crime, and squalor. (*The Granger Collection, New York*)

in the home, but the pace of the machine and the routine made factory work even more oppressive.

Once technological advances became an important aspect of industrialization, the machines required highly regulated human labor—generally menial, often dangerous, but definitely routine. In Britain's coal mines, for example, steam engines did not chop the coal from the veins; they did not even haul the coal wagons to the main shaft. Men, women, and small children hacked the coal out and sorted it, while horses and mules—and sometimes human beings—pulled coal wagons on rails to the main shaft, where steam-powered engines lifted the coal to the surface. The workers in Britain's mines labored under the hazards of cave-ins, explosions, and deadly gas fumes. Deep under the earth's surface, life was dark, cold, wet, and tenuous. Their bodies stunted and twisted, their lungs wrecked, miners labored their lives away in "the pits."

Factory workers fared a little better than the miners. Sometimes, compared to their lives in the country, the workers' standard of living rose, particularly if they were part of a whole family that found work; the pay for a family might be better than they could have earned for agricultural labor. But working conditions were terrible, as were living conditions. The factories were dirty, hot, unventilated, and frequently dangerous. Workers often lived in overcrowded and dirty housing. If they were unmarried or had left their family in the country, they often lived in a barracks with other members of their sex. If they lost their jobs, they also lost their shelter.

Factory workers' lives were depressing. They had very little connection with their surroundings, and like immigrants to a new country, they lived with hardship and deprivation. In the villages they had left, they had been poor but were socially connected to family, church, and even to local landlords. But in the cities, factory workers labored in plants with twenty to a hundred workers and had little contact with their employers; instead, they were pushed by foremen to work hard and efficiently, to keep up with the machines. Workers had little time on the job to socialize with others; they were fined for talking to one another, for lateness, and for many petty infringements. They often became competitors in order to keep their jobs. Lacking organization, a sense of comradeship, education, and experience of city life, factory workers found little succor when times were bad.

But factory workers did make lives for themselves. They married or entered into some relationship at a younger age than artisans did, and they had more children on the average than other classes did. A wife and children were an economic asset because they worked to help the family. When workers grew old or were disabled, their children became their only "pension." As mechanization progressed, women and children were generally driven out of the factory labor force, but in the early factory system, they were the mainstay of the industrial process.

Many workers developed a life around the pub, the café, or some similar gathering place, where there were drinks and games and the gossip and news of the day. On Sundays, their one day off, workers drank and danced; absenteeism was so great on Monday that the day was called "holy Monday." Gin drinking was denounced on all sides; workers and reformers alike urged temperance. Most workers did not attend church, but when they did, they frequented those churches that tried to reach out to them—not usually the established churches, which seemed to them only for the wealthy. In England, workers attended revivals, the Methodists and the Dissenters welcomed them, and the Catholic church sought out Irish workers. Many workers played sports, and some social organizations grew up around their sporting games. In these and other ways, workers developed a culture of their own—a culture that was misunderstood and often deplored by middle-class reformers.

For the most part, industrial workers did not protest their conditions violently, although sometimes they did—and in some countries more than others. In general, factory workers endured their lack of political and economic rights. They worked long hours, were fined for mistakes and even for accidents, were fired at the will of the employer or the foreman, and suffered from work insecurity. Yet, they rarely broke machines—unlike country laborers who protested the mechanization of agriculture in this way. Factory workers had few organizations and no political rights. They lacked the traditions and organizations of the craftsmen, but they did join with artisans in movements for political rights—the Chartists in England and the republicans in France. When workers protested, they were repressed. Even a peaceful demonstration, during which they sang hymns and prayed, might be disrupted by soldiers and gunfire. Workers who did protest lost their jobs and were *blackballed* (employers circulated their names so that other employers would not hire them). Workers were neither wealthy enough nor organized enough to take offending employers to court for violations of the law.

Many workers and radicals believed that the only hope for their class lay in unified action through trade unions, mutual-aid societies, co-operatives, and political organizations. In England and western Europe after the middle of the nineteenth century, trade unions began to appear, despite the fact that they were illegal. Unions made some headway in protecting their members from unemployment and dangerous working conditions. But strikes were rarely successful; they were usually misunderstood by the general public and often suppressed by force. Not until the 1870s and 1880s was widespread discontent expressed by militant trade unions. (See Chapter 26.)

Although political agitation was not effective in achieving workers' goals in the first half of the nineteenth century, they made some progress in obtaining a little economic security. Workers formed "friendly societies" or mutual-aid and cooperative organizations to help themselves when they were out of work or sick. They paid some dues or took up special collections when one of their members died or was killed on the job. They also created clubs where they could learn to read and write or have someone read to them or write a letter for them. Self-help organizations often grew into unions; sometimes they were unions in disguise as a way of circumventing the law.

In England, unions were legal in 1825, but they were forbidden to strike. If a union's officer ran away with its treasury, the law did not protect the workers' dues. Small unions were powerless. An 1834 attempt to gain strength by joining all unions together in a Grand National Consolidated Trade Union failed because measures that would help one trade would not necessarily help another. In the 1850s, highly skilled workers joined together in a single craft union, which was a more successful tactic because employers found it difficult to replace a skilled worker. Still, the vast majority of workers were not organized during much of the nineteenth century.

Relief and Reform

Poverty became an issue with the onset of industrialization. True, there had always been poor people, but with industrialization the economic and psychological hardships borne by the work force seemed to increase. Many people felt that the poor—those who were so unfortunate that they needed the assistance of others—were growing in numbers, that their condition was deplorable, and that it had actually deteriorated in the midst of increased wealth. If machines could produce so much wealth and so many products, social observers wondered why poor people were so numerous.

Britain was the first nation to face the worsening condition of the poor. In the eighteenth century, English agricultural laborers had had a higher standard of living than their counterparts on the Continent. As Britain rapidly industrialized, however, the changing conditions convinced observers that both rural and urban workers' lives had worsened. Parliamentary reports and investigations of civic-minded citizens documented the suffering for all to read. These parliamentary reports did initiate some reforms—for example, the Factory Acts were a series of measures, beginning in 1802, that limited the hours of those (especially women and children) who labored in mines and factories (see Chapter 23).

The Factory Acts also required children to spend time in school. Reformers felt that one way to protect working-class children—to hold them responsible for their lives and yet to give them the opportunity to change—was to educate them. England was much slower than France or Germany to provide state schools. British private enterprise and charities, rather than the government, took the initiative; controversy grew among the religious sects about which of them should educate the children. Sometimes there were schools for boys and not for girls, and it was often argued that for moral reasons the sexes should not mix in the same classroom, even though they worked side by side in the factory. Under the first compulsory-education provisions of English law (which did not provide for the schools), children often worked ten or twelve hours a day and then had to attend rudimentary schools.

Other legislation was passed in 1834. A reform of the Poor Law, the New Poor Law, tried to differentiate between the "deserving" poor and the "undeserving" poor by requiring any recipient of assistance to live in a workhouse. Legislators usu-ally held the poor responsible for their plight and thought that only those who were truly needy—those who were unable to labor because they were disabled, too old, or too young—would submit to the prisonlike conditions of the workhouse to receive a meal and shelter. In general, the legislators were right. The poor and the unemployed working class hated and feared the workhouse, where families were separated into separate buildings by age and sex, miserably fed, and hired out to manufacturers and farmers for less than the going wage. They feared "pauperization." Humanitarians railed against these harsh, inhumane, and inadequate reforms.

In contrast to Britain, in much of Europe the people more readily accepted the idea that the state could interfere with the market to protect labor. Also, most states in Europe had larger bureaucracies to enforce regulations and to carry out relief measures. Statesmen on the Continent, however, worried that too much interference with employers would handicap their nation in the economic competition with countries that had industrialized earlier. They were vulnerable to arguments against the protection of labor, because its cost would make their labor and goods uncompetitive with Britain's. Governments in Germany, France, and Belgium did not always follow the logic of these arguments to endorse a policy of unrestricted industry, but sometimes they did. Such policies deepened class bitterness.

Historians still debate about how bad workers' conditions were in the early stages of industrialization. Although most workers experienced periods of acute distress, particularly during and immediately after the French Revolution and Napoleonic wars, historians generally conclude that the standard of living slowly improved during the eighteenth and nineteenth centuries. Although historians may take an optimistic view about the long-range effects of industrialization, nonetheless the rapidity of change worked great hardships on the workers of all countries. They endured cruel conditions in factories and slums. British craft workers faced competition from machines and displacement; Irish farm laborers and their families starved during the midcentury Great Famine that decimated their population. Emigration to England, Britain's colonies, or the United

The Great Exhibition of 1851 by Dickinson. The Great Exhibition at the Crystal Palace drew millions to see the products and processes of machine and craft industries. The building itself was a glass palace supported by a cast-iron frame, a construction imitated in many grand railroad terminals, department stores, and auditoriums throughout Europe and the United States. (*By permission of the Houghton Library, Harvard University*)

States might mean escape from starvation, but workers still lived desperately hard lives. For those British workers who did not emigrate, statistical evidence showing an increase in the living standard does not reveal much about the radically reduced quality of life that men, women, and children experienced in moving from rural communities to work in urban factories and live in slums. Their cruel experiences were relived by workers in the rest of Europe and the United States later in the nineteenth century and in many countries in the twentieth century.

Industrialization in Perspective

In 1851, the people who attended the great Crystal Palace exhibition in London knew that they were on the threshold of a new age of industrialization. The Crystal Palace was a gigantic temple of glass and cast iron, built to glorify the industrial greatness of the nations that entered exhibits and sent delegates. The spectators marveled at the displays of inventions like the sewing machine and the McCormick reaper, and gazed at the quality goods from many nations. Though most of the goods were made by craftsmen rather than factory workers, the new labor-saving devices captured the visitors' attention. Princes, princesses, and potentates joined the throngs celebrating the Industrial Revolution that was transforming Europe and the United States.

In 1851, the total legacy of industrialization was unclear to these spectators, and even its most enthusiastic supporters could not imagine what its future would be. In the long run, industrialization became a great force for democratization, even though democratization took place only very slowly over the nineteenth and twentieth centuries. Members of the French working class, who won the right to vote in 1848, did so because of the political tradition of their nation, not because of their economic role in industrialization. (Economic power would not come for more than a generation after midcentury.) In no other country did workers win the right to vote by midcentury. The middle class, however, had won political representation in France, Britain, and parts of central Europe by that time; this development indicated that the social power of landowners was gradually losing ground to forces arising from industrialization. First the middle class and later the working class gained the right to participate in the political life of their countries. Another slow process involved the secularization of society—that is, the movement away from belonging to a community of families united by religious belief and customary ceremony. In most of Europe, the priest, the village, and the family were still the dominant social forces and they would remain so until urbanization, which accompanied industrialization, had progressed a great deal further than it had by the middle of the century.

Although the urbanization of Europe and America had barely begun, people were aware of the problems of industrialization and were trying to adopt reform measures. Sometimes the social thought of liberals, conservatives, and radicals was brilliantly prescient about the problems facing modern industrial society. But some social thinkers were nostalgic for the good old days when "a master knew his man" and both had obligations to one another. Faith in progress, inspired in part by the achievements exhibited in the Great Exhibition, convinced other reformers that they could develop the tools to resolve the era's problems. Still others, "revolutionary realists" as they liked to call themselves, distrusted the sentimental social thinkers and the believers in progress, though the realists incorporated in their vision of the future a romantic nostalgia for working conditions that had not existed for more than a century. Yet these social thinkers of the nineteenth century supplied the ideas and analysis with which, until deep into the twentieth century, men and women tried to understand and to mold their industrializing world.

Although their analysis of social ills might be penetrating and their will to effect change might be sincere, the best-intentioned reformers had to work with governmental and private institutions that were survivals of the Old Regime. Although adapted and modified, these institutions were still tools for governing another kind of society, not an industrialized one. As people tried to deal with the problems of industrial urban society, the power of the state grew. Its influence on everyone's lives developed in the second half of the nineteenth century and drastically altered political life in the twentieth. Such a change could not have been foreseen nor could the far-flung Westernization of the globe have been predicted by those who attended the 1851 Crystal Palace exhibition.

Suggested Reading

The Cambridge Economic History of Europe, vol. 6 (1965). Includes several fine essays on industrialization, by specialists in central and eastern Europe.

Cameron, Rondo, *France and the Economic Development of Europe, 1800–1914* (1975). Puts emphasis on France's role as investor in the development of the rest of Europe.

Deane, Phyllis, *The First Industrial Revolution, 1750–1850* (1965). An excellent introduction.

Floud, Roderick, and Donald McCloskey, *The Eco-*

nomic History of Britain Since 1900, 2 vols. (1981). This work incorporates the latest scholarship on British industrialization.

Halévy, Elie, A History of the English People in the Nineteenth Century, vols. 1–3, rev. ed. (1987). A classic work.

Himmelfarb, Gertrude, The Idea of Poverty: England in the Early Industrial Age (1983). A brilliant history of English social thought focused on the condition of the poor.

Hobsbawm, Eric, The Age of Revolution: 1789–1848 (1964). A survey of this tumultuous period, stressing the connections between economic, social, and political revolution.

——, Labouring Men (1964). A number of controversial essays on labor and social history.

——, The Age of Capital (1988). A general survey from a Marxist viewpoint of the political and economic history of the period.

Landes, David, The Unbound Prometheus: Technological Change and Industrial Development in Western Europe from 1750 to the Present (1969). A classic treatment of a complex subject, beautifully and intelligently written.

Langer, William L., Political and Social Upheaval: 1832–1852 (1969). An excellent source with good references and bibliography.

Sewell, William H., Jr., Work and Revolution in France: The Language of Labor from the Old Regime to 1848 (1980). A review of labor's involvement in this turbulent period.

Thompson, E. P., Making of the English Working Class (1966). A very readable, dramatic, enormously influential, and controversial book.

Webb, R. K., Modern England from the Eighteenth Century (1967 and 1980). A text that is balanced, well-written, well-informed, and up-to-date on historical controversies.

Novels of special note:

Balzac, Honoré de, Eugenie Grandet; Père Goriot. A great novelist's studies of the decay of human character under social and economic pressures.

Dickens, Charles, Hard Times; Our Mutual Friend; Oliver Twist. The great humanitarian's social protest novels.

Disraeli, Benjamin, Sybil. A politician's program in novel form.

Gaskell, Elizabeth, North and South (1968 reprint of 1914 ed.). A woman's vision of industrial and social change.

Zola, Émile, Germinal. Describes the condition of miners in the 1850s and 1860s. Very interesting to compare with Richard Llewellyn's novel of Welsh miners, How Green Was My Valley.

Review Questions

1. Why did England experience industrialization before the rest of Europe? How did political and social factors influence industrialization in England?

2. How did political and social factors influence industrialization, or the lack of it, in France, in the German states, in the Netherlands?

3. How did changes in European agriculture in the early nineteenth century reflect the impact of capitalism and of industrialization?

4. Historians argue about the relative importance of labor, capital, government, technological invention, and natural resources and geography in the process of industrialization. Construct arguments for the primacy of each of these factors.

5. What factors promoted the growth of cities between 1800 and 1860?

6. Historians argue for and against the concept of the Industrial Revolution. What arguments could be made that industrialization is a slow process? What arguments could be made that industrialization as experienced by 1850 was rapid?

7. What groups were designated middle class in nineteenth-century Europe? What groups were designated working class, or lower orders, in nineteenth-century Europe? Why did contemporaries and some historians make the terms plural?

8. Why did organized religion play a decreasing role or a role different from its spiritual one in the lives of working-class people in the middle of the nineteenth century?

9. What aspects of working-class life and culture did the middle class try to change in the nineteenth century?

10. How did the law discriminate against and punish the working class during the early stages of industrialization? How did it try to protect it?

22

Ferment of Ideas: Romanticism, Conservatism, Liberalism, Radicalism, Early Socialism, Nationalism

I n 1815, the armies of France no longer marched across the Continent, and Napoleon was imprisoned on an island a thousand miles off the coast of Africa. The traditional rulers of Europe, some of them just restored to power, were determined to protect themselves and society from future Robespierres who organized reigns of terror and Napoleons who obliterated traditional states. As defenders of the status quo, they attacked the reformist spirit of the philosophes that had produced the Revolution. In *conservatism,* which championed tradition over reason, hierarchy over equality, and the community over the individual, they found a philosophy to justify their assault on the Enlightenment and the French Revolution.

But the forces unleashed by the French Revolution had penetrated European consciousness too deeply to be eradicated. One force for revolution was *liberalism,* which aimed to secure the liberty and equality proclaimed by the French Revolution. Another was *nationalism,* which called for the liberation of subject peoples and the unification of broken nations.

The postrevolutionary period also saw a new cultural orientation. *Romanticism,* with its plea for the liberation of human emotions and the free expression of personality, challenged the Enlightenment stress on rationalism. Although primarily a literary and artistic movement, Romanticism also permeated philosophy and political thought, particularly conservatism.

Still another force emerging in the post-Napoleonic period was socialism. Reacting to the problems created by the Industrial Revolution, socialists called for creating a new society based on cooperation rather than on capitalist competition. A minor movement in the era from 1815 to 1848, socialism in its Marxist version became a major intellectual and social force in the last part of the century.

William Blake (1757–1827): *Circle of the Lustful, Paolo and Francesca, Dante's "Divine Comedy,"* 1827. (*National Gallery of Art, Washington, D.C., Gift of W. G. Russell Allen* B-238, pl. 1.)

Romanticism: A New Cultural Orientation

The Romantic Movement, which began in the closing decades of the eighteenth century, dominated European cultural life in the first half of the nineteenth century. Historians recognize the prominence of romanticism in nineteenth-century cultural life, but the movement was so complex, and the differences among the various romantic writers, artists, and musicians so innumerable, that historians cannot agree on a definition of romanticism. Romantics were both liberals and conservatives, revolutionaries and reactionaries; some were preoccupied with religion and God, while others paid little attention to faith.

Most of Europe's leading cultural figures came under the influence of the Romantic Movement. Among the exponents of romanticism were the poets Shelley, Wordsworth, Keats, and Byron in England; the novelist Victor Hugo and the Catholic philosopher Chateaubriand in France; the writers A. W. and Friedrich Schlegel and philosophers Schiller and Schelling in Germany. Caspar David Friedrich in Germany and John Constable in England expressed the romantic mood in art, and the later Beethoven, Schubert, Chopin, and Wagner expressed it in music.

Exalting Imagination and Feelings

Perhaps the central message of the romantics was that the imagination of the individual should determine the form and content of an artistic creation. This outlook ran counter to the rationalism of the Enlightenment, which itself had been a reaction against the otherworldly Christian orientation of the Middle Ages. The philosophes had attacked faith because it thwarted and distorted reason; romantic poets, philosophers, and artists now denounced the rationalism of the philosophes because it crushed the emotions and impeded creativity. The philosophes, said the romantics, had turned flesh-and-blood human beings into soulless thinking machines, and vibrant nature into lifeless wheels, cogs, and pulleys. The reign of reason had diminished the individual. It had separated individuals from their feelings; it had prevented them from realizing their human nature; it had deadened their hearts and paralyzed their wills. To restore human beings to their true nature, to make them whole again, they must be emancipated from the tyranny of excessive intellectualizing; their feelings must be nourished and expressed. Taking up one of Rousseau's ideas, romantics yearned to rediscover a pristine freedom and creativity in the human soul that had been squashed by habits, values, rules, and standards imposed by civilization.

The philosophes had concentrated on people in general—those elements of human nature shared by all people. Romantics, on the other hand, emphasized human uniqueness—those distinctive traits that set each human being apart. Each person yearns to discover and to express his or her true self. Each plays his or her own music; each writes his or her own poetry; each paints his or her own personal vision of nature. Each experiences love and suffering in his or her own way. In the opening lines of his autobiography, *Confessions,* Jean Jacques Rousseau, a romantic in an age of reason, expressed the intense subjectivism that characterized the Romantic Movement:

> *I am commencing an undertaking, hitherto without precedent and which will never find an imitator. I desire to set before my fellows the likeness of a man in all the truth of nature, and that man myself. Myself alone! I know the feelings of my heart, and I know men. I am not made like any of those I have seen. I venture to believe that I am not made like any of those who are in existence. If I am not better, at least I am different.*[1]

Whereas the philosophes had regarded the feelings as an obstacle to clear thinking, to the romantics they were the human essence. People could not live by reason alone, said the romantics. They agreed with Rousseau, who wrote: "For us, to exist is to feel and our sensibility is incontestably prior to our reason."[2] For the romantics, reason was cold and dreary, its understanding of people and life meager and inadequate. Reason could not comprehend or express the complexities of human nature nor the richness of human experience. By always dissecting and analyzing, by imposing deadening structure and form, and by demanding adherence to strict rules, reason crushed inspiration and creativity and barred true understanding. "The Reasoning Power in Man," said William Blake, the British poet, artist, and mystic, is "an incrustation over my immortal Spirit."[3]

For the romantics, the avenue to truth was not the intellect but spontaneous human emotions. By cultivating instincts and imagination, individuals could experience reality and discover their authentic selves. The romantics wanted people to feel and to experience—to "bathe in the waters of life," said Blake.[4] Or as Johann Goethe, Germany's great poet, wrote in *Faust*: "My worthy friend, gray are all theories,/And green alone Life's golden tree."[5]

For this reason, the romantics insisted that imaginative poets had a greater insight into life than analytical philosophers did. Poetry is a true philosophy, the romantics said; it can do what rational analysis and geometric calculations cannot—speak directly to the heart, clarify life's deepest mysteries, participate in the eternal, and penetrate to the depths of human nature. To think profoundly, one has to feel deeply, said the romantics. For reason to function best, it must be nourished by the poetic imagination; that alone extricates and ennobles feelings hidden in the soul. "I am certain of nothing but of the holiness of the Heart's affections and the truth of Imagination," wrote John Keats. "O for a Life of Sensations rather than of Thoughts."[6]

The Enlightenment mind had been clear, critical, and controlled. It had adhered to standards of esthetics, thought to be universal, that had dominated European cultural life since the Renaissance. That mind stressed technique, form, and changeless patterns, and tended to reduce the imagination to mechanical relationships. "Analysis and calculation make the poet, as they make the mathematician," wrote Étienne Condillac, a prominent French philosophe. "Once the material of a play is given, the invention of the plot, the characters, the verse, is only a series of algebraic problems to be worked out."[7] Following in this tradition, Népomucène Lemercier determined that there were twenty-six rules for tragedy, twenty-three for comedy, and twenty-four for the epic; he

Francisco Goya (1746–1828): The Sleep of Reason Produces Monsters. Romantic writers and artists explored the world of dreams and fantasy that Freud would later call the unconscious. Goya's work shows that when a man permits his reason to sleep, he is controlled by creatures from an irrational world. (*Courtesy Museum of Fine Arts, Boston*)

proceeded to manufacture plays and epics according to this formula.

Romantic poets, artists, and musicians broke with the traditional styles and austere rules and created new cultural forms and techniques. "We do not want either Greek or Roman Models," said Blake, but should be "just and true to our own Imaginations."[8] Victor Hugo, the dominant figure among French romantics, declared: "Freedom in art! . . . Let us take the hammer to the theories, the poetics [the analysis of poetry] and the systems."[9] For the romantics, one did not learn how to write poetry or paint pictures by following textbook rules; one could not comprehend the poet's or artist's intent by judging works according to fixed standards. Only by trusting to their own feelings could individuals attain their creative potential and achieve self-realization. The most beautiful works of art, for example, were not photographic imitations of nature but authentic and spontaneous expressions of the artist's feelings, fantasies, and dreams. Similarly, the romantics were less impressed by Beethoven's constructions than by the intensity and power that his music embodied.

The romantics explored the inner life of the mind, which Freud would later call *the unconscious.* "It is the beginning of poetry," wrote Friedrich Schlegel, "to abolish the law and the method of the rationally proceeding reason and to plunge us once more into the ravishing confusion of fantasy, the original chaos of human nature."[10] It was this layer of the mind—mysterious, primitive, more elemental and more powerful than reason, the wellspring of creativity—that the romantics yearned to revitalize and release.

Nature, God, History

The philosophes had viewed nature as a lifeless machine—a giant clock, all of whose parts worked together in perfect precision and harmony. Nature's laws, operating with mathematical certainty, were uncovered by the methodology of science. Rejecting this impersonal, mechanical model, romantics reacted to nature in an emotional way, inspired and awed by its beauty and majesty. To the romantics, nature was alive and suffused with God's presence. Nature stimulated the creative energies of the imagination; it taught human beings a higher form of knowledge, as William Wordsworth wrote:

> One impulse from a vernal wood
> May teach you more of man,
> Of moral evil and of good,
> Than all the sages can.[11]

Interaction with nature fostered self-discovery. Thus, Wordsworth saw in nature

> The anchor of my purest thoughts, the nurse,
> The guide, the guardian of my heart, and soul
> Of all my moral being.[12]

For the romantics, nature did not consist of mechanical parts but of trees, lakes, mountains, clouds, and stars; one experienced nature with feeling, seeking mystical union. Not the mathematician's logic but the poet's imagination unlocked nature's most important secrets. In perhaps the most impassioned application of this principle, English romantics decried their country's drab factories—the "dark satanic mills" that deprived life of its joy and separated people from nature.

The philosophes had seen God as a great watchmaker—a detached observer of a self-operating mechanical universe—and they tried to reduce religion to a series of scientific propositions. Many romantics viewed God as a spiritual force that inspired people, and they deplored the decline of Christianity. The cathedrals and ceremonies, poetic and mysterious, satisfied the esthetic impulse; Christian moral commands, compassionate and just, elevated human behavior to a higher level. The romantics condemned the philosophes for weakening Christianity by submitting its dogmas to the test of reason. For the romantics, religion was not science and syllogism but a passionate and authentic expression of human nature. The romantics' call to acknowledge that the individual is a spiritual being and to cultivate the religious side of human nature accorded with their goal of restoring the whole personality, which had been fragmented by the philosophes' excessive emphasis on the intellect.

The philosophes had viewed the Middle Ages as an era of darkness, superstition, and fanaticism and regarded surviving medieval institutions and traditions as barriers to progress. The romantics, on the other hand, revered the Middle Ages. The wars of the French Revolution, Napoleon, and the breakdown of political equilibrium had produced a sense of foreboding about the future. Some sought spiritual security by looking back to the Middle Ages, when Europe was united by a single faith. Then, said romantics, no rationalist's blade dissected and slashed Christian mysteries; no wild-eyed revolutionaries tore apart the fabric of society. To the romantic imagination, the Middle

Ages abounded with heroic deeds, noble sentiments, and social harmony.

Romantics and philosophes held differing conceptions of history. For the philosophes, history served a didactic purpose by providing examples of human folly. Such knowledge assisted people in preparing for a better future, and for that reason alone history should be studied. To the romantics, a historical period, like an individual, was a unique entity with its own soul. They wanted the historian to portray and analyze the variety of nations, traditions, and institutions that constituted the historical experience. The command of the romantics to study the specific details of history and culture and to comprehend them within the context of their times is the foundation of modern historical scholarship.

Searching for universal principles, the philosophes had dismissed folk traditions as peasant superstitions and impediments to progress. The romantics, on the other hand, rebelling against the standardization of culture, saw native languages, songs, and legends as the unique creations of a people and the deepest expression of national feeling. The romantics regarded the legends, myths, and folk traditions of a people as the wellspring of poetry and art, the spiritual source of a people's cultural vitality, creativity, and identity. Hence they examined these earliest cultural expressions with awe and reverence. In this way, romanticism was instrumental in the shaping of modern nationalism.

Lord Byron (1788–1824). One of the leading romantic poets, Byron created the "Byronic hero," a lonely and mysterious figure. His own short life exalted the emotions and the senses. He went to Greece in 1824 to aid the revolutionaries and died there from poor health. (*Historical Pictures Service, Chicago*)

The Impact of the Romantic Movement

The romantic revolt against the Enlightenment had an important and enduring impact on European history. By focusing on the creative capacities inherent in the emotions—intuition, spontaneity, instinct, passion, will, empathy—the romantics shed light on a side of human nature that the philosophes had often overlooked or undervalued. By encouraging personal freedom and diversity in art, music, and literature, they greatly enriched European cultural life. Future artists, writers, and musicians would proceed along the path cleared by the romantics. Modern art, for example, owes much to the Romantic Movement's emphasis on the legitimacy of human feeling and its exploration of the hidden world of dreams and fantasies. The romantic emphasis on feeling sometimes found expression in humanitarian movements that fought slavery, child labor, and poverty. By recognizing the distinctive qualities of historical periods, peoples, and cultures, the romantics helped to create the modern historical outlook. By valuing the nation's past, romanticism contributed to modern nationalism and conservatism.

But there was a potentially dangerous side to the Romantic Movement. By waging their attack on reason with excessive zeal, the romantics undermined the rational foundations of the West. The romantic idealization of the past and glorification of ancient folkways, native soil, and native language introduced a highly charged, nonrational component into political life. In the decades to come, romanticism, particularly in Germany, fused with political nationalism and "created a general climate of inexact thinking, an intellectual . . . dream world and an emotional approach to problems of political action to which sober reasoning should have been applied."[13]

The philosophes would have regarded the romantics' veneration of a people's history and traditions, their search for a nation's soul in an archaic culture, as barbarous—a regression to superstition, the triumph of myth over philosophy. Indeed, when transferred to the realm of politics, the romantics' idealization of the past and fascination for inherited national myths as the source of wisdom did reawaken a way of thinking about the world that rested more on feeling than on reason. In the process, people became committed to ideas that were fraught with danger.

Conservatism: The Value of Tradition

To the traditional rulers of Europe—kings, aristocrats, clergy—the French Revolution was a great evil that had inflicted a near-fatal wound on civilization. As far as they were concerned, the revolutionaries heralded chaos when they executed Louis XVI, confiscated the land of the church, destroyed the special privileges of the aristocracy, and instituted the Reign of Terror. Then the Revolution gave rise to Napoleon, who deposed kings, continued the assault on the aristocracy, and sought to dominate Europe. Disgusted and frightened by the revolutionary violence, terror, and

warfare, the traditional rulers sought to refute the philosophes' world-view that had spawned the Revolution. To them, natural rights, equality, the goodness of man, and perpetual progress were perverse doctrines that had produced the Jacobin "assassins." In conservatism they found a political philosophy to counter the Enlightenment ideology.

Edmund Burke's *Reflections on the French Revolution* (1790) was instrumental in shaping conservative thought. Burke (1729–1797), a British philosopher and statesman, wanted to warn his countrymen of the dangers inherent in the ideology of the revolutionaries. Although writing in 1790, Burke astutely predicted that the Revolution would lead to terror and military dictatorship. To Burke, fanatics armed with pernicious principles—abstract ideas divorced from historical experience—had dragged France through the mire of revolution. Burke developed a coherent political philosophy that served as a counterweight to the ideology of the Enlightenment and the Revolution.

Hostility to the French Revolution

The philosophes and French reformers, entranced by the great discoveries in science, had believed that the human mind could also transform social institutions and ancient traditions according to rational models. Progress through reason became their faith. Dedicated to creating a new future, the revolutionaries abruptly dispensed with old habits, traditional authority, and familiar ways of thought.

To conservatives, who like the romantics venerated the past, this was supreme arrogance and wickedness. They regarded the revolutionaries as presumptuous men who recklessly severed society's links with ancient institutions and traditions and condemned venerable religious and moral beliefs as ignorance. Moreover, the revolutionaries forgot—or never knew—that the traditions and institutions they wanted to destroy did not belong solely to them. Past generations and indeed future generations had a claim to these creations of French genius. By attacking time-honored ways, the revolutionaries had deprived French society of moral leadership and had opened the door to anarchy and terror. "You began ill," said Burke of the revolutionaries, "because you began by despising everything that belonged to you. . . . When ancient opinions and rules of life are taken away, the loss cannot possibly be estimated. From that moment we have no compass to govern us; nor can we know distinctly to what port we steer."[14]

The philosophes and French reformers had expressed unlimited confidence in the power of human reason to understand and to change society. Although they appreciated human rational capacities, conservatives also recognized the limitations of reason. "We are afraid to put men to live and trade each on his own private stock of reason," said Burke, "because we suspect that this stock in each man is small, and that the individuals would do better to avail themselves of the general bank and capital of nations and of ages."[15] Conservatives saw the Revolution as a natural outgrowth of an arrogant Enlightenment philosophy that overvalued reason and sought to reshape society in accordance with abstract principles.

For conservatives, human beings were not by nature good. Human wickedness was not due to a faulty environment, as the philosophes had proclaimed, but was at the core of human nature, as Christianity taught. Evil was held in check not by reason but by tried and tested institutions, traditions, and beliefs. Without these habits inherited from ancestors, said conservatives, the social order was threatened by sinful human nature.

Because monarchy, aristocracy, and the church had endured for centuries, argued the conservatives, they had worth. The clergy taught proper moral values; monarchs preserved order and property; aristocrats guarded against despotic kings and the tyranny of the common people. All protected and spread civilized ways. By despising and uprooting these ancient institutions, the revolutionaries had hardened the people's hearts, perverted their morals, and caused them to commit terrible outrages on each other and society.

Conservatives detested attempts to transform society according to a theoretical model. They felt that human nature was too intricate and that social relations were too complex for such social engineering. For conservatives, the revolutionaries had reduced people and society to abstractions divorced from their historical settings; consequently, they had destroyed ancient patterns that seemed inconvenient and had drawn up constitutions based on the unacceptable principle that government derives its power from the consent of the governed.

For conservatives, God and history were the only legitimate sources of political authority; states were not made but were an expression of the nation's moral, religious, and historical experience. No legitimate or sound constitution could be drawn up by a group assembled for that purpose. Scraps of paper with legal terminology and philosophic visions could not produce an effective government; instead, a sound political system evolved gradually and inexplicably in response to circumstances. For this reason, conservatives admired the English constitution. It was not a product of abstract thought; no assembly had convened to fashion it. Because it grew imperceptibly out of the historical experience and needs of the English people, it was durable and effective.

For conservatives, society was not a machine with replaceable parts but a complex and delicate organism. Tamper with its vital organs, as the revolutionaries had done, and it would die.

The Quest for Social Stability

The liberal philosophy of the Enlightenment and the French Revolution started with the individual. The philosophes and the revolutionaries envisioned a society in which the individual was free and autonomous. Conservatives believed that society was not a mechanical arrangement of disconnected individuals but a living organism held together by centuries-old bonds. Alone, a person would be selfish, unreliable, frail; it was only as a member of a social group—family, church, or state—that one acquired the ways of cooperation and the manners of civilization. By exalting the individual, the revolutionaries had threatened to dissolve society into disconnected parts. Individualism would imperil social stability, destroy obedience to law, and fragment society into self-seeking isolated atoms.

Holding that the community was more important than the individual, conservatives rejected the philosophy of natural rights. Rights were not abstractions that preceded an individual's entrance into society and pertained to all people everywhere. Rather, the state, always remembering the needs of the entire community and its links to past generations, determined what rights and privileges its citizens might possess. There were no "rights of man," only rights of the French, the English, and so forth, as determined and allocated by the particular state.

Conservatives viewed equality as another pernicious abstraction that contradicted all historical experience. For conservatives, society was naturally hierarchical, and they believed that some men by virtue of their intelligence, education, wealth, and birth were best qualified to rule and instruct the less able. They said that by denying the existence of a natural elite and uprooting a long-established ruling elite that had learned its art through experience, the revolutionaries had deprived society of effective leaders, brought internal disorder, and prepared the way for a military dictatorship.

Whereas the philosophes had attacked Christianity for promoting superstition and fanaticism, conservatives saw religion as the basis of civil society. Excess liberty and the weakening of religion had brutalized people and shattered the foundations of society. Catholic conservatives, in particular, held that God had constituted the church and monarchy to check sinful human nature. "Christian monarchs are the final creation of the development of political society and of religious society," said Louis de Bonald, a French émigré. "The proof of this lies in the fact that when monarchy and Christianity are both abolished society returns to savagery."[16]

Conservatism pointed to a limitation of the Enlightenment. It showed that human beings and social relationships are far more complex than the philosophes had imagined. People do not always accept the rigorous logic of the philosopher and are not eager to break with ancient ways, however illogical they appear to the intellect. They often find familiar customs and ancestral religions more satisfying guides to life than the blueprints of philosophers. The granite might of tradition remains an obstacle to all the visions of reformers.

Liberalism: The Value of the Individual

The decades after 1815 saw a spectacular rise of the bourgeoisie. Talented and ambitious bankers, merchants, manufacturers, professionals, and officeholders wanted to break the stranglehold that the landed nobility, the traditional elite, held on political power and social prestige; they also wanted to eliminate restrictions on the free pursuit of profits.

The political philosophy of the bourgeoisie was most commonly liberalism. While conservatives sought to strengthen the foundations of traditional society, which had been severely shaken in the period of the French Revolution and Napoleon, liberals wanted to alter the status quo and to carry out the promise of the Enlightenment and the French Revolution. Conservatives extolled the community, but liberals gave central concern to individual freedom. Conservatives tried to preserve a social hierarchy based on inherited aristocracy, but liberals insisted that a person's value was measured not by birth but by achievement. Conservatives held that the state rests on tradition, but liberals sought the rational state in which political institutions and procedures were based on intelligible principles. Conservatives wanted individuals, inherently evil, to obey their betters. Liberals, on the other hand, had confidence in the capacity of individuals to control their own lives.

The Sources of Liberalism

In the long view of Western civilization, liberalism is an extension and development of the democratic practices and rational outlook that originated in ancient Greece. Also flowing into the liberal tradition is Judeo-Christian respect for the individual. But the immediate historical roots of nineteenth-century liberalism extended back to seventeenth-century England. At that time, the struggle for religious toleration by English Protestant dissenters established the principle of freedom of conscience, which is easily transferred into freedom of opinion and expression in all matters.

The Glorious Revolution of 1688 set limits on the power of the English monarchy. In that same century John Locke's natural-rights philosophy declared that the individual was by nature entitled to freedom, and it justified revolutions against rulers who deprived citizens of their lives, liberty, or property.

The French philosophes were instrumental in the shaping of liberalism. From Montesquieu, liberals derived the theory of the separation of powers and of checks and balances—principles intended to guard against autocratic government. The philosophes had supported religious toleration and freedom of thought, expressed confidence in the capacity of the human mind to reform society, maintained that human beings are essentially good, and believed in the future progress of humanity—all fundamental principles of liberalism.

The American and French revolutions were crucial phases in the history of liberalism. The Declaration of Independence gave expression to Locke's theory of natural rights; the Constitution of the United States incorporated Montesquieu's principles and demonstrated that people could create an effective government; the Bill of Rights protected the person and rights of the individual. In destroying the special privileges of the aristocracy and opening careers to talent, the French National Assembly of 1789 implemented the liberal ideal of equality under the law. It also drew up the Declaration of the Rights of Man and of the Citizen, which affirmed the dignity and rights of the individual, and a constitution that limited the king's power. Both the American and French revolutions explicitly called for the protection of property rights, another basic premise of liberalism.

Individual Liberty

The liberals' primary concern was the enhancement of individual liberty. They agreed with the German philosopher Immanuel Kant that every person exists as an end in himself or herself and not as an object to be used arbitrarily by others. If uncoerced by government and churches and properly educated, a person could develop into a good, productive, and self-directed human being. People could make their own decisions, base actions on universal moral principles, and respect one anothers' rights.

Liberals rejected a legacy of the Middle Ages, the classification of the individual as a commoner or aristocrat on the basis of birth. They held that a man was not born into a certain station in life but made his way through his own efforts. Taking their cue from the French Revolution, liberals called for an end to all privileges of the aristocracy.

In the tradition of the philosophes, liberals stressed the pre-eminence of reason as the basis of political life. Unfettered by ignorance and tyranny, the mind could eradicate evils that had burdened people for centuries and begin an age of free institutions and responsible citizens. For this reason, liberals supported the advancement of education. They believed that educated people apply reason to their political and social life, and thus they act in ways beneficial to themselves and society and are less likely to submit to tyrants.

Liberals attacked the state and other authorities that prevented the individual from exercising the right of free choice, that interfered with the right of free expression, and that prevented the individual from self-determination and self-development. They agreed with John Stuart Mill, the British philosopher, who declared that "over his own body and mind, the individual is sovereign. . . . that the only purpose for which power can be rightly exercised over any member of a civilized community, against his will, is to prevent harm to others."[17]

The great question that confronted nineteenth-century liberals was the relationship between state authority and individual liberty. To guard against the absolute and arbitrary authority of kings, liberals demanded written constitutions that granted freedom of speech, the press, and religion; freedom from arbitrary arrest; and the protection of property rights. To prevent the abuse of political authority, liberals called for a freely elected parliament and the distribution of power among the various branches of government. Liberals held that a government that derived its authority from the consent of the governed, as given in free elections, was least likely to violate individual freedom. A corollary of this principle was that the best government is one that governs least—that is,

Nicolò Paganini (1782–1840) by Jean Auguste Dominique Ingres (1780–1867). The structure and order of classical music gave way to sweeping melodies and rich harmonies. Paganini, the composer-performer, stunned audiences with his virtuosity. Paganini's name became synonymous with the violin, as Franz Liszt's was with the piano. (*Louvre/Cliché des Musées Nationaux*)

one that interferes as little as possible with the economic activities of its citizens and does not involve itself in their private lives or their beliefs.

Liberal Economic Theory

Liberals held that the economy, like the state, should proceed according to natural laws rather than the arbitrary fiat of rulers. Adopting the laissez-faire theory of Adam Smith, they maintained that a free economy, in which private enterprise was unimpeded by government regulations, was as important as political freedom to the well-being of the individual and the community. When people acted from self-interest, the liberals said, they worked harder and achieved more; self-interest and natural competitive impulses spurred economic activity and ensured the production of more and better goods at the lowest possible price, thereby benefiting the entire nation. For this reason, the government must neither block free competition nor deprive individuals of their property, which was their incentive to work hard and efficiently. The state contributed to the nation's prosperity when it maintained domestic order; it endangered economic development when it tampered with the free pursuit of profits. Believing that individuals were responsible for their own misfortunes, liberals were often unmoved by the misery of the poor and considered social reforms to alleviate poverty as unwarranted and dangerous meddling with the natural laws of supply and demand.

Two attitudes emerged from liberal economic principles—one optimistic, hoping for the expansion of human productive capacities and the end of want; and the other pessimistic, predicting a cycle of increasing pressure on scarce resources and deepening competition among workers for the necessities of life. For the first half of the nineteenth century, Thomas Malthus (1766–1834), author of the *Essay on the Principle of Population,* had an impact as great as Adam Smith's on the lives of workers and the thought of reformers. Malthus argued that population increase would outstrip increases in food production, which suggested that the poverty of the working class was permanent. Malthus reasoned that if wages were raised, workers' families would grow and the extra wages would be used to support the added members. This doctrine was called Malthusianism and seemed to supply "scientific" justification for opposing governmental action to aid the poor. Poverty, argued Malthusians, was an iron law of nature, the result of population pressure on resources; it could not be eliminated by government reforms.

Fellow economist David Ricardo (1772–1823) used Malthus's idea to form another theory that also made poverty seem inevitable and irremediable. Wages, he said, tended to remain at the minimum needed to maintain workers. An increase in wages encouraged laborers to increase their families. As the supply of workers increased, competition for jobs also increased, causing wages to decline. Ricardo's disciples made his law inflexible—an "Iron Law of Wages" offered dismal prospects.

Many workers felt the new science of economics offered little hope for them. They argued that the liberals were only concerned with their class and national interests, that they were hard, callous, and apathetic toward the sufferings of the poor. The liberals responded that the cure for the evils of industrialization was more industrialization.

Early in the nineteenth century, liberals feared that state interference in the economy to redress social ills would threaten individual rights and the free market that they thought was essential to personal liberty. They also feared privileged groups and preferred a weak state to a powerful one in the hands of the elite. In time, the liberals modified their position, first supporting government action to provide education or opportunity for all and then accepting the principle of state aid to the poor. They came to believe that justice required some protection against the economy's ravages for those who were powerless. They thought reform was possible without losing the advantages of capitalism and without sacrificing personal liberty.

Liberalism and Democracy

The French Revolution presented a dilemma for liberals. They supported the reforms of the moderate stage: the destruction of the special privileges of the aristocracy, the drawing up of a declaration of rights and a constitution, the establishment of a parliament, the opening of careers to talent; but they repudiated Jacobin radicalism. Liberals were frightened by the excesses of the Jacobin regime: its tampering with the economy, which liberals felt violated the rights of private property; its appeal to the "little people," which they felt invited mob rule; its subjection of the individual to the state, which they regarded as the denial of individual rights; its use of the guillotine, which awakened the basest human feelings.

Although many liberals still adhered to the philosophy of natural rights, some who were disturbed by the Jacobin experience discarded the theory underlying the reforms of the Revolution. These liberals, fearing social disorder as much as conservatives did, did not want to ignite revolutions by the masses. In the hands of the lower classes, the natural-rights philosophy was too easily translated into the democratic creed that all people should share in political power, a prospect that the bourgeois regarded with horror. To them, the participation of commoners in politics meant a vulgar form of despotism and the end to individual liberty. The masses—uneducated, unpropertied, inexperienced, and impatient—had neither the ability nor the temperament to maintain liberty and protect property.

In this new age, said Alexis de Tocqueville, a French political theorist, the masses had a passion for equality, not liberty. They demanded that the avenue to social, economic, and political advancement be opened to all; they no longer accepted disparity in wealth and position as part of the natural order. They would willingly sacrifice political liberty to improve their material well-being. Looking to the state as the guarantor of equality, said de Tocqueville, the people would grant it ever more power. The state then would regulate its citizens' lives, crush local institutions impeding centralized control, and impose the beliefs of the majority on the minority. Liberty would be lost not to the despotism of kings but to the tyranny of the majority. (See pages 540–541.)

Because bourgeois liberals feared that democracy could crush personal freedom as ruthlessly as any absolute monarch could, they called for property requirements for voting and officeholding. They wanted political power to be concentrated in the hands of a safe and reliable—that is, a propertied and educated—middle class. Such a government would prevent revolution from below, a prospect that caused anxiety among bourgeois liberals.

Early nineteenth-century liberals engaged in revolutions, to be sure, but their aims were always limited. Once they had destroyed absolute monarchy and gained a constitution and a parliament or a change of government, they quickly tried to terminate the revolution. When the fever of revolution spread to the masses, liberals either withdrew or turned counterrevolutionary, for they feared the stirrings of the multitude.

Although liberalism was the political philosophy of a middle class generally hostile to democracy, the essential ideals of democracy flowed logically from liberalism. Eventually, democracy became a later stage in the evolution of liberalism, because the masses, their political power enhanced by the Industrial Revolution, would press for greater social, political, and economic equality. Thus, by the early twentieth century, many European states had introduced universal suffrage, abandoned property requirements for officeholding, and improved conditions for workers.

But the fears of nineteenth-century liberals were not without foundation. In the twentieth century, the participation of common people in politics has indeed threatened freedom. Impatient with parliamentary procedures, the masses, particularly when troubled by economic problems, have in some instances given their support to demagogues who promise swift and decisive action. The granting of political participation to the masses has not always made people more free. The confidence of democrats has been shaken in the twentieth century by the seeming willingness of common people to trade freedom for authority, order, economic security, and national power. Liberalism is based on the assumption that human beings can and do respond to rational argument, that reason will prevail over base human feelings. The history of our century shows that this may be an overly optimistic assessment of human nature.

Radicalism and Democracy: The Expansion of Liberalism

In the early nineteenth century democratic ideals were advanced by thinkers and activists called radicals. Inspired by the democratic principles expressed in Rousseau's *Social Contract* and by the republican stage of the French Revolution, French radicals championed popular sovereignty—rule by the people. In contrast to liberals, who feared the masses, French radicals trusted the common person. Advocating universal suffrage and a republic, radicalism gained the support of French workers in the 1830s and 1840s.

English radicals, like their liberal cousins, inherited the Enlightenment's confidence in reason and its belief in the essential goodness of the individual. In the first half of the nineteenth century, English radicals sought parliamentary reforms, because some heavily populated districts were barely represented in Parliament, while lightly populated districts were overrepresented; they demanded payment for members of Parliament to permit the nonwealthy to hold office; they sought universal manhood suffrage to give the masses representation in Parliament; and they insisted on the secret ballot to prevent intimidation. Radicals attacked the aristocracy and the privileged, and many supported the working-class struggle for reform.

British radicalism was inspired by Tom Paine (1737–1809) and Jeremy Bentham (1748–1832). Responding to Burke's *Reflections on the French Revolution,* Paine, in *The Rights of Man* (published in two parts in 1791 and 1792), denounced reverence for tradition, defended the principle of natural rights, and praised as progress the destruction of the Old Regime. From Paine, the English radical tradition acquired a faith in reason and human goodness, a skeptical attitude toward established institutions, a dislike of organized religion, the belief that the goal of government was the greater happiness of ordinary people, and the conviction that the exclusion of common people from political participation was an injustice.

In contrast to Paine, Jeremy Bentham rejected the doctrine of natural rights as an abstraction that had no basis in reality, and he regarded the French Revolution as an absurd attempt to reconstruct society on the basis of principles as misguided as those that had supported the Old Regime. Bentham's importance to the English radical tradition derives from the principle of *utility,* which he offered as a guide to reformers. The central fact of human existence, said Bentham, is that human beings seek to gratify their desires, that they prefer pleasure to pain. Consequently any political, economic, judicial, or social institution and any legislation should be judged according to a simple standard: does it bring about the greatest happiness for the greatest number? If not, it should be swept away. By focusing on the need for reform on every level of society and by urging a careful and objective analysis of social issues, Bentham contributed substantially to the shaping of British radicalism.

Bentham said that those in power had always used what they considered the highest principles—God's teachings, universal standards, honored traditions—to justify their political and social systems, their moral codes, and their laws. On the highest grounds, they persecuted and abused people, instituted practices rooted in ignorance and superstition, and imposed values that made people miserable because they conflicted with human nature and the essential needs of men and women.

The principle of utility, said Bentham, permits the reforming of society in accordance with people's true nature and needs. It does not impose unrealistic standards on men and women but accepts people as they are. Utilitarianism, he declared, bases institutions and laws on an objective study of human behavior rather than on unsubstantiated religious beliefs, unreliable traditions, and philosophical abstractions. Bentham's utilitarianism led him to support both extending the suffrage and the secret ballot and to attack political corruption and clerical control of education. In contrast to laissez-faire liberals, Bentham and his followers argued for some legislation to protect women and children in the factories and for sanitation reform to improve the conditions in the cities. The utilitarians also demanded that the archaic English penal system be reformed.

Early Socialism: New Possibilities for Society

A new group called socialists went further than either the liberals or the radicals, demanding the creation of a new society based on the spirit of cooperation rather than on competition. Reflecting the spirit of the Enlightenment and the French Revolution, they were convinced that people could create a better world according to the principles of reason, and that they could do it in a relatively short time. The socialists' thought was romantic as well, in that they dreamed of a new social order in which each individual could fulfill his or her own nature. The most important early socialist thinkers—Saint-Simon, Fourier, and Owen—espoused a new social and economic system in which production and distribution of goods would be planned for the general good of society. Their thought influenced Karl Marx and Friedrich Engels, who in the second half of the nineteenth century became the most influential formulators and propagators of socialism. (See pages 534–538.) There were also Christian communitarians, who protested the unsettling conditions caused by industrialization and the treatment of the poor; these Christian "socialists" urged believers to share their property and labor and live together in model communities.

Socialists questioned the assumption that society was made up of isolated and self-seeking individuals, and challenged the laws of economics as they were formulated by the laissez-faire economists. They denied that human beings reached the peak of their achievements as individuals, arguing that people achieved more happiness for themselves and for others as a community that worked together and experienced solidarity. Some socialists urged voluntary divorce from the larger society; they proposed communes or model factory towns as places to apply the principles of socialism or communitarianism. Some were very perceptive about the nature of industrialization and the future of industrial society; others romantically longed for the past and created schemes that would preserve the values and ethics of village life as it existed before industrialization and urbanization.

Saint-Simon: Technocratic Socialism

Descended from a distinguished French aristocratic family, Henri Comte de Saint-Simon

(1760–1825) renounced his title during the French Revolution and enthusiastically preached the opportunity for a new society. He regarded his own society as defective and in need of reorganization: the critical philosophy of the Enlightenment had shattered the old order, but it had not provided a guide for reconstructing society. Saint-Simon believed that he had a mission to set society right by providing an understanding of the new age being shaped by science and industry. Many of the brightest young people in France believed in his mission.

Like the romantics, Saint-Simon saw the importance of religion. He argued that just as Christianity had provided social unity and stability during the Middle Ages, scientific knowledge would bind the society of his time. The scientists, industrialists, bankers, artists, and writers would replace the clergy and the aristocracy as the social elite; Saint-Simon had a romantic love of genius and talent. In the new industrial age, he thought, the control of society must pass to the *industriels*—those who produce or who make it possible to produce. These manufacturers, bankers, engineers, intellectuals, and scientists would harness technology for the betterment of humanity. Saint-Simon's disciples championed efforts to build great railway and canal systems, including the Suez and Panama canals. His vision of a scientifically organized society led by trained experts was a powerful force among intellectuals in the nineteenth century and is very much alive today among those who believe in a technocratic society.

Like the philosophes, Saint-Simon valued science, had confidence in the power of reason to improve society, and believed in the certainty of progress according to laws of social development. Also like the philosophes, he attacked the clergy for clinging to superstition and dogma at the expense of the common people. The essence of Christianity was the Golden Rule—the sublime command that people should treat each other like brothers and sisters. According to Saint-Simon, the traditional clergy, having placed dogma above moral law, had forfeited their right to lead Europe, just as the aristocracy had before the French Revolution forfeited its right to rule. He called for "a new Christianity" (the title of one of his books) to serve as an antidote to selfish interests and to abjure the narrow nationalism that divided the peoples of Europe.

Fourier: Psychological Socialism

Another early French socialist was Charles Fourier (1772–1837), who believed, as the romantics did, that society conflicted with the natural needs of human beings and that this tension was responsible for human misery. Only the reorganization of society so that it would satisfy people's desire for pleasure and satisfaction would end that misery. Whereas Saint-Simon and his followers had elaborate plans to reorganize society on the grand scale of large industries and giant railway and canal systems, Fourier sought to create small communities to allow men and women to enjoy life's simple pleasures. These communities of about 1,600 people, called *phalansteries*, would be organized according to the unchanging needs of human nature.

Fourier was not greatly concerned about the realities of industrialization, and his ideas reflect the artisan society that still existed in France when he was growing up. In phalansteries, no force would coerce or thwart innocent human drives. Everyone would work at tasks that interested them and would produce things that brought themselves and others pleasure. Like Adam Smith, Fourier understood that specialization bred boredom and alienation from work and life. Unlike Smith, he did not believe that vastly increased productivity compensated for the evils of specialization. In the phalansteries, money and goods would not be equally distributed; those with special skills and responsibilities would be rewarded accordingly. This system of rewards accorded with nature because people have a natural desire to be rewarded.

Both Fourier and the Saint-Simonians supported female equality, placing them among the first social thinkers to do so. Fourier did not define female equality merely in political terms. He thought that marriage distorted the natures of both men and women because monogamy restricted their sexual needs and narrowed their lives' scope to the family alone. Instead, people should think of themselves as part of the family of all humanity. Because married women had to devote all their strength and time to household and children, they had no time or energy left to enjoy life's pleasures. Fourier did not call for the abolition of the family, but he did hope that it would disappear of its own accord as society adjusted to his theories. Men and women would find new ways of fulfilling themselves sexually, and the community would be organized so that it could care for the children. Fourier's ideas found some reception in the United States, where in the 1840s at least twenty-nine communities were founded on Fourierist principles. None, however, lasted more than five or six years.

Owen: Industrial Socialism

In 1799, Robert Owen (1771–1858) became part owner and manager of the New Lanark cotton mills in Scotland. Distressed by widespread mistreatment of workers, Owen resolved to improve the lives of his employees and to prove that it was possible to do so without destroying profits. He raised wages, upgraded working conditions, refused to hire children under ten, and provided workers with neat homes, food, and clothing, all at reasonable prices. He set up schools for children and for adults. In every way, he demonstrated his belief that healthier, happier workers produced more than the less fortunate ones. Like Saint-Simon, Owen believed industry and technology could and would enrich humankind, if organized according to the proper principles. Visitors came from all over Europe to see Owen's factories.

Just like many philosophes, Owen also held that the environment was the principal shaper of character—that the ignorance, alcoholism, and crime of the poor derived from bad living conditions. Public education and factory reform, said Owen, would make better citizens of the poor. When Parliament balked at reforms, Owen even urged the creation of a grand national trade union of all the workers in England. In the earliest days of industrialization, with very few workers organized in unions, this dream seemed an impossible one. Owen came to believe that the entire social and economic order must be replaced by a new system based on harmonious group living rather than on competition. He established a model community at New Harmony, Indiana, but it was short-lived. Even in his factory in England, Owen had some difficulty holding on to workers, many of whom were devout Christians and resented his secular ideas and the dancing taught to their children in his schools.

Nationalism: The Sacredness of the Nation

Nationalism is a conscious bond shared by a group of people who feel strongly attached to a particular land and who possess a common culture and history marked by shared glories and sufferings. Nationalism is accompanied by a conviction that one's highest loyalty and devotion should be given to the nation. Nationalists exhibit great pride in their people's history and traditions and often feel that their nation has been specially chosen by God or history. Like a religion, nationalism provides the individual with a sense of community and with a cause worthy of self-sacrifice.

Thus, in an age when Christianity was in retreat, nationalism became the dominant spiritual force in nineteenth-century European life. Nationalism provided new beliefs, martyrs, and "holy" days that stimulated reverence; it offered membership in a community, which satisfied the overwhelming psychological need of human beings for fellowship and identity. And nationalism supplied a mission—the advancement of the nation—to which people could dedicate themselves.

The Emergence of Modern Nationalism

The essential components of nationalism emerged at the time of the French Revolution. The Revolution asserted the principle that sovereignty derived

Eugène Delacroix (1799–1863): Liberty Leading the People, 1830. Early nineteenth-century reformers found their rallying call in liberty, a legacy of the French Revolution. In this painting, Delacroix, the leader of French romantic artists, glorifies liberty. (*Louvre/Cliché des Musées Nationaux*)

from the nation, from the people as a whole—the state was not the private possession of the ruler but the embodiment of the people's will. The nation-state was above king, church, estate, guild, or province; it superseded all other loyalties. The French people must view themselves not as subjects of the king, not as Bretons or Normans, not as nobles or bourgeois, but as citizens of a united fatherland, *la patrie*. These two ideas—that the people possess unlimited sovereignty and that they are united in a nation—were crucial in fashioning a nationalist outlook.

As the Revolution moved from the moderate to the radical stage, French nationalism gained in intensity. In 1793–94, when the republic was threatened by foreign invasion, the Jacobins created a national army, demanded ever greater allegiance to and sacrifice for the nation, and called for the expansion of France's borders to the Alps and the Rhine. With unprecedented success, the Jacobins used every means—press, schoolroom, rostrum—to instill a love of country.

The Romantic Movement also awakened nationalist feelings. By examining the language, literature, and folkways of their people, romantic thinkers instilled a sense of national pride in their compatriots. Johann Gottfried Herder (1744–1803) conceived the idea of the *Volksgeist*—the soul of the people. For Herder, each people was unique and creative; each expressed its genius in language, literature, monuments, and folk traditions. Herder did not make the theoretical jump from a spiritual or cultural nationalism to political nationalism; he did not call for the formation of states based on nationality. But his emphasis on the unique culture of a people stimulated a national consciousness among Germans and the various Slavic peoples who lived under foreign rule. Fascination with the Volksgeist prompted intellectuals to investigate the past of their own people, to rediscover their ancient traditions, and to extol their historic language and culture. From this cultural nationalism it was only a short step to a political nationalism that called for national liberation, unification, and statehood.

The romantics were the earliest apostles of German nationalism. They restored to consciousness memories of the German past, and they emphasized the peculiar qualities of the German folk and the special destiny of the German nation. The romantics glorified medieval Germany and valued hereditary monarchy and aristocracy as vital links to the nation's past. They saw the existence of each individual as inextricably bound up with folk and fatherland, and they found the self-realization for which they yearned in the unification of their own egos with the national soul. To these romantics, the national community was a vital force that gave the individual both an identity and a purpose in life. And the nation stood above the individual; the national spirit bound isolated souls into a community of brethren. In unmistakably romantic tones, Ernst Moritz Arndt urged Germans to unite against Napoleon:

> German man, feel again God, hear and fear the eternal, and you hear and fear also your Volk [*people*], you feel again in God the honor and dignity of your fathers, their glorious history rejuvenates itself in you, their firm and gallant virtue reblossoms in you, the whole German Fatherland stands again before you in the august halo of past centuries. . . .
> No longer Catholics and Protestants, no longer Prussians and Austrians, Saxons and Bavarians, Silesians and Hanoverians, no longer of different faith, different mentality, and different will—be Germans, be one, will to be one by love and loyalty, and no devil will vanquish you.[18]

Most German romantics expressed hostility to the liberal ideals of the French Revolution. They condemned the reforms of the Revolution for trying to reconstruct society by separating individuals from their national past, for treating them as isolated abstractions. They held that the German folk spirit should not be polluted by foreign French ideas.

To the philosophes, the state was a human creation that provided legal safeguards for the individual. To the romantics, the state was something holy, the expression of the divine spirit of a people; it could not be manufactured to order by the intellect. The state's purpose was not the protection of natural rights nor the promotion of economic well-being; rather, the state was a living organism that linked each person to a sacred past, imbued individuals with a profound sense of community, and subordinated the citizen to the nation.

Nationalism and Liberalism

In the early nineteenth century, liberals were the principal leaders and supporters of nationalist movements. They viewed the struggle for national rights—the freedom of a people from foreign rule—as an extension of the struggle for the rights of the individual. There could be no liberty, said nationalists, if people were not free to rule themselves in their own land.

Liberals called for the unification of Germany and Italy, the rebirth of Poland, the liberation of Greece from Turkish rule, and the granting of autonomy to the Hungarians of the Austrian Empire. Liberal nationalists envisioned a Europe of independent states based on nationality and popular sovereignty. Free of foreign domination and tyrant princes, these newly risen states would protect the rights of the individual and strive to create a brotherhood of nationalities in Europe.

In the first half of the nineteenth century, few intellectuals recognized the dangers inherent in nationalism or understood the fundamental conflict between liberalism and nationalism. For the liberal, the idea of universal natural rights transcended all national boundaries. Inheriting the cosmopolitanism of the Enlightenment, liberalism emphasized what all people had in common, called for all individuals to be treated equally under the law, and preached toleration. Nationalists, manifesting the particularist attitude of the in-group and the tribe, regarded the nation as the essential fact of existence. Consequently, they often willingly subverted individual liberty for the sake of national grandeur. Whereas the liberal sought to protect the rights of all within the state, the nationalist often ignored or trampled on the rights of individuals and national minorities. Whereas liberalism grew out of the rational tradition of the West, nationalism derived from the emotions. Because it fulfilled an elemental yearning for community and kinship, nationalism exerted a powerful hold over human hearts, often driving people to political extremism. Liberalism demanded objectivity in analyzing tradition, society, and history, but nationalism evoked a mythic and romantic past that often distorted history.

In the last part of the nineteenth century, the irrational and mythic quality of nationalism would intensify. By stressing the unique qualities and history of a particular people, nationalism would promote hatred between nationalities. By kindling deep love for the past, including a longing for community and kinship, nationalism exerted a powerful hold over human hearts; often arousing the emotions to a fever pitch, nationalism would shatter rational thinking, drag the mind into a world of fantasy and myth, and introduce extremism into politics. Love of nation would become an overriding passion threatening to extinguish the liberal ideals of reason, freedom, and equality.

Notes

1. Jean Jacques Rousseau, *The Confessions* (New York: Modern Library, 1950), p. 2.

2. Quoted in H. G. Schenk, *The Mind of the European Romantics* (Garden City, N.Y.: Doubleday, 1969), p. 4.

3. William Blake, *Milton*, 40. 34–35.

4. Ibid., 41. 1.

5. Goethe, *Faust*, trans. by Bayard Taylor (New York: Modern Library, 1950), pt. 1, sc. 4.

6. Letter of Keats, November 22, 1817, in Hyder E. Rollins, ed., *The Letters of John Keats* (Cambridge, Mass.: Harvard University Press, 1958), 1: 184–185.

7. Quoted in John Herman Randall, Jr., *The Career of Philosophy* (New York: Columbia University Press, 1965), 2: 80.

8. Blake, *Milton*, Preface.

9. Quoted in Robert T. Denommé, *Nineteenth-Century French Romantic Poets* (Carbondale: Southern Illinois University Press, 1969), p. 28.

10. Quoted in Ernst Cassirer, *An Essay on Man* (New York: Bantam Books, 1970), p. 178.

11. From "The Tables Turned," in *The Complete Poetical Works of Wordsworth*, Andrew J. George, ed. (Boston: Houghton Mifflin, 1904, rev. ed. 1982), p. 83.

12. From "Lines Composed a Few Miles Above Tintern Abbey," *The Complete Poetical Works of William Wordsworth* (Philadelphia: Porter and Coates, 1851), p. 194.

13. Horst von Maltitz, *The Evolution of Hitler's Germany* (New York: McGraw-Hill, 1973), p. 217.

14. Edmund Burke, *Reflections on the Revolution in France* (New York: Liberal Arts Press, 1955), pp. 40, 89.

15. Ibid., p. 99.

16. Quoted in Frederick B. Artz, *Reaction and Revolution, 1814–1832* (New York: Harper Torchbooks, 1963), p. 73.

17. John Stuart Mill, *On Liberty,* Currin V. Shields, ed. (Indianapolis: Bobbs-Merrill, 1956), ch. 1.

18. Quoted in Hans Kohn, *Prelude to Nation-States* (Princeton, N.J.: D. Van Nostrand, 1967), p. 262.

Suggested Reading

Arblaster, Anthony, *The Rise and Decline of Western Liberalism* (1984). A critical analysis of liberalism, its evolution and characteristics.

Bullock, Alan, and Maurice Shock, eds., *The Liberal Tradition* (1956). Selections from the works of British liberals, preceded by an essay on the liberal tradition.

Denommé, Robert T., *Nineteenth-Century French Romantic Poets* (1969). The genesis of Romanticism in France; an analysis of several French romantic poets.

de Ruggiero, Guido, *The History of European Liberalism* (1927). A classic study.

Epstein, Klaus, *The Genesis of German Conservatism* (1966). An analysis of German conservative thought as a response to the Enlightenment and the French Revolution.

Fried, Albert, and Ronald Sanders, eds., *Socialist Thought* (1964). Selections from the writings of socialist theorists.

Harris, R. W., *Romanticism and the Social Order, 1780–1830* (1969). Involvement of English romantics in social and political questions.

Hayes, Carlton J. H., *Historical Evolution of Modern Nationalism* (1931). A pioneering work in the study of nationalism.

Honour, Hugh, *Romanticism* (1979). A study of the influence of Romanticism on the visual arts.

Kohn, Hans, *The Idea of Nationalism* (1961). A comprehensive study of nationalism from the ancient world through the eighteenth century by a leading student of the subject.

———, *Prelude to Nation-States* (1967). The emergence of nationalism in France and Germany.

MacCoby, S., ed., *The English Radical Tradition, 1763–1914* (reprint 1978). Selections from the writings of English radicals.

Manuel, Frank, *The Prophets of Paris* (1962). Good discussions of Saint-Simon and Fourier.

Markham, F. M. H., ed., *Henri Comte de Saint-Simon* (1952). Selected writings.

Poster, Mark, ed., *Harmonian Man* (1971). Selected writings of Fourier.

Schapiro, J. S., *Liberalism: Its Meaning and History* (1958). A useful survey with readings.

Schenk, H. G., *The Mind of the European Romantics* (1966). A comprehensive analysis of the Romantic Movement.

Shafer, B. C., *Faces of Nationalism* (1972). The evolution of modern nationalism in Europe and the non-European world; contains a good bibliography.

Simon, W. M., *French Liberalism 1789–1848* (1972). Selections from the writings of French liberals.

Smith, A. D., *Theories of Nationalism* (1972). The relationship between nationalism and modernization.

Weiss, John, *Conservatism in Europe, 1770–1945* (1977). Conservatism as a reaction to social modernization.

Review Questions

1. The Romantic Movement was a reaction against the dominant ideas of the Enlightenment. Discuss this statement.

2. What was the significance of the Romantic Movement?

3. What were the attitudes of the conservatives toward the philosophes and the French Revolution?

4. "It is with infinite caution that any man ought to venture upon pulling down an edifice which had answered in any tolerable degree for ages the common purposes of society." How does this statement by Burke represent the conservative viewpoint?

5. Why did conservatives reject the philosophy of natural rights?

6. What were the sources of liberalism?

7. The central concern of liberals was the enhancement of individual liberty. Discuss this statement.

8. What was a fundamental difference between French radicals and liberals?

9. What did British radicalism owe to Paine and Bentham?

10. What basic liberal-capitalist doctrines were attacked by early socialists?

11. Why are Saint-Simon, Fourier, and Owen regarded as early socialists? Discuss their ideas.

12. Define nationalism.

13. How did the French Revolution and romanticism contribute to the rise of modern nationalism?

14. What is the relationship between nationalism and liberalism?

15. Account for nationalism's great appeal.

23

Europe, 1815–1848: Revolution and Counterrevolution

A clash between the forces unleashed by the French Revolution and the traditional outlook of the Old Regime took place during the years 1815 through 1848. The period opened with the Congress of Vienna, which drew up a peace settlement after the defeat of Napoleon, and closed with the revolutions that swept across most of Europe in 1848.

Much of the Old Regime outside France survived the stormy decades of the French Revolution and Napoleon. Monarchs still held the reins of political power. Aristocrats, particularly in central and eastern Europe, retained their traditional hold over the army and administration, controlled the peasantry and local government, and enjoyed tax exemptions. Determined to enforce respect for traditional authority and to smother liberal ideals, the conservative ruling elites resorted to censorship, secret police, and armed force.

The French Revolution, however, had shown that absolutism could be challenged successfully and feudal privileges abolished. Inspired by the revolutionary principles of liberty, equality, and fraternity, liberals and nationalists continued to engage in revolutionary activity.

The Congress of Vienna, 1814–1815

Metternich: Arch-Conservative

After the defeat of Napoleon, a congress of European powers met at Vienna to draw up a peace settlement. The pivotal figure at the Congress of Vienna was Prince Klemens von Metternich (1773–1859) of Austria, who had organized the coalition that triumphed over Napoleon. Belonging to the old order of courts and kings, Metternich hated the new forces of nationalism and

Honoré Daumier (1808–1879): *The Uprising.* (*The Phillips Collection, Washington, D.C.*)

liberalism. He regarded liberalism as a dangerous disease carried by middle-class malcontents and believed that domestic order and international stability depended on rule by monarchy and respect for aristocracy. The misguided liberal belief that society could be reshaped according to the ideals of liberty and equality, said Metternich, had led to twenty-five years of revolution, terror, and war. To restore stability and peace, the old Europe must suppress liberal ideas and quash the first signs of revolution. If the European powers did not destroy the revolutionary spirit, they would be devoured by it.

Metternich also feared the new spirit of nationalism. As a multinational empire, Austria was particularly vulnerable to nationalist unrest. If its ethnic groups—Poles, Czechs, Magyars, Italians, South Slavs, Rumanians—became infected with the nationalist virus, they would shatter the Hapsburg Empire. A highly cultured, multilingual, and cosmopolitan aristocrat, Metternich considered himself the defender of European civilization. He felt that by arousing the masses and setting people against people, nationalism could undermine the foundations of the European civilization that he cherished.

Metternich's critics accuse him of shortsightedness. Instead of harnessing and directing the new forces let loose by the French Revolution, he thought that he could stifle them. Instead of trying to rebuild and remodel, he thought only of propping up dying institutions. Regarding any attempt at reform as opening the door to radicalism and revolution, he refused to make any concessions to liberalism.

Metternich sought to return to power the ruling families deposed by more than two decades of revolutionary warfare, and to restore the balance of power so that no one country could be in a position to dominate the European continent as Napoleon had. Metternich was determined to end the chaos of the Napoleonic period and restore stability to Europe. There must be no more Napoleons who obliterate states, topple kings, and dream of European hegemony. Although he served the interests of the Hapsburg monarchy, Metternich also had a sense of responsibility to Europe as a whole. He sought a settlement that would avoid the destructiveness of a general war.

Representing Britain at the Congress of Vienna

was Robert Stewart Viscount Castlereagh (1769–1822), the British foreign secretary, who was realistic and empirically minded. Although an implacable enemy of Napoleon, Castlereagh demonstrated mature statesmanship in his attitude toward defeated France: "It is not our business to collect trophies, but to try . . . to bring the world back to peaceful habits. I do not believe this to be compatible with any attempt . . . to affect the territorial character of France . . . neither do I think it a clear case . . . that France . . . may not be found a useful rather than a dangerous member of the European system."[1]

Tsar Alexander I (1777–1825) attended the Congress himself. Showing signs of mental instability and steeped in Christian mysticism, the Russian tsar wanted to create a European community based on Christian teachings. Influenced by Baroness von Kruedener, a religious fanatic, Alexander regarded himself as the savior of Europe, an attitude that caused other diplomats to regard him with distrust.

Representing France was Prince Charles Maurice de Talleyrand-Périgord (1754–1838). He had served Napoleon as foreign minister, but when the emperor's defeat seemed imminent, he worked for the restoration of the Bourbon monarchy. A devoted patriot, Talleyrand sought to remove from France the stigma of the Revolution and Napoleon and to restore its respectability in the international arena.

The aging Prince Karl von Hardenberg (1750–1822) represented Prussia. Like Metternich, Castlereagh, and Talleyrand, the Prussian statesman believed that the various European states, in addition to pursuing their own national interests, should concern themselves with the well-being of the European community as a whole.

Crisis over Saxony and Poland

Two interrelated issues threatened to disrupt the conference and enmesh the Great Powers in another war. One was Prussia's intention to annex the German kingdom of Saxony; the other was Russia's demand for Polish territories. The tsar wanted to combine the Polish holdings of Russia, Austria, and Prussia into a new Polish kingdom under Russian control. Both Britain and

An Age of Revolution: Liberal, National, Industrial

Congress of Vienna, 1815, by Jean Baptiste Isabey (1767–1855). The delegates to the Congress of Vienna (Metternich is standing before a chair at the left) in 1815 sought to re-establish many features of the Europe that existed before the French Revolution and Napoleon. The delegates can be called shortsighted; nevertheless, the balance of power that they formulated preserved international peace. (*The New York Public Library*)

Austria regarded such an extension of Russia's power into central Europe as a threat to the balance of power. Metternich declared that he had not fought Napoleon to prepare the way for the tsar. Britain agreed that Russia's westward expansion must be checked.

Prince Talleyrand of France suggested that Britain, Austria, and France conclude an alliance to oppose Prussia and Russia. This clever move by Talleyrand restored France to the family of nations. Now France was no longer the hated enemy but a necessary counterweight to Russia and Prussia. Threatened with war, Russia and Prussia moderated their demands and the crisis ended.

The Settlement

After months of discussion, quarrels, and threats, the delegates to the Congress of Vienna finished their work. Resisting Prussia's demands for a punitive peace, the allies did not punish France severely. They feared that a humiliated France would only prepare for a war of revenge. Moreover, Metternich continued to need France to balance the power of both Prussia and Russia. France had to pay a large indemnity over a five-year period and submit to allied occupation until the obligation was met.

The peace settlement changed the borders

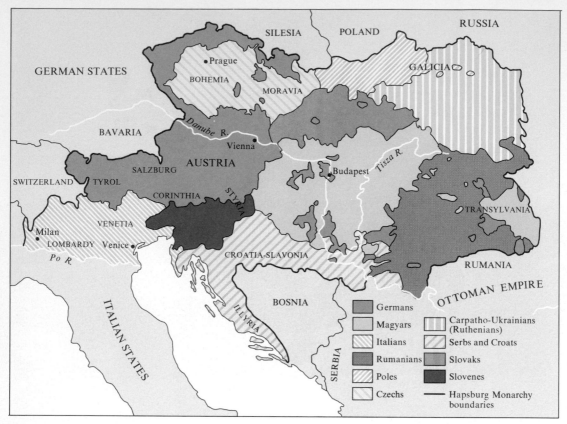

Map 23.1 Peoples of the Hapsburg Monarchy, 1815

throughout Europe. Although it lost most of its conquests, France emerged with somewhat more land than it possessed before the Revolution. To guard against a resurgent France, both Prussia and Holland received territories on the French border. Holland obtained the southern Netherlands (Belgium); Prussia gained the Rhineland and part of Saxony, but not as much as the Prussians had desired. Nevertheless, Prussia emerged from the settlement significantly larger and stronger. Russia obtained Finland and a considerable part of the Polish territories, but not as much as the tsar had anticipated; the Congress prevented further Russian expansion into central Europe. The northern Italian province of Lombardy was restored to Austria, which also received adjacent Venetia. England obtained strategic naval bases: Helgoland in the North Sea, Malta and the Ionian Is-

lands in the Mediterranean, the Cape Colony in South Africa, and Ceylon in the Indian Ocean. Germany was organized into a confederation of thirty-eight (later thirty-nine) states. Norway was given to Sweden. The legitimate rulers, who had been displaced by the Revolution and the wars of Napoleon, were restored to their thrones in France, Spain, Portugal, the Kingdom of the Two Sicilies, the Papal States, and many German states.

The conservative delegates at the Congress of Vienna have often been criticized for ignoring the liberal and nationalist aspirations of the different peoples and turning the clock back to the Old Regime. Critics have castigated the Congress for dealing only with the rights of thrones and not the rights of peoples. But, after the experience of two world wars in the twentieth century, some historians today are impressed with the peacemakers' success in restoring a balance of power that effectively stabilized international relations. No one country was strong enough to dominate the Continent; no Great Power was so unhappy that it resorted to war to undo the settlement. Not until the unification of Germany in 1870–71 was the balance of power upset; not until World War I in 1914 did Europe have another general war of the magnitude of the Napoleonic wars.

Revolutions, 1820–1829

Russia, Austria, Prussia, and Great Britain agreed to act together to preserve the territorial settlement of the Congress of Vienna and the balance of power. After paying its indemnity, France was admitted into this Quadruple Alliance, also known as the Concert of Europe. Metternich intended to use the Concert of Europe to maintain harmony between nations and internal stability within nations. Toward this end, conservatives in their respective countries censored books and newspapers, imprisoned liberal activists, and suppressed nationalist uprisings. In 1819, Metternich and representatives from the leading German states met at Karlsbad and drew up several decrees calling for the dissolution of the *Burschenschaft*, a student fraternity that favored German national unity, for the imposition of strict censorship over the press, and for the dismissal of professors who disseminated liberal ideas.

But repression could not contain the liberal and nationalist ideals unleashed by the French Revolution; nothing could halt the transformation of European society. The first revolution after restoration of the legitimate rulers occurred in Spain in 1820. The uprising was essentially a military revolt by infrequently paid and poorly fed soldiers who were being sent to Latin America to win back Spain's colonies that, partly under the inspiration of the American and French revolutions, had revolted against Spanish rule. King Ferdinand VII attempted to appease the soldiers by reinstating the liberal constitution of 1812, which had been promulgated during the struggle against Napoleon and revoked two years later. Both Metternich

Giuseppe Verdi (1813–1901). Verdi and Richard Wagner divide the operatic world of the mid-nineteenth century. Verdi, however, was deeply concerned with the future and fate of Italy. His name became an acronym for explosive sentiment. As the audience cheered, "Viva Verdi," they cheered for a unified monarchy: V̲ittorio, E̲mmanuele, R̲e D̲' I̲talia (Victor Emmanuel, King of Italy). (*The Mansell Collection*)

and Tsar Alexander were alarmed. Fearing that the Spanish uprising, with its quasi-liberal overtones, would inspire revolutions in other lands, the Concert of Europe empowered France to intervene. In 1823, 100,000 French troops crushed the revolution. King Ferdinand dismissed the liberal constitution and brutally punished the leaders of the insurrection.

Revolutionary activity in Italy also frightened the Concert of Europe. In 1821, it authorized Austria to extinguish a liberal uprising in the Kingdom of the Two Sicilies. The Austrians also crushed an uprising in Piedmont, in northern Italy (see Chapter 25). Rulers in other Italian states jailed and executed liberal leaders, and several thousand Italians went into exile.

In both instances, Britain strongly opposed the actions of the alliance; it interpreted the alliance differently from the way that Austria, Prussia, and Russia did. The three eastern powers wanted the alliance to smother in the cradle all subversive movements that threatened the old order. To Metternich, the central problem of the age was suppressing revolutions, and he regarded the alliance as a means of preserving the status quo. Britain, however, viewed the alliance solely as a means of guarding against renewed French aggression. It had no desire to intervene in the domestic affairs of other nations.

A revolution also failed in Russia. During the Napoleonic wars and the occupation of France, Russian officers were introduced to French ideas. Contrasting French liberal ideas and ways with Russian autocracy, some officers resolved to change conditions in Russia. Like their Western counterparts, they organized secret societies and disseminated liberal ideas within Russia. When Alexander I died, these liberal officers struck. But representing only a fraction of the aristocracy and with no mass following among the soldiers, they had no chance of success. Their uprising in December 1825 was easily smashed by the new tsar, Nicholas I, and the leaders were severely punished. To prevent Western ideas from infiltrating into his realm, Nicholas imposed rigid censorship and organized the Third Section, a secret police force that spied on suspected subversives. The Decembrists had failed, but their courage would inspire future opponents of tsarist autocracy.

The revolutions in Spain, Italy, and Russia failed, but the Concert of Europe also suffered setbacks. Stimulated by the ideals of the French Revolution, the Greeks revolted against their Turkish rulers in 1821. Although the Turkish sultan was the legitimate ruler, Russia, France, and Britain aided the Greek revolutionaries, for they were Christians, while the Turks were Muslims; moreover, pro-Greek sentiments were very strong among educated western Europeans who had studied the literature and history of ancient Greece. To them the Greeks were struggling to regain the freedom of their ancient forebears. Not only the pressure of public opinion but fear of Russian motives led Britain to join in intervention. If Russia carried out its intention of aiding the Greeks on its own, no doubt the Russian bear would never release Greece from its hug. Britain could not permit this extension of Russian power in the eastern Mediterranean. Despite Metternich's objections, Britain, France, and Russia took joint action against the Turks.

In 1829, Greece gained its independence. The Metternich system, which aimed to preserve the territorial settlements made at Vienna and to protect traditional and legitimate rulers against liberal and nationalist revolutions, had been breached. The success of the Greeks heartened liberals in other lands.

Revolutions, 1830–1832

After Napoleon's defeat, a Bourbon king, Louis XVIII (1814–1824), ascended the throne of France. Louis XVIII's heart belonged to the Old Regime, but his intellect told him that twenty-five years of revolutionary change could not be undone. Recognizing that the French people would not accept a return to the old order, Louis pursued a moderate course. Although his pseudoconstitution, the Charter, declared that the king's power rested on divine right, it also stipulated that citizens possessed fundamental rights—freedom of thought and religion and equal treatment under the law—and it set up a two-house parliament. But peasants, urban workers, and most bourgeois could not meet the property requirements for voting.

Aided by competent ministers and committed to a policy of moderation, Louis XVIII governed effectively, although he was resisted by diehard aristocrats, called *ultras*. These aristocrats, many of them returned émigrés, wanted to erase the past twenty-five years of French history and restore the power and privileges of church and aristocracy. Their leader was the king's younger brother, the Comte d'Artois, who after Louis' death in 1824 ascended the throne as Charles X (1824–1830).

The new government aroused the hostility of the bourgeoisie by indemnifying the émigrés for the property they had lost during the Revolution, by censoring the press, and by giving the church greater control over education. In the election of 1830, the liberal opposition to Charles X won a decisive victory. Charles responded with the July Ordinances, which dissolved the newly elected Chamber of Deputies; the ordinances also deprived rich bourgeois of the vote and severely curtailed the press.

The bourgeoisie, students, and workers rebelled. They engaged in street demonstrations and put up barricades. Army regiments that had deserted Charles joined the rebels. In the fighting that followed, some 2,000 Parisians were killed.

The insurgents hoped to establish a republic, but the wealthy bourgeois who took control of the revolution feared republican radicalism. They offered the throne to the Duc d'Orléans; Charles X abdicated and went into exile in Britain. The new king, Louis Philippe (1830–1848), never forgot that he owed his throne to the rich bourgeois. And the Parisian workers who had fought for a republic and economic reforms to alleviate poverty felt betrayed by the outcome, as did the still-disenfranchised petty bourgeois.

The Revolution of 1830 in France set off shock waves in Belgium, Poland, and Italy. The Congress of Vienna had assigned Catholic Belgium to Protestant Holland; from the outset the Belgians had protested. Stirred by the events in Paris, Belgian patriots proclaimed their independence from Holland. The Dutch could not suppress the insurgents, and the Quadruple Alliance did not act, largely because Russia was tied down by a revolution in Poland. Thus, liberal government was established in Belgium.

Inspired by the uprisings in France and Belgium, Polish students, intellectuals, and army officers took up arms against their Russian overlords. The peasants refused to join the insurrection because the revolutionaries did not promise land reform. The revolutionaries wanted to restore Polish independence, a dream that poets, musicians, and intellectuals had kept alive. Polish courage, however, was no match for Russian might, and Warsaw fell in 1831. The tsar took savage revenge on the revolutionaries; those who failed to escape to the West were executed. Subsequently the tsar's government made strenuous efforts to impose Russian language and culture on Polish students.

In 1831–1832, Austrian forces again extinguished a revolution in Italy. Here, too, revolutionary leaders had failed to stir the great peasant masses to the cause of Italian independence and unity.

The Rise of Reform in Britain

Although it was the freest state in Europe in the early decades of the nineteenth century, Britain was far from democratic. A constitutional monarchy, with many limits on the powers of king and state, Britain was nonetheless dominated by aristocrats. Landed aristocrats controlled both the House of Lords and the House of Commons—the House of Lords because they constituted its membership and the House of Commons because they patronized or sponsored men favorable to their interests. The vast majority of people, middle class as well as working class, could not vote. Many towns continued to be governed by corrupt groups. New industrial towns were not allowed to elect representatives to Parliament; often lacking a town organization, they could not even govern themselves effectively. Without a voice in the government, the working classes at times resorted to protesting by riot and rampage.

The social separation of noble and commoner was not as rigid in Britain as on the Continent. Younger sons of aristocrats did not inherit titles and were, therefore, obliged to make careers in law, business, the military, and the church. The upper and middle classes mingled much more freely than on the Continent, and the wealthiest merchants tended to buy lands, titles, and husbands for their daughters. Nonetheless, Parliament, the courts, local government, the established Anglican church, the monarch—all were a part of a social and political system dominated by aristocratic interests and values. This domination had changed little despite the vast changes in social and economic structure that had taken place in the process of industrialization during the second half of the eighteenth century.

The two political parties in Britain, the Whigs and the Tories, were separated not by class but by ideas and values and by family connections and patronage. The Whigs saw themselves as champions of civil, political, and religious liberties—as defenders of Parliament and the nation against any tyranny of king and state. The Tories saw themselves as defenders of royal authority, the Anglican church, the empire, and national and imperial glory; they believed that some are born to rule and most to follow. Neither party was democratic, and at the end of the eighteenth century during the American and French revolutionary wars, a group of reformers criticized both parties as part of a corrupt oligarchy that deprived the people of ancient liberties and a voice in government.

In 1815, Britain faced depression in industrial areas, and unrest brewed in the rural districts when veterans returning from the Napoleonic wars could find no work. Already, during the last years of the Napoleonic wars, there had been an outbreak of rural unrest brought on by high prices and unemployment and low wages. Some craftsmen and farmworkers called Luddites reacted to the introduction of machinery by destroying it. Both the Whigs and the Tories urged strict measures repressing any agitation or violence. The law forbade conspiracies to restrain trade, which included the organization of unions and self-help societies; crimes against property, such as theft, destroying machinery, or poaching (hunting on private property), were severely punished.

Artisans and craftsmen began to agitate for the right to vote. In 1819, at St. Peter's Fields near Manchester, a peaceful crowd of perhaps 50,000 gathered to demand changes in the suffrage law and to listen to radical reformers. The militia charged, killing eleven and wounding hundreds. Nicknamed the "Peterloo Massacre" in derisive comparison to the great victory of Waterloo, the incident provoked increased government repression, which differed little from that used in the autocratic states of Europe to stamp out the ideas of the French Revolution. Many British radicals

were imprisoned and some deported. Large meetings were forbidden, seditious libel was severely punished, and many political agitators were hastily tried without due process of law. Newspapers and pamphlets were taxed and homes searched, which violated the English birthright to speak and meet freely, to due process of law, and to the privacy of one's own home.

Some members of Parliament urged timely reforms. Two traditions strengthened the reformers. One was the commitment of liberal aristocrats to political, religious, and civil liberty; the other was a pragmatic approach to politics that permitted Whigs, Tories, and radicals to reach compromises and to solve some specific problems without bringing in ideology.

In the 1820s, Robert Peel (1788–1850) made some economic and legal reforms that lowered taxes and stimulated the economy and reduced the number of crimes subject to the death penalty. Reformers also pressed for the end of legal discrimination against Catholics and Nonconformists (non-Anglican Protestants). The English could worship as they pleased, but the Corporation Act (1661) and the Test Act (1673) required that holders of public office take communion in the Anglican church. This barred Nonconformists and Catholics from government positions and from the universities. The laws were often ignored, but they still provoked unrest among the lower classes, who were often Nonconformists or, if Irish, Catholics. In 1828, the acts were repealed and public offices were opened to Nonconformists and Catholics. Catholics were still denied seats in Parliament, though, because members of Parliament were required to express opposition to two basic Catholic principles—transubstantiation and the reverence for the Virgin. Liberal Whigs campaigned for "Catholic emancipation." Tories, defenders of the established church, were torn when the Duke of Wellington (the hero of Waterloo) and Robert Peel—both devout Anglicans—decided they must support the removal of the restrictions on Catholics to avoid civil war in Ireland. After 1829, Catholics and Nonconformist Protestants participated in the nation's political life as equals to the Anglicans, although they still suffered from social discrimination.

During the 1830s and 1840s, the liberal reform movement continued and accomplished a number of measures, some principled and others pragmatic. In 1833, slavery was abolished within the British Empire. (The British slave trade had been abolished earlier.) The owners of slaves were compensated for the loss of their property. Humanitarians, pragmatists, and defenders of private property could all champion the reform. The Municipal Corporations Act (1835) granted towns and cities greater authority over their affairs, a first step toward ending corruption and beginning the democratization of town government. The measure created town and city governments that could, if they wished, begin to solve some problems of urbanization and industrialization. These municipal corporations could institute reforms such as sanitation, which Parliament encouraged by passing in 1848 the first Public Health Act.

Increasingly, reform centered on extension of the suffrage and enfranchisement of the new industrial towns. Middle-class men, and even workers, hoped to gain the right to vote. Because of population shifts, some sparsely populated regions—called *rotten boroughs*—sent representatives to the House of Commons, while many densely populated factory towns had little or no representation; and in many cases a single important landowner controlled many seats in the Commons. Voting was public, which allowed for intimidation, and candidates frequently tried to influence voters with drinks, food, and even money.

Intense and bitter feelings built up during the campaign for the Reform Bill of 1832. The very process of passing the Reform Bill created a precedent for party politics and cabinet government for the remainder of the century. The House of Commons, dominated by the Whigs since 1830, passed the bill to extend the suffrage by some 200,000, almost double the number who were then entitled to vote. These new voters would be middle class. The House of Lords, however, refused to pass the bill. There were riots and strikes in many cities, and mass meetings, both of workers and of middle-class people, took place all over the country. King William IV (1830–1837) became convinced, along with many Whig and even some Tory politicians, that the situation was potentially revolutionary. To defuse it, he threatened to increase the number of the bill's supporters in the House of Lords by creating new peers. This threat brought

reluctant peers into line, and the bill was passed. The Reform Act of 1832 extended the suffrage to the middle class and made the House of Commons more representative. The rotten boroughs lost their seats, which were granted to towns. Suffrage did not extend to workers, however, because there were high property qualifications.

Workers did gain some relief, however, when humanitarians pressured Parliament to pass the Factory Act (1833), which legislated that no child under thirteen could work more than nine hours a day and that no one aged thirteen to eighteen could work more than sixty-nine hours a week. The act also provided some inspectors to investigate infractions and to punish offenders. In 1842, an investigation of child labor in the mines shocked the public with graphic descriptions:

> A girdle is put round the naked waist, to which a chain from the carriage is hooked and passed between the legs, and the boys crawl on their hands and knees drawing the carriage after them.
>
> The children are well tired at night. . . . Many fall ill. They work from 7 to 5 o'clock.
>
> When the nature of this horrible labour is taken into consideration . . . a picture is presented of deadly physical oppression and systematic slavery.[2]

Parliament responded in the same year by banning children under ten from the mines. The Factory Act of 1847 stipulated that boys under eighteen and women could work no more than ten hours a day in the mines and factories. At first workers resented the prohibition of child labor because it would greatly reduce their family income if their children could not work. Gradually, however, they realized that the humanitarian protection of the children might make their own lives easier and safer, and their wages higher. The ten-hour day for adult male workers would not be enacted until 1874, however.

The Chartist movement—a very diverse and complicated affair—attracted very different kinds of people with widely varying visions of the future. Its adherents came from the ranks of both intellectual radicals and workers. They pressed for political, not economic, reforms. During the 1830s and 1840s the Chartists agitated for democratic measures, such as universal manhood suffrage, the secret ballot, salaries and the abolition of property qualifications for members of Parliament, and annual meetings of Parliament. For most of the 1830s, these political demands united reformers whose aspirations were in reality very different, and the Chartist platform remained the democratic reform program for the rest of the century, long after the death of Chartism itself at midcentury.

During the "hungry forties," the severe economic hardships added to the numbers of Chartists, but the leaders of the movement split into two groups, one favoring radical and revolutionary action and the other continuing to advocate peaceful tactics. Some Chartists spent their efforts, allied to middle-class reformers in the Anti-Corn Law League, in agitating to remove tariffs on grain in order to lower food prices and strike a blow at the great landowners who dominated British political life. The league succeeded in repealing the Corn Laws in 1846, which effectively established free trade for Britain. Other Chartists who were craftsmen and artisans devoted their efforts to trade unions, cooperatives, and mutual aid societies.

England shared in a general European economic slump from 1846 to 1848. It too suffered from depression and harvest failures, particularly of potatoes blighted by fungus, but there was an upturn in the economy in 1848. The last political effort by the Chartists was led by Feargus O'Connor, a charismatic Irishman, who organized a mass demonstration to present a huge petition of six demands to Parliament in 1848. The cabinet ignored the great charter, which had signatures of at least 2 million names. The movement died out just as most of Europe burst into revolution. The working-class leadership of Chartism turned away from political programs to almost exclusively economic activity, such as trade unions that could bring immediate benefits to workers. Others dispersed into other causes.

Unlike the continental states, England avoided revolution. British politicians thought it was because they had made timely reforms in the 1830s and 1840s, and that belief itself became a force in political life. Whenever times were hard there were always political leaders who would say the remedy was reform and that reform would prevent revolution. The political experience of the first half of the nineteenth century laid the foundation for British parliamentary practices, which came to be the model of liberal, progressive, and stable politics. Britain was the symbol for all those who argued for reform rather than revolution. In the rest of Europe in 1848, however, such arguments were meeting with little success.

The Revolutions of 1848: France

Eighteen forty-eight is often called *the year of revolution,* for throughout Europe, uprisings for political liberty and nationhood took place. The economic crisis of the previous two years had intensified political and national unrest. Food riots broke out in many places. The decimation of the potato crop by disease and the grain harvest by drought had caused terrible food shortages. Also, a financial crisis precipitated by overspeculation had caused business failures, unemployment, and reduced wages. The common people blamed their governments for their misery and sought redress. Although economic hardship aggravated discontent with the existing regimes, "it was the absence of liberty," concludes historian Jacques Droz, "which . . . was most deeply resented by the peoples of Europe and led them to take up arms."[3]

The February Revolution

An uprising in Paris set in motion the revolutionary tidal wave that was to engulf much of Europe in 1848. The Revolution of 1830 had broken the back of the ultras in France. There would be no going back to the Old Regime.

But King Louis Philippe and his ministers, moderates by temperament and philosophy, had no intention of going forward to democracy. A new law in 1831 broadened the franchise from fewer than 100,000 voters to 248,000 by 1846.

Jean François Millet (1814–1875): Planting Potatoes (detail). Concentrating mainly on peasant life, Millet expressed the romantic view of the sanctity of humanity's bond with nature. (*Courtesy Museum of Fine Arts, Boston*)

Even so, only about 3 percent of adult males qualified to vote. The government of Louis Philippe was run by a small elite consisting of wealthy bourgeois bankers, merchants, and lawyers, and aristocrats who had abandoned the hope of restoring the Old Regime. This ruling elite championed the revolutionary ideas of equal treatment under the law and of careers open to talent, but feared democracy and blocked efforts to broaden the franchise. When the poorer bourgeoisie protested against the limited franchise, which still excluded professionals and small tradesmen, François Guizot, the leading minister, arrogantly proclaimed: "Get rich, then you can vote." The ruling elite had become a selfish and entrenched oligarchy, unresponsive to the aspirations of the rest of the nation. Articulate intellectuals denounced the government for its narrow political base and voiced strong republican sentiments. To guard against republicanism and as a reaction to repeated attempts to assassinate the king, the government cracked down on radical societies and newspapers.

Radical republicans, or democrats, wanted to abolish monarchy and grant all men the vote. They had fought in the Revolution of 1830 but were disappointed with the results. Patriots and romantics who looked back longingly on the glory days of Napoleon also hated Louis Philippe's government. These French nationalists complained that the king, who dressed like a businessman and pursued a pacifist foreign policy, was not fit to lead a nation of patriots and warriors. Under Louis Philippe, they said, France could not realize its historic mission of liberating oppressed nationalities throughout Europe.

The strongest rumblings of discontent, barely heeded by the ruling elite, came from the laboring poor. Many French workers, still engaged mainly in pre–Industrial Revolution occupations, were literate and concerned with politics; they read the numerous books and newspapers that denounced social injustice and called for social change. Artisans and their families had participated in the great revolutionary outbreaks of 1789 and had defended the barricades in 1830. Like their sans-culotte forebears, they favored a democratic republic that would aid the common people. These people felt betrayed by the regime of Louis Philippe, which had brought them neither political representation nor economic reform.

The few factory workers and the artisans in small workshops were becoming attracted to socialist thinkers who attacked capitalism and called for state programs to deal with poverty. Louis Blanc, a particularly popular socialist theorist, denounced capitalist competition and demanded that the government establish cooperative workshops. Owned by the workers themselves, these workshops would assure employment for the jobless.

A poor harvest in 1846 and an international financial crisis in 1847, which drastically curtailed French factory production, aggravated the misery of the laboring poor. Prevented by law from striking, unable to meet the financial requirements for voting, and afflicted with unemployment, the urban workers wanted relief. Alexis de Tocqueville, in a speech before the Chamber of Deputies on January 29, 1848, captured the mood of the working class:

> Do you not hear them repeating unceasingly that all that is above them is incapable and unworthy of governing them; that the present distribution of goods throughout the world is unjust; that property rests on a foundation which is not an equitable foundation? And do you not realize that when such opinions take root, when they spread in an almost universal manner, when they sink deeply into the masses, they are bound to bring with them sooner or later, I know not when nor how, a most formidable revolution?
>
> This, gentlemen, is my profound conviction: I believe that we are at this moment sleeping on a volcano. I am profoundly convinced of it. . . .[4]

The government, however, steadfastly refused to pass reforms. Its middle-class opponents sidestepped regulations against political assemblies and demonstrations by gathering at large banquets to protest. When the government foolishly tried to block future banquets, students and workers took to the streets in February 1848, denouncing Guizot and demanding reforms. Barricades began to go up. Attempting to defuse an explosive situation, Louis Philippe dismissed the unpopular Guizot. But the barricades, commanded by republicans, did not come down, and the antigovernment demonstrations continued. When soliders, confused by a shot that had perhaps gone off accidentally, fired directly into a crowd and killed fifty-two Parisians, the situation got out of hand. Unable to pacify the enraged Parisians, Louis Philippe abdicated. France became a republic, and the people of Paris were jubilant.

The June Days: Revolution of the Oppressed

Except for one workingman, the leadership of the provisional government established in February consisted of bourgeoisie. The new leaders were committed to political democracy, but only some, notably the socialist Louis Blanc, favored social reforms. These ministers had little comprehension of or sympathy for the plight of the laboring poor; they regarded socialist ideas as a threat to private property. Although they condemned the inherited privileges of aristocracy, these leaders never questioned the privileges that derived from inherited wealth.

Map 23.2 Europe, 1815 ▶

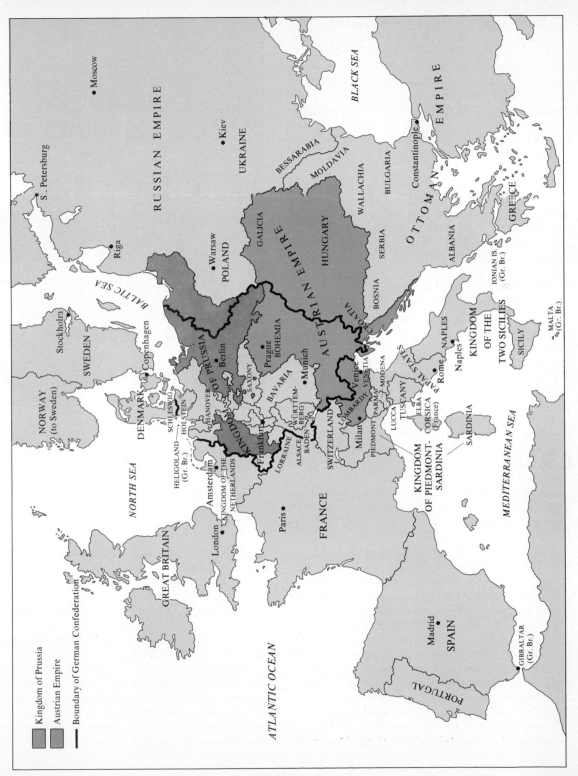

Kingdom of Prussia
Austrian Empire
Boundary of German Confederation

RUSSIAN EMPIRE

OTTOMAN EMPIRE

AUSTRIAN EMPIRE

Moscow

S. Petersburg

Riga

Warsaw
POLAND

Kiev
UKRAINE

BESSARABIA

MOLDAVIA

WALLACHIA

BULGARIA

SERBIA

BOSNIA

ALBANIA

GREECE

Constantinople

BLACK SEA

GALICIA

HUNGARY

CROATIA

BOHEMIA

Prague

BALTIC SEA

SWEDEN

Stockholm

Copenhagen

DENMARK

SCHLESWIG
HOLSTEIN

HELIGOLAND
(Gr. Br.)

NORWAY
(to Sweden)

NORTH SEA

GREAT BRITAIN

London

Amsterdam
KINGDOM OF THE
NETHERLANDS

HANOVER

KINGDOM OF PRUSSIA

Berlin

SAXONY

Frankfurt

LORRAINE

ALSACE

BADEN

WÜRTTEM-
BERG

BAVARIA

Munich

SWITZERLAND

Paris

FRANCE

PIEDMONT

Milan

LOMBARDY

VENETIA

Venice

PARMA

MODENA

LUCCA

TUSCANY

PAPAL STATES

Rome

ELBA

CORSICA
(France)

SARDINIA

KINGDOM
OF PIEDMONT-
SARDINIA

NAPLES

Naples

KINGDOM
OF THE
TWO SICILIES

SICILY

MALTA
(G.: Br.)

IONIAN IS.
(Gr. Br.)

MEDITERRANEAN SEA

ATLANTIC OCEAN

Madrid
SPAIN

PORTUGAL

GIBRALTAR
(Gr. Br.)

23 *Europe, 1815–1848: Revolution and Counterrevolution*   **513**

These bourgeois liberals passionately denounced oppressive rulers, but they could not grasp that, to the working class, *they* had become the oppressors. They considered it a sacred duty to fight for the rights of the individual, but they did not include freedom from hunger and poverty among these rights. By occupation and wealth, the middle class considered itself to be apart from the working class. To the bourgeoisie, the workers were dangerous creatures, "the wild ones," "the vile mob."

Meanwhile, workers who could find jobs labored twelve and fourteen hours a day under brutalizing conditions. In some districts, one out of three children died before the age of five. Everywhere in France, beggars, paupers, prostitutes, and criminals were evidence of the struggle to survive.

The urban poor were desperate for jobs and bread. Socialist intellectuals, sympathetic to the plight of the workers, proposed that the state organize producer cooperatives run by workers. Some wanted the state to take over insurance companies, railroads, mines, and other key industries. To the property owners of all classes, such schemes smacked of madness.

The middle-class leaders of the new republic gave all adult males the vote and abolished censorship; however, their attempts to ease the distress of the urban poor were insincere and halfhearted. The government limited the workday to ten hours and legalized labor unions, but it failed to cope effectively with unemployment. Louis Blanc called for the creation of producers' cooperatives in order to guarantee employment for the city poor. The republic responded by establishing national workshops that provided some employment on public works projects. Most workers, however, received wages for doing nothing. Drawn by the promise of work, tens of thousands of laborers left the provinces for Paris, swelling the ranks of the unemployed. The national workshops provided work, food, and medical benefits for some of the unemployed. But to the workers, this was a feeble effort to deal with their monumental distress. To the property-owning peasantry and bourgeoisie, the national workshops were a hateful concession to socialism and a waste of government funds. They viewed the workshops as nests of working-class radicalism, where plans were be-

The Barricade by Adolphe Hervier. Although this painting is supposed to capture a precise moment: six o'clock in the evening, June 24, 1848, it is symbolic of revolutions that erupted that year in France, Germany, Austria, and Germany. (*Photo Jean-Loup Charmet*)

ing hatched to change the economic system and seize their property.

For their participation in the February uprising against Louis Philippe, the workers had obtained meager benefits. When the government closed the workshops, working-class hostility and despair turned to open rebellion. Again barricades went up in the streets of Paris.

The June Revolution in Paris was unlike previous uprisings in France. It was a revolt against poverty and a cry for the redistribution of property; as such, it foreshadowed the great social revolutions of the twentieth century. The workers stood alone. To the rest of the nation, they were barbarians attacking civilized society. Aristocrats, bourgeois, and peasants feared that no one's property would be safe if the revolution succeeded. From hundreds of miles away, Frenchmen flocked to Paris to crush what they considered to be the madness within their midst.

Although they had no leaders, the workers showed remarkable courage. Women and children fought alongside men behind the barricades. After three days of vicious street fighting and atrocities on both sides, the army extinguished the revolt. Some 1,460 lives had been lost, including four generals. The June Days left deep scars on French society. For many years, workers would never forget that the rest of France had united against them; the rest of France would remain terrified of working-class radicalism.

In December 1848, the French people in overwhelming numbers elected Louis Napoleon, nephew of the great emperor, as president of the Second Republic. They were attracted to the magic of Louis Napoleon's name, and they expected him to prevent future working-class disorders. The election, in which all adult males could vote, demonstrated that most Frenchmen were socially conservative; they were unsympathetic to working-class poverty and deeply suspicious of socialist programs.

The Revolutions of 1848: Germany, Austria, and Italy

Like an epidemic, the fever of revolution that broke out in Paris in February raced across the Continent. Liberals, excluded from participation in political life, fought for parliaments and constitutions; many liberals were also nationalists who wanted unity or independence for their nations. Some liberals had a utopian vision of a new Europe of independent and democratic states. In this vision, reactionary rulers would no longer stifle individual liberty; no longer would a people be denied the right of nationhood.

The German States: Liberalism Discredited

After the Congress of Vienna, Germany consisted of a loose confederation of thirty-nine independent states, of which Austria and Prussia were the most powerful. Jealous of their independence and determined to preserve their absolute authority, the ruling princes detested liberal and nationalist ideals. In the southern German states, which had been more influenced by the French Revolution, princes did grant constitutions and establish parliaments to retain the loyalty of their subjects. But even in these states the princes continued to hold the reins of authority.

The German nationalism that had emerged during the French occupation gained in intensity during the restoration (the post-Napoleonic period), as intellectuals, inspired in part by the ideas of the romantics, insisted that Germans, who shared a common language and culture, should also be united politically. During the restoration, the struggle for German unity and liberal reforms continued to be waged primarily by students, professors, writers, lawyers, and other educated people. The great mass of people, knowing only loyalty to their local prince, remained unmoved by appeals for national unity.

The successful revolt against Louis Philippe, hostility against absolute princes, and the general economic crisis combined to produce uprisings in the capital cities of the German states in March 1848. Throughout Germany, liberals clamored for constitutions, parliamentary government, freedom of thought, and an end to police intimidation. Some called for the creation of a unified Germany governed by a national parliament and headed by a constitutional monarch. The poor of town and countryside joined the struggle. The great depression of the 1840s had aggravated the misery of the German peasant and urban masses, and as the pressures of hunger and unemployment worsened, their discontent exploded into revolutionary fervor.

In the spring of 1848, downtrodden artisans, who faced severe competition from the new factories, served as the revolution's shock troops. Unable to compete with the new machines, artisans saw their incomes fall and their opportunities for work decrease. For example, skilled weavers at home earned far less than factory hands did, and some jobless craftsmen were forced to take factory jobs, which they regarded as a terrible loss of status. These craftsmen wanted to restrict the growth of factories, curtail capitalist competition, and restore the power of the guilds that gave them security and status.

Having lost hope that the absolute princes would aid them, craftsmen gave their support to bourgeois liberals who, without their support, could not challenge the throne or wrest power from the aristocrats. In many German states, the actions of the embittered urban craftsmen determined the successful outcome of the insurrections. (The factory workers in the emerging industries, on the other hand, showed no enthusiasm for revolution, despite the appeals of radical socialists.) Adding to the discomfort of the ruling princes was rioting in the countryside by peasants goaded by crop failure, debt, and oppressive demands from the aristocracy.

Terrified that these disturbances would lead to anarchy, the princes made concessions to the liberals, whom they previously had censored, jailed, and exiled. During March and April 1848, the traditional rulers in Baden, Württemberg, Bavaria, Saxony, Hanover, and other states replaced reactionary ministers with liberals, eased censorship, established jury systems, framed constitutions, formed parliaments, and ended peasant obligations to lords.

In Prussia, Frederick William IV was slow to make concessions, and his troops treated the people of Berlin, who had long hated the army quartered in their city, with contempt. On March 18, as tension in Berlin mounted, the king proclaimed reforms. The Berliners gathered in the palace square to applaud Frederick William's decision. But the hostilities between civilians and soldiers led to pushing and the unintentional firing of two shots by two soldiers. The enraged Berliners armed themselves and hurriedly constructed barricades from anything they could find—barrels, pavement stones, fire pumps, bedding, sacks of flour, fruit stalls. Most insurgents were artisans, but merchants and students also participated in the fighting. Unable to subdue the insurgents, the army urged bombarding the city with artillery. Frederick William opposed the idea and ordered the troops to leave Berlin. The insurgents had won the first round.

The jubilant Berliners paraded the bodies of their fallen fighters in the palace courtyard, demanding that the king come to the window. Frederick William removed his hat and the queen fainted. Recalling that day, the king would later remark: "We all crawled on our stomachs." The Prussian king, like the other German princes, had to agree to the formation of a parliament and the admission of prominent liberals into the government.

But the triumph of the liberals in Prussia and the other German states was not secure. Although reforms liberalized the governments of the German states, the insurrections had not toppled the ruling dynasties. Moreover, the alliance between the bourgeois and the artisans was tenuous. The violence of the artisans frightened the property-owning middle class, which sought only moderate political reforms, preferably through peaceful means. In addition, restoration of the guild system was to the middle class a reactionary economic measure.

Liberals took advantage of their successes in Prussia and other German states to form a national assembly charged with the task of creating a unified and liberal Germany. Representatives from all the German states attended the assembly, which met at Frankfurt. The delegates, including many articulate lawyers and professionals, came predominantly from the educated middle class; only a handful were drawn from the lower classes. After many long debates, the Frankfurt Assembly approved a federation of German states. The German union would have a parliament and would be headed by the Prussian king. Austria, with its many non-German nationalities, would be excluded from the federal union. Some radical democrats wanted to proclaim a German republic, but they were an ineffective minority. Most delegates were moderate liberals who feared that universal (male) suffrage and the abolition of monarchy would lead to plebeian rule and the destruction of the social order. The deputies selected Frederick William as emperor of the new Germany, but the Prussian king refused; he would never wear a crown given to him by common people during a period of revolutionary agitation.

Map 23.3 Europe's Age of Revolutions ▶

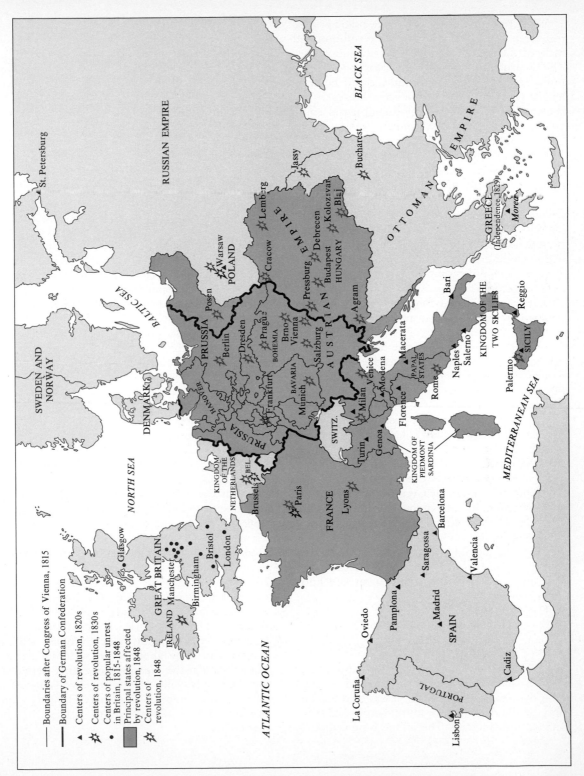

Boundaries after Congress of Vienna, 1815

Boundary of German Confederation

▲ Centers of revolution, 1820s

✹ Centers of revolution, 1830s

● Centers of popular unrest in Britain, 1815–1848

Principal states affected by revolution, 1848

✹ Centers of revolution, 1848

SWEDEN AND NORWAY

St. Petersburg

RUSSIAN EMPIRE

BALTIC SEA

NORTH SEA

ATLANTIC OCEAN

DENMARK

GREAT BRITAIN

Glasgow

IRELAND

Manchester

Birmingham

Bristol

London

HANOVER

KINGDOM OF THE NETHERLANDS

BEL.

Brussels

PRUSSIA

Berlin

Dresden

Frankfurt

BAVARIA

Munich

Posen

Warsaw

POLAND

Cracow

BOHEMIA

Prague

Brno

Vienna

Salzburg

SWITZ.

Paris

Lyons

FRANCE

Turin

Genoa

KINGDOM OF PIEDMONT SARDINIA

Lemberg

AUSTRIAN EMPIRE

Pressburg

Budapest

HUNGARY

Debrecen

Kolozsvár

Blej

Agram

Jassy

Bucharest

OTTOMAN EMPIRE

BLACK SEA

GREECE
(Independence, 1829)

Morea

Milan

Venice

Modena

Macerata

PAPAL STATES

Florence

Rome

Bari

Naples

Salerno

KINGDOM OF THE TWO SICILIES

Palermo

SICILY

Reggio

MEDITERRANEAN SEA

SPAIN

Madrid

Pamplona

Saragossa

Barcelona

Valencia

Oviedo

La Coruña

PORTUGAL

Lisbon

Cadiz

23 Europe, 1815–1848: Revolution and Counterrevolution   517

While the delegates debated, the ruling princes recovered from the first shock of revolution and ordered their armies to crush the revolutionaries. The February Revolution in Paris had shown European liberals that authority could be challenged successfully; the June Days, however, had shown the authorities that revolutionaries could be beaten by professional soldiers. Moreover, the German middle class, frightened by lower-class agitation and unsympathetic to the artisans' demands to restrict capitalism and restore the authority of the old guilds, was losing enthusiasm for revolution—so, too, were the artisans. The disintegration of the alliance between middle-class liberals and urban artisans deprived the revolutionaries of mass support. A revival of the old order would not face much resistance.

In Prussia, a determined Frederick William ordered his troops to reoccupy Berlin. In March the citizens of Berlin had fought against the king's troops, but in November, no barricades went up in Berlin. Prussian forces also assisted the other German states in crushing the new parliaments. The masses of workers and peasants did not fight to save the liberal governments, which fell one by one. A small minority of democrats resisted, particularly in Baden; many of these revolutionaries died in the fighting or were executed.

German liberalism had failed to unite Germany or to create a constitutional government dominated by the middle class. Liberalism, never securely rooted in Germany, was discredited. In the following decades, many Germans, identifying liberalism with failure, abandoned liberal values and turned to authoritarian Prussia for leadership in the struggle for unification. The fact that authoritarians hostile to the spirit of parliamentary government eventually united Germany had deep implications for future German and European history.

Austria: Hapsburg Dominance

The Hapsburg (Austrian) Empire, the product of dynastic marriage and inheritance, had no common nationality or language; it was held together only by the reigning Hapsburg dynasty, its army, and its bureaucracy. The ethnic composition of the empire was enormously complex. The Germans dominated; concentrated principally in Austria, they constituted about 25 percent of the empire's population. The Magyars predominated in the Hungarian lands of the empire. The great bulk of the population consisted of Slavs—Czechs, Poles, Slovaks, Slovenes, Croats, Serbs, Ruthenians. In addition, there were Italians in northern Italy and Rumanians in Transylvania. The Hapsburg dynasty, aided by the army and the German-dominated civil service, prevented the multinational empire from collapsing into anarchy.

Metternich, it is often said, suffered from a "dissolution complex": he understood that the new forces of nationalism and liberalism could break up the Austrian Empire. Liberal ideas could lead Hapsburg subjects to challenge the authority of the emperor, and nationalist feelings could cause the different peoples of the empire to rebel against German domination and Hapsburg rule. To keep these ideas from infecting Austrian subjects, Metternich's police imposed strict censorship, spied on professors, and expelled from the universities students caught reading forbidden books. Despite Metternich's political police, the universities still remained hotbeds of liberalism.

In 1848, revolutions spread throughout the Austrian Empire, starting in Vienna. Aroused by the abdication of Louis Philippe, Viennese liberals denounced Hapsburg absolutism and demanded a constitution, relaxation of censorship, and restrictions on the police. The government responded with hesitance and limited force to the demonstrations of students and workers, and many parts of Vienna fell to the revolutionaries. The authorities used force that was strong enough to arouse the insurrectionists and create martyrs but not strong enough to subdue them. Confused and intimidated by the revolutionaries, the government allowed freedom of the press, accepted Metternich's resignation, and promised a constitution. The Constitutional Assembly was convened and in August voted the abolition of serfdom. At the same time that the Viennese insurgents were tasting the heady wine of reform, revolts in other parts of the empire—Bohemia, Hungary, and northern Italy—added to the distress of the monarchy.

But the revolutionaries' victory was only temporary, and the defeat of the old order only illusory; the Hapsburg government soon began to recover its balance. The first government victory came with the crushing of the Czechs in Bohemia. In 1848, Czech nationalists wanted the Austrian Empire reconstructed along federal lines that would give the Czechs equal standing with Germans. The Czechs called for a constitution for Bohemia and equal status for the Czech language in all official business. In June, students and destitute workers engaged in violent demonstrations that frightened the middle and upper classes—both Czech and German. General Alfred zu Windischgrätz bombarded Prague, the capital of Bohemia, into submission and re-established Hapsburg authority.

In October 1848, the Hapsburg authorities ordered the army to bombard Vienna. Against the regular army, the courageous but disorganized and divided students and workers had little hope. Imperial troops broke into the city, overcame resistance, and executed several of the revolutionary leaders. In March 1849, the Hapsburg leaders replaced the liberal constitution drafted by the popularly elected Constitutional Assembly with a more conservative one drawn up by its own ministers.

The most serious threat to the Hapsburg realm came from the Magyars in Hungary. Some 12 million people lived in Hungary, 5 million of whom were Magyars. The other nationalities consisted of South Slavs (Croats and Serbs) and Rumanians. The upper class were chiefly Magyar landowners, who enjoyed tax exemptions and other feudal privileges. Drawn to liberal and modern ideas and fearful of peasant uprisings, some Hungarian nobles pressed for an end to serfdom and the tax exemptions of the nobility. Louis Kossuth (1802–1894), a member of the lower nobility, called for both social reform and a deepening of national consciousness. The great landowners, determined to retain their ancient privileges, resisted liberalization.

Led by Kossuth, the Magyars demanded local autonomy for Hungary. Hungary would remain within the Hapsburg Empire, but would have its own constitution and national army and would control its own finances. The Hungarian leadership introduced liberal reforms—suffrage for all males who could speak Magyar and owned some property, freedom of religion, freedom of the press, the termination of serfdom, and the end of the privileges of nobles and church. Within a few weeks, the Hungarian parliament changed Hungary from a feudal to a modern liberal state.

But the Hungarian leaders' nationalist dreams towered above their liberal ideals. The Magyars intended to incorporate lands inhabited by Serbs, Slovaks, and Rumanians into their kingdom and transform these people, whom they regarded as ethnic inferiors, into Hungarians. As historian Hugh Seton-Watson has written,

> *Kossuth and his friends genuinely believed that they were doing the non-Hungarians a kindness by giving them a chance of becoming absorbed in the superior Hungarian culture. To refuse this kindness was nationalist fanaticism; to impose it by force was to promote progress. The suggestion that Romanians, Slovaks, or Serbs were nations, with a national culture of their own, was simply ridiculous nonsense.*[5]

In the spring of 1849, the Hungarians renounced their allegiance to the Hapsburgs and proclaimed Hungary an independent state with Kossuth as president.

The Hapsburg rulers took advantage of the ethnic animosities inside and outside Hungary. They encouraged Rumanians and South Slavs to resist the new Hungarian government. When Hapsburg forces moved against the Magyars, they were joined by an army of South Slavs, whose nationalist aspirations had been flouted by the Hungarians. The recently ascended Hapsburg emperor, Francis Joseph, also appealed to Tsar Nicholas I for help. The tsar complied, fearing that a successful revolt by the Hungarians might lead the Poles to rise up against their Russian overlords. The Hungarians fought with extraordinary courage but were overcome by superior might. Kossuth and other rebel leaders went into exile; about one hundred rebel leaders were executed. Thus, through division and alliance, the Hapsburgs prevented the disintegration of the empire.

Italy: Continued Fragmentation

Italian nationalists, eager to end the humiliation of Hapsburg occupation and domination and to unite the disparate states into a unified and liberal nation, also rose in rebellion in 1848. Revolution broke out in Sicily six weeks before the February Revolution in Paris. Bowing to the revolutionaries' demands, King Ferdinand II of Naples granted a liberal constitution. The Grand Duke of Tuscany, King Charles Albert of Piedmont-Sardinia, and Pope Pius IX, ruler of the Papal States, also felt compelled to introduce liberal reforms.

Then the revolution spread to the Hapsburg lands in the north. The citizens of Milan, in Lombardy, built barricades and stood ready to fight the Austrian oppressor. When the Austrian soldiers attacked, they were fired on from nearby windows. From rooftops, Italians hurled stones and boiling water. After "Five Glorious Days" (March 18–22) of street fighting, the Austrians withdrew. The people of Milan had liberated their city. On March 22, the citizens of Venice declared their city free of Austria and set up a republic. King Charles Albert, who hoped to acquire Lombardy and Venetia, declared war on Austria. Intimidated by the insurrections, the ruling princes of the Italian states and Hapsburg Austria had lost the first round.

But soon everywhere in Italy the forces of reaction recovered and reasserted their authority. The Austrians defeated the Sardinians and reoccupied Milan, and Ferdinand II crushed the revolutionaries in the south. Revolutionary disorders in Rome had forced Pope Pius IX to flee in November 1848; in February 1849 the revolutionaries proclaimed Rome "a pure democracy with the glorious title of the Roman Republic." Heeding the pope's call for assistance, Louis Napoleon attacked Rome, destroyed the infant republic, and allowed Pope Pius to return. The last city to fall to the reactionaries was Venice, which the Austrians subjected to a merciless bombardment. After six weeks, the Venetians, weakened by starvation and cholera, surrendered. Reactionary princes still ruled in Italy; the Hapsburg occupation persisted in the north. Italy was still a fragmented nation.

The Revolutions of 1848: An Assessment

The revolutions of 1848 began with much promise, but they all ended in defeat. The revolutionaries' initial success was due less to their strength than to the governments' hesitancy to use their superior force. The reactionary leaders of Europe overcame their paralysis, however, and moved decisively to smash the revolutions. The courage of the revolutionaries was no match for regular armies. Thousands were killed and imprisoned; many fled to America.

Class divisions weakened the revolutionaries. The union between middle-class liberals and workers, which brought success in the opening stages of the revolutions, was only temporary. Bourgeois liberals favoring political reforms—constitution, parliament, and protection of basic rights—grew fearful of the laboring poor, who demanded social reforms—jobs and bread. To the bourgeois, the workers were an uneducated mob driven by dark instincts. When the working class engaged in revolutionary action, a terrified middle class deserted the cause of revolution or joined the old elites in subduing the workers.

Intractable nationalist animosities helped to destroy all the revolutionary movements against absolutism in central Europe. In many cases the different nationalities hated each other more than they hated the reactionary rulers. Hungarian revolutionaries dismissed the nationalist yearnings of the South Slavs and Rumanians living in Hungary, who in turn helped the Hapsburg dynasty to extinguish the nascent Hungarian state. The Germans of Bohemia resisted Czech demands for self-government and the equality of the Czech language with German. When German liberals at the Frankfurt Convention debated the boundary lines of a united Germany, the problem of Prussia's Polish territories emerged. In 1848, Polish patriots wanted to re-create the Polish nation, but German delegates at the convention by an overwhelming majority opposed returning the Polish lands seized by Prussia in the late eighteenth century. In addressing the delegates, Wilhelm Jordan described

Chronology 23.1 Revolution and Reaction

1819	The Peterloo Massacre; troops fire on English workers
1820	Military revolt in Spain
1821	Austria crushes revolts in Italy
1823	French troops crush revolt in Spain
1825	Uprising in Russia crushed by Nicholas I
1829	Greece gains its independence from Turkey
1830	The July Ordinances in France are followed by a revolution that forces Charles X to abdicate
August 1830	The Belgian revolution
October 1830	Belgians declare their independence from Holland, establishing a liberal government
1831	The Polish revolution fails
1831–32	Austrian forces crush a revolution in Italy
1832	The Reform Act extends suffrage to the middle class in Britain
1848	The year of revolution
February 1848	Revolution in Paris—Louis Philippe abdicates, and France becomes a republic
March 1848	Uprisings in capital cities of the German states; liberal reforms follow
March 18–22, 1848	"Five Glorious Days" in Milan
March 22, 1848	Citizens of Venice declare their freedom from Austria and establish a republic
June 1848	June Days of Paris—revolutionaries are beaten by professional soldiers
August 1848	The Constitutional Assembly meets in Vienna; serfdom is abolished
December 1848	Louis Napoleon is elected president of the Second Republic of France
August 1849	The Hungarians' bid for independence is crushed by the Hapsburg forces, aided by Russian troops

the Poles as a people "which does not possess the same measure of human content as is given to the German kind," and denounced those Germans who would permit their kinsmen to live under Polish rule as traitors to their people. Then he justified Germany's claim to the Polish lands.

> *It is high time for us to wake up . . . to a healthy national egoism . . . which places the welfare and honor of the fatherland above everything else. . . . Frankly, the rules of theoretical justice never seem more pitiful to me than when they presume to fix the fate of nations. . . . No, I admit without blinking, our right is no other than the right of the stronger, the right of conquest.*[6]

Before 1848, democratic idealists envisioned the birth of a new Europe of free people and liberated nations. The revolutions in central Europe showed that nationalism and liberalism were not natural allies, that nationalists were often indifferent to the rights of other peoples. Disheartened by these nationalist antagonisms, John Stuart Mill, the English liberal statesman and philosopher, lamented that "the sentiment of nationality so far outweighs the love of liberty that the people are willing to abet their rulers in crushing the liberty and independence of any people not of their race or language."[7]

The liberal and nationalist aims of the revolutionaries were not realized, but liberal gains were not insignificant. All French men obtained the right to vote; the labor services of peasants were abolished in Austria and the German states; parliaments, dominated to be sure by princes and aristocrats, were established in Prussia and other German states. In the decades to come, liberal reforms would become more widespread. These reforms would be introduced peacefully, for the failure of the Revolutions of 1848 convinced many people, including liberals, that popular uprisings were ineffective ways of changing society. The Age of Revolution initiated by the French Revolution of 1789 had ended.

Notes

1. Quoted in Henry A. Kissinger, *A World Restored* (New York: Grosset & Dunlap, The Universal Library, 1964), p. 183.

2. From Great Britain, *Parliamentary Papers: Report of the Commissioners: Children's Employment* (*Mines*), session 3 February–12 August, 1842, 15:52, 67, 94.

3. Jacques Droz, *Europe Between Revolutions, 1815–1848* (New York: Harper Torchbooks, 1968), p. 248.

4. *The Recollections of Alexis de Tocqueville,* trans. by Alexander Teixeira de Mattos (Cleveland: Meridian Books, 1969), pp. 11–12.

5. Hugh Seton-Watson, *Nations and States* (Boulder, Colo.: Westview Press, 1977), p. 162.

6. Quoted in J. L. Talmon, *Political Messianism: The Romantic Phase* (New York: Praeger, 1960), p. 482.

7. Quoted in Hans Kohn, *Nationalism: Its Meaning and History* (Princeton, N.J.: D. Van Nostrand, 1965), pp. 51–52.

Suggested Reading

Deak, Istvan, *The Lawful Revolution* (1979). A review of the Hungarian revolution.

Droz, Jacques, *Europe Between Revolutions* (1967). A fine survey of the period 1815–1848.

Duveau, Georges, *1848: The Making of a Revolution* (1967). A valuable history of the two revolutions in France in 1848.

Fasel, George, *Europe in Upheaval: The Revolutions of 1848* (1970). A good introduction.

Fejtö, François, ed., *The Opening of an Era: 1848* (1973). Contributions by nineteen eminent European historians.

Halévy, Elie, *A History of the English People in the Nineteenth Century*, vols. 1–3, rev. ed. (1987). A must for anyone who wants to know about England's experience from 1815 to the 1840s.

Jelavich, Barbara, *The Hapsburg Empire in Euro-*

pean Affairs, 1814–1918 (1969). The opening chapters cover the period discussed in this chapter.

Kissinger, Henry A., A World Restored (1964). A study of the statesmen and their statesmanship during and immediately after the Congress of Vienna.

Langer, W. L., Political and Social Upheaval, 1832–1852 (1969). Another volume in The Rise of Modern Europe series by its editor. Rich in data and interpretation; contains a valuable bibliographical essay.

Robertson, Priscilla, Revolutions of 1848 (1960). Vividly portrays the events and the personalities involved.

Sigmann, Jean, 1848: The Romantic and Democratic Revolutions in Europe (1970). A useful survey.

Stearns, Peter N., 1848: The Revolutionary Tide in Europe (1974). Strong on social factors.

Talmon, J. L., Romanticism and Revolt (1967). The forces shaping European history from 1815 to 1848.

Thompson, E. P., Making of the English Working Class (1966). A very readable, dramatic, enormously influential, and controversial book.

Webb, R. K., Modern England from the Eighteenth Century (1968). A balanced and well-informed book.

Review Questions

1. What was Metternich's attitude toward the French Revolution? What was his attitude toward Napoleon?

2. How did the Congress of Vienna violate the principle of nationalism? What was the principal accomplishment of the Congress?

3. Between 1820 and 1832, where were revolutions suppressed, and how? Where were revolutions successful, and why?

4. How did Britain's social structure differ from the Continent's in the period following the French Revolution?

5. How did Parliament respond to demands for economic and political reforms from 1815 to 1848?

6. What were the complaints of the urban poor to the new French government after the February Revolution in 1848? What was the significance of the June Days in French history?

7. Why did the Revolutions of 1848 fail in the German states, the Austrian Empire, and Italy?

8. What were the liberal gains of the Revolutions of 1848? Why were liberals and nationalists disappointed with the results of the Revolutions of 1848?

V

An Age of Contradiction:
Progress and Breakdown

1848–1914

24

Thought and Culture in the Mid-Nineteenth Century: Realism and Social Criticism

The second half of the nineteenth century was characterized by great progress in science, a surge in industrialism, and a continuing secularization of life and thought. The principal intellectual currents of the century's middle decades reflected these trends. Realism, positivism, Darwinism, Marxism, and liberalism all reacted against romantic, religious, and metaphysical interpretations of nature and society and focused on the empirical world; adherents of these movements relied on careful observation and strove for scientific accuracy. This emphasis on objective reality helped to stimulate a growing criticism of social ills; for despite unprecedented material progress, reality was often sordid, somber, and depressing. In the last part of the century, reformers motivated by an expansive liberalism, a socially committed Christianity, or both, pressed for the alleviation of social injustice.

Realism and Naturalism

Realism, the dominant movement in art and literature in the mid-nineteenth century, opposed the romantic veneration of the inner life and romantic sentimentality. The romantics exalted passion and intuition, let their imaginations transport them to a presumed idyllic medieval past, and sought subjective solitude amid nature's wonders. Realists, on the other hand, were preoccupied with the external world, with social conditions and contemporary manners, with the familiar details of everyday life. With clinical detachment and meticulous care, they analyzed how people looked, worked, and behaved.

Like scientists, realist writers and artists carefully investigated the empirical world. For ex-

Gustave Courbet: *The Stone Breakers*, 1849; (*Gemäldegalerie Neue Meister/Staatliche Kunstsammlungen Dresden/Deutsche Fotothek Dresden*)

ample, Gustave Courbet (1819–1877), who exemplified realism in painting, sought to practice what he called a "living art," painting common people and commonplace scenes—laborers breaking stones, peasants tilling the soil or returning from a fair, a country burial, wrestlers, bathers, family groups. In a matter-of-fact style, without any attempt at glorification, realist artists also depicted floor scrapers, rag pickers, prostitutes, and beggars. Émile de Vogüé, a nineteenth-century French writer, described realism as follows:

> They [realists] have brought about an art of observation rather than of imagination, one which boasts that it observes life as it is in its wholeness and complexity with the least possible prejudice on the part of the artist. It takes men under ordinary conditions, shows characters in the course of their everyday existence, average and changing. Jealous of the rigour of scientific procedure, the writer proposes to instruct us by a perpetual analysis of feelings and of acts rather than to divert us or move us by intrigue and exhibition of the passions. . . . The new art seeks to imitate nature.[1]

Romantic writers had written lyrics, for lyric poetry is the language of feeling; the novel, because it lends itself admirably to depicting human behavior and social conditions, was the literary genre used by realist writers. Many realist novels were serialized in the inexpensive newspapers and magazines that the many newly literate common people could read. Thus the commoners' interests helped to shape the content of the novels. Seeking to portray reality as it is, realist writers frequently dealt with social abuses and the sordid aspects of human behavior and social life. Harriet Beecher Stowe's *Uncle Tom's Cabin* (1852) graphically described the horrors of slavery. Ivan Turgenev's *Sketches* (1852) described rural conditions in Russia and expressed compassion for the brutally difficult life of serfs. In *War and Peace* (1863–1869), Leo Tolstoy vividly described the manners and outlook of the Russian nobility and the tragedies that attended Napoleon's invasion of Russia. In *Anna Karenina* (1873–1877), he treated the reality of class divisions and the complexities of marital relationships. Fëdor Dostoevski's *Crime and Punishment* (1866) is a psychological novel

Auguste Rodin (1840–1917): Balzac, 1893. The poem embodied the outlook of Romanticism; the novel containing social criticism, however, satisfied the concern of nineteenth-century realists because it could portray the "real" world through careful, empirical observation. Honoré de Balzac wrote nearly a hundred novels, novellas, and short stories that explored French life in the late eighteenth and early nineteenth centuries. (*Museum of Art, Rhode Island School of Design, Rodin Fund*)

that provides penetrating insights into human behavior. Eugène Sue's serialized novel, *Les Mystères de Paris* (1842–1843), contains harrowing accounts of slum life and crime in Paris. George Sand's *Indiana* (1832), which portrayed the married woman as a victim, was praised by a reviewer for presenting

> a true, living world, which is our world . . . characters and manners just as we can observe them around us, natural conversations, scenes in familiar settings, violent, uncommon passions, but sincerely felt or observed and such as are still aroused in many hearts, under the apparent uniformity and monotonous frivolity of our lives.[2]

Many regard Gustave Flaubert's *Madame Bovary* (1857) as the prototype of the realistic novel; it tells the story of a self-centered wife who shows her hatred for her devoted, hardworking, but dull husband by committing adultery. In *Bleak House* (1853), *Hard Times* (1854), and several other works, Charles Dickens portrayed the squalor of life, the hypocrisy of society, and the drudgery of labor in British industrial cities. In *Mary Barton* (1848) and *North and South* (1855), Elizabeth Gaskell, the wife of a Unitarian minister in Manchester, dealt compassionately with the plight of industrial workers.

Literary realism evolved into naturalism when writers tried to demonstrate that there was a causal relationship between human character and the social environment—that certain conditions of life produced predictable character traits in human beings. This belief that human behavior was governed by a law of cause and effect reflected the immense prestige attached to science in the closing decades of the nineteenth century. Émile Zola, the leading naturalist novelist, had an unreserved confidence in the scientific method; he described the task of the writer in an age of science as follows:

> Man is not alone; he lives in society, in a social condition; and consequently, for us novelists, this social condition unceasingly modifies the phenomena. Indeed our great study is just there, in the reciprocal effect of society on the individual and the individual on society. . . .

> And this is what constitutes the experimental novel: . . . to exhibit man living in social conditions produced by himself, which he modifies daily, and in the heart of which he himself experiences a continual transformation. . . .
>
> I have reached this point: the experimental novel is a consequence of the scientific evolution of the century; it continues and completes physiology, which itself leans for support on chemistry and medicine; it substitutes for the study of the abstract and the metaphysical man the study of the natural man, governed by physical and chemical laws, and modified by the influences of his surroundings; it is in one word the literature of our scientific age, as the classical and romantic literature corresponded to a scholastic and theological age.[3]

In his novels, Zola probed the slums, brothels, mining villages, and cabarets of France, examining how people were conditioned by the squalor of their environment. The Norwegian Henrik Ibsen, the leading naturalist playwright, examined with clinical precision the commercial and professional classes, their personal ambitions and family relationships. In the *Pillars of Society* (1877), Ibsen treated bourgeois social pretensions and hypocrisy; in *A Doll's House* (1879) a woman leaves her husband in search of a more fulfilling life—a theme that shocked the late-nineteenth-century bourgeois audience.

In aiming for a true-to-life portrayal of human behavior and the social environment, realism and naturalism coincided with an attitude of mind shaped by science, industrialism, and secularism. Both movements reasserted the importance of the external world. The same outlook also gave rise to positivism in philosophy.

Positivism

In the nineteenth century, science and technology continued to make astonishing strides, which, combined with striking economic advancement, led many Westerners to believe that they were living in an age of such progress that a golden age was on the horizon. Viewing science as the highest achievement of the mind, many intellectuals sought to apply the scientific method to other areas of thought. They believed that this method was a reliable way to approach all problems. They insisted that history could be studied scientifically and society reorganized in accordance with scientific laws of social development. Marxism was one attempt to fashion a science of society; another attempt was positivism.

Positivists held that whereas people's knowledge of nature was vastly expanding, their understanding of society was deficient. This deficiency could be remedied by applying a strict empirical approach to the study of society. The philosopher must proceed like a scientist, carefully assembling and classifying data and formulating general rules that demonstrate regularities in the social experience. Such knowledge based on concrete facts would provide the social planner with useful insights. Positivists rejected metaphysics, which in the tradition of Plato tried to discover ultimate principles through reason alone, rather than through observation of the empirical world. For the positivist, any effort to go beyond the realm of experience to a deeper reality would be a mistaken and fruitless endeavor. The positivist restricted human knowledge only to what could be experienced, and saw the method of science as the only valid approach to knowledge.

A leading figure in the emergence of positivism was Auguste Comte (1798–1857), an engineer with thorough scientific training. Comte served as secretary to Saint-Simon (see page 494) until their association, punctuated by frequent quarrels, ended in 1824. But much of Saint-Simon's thought found its way into Comte's philosophy. Like Saint-Simon (and Marx), Comte called for a purely scientific approach to history and society: only by a proper understanding of the laws governing human affairs could society, which was in a state of intellectual anarchy, be rationally reorganized.

Again like Saint-Simon, Comte held that the Enlightenment and the French Revolution had shattered the Old Regime but had not replaced it with new institutions and a new ideology; this was the pressing need of the age.

Comte called his system *positivism,* because he believed it rested on sure knowledge derived from observed facts and was therefore empirically verifiable. Like others of his generation Comte believed that scientific laws underlay human affairs and that they were discoverable through the methods of the geologist and the chemist—that is, through recording and systematizing observable data. "I shall bring factual proof," he said, "that there are just as definite laws for the development of the human race as there are for the fall of a stone." [4]

One of the laws that Comte believed he had discovered was the "law of the three stages." Comte held that the human mind had progressed through three broad historical stages—the theological, the metaphysical, and the scientific. In the theological stage, the most primitive, the mind found a supernatural explanation for the origins and purpose of things, and society was ruled by priests. In the metaphysical stage, which included the Enlightenment, the mind tried to explain things through abstractions—"nature," "equality," "natural rights," "popular sovereignty"— that rested on hope and belief rather than on empirical investigation. The metaphysical stage was a transitional period between the infantile theological stage and the highest stage of society, the scientific or positive stage. In this culminating stage the mind breaks with all illusions inherited from the past, formulates laws based on careful observation of the empirical world, and reconstructs society in accordance with these laws. People remove all mystery from nature and base their social legislation on laws of society similar to the laws of nature discovered by Newton. Recognizing that religion is an outlet for human emotional needs, Comte proposed a Religion of Humanity in which the human race, its past and future, would be venerated, replacing Christian teachings.

Because Comte advocated the scientific study of society, he is regarded as a principal founder of sociology, but he influenced other fields as well. Comte's effort inspired many thinkers to collect and analyze critically all data pertaining to social phenomena. An English historian, Henry T. Buckle (1821–1862), for example, tried to make the study of civilization an exact science. Buckle saw human culture as a product of climate, soil, and food, so that the achievements of western Europe were due to a favorable environment, the backwardness of Russia and Africa to an unfavorable one. Buckle believed that rigorous laws operated in the social world and that they could be uncovered best through statistical studies.

Although Comte attacked the philosophes for delving into abstractions instead of fashioning laws based on empirical knowledge, he was also influenced by the spirit of eighteenth-century philosophy. Like the philosophes he valued science, criticized supernatural religion, and believed in progress. In this way he accepted the Enlightenment's legacy, including the empirical and anti-theological spirit of Diderot's *Encyclopedia* and Montesquieu's quest for historical laws governing society.

Darwinism

Many contributed to the steady advance of science in the nineteenth century. In 1808, John Dalton, an English chemist, formulated the atomic theory. In 1831, another English chemist, Michael Faraday, discovered the principle of electromagnetic induction on which the electric generator and electric motor are based. In 1847, Hermann von Helmholtz, a German physicist, formulated the law of conservation of energy, which states that the total amount of energy in the universe is always the same; energy that is used up is not lost but is converted into heat. In 1887, another German physicist, Heinrich Hertz, discovered electromagnetic waves, which later made possible the invention of radio, television, and radar. In 1869, Dmitri Mendeleev, a Russian chemist, constructed a periodic table for the elements that helped make chemistry more systematic and mathematical. In 1861, Louis Pasteur, a French scientist, proved that diseases were caused by microbes and devised vaccines to prevent them.

Perhaps the most important scientific advance was the theory of evolution formulated by Charles Darwin (1809–1882), an English naturalist. Darwin did for his discipline what Newton had done for physics; he made biology an objective science based on general principles. The Scientific Revolution of the seventeenth century had given people a new conception of space; Darwin radically altered our conception of time.

Charles Darwin with His Eldest Son, William. Darwin's theory of evolution was grounded in empirical observation and sound scientific reasoning. His theory also had a revolutionary impact on religion and social philosophy. (*Courtesy of Down House, Kent*).

Natural Selection

During the eighteenth century, almost all people had adhered to the biblical account of creation contained in Genesis: God had instantaneously created the universe and the various species of animal and plant life; and he had given every river and mountain and each species of animal and plant a finished and permanent form distinct from every other species. God had designed the bird's wings so that it could fly, the fish's eyes so that it could see under water, and the human legs so that people could walk. All this, it was believed, had occurred some six thousand years ago.

Gradually, this view was questioned. In 1830–1833, Sir Charles Lyell published his three-volume

Principles of Geology, which showed that the planet had evolved slowly over many ages. In 1794, Erasmus Darwin, the grandfather of Charles Darwin, published *Zoonomia, or the Laws of Organic Life,* which offered evidence that the earth had existed for millions of years before the appearance of people and that animals experienced modifications that they passed on to their offspring.

In December 1831, Darwin sailed as a naturalist on the H.M.S. *Beagle,* which surveyed the shores of South America and some Pacific islands. During the five-year expedition, Darwin collected and examined specimens of plant and animal life; he concluded that many animal species had perished, that new species had emerged, and that there were links between extinct and living species.

Influenced by Lyell's achievement, Darwin sought to interpret distant natural occurrences by means of observable processes still going on today. He could not accept that a fixed number of distinct and separate species had been instantaneously created a mere six thousand years ago. In the *Origin of Species* (1859), and the *Descent of Man* (1871), Darwin used empirical evidence to show that the wide variety of animal species was due to a process of development over many millennia, and he supplied a convincing theory that explained how evolution operates.

Darwin adopted the Malthusian idea (see page 490) that the population reproduces faster than the food supply, causing a struggle for existence. Not all infant organisms grow to adulthood; not all adult organisms live to old age. The principle of *natural selection* determines which members of the species have a better chance for survival. The offspring of a lion, giraffe, or insect are not exact duplications of their parents. A baby lion might have the potential for being slightly faster or stronger than its parents; a baby giraffe might grow up to have a longer neck than its parents; an insect might have a slightly different color. These small variations give the organism a crucial advantage in the struggle for food and against natural enemies. The organism favored by nature is more likely to reach maturity, to mate, and to pass on its superior qualities to its offspring, some of which will acquire the advantageous trait to an even greater degree than the parent. Over many generations the favorable characteristic becomes more pronounced and more widespread within the species. Over millennia, natural selection causes the death of old species and the creation of new ones. Very few of the species that dwelt on earth 10 million years ago still survive today, and many new ones, including human beings, have emerged. People themselves are products of natural selection, evolving from earlier, lower, non-human forms of life.

Darwinism and Christianity

Like Newton's law of universal gravitation, Darwin's theory of evolution had revolutionary consequences in areas other than science. Evolution challenged traditional Christian belief. To some, it undermined the infallibility of Scripture and the conviction that the Bible was indeed the Word of God. Darwin's theory touched off a great religious controversy between fundamentalists who defended a literal interpretation of Genesis and advocates of the new biology. In time, most religious thinkers tried to reconcile evolution with the Christian view that there was a Creation and that it had a purpose. These Christian thinkers held that God was the creator and the director of the evolutionary processes.

Darwinism ultimately helped end the practice of relying on the Bible as an authority in questions of science, completing a trend initiated by Galileo. Darwinism thus contributed to the waning of religious belief and to a growing secular attitude; the new secularism dismissed or paid scant attention to the Christian view of a universe designed by God and a soul that rises to heaven. For many, the conclusion was inescapable: nature contained no divine design or purpose, and the human species itself was a chance product of impersonal forces. The core idea of Christianity—that people were children of God participating in a drama of salvation—rested more than ever on faith rather than reason. Some even talked openly about the death of God. The notion that people are sheer accidents of nature was shocking. Copernicus had deprived people of the comforting belief that the earth had been placed in the center of the universe just for them; Darwin deprived people of the privilege of being God's special creation, thereby contributing to the feeling of anxiety that characterizes the twentieth century.

Social Darwinism

Darwin's theories were extended by others beyond the realm in which he had worked. Social thinkers, who recklessly applied Darwin's conclusions to the social order, produced theories that had dangerous consequences for society. Social Darwinists—those who transferred Darwin's scientific theories to social and economic issues—used the terms "struggle for existence" and "survival of the fittest" to buttress economic individualism and political conservatism. Successful businessmen, they said, had demonstrated their fitness to succeed in the competitive world of business. Their success accorded with nature's laws and therefore was beneficial to society; those who lost out in the social-economic struggle demonstrated their unfitness. Using Darwin's model of organisms evolving and changing slowly over tens of thousands of years, conservatives insisted that society too should experience change at an unhurried pace. Instant reforms conflicted with nature's laws and wisdom and resulted in a deterioration of the social body.

The application of Darwin's biological concepts to the social world, where they did not apply, also buttressed imperialism, racism, nationalism, and militarism. Social Darwinists insisted that nations and races were engaged in a struggle for survival in which only the fittest survive and deserve to survive. Karl Pearson, a British professor of mathematics, stated in *National Life from the Standpoint of Science* (1900):

> History shows me only one way, and one way only in which a higher state of civilization has been produced, namely the struggle of race with race, and the survival of the physically and mentally fitter race. . . . The path of progress is strewn with the wrecks of nations; traces are everywhere to be seen of the [sacrifice] of inferior races, and of victims who found not the narrow way to perfection. Yet these dead people are, in very truth, the stepping stones on which mankind has arisen to the higher intellectual and deeper emotional life of today.[5]

"We are a conquering race," said U.S. Senator Albert J. Beveridge. "We must obey our blood and occupy new markets, and if necessary, new lands."[6] "War is a biological necessity of the first importance,"[7] exclaimed the Prussian General von Bernhardi in *Germany and the Next War* (1911).

Darwinian biology was used to promote the belief in Anglo-Saxon (British and American) and Teutonic (German) racial superiority. These peoples attributed the growth of the British Empire, the expansion of the United States to the Pacific, and the extension of German power to their racial qualities. The domination of other peoples—American Indians, Africans, Asians, Poles—was regarded as the natural right of the superior race. British naturalist Alfred Russel Wallace, who arrived at the theory of evolution independently of Darwin, wrote in 1864:

> The intellectual and moral, as well as the physical qualities of the European are superior; the same power and capacities which have made him rise in a few centuries from the condition of the wandering savage . . . to his present state of culture and advancement . . . enable him when in contact with savage man, to conquer in the struggle for existence and to increase at his expense.[8]

The theory of evolution was a great achievement of the rational mind, but in the hands of the Social Darwinists it served to undermine the Enlightenment tradition. Whereas the philosophes emphasized human equality, Social Darwinists divided humanity into racial superiors and inferiors. Whereas the philosophes believed that states would increasingly submit to the rule of law to reduce violent conflicts, Social Darwinists regarded racial and national conflict as a biological necessity, a law of history, and a means to progress. In propagating a tooth-and-claw version of human and international relations, Social Darwinists dispensed with the humanitarian and cosmopolitan sentiments of the philosophes and distorted the image of progress. Their views promoted territorial aggrandizement and military build-up and led many to welcome World War I. The Social Darwinist notion of the struggle of races for survival became a core doctrine of the Nazi party after World War I and provided the "scientific" and "ethical" justification for genocide.

Karl Marx (left) and Friedrich Engels (right) with Marx's Three Daughters, 1860s. Marx saw history solely in terms of economic and social interrelationships, a struggle between laborers and the owners of the means of production. He called for the proletariat to overthrow capitalism and to establish a classless society. (*Culver Pictures*)

Marxism

Karl Marx (1818–1883) was born of German-Jewish parents (both descendants of prominent rabbis). To save his job as a lawyer, Marx's father converted to Protestantism. Enrolled at a university to study law, Marx switched to philosophy. In 1842, Marx was editing a newspaper that was soon suppressed by the Prussian authorities for its outspoken ideas. Leaving his native Rhineland, Marx went to Paris where he met another German, Friedrich Engels (1820–1895), who was the son of a prosperous textile manufacturer. Marx and Engels entered into a lifelong collaboration and became members of socialist groups. In February 1848 they published the *Communist Mani-*

festo, which called for a working-class revolution to overthrow the capitalist system. Forced to leave France in 1849 because of his political views, Marx moved to London, where he spent the rest of his life.

Although supported by Engels, Marx was continually short of funds, and at times he and his wife and daughters lived in dreadful poverty. In London, Marx spent years writing *Capital*—a study and critique of the modern capitalistic economic system that he predicted would be destroyed by a socialist revolution.

A Science of History

As did so many thinkers influenced by the Enlightenment, Marx believed that human history, like the operations of nature, was governed by scientific law. Marx was a strict materialist; rejecting all religious and metaphysical interpretations of both nature and history, he sought to fashion an empirical science of society. He viewed religion as a human creation—a product of people's imagination and feelings, a consolation for the oppressed—and the happiness it brought as an illusion. Real happiness would come, said Marx, not by transcending the natural world but by improving it. Rather than deluding oneself by seeking refuge from life's misfortunes in an imaginary world, one must confront the ills of society and reform them. This last point is crucial. "The philosophers have only *interpreted* the world in different ways; the point is to *change* it."[9]

The world could be rationally understood and changed, said Marx. People were free to make their own history, but to do so effectively, they must comprehend the inner meaning of history—the laws governing human affairs in the past and operating in the present. To Marx, history was not an assortment of unrelated and disconnected events; rather, like the growth of a plant, it proceeded according to its own inner laws. Marx claimed to have uncovered these laws. He said that economic and technological factors—the way in which goods are produced and wealth is distributed—were the moving forces in history. They accounted for historical change and were the basis of all culture—politics, law, religion, morals, and philosophy. "The history of humanity," concluded Marx, "must therefore always be studied and treated in relation to the history of industry and exchange."[10]

Marx said that material technology—the methods of cultivating land and the tools for manufacturing goods—determined society's social and political arrangements and its intellectual outlooks. For example, the hand mill, the loose yoke, and the wooden plow had given rise to feudal lords, whereas power-driven machines had spawned the industrial capitalists. As material technology expanded, it came into conflict with established economic, social, and political forms, and the resulting tension produced change. Thus, feudal patterns could not endure when power machinery became the dominant mode of production. Consequently, medieval guilds, communal agriculture, even the domestic production of goods gave way to free labor, private property, and the factory system of manufacturing. As Marx put it, the expansion of technology triggered a change from feudal social and economic relationships to capitalist ones. Ultimately, the change in economic-technological conditions would become the cause for great political changes.

This process was most clearly demonstrated by the French Revolution. Radical changes in the economic foundations of society had taken place since the Middle Ages without corresponding political changes. However, the forces of economic change could not be contained in outdated political forms. In France this tension exploded into revolution. Whatever their conscious intentions, said Marx, the bourgeois leaders of the French Revolution had scattered feudal remnants to the wind; they had promoted free competition and commercial expansion and transferred power from the landed aristocracy to the leaders of finance and industry. Not every revolutionary change in history is explosive, according to Marx, but whenever major economic changes take place, political and social changes must follow.

Class Conflict

Throughout history, said Marx, there has been a class struggle between those who own the means of production and those whose labor has been exploited to provide wealth for this upper class. This opposing tension between classes has pushed history forward into higher stages. In the ancient world, when wealth was based on land, the struggle was between master and slave, patrician and plebeian; during the Middle Ages, when land was still the predominant mode of production, the struggle was between lord and serf. In the modern industrial world, two sharply opposed classes were confronting each other—the capitalists owning the factories, mines, banks, and transportation systems, and the exploited wage earners (the proletariat).

The class with economic power also controlled the state, said Marx and Engels. That class used political power to protect and increase its property and to hold down the laboring class. "Thus the ancient State was above all the slaveowners' state for holding down the slaves," said Engels, "as a feudal State was the organ of the nobles for holding down the . . . serfs, and the modern representative State is the instrument of the exploitation of wage-labor by capital."[11]

Marx and Engels said, too, that the class that controlled material production also controlled mental production, that is, the ideas held by the ruling class became the dominant ideas of society. These ideas, presented as laws of nature or moral and religious standards, were regarded as the truth by oppressor and oppressed alike. In reality, however, these ideas merely reflected the special economic interests of the ruling class. Thus, said Marx, bourgeois ideologists would insist that natural rights and laissez faire were laws of nature having universal validity. But these "laws" were born of the needs of the bourgeoisie in its struggle to wrest power from an obsolete feudal regime and to protect its property from the state. Similarly, nineteenth-century slaveholders convinced themselves that slavery was morally right—that it had God's approval and was good for the slave. Slaveowners and capitalist employers alike may have defended their labor systems by citing universal principles that they thought were true, but in reality their systems rested on a simple economic consideration—slave labor was good for the pocketbook of the slaveowner, and wage labor was good in the same way for the capitalist.

The Destruction of Capitalism

Under capitalism, said Marx, the worker knew only poverty. He worked long hours for low wages, suffered from periodic unemployment, and lived in squalid, overcrowded dwellings. Most monstrous of all, he was forced to send his young children into the factories.

> *Children of nine or ten years are dragged from their squalid beds at two, three, or four o'clock in the morning and compelled to work for a bare subsistence until ten, eleven, or twelve at night, their limbs wearing away, their frames dwindling, their faces whitening, and their humanity absolutely sinking into a stone-like torpor, utterly horrible to contemplate.*[12]

Capitalism also produced another kind of poverty, said Marx—poverty of the human spirit. Under capitalism the factory worker was reduced to a laboring beast, performing tedious and repetitive tasks in a dark, dreary, dirty cave, an altogether inhuman environment that deprived people of their human sensibilities. Unlike the artisans in their own shops, factory workers found no pleasure and took no pride in their work; they did not have the satisfaction of creating a finished product that expressed their skills. Work, said Marx, should be a source of fulfillment for people. It should enable people to affirm their personalities and develop their potential. By treating people not as human beings but as cogs in the production process, capitalism alienated people from their work, themselves, and one another. Marx wrote:

> *[T]he worker . . . does not fulfil himself in his work but denies himself, has a feeling of misery rather than well-being, does not develop freely his mental and physical energies but is physically exhausted and mentally debased. . . . His work is not voluntary but imposed,* forced labour. *It is not the satisfaction of a need, but only a* means *for satisfying other needs. Its alien character is clearly shown by the fact that as soon as there is no physical or other compulsion it is avoided like the plague. . . .*
> *. . . [T]he more the worker expends himself in work, . . . the poorer he becomes in his inner life, and the less he belongs to himself. . . . The worker puts his life into the object, and his life then belongs no longer to himself but to the object.*[13]

Marx believed that capitalist control of the economy and the government would not endure forever. The capitalist system would perish just as the feudal society of the Middle Ages and the slave society of the ancient world had perished. From the ruins of a dead capitalist society a new economic-social system, socialism, would emerge.

Marx predicted how capitalism would be destroyed. Periodic unemployment would increase the misery of the workers and intensify their hatred of capitalists. Small businessmen and shopkeepers, unable to compete with the great capitalists, would sink into the ranks of the working class, greatly expanding its numbers. Society would become polarized into a small group of immensely wealthy capitalists and a vast proletariat, poor, embittered, and desperate. This monopoly of capital by the few would become a brake on the productive process. Growing increasingly conscious of their misery, the workers—aroused, educated, and organized by communist intellectuals—would revolt. "Revolution is necessary," said Marx, "not only because the *ruling* class cannot be overthrown in any other way, but also because only in a revolution can *the class which overthrows it* rid itself of the accumulated rubbish of the past and become capable of reconstructing society."[14] The working-class revolutionaries would smash the government that helped the capitalists maintain their dominance. Then they would confiscate the property of the capitalists, abolish private property, place the means of production in the workers' hands, and organize a new society. The *Communist Manifesto* ends with a ringing call for revolution:

> *The Communists . . . openly declare that their ends can be attained only by the forcible overthrow of all existing social conditions. Let the ruling classes tremble at a Communist revolution. The proletarians have nothing to lose but their chains. They have a world to win.*
> *Workingmen of all countries, unite!*[15]

Marx did not say a great deal about the new society that would be ushered in by the socialist revolution. With the destruction of capitalism, the distinction between capitalist and worker would cease and with it the class conflict. No longer would society be divided into haves and havenots, oppressor and oppressed. Since this classless society would contain no exploiters, there would be no need for a state, which was merely an instrument for maintaining and protecting the power of the exploiting class. Thus, the state would eventually wither away. The production and distribution of goods would be carried out through community planning and communal sharing, replacing the capitalist system of competition. People would work at varied tasks, rather than being confined to one form of employment, just as Fourier had advocated (see Chapter 22). No longer factory slaves, people would be free to fulfill their human potential, to improve their relationships on a basis of equality with others, and to work together for the common good.

The Influence of Marx

Marxism had immense appeal for both the downtrodden and intellectuals. It promised to end the injustices of industrial society; it claimed the certainty of science; it assured adherents that the triumph of their cause was guaranteed by history. In many ways, Marxism was a secular religion—the proletariat become a chosen class endowed with a mission to achieve worldly salvation for humanity.

Marx's influence grew during the second wave of industrialization in the closing decades of the nineteenth century, when class bitterness between the proletariat and the bourgeoisie seemed to worsen. Many workers thought that liberals and conservatives had no sympathy for their plight and that the only way to improve their lot was through socialist parties. It seemed to Marx's advocates that his predictions would be realized: monopoly capitalist firms in the advanced nations would swallow small competitors and, for the sake of profit, draw all the world into capitalism. Moreover, severe economic depressions seemed to force more and more people out of farming or small business and into the working class. Others disagreed with this scenario, pointing out that the workers were not getting poorer and that Marx's picture may have been accurate for the midcentury but not for the end of the century, that workers, because of their unions, increased productivity, and protection by the state had improved their lives considerably (see Chapter 26).

Marx's emphasis on economic forces has im-measurably broadened the perception of historians, who now explore the economic factors in historical developments. This approach has greatly expanded our understanding of Rome's decline, the outbreak of the French Revolution and the American Civil War, and other crucial developments. Marx's theory of class conflict has provided social scientists with a useful tool for analyzing social process. His theory of alienation has been absorbed by sociologists and psychologists. Of particular value to social scientists is Marx's insight that the ideas people hold to be true and the values they consider valid often veil economic interests. On the political level, both the socialist parties of western Europe, which pressed for reform through parliamentary methods, and the communist regimes in Russia and China, which came to power through revolution, claimed to be heirs of Marx.

Critics of Marx

Critics point out serious weaknesses in Marxism. The rigid Marxist who tries to squeeze all historical events into an economic framework is at a disadvantage. Economic forces alone will not explain the triumph of Christianity in the Roman Empire, the fall of Rome, the Crusades, the French Revolution, modern imperialism, World War I, or the rise of Hitler. Economic explanations fall particularly flat in trying to account for the emergence of modern nationalism, whose appeal, resting on deeply ingrained emotional needs, crosses class lines. The great struggles of the twentieth century have not been between classes but between nations.

Many of Marx's predictions or expectations have not materialized. Workers in Western lands did not become the oppressed and impoverished working class that Marx described in the mid-nineteenth century. Western workers, because of increased productivity and the efforts of labor unions and reform-minded governments, improved their lives considerably, so that they now enjoy the highest standard of living in history. The tremendous growth of a middle class of professionals, civil service employees, and small-business persons belies Marx's prediction that capitalist society would be polarized into a small group of very rich capitalists and a great mass of destitute workers. Marx believed that socialist revolutions would break out in the advanced industrialized lands. But the socialist revolutions of the twentieth century have occurred in underdeveloped, predominantly agricultural states. The state in communist lands, far from withering away, has grown more centralized, powerful, and oppressive. In no country where communist revolutionaries have seized power have people achieved the liberty that Marx desired. All these failed predictions and expectations seem to contradict Marx's claim that his theories rested on an unassailable scientific foundation.

Anarchism

Anarchism was another radical movement that attacked capitalism. Like Marxists, anarchists protested the exploitation of workers, denounced the coercive authority of government, and envisioned a stateless society. Only by abolishing the state, said anarchists, could the individual live a free and full life. To achieve these ends, a small number of anarchists advocated revolutionary terrorism; others, like the great Russian novelist Leo Tolstoy, rejected all violence. These anarchists sought to destroy the state by refusing to cooperate with it.

Pierre Joseph Proudhon

Anarchists drew inspiration from Pierre Joseph Proudhon (1809–1865), a self-educated French printer and typesetter. Proudhon criticized social theorists who devised elaborate systems that regimented daily life, conflicted with human nature, and deprived people of their personal liberty. He desired a new society that maximized individual freedom. He looked back longingly to preindustrial society, free of exploitation and corruption and of great manufacturers and financiers. He had great respect for the dignity of labor and wanted to liberate it from the exploitation and false values of industrial capitalism. An awakened working class would construct a new moral and social order. Proudhon believed that people would deal justly with one another, respect one another, and

develop their full potential in a society of small peasants, shopkeepers, and artisans. Such a society would not require a government; government only fosters privilege and suppresses freedom:

> To be governed is to be watched over, inspected, spied on, directed, legislated at, regulated, docketed, indoctrinated, preached at, controlled . . . censored, ordered about, by men who have neither the right nor the knowledge nor the virtue. To be governed means to be, at each operation, at each transaction, at each movement . . . registered, controlled, taxed . . . hampered, reformed, rebuked, arrested. It is to be, on the pretext of the general interest, taxed, drilled . . . exploited . . . repressed, fined, abused. . . . That's government, that's its justice, that's its morality.[16]

Proudhon was less a theorist than a man who could express passionately the disillusionment and disgust with the new industrial society that was developing in Europe.

Mikhail Bakunin

Anarchism had a particular appeal in Russia, where there was no representative government and no way, other than petitions to the tsar, to legally redress injustice. A repressive regime, economic backwardness, a youth movement passionately committed to improving the lives of the masses, and a magnetic leader, Mikhail Bakunin (1814–1876), all contributed toward shaping the Russian anarchist tradition. Bakunin was a man of action who organized and fought for revolution and set an example of revolutionary fervor. The son of a Russian noble, he left the tsar's army to study philosophy in the West, where he was attracted to the ideas of Proudhon and Marx. He was arrested for participating in the German revolution of 1848 and turned over to tsarist officials. He served six years in prison and was then banished to Siberia, from which he escaped in 1861.

Bakunin devoted himself to organizing secret societies that would lead the oppressed in revolt. Whereas Marx held that revolution would occur in the industrial lands through the efforts of a

Gustave Courbet (1819–1877): Proudhon and His Daughters. Pierre Joseph Proudhon condemned the new industrial society, which he believed restricted workers and spread poverty. He sought a society that would maximize individual freedom. His call for freedom influenced many social thinkers and was adopted by nineteenth-century anarchists. (*Historical Pictures Service, Chicago*)

class-conscious proletariat, Bakunin wanted all oppressed people to revolt, including the peasants (the vast majority of the population in central and eastern Europe). Toward this end, he favored secret societies and terrorism. He argued that a single act of terrorism, such as an assassination of a hated official, could spark the revolution.

Marx and Bakunin disagreed on one crucial issue of strategy. Marx wanted to organize the workers into mass political parties; Bakunin, on the other hand, held that revolutions should be fought by secret societies of fanatic insurrectionists. Bakunin feared that after the Marxists overthrew the capitalist regime and seized power, they would become the new masters and exploiters, using the state to enhance their own power. They would, said Bakunin, become a "privileged minority . . . of *ex-workers,* who, once they become

rulers or representatives of the people, cease to be workers and begin to look down upon the toiling people. From that time on they represent not the people but themselves and their claims to govern the people."[17] Therefore, said Bakunin, once the workers capture the state, they should destroy it forever. Bakunin's astute prediction that a socialist revolution would lead state power to intensify rather than disappear has been borne out in the twentieth century.

Anarchists engaged in several acts of political terrorism, including the assassination or attempted assassination of heads of state and key ministers, but they never waged a successful revolution. They failed to reverse the trend toward the concentration of power in industry and government that would characterize the twentieth century. But the motives that impelled them to challenge the values and institutions of modern society and to engage in acts of terror express emotional conditions that have not disappeared with the waning of anarchism.

Liberalism in Transition

In the early part of the nineteenth century, European liberals were preoccupied with protecting the rights of the individual against the demands of the state. They championed laissez faire because they feared that state interference in the economy to redress social evils would threaten individual rights and the free market that they thought were essential to personal liberty; they favored property requirements for voting and office holding, because they were certain that the unpropertied and uneducated masses lacked the wisdom and experience to exercise political responsibility.

In the last part of the century, liberals began— not without reservation and qualification—to support extended suffrage and government action to remedy the abuses of unregulated industrialization. This growing concern for the welfare of the laboring poor coincided with and was influenced by an unprecedented proliferation of humanitarian movements on both sides of the Atlantic. Nurtured by both the Enlightenment and Christian traditions, reform movements called for the prohibition of child labor, schooling for the masses, humane treatment for prisoners and the mentally ill, equality for women, the abolition of slavery, and an end to war. By the beginning of the twentieth century, liberalism had evolved into liberal democracy, and laissez faire had been superseded by a reluctant acceptance of social legislation and government regulation. But from beginning to end, the central concern of liberals remained the protection of individual rights.

Alexis de Tocqueville

Few mid-nineteenth century thinkers grasped the growing significance of democracy as did Alexis de Tocqueville, the French aristocrat and statesman. In *Democracy in America* (1835–1840), based on his travels in the United States, de Tocqueville analyzed, with cool detachment and brilliance, the nature, merits, and weaknesses of his subject. In contrast to France of the Old Regime, said de Tocqueville, American society had no hereditary aristocracy with special privileges; the avenues to social advancement and political participation were open to all. De Tocqueville held that democracy was more just than aristocratic government, and he predicted that it would be the political system of the future.

But de Tocqueville also recognized and explored a core problem of democracy: in a democratic society people's passion to be equal outweighs their commitment to liberty. Spurred by the ideal of equality, said de Tocqueville, people in a democracy desire the honors and possessions that they think are their due. But since people are not naturally equal in ability, many are frustrated and turn to the state to secure for them those advantages that they cannot obtain for themselves. Consequently, there is an ever-present danger in a democracy that people, driven by a passion for equality, will surrender their liberty to a central state that promises to provide the privileges they seek. To prevent democracy from degenerating into state despotism, de Tocqueville urged strengthening institutions of local government, forming numerous private associations over which the state has no control, protecting the independence of the judiciary, and preserving a free press.

Another danger in a democratic society, said de Tocqueville, is the tendency of the majority to impose its viewpoint over the minority. The majority demands conformity of belief. Its power is so absolute and irresistible, held de Tocqueville, that the minority is fearful to stray from the track which the majority prescribes. De Tocqueville declared: "I think that liberty is endangered when this power [of the majority] is checked by no obstacles which may retard its course, and force it to moderate its own vehemence."[18]

Although recognizing the limitations of democracy, de Tocqueville did not seek to reverse its growth. In this new age that is dawning, he said,

all who shall attempt . . . to base freedom upon aristocratic privilege will fail . . . all who shall attempt to draw and to retain authority within a single class, will fail. . . . All . . . who would establish or secure the independence and the dignity of their fellow-men, must show themselves the friends of equality. . . . Thus the question is not how to reconstruct aristocratic society, but how to make liberty proceed out of that democratic state of society in which God has placed us.[19]

John Stuart Mill

The transition from laissez-faire liberalism to a more socially conscious and democratic liberalism is seen in the thought of John Stuart Mill, a British philosopher and statesman. Mill's *On Liberty* (1859) is the classic statement of individual freedom—that the government and the majority have no right to interfere with the liberty of another human being whose actions do no injury to others. Mill regarded freedom of thought and expression, the toleration of opposing and unpopular viewpoints, as a necessary precondition for the shaping of a rational, moral, and civilized citizen. Like other liberals, Mill would place limits on the power of government, for in an authoritarian state citizens cannot develop their moral and intellectual potential.

Although he feared the state, Mill also recognized the necessity for state intervention to promote the general good. For example, he maintained that it was permissible for the state to require children to attend school against the wishes of their parents, to regulate hours of labor, to promote public health, and to provide workers' compensation and old age insurance.

In *Considerations on Representative Government* (1861), Mill endorsed the active participation of all citizens, including the lower classes, in the political life of the state. However, he also proposed a system of plural voting in which education and character would determine the number of votes each person was entitled to cast. In this way Mill, a cautious democrat, sought to protect the individual from the tyranny of a politically unprepared majority.

In contrast to most of his contemporaries, Mill felt that differences between the sexes (and between the classes) were due far more to education than to inherited inequalities. Believing that all

John Stuart Mill. Mill's *On Liberty* is regarded as the classic defense of individual liberty. He also concerned himself with most of the major issues of industrialization, including the definition of productive and unproductive labor, the distribution of gains from international commerce, and the precise relationship between profits and wages. (*The Granger Collection, New York*)

people—women as well as men—should be able to develop their talents and intellects as fully as possible, Mill was an early champion of female equality, including the suffrage: In the *Subjection of Women* he wrote:

. . . the principle which regulates the existing social relations between the two sexes—the legal subordination of one sex to the other—is wrong in itself, and now one of the chief hindrances to human improvement: and . . . it ought to be replaced by a principle of perfect equality, admitting no power or privilege on the one side, nor disability on the other.[20]

Thomas Hill Green

Thomas Hill Green, an Oxford University professor, argued that laissez faire protected the interests of the economically powerful class and ignored the welfare of the nation. Accordingly he approved of legislation to promote better conditions of health, labor, and education. Green valued private property but could not see how this principle helped the poor. "A man who possesses nothing but his powers of labor and who has to sell these to a capitalist for bare daily maintenance, might as well . . . be denied rights of property altogether."[21]

For Green, liberalism encompassed more than the protection of individual rights from an oppressive government; a truly liberal society, he said, gives people the opportunity to fulfill their moral potential and human capacities. The liberal state, said Green, has a moral obligation to create social conditions that permit the individual to pursue this self-development. Toward that end, said Green, the state should promote public health, ensure decent housing, and provide for education. An ignorant person, Green held, cannot be a good citizen and cannot be morally self-sufficient. Since many parents will not voluntarily make provisions for the education of their children, it behooves the state to install a system of compulsory education.

Green remained an advocate of capitalism but rejected strict laissez faire which, he said, benefited only a particular class. For Green, the liberal state must concern itself with the common good:

If the ideal of true freedom is the maximum of power for all members of human society alike to make the best of themselves, we are right in refusing to ascribe the glory of freedom to a state in which the apparent elevation of the few is founded on the degradation of the many.[22]

To be sure, many liberals regarded state intervention as a betrayal of the liberal principle of individual freedom and held to the traditional liberal view that the plight of the downtrodden was not a legitimate concern of the state. In *Man Versus the State* (1884) British philosopher Herbert Spencer rejected the idea "that evils of all kinds should be dealt with by the State." The outcome of state intervention, he said, is that "each member of the community as an individual would be a slave to the community as a whole . . . and the slavery will not be mild."[23] Committed to a philosophy of extreme individualism, Spencer never abandoned the view that the state was an evil and oppressive institution.

In general, however, by the beginning of the twentieth century, liberals in Britain increasingly acknowledged the need for social legislation; the foundations for the British welfare state were being laid. On the Continent, too, social welfare laws were enacted. To be sure, the motives behind such legislation were quite diverse and often had little to do with liberal sentiments (see Chapter 26). Nevertheless, in several countries liberalism was expanding into political and social democracy, a trend that would continue in the twentieth century.

Notes

1. Cited in Damian Grant, *Realism* (London: Methuen, 1970), pp. 31–32.

2. Cited in F. W. J. Hemmings, ed., *The Age of Realism* (New Jersey: Humanities Press, 1978), p. 152.

3. Émile Zola, *The Experimental Novel*, trans. by Belle M. Sherman (New York: Haskell House, 1964), pp. 20–21, 23.

4. Quoted in Ernst Cassirer, *The Problem of Knowledge*, trans. by William H. Woglom and Charles W. Hendel (New Haven: Yale University Press, 1950), p. 244.

5. Karl Pearson, *National Life from the Standpoint of Science* (London: Adam and Charles Black, 1905), pp. 21, 64.

6. Quoted in H. W. Koch, "Social Darwinism in the 'New Imperialism,'" in H. W. Koch, ed., *The*

Origins of the First World War (New York: Taplinger, 1972), p. 341.

7. Ibid., p. 345.

8. Quoted in John C. Greene, *The Death of Adam* (New York: Mentor Books, 1961), p. 313.

9. Karl Marx, *Theses on Feuerbach,* excerpted in T. B. Bottomore and Maximilien Rubel, eds., *Karl Marx: Selected Writings in Sociology and Social Philosophy* (London: Watts, 1956), p. 69.

10. Karl Marx, *The German Ideology* (New York: International Publishers, 1939), p. 18.

11. Friedrich Engels, *The Origin of the Family, Private Property and the State,* in Emile Burns, *A Handbook of Marxism* (New York: Random House, 1935), p. 330.

12. Karl Marx, *Capital* (Chicago: Charles H. Kerr, 1912), 1:268.

13. Karl Marx, *Economic and Philosophical Manuscripts,* in T. B. Bottomore, ed., *Karl Marx Early Writings* (New York: McGraw-Hill, 1963), pp. 124–125, 122.

14. Marx, *The German Ideology,* p. 69.

15. Karl Marx, *The Communist Manifesto,* trans. by Samuel Moore (Chicago: Henry Regnery, 1954), pp. 81–82.

16. Quoted in James Joll, *The Anarchists* (New York: Grosset & Dunlap, 1964), pp. 78–79.

17. Excerpted in G. P. Maximoff, ed., *The Political Philosophy of Bakunin* (Glencoe, Ill.: The Free Press, 1953), p. 287.

18. Alexis de Tocqueville, *Democracy in America,* trans. by Henry Reeve (New York: Oxford University Press, 1947), p. 162.

19. Ibid., pp. 493–494.

20. John Stuart Mill, *The Subjection of Women* in *On Liberty, Etc.* (London: Oxford University Press, 1924), p. 427.

21. Thomas Hill Green, *Lectures on the Principles of Political Obligation* (Ann Arbor, Mich.: The University of Michigan Press, 1967), p. 219.

22. Thomas Hill Green, "Liberal Legislation or Freedom of Contract," a lecture given at Leicester, 1881, excerpted in Alan Bullock and Maurice Shock, eds. *The Liberal Tradition* (London: Adam and Charles Black, 1956), p. 181.

23. Herbert Spencer, *Man Versus the State* (London: Watts, 1940), pp. 34, 49–50.

Suggested Reading

Andreski, Stanislav, ed., *The Essential Comte* (1974). Excerpts from Comte's works.

Bullock, Alan, and Maurice Shock, eds., *The Liberal Tradition* (1956). Well-chosen selections from the writings of British liberals; the introduction is an excellent survey of liberal thought.

de Ruggiero, G., *The History of European Liberalism* (1927). A good starting point.

Farrington, Benjamin, *What Darwin Really Said* (1966). A brief study of Darwin's work.

Grant, Damian, *Realism* (1970). A good short survey.

Greene, J. C., *The Death of Adam* (1961). The impact of evolution on Western thought.

Hemmings, F. W. J., ed., *The Age of Realism* (1978). A series of essays on realism in various countries.

Hofstadter, Richard, *Social Darwinism in American Thought* (1955). A classic treatment of the impact of evolution on American conservatism, imperialism, and racism.

Joll, James, *The Anarchists* (1964). A fine treatment of anarchists, their lives, and thought.

McLellan, David, *Karl Marx: His Life and Thought* (1977). A highly regarded biography.

———, ed., *Karl Marx: Selected Writings* (1977). A balanced selection of Marx's writings.

Manuel, Frank E., *The Prophets of Paris* (1965). Contains a valuable chapter on Comte.

Matthews, Betty, ed., *Marx: A Hundred Years On* (1983). Eleven essays by authorities.

Nochlin, Linda, *Realism* (1971). The nature of realism; realism in art.

Richter, Melvin, *The Politics of Conscience* (1964). A study of T. H. Green and his age.

Tucker, Robert, *The Marxian Revolutionary Idea* (1969). Marxism as a radical social philosophy.

———, ed., *The Marx-Engels Reader* (1972). An anthology of Marx's essential writings.

Review Questions

1. How did realism differ from romanticism?

2. Realism and naturalism coincided with an at-

titude of mind shaped by science, industrialism, and secularism. Discuss this statement.

3. What is the relationship between positivism and science?

4. What was Comte's "law of the three stages"?

5. The theory of evolution had revolutionary consequences in areas other than science. Discuss this statement.

6. Why were Social Darwinist theories so popular?

7. What was Marx's philosophy of history?

8. What did Marx have in common with the philosophes of the Enlightenment?

9. Why did Marx think that capitalism was doomed? How would its destruction happen?

10. Why did Proudhon hate government?

11. In what ways did Bakunin and Marx differ?

12. Relate the theories of de Tocqueville, Mill, Green, and Spencer to the evolution of liberalism. Draw relevant comparisons and contrasts regarding their theories.

25

The Surge of Nationalism: From Liberal to Extreme Nationalism

The Revolutions of 1848 ended in failure, but nationalist energies were too powerful to contain. In 1867, Hungary gained the autonomy it had sought in 1848, and by 1870, the unification of both Italy and Germany was complete.

The leading architects of Italian and German unification were not liberal idealists or romantic dreamers of the type who had fought in the Revolutions of 1848; they were tough-minded practitioners of *Realpolitik,* "the politics of reality." Shrewd and calculating statesmen, they respected power and knew how to wield it; focusing on the world as it actually is, they dismissed ideals as illusory, noble sentiments that impeded effective action. *Realpolitik* was the political counterpart of realism and positivism. All three outlooks shared the desire to view things coldly and objectively as they are, rather than as idealists would like them to be.

Nationalism, gaining in intensity in the last part of the nineteenth century, was to become the dominant spiritual force in European life. Once Germany was unified, Pan-Germans sought to incorporate Germans living outside the Reich into the new Germany and to build a vast overseas empire. Russian Pan-Slavs dreamed of bringing the Slavs of eastern Europe under the control of "Mother Russia." Growing increasingly resentful of Magyar and German domination, the Slavic minorities of the Hapsburg Empire agitated for recognition of their national rights. In the late nineteenth century, nationalism became increasingly belligerent, intolerant, and irrational, threatening both the peace of Europe and the liberal-humanist tradition of the Enlightenment.

Victor Emmanuel and Garibaldi at the Bridge of Teano, 1860. (*Scala/Art Resource*)

The Unification of Italy

In 1848, liberals had failed to drive the Austrians out of Italy and to unite the Italian nation. By 1870, however, Italian unification had been achieved. But the movement for unification had faced many obstacles.

Forces For and Against Unity

In 1815, Italy consisted of several separate states. In the south, a Bourbon king ruled the Kingdom of the Two Sicilies; the pope governed the Papal States in central Italy; Hapsburg Austria ruled Lombardy and Venetia in the north; Hapsburg princes subservient to Austria ruled the duchies of Tuscany, Parma, and Modena. Piedmont in the northwest and the island of Sardinia were governed by an Italian dynasty—the House of Savoy.

Besides all these political divisions, Italy was divided economically and culturally. Throughout the peninsula, attachment to the local region was stronger than devotion to national unity. Economic ties between north and south were weak; inhabitants of the northern Italian cities felt little closeness to Sicilian peasants. Except for the middle class, most Italians clung to the values of the Old Regime. Believing that society was ordered by God, they accepted without question rule by prince and pope and rejected the values associated with the French Revolution and the Enlightenment. To these traditionalists, national unity was also hateful. It would deprive the pope of his control over central Italy, introduce liberal ideas that would undermine clerical and aristocratic authority, and depose legitimate princes.

During the wars of the French Revolution, France had occupied Italy. The French eliminated many barriers to trade among the Italian states; they built roads that improved links between the various regions, and they introduced a standard system of law over most of the land. The French had also given the Italian states constitutions, representative assemblies, and the concept of the state as a community of citizens.

The Italian middle class believed that expelling foreign rulers and forging national unity would continue the process of enlightened reform initiated by the French occupation, and that this process would promote economic growth. Merchants and manufacturers wanted to abolish taxes on goods transported from one Italian state to another; they wanted roads and railways built to link the peninsula together; they wanted to do away with the numerous systems of coinage and weights and measures that complicated business transactions. Italians who had served Napoleon as local officials, clerks, and army officers resisted the restoration of clerical and feudal privileges that denied them career opportunities.

An expanding intellectual elite, through novels, poetry, and works of history, awakened interest in Italy's glorious past. They insisted that a people who had built the Roman Empire and had produced the Renaissance must not remain weak and divided, their land occupied by Austrians. These sentiments appealed particularly to university students and the middle class. But the rural masses, illiterate and preoccupied with the hardships of daily life, had little concern for this struggle for national revival.

Failed Revolutions

Secret societies kept alive the hopes for liberty and independence from foreign rule in the period after 1815. The most important of these societies was the Carbonari, which had clubs in every state in Italy. In 1820, the Carbonari, its members drawn largely from the middle class and the army, enjoyed a few months of triumph in the Kingdom of the Two Sicilies. Supported by the army and militia, they forced King Ferdinand I to grant a constitution and a parliamentary government. But Metternich feared that the germ of revolution would spread to other countries. Supported by Prussia and Russia, Austria suppressed the constitutional government in Naples and another revolution that broke out in Piedmont. In both cases, Austria firmly fixed an absolute ruler on the throne. In 1831–32, the Austrians suppressed another insurrection by the Carbonari in the Papal States. During these uprisings the peasants had given little support; indeed, they seemed to side with the traditional rulers.

Map 25.1 Unification of Italy, 1859–1870

After the failure of the Carbonari, a new generation of leaders emerged in Italy. One of them, Giuseppe Mazzini (1805–1872), dedicated his life to the creation of a united and republican Italy—a goal he pursued with extraordinary moral intensity and determination. Mazzini was both a romantic and a liberal. As a liberal, he fought for republican and constitutional government and held that national unity would enhance individual liberty. As a romantic, he sought truth through heightened feeling and intuition and believed that an awakened Italy would lead to the regeneration of humanity. Just as Rome had provided law and unity in the ancient world, and the Roman pope had led Latin Christendom during the Middle Ages, Mazzini believed that a third Rome, a newly united Italy, would usher in a new age of free nations, personal liberty, and equality. This era would represent great progress for humanity: peace, prosperity, and universal happiness would replace conflict, materialism, and self-interest. Given to religious mysticism, Mazzini saw a world of independent states founded on nationality, republicanism, and democracy as the fulfillment of God's plan.

After his release from prison for participating in the insurrection of 1831, Mazzini went into exile and founded a new organization—Young Italy. Consisting of dedicated revolutionaries, many of them students, Young Italy was intended to serve as the instrument for the awakening of Italy and the transformation of Europe into a brotherhood of free peoples. This sacred struggle, said Mazzini, demanded heroism and sacrifice.

Mazzini believed that a successful revolution must come from below—from the people, moved by a profound love for their nation. They must overthrow the Hapsburg princes and create a democratic republic. The Carbonari had failed, he said, because they had staged only local uprisings and had no overall plan for the liberation and unification of Italy. This could be achieved only by a revolution of the masses. Mazzini had great charisma, determination, courage, and eloquence; he was also a prolific writer. His idealism attracted the intelligentsia and youth and kept alive the spirit of national unity. He infused the *Risorgimento,* the movement for Italian unity, with spiritual intensity.

Mazzini's plans for a mass uprising against Austria and the princes failed. In 1834, a band of Mazzini's followers attempted to invade Savoy from bases in Switzerland. But everything went wrong, and the invasion collapsed. Other setbacks were suffered in 1837, 1841, and 1843–44. During the Revolutions of 1848, however, Italian liberal-nationalists enjoyed initial successes (see Chapter 23). In Sicily, revolutionaries forced King Ferdinand to grant a liberal constitution. The rulers of Tuscany and Piedmont-Sardinia promised constitutions. After five days of fighting, revolutionaries drove the Austrians out of Milan in Lombardy. The Austrians were also forced to evacuate Venice, where a republic was proclaimed. The pope fled Rome, and Mazzini was elected to an executive office in a new Roman Republic. However, the forces of reaction led by Hapsburg Austria regained their courage and their authority, and one by one, they crushed the revolutionary movements. Louis Napoleon's troops dissolved the infant Roman Republic and restored Pope Pius IX to power. Italy remained divided, and Austria still ruled the north.

Cavour and Victory over Austria

The failure of the Revolutions of 1848 contained an obvious lesson: that Mazzini's approach—an armed uprising by aroused masses—did not work. It failed because the masses were not deeply committed to the nationalist cause and the revolutionaries were no match for the Austrian army. Italian nationalists now hoped that the Kingdom of Piedmont-Sardinia, ruled by an Italian dynasty, would expel the Austrians and lead the drive for unity. Count Camillo Benso di Cavour (1810–1861), the chief minister of Piedmont-Sardinia, became the architect of Italian unity.

Cavour, unlike Mazzini, was neither a dreamer nor a speechmaker, but a cautious and practical politician who realized that mass uprisings could not succeed against Austrian might. Moreover, mistrusting the common people, he did not approve of Mazzini's goal of a democratic republic. Cavour had no precise blueprint for unifying Italy. His immediate aim was to increase the territory of Piedmont by driving the Austrians from northern Italy and incorporating Lombardy and Venetia into Piedmont-Sardinia. But this expulsion could not be accomplished without allies, for Austria was a great power and Piedmont a small state. To improve Piedmont's image in foreign affairs, Cavour launched a reform program to strengthen the economy. He reorganized the currency, taxes, and the national debt; in addition, he had railways and steamships built, fostered improved agricultural methods, and encouraged new businesses. Within a few years, Piedmont had become a progressive modern state.

In 1855, Piedmont joined England and France in the Crimean War against Russia. Cavour had no quarrel with Russia, but sought the friendship of Britain and France and a chance to be heard in world affairs. At the peace conference, Cavour was granted an opportunity to denounce Austria for occupying Italian lands.

After the peace conference, Cavour continued to encourage anti-Austrian feeling among Italians and to search for foreign support. He found a supporter in Napoleon III (1852–1870), the French emperor, who hoped that a unified northern Italy would become an ally and client of France.

In 1858, Cavour and Napoleon III reached an agreement. If Austria attacked Piedmont, France would aid the Italian state. Piedmont would annex Lombardy and Venetia and parts of the Papal States. For its assistance, France would obtain Nice and Savoy from Piedmont. With this agreement in his pocket, Cavour cleverly maneuvered Austria into declaring war, for it had to appear that Austria was the aggressor.

Supported by French forces and taking advantage of poor Austrian planning, Piedmont conquered Lombardy and occupied Milan. But Napoleon III quickly had second thoughts. If Piedmont took any of the pope's territory, French Catholics would blame their own leader. Even more serious was the fear that Prussia, suspicious of French arms, would aid Austria. For these reasons Napoleon III, without consulting Cavour, signed an armistice with Austria. Piedmont would acquire Lombardy, but no more. An outraged Cavour demanded that his state continue the war until all northern Italy was liberated, but King Victor Emmanuel of Piedmont accepted the Austrian peace terms.

The victory of Piedmont-Sardinia, however, proved greater than Cavour had anticipated. During the conflict, patriots in Parma, Modena, Tuscany, and Romagna (one of the Papal States) had seized power. These new revolutionary governments voted to join with Piedmont. Neither France nor Austria would risk military action to thwart Piedmont's expansion. In return for Napoleon III's acquiescence, Piedmont ceded Nice and Savoy to France.

Garibaldi and Victory in the South

Piedmont's success spurred revolutionary activity in the Kingdom of the Two Sicilies. In the spring of 1860, some one thousand red-shirted adventurers and patriots led by Giuseppe Garibaldi (1807–1882) landed in Sicily. They were determined to liberate the land from its Bourbon ruler, and they succeeded.

An early supporter of Mazzini, Garibaldi had been forced to flee Italy to avoid arrest for his revolutionary activities. He spent thirteen years in South America, where he participated in revolutionary movements. There he learned the skills of the revolutionary's trade and toughened his body and will for the struggle that lay ahead.

Garibaldi held exceptional views for his day. He supported the liberation of all subject nationalities, female emancipation, the right of workers to organize, racial equality, and the abolition of capital punishment. But the cause of Italian national unity was his true religion. Whereas Cavour set his sights primarily on extending Piedmont's control over northern Italy, Garibaldi dedicated himself to the creation of a unified Italy.

Garibaldi returned to Italy just in time to fight in the Revolution of 1848. He was an extraordinary leader who captivated the hearts of the people and won the poor and illiterate to the cause of Italian nationality. A young Italian artist who fought beside Garibaldi in 1849 said of his commander:

> I shall never forget that day when I first saw him on his beautiful white horse. He reminded us of . . . our Savior . . . everyone said the same. I could not resist him. I went after him; thousands did likewise. He only had to show himself. We all worshipped him. We could not help it.[1]

After the liberation of Sicily in 1860, Garibaldi invaded the mainland. He occupied Naples without a fight and prepared to advance on Rome.

Chronology 25.1 Unification of Italy

1821	Austria suppresses a rebellion by the Carbonari
1831–32	Austria suppresses another insurrection by the Carbonari
1832	Mazzini forms Young Italy
March 1848	Austrians are forced to withdraw from Milan and Venice
November 1848	Pope forced to flee Rome
1848–49	Austria reasserts its authority in Milan and Venice; Louis Napoleon crushes revolutionaries in Rome
1858	Napoleon III agrees to help Piedmont-Sardinia against Austria
1859	Austro-Sardinian War; Piedmont obtains Lombardy from Austria; Parma, Modena, Tuscany, and Romagna vote to join with Sardinia
1860	Garibaldi invades the Kingdom of the Two Sicilies
March 17, 1861	Victor Emmanuel of Piedmont is proclaimed king of Italy
1866	Italy's alliance with Prussia against Austria results in the annexation of Venetia by Italy
1870	Rome is incorporated into the Italian state and unity is achieved

In this particular instance, Garibaldi's success confirmed Mazzini's belief that a popular leader could arouse the masses to heroic action.

Cavour feared that an assault on Rome by Garibaldi would lead to French intervention. Napoleon III had pledged to defend the pope's lands, and a French garrison had been stationed in Rome since 1849. Moreover, Cavour considered Garibaldi too impulsive and rash, too attracted to republican ideals, too popular to lead the struggle for unification.

Cavour persuaded Napoleon III to approve an invasion of the Papal States by Piedmont to head off Garibaldi. A papal force offered only token opposition, and the Papal States of Umbria and the Marches soon voted for union with Piedmont, as did Naples and Sicily. Refusing to trade on his prestige with the masses to fulfill personal ambition, Garibaldi turned over his conquests to the Sardinian king, Victor Emmanuel, who was declared king of Italy in 1861.

Italian Unification Completed

Two regions still remained outside the control of the new Italy: the city of Rome, ruled by the pope and protected by French troops; and Venetia, occupied by Austria. Cavour died in 1861, but the march toward unification continued. During the conflict between Prussia and Austria in 1866, Italy sided with the victorious Prussians and was rewarded with Venetia. During the Franco-Prussian War of 1870, France withdrew its garrisons from Rome; much to the anger of the pope, Italian troops marched in, and Rome was declared the capital of Italy.

Map 25.2 Unification of Germany, 1866–1871

The following legend appears on the map:

— German Confederation boundary, 1815–1866

— Bismarck's German Empire

Prussia before 1866

Conquered by Prussia, 1866

Austrian territories excluded from German Confederation, 1867

Joined with Prussia to form German Confederation, 1867

South German States joining to form German Empire, 1871

Conquered from France, 1871

✕ Major battle

The Unification of Germany

In 1848, German liberals and nationalists, believing in the strength of their ideals, had naively underestimated the power of the conservative old order. After the failed revolution, some disenchanted revolutionaries retained only a half-hearted commitment to liberalism or embraced conservatism; others fled the country, weakening the liberal leadership. All liberals came to doubt the effectiveness of revolution as a way to transform Germany into a unified state; all gained a new respect for the realities of power. Abandoning idealism for realism, liberals now thought that German unity would be achieved through Prussian arms, not liberal ideals.

Prussia, Agent of Unification

During the late seventeenth and eighteenth centuries, Prussian kings had fashioned a rigorously trained and disciplined army. The state bureaucracy, often staffed by ex-soldiers, perpetuated the military mentality. As the chief organizations in the state, the army and the bureaucracy drilled into the Prussian people a respect for discipline and authority.

The Prussian throne was supported by the Junkers; these powerful aristocrats, who owned vast estates farmed by serfs, were exempt from most taxes, and dominated local government in their territories. The Junkers' commanding position made them officers in the royal army, diplomats, and leading officials in the state bureaucracy. The Junkers knew that a weakening of the king's power would lead to the loss of their own aristocratic prerogatives.

In late-eighteenth-century France, a powerful and politically conscious middle class had challenged aristocratic privileges. The Prussian monarchy and the Junkers had faced no such challenge, for the Prussian middle class at that time was small and without influence. The idea of the rights of the individual did not deeply penetrate Prussian consciousness, nor did it undermine the Prussian tradition of obedience to military and state authority.

Reforms from Above The reform movement that began after Napoleon had completely routed the Prussians at Jena arose from distress with the military collapse and the apathy of the Prussian population. High bureaucrats and military men demanded reforms that would draw the people closer to their country and king. These leaders had learned the great lesson of the French Revolution: a devoted citizen army fights more effectively than oppressed serfs. To imbue all classes with civic pride, the reformers abolished hereditary serfdom, gave the urban middle class a greater voice in city government, laid the foundations for universal education, and granted full citizenship to Jews. To improve the army's morale, they eliminated severe punishments and based promotions on performance rather than birth.

But the reformers failed to give Prussia a constitution and parliamentary institutions. The middle class still had no voice in the central government; monarchical power persisted, and the economic, political, and military power of the Junkers remained unbroken. Thus, liberalism had an unpromising beginning in Prussia. In France, the bourgeoisie had instituted reforms based on the principles of liberty and equality; in Prussia, the bureaucracy introduced reforms to strengthen the state, not to promote liberty. A precedent had been established: reform in Prussia would come from conservative rulers, not from the efforts of a middle class aroused by liberal ideals.

In 1834, under Prussian leadership, the German states, with the notable exception of Austria, established the *Zollverein,* a customs union that abolished tariffs between the states. The customs union stimulated economic activity and promoted a desire for greater unity. Businessmen, particularly, felt that having thirty-nine states in Germany was an obstacle to economic progress. The Zollverein provided the economic foundations for the political unification of Germany, and it led many Germans to view Prussia, not Austria, as the leader of the unification movement.

Failure of Liberals During the restoration the ideas of legal equality, political liberty, and careers open to talent found favor with the Prussian bourgeoisie. Like the French bourgeois of the Old Regime, Prussian bankers, manufacturers, and lawyers hated a system that denied them social recognition and political influence and rewarded idle sons of the nobility with the best positions. They also denounced government regulations and taxes that hampered business, and hated the rigorous censorship that stifled free thought. The peasants and artisans—concerned with economic survival, respectful of tradition, and suspicious of new ideas—had little comprehension of nor sympathy for liberal principles.

During the Revolution of 1848, liberals failed to wrest power from the monarchy and aristocracy and to create a unified Germany. Frederick William IV (1840–1861) had refused the crown offered him by the Frankfurt Assembly (see Chapter 23). The Prussian monarch could not stomach a German unity created by a revolution of commoners. But a German union fashioned and headed by a conservative Prussia was different and attractive to Frederick. In 1849, Prussia initiated a diplomatic campaign toward this end. Austria resisted this maneuver because it was determined to retain its pre-eminence in German affairs. Faced with Hapsburg resistance, Prussia renounced its plans for a German union and agreed to the re-establishment of the German Confederation (see Chapter 23). This political humiliation taught Frederick William an obvious lesson: before Prussia could extend its hegemony over the other German states, Austrian influence in German affairs would have to be eliminated.

Bismarck and the Road to Unity

In 1858, Frederick William IV, by then mentally deranged, surrendered control of the government to his brother, who became William I (1861–1888), king of Prussia, when Frederick William died. William also regarded Austria as the principal barrier to the extension of Prussian power in Germany. This was one reason why he called for a drastic reorganization of the Prussian army. But the liberals in the lower chamber of the Prussian parliament blocked passage of the army reforms, for they feared that the reforms would greatly increase the power of the monarchy and the military establishment. Unable to secure passage, William withdrew the reform bill and asked the lower chamber for additional funds to cover government expenses. When parliament granted these funds, he used the money to institute the army reforms. Learning from its mistake, the lower chamber would not approve the new budget in 1862 without an itemized breakdown.

A conflict had arisen between the liberal majority in the lower chamber and the Crown. If the liberals won, they would, in effect, establish parliamentary control over the king and the army. At this critical hour, King William asked Otto von Bismarck (1815–1898) to lead the battle against parliament.

Descended on his father's side from an old aristocratic family, Bismarck was a staunch supporter of the Prussian monarchy and the Junker class and a devout patriot. He yearned to increase the territory and prestige of his beloved Prussia and to protect the authority of the Prussian king who,

Bismarck believed, ruled by the grace of God. Liberals were outraged by Bismarck's domineering and authoritarian manner and his determination to preserve monarchical power and the aristocratic order. Set on continuing the reorganization of the army and not to bow to parliamentary pressure, Bismarck ordered the collection of taxes without parliament's approval—an action that would have been unthinkable in Britain or the United States.

When the lower chamber continued to withhold funds, Bismarck took action. He dismissed the chamber, imposed strict censorship on the press, arrested outspoken liberals, and fired liberals from the civil service. The liberals protested against these arbitrary and unconstitutional moves, but they did not use force. Since the army fully supported the government, and there was no significant popular support for challenging the government, an armed uprising would have failed. What led to a resolution of the conflict was Bismarck's extraordinary success in foreign affairs.

Wars with Denmark and Austria To Bismarck a war between Austria and Prussia seemed inevitable, for only by removing Austria from German affairs could Prussia extend its dominion over the other German states. Bismarck's first move, however, was not against Austria but against Denmark. The issue that led to the war in 1864 was enormously complex. Simplified, the issue was that Bismarck (and German nationalists) wanted to free the two duchies of Schleswig and Holstein from Danish control—both territories, which contained a large number of Germans, had been administered by Denmark, but in 1863, Schleswig was incorporated into the Danish realm. Austria joined as Prussia's ally, because it hoped to prevent Prussia from annexing the territories. After Denmark's defeat, Austria and Prussia tried to decide the ultimate disposition of the territory. What Austria wanted was a joint Austrian and Prussian occupation of the disputed regions. But the negotiations broke down. Bismarck used the dispute to goad Austria into war. The Austrians, on their side, held that Prussia must be defeated for Austria to retain its influence over German affairs.

In 1866, with astonishing speed, Prussia assembled its forces and overran Austrian territory. At the battle of Sadowa (or Königgrätz), Prussia

Otto von Bismarck and William II, 1888. Between 1862 and 1871, Bismarck worked tirelessly to unite Germany under the Prussian monarchy. Bismarck's wars against Denmark, Austria, and France led to the unification of Germany and earned him the admiration of the German people. (*Bildarchiv Preussischer Kulturbesitz*)

decisively defeated the main Austrian forces and the Seven Weeks' War ended. Prussia took no territory from Austria, but the latter agreed to Prussia's annexation of Schleswig and Holstein and a number of small German states. And Prussia organized a Confederation of North German States from which Austria was excluded. In effect, Austria was removed from German affairs, and Prussia became the dominant power in Germany.

The Triumph of Nationalism and Conservatism over Liberalism The Prussian victory had a profound impact on political life within Prussia. Bismarck was the man of the hour, the great hero who had extended Prussia's power. Most liberals forgave Bismarck for his authoritarian handling of parliament. The liberal press that had previously denounced Bismarck for running roughshod over the constitution embraced him as a hero. Prussians were urged to concentrate on the glorious tasks ahead and to put aside the constitutional struggle, which in contrast appeared petty and insignificant.

Bismarck recognized the great appeal of nationalism and used it to expand Prussia's power over other German states and to strengthen Prussia's voice in European affairs. By heralding his state as the champion of unification, Bismarck gained the support of nationalists throughout Germany. In the past, the nationalist cause had been the property of liberals, but Bismarck appropriated it to promote Prussian expansion and conservative rule.

Prussia's victory over Austria, therefore, was a

triumph for conservatism and nationalism and a defeat for liberalism. The liberal struggle for constitutional government in Prussia collapsed. The Prussian monarch retained the right to override parliamentary opposition and act on his own initiative. In 1848, Prussian might had suppressed a liberal revolution; in 1866, liberals beguiled by Bismarck's military triumphs gave up the struggle for responsible parliamentary government. They had traded political freedom for Prussian military glory and power.

The capitulation of Prussian liberals demonstrated the essential weakness of the German liberal tradition. German liberals displayed a diminishing commitment to the principles of parliamentary government, and a growing fascination with force, military triumph, and territorial expansion. Bismarck's words, written in 1858, turned out to be prophetic: "Exalt his self-esteem toward foreigners and the Prussian forgets whatever bothers him about conditions at home."[2] The liberal dream of a united Germany had been pre-empted by conservatives. Enthralled by Bismarck's achievement, many liberals abandoned liberalism and threw their support behind the authoritarian Prussian state. And Germans of all classes acquired an adoration for Prussian militarism and for the power state, with its machiavellian guideline that all means are justified if they result in the expansion of German power. In 1848, German liberals had called for "Unity and Freedom." What Bismarck gave them was unity and authoritarianism.

War with France   Prussia emerged from the war with Austria as the leading power in the North German Confederation; the Prussian king controlled the armies and foreign affairs of the states within the confederation. To complete the unification of Germany, Bismarck would have to draw the South German states into the new German Confederation. But the South German states, Catholic and hostile to Prussian authoritarianism, feared being absorbed by Prussia.

Bismarck hoped that a war between Prussia and France would ignite the nationalist feelings of the South Germans, causing them to overlook the differences that separated them from Prussia. If war with France would serve Bismarck's purpose, it was also not unthinkable to Napoleon III, the

emperor of France. The creation of a powerful North German Confederation had frightened the French, and the prospect that the South German states might one day add their strength to the new Germany was terrifying. Both France and Prussia had parties who advocated war.

A cause for war arose over the succession to the vacated Spanish throne. Under strong consideration was Prince Leopold of Hohenzollern-Sigmaringen, a distant relative of King William of Prussia. France vehemently opposed the candidacy of Leopold, for his accession might lead to Prussian influence being extended into Spain. William, seeking to preserve the peace, urged Prince Leopold to withdraw his name from consideration.

The French ambassador then demanded that William give formal assurance that no Hohenzollern would ever again be a candidate for the Spanish crown. William refused. In a telegram sent from Ems to Berlin, he informed Bismarck of his conversation with the French ambassador. With the support of high military leaders, Bismarck edited the telegram. The revised version gave the impression that the Prussian king and the French ambassador had insulted each other. Bismarck wanted to inflame French feeling against Prussia and arouse German opinion against France. He succeeded. In both Paris and Berlin, crowds of people, gripped by war fever, demanded satisfaction. When France declared a general mobilization, Prussia followed suit; Bismarck had his war.

With the memory of the great Napoleon still strong, the French expected a quick victory. But the poorly prepared and incompetently led French army could not withstand the powerful Prussian military machine. The South German states, as Bismarck had anticipated, came to the aid of Prussia. Quickly and decisively routing the French forces and capturing Napoleon III, the Prussians went on to besiege Paris. Faced with starvation, Paris surrendered in January 1871. France was compelled to pay a large indemnity and to cede to Germany the border provinces of Alsace and Lorraine—a loss that French patriots could never accept.

The Franco-Prussian War completed the unification of Germany. On January 18, 1871, at Versailles, the German princes granted the title of German kaiser (emperor) to William I. A power-

Chronology 25.2 Unification of Germany

1815	Formation of the German Confederation
1834	Establishment of the Zollverein under Prussian leadership
1848	Failure of the liberals to unify Germany
1862	Bismarck becomes chancellor of Prussia
1864	Austria and Prussia defeat Denmark in a war over Schleswig-Holstein
1866	Seven Weeks' War between Austria and Prussia; Prussia emerges as the dominant power in Germany
1866	Formation of North German Confederation under Prussian control
1870–71	Franco-Prussian War
January 18, 1871	William I becomes German kaiser

ful nation had arisen in central Europe. Its people were educated, disciplined, and efficient; its industries and commerce were rapidly expanding; its army was the finest in Europe. Vigorous, confident, and intensely nationalistic, the new German Empire would be eager to play a greater role in world affairs. No nation in Europe was a match for the new Germany. Metternich's fears had been realized—a Germany dominated by Prussia had upset the balance of power. The unification of Germany created fears, tensions, and rivalries that would culminate in world war.

Nationality Problems in the Hapsburg Empire

In Italy and Germany, nationalism had led to the creation of unified states; in Austria, nationalism eventually caused the destruction of the centuries-old Hapsburg dynasty. A mosaic of different nationalities, each with its own history and traditions, the Austrian Empire could not survive in an age of intense nationalism. England and France had succeeded in unifying peoples of different ethnic backgrounds, but they did so during the Middle Ages, when ethnic consciousness was still rudimentary. The Austrian Empire, on the other hand, had to weld together and reconcile antagonistic nationalities when nationalistic consciousness was high. The empire's collapse in the final stages of World War I was the culmination of years of antagonism between its different peoples.

In the first half of the nineteenth century, the Germans, constituting less than one-quarter of the population, were the dominant national group in the empire. But Magyars, Poles, Czechs, Slovaks, Croats, Rumanians, Ruthenians, and Italians were experiencing national self-awareness. Poets and writers who had been educated in Latin, French, and German began to write in their mother tongues and extol their splendor. By searching their past for glorious ancestors and glorious deeds, writers kindled pride in their native history and folklore and aroused anger against past and present injustices.

In 1848–49, the Hapsburg monarchy had extinguished the Magyar bid for independence, the Czech revolution in Prague, and the uprisings in the Italian provinces of Lombardy and Venetia. Gravely frightened by these revolutions, the Austrian power structure resolved to resist pressures for political rights by strengthening autocracy and tightening the central bureaucracy. German and Germanized officials took over administrative and judicial duties formerly handled on a local level. An expanded secret police stifled liberal and nationalist expressions. The various nationalities, of course, resented these efforts at centralization and repression.

Magyarization

The defeats by France and Piedmont in 1859 and by Prussia in 1866 cost Austria its two Italian provinces. The defeat by Prussia also forced the Hapsburg monarchy to make concessions to the Magyars, the strongest of the non-German nationalities; for without a loyal Hungary, the Hapsburg monarchy could suffer other humiliations. The Settlement of 1867 split the Hapsburg territories into Austria and Hungary. The two countries retained a common ruler, Francis Joseph (1848–1916), who was emperor of Austria and king of Hungary. Hungary gained complete control over its internal affairs—the administration of justice and education. Foreign and military affairs and common financial concerns were conducted by a ministry consisting of delegates from both lands.

With the Settlement of 1867, Magyars and Germans became the dominant nationalities in the empire. The other nationalities felt that the German-Magyar political, economic, and cultural domination blocked their own national aspirations. Nationality struggles in the half-century following the Settlement of 1867 consumed the energies of the Austrians and Hungarians. In both lands, however, the leaders failed to solve the minority problems, a failure that ultimately led to the dissolution of the empire during the last weeks of World War I.

The nationality problems in Hungary differed substantially from those in Austria. Constituting slightly less than half the population of Hungary, the Magyars were determined to retain their hegemony over the other minorities—Rumanians, Slovaks, Ruthenians, Serbs, Croats, and Jews. In the first phase of their national struggle, the Hungarians had sought to liberate their nation from German domination. In the second phase, after 1867, the landholding aristocracy that ruled Hungary tried to impose the Magyar language and traditions on the other nationalities. Non-Magyars who learned the Magyar language and considered themselves Hungarians could participate as equals in Hungarian society. Those who resisted were viewed as traitors and conspirators and faced severe penalties. Non-Magyars were largely excluded from voting and virtually barred from government jobs, which were reserved for Magyars or those who had adopted Magyar language and culture.

The government tightly controlled the non-Magyar peoples. It suppressed their cultural organizations and newspapers, and the great majority of public schools, even in predominantly non-Magyar regions, carried on instruction largely in Magyar. Because of limited suffrage, the manipulation of districts, and threats of violence, non-Magyars were barely represented in the Hungarian parliament. Protests by the nationalities against this forced Magyarization often led to jail sentences. The repressive measures strengthened the Slavs' and Rumanians' hatred of the regime. At the same time, however, Magyarization brought economic and cultural opportunities. Jews in particular accepted the Magyar government and took advantage of what it offered.

But nationality movements within Hungary constituted less of a threat to the preservation of the Austro-Hungarian Empire than Magyar nationalism itself did. The Independence party, whose influence grew after 1900, began to demand a complete end to the link with Austria and the "cursed common institutions."

German Versus Czech

The Austrian population of the Dual Monarchy was made up of Germans (one-third) and Slavs (two-thirds). Hungary tried to forge a unified state by assimilating the non-Magyars; Austria, on the other hand, made no deliberate effort to Ger-

A Bohemian Funeral Procession, 1899. The Hapsburg Empire was burdened by conflicts between its
different nationalities. In Bohemia, Czechs and
Germans often engaged in violent confrontations,
as Czechs pressed for recognition of their language
and rights. This funeral is for victims of a nationalistic riot. (*Bilderdienst Süddeutscher Verlag*)

manize the Slavs. No attempt was made to make
German the official language of the state or to
dissociate non-Germans from their native traditions. In Austria, elementary school students were
usually taught in their mother tongues. The state
acknowledged the equal right of all the country's
languages in the schools, in administration, and in
public life.

But the nationality problem was aggravated by
the haughty attitude of the German Austrians,
who considered themselves culturally superior to
the Slavic peoples. Neither the Germans nor the
Magyars would allow the Czechs and the South
Slavs the same control over domestic affairs that
had been granted the Magyars in the Settlement of
1867. The Germans believed that they had a
historic mission to retain their dominance, an
attitude that clashed with the Slavs' growing national consciousness. And the Slavic masses were
not only aroused by nationalism but, with the
spread of liberal-democratic ideas, were also gaining the vote.

The most serious conflict occurred in Bohemia between the Germans and the Czechs, the largest group of Slavs. The Czechs had the highest literacy rate in the Dual Monarchy, and Bohemia had become the industrial heartland of the empire. The emergence of a Czech university and Czech youth associations and the growth of the Czech literature stimulated a national consciousness. Championed by a growing middle class that had made considerable economic and cultural gains, nationalism among the Czechs of Bohemia gained in intensity in the final decades of the nineteenth century. Between the Czechs and the Germans, there was great animosity.

Concentrated primarily in the Sudetenland, the German Bohemians regarded themselves as culturally and morally superior to the Czechs and wanted to preserve their predominance in the government's administration. Considering the Czech language fit only for peasants and servants, the Sudeten Germans felt it ridiculous that Czech be placed on an equal level with the German tongue. The two groups argued over whether street signs and menus should be written in German or Czech. Czech nationalists wanted the same constitutional independence that had been granted to the Hungarians; Sudeten Germans demanded that Austria remain a centralized state governed by a German-dominated bureaucracy. Violent demonstrations, frenzied oratory, and strident editorials fanned the flames of hatred. A growing resentment against the Czechs and a growing admiration for Bismarck's new Germany led some Austrian Germans, particularly the Sudeten Germans, to seek union with Germany. Georg von Schönerer, the leader of the Austrian Pan-German movement, denounced both Slavs and Jews as racial inferiors, and called for the creation of a Greater Germany.

The clash between Czech and German grew uglier when in 1897 a new prime minister, Count Casimir Badeni, required government officials in Bohemia to know both the German and the Czech languages. This requirement was no hardship for Czech officials, since most of them already knew German. Few German officials, however, knew Czech or cared to learn it. Riots broke out in various cities, German and Czech deputies in parliament engaged in fist fights, and the emperor was forced to dismiss Badeni. Eventually the reform was dropped, but Czech-German hostilities remained intense.

South Slavs

The problem of the South Slavs—Serbs, Croats, Slovenes—differed from that of the Czechs. No Czech state served as a magnet for the Czechs living within Austria, whereas in the Kingdom of Serbia (which gained full independence from the Ottoman Turks in 1878), the South Slavs had a foreign power to encourage their nationalist hopes. Serbian nationalists dreamed of extending their rule over their ethnic cousins, the South Slavs of Austria-Hungary. The Hapsburg monarchy viewed this vision of a Greater Serbia as a threat to its existence. This conflict between Serbia and Austria-Hungary was to trigger World War I.

The awakening of nationalism in the multi-ethnic Austro-Hungarian Empire raised the specter of dissolution. Could the forces of unity—the army, the bureaucracy, and loyalty to the Hapsburg dynasty—contain the centrifugal forces that threatened to shatter the empire into separate parts? A restructuring of the Dual Monarchy into a federated state that would give equality to the Slavs might have eased the pressures within the empire, particularly since only extremists among the minorities were calling for independence. But the leading statesmen resisted the Slavs' demands. At the end of World War I, the empire was fractured into separate states based on nationality.

The Rise of Racial Nationalism

In the first half of the nineteenth century, nationalism and liberalism went hand in hand. Liberals sought both the rights of the individual and national independence and unification. Liberal nationalists believed that a unified state free of foreign subjugation was in harmony with the principle of natural rights, and they insisted that love of country led to love of humanity. "With all my ardent love of my nation," said Francis Palácky, a Czech patriot, "I always esteem more highly the good of mankind and of learning than the good of the nation."[3] Addressing the Slavs, Mazzini declared: "We who have ourselves arisen in the name of our national right, believe in your right,

An Age of Contradiction: Progress and Breakdown

and offer to help you to win it. But the purpose of our mission is the permanent and peaceful organization of Europe."[4]

As nationalism grew more extreme, however, its profound difference from liberalism became more apparent. The extreme nationalism of the late nineteenth and early twentieth centuries was the seedbed of totalitarian nationalism. It contributed to World War I and to the rise of fascism after the war.

Concerned exclusively with the greatness of the nation, extreme nationalists rejected the liberal emphasis on political liberty. They regarded liberty as an obstacle to national power and maintained that authoritarian leadership was needed to meet national emergencies. The needs of the nation, they said, transcended the rights of the individual. Extreme nationalists also rejected the liberal ideal of equality. Placing the nation above everything, nationalists became increasingly intolerant of minorities within the nation's borders and hateful of other peoples. In the name of national power and unity, they persecuted minorities at home and stirred up hatred against other nations. In the pursuit of national power, nationalists increasingly embraced militaristic, imperialistic, and racist doctrines. At the founding of the Nationalist Association in Italy in 1910 one leader declared:

> Just as socialism teaches the proletariat the value of class struggle, so we must teach Italy the value of international struggle. But international struggle is war? Well, then, let there be war! And nationalism will arouse the will for a victorious war, . . . the only way to national redemption.[5]

Interpreting politics with the logic of emotions, extreme nationalists insisted that they had a sacred mission to regain lands once held in the Middle Ages, to unite with their kinfolk in other lands, or to rule over peoples considered inferior. They organized patriotic societies, denounced national minorities, particularly Jews, and created a cult of ancestors and a mystique of blood, soil, and a sacred national past. In these ancestral traditions and attachments, the nationalist found a higher reality akin to religious truth. Loyalty to the nation-state was elevated above all other allegiances. The ethnic state became an object of religious reverence; the spiritual energies that formerly had been dedicated to Christianity were now channeled into the worship of the nation-state.

By the beginning of the twentieth century, conservatives had become the staunchest advocates of nationalism, and the nationalism preached by conservative extremists was stripped of Mazzinian ideals of liberty, equality, and the fellowship of nations. Landholding aristocrats, generals, and clergy, often joined by big industrialists, saw nationalism as a convenient instrument for gaining a mass following in their struggle against democracy and socialism. Championing popular nationalist myths and dreams, and citing Social Darwinist doctrines, a newly radicalized right hoped to harness the instinctual energies of the masses, particularly the peasants and the lower middle class—shopkeepers, civil servants, white-collar workers—to conservative causes. Peasants viewed liberalism and socialism as threats to traditional values, while the lower bourgeoisie feared the proletariat. These people were receptive to the rhetoric of ultranationalists who denounced democracy and socialism as threats to national unity and Jews as aliens who endangered the nation.

Volkish Thought

Extreme nationalism was a general European phenomenon, but it was especially dangerous in Germany. Bismarck's triumphs lured Germans into a dreamworld. Many started to yearn for the extension of German power throughout the world. The past, they said, belonged to France and Britain; the future, to Germany.

The most ominous expression of German nationalism (and a clear example of mythical thinking) was *Volkish* thought.[6] (*Volk* means "folk" or "people.") German Volkish thinkers sought to bind together the German people through a deep love of their language, traditions, and fatherland. These thinkers felt that Germans were animated by a higher spirit than that found in other peoples. To Volkish thinkers the Enlightenment and parliamentary democracy were foreign ideas that corrupted the pure German spirit. With fanatical devotion, Volkish thinkers embraced all things German—the medieval past, the German landscape, the simple peasant, the vil-

Richard Wagner, 1849, by Ernst Benedikt Kietz.
Wagner was a crucial figure in the shaping of German romanticism. His operas, glorifying a mythic German past, contributed to the Volkish outlook. (*Nationalarchiv der Richard-Wagner-Stiftung/ Richard-Wagner-Gedenkstätte Bayreuth*)

lage—and denounced the liberal-humanist tradition of the West as alien to the German soul.

One shaper of the Volkish outlook was Wilhelm von Riehl (1823–1897), a professor at the University of Munich. He contrasted the artificiality of modern city life with the unspoiled existence in the German countryside. Another was Berthold Auerbach (1812–1882), who glorified the peasant as the ideal German. Paul de Lagarde (1827–1891), a professor of oriental languages, called for a German faith, different from Christianity, that would unite the nation; he saw the Jews as enemies of Germany. Julius Langbehn (1851–1907) lauded a mystical and irrational life force as superior to reason and held that the Jews corrupted the German spirit.

Volkish thought attracted Germans frightened by all the complexities of the modern age—industrialization, urbanization, materialism, class conflicts, alienation. Seeing their beloved Germany transformed by these forces of modernity, Volkish thinkers yearned to restore the sense of community that they attributed to the preindustrial age. Only by identifying with their sacred soil and sacred traditions could modern Germans escape from the evils of industrial society. Only then could the different classes band together in an organic unity.

The Volkish movement had little support from the working class, which was concerned chiefly with improving its standard of living. It appealed mainly to farmers and villagers who regarded the industrial city as a threat to native values and a catalyst for foreign ideas; to artisans and small shopkeepers threatened by big business; and to scholars, writers, teachers, and students, who saw in Volkish nationalism a cause worthy of their idealism. The schools were leading agents for the dissemination of Volkish ideas.

Volkish thinkers looked back longingly to the Middle Ages, which they viewed as a period of social and spiritual harmony and reverence for national traditions. They also glorified the ancient Germanic tribes that overran the Roman Empire; they contrasted their courageous and vigorous German ancestors with the effete and degenerate Romans. A few tried to harmonize ancient Germanic religious traditions with Christianity.

Such attitudes led Germans to see themselves as a heroic people fundamentally different from and better than the English and French. It also led them to regard German culture as unique—innately superior to and in opposition to the humanist outlook of the Enlightenment. Volkish thinkers, like their romantic predecessors, held that the German people and culture had a special destiny and a unique mission. They pitted the German soul against the Western intellect, feeling and spirit against a drab rationalism. To be sure, the Western humanist tradition still had its supporters in Germany, but the counterideology of Volkish thought was becoming increasingly widespread.

Volkish thinkers were especially attracted to racist doctrines. Racist thinkers held that race was the key to history, and that not only physical features but moral, esthetic, and intellectual qualities distinguished one race from another. In their view, a race demonstrated its vigor and achieved greatness when it preserved its purity; intermarriage between races was contamination that would result in genetic, cultural, and military decline. Like their Nazi successors, Volkish thinkers claimed that the German race was purer than, and therefore superior to all other races. Its superiority was revealed in such physical characteristics as blond hair, blue eyes, and fair skin—all signs of inner qualities lacking in other races. German racists claimed that Germans were descendants of ancient Aryans.* They held that the Aryans were a superior race and the creators of European civilization and that the Germans had inherited their superior racial qualities.

Volkish thinkers embraced the ideas of Houston Stewart Chamberlain (1855–1927), an Englishman whose fascination for Germanism led him to adopt German citizenship. In *The Foundations of the Nineteenth Century,* published in 1899, Chamberlain asserted in pseudoscientific fashion that the inner qualities of a people were related to such physical characteristics as the size of the skull. Germans had a superior physical form; consequently they were esthetically, morally, and intellectually superior and the bearers of a higher culture—in short, members of a master race. Chamberlain's book was enormously popular in Germany; the kaiser read it aloud to his children.

German racial nationalists insisted that as a superior race, Germans had a national right to dominate other peoples, particularly the "racially inferior" Slavs of the East. The Pan-German Association, whose membership included professors, schoolteachers, journalists, lawyers, and aristocrats, spread racial and nationalist theories and glorified war as an expression of national vitality. The association's philosophy is expressed in the following statement from its journal:

> *The racial-biological ideology tells us that there are races that lead and races that follow. Political history is nothing but the history of struggles among the leading races. Conquests, above all, are always the work of the leading races. Such men can conquer, may conquer, and shall conquer.*[7]

*The Aryans emerged some 4,000 years ago, probably between the Caspian Sea and the Hindu Kush Mountains. An Aryan tongue became the basis of most European languages. Intermingling with others, the Aryans lost their identity as a people.

Anti-Semitism

German racial nationalists singled out Jews as the most wicked of races and a deadly enemy of the German people. Anti-Semitism, which was widespread in late-nineteenth-century Europe, provides a striking example of the perennial appeal, power, and danger of mythical thinking. Anti-Semitic organizations and political parties sought to deprive Jews of their civil rights, and anti-Semitic publications proliferated.

Edouard Drumont, a French journalist, held that the Jews, racially inferior and believers in a primitive religion, had gained control of France. Like medieval Christian anti-Semites, Drumont accused Jews of deicide and of using Christian blood for ritual purposes. During the anti-Semitic outbursts accompanying the Dreyfus affair (see page 587), when the French right was shouting "Death to the Jews," Drumont's newspaper (founded with Jesuit funds) blamed all the ills of France on the Jews, called for their expulsion from the country, and predicted that they would be massacred.

Rumania barred most Jews from holding office and from voting, imposed various economic restrictions on them, and restricted their admission into secondary schools and universities. The Rumanian government even financed an international congress of anti-Semites that met in Bucharest in 1886.

Russia placed a quota on the number of Jewish students admitted to secondary schools and higher educational institutions, confined Jews to certain regions of the country, and "to purify the sacred historic capital" expelled some 20,000 Jews from Moscow. Some government officials encouraged and even organized *pogroms* (mob violence) against Jews. Between 1903 and 1906, pogroms broke out in 690 towns and villages, most of them in the Ukraine, traditionally a hotbed of anti-Semitism. (Ukrainian folk songs and legends glorified centuries-old massacres of Jews.) The attackers looted, burned, raped, and murdered, generally with impunity. In Russia, and several other lands, Jews were put on trial for slaughtering Christian children as part of a Passover ritual—a deranged accusation that survived from the Middle Ages.

In Germany and Austria hatred of the Jews developed into a systematic body of beliefs. As historian Hans Kohn says: "Germany became the fatherland of modern anti-Semitism; there the systems were thought out and the slogans coined. German literature was the richest in anti-Jewish writing."[8] Like conservatives in other lands, German conservatives deliberately fanned the flames of anti-Semitism to win the masses over to conservative causes. The Christian Social Workers' party, founded in 1878 by Adolf Stöcker, a prominent Protestant preacher, engaged in anti-Semitic agitation in order to recruit the lower bourgeoisie to the cause of Protestant church and the Prussian monarchy. In German-speaking Austria, Karl Lueger, a leader of the Christian Socialist party founded by conservative German nationalists, exploited anti-Semitism to win elections in overwhelmingly Catholic Vienna. Georg von Schönerer, founder of the German National party in Austria, wanted to eliminate Jews from all areas of public life.

Anti-Semitism and the success of the Italians, Germans, Serbians, and others in achieving political independence stirred nationalist feelings among Jews. Jewish nationalism took the form of Zionism—a return to Palestine, the historic homeland of the Jews. A key figure in the emergence of Zionism was Dr. Theodor Herzl (1860–1904), an Austrian journalist, who was horrified by the anti-Semitism he witnessed in Paris during the Dreyfus trial. In *The Jewish State* (1896), he argued that the creation of a Jewish state was the best solution to the Jewish question. In 1897 in Switzerland, the First Zionist Congress called for the establishment of a Jewish homeland in Palestine, which was then a province of the Turkish empire.

Anti-Semitism had a long and bloodstained history in Europe, stemming both from an irrational fear and hatred of outsiders with noticeably different ways and from the commonly accepted myth that the Jews as a people were collectively and eternally cursed for rejecting Christ. Christians saw Jews as the murderers of Christ—an image that promoted terrible anger and hatred.

During the Middle Ages, people believed and spread incredible tales about Jews. They accused Jews of torturing and crucifying Christian children in order to use their blood for religious ceremonies, of poisoning wells to kill Christians, of worshiping the Devil, and of organizing a secret government that conspired to destroy Christianity. Jews were thought to be physically different from other people—they were said to have tails, horns, and a distinctive odor. Serving to propagate this myth was the decision of the Fourth Lateran Council (1215) that required Jews to wear a distinguishing mark on their clothing.

Although some medieval popes and bishops condemned these fables and sought to protect Jews from mob violence, the lower clergy and popular preachers spread them to the receptive masses. Periodically mobs humiliated, tortured, and massacred Jews, and rulers expelled them from their kingdoms. Often barred from owning land and excluded from the craft guilds, medieval Jews concentrated in trade and moneylending—occupations that frequently earned them greater hostility. By the sixteenth century, Jews in a number of lands were forced by law to live in separate quarters of the town called *ghettos*. Medieval Christian anti-Semitism, which depicted the Jew as vile and Judaism as repulsive, fertilized the soil for modern anti-Semitism.

In the nineteenth century, under the aegis of the liberal ideals of the Enlightenment and the French Revolution, Jews gained legal equality in most European lands. They could leave the ghetto and participate in many activities that had been closed to them. Traditionally an urban people, the Jews, who were concentrated in the leading cities of Europe, took advantage of this new freedom and opportunity. Motivated by the fierce desire of outsiders to prove their worth and aided by deeply embedded traditions that valued education and family life, many Jews achieved striking success as entrepreneurs, bankers, lawyers, journalists, doctors, scientists, scholars, and performers. For example, in 1880, Jews, who constituted about 10 percent of the Viennese population, accounted for 38.6 percent of the medical students and 23.3 percent of the law students in Vienna. Viennese cultural life before World War I was to a large extent shaped by Jewish writers, artists, musicians, critics, and patrons. All but one of the major banking houses were Jewish.

But most European Jews—peasants, peddlers, and laborers—were quite poor. Perhaps 5,000 to 6,000 Jews of Galicia in Austria-Hungary died of starvation annually, and many Russian Jews fled to the United States to escape from desperate

Anti-Semitism: Bodies of Jewish Fugitives, Shot While Crossing the Dniester Between the Ukraine and Rumania. In Russia, some government officials at times encouraged and supported anti-Semitic outrages. (*Brown Brothers*)

poverty. But the anti-Semites saw only "Jewish influence," "Jewish manipulation," and "Jewish domination." Aggravating anti-Semitism among Germans was the flight of thousands of Russian Jews into Austria and Germany. Poor, speaking a different language (Yiddish), and having noticeably different customs, these Jews offended Germans and triggered primitive fears and hates.

Those Jews who were members of the commercial and professional classes, like other bourgeois, gravitated toward liberalism. Moreover, as victims of persecution, they naturally favored societies that were committed to the liberal ideals of legal equality, toleration, the rule of law, and equality of opportunity. As strong supporters of parliamentary government and the entire system of values associated with the Enlightenment, the Jews became targets for conservatives and Volkish thinkers who repudiated the humanist and cosmopolitan outlook of liberalism and professed a militant nationalism. German historian Karl Dietrich Bracher concludes: "Anti-Semitism was a manifestation of a rejection of the 'West' with which the Jews were identified . . . because the Enlightenment and democracy were essential preconditions for their acceptance and progress."[9]

Anti-Semites blamed the Jews for all the social and economic ills caused by the rapid growth of industries and cities and for all the new ideas that were undermining the old order. Their anxieties and fears concentrated on the Jews, to whom they attributed everything they considered evil in the modern age, all that threatened the German Volk.

The thought processes of Volkish anti-Semites

demonstrate the mind's monumental capacity for irrational thinking. In the mythical world of Volkish thinkers, Jews were regarded as evil entrepreneurs and financiers who exploited hardworking and decent Germans, manipulated the stock exchange, and caused depressions; as international socialists who were dragging Germany into class war; as democrats who were trying to impose an alien system of parliamentary democracy on Germany; as intellectuals who undermined traditional German culture; as city people who had no ties to or love for the German soil; as materialists who were totally without German spiritual qualities; as foreign intruders who could never be loyal to the fatherland; as racial inferiors whose genes could infect and weaken the German race; and as international conspirators who were plotting to dominate Germany and the world. This last accusation was a secularized and updated version of the medieval myth that Jews were plotting to destroy Christendom. In an extraordinary display of irrationality, Volkish thinkers held that Jews throughout the world were gaining control over political parties, the press, and the economy in order to dominate the planet.

In the Middle Ages, Jews had been persecuted and humiliated primarily for religious reasons. In the nineteenth century, national-racial considerations supplemented a traditional, biased Christian perception of Jews and Judaism. However, whereas Christian anti-Semites believed that through conversion, Jews could escape the curse of their religion, racial anti-Semites, who used the language of Social Darwinism, said that Jews were indelibly stained and eternally condemned by their genes. Their evil and worthlessness derived from inherited racial characteristics, which could not be altered by conversion. As one anti-Semitic deputy stated in a speech before the German Reichstag in 1895:

> If one designates the whole of Jewry, one does so in the knowledge that the racial qualities of this people are such that in the long run they cannot harmonize with the racial qualities of the Germanic peoples and that every Jew who at this moment has not done anything bad may nevertheless under the proper conditions do precisely that, because his racial qualities drive him to do it. . . . the Jews . . . operate like parasites . . . the Jews are cholera germs.[10]

The Jewish population of Germany was quite small: in 1900 it was only about 497,000, or 0.95 percent, of the total population of 50,626,000. Jews were proud of their many contributions to German economic and intellectual life (by the 1930s, 30 percent of the Nobel Prize winners in Germany were Jews); they considered themselves patriotic Germans and regarded Germany as an altogether desirable place to live—a place of refuge in comparison to Russia, where Jews lived in terrible poverty and suffered violent attacks. German Jews, who felt that they already had a homeland, had little enthusiasm for Zionism.

German anti-Semitic organizations and political parties failed to get the state to pass anti-Semitic laws, and by the early 1900s these groups had declined in political power and importance. But the mischief had been done. In the minds of many Germans even in respectable circles, the image of the Jew as an evil and dangerous creature had been firmly planted. It was perpetuated by the schools, youth groups, the Pan-German Association, and an array of racist pamphlets and books. Late-nineteenth-century racial anti-Semites had constructed an ideological foundation on which Hitler would later build his movement. In words that foreshadowed Hitler, Paul de Lagarde said of the Jews: "One does not have dealings with pests and parasites; one does not rear them and cherish them; one destroys them as speedily and thoroughly as possible."[11]

It is, of course, absurd to believe that a nation of 50 million was threatened by a half-million citizens of Jewish birth, or that the 11 million Jews of the world (by 1900) had organized to rule the planet. The Jewish birthrate in Germany was low, the rate of intermarriage high, and the desire for complete assimilation into German life great. Within a few generations the Jewish community in Germany might well have disappeared. Moreover, despite the paranoia of the anti-Semite, the German Jews and the Jews in the rest of Europe were quite powerless. There were scarcely any Jews in the ruling circles of governments, armies, civil services, or heavy industries. As events were to prove, the Jews, with no army or state and dwelling among people many of whom despised them, were the weakest of peoples. But the race mystics, convinced that they were waging a war of self-defense against a satanic foe, were impervious to rational argument. Anti-Semites, said Theodor

Mommsen, the great nineteenth-century German historian, would not listen to

> logical and ethical arguments. . . . They listen only to their own envy and hatred, to the meanest instincts. Nothing else counts for them. They are deaf to reason, right, morals. One cannot influence them. . . . [Anti-Semitism] is a horrible epidemic, like cholera—one can neither explain nor cure it.[12]

Thus racial nationalists attacked and undermined the Enlightenment tradition. They denied equality, scorned toleration and cosmopolitanism, and made myth and superstition vital forces in political life. That many people believed these racial theories was an ominous sign for Western civilization. It showed how tenuous the rational tradition of the Enlightenment is, how receptive the mind is to dangerous myths, and how easily human behavior can degenerate into inhumanity.

Notes

1. Quoted in Christopher Hibbert, *Garibaldi and His Enemies* (Boston: Little, Brown, 1965), p. 45.

2. Otto Pflanze, *Bismarck and the Development of Germany: The Period of Unification* (Princeton, N.J.: Princeton University Press, 1963), p. 232.

3. Hans Kohn, *Pan-Slavism* (Notre Dame, Ind.: University of Notre Dame Press, 1953), pp. 66–67.

4. Quoted ibid., p. 44.

5. Cited in Edward R. Tannenbaum, *1900: The Generation Before the Great War* (Garden City, N.Y.: Doubleday, 1976), p. 337.

6. This discussion is based largely on the works of George L. Mosse, particularly *The Crisis of German Ideology* (New York: Grosset & Dunlap Universal Library, 1964).

7. Cited in Horst von Maltitz, *The Evolution of Hitler's Germany* (New York: McGraw-Hill, 1973), p. 33.

8. Hans Kohn, *Nationalism: Its Meaning and History* (Princeton, N.J.: D. Van Nostrand, Anvil Books, 1955), p. 77.

9. Karl Dietrich Bracher, *The German Dictatorship*, trans. by Jean Steinberg (New York: Praeger, 1970), p. 36.

10. Quoted in Raul Hilberg, *The Destruction of the European Jews* (Chicago: Quadrangle, 1967), pp. 10–11.

11. Quoted in Helmut Krausnick, Hans Buchheim, Martin Broszat, and Hans-Adolf Jacobsen, *Anatomy of the SS State,* trans. by Richard Barry, et al. (London: William Collins Sons, 1968), p. 9.

12. Quoted in Peter G. J. Pulzer, *The Rise of Political Anti-Semitism in Germany and Austria* (New York: Wiley, 1964), p. 299.

Suggested Reading

Beales, Derek, *The Risorgimento and the Unification of Italy* (1971). A comprehensive overview followed by documents.

Hamerow, T. S., *Restoration, Revolution, Reaction* (1958). An examination of economics and politics in Germany, 1815–1871, stressing the problems caused by the transition from agrarianism to industrialism.

———, ed., *Otto von Bismarck* (1962). A collection of readings from leading historians.

Hibbert, Christopher, *Garibaldi and His Enemies* (1965). A vivid portrait of the Italian hero.

Holburn, Hajo, *A History of Modern Germany, 1840–1945* (1969). A standard reference work.

Jászi, Oscar, *The Dissolution of the Habsburg Monarchy* (1961). Originally published in 1929, this volume examines how nationalist animosities contributed to the dissolution of the Hapsburg monarchy.

Katz, Jacob, *From Prejudice to Destruction* (1980). A survey of modern anti-Semitism; holds that modern anti-Semitism is an outgrowth of traditional Christian anti-Semitism.

Kohn, Hans, *Nationalism: Its Meaning and History* (1955). A concise history of modern nationalism by a leading student of the subject.

Mack Smith, Denis, ed., *Garibaldi* (1969). A collection of readings: Garibaldi as he saw himself, how his contemporaries saw him, how nineteenth- and twentieth-century historians have viewed him; preceded by a valuable introduction.

Mosse, George L., *Toward the Final Solution* (1978). An analysis of European racism.

——, *The Crisis of German Ideology* (1964). Explores the dark side of German nationalism; an excellent study of Volkish thought.

Pauley, B. F., *The Habsburg Legacy, 1867–1939* (1972). A good brief work on a complex subject.

Pflanze, Otto, *Bismarck and the Development of Germany* (1963). An excellent study of the political history of Germany during the period 1815–1871.

Pulzer, Peter G. J., *The Rise of Political Anti-Semitism in Germany and Austria* (1964). Relationship of anti-Semitism to changing socioeconomic conditions; impact of anti-Semitism on politics.

Rodes, John E., *The Quest for Unity: Modern Germany, 1848–1970* (1971). A good survey of German history.

Review Questions

1. What forces worked for and against Italian unity?

2. Mazzini was the soul, Cavour the brains, and Garibaldi the sword in the struggle for the unification of Italy. Discuss their participation in and contributions to the struggle.

3. Why is it significant that Prussia served as the agent of German unification rather than the Frankfurt Assembly in 1848?

4. Prussia's victory over Austria was a triumph for conservatism and a defeat for liberalism. Discuss this statement.

5. What was the significance of the Franco-Prussian War for European history?

6. In the Hapsburg Empire, nationalism was a force for disunity. Discuss this statement.

7. To whom did Volkish thought appeal? Describe why.

8. Why is racial nationalism a repudiation of the Enlightenment tradition and a regression to mythical thinking?

9. What is the relationship between medieval and modern anti-Semitism?

10. Anti-Semites attributed to Jews everything that they found repellent in the modern world. Discuss this statement.

11. Anti-Semitism demonstrates the immense power and appeal of mythical thinking. Discuss this statement.

26

The Industrial West: Responses to Modernization

I n the last part of the nineteenth century, the accelerated pace of industrialization transformed European and American societies. Simultaneously, Western nations built governmental machinery for including and controlling great numbers of citizens. This strengthening and centralizing process—*state-building* in modern terminology—is an important part of modernization. European nations and the United States experienced the process of industrialization, urbanization, and democratization differently, according to their political and social institutions and the rapidity of their industrialization. Nevertheless, all reacted to the transformation of their societies by modifying traditional institutions to meet these new circumstances. The old power structures of rural, agrarian, privileged society endured, reacting to the new era by resisting and repressing emerging forces, but reshaping basic institutions nonetheless.

The major activity of Western governments became state-building, which meant not only strengthening central authority but also absorbing previously excluded classes into the community, primarily through the power of nationalism. Governments created and reinforced popular expressions of nationalism. Masses of people who had never been involved in the political life of their country converted to enthusiastic nationalists. The state's power differed from country to country, but it grew enormously as government affected the lives of ordinary citizens through military conscription, public education, and broad taxation.

Industrialization facilitated trends toward centralization with the concentration of factory workers in cities and the loosening of traditional rural ties. Civil wars, unification movements, and struggles for political representation ended usually with even greater power in the hands of the government. A new balance of classes and regions in the modern centralized state was achieved through

British Women in a Factory, 1902. (*Mary Evans Picture Library*)

repression of dissent. This happened in the U.S. Civil War, in the suppression of the Irish struggle for Home Rule, in the subjection of southern Italy to the north, in the repression of Catholics and socialists in unified Germany, and in the persecution of minorities in czarist Russia.

Industrialization greatly affected international relations as well. National power was no longer measured by population, area, and the size of the army. The amount of coal and iron production, the mileage and tonnage of railways and navies, the mechanization of industry, and the skill of the populace became important components of national power. Russia's giant army could not compensate for French, British, or even Belgian industrial power. Production, trade, foreign markets, and political empires altered the balance of power among nations; the preeminent positions of France, Russia, and Austria changed, as Germany and the United States threw their industrial weights onto the scale of world power in the generation before 1914.

The Advance of Industry

Industry had developed on the foundation of cheap labor and plentiful agricultural commodities, which were made even more easily and cheaply available by the development of a relatively inexpensive transportation and communication system. It took more than a century for that foundation to be built, but it was in place for almost all of Europe and parts of the Americas by midcentury. (See Chapter 21.) Beginning in the second half of the nineteenth century, the structure of a new economic world began to be built on that foundation. Many historians have called this period the Second Industrial Revolution because the great increase in the speed, scale, and scope of change seemed a totally new social and economic development, differing from the slower change that had been taking place since the eighteenth century. This changed world was characterized by new forms of business and labor organization, by the rise of the middle class to political and social power corresponding to its economic power, by the decline of traditional groups or classes, by dramatic changes in the role of women and children in the family, and by technological change based on the application of inventions and scientific discoveries to industrial production.

It is important to understand how little appeared to have changed for much of the Western world by the Crystal Palace exhibition of 1851, which symbolized the pride and exuberance of the new industrial society. Farming was still the main occupation of people everywhere, including Britain, where industrialization was most advanced. Even in Britain there were more domestic servants than factory workers and twice as many agricultural laborers as textile and clothing workers. Large factories were few, and handicrafts still flourished. Electricity was too fragile to power lighting or drive machines and was used only in signaling. Steel was so expensive to manufacture that it was treated almost as a precious metal. Sailing ships still outnumbered steamships, and horses carried more freight than trains. On-the-job training was more common than schooling, and construction and machine making still relied on trial and error rather than on architecture and engineering.

After midcentury, however, much changed radically during two important spurts. First, between 1850 and 1870 in Europe and America the shift from hand to machine production took hold, leading to the concentration of factory workers in industrial cities and to the growth of unions. The standard of living for most workers rose. New machines and processes, legislation, and trade-union bargaining relieved the worst conditions of early industrialization; also, the first regulations of urban development and sanitation began to improve living conditions. In the more advanced industrial areas the social organization of the workplace changed, as the introduction of heavy equipment resulted in men replacing women and children in the factories and the somewhat higher wages for skilled male laborers meant that women in their families no longer were compelled by dire necessity to work in factories. Women forced out of factories (they would return during World War I) were not freed for a life of leisure, however; they worked as domestics, pieceworkers, seamstresses, laundresses, and similar jobs. Children became students as the state and the economy demanded that they acquire at least a minimal education.

Consumers and investors adjusted to the industrial world with new patterns of investment and consumption, which further influenced the organization of society and economy toward mass production.

Then, in the second period of change, following the severe economic depression of 1873, which affected all major countries, came the development of *cartels* and *monopolies*—giant firms able to dominate entire industries nationally and internationally. This phenomenon was particularly striking in Germany and the United States, but it affected most of the industrialized countries. From the 1890s to World War I, there was a marked change in the scale of development: giant firms run by boards of directors, including financiers, operated far-flung enterprises of enormous, mechanized factories manned by unskilled, low-paid, often seasonal workers. These industrial giants were able to control the output, price, and distribution of commodities; they dominated smaller firms, financed and controlled research and development, and expanded far beyond their national frontiers. The "captains of industry," the owners or managers of these large firms, possessed such extraordinary economic power that they often commanded political power as well. In the United States, for example, certain senators were known as the "oil senator," the "railroad senator," or the "cotton senator" because they were backed by particular industries to protect their interests. This situation was common in all the industrial states.

The emergence and concentration of heavy industry in large firms, capitalized by specialist banks, characterized the post-1890 period all over Europe. This tendency was marked in Austria-Hungary, Russia, and Italy because the costs of development to compete with advanced countries were so high that small entrepreneurs could not meet them. In Austria-Hungary one or two giant entrepreneurs dominated steel, mines, and munitions operations, having absorbed many competitors in a single generation. (In Britain and France, in contrast, the trend toward concentration stretched across several generations.) Such rapid growth caught the imagination of businessmen as well as socialist critics. Few noticed that small business was expanding along with big business in central Europe—the growth of the 1890s and the following decade was general and not limited to monopolies and cartels.

Economic development was extremely uneven, though. Central, southern, and eastern Europe remained backward areas in many respects and stayed so until World War I and after. In these areas, governments did not rely on private enterprise to build "essential" industries (broadly defined to include transportation, communication, national banks, and the production of war goods). War industries had been state enterprises for a long time. Britain's essential industries alone had developed under laissez-faire policies, though such policies were popular in the United States and France at times during the nineteenth century. In these industries, government encouraged the tendency to monopoly and large-scale operations. Nonetheless, the eastern empires were economically backward; in these overwhelmingly agricultural societies, manufacturing consisted for the most part of consumer-oriented, small-scale operations in textiles and food processing, in which craftsmen maintained their place. In Austria, for example, of almost a million firms in 1912 (more than 75 percent) were very small businesses based on agricultural commodities. In that year, 5,000 registered artisan guilds with a half-million masters and a half-million journeymen still existed, whereas guilds had disappeared a half-century earlier in England, Belgium, and France.

In the first period of consolidation, from 1850 to 1870, the standard of living of many workers went up. Labor tried to protect itself with craft unions, craft organizations, and social clubs, which helped in times of unemployment, sickness, or accidents. Later, labor responded to structural change in the economy by organizing on an industry-wide basis and voting for candidates who were sympathetic to their plight. In the second period of change, from 1870 to 1914, the standard of living for workers in western Europe rose, although in the decade before World War I, the cost of living also rose by as much as 10 percent. A wave of strikes, often punctuated by violence, swept through every industrial and industrializing country in the 1890s. Many of these strikes, such as the dockworkers' strikes in London and Liverpool, the railroad workers' strike in France, and the miners' strikes in England and France, were repressed violently. The striking French railroad

Claude Monet (1840–1926): The Gare St.-Lazare, Paris: Arrival of a Train, 1877. The fascination with railroads, visible in the work of painters as realists, naturalists, impressionists, and post-impressionists, is apparent in Monet's treatment. The railroad boom in the Second Empire was fostered by Napoleon III. (*Courtesy of The Harvard University Art Museums, Fogg Art Museum, Bequest—Collection of Maurice Wertheim, Class of 1906*)

workers were drafted and forced to return to work as soldiers. On the eve of the war, the political power of industrialists was so great that, even with the vote, labor had little success in alleviating the sources of its discontent.

Fifty Years of Technological Change

Laying the foundations of industrial development had taken more than a century. In the next half-century, technological change was revolutionary.

At midcentury, all Europe caught the railroad mania that had seized Britain in the 1840s. Railroads became the moving force of many other industries as well, particularly coal, iron, gravel, wood, and tar. More than a century of iron metallurgy was capped by the improved processes of Bessemer and Siemens, which made quality steel cheaply and available for use in railroads and construction. Stronger steel in machinery allowed for the wider application of steam in mines, construction, and other industries. New forms of capitalization or finance fueled the rail expansion. The public, including the investors, was thrilled by railroad building, which had the aura of progress that canal and road building did not have, despite the fact that they provided cheaper transportation. In Britain, at first, many railroad firms competed, but those that could draw in the greatest amounts of capital soon swallowed up their competitors.

In the other nations of Europe, government fostered railroad building. In France, railroads further centralized the country's society because all tracks led to Paris; the mobility provided by trains contributed to the turning of peasants into Frenchmen, ending regional loyalties. In the German and Italian states too, railroads contributed to unification. The citizens' vision widened to include the nation and beyond, just as the economic markets did.

The nations most transformed by railways were in North America and Eurasia. By 1870, the United States contained more miles of railway (176,000) than all of Europe did; the American transcontinental railroad offered an avenue into vast, unsettled areas. Canada repeated the story. In Russia in the 1890s, the Trans-Siberian Railroad opened up the tsar's hinterland, carrying millions of settlers east to the desolate stretches of Central Asia.

The epic expansion of railroads was paralleled in shipping. In 1850, 5 percent of the world's tonnage of ships were steam-powered; by 1893, the figure had advanced to half of all tonnage. The shift brought changes in marine technology, such as the replacement of iron with steel and the substitution of screw propellers for the paddle wheels that moved riverboats. In 1870, 4.5 million tons of goods were shipped by sailboat and less than a million tons by steamship; by 1881, the tonnage was about equal; and by 1885, steam surpassed sail. By 1913, steam carried 11 million tons of goods and sail only 800,000. The whole world had been accessible to Westerners for some time, but by the 1880s, thanks to steam and railroad transportation, it was open as well to the cheap, plentiful goods of European and American manufacturers.

At the turn of the century, however, the age of steam would come to a close. Two German engineers, Gottfried Daimler and Carl Benz, joined to perfect the internal combustion engine. They produced a luxury automobile named for Daimler's daughter, Mercedes. The American Henry Ford used mass-production assembly-line techniques to produce his Model T for "the ordinary man," and the automobile age was born. The invention of the diesel engine by another German in 1897 meant cheaper, more efficient fuel could be used. Diesel engines soon replaced steam engines on giant cargo ships, warships, and luxury liners.

In communications, the invention of the telegraph stimulated industrial expansion for more than a generation. At the time, the undramatic but rapid improvement of postal services was much more important to industrial growth than the spectacular inventions like the telephone and the radio. Development costs were so prohibitive for the telephone (invented by Alexander Graham Bell in 1876) and the wireless, or radio (invented by Guglielmo Marconi in 1895), that it took twenty-five years after their invention for either device to be widely used, even in industrial countries.

Advances in electronics illustrate a general trend of the second half of the nineteenth century. After a long lag, the Scientific Revolution and the Industrial Revolution joined forces. Inventions played a greater and more visible role in the late-nineteenth-century industrial expansion than they had in the much slower, more cumulative earlier growth. More than a half century elapsed between Michael Faraday and James Maxwell's discovery of the fundamentals of electricity and the inventions of Thomas Edison, Bell, and Marconi. In a much shorter span of time—by the end of the century—electricity was providing power for lights, trains for urban and suburban use, and some factory engines. This same trend is also evident in industrial chemistry, which revolutionized many products. In 1850 almost all industrial materials were the ones people had been using for centuries—wood, stone, cotton, wool, flax, hemp, leather, and the base metals like copper, iron, lead, and tin and their alloys. Even dyes and drugs were the products of plants or animals. However, from midcentury, building on the general framework provided by John Dalton's theory of molecular structure and Dmitri Mendeleev's classification of elements by valence, chemists discovered new elements and perfected formulas for alloys and other combinations. Dyes and coal-tar

Map 26.1 Expansion of Europe's Rail System ▶

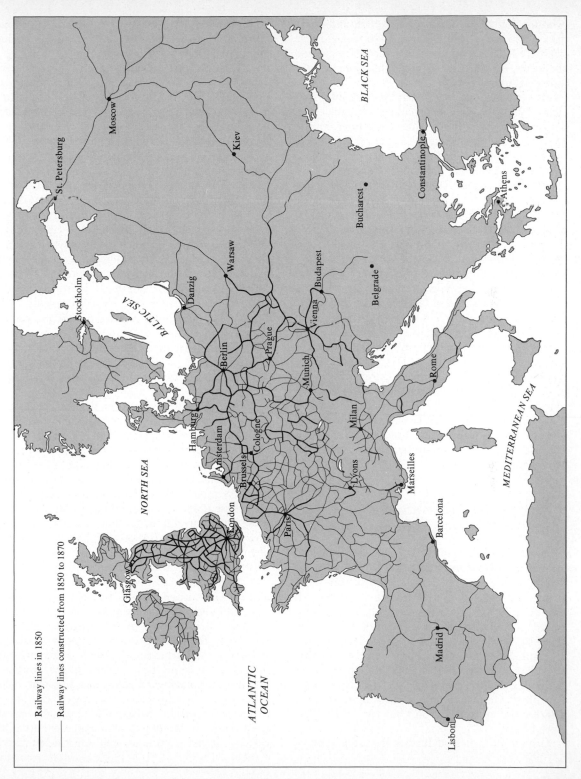

BLACK SEA

Moscow

Kiev

St. Petersburg

Constantinople

Athens

Bucharest

Warsaw

Danzig

Budapest

Belgrade

Stockholm

BALTIC SEA

Vienna

Berlin

Prague

Munich

Rome

Hamburg

Milan

MEDITERRANEAN SEA

Amsterdam

Cologne

Brussels

Lyons

Marseilles

NORTH SEA

Barcelona

London

Paris

Glasgow

Railway lines in 1850

Railway lines constructed from 1850 to 1870

Madrid

ATLANTIC
OCEAN

Lisbon

products (such as liquid fuel), aspirin and other drugs, saccharin, and disinfectants were developed. By 1900, Germany was the center of applied chemistry, an important segment of that country's industrial expansion.

In medicine, too, the marriage of science and technology produced miraculous progeny. The discovery of anesthetics and antiseptics in the 1850s and the passionate insistence on cleanliness by the English surgeon Joseph Lister made it possible for many more patients to survive surgery and hospitalization. The discovery and isolation of disease-causing bacteria by Louis Pasteur, a French chemist, made it possible to pinpoint the causes of some diseases, to isolate or quarantine the diseased, and to immunize or inoculate the healthy against disease. By the end of the century, researchers had identified the causes of several killer diseases—typhoid, tuberculosis, cholera, tetanus, diphtheria, and leprosy. Science had exposed poor sanitation and squalor as the breeders of disease, and industrialized countries worked harder and more efficiently than before to ameliorate these conditions. Death rates dropped precipitously; life expectancy increased, as did population numbers. In the more industrialized nations the birthrate declined as the population rose, because many people believed that having large families lowered their standard of living and because they knew about health measures and birth control.

The Acceleration of Urbanization

More rapid industrialization increased the numbers of northwestern Europeans and Americans who lived in cities, which became more numerous, larger, and more densely populated. London, although not an industrial city, had become a megalopolis of 5 million people by 1880 and was home to 7 million by 1914. Paris increased from 2 to 3 million between midcentury and World War I. Berlin, a city of only half a million in 1866, reached 2 million by World War I. There were only three German cities of more than 100,000 on the eve of unification, but by 1903 there were fifteen.

Urbanization helped further the integration of the citizen into the nation. In the cities, people responded to various pressures of education, the press, and patriotic campaigns; they became conscious of national loyalties and slowly moved away from regional, class, and religious loyalties. In the cities, the middle class rose to political, economic, and social prominence, often expressing its newfound importance and prosperity by civic activity. As machinery replaced handcraftsmen, the artisan working class experienced a sharp decline. Many towns that had been craft centers decayed as artisans moved to larger urban areas in search of employment. Factory workers, their ranks swelled by peasants and artisans, emerged as an important social group in cities. A city culture developed, although some observers who remembered the old regional, religious, and occupational loyalties did not consider it to be a culture. Cut off from the regions of their birth, factory-working peasants and artisans shed their old loyalties; in the cities, some found a place for themselves in their neighborhoods, some in union and party activities, and some not at all. Industrialization also created a new "white collar" group of clerks who tried to differentiate themselves from factory workers.

Industrialization and urbanization played a much more important part in national integration than did government campaigns to create homogeneity. Often the success of minority cultural resistance to the pressures for integration depended on the relative economic backwardness of the area. As industrialization and urbanization proceeded, maintaining traditional loyalties became more and more difficult. There were exceptions, however: industrialization heightened minority identity among such peoples as the Czechs in Austria-Hungary and the Basques in Spain.

In contrast to northwestern Europe, southern and eastern Europe remained overwhelmingly agricultural until the twentieth century. In Russia, in the Balkans and parts of the Austro-Hungarian Empire, in the Iberian peninsula, and in southern Italy, peasant discontent undermined the national integration that political leaders sought. In these economically backward areas, peasants who held small pieces of land could not always eke out a living; other peasants without holdings labored on great estates for landlords who paid them little. In eastern Germany, Russia, and Austria-Hungary, the agricultural sector followed the rest of the economy in producing for export rather than for home consumption, which meant that the peasants' standard of living in terms of food and steady employment sometimes declined.

The Rise of Unions and Socialist Parties

The formation of giant enterprises, which used the technology of the second wave of industrialization, required armies of unskilled workers, who did not fit in the trade or craft unions or syndicates of skilled craftsmen organized during the prosperous years in the mid-nineteenth century. From the 1880s, skilled craftsmen, trained factory workers, and organized union workers watched as machines and unskilled workers took their places. The years of struggle to organize and to get legal recognition for unions seemed fruitless as workers faced the results of technological change, which had made their skills obsolete. The new unskilled laborers worked for low pay, usually by the day or the job, if they were lucky enough (or shared enough of their wages with the foreman) to be chosen to work. With pay so low, work so irregular, and skills so minimal, unions (which depended on control of the labor supply) seemed almost impossible to organize. The corporate giants stuck together to defeat attempts at unionization, and used their political power to keep the union movement weak. As a result, work conditions were terrible, hours were long, and work remained irregular and low-paying in the new industries.

By the 1890s, however, unskilled workers in England, the United States, France, and Germany began the difficult task of organizing unions based on an industry, not on a single skill or craft. In England, women and girls who worked in match factories, where phosphorus endangered their health, went on strike in 1888; they won the attention of the press and the public, which deplored their miserable conditions and wages. Their strike succeeded because other workers called sympathy strikes; workers had begun to recognize the importance of solidarity. When impoverished British dockworkers struck in 1889,

they were rescued from sure defeat by support from Australian and American dockworkers.

In their efforts at organized political activity, workers used their suffrage to pressure government for reform. Beginning in the 1860s and 1870s, they demanded legislation for minimum wages, maximum hours, and better working conditions. They pushed government to deal with the social consequences of industrialization and urbanization, and government paid attention. In the 1880s, Bismarck instituted reforms (see page 589), and by 1914, Britain, France, Austria, Italy, Denmark, and Switzerland were providing some benefits for sick, injured, and elderly workers. In some countries, such as the United States, workers voted for the same political parties that other classes voted for, and the candidates competed with one another for their votes. In other countries, such as Britain, workers at first followed that policy, and then organized a separate party pledged to their interests. In France, Germany, and Italy, workers were drawn to socialist parties or to anarchist parties that called for the end of capitalism.

Over the years from 1850 to 1914, workers' lives improved due to trade-union organization, government intervention in the economy, and the general increase in productivity brought on by industrialization. Still, members of the working class faced problems and inequities that drew them to socialist parties that strove for state control of industry and worker control of government and workplace. Most workers—and their families—lived in overcrowded, bleak tenements, without central heating or running water. They worked long hours, as much as 55 hours a week in trades where governments restricted the length of the work week, and as much as 70 to 75 hours in unregulated trades. Their jobs were exhausting and monotonous. They suffered from malnutrition; the English men and boys who appeared for medical exams to serve in the Boer War were found to be so physically unfit that their condition prompted reforms to improve the health and education of the laboring class. The working class as a whole suffered from diseases, particularly tuberculosis, and from lack of medical care. Women often died in childbirth due to inadequate treatment, and men, particularly miners and dockworkers, commonly experienced job accidents that maimed and killed. Socialists believed that these conditions were due to the capitalist profit system that exploited and impoverished workers and enriched the owners.

Socialist parties, which by the 1890s were influenced by Marx and his followers (see Chapter 24), grew phenomenally in Germany and rapidly in much of the rest of Europe. Even Russia, which was scarcely industrial, had a Marxist socialist party. The growth of socialism reflected changes in the industrial sector: increasing unionization, and workers' growing consciousness that they had special needs that other political parties did not fulfill. Socialists were divided about tactics for change, however, depending on their ideology and their country's political environment. Some socialists, who insisted that they were "orthodox" Marxists, believed that socialist-led revolution was the necessary first step for change; among the orthodox Marxists were Wilhelm Liebknecht and August Bebel of Germany and Jules Guesde of France. Others, "revisionist" Marxists, argued that Marx's predictions and theory needed to be adapted to new conditions, such as an improving standard of living and universal manhood suffrage; in Germany, Eduard Bernstein, a "revisionist," urged socialists to use the political and economic system to build socialism without revolution. In England, where Marxism had not gained much influence, the labor movement and the newly formed Independent Labour party used the political system to bring about change. In France, where the official party position was orthodox, the brilliant and popular socialist leader Jean Jaurès was a gradualist, who believed socialism could be achieved by democratic means of education and elections.

On the eve of World War I, signs appeared of increasing militance by workers, who had suffered from a decline in real wages in a period of inflation. A wave of strikes and labor violence took place throughout the industrialized world. The socialist parties and trade union congresses, which belonged to the Second International (successor to Marx's First International Workingmen's Associations), annually voted for the "hard line" of revolutionary activity to bring about socialism. The revolutionary position was internationalist as well, holding that workers should refuse to support their nations in imperialistic wars. Many middle- and upper-class people in every European state feared the organized workers' position. But workers felt themselves to be as patriotic and as much a part of their nation as any other group, despite the yearly declarations of the International.

Great Britain, 1847–1914

England appeared to be the most modern and progressive of states at midcentury. It had made phenomenal industrial progress, and most of its people began to share a higher standard of living in the era of free trade after 1847. The British elite, as well as foreigners, believed England to be the model parliamentary government, balancing an uncomparable degree of political liberty with economic and social reforms, which enabled it to avoid the extremes of revolution and reaction that other nations experienced in the nineteenth century. Political parties competed with one another to govern, and in the competition reformed evils and extended membership in the political community to previously excluded groups.

That was the appearance. The reality differed. "Country gentlemen" dominated British politics: titled aristocrats manned the cabinets and commanded the army and navy. (A gentleman's manners and education were thought to be the "good breeding" expected for the civil service, for any public and private promotion, and for social acceptance.) Great social mobility existed, but the wealthy industrialists, merchants, and entrepreneurs had to acquire a gentleman's manners in order to become influential in political and social life.

Reform and Progress

The effect of almost a century of industrial and commercial changes—and some fortuitous events, like the discovery of gold in California, Alaska, and Australia—brought prosperity, and confidence. A sense of well being shaped the politics of the time. Two men of two quite different personalities and values were the central political figures of this period: William E. Gladstone (1809–1898), a pious, sober man and an orator who could inspire people over issues of taxes and revenues, and Benjamin Disraeli (1804–1881), a flamboyant personality—a novelist and a dreamer who talked of the greatness of empire. Gladstone, the Liberal, saw politics as the struggle between the forces of good and evil and believed that God had chosen him to carry out his divine will. Disraeli, the Conservative, thought politics a fascinating game and loved the role of courtier to Queen Victoria. Their competition stimulated reform and laid down the rules of the parliamentary game for others to admire and imitate.

Such was the case with the Reform Bill of 1867. Gladstone moved to extend the suffrage, but failed to get the bill passed, forcing his resignation according to the custom of cabinet responsibility (by which the cabinet must resign if it fails to pass its measures). Then Disraeli proposed giving the vote to the great majority of city workers—many more than Gladstone had envisioned. The Conservatives carried the measure, and suddenly the electorate was doubled. Liberals and Conservatives alike had feared democracy, yet in a moment it had become a reality. Disraeli claimed that he was not afraid of the masses because the Conservative social program and imperialistic foreign policy would attract the poor. However, most of his followers, and many Liberals as well, thought his eagerness to win the game of passing bills and maintaining majorities had carried him away.

Suddenly, enfranchised masses had to be educated. Religious controversy had defeated earlier attempts to require elementary education, but the prospect of uneducated voters pushed Parliament to require compulsory elementary education. Gladstone's Reform Bill of 1884 enfranchised rural laborers; now most English *men* could vote. Women and many Irishmen still could not, but many believed it was only a matter of time until democracy would include even them.

Britain's prosperity seemed to provide a good environment for political and social progress, but this complacent era was shattered in 1873, when a severe depression led people of all classes to question economic policy and to fear class antagonisms. Britons realized that Germany and the United States were keen industrial competitors

Isambard Kingdom Brunel, 1857. Brunel, an engineer, was photographed in front of the chains of a checking drum belonging to the steamship the *Great Eastern*. In the 1840s, the railroads had transformed the face of Europe. Countries were unified, and economies expanded. The steamship came to the fore during the last decades of the nineteenth century. The world now had easy access to goods of European and U.S. industry, transported by steamship speed and efficiency. (*Victoria and Albert Museum*)

who had surpassed them in important fields. And at the very moment that British confidence was shaken by economic depression, industrial rivalry, and the unresolvable Irish question, labor and feminists militantly demanded political and economic reform.

Social and Political Unrest

Labor Discontent For a generation after the failure of the Chartists' democratic demands of the 1840s, labor militancy subsided. Unlike many European workers, the English could organize legal unions along craft lines to raise their standard of living and improve their working conditions. Skilled workers improved their position and England's labor movement became the strongest in Europe. Real purchasing power increased due to the repeal of grain tariffs in 1847 and higher productivity; the quality of life rose as government responded to improve urban conditions. After the Depression of 1873, however, in England as in all the other European countries technological change led in the 1880s to a rise in militant industrial unions, "new unions."

Unlike their continental brothers, British workers on the whole had never been attracted to socialism, particularly not to Marxism. There were working-class socialists (Utopian Owenites and nonconformist, dissenting Christians), but they managed to express their protests against injustice in the Liberal party. In the 1880s, widespread poverty and new trends in industry—particularly monopolies, cartels and foreign competition—led some labor leaders to urge greater militancy; they espoused an English brand of socialism. Keir Hardie, a colorful speaker who insisted on wearing a worker's cap and jacket when he took his seat in the House of Commons to represent a poor Welsh mining district, created the Independent Labour party in 1893 to fight for workers' interests. He and other union leaders, sometimes in alliance with middle-class socialists like the Fabians, sometimes with Liberals, hammered out a political and economic program that developed into a platform for a separate Labour party.

The Labour party might never have grown without the Taff Vale decision (1901), which awarded damages to an employer picketed by a union. If workers could be fined for picketing or other actions restraining trade, their unions could be broken and they would lose the economic gains of half a century. And there were reforms to be won. German workers had gained some measures protecting them from unemployment and old age.

Labor took to politics, and in the elections of 1906, although Gladstone's heirs were overwhelmingly elected to the House of Commons, the new Labour party gained twenty-nine members, an important faction when Conservatives and Liberals were almost equal in number.

A wave of labor unrest at the turn of the century included strikes and violence. The miners, the dockworkers, and the railway workers allied, urging a general strike for minimum wages. Worker discontent pushed the traditional trade-union movement and the new unions of unskilled industrial labor to greater militancy.

The Irish Question The great famine of 1846–47, in which a million Irish died and another million emigrated, brought unparalleled suffering to the Irish. Parliament responded to this major catastrophe by callously repressing discontent and refusing to help the starving Irish. A revolutionary republican army—the Fenians—was born from the hatred caused by this treatment. Throughout the prosperous 1860s, this group engaged in terrorism to disrupt British stability and parliamentary politics. They demanded Irish independence. Hoping for reconciliation, Gladstone staked the Liberal party's future on Irish reform. In 1869 he ended the taxes the Catholic Irish paid for a church (the Anglican) they did not attend. He also passed a land act that forced landlords to compensate tenant farmers, if they were evicted, for any improvements they had made on the land. Until then, renters had no incentive to improve land or farm buildings, which meant the Emerald Isle was not producing enough food. Despite the reforms, Irish Protestants (called Anglo-Irish) still held economic power and social privilege.

These reforms might have reconciled the Irish if they had been made in the 1840s and 1850s. By the 1880s they were too late; the issue had become *home rule* (self-government within the British Empire). In the Commons the Irish, led by Charles Stewart Parnell, formed a separate bloc to force the Conservatives and the Liberals to reckon with the issue of home rule. The Irish used every known parliamentary tactic, and invented some new ones, to secure a separate legislature and executive for Ireland. (The Irish had had no parliament of their own since the union with England and Scotland in 1801.) But Parnell's supporters were hurt by the terrorist acts of other nationalists, even though they denounced violent action. Gladstone urged home rule, but his party split over the issue, and as public passions were aroused, Parliament enacted extreme measures, suspending trial by jury and many other liberties in Ireland. At the end of his career, Gladstone knew that he had failed his most important task. The reconciliation of the Irish, which even independence after World War I could not accomplish, was not to be achieved.

Feminist Agitation   Other issues threatened the forms of parliamentary government that Gladstone and Disraeli had developed. The campaign for female suffrage was particularly explosive, as feminist tactics and government repression steadily escalated in violence. Women were allowed to vote for and serve on school and local government boards; in both arenas they were very active—they were, in fact, the backbone of school boards and the charity organizations that were responsible for poverty relief. The right of voting for members of the House of Commons was denied them, however, despite their peaceful petitions.

Some feminists thought that women should concentrate their efforts on improving themselves and making legal efforts to improve their status in society; others found that approach was too slow and proposed radical action to reach equality. Still others thought the political road was the wrong one to take; if women wanted to be free, they needed to liberate themselves economically and socially from their dependence on men. Many Liberals and some Labourites favored women's suffrage, but women were advised by the leader of the Liberals "to keep on pestering . . . but exercise the virtue of patience." For those women who felt the advice patronized them and whose patience was running out, a family of feminists advocated a more militant course of action. Emmeline Pankhurst and her daughters Sylvia and Christabel urged demonstrations, invasions of the House of Commons, destruction of property, and hunger strikes. They did not urge these dramatic actions all at once, but when their petitions and demands were ignored, they moved to more and more shocking actions. Suffragettes began a cam-

Irish Immigrants Aboard Ship, 1870s. The great famine of 1846–47 opened the floodgates of Irish immigration. The English lacked government machinery, an economic philosophy of intervention when faced with disaster, and sufficient will to ease the suffering of the Irish. The Irish streamed into England and English colonies, as well as to America, in search of a livelihood. The Irish who remained at home demanded Home Rule and then independence. (*Library of Congress*)

paign of breaking windows, starting fires in mailboxes, and chaining themselves to the gates at Parliament. As a gesture of protest, in 1913 one militant threw herself to her death under King Edward VII's horse at the races.

When feminists were arrested for violating the law, they staged hunger strikes. Ugly situations resulted, with the police force-feeding the demonstrators and subjecting them to ridicule and rough treatment. Often the police would release half-starved feminists and, when they had recovered their health, would reimprison them. Ridiculed, humiliated, and punished—but above all legally ignored—the feminists refused to accept the passive role that a male-dominated society had assigned them. When women played a major part on the home front in World War I, many of the elite changed their minds, and in 1918, women over 30 years old were enfranchised. Finally, in 1928, women gained the right to vote on the same terms as men, that is, they had to be 21 years of age and to have six months' residency.

Britain on the Eve of War

Between 1906 and 1911, the Liberals, led by David Lloyd George (1863–1945) and the then-Liberal Winston Churchill (1874–1965), introduced a series of important social measures. Aided by the Labour party, they enacted a program of old-age pensions, labor exchanges to help the unemployed find work, unemployment and health insurance (a program deeply influenced by Bismarckian social legislation), and minimum wages for certain industries. Parliament also repealed the Taff Vale decision. In the process, however, a constitutional crisis developed between the Liberals, who had Labour support, and the Conservatives, who dominated the House of Lords.

When Lloyd George introduced the "people's budget" of 1909, the House of Lords refused to accept it, although the House of Commons was traditionally responsible for financial measures. In the people's budget, social legislation was to be financed by raising the income tax and by levying heavier inheritance taxes ("death duties") and "unearned" income taxes on rents, investments, and increases in the value of land; all of these taxes were directed toward the wealthy and the privileged. The Liberals waged an all-out political fight with the lords, whom they called "diehards" and "last ditchers" for their intransigence. Many lords saw their struggle as the defense of Britain and its empire against the Liberals' "socialist" campaign.

As with the Reform Bill of 1832, the king threatened to create peers who would vote to pass the budget in the House of Lords. Such an action

seemed likely to shake the parliamentary system—certainly to destroy the status of hereditary membership in the House of Lords. Lloyd George sarcastically described the dukes as "five hundred men, ordinary men, chosen accidentally from among the unemployed." During the bitter campaign for the budget, class antagonisms unacknowledged for a couple of generations were freely expressed, but the people's budget was finally passed. Later, the Parliament Act of 1911 stipulated that the House of Lords could only delay the passage of a bill that the Commons wanted, not prevent it. On the eve of World War I, the machinery for democratic government in Britain was in place.

The continuing bitter struggle for Irish home rule made the explosive environment in prewar Britain still more volatile. The House of Lords, dominated by Tory imperialists (disciples of Disraeli's vision of imperial greatness), used every possible tactic against home rule, but, after the Parliament Act of 1911, could not prevent its passage. The Liberals (disciples of Gladstone) pushed for home rule, but their opponents were so angry that they threatened to refuse to accept Parliament's decision, arguing that the British Empire was too important to be broken up by party politics, elections, and mere majority rule.

Outside Parliament, militant groups took the law into their own hands. The situation was more violent and revolutionary than in Gladstone's day. Irish Catholic extremists, such as the Irish Republican Brotherhood and the Gaelic League, pressed for full independence; among the Protestant Irish (Ulstermen), the Ulster Volunteers recruited a large private army and openly trained it for revolution in the event that home rule was enacted. Gangs smuggled guns, soldiers fired on demonstrators, violence bred violence, and civil war seemed close. English Tory leaders threatened mutiny—one going so far as to review 80,000 volunteers in defiance of Parliament and to urge mutiny on the army officers sent to subdue rebellion in Ireland.

At the very moment in 1914 that Great Britain was declaring war in Europe, Ireland was uppermost in British minds. With the onset of war, women and labor suspended their militant campaigns, pledging their loyalty to king and country "for the duration." Many Irish fought for Britain

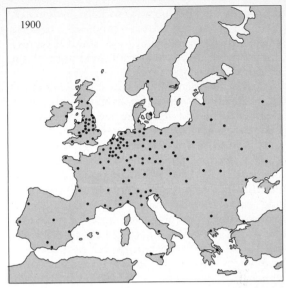

Map 26.2 European Cities of 100,000 or More, 1800–1900

in World War I, but the deferred promise of home rule angered many others, who continued their struggle for independence. In 1916, the Easter Rebellion, an Irish insurrection led by Sir Roger Casement, was suppressed and its leaders executed. At that moment Lloyd George negotiated a settlement that was carried out after the war: Ireland was divided, the south gaining independence and a republican government, and the six counties of Ulster remaining part of the United Kingdom.

The bitter conflicts of prewar Britain showed the cracks in the country's self-image as a stable, liberal, constitutional regime. Parliamentary liberal government proved itself able to conduct and win a grueling world war, but issues of empire and depression would try the constitutional forms again.

France, 1848–1914

The political fortunes of France from midcentury on swung from democratic revolution to authoritarian stability, from active participation of the

people to their domination by a single man or a small group of men. At the same time, France's industrialization proceeded much more slowly than that in Germany or in the United States, a lag that greatly affected the nation's place in the balance of power.

The Era of Napoleon III

The personality and politics of Louis Napoleon Bonaparte (1808–1873), nephew of Napoleon I, dominated France at midcentury. By an overwhelming majority, Bonaparte was elected president of the Second French Republic, which a democratic and social revolution had established in 1848. Within three years, he had made himself dictator—the Second Republic became the Second Empire—and ratified his destruction of the republic by a plebiscite. This vote and subsequent elections were usually rigged and the opposition was controlled.

Bonaparte outraged liberals and republicans, including Alexis de Tocqueville and Victor Hugo and much of the working class, but most of the other French citizens accepted the "little Napoleon." Many thought that Louis Bonaparte's politics—a mix of democratic, socialist, nationalist, and authoritarian ideas—promised national glory, strong leadership, and social progress. Bonaparte seemed a man who could unite all the French classes and groups.

The governments of the Great Powers did not see Napoleon as a force for stability, with reason. Between 1852 and 1870, the new emperor promised peace and economic progress but waged war: the Crimean War (see page 595) forced Russia to make wide-ranging reforms and the battles of the unification of Italy humiliated and diminished Austria. In both affairs, Bonaparte's progressive and liberal policies allied France with Britain, whose enmity had plagued France for more than a century. Actively supporting Italian unification, he won Italian friendship, though he left troops in Rome to protect the pope from zealous Italian nationalists. Even his adventurism in Mexico, when he tried unsuccessfully to place the Hapsburg Archduke Maximilian on a nonexistent Mexican throne, which upset the Great Powers, including the United States, did not alienate French public opinion because it did not cost France much. He furthered French imperialism, joining Britain in the opening of China and claiming portions of Africa. These moves did not upset European stability in the way that European wars did.

Midcentury was a period of prosperity, confidence, and political apathy, particularly when compared to the radical 1840s. The general inflation and economic growth that followed the discovery of gold in California and Alaska helped Bonaparte, who claimed to be a socialist because he accepted Saint-Simonian ideas of state-sponsored building of canals and railroads on cheap credit from government banks. He also expressed concern for the plight of the workers, whose suffering became acute as industrialization took hold in France. Construction projects on cheap credit may have been regarded by liberals as socialistic, but few socialists were, in fact, willing to claim Bonaparte as one of theirs. Many voters, however, believed that he was more concerned with the masses than the predominantly middle-class governments before him had been.

Thus, Bonaparte combined the appearance of democracy—elections, plebiscites, a press and intellectual debate (though he intervened in all these activities)—with economic expansion, which was beneficial to the bourgeois and the workers. He made appeals to national glory with a liberal and not-too-costly foreign policy at the same time that he suppressed legislative opposition, rarely convened the parliament, and manipulated both elections and debate. He censored the press and harassed his critics. He chose his close friends and his relatives as advisers and administrators.

For a generation, his government was popular among property owners, including the majority of peasants, business groups, and Roman Catholics (all had feared the social change demanded in 1848). They approved of stability at home and expansion abroad and of the economic development stimulated by railroad construction and the rebuilding of Paris. This period found enormous creativity in France—in the arts, France's Edgar Degas, Auguste Rodin, Georges Bizet, and Camille Pissaro had few equals, and in the sciences, Louis Pasteur and Claude Bernard were major contributors.

The tide turned in the 1860s. Bonaparte loosened the controls on the press and the legislature, and the scandals associated with his rebuilding of Paris received wide publicity. In 1864, strikes were legalized, and in 1868, workers were given a limited right to unionize. But the emperor did not win workers' loyalty by these reforms. When many members of the opposition were elected in 1869, Napoleon III accepted a new constitution with liberal safeguards for individual liberties, which made his role in government much like that of Queen Victoria: a constitutional parliamentary monarch.

Was Napoleon III, after all, a sincere liberal who wanted first to establish his power and then to give France reforms? Or did he take after the great Napoleon, being more concerned with his personal power and glory and only succumbing to liberalism because he feared revolution? Did he see the era of mass politics as an opportunity for a strong man to rule by providing some modicum of economic security and symbols of national glory to the majority? Was he just another of the strong men in politics after the 1860s who practiced Realpolitik abroad and authoritarian or paternalistic democracy at home—another Bismarck, another Cavour, another Disraeli? The question of Napoleon's goals still perplexes historians. He interests them because his goals and methods seem to foreshadow twentieth-century developments, but whatever his ambitions, they were undermined by his foreign policy, which drew France into war with Prussia in 1870.

After the Fall

Defeat in the Franco-Prussian War, which began on a pretext but ended with a unified and powerful German Empire in possession of the French territory of Alsace and Lorraine, brought down the empire of Napoleon III. Bitter frustration with defeat and hatred of the Prussian invaders led the people of Paris to rise against the armistice signed by the provisional government—the politicians who had replaced Napoleon. The Paris Commune (1871) began as a patriotic refusal to accept defeat and a rejection of the corrupt Second Empire, but became a rejection of the provisional government as well. Ultimately, the Communards (as those who resisted the Prussians and the provisional government were called) challenged property owners and those in the French countryside.

When the provisional government agreed to peace terms with Germany and demanded that the rent and debts not collected during the war be paid, the Communards refused to obey. The revolutionary forces that had been growing for a generation came to the fore; they differed greatly in their programs for the future, but were all republicans. They included the followers of Pierre Joseph Proudhon (see page 538), who were very influential among the artisans and small entrepreneurs. Also, groups of republican and socialist veterans of the Revolution of 1848 gathered, from prisons, from hiding, and from exile. An additional unit included the disciples of Auguste Blanqui, an old insurrectionist. For two months in the spring of 1871, the revolutionaries ruled Paris, always guided by the heroic precedents of the Jacobins of 1793 and the radicals of June 1848. Then, Adolphe Thiers, head of the provisional government that still governed the rest of France and the man who had accepted Bismarck's peace terms for lifting the Prussian siege, himself ordered a siege of Paris. The fighting was bitter and desperate, with many acts of terrorism and violence. Both sides in this civil war set fires that destroyed large parts of the city they loved. The Communards were defeated and treated as traitors: 20,000 of them were executed without trial; and those who were tried received harsh sentences (death, life imprisonment, and transportation to prison colonies).

The Commune became legendary. Across Europe, governing classes were terrified by the hatred that they imagined the masses to feel. But most Communards were ardent French patriots, not international revolutionaries; their desperate economic plight had driven them to action, not some ideological commitment to the abolition of private property. Nevertheless, many of the governing elite decided that the people should be ruled with an iron fist.

International revolutionaries, both socialists and anarchists, thought they saw a radicalization of the people in the desperate acts of the Communards. These revolutionaries also became convinced that the political leaders of other countries would be just as hard as Thiers had been when he used French troops against the French people, and they doubted that society would evolve toward socialism. The masses, said revolutionaries like Marx, must perfect their organizations for insurrections and violent seizure of power. Workers must learn to be as ruthless as Thiers. Other radicals, appalled by the bloodbath, argued for using the ballot box and organizing political parties; in their view, the power of the modern state had become too great for insurrection to lead to revolution as it had in 1789, 1830, and 1848.

The Paris Commune and its brutal suppression by the government did not create social and political differences among the French, but what happened dramatized existing distinctions and intensified the hatred between social groups. With the empire defeated and the Commune suppressed, law and order were re-established under a harsh peace treaty. Burdened by an indemnity and the loss of Alsace and part of Lorraine, embittered by the experience of war and civil war, France slowly rebuilt its national unity and regained its place in Europe.

The Emergence of the Third Republic

At the time, no one expected that the government emerging from the next few years of political crisis would be another republic—and the longest one in the history of France (1870–1940). The monarchists formed the most numerous and most

Edouard Manet (1832–1883): Portrait of Émile Zola. Many intellectuals and students defended an Alsatian Jew, Captain Dreyfus, falsely convicted of treason. France was a battleground of demonstrations and riots over the Dreyfus affair. Among the Dreyfusards were novelists Émile Zola, Anatole France, Marcel Proust, and Charles Péguy; painter Paul Cézanne; and political figures Georges Clemenceau and Jean Jaurès. (*Alinari, Brogi/Art Resource*)

powerful political group; they seemed to offer stability and order without the dangers of radical, or even liberal, republicanism. But there were *two* conflicting monarchist parties: the Legitimists and the Orléanists. The Orléanists agreed to compromise, but the Legitimists refused to accept the tricolor, which symbolized the liberties won in the French Revolution.

The disunity among the monarchists enabled France to become a republic by default. However,

the French government did not become wholly republican until 1879. Until then, the constitution was monarchist and Marshal Marie Edmé MacMahon as president held executive authority. With no king willing to rule, the republicans gained power.

Somewhat in imitation of the British system, the republican government was made up of a powerful bicameral legislature—a senate and a chamber of deputies, which resembled the House of Commons—and a prime minister who had to have its support. Frenchmen had gained the right to vote in 1848 when the Second Republic had enacted the most democratic suffrage in Europe. The president was a figurehead, indicating the hope that no new Napoleon would rise to overthrow the regime; the result was an office that no talented politician wanted. Unlike Britain with its two-party system, France had many political parties, which exaggerated the differences between the French rather than modifying them, and contributed to instability. No one party had sufficient strength within parliament to provide strong leadership. Prime ministers resigned in rapid succession; cabinets rose and fell frequently, giving the impression of a state without direction. Political life seemed to be one of wheeling and dealing, but in the process, legislation was enacted that made elementary education free and compulsory and legalized trade unions. The Third Republic survived, but not without major crises.

Threats to the Republic

At times during the first generation of the Third Republic, dissatisfaction seemed to unite the right and the left. In the 1880s, scandals and corruption threatened to undermine the republic. Opposition centered around a dashing general, Georges Boulanger (1837–1891), whose popularity reminded many of Napoleon III. Was France to swing back to authoritarianism from its brief experiment with democratic republicanism? But Boulanger was a republican, and at the moment he was expected to seize power he fled to Belgium, where he committed suicide on the grave of his former mistress. The crisis forced radicals and moderates together in defense of the republic.

Almost immediately, another scandal was exposed. Several republican deputies were implicated in a giant stock swindle in the financing and building of the Panama Canal. They had taken bribes, then tried to cover this up. The low level of public morality shocked the people; many thought that all politics was immoral, and others believed specifically that democratic politics was. Neither attitude helped build a republican morality.

The crisis that tore France in two for over a decade—the Dreyfus affair—came closely on the heels of the Boulanger affair and the Panama Canal scandals. In 1894, Captain Alfred Dreyfus, an Alsatian-Jewish artillery officer, was wrongly accused of having sold secrets to the Germans. After a court martial, he was condemned to life imprisonment on Devil's Island. Anti-Semitic elements joined with the republic's opponents, including the army, the clergy, and monarchists, to denounce and block every attempt to clear Dreyfus of the charges against him. In the beginning, few people defended Dreyfus; the vast majority felt that the honor of France and the army was at stake. Then individuals, mainly radical republicans, came to his defense, including the writers Anatole France and Émile Zola and the future republican leader Georges Clemenceau, along with university students. They protested and demonstrated, insisting on a retrial and a revision of the verdict. After many humiliations, Dreyfus was finally cleared in 1906.

The result of the victory of the radical republicans, however, was a fierce campaign to root out those opposing the republic. The radicals attacked the church, expelled religious orders, confiscated their property, and waged a vigorous campaign to replace the influence of the parish priest with that of the district schoolmaster. Complete separation of church and state was ordered. France became a secular state, and taxes no longer supported the parishes and schools.

France on the Eve of War

The Dreyfus case exposed and exaggerated the problems of French society. The struggle for the control of education—the secularization of France, as it was called—revealed the gulf between the issues that agitated the elite from those that concerned the masses. In England and Germany at the turn of the twentieth century, the parliaments were beginning to make reforms calculated to have mass appeal. The governments were providing some rudiments of a state-supported welfare system for working people and were backing their programs with a fairer tax structure. But France had no income tax and no national pension scheme until World War I.

Despite progress in the middle of the nineteenth century, French economic development lagged. France had fewer and smaller industries than Britain or Germany; more French people lived in rural areas or in small communities; in general, industry, trade unions, and socialist groups tended to be decentralized rather than national; artisans were much more influential than proletarians. For a generation after the bitter suppression of the Paris Commune, French labor was markedly antipolitical. For a decade, its leadership was broken and dispersed within France or in exile. Militants argued against cooperating with the republic or with any bourgeois government.

In the 1880s, both trade unionism and political parties with a socialist program began to make headway and to press for social reform through the democratic parliamentary institutions of the republic. France was very slow, however, to enact social measures such as pensions and regulations governing working conditions, wages, and hours. Such measures, which might have improved the lives of ordinary people, were regarded by the ruling class as socialism and by the socialists as tokens to buy off workers. Radical syndicalism (which advocated bringing industries and government under the control of workers) and even anarchism had many supporters among workers and intellectuals; instead of political action, they preferred to wage economic war against the state through strikes. A wave of strikes beginning in 1909 ended the following year with the government suppressing a national railway strike. Not surprisingly, socialists, syndicalists, and anarchists were all suspicious of politics and politicians.

France was a troubled country, and the Third Republic was not a popular regime. The church, the army, socialism, and even memories of the monarchy and the empire inspired deeper passions than the republic, which survived only because the dissension among its enemies allowed it to. France approached World War I as a deeply divided country; at the time, few would have believed that the war would reveal that the French nation had united despite the scandals and conflicts.

Germany, 1870–1914

Midcentury Germany was dominated by the struggle for unification. (See Chapter 25.) The result of unification was a German Empire that enabled Prussia to control all the German states and European politics as well. The king of Prussia was emperor, and Bismarck, the "Iron Chancellor," was responsible only to the emperor. Bismarck was the man of the hour for German conservatives and liberals alike.

The Bismarckian Constitution

Bismarck's constitution, like Bonaparte III's, was hardly liberal, though it granted universal manhood suffrage and allowed the Reichstag (lower house) to discuss all topics. The government was federal, so the twenty-four states had some powers, while foreign affairs and defense were in the hands of the emperor and his chancellor. Aristocrats staffed the military, the foreign service, and the top echelon of the bureaucracy; they rejected contact with the bourgeoisie and the lower bureaucrats. The German kaiser, unlike the British monarch, had considerable control over lawmaking and foreign affairs and commanded the army and navy.

The German Empire did not have two-party government or guarantees of civil liberties. The only control over Bismarck was the Reichstag's refusal to pass the budget, an extreme measure the politicians were usually unwilling to take. Only the king-emperor could remove the chancellor or the cabinet members from office. German liberals did not vigorously struggle for basic political and civil liberties. They tolerated evasions of principle and practices that British liberals would never have allowed. Germany never developed a truly parliamentary system, and certainly not a liberal

society. Bismarck's political practices weakened liberal and democratic elements. He cared little for principle and regarded parties as mere interest groups; he believed they were incapable of making policy for the country. As a result of their experience in Bismarckian Germany, or their lack of it, political parties, with the exception of the Catholics and the socialists, tended to represent single issues or regional interests.

Bismarck's Kulturkampf

In Bismarck's mind, the Catholics and the socialists were internationalists who did not place the interests of Germany first. Almost 40 percent of Germany was Roman Catholic. Taking advantage of a split in the Catholic church over the question of papal infallibility, and of the prejudice stimulated by that doctrine among non-Catholics, Bismarck began to persecute Catholics. The Kulturkampf, struggle for culture, was a series of laws passed in 1873 that tried to subject the church to the state. The laws discriminated against the Jesuits and required state supervision of the church and training of priests in state schools. Catholics were required to be married by the state. Churchmen who refused to accept these laws were imprisoned or exiled. The German liberals did not defend the civil liberties of the Catholics against these laws.

Persecution only strengthened the German Catholics' loyalty, however; the Catholic Center party gained support. Prussian conservatives, though Protestant in religion, resented Bismarck's anticlerical policy, which could hurt Lutherans as well as Catholics. With the succession of Leo XIII to the papacy in 1878, Bismarck quietly opened negotiations for peace with the church.

Bismarck Versus the Socialists

In the late 1870s, Bismarck attacked the socialists. Ferdinand Lassalle (1825–1864), a charismatic lawyer-reformer who had support from workers and trade unionists and influence with Bismarck himself, formed a German Workers' Association, which he hoped would join patriotism to unionism among the workers. Marx and followers August Bebel and Wilhelm Liebknecht scoffed at Lassalle's program. They opposed attempts to get support from the emperor, the military, or the bureaucracy. Nevertheless, there were more Lassalleans than Marxists, so in 1875 they joined forces to create a German socialist party. The compromises made by socialist groups made little difference, however, because Bismarck intended to separate workers from their leaders and to crush the socialists. He was sure the liberals would fail to defend the socialists too.

Bismarck knew how to manipulate public opinion. When two attempts on the emperor's life occurred in 1878, he demanded that the socialists be suppressed. In reality, the socialists, few in number, were not a threat—their immediate practical program was a demand for civil liberties and democracy in Germany. Only the narrowest of conservative views would have seen the socialists as a danger, but many in Germany, particularly the Prussian Junker class, held such a narrow view. The liberals once again did not oppose Bismarck's special legislation outlawing subversive organizations and authorizing the police to ban meetings and newspapers. The Social Democratic party, like the Catholic Center party before, survived the persecution; it grew stronger and better disciplined as the liberals grew weaker, discredited by their unwillingness to act.

Bismarck's policy was not merely repressive. He tried to win the workers by paternalistic social legislation. Like many conservatives, he was disturbed by the effects of industrialization, which had developed at a rapid pace in the 1850s and 1860s. Germany was the first state to enact a program of social legislation for the proletariat, which included insurance against sickness, disability, accidents, and old age. The employer, the state, and the worker each contributed small amounts to an insurance fund. Many people called the legislation *state socialism*. Like socialists in every other nation, German socialists vehemently debated over whether they should cooperate with the state or try to use the state's power to enact socialism. These debates overestimated their power, which would not emerge until just before World War I.

Despite Bismarck's attempts to woo the workers away from socialism, the German working class continued to support the Social Democratic party in elections. It was a party and a way of life; its members belonged to the many socialist political organizations, youth and women's divisions, athletic leagues, and cultural societies. On the eve of World War I, union membership was roughly 3 million, and the Social Democratic party was the largest single party in Germany. The socialists talked revolution, but the unions and many party members favored policies of gradual reform. Great numbers of German workers were patriotic, even imperialistic, and thought their government deserved their loyalty.

Germany on the Eve of War

After the crash of 1873, Germany's economic growth was steady but not rapid. By the century's end, Germany had caught, and in some areas surpassed, the British. When Kaiser William II (1889–1918) ascended the throne, Germany possessed the most extensive sector of large-scale and concentrated industrial and corporate capitalism of any Great Power, with the largest and most powerful unions.

Germany's industrial growth was uneven, however. Though the heavy industries were quickly developing into giant monopolies or cartels, and mining and railroads were state-owned and state-operated, the rapidity of expansion from craft to giant monopoly in some industries was more important than the percentage of the German economy controlled by such industries. Many small firms were operating as well, and large-scale agricultural producers were still very powerful. Large unions had arisen to deal with the monopolies, but workers in smaller firms were still organized by craft.

The population rose one-third in the single generation of 1882 to 1902, but the industrial work force increased by 180 percent in that time, becoming 35 percent of the active labor force of 27 million people. Many of these people were called directly from the farm to work in heavily concentrated industries in alien urban environments. Only the peasants in Russia or peasant-immigrants in the United States experienced comparable dislocation. The conflicts between traditional sources of political and social power and the new organizations of industry and labor

German Industry: Krupp Works at Essen, Manufacturing Guns. The beginning of Kaiser William II's reign coincided with the explosion of German industrial and corporate capitalism. Calls for expansionist colonial policies were complemented by heavy industry that was willing and able to support German imperialism. (*Culver Pictures*)

contributed to great social dissatisfaction on the eve of World War I.

The kaiser was a brash, outspoken young man who alienated the leaders of the other powers. He dismissed Bismarck in order to pursue his own domestic and foreign policies, both of which were popular with the new industrialists. Because these policies led to World War I, the kaiser is held in disrepute, but two facts should be remembered. First, Germans were not as horrified by the kaiser's statements as foreigners were (or as historians have been since). Second, Bismarck had prepared the way for William II; Bismarck might have withstood the clamor for colonies, but did not. The alliance system that played an important part in touching off the declaration of war in 1914 was Bismarck's. Also the constitution—a peculiar mixture of aristocratic Prussian power in the upper house, democratic universal male suffrage that was manipulated to nonliberal ends, and an unassailable chancellor and military—was Bismarck's creation. His opportunistic maneuvers against Catholics, liberals, and socialists undermined the development of a viable parliamentary government. The bureaucracy, the military, and the chancellor remained out of the reach of the voting populace.

A symptom of the peculiar political system that governed this rapidly expanding economy was the fact that the Social Democrats were the one party that campaigned for chancellor responsibility, that is, for the ability of the legislature to reject the chancellor. Social Democrats urged many democratic measures. As their political leaders called for revolution, their followers urged their unions to win from the government those measures that would improve everyday life. In 1914 the most highly industrialized and powerful European nation with the largest and most successful socialist party was nevertheless subject to a political regime that preserved aspects of an absolute monarchy.

Austria-Hungary, 1866–1914

Following the Austro-Prussian War, Magyars and Germans became the dominant nationalities in the empire (see Chapter 25), but nationality struggles were not over. In succeeding decades, they consumed the Dual Monarchy's energies and obscured other issues, particularly economic backwardness.

Social and Economic Development

In Austria-Hungary, as in Italy and Russia, the government, which needed heavy industries for war and defense, played an important role in industrialization. The government gave tax incentives, tariff protection, and direct subsidies to the industries it favored. The defense sectors of the economy were the largest-scale operations in the empire; in this sector the government fostered the tendency toward monopoly and favoritism.

Other segments of the empire's economic system reflected the economic backwardness of the area. Most industry was consumer-oriented—small-scale operations in textiles and food processing. Craftsmen maintained their importance in central and southern Europe in general, and in Austria in particular. On the eve of World War I, Vienna was a large, intellectually and artistically brilliant, beautiful capital city with 2 million inhabitants who earned their living in much the same ways as, and on the same economic scales as they had in the previous century.

In Hungary a large percentage of the population worked in agriculture. About 30 percent of the urban population were independent artisans who did not hire any laborers; another 30 percent were employed in small workshops of not more than twenty workers, and usually fewer than ten.

The European-wide tendency toward heavy industry concentration in large firms capitalized by specialist banks, which characterized the post-1890s, was exaggerated in the underdeveloped states, such as Austria-Hungary. In Austria, as in Russia, this economic concentration reinforced the state's extraordinary power, but the most striking aspect of this development is that it took place in a society in which the court and the old aristocracy were almost totally closed to new ideas and new blood. Three or four hundred aristocratic families whose lives centered on the Hapsburg court dominated government and society. The German-speaking owners of great estates maintained splendid palaces in Vienna and elegant country homes for weekends. Unlike aristocracies in the rest of Europe, Austria's upper crust excluded the artistic and intellectual elites as well as the lower-level aristocracy—at a time when Vienna's intellectual circle was one of the world's most brilliant. The lesser aristocracy were ennobled for serving the state in the military, the bureaucracy, or other ways. Some very important bankers and industrialists reached this lower level, but the aristocracy's upper rank was closed to them. Yet the values of the upper rank were accepted by the lower, which meant that the Hapsburgs themselves remained the source of authority and prestige throughout Austrian society, in much the same fashion as the Romanovs in Russia.

In Hungary, the entrepreneurial and business classes were even less respected than they were in Austria, a reflection of the backward state of Hungary's industrial development. The dominant Magyar landed magnates and gentry cared so little for commerce and industry that the field was left open to non-Magyar subjects, in particular, Austrian Germans, Czechs, and Jews. Non-Magyars were constrained from political activity, but economic development was almost totally in their hands. In this instance, the minorities benefited greatly from Magyar prejudices.

Politics in the Dual Monarchy

Nothing in the dualist political system excluded the possibility of representation or even autonomy for other minority nationalities, such as the Czechs, the Poles, or the South Slavs. From 1870 to 1914, the emperor's advisers, responding to the demands of Magyars and Germans or those of Slavic minorities, shifted back and forth between policies of decentralization (to conciliate real national grievances) and centralization, or at best of dualism. At times, the two segments of the monarchy pursued very different domestic policies.

In the wake of German unification and the establishment of a new constitution, Austria centralized, hoping to control and suppress Slavic nationalist aspirations. One of the measures of centralization (opposition to regionalism) in Germany, Italy, and other states was to practice secularization, which in other states usually meant the pursuit of anticlerical policies. Liberal governments instituted civil marriage and restrictions on the papacy, expressing their disapproval of the doctrines of papal infallibility promulgated in 1870. In Austria, however, Emperor Franz Joseph, a devout Catholic, called a halt to the liberal centralization policies of the dominant German ethnic group so long as they were tied to anticlericalism; this act strengthened the minority groups' hopes of achieving national autonomy.

For more than a decade, from 1879 to 1893, a coalition of national minorities, conservatives, and Catholic clerics won concessions from the government. A socialist labor movement also developed during that period. The government chose to follow a Bismarckian policy of suppressing the Socialist party while enacting social legislation to protect workers. In the Dual Monarchy, as in Germany, the Socialist party fought for fundamental political rights, such as universal manhood suffrage. Socialists argued that the class struggle was the primary issue and the nationality question secondary. The universal suffrage measure was overwhelmingly defeated because virtually every national group decided that it was more important to keep their national rivals from voting than to extend the vote among themselves. Rather than advocate universal representation, each group insisted on its special right to political autonomy, comparable to the special position of the Magyars. Not until 1907 did universal manhood suffrage pass, and then only in the Austrian half of the empire. From this experience, the Austrian Social Democrats developed a program that tried to counteract intense nationalism, particularly of the racial stripe practiced by German and Magyar ruling national groups. In the Second International (1889–1914), the Austrians were leading spokespersons for reconciling the national aspirations of repressed minorities with socialist demands at a time when many of their European colleagues thought socialists had to oppose any manifestation of nationalism.

Meanwhile, throughout the period from 1867 to the outbreak of World War I, Hungary moved toward greater centralization, demanding more room for independent action. The hottest issue revolved around the army, where the Magyars insisted on separate Magyar regiments with Magyar, rather than German, as the language of command. The emperor insisted on a unified army and refused to accept the Magyar's demands. The Magyars finally relented, but not until legislative debate on the issue had nearly ended in violence.

Austria-Hungary on the Eve of War

In the decade immediately before the outbreak of World War I, class conflict became as great an issue as the nationality struggles. In Austria, the working class demanded social change. In Hungary, oppressed peasantry, usually Slavs, challenged all-powerful Magyar landlords whose great wealth was based on export agriculture. In Bohemia, industrialization on a grand scale exacerbated class separation, which intensified the nationality struggle between Czechs and the dominant Germans.

The Hapsburg Empire's breakdown in World War I frequently obscures for some people the fact of its great endurance. The empire had existed for centuries. Even as nationalism burst on the scene in the nineteenth century, the Hapsburgs continued to rule. With industrialization, class antagonisms intensified; still the empire survived. But in 1914 the Hapsburg military high command advocated war in the hope of fortifying the emperor and the army—the only remaining institutions of unity. They lost that gamble.

Italy, 1870–1914

Italian nationalists expected greatness from the unification of their country, so long conquered, plundered, divided, and ruled by absolute princes. In each cause for rejoicing, however, Italians had to face a nagging doubt as well. The economic backwardness of the nation forestalled industrial and political development. The impoverished and illiterate people and their republican leaders expected much of the Italian state, but their expectations would not be fulfilled.

Italy, an overwhelmingly Roman Catholic country, was split by religious controversy. Many Italians wanted a unified Italy in which the pope played less of a political role. Liberals and republicans wanted a secular state, with civil marriage and public education, which was anathema to the church. Pope Pius IX refused to accept this new Italy, whose leaders confiscated papal territories, closed religious houses, and took church properties.

Another divisive factor was Italy's long tradition of separate and often rival states. Some principalities resisted unification under Victor Emmanuel, the Piedmontese king. Numerous Italians doubted the central government would deal justly with every region. Many Italians argued for federalism, wherein some government powers—defense, foreign affairs, and perhaps railroad building—would fall to the central government, but many important aspects of life, such as education, would remain in the hands of local governments.

Furthermore, few Italians could participate in the constitutional monarchy. Of the 27 million citizens, only about 2 million could vote—even after the reforms of 1881 that tripled the electorate. Liberals could point out that almost every literate male could vote, but this achievement was small consolation to those who had fought for unification but now were denied voting privileges because they did not pass a literacy test. The government was comprised of ministers responsible to the king (as in Germany), an upper house of appointed members, and an elected lower house. The political parties were small groups gathered around a few personalities; parties and ideologies did not mean much when an ambitious politician wanted to take office. For example, a man might be elected to the lower house as a member of the left, only to move to the center in order to hold cabinet office. To Italians, parliament seemed to be a place where deals were made and corruption prevailed.

Among Italian workers, cynicism about the government was so deep that many turned to anarchism and syndicalism, attracted by the rejection of authority and the tactics of terrorism, assassination, and general strikes. Such workers shared many of the class feelings that French workers expressed after the Paris Commune. Strong unions, socialist ideals, and disgust with parliamentary government led the workers to believe that direct action would gain more than elections and parties.

In some rural areas, particularly in the south, the peasants were so isolated from the national political and economic life that traditional patterns of loyalty to the local landowner, now also a political leader, persisted. Catholic, loyal to their landlord, and bitterly unhappy with their economic situation, they saw few signs of the new state other than taxation and conscription. Often their children migrated to the north to work in factories or moved even farther—to the New World.

The ruling elite brushed aside Italy's difficult social and economic problems and concentrated instead on issues more easily expressed to an inexperienced political nation: nationalism, foreign policy, and military glory. The politicians trumpeted Italy's ambitions for Great Power status to justify military expenditures beyond the means of such a poor state. They furnished the rationale for Italy's scramble for African and Mediterranean territories by promising that their expansionist foreign policy would provide the solution to all Italy's social ills: the profits from exploiting others would pay for badly needed social reforms, and the raw materials gained would fuel industrialization. None of these promises came true, which deepened the cynicism of a disillusioned people. As a foreign and as a domestic policy, this pursuit of glory was too costly for the fragile nation.

Before World War I, Italy was deeply divided politically. A wave of strikes and rural discontent gave sufficient warning to political leaders that they declared neutrality, deciding, unlike Russia, not to risk the shaky regime by entering the war. But the appeals of expansionism were too great for them to maintain this policy.

Russia, 1825–1914

Of far greater diversity and territorial sway than even the Hapsburg monarchy, nineteenth-century Russia spread from the Prussian border to the Pacific Ocean, a Eurasian giant. The huge borderlands and the diversity of peoples inhabiting them reaffirmed the autocratic tradition of the Russian state. Russia possessed neither a loyal and intelligent nobility of independent means nor an enterprising and well-to-do middle class; it also lacked the creative competition of free citizens. For several centuries the state itself had taken over the responsibility for mobilizing resources, growing all-powerful while reducing its subjects to pawns. Even in the early nineteenth century, only two classes of people were said to exist in the Russian Empire: the servitors of the tsar—army officers, officials, and the landed nobility from which they sprang—and the serfs who served the servitors. The urban people, merchants and craftsmen who had been forcibly organized into guilds in the late eighteenth century, enjoyed little freedom; they were few in number and generally despised like the common folk by the nobility.

The servitors, Europeanized since the time of Peter the Great, constituted a small privileged minority. They were separated from the mass of the population by barriers of education, culture, and experience that were more profound than any class distinctions in Europe. Like the tsar himself, they lived in fear of popular uprisings. The tsar had additional reasons for fear: the country suffered from external insecurity, especially in its relations with the Great Powers of Europe, which were better armed, more prosperous, and above all, had popular support for their foreign policies.

Nicholas I: Progress and Repression

Russia's fortunes depended on its political order, which centered more than in western Europe on the rulers. The tsarist government, its central institutions reorganized on the lines of Western models in the wake of the French Revolution, took a decidedly conservative turn after Napoleon's defeat, and for good reason. Many returning Russian officers, asking why Russia could not share the civilized life they had seen in western Europe, turned revolutionary. The unsuccessful Decembrist uprising in 1825, during the brief interlude between the death of Alexander I (1801–1825) and the accession of Nicholas I (1825–1855), was the effort of a small group of conspirators demanding a constitution. Fear of revolution determined the character of the reign of Nicholas I and of tsarist governments thereafter.

Aware of the subversive influence of foreign ideas and conditions, Nicholas decreed an ideology of Russian superiority, called *official nationality*. The Russian people were taught to believe that the Orthodox creed of the Russian church, the autocratic rule of the tsar, and Russia's Slavic culture made the Russian Empire superior to the West. To enforce this contrived invincibility, Nicholas I created the Third Section, a secret agency of police spies, and controlled access to his country from Europe, drawing toward the end of his reign a virtual iron curtain to keep out dangerous influences. His ideal was a monolithic country run, like an army, by a vigorous administration centered on the monarch; all Russians were to obey his wise and fatherly commands.

However, in Nicholas's reign, corruption and deceit pervaded the bureaucracy. Society stagnated except for intense intellectual agitation

Russians Building the Trans-Siberian Railroad.
This scene of railroad building could have been
taken in North or South America, in India or
China, or in northern or southern Africa in the
nineteenth century. Railroads made vast stretches
of land accessible to many settlers. Building the
great railroads often brought together laborers
from diverse nationalities and races. The Trans-
Siberian Railroad, begun in 1891 in the hope that
it would usher in an era of heavy industrialization,
was completed in 1903, on the eve of the Russo-
Japanese War. (*The Bettmann Archive/BBC Hulton*)

among small circles of students. Yet the tsar also
promoted innovation. He ordered a railway built
between St. Petersburg and Moscow; he opened
schools and universities, hoping in vain to encourage Russian participation in the European
advance of knowledge without encouraging subversive comparison with the West.

The Crimean War (1854–1856) deflated
Nicholas I's ambition to make Russia victorious in
all comparisons with western Europe. Russian
threats to the Ottoman Empire and to Anglo-
French domination of the eastern Mediterranean
led to armed conflict fought on Russian soil. The
English and French expeditionary forces defeated
the Russian army. During the war, in a mood of
profound crisis, a new regime began under Alexander II (1855–1881).

Alexander II: Reforms and Westernization

Alexander II was hailed as "tsar liberator," but
suffered from an emotional instability that reflected the dilemma of his reign. On one hand, he
was determined to preserve autocratic rule; his
country lacked all prerequisites for constitutional
government. On the other hand, he wanted Rus-

sia to achieve what had made western Europe strong—the energetic support and free enterprise of its citizens. Whether stimulating popular initiative was possible without undermining autocracy was the key puzzle for him and for his successors to the end of the tsarist regime.

Alexander's boldest reform was the emancipation of the serfs in 1861. The serfs were liberated from bondage to the nobility and given land of their own, but not individual freedom. They remained tied to their village and to their households, which owned the land collectively. Emancipation did not transform the peasants into enterprising and loyal citizens.

For the nonpeasant minority, a package of other reforms brought new opportunities: limited self-government for selected rural areas and urban settlements, an independent judiciary, and the rule of law. Trial by jury was introduced, as well as a novel profession—lawyers. Military service also underwent reform, so that all male Russians, regardless of status, were drafted into a citizen army granting as much equality as Russian conditions would permit.

Meanwhile, Alexander reopened the borders, allowing closer ties with Europe and westernizing Russian society. The rising class of business people and professional experts looked west and conformed to Western middle-class standards. There was some relaxation in the repression of non-Russian minorities. Railroads were constructed, which facilitated agricultural exports and permitted the import of Western goods and capital. For some years the economy boomed.

More significant in the long run was the flowering of Russian thought and literature. Since the late eighteenth century, the impact of Western culture on Russian life had created an extraordinary intellectual ferment; it came to a climax under Alexander II among a slowly growing group known as the *intelligentsia*. The intelligentsia's members were educated Russians whose minds were shaped by Western schooling and travel, yet who still were prompted by the "Russian soul." Caught between two conflicting cultures, their critical awareness was heightened by alienation. They examined Russian life with Western sensibilities and the West with Russian sensibilities. Members of the privileged classes, they tried to ease their troubled conscience by service to the common people, whom they idealized; at their best, they produced a brilliant literature that became a source of intense national pride and exerted a profound influence around the world. Fëdor Dostoevski and Leo Tolstoy wrote their greatest novels in the 1860s and 1870s. The intelligentsia quarreled with fierce sincerity over whether Russia should pursue superiority by imitating the West or by cultivating its own Slavic genius, possibly through a Pan-Slavic movement. Pan-Slavism, which glorified the solidarity of Russians with other Slavic peoples of eastern Europe, was a popular cause. Even more than the tsars, the intelligentsia hoped for a glorious Russia that would outshine the West.

Yet tsarist autocracy undercut their hopes. The tsar would not permit open discussion likely to provoke rebellion. Liberals advocating gradual change were thwarted by censorship and the police. The 1860s saw the rise of self-righteous fanatics ready to match the chicanery of the police and foment social revolution. By the late 1870s, they organized themselves into a secret terrorist organization. In 1881, they assassinated the tsar. The era of reforms ended.

The next tsar, Alexander III (1881–1894), a firm if unimaginative ruler, returned to the principles of Nicholas I. In defense against the revolutionaries, he perfected the police state, adapting Western methods and even enlisting anti-Semitism in its cause. He updated autocracy and stifled dissent, but he also promoted the economy. Russia had relied too heavily on foreign loans and goods; it had to build up its own resources. It also needed more railroads to bind its huge empire together. So in 1891 the tsar ordered construction of the Trans-Siberian Railroad. Soon afterward, Minister of Finance Sergei Witte used railroad expansion to boost heavy industry and industrialization generally.

Nicholas II: Industrialization and a Constitutional Experiment

In 1900, Witte addressed a far-sighted memorandum to the young Nicholas II (1894–1917), who, hopelessly unprepared and out of tune with the times, had succeeded his father in 1894:

Russia more than any other country needs a proper economic foundation for its national policy and culture. . . . International competition does not wait. If we do not take energetic and decisive measures so that in the course of the next decade our industry will be able to satisfy the needs of Russia and of the Asiatic countries which are—or should be—under our influence, then the rapidly growing foreign industries will . . . establish themselves in our fatherland and the Asiatic countries mentioned above. . . . Our economic backwardness may lead to political and cultural backwardness as well.[1]

Yet forced industrialization also brought perils. It propelled the country into alien and often hated ways of life; it created a discontented new class of workers and it impoverished agriculture; it promoted mobility, literacy, and contact with western Europe, thereby increasing political agitation among the professional classes, intelligentsia, workers, peasants, and subject nationalities. Indispensable for national self-assertion and survival, industrialization strained the country's fragile unity.

The first jolt, the Revolution of 1905, followed Russia's defeat by Japan in the Russo-Japanese War. (See Chapter 27.) Fortunately for the tsar, his soldiers stayed loyal. The autocracy survived, although now saddled with a parliament called the Imperial Duma, a concession to the revolution. The new regime, inwardly rejected by Nicholas II, started auspiciously. Under its freedoms, Russian art and literature flourished and the economy progressed. Agrarian reforms introduced the incentives of private property and individual enterprise into the villages. The supporters of the constitutional experiment hoped for a liberal Russia at last, but in vain.

The rulers of Russia between 1825 and 1914 had labored under enormous difficulties in their efforts to match the power and prestige of the great states of Europe. Two of them (Alexander II and Nicholas II) came to violent ends; the other two died in weariness and failure. Although the fear that the tsars inspired was real, their splendor was hollow. Their tragedy—the incompatibility of high hopes for their country's prominence in the world with the reality of limited resources, their own and those of their peoples—was understood neither by the liberal West nor by their critics among the intelligentsia, with whom they shared the vision of a superior Russia.

A Golden Age?

To thoughtful Europeans living in 1915, after a year of World War I the nineteenth century must have seemed a golden era. They might have viewed it as a period of unparalleled peace and progress, full of the promise of all that well-meaning people considered modern—liberal institutions and democratic movements, autonomous nations, scientific and industrial progress, and individual human development. The century just passed seemed one of progress in the production of goods, the alleviation of want, the development of technology, and the application of science to industry and medicine.

Part of that progress, in most minds, was the extension of constitutional and liberal government and the expression of humanitarian concern for others. Serfdom had been abolished in Europe; so had slavery in the United States and Brazil. Europeans spoke of self-government as a right. The importance of democracy had been acknowledged, and in most of Europe, universal manhood suffrage was in effect before the outbreak of the war.

The world had become smaller, more interdependent and cosmopolitan. Many Westerners were better educated and probably better fed, housed, and clothed than their counterparts in preceding eras. Europe was at the height of its power in the nineteenth century. European productive capacities had reached out to most areas of the world, and whether considered in aggregate as European culture or individually as German, French, English, or Italian culture, it was brilliant.

Yet people looking back from the vantage point of 1915 must have realized, too, that something had gone wrong in the nineteenth century. Authoritarian governments persisted in central, eastern, and southern Europe. Traditional institutions and groups still exercised their privileges at the expense of others, often by brutally repressing

Chronology 26.1 Europe in the Age of Industrialization

1846–47	Great famine in Ireland
1851	Louis Napoleon Bonaparte overthrows the Second Republic, becoming Emperor Napoleon III
1854–56	The Crimean War
1860s	Irish movement for republican form of government (the Fenians); Civil War in the United States; unification movements in German and Italian states
1861	Kingdom of Italy is formed; Alexander II, Russian tsar, emancipates the serfs and institutes reforms
1863	Emancipation of slaves in the United States
1867	Second Reform Bill doubles the English electorate
1870	The Third French Republic is established
1870–71	The Franco-Prussian War; the Paris Commune; creation of the German Empire with William I as kaiser and Bismarck as chancellor
1873	The Great Depression
1880s	Charles Stewart Parnell leads the Irish home rule movement in the British Parliament
1881	Tsar Alexander II is assassinated
1884	Reform Bill grants suffrage to most English men
1894–1906	The Dreyfus affair in France
1905	Revolution in Russia—Nicholas II grants the formation of the Imperial Duma; separation of church and state in France
1909	Lloyd George introduces "people's budget"
1911	Parliament Act limits the power of the House of Lords

opposition. Doubts had been stirred when the revolutions of 1848 had failed to reconcile national and class conflicts. Perhaps the bitter reaction to 1848 and the harsh reality of the midcentury wars of unification had perverted the ideals of liberal government and individual freedom. Many doubted the wisdom of democratic government as they saw the passions of the masses manipulated by cynical leadership. Perhaps the ideals of liberal government, individual freedom, national autonomy, and economic progress were not equally suited to every situation.

In the last part of the nineteenth century and the first part of the twentieth, liberal-democratic ideals fell prey to authoritarianism, extreme nationalism, imperialism, class conflict, and racism. But despite world war, mass destruction, and the manipulation of humanity in the name of nationalist passions, these ideals would survive and spread.

Note

1. Theodore H. Von Laue, *Sergei Witte and the Industrialization of Russia* (New York: Columbia University Press, 1963), p. 3.

Suggested Reading

Blake, R., *Disraeli* (1967). An excellent one-volume biography.

Chekhov, Anton, *Selected Stories,* especially "The Peasants," "Three Years," and "In Exile."

Dostoevsky, Fyodor, *Notes from the Underground.*

Eyck, Erich, *Bismarck and the German Empire* (1950). A very critical biography; an abridgment of a larger work.

Ford, Colin, and Brian Harrison, *A Hundred Years Ago* (1983). An excellent social history of Britain with fine photographs.

Goldberg, Harvey, *The Life of Jean Jaurès* (1962). The most readily available work on this important man.

Gordon, Craig, *Politics of the Prussian Army* (1955). A very valuable study with important implications for German and European history.

Gorky, Maxim, *My Childhood.*

Hobsbawm, Eric, *The Age of Capital* (1988). A Marxist interpretation of mid-nineteenth-century Europe.

Holborn, Hajo, *History of Modern Germany, 1840–1945,* vol. 3 (1969). A definitive work.

Johnson, D., *France and the Dreyfus Affair* (1967). The best of many books on the controversial affair.

Joll, James, *Europe Since 1870* (1973). A valuable general survey, particularly good on socialism in the individual nations.

Kann, Robert, *The Multinational Empire: Nationalism and National Reform in the Hapsburg Monarchy, 1840–1918,* 2 vols. (1950–1964). A definitive text.

Mack Smith, Denis, *Italy: A Modern History,* rev. ed. (1969). An excellent survey, with emphasis on the theme of the failure of Italy to develop viable liberal institutions or economic solutions.

Mayer, Arno, *The Persistence of the Old Regime* (1981). His theme is how much of traditional Europe survived to the eve of World War I.

Mosse, W. E., *Liberal Europe, 1848–1875* (1974). A comparative history of Europe in the liberal era.

Noland, Aaron, *The Founding of the French Socialist Party, 1893–1905* (1956). A well-informed study of the origins of the Socialist party in France.

O'Brien, C. C., *Parnell and His Party, 1880–90* (1957). A good book on this important Irish leader.

Seton-Watson, Christopher, *Italy from Liberalism to Fascism* (1967). An excellent survey of Italian history.

Taylor, A. J. P., *The Hapsburg Monarchy, 1809–1918* (1965). A well-written, incisive, brief history.

———, *Bismarck: The Man and the Statesman* (1967). A brilliant portrait of the complicated man who dominated the second half of the nineteenth century.

Webb, R. K., *Modern England from the Eighteenth Century to the Present* (1968). A well-informed, readable book that is balanced on controversial issues.

Williams, Roger, *The World of Napoleon III,* rev. ed. (1965). An indispensable fresh look at this fascinating man.

Wright, Gordon, *France in Modern Times,* 2nd ed. (1974). A good survey of the entire period.

Zeldin, Theodore, *France, 1848–1945: Ambition, Love, and Politics,* vol. 1 (1973). An explanation of the forces that held France together.

Review Questions

1. Why was England seen by many as the model liberal nation in the middle decades of the nineteenth century?

2. How did the competition between political parties further reform in Victorian England?

3. How did the Reform Bill of 1867 usher in a new era in British politics?

4. In England, the middle class and the workers often worked together for reform in the period from 1860 to 1914. In France they rarely did. Why?

5. How did Napoleon III's domestic and foreign policies conflict?

6. What was the general crisis of liberalism after 1870?

7. How did the conservatives attempt to win over the masses after 1870?

8. Historians disagree about the merits of the Bismarckian legacy to Germany. Discuss evidence for this disagreement.

9. What social problems did unified Italy fail to resolve?

10. How did its social system hold Austria-Hungary together against the disruptive effect of national conflict and government structure?

11. On the eve of World War I, most of the European states were threatened by a crisis, either political or social. Discuss the threat of revolution or social change among the Great Powers on the eve of the war.

12. What problems did the tsars from Nicholas I to Nicholas II face in ruling Russia? Given the conditions of their country, could they have become constitutional monarchs?

27

Western Imperialism: Global Dominance

From the long perspective, European history has been one of expansion. In the sixteenth century, Europeans conquered and settled substantial regions of the Americas; from the sixteenth to the eighteenth centuries, Europeans made inroads in southeast Asia and Africa for lucrative trade in spices, silks, finished goods, and slaves; in the eighteenth century, Europeans fought a series of wars with one another for the rights to trade in Asia and the Americas. By the end of the eighteenth century, though, the old slaving stations in Africa had declined, as had the Caribbean sugar trade and the mines of Central and South America. Revolutionary wars for independence in the United States and Latin America seemed to bring an end to colonialism and to usher in a new era of trade and investment without political control. Trade with former colonies was no less profitable, and scarcely less secure, than trade with colonies.

For much of the nineteenth century, Europeans showed little interest in adding to the remnants of the eighteenth-century empires. Advocates of free trade argued that commerce would go to whichever country could produce the best goods most cheaply. Efforts to add colonies would be better expended in improving industry, they said. They also hoped Europeans had grown too civilized to fight over trade networks. European liberals, in particular, believed a major war would destroy the livelihoods of too many people because commerce was so interdependent.

Nonetheless, European influence over the rest of the world grew in the nineteenth century. Masses of European immigrants made new homes in North and South America, Australia, and New Zealand. As European nations industrialized, world trade expanded greatly, drawing previously untouched peoples into the network of supply and demand of raw materials, finished goods, and capital. The expansion of world trade and the spread

The First Ships Through the Suez Canal. (*The Bettmann Archive/BBC Hulton*)

of Western ideas along with Western technology continued to take place even without extension of political empire.

Yet at the end of the century, the European presence shifted abruptly from commercial penetration to active conquest, political control, and exploitation of previously unclaimed and in many ways untouched territories. From about 1880 to 1914, Europeans confronted each other, willing to fight over stretches of desert or rain forest that they could scarcely locate on the map. Asians and Africans who could not resolve conflicts among themselves found their lives controlled and their lands occupied. Even those who were able to unite found themselves unable to counter Western military and technological superiority.

In the last two decades of the nineteenth century, European nations very rapidly laid claim to Africa, seizing goods, annexing territories, and carving out empires if local rulers were too weak or too self-interested to prevent it. Westerners exploited the weakness of the Japanese and Chinese dynasties, forcing commercial connections and the cession of treaty ports and territory to gain economic and political advantage in the Far East. In the second half of the century, the British deprived India of all semblance of independence, ruling it both directly and indirectly, but ruling it nonetheless. Latin American development and prosperity became so dependent on Europe and the United States that many people questioned the appearance of political autonomy maintained by Latin American governments.

European domination of most of the world persisted until after World War II, and the impact of *imperialism*—the domination by one country of the political, economic, or cultural life of another country or region—is felt in our own day.

The Emergence of the New Imperialism

What accounted for the struggle of Europeans to claim and control the entire world? Some historians suggest that the *new* imperialism (to differentiate it from the *colonialism* of settlement and trade of the sixteenth to eighteenth centuries) was a direct result of industrialization. With intensified economic activity and competition, Europeans struggled for raw materials, markets for their commodities, and places to invest their capital. In the late nineteenth century, many politicians and industrialists believed that the only way their nation could ensure the economic necessities was the annexation of overseas territories; if they trusted their nations' economies to the free market, competitor states might triumph instead. Captains of industry defended the new empires to their sometimes reluctant governments and countrymen, predicting dire consequences if their nation failed to get its share of the world markets.

Other historians are more skeptical. They point to the fact that most areas claimed by Europeans and Americans were not profitable sources of raw materials or wealthy enough to be good markets. For Europeans and Americans the primary trading and investment venues were Europe and America rather than Asia or Africa. Some individual businesses made colonial profits, but most colonies proved unprofitable for the western taxpayer. Between 1865 and 1914, for example, only 39 percent of British investment went to lands of the Empire outside the British Isles, 28 percent of that amount going to self-governing dominions. The rate of return on the average did not surpass that from home investments. In general, the colonies did not attract surplus European population that could contribute to the mother country's economy. The United States tended to draw most of the European emigration, which also streamed to Australia, Canada, New Zealand, and South America. Two-thirds of British emigration went outside the empire, mostly to the United States. Italians certainly did not migrate to Italy's African territories, and the French scarcely migrated at all. But the historians' skepticism does not lead them to doubt that the new imperialism resulted from a mix of industrialization and nationalism. Neither do they doubt that policymakers hoped empire would solve economic problems, which were particularly pressing after the great crash of 1873.

The economic justifications of imperialism are inseparable from the intensely nationalistic ones. Newly unified states, Germany and Italy demanded colonies as recognition of their Great Power status; leaders in those two nations were convinced that Britain's status depended on colonies and naval power. Awareness of the heavier

A Christian Missionary in Togoland (Ghana).
Throughout the nineteenth century, Christian missionaries had gone to Asia, Africa, and Latin America to preach and to carry on the crusade against slavery. Many of these Christians devoted their lives to accomplishing their goals; at the same time, many carried with them the ethnocentric values and judgments of their compatriots who thought that non-Europeans were backward and uncivilized. (*Culver Pictures*)

tax burden of British subjects, the expenses of empire, and the greatly increased possibility of war with rival nations or resistant subjects could not dissuade these leaders from an imperial course. Having lost ingloriously to Prussia in 1870, France also turned overseas, hoping to recoup some prestige and to add to its manpower and wealth for future European struggles. Many leaders hoped that a policy of imperialism would win them the loyalty of their own people; some argued that the well-being of the workers depended on colonies. Americans, who had built one of the world's great industrial powers after the Civil War, trumpeted their achievements by defeating once-imperial Spain in Cuba and the Philippines. Economically backward Russia pushed east to the

Pacific and south toward India for ports and resources to develop its commerce and industry. In the 1890s, the Japanese announced that they had joined the world's Great Powers and fought with China to win control of Korea's raw materials and markets.

The nationalistic competition between the Europeans led them, for a time, to extend their power struggles to Africa and Asia. Far away from their European boundaries, leaders acquired territories for strategic reasons or sometimes just to keep competitors from doing so. Britons reasoned that they had to keep the Germans from gaining a foothold in the Middle East because it might open the Indian Ocean—and the British-dominated Indian subcontinent—to them, and to keep the Russians out of Afghanistan because they might push into India. Bismarck, the master diplomat, encouraged the French to expand in Africa, knowing full well that this course would bring them into conflict with the Italians and the English. Pursuit of empire would distract the French from Alsace and Lorraine, which Germany had taken from them in 1870, he thought, and it would divide Frenchmen into imperialists and anti-imperialists, creating another political rift to weaken the French government. Sometimes even a master game player can fumble, though; when Germany's shift to colonialism called for naval expansion after Bismarck's dismissal, Britain began to ally in European politics with its colonial rival France.

The British like to think that they were not aggressively imperialistic but were merely defending the responsibilities of an empire they already possessed. They tended to define enormous amounts of territory and water as essential to the defense of their Indian colony. But nations with less extensive or less lucrative empires saw Britain as their primary rival for the spoils of imperialism—for "a place in the sun," as the Germans liked to phrase it. In Russia, a small clique of nobles and officers urged expansion, knowing that their move into Asia would bring them into conflict with Britain (and, later, that it would mean confronting the Japanese). Thus, the conflicts between Europeans were played out for a while in Asia and Africa, perhaps contributing to the relative peace of Europe itself. In the long run, the tense atmosphere of imperialism—the militarism and the racism—contributed to a more devastating conflict in Europe, World War I, which engaged the empires as well.

The most extreme ideological expression of nationalism was Social Darwinism (see Chapter 24), with its image of national vitality and competition between fit and unfit. Social Darwinists vigorously advocated empire. They argued that the strong nations—by definition, those that were successful at expanding industry and empire—would survive and that others would not. To these elitists, all white men were better fit than nonwhites to prevail in the struggle for dominance, but among Europeans, some nations were deemed more fit than others for the competition. Usually, Social Darwinists thought their nation the best, which sparked their competitive enthusiasm, but some feared that their people were incapable of the endurance and sacrifice necessary to win. Their fears did not tame their imperialism, however, as they called for colonies to test and train the people for the struggles ahead. Social Darwinists were not embarrassed by the fact that their arguments were blatantly racist; they even applied racial terms to their own people when expressing class inequality. When working-class men proved physically unfit to serve in the Boer War, British imperialists became advocates of health and education reforms to improve the British "race" so that it could rule an empire. In the popular mind, the concepts of evolution justified the exploitation of "lesser breeds without the law" by superior races. This language of race and conflict, of superior and inferior people, was widely expressed in the Western states.

Not all advocates of empire were Social Darwinists, however. Some did not think of themselves as racists. In fact, they believed that the extension of empire, law, order, and industrial civilization would raise "backward peoples" up the ladder of evolution and civilization. In the nineteenth century, Europeans, except for missionaries, rarely adopted the customs or learned the languages of local people when they did business in Asia, Africa, or Latin America. They had little or no sense that other cultures and other peoples had merit and deserved respect. In contrast, in the seventeenth and eighteenth centuries, traders had often adopted the ways of the people with whom they came into contact. The European attitude toward other cultures had clearly changed.

Many Westerners believed it was their duty as Christians to set an example and to educate others. Missionaries were the first to meet and learn about many peoples and the first to develop writing for those without a written language. Christian missionaries were ardently opposed to slavery, and throughout the century they had gone to unexplored African regions to preach against slavery, which was still carried on by Arab and African traders. But to end slavery, many of them believed that Europeans must furnish law, order, and stability. They thought the extension of the world market economy would create alternatives to the ancient occupations of war, pillage, and enslavement of the vanquished.

Every country contained persons who thought that imperial glory was good for the masses, bringing democracy in line with the grand purposes of the state. Still others thought that glory was good for the classes because the traditional elite in the military, diplomatic corps, and civil service would have prestigious positions in a great empire. And, of course, some believed that their culture, religion, and civilization ought to be spread to other peoples of the world for their own good.

Some of the passion for imperialism was sparked by interest in exotic places. At the turn of the nineteenth century, the expeditions by Mungo Park, a Scottish explorer, on the Niger River in West Africa stimulated the romantic imagination. The explorations of David Livingstone in the Congo Basin and of Richard Burton and John Speke (who raced with each other and with Livingstone to find the source of the Nile River) fascinated many Europeans. In the beginning of the century, expeditions were a matter of adventure and scientific curiosity; they often included explorers from several countries. After midcentury, national prestige became a goal in these forays. Sponsored by national geographic and exploratory societies and encouraged by their nation's military, explorers captured the public imagination in much the same way that astronauts do today. Individual personalities, who seemed larger than life to their contemporaries, often saw exploration as an escape from a humdrum or stultifying existence at home.

Individuals and nations competed to find the highest mountain, the longest river, the highest waterfall, the land never before seen by white men. Such superlatives called men and women away from their ordinary lives to adventure—if not to experience it, at least to dream of it. The fiction of English authors Rudyard Kipling (1865–1936) and H. Rider Haggard (1856–1925) and their many inferior imitators stimulated the passion for faraway places and unknown peoples. Writers told of European bravery and sacrifice in the colonies; in books for young people, they wrote inspirationally of heroes, adventures, and achievements and helped shape the attitudes of the next generation. Kipling wrote: "Take up the White Man's Burden—/Send forth the best ye breed—/Go bind your sons to exile/To serve your captives' need." He also wrote of the Indian Gunga Din, whose faithful service to his white masters, some British soldiers in battle, won him their respect. Until twentieth-century writers like Joseph Conrad, George Orwell, Olive Schreiner, and E. M. Forster, authors rarely described the exploitation, cruelty, and abuses of empire.

A Global Economy

The Western economy became truly global by the end of the nineteenth century. New markets, new technology, and overseas trade and investment were moving toward a world market economy, although untouched and undeveloped areas did exist. As the Western powers industrialized, even the small and backward European countries exploited raw materials and markets in the rest of the world. In many parts of Europe, even the working classes and the peasantry were able to buy goods from faraway places that had previously been available only to the very wealthy.

The underdeveloped areas of the world, in turn, found markets for their crops and were able to buy European commodities—at least, the wealthy could. But being part of the world economy also made these areas subject to the smallest tremors on the European and American stock exchanges and to changing fashions of consumption. Participation in the world market brought wealth to a few people, but it meant hardship for many, as well as loss of traditional customs and social relationships.

Increasing crop production to satisfy European and American markets often created problems. Producing for the Western market meant turning land that had grown food for families over to export crops like coffee or indigo, thus reducing the food supply; it often meant consolidation of small peasant holdings in the hands of richer peasants or landlords. Thus, market forces drove the poorer peasants off the land, into debt to the landlord or to the usurer, and into cities. For most of the nineteenth century, the peasants felt bonded to their traditional masters, but in the twentieth century, they came to see themselves as enslaved by foreigners who either controlled the government or the world market. The passionate desire to escape this bondage has fueled revolutionary movements throughout the world.

Economic interdependence operated to the great advantage of Europeans and Americans; the world economy enriched and eased the lives of consumers as early as the beginning of the twentieth century. Many Europeans and Americans dressed in Egyptian cotton, Australian wool, Chinese silk, and Argentinian leather and consumed Chinese tea or Colombian coffee; some had homes or offices furnished in hardwoods from Burma, Malaya, or Africa. Westerners could purchase all these goods, and many more, at prices so favorable that many luxury items became available to those who were not rich. Europeans and Americans could travel anywhere, using gold or easily available foreign currency exchanged at a rate almost always favorable to them. They could invest their money in the raw materials or the government bonds of virtually any area of the world and expect a good return. They also expected their investments to be secure and their property and person to be protected. Non-Western political authorities who could not guarantee that security, for whatever reason, risked intervention, perhaps occupation, by European or American forces. In some non-Western areas the governors had to grant *extraterritoriality,* or the right of Europeans to trial by their own laws in foreign countries. Europeans often also lived a segregated and privileged life in quarters, clubs, and whole sections of foreign lands or cities in which no native was allowed to live.

Control and Resistance

In the nineteenth century, changing technology widened the gap between Europe and other areas, making industrialized states for the first time clearly more powerful than the states in Asia and Africa. Europeans could bring to bear the enormous power of industry and of military technology, and European nation-states could mobilize the support of all their citizens. These facts made it unlikely that a non-European country or people could successfully resist a European state intent on conquest, although Ethiopia was able to resist Italy's incursions, North Africans kept the French on the defensive in Algeria and Morocco, and the Japanese held off potential invaders.

Europeans established varying degrees of political control over much of the rest of the world. Control could mean outright annexation and the governing of a territory as a colony. In this way Germany controlled Tanganyika (East Africa) after 1886, and Britain ruled much of India. Control could also mean status as a protectorate, in which the local ruler continued to rule but was directed, or "protected," by a Great Power. In this way the British controlled Egypt after 1882 and maintained authority over their dependent Indian princes, and France guarded Tunisia. There were also spheres of influence, in which, without military or political control, a European nation had special trading and legal privileges other Europeans did not have. At the turn of the century the Russians in the north and the British in the south, each recognizing the other's sphere of influence, divided Persia (Iran). Some peoples were so completely dependent on foreigners to buy their goods or to loan money that they seemed politically independent only in the most technical sense; they dared take no action that might upset their economic connections, not even action that might ease their debt crisis.

Nevertheless, many non-Europeans resisted American and European economic penetration and political control in varied ways, and the very process of resistance shaped their history and their self-awareness. In many areas, such as the Ottoman Empire, China, and Japan, ruling governments found ways of limiting the political influence of Western trading interests. Some countries tried, as Egypt did, to seek economic independence through modernization. The Turks played Europeans off against one another and maintained control over their lands outside Europe, if not in the Balkans. The Chinese emperor granted trading privileges or concessions, even control of cities to Europeans, but he kept China under his rule. The Japanese, responding to European and American commercial incursions, drastically changed their economy, their government, even aspects of their social structure, but they continued to control their territory.

These forms of resistance were carried out by rulers who could command loyal subjects. Other resisters—individuals, groups, and regional communities—sometimes retained traditional ways, rejecting Western education and secularization and often renewing institutions, particularly religious ones, that were falling into disuse when the Europeans arrived. Such resistance became a statement of both national and individual identity. A few out of the many instances of such resistance include the Sudanese Muslims' holy war led by the Mahdi Mohammed Ahmed against both Egyptian fellow Muslims, who were regarded as agents of the European nonbelievers, and the Europeans; the Boxer Rebellion in China; and the Sepoy Mutiny in India. Still others reacted to Western penetration with strongly nationalistic feelings and fought to strengthen the nationalism of their people, sometimes even going to Western universities, military schools, and factories to master the advanced technology. Mohandas Gandhi, Jawaharlal Nehru, Sun Yat-sen, Chiang Kai-shek, and Mustapha Kemal Atatürk are the most famous examples of nationalistic resistance to the West.

In most cases, however, efforts at resistance brought non-European peoples more firmly under Western control. When their interests were threatened, Europeans generally responded by annexing the offending region or establishing a protectorate. Resistance continued, nonetheless: whole peoples in Africa moved from place to place to escape European religion, taxes, and laws; and insurgent mountain people in Indochina and Algeria evaded French cultural influence or restricted it to the coastline. In some places Europeans were never fully secure in their control, but Western domination seemed a relentless global force at the time.

European Domination of Asia

The story of European imperialism in Asia is complicated. In India, China, and Japan, powerful kingdoms existed when the first European traders arrived. For several hundred years, there were trading connections in which the European was usually the weaker party, dependent on the good will and interest of the Asians. In China and India, native craftsmen produced goods superior to European products, so Asians had little reason to trade with the West, whereas Europeans had many incentives for commerce with the East. The Asian kingdoms possessed a sense of cultural unity arising from tradition and from loyalty to the great religious and ethical systems of Hinduism, Buddhism, Islam, and Confucianism. When as a result of industrialization in the nineteenth century the Europeans came in much greater numbers with greater power, the Chinese and Mogul empires were weakened by internal problems. Indian, Chinese, and Japanese cultural identities were not nationalism as Europeans knew it, but within a short time, resentment of European domination developed into national feeling, unifying diverse social and religious communities.

India

The Indian subcontinent became the scene of intense European competition in the eighteenth century. At that time the highly advanced and religiously tolerant Mogul Empire disintegrated in part as the result of the policies of Aurangzeb Alamgir (1658–1707), a Muslim zealot who tried to end religious toleration and, in fact, began a half-century of civil war. Internally torn by religious conflict between Hindus and Muslims, as well as Sikhs, and by rivalries of powerful native princes, India fell prey to the Europeans. By the end of the century, the British had cleared out their rivals—the Portuguese, the Dutch, and the French—one by one.

British Rule The British East India Company gained the upper hand in India by making alliances with warring princes, by carrying on trade and collecting taxes, and by commanding armies of *sepoys* (native soldiers). Parliament regulated the chartered monopoly enterprise, but in fact did not control it much until the Sepoy Mutiny of

Map 27.1 Asia in 1914 ▶

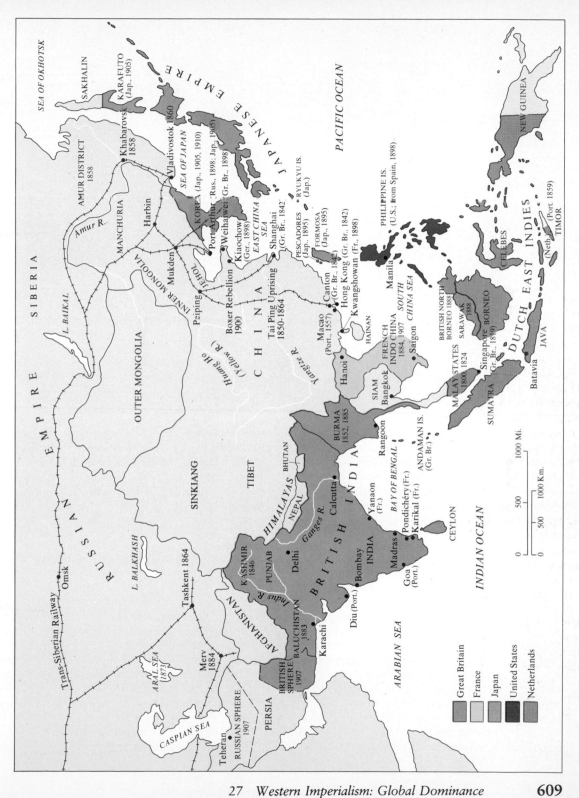

SEA OF OKHOTSK

SAKHALIN

KARAFUTO (Jap., 1905)

JAPANESE EMPIRE

AMUR DISTRICT 1858

Khabarovsk 1858

Vladivostok 1860

SEA OF JAPAN

SIBERIA

Amur R.

MANCHURIA

Harbin

L. BAIKAL

KOREA (Jap., 1905, 1910)

Port Arthur (Rus., 1898; Jap., 1905)

Weihaiwei (Gr. Br., 1898)

PACIFIC OCEAN

NEW GUINEA

RUSSIAN EMPIRE

INNER MONGOLIA

Mukden

JEHOL

Peiping

Kiaochow (Ger., 1898)

Shanghai (Gr. Br., 1842)

EAST CHINA SEA

RYUKYU IS. (Jap.)

PHILIPPINE IS. (U.S.: from Spain, 1898)

OUTER MONGOLIA

Boxer Rebellion 1900

Huang Ho (Yellow R.)

Tai Ping Uprising 1850-1864

C H I N A

Yangtze R.

PESCADORES (Jap., 1895)

FORMOSA (Jap., 1895)

Canton

Macao (Port., 1557)

Hong Kong (Gr. Br., 1842)

Kwangshowan (Fr., 1898)

Manila

SOUTH CHINA SEA

HAINAN

Hanoi

FRENCH INDO CHINA 1884, 1907

Saigon

BRITISH NORTH BORNEO 1888

SARAWAK 1888

BORNEO

Singapore (Gr. Br., 1819)

DUTCH EAST INDIES

CELEBES

TIMOR (Port. 1859)

(Neth.)

SINKIANG

TIBET

BHUTAN

NEPAL

HIMALAYAS

SIAM

Bangkok

MALAY STATES 1800, 1824

SUMATRA

JAVA

Batavia

BURMA 1852, 1885

Rangoon

BAY OF BENGAL

ANDAMAN IS. (Gr. Br.)

B R I T I S H   I N D I A

Calcutta

Ganges R.

Yanaon (Fr.)

Pondichéry (Fr.)

Karikal (Fr.)

CEYLON

INDIAN OCEAN

1000 Mi.

1000 Km.

KASHMIR 1846

PUNJAB

Delhi

Indus R.

INDIA

Bombay

Madras

Goa (Port.)

500

500

R U S S I A N   E M P I R E

L. BALKHASH

Omsk

Trans-Siberian Railway

Tashkent 1864

AFGHANISTAN

BALUCHISTAN

BRITISH SPHERE 1907

Karachi

Diu (Port.)

ARABIAN SEA

Merv 1884

ARAL SEA (1873)

RUSSIAN SPHERE 1907

PERSIA

Teheran

CASPIAN SEA

Great Britain

France

Japan

United States

Netherlands

A Tiger Hunt in the Raj in the 1870s with the Prince of Wales (later Edward VII). Unity was imposed on the diverse Indian peoples by British imperialism. A handful of British administrators and soldiers, with the assistance of an English-educated elite and well-trained regiments of native and British troops, ruled over 300 million Indians. After the Great Rebellion of 1857 (the Sepoy Mutiny), the British lived a separate existence in the subcontinent, widening the distance between themselves and their subjects by their attitude of racial and national superiority. (*The Bettmann Archive/BBC Hulton*)

1857–58. (The Indians call this massive act of resistance the Great Rebellion.) This major popular uprising joined Muslim and Hindu soldiers with some native princes who finally perceived that the British, rather than neighboring princes, were the true threat to their authority. Peasants, too, who were victims of both their local landlords and the market forces, participated in the uprising. In a fierce war, with many wanton attacks on peaceful and loyal Indian villages, the British with the aid of faithful troops from the Punjab repressed the uprising. Unlike the Chinese and the Japanese, the peoples of India lost all semblance of independence. The British ruled some states through dependent Indian princes, but about two-thirds of the subcontinent was ruled directly by about a thousand British officials.

The British governed India through a civil service. Employees of the East India Company had first mixed with the local populace, often marrying Indian women and adopting Indian customs and languages. The sepoy uprising so threatened the British community, however, that it took all the authority that it could into its hands and maintained a social and legal separation from Indians. At first, the civil service was entirely British, its officials confident of the superiority of their people, law, and society. Later, an elite of Indians educated in English and trained in administration became part of the civil service. Indian civil servants, along with soldiers who were recruited from peoples with military traditions, such as the Gurkhas and the Punjabis, carried out British laws, adding their interpretations, customs, and traditions. By 1900, a civil service of 4,000 Europeans and half a million Indians ruled over more than 300 million Indians representing almost 200 language groups and several religions, races, and cultures, and living in territories that today make up India, Pakistan, and Bangladesh. For a time, Burma too came under this administration. The British created a powerful state with a single system of law, administration, and language that showed little regard for the diversity of the peoples ruled, but many Indians accepted the system as just and longed for the day they would administer it. (The British allowed native princes to rule if they followed British policies.) Under the impact of British imperialism the subcontinent gained some political unity, an English-educated elite, and a focus for discontent—the common resentment of the British.

The British built a modern railroad and communications system and developed agriculture and industry to meet the needs of the world market. The railroad, as a link to areas of food surplus, reduced the incidence and impact of local famines, which had plagued India's history. British rule ended the century of war and disorder after the disintegration of the Mogul Empire, although it did not end the control local landlords and usurers had over the lives of peasants. Population increased as fewer people died of starvation and lives were saved due to Western medical practices. But many students of history believe that the Indian masses did not benefit from economic progress because they could not pay their debts in money as their landlords demanded, and because the increase in population more than matched the increase in food; rather than starvation for some, malnutrition for most became the rule, they argue. Further aggravating the situation, the British flooded the Indian market with cheap, machine-produced English goods, which drove native artisans out of business or even deeper into debt.

The racism that excluded the Indian elite from British clubs, hotels, and social gatherings and from top government positions alienated the leaders that British rule had created. Many of the older elite of princes and landlords who may have profited from British connections resented the lack of respect for Indian traditions and culture. Educated Indians, demanding equality and self-government, created the Indian National Congress in the 1880s. This organization was not national, because its members were upper-class Hindus, and not a congress, because it had no representative authority. Despite its narrow membership, this group would free India from the British after World War II. At first the Congress party demanded representation for Indians; later it sought home rule, or equal self-government within the British Empire; ultimately it organized masses of Indians to gain independence.

Independence The Russo-Japanese War of 1904–1905 sparked militant resistance throughout much of Asia. Radical nationalists in India were inspired to struggle for independence when they saw Russia humiliated by the Japanese. Similarly World War I brought greater solidarity among Indians who, although alike in their opposition to British rule, had been far from united. The Muslims had founded their own Muslim League in 1912 to voice the fears and demands of their minority community to the British governors; many Hindus believed that the British favored the Muslim community as part of a divide-and-conquer theory of government. The Indian elite were able to find grounds for cooperation among the disparate communities, but the masses continued to be divided by differences of religion, class, and culture. These differences made Indian self-government seem distant even to those British who thought it desirable. To undermine opposition, some British governors played on communal differences. In 1919, partly in response to agitation and partly as a reward for loyal Indian service during the war, the British granted India a legislative assembly representing almost a million of the 247 million in the subcontinent. An elaborate scheme allotted representation by groups (that is, to Hindus, Muslims, Europeans, Anglo-Indians, and Sikhs) and by economic and social functions (that is, to rural, urban, university, landholding, and commercial classes). The British granted some powers to this assembly, but retained most.

At the very time that the British granted the legislature, agitation and unrest became most bitter. In 1919, at Amritsar in Punjab, a British officer commanded his Gurkha troops to fire into a peaceful demonstration until their ammunition was exhausted. Three hundred seventy-nine Indians died and twelve hundred were wounded; women and children were among the victims. The government punished the officer, but the British community in India gave him a fortune, honoring him for what he had done. The massacre and the behavior of the Britons stung Indians to action, including former supporters of the British and advocates of self-government within the British Empire.

Out of this feverish period emerged a gentle but nonetheless determined revolutionary leader, Mohandas K. Gandhi (1869–1948). In South Africa he had led the resistance of Indians to the vicious system of racial discrimination there, and in the process developed a doctrine of civil disobedience and nonviolent resistance. He believed that the power of love and spiritual purity would ultimately overthrow British rule in India. His was a spiritually uplifting message—and a shrewd political tactic as well. Gandhi called on the Indian elite to give up the privileges allotted by the British—to resign their positions, to boycott British schools, and finally, to boycott all foreign goods. The elite's sacrifice of privilege would not have freed India by itself; mass support was also required. Gandhi rallied this support dramatically with "the march to the sea"—a mass refusal to pay taxes on salt. When imprisoned, Gandhi and his followers fasted for spiritual discipline, but their tactic also threatened the British with the possibility that the confined leaders would starve to death, setting off more civil disturbances. Gandhi also emphasized the boycott of foreign goods by spinning cottons and wearing simple native dress. To gain independence, Gandhi was even willing to sacrifice the higher standard of living that an industrial economy could bring to India.

After World War II had exhausted British resources and reduced British power, independence came: India was partitioned into Muslim Pakistan and predominantly Hindu India. Independence was achieved without a war between Britain and India, an accomplishment that many credit to the strength of Gandhi's moral leadership. But even his leadership could not prevent conflict between Hindu and Muslim, as bloody massacres at independence so clearly revealed.

China

For centuries, Europeans had admired China for its wealth, art, and culture. The Enlightenment philosophes had admired China's imperial government for its mandarin rule (mandarins were men who had passed tests of Chinese learning). In the nineteenth century, China excluded foreigners, whether they were missionaries, traders, or soldiers and sailors, in an effort to preserve the traditional ruling class, economy, and beliefs against Christianity, Western science, and secular ideologies.

Defeat by the British in the Opium War of 1839–1842 forced the Manchu Dynasty to open trade with the West. Before the war, any commerce had been limited, controlled by native monopolists who were granted trading privileges by the emperor. When the Chinese government destroyed Indian opium being traded by the East India Company, the British aggressively asserted their right to free trade and demanded compensation. In the subsequent war, Britain seized several trading cities along the coast, including Hong Kong, and the Chinese capitulated. In the Treaty of Nanking (1842), the British insisted that they determine the tariffs the Chinese might charge them and that British subjects in China have the right to be tried according to their own law (the right of extraterritoriality). Both provisions undermined the emperor's ability to control the foreigners in his country.

Defeat in the Opium War also forced change on the emperor. He drew on China's mandarins to revitalize the Manchu bureaucracy by cleaning out much of the official corruption that weighed heavily on the poorest taxpayers and by strengthening China against the Westerners, sometimes hiring Westerners to train Chinese armies. Nevertheless, widespread economic discontent, hatred of the Manchu (who were regarded by many Chinese as foreign conquerors even though the conquest had taken place some two hundred years earlier), and religious mysticism inspired the Taiping Rebellion of 1850–1864. This uprising seriously

"The Real Trouble Will Come with the 'Wake' " by Joseph Keppler, 1900. The Great Powers were unable to carve up China as they had Africa. The Europeans were able to wring such concessions as Hong Kong, trading, and special privileges from the weak empire. The American late-comers insisted that China be kept open for the trade of all—the Open Door policy. With the overthrow of the Manchu Dynasty in 1911, China became a republic, plagued by civil war and foreign aggression until the end of World War II. This lithograph from the August 1900 issue of *Puck* shows the Chinese dragon being fought over by the Great Powers. (*Library of Congress*)

threatened the dynasty, but it was able to suppress the rebels with Western assistance. Britain and France extorted additional concessions. They forced the emperor to allow Chinese to emigrate freely, especially to South Africa and the United States, where they were exploited to build railroads.

For a time the Europeans seemed content with trading rights in coastal towns and preferential treatment for their subjects. But the Sino-Japanese War of 1894–95, which Japan won easily because of China's weakness, encouraged the Europeans to mutilate China. Britain, France, Russia, and Germany all scrambled for concessions, protectorates, and spheres of influence. China might have

been carved up like Africa but each Western nation, afraid of its rivals, resisted any partition that might possibly give another state an advantage. The United States, which insisted that it be given any trading concession that any other state received, proclaimed an "Open Door" policy that trade should be open to all; it said that the Great Powers should respect the territorial integrity of China. The U.S. action may have restrained the Western powers from partitioning China; it was also a way to ensure American interests in China. Perhaps this U.S. policy did little; the important treaty ports were already apportioned, and capitalism, the most powerful threat to China's independent status, continued to make major inroads.

Chinese traditionalists organized secret societies to expel foreigners and to punish Chinese who accepted Christianity or any other form of westernization. Usually, these societies opposed the Manchu Dynasty, particularly if it tried to make any reforms that would undermine traditional China, but sometimes they allied themselves with it. In 1900, encouraged by the Empress Tzuhsi, the Society of Righteous and Harmonious Fists (called the Boxers by Europeans) attacked foreigners throughout the north of China. An international army of Europeans, Japanese, and Americans suppressed the rebellion, seized Chinese treasures, and forced China to pay an indemnity. They also made China accede to foreign troops stationed on its soil.

Chinese discontent with the dynasty deepened, as did unrest and nationalistic opposition to the foreigners. When the Japanese defeated the Russians in 1905, many Chinese argued that the only way to protect their country was to imitate the West, as the Japanese had done. Many signs of growing nationalism appeared, particularly the widespread support given a Chinese boycott of American goods in 1905 to protest the U.S. refusal to accept any more Chinese immigrants. In 1911, nationalist revolutionaries, strongly present among soldiers, workers, and students, overthrew the Manchu and declared a republic. Sun Zhongshan (Sun Yat-sen, 1866–1925), who was in the United States when the revolution broke out, returned to China to become the first president of the republic and the head of the Nationalist party.

Espousing the Western ideas of democracy, nationalism, and social welfare (the three principles of the people, as Sun called them), the republic struggled to establish its authority over a China torn by civil war and ravaged by foreigners—Russia was claiming Mongolia and Britain was claiming Tibet. The northern warlords, who were regional leaders with private armies, resisted any attempt to strengthen the republic's army because it might diminish their power. In the south, the republic more or less maintained control. After Sun's death, the Guomindong (Kuomintang), under the authoritarian leadership of Jiang Jieshi (Chiang Kai-shek, 1887–1975), tried to westernize by using the military power of the state and introducing segments of a modern economic system. But faced with civil war, attacked from both the right and the communist left under Mao Zedong (Mao Tse-tung, 1893–1976), and by the Japanese after 1931, the Kuomintang made slow progress. A divided China continued to be at the mercy of outside interests until after World War II.

Japan

Japan, like China, was opened to the West against its will. The Japanese had expelled Europeans in the seventeenth century and kept isolated for the next two centuries. By the 1850s, as in India and China, social dissension within Japan and foreign pressure combined to force the country to admit outside trade. Americans in particular refused to accept Japanese prohibitions on commercial and religious contacts. Like China, Japan succumbed to superior technological power. In 1853, Commodore Matthew C. Perry sailed into Tokyo Bay, making a show of American strength and forcing the Japanese to sign a number of treaties that granted Westerners extraterritoriality and control over tariffs.

A flood of unrest was unleashed. The warrior nobility, the *samurai*, who feared for their social status, attacked foreigners and murdered members of their own government. The samurai thought that trade would enhance the status of merchants, a social class they despised. In response to samurai belligerence, a fleet of U.S. and European ships attacked and destroyed important Japanese fortresses. A group of samurai seized the government, determined to preserve Japan's independence. This takeover—the Meiji Restoration of 1867—returned power to the emperor, or Meiji, from the feudal aristocracy that had ruled in his name for almost seven hundred years. The new government enacted a series of reforms turning Japan into a powerful modern unitary state. Large landowners were persuaded to turn their estates over to the emperor in exchange for compensation and high-level positions in the government. All classes were made equal before the law. Universal military service was required, as in France and Germany, which diminished social privilege and helped to imbue Japanese of all classes with nationalism. The Japanese modeled

Commodore Perry and the U.S. Squadron Meeting Japanese Imperial Commissioners at Yokohama, 1854. Commodore Matthew Perry had opened Japan against its will to the West the preceding year. With the Meiji Restoration of 1867, a strong central government pushed Japan to become one of the top ten industrial nations by 1900. Japan began imperialistic expansion, coming into conflict with China and Russia. Western imperialism found itself successfully challenged. (*Culver Pictures*)

their constitution on Bismarck's: there was a bicameral diet, or parliament, but the emperor held the most authority, which he delegated to his ministers to govern in his name without much control from the parliament.

The Meiji regime introduced modern industry and economic competition. Japanese visited factories all over the West and hired Westerners to teach industrial skills. The government, like central and eastern European governments, built defense industries, backed heavy industry and mining, and developed a modern communication system of railroads, roads, and telegraph. State moneys and government initiative created this economic development. The government encouraged competitive consumer industries as well.

During the 1880s, it sold factories to wealthy family monopolies, the *zaibatsu,* which came to dominate the Japanese economy. Industry in Japan adopted traditional Japanese values and emphasized cooperation more than competition; relations between employer and employee were paternalistic rather than individualistic, and deferential rather than antagonistic. Within little more than a generation of the Meiji Restoration, Japan moved from economic backwardness to a place among the top ten industrial nations. To underdeveloped countries, Japan became a model of a nation that borrowed from the West yet preserved its traditional values and social structure.

By 1900, Japan had ended the humiliating treaties with the West and become an imperialist power in its own right. It had won Taiwan and Korea in its war with China (1894–95), although the Great Powers intervened, forcing the Japanese to return some of the spoils of victory while they themselves grabbed greater spheres of influence from the helpless Chinese. Their self-serving maneuvering infuriated the Japanese. Finally, in 1904, conflict over influence in Manchuria brought Japan and Russia to war, which Japan won. The victory of an Asian power over a Western power had a tremendous impact on Asian nationalists. If Japan could unite its people with nationalism and strong leadership, others should be able to do so. Japan's victory inspired anti-Western and nationalist movements throughout China, Indochina, India, Iran, the Middle East, and even among South African Indians who had emigrated from one British colony to another but preserved their cultural identity.

Japan earned the respect of the imperialists as well as the anti-imperialists. The first alliance that Britain negotiated when it moved from a policy of "splendid isolation" (a policy of avoiding alliances) was the 1902 naval alliance with Japan. U.S. President Theodore Roosevelt offered to arbitrate the Russo-Japanese War. In World War I, Japan fought on the side of the Allies and emerged as the most powerful Asian state. It took over the former German holdings north of the Equator, except for Germany's sphere of influence in China. (U.S. President Woodrow Wilson blocked that move at the Paris peace conference.)

How Japan would exercise its hard-won power was an open question in the post–World War I era. In the 1920s, the prosperous economy fortified the middle class and increased the importance of the working class, strengthening democratic institutions. But Japan's dependence on foreign trade meant the nation was hard hit by the Great Depression of 1929, when the major states subjected its trade to tariffs. The depression weakened the elements that contributed to peace, stability, and democracy in Japan and strengthened the militarist and fascist groups that were set on imperialism in Manchuria and China. To Asians in the 1930s, Japan seemed to champion Asian racial equality and to oppose Western imperialism. Many leaders of nationalist movements in Burma, India, Indochina, and Indonesia were attracted for a time by Japan's pose. World War II, however, brought Japanese occupation and exploitation, not freedom and equality for Asians.

Southeast Asia

On the peripheries of the once-great Chinese and Indian empires, Europeans gained control and influence in Southeast and Central Asia. In Southeast Asia, the French claimed Indochina (Vietnam, Laos, and Cambodia today) in a war with China (1883–1885). The French parliament rejected the government of Jules Ferry for pursuing a war for a faraway and not obviously valuable territory, but annexed the territory nonetheless. Indochina was a prosperous country, but it traded mostly with Asia and very little with France. Some individuals profited economically from the colony, and some civil servants, soldiers, priests, and scholars were interested in it, but as a whole France was indifferent to its new acquisition.

French expansion might have continued into Siam (Thailand), just as the British might have expanded from their base in Burma. Neither of the two Great Powers was willing to let the other take Siam over. It remained an area of conflict between France and Britain until the Entente Cordiale of 1904 (see Chapter 29), when fear of Germany led Britain and France to put colonial differences aside. In general, Siam, like Turkey in the Middle East, was able to play the powers off against one another and to preserve some territorial integrity. Siam belied the imperialist claim that European rule improved the economies of backward countries. During the nineteenth century an independent Siam became more prosperous than neighboring Burma or Indochina, which were colonies.

Elsewhere in Southeast Asia, the United States and Germany challenged British and French preeminence. During the Spanish-American War, the Americans seized and annexed the Philippines and Guam. (Although the war was ostensibly fought to free Cuba, the first battle took place at Manila Bay.) Once taken, the islands proved difficult to pacify. Germany, the United States, Britain, and France laid claim to various other Pacific islands, where they built naval stations to symbolize their presence in the East. Throughout the period the Netherlands maintained its holdings in the East

Indies (Indonesia)—the remnant of the once-great seventeenth-century Dutch empire. Even colonies began to acquire colonies, as New Zealand and Australia pushed claims to Borneo and Tasmania, and, after World War I, to German colonies south of the Equator. They had some economic reasons for staking these claims, but asserting their national identity was equally important.

Central Asia

As China, India, and the Ottoman Empire lost their ability to control their border territories, European states tried to grab them. Indochina, Tibet, Korea, Burma, Afghanistan, and Persia found themselves the objects of Great Power competition. The ensuing struggles for domination of Southeast and Central Asia offer important insights into imperialism as an outcome of intense nationalism.

As France and Britain competed in Southeast Asia, and Japan and the great European powers over northern China, Russia and Britain opposed one another in Central Asia. In the last decades of the nineteenth century, Russia expanded in three areas: the Balkans in southeastern Europe, Persia and Afghanistan in Central Asia, and Manchuria and Korea in East Asia. In eastern Europe, Russia's push meant conflict with Austria-Hungary, Turkey, and their ally Germany. In East Asia, Russians ran into the Japanese, leading to the Russo-Japanese War. In Central Asia, Russia and Britain opposed one another.

In Central Asia, Russia's moves south into Afghanistan and Persia (Iran), both of which bordered India, alarmed the British. They believed the greatest danger to their position in India lay in internal uprisings, and a hostile force on the Indian border might inspire rebellious Indians. After 1889, Britain and Russia vied in loaning the shah of Persia money to build a railroad to Teheran. The Russians were then borrowing money from the French for their own industrialization, but they nonetheless offered capital to create a dependency in Persia. The British moved to stop the Russians, whose aim appeared to be the acquisition of a warm-water port on the Persian Gulf—too close to India for British comfort. The years 1878–1881 and 1884–1885 saw British and Russian troops engaged in Afghanistan, trying to dominate the rim of Asia.

The Russians took advantage of the Boer War (see page 623) to advance into Persia, Tibet, and Afghanistan. In 1904, the British moved on Tibet to prevent the ruling Dalai Lama's tutor from negotiating special trade agreements with the Russians, even though the total volume of trade would have been infinitesimally small. By 1906, however, both Russia and Britain were afraid of the rise of German power in Europe and were willing to compromise. The Russians agreed to leave the British puppet ruler of Afghanistan alone. Persia would be divided into three zones: one in the north for the Russians, one in the south for the British, and one for the Persians in the middle to keep the two powers separate.

This resolution of difficulties made possible the British and Russian alliance in Europe, and had tremendous impact on Persia as well. The shah, his country's finances in distress and made worse by Russian loans, responded to uprisings by granting a constitution—including a National Assembly—in 1906. His successor, with Russian help, fought a civil war with the nationalistic Persian elite. But he was deposed in 1909 for granting too many favors to the Europeans, particularly the Russians, and the National Assembly revived under another Qājār shah. Torn by the conflicting interests of Britain and Russia, Persia maintained neither independence nor stability. Its situation was further complicated after World War I when its vast reserves of oil became valuable to the Great Powers. Reza Shah of the Pahlavi family gained control of Persia in 1925 and abolished the special privileges that had been granted to foreigners. In 1934, the shah granted the concession over the Bahrain Islands to the American firm of Standard Oil, thinking that foreigners whose interests seemed to be merely economic might be more easily controlled than foreigners with geopolitical designs. Yet as British power receded in the area during and after World War II, U.S. power took its place.

The Ottoman Empire

Throughout the nineteenth century the Ottoman Empire was an area of conflict. The Russians, who liked to pose as the defenders of Orthodox Christian peoples in Turkish Europe and of the shrines in the Holy Land, pressured the Turks because the Russians wanted a warm-water port on the Mediterranean. The British supported the Turks because Britain wanted to block Russian access to the sea and, in 1854, they and the French joined the Turks in the Crimean War to deny the Russians their goal.

The development of Slavic nationalism and Austrian interest in the Balkans altered the diplomatic picture. Attempts to reform and westernize the Ottoman Empire and to give some autonomy to Slavic peoples aroused Turkish traditionalism. Abdul Hamid II (1876–1909), who was as harsh and autocratic as any Ottoman ruler before him, made reforms and allowed, even encouraged, harsh treatment of Christian subjects within his empire. In 1876, the Ottomans warred with the Serbs, who laid claim to two provinces of Slavic peoples still under Ottoman control. The Serbs were defeated, and Abdul Hamid ordered the mass murder of some 12,000 Christian Bulgarians because he feared that their religion and their nationalism made them doubly unreliable subjects.

British policy shifted abruptly toward intervention, while the Russians declared war and then handed the Turks the Treaty of San Stefano, highly favorable to Russia. Austria immediately called a conference of the Great Powers—the Congress of Berlin of 1878—where Bismarck, playing the "honest broker," redressed the balance of power in favor of Austria and Britain to avoid war in Europe. Britain said its true interests were Egypt and the Suez Canal—the route to India—but Disraeli nonetheless left the conference having acquired the island of Cyprus for Britain.

At the turn of the century, Anglo-Russian rivalry over the "sick man of Europe" (as Turkey was called because the Great Powers were all eagerly awaiting his death to divide the spoils) was overshadowed by Britain's rivalry with Germany. The conflict's origins seemed quite innocent, certainly not political. A group of German financiers proposed a railroad from central Turkey to Baghdad on the Tigris River, with a connection down the Euphrates River to Basra and the Persian Gulf. A railroad already existed from Berlin through the Balkans to Istanbul and central Turkey. Because the proposed new railroad would further open Turkey and its empire to the world market, the sultan was enthusiastic and offered to subsidize the project by guaranteeing the bonds and profits for the syndicate. The German backers of the railroad offered British and French investment groups a 25 percent share each, with 25 percent control to the Turks; the Germans kept the final quarter for themselves.

The British government, however, refused to allow British citizens to invest in the railroad. Politics dominated economics; the British feared German ascendancy in an area so close to India and the Suez Canal. Britain's action, together with German naval expansion, aggravated Anglo-German relations. The Germans came to see the British as their number one rival. In World War I, the Ottomans sided with the Germans, partly because of German influence over a generation of the Turkish elite and partly out of fear of the Russian presence in the Caucasus and the Black Sea areas.

Throughout World War I, the Allies secretly negotiated the division of the Ottoman Empire. Hoping to weaken its contribution to the German war effort, Britain sponsored Arab independence movements in the Arabian peninsula and in the territories that are today Iraq, Syria, Lebanon, Jordan, and Israel. In the Balfour Declaration of 1917, the British also promised the Zionists a Jewish homeland in Palestine.

When the war was over, the Turks, led by Kemal Atatürk, refused to accept the dismemberment of Turkish-speaking territory, although they did accept the loss of Arab lands and some islands off their southwestern coast. The Turks drove the Allies out of Anatolia, declared a republic in 1923 under Atatürk's presidency, and moved the capital to Ankara, far away from the Europeanized city of Constantinople (Istanbul). Turkey, which became a secular state, was no longer the spiritual leader of millions of Muslims throughout the world. During Atatürk's presidency (1923–1938) the Turkish government ended many ancient practices, such as veils for women, harems, and polygamy. European education and ideas flourished in the new republic. The conflict between the modern and the traditional in Turkey was resolved by war and revolution in favor of modern nationalism.

Map 27.2 The Middle East, Post–World War I ▶

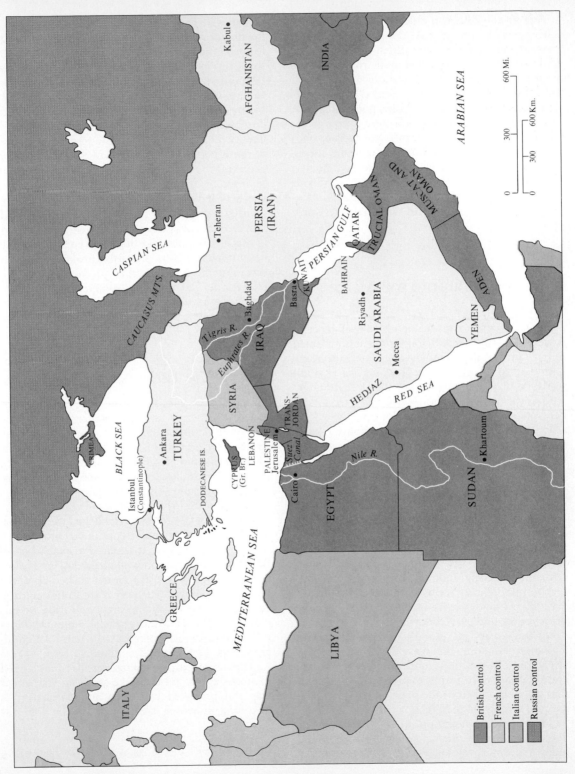

KABUL •

AFGHANISTAN

INDIA

ARABIAN SEA

600 Mi.

600 Km.

300

300

MUSCAT AND OMAN

TRUCIAL OMAN

•Teheran

PERSIA (IRAN)

PERSIAN GULF

QATAR

CASPIAN SEA

CAUCASUS MTS.

Baghdad•

Tigris R.

Euphrates R.

•Basra

KUWAIT

BAHRAIN

•Riyadh

SAUDI ARABIA

•Mecca

ADEN

YEMEN

IRAQ

SYRIA

HEDJAZ

RED SEA

CRIMEA

BLACK SEA

•Ankara

TURKEY

DODECANESE IS.

LEBANON

CYPRUS
(Gr. Br.)

TRANS-JORDAN

PALESTINE
Jerusalem•

Suez Canal

Nile R.

•Khartoum

Istanbul
(Constantinople)•

Cairo•

EGYPT

SUDAN

GREECE

MEDITERRANEAN SEA

LIBYA

ITALY

British control

French control

Italian control

Russian control

Among the Arabs, the desire for national self-determination, which arose around World War I, grew stronger after the war. Britain schemed for a while to establish a puppet Arab ruler but was rebuffed. The Arab chiefs welcomed British aid against the Turks but deeply resented British intervention in their spiritual and local political affairs. They suspected the Europeans were primarily interested in the area's oil. Arab nationalism, once encouraged against the Ottomans, could not be controlled when the Turks ceased to be a power. As nationalism developed, it often combined with religion to foment opposition that plagued the imperialists between the world wars and afterward.

The Scramble for Africa

The most rapid European expansion took place in Africa. As late as 1880, European nations ruled only a tenth of the continent. By 1914, Europeans had claimed all of Africa except Liberia (a small territory of freed slaves from the United States) and Abyssinia (Ethiopia), which had successfully held off Italian invaders at Adowa in 1896. The only Great Powers that did not play a part in carving up Africa were Russia, Austria-Hungary, and the United States.

European powers had occasionally been involved in Africa early in the century. The French had moved into Algeria in 1830. During the Napoleonic wars the British had gained Cape Town in South Africa, a useful provisioning place for trading ships bound for India and the East. Dutch cattlemen and farmers (Boers), who had settled in the Cape Town area starting in the mid-seventeenth century, refused to accept the British abolition of slavery in 1834. To get away from the British, they had moved northward in a migration called the Great Trek (1835–1837), warring with native tribes along the way. The Boers aggressively asserted their independence from the British and by 1880 were firmly established in the territory they had taken in the interior, the Transvaal and the Orange Free State.

In general, though, up to the 1870s, Great Power interest in Africa seemed marginal and likely to decline even further. Then the astounding

activities of Leopold II, king of Belgium, changed the picture. In 1876, as a private entrepreneur, he formed the International Association for the Exploration and Civilization of Central Africa. Leopold sent Henry Stanley (1841–1904) to the Congo River basin to establish trading posts, sign treaties with the chiefs, and claim the territory for the association. Stanley, an adventurer and a newspaper reporter who had fought on both sides of the American Civil War, had earlier led an expedition to central Africa in search of David Livingstone, the popular missionary-explorer who was believed to be in danger. When Stanley found Livingstone in 1871, the human-interest and adventure story was calculated to delight thousands of readers. For men like Stanley, Leopold's private development efforts promised profit and adventure. For the Africans, they promised brutal exploitation. The French responded to Leopold's actions by immediately establishing a protectorate on the north bank of the Congo. The scramble was on.

The Berlin Conference

Bismarck and Jules Ferry, the premier of France, called an international conference of the Great Powers in Berlin in 1884 to lay some ground rules for the development of Africa south of the Sahara. Leopold (as an individual, not as the king of Belgium) was declared the personal ruler of the Congo Free State. The Congo basin was made a free trade zone for merchants of every nation.

The Berlin Conference established the rule that a European country had to occupy territory effectively in order to claim it. This led to a mad race to the interior of Africa; it was a field day for explorers and soldiers. As Europeans rushed to claim territory, they ignored both natural and cultural frontiers. Even today the map of Africa reveals many straight (and thus artificial) boundary lines rather than the irregular lines of natural boundaries, such as rivers and mountains.

The nations at the conference also had agreed to stop slavery and the slave trade in Africa that was still practiced by Arabs and Africans. Before long, however, the Congo Association was

Map 27.3 Africa in 1914 ▶

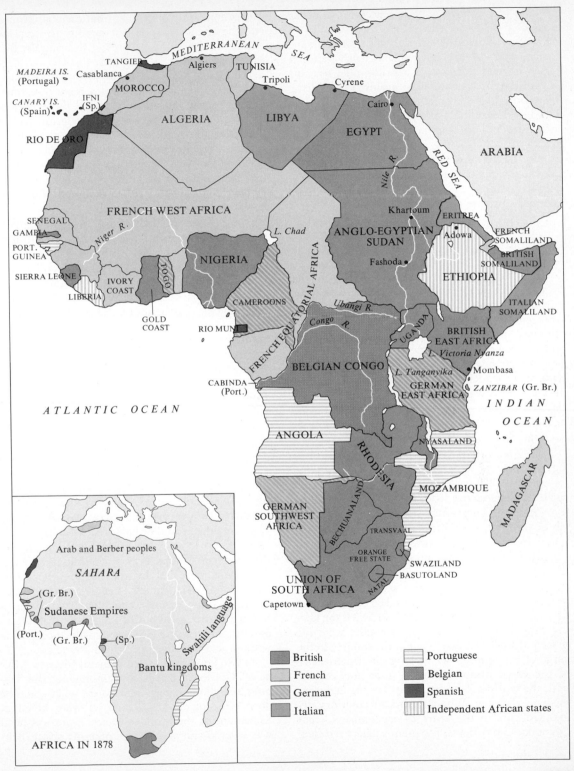

MADEIRA IS.
(Portugal)

CANARY IS.
(Spain)

MEDITERRANEAN   SEA

TANGIER
Casablanca   Algiers   TUNISIA
MOROCCO   Tripoli   Cyrene

IFNI
(Sp.)

RIO DE ORO

ALGERIA   LIBYA   EGYPT   Cairo

ARABIA

RED SEA

Nile R.

FRENCH WEST AFRICA

SENEGAL
GAMBIA
PORT.
GUINEA

Niger R.

L. Chad

Khartoum

ANGLO-EGYPTIAN
SUDAN

ERITREA
Adowa   FRENCH
SOMALILAND
BRITISH
SOMALILAND

SIERRA LEONE

NIGERIA

IVORY
COAST

TOGO

Fashoda

ETHIOPIA

LIBERIA

GOLD
COAST

CAMEROONS

RIO MUNI

FRENCH EQUATORIAL AFRICA

Ubangi R.

Congo   R.

ITALIAN
SOMALILAND

UGANDA

BRITISH
EAST AFRICA

L. Victoria Nyanza

ATLANTIC   OCEAN

CABINDA
(Port.)

BELGIAN CONGO

L. Tanganyika   Mombasa

GERMAN
EAST AFRICA

ZANZIBAR (Gr. Br.)

INDIAN

OCEAN

ANGOLA

NYASALAND

RHODESIA

MOZAMBIQUE

MADAGASCAR

GERMAN
SOUTHWEST
AFRICA

BECHUANALAND

TRANSVAAL

ORANGE
FREE STATE

SWAZILAND
BASUTOLAND

UNION OF
SOUTH AFRICA

NATAL

Capetown

Arab and Berber peoples

SAHARA

(Gr. Br.)

Sudanese Empires

(Port.)

(Gr. Br.)   (Sp.)

Bantu kingdoms

Swahili language

AFRICA IN 1878

British

French

German

Italian

Portuguese

Belgian

Spanish

Independent African states

trying to turn a profit with practices as vicious as those of the African slave traders. At the turn of the century, Edward D. Morel, an English humanitarian, and Roger Casement, an Irish national hero who was at the time a British civil servant, waged a vigorous campaign against Leopold for the Aborigines' Protection Society. They produced evidence that slavery, mutilation, brutality, and murder were commonly practiced to force blacks to work for the rubber plantations in the Congo. In response to the outcry of public opinion, the Belgian parliament declared the territory a Belgian colony in 1908, putting an end to Leopold's private enterprise.

The British in Africa

Great Britain's activities in Africa exemplify the complicated motives, operations, and results of European imperialism. In the second half of the nineteenth century, Britain maintained only a few outposts along the coast of West Africa; even its hold on South Africa appeared to be loosening. The British navy, from time to time, interfered with slave traders in Africa, but overall British interest there was minimal. In principle, Britain rejected empire. Then, local conditions in Egypt, home of the Suez Canal, resulted in British occupation.

Egypt For a generation (1805–1847), Mohammed Ali, governor of Egypt, had struggled for his independence from the sultan of the Ottoman Empire. Thereafter, strong *khedives* (Turkish governors), with British and French support, had maintained Egypt's autonomy. But foreign investment and influence grew, as successive khedives spent lavishly in attempts to maintain their position and to modernize the land. Egypt fell deeply into debt to Europeans. Then the building of the Suez Canal (1859–1869), in which the khedive and British and French capitalists were the principal stockholders, brought the country to the verge of bankruptcy. In the long run the existence of the canal promised Egypt trade and contact with the world economy, but its cost brought immediate disaster. When European creditors demanded cuts in the army to economize so that Egypt could pay debts, Egyptian soldiers rebelled.

The combination of probable national bankruptcy and the khedive's apparent inability to keep law and order was sufficient pretext to bring the British in as "protectors" in 1882.

The canal was important to the British as a waterway to India, but it was a mere investment to the French. The British invited the French to join their invasion to protect the investments, but the latter could not do so for domestic political reasons. Despite this inability, the French deeply resented the fact that the British took action without them; patriotic organizations vehemently protested the "insult" to French national honor and demanded government action.

Prime Minister Gladstone, a "little Englander" (one who opposed empire), promised to withdraw British troops once the situation stabilized, but every day that the British remained, Egyptian discontent mounted against them, threatening the stability of markets and investments and even of government. Furthermore, Egyptian opposition took two irreconcilable forms. Some Egyptians wanted to modernize their nation with a strong government and army so that they could throw the British out. Others hated all aspects of westernization because it drew Egypt further away from Islam. As the British became entrenched, vain attempts at resistance became more violent.

Not only did the British not withdraw from Egypt, they also moved farther south. In the Sudan, devout Muslims were waging holy war against Egyptian authority because they resented foreign and non-Muslim influence over the khedive. The British were trying to strengthen the khedive's authority so that taxes would be paid, Egypt's budget could be balanced, and debts could be paid. When an English general led 10,000 of the khedive's troops against the Sudanese Muslims, who were led by the Mahdi, they were annihilated. Gladstone's liberal party argued against further action in the Sudan, which Egyptian troops occupied but could not control. Occupation angered the French; costly occupation without stability angered British financiers.

In 1885, Gladstone sent General Charles "Chinese" Gordon, famous for suppressing the Taiping Rebellion, to the Sudan to see what could be done. Gordon and the garrison were killed at Khartoum by the Mahdi's forces; Gordon's head was severed and placed on a pike. A furious British public accused Gladstone of martyring the famous hero by forbidding him to wage war while sending him to the war zone to take charge. Gladstone refused to annex the Sudan, but in 1898 when the Conservatives were in power, General Herbert Kitchener was sent there, and his men armed with machine guns mowed down charging Muslims at Omdurman. The casualties were reported to be 11,000 Muslims and 28 Britons, which many Britons felt was appropriate revenge for the death of Gordon.

The battle of Omdurman was an ugly victory, and 1898 became a year of ugly confrontations and dubious victories for the British Empire. Immediately after the battle, British forces confronted the French at Fashoda in the Sudan. Major Jean-Baptiste Marchand had marched a French exploratory expedition all the way from West Africa to the Sudan in order to lay claim to the territory from West Africa to Somaliland on the Red Sea. The British were moving south from Egypt and north from Kenya into the same territory. In the diplomatic crisis that followed, Britain and France were brought to the brink of war, and public passions were inflamed. Too divided by the Dreyfus affair at home (see Chapter 26) to risk a showdown with Britain, however, the French cabinet ordered Marchand to retreat. Behind the scenes, French statesmen began to negotiate with Britain to reconcile their two nations' ambitions. France did not have the resources to challenge both Germany across the Rhine and Britain in Africa and Asia. The British, too, faced with conflict in the Sudan and mounting troubles in South Africa, realized their limits. They began to see their "splendid isolation" as a risky policy that might make the whole world their enemy (with the possible exception of the United States, at that moment also isolated by its war with Spain).

South Africa Nothing underlined Britain's isolation and the widespread distrust of British motives more than the Boer War, which began in 1899. British relations with the settlers of the Boer territories of Transvaal and the Orange Free State had been difficult since the Great Trek; they were aggravated by the discovery of rich deposits of gold and diamonds in Boer territory.

The early opposing leaders were strong and unyielding. Paul Kruger (1825–1904), the Boer president of the Transvaal, was trying to gain independence, power, and access to the sea for the Boers and to restrict the foreign prospectors who were flooding into Boer territory by the thousands. The prime minister of Cape Colony, Cecil Rhodes (1853–1902), was a British subject who had made a fortune in diamonds and gold in South Africa. He was responsible for acquiring Rhodesia, a sizable and wealthy territory, for Britain. He dreamed of British red coloring the map of Africa from Cape Town to Cairo, and he built a railroad from the Cape to Rhodesia.

In 1895, Rhodes's close friend Leander Jameson led about six hundred armed men into the Transvaal to spark an uprising against Kruger, an event that would give the British a pretext to invade. The raid failed, both Jameson and Rhodes were disgraced for their part in the plot, and Rhodes had to resign. The scandal reached all the way to Joseph Chamberlain, the imperialist colonial secretary in the British cabinet. Kaiser William II of Germany impetuously sent President Kruger a congratulatory telegram after the Boers had repulsed the Jameson raid. The British took this diplomatic insult as a symbol of their isolation, which it most certainly was.

Everything about the Boer War was unfortunate for the British. The Boers were formidable opponents—farmers by day and commandos by night, armed with the latest French and German rifles. Hatred for the British in the press of other European countries was almost universal. The war was exceptionally costly in both money and lives; it aroused many Britons to a fever pitch of patriotism. At the same time, anti-imperialism gained strength, and the war produced an outcry within Britain against the direction British policy had taken. Humanitarians in London found some British tactics shameful. To deal with their stubborn foe, for example, the British herded, or "concentrated," whole settlements of Boers into compounds surrounded by barbed wire. The British won the major battles but faced stiff guerrilla resistance.

After three years, the nasty war ended in 1902. The British, hoping to live together in peace with the Boers, drew up a conciliating treaty. The peace treaty made many concessions to the Boers, including the right to use their own language, Afrikaans (although English remained the official language), and the offer of amnesty to any Boer who would swear allegiance to the British king. But the settlement that appeared to be generous and just to the belligerents boded ill for other people who were not involved in the war. Justice, equality, and self-government for the Boers and the British did not help the majority black population of South Africa. In fact, Boer autonomy meant that the government in London could do little to protect the rights of black Africans in Boer territories. Few safeguards for blacks were written into the treaty or the constitution of the new Union of South Africa.

Other European Countries in Africa

The cost of imperialism in Africa seemed high not only to the British and French but to other imperialists as well. The Italians' defeat at Adowa (1896) by Ethiopians belied Italian dreams of empire and national glory. (Bismarck scoffed that the Italians had enormous appetites but very poor teeth.) Victory would not have alleviated Italy's economic problems, although it might have reduced political discontent. Germans could take little heart from their African acquisitions—Southwest Africa (Namibia), Southeast Africa (Tanzania, but not Zanzibar, which was British), the Cameroons, and Togo (part of Ghana today). The German colonies were the most efficiently governed (critics said the most ruthlessly controlled), but they yielded few benefits other than pride of ownership because they were costly to govern. And the Belgians had obviously gained no prestige from the horrors perpetrated in the Congo. Serious thinkers, contemplating the depths to which Europeans would sink in search of fortune and fame, began to suggest that barbarity characterized the Europeans more than the Africans. The Europeans seemed to be the moral barbarians, as novelist Joseph Conrad and others pointed out. Honor was fleeting and profits illusory, for the most part, in these new African empires.

Yet, it appeared that Europeans might go to war with each other for those African lands with few people and fewer resources. Such a war promised to be more deadly than the colonial conflicts

Yoruba Carving of a European. The African artist who carved this figure has captured the spirit of the old colonialism and the new imperialism with the symbols of the European man with a gun and a horse. Aztec, Chinese, Japanese, and Indian artists also conveyed in their works the sense of the intruder with power. (*Neg. #327026, Courtesy Department of Library Services, American Museum of Natural History*)

between the technologically superior Europeans and the Africans and Asians. Germany expressed its aggressive imperialism in a naval arms race with the British that threatened the latter's power and national self-image. The "Teutonic cousins" eyed each other with deepening suspicion. This tension contributed to the alliances the Great Powers made in the decade before World War I.

Latin America

Early in the nineteenth century, Latin American colonists rebelled against Spain to gain political independence. Their rebellion was part of the same era of democratic revolution as the American revolution in 1776 and the French Revolution in 1789. The colonists, who were active in trade, were encouraged by Britain and the United States, both of which wanted a free hand for their commerce. British Prime Minister George Canning and U.S. President James Monroe issued warnings to the Concert of Europe (Russia, Austria, Prussia, Great Britain, and France) not to intervene or to colonize the Americas. For the entire nineteenth century, Latin America was the object of European trade and immigration. Argentina, Brazil, Chile, and the other countries took in Irish, Germans, Italians, eastern Europeans and Spaniards; much the same as the United States, they became primarily immigrant nations. (A few nations—Mexico and Peru, for example—resisted the Atlantic migration, preserving an Amerindian or mestizo society.)

Europeans also invested heavily in both Latin and North America. For much of the nineteenth century, Britain and, to a lesser degree, France were the dominant economic powers in Latin America; they cooperated commercially with local merchants, loaned money, and arranged for treaties favorable to the business interests of their citizens. Toward the end of the century, investments and commerce from the United States became powerful forces in the Caribbean islands and Latin America.

Both the Europeans and the local merchants and landowners exploited the lower classes. Brazil relied on African slave labor to produce for European markets; it was, in fact, the last American nation to abolish slavery. Native Indians were pushed off their lands in Argentina, Brazil, and Chile just as ruthlessly as in North America.

Europe dominated the Western Hemisphere culturally, too. In Latin America a small, wealthy upper class benefited from its connection with Europe and imitated continental culture. At Manaus in the Amazon region, rich South Americans built an ornate opera house, resembling Milan's La Scala, from profits of rubber farms worked by enslaved Indians. Wealthy North Americans lived like the British gentry, using the profits of cotton or coffee labor. In Buenos Aires, Rio de Janeiro, and Santiago, merchants discussed the latest European intellectual fad. Upper-class Latin and North Americans sent their children to Europe to attend school and to acquire "culture" before they entered business, agriculture, and government in their native lands. In these matters, the Latin American elite behaved much the same as the westernizers among the elite of India, the Middle East, or Southeast Asia. In both Latin and North America, however, some people felt that New World countries must develop their own cultures, not imitate Britain or France, and significant cultures did develop.

The wealthy classes in Latin America depended on Europe for trade as well as culture. They became indebted to Europeans for funds to support their governments and to build their railroads. For their part, the Europeans were content to gain the profits from commerce without direct colonization. If political dissension threatened to interfere with peaceful trade, Europeans had ways of letting the merchant class know the costs of that dissension. In general, dependent merchants maintained the conditions that Europeans thought were desirable for business. When the rules of free trade were violated, European vessels might blockade harbors or seize customs houses. But unlike the British in Egypt, Europeans in the Americas usually withdrew their troops or ships as soon as they had enforced their will.

An exception to this general policy of nonintervention was Napoleon III's attempt in 1867 to conquer Mexico and to install an Austrian archduke (Maximilian) on a bogus throne. The Mexicans, led by Benito Juárez (1806–1872), resisted the French invasion. Napoleon thought better of his dreams of easy glory and abandoned the campaign, which was undertaken more to please members of his military than the French business community. The Mexicans captured and executed Emperor Maximilian, and the experience intensified Mexican nationalism.

Although Latin Americans were sheltered from direct European imperialism by the business interests of Britain and the United States, they had little protection against the aggressions of the lat-

Slaves Drying Coffee on a Plantation in Terreiros, Rio de Janeiro, c. 1882. Slaves in Brazil (slavery was not abolished there until 1888) toiled to produce one of its main exports to a world market. The world economy, which began with the Commercial Revolution, emerged full force with the Age of Imperialism, as more and more resources of the non-European world were produced, bought, and sold for overseas consumption. (*Photograph by Marc Ferrez; courtesy of Gilberto Ferrez*)

ter. By the end of the nineteenth century, the United States was able to push the British aside and energetically pursue its own interests, first in the Caribbean and Central America and then throughout Latin America. Growing economic power brought the United States into the field of Great Powers. After the Spanish-American War (1898), the United States occupied Cuba and annexed Puerto Rico and the Philippines; it also restated the Monroe Doctrine, which prohibited colonization of the Americas by foreign nations but did not inhibit U.S. expansionism. In the Roosevelt Corollary (1904), the United States announced that Europeans could not intervene in the Western Hemisphere even to protect their citizens or their business interests. Such intervention was too often the pretext for imperial control of one form or another, which the United States felt would jeopardize its interests.

Yet U.S. citizens continued to interfere freely in Latin American affairs. They engineered the secession of Panama from Colombia in 1903 to obtain the rights to build the Panama Canal on favorable terms. For the next three decades the United States intervened repeatedly in the Caribbean, sending marines to occupy the Dominican Republic, Haiti, Nicaragua, and the port of Veracruz in Mexico, seizing customs revenues for payment of debts, and threatening Latin American governments. American "gunboat diplomacy" replaced English and French commercial power in northern Latin America. Like Britain, the United States used force to maintain its interests while, at the same time, articulating a policy of free competition for trade and commerce—of open doors around the world, including Latin America.

In many ways, U.S. behavior resembled European imperialism. Like the European nations who acquired bases in China, the United States took Guantanamo Bay in Cuba, Fonseca in Nicaragua, and the Canal Zone in Panama, which was originally leased to the United States in perpetuity. Like European businesses, U.S. entrepreneurs invested so heavily in underdeveloped areas that they frequently controlled governments and ruling elites. In 1923, 43 percent of all U.S. foreign investment went to Latin America, 27 percent to Canada, 22 percent to Europe (at a time when the United States was underwriting German recovery from World War I), and 8 percent to Asia and Africa. Foreign investment may have been a mere fraction of total American wealth, but it was significant to important segments of the national economy.

The United States practiced "dollar diplomacy" (exercising political influence over nations through economic investment) just as Europeans had in Morocco, Tunisia, Egypt, Persia, Turkey, and China. Corrupt members of dictatorial regimes in Latin America borrowed money from the United States for national development or for their own personal use. When repayment was not forthcoming, the United States treated these governments like private companies in default, sending in U.S. marines to take customs, taxes, and treasuries until debts were repaid. The United States put the customs revenues of Haiti (1915) and Santo Domingo (1904, 1916–1924) into receivership, just as the British and French had done to Egyptian customs. In Central America the United States controlled the governments as puppet or client states, just as the European countries

directed the governments of the Middle East or Central Asia. And early in the twentieth century, U.S. influence over Mexico under the presidency of Porfirio Díaz (1876–1880, 1884–1911) was very similar to German and British controls over the Ottoman Empire.

The Latin American response to U.S. imperial actions was very like Asian and African responses to European imperialism. The strongest challenge to U.S. interests before World War I came with the Mexican Revolution in 1911. Its leaders, Emiliano Zapata, Victoriano Huerta, and Francisco "Pancho" Villa, differed in their motives for the overthrow of Díaz, but together they upset Mexican–U.S. relations. Zapata's goal was to break up great estates and give them to the peasantry; Huerta, who was encouraged by the British, hoped to strengthen Mexico by increasing foreign investment in industry. In 1916, Villa angered the United States by killing several U.S. engineers and making a raid across the border. President Woodrow Wilson, who was at that time offering to mediate between the warring European states, ordered U.S. troops into Mexico to pursue Villa. Thus, while Wilson was preaching self-determination of European nations, sympathetically concerned with the wrongs done to the weak by the strong powers, he was also violating the sovereignty of Mexico, which was torn in pieces by civil war.

After World War I, relations between the United States and Latin America remained troubled, particularly during the Great Depression of 1929, which had devastating effects on those countries that had begun to industrialize and to build an export market. Some Latin American nations responded to the Depression much as Italy, Germany and eastern European states did. Unable to cope with the economic disaster, Argentina and Brazil, for example, experimented with authoritarian nationalist governments that resembled the fascist regimes in Europe. President Franklin D. Roosevelt announced a U.S. policy of cooperation with the South Americans—a "good neighbor" policy underlined by the Pan American Union—in the hope of improving relations and increasing trade between the two continents.

Not until the post–World War II era, however, did Latin American states begin to make serious headway with industrialization and economic expansion. Still, for many Latin Americans who wanted to reform social inequality, the enrichment of the few seemed the major result of economic growth, which depended on the United States for capital, machinery, and markets. The troubled relations between the United States and Latin America continue today—a legacy of the distrust that grew out of U.S. imperialism.

The Legacy of Imperialism

World War I was a turning point in the history of imperialism, though neither mother countries nor colonies, seemed aware of it at the time. Britain and France divided the German colonial spoils and replaced Turkish power in the Middle East. Both empires were at their peak in 1919, and even more than before the war, leaders in both countries thought colonies essential to the well-being of their nations—for prestige, for manpower, and for trade.

But the origins of decolonization date from the postwar era. Wilson and Lloyd George, who championed national self-determination at Versailles, may not have meant their slogans to apply to the colonial world, but many intellectuals, both in the colonies and in Europe, could not easily draw lines to separate European nationalism from Indian or Chinese patriotism. Liberal democrats in the West began to talk of training the colonies for eventual self-government or independence. In France, democrats talked of French citizens of all colors within the empire. In the colonies, forces for independence grew, and intellectuals in the colonies for whom the democrats' timetable for equality or for self-government was too slow found leadership in the anti-imperialist campaign of Lenin and the Bolsheviks.

Less than three decades later, World War II exhausted the European colonial powers. It depleted their soldiery, their financial resources, and their willingness to wage war against their rebellious colonies. During this war, the Allies relied on colonies for labor, soldiers, bases, and supplies. Colonies and British Commonwealth states like Australia made giant strides toward industrialization to meet the Allies' demand for supplies. At the very moment that colonies were most important to their mother countries, they were taking steps toward greater economic independence. Furthermore, the inability of the Europeans to avoid the war's slaughter and the racist destruction of the Jews undercut any moral authority Westerners might have claimed. For British and French citizens the postwar task was to realize peace, democracy, and social welfare at home. For many, this meant that the colonies, or at least some of them, would have to have self-determination, perhaps even independence. The question was not *if* there would be self-determination, but *when, where,* and *how* it would occur.

Today, almost a century after the rapid division of the world among the European and U.S. powers and decades after the decolonization of most of the world, the results of imperialism persist. Imperialism has left a legacy of deep animosity in countries of Asia, Africa, and Latin America. Although most nations have political independence, Western economic and cultural domination still exists and often influences the policies of autonomous governments. Much of the world is still poor and suffers from insufficient capital, unskilled leaders, and unstable governments. Many people in these poor areas believe that their countries' condition has resulted from a century of Western exploitation. They also believe that any political turmoil in their areas is due to the fact that the superpowers regard the areas as strategic to their interests or important in their ideological power struggle.

Many people in the non-Western world, which some call the Third World, believe that Lenin's analysis of imperialism explains the continuing poverty and dependence of their nations. On the eve of World War I, Lenin, a revolutionary Marxist who was one of the architects of the Russian Revolution, argued that imperialism was necessary to the capitalist economy. He said that the only way that capitalist nations could maintain their economic and social organizations in an era of monopoly of production and finance was through exploiting the less developed world. Monopolistic capitalism was condemned to periodic depressions for lack of materials, markets, and capital, he said. Unless the governments of capitalist countries could ensure high wages and profits for their own people by exploiting colonial peoples, working-class revolutions would break

Chronology 27.1 Expansion of Western Dominance

1830	The French move into Algeria
1839–1842	The Opium War—defeat of the Chinese by the British, resulting in their annexing treaty ports in China and opening it to Western trade
1853	Commodore Perry, with U.S. naval forces, opens Japan to trade
1857–58	The Sepoy Mutiny—Britain replaces the East India Company and governs India through a viceroy
1867	Mexicans led by Juárez execute Emperor Maximilian; the Meiji Restoration in Japan
1869	The opening of the Suez Canal
1876	Stanley sets up posts in the Congo for Leopold II of Belgium
1878	Congress of Berlin—meeting of the Great Powers to prevent Russia from upsetting the balance of power in the Near East
1878–1881	British and Russian troops occupy Afghanistan
1881	The French take control of Tunisia
1882	Britain occupies Egypt
1883–1885	The French fight the Chinese to claim Indochina
1884	The Berlin Conference on Africa
1894–1895	Sino-Japanese War—the British, Russians, and French intervene to take away Japan's gains
1896	Ethiopians defeat Italian invaders at Adowa
1898	The Spanish-American War—the United States annexes the Philippines and Puerto Rico and occupies Cuba; the battle of Omdurman
1899–1902	The Boer War between the British and the Afrikaners
1900	The Boxers rebel against foreign presence in China
1904–1905	Russo-Japanese War—the Japanese defeat the Russians
1911	The Mexican Revolution; the Manchu Dynasty is overthrown and a republic formed; Sun Yat-sen becomes president; civil war breaks out in China
1919	Britain grants a legislative assembly in India; Gandhi's passive resistance movement broadens with the Amritsar Massacre; Kemal Atatürk emerges as the Turkish national leader; League of Nations mandate system established

out. Powerful business interests also pushed their governments to the verge of war to safeguard their profits. Lenin said that at the same time, imperialism greatly accelerated both development of capitalism and opposition to it among its victims in Asia, Africa, and Latin America. He predicted that struggle for empire would end in war between the Great Powers, a conflict that would draw the colonies into European affairs even faster than the operations of the market. Many people in the Third World use this analysis to explain the great events of the twentieth century, including the two world wars and the Great Depression.

Imperialism has been a source of great bitterness to former colonial peoples not only because of its economic exploitation but also because of its encouragement of racism and callous disregard of other cultures. Thus, non-Western nationalism has often possessed anti-Western elements. Today, European nations and the United States must deal in the areas of economics and politics with nations acutely conscious of their nationhood and quick to condemn any policy that they perceive as imperialistic.

World War II may have brought an end to the age of Western imperialism. But the world's dependence on European and U.S. industry and technology has not diminished. Out of the Industrial Revolution grew a global economy that has enveloped every part of the world. For food, for manufactured goods, for energy, for technology, all nations and peoples depend on forces beyond the control of any one country. This dependence, complicated by imperialism's legacy of bitterness and distrust, forms the heart of the world order today.

Suggested Reading

Baumgart, Winfried, *Imperialism* (1982). A critical examination of arguments and issues on the subject.

Betts, Raymond, *The False Dawn* (1975).

Brodie, Fawn, *Devil Drives: A Life of Sir Richard Burton* (1967). A fine biography of the great explorer.

Brunschwig, Henri, *French Colonialism: 1871–1914. Myths and Realities* (trans. 1964). His general thesis is similar to Robinson, Gallagher, and Denny (see below); the best book on French imperialism.

Headrick, Daniel, *The Tools of Empire* (1981). Interesting argument for the role of technology in imperialism.

———, *Tentacles of Progress: Technological Transfer in the Age of Imperialism, 1850–1940* (1988). Accompanies and expands his emphasis in *The Tools of Empire*.

Henderson, W. O., *Studies in German Colonial History* (1963). Several interesting essays on this topic, which is difficult to research in English sources.

Hobsbawm, Eric, *The Age of Empire* (1988). The third volume in his Marxist interpretation of that age.

Hobson, J. A., *Imperialism: A Study* (1902). This book and those of Luxemburg and Lenin (see below) are highly controversial and influential theoretical analyses.

Jeal, Tim, *Livingstone* (1974). A very readable biography of a fascinating life, with good background on Africa.

Langer, William, *European Alliances and Alignments, 1871–1890* and *Diplomacy of Imperialism, 1890–1902*, 2 vols. (1950). Indispensable sources for information about imperialism from the perspective of diplomatic history.

Lenin, V. I., *Imperialism: The Highest Stage in Capitalism* (1917). Classic debate.

Luxemburg, Rosa, *The Accumulation of Capital* (trans. 1963).

May, Ernest, *Imperial Democracy* (1961). American expansionism discussed more thoroughly and less controversially than is usual.

Porter, Bernard, *The Lion's Share: A Short History of British Imperialism, 1850–1970* (1975). A good survey history.

Robinson, R. E., John Gallagher, and Alice Denny, *Africa and the Victorians: The Official Mind of Imperialism* (1961). An essential book for this fascinating subject; well-written and controversial.

Thornton, A. P., *The Imperial Idea and Its Enemies: A Study in British Power*, 2nd ed. (1985). An interesting study of the ideas and policies of British imperialism.

Review Questions

1. How did industrialization change Europeans' relations with China, India, and Japan?

2. Why did imperialism grow after 1880? What rationalizations for European expansion were usually offered at the end of the nineteenth century?

3. What examples are there of successful resistance to Western imperialism?

4. How did imperialism fit in with the European alliance system? How did it cause it? How did imperialism undermine European stability under the alliance system?

5. What were the obstacles preventing Indian independence?

6. Why were Japan and China able to withstand imperialist expansion?

7. Why was Africa divided up in such a brief time?

8. How did imperialism threaten world peace in the early twentieth century?

9. Why did England and France (which seemed on the verge of war in 1898) make peace and form an alliance?

10. How was Turkey able to maintain itself in the nineteenth century against the encroachments of Europeans? Why did it fail to do so in the twentieth century?

11. What problems in the Middle East and Central Asia appear to have been resolved because Russia was defeated in World War I?

28

Modern Consciousness:
New Views of Nature,
Human Nature, and the Arts

T he modern mentality may be said to have passed through two broad phases: early modernity and late modernity. Formulated during the era of the Scientific Revolution and the Enlightenment, early modernity stressed confidence in reason, science, human goodness, and humanity's capacity to improve society for human betterment. Then in the late nineteenth and early twentieth centuries, a new outlook took shape. Late modern thinkers and scientists achieved revolutionary insights into human nature, the social world, and the physical universe; writers and artists opened up hitherto unimagined possibilities for artistic expression. These developments produced a shift in European consciousness. The mechanical model of the universe that had dominated the Western outlook since Newton had to be altered; the Enlightenment view of human rationality and goodness was questioned; the belief in natural rights and objective standards governing morality was attacked; rules of esthetics that had governed the arts since the Renaissance were dispensed with. Shattering old beliefs, late modernity left Europeans without landmarks, without generally accepted cultural standards or agreed upon conceptions about human beings and life's meaning.

The late modern period was marked by extraordinary creativity in thought and the arts. However imaginative and fruitful these changes were for Western intellectual and cultural life, though, they also helped to create the disoriented, fragmented, and troubled era that is the twentieth century.

Vincent van Gogh (1853–1890): *The Starry Night* 1889. Oil on canvas, 29 × 36¼". (*Collection, The Museum of Modern Art, New York. Acquired through the Lillie P. Bliss Bequest.*)

Irrationalism

Some late-nineteenth-century thinkers challenged the basic premises of the philosophes and their nineteenth-century heirs. They repudiated the Enlightenment conception of human rationality, stressing instead the irrational side of human behavior. For these thinkers it seemed that reason exercised a very limited influence over human conduct; impulses, drives, instincts—all forces below the surface—determined behavior much more than did logical consciousness. Like the romantics, proponents of the irrational placed more reliance on feeling and intuition than on reason. They belittled the intellect's attempt to comprehend nature and society, praised outbursts of the irrational, and in some instances exalted violence.

Nietzsche

The principal figure in the "dethronement of reason" and the glorification of the irrational was the German philosopher Friedrich Nietzsche (1844–1900). Nietzsche's writings are not systematic treatises but collections of aphorisms, often containing internal contradictions. For this reason his philosophy lends itself to misinterpretation and misapplication, as manifested by Nazi theorists who distorted Nietzsche to justify their theory of the German master race.

Nietzsche attacked the accepted views and convictions of his day as a hindrance to a fuller and richer existence. He denounced social reform, parliamentary government, and universal suffrage, ridiculed the vision of progress through science, condemned Christian morality, and mocked the liberal belief in man's essential goodness and rationality. He said that man must understand that life, which is replete with cruelty, injustice, uncertainty, and absurdity, is not governed by rational principles. There exist no absolute standards of good and evil whose truth can be demonstrated by reflective reason. There is only naked man living in a godless and absurd world.

Modern bourgeois society, said Nietzsche, was decadent and enfeebled—a victim of the excessive development of the rational faculties at the expense of will and instinct. Against the liberal-rationalist stress on the intellect, Nietzsche urged recognition of the dark, mysterious world of instinctual desires—the true forces of life. Smother the will with excessive intellectualizing and you destroy that spontaneity that sparks cultural creativity and ignites a zest for living. The critical and theoretical outlook destroyed the creative instincts. For man's manifold potential to be realized, he must forgo relying on the intellect and nurture again the instinctual roots of human existence.

Christianity, with all its prohibitions, restrictions, and demands to conform, also crushes the human impulse for life, said Nietzsche. Christian morality must be obliterated, for it is fit only for the weak, the slave. The triumph of Christianity in the ancient world, said Nietzsche, was a revolution of the meek to inherit the earth from the strong. Christian otherworldliness undermined man's will to control the world; Christian teachings saddled man with guilt, preventing him from expressing his instinctual nature. In *The Anti-Christ,* Nietzsche wrote:

> *Christianity has waged a* war to the death *against this* higher *type of man. . . . Christianity has taken the side of everything weak, base, ill-constituted, it has made an ideal out of opposition to the preservative instincts of strong life. . . . Christianity is a revolt of everything that crawls along the ground directed against that which is elevated. . . . Christianity is called the religion of* pity.— *Pity stands in antithesis to the basic emotions which enhance the energy of the feeling of life: it has a depressive effect. One loses force when one pities.*[1]

Although the philosophes had rejected Christian doctrines, they had largely retained Christian ethics. Nietzsche, however, did not attack Christianity because it was contrary to reason, as the philosophes had. He attacked Christianity because he said it gave man a sick soul. It was life-denying; it blocked the free and spontaneous exercise of human instincts and made humility and self-abnegation virtues and pride a vice; in short, Christianity extinguished the spark of life.

This spark of life, this inner yearning that is man's true essence, must again burn.

"God is dead," proclaimed Nietzsche. God is man's own creation; there are no higher worlds. Christian morality is also dead. The death of God and Christian values can mean the liberation of man, insisted Nietzsche. Man can surmount *nihilism* (the belief that moral and social values have no validity); he can create new values and achieve self-mastery. He can overcome the deadening uniformity and mediocrity of modern civilization. He can undo democracy and socialism, which have made masters out of cattlelike masses, and the shopkeeper's spirit, which has made man soft and degenerate. European society is without heroic figures; all belong to a vast herd but there are no shepherds. Europe can only be saved by the emergence of a higher type of man, the *superman* or *overman,* who will not be held back by the egalitarian rubbish preached by democrats and socialists. "It is necessary for *higher* man to declare war upon the masses," said Nietzsche, to end "the dominion of *inferior* men." Europe requires "the annihilation of universal suffrage—this is to say, that system by means of which the lowest natures prescribe themselves as a law for higher natures."[2] Europe needs a new breed of rulers, a true aristocracy of masterful men. The superman is a new kind of man who breaks with accepted morality and sets his own standards. He does not repress his instincts but asserts them. He destroys old values and asserts his prerogative as master. Free of Christian guilt, he proudly affirms his own being; dispensing with Christian "thou shalt not," he instinctively says "I will." He dares to be himself. Because he is not like other people, traditional definitions of good and evil have no meaning for him. He does not allow his individuality to be stifled. He makes his own values, those that flow from his very being. He knows that life is meaningless but lives it laughingly, instinctively, fully. The masses, cowardly and envious, will condemn the superman as evil; this has always been their way.

The superman grasps that "the most fundamental desire in man [is] his drive for power,"[3] that human beings crave and strive for power ceaselessly and uncompromisingly. This will to power governs everyday life and is the determining factor in international affairs. The enhancement of power brings supreme enjoyment: "The love of power is the demon of men. Let them have everything—health, food, a place to live, entertainment—they are and remain unhappy and low-spirited; for the demon waits and waits and will be satisfied. Take everything from them and satisfy this and they are almost happy—as happy as men and demons can be."[4]

The German philosopher Arthur Schopenhauer (1788–1860) had declared that beneath the conscious intellect is the will, a striving, demanding, and imperious force that is the real conductor of human behavior. Schopenhauer sought to repress the will. He urged people to stifle desires and retreat into quietude to escape from life's misfortunes. Nietzsche learned from Schopenhauer to appreciate the unconscious strivings that dominate human behavior, but Nietzsche called for the heroic and joyful assertion of the will to redeem life from nothingness.

Supermen are free of all restrictions, rules, and codes of behavior imposed by society. They burst upon the world propelled by that something that urges people to want, take, strike, create, struggle, seek, dominate. Supermen are people of restless energy who enjoy living dangerously, have contempt for meekness and humility, and dismiss humanitarian sentiments. At times Nietzsche declares that supermen, a new breed of nobles, will rule the planet; at other times he states that they will demonstrate their superiority by avoiding public life, ignoring established rules, and refraining from contact with inferiors.

The influence of Nietzsche's philosophy is still a matter of controversy and conjecture. Perhaps better than anyone else, Nietzsche recognized the ills of modern Western civilization and urged confronting them without hypocrisy or compromise. But he had no constructive proposals for dealing with the malaise of modern society. No social policy could be derived from his radical individualism. And his vitriolic attack on European institutions and values, immensely appealing to central European intellectuals, helped to erode the rational foundations of Western civilization. Many young people, attracted to Nietzsche's philosophy, welcomed World War I because they thought that it would forge a path to a new heroic age. They could not be blamed for taking literally Nietzsche's words: "A society that definitely and *instinctively* gives up war and conquest is in decline."[5]

The Nazis regarded themselves as embodiments of Nietzsche's superman. Nietzsche himself, who detested German nationalism and militarism, would have rejected Hitler; but Nietzsche's extreme and violent attack on Western values and his praise of power provided a breeding ground for violent and irrational ideologies.

Dostoevski

Like Nietzsche, Fëdor Dostoevski (1821–1881), a Russian novelist and essayist, attacked the rational-scientific tradition enshrined by the Enlightenment. In *Notes from the Underground* (1864), the narrator (the Underground Man) rebels against the efforts of rationalists, humanists, positivists, liberals, and socialists to define human nature according to universal principles and to reform society so as to promote greater happiness. He rebels against science and reason—against the entire liberal and socialist vision—and he does this in the name of human subjectivity—the uncontainable, irrepressible, whimsical, and foolish human will. Human nature, says the Underground Man, is too volatile, too diversified, to be schematized by the theoretical mind.

For the Underground Man, there are no absolute and timeless truths that precede the individual and to which the individual should conform. There is only a terrifying world of naked wills vying with one another. In such a world, people do not necessarily seek happiness, prosperity, and peace—all that is good for them, according to "enlightened" thinkers. To the rationalist who aims to eliminate suffering and deprivation, Dostoevski replies that some people freely choose suffering and depravity because it gratifies them—for some, "even in a toothache there is enjoyment"—and they are repelled by wealth, peace, security, and happiness. They do not want to be robots in a stringently regulated social order that creates a slot for everything, and they consider excessive intellectualizing—"over-acute consciousness"—a disease that keeps the individual from living fully.

> . . . it seems that something that is dearer to almost every man than his greatest advantages must really exist, . . . for which, if necessary, a man is ready to act in opposition to all laws, that is, in opposition to reason, honor, peace, prosperity. . . . One's own free unfettered choice, one's own fancy, however wild it may be, one's own fancy worked up at times to frenzy—why that is that very "most advantageous advantage" which we have overlooked, which comes under no classification and through which all systems and theories are continually being sent to the devil. . . . What man needs is simple independent choice, whatever that independence may cost and wherever it may lead.[6]

The Underground Man struggles to define his own existence according to his own needs, rather than in accordance with standards and values created by others. He regards freedom of choice as a human being's most priceless possession and holds that choice derives not from the intellect but from impulses and feelings that account for our essential individuality. For him, the "rational faculty . . . is . . . simply one-twentieth of all my faculties of life"; life is more than reasoning, more than "simply extracting square roots."[7]

Bergson

Another thinker who reflected the growing irrationalism of the age was Henri Bergson (1859–1941), a French philosopher of Jewish background. Originally attracted to positivism, Bergson turned away from the positivistic claim that science could explain everything and fulfill all human needs. Such an emphasis on the intellect, said Bergson, sacrifices spiritual impulses, imagination, and intuition and reduces the soul to a mere mechanism.

The methods of science cannot reveal ultimate reality, Bergson insisted. European civilization must recognize the limitations of scientific rationalism. The method of intuition, whereby the mind strives for an immanent relationship with the object, to become one with it, can tell us more about reality than the method of analysis employed by science. Entering into the object through an intuitive experience is an avenue to truth that is closed to the calculations and measurements of science. Although not based on scientific procedures, Bergson insisted, the method of intuition is a superior avenue to knowledge. The mind is not a collection of atoms operating according to mechanical principles but an active consciousness with profound intuitive capacities. Bergson's philosophy pointed away from science toward religious mysticism.

Sorel

Nietzsche proclaimed that irrational forces constitute the essence of human nature; Bergson held that a nonrational intuition provided insights unattainable by the scientific mentality. Georges Sorel (1847–1922), who gave up engineering to follow intellectual pursuits, was a French philosopher who recognized the political potential of the nonrational. Like Nietzsche, Sorel was disillusioned with contemporary bourgeois society, which he considered decadent, soft, and unheroic. Whereas Nietzsche called for the superman to rescue society from decadence and mediocrity, Sorel placed his hopes in the proletariat, whose position made them courageous, virile, and determined.

Sorel wanted the proletariat to destroy the existing order and make the workshop the model of a new society. This overthrow, said Sorel, would be accomplished through a general strike—a universal work stoppage that would bring down the government and give power to the workers.

The general strike had all the appeal of a great myth, said Sorel. What is important is not that the general strike will actually take place, but that its image stirs all the anticapitalist resentments of the workers and inspires them to their revolutionary responsibilities. Sorel understood the extraordinary potency of myths for eliciting total commitment and inciting heroic action. Because they appeal to the imagination and feelings, myths are an effective way of moving the masses to revolt. By believing in the myth of the general strike, workers would soar above the moral decadence of bourgeois society and bear the immense sacrifices that their struggle calls for.

Like Marx, Sorel believed that the goals of the worker could not be achieved through peaceful parliamentary means; he too wanted no reconciliation between bourgeois exploiters and oppressed workers. The only recourse for workers was direct action and violence, which Sorel regarded as en-

nobling, heroic, and sublime—a means of restoring grandeur to a flabby world.

Sorel's exaltation of violence and mass action, his condemnation of liberal democracy, and his recognition of the power and political utility of fabricated myths would find concrete expression in the fascist movements after World War I. Sorel heralded the age of mass political movements and myths manufactured by propaganda experts.

Freud: A New View of Human Nature

In many ways Sigmund Freud (1856–1939), an Austrian-Jewish doctor who spent most of his adult life in Vienna, was a child of the Enlightenment. Like the philosophes, Freud identified civilization with reason and regarded science as the avenue to knowledge. But unlike the philosophes, Freud focused on the massive power and influence of nonrational drives. Whereas Nietzsche glorified the irrational and approached it with a poet's temperament, Freud recognized its potential danger, sought to comprehend it scientifically, and wanted to regulate it in the interests of civilization. Unlike Nietzsche, Freud did not belittle the rational but always sought to salvage respect for reason.

Freud held that people are not fundamentally rational; human behavior is governed primarily by powerful inner forces that are hidden from consciousness. These instinctual strivings, rather than rational faculties, constitute the greater part of the mind. Freud's great achievement was to explore the world of the unconscious with the tools and temperament of a scientist. He considered not just the external acts of a person but also the inner psychic reality that underlies human behavior.

Freud sought to comprehend neuroses—disorders in thinking, feeling, and behavior that interfere with everyday acts of personal and social life. Neuroses can take several forms, including hysteria, anxiety, depression, and so on. To understand neuroses, said Freud, one had to look beyond a patient's symptoms and discover those unconscious factors, generally sexual in nature, that are at the root of the person's distress. The

Freud and His Daughter Anna in the Dolomites, 1912. Sigmund Freud, the father of psychoanalysis, penetrated the world of the unconscious in a scientific way. He concluded that powerful drives govern human behavior more than reason does. His explorations of the unconscious produced an image of the human being that broke with the Enlightenment's view of the individual's essential rationality. (*Mary Evans Picture Library*)

key to the unconscious, he said, was the interpretation of dreams.

The *id*, the unconscious seat of the instincts, constantly demands gratification, said Freud. Unable to endure tension, it demands sexual release, the termination of pain, the cessation of hunger. When the id is denied an outlet for its instinctual energy, people become frustrated, angry, and unhappy. Gratifying the id is our highest pleasure.

But the full gratification of instinctual demands is detrimental to civilized life.

Freud postulated a terrible conflict between the relentless strivings of our instinctual nature and the requirements of civilization. Civilization, for Freud, requires the renunciation of instinctual gratification and the mastery of animal instincts, a thesis he developed in *Civilization and Its Discontents* (1930). Although Freud's thoughts in this work were no doubt influenced by the great tragedy of World War I, the main theme could be traced back to his earlier writings. Human beings derive their highest pleasure from sexual fulfillment, said Freud, but unrestrained sexuality drains off psychic energy needed for creative artistic and intellectual life. Hence society, through the family, the priest, the teacher, and the police, imposes rules and restrictions on our animal nature. But this is immensely painful. People are caught in a tragic bind. Society's demand for the denial of full instinctual gratification causes terrible frustration; equally distressing, the violation of society's rules under the pressure of instinctual needs evokes terrible feelings of guilt. Either way people suffer; civilized life simply entails too much pain for people. It seems that the price we pay for civilization is neurosis. Most people cannot endure the amount of instinctual renunciation that civilization requires. There are times when our elemental human nature rebels against all the restrictions and "thou shalt nots" demanded by society, against all the misery and torment imposed by civilization.

"Civilization imposes great sacrifices not only on man's sexuality but also on his aggressivity,"[8] said Freud. People are not good by nature, as the philosophes had taught; on the contrary, they are "creatures among whose instinctual endowments is to be reckoned a powerful share of aggressiveness." Their first inclination is not to love their neighbor but to "satisfy their aggressiveness on him, to exploit his capacity for work without compensation, to use him sexually without his consent, to seize his possessions, to humiliate him, to cause him pain, to torture and to kill him."[9] Man is wolf to man, concluded Freud. "Who has the courage to dispute it in the face of all the evidence in his own life and in history?"[10] Civilization "has to use its utmost efforts in order to set limits to man's aggressive instincts," but "in spite of every effort these endeavors of civilization have not so far achieved very much."[11] People find it difficult to do without "the satisfaction of this inclination to aggression."[12] When circumstances are favorable, this primitive aggressiveness breaks loose and "reveals man as a savage beast to whom consideration towards his own kind is something alien."[13] For Freud, "the inclination to aggression is an original self-subsisting disposition in man . . . that . . . constitutes the greatest impediment to civilization." Civilization attempts "to combine single human individuals and after that families, then races, peoples and nations into one great unity. . . . But man's natural aggressive instinct, the hostility of each against all and of all against each, opposes this program of civilization."[14] Aggressive impulses drive people apart, threatening society with disintegration. For Freud an unalterable core of human nature is ineluctably in opposition to civilized life. To this extent everyone is potentially an enemy of civilization.

Freud's awareness of the irrational and his general pessimism regarding people's ability to regulate it in the interests of civilization did not lead him to break faith with the Enlightenment tradition, for Freud did not celebrate the irrational. He was too aware of its self-destructive nature for that. Civilization is indeed a burden, but people must bear it, for the alternative is far worse. In the tradition of the philosophes, Freud sought truth based on a scientific analysis of human nature and believed that reason was the best road to social improvement. Like the philosophes, he was critical of religion, regarding it as a pious illusion—a fairy tale in conflict with reason. Freud wanted people to throw away what he believed was the crutch of religion—to break away from childlike dependency and stand alone. Also like the philosophes, Freud was a humanitarian who sought to relieve human misery by making people aware of their true nature, particularly their sexuality. He wanted society to soften its overly restrictive sexual standards because they were injurious to mental health. As a practicing psychiatrist, he tried to assist his patients in dealing with emotional problems. Freud wanted to raise to the level of consciousness hitherto unrecognized inner conflicts that caused emotional distress.

Although Freud undoubtedly was a child of the Enlightenment, in crucial ways he differed from the philosophes. Regarding the Christian doctrine of original sin as myth, the philosophes had believed that people's nature was essentially good. If people took reason as their guide, evil could be eliminated. Freud, however, asserted, in secular and scientific terms, a pessimistic view of human nature. Freud saw evil as rooted in human nature rather than as a product of a faulty environment. Education and better living conditions will not eliminate evil, as the philosophes expected, nor will abolition of private property, as Marx had declared. The philosophes venerated reason; it had enabled Newton to unravel nature's mysteries and would permit people to achieve virtue and reform society. Freud, who wanted reason to prevail, understood that its soft voice had to compete with the thunderous roars of the id. Freud broke with the optimism of the philosophes. His awareness of the immense pressures that civilization places on our fragile egos led him to be generally pessimistic about the future. Unlike Marx, Freud had no vision of utopia.

The Modernist Movement
Breaking with Conventional Modes of Esthetics

At the same time that Freud was breaking with the Enlightenment view of human nature, artists and writers were rebelling against traditional forms of artistic and literary expression that had governed European cultural life since the Renaissance. Their experimentations produced a great cultural revolution called *modernism*, which still profoundly influences the arts. In some ways, modernism was a continuation of the Romantic Movement that had dominated European culture in the early nineteenth century. Both movements subjected to searching criticism cultural styles that had been formulated during the Renaissance and had roots in ancient Greece.

But even more than romanticism, modernism aspired to an intense introspection—a heightened awareness of self—and saw the intellect as a barrier to the free expression of elemental human emotions. More than their romantic predecessors, modernist artists and writers abandoned conventional literary and artistic models and experimented with new modes of expression. The consequence of their bold venture, says literary critic and historian Irving Howe, was nothing less than the "breakup of the traditional unity and continuity of Western culture."[15]

Like Freud, modernist artists and writers went beyond surface appearances in search of a more profound reality hidden in the human psyche. Writers like Thomas Mann, Marcel Proust, James Joyce, August Strindberg, D. H. Lawrence, and Franz Kafka explored the inner life of the individual and the psychopathology of human relations; they dealt with the predicament of men and women who rejected the values and customs of their day, and they depicted the anguish of people burdened by guilt, torn by internal conflicts, and driven by an inner self-destructiveness; they showed the overwhelming might of the irrational and the seductive power of the primitive and broke the silence about sex that had prevailed in Victorian literature.

From the Renaissance through the Enlightenment and into the nineteenth century, Western esthetic standards had been shaped by the conviction that the universe embodied an inherent mathematical order. A corollary of this conception of the outer world as orderly and intelligible was the view that art should imitate reality. From the Renaissance on, says sociologist Daniel Bell, art was seen as "a mirror of nature, a representation of life. Knowledge was a reflection of what was 'out there', . . . a copy of what was seen."[16] Since the Renaissance, artists had deliberately made use of laws of perspective and proportion; musicians had used harmonic chords that brought rhythm and melody into a unified whole; writers had produced works according to a definite pattern that included a beginning, middle, and end.

Modernist culture, however, acknowledged no objective reality of space, motion, and time that means the same to all observers. Rather, reality can be grasped in many ways; a multiplicity of frames of reference apply to nature and human experience. Reality is what the viewer perceives it to be through the prism of the imagination. "There is no outer reality," said the modernist German poet Gottfried Benn, "there is only human consciousness, constantly building, modifying, rebuilding new worlds out of its own

creativity."[17] Modernism is concerned less with the object itself than with how the artist experiences it, with the sensations that an object evokes in the artist's very being, with the meaning the artist's imagination imposes on reality. Bell expresses this point in reference to painting:

> Modernism . . . denies the primacy of an outside reality, as given. It seeks either to rearrange that reality, or to retreat to the self's interior, to private experience as the source of its concerns and aesthetic preoccupations. . . . There is an emphasis on the self as the touchstone of understanding and on the activity of the knower rather than the character of the object as the source of knowledge. . . . Thus one discerns the intentions of modern painting . . . to break up ordered space. . . . to bridge the distance between object and spectator, to "thrust" itself on the viewer and establish itself immediately by impact.[18]

Dispensing with conventional forms of esthetics that stressed structure and coherence, modernism propelled the arts into uncharted seas. Recoiling from a middle-class, industrial civilization that valued rationalism, organization, clarity, stability, and definite norms and values, modernist writers and artists were fascinated by the bizarre, the mysterious, the unpredictable, the primitive, the irrational, the formless. Writers, for example, experimented with new techniques to convey the intense struggle between the conscious and the unconscious, to connote the aberrations and complexities of human personality and the irrationality of human behavior. In particular they devised a new way—the stream of consciousness—to exhibit the mind's every level—both conscious reflection and unconscious strivings—and to capture how thought is punctuated by spontaneous outbursts, disconnected assertions, random memories, hidden desires, and persistent fantasies. Musicians like Igor Stravinsky and Arnold Schoenberg experimented with dissonance and primitive rhythms. When Stravinsky's ballet *The Rite of Spring* was performed in Paris in 1913, the theater audience rioted to protest the composition's break with tonality, its use of primitive, jazzlike rhythms, and its theme of ritual sacrifice.

The modernist movement, which began near the end of the nineteenth century, was in full bloom before World War I and would continue to flower in the postwar world. Probably the clearest expression of the modernist viewpoint is found in art.

Modern Art

In the late nineteenth century, artists began to turn away from the standards that had characterized art since the Renaissance. No longer committed to depicting how an object appears to the eye, they searched for new forms of expression.

The history of modern painting begins with impressionism, which covered the period 1860–1886 and broke with traditional formulas of composition (the arrangement of figures and objects) and treatments of color and light. Impressionism centered in Paris and its leading figures were Edouard Manet, Claude Monet, Camille Pissaro, Edgar Degas, and Pierre Auguste Renoir. Taking Pissaro's advice—"Don't proceed according to rules and principles but paint what you observe and feel"—impressionists tried to give their own immediate and personal impression of an object or an event. They tried to capture how movement, color, and light appeared to the eye at a fleeting instant.

Intrigued by the impact that light has on objects, impressionists left their studios for the countryside, where they painted nature under an open sky. They used bold colors and drew marked contrasts between light and dark to reflect how objects in intense sunlight seem to shimmer against their background.

In addition to landscapes, the impressionists painted railways, bridges and boulevards, and people—in dance halls, in cafés, in theaters, in public gardens. Impressionistic painters wanted to portray life, as it was commonly experienced in a rapidly industrializing and urbanizing world. And always they tried to convey their momentary impression of an event or figure.

In the late 1880s and the 1890s, several artists went beyond impressionism. Called postimpressionists, they further revolutionized the artist's sense of space and color. Even more than the impressionists, they tried to make art a vivid emotional experience and to produce a personal

Igor Stravinsky (1882–1971), sketched by Pablo Picasso (1881–1973). Although Picasso's sketch of Stravinsky is conservative in style, Stravinsky himself introduced revolutionary innovations in music, as Picasso did in art. Stravinsky experimented with dissonance and primitive rhythms. The premiere of his ballet, *The Rite of Spring,* was marked by a riot. (*Cliché: Musée Picasso/© ARS N.Y./ SPADEM 1988*)

impression of reality rather than a photographic copy of objects.

Paul Cézanne (1839–1906) was born in the south of France and came to Paris, the center of the Western art world. In 1882, he returned to the region of his birth, where he painted its natural scenery. Cézanne sought to portray his visual perception of an object, not the object itself. In other words, to what is seen, the artist brings a personal apperception, which his or her intelligence organizes into a work of art. When painting objects in a group, Cézanne deliberately distorted perspective, subordinating the appearance of an individual object to the requirements of the total design. Cézanne tried to demonstrate that an object, when placed together with other objects, is seen differently than when it stands alone. His concern with form and design influenced the cubists. (See color insert, "The Emergence of Modern Art," Figure 3.)

No longer bound by classical art forms, artists examined non-Western art, searching for new forms of beauty and new ways of expression. A large number of artifacts and art objects from Asia, Africa, and the Pacific area coming into European capitals as souvenirs of nineteenth-century imperialist ventures and from anthropologists and ethnographers stimulated interest in non-Western art. Paul Gauguin (1848–1903) saw beauty in carvings and fabrics made by such technologically backward people as the Marquesas Islanders. He also discovered that art did not depend on skilled craftsmanship for its power. Very simple, even primitive, means of construction could produce works of great beauty.

A successful Parisian stockbroker, Gauguin abandoned the marketplace for art. He came to view bourgeois civilization as artificial and rotten. By severing human beings from the power of their own feelings, industrial civilization blunted the creative expression of the imagination and prevented people from attaining a true understanding of themselves. For these reasons Gauguin fled to Tahiti. On this picturesque island, which was largely untouched by European ways, he hoped to discover humanity's original nature without the distortion and corruption of modern civilization. (See color insert, Figure 2.)

The postimpressionists produced a revolution not only of space but also of color, as exemplified by Vincent van Gogh (1853–1890). The son of a Dutch minister, van Gogh was a lonely, tortured, and impetuous soul. For a short period he served as a lay preacher among desperately poor coal miners. Moving to Paris in 1886, van Gogh came under the influence of the French impressionists. Desiring to use color in a novel way—his own way—van Gogh left Paris for the Mediterranean countryside, where he hoped to experience a new vision of sunlight, sky, and earth. Van Gogh used purer, brighter colors than artists had used before. He also recognized that color, like other formal qualities, could act as a language in and of itself.

He believed that the local or "real" color of an object does not necessarily express the artist's experience. Artists, according to van Gogh, should seek to paint things not as they are, but as the artists feel them. *The Starry Night* (see page 632) conveys his vision of a night sky, not with tiny points of lights, but with exploding and whirling stars in a vast universe, overwhelming the huddled dwellings built by human beings. The foreboding dark cypress intrudes into the sky's turbulence of intense yellow lights.

Practically unknown in his lifetime, van Gogh's art became extremely influential soon after his death in 1890. One of the first artists to be affected by his style was the Norwegian artist Edvard Munch (1863–1944), who saw van Gogh's use of color while in Paris. In *The Dance of Life,* for example, Munch used strong, simple lines and intense color to explore unexpressed sexual stresses and conflicts. In *The Scream,* he deliberately distorted the human face and the sky, ground, and water to portray terror.

After the postimpressionists, art moved still further away from reproducing an exact likeness of a physical object or human being. Increasingly, artists sought to penetrate the deepest recesses of the unconscious, which they saw as the wellspring of creativity and the dwelling place of a higher truth. Paul Klee, a prominent twentieth-century artist, described modern art as follows:

> *Each [artist] should follow where the pulse of his own heart leads. . . . Our pounding heart drives us down, deep down to the source of all. What springs from this source, whether it may be called dream, idea or phantasy—must be taken seriously. . . .*[19]

In Germany the tendency to use color for its power to express psychological forces continued in the work of artists known as the German expressionists. In Ernst Ludwig Kirchner's (1880–1938) *Reclining Nude* of 1909, strong, acid yellows and greens evoke feelings of tension, stress, and isolation. Kirchner also used bold, rapid lines to define flat shapes, a technique borrowed from folk art and from non-Western native traditions. (See color insert, Figure 5.)

In France, another group of avant-garde artists called the *fauves* ("the wild beasts") used color with great freedom to express intense feelings and heightened energy. After examining the works of the fauves, a French critic wrote: "What is presented here . . . has nothing to do with painting; some formless confusion of colors, blue, red, yellow, green, the barbaric and naive spirit of the child who plays with the box of colors he has just got as a Christmas present."[20] Rebelling against new currents in painting, critics failed to recognize the originality and genius of the fauves.

Henri Matisse (1869–1954), the leading fauvist painter, freed color from every restriction. He painted broad areas with stunning pigment unrelated to the real colors of the subject. His brilliant use of color and design aroused a violent reaction; one New York critic said of a Matisse exhibition: "ugliness that is most appalling . . . artistic degeneration . . . hideousness."[21]

Between 1909 and 1914, a new style called *cubism* was developed by Pablo Picasso (1881–1973) and Georges Braque (1882–1963). They explored the interplay between the flat world of the canvas and the three-dimensional world of visual perception. Like the postimpressionists, they sought to paint a reality deeper than what the eye sees at first glance.

In a typical Renaissance or baroque painting, objects are set inside an imaginary block of space, and they are represented from a single, stationary point of view. A cubist work is constructed on a different system, so that it re-creates the experience of seeing in a space of time. One can only know the nature of a volume by seeing it from many angles. Therefore, cubist art presents objects from multiple viewpoints. The numerous fragmentary images of cubist art make one aware of the complex experience of seeing. One art historian describes cubism as follows: "The cubist is not interested in usual representational standards. It is as if he were walking around the object he is analyzing, as one is free to walk around a piece of sculpture for successive views. But he must represent all these views at once."[22]

The colors used in early cubist art are deliberately banal, and the subjects represented are ordinary objects from everyday life. Picasso and Braque wanted to eliminate eye-catching color and intriguing subject matter so that their audiences would focus on the process of *seeing* itself.

In *Les Demoiselles d'Avignon*, Picasso painted

Edvard Munch (1863–1944): The Scream, 1893. The dark forces of emotional pain and sexual aberration fill the canvasses of Norwegian postimpressionist Edvard Munch. The tormented human being in *The Scream* reshapes both the world and its very own form in a blinding cry of psychic anguish. (*Nasjonalgalleriet, Oslo*)

five nudes. In each instance the body is distorted in defiance of classical and Renaissance standards of beauty. The masklike faces show Picasso's debt to African art and together with the angular shapes deprive the subjects of individuality and personality. The head of the squatting figure combines a profile with a full face—Picasso's attempt to present multiple aspects of an object at the same time. (See color insert, Figure 4.)

Throughout the period from 1890 to 1914, avant-garde artists were de-emphasizing subject matter and stressing the expressive power of such formal qualities as line, color, and space. It is not surprising that some artists finally began to create work that did not refer to anything seen in the real world. Piet Mondrian (1872–1944), a Dutch artist, came to Paris shortly before World War I. There he saw the cubist art of Picasso and Braque. The cubists had compressed the imaginary depth in their paintings so that all the objects seemed to be contained within a space only a few inches deep. They had also reduced subject matter to insignificance. It seemed to Mondrian that the next step was to get rid of illusionistic space and subject matter entirely. His painting *Broadway Boogie Woogie,* for example, appears flat. Looking at Mondrian's paintings is a kinesthetic experience, as one senses the delicate interplay of balances and counterweights. By eliminating from his painting any reference to the visible world, Mondrian helped to inaugurate abstract art. (See color insert, Figure 8.)

Another founder of abstract art was Wassily Kandinsky (1866–1944), a Russian residing in Germany. Kandinsky gradually came to remove all traces of the physical world from his paintings, to create a nonobjective art that bears no resemblance to the natural world. In stating that he "painted . . . subconsciously in a state of strong inner tension,"[23] Kandinsky explicitly expressed a principal quality of modern art.

Just before World War I, a young French artist named Marcel Duchamp (1887–1968) observed that things become art when the artist designates them as such, usually by placing them in an art context. *Art,* in other words, can be defined as a mode of perception. As the cubists had demonstrated, objects are always seen in relation to other objects in the environment. With *Bicycle Wheel,* Duchamp pairs two familiar objects (a bicycle wheel and a wooden stool) in a bizarre, unfamiliar way. Most people associate speed, movement, and transportation with bicycle wheels. Stools, however, must remain stationary in order to function as seats. In attaching the wheel to the stool, Duchamp robbed both utilitarian objects of their functions: the wheel can only spin aimlessly in the air, and the stool is no longer suitable for sitting. The resulting assemblage, when seen in The Museum of Modern Art equipped with stand and label, has become art. Duchamp's *Bicycle Wheel* is a sculpture that amuses, disturbs, and challenges viewers (see page 750).

The revolution in art that took place near the turn of the twentieth century is reverberating still. After nearly a hundred years, these masters of modern art continue to inspire their audiences with their passion and vision. In breaking with the Renaissance view of the world as inherently orderly and rational, modern artists opened up new possibilities for artistic expression. They exemplified the growing power and appeal of the nonrational in European life.

Social Thought: Confronting the Irrational and the Complexities of Modern Society

The end of the nineteenth and the beginning of the twentieth centuries mark the great age of sociological thought. The leading sociological thinkers of the period all regarded science as the only valid model for correct thinking and all claimed that their thought rested on a scientific foundation. They struggled with some of the crucial problems of modern society. How can society achieve coherence and stability when religion no longer unites people? What are the implications of the nonrational for political life? How can people preserve their individuality in a society that is becoming increasingly regimented?

Durkheim

Émile Durkheim (1858–1917), a French scholar of Jewish background, and heir to Comte's positivism, was an important founder of modern sociology. Like Comte, he considered scientific thought the only valid model for modern society. A crucial element of Durkheim's thought was the effort to show that the essential ingredients of modern times—secularism, rationalism, and individualism—threaten society with disintegration. In traditional society a person's place and function were determined by birth. Modern people, how-

Georges Seurat (1859–1891): Invitation to the Sideshow. Although late-nineteenth-century art often mirrors the instability of society and the individual, many artists sought a mathematical, concrete view of reality. Seurat was a sober, scientific artist who studied the underlying structure of objects and light. His style, characterized by thousands of dots of color, captures solidity and luminosity. (*The Metropolitan Museum of Art, Bequest of Stephen C. Clark, 1960. 61.101.17*)

ever, captivated by the principle of individualism, will not accept such restraints. They seek to uplift themselves and demand that society allow them the opportunity. In the process, they reject or ignore the social restraints that society so desperately requires, thereby giving rise to a spirit of anarchy.

The weakening of those traditional ties that bind the individual to society constituted, for Durkheim, the crisis of modern society. Without collective values and common beliefs, he felt, society was threatened with disintegration and the individual with disorientation. To a Western world intrigued by scientific progress, Durkheim emphasized the spiritual malaise of modern society. Modern people, said Durkheim, suffer from

anomie—a collapse of values. They do not feel integrated into a collective community and find no purpose in life. In *Suicide* (1897), Durkheim maintained that the pathology of modern society is demonstrated by its high rate of suicide. Modern people are driven to suicide by intense competition and the disappointment and frustration resulting from unfulfilled expectations and lack of commitment to moral principles. People must limit their aspirations and exercise discipline over their desires and passions. They must stop wanting more. Religion once could spur people to do these things, but it no longer can.

Durkheim approved of modernity, but he noted that modern ways have not brought happiness or satisfaction to the individual. Modern scientific and industrial society requires a new moral system that will bind together the various classes into a cohesive social order and help to overcome those feelings of restlessness and dissatisfaction that torment people. Like Saint-Simon, Durkheim called for a rational and secular system of morals to replace Christian dogma, which had lost its power to attract and to bind. If a rational and secular replacement for Christianity is not found, society runs the risk of dispensing with moral beliefs altogether and this vacuum it could not endure. Like the positivists, Durkheim insisted that the new moral beliefs must be discovered through the methods of science.

Durkheim hoped that occupational and professional organizations—updated medieval guilds—would integrate the individual into society and provide the moral force able to restrain the selfish interests of both employer and worker. By curbing egoism, fostering self-discipline, and promoting altruism, these organizations could provide substitutes for religion.

Pareto

Like Comte, Vilfredo Pareto (1848–1923), an Italian economist and sociologist, aimed to construct a system of sociology on the model of the physical sciences. His studies led him to conclude that social behavior does not rest primarily on reason but on nonrational instincts and sentiments. These deeply rooted and essentially changeless feelings are the fundamental elements in human behavior. Although society may change, human nature remains essentially the same. Whoever aims to lead and to influence people must appeal not to logic but to elemental feelings. Most human behavior is nonrational; nonlogical considerations also determine the beliefs that people hold. Like Marx and Freud, Pareto believed that we cannot accept a person's word at face value; in human instincts and sentiments we find the real cause of human behavior. People do not act according to carefully thought-out theories; they act first from nonlogical motivations and then construct a rationalization to justify their behavior. Much of Pareto's work was devoted to studying the nonrational elements of human conduct and the various beliefs invented to give the appearance of rationality to behavior that derives from feeling and instinct.

Pareto divided society into two strata—an elite and the masses. In the tradition of Machiavelli, Pareto held that a successful ruling elite must, with cunning, and if necessary violence, exploit the feelings and impulses of the masses to its own advantage. Democratic states, he said, delude themselves in thinking that the masses are really influenced by rational argument. Pareto predicted that new political leaders would emerge who would master the people through propaganda and force, appealing always to sentiment rather than reason. To this extent, Pareto was an intellectual forerunner of fascism.

Weber

Probably the most prominent social thinker of the age and a leading shaper of modern sociology was Max Weber (1864–1920). To Weber, a German academic, Western civilization, unlike the other civilizations of the globe, had virtually eliminated myth, mystery, and magic from its conception of nature and society. This process of rationalization—the "disenchantment of the world," as Weber called it—was most conspicuous in Western science, but it was also evident in politics and economics. Weber considered Western science an attempt to understand and master nature through reason, and Western capitalism an attempt to organize work and production in a rational manner. The Western state has a rational written constitution, rationally formulated law, and a bureaucracy of trained government officials that administers the affairs of state according to rational rules and regulations.

The question of why the West, and not China or India, engaged in this process of rationalization intrigued Weber, and much of his scholarly effort went into answering it. Weber showed how various religious beliefs have influenced people's understanding of nature and their economic behavior. Weber's most famous thesis is that Protestantism produced an outlook that was conducive to the requirements of capitalism (see page 306). Weber also explained how religious values hindered the process of rationalization in China and India.

Weber understood the terrible paradox of reason. Reason accounts for brilliant achievements in science and economic life, but it also despiritualizes life by ruthlessly eliminating centuries-old traditions, denouncing deeply felt religious beliefs as superstition, and regarding human feelings and passions as impediments to clear thinking. The process of disenchantment has given people knowledge, but it has also made people soulless and life meaningless. This is the dilemma of modern individuals, said Weber. Science cannot give people a purpose for living and the burgeoning of bureaucracy in government, business, and education stifles individual autonomy.

> It is horrible to think that the world could one day be filled with nothing but those little cogs, little men clinging to little jobs and striving towards bigger ones. . . . This passion for bureaucracy . . . is enough to drive one to despair. . . . That the world should know no men but these: it is in such an evolution that we are already caught up, and the great question is, therefore, not how we can promote and hasten it, but what can we oppose to this machinery in order to keep a portion of mankind free from this parceling-out of the soul, from this supreme mastery of the bureaucratic way of life.[24]

The prospect existed that people would refuse to endure this violation of their spiritual needs and would reverse the process of disenchantment by seeking redemption in the irrational. Weber himself, however, was committed to the ideals of the Enlightenment and to perpetuating the rational scientific tradition, which he felt was threatened by bureaucratic regimentation on the one hand and irrational human impulses on the other.

Like Freud, Weber believed that to safeguard reason, it was necessary to comprehend human irrationality. One expression of the irrational that Weber analyzed in considerable depth was the charismatic leader who attracts people by force of personality. Charismatic leaders may be religious prophets, war heroes, demagogues, or others who possess this extraordinary personality that attracts and dominates others. People yearn for charismatic leadership, particularly during times of crisis. The leader claims a mission—a sacred duty—to lead the people during the crisis; the leader's authority rests on the people's belief in the mission and their faith in the leader's extraordinary abilities. A common allegiance to the charismatic leader unites the community. Weber's analysis of this phenomenon throws light on the popularity of twentieth-century dictators and demagogues.

Modern Physics

Until the closing years of the nineteenth century the view of the universe held by the Western mind rested largely on the classical physics of Newton and included the following principles: (1) Time, space, and matter were objective realities that existed independently of the observer. (2) The universe was a giant machine whose parts obeyed strict laws of cause and effect. (3) The atom, indivisible and solid, was the basic unit of matter. (4) Heated bodies emitted radiation in continuous waves. (5) Through further investigation it would be possible to gain complete knowledge of the physical universe.

Between the 1890s and the 1920s, this view of the universe was shattered by a second Scientific Revolution. The discovery of x-rays by Wilhelm Konrad Roentgen in 1895, of radioactivity by Henri Bequerel in 1896, and of the electron by J. J. Thomson in 1897 led science to abandon the conception of the atom as a solid and indivisible particle. Rather than resembling a billiard ball, the atom consisted of a nucleus of tightly packed protons separated from orbiting electrons by empty space.

In 1900, Max Planck, a German physicist, proposed the quantum theory, which holds that a heated body does not radiate energy in a continuous unbroken stream, as had been believed, but in intermittent spurts, or jumps, called quanta. Planck's theory of discontinuity in energy radiation challenged a cardinal principle of classical physics that action in nature was strictly continuous.

In 1905, Albert Einstein, a German-Swiss physicist of Jewish lineage, substantiated and elaborated on Planck's theory by suggesting that

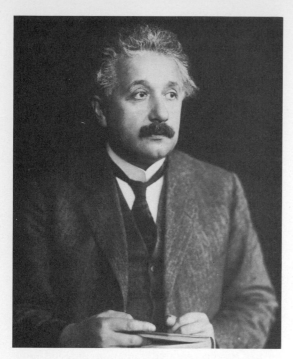

Albert Einstein. Einstein was a principal architect of modern physics. Forced to flee Nazi Germany before World War II, he became a United States citizen. He was appointed to the Institute for Advanced Study at Princeton, N.J. (*Culver Pictures*)

all forms of radiant energy—light, heat, x-rays—moved through space in discontinuous packets of energy. Then, in 1913, Niels Bohr, a Danish scientist, applied Planck's theory of energy quanta to the interior of the atom and discovered that the Newtonian laws of motion could not fully explain what happened to electrons orbiting an atomic nucleus.

As physicists explored the behavior of the atom further, it became apparent that its nature was fundamentally elusive and unpredictable. They soon observed that radioactive atoms threw off particles and transformed themselves from atoms of one element into atoms of an entirely different element. But the transformation of a single atom in a mass of radioactive material could not be predicted according to inexorable laws of cause and effect. For example, it is known that over a period of 1,620 years, half the atoms of the element radium decay and transform themselves

into atoms of another element. It is impossible, however, to know when a particular atom in a lump of radium will undergo this transformation. Scientists can only make accurate predictions about the behavior of an aggregate of radium atoms; the transformation of any given radium atom is the result of random chance rather than of any known physical law. That we cannot predict when a particular radioactive atom will decay calls into question the notion of classical physics that physical nature proceeds in an orderly fashion in accordance with strict laws of cause and effect.

Newtonian physics says that given certain conditions, we can predict what will follow. For example, if an airplane is flying north at 400 miles per hour, we can predict its exact position two hours from now, assuming that the plane does not alter its course or speed. Quantum mechanics teaches that in the subatomic realm, we cannot predict with certainty what will take place; we can only say that given certain conditions, it is *probable* that a certain event will follow. This principle of uncertainty was developed in 1927 by the German scientist Werner Heisenberg, who showed that it is impossible to determine at one and the same time both an electron's precise speed and its position. Science writer Alan E. Nourse explains:

> [*Heisenberg showed*] *that the very act of attempting to examine an electron any more closely in order to be* more certain *of where it was and what it was doing at a given instant* would itself alter where the electron was and what it was doing at the instant in question. *Heisenberg, in effect, was saying that in dealing with the behavior of electrons and other elementary particles the laws of cause and effect do not and cannot apply, that all we can do is make predictions about them on the basis of probability and not a very high degree of probability at that. . . . the more certain we try to become about a given electron's* position *at a given instant, the wider the limits of probability we must accept with regard to what its* momentum [*speed*] *is at the same time, and vice versa. The more closely either one property of the electron or the other is examined, the more closely we approach certainty with regard to one property or the*

other, the more wildly uncertain the other property becomes. And since an electron can really only be fully described in terms of both its position and its momentum at any given instant, it becomes utterly impossible to describe an electron at all in terms of absolute certainties. We can describe it only in terms of uncertainties or probabilities.[25]

In the small-scale world of the electron, we enter a universe of uncertainty, probability, and statistical relationships. No improvement in measurement techniques will dispel this element of chance and provide us with complete knowledge of the universe.

Although Einstein could not accept that a complete comprehension of reality was unattainable, his theory of relativity was instrumental in the shaping of modern physics; it altered classical conceptions of space and time. Newtonian physics had viewed space as a distinct physical reality, a stationary and motionless medium through which light traveled and matter moved. Time was viewed as a fixed and rigid framework that was the same for all observers and existed independently of human experience. For Einstein, however, neither space nor time had an independent existence; neither could be divorced from human experience. Once asked to explain briefly the essentials of relativity, Einstein replied: "It was formerly believed that if all material things disappeared out of the universe, time and space would be left. According to the relativity theory, however, time and space disappear together with the things."[26]

Contrary to all previous thinking, relativity theory holds that time differs for two observers traveling at different speeds. Imagine twin brothers involved in space exploration, one as an astronaut, the other as a rocket designer who never leaves earth. The astronaut takes off in the most advanced space ship yet constructed, one that achieves a speed close to the maximum attainable in our universe—the speed of light. After traveling several trillion miles, the spaceship turns around and returns to earth. According to the experience of the ship's occupant, the whole trip took about two years. But when the astronaut lands on earth, he finds totally changed conditions. For one thing, his brother has long since died, for according to earth's calendars some two

hundred years have elapsed since the rocket ship set out on its journey. Such an occurrence seemed to defy all common-sense experience, yet experiments supported Einstein's claims.

Motion, too, is relative. The only way we can describe the motion of one body is to compare it with another moving body. This means that there is no motionless, absolute, fixed frame of reference anywhere in the universe. The following illustration by science writer Isaac Asimov illustrates Einstein's theory of the relativity of motion:

Suppose we on the earth were to observe a strange planet ("Planet X"), exactly like our own in size and mass, go whizzing past us at 163,000 miles per second relative to ourselves. If we could measure its dimensions as it shot past, we would find that it was foreshortened by 50 per cent in the direction of its motion. It would be an ellipsoid rather than a sphere and would, on further measurement, seem to have twice the mass of the earth.

Yet to an inhabitant of Planet X, it would seem that he himself and his own planet were motionless. The earth would seem to be moving past him at 163,000 miles per second, and it would appear to have an ellipsoidal shape and twice the mass of his planet.

One is tempted to ask which planet would really be foreshortened and doubled in mass, but the only possible answer is: that depends on the frame of reference.[27]

In his famous equation, $E = mc^2$, Einstein showed that matter and energy are not separate categories but two different expressions of the same physical entity. The source of energy is matter; and the source of matter is energy. Tiny quantities of matter could be transformed into staggering amounts of energy. The atomic age was dawning.

The discoveries of modern physics transformed the world of classical physics. Whereas nature had been regarded as something outside of the individual—an objective reality that existed independently of ourselves—modern physics teaches that our position in space and time determines what we mean by reality and our very presence affects reality itself. When we observe a particle with our measuring instruments, we are interfering with it, knocking it off its course; we are participating in reality. Nor is nature fully knowable, as the classical physics of Newton had presumed; uncertainty, probability, and even mystery are inherent in the universe.

We have not yet felt the full impact of modern physics, but there is no doubt that it has been part of a revolution in human perceptions. Jacob Bronowski, a student of science and culture concludes:

> One aim of the physical sciences has been to give an exact picture of the material world. One achievement of physics in the twentieth century has been to prove that that aim is unattainable. . . . There is no absolute knowledge. . . . All information is imperfect. We have to treat it with humility. That is the human condition; and that is what quantum physics says. . . . The Principle of Uncertainty . . . fixed once and for all the realization that all knowledge is limited.[28]

That we cannot fully comprehend nature must inevitably make us less certain about our theories of human nature, government, history, and morality. That scientists must qualify and avoid absolutes has no doubt made us more cautious and tentative in framing conclusions about the individual and society. Like Darwin's theory of human origins, Freud's theory of human nature, and the transformation of classical space by modern artists, the modifications of the Newtonian picture by modern physicists contributed to the sense of uncertainty and disorientation that characterizes the twentieth century.

The Enlightenment Tradition in Disarray

Most nineteenth-century thinkers carried forward the spirit of the Enlightenment, particularly in its emphasis on science and its concern for individual liberty and social reform. In the tradition of the philosophes, nineteenth-century thinkers regarded science as humanity's greatest achievement and believed that through reason society could be reformed. The spread of parliamentary government and the extension of education, along with the many advances in science and technology, seemed to confirm the hopes of the philosophes in humanity's future progress.

But at the same time, the Enlightenment tradition was being undermined. In the early nineteenth century, the romantics revolted against the Enlightenment's rational-scientific spirit. In the closing decades of the century the Enlightenment tradition was challenged by Social Darwinists who glorified violence and saw conflict between individuals and between nations as a law of nature. A number of thinkers, rejecting the Enlightenment view of people as fundamentally rational, held that subconscious drives and impulses govern human behavior more than reason. These thinkers urged celebrating and glorifying the irrational, which they regarded as the true essence of human beings.

Even theorists who studied the individual and society in a scientific way pointed out that below a surface of rationality lies a substratum of irrationality that constitutes a deeper reality. The conviction was growing that reason was a puny instrument in comparison to the volcanic strength of nonrational impulses, that these impulses pushed people toward destructive behavior and made political life precarious, and that the nonrational did not bend very much to education.

At the beginning of the twentieth century the dominant mood remained that of confidence in Europe's future progress and in the values of European civilization. However, certain disquieting trends were evident that would grow to crisis proportions in succeeding decades. Although few people may have realized it, the Enlightenment tradition was in disarray.

The Enlightenment conceived of an orderly, machinelike universe—of natural law and natural rights operating in the social world, of objective rules that gave form and structure to artistic productions, of the essential rationality and goodness of the individual, and of science and technology as instruments of progress. This coherent worldview, which had produced an attitude of certainty, security, and optimism, was in the process of dissolution by the early twentieth century. The common-sense Newtonian picture of the physical universe, with its inexorable laws of cause and effect, was altered; the belief in natural rights and objective standards governing morality was undermined; confidence in human rationality and goodness, the efficacy of science and technology, and the inevitability of human progress were being questioned. Rules and modes of expression that lay at the very heart of Western esthetics were abandoned.

By the early twentieth century the universe no longer seemed an orderly system, an intelligible whole, but something fundamentally inexplicable. Human nature, too, seemed intrinsically unfathomable and problematic. To the question "Who is man?" Greek philosophers, medieval scholastics, Renaissance humanists, and eighteenth-century philosophes had provided a coherent and intelligible answer. By the early twentieth century, Western intellectuals no longer possessed a clear idea of the human being; the individual seemed a stranger unto himself or herself, and life seemed devoid of an overriding purpose, as Nietzsche sensed:

> *Disintegration characterizes this time, and thus uncertainty: nothing stands firmly on its feet or on a hard faith in itself; one lives for tomorrow as the day after tomorrow is dubious. Everything on our way is slippery and dangerous, and the ice that still supports us has become thin: all of us feel the warm, uncanny breath of the thawing wind; where we still walk, soon no one will be able to walk.*[29]

This radical new disorientation led some intellectuals to feel alienated from and even hostile toward Western civilization. At the beginning of the twentieth century, says Dutch historian Jan Romein, "European man, who only half a century earlier had believed he was about to embrace an almost totally safe existence, and paradoxically enough did so in many ways, found himself before the dark gate of uncertainty."[30]

When the new century began, most Europeans were optimistic about the future, some even holding that European civilization was on the threshold of a golden age. Few suspected that European civilization would soon be gripped by a crisis that threatened its very survival. The powerful forces of irrationalism that had been celebrated by Nietzsche, analyzed by Freud, and creatively expressed in modernist culture would erupt with devastating fury in twentieth-century political life, particularly in the form of extreme nationalism and racism that extolled violence. Disoriented and disillusioned people searching for new certainties and values would turn to political ideologies that openly rejected reason, lauded war, and scorned the inviolability of the human person. These currents began to form at the end of the nineteenth century, but World War I brought them together into a tidal wave.

World War I accentuated the questioning of established norms and the dissolution of Enlightenment certainties and caused many people to regard Western civilization as dying and beyond recovery. The war not only exacerbated the spiritual crisis of the preceding generation, it also shattered Europe's political and social order and gave birth to totalitarian ideologies that nearly obliterated the legacy of the Enlightenment.

Notes

1. Friedrich Nietzsche, *Twilight of the Idols* and *The Anti-Christ,* trans. by R. J. Hollingdale (New York: Penguin, 1972), pp. 117–118.

2. Friedrich Nietzsche, *The Will to Power,* trans. by A. M. Ludovici (New York: Russell & Russell, 1964), vol. 2, sec. 861–862, pp. 297–298.

3. Friedrich Nietzsche, *The Will to Power,* trans. by Walter Kaufmann and R. J. Hollingdale, and ed. by Walter Kaufmann (New York: Vintage Books, 1968), pp. 383–384.

4. Quoted in R. J. Hollingdale, *Nietzsche* (London: Routledge and Kegan Paul, 1973), p. 82.

5. Nietzsche, *The Will to Power,* p. 386.

6. Fyodor Dostoevski, *Notes from the Underground* and *The Grand Inquisitor,* trans. by Ralph E. Matlaw (New York: E. P. Dutton, 1960), pp. 20, 23.

7. Ibid., p. 25.

8. Sigmund Freud, *Civilization and Its Discontents* (New York: Norton, 1961), p. 62.

9. Ibid., p. 58.

10. Ibid.

11. Ibid., p. 59.

12. Ibid., p. 61.

13. Ibid., p. 59.

14. Ibid., p. 69.

15. Irving Howe, ed., *The Idea of the Modern in Literature and the Arts* (New York: Horizon Press, 1967), p. 16.

16. Daniel Bell, *The Cultural Contradictions of Capitalism* (New York: Basic Books, 1976), p. 110.

17. Quoted in Howe, *The Idea of the Modern,* p. 15.

18. Bell, *The Cultural Contradictions of Capitalism,* pp. 110, 112.

19. Paul Klee, *On Modern Art,* trans. by Paul Findlay (London: Faber & Faber, 1948), p. 51.

20. Quoted in Alfred H. Barr, Jr., ed., *Masters of Modern Art* (New York: Museum of Modern Art, 1954), p. 46.

21. Quoted in ibid., p. 47.

22. John Canaday, *Mainstreams of Modern Art* (New York: Holt, 1961), p. 458.

23. Quoted in G. H. Hamilton, *Painting and Sculpture in Europe, 1880–1940* (Baltimore: Penguin Books, 1967), p. 133.

24. Quoted in Robert Nisbet, *The Social Philosophers* (New York: Crowell, 1973), p. 441.

25. Alan Nourse, *Universe, Earth, and Atom* (New York: Harper & Row, 1969), pp. 554–555, 560.

26. Quoted in A. E. E. McKenzie, *The Major Achievements of Science* (New York: Cambridge University Press, 1960), I, 310.

27. Isaac Asimov, *Asimov's Guide to Science* (New York: Basic Books, 1972), pp. 354–355.

28. Jacob Bronowski, *The Ascent of Man* (Boston: Little, Brown, 1973), p. 353.

29. Nietzsche, *The Will to Power,* sec. 57, p. 40.

30. Jan Romein, *The Watershed of Two Eras,* trans. by Arnold J. Pomerans (Middletown, Conn.: Wesleyan University Press, 1978), p. 658.

Suggested Reading

Baumer, Franklin, *Modern European Thought* (1977). A well-informed study of modern thought.

Biddiss, Michael D., *The Age of the Masses* (1977). Useful survey of ideas and society in Europe since 1870.

Bradbury, Malcolm, and James McFarlane, eds., *Modernism, 1890–1930* (1974). Essays on various phases of modernism; valuable bibliography.

Coates, W. H., and H. V. White, *The Ordeal of Liberal Humanism,* vol. 2 (1970). A standard survey of intellectual history since the French Revolution.

Cruickshank, John, ed., *Aspects of the Modern European Mind* (1969). A useful collection of sources in modern intellectual history.

Hamilton, G. H., *Painting and Sculpture in Europe, 1880–1940* (1967). An authoritative study.

Hollingdale, R. J., *Nietzsche* (1973). A lucid and insightful study.

Hughes, H. Stuart, *Consciousness and Society* (1958). An excellent survey of thought from the 1890s to 1930.

Kaufmann, Walter, *Nietzsche* (1956). An excellent analysis of Nietzsche's thought.

Masur, Gerhard, *Prophets of Yesterday* (1961). Studies in European culture, 1890–1914.

Monaco, Paul, *Modern European Culture and Consciousness, 1870–1980* (1983). A useful survey.

Nelson, Benjamin, ed., *Freud and the Twentieth Century* (1957). A valuable collection of essays.

Rieff, Philip, *Freud: The Mind of the Moralist* (1961). A well-informed study of Freud's thought and influence.

Roazen, Paul, *Freud's Political and Social Thought* (1968). The wider implications of Freudian psychology.

Rosenthal, Bernice, ed., *Nietzsche in Russia* (1986). A collection of essays detailing Nietzsche's impact on Russian thought; good introduction by the editor.

Stromberg, Roland N., *An Intellectual History of Modern Europe* (1975). A fine text.

Zeitlin, I. M., *Ideology and the Development of Sociological Theory* (1968). Examines in detail the thought of major shapers of sociological theory.

Review Questions

1. What were Nietzsche's attitudes toward Christianity and democracy?

2. What was the significance of Nietzsche's thought?

3. What does Dostoevski's Underground Man mean when he says that life is more than "simply extracting square roots"?

4. How did Bergson reflect the growing irrationalism of the age?

5. How did Sorel show the political potential of the nonrational?

6. In what way was Freud a child of the Enlightenment? How did he differ from the philosophes?

7. What were the standards of esthetics that had governed Western literature and art since the Renaissance? How did the modernist movement break with these standards?

8. For Durkheim, what constituted the crisis of modern society? How did he attempt to cope with crisis?

9. What do you think of Pareto's judgment that the masses in a democratic state are not really influenced by rational argument?

10. For Weber, what was the terrible paradox of reason?

11. Describe the view of the universe held by Westerners about 1880. How was this view altered by modern physics? What is the significance of this revolution to our perception of the universe?

12. In what ways was the Enlightenment tradition in disarray by the early years of the twentieth century?

VI

World Wars and Totalitarianism: The West in Crisis

1914–1945

29

The Road to World War I:
Failure of the European
State System

Prior to 1914, the dominant mood in Europe was one of pride in the accomplishments of Western civilization and confidence in its future progress. Advances in science and technology, the rising standard of living, the spread of democratic institutions, the expansion of social reform, the increase in literacy for the masses, Europe's position of power in the world—all contributed to a sense of optimism. Other reasons for optimism were that since the defeat of Napoleon, Europe had avoided a general war, and since the Franco-Prussian War (1870–71), the Great Powers had not fought one another. Reflecting on the world he knew before World War I, Arnold Toynbee recalled that his generation

> expected that life throughout the World would become more rational, more humane, and more democratic and that, slowly, but surely, political democracy would produce greater social justice. We had also expected that the progress of science and technology would make mankind richer, and that this increasing wealth would gradually spread from a minority to a majority. We had expected that all this would happen peacefully. In fact we thought that mankind's course was set for an earthly paradise, and that our approach towards this goal was predestined for us by historical necessity.[1]

Few people recognized that the West's outward achievements masked an inner turbulence that was propelling Western civilization toward a cataclysm. The European state system was failing. In the early nineteenth century, liberals had believed that redrawing the political map of Europe on the basis of nationality would promote peaceful relations among states. But quite the reverse occurred. By 1914, national states, answering to no higher power, were fueled by an explosive nationalism and were grouped into alliances that faced each other with ever-mounting hostility. Nationalist

William II with His Sons. (*Culver Pictures*)

657

passions, overheated by the popular press and expansionist societies, poisoned international relations. Nationalist thinkers propagated pseudoscientific racial and Social Darwinist doctrines that glorified conflict and justified the subjugation of other peoples. Committed to enhancing national power, statesmen lost sight of Europe as a community of nations sharing a common civilization. Caution and restraint gave way to belligerency in foreign relations.

The failure of the European state system was paralleled by a cultural crisis. Some European intellectuals attacked the rational tradition of the Enlightenment and celebrated the primitive, the instinctual, and the irrational. Increasingly, young people grew attracted to philosophies of action that ridiculed liberal bourgeois values and viewed war as a purifying and ennobling experience. Colonial wars, colorfully portrayed in the popular press, ignited the imagination of bored factory workers and daydreaming students and reinforced a sense of duty and an urge for gallantry among soldiers and aristocrats. These "splendid" little colonial wars helped fashion an attitude that made war acceptable, if not laudable. Yearning to break loose from their ordinary lives and to embrace heroic values, many Europeans regarded violent conflict as the highest expression of individual and national life. German historian Heinrich von Treitschke (1834–1896) expressed the prevailing mood when he wrote: "Those who preach the nonsense about everlasting peace do not understand the life of the [German] race. . . . [T]o banish war from history would be to banish all progress and becoming. It is only the periods of exhaustion, weariness and mental stagnation that have dallied with the dream of everlasting peace."[2]

Although technology was making warfare more brutal and dangerous, Europe retained a romantic illusion about combat. "Even if we end in ruin it was beautiful," exclaimed General Erich von Falkenhayn, the future chief of the German General Staff, at the outbreak of World War I.[3]

Although Europe was seemingly progressing in the art of civilization, the mythic power of nationalism and the primitive appeal of conflict were driving European civilization to the abyss. Few people recognized the potential crisis— certainly not the statesmen whose reckless blundering allowed the Continent to stumble into war.

Aggravated Nationalist Tensions in Austria-Hungary

On June 28, 1914, a young terrorist with the support of The Black Hand, a secret Serbian nationalist society, murdered Archduke Francis Ferdinand, heir to the throne of Austria-Hungary. Six weeks later the armies of Europe were on the march; an incident in the Balkans had sparked a world war. An analysis of why Austria-Hungary felt compelled to attack Serbia, and why the other powers became enmeshed in the conflict, shows how explosive Europe was in 1914. And nowhere were conditions more volatile than in Austria-Hungary, the scene of the assassination.

With its numerous nationalities, each with its own national history and traditions and often conflicting aspirations, Austria-Hungary stood in opposition to nationalism, the most powerful spiritual force of the age. Perhaps the supranational Austro-Hungarian Empire was obsolete in a world of states based on the principle of nationality. Dominated by Germans and Hungarians, the empire remained unable either to satisfy the grievances or to contain the nationalist aims of its minorities, particularly the Czechs and South Slavs (Croats, Slovenes, Serbs).

Austria-Hungary's failure to solve its minority problems had significant repercussions for international relations. The more moderate leaders of the ethnic minorities did not call for secession from the empire. Nevertheless, heightened agitation among the several nationalities, which worsened in the decade before 1914, created terrible anxieties among Austrian leaders. The fear that the empire would be torn apart by rebellion caused Austria to pursue a more forceful policy against any nation that fanned the nationalist feelings of its Slavic minorities. In particular, this policy meant worsening tensions between Austria and small Serbia, which had been independent of the Ottoman Empire since 1878.

Captivated by Western ideas of nationalism, the Serbs sought to create a Greater Serbia by uniting with their racial kin, the South Slavs who dwelt in Austria-Hungary. Since some 7 million South Slavs lived in the Hapsburg Empire, the dream of a Greater Serbia, shrilly expressed by Serbian nationalists, caused nightmares in Austria. Austrian leaders feared that continued Serbian agitation would encourage the South Slavs to press for secession. Regarding Serbia as a grave threat to Austria's existence, such leaders as Foreign Minister Count Leopold von Berchtold and Field Marshal Franz Conrad von Hötzendorf urged the destruction of the Serbian menace.

Another irritant to Austria-Hungary was Russian Pan-Slavism, which called for the solidarity of Russians with their Slavic cousins in eastern Europe—Poles, Czechs, Slovaks, South Slavs, and Bulgarians. Pan-Slavism was based on a mystic conception of the superiority of Slavic civilization to Western civilization and of Russia's special historic mission to liberate its kin from Austrian and Turkish rule. Although Russian Pan-Slavs were few and did not dictate foreign policy, they constituted a significant pressure group. Moreover, their provocative and semireligious proclamations frightened Austria-Hungary, which did not draw a sharp line between Pan-Slavic aspirations and official Russian policy.

The tensions arising out of the multinational character of the Austro-Hungarian Empire in an age of heightened nationalist feeling set off the explosion in 1914. Unable to solve its minority problems and fearful of Pan-Slavism and Pan-Serbism, Austria-Hungary felt itself in a life-or-death situation. This sense of desperation led it to lash out at Serbia after the assassination of Archduke Francis Ferdinand.

The German System of Alliances

The war might have been avoided, however, or might have remained limited to Austria and Serbia had Europe in 1914 not been divided into two hostile alliance systems. Such a situation contains inherent dangers. For example, knowing that it has the support of allies, a country might pursue a more provocative and reckless course and be less conciliatory during a crisis. Second, a conflict between two states might spark a chain reaction that will draw in the other powers, thereby transform-

ing a limited war into a general war. This course is precisely what followed the assassination. The origins of this dangerous alliance system go back to Bismarck and the Franco-Prussian War.

The New German Empire

The unification of Germany in 1870–71 turned the new state into an international power of the first rank, upsetting the balance of power in Europe. For the first time since the wars of the French Revolution, one nation was in a position to dominate the European continent. How a united and powerful Germany would fit into European life was the crucial problem in the decades following the Franco-Prussian War.

To German nationalists, the unification of Germany was both the fulfillment of a national dream and the starting point for an even more ambitious goal—the extension of German power in Europe and the world. As the nineteenth century drew to a close, German nationalism grew more extreme. Believing that Germany must either grow or die, nationalists pressed the government to build a powerful navy, acquire colonies, gain a much greater share of the world's markets, and expand German interests and influence in Europe. Sometimes these goals were expressed in the language of Social Darwinism—nations are engaged in an eternal struggle for survival and domination.

The Pan-German Association, which included among its members some prominent intellectuals, journalists, and politicians, preached the special destiny of the German race and advocated German expansion in Europe and overseas. Pan-Germans probably had less power than Russian Pan-Slavs. Nevertheless, like their Pan-Slav counterparts, they engaged in shrill propaganda, included people of influence, and frightened observers in other countries. Decisive victories against Austria (1866) and France (1871), the formation of the German Reich, rapid industrialization, and the impressive achievements of German science and scholarship had molded a powerful and dynamic nation. Imbued with great expectations for the future, Germans became increasingly impatient to see the fatherland gain its "rightful" place in world affairs—an attitude that frightened non-Germans.

Bismarck's Goals

Under Bismarck, who did not seek additional territory but wanted only to preserve the recently achieved unification, Germany pursued a moderate and cautious foreign policy. One of Bismarck's principal goals was to keep France isolated and friendless. France had suffered deep humiliation as a result of its defeat in the Franco-Prussian War. Prussia's quick and decisive victory shocked the French, who had entered the war brimming with confidence. Compounding French humiliation was the loss of Alsace and Lorraine to Germany. Victor Hugo expressed the "sacred anger" of the French: "France will have but one thought: to reconstitute her forces, gather her energy . . . raise her young generation to form an army of the whole people . . . to become again a great France, the France of 1792, the France of an idea with a sword. Then one day she will be irresistible. Then she will take back Alsace-Lorraine."[4] While French nationalists yearned for a war of revenge against Germany, the government, aware of Germany's strength, was unlikely to initiate such a conflict. Still, the issue of Alsace-Lorraine increased tensions between France and Germany. Germany's annexation of the French provinces proved to be a serious blunder, for it precluded any reconciliation between the two countries.

Bismarck also hoped to prevent a war between Russia and Austria-Hungary, for such a conflict could lead to German involvement, to the breakup of Austria-Hungary, and to Russian expansion in eastern Europe. To maintain peace and Germany's existing borders, Bismarck forged complex alliances. In the decade of the 1880s Bismarck created the Triple Alliance—consisting of Germany, Austria-Hungary, and Italy—and an alliance with Russia.

There was one major weakness to Germany's alliance system: Austria and Russia were potential enemies. Austria feared Russian ambitions in the Balkans and felt threatened by Russian Pan-Slavs. Bismarck knew that an alliance with Austria was essentially incompatible with Germany's treaty obligations to Russia, but he hoped that the arrangement would enable him to exercise a moderating influence over both eastern powers, thereby forestalling a war that would upset the status quo. An additional reason for the treaty with Russia was that it denied France a valuable ally.

Bismarck conducted foreign policy with restraint. He formed alliances not to conquer new lands but to protect Germany from aggression from either France or Russia, not to launch war but to preserve order and stability in Europe. In 1888, however, a new emperor ascended the German throne. When the young Kaiser William II (1888–1918) clashed with his aging prime minister, Bismarck was forced to resign (1890). Lacking Bismarck's diplomatic skills, his cool restraint, and his determination to keep peace in Europe, the new German leaders pursued a belligerent and imperialistic foreign policy in the following decades that frightened other states, particularly Britain. Whereas Bismarck considered Germany a satiated power, these men insisted that Germany must have its place in the sun.

The first act of the new leadership was to permit the treaty with Russia to lapse, thereby allowing Germany to give full support to Austria, which was considered a more reliable ally. Whereas Bismarck had warned Austria to act with moderation and caution in the Balkans, his successors not only failed to hold Austria in check but actually encouraged Austrian aggression. This proved fatal to the peace of Europe.

The Triple Entente

Fear of Germany

When Germany broke with Russia in 1890, France was quick to take advantage of the situation. Frightened by Germany's increasing military strength, expanding industries, growing population, and alliance with Austria and Italy, France eagerly coveted Russia as an ally. The French government urged its bankers to invest in Russia, supplied weapons to the tsar, and arranged for the French and Russian fleets to exchange visits. In 1894, France and Russia entered into an alliance; the isolation forced on France by Bismarck had ended.

Like France and Russia, Great Britain was alarmed by Germany's growing military might.

Map 29.1 Ethnic Groups in Germany, Austria, and the Balkans Before World War I ▶

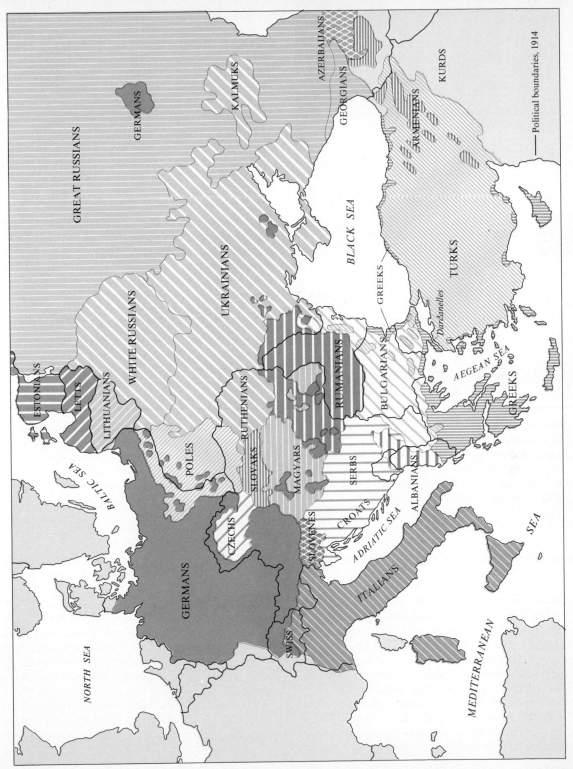

GREAT RUSSIANS

GERMANS

KALMUKS

AZERBAIJANS

GEORGIANS

KURDS

ARMENIANS

Political boundaries, 1914

BLACK SEA

TURKS

UKRAINIANS

Dardanelles

GREEKS

WHITE RUSSIANS

BULGARIANS

AEGEAN SEA

GREEKS

ESTONIANS

LETTS

LITHUANIANS

RUTHENIANS

RUMANIANS

POLES

SLOVAKS

MAGYARS

SERBS

ALBANIANS

BALTIC SEA

CZECHS

SLOVENES

CROATS

ADRIATIC SEA

SEA

GERMANS

ITALIANS

NORTH SEA

SWISS

MEDITERRANEAN

SEA

Nicholas II and His Family. Nicholas II, the last tsar of Russia, ruled from 1894 to 1917. The sufferings brought on by World War I led to revolution and he was forced to abdicate. The tsar and his family were shot by the Bolsheviks in July 1918. (*The Bettmann Archive/BBC Hulton*)

Furthermore, because of its spectacular industrial growth, Germany had become a potent trade rival of England. Britain was also distressed by Germany's increased efforts to become a great colonial power—a goal demanded by German nationalists. But most alarming was Germany's decision to build a great navy, for it could interfere with British overseas trade or even blockade the British Isles. Germany's naval program was the single most important reason that Britain moved closer first to France and then to Russia. Germany's naval construction, designed to increase its stature as a Great Power but not really necessary for its security, was one indication that German leaders had abandoned Bismarck's policy

of good sense. Eager to add the British as an ally and demonstrating superb diplomatic skill, France moved to end long-standing colonial disputes with Britain. The Entente Cordiale of 1904 accomplished this conciliation. England had emerged from its self-imposed splendid isolation.

The Franco-British understanding increased German anxiety, but Germany also doubted that France and England, who had almost gone to war in 1898 over regions in the Sudan, had overcome their deep animosities. Consequently, Chancellor Bernhard von Bülow (1849–1929) decided to provoke a crisis in Morocco that would test the Anglo-French Entente Cordiale. Von Bülow chose Morocco because earlier the British had resisted French imperialist designs there. He prodded a reluctant Kaiser William II to visit the Moroccan port of Tangier, a sign that Germany would support the Moroccan sultan against France; von Bülow had his crisis. In January 1906, a conference was held in Algeciras, Spain, to resolve it; the outcome was a defeat for Germany, for Britain sided with France, which was given special rights in Morocco. Germany's efforts to disrupt the Anglo-French Entente Cordiale failed; the two former enemies demonstrated their solidarity.

Eager to erect a strong alliance to counter Germany's Triple Alliance, French diplomats now sought to ease tensions between their Russian ally and their new British friend. Two events convinced Russia to adopt a more conciliatory attitude toward Britain: a disastrous and unexpected defeat in the Russo-Japanese War of 1904–1905 and a working-class revolution in 1905. Shocked by defeat, its army bordering on disintegration, its workers restive, Russia was now receptive to settling its imperial disputes with Britain over Persia, Tibet, and Afghanistan, a decision encouraged by France. In the Anglo-Russian Entente of 1907, as in the Anglo-French Entente Cordiale of 1904, the former rivals conducted themselves in a conciliatory if not friendly manner. In both instances, what engendered this spirit of cooperation was fear of Germany; both agreements represented a triumph for French diplomacy. The Triple Entente, however, was not a firm alliance, for there was no certainty that Britain, traditionally reluctant to send its troops to the Continent, would give any more than diplomatic support to France and Russia in case there was a showdown with Germany.

Europe was now broken into two hostile camps: the Triple Entente of France, Russia, and Britain and the Triple Alliance of Germany, Austria-Hungary, and Italy. Serving to increase fear and suspicion between the alliances was the costly arms race and the maintenance of large standing armies by all the states except Britain.

German Reactions

Germany denounced the Triple Entente as a hostile anti-German coalition designed to encircle and crush Germany. If Germany were to survive, it must break this ring. In the past, German arms had achieved unification; German military might would also end this threat to the fatherland. Considering Austria-Hungary as its only reliable ally, Germany resolved to preserve the power and dignity of the Hapsburg Empire. If Austria-Hungary fell from the ranks of the Great Powers, Germany would have to stand alone against its enemies. At all costs Austria-Hungary must not be weakened.

But this assessment suffered from dangerous miscalculations. First, Germany overstressed the hostile nature of the Triple Entente. In reality, France, Russia, and Britain drew closer together not to wage aggressive war against Germany but to protect themselves against burgeoning German military, industrial, and diplomatic power. Second, by linking German security to Austria, Germany greatly increased the chance of war. Becoming increasingly fearful of Pan-Serbism and Pan-Slavism, Austria might well decide that only a war could prevent its empire from disintegrating. Confident of German support, Austria would be more likely to resort to force; fearful of any diminution of Austrian power, Germany would be more likely to give Austria that support. Unlike Bismarck, the new leadership did not think in terms of restraining Austria but of strengthening it, by war if necessary.

The Drift Toward War

The Bosnian Crisis

After 1908, several crises tested the competing alliances, pushing Europe closer to war. Particularly significant was the Bosnian affair, for it contained many of the ingredients that eventually ignited the war in 1914. The humiliating defeat by Japan in 1905 had diminished Russia's stature as a Great Power, and the abortive revolution in the same year had weakened the government's authority at home. The new Russian foreign minister, Alexander Izvolsky, hoped to gain a diplomatic triumph by compelling Turkey to allow Russian warships to pass through the Dardanelles, fulfilling a centuries-old dream of extending Russian power into the Mediterranean. Izvolsky hoped that England and France, traditional opponents of Russia's Mediterranean ambitions but now Russia's allies, would not block the move. But certainly Austria would regard it as a hostile act.

Like Izvolsky, Baron Lexa von Aehrenthal, the new Austrian foreign minister, sought to restore his country's flagging prestige. The goals of both foreign ministers made an agreement possible. In particular, Aehrenthal desired the annexation of the provinces of Bosnia and Herzegovina. Officially a part of the Ottoman Empire, these provinces had been administered by Austria-Hungary since 1878. The population consisted mainly of ethnic cousins of the Serbs. A formal annexation would certainly infuriate the Serbs, who hoped one day to make the region part of a Greater Serbia. Russia and Austria made a deal. Russia would permit Austrian annexation of Bosnia and Herzegovina, and Austria would support Russia's move to open the Dardanelles. In 1908, Austria proceeded to annex the provinces, but Russia met stiff resistance from England and France when it presented its case for opening the Straits to Russian warships.

Austria had gained a diplomatic victory, while Russia suffered another humiliation. Even more enraged than Russia was Serbia, which threatened to invade Bosnia to liberate its cousins from Austrian oppression. The Serbian press openly declared that Austria-Hungary must perish if the South Slavs were to achieve liberty and unity. A fiery attitude also prevailed in Vienna—Austria-Hungary could not survive unless Serbia was destroyed. One Austrian newspaper that often reflected official thinking declared: "The hour has struck. War is inevitable. . . . Our blood throbs in our veins, we strain at the leash. Sire! Give us the signal."

During this period of intense hostility between Austria-Hungary and Serbia, Germany supported

Map 29.2 The Balkans, 1914

Constantinople. Because it was on the victorious side, landlocked Serbia gained the Albanian coast, which gave it a long-desired outlet to the sea. Austria was determined to keep its enemy from reaping this reward, and Germany, as in the Bosnian crisis, supported its ally. Unable to secure Russian support, an enraged Serbia was forced to surrender the territory, which became the state of Albania.

Thus, during a five-year period, Austria-Hungary inflicted on Serbia two terrible humiliations. Russia shared these humiliations, for it had twice failed to help its small Slavic friend and had been denied access to the Dardanelles at the time of the Bosnian crisis. Incensed Serbian nationalists accelerated their campaign of propaganda and terrorism against Austria. Believing that another humiliation would irreparably damage its prestige, Russia vowed to back Serbia in its next confrontation with Austria. And Austria had reached the end of its patience with Serbia. Emboldened by German encouragement, Austria wanted to end the Serbian threat once and for all. Thus the ingredients for war between Austria and Serbia, a war that might easily draw in Russia and Germany, were present. Another incident might well start a war. It came on June 28, 1914.

its Austrian ally. To keep Austria strong, Germany would even agree to the dismemberment of Serbia and to its incorporation into the Hapsburg Empire. As a result of this crisis, Austria and Germany coordinated battle plans in case a conflict between Austria and Serbia involved Russia and France. Unlike Bismarck, who tried to hold Austria in check, German leadership now coolly envisioned an Austrian attack on Serbia, and just as coolly offered German support if Russia intervened.

Balkan Wars

The Bosnian crisis pushed Germany and Austria closer together, brought relations between Austria and Serbia to the breaking point, and inflicted another humiliation on Russia. The first Balkan War (1912) continued these trends. The Balkan states of Montenegro, Serbia, Bulgaria, and Greece attacked a dying Ottoman Empire. In a brief campaign, the Balkan armies captured the Turkish empire's European territory, with the exception of

Assassination of Francis Ferdinand

Archduke Francis Ferdinand (1863–1914), heir to the throne of Austria, was sympathetic to the grievances of the South Slavs and favored a policy that would place the Slavs on an equal footing with Hungarians and Germans within the Hapsburg Empire. If such a policy succeeded, it could soothe the feelings of the Austrian Slavs and reduce the appeal of a Greater Serbia, the aim of The Black Hand.

On June 28, 1914, Francis Ferdinand was assassinated while making a state visit to Sarajevo, capital of Bosnia. Young Gavrilo Princip, part of a team of Bosnian terrorists, fired two shots at close range into the archduke's car. Francis Ferdinand and his wife died within fifteen minutes. The conspiracy was organized by Dragutin Dimitrijevic, chief of intelligence of the Serbian army, who was

The Assassins of the Archduke Francis Ferdinand and His Wife Being Captured in Sarajevo, June 28, 1914. The assassination of the archduke and his wife was the spark that ignited World War I. The adversaries looked forward to a short, decisive conflict. Emotions ran high with visions of gallantry. Only a few foresaw the collapse of a Western ideal: a world ruled by reason and morality. (*The Granger Collection, New York*)

linked to the Black Hand.* By killing the archduke, the terrorists hoped to bring to a boiling point tensions within the Hapsburg Empire and to prepare the way for revolution.

Feeling that Austria's prestige as a Great Power, and indeed its very survival as a supra-national empire, were at stake, key officials, led by the foreign minister, Count Leopold von Berchtold, decided to use the assassination as a pretext to crush Serbia. For many years leaders of Austria had yearned for war with Serbia in order to end the agitation for the union of the South Slavs. Now, they reasoned, the hour had struck. But war with Serbia would require the approval of Germany. Believing that Austria was Germany's only reliable ally and that a diminution of Austrian power and prestige threatened German security, German statesmen decided to support Austria. Rather than urging a peaceful settlement

*Serbia's prime minister, Nikola Pašić, learned of the plot and through the Serbian envoy in Vienna tried to get Austria to cancel Francis Ferdinand's visit. The Austrians, however, were not told of a specific assassination attempt, for Pašić did not want to admit that such an act of terrorism was being plotted on Serbian soil.

of the issue they encouraged their ally to take up arms against Serbia. Germany and Austria wanted a quick strike to overwhelm Serbia before other countries were drawn in.

Germany Encourages Austria

Confident of German backing, on July 23 Austria presented Serbia with an ultimatum and demanded a response within forty-eight hours. The terms of the ultimatum were so harsh that it was next to impossible for Serbia to accept them. This reaction was the one that Austria intended, as it sought a military solution to the crisis rather than a diplomatic one. But Russia would not remain indifferent to an Austro-German effort to liquidate Serbia. Russia feared that an Austrian conquest of Serbia was just the first step in an Austro-German plan to dominate the Balkans. Such an extension of German and Austrian power in a region bordering Russia was unthinkable to the tsar's government. Moreover, after suffering repeated reverses in foreign affairs, Russia would not tolerate another humiliation. As Germany had resolved to back its Austrian ally, Russia determined not to abandon Serbia.

Serbia responded to Austria's ultimatum in a conciliatory manner, agreeing to virtually all Austria's demands. But Serbia would not allow Austrian officials into Serbia to investigate the assassination. Having already decided against a peaceful settlement, Austria insisted that Serbia's failure to accept one provision meant that the entire ultimatum had been rejected and ordered mobilization of the Austrian army.

This was a crucial moment for Germany. Would it continue to support Austria, knowing that an Austrian attack on Serbia would most likely bring Russia into the conflict? Determined not to desert Austria and believing that a showdown with Russia was inevitable anyway, the German war party continued to urge Austrian action against Serbia. They argued that it was better to fight Russia in 1914 than a few years later, when the tsar's empire would be stronger. Confident of the superiority of the German army, the war party held that Germany could defeat both Russia and France, that Britain's army was too weak to make a difference, and that, in any case, Britain might remain neutral. Although Germany would have preferred a limited war involving only Austria and Serbia, it was not dismayed by the idea of a general war. Indeed, some military leaders and statesmen were exhilarated by the prospect of a war with Russia and France. The defeat of Germany's enemies would break the ring of encirclement, increase German territory, and establish Germany as the foremost power in the world.

On July 24–25, Russia took preliminary steps toward mobilizing against Austria. Russia felt compelled to act immediately because its vast size, inadequate transportation system, and inefficient bureaucracy were major obstacles to effective mobilization. On July 28, 1914, Austria declared war on Serbia; Russia, with the assurance of French support, proclaimed partial mobilization aimed at Austria alone. But the military warned that partial mobilization would throw the slow-moving Russian war machine into total confusion if the order had to be changed suddenly to full mobilization. Moreover, the only plans the Russian general staff had drawn up called for full mobilization, that is, for war against both Austria and Germany. The tsar, pressured by his generals, gave the order for full mobilization on July 30. Russian forces would be arrayed against Germany as well as Austria.

Thus the prevailing military theory worked against peace. Germany could not allow Russia the advantage of mobilizing first. Battle plans, worked out years in advance, required the mobilization of huge numbers of soldiers and were geared to tight railroad timetables. Because the country that struck first had the advantage of fighting according to its own plans rather than having to improvise in response to the enemy's attack, generals regarded mobilization by the enemy as an act of war. Therefore, when Russia refused a German warning to halt mobilization, Germany, on August 1, ordered a general mobilization and declared war on Russia. Two days later Germany also declared war on France, believing that France would most likely support its Russian ally. Moreover, German battle plans were based on a war with both Russia and France. Thus a war between Germany and Russia automatically meant a German attack on France.

When Belgium refused to allow German troops

to march through Belgian territory into France, Germany invaded the small nation, which brought Britain, pledged to guarantee Belgian neutrality, into the war. Britain could never tolerate German troops directly across the English Channel in any case, nor could it brook German mastery of western Europe. A century before, Britain had fought Napoleon to prevent France from becoming master of Europe. In 1914, it would fight Germany for the same reason. Moreover, British and French military and naval commands had entered into joint planning that linked the two powers closer together. If France were attacked, it would be unlikely that Britain would remain neutral.

Responsibility

The question of whether any one power was mainly responsible for the war has intrigued historians. In assessing blame, historians have been principally concerned with Germany's role. German historian Fritz Fischer argues that Germany's ambition to dominate Europe was the underlying cause of the war. Germany encouraged Austria to strike at Serbia knowing that an attack on Serbia could mean war with Russia and its French ally. Believing that it had the military advantage, Germany was willing to risk such a war. "As Germany willed and coveted the Austro-Serbian war and, in her confidence in her military superiority, deliberately faced the risk of a conflict with Russia and France, her leaders must bear a substantial share of the historical responsibility for the outbreak of general war in 1914."[5]

Attracted by Social Darwinist and militarist doctrines, continues Fischer, Germany aimed to become the foremost economic and political power in Europe and to play a far greater role in world politics; to achieve this goal Germany was willing to go to war. Critics of Fischer point out that other nations, not merely Germany, were enthralled by Social Darwinism and militarism, that this was not a particularly German mode of thinking but part of a general European sickness. They argue further that Germany would have preferred a limited war between Austria and Serbia and in 1914 had no plans to dominate Europe.

The other powers have also come in for a share of the blame. Austria bears responsibility for its determination to crush Serbia and its insistence on avoiding a negotiated settlement. Serbia's responsibility stems from pursuing an aggressive Pan-Serbian policy that set it on a collision course with Austria-Hungary. In 1913, Sir Fairfax Cartwright, the British ambassador to Vienna, warned: "Serbia will some day set Europe by the ears, and bring about a universal war on the Continent. I cannot tell you how exasperated people are getting here at the continual worry which that little country causes to Austria."[6] Russia bears responsibility for instituting general mobilization, thereby turning a limited war between Austria-Hungary and Serbia into a European war; France for failing to restrain Russia and indeed for encouraging its ally to mobilize; and England for failing to make clear that it would support its allies, for had Germany seen plainly that Britain would intervene, it might have been more cautious.

Other historians, dismissing the question of responsibility, regard the war as an obvious sign that European civilization was in deep trouble. Viewed in the broad perspective of European history, the war marked a culmination of dangerous forces in European life: the glorification of power; the fascination with violence; the celebration of the nonrational; the diminishing confidence in the capacity of reason to solve the problems created by the Industrial Revolution; the general dissatisfaction and disillusionment with bourgeois society; the alliance system; and above all, the explosive nationalism.

War as Celebration

When war was certain, an extraordinary phenomenon occurred. Crowds gathered in capital cities and expressed their loyalty to the fatherland and their readiness to fight. Even socialists, whose loyalty was supposed to be given to an international workers' movement, devoted themselves to their respective nations. It seemed as if people wanted violence for its own sake. It was as if war provided an escape from the dull routine of classroom, job, and home; from the emptiness, drabness, medioc-

Troops Leaving Berlin, 1914. "The sword has been forced into our hand," said Germans at the outbreak of war. German troops mobilized eagerly and efficiently; here a trainload is leaving for the western front. (*Historical Pictures Service, Chicago*)

rity, and pointlessness of bourgeois society; from "a world grown old and cold and weary," said Rupert Brooke, a young British poet.[7] To some, war was a "beautiful . . . sacred moment" that satisfied an "ethical yearning."[8] But more significantly, the outpouring of patriotic sentiments demonstrated the immense power that nationalism exercised over the European mind. With extraordinary success, nationalism welded millions of people into a collectivity ready to devote body and soul to the nation, especially during its hour of need.

In Paris, men marched down the boulevards singing the stirring words of the French national anthem, the "Marseillaise," while women showered young soldiers with flowers. A participant in these days recalls: "Young and old, civilians and military men burned with the same excitement. . . . Beginning the next day, thousands of men eager to fight would jostle one another outside recruiting offices, waiting to join up. . . . The word 'duty' had a meaning for them, and the word 'country' had regained its splendor."[9] Similar scenes occurred in Berlin. "It is a joy to be alive," editorialized one newspaper. "We wished so much for this hour. . . . The sword which has been forced into our hand will not be sheathed until our aims are won and our territory extended as far as necessity demands."[10]

Soldiers bound for battle acted as if they were going off on a great adventure. "My dear ones, be proud that you live in such a time and in such a nation and that you . . . have the privilege of sending those you love into so glorious a battle," wrote a young German law student to his family.[11] The young warriors yearned to do something noble and altruistic, to win glory, and to experience life at its most intense.

Many of Europe's most distinguished intellectuals were also captivated by the martial mood, sharing Rupert Brooke's sentiments: "Now God be thanked Who has matched us with His hour,/ And caught our youth, and wakened us from sleeping."[12] To the prominent German historian Friedrich Meinecke, August 1914 was "one of the great moments of my life which suddenly filled my soul with the deepest confidence in our people and the profoundest joy."[13] Besides being gripped by a thirst for excitement and a quest for the heroic, some intellectuals welcomed the war because it unified the nation in a spirit of fraternity and self-sacrifice. It was a return, some felt, to the organic roots of human existence, a way of overcoming a sense of individual isolation. Stefan Zweig (1881–1942), an Austrian writer, recalls how news of the war was greeted in Vienna:

> As never before, thousands and hundreds of thousands felt what they should have felt in peace time, that they belonged together. A city of two million, a country of nearly fifty million, in that hour felt that they were participating in world history, in a moment which would never recur, and that each one was called upon to cast his infinitesimal self into the glowing mass, there to be purified of all selfishness. All differences of class, rank, and language were flooded over at that moment by the rushing feeling of fraternity. Strangers spoke to one another in the streets, people who had avoided each other for years shook hands, everywhere one saw excited faces. Each individual experienced an exaltation of his ego, he was no longer the isolated person of former times, he had been incorporated into the mass, he was part of the people, and his person, his hitherto unnoticed person, had been given meaning.[14]

Some intellectuals believed the war would spiritually regenerate European society. It would resurrect glory, nobility, and heroism; it would awaken a spirit of self-sacrifice and give life an overriding purpose; it would rid the nation of wickedness, selfishness, and hypocrisy and cleanse Europe of its spiritual and racial impurities. From the war would emerge a higher civilization, morally reborn.

But it must be emphasized that the soldiers who went off to war singing and the statesmen and generals who welcomed war or did not try hard enough to prevent it expected a short, decisive, gallant conflict. Virtually no one envisioned what World War I turned out to be—four years of frightful, barbaric, indecisive, senseless bloodletting. But although their gloomy words were drowned out by the cheers of chauvinists and fools, there were prophets who realized that Europe was stumbling into darkness. "The lamps are going out all over Europe," said British Foreign Secretary Edward Grey. "We shall never see them lit again in our lifetime."

Notes

1. Arnold Toynbee, *Surviving the Future* (New York: Oxford University Press, 1971), pp. 106–107.

2. Heinrich von Treitschke, *Politics,* excerpted in *Germany's War Mania* (New York: Dodd, Mead, 1915), pp. 222–223.

3. Quoted in James Joll, "The Unspoken Assumptions," in H. W. Koch, ed., *The Origins of the First World War* (New York: Taplinger, 1972), p. 325.

4. Quoted in Barbara Tuchman, *The Guns of August* (New York: Macmillan, 1962), pp. 46–47.

5. Fritz Fischer, *Germany's Aims in the First World War* (New York: W. W. Norton, 1967), p. 88.

6. Quoted in Joachim Remak, *The Origins of World War I* (New York: Holt, 1967), p. 135.

7. From "Peace," in *Collected Poems of Rupert Brooke* (New York: Dodd, Mead, 1941), p. 111.

8. Quoted in Joachim C. Fest, *Hitler* (New York: Harcourt Brace Jovanovich, 1973), p. 66.

9. George A. Panichas, ed., *Promise of Greatness* (New York: John Day, 1968), pp. 14–15.

10. Quoted in Tuchman, *The Guns of August,* p. 145.

11. Quoted in Robert G. L. Waite, *Vanguard of Nazism* (New York: W. W. Norton, 1969), p. 22.

12. From "Peace," in *Collected Poems of Rupert Brooke,* p. 111.

13. Quoted in Koch, *The Origins of the First World War,* p. 318.

14. Stefan Zweig, *The World of Yesterday* (New York: Viking, 1970), p. 223.

Lafore, Laurence, *The Long Fuse* (1971). A beautifully written study of the causes of the conflict.

Langer, W. L., *European Alliances and Alignments* (1964). Originally published in 1931, this now-classic work treats the major international issues between 1871 and 1890.

Laqueur, Walter, and George Mosse, eds., *1914* (1966). A valuable collection of essays on the coming of war.

Leed, Eric J., *No Man's Land: Combat and Identity in World War I* (1979). The impact of the war on the men who participated in it.

Remak, Joachim, *The Origins of World War I* (1967). A fine introduction.

Stromberg, Roland N., *Redemption by War: The Intellectuals and 1914* (1982). A superb analysis of the reason why so many intellectuals welcomed the war.

Thomson, G. M., *The Twelve Days* (1964). An account of the twelve days preceding the outbreak of war.

Suggested Reading

Berghahn, V. R., *Germany and the Approach of War in 1914* (1975). Relates German foreign policy to domestic problems.

Fay, Sidney, *The Origins of the World War,* 2 vols. (1966). A comprehensive study of the underlying and immediate causes of the war; first published in 1928.

Fischer, Fritz, *Germany's Aims in the First World War* (1967). A controversial work, stressing Germany's responsibility for the war.

Geiss, Imanuel, ed., *July 1914* (1967). Selected documents.

Koch, H. W., ed., *The Origins of the First World War* (1972). Useful essays, particularly those dealing with the glorification of war before 1914.

Review Questions

1. How did the nationality problems in Austria-Hungary contribute to the outbreak of World War I?

2. What were the principal purposes of Bismarck's system of alliances?

3. What conditions led to the formation of the Triple Entente? How did Germany respond to it?

4. After the assassination of Archduke Francis Ferdinand, what policies were pursued by Austria-Hungary, Germany, Russia?

5. Was World War I inevitable?

6. In assessing responsibility for the war, what arguments have been advanced by historians?

7. Why did many Europeans welcome the war?

30

World War I: The West in Despair

There will be wars as never before on earth," predicted Nietzsche. World War I bore him out. Modern technology enabled the combatants to kill with unprecedented efficiency; modern nationalism infused both civilians and soldiers with the determination to fight until the enemy was totally beaten. The modern state, exercising wide control over its citizens, mobilized its human, material, and spiritual resources to wage total war. As the war hardened into a savage and grueling fight, the statesmen did not press for a compromise peace but rather demanded ever more mobilization, ever more escalation, and ever more sacrifices. The Great War profoundly altered the course of Western civilization, deepening the spiritual crisis that had produced it. How could one speak of the inviolability of the individual when Europe had become a slaughterhouse? Or of the primacy of reason when nations permitted slaughter to go unabated for four years? Now only the naive could believe in continuous progress. Western civilization had entered an age of violence, anxiety, and doubt that still persists.

Stalemate in the West

On August 4, 1914, the German army invaded Belgium. German war plans, drawn up years earlier, principally by General Alfred von Schlieffen, called for the army to swing through Belgium to outflank French border defenses, envelop the French forces, and destroy the enemy by attacking their rear. With the French army smashed and Paris isolated, German railroads would rush the victorious troops to the eastern front to reinforce the small force that had been assigned to hold off the Russians. The German military felt certain that

Allied Soldiers in the Trenches During World War I. (*Imperial War Museum, London*)

the spirit and skill of the German army would ensure victory over the much larger Russian forces. But everything depended on speed. France must be taken before the Russians could mobilize sufficient numbers to invade Germany. The Germans were confident that they would defeat France in two months or less.

French strategy called for a headlong attack into Alsace and Lorraine. Believing that French strength lay in the spiritual qualities of the French soldier—in the will to victory that had inspired Republican arms in 1792—the French generals completely embraced an offensive strategy. "The French Army returning to its tradition henceforth admits no law but the offensive," began the field regulations drawn up in 1913. Inspired by Napoleon's stress on offensive warfare and convinced that French soldiers possessed an unconquerable will and an irresistible nerve, the French army prepared its soldiers only for offensive warfare. The field regulations proclaimed: "Battles are beyond anything else struggles of morale. Defeat is inevitable as soon as the hope of conquering ceases to exist. Success comes not to him who has suffered the least but to him whose will is firmest and morale strongest."[1]

The French doctrine proved an instant failure. Although bayonet charges against machine-gun emplacements demonstrated the valor of French soldiers, they also revealed the incompetence of French generals. Making no effort at concealment or surprise and wearing striking red and blue uniforms, French soldiers were perfect targets. Marching into concentrated fire, they fell like pins. Everywhere the audacious attack was failing, but French generals, beguiled by the mystique of the offensive, would not change their tactics.

German success was not complete, however. Moving faster than anticipated, the Russians invaded East Prussia, which forced General Helmuth von Moltke to transfer troops from the French front, hampering the German advance. By early September the Germans had reached the Marne River, 40 miles from Paris. With their capital at their backs, the regrouped French forces, aided by the British, fought with astounding courage. Meanwhile the Germans were exhausted by long marches and had outrun their supplies. Moreover, in their rush toward Paris, they had unknowingly exposed their flank, which the French attacked. The British then penetrated a gap

that opened up between the German armies, forcing the Germans to retreat. The First Battle of the Marne had saved Paris. Now the war entered a new and unexpected phase—the deadlock of trench warfare.

For 400 miles across northern France, from the Alps to the North Sea, the opposing sides both constructed a vast network of trenches. These trenches had underground dugouts, and barbed wire stretched for yards before the front trenches as a barrier to attack. Behind the front trenches were other lines to which soldiers could retreat and from which support could be sent. Between the opposing armies lay "no man's land," a wasteland of mud, shattered trees, torn earth, and broken bodies. Trench warfare was a battle of nerves, endurance, and courage, waged to the constant thunder of heavy artillery. It was also butchery. As attacking troops climbed over their trenches and advanced bravely across no man's land, they were decimated by heavy artillery and chewed up by machine-gun fire. If they did penetrate the front-line trenches of the enemy, they were soon thrown back by a counterattack.

Despite a frightful loss of life, little land changed hands. So much heroism, sacrifice, and death achieved nothing. The generals ordered still greater attacks to end the stalemate; this only increased the death toll, for the advantage was always with the defense, which possessed machine guns, magazine rifles, and barbed wire. Tanks could redress the balance, but the generals, committed to old concepts, did not make effective use of them. And whereas the technology of the machine gun had been perfected, the motorized tanks often broke down.

Gains and losses of land were measured in yards, but the lives of Europe's youth were squandered by the hundreds of thousands. In 1915, for example, France launched numerous attacks against German lines but never gained more than three miles in any one place. Yet these small gains cost France 1,430,000 casualties. Against artillery, barbed wire, and machine guns, human courage had no chance; the generals—uncomprehending, unfeeling, and incompetent—persisted in their mass attacks. This futile effort at a breakthrough wasted untold lives to absolutely no purpose.

In 1915, neither side could break the deadlock. Hoping to bleed the French army dry and force

British Munitions Workers. With millions of men in the military, women took jobs formerly held only by men. Women drove trucks and buses, operated cranes, and worked in armament factories. Resistance to granting them equal rights diminished, as politicians recognized the essential contribution of women to the war effort. (*Brown Brothers*)

its surrender, the Germans in February 1916 attacked the town of Verdun, which was protected by a ring of forts. They chose Verdun because they knew the French could never permit a retreat from this ancient fortress. The Germans hoped that France, compelled to pour more and more troops into battle, would suffer such a loss of men that it would be unable to continue the war. Verdun was World War I's bloodiest battle. The leadership of General Henri Philippe Pétain, the tenacity of the French infantry, and the well-constructed concrete and steel forts enabled the French to hold on. When the British opened a major offensive on July 1, the Germans had to channel their reserves to the new front, relieving the pressure on Verdun.

France and Germany suffered more than a million casualties at Verdun, which one military historian calls "the greatest battle in world history."[2] No longer was the war a romantic adventure. A young French soldier, shortly before he was killed, expressed the mood of disillusionment that gripped the survivors of trench warfare: "Hu-

Map 30.1 World War I, 1914–1918 ▶

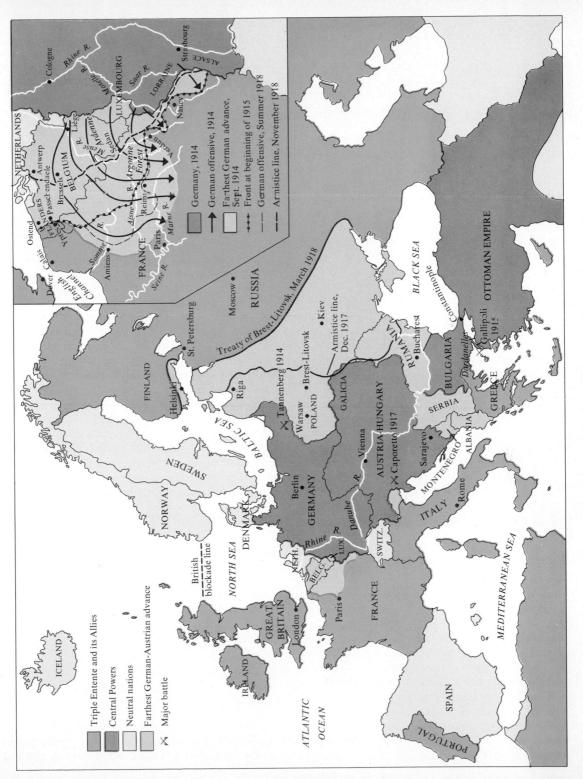

Germany, 1914

German offensive, 1914

Farthest German advance,
Sept. 1914

Front at beginning of 1915

German offensive, Summer 1918

Armistice line, November 1918

Cologne
Rhine R.
Strasbourg
ALSACE
Saar R.
LUXEMBOURG
LORRAINE
Moselle R.
Nancy
NETHERLANDS
Liège
R. Meuse
ARDENNES
Sedan
BELGIUM
Antwerp
Brussels
R. Argonne Forest
Passchendaele
Reims
FLANDERS
Ypres
Aisne R.
Verdun
Ostend
Somme R.
Marne R.
Dover
Calais
Amiens
FRANCE
Paris
Seine R.
English Channel

Triple Entente and its Allies

Central Powers

Neutral nations

Farthest German-Austrian advance

✕ Major battle

British
blockade line

ICELAND

NORWAY

SWEDEN

FINLAND

Helsinki

St. Petersburg

Moscow

RUSSIA

Treaty of Brest-Litovsk, March 1918

Armistice line,
Dec. 1917

Kiev

Riga

Tannenberg 1914 ✕

Warsaw
Brest-Litovsk

POLAND

GALICIA

Vienna

R.

AUSTRIA-HUNGARY

✕ Caporetto 1917

Sarajevo

MONTENEGRO

ALBANIA

BALTIC SEA

NORTH SEA

DENMARK

Berlin

GERMANY

Danube R.

Rhine R.

NETH.

BELG.

LUX.

SWITZ.

ITALY

Rome

RUMANIA

Bucharest

BULGARIA

SERBIA

GREECE

BLACK SEA

Constantinople

Dardanelles

Gallipoli 1915

OTTOMAN EMPIRE

GREAT BRITAIN

London

IRELAND

Paris

FRANCE

ATLANTIC OCEAN

SPAIN

PORTUGAL

MEDITERRANEAN SEA

manity is mad! It must be mad to do what it is doing. What a massacre! What scenes of horror and carnage. I cannot find words to translate my impressions. Hell cannot be so terrible. Men are mad!" [3]

At the end of June 1916, the British, assisted by the French, attempted a breakthrough at the Somme River. On July 1, after seven days of intense bombardment intended to destroy German defenses, the British climbed out of their trenches and ventured into no man's land. But German positions had not been destroyed. Emerging from their deep dugouts, German machine gunners fired repeatedly at the British, who had been ordered to advance in rows. Marching into concentrated machine-gun fire, few British troops ever made it across no man's land. Out of 110,000 who attacked, 60,000 fell dead or wounded, "the heaviest loss ever suffered in a single day by a British army or by any army in the First World War," observes British historian A. J. P. Taylor.[4] Some reached the German wire, only to become entangled in it. The Germans killed them with rifle fire and bayonets. For days the wounded lay in no man's land, their shrieks unheeded.

After this initial disaster, common sense and a concern for human life demanded that the attack be called off, but the generals continued to feed soldiers to the German guns. When the battle of the Somme ended in mid-November, Britain and France had lost over 600,000 men; and the military situation remained essentially unchanged. Soldiers in the trenches could see no end to the slaughter. The only victor was the war itself, which was devouring Europe's youth at an incredible rate.

In December 1916, General Robert Nivelle was appointed commander in chief of the French forces. Having learned little from past French failures to achieve a breakthrough, Nivelle ordered another mass attack for April 1917. The Germans discovered the battle plans on the body of a French officer and withdrew to a shorter line on high ground, constructing the strongest defense network of the war. Knowing that the French had lost the element of surprise and pushing aside the warnings of leading statesmen and military men, Nivelle went ahead with the attack. "The offensive alone gives victory; the defensive gives only defeat and shame," he told the president and the minister of war.[5]

The Nivelle offensive, which began on April 16, was another blood bath. In many places French artillery had not cut the German barbed wire. As the soldiers tried to grope their way through, they were chewed up by German machine-gun fire. Sometimes the fire was so intense that the French could not make it out of their own trenches. Although French soldiers fought with courage, the situation was hopeless. Still Nivelle persisted with the attack; after ten days French casualties numbered 187,000.

The soldiers could endure no more. Spontaneous revolts, born of despair and military failure, broke out in rest areas as soldiers refused to return to the slaughter ground. In some instances they shouted "Peace" and "To hell with the war." Mobs of soldiers seized trains to reach Paris and stir up the population against the war. Mutineers took control of barracks and threatened to fire on officers who interfered. The mutiny spread to the front lines as soldiers told their officers they would defend the trenches but not attack. The French army was disintegrating. "The slightest German attack would have sufficed to tumble down our house of cards and bring the enemy to Paris," recalled a French officer.[6]

General Pétain, the hero of Verdun, replaced the disgraced Nivelle. To restore morale, Pétain granted more leave, improved the quality of food, made the rest areas more comfortable, and ordered officers to demonstrate a personal concern for their men. He visited the troops, listened to their complaints, and told them that France would engage in only limited offensives until the United States, which had just entered the war, reinforced the allies in large numbers. These measures, combined with imprisonments and executions, restored discipline. The Germans, unaware of the full magnitude of the mutiny, had not put pressure on the front; by the time the Germans attacked, Pétain had revitalized the army.

Other Fronts

While the western front hardened into a stalemate, events moved more decisively on the eastern front. In August 1914, according to plan, the bulk

War in the North Sea. In January 1917, Germany decided to launch a campaign of unrestricted submarine warfare to deprive Britain of war supplies. U.S. ships, as Britain's principal supplier, came under attack by German submarines, as well as by ships and dirigibles like those pictured here. The U.S. Congress declared war on April 6. (*Bildarchiv Preussischer Kulturbesitz*)

of the German army invaded France hoping for a speedy victory, while a small force defended the eastern frontier against Russia. Responding to French requests to put pressure on Germany, the Russians, with insufficient preparation, invaded East Prussia. After some initial successes, which sent a scare into the German general staff, the Russians were soundly defeated at the battle of Tannenberg (August 26–30, 1914) and forced to withdraw from German territory, which remained inviolate for the rest of the war.

Meanwhile, Germany's ally Austria was having no success against Serbia and Russia. An invasion of Serbia was thrown back, and an ill-conceived offensive against Russia cost Austria its Galician provinces. Germany had to come to Austria's rescue. In the spring of 1915, the Germans made a breakthrough that forced the Russians to abandon Galicia and most of Poland. Outrunning their supplies, the Germans and Austrians had to slow down their pursuit of the retreating Russians, who were able to build a new line. Germany did not gain the decisive victory it had sought; although badly battered, Russia remained in the war, forcing Germany to fight on two fronts.

In June 1916, the Russians launched an offensive under General Aleksei Brusilov that opened a wide breach in the Austrian lines. Brusilov proved to be a brilliant commander, but he did not get sufficient help from other Russian armies. Hampered by this lack of support and by the inability of the Russian railways to transport his reserves, Brusilov could not maintain the offensive. A German counteroffensive forced a retreat and cost the Russians over a million casualties. After the winding down of the Brusilov offensive, Russia's military position deteriorated and domestic unrest worsened.

In March 1917, food shortages and disgust with the great loss of life exploded into a spontaneous revolution; the tsar was forced to abdicate. The new government, dominated by liberals, opted to continue the war despite the weariness of the Russian masses. In November 1917, a second revolution brought into power the Bolsheviks, or communists, who promised "Peace, Land, Bread" (see Chapter 31). In March 1918, the Bolsheviks ended Russia's role in the war by signing the punitive Treaty of Brest-Litovsk in which Russia surrendered Poland, the Ukraine, Finland, and the Baltic provinces. An insatiable Germany gained 34 percent of Russia's population, 32 percent of its farmland, 54 percent of its industrial enterprises, and 89 percent of its coal mines.

Several countries, which were not belligerents in August 1914, joined the war later. That autumn, the Ottoman Turks entered the conflict as an ally of Germany. Prior to the war, Germany had cultivated the Ottoman Empire's friendship by training the Turkish army; on their part, the Turks wanted German help in case Russia attempted to seize the Dardanelles. To relieve the pressure on Russia, the British planned to seize the Dardanelles and Constantinople. Although the Turks retreated from the Caucasus, Britain persisted with the plan. Its supporters, including Winston Churchill, First Lord of the Admiralty, argued that the opening of another front in the Balkans might compel Germany to withdraw forces from the west. Even more important, the capture of the Dardanelles would enable the Allies to supply Russia and, in turn, to obtain badly needed Russian grain.

In April 1915, a combined force of British, French, Australian, and New Zealander troops stormed the Gallipoli Peninsula on the European side of the Dardanelles. Ignorance of amphibious warfare, poor intelligence, and the fierce resistance of the Turks prevented the Allies from getting off the beaches and taking the heights. Some of the hardest fighting of the war took place on the beaches and cliffs of Gallipoli. The Gallipoli campaign cost the Allies 252,000 casualties, and they had gained nothing.

Although a member of the Triple Alliance, Italy remained neutral when war broke out. In May 1915, on the promise of receiving Austrian territory, Italy entered the war on the side of the Allies. The Austrians repulsed a number of Italian offensives along the frontier and in 1916 took the offensive against Italy. A combined German and Austrian force finally broke through the Italian lines in the fall of 1917 at Caporetto, and the Italians retreated in disorder, leaving behind huge quantities of weapons. Germany and Austria took some 275,000 prisoners.

The Collapse of the Central Powers

American Entry

The year 1917 seemed disastrous for the Allies. The Nivelle offensive had failed, the French army had mutinied, a British attack at Passchendaele did not bring the expected breakthrough and added some 300,000 casualties to the list of butchery, and the Russians, torn by revolution and gripped by war weariness, were close to making a separate peace. But there was one encouraging development for the Allies. In April 1917, the United States declared war on Germany.

From the outset America's sympathies lay with the Allies. To most Americans, Britain and France were democracies, threatened by an autocratic and militaristic Germany. These sentiments were reinforced by British propaganda that depicted the Germans as cruel "Huns." Since most war news came to the United States from Britain, anti-German feeling gained momentum. What precipitated American entry was the German decision of January 1917 to launch a campaign of unrestricted submarine warfare. The Germans were determined to deprive Britain of war supplies and to starve it into submission. Their resolve meant that German U-boats would torpedo both enemy and neutral ships in the war zone around the British Isles. Since the United States was Britain's principal supplier, American ships became a target of German submarines.

Angered by American loss of life and materiel and by the violation of the doctrine of freedom of the seas, and fearful of a diminution of prestige if the United States took no action, President Woodrow Wilson (1856–1924) pressed for American entry. Also at stake was American security, which would be jeopardized by German domination of western Europe. Leading American statesmen and diplomats feared that such a radical change in the balance of power threatened American national interests. Some argued that a Germany bloated with victory in Europe might one day seek conquests in the Western Hemisphere. As Secretary of State Robert Lansing wrote in a private memorandum just prior to American entry: "The Allies must *not* be beaten. It would mean the triumph of Autocracy over Democracy; the shattering of all our moral standards; and a real, though it may seem remote, peril to our independence and institutions."[7] Not only would a German triumph destroy the balance of power and foment global German expansion, it would also shatter any hopes of building a peaceful and democratic world after the war, which was the idealistic Wilson's principal hope.

In initiating unrestricted submarine warfare, Germany gambled that the United States, even if it became a belligerent, could not intervene in sufficient numbers quickly enough to make a difference. The Germans lost their gamble. The United States broke diplomatic relations with Germany immediately upon learning of the submarine campaign. Three weeks later the British turned over to the Americans a message sent by Berlin to the German ambassador in Mexico City and deciphered by British code experts. Germany proposed that in case of war between Germany and the United States, Mexico should join Germany as an ally; in return Mexico would receive Texas, New Mexico, and Arizona. This fantastic proposal further exacerbated anti-German feeling in the United States. As German submarines continued to attack neutral shipping, President Wilson, on April 2, 1917, urged Congress to declare war on Germany, which it did on April 6.

Although the United States may have entered the war to protect its own security, President Wilson told the American people and the world that the United States was fighting "to make the world safe for democracy." With America's entry, the war was transformed into a moral crusade—an ideological conflict between democracy and autocracy. In January 1918, Wilson enunciated American war aims in the Fourteen Points, which called for territorial changes based on nationality and the application of democratic principles to international relations. An association of nations would be established to preserve peace; it would conduct international relations with the same respect for law evidenced in democratic states. In nationalism and democracy, the two great legacies of the nineteenth century, Wilson placed his hope for the future peace of the world.

Germany's Last Offensive

With Russia out of the war, General Erich Ludendorff prepared for a decisive offensive before the Americans could land sufficient troops in France to help the Allies. A war of attrition now favored the Allies, who could count on American supplies and manpower. Without an immediate and decisive victory, Germany could not win the war. Ludendorff hoped to drive the British forces back to the sea, forcing them to withdraw from the Continent. Then he would turn his full might against the French.

On March 21, 1918, the Germans launched the *Kaiserschlacht*—the Emperor's Battle—which was intended to bring victory in the west. Just before dawn, the Germans began bombarding British lines. After hitting the British with artillery, gas, and mortar shells, the Germans climbed out of their trenches and moved across a no man's land enveloped by fog; the attackers could not be seen as they advanced toward the British trenches. They breached the enemy lines, and the British retreated. Expanding their offensive, the Germans now sought to split the British and French forces by capturing Amiens, the major allied communications center, and to drive the British back to the channel ports.

Suddenly the deadlock had been broken; it was now a war of movement. Within two weeks the Germans had taken some 1,250 square miles. But British resistance was astonishing, and the Germans, exhausted and short of ammunition and food, called off the drive. A second offensive against the British in April also had to be called off, as the British contested every foot of ground. Both campaigns depleted German manpower while the Americans were arriving in great numbers to strengthen Allied lines and uplift morale.

At the end of May, Ludendorff resumed his offensive against the French. Attacking unexpectedly, the Germans broke through and advanced to within 56 miles of Paris by June 3. General John Pershing, head of the American forces, cabled Washington that "the possibility of losing Paris has become apparent."[8] But the offensive was already winding down as reserves braced the French lines. In the Battle of Belleau Wood (June 6–25, 1918), the Americans checked the Germans. There would be no open road to Paris.

In mid-July the Germans tried again, crossing the Marne River in small boats. Although in one area they advanced 9 miles, the offensive failed against determined American and French opposition. On July 18 the French mounted a mass tank attack against the flank of the advancing Germans and punctured the German lines. The Germans tried to keep the offensive going but were unable to widen the salient, and Ludendorff ordered a pullback. By August 3, the Second Battle of the Marne had come to an end. The Germans had thrown everything they had into their spring and summer offensive, but it was not enough. The Allies had bent, but reinforced and encouraged by American arms, they did not break. Now they began to counterattack.

On August 8 the British, assisted by the French and using tanks to great advantage, broke through east of Amiens. Ludendorff said that "August 8th was the black day of the German Army. . . . Our war machine was no longer efficient."[9] And the kaiser himself declared to his generals: "We have nearly reached the limit of our powers of resistance. The war must be ended."[10] The Allies, their confidence surging, continued to attack with great success in August and September.

Meanwhile German allies, deprived of support from a hard-pressed Germany, were unable to cope. An Allied army of French, Britons, Serbs, and Italians compelled Bulgaria to sign an armistice on September 29. Shortly afterward, British successes in the Middle East compelled Turkey to withdraw from the war. In the streets of Vienna people were shouting "Long live peace! Down with the monarchy!" The Austro-Hungarian Empire was rapidly disintegrating into separate states based on nationality.

At the end of September, Ludendorff concluded: "The enemy had to be asked for peace and an armistice. . . . The military position, which would all too probably get worse, demanded this."[11] By early October, the last defensive position of the Germans crumbled. Fearful that the Allies would invade the fatherland and shatter the reputation of the German army, Ludendorff wanted an immediate armistice. But he needed a way to obtain favorable armistice terms from President Wilson and to shift the blame for the lost war away from the military and the kaiser to the civilian leadership. Cynically, he urged the creation of a popular parliamentary government in Germany. But events in Germany went further than the general had anticipated. Whereas Ludendorff sought a limited monarchy, the shock of defeat and hunger sparked a revolution that forced the kaiser to abdicate. On November 11, the new German Republic signed an armistice ending the hostilities. At 11 A.M., the soldiers from both sides walked into no man's land and into the daylight. A newspaper correspondent with the British army in France wrote: "Last night for the first time since August in the first year of the war, there was no light of gunfire in the sky, no sudden stabs of flame through darkness, no spreading glow above black trees where for four years of nights human beings were smashed to death. The Fires of Hell had been put out."[12]

The Peace Conference

Wilson's Hope for a New World

In January 1919, representatives of the Allied powers assembled in Paris to draw up peace terms; President Wilson was also there. The war-weary masses turned to Wilson as the prophet who would have the nations beat their swords into plowshares. In Paris, 2 million people lined the streets to cheer Wilson and throw bouquets; his carriage passed under a huge banner proclaiming "Honor to Wilson the Just." In Rome, hysterical crowds called him the god of peace; in Milan, wounded soldiers sought to kiss his clothes; in Poland, university students spoke his name when they shook hands with each other.

For Wilson the war had been fought against autocracy. A peace settlement based on liberal-democratic ideals, he hoped, would sweep away the foundations of war. Wilson proclaimed his message with a spiritual zeal that expressed his Presbyterian background and his faith in American democracy.

None of Wilson's principles seemed more just than the idea of self-determination—the right of a people to have its own state, free of foreign domination. In particular, this goal meant (or was interpreted to mean) the return of Alsace and Lorraine to France, the creation of an independent Poland, a readjustment of the frontiers of Italy to incorporate Austrian lands inhabited by Italians, and an opportunity for Slavs of the Austro-Hungarian Empire to form their own states. Although Wilson did not demand the liberation of all colonies, the Fourteen Points did call for "a free, open-minded and absolutely impartial adjustment of all colonial claims" and a territorial settlement "made in the interest and for the benefit of the population concerned."

Aware that a harshly treated Germany might well seek revenge, thereby engulfing the world in another cataclysm, Wilson insisted that there should be a "peace without victory." A just settlement would encourage a defeated Germany to work with the victorious Allies in building a new Europe. But on one point he was adamant: Prussian militarism, which he viewed as a principal cause of the war, must be eliminated.

To preserve peace and to help remake the world, Wilson urged the formation of a League of Nations, an international parliament to settle disputes and discourage aggression. Wilson wanted a peace of justice to preserve Western civilization in its democratic and Christian form.

Problems of Peacemaking

But how could such high-sounding, moralistic proclamations be translated into concrete peace provisions? "Obviously no mortal man this side of the millennium could have hoped to bring about all the things that the world came to expect of Wilson," concludes American historian Thomas

Woodrow Wilson and the King of Italy Greeting Crowds in Italy After Signing the Peace Treaty. Woodrow Wilson was greeted in Europe as the bringer of peace. His presence at the peace conference, where he had to haggle over points, and the Republican victory in the U.S. congressional election in November 1918, soon tarnished his image. (*Culver Pictures*)

A. Bailey. "Wilson's own people were bound to feel disillusioned; the peoples of the neutral and Allied countries were bound to feel deceived; and the peoples of the enemy countries were bound to feel betrayed."[13]

Wilson's negotiating position was undermined by the Republican party's victory in the congressional elections of November 1918. Before the election, Wilson appealed to the American people to vote for Democrats as a vote of confidence in his diplomacy. But Americans elected twenty-five Republicans and fifteen Democrats to the Senate. Whatever the motives of the American people in voting Republican—apparently their decision rested on local and national, not international, issues—the outcome diminished Wilson's prestige at the conference table. To his fellow negotiators, Wilson was trying to preach to Europe when he could not command the support of his own country. Since the Senate must ratify any American treaty, European diplomats had the terrible fear that what Wilson agreed to the Senate might reject—which is precisely what happened.

It has been suggested that Wilson's very presence at the conference table also diminished his prestige. As president of the nation that had rescued the Allies and as initiator of a peace program that held the promise of a new world, Wilson occupied a position of honor from which he could exert considerable influence and authority. But by attending the conference in person and haggling with the other representatives, he was knocked from his lofty pedestal and became all too human. "Messiahs tend to arouse less enthusiasm the more they show themselves," observes Bailey; "the role requires aloofness and the spell of mystery."[14]

Another obstacle to Wilson's peace program was France's demand for security and revenge. Nearly the entire war on the western front had been fought in French territory. Many French industries and farms had been ruined; the country mourned the loss of half its young men. To many in France the Germans were savages, vandals, assassins. The French people were skeptical of Wilson's idealism. "Let us try out the new order," said a French editorial in the *Echo de Paris,* "but so long as we are not assured of its absolute success . . . let us maintain . . . unsatisfactory though they may be, the pillars of the old order . . . which will seek to maintain peace by the aid of military, political and economic guarantees."[15]

Representing France at the conference table was Georges Clemenceau (1841–1929), nicknamed "the Tiger." Nobody loved France or hated Germany more. Cynical, suspicious of idealism, and not sharing Wilson's hope for a new world or his confidence in the future League of Nations, Clemenceau demanded that Germany be severely punished and its capacity to wage war destroyed. Fearful of Germany's greater population and superior industrial strength, and of its military tradition that would not resign itself

to defeat, Clemenceau wanted guarantees that the wars of 1870–71 and 1914–1918 would not be repeated. The war had shown that without the help of Britain and the United States, France would have been at the mercy of Germany. Because there was no certainty that these states would again aid France, Clemenceau wanted to use his country's present advantage to cripple Germany.

The intermingling of European nationalities was another barrier to Wilson's program. Because in so many regions of central Europe there was a mixture of nationalities, no one could create a Europe completely free of minority problems; some nationalities would always feel that they had been treated shabbily. And the various nationalities were not willing to moderate their demands or lower their aspirations. "To most Europeans," states German-American historian Hajo Holborn, "the satisfaction of their national dreams was an absolute end even when their realization violated the national determination of others."[16] For example, the Fourteen Points called for the creation of an independent Poland with secure access to the sea. But between Poland and the sea lay territory populated by Germans. Giving this land to Poland would violate German self-determination; denying it to Poland would mean that the new country had little chance of developing a sound economy. No matter what the decision, one people would regard it as unjust. Similarly, to provide the new Czechoslovakia with defensible borders, it would be necessary to give it territory inhabited principally by Germans. This too could be viewed as a denial of German self-determination, but not granting it to Czechoslovakia would mean that the new state would not be able to defend itself against Germany.

Also serving as a barrier to Wilson's program were the secret treaties drawn up by the Allies during the war. These agreements, dividing up German, Austrian, and Ottoman territory, did not square with the principle of self-determination. For example, to entice Italy into entering the war, the Allies had promised it Austrian lands that were inhabited predominantly by Germans and Slavs. Italy was not about to repudiate its prize because of Wilson's principles.

Finally, the war had aroused great bitterness that persisted after the guns had been silenced.

Both the masses and their leaders demanded retribution and held exaggerated hopes for territory and reparations. In such an atmosphere of postwar enmity, the spirit of compromise and moderation could not overcome the desire for spoils and punishment. A century earlier, when the monarchs had defeated Napoleon, they sought a peace of reconciliation with France. But democratic statesmen and nations found it harder to set aside their hatreds than had despotic monarchs and aristocratic diplomats.

The Settlement

After months of negotiations, punctuated often by acrimony, the peacemakers hammered out a settlement. Five treaties made up the Peace of Paris—one each with Germany, Austria, Hungary, Bulgaria, and Turkey. Of the five, the Treaty of Versailles, which Germany signed on June 28, 1919, was the most significant.

France regained Alsace and Lorraine, territory lost to Germany in the Franco-Prussian War of 1870–71. The Treaty of Versailles also barred Germany from placing fortifications in the Rhineland. The French military had wanted to take the Rhineland from Germany and break it up into one or more republics under French suzerainty. The Rhine River was a natural defensive border; one had only to destroy the bridges to prevent a German invasion of France. With Germany deprived of this springboard for invasion, French security would be immensely improved. Recognizing that the German people would never permanently submit to the amputation of the Rhineland, which was inhabited by more than 5 million Germans and contained key industries, Wilson and British Prime Minister David Lloyd George (1863–1945) resisted these French demands. They did not want to create an Alsace-Lorraine in reverse by awarding France a region that was overwhelmingly German. Nor could Wilson ever agree to such a glaring violation of the principle of self-determination.

But Clemenceau did not willingly agree to give up France's demand for control of the Rhineland. The confrontation between Wilson and Clemenceau was so bitter that the president made plans to return to the United States, threatening to disrupt the conference. Faced with the opposition of Wilson and Lloyd George, Clemenceau backed down and agreed instead to Allied occupation of the Rhineland for fifteen years, the demilitarization of the region, and an Anglo-American promise of assistance if Germany attacked France in the future. This last point, considered vital by France, proved useless. The alliance went into effect only if both the United States and Britain ratified it. Since the Security Treaty did not get past the United States Senate, Britain also refused to sign it. France had made a great concession on the Rhineland issue but received nothing in exchange; the French people felt that they had been duped and wronged.

A related issue concerned French demands for annexation of the coal-rich Saar Basin, which adjoined Lorraine. By obtaining this region, France would weaken Germany's military potential and strengthen its own. France argued that this would be just compensation for the deliberate destruction of the French coal mines by the retreating German army at the end of the war. But here too France was disappointed. The final compromise called for a League of Nations commission to govern the Saar Basin for fifteen years, after which the inhabitants would decide whether their territory would be ceded to France or returned to Germany.

In eastern Germany, in certain districts of Silesia that had a large Polish population, a plebiscite determined the future of the region. As a result, part of Upper Silesia was ceded to Poland. The settlement also gave Poland a corridor cut through West Prussia and terminating in the Baltic port of Danzig, and Danzig itself was declared an international city to be administered by a League of Nations commission. The Germans would never resign themselves to this loss of territory that separated East Prussia from the rest of Germany, especially since it was awarded to the Poles, whom many Germans viewed as cultural and racial inferiors.

Regarding the Germans as unfit to care for colonial peoples, Wilson supported stripping Germany of its overseas possessions, all of which had been seized by the Allies during the war. The disposition of Ottoman colonies was also at issue. But instead of the outright annexation of colonies by the victorious powers, Wilson proposed the mandate system, whereby small nations would be entrusted with the administration of the colonies under the guidance of the League of Nations. Such an arrangement would accord with the spirit of the Fourteen Points. Here too, Wilson's proposal conflicted with secret agreements made by Britain with its dominions—the Union of South Africa, Australia, New Zealand—and with Japan.

Backing down from his position on the German and Ottoman colonies, Wilson permitted the victorious nations to be awarded control. However, these nations held the colonies not outright but as mandates under the supervision of the League, which would protect the interests of the native peoples. Thus the division of Ottoman and German colonies represented a compromise between traditional imperialism and Wilsonian idealism. The mandate system implied the ultimate end of colonialism, for it clearly opposed the exploitation of colonial peoples and asserted independence as the rightful goal for subject nations.

To prevent a resurgence of militarism, the settlement abolished the German general staff and forbade military conscription in Germany. The German army was limited to 100,000 volunteers and deprived of heavy artillery, tanks, and warplanes. The German navy was limited to a token force that did not include submarines.

The issue of war reparations (compensation) aroused terrible bitterness between Wilson and his French and British adversaries. Goaded by public opinion and enticed by Germany's helplessness, Lloyd George and Clemenceau sought to make Germany pay the total costs of the war. Although Wilson resisted such an impossible demand, he did make considerable concessions on exacting vast reparations from the defeated Germans. Wilson agreed that the costs of pensions paid to Allied veterans and their families should be borne by Germany, an inclusion that nearly tripled the bill. The American delegation wanted the treaty to fix a reasonable sum that Germany would have to pay and specify the period of years allotted for payment. But no such items were included; they were left for future consideration. The Treaty of Versailles left Germany with an open-ended bill that would probably take generations to pay; nor had the Allies considered Germany's capacity to pay. Wilson had lost on the issue of reasonable reparations.

Moreover, Article 231, which preceded the reparation clauses, placed sole responsibility for the war on Germany and its allies. The Germans responded to this accusation with contempt. Clearly the German government would feel little incentive to pay the reparations and considerable moral justification in evading them.

In separate treaties the conference dealt with the dissolution of the Hapsburg Empire. In the closing weeks of the war, the Austro-Hungarian Empire had crumbled as the various nationalities proclaimed their independence from Hapsburg rule. In most cases, the peacemakers ratified with treaties what the nationalities had already accomplished in fact. Serbia joined with Austrian lands inhabited by Croats and Slovenes to become Yugoslavia. Czechoslovakia arose from the predominantly Czech and Slovak regions of Austria. Hungary, which broke away from Austria to become a separate country, had to concede considerable land to Rumania and Yugoslavia. Austria had to turn over to Italy the South Tyrol, which was inhabited by 200,000 Austrian Germans. This clear violation of the principle of self-determination greatly offended liberal opinion. Deprived of its vast territories and prohibited from union with Germany, the new Austria was a third-rate power.

Assessment and Problems

The Germans unanimously denounced the Treaty of Versailles, for in their minds the war had ended not in German defeat but in a stalemate. They regarded the armistice as the prelude to a negotiated settlement among equals based on Wilson's call for a peace of justice. Instead the Germans were barred from participating in the negotiations. And they viewed the terms of the treaty as humiliating and vindictive—designed to keep Germany militarily and economically weak. What standard of justice, they asked, allowed the Allies to take the German colonies for themselves, to reduce the German military to a pitiful size without themselves disarming, to ban Germany from the League of Nations, to saddle Germany with impossible reparations, to take away approxi-

Map 30.2 Post–World War I: Broken Empires and Changed Boundaries ▶

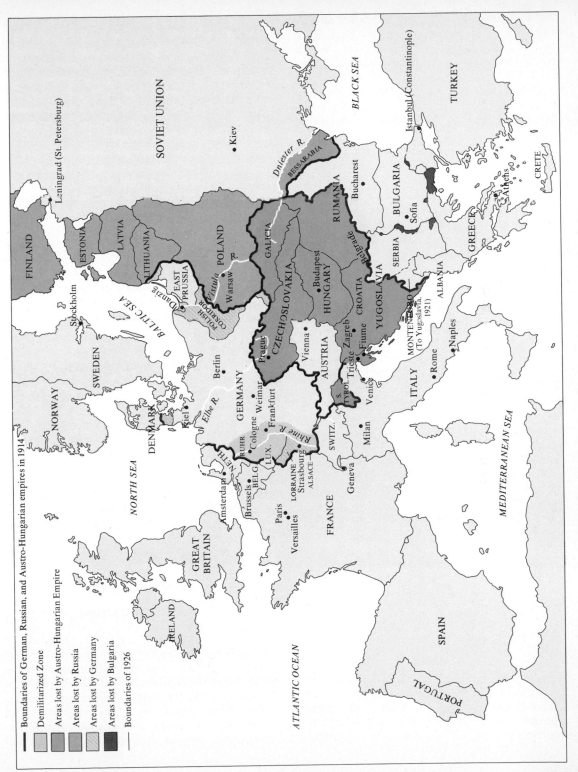

Boundaries of German, Russian, and Austro-Hungarian empires in 1914

Demilitarized Zone

Areas lost by Austro-Hungarian Empire

Areas lost by Russia

Areas lost by Germany

Areas lost by Bulgaria

Boundaries of 1926

SOVIET UNION

BLACK SEA

TURKEY

Istanbul (Constantinople)

CRETE

Kiev

Leningrad (St. Petersburg)

FINLAND

ESTONIA

LATVIA

LITHUANIA

POLAND

Vistula R.

Warsaw

Dniester R.

BESSARABIA

RUMANIA

Bucharest

BULGARIA

Sofia

SERBIA

GREECE

Athens

Stockholm

SWEDEN

BALTIC SEA

Danzig

EAST PRUSSIA

POLISH CORRIDOR

GALICIA

CZECHOSLOVAKIA

Prague

Budapest

HUNGARY

CROATIA

Belgrade

YUGOSLAVIA

Zagreb

MONTENEGRO (To Yugoslavia, 1921)

ALBANIA

Naples

NORWAY

DENMARK

Kiel

Elbe R.

Berlin

GERMANY

Weimar

Cologne

Frankfurt

Rhine R.

RUHR

Vienna

AUSTRIA

TYROL

Trieste

Fiume

Venice

S.

ITALY

Rome

Milan

NORTH SEA

NETH.

Amsterdam

BELG.

Brussels

LUX.

LORRAINE

Strasbourg

ALSACE

SWITZ.

Geneva

FRANCE

Paris

Versailles

GREAT BRITAIN

IRELAND

ATLANTIC OCEAN

SPAIN

PORTUGAL

MEDITERRANEAN SEA

mately one-eighth of German territory and deprive it of one-tenth of its population, to blame the war on Germany, to provide for the self-determination of Poles while precluding the union of German-speaking Austria with Germany, to hand over to Italy some 200,000 Austrian Germans, to place Germans under Polish rule, and to declare the German port of Danzig a free city?

The Germans protested that when the United States entered the war, Wilson had stated that the enemy was not the German people, but their government. Surely, the Germans now argued, the new German democracy should not be punished for the sins of the monarchy and the military. To the Germans, the Treaty of Versailles was not the dawning of the new world that Wilson had promised, but an abomination—a vile crime.

War-weary, torn by revolutionary unrest, desperately short of food, its economy in disarray, and with the Allies poised to invade, the new German Republic had no choice but to sign the treaty. However, the sentiments of the German people were clearly and prophetically expressed by the Berlin *Vorwärts,* the influential Social Democratic newspaper: "We must never forget it is only a scrap of paper. Treaties based on violence can keep their validity only so long as force exists. Do not lose hope. The resurrection day comes."[17]

Critics in other lands also condemned the treaty as a punitive settlement in flagrant violation of Wilsonian idealism. The peacemakers, they argued, should have set aside past hatreds and, in cooperation with the new democratic German Republic, forged a just settlement that would serve as the foundation of a new world. Instead they burdened the fledgling German democracy with reparations that were impossible to pay, insulted it with the accusation of war guilt, and deprived it of territory in violation of the principle of self-determination. All these provisions, said the critics, would only exacerbate old hatreds and fan the flames of German nationalism. This was a poor beginning for democracy in Germany and for Wilson's new world.

Defenders of the peace settlement insisted that had Germany won the war it would have imposed a far harsher settlement on the Allies. They pointed to German war aims, which called for the annexation of parts of France and Poland, the reduction of Belgium and Rumania to satellites,

and German expansion in central Africa. They pointed also to the Treaty of Brest-Litovsk, which Germany compelled Russia to sign in 1918, as an example of Germany's ruthless appetite. Moreover, they insisted that the peace settlement was by no means a repudiation of Wilson's principles. The new map of Europe was the closest approximation of the ethnic distribution of its peoples that Europe had ever known.

What is most significant about the Treaty of Versailles is that it did not solve the German problem. Germany was left weak but unbroken—its industrial and military power only temporarily contained, its nationalist fervor undimmed. The real danger in Europe was German unwillingness to accept defeat or surrender the dream of expansion.

Would France, Britain, and the United States enforce the treaty against a resurgent Germany? The war had demonstrated that an Allied victory depended on American intervention. But in 1920, the U.S. Senate, angry that Wilson had not taken Republicans with him to Paris and fearing that membership in the League of Nations would involve America in future wars, refused to ratify the Treaty of Versailles. Britain, feeling guilty over the treatment of Germany, lacked the will for enforcement and even came to favor treaty revision. The responsibility for preserving the settlement therefore rested primarily with France, which was not encouraging. The Paris peace settlement left Germany resentful but potentially powerful, and to the east lay small and weak states, some of them with sizable German minorities, that could not check a rearmed Germany.

The War and European Consciousness

World War I was a great turning point in the history of the West. The war left many with the gnawing feeling that Western civilization had lost its vitality and was caught in a rhythm of breakdown and disintegration. It seemed that Western civilization was fragile and perishable, that Western people, despite their extraordinary accom-

Käthe Kollwitz: The Survivors. With an estimated 10 million dead and 21 million wounded, World War I shattered the hope that western Europe had been making continuous progress toward universal peace and a rational and enlightened civilization. (*National Gallery of Art, Washington, D.C., Rosenwald Collection*)

plishments, were never more than a step or two away from barbarism. Surely any civilization that could allow such senseless slaughter to last four years had entered its decline and could look forward to only the darkest of futures.

European intellectuals were demoralized and disillusioned. The orderly, peaceful, rational world of their youth had been destroyed. The Enlightenment world-view, weakened in the nineteenth century by the assault of romantics, Social Darwinists, extreme nationalists, race mystics, and glorifiers of the irrational, was now disintegrating. The enormity of the war had shattered faith in the capacity of reason to deal with crucial social and political questions. It appeared that civilization was fighting an unending and seemingly hopeless battle against the irrational elements in human nature and that war would be a continuous phenomenon in the twentieth century.

Confidence in the future gave way to doubt. The old beliefs in the perfectibility of humanity, the blessings of science, and ongoing progress now seemed an expression of naive optimism. A. J. P. Taylor concludes:

> The First World War was difficult to fit into the picture of a rational civilization advancing by ordered stages. The civilized men of the

Chronology 30.1 World War I

June 28, 1914	Archduke Ferdinand of Austria is assassinated at Sarajevo
August 4, 1914	The Germans invade Belgium
August–September 1914	The Russians invade East Prussia, and are defeated by the Germans at the battle of Tannenberg
September 1914	The first battle of the Marne saves Paris
April 1915	The Allies storm Gallipoli Peninsula, withdrawing after 252,000 casualties are suffered
May 1915	Italy enters the war on the Allies' side
1915	Germany forces Russia to abandon Galicia and most of Poland
February 1916	General Pétain leads French forces at Verdun; Germans fail to capture the fortress town
June 1916	General Brusilov leads a Russian offensive against Austrian lines; a million casualties are suffered
July–November 1916	The battle of the Somme—the Allies suffer 600,000 casualties
January 1917	Germany launches unrestricted submarine warfare
April 6, 1917	The United States declares war on Germany

twentieth century had outdone in savagery the barbarians of all preceding ages, and their civilized virtues—organization, mechanical skill, self-sacrifice—had made war's savagery all the more terrible. Modern man had developed powers which he was not fit to use. European civilization had been weighed in the balance and found wanting.[18]

Western civilization had lost its spiritual center. The French writer Paul Valéry summed up the mood of a troubled generation for whom the sun seemed to be setting on the Enlightenment.

The storm has died away, and still we are restless, uneasy as if the storm were about to break. Almost all the affairs of men remain in a terrible uncertainty. We think of what has disappeared, and we are almost destroyed by what has been destroyed; we do not know what will be born, and we fear the future, not without reason. We hope vaguely, we dread precisely; our fears are infinitely more precise than our hopes; we confess that the charm of life is behind us. There is no thinking man . . . who can hope to dominate this anxiety, to escape from this impression of darkness. . . . But among all these injured things is the Mind. The Mind has indeed been cruelly wounded; its complaint is heard in the hearts of intellectual men; it passes a mournful judgment on itself. It doubts itself profoundly.[19]

Chronology 30.1 continued

May 1917	General Pétain restores morale and discipline in the French army
July–November 1917	The British are defeated at Passchendaele
Fall 1917	The Italians are defeated at Caporetto
November 1917	The Bolsheviks take power in Russia
January 1918	U.S. President Woodrow Wilson announces his Fourteen Points
March 1918	Russia signs the Treaty of Brest-Litovsk, losing territory to Germany and withdrawing from the war
March 21, 1918	The Germans launch a great offensive to end the war
June 3, 1918	The Germans advance to within 56 miles of Paris
August 8, 1918	The British win the battle of Amiens
October 1918	Turkey is forced to withdraw from the war after several British successes
November 3, 1918	Austria-Hungary signs an armistice with the Allies
November 11, 1918	Germany signs an armistice with the Allies, ending World War I
January 1919	Paris Peace Conference
June 28, 1919	Germany signs the Treaty of Versailles

This disillusionment heralded a loss of faith in liberal-democratic values that contributed to the widespread popularity of fascist ideologies in the postwar world. Having lost confidence in the power of reason to solve the problems of the human community, in liberal doctrines of individual freedom, and in the institutions of parliamentary democracy, many people turned to fascism as a simple saving faith. Far from making the world safe for democracy as Wilson and other liberals had hoped, World War I gave rise to totalitarian movements that would nearly destroy democracy.

The war produced a generation of young people who had reached their maturity in combat. Violence had become a way of life for millions of soldiers hardened by battle and for millions of civilians aroused by four years of propaganda. The astronomical casualty figures—some 10 million dead and 21 million wounded—had a brutalizing effect. Violence, cruelty, suffering, and even wholesale death seemed to be natural and acceptable components of human existence; the sanctity of the individual seemed to be liberal and Christian claptrap.

The fascination with violence and contempt for life lived on in the postwar world. Many returned veterans yearned for the excitement of battle and the fellowship of the trenches. The brutalizing effect of the war is seen in the following statement by a German soldier for whom the war never ended:

People told us that the War was over. That made us laugh. We ourselves are the War. Its flame burns strongly in us. It envelops our whole being and fascinates us with the enticing urge to destroy. We ... marched onto the battlefields of the postwar world just as we had gone into battle on the Western Front: singing, reckless, and filled with the joy of adventure as we marched to the attack; silent, deadly, remorseless in battle.[20]

The Great War's veterans made ideal recruits for extremist political movements that glorified action and promised to rescue society from a decadent liberalism.

Both Hitler and Mussolini, themselves ex-soldiers imbued with the ferocity of the front, knew how to appeal to veterans. The lovers of violence and the harbingers of hate who became the leaders of fascist parties would come within a hairsbreadth of destroying Western civilization. The intensified nationalist hatreds following World War I also helped to fuel the fires of World War II. The Germans swore to regain lands lost to the Poles; some Germans dreamed of a war of revenge. Italy, too, felt aggrieved because it had not received more territory from the dismembered Austro-Hungarian Empire.

However, while the experience of the trenches led some veterans to embrace an aggressive militarism, others were determined that the horror should never be repeated. Tortured by the memory of the Great War, European intellectuals wrote pacifist plays and novels and signed pacifist declarations. In the 1930s, an attitude of "peace at any price" discouraged resistance to Nazi Germany in its bid to dominate Europe.

World War I was total war—it encompassed the entire nation and had no limits. States demanded total victory and total commitment from their citizens. They regulated industrial production, developed sophisticated propaganda techniques to strengthen morale, and exercised ever greater control over the lives of their people, organizing and disciplining them like soldiers. This total mobilization of nations' human and material resources provided a model for future dictators. With ever greater effectiveness and ruthlessness, dictators would centralize power and manipulate thinking. The first indication that the world would never be the same again, and perhaps the most important consequence of the war, was the Russian Revolution in 1917 and the Bolshevik seizure of power.

Notes

1. Quoted in Barbara Tuchman, *The Guns of August* (New York: Macmillan, 1962), p. 51.

2. S. L. A. Marshall, *The American Heritage History of World War I* (New York: Dell, 1966), p. 215.

3. Quoted in Alistair Horne, *The Price of Glory* (New York: Harper, 1967), p. 240.

4. A. J. P. Taylor, *A History of the First World War* (New York: Berkeley, 1966), p. 84.

5. Quoted in Richard M. Watt, *Dare Call It Treason* (New York: Simon & Schuster, 1963), p. 169.

6. Quoted in ibid., p. 215.

7. Quoted in Daniel M. Smith, *The Great Departure* (New York: Wiley, 1965), p. 20.

8. Quoted in Marshall, *The American Heritage History of World War I*, p. 334.

9. Erich Ludendorff, *My War Memories* (London: Hutchinson, 1919), p. 679.

10. Quoted in John Terraine, *To Win a War: 1918, the Year of Victory* (Garden City, N.Y.: Doubleday, 1981), p. 102.

11. Ibid., p. 141.

12. Excerpted in Louis L. Snyder, ed., *Historic Documents of World War I* (Princeton: D. Van Nostrand, 1958), p. 183.

13. Thomas A. Bailey, *Woodrow Wilson and the Lost Peace* (Chicago: Quadrangle Books, 1963), p. 29.

14. Ibid., p. 209.

15. Quoted in *The Nation*, 108 (January 18, 1919): 86.

16. Hajo Holborn, *The Political Collapse of Europe* (New York: Alfred A. Knopf, 1966), p. 102.

17. Quoted in Bailey, *Woodrow Wilson and the Lost Peace,* p. 303.

18. A. J. P. Taylor, *From Sarajevo to Potsdam* (New York: Harcourt, Brace and World, 1966), pp. 55–56.

19. Paul Valéry, *Variety* (New York: Harcourt, Brace, 1927), pp. 27–28.

20. Quoted in Robert G. L. Waite, *Vanguard of Nazism* (New York: W. W. Norton, 1969), p. 42.

Suggested Reading

Albrecht-Carrie, René, *The Meaning of the First World War* (1965). How the war upset the delicate equilibrium of Europe.

Bailey, Thomas, *Woodrow Wilson and the Lost Peace* (1963). A critical interpretation of the role of the United States at the peace conference.

Essame, H., *The Battle for Europe, 1918* (1972). The last campaign.

Falls, Cyril, *The Great War* (1961). A good narrative of the war.

Fussell, Paul, *The Great War and Modern Memory* (1977). The influence of the Great War on British writers.

Horne, Alistair, *The Price of Glory* (1967). Brilliantly recaptures the battle of Verdun.

Marshall, S. L. A., *The American Heritage History of World War I* (1966). Probably the best account available.

Panichas, George A., ed., *Promise of Greatness* (1968). Recollections of the war by people of prominence.

Remarque, Erich Maria, *All Quiet on the Western Front* (1969). A novel that has become a classic.

Terraine, John, *To Win a War: 1918, the Year of Victory* (1981). The final campaign; contains numerous passages from primary sources.

Tuchman, Barbara, *The Guns of August* (1962). A beautifully written account of the opening weeks of the Great War.

Watt, R. M., *Dare Call It Treason* (1963). A brilliant study of the French army mutinies of 1917.

Williams, John, *The Other Battleground* (1972). A comparison of the home fronts in Britain, France, and Germany.

Review Questions

1. What battle plans did Germany and France implement in 1914? What prevented Germany from reaching Paris in 1914?

2. Describe trench warfare.

3. Identify and explain the historical significance of the battles of Verdun, the Somme, and Gallipoli.

4. Why did the United States enter the war?

5. Why did General Ludendorff seek an armistice?

6. What was Wilson's peace program? What obstacles did he face?

7. What were the provisions of the Treaty of Versailles regarding Germany? How was Austria-Hungary affected by the war? What was the German reaction to the treaty?

8. Why was World War I a great turning point in the history of the West?

31

The Soviet Union: Modernization and Totalitarianism

A fateful consequence of World War I, even before its final battles were fought, was the Russian Revolution of 1917. The Revolution occurred in two stages. In March, the tsarist regime was overthrown. The March revolution ushered in a period of liberal government and freedom, which soon led to a complete breakdown of law and order. Taking advantage of the chaos, the Bolsheviks, in a second stage of the Revolution, seized power in November and established a communist dictatorship.[*]

These events were fateful not only for Russia but also for Europe and the world; they foreshadowed basic trends of the twentieth century. More than ever, the victory of the Western powers in the war carried Western institutions and values beyond the territorial base of Western civilization. In Asia and Africa, as in many parts of Europe, indigenous tradition did not fit the Western heritage; democracy, industrialism, and social justice were alien imports that undermined the bonds holding society together. How could unprepared peoples run their society in the Western manner? How could their governments hold their unruly subjects together and build up their skills for survival in times of social change and worldwide competition for power? The Russian Revolution of 1917 highlighted the problems caused by the expansion of Western civilization and Western power into the non-Western world.

The overthrow of the tsar showed that governments without a base of support among the mass of their people could not survive. The collapse of Russian liberalism in the first stage of the Revolution demonstrated the difficulty of establishing

[*]Until March 1918, events in Russia were dated by the Julian calendar, 13 days behind the Gregorian calendar used in the West.

Peasant Woman on a Tractor at a Soviet Collective Farm. (*UPI/Bettmann Newsphotos*)

Western liberal-democratic forms of government in countries lacking a sense of unity, a strong middle class, and a tradition of responsible participation in public affairs. After World War I, the weaknesses of liberal government became more glaring. In one country after another in central, eastern, and southern Europe, liberal governments were replaced by authoritarian regimes. European—and later, non-Western—dictators copied the Russian communists, who pioneered the first experiment of trying to match the accomplishments of Western civilization, including its power, with the culturally unprepared human resources at their disposal.

The Russian Revolution of 1917

The Collapse of Autocracy

Fears of revolution had long troubled foresighted Russians. In the opening years of the twentieth century they sat, as some of them put it, on a volcano ready to explode. Their country, a huge multinational empire held together by force, was in mortal crisis. The mass of the people were peasants, who provided the workers for food production as well as for factories. Illiterate and resentful of the controls foisted upon them by the tsars in the past, workers and peasants had shown their hatred in the revolution of 1905. They also disliked the Westernized minority that dominated the country's finance, industry, and professions; those comfortable people were the agents of the tsars. The educated elite, sharply splintered in its own ranks and dreading the "dark" masses, likewise opposed the tsar; the elite called for constitutional government and freedom. Most non-Russian nationalities in the empire felt imprisoned and demanded freedom too. Increased contact with "the West," as Russians called Europe, raised expectations and deepened dissatisfaction among all classes, as did the spread of Western ideas promoted by rising literacy and the freer movement offered by the new railways. It seemed that only the tsar could be responsible for the country's poverty and backwardness. Threatened by rising dissatisfaction, the tsarist regime had turned into a police state—not very effectively, as the events of 1905 showed.

Russian backwardness and disaffection undermined Russian power in the world at large. The country lacked the industries needed for modern war; it also lacked the necessary political unity. Defeat by Japan, followed by the revolution of 1905, raised an ominous specter: external humiliation aggravated by internal revolution might destroy the empire. In 1905, the army remained intact and quelled the revolution. But what about the next crisis?

After the outbreak of war in 1914, the volcano came to life. On the German front, the Russian armies—ill-equipped, poorly led, and suffering huge losses—were soon defeated and, never regaining the initiative, began a long retreat to the east. The German government prepared plans for dismembering the Russian Empire. By 1916, the home front began to fall apart. Shops were empty, money valueless, and hunger and cold stalked the working quarters of cities and towns. But Tsar Nicholas II (1868–1918), who was determined to preserve autocracy, resisted any suggestion that he liberalize the regime for the sake of the war effort.

The people of Russia had initially responded to the war with a show of patriotic fervor. They russianized the German name of their capital, St. Petersburg, renaming it Petrograd. But by January 1917, virtually all Russians, and foremost the soldiers, despaired of autocracy: it had failed to protect the country from the enemy, and economic conditions had deteriorated. Autocracy was ready to collapse at the slightest adversity. In early March (February 23 by the calendar then in use) a strike, riots in the food lines, and street demonstrations in Petrograd flared into sudden unpremeditated revolution. The soldiers, who in 1905 had stood by the tsar, now rushed to support the striking workers. The Romanov dynasty, after three hundred years of rule (1613–1917), came to a petty and inglorious end a month before the United States entered the war "to make the world safe for democracy."

Even before the tsar had abdicated, two rival centers of government sprang up in Petrograd: first a council of soldiers and workers called the Petrograd *Soviet* (council), representing those who had fought in the streets and risked their lives; and soon thereafter a committee of various liberals afraid of revolution and the soviet. The latter claimed office as the Provisional Government—provisional until a representative Constituent Assembly (to be elected as soon as possible) could establish a permanent regime. Both the Petrograd Soviet and the Provisional Government agreed that henceforth all Russians should enjoy full freedom.

Thus, at the height of a disastrous war, mounting shocks mobilized the unresolved social and political tensions of many centuries, and the long-dreaded volcano exploded. Liberty came, hot and furious, to an utterly unprepared Russia, which soon reduced it to hopeless anarchy. Liberal democrats in Western countries had never suffered conditions like those now emerging in Russia.

The Problems of the Provisional Government

The collapse of autocracy was followed by what supporters in Russia and the West hoped would be a liberal-democratic regime pledged to give Russia a constitution. In reality, however, the course of events from March to November 1917 resembled a free-for-all, a no-holds-barred fight for the succession to autocracy, with only the fittest surviving. Events also demonstrated, under conditions of exceptional popular agitation and mobility, the desperate state of the Russian Empire, its internal disunity, and the furies of the accumulated resentments. Both Germany and national minorities in Russia took advantage of the anarchy to dismember the country.

Among the potential successors to the tsars, the liberals of various shades seemed at first to enjoy the best chances. They represented the educated and forward-looking elements in Russian society that had arisen after the reforms of the 1860s—lawyers, doctors, professional people of all kinds, intellectuals, businesspeople and industrialists, many landowners, and even some bureaucrats. Liberals had opposed autocracy and earned a reputation for leadership. Their strength lay in the Party of Popular Freedom, generally known by its previous name of Constitutional Democrats (or Cadets). The liberals had joined the March revolution only reluctantly, for they were

afraid of the masses and the violence of the streets; they dreaded social revolution that could result in the seizure of factories, dispossession of landowners, and tampering with property rights. Although most leaders of the Provisional Government had only modest means, they were "capitalists," believing in private enterprise as the source of economic progress. Their ideal was a constitutional monarchy, its leadership entrusted to the educated and propertied elite familiar with the essentials of statecraft. For them, freedom meant rule by the educated minority.

Unfortunately, the liberals deceived themselves about the mood of the people. Looking to the Western democracies—including, after April 1917, the United States—for political and financial support, they were eager to continue the war on the side of the Allies, which discredited them among the war-weary masses. The liberals also antagonized the peasants by not giving them landlords' lands free of charge. As nationalists, the liberals also opposed the self-determination sought by national minorities; their Russia was to remain whole and undivided.

In all their plans, the liberals acted as if conditions were normal and Russia still had a chance of winning the war. In fact, not enough steel was produced to supply both the railroads with rails and the army with artillery shells. Almost 2 million soldiers had deserted, "voting for peace with their legs," as Lenin, leader of the opposition Bolsheviks, said; more were to be demobilized for lack of food.

The Provisional Government swept away the oppressive restrictions of tsarism, including discrimination on grounds of religion or nationality, and ended the death penalty. Now Russians could speak and act freely. Yet the new freedoms intensified the accumulated tensions in Russian life. As the old order crumbled, the Provisional Government could not create an administrative network capable of taking the place of the tsarist bureaucracy, nor did it convene the promised Constituent Assembly. Consequently the Russian Empire ceased to function as a state. More soviets of workers and soldiers sprang up; some villages even declared themselves independent. In the face of the rising chaos, many liberals gave up all hope for a free Russia; said one of them in early May: " . . . on the day of the revolution Russia received more liberty than she could take, and the revolution has destroyed Russia. Those who made it will be cursed. . . ."[1]

To workers, soldiers, and peasants—all classified as peasants before 1917—freedom meant for once speaking their own untrained minds. The government created by the soldiers and workers after their own liking was the Petrograd Soviet. It spoke for the Russian masses. Feeling incapable with its untrained constituency to take the lead, it tolerated the Provisional Government as long as it respected its sentiments. Some Soviet leaders eventually joined the Provisional Government in a series of coalitions between "capitalists" and "socialists." In July, Aleksandr Kerensky (1881–1970), a radical lawyer of great eloquence who from the start had belonged to both camps, became the leader of the Provisional Government, the symbol of a liberal-democratic Russia determined to continue the war. The coalitions, however, did not halt the drift toward soviet democracy.

That drift, swelling to a mighty tide of spontaneous social revolution in midsummer, was fed from many sources. The war brought further disasters; the army disintegrated, sending its deserters into the countryside as armed agitators. The peasants began to divide the landlords' land among themselves, which encouraged more soldiers to desert in order to claim a share of the land. The breakdown of the railways stopped factory production; enraged workers ousted factory managers and owners. Consumer goods grew scarce and prices soared, and the peasants could see no reason to sell their crops if they could buy nothing in return. Thus the specter of famine in the cities arose. Hardships, and anger, mounted.

The suffering of the people was blamed on the "capitalists," all those who had been associated with the Europeanized elite—anybody with clean fingernails and soft hands. The popular mood turned ugly; now at last it was time to settle age-old scores. Among the groups carried away by the tide were the non-Russian nationalities—Finns, Ukrainians, Georgians, and others. Sometimes supported by German money, they demanded self-determination and even secession. Freedom obviously was not leading to a grand upsurge of patriotic resolve to drive out the enemy, as had happened in the course of the French Revolution, but rather to dissolution and chaos.

By July 1917, it had become clear that law and order could be upheld only by brute force. In late August and early September, a conspiracy led by an energetic young general, Lavr Kornilov, aimed at setting up a military dictatorship. Kornilov had the support not only of the officer corps and the tsarist officials but also of many liberals fed up with anarchy. What stopped the general was not Kerensky's government (which had no troops), but the workers of Petrograd. Their agitators demoralized the soldiers sent to suppress the Soviet, thereby proving that a dictatorship of the right had no mass support. The workers also repudiated Kerensky and the Provisional Government as well as their own moderate leaders; henceforth they voted for the Bolsheviks.

In this setting the Bolsheviks, under Lenin, were ready to attempt their solution for Russia's supreme crisis: a dictatorship of the left exclusively based on the soviets, with mass support from the peasants in uniform, the peasants at the factory, and to some extent, even the peasants in the villages. Thus entered the Bolsheviks—communists, as they soon called themselves—a small band of unknown but surprisingly well-prepared political soldiers.

The Bolshevik Revolution

Lenin and the Rise of Bolshevism

By the fall of 1917, revolutionary Bolshevism had a long history. Rooted in the Russian revolutionary tradition, it harked back to the early nineteenth century, when educated Russians began to compare their country unfavorably with western Europe. They too wanted constitutional liberty, the rights to free speech and political agitation, in order to make their country modern. Prohibited from speaking out in public, the critics went underground, giving up their original liberalism as too pacifist and narrow for their ends. Revolutionary socialism, with its idealistic vision and compassion for the multitude, was a better ideology in the harsh struggle with the police. By the 1870s, many socialists had evolved into austere and self-denying professional revolutionaries

Lenin with Stalin, 1922. This faked photograph was arranged by Stalin to show his close association with Lenin. Lenin, the architect of the Russian Revolution, is shown two years before his death. He was a visionary with intelligence, discipline, and dedication to his goals. Stalin, although often idealized in patriotic posters, was ruthless. He was determined to reshape the Soviet people's consciousness through the revolution of totalitarianism, laying the foundation for Soviet Russia's emergence as a superpower. (*The Mansell Collection*)

who, in the service of the cause, had no moral scruples, just as the police had no scruples in the defense of the tsars. Bank robbery, murder, assassination, treachery, and terror were not immoral if they served the revolutionary cause.

At first the revolutionaries had staked their hopes on the Russian peasants as a progressive force capable of transforming peasant communal life into a superior socialist society. Peasant-oriented socialists, gathered in the Social Revolutionary party, remained a large but ineffectual part of the revolutionary movement until the early Soviet regime. Yet already in the 1880s and 1890s, the more alert revolutionaries had learned industrial economics and sociology from Marx; from Marxism they had also acquired a vision of a universal and inevitable progression toward socialism and communism, which satisfied their semireligious craving for salvation in this world, not the next. Marxism also allied them with socialist movements in other lands, giving them an internationalist outlook. History, they believed, was on their side, as it was for all the proletarians and oppressed peoples in the world. There throbbed among all Russian revolutionaries a deep patriotic urge to end their country's inferiority. They dreamed of enabling their country one day to surpass the strongest Western nations in the name of the highest ideals drawn from Western civilization and enshrined in their socialist (or communist) vision.

By 1900, a number of able young Russians had rallied to revolutionary Marxism, almost all of them from privileged families or favored by education. The most promising was Vladimir Ilyich Ulyanov, known as Lenin (1870–1924), the son of a teacher and school administrator who had attained the rank of a nobleman. Lenin had studied law, but he practiced revolution instead. His first contribution to the Revolution lay in adapting Marxism to Russian conditions, taking considerable liberties with the master's teaching. His second followed from the first: outlining the organization of an underground party capable of surviving against the tsarist police. It was to be a tightly knit conspiratorial elite of professional revolutionaries; its headquarters would be safely located abroad, and it would have close ties to the masses, that is, to the workers and other potentially revolutionary elements. To protect against police infiltration, Lenin rejected the formal democracy within the party practiced by Western Marxist parties. He trusted that an informal give-and-take among comrades would occur, never admitting that the lack of checks and balances promoted abuses of personal power.

Two prominent Marxists close to Lenin were Leon Trotsky (1879–1940) and Joseph Stalin (1879–1953). Trotsky, whose original name was Lev Bronstein, was the son of a prosperous Jewish farmer from southern Russia and was soon known for his brilliant pen. Stalin (the man of steel) was originally named Iosif Dzhugashvili; he was from Georgia, beyond the Caucasus mountains. Bright enough to be sent to the best school in the area, he dropped out for a revolutionary career. While they were still young, Lenin, Trotsky, and Stalin were all hardened by arrest, lengthy imprisonments, and exile to Siberia. Lenin and Trotsky later lived abroad, while Stalin, following a harsher course, stayed in Russia; for four years before 1917 he was banished to bleakest northern Siberia, conditioned to ruthlessness for life.

In 1903, the Russian Marxists had split into two factions, the moderate Mensheviks, so named after finding themselves in a minority (*menshinstvo*) at a rather unrepresentative vote at the Second Party Congress, and the extremist Bolsheviks, who at that moment were in the majority (*bolshinstvo*). They might more accurately have been called the "softs" and the "hards." The "softs" (Mensheviks) preserved basic moral scruples; they would not stoop to crime or undemocratic methods for the sake of political success. For that the "hards" (Bolsheviks) ridiculed them, noting that a dead, imprisoned, or unsuccessful revolutionary was of little use.

Meanwhile, Lenin perfected Bolshevik revolutionary theory. He violated Marxist tradition by paying close attention to the revolutionary potential of peasants (thereby anticipating Mao Zedong). Lenin also looked closely at the numerous peoples in Asia who had recently fallen under Western imperialist domination. These people, he sensed, constituted a potential revolutionary force. In alliance with the Western—and Russian—proletariat, they might overthrow the worldwide capitalist order. Imperialism, he said, was caused by the giant monopolies of the Great Powers. Driven by their rivalry for profits, they had pushed their countries into colonial expansion and now into suicidal war. Lenin overlooked the fact that the financing of colonial ventures was but a minute part of capitalist enterprise and that the international monopolies, handling business in many different states, were bound to suffer by war. He did, however, anticipate the anti-Western groundswell that arose from the great outpouring of European power and culture in the decades before the war; he envisioned that tide rising to a mighty world revolution. The Bolsheviks, the most militant of all revolutionary socialists, were ready to assist in that gigantic struggle.

Lenin's Opportunity

On April 16, 1917, Lenin, with German help, arrived in Petrograd from exile in Switzerland. Of all Russian political leaders, Lenin possessed the clearest insight into his country's condition. Russia was, he said, the freest country in the world, but the Provisional Government could not possibly preserve Russia from disintegration. The bulk of the soldiers, workers, and peasants would repudiate the Provisional Government's cautious liberalism in favor of a regime expressing their demand for peace and land. Nothing would stop them from avenging themselves for centuries of oppression. Lenin also felt that only complete state control of the economy could rescue the country from disaster. The sole way out, he insisted, was the "dictatorship of the proletariat" backed by the soviets of soldiers, workers, and peasants, particularly the poorer peasants.

Lenin was a Russian nationalist as well as a socialist internationalist; he stepped forward with a vision of a modern and powerful Russian state destined to be a model in world affairs. As he boasted in October 1917: "The [March] revolution has resulted in Russia catching up with the advanced countries in a few months, as far as her political system is concerned. But that is not enough. The war is inexorable; it puts the alternative with ruthless severity; either perish or overtake and outstrip the advanced countries *economically* as well."[2] Russian communism was thus nationalist communism; the Bolsheviks saw the abolition of income-producing property by the dictatorship of the proletariat as the most effective way of mobilizing the country's resources. Yet in twentieth-century style, the Bolshevik mission was also internationalist. The Russian Revolution was to set off a world revolution, liberating all oppressed classes and peoples around the world, thereby achieving a higher stage of civilization.

With arguments like these, Lenin prepared his party for the second stage of the Revolution of 1917—the seizure of power by the Bolsheviks. Conditions favored him, as he had predicted. The Bolsheviks obtained majorities in the soviets everywhere. The peasants were in active revolt, seizing the land themselves. The Provisional Government lost all control over the course of events.

The planning and execution of the Bolshevik coup was entrusted to Trotsky, who gloried in his role as a revolutionary leader. As a Marxist theorist, he made the overthrow of the Provisional Government into a universal model for proletarian revolutions. The coup's details were subsequently dramatized in Soviet literature and art as the grand opening of a new era. Thus dressed up it has also impressed people in the West. At the time, however, the Bolshevik coup was a minor event. On November 6 and 7 (October 24 and 25 by the old calendar), the Bolsheviks hardly "seized" power; rather, it fell into their laps.

In the name of the Second All-Russian Congress of Soviets that was just assembling in Petrograd, the Bolsheviks quickly organized a government proclaiming "soviet democracy" but determined to establish a dictatorship. Only a dictatorship of the left, they said, had a chance of restoring government authority. The rest of the world, preoccupied with war, paid little attention. The *New York Times* on November 10 called the Bolsheviks "political children, without the slightest understanding of the vast forces they are playing with." Thus began a novel political experiment destined to change the world. Its ultimate aims were nothing less than to end class exploitation and to raise the poor and helpless peoples of backward lands to the power and wealth of Western countries.

Its immediate necessity, however, was merely to survive. The Bolshevik seizure of power in Petrograd was another step toward civil war—the real test of power for all forces eager to take the place of the tsars. The credit for Bolshevik survival belongs to Lenin.

The Bolsheviks Survive

Lenin as Leader

Lenin is most commonly remembered in Soviet Russia from the ever-present, eye-catching posters framed with slogans addressed to the masses. The posters show Lenin in a dark business suit and sport cap, addressing a spellbound audience of workers and soldiers. His sweeping gestures, right arm outstretched as if to drive home his point, show him not commanding like Peter the Great, but pleading, persuading, cajoling, and sometimes threatening—a symbol to idolize. Lenin looked like a source of inexhaustible energy and confidence—he alone had grasped the opportunity for a socialist revolution; he had sustained a wavering, uncertain party and had led the advance into a totally unknown and risky future.

Lenin pleaded that he was guiding the Russian proletariat and all humanity toward a higher social order, symbolizing—in Russia and much of the world—the rebellion of the disadvantaged against Western (or "capitalist") superiority. That is why, in 1918, he changed the name of his party from Bolshevik to Communist. For Lenin, as for Marx, a world without exploitation was humanity's noblest ideal. Under this creed he matched his mission against that of Woodrow Wilson, who wanted to make the world safe for democracy. There were now two ideals of democracy—soviet style and American style. If individuals can be taken as symbols of historic turning points, Lenin counts among the most influential men of the twentieth century.

Dismemberment, Civil War, and Foreign Intervention

Staggering adversity confronted Lenin after his seizure of power. In the prevailing anarchy, Russia lay open to the German armies. Invoking the plea for national self-determination, the German government was quick to demand the liberation of territories held by Russia for its own benefit. Under the Treaty of Brest-Litovsk, signed in March 1918, the lowest point in Russian history for over two hundred years, Russia lost Finland, Poland, the Baltic provinces—regions inhabited largely by non-Russians—plus the rebellious Ukraine, its chief industrial base and breadbasket. Yet Lenin had no choice but to accept the humiliating terms.

After the Treaty of Brest-Litovsk was signed, the civil war that had been brewing since the summer of 1917 broke out in full. In the winter of 1917–18, tsarist officers had been gathering troops in the south, counting on the loyalty of the Cossacks; they also found allies in other parts of the country. The political orientation of these anticommunist groups, generally called Whites in contrast to the Communist Reds, combined all shades of opinion from moderate socialist to reactionary, the latter usually predominating. All received support from foreign governments that freely intervened in Russia's agony. The Germans, until their own revolution in November 1918, occupied much of southern Russia. England, France, and the United States sent troops to points in northern and southern European Russia; England, Japan, and the United States also sent troops to Siberia. At first they hoped to offset German expansion, later to overthrow the communist re-

gime. In May and June 1918, Czech prisoners of war, about to be evacuated, precipitated anti-communist uprisings along the Siberian railway, bringing the civil war to fever pitch.

In July 1918, Nicholas II and his entire family were murdered by communists. In August, a non-communist socialist nearly assassinated Lenin, while the White forces in the south moved to cut off central Russia from its food supply. The communists, meanwhile, built up their own Red Army. Recruited from the remnants of the tsarist army and its officer corps, the Red Army was reinforced by compulsory military service and strict discipline; Trotsky reintroduced the death penalty, which had been outlawed by the Provisional Government. He also appointed political commissars to be responsible for the political reliability and morale of the troops. But the Red Army, like the armies of the Whites, lacked discipline; soldiers butchered their own comrades as well as civilians. Their leaders, too, spared no lives to maintain control. Only the most ruthless commanders, including Trotsky and Stalin, prevailed.

In 1919, thanks to the Allied victory and the American contribution to it, the German menace ended. Yet foreign intervention stepped up in response to the formation of the Communist International (Comintern), an organization founded in 1918 by Lenin to guide the international revolutionary movement that he expected to issue from the world war. Lenin sought revolutionary support from abroad for strengthening his hand at home; his enemies reached into Russia to defeat at its source the revolution that they feared in their own countries.

Gradually the Red Army defeated its enemies. The last White forces, entrenched on the Crimean peninsula, were evacuated with British help in November 1920. At the same time, foreign interventionists called off their efforts. War-weariness and communist propaganda undermined the morale of Allied soldiers, and public opinion demanded their return.

Before winning the civil war, the communists faced a sudden invasion from Poland. After initial victories, the Red Army was routed and Lenin was forced to accept a new Polish-Russian boundary running deep inside Russian territory. By

Map 31.1 Russian Civil War, 1918–1920 ▶

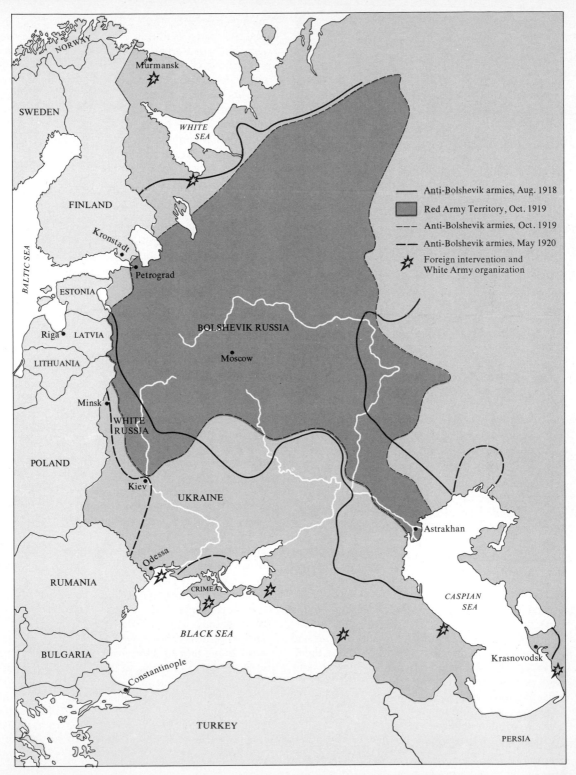

NORWAY

SWEDEN

Murmansk

WHITE
SEA

FINLAND

BALTIC SEA

Kronstadt

Petrograd

ESTONIA

Riga · LATVIA

LITHUANIA

Minsk ·

WHITE
RUSSIA

POLAND

Kiev ·

UKRAINE

RUMANIA

Odessa ·

CRIMEA

BLACK SEA

BULGARIA

Constantinople ·

TURKEY

BOLSHEVIK RUSSIA

Moscow ·

Astrakhan

CASPIAN
SEA

Krasnovodsk

PERSIA

———— Anti-Bolshevik armies, Aug. 1918

Red Army Territory, Oct. 1919

– – – Anti-Bolshevik armies, Oct. 1919

━ ━ Anti-Bolshevik armies, May 1920

✪ Foreign intervention and
White Army organization

Starving Children in a Famine Region of Russia, 1921. The privations suffered by the Russian people in the years immediately following World War I and the Bolshevik Revolution were incalculable. The first four years of the new Communist regime, 1917–1921, were marked by civil war and foreign invasion. Cities faced starvation and food was taken from peasants at gunpoint. Several million lives were lost. (*Historical Pictures Service, Chicago*)

a staggering price. Reds and Whites alike had carried the tsarist tradition of political violence to a new pitch of horror (some of it described in famous novels by Pasternak and Sholokhov). The entire population, including the Communist party and its leaders, suffered in the war, which was followed in 1921–22 by a famine that took still more millions of lives.

World war and civil war had brought terrible suffering to the Russian people. Adding to their misery was the policy known as war communism, introduced in 1918 to deal with plummeting agricultural and economic production, rampant inflation, and desperate hunger in the cities. Under war communism, the state took over the means of production and greatly limited the sphere of private ownership; it conscripted labor and, in effect, confiscated grain from the peasants. War communism devastated the economy even further and alienated workers and peasants. Factories were mismanaged, workers stayed away from their jobs or performed poorly, and peasants resisted the food requisition detachments that seized their grain. Sometimes there were rebellions. In March 1921, an uprising of sailors at the Kronstadt naval base and of workers in nearby Petrograd indicated the need for a change of course. The people who in 1917 had been ready to give their lives for the Revolution now rose against the repression that had been introduced during the civil war; they called for a restoration of soviet democracy. Trotsky ruthlessly suppressed that uprising, but the lesson was clear: the communist regime had to retreat from war communism and to restore a measure of stability to the country.

In 1921, the Communist party adopted the New Economic Policy, generally called NEP, which lasted until 1928. Under a system that Lenin characterized as "state socialism," the government retained control of finance, industry, and transportation—"the commanding heights" of the economy—but allowed the rest of the economy to return to private enterprise. The peasants, after giving part of their crops to the government, were free to sell the rest in the open market; traders could buy and sell as they pleased. With the resumption of small-scale capitalism, an air of normal life returned, which allowed the key institutions of the new regime to establish their routines.

1921, Soviet Russia had been virtually ejected from eastern Europe, yet the major parts of Russia had at last been brought under communist control.

Hard-pressed as Lenin's party had been, it had prevailed. The Whites were divided among themselves and lacked their opponents' political skills and experience with terror. The Bolsheviks had the advantage of interior communications and enjoyed greater popular support than the Whites, who were identified with the tsarist regime. But the communist victory in the civil war had exacted

The Communist Party

While the communists were waging a fierce struggle against the Whites, they instituted a militant dictatorship run by their party. Numbering about 500,000 in 1921, the Communist party was indeed remarkable. It was controlled by a small, close-knit core of professional political leaders, the best of them unusually disciplined in personal dedication. This new elite's organizational skills permitted them to preserve their revolutionary drive in the face of both failure and success. From the start, those who did not pull their weight were purged.

Despite the lack of discipline in its ranks, the Communist party was more adaptable, energetic, and effective than the tsarist bureaucracy; shaped by war, revolution, and civil war, it was also more ruthless. The savagery of the times and the backwardness of the people undermined or even destroyed the human values that Marx had channeled from the Enlightenment into his vision of the socialist society. These values, however, remained part of Lenin's dream of human happiness under communism.

For most Russians, being a good Communist was not easy. They had to be political activists well versed in Marxism-Leninism, and they were continually admonished to observe strict party discipline, to toe the party line, and to set a model of communist dedication in every job they held. Reality, however, was somewhat different. Especially in the lower ranks, sloppiness, corruption, and abuse of authority spoiled the high ideals.

The top leaders, however, were superior to tsarist officials. They combined a long experience of working with the masses and a fierce patriotic ambition to rescue their country from defeat and backwardness. They were inexperienced in statecraft, but they were ready to learn and explosively energetic.

Under its constitution, the "Russian Communist Party (Bolshevik)," as its formal title read, was a democratic body. Its members elected delegates to periodic party congresses, which in turn elected the membership of the central committee, where leadership originally centered. However, under the pressure of the civil war, power soon shifted to a smaller and more intimate group—the *politburo* (political bureau). There the key leaders, Lenin, Trotsky, Stalin, and a few others, determined policy, assigned tasks, and appointed key officials. Ideally, their leadership was democratic in the sense that the flow of decisions from the top down was matched by an upward flow of information and opinion—a system called "democratic centralism." In the face of continuing crises, however, individual leaders like Lenin, or later Stalin, dominated their associates. And as the party grew, so did the need for centralization and bureaucratic organization; the higher echelons controlled the lower; there was never time for consensus-building consultation.

Thus the conditions favoring one-party dictatorship in Russia also shaped the Communist party. To guarantee the unity of the country, the party had to be monolithic itself. For that reason, the politburo assumed a dictatorial role. Impatient with unending disputes among righteous and strong-willed old revolutionaries, Lenin, in agreement with other top leaders, demanded unconditional submission to his decisions. He even ordered that dissidents be disciplined and political enemies be terrorized. No price was too high for the sake of unity.

The party dominated all public agencies; its key leaders held the chief positions in goverment. No other political parties were tolerated, and trade unions became agents of the regime. Never before had the people of Russia been so dominated by government.

The drastic escalation of governmental power showed that the Bolshevik Revolution had a double—and contradictory—objective. Its first aim was to overthrow the Europeanized elite by an uprising from below, making the people of Russia feel more in control of their country. In that respect the Bolshevik Revolution resembled the French Revolution. Its second objective, however, ran against the grain of the first. In attempting to transform their Soviet Russia into a modern industrialized state that would serve as a model for the world, the Bolsheviks imposed a new autocracy even more authoritarian than the old. Russia must be rebuilt on an uncongenial design adapted from the West—against the people's will, if necessary.

The second objective recreated, with twentieth-century refinements, the service state of Peter the Great. It was led by a revolutionary party in close touch with the masses. Yet it also worked for their long-range betterment in terms that they could not grasp and that required a discipline they resented. In the view of the party leaders, the masses always needed firm guidance.

The One-Party Dictatorship

It was with the help of the Communist party, then, that Lenin from the start imposed his communist dictatorship. Almost immediately after the seizure of power, the communists, in a temporary coalition with radical peasant-oriented socialists, outlawed all other political parties and suppressed their newspapers. In January 1918, the communists dispersed the Constituent Assembly, the last vestige of the Provisional Government. Then, losing their peasant-socialist partners after the Treaty of Brest-Litovsk, they established a full-blown one-party state. Already in November 1917 they had set up an Extraordinary Commission (called the *Cheka*) to ferret out all counterrevolutionary activity. Staffed by hardened revolutionaries, it engaged in extreme terror not only against enemies of the regime but also against the population at large. The Cheka founded the forced-labor camps that became notorious under Stalin's regime.

As former victims of tsarist repression, the communists felt no moral objection to the use of force or even of stark terror. As Lenin admonished his followers: "cleanse the land of Russia of all sorts of harmful insects, of crook-fleas, and bedbugs," by which he meant "the rich, the rogues, and the idlers." He even suggested that "one out of every ten idlers be shot on the spot."[3] Those not shot found themselves, with Lenin's blessings, in the Cheka's forced-labor camps.

The communists also made sure of continued popular support. Caught between Red and White, most of the people tended to favor the Reds because they offered more. Out of respect for the ideal of self-determination, the communists held out hope for cultural and administrative autonomy among non-Russian minorities. At the same time, they pleased Russian nationalists by forcibly bringing back most of those nationalities that had tried to escape from the empire. By warding off foreign intervention, the communists also claimed credit for defending Mother Russia.

More important, in their bid for popular support, the communists endorsed the peasant seizure of nonpeasant lands, although with reservations about the peasants' preference for farming the land by their own backward methods. They initially allowed workers to control factories but soon strengthened managerial control through party-led trade unions and nationalization of industry.

The communists abolished the power of the Orthodox church, the traditional ally of tsarism and the enemy of innovation. They were militant atheists, believing with Marx that religion was "opium of the people"; God had no place in their vision for a better society. Yet the Orthodox church and other religions survived, much reduced in influence and closely watched, an enduring target for atheist propaganda.

The communists also simplified the alphabet, changed the calendar to the Gregorian system prevailing in the capitalist West, and brought theater and all arts, hitherto reserved for the elite, to the masses. Above all, they wiped out—by expropriation of property and discrimination, expulsion, and execution—the educated upper class of bureaucrats, landowners, professional people, and industrialists. Their Russia was more than ever a country of peasants.

Shaping Soviet Society

The Russia of the communists was "Soviet" Russia. It was the first regime in Russian history to derive its power and legitimacy from below—from the toiling masses—and it spoke their rough language and expressed their crude sense of social justice. The communists' constituency, significantly, was both men and women. The party promised "to liberate woman from all the burdens of antiquated methods of housekeeping, by replacing them by house-communes, public kitchens, central laundries, nurseries, etc."[4] Traditional values, particularly in the Asian parts of the Soviet Union, hardly favored equality between the sexes, especially in political work. The practical necessity of combining work with family responsibility, moreover, tended to keep women out of managerial positions in the party and the organizations of the state, but the ideal remained alive.

The Bolsheviks derived much acclaim from their emphasis on redistributing housing, food, and clothing and making education available to the masses. They were not opposed to some private property; they allowed items for personal use, provided they were in keeping with the standards of the common people. But they outlawed income-producing private property that enabled capitalists to employ (or exploit, as the communists said) others for their own profit. With the disappearance of private enterprise, the state gradually became the sole employer, thereby forcefully integrating the individual into the reconstruction of the country. Socialism promised a far more intense mobilization of the country than a system based on private property. The Bolsheviks never ceased to stress that they worked strenuously for the welfare of the vast majority of the population.

The latter point, unfortunately, was not easily proved, for Lenin's views of the country's needs differed sharply from common opinion. The working people wanted democracy, by which they meant governing themselves in their own customary ways. Lenin, on the other hand, wanted socialism, re-educating the masses to a higher standard of individual conduct and economic productivity that would be superior even to capitalism. In the spring of 1918, he argued that the Russian workers had not yet matched capitalist performance: "The Russian worker is a bad worker compared with the workers of the advanced, i.e., western countries." To overcome this fatal handicap, Lenin urged competition—socialist competition—and relentlessly hammered home the need for "iron discipline at work" and "unquestioning obedience" to a single will—that of the Communist party. There was no alternative: "Large-scale machinery calls for absolute and strict unity of will, which directs the joint labors of hundreds and thousands and tens of thousands of people. A thousand wills are subordinated to one will. . . ."[5]

In these words lay the essence of subsequent Soviet industrialization. The entire economy was to be monolithic, rationally planned in its com-plex interdependence, and pursuing a single goal: overcoming the weaknesses of Russia so disastrously demonstrated in the war. Leaving the workers to their own spontaneity, Lenin realized, would merely perpetuate Russian backwardness. Instead he called for a new "consciousness," a hard-driving work ethic expressed in the Russian Marxist revolutionary vocabulary.

The minds of the people, therefore, came under unprecedented government control. In education from the kindergarten through the university, in press and radio, and in literature and the arts, the Communist party tried to fashion people's thoughts to create the proper "consciousness." The party made Marxism-Leninism the sole source of inspiration, eliminating as best it could all rival creeds—whether religious, political, or philosophical. Minds were to be as reliably uniform as machine processes and totally committed to the party as well as to the new Soviet Union.

Soviet patriotism was always a prime concern of ideological indoctrination. The communists were determined to strengthen the unity of the Russian multinational empire endangered by the Revolution. They propagated Marxism-Leninism as a universal creed. All proletarians, they argued, shared a common class bond transcending ethnic and national differences. Proceeding from this assumption, the party promulgated in 1924 the first Soviet constitution, creating the Union of Soviet Socialist Republics (U.S.S.R.). It was a federation of four ethnically distinct states, called union republics: Russia proper, the Ukraine, White Russia (the westernmost parts of the country, near Poland), and the Transcaucasian Federation (containing Armenia, Azerbaijan, and Georgia). Each union republic enjoyed cultural and administrative autonomy under the common Soviet socialist form of government and party control. Rallying patriotic pride, party leaders boasted that by its new constitution the country demonstrated its advanced level of social existence; it would attract other Soviet socialist states, until eventually it provided peace to the entire world through "the pacific co-existence and fraternal collaboration of peoples."[6] To prevent Soviet citizens from doubting their new superiority, the party prohibited all uncontrolled comparison with capitalist countries.

An Ideology for World Revolution

In foreign policy, Lenin was far bolder than any tsar: he turned Russian state ambition into an international revolutionary force.

The Russian Revolution deeply touched hitherto suppressed nationalistic ambitions for political self-determination and cultural self-assertion among a growing number of peoples around the world, especially in Asia. It appealed particularly to intellectuals educated in the West (or in Westernized schools) yet who identified themselves with their downtrodden compatriots. Taught to worship the ideals of the French Revolution—liberty, equality, and fraternity—they noted that the Europeans (or white people everywhere) did not apply these ideals to people of different cultures and colors (if indeed they applied them among themselves). These intellectuals were determined to turn these ideals to their own advantage, if necessary by revolution. Like Lenin, they were of a double mind: they spoke for their own peoples, but they also were eager to make their countries and cultures modern, that is, to reshape them in some form after the model of Western power. These patriots included moderates like Gandhi and Nehru in India, who soon repudiated Lenin, and radicals like Ho Chi Minh in Vietnam, and Zhou Enlai (Chou En-lai) and Mao Zedong in China, who became his disciples. Lenin made himself the spokesman for the rising tide of anti-Westernism, soliciting support for the common aim of unhinging the capitalist world order based on Western superiority.

As a political tool for this purpose, Lenin created the Communist—or Third—International (Comintern). The most radical successor to earlier socialist international associations, it helped raise small communist parties in western Europe which, in time, became dependable, although rather powerless, agents of Soviet Russia. In Asia, where no proletariat existed, Lenin tried to work closely with incipient nationalist movements and even envisaged setting up peasant soviets. He also held out the possibility that backward countries might skip the hated capitalist phase altogether, provided they allied themselves with the "leading socialist country," namely the Soviet Union.* It was soon clear that the anti-Western agitation of the twentieth century would not follow the path of world revolution predicted by Lenin. Yet Lenin and the Bolshevik Revolution inspired admiration and instinctive loyalty among the colonial and semicolonial peoples in what would come to be called the Third World.

Unwittingly, Lenin also contributed to a novel division in the world. In the uncertain times following World War I, the specter of world revolution created extravagant hopes and fears. Some people believed in the communist vision; others were thrown into a panic by it. The spread of communism was more than matched in western and central Europe, and in the Americas as well, by a vigorous anticommunism that, in turn, contributed to the rise of right-wing or fascist movements. Propertied and patriotic men and women had good reason to be scared; world revolution threatened their sense of security, their religion, their very sanity. World opinion became polarized: fear of communism became an obsession in the West, as did the fear of capitalism in Russia and many poor countries around the world.

World revolution, however, was never a realistic prospect. The tide of Western ascendancy was running strong. Moreover, the Comintern was never a truly international force; it remained a tool of the Russian Communist party. But the fear it aroused served Lenin well: it made Soviet Russia appear strong when in fact the country was exhausted. At very little cost, the Comintern put prestige-conscious Russia back on the map of world politics. Having captured the attention of the world, Soviet Russia now stood out as the communist alternative to the capitalist West, re-

---

*Western Marxists believed that in the progression from feudalism to capitalism, and from capitalism to socialism and communism, no stage could be omitted. A country could start on a higher stage of development only if it had acquired all the social and technical skills of the preceding stage. Having argued, in contrast, that Russia could advance to socialism even though it had not matched the achievements of capitalism, Lenin advocated an even quicker shortcut for underdeveloped countries under Soviet leadership. He argued this case in his "Theses on the National and Colonial Question" (1920).

jecting the West and yet following it. Like the Western countries, the U.S.S.R. believed in industrial progress. Like them, it wanted to feel superior, above all in its vision of the future—a vision that, beyond the dark realities of Soviet life, held out hope for a social order more humane than Western capitalism.

The Stalin Revolution

Stalin's Rise to Power

Secure after the end of the civil war, the communist service state gradually embarked on the daring experiment of social engineering envisaged in November 1917. Having set forth a master plan, Lenin was not destined to see it carried into action. Incapacitated by strokes soon after the NEP was adopted, he relinquished control of the party. In the leisure of his sickroom, he began to realize how little his backward country was prepared for building a superior society. His last words urged patient, hard work in learning from capitalism. He died in January 1924.

The task of achieving the goal that Lenin had set in his impatient prime was taken up by Stalin. The "man of steel" was crude and vulgar, toughened by the revolutionary underground and tsarist prisons and by the roughest aspects of Russian life. Nobody in 1917 would have foreseen this high-ranking Bolshevik as the successor to the university-trained, cosmopolitan Lenin. Relentlessly energetic, but relatively inconspicuous among the more temperamental and intellectual key Bolsheviks, Stalin was given, in 1922, the unwanted and seemingly routine task of general secretary of the party. It became his responsibility, in the chaotic aftermath of the Revolution and the civil war, to give reality to the Leninist vision of the monolithic party as the ultimate guaranty of effective legislation. He did so to his own advantage, building up a reliable party cadre—apparatus men, or *apparatchiki,* as they came to be called—and dominating the party as not even Lenin had. When in the protracted struggles for the succession to Lenin he was challenged, particu-

larly by Trotsky and his associates, it was too late to unseat him. None of Stalin's rivals could rally the necessary majorities at the party congresses. Although equally ruthless, none could match Stalin's drive and skill in party infighting or in making rough and anarchic people into docile members of the Communist party apparatus.

Stalin, like Lenin, is best known from his poster image. Soviet citizens saw him as an energetic man clad in a simple military tunic, devoid of show or pomp, a fatherly figure, a good conciliatory chairman signifying a mood of bureaucratic control suitable to the industrial era. Yet the image was a façade. Behind it lay a coarse, vindictive, impatient temperament cast in preindustrial times, surcharged with the furies of a lost war, a victorious revolution, and a protracted civil war. He represented a brutalized raw society rebelling against authority and wanting to rise to prosperity and glory. The real Stalin was an appalling mixture of contradictory qualities, raised to superhuman proportions by his office as the dictator of Soviet Russia. To this day he is a fiercely controversial figure, but nobody has ever suggested that he took his tasks lightly.

Modernizing Russia: Industrialization and Collectivization

To Stalin, Russia's most pressing need was not world revolution but the fastest possible buildup of Soviet power through industrialization. The country could not afford another near-annihilation as it had suffered in the war and the civil war that followed. Bolshevik pride dictated that the country be made strong as much as possible by Russian efforts. Stalin's slogan was "socialism in one country," which signified that Soviet Russia by itself possessed all the necessary resources for "surpassing and overtaking" capitalism in the shortest time possible. It was a staggering job.

Stalin decided on all-out industrialization at the expense of the toiling masses. Peasants and workers, already poor, would be required to make tremendous sacrifices of body and spirit to overcome the nation's weaknesses. The Bolshevik Rev-

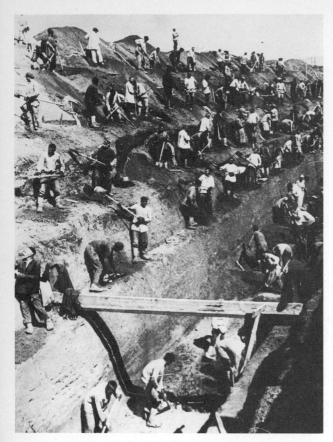

Soviet Construction Workers at Magnitka Hill in 1929. A city of metallurgists was built at this site. The task of industrializing the Soviet Union was staggering. The subsequent hardships endured by its people during the 1920s and 1930s are hard to imagine. For decades, the working masses were rewarded with nothing more than hope for a vague future success. (*Novosti from Sovfoto*)

olution had cleared the way for decisive action. Dependent on and controlled by their government as never before, the Russian people could offer little resistance.

Stalin decided to end the NEP and decreed a series of Five-Year Plans, the first and most experimental one commencing in 1928. The industrialization drive was heralded as a vast economic and social revolution, undertaken by the state on a rational plan. The emphasis lay on heavy industry, the construction of railroads, power plants, steel mills, and military hardware like tanks and warplanes. Production of consumer goods was cut down to the minimum. All small-scale private trading, revived under the NEP, came to an end; the state shops and cooperatives were bare, the service in them poor. Russians who had just come within sight of their pre-1914 standard of living now found their expectations dashed for decades to come.

Thus a new grim age began with drastic material hardships and profound mental anguish. Few Soviet citizens understood the necessities for the Five-Year Plan, but in the early years, young people particularly were fired to heroic exertions. They were proud to sacrifice themselves for the building of a superior society. When the Great Depression in the capitalist countries put millions out of work, no Soviet citizen suffered from unemployment; gloom pervaded the West, but confidence and hope, artificially fostered by the party, buoyed up Soviet Russia. Because of flaws caused by lack of experience, the first Five-Year Plan had to be scrapped before running its course. Subsequent Five-Year Plans, however, gradually improved the quality of planning as well as of production. At no time, though, did the planning produce Western-style industrial efficiency.

Meanwhile, a related and far more brutal revolution overtook Soviet agriculture, for the peasants had to be forcibly integrated into the planned economy through collectivization. Agriculture—the peasants, their animals, their fields—had to submit to the same rational control as industry. Collectivization meant the pooling of farmlands, animals, and equipment for the sake of more efficient large-scale production. The Bolshevik solution for the backwardness of Russian agriculture had long been that the peasants should become like workers. But knowing the peasants' distaste for the factory, their attachment to their own land, and their stubbornness, the party had hesitated to carry out its ambition. In 1929, however, Stalin realized that for the sake of industrialization he had no choice. If the Five-Year Plan were to succeed, the government had to receive planned crops of planned size and quality at planned times. With collectivization, the ascendancy of the party over the people of Russia became almost complete.

For the peasants, the price was horrible. Stalin declared war on the Russian countryside. The *kulaks* (the most enterprising and well-to-do peasants) were sent to forced labor camps or killed outright. Their poorer and less efficient neighbors were herded onto collective farms at the point of a bayonet. The peasants struck back, sometimes in pitched battles. The horror of forced collectivization broke the spirit even of hardened officials. "I am an old Bolshevik," sobbed a secret police colonel to a fellow passenger on a train; "I worked in the underground against the Tsar and then I fought in the civil war. Did I do all that in order that I should now surround villages with machine-guns and order my men to fire indiscriminately into crowds of peasants? Oh, no, no!"[7]

Defeated but unwilling to surrender their livestock, the peasants slaughtered their animals, gorging themselves in drunken orgies against the days of inevitable famine. The country's cattle herds declined to one-half, inflicting irreparable secondary losses as well. The number of horses, crucial for rural transport and farm work, fell by one-third. Crops were not planted or not harvested, the Five-Year Plan was disrupted, and during 1931–1933 untold millions starved to death.

The suffering was most cruel in the Ukraine, where famine killed approximately 7 million helpless people, many after extreme abuse and persecution.[8] For the sake of buying industrial equipment abroad so that industrialization could proceed on target, the Soviet Union had to export food, as much of it as possible and for prices disastrously lowered by the Great Depression. Let the peasants in the Ukrainian breadbasket perish so that the country could grow strong! Moreover, Stalin relished the opportunity to punish the Ukrainians for their disloyalty during the civil war and their resistance to collectivization. Typically, the local officials and activists who stripped the peasants of their possessions and searched for hidden grain viewed themselves as idealists building a new society; they infused their own ruthlessness into the official orders. Their dedication to the triumph of communism overcame all doubts caused by the sight of starving people and the sounds of wailing women and children.

By 1935, practically all farming in Russia was collectivized. In theory, the collective farms were run democratically, under an elected chairman; in practice, the peasants followed, as best they could, the directives handed down from the nearest party office. People grumbled about the rise of a new serfdom; agricultural development had been stifled. Nevertheless, Stalin had reason to rejoice as he counted the results of collectivization: the kulaks had been wiped out as a class, and the peasants, ever rebellious under the tsars, had been cowed into permanent submission.

Total Control

To quash resistance and mold a new type of suitably motivated and disciplined citizen, Stalin unleashed a third revolution, the revolution of totalitarianism. It aimed at a total reconstruction of state and society down to the innermost recesses of human consciousness. It called for "a new man" suited to the needs of Soviet industrialism. Society was reshaped for the utmost productivity. In the process, the hallowed revolutionary ideal of equality was abandoned.

Soviet citizens had to work as hard as they could, with the rewards going to those who made special contributions toward plan fulfillment, to engineers, scientists, managers, and certain heroes of labor, like the famous miner Stakhanov, who set artificially inflated records of output. Workers were paid piece wages; the trade unions henceforth became tools of the state, enforcing work discipline. A new elite of party-trained industrial managers rose. In addition, family discipline and sexual mores, which had become lax after the Revolution, were tightened by decree into a new work-oriented ethic.

In 1935, Stalin, summing up these changes, officially declared that socialism had been achieved in the Soviet Union. Extending the number of union republics to eleven, the Soviet Constitution of 1936 set forth major institutions and principles guiding the new society, often in terms reminiscent of Western constitutions. But the wording left no doubt about what was expected of Soviet citizens. They must "abide by the Constitution, observe the laws, maintain labor discipline, honestly perform public duties, respect the rules of socialist intercourse, and safeguard and strengthen public property" (theft of state

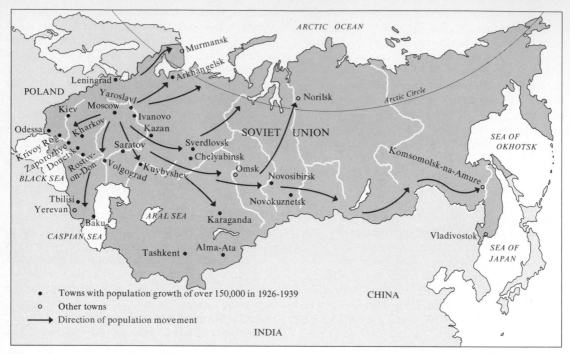

Map 31.2 Soviet Population Growth and Movement, 1926–1939

property was a widespread practice). All offenders were called "enemies of the people" and threatened with dire punishment. The list of duties ended with the words "treason is the most heinous of crimes. The defense of the Fatherland is the most sacred duty of every citizen"—ominous words indeed.

The revolution of totalitarianism extended even further. All media of communications— literature, the arts, music, the stage—were forced into subservience to the Five-Year Plan and Soviet ideology. In literature, as in all art, an official style was promulgated called *socialist realism*. It aimed at describing the world as the party hoped to shape it.

Novels in the socialist realist manner told how the romances of tractor drivers and milkmaids, or of lathe operators and office secretaries, led to new victories of production under the Five-Year Plan. Composers found their music examined for remnants of bourgeois spirit; they were to write simple tunes suitable for heroic times. Everywhere, huge, high-color posters showed men and women hard at work with radiant faces calling others to join them; often Stalin, the wise father and leader, was shown taking the salute among them. In this manner artistic creativity was locked into a dull, utilitarian straitjacket of official cheerfulness; creativity was allowed only to boost industrial productivity. Behind the scenes, all artists were disciplined to conform to the will of the party or be crushed.

Education, from nursery school to university, was likewise harnessed to train dutiful and loyal citizens. Said one text on Soviet pedagogy:

We must cultivate in our children the realization that the Union of Soviet Socialist Republics is a land where a socialist society is being constructed for the first time in history. We must develop in them a feeling of pride in the most revolutionary class, the working class, and in its vanguard, the Communist Party. This party, the party of Lenin and Stalin, was able to organize the toiling masses for the construction of a new communist society. Through the victories of the Stalin five-year plans, our land was transformed into a mighty industrial country, the most advanced and most cultured. We must make every school child aware of the grandeur of our struggle and our victories; we must show him the cost of these great successes in labor and blood; we must tell him how the great people of our epoch—Lenin, Stalin, and their companions in arms—organized the workers in the struggle for a new and happy life.[9]

Endeavoring to rally all Soviet people for that heroic struggle, Stalin gave communist political education a personal twist. He mobilized popular habits of hero worship, creating an image of himself as "The Greatest Genius of All Times and Peoples." Personal allegiance to a great man still counted as a political force among common folk; under Stalin, who in private remained rather modest, it became a tool of social engineering, part of his revolution of modernization. Projecting a superior leader as a symbol of unity and common purpose helped to overcome deep-seated doubts and divisions among the people. Never before had the glorification of a political figure (denounced by Stalin's successors as "the cult of personality") been carried to such extremes.

Stalin's Terror

Communist indoctrination, however, remained ineffectual. Peasant tradition rebelled against the large-scale, rigidly enforced cooperation of modern industrialism. Against that ingrained resistance, Stalin unleashed raw terror to break stubborn wills and compel conformity. Terror had been used as a tool of government ever since the Revolution (and the tsars had also used it, moderately and intermittently). After the start of the first Five-Year Plan, show trials were staged that denounced as saboteurs the engineers who found Stalin's tempo counterproductive. The terror used to herd the peasants onto collective farms was of a larger scale. Stalin also used terror to crush opposition and to instill an abject fear not only in the ranks of the party but also in Russian society at large. Through terror, society had to be purged of all resistance to Stalin's policies.

Purges had long been used to rid the party of

weaklings. After 1934, however, the purges became an instrument of Stalin's drive for unchallenged personal power. A party congress in that year had expressed doubts about Stalin's brutality in dealing with the peasants; it advanced a potential rival, Sergei Kirov. Soon thereafter, Kirov was murdered at Stalin's request. In 1936, Stalin's vindictive terror broke into the open. The first batch of victims, including many founders of the Communist party, was accused of conspiring with the exiled Trotsky to set up a "terrorist center" and of scheming to terrorize the party; they were blamed for the murder of Kirov. The world watched the great show trials with amazement and horror as Stalin intimidated his people. After being sentenced to death, the first group was immediately executed. In 1937, the next group, including prominent communists of Lenin's day, was charged with cooperating with foreign intelligence agencies and wrecking "socialist reconstruction," the term for Stalin's revolution; they too were executed. Shortly afterward, a secret purge wiped out the military high command, leaving the Soviet army without leadership for years.

In 1938, the last and biggest show trial advanced the most monstrous accusation of all: sabotage, espionage, and attempting to dismember the Soviet Union and kill all its leaders (including Lenin in 1918). In the public hearings some defendants refuted the public prosecutor, but in the end all confessed before being executed. Western observers were aghast at the cynical charges and the tortures used to obtain the confessions.

The great trials, however, involved only a small minority of Stalin's victims; many more perished in silence. The terror hit first of all members of the party, especially the Old Bolsheviks, who had joined before the Revolution; they were the most independent-minded members and therefore the most dangerous to Stalin. But Stalin also diminished the cultural elite that had survived the Lenin revolution. Thousands of engineers, scientists, industrial managers, scholars, and artists disappeared; they were shot or sent to forced-labor camps where most of them perished. No one was safe. To frighten the common people in all walks of life, men, women, and even children were dragged into the net of Stalin's secret police—a soul-killing reminder to the survivors: submit or else.

The Human Price

The toll of the purges is reckoned in the tens of millions; it included Trotsky, who in 1940 was murdered in Mexico. The bloodletting was ghastly, as Stalin's purge officials themselves followed each other into death and ignominy.

The human price that Soviet Russia paid for Stalin's effort to wipe out his country's inferiority has been documented by the great Russian writer Aleksandr Solzhenitsyn in his work *The Gulag Archipelago*. Yet by Solzhenitsyn's own testimony, the responsibility for the atrocities was not Stalin's alone; the "wolfishness" of the terror flowed from Russian life itself. Speaking of the torturers, the "Blue Caps" who interrogated and often killed innocent victims of the terror, Solzhenitsyn asks: "Where did this wolf-tribe appear from among our people? Does it really stem from our own roots? Our own blood?" Devastatingly he answers: "It is our own."[10]

Stalin, who had passed through the hands of the tsarist police and had participated in the carnage of the civil war, was untroubled by the waste of life. He believed that without the total obedience of the Russian people, the Soviet economy could not be effectively and quickly mobilized and that terror was necessary to compel compliance. By showing party officials and the Russian masses how vulnerable they were, how dependent on his will, Stalin intended to frighten them into servility. No doubt, the terror was also an expression of Stalin's sickly suspicious and vengeful nature. He saw enemies everywhere, took pleasure in selecting victims, and reveled in the show of his omnipotence. But he was fully aware that his power was never as complete as it was advertised.

In foreign even more than in internal affairs, Stalin's policy was marked by fear; the danger of war was always uppermost in his mind. It was to Soviet advantage to make a show of strength, but underneath this façade Stalin pursued a conservative policy, husbanding Russia's resources for internal reconstruction and hoping that the capitalist states would fall out among themselves, allowing him to play the happy bystander, entering the fray only for the kill. Stalin did not follow up Lenin's teaching about world revolution. He realized that the key to the future of Soviet communism lay in the power of the Soviet Union and

that its power was never sufficient amid the dangers it confronted in the world. His personal sense of insecurity reflected the persistent insecurity of his country. By the end of the 1930s, after the Stalin revolution, yet another era of profound and cruel perils began for his country—World War II and the battle with Nazi Germany. If Hitler had won that war, the human devastation in Russian lands would have been infinitely worse than the suffering caused by Stalin's brutish efforts to prevent such a catastrophe.

Leninism and Stalinism in Perspective

The fateful events in Russia from the end of World War I to the late 1930s profoundly excited opinion everywhere. Some Marxists saw their ideals realized; others felt that Stalin had betrayed the cause of socialism. Some hopeful Western liberals agreed with the American visitor to the Soviet Union who said that he "had seen the future and it worked."[11] But most Westerners were appalled by Soviet theory and practice, although for profit or political expediency some came to terms with the regime. In the face of the Great Depression and Japanese expansion, for instance, the United States officially recognized the Soviet Union in 1933. The purges disenchanted many early communist sympathizers, including George Orwell, who in revulsion wrote *Animal Farm* and *1984*. In the countries of Asia, on the other hand, the progress of the Five-Year Plans was watched with envy and admiration: if Russia could raise itself by its bootstraps, why could others not follow its example?

In retrospect, Nikita Khrushchev's attack (see page 808) on the cult of personality and the works of Solzhenitsyn have driven home Stalin's inhumanity. And under Mikhail Gorbachev, the denunciation of Stalin has intensified. Yet placing Stalin in the context of the extreme crisis prevailing in Russia after World War I makes clearer the continuity from Lenin to Stalin and their place in the course of Russian history. Both men, but Stalin especially, fitted into the tradition of cruel

Chronology 31.1 The Rise of the Soviet Union

March 1917	The tsarist regime is overthrown
November 1917	The Bolsheviks, led by Lenin, seize power
1918–1920	Civil war and foreign intervention
January 1918	The Bolsheviks disband the Constituent Assembly
March 1918	Treaty of Brest-Litovsk; the Communist International is formed
July 1918	Nicholas II and his family are executed
April 1920	Poland invades Russia, annexes Russian territory
November 1920	The remnants of the White Army are evacuated from the Crimean peninsula
1921–1928	The New Economic Policy
1922	Stalin becomes general secretary of the Communist party
January 1924	Lenin dies
1924	The constitution of the Union of Soviet Socialist Republics takes effect
1928	The first Five-Year Plan starts rapid industrialization
1929	Stalin in sole command; collectivization of agriculture starts
1936	The Stalin constitution: socialism achieved
1936–1938	Stalin's terror purges
June 1941	Hitler invades the Soviet Union

and overbearing state-building tsars like Peter the Great.

Stalin left no doubt about the ultimate justification for such policy. In 1931, bluntly disregarding Marxist-Leninist jargon and forgetting about Russian expansion into Asia, he said:

> *Those who fall behind get beaten. But we do not want to be beaten. No, we refuse to be beaten. One feature of the history of old Russia was the continual beatings she suffered for falling behind, for her backwardness. All beat her—for her backwardness, for military backwardness, cultural backwardness, political backwardness, for industrial backwardness, for agricultural backwardness. She was beaten because to do so was profitable and could be done with impunity. . . . You are backward, you are weak—therefore you are wrong, hence you can be beaten and enslaved. You are mighty, therefore you are right, hence we must be wary of you. Such is the law of the exploiters. . . . That is why we must no longer lag behind.[12]*

He set forth the stark reckoning of Russian history: the cost of foreign enslavement against the costs of a terror-driven mobilization; the dream of a Russia liberated from inferiority against the human price of totalitarianism.

Westernizing an unprepared Russia was bound to be a wasteful and cruel experiment. It was made more cruel by the tradition of violence in Russian statecraft—no wonder that Stalin was an admirer of Ivan the Terrible. The ruthlessness of the revolutionary movement, the battles of World War I, the excitements of revolution, and the passions of civil war added their share of inhumanity. In his own part of that experiment, Stalin worked with unruly and untrained people to make his country conform to essential aspects of the modern West. Marxism-Leninism adapted Western models to the conditions of the Russian Empire. The Stalin constitution imitated Western constitutional language. Soviet industrialization took its lead from Western urban-industrial society. And above all, Soviet international political ambition was patterned after the fullness of Western power around the world. In these essentials, Stalin modernized his country and laid the foundations for the rise of Soviet Russia into a superpower, more secure and respected in the world than any previous Russian regime. Monstrous indeed are the stakes of twentieth-century power politics, but it is in this perspective that Stalin must be understood.

Notes

1. V. A. Maklakov, quoted in *The Russian Provisional Government 1917,* III, documents selected and edited by Robert Paul Browder and Aleksandr F. Kerensky (Stanford, Calif.: Stanford University Press, 1961), p. 1276.

2. V. I. Lenin, "The Impending Catastrophe and How to Combat It," *Lenin on Politics and Revolution,* selected writings, ed. by James E. Connor (New York: Pegasus, 1968), p. 183.

3. V. I. Lenin, "On Revolutionary Violence and Terror," *The Lenin Anthology,* ed. by R. C. Tucker (New York: Norton, 1975), p. 432.

4. "All-Russian Communist Party (Bolsheviks), 1919," in *Soviet Communism: Programs and Rules. Official Texts of 1919, 1952, (1956), 1961,* ed. by Jan F. Triska (San Francisco: Chandler, 1962), p. 23.

5. V. I. Lenin, "The Immediate Tasks of the Soviet Government," *The Lenin Anthology,* pp. 448ff.

6. "Constitution of the Union of Soviet Socialist Republics, Part I: Declaration," *A Documentary History of Communism,* ed. by Robert V. Daniels (New York: Random House, 1960), 1:249.

7. Quoted in Isaac Deutscher, *Stalin: A Political Biography* (New York: Oxford University Press, 1966), p. 325.

8. Robert Conquest, *The Harvest of Sorrow: Soviet Collectivization and the Terror-Famine* (New York: Oxford University Press, 1986), p. 304.

9. "I Want to Be Like Stalin," from the *Russian Text on Pedagogy* by B. P. Yesipov and N. K. Goncharov, trans. by George S. Counts and Nucia P. Lodge, with an introduction by George S. Counts (New York: John Day, 1947), pp. 36–37.

10. Aleksandr I. Solzhenitsyn, *The Gulag Archipelago.* Vol. I (New York: Harper & Row, 1974), p. 160.

11. Lincoln Steffens, "I have been over into the future, and it works." In *Autobiography* (New York: Harcourt, Brace, 1931), p. 799.

12. J. V. Stalin, "Speech to Business Executives" (1931), in *A Documentary History of Communism,* 2:22.

Suggested Reading

Antonov-Ovseenko, Anton, *The Time of Stalin: Portrait of a Tyranny* (1981). A recent anti-Stalinist treatment by a Soviet author.

Carr, E. H., *The Russian Revolution from Lenin to Stalin* (1970). A brief summary based on the author's multivolume study of the years 1917–1929.

Cohen, Stephen, *Bukharin and the Bolshevik Revolution* (1980). Argues that there existed more moderate alternatives to Stalin's policies.

Conquest, Robert, *The Harvest of Sorrow: Soviet Collectivization and the Terror-Famine* (1986). The human consequences of collectivization.

Deutscher, Isaac, *Trotsky: 1879–1940,* 3 vols., *The Prophet Armed* (1954), *The Prophet Unarmed* (1959), *The Prophet Outcast* (1963). The classic work on Trotsky.

Ginzburg, Eugenia, *Journey into the Whirlwind* (1967). A woman's experiences under the terror.

Koestler, Arthur, *Darkness at Noon* (1941). A revealing novel about the fate of an Old Bolshevik in the terror purge.

Lewin, Moshe, *The Making of the Soviet System: Essays in the Social History of Interwar Russia* (1985). A thoughtful analysis by a noted scholar.

Mandelstam, Nadezhda, *Hope Against Hope: A Memoir* (1976). A searing account of life during the purges by the widow of one of the victims.

Nove, Alec, *Stalinism and After* (1975). An excellent short work from an economist's perspective.

Pasternak, Boris, *Doctor Zhivago* (1958). The tragedies of Russian life from Nicholas II to Stalin as seen through the eyes of a superbly sensitive and observant poet.

Scott, John, *Behind the Urals: An American Worker in Russia's City of Steel* (1942, reprint 1973). A firsthand account of life under the first Five-Year Plan.

Sholokhov, Mikhail, *And Quiet Flows the Don; The Don Flows Home to the Sea*, 2 vols. (1934, 1940). A Nobel Prize-winning novel about the brutalizing effects of war, revolution, and civil war.

Solzhenitsyn, Aleksandr I., *One Day in the Life of Ivan Denisovich* (1963). The first account of life in one of Stalin's forced-labor camps to reach the public.

———, *The First Circle* (1968). The life of privileged victims of the terror.

———, *The Gulag Archipelago,* 3 vols. (1973–1975). The classic account of Stalin's terror, especially vol. I.

Trotsky, Leon, *The Russian Revolution: The Overthrow of Tsarism and the Triumph of the Soviets* (1932). A classic account of the Bolshevik Revolution by its chief organizer. Read especially the chapters entitled "Five Days" and "The Seizure of the Winter Palace."

Tucker, Robert C., *Stalin as a Revolutionary* (1973). A psychological study of the young Stalin.

———, *The Lenin Anthology* (1975). For those who want a taste of Lenin's writings.

———, ed., *Stalinism: Essays in Historical Interpretation* (1977). Essays on Stalin by prominent scholars.

Ulam, Adam B., *The Bolsheviks: The Intellectual and Political History of the Triumph of Communism in Russia* (1965). A full account built around Lenin.

———, *Stalin: The Man and His Era* (1973). The best biography to date.

Von Laue, Theodore H., *Why Lenin? Why Stalin?* (1970). A readable survey emphasizing the global contexts.

Review Questions

1. Why did the tsarist regime collapse in March 1917?

2. Why did the Provisional Government and liberal democracy fail in 1917?

3. Why, by contrast, were the Bolsheviks successful in seizing and holding power from 1917 to 1921?

4. By what institutions and methods did Lenin build the Soviet state? What innovations did he introduce after the collapse of the tsarist regime and the failure of the Provisional Government?

5. How did the peasants fare through war, revolution, and the rise of the Soviet state? Why did Stalin collectivize agriculture?

6. How did the Soviet leaders view the position of Russia in the world? What were their aims and ambitions? How did their goals compare with those of other states?

7. What were Stalin's motives and justifications for the terror purge?

8. How do you explain the fact that the communist regime was far more ruthless in its methods of government than the tsarist regime? Which regime accomplished more for the power of Russia?

9. Compare and contrast the treatment of religion in American life with its treatment under Soviet rule. How do you account for the differences? Likewise, compare and contrast the organization of agriculture and industry in the United States with the organization of their counterparts under Soviet rule. Again, how do you account for the differences?

10. How would you define the differences between the conditions shaping American history and the conditions shaping Russian history in the years covered by this chapter? Can you see any of the conditions that shaped the Soviet regime at work in American society and government? Or, to put the question differently, to what extent do you think American ways of thinking are applicable to the conditions prevailing in Russia?

32

The Rise of Fascism: The Attack on Democracy

Liberals viewed the Great War as a conflict between freedom and autocracy and expected an Allied victory to accelerate the spread of democracy throughout Europe. In the immediate aftermath of the war it seemed that liberalism would continue to advance as it had in the nineteenth century. The collapse of the autocratic German and Austrian empires had led to the formation of parliamentary governments throughout eastern and central Europe. Yet within two decades, in an extraordinary turn of events, democracy seemed in its death throes. In Spain, Portugal, Italy, and Germany, and in all the newly created states of central and eastern Europe except Czechoslovakia, democracy collapsed and various forms of authoritarian governments emerged. The defeat of democracy and the surge of authoritarianism was best exemplified by the triumph of totalitarian fascist movements in Italy and Germany.

The emergence of fascist movements in more than twenty European lands after World War I was a sign that liberal society was in a state of disorientation and dissolution. Fascism was a response to a postwar society afflicted by spiritual disintegration, economic dislocation, political instability, and thwarted nationalist hopes. It was an expression of fear that the Bolshevik Revolution would spread westward. It was also an expression of hostility to democratic values and a reaction to the failure of liberal institutions to solve crushing problems of modern industrial society. To fascists and their sympathizers, democracy seemed an ineffective, spiritless, and enfeebled old regime ready to topple.

In their struggle to bring down the liberal state, fascist leaders aroused primitive impulses, resurrected ancient folkways and tribal loyalties, and made use of myths and rituals to mobilize and manipulate the masses. Organizing propaganda campaigns with the thoroughness of a military

Adolf Hitler (right) Before His Labor Army at Nuremberg, Germany, September 1938. (UPI/Bettmann Newsphotos)

operation, fascists stirred and dominated the masses and confused and undermined their democratic opposition, breaking its will to resist. Fascists were most successful in countries with weak democratic traditions. When parliamentary government faltered, it had few staunch defenders and many who yearned to dance at its death.

The proliferation of fascist movements demonstrated that the habits of democracy are not quickly learned or easily retained. Particularly during times of crisis, people lose patience with parliamentary discussion and constitutional procedures, sink into nonrational modes of thought and behavior, and are easily manipulated by unscrupulous politicians. For the sake of economic or emotional security and national grandeur, they will often willingly sacrifice political freedom. Fascism starkly manifested the immense power of the irrational; it humbled liberals, making them permanently aware of the limitations of reason and the fragility of freedom.

The fascist goal of maximum centralization of power was furthered by developments during World War I—the expansion of bureaucracy, the concentration of industry into giant monopolies, and the close cooperation between industry and the state. The instruments of modern technology—radio, motion pictures, public address systems, telephone, teletype—made it possible for the state to indoctrinate, manipulate, and dominate its subjects.

Elements of Fascism

Fascist movements were marked by an extreme nationalism and a determination to eradicate liberalism and Marxism—to undo the legacy of the French Revolution of 1789 and the Bolshevik Revolution of 1917. Fascists believed that theirs was a spiritual revolution, that they were initiating a new era in history, that they were building a new civilization on the ruins of liberal democracy. "We stand for a new principle in the world," said Mussolini. "We stand for the sheer, categorical, definitive antithesis to the world of democracy . . . to the world which still abides by the fundamental principles laid down in 1789."[1] The chief principle of Nazism, said Hitler, "is to abolish the liberal concept of the individual and the Marxist concept of humanity, and to substitute for them the *Volk* community, rooted in the soil and united by the bond of its common blood."[2]

Fascists accused liberal society of despiritualizing human beings, of transforming them into materialistic creatures who knew no higher ideal than profit—whose souls were deadened to noble causes, heroic deeds, and self-sacrifice. Idealistic youth and intellectuals rejoiced in fascism's activism; they saw it as a revolt against the mediocrity of mass society, as a reaffirmation of the highest human spiritual qualities, as an answer to despair.

Fascists regarded Marxism as another enemy, for class conflict divided the nation. To fascists, the Marxist call for workers of the world to unite meant the death of the national community. Fascism, in contrast, would reintegrate the proletariat into the nation and end class hostilities that divide and weaken the state and its people. By making people of all classes feel that they were a needed part of the nation, fascism offered a solution to the problem of insecurity and isolation in modern industrial society.

In contrast to liberalism and Marxism, fascism attacked the rational tradition of the Enlightenment and exalted will, blood, feeling, and instinct. Intellectual discussion and critical analysis, said fascists, cause national divisiveness; reason promotes doubt, enfeebles the will, and hinders instinctive, aggressive action. Glorifying action for its own sake, fascists aroused and manipulated brutal and primitive impulses and carried into politics the combative spirit of the trenches. They formed private armies that attracted veterans—many of them rootless, brutal, and maladjusted men who sought to preserve the loyalty, camaraderie, and violence of the front.

Fascism exalted the leader, who intuitively grasped what was best for the nation, and called for rule by an elite of dedicated party members. The leader and the party would relieve the individual of the need to make decisions. Holding that the liberal stress on individual freedom promoted competition and conflict that shattered national unity, fascists pressed for monolithic unity—one leader, one party, and one national will.

Fascism drew its mass support from the lower

middle class—small merchants, artisans, white-collar workers, civil servants, peasants of moderate means—who were frightened by both big capitalism and socialism. They hoped that fascism would protect them from the competition of big business and prevent the hated working class from establishing a Marxist state that would threaten their property. The lower middle class saw in fascism a noncommunist way of overcoming economic crises and restoring traditional respect for family, native soil, and nation. Many of these people also saw in fascism a way of attacking the existing social order, which denied them opportunities for economic advancement and social prestige. Having no patience for parliamentary procedures or sympathy for democratic principles, they were drawn to demagogues who exuded confidence and promised direct action.

Although a radicalized middle class gave fascist movements their mass support, the fascists could not have captured the state without the aid of existing ruling elites—landed aristocrats, industrialists, and army leaders. In Russia, the Bolsheviks had to fight their way into power; in Italy and Germany, the old ruling order virtually handed power to the fascists. In both countries, fascist leaders succeeded in reassuring the conservative elite that they would not institute widespread social reforms or interfere with private property and would protect the nation from communism. The old elite abhorred the violent activism and demagoguery of fascism and had contempt for fascist leaders, who were often brutal men without breeding or culture. Yet to protect their interests, the old ruling class entered into an alliance with the fascists.

The Rise of Fascism in Italy

Postwar Unrest

Although Italy had been on the winning side in World War I, it had the appearance of a defeated nation. Food shortages, rising prices, massive unemployment, violent strikes, workers occupying factories, and peasants squatting on the unculti-vated periphery of large estates created a climate of crisis. These dismal conditions contrasted sharply with the vision of a postwar world painted by politicians during the war. Italy required effective leadership and a reform program, but the liberal government was paralyzed by party disputes; with several competing parties, the liberals could not organize a solid majority that could cope with the domestic crisis.

The middle class was severely stressed. To meet its accelerating expenses, the government had increased taxes, but the burden fell unevenly on small landowners, small businessowners, civil-service workers, and professionals. Moreover, the value of war bonds, purchased primarily by the middle class, had declined considerably because of inflation. Instead of finding a return to the good days and their former status once the war ended, these solid citizens found their economic position continuing to deteriorate.

Large landowners and industrialists feared that their nation was on the verge of a Bolshevik-style revolution. They took seriously the proclamations of the socialists: "The proletariat must be incited to the violent seizure of political and economic power and this must be handed over entirely and exclusively to the Workers' and Peasants' Councils."[3] In truth, Italian socialists had no master plan to seize power. Peasant squatters and urban strikers were responding to the distress in their own regions and did not significantly coordinate their efforts with those in other localities. Moreover, when the workers realized that they could not keep the factories operating, their revolutionary zeal waned and they started to abandon the plants. The workers' and peasants' poorly led and futile struggles did not portend a Red Revolution. Nevertheless the industrialists and landlords, with the Bolshevik Revolution still vivid in their minds, were taking no chances.

Adding to the unrest was national outrage at the terms of the peace settlement. Italians felt that despite their sacrifices—500,000 dead and 1 million wounded—they had been robbed of the fruits of victory. Although Italy had received the Brenner Pass and Trieste, it had been denied the Dalmatian coast, the Adriatic port of Fiume, and territory in Africa and the Middle East. Nationalists blamed the liberal government for what they called a "mutilated victory." In 1919, a force of

Mussolini at Rome, Celebrating the Tenth Anniversary of the Fascist Gathering in Milan for the March on Rome. Initially, Mussolini was able to bluff his way to power because an indecisive liberal regime did not counter force with force. Although Mussolini established a one-party state and manipulated mass organizations and the mass media, he was less successful than Hitler or Stalin in creating a totalitarian regime. (*AP/Wide World Photos*)

war veterans led by the poet and adventurer Gabriele D'Annunzio (1863–1938) seized Fiume, to the delirious joy of Italian nationalists and the embarrassment of the government. D'Annunzio's occupation of the port lasted more than a year, adding fuel to the flames of Italian nationalism and demonstrating the weakness of the liberal regime in imposing its authority over rightist opponents.

Mussolini's Seizure of Power

Benito Mussolini (1883–1945) was born in a small village in east central Italy. Proud, quarrel-some, violent, and resentful of the humiliation he suffered for being poor, the young Mussolini was a troublemaker and was often brought before school authorities. But he was also intelligent, ranking first on final examinations in four subjects. After graduation, Mussolini taught in an elementary school, but this did not suit his passionate temperament. From 1902 to 1904, he lived in Switzerland, where he broadened his reading, lectured, and wrote. He also came under the influence of anarchists and socialist revolutionaries. Returning to Italy, he was labeled a dangerous revolutionary by the police. As a reward for his zeal and political agitation, which led to five months in prison for inciting riots, Mussolini in

1912 was made editor of *Avanti*, the principal socialist newspaper. During the early days of World War I he was expelled from the Socialist party for advocating Italian intervention in the war. After Italy entered the war, Mussolini served at the front and suffered a serious wound during firing practice, for which he was hospitalized.

In 1919, Mussolini organized the Fascist party to realize his immense will to power; this quest for power, more than a set of coherent doctrines, characterized the young movement. A supreme opportunist rather than an ideologist, Mussolini exploited the unrest in postwar Italy in order to capture control of the state. He attracted converts from the discontented, disillusioned, and uprooted. Many Italians, particularly the educated bourgeoisie who had been inspired by the unification movement of the nineteenth century, viewed Mussolini as the leader who would gain Fiume, Dalmatia, and colonies and win Italy's rightful place of honor in international affairs. Hardened battle veterans joined the Fascist movement to escape the boredom and idleness of civilian life. They welcomed an opportunity to wear the uniforms of the Fascist militia (Black Shirts), parade in the streets, and do battle with socialist and labor-union opponents. Squads of Fascist Black Shirts (*squadristi*) raided socialist and trade-union offices, destroying property and beating the occupants. It soon appeared that Italy was drifting toward civil war as socialist Red Shirts responded in kind.

Industrialists and landowners, hoping that Mussolini would rescue Italy from Bolshevism, contributed large sums to the Fascist party. The lower middle class, fearful that the growing power of labor unions and the Socialist party threatened their property and social prestige, viewed Mussolini as a protector. Middle-class university students, searching for adventure and an ideal, and army officers, dreaming of an Italian empire and hateful of parliamentary government, also were receptive to Mussolini's party. Intellectuals disenchanted with liberal politics and parliamentary democracy were intrigued by Mussolini's philosophy of action. Mussolini's nationalism, activism, and anticommunism gradually seduced elements of the power structure—capitalists, aristocrats, army officers, the royal family, the church. Regarding liberalism as bankrupt and parliamentary government as futile, many of these people yearned for a military dictatorship.

In 1922, Mussolini made his bid for power. Speaking at a giant rally of his followers in late October, he declared: "Either they will give us the government or we shall take it by descending on Rome. It is now a matter of days, perhaps hours." A few days later thousands of Fascists began the March on Rome. Some members of parliament demanded that the army defend the government against a Fascist coup. It would have been a relatively simple matter to crush the 20,000 Fascist marchers armed with little more than pistols and rifles, but King Victor Emmanuel III (1869–1947) refused to act. The king's advisers, some of them sympathetic to Mussolini, exaggerated the strength of the Fascists. Believing that he was rescuing Italy from terrible violence, the king appointed Mussolini prime minister.

Mussolini had bluffed his way into power. Fascism had triumphed not because of its own strength—the Fascists had only 35 of 535 seats in parliament—but because the liberal regime, irresolute and indecisive, did not counter force with force. In the past, the liberal state had not challenged Fascist acts of terror; now it feebly surrendered to Fascist blustering and threats. No doubt liberals hoped that once in power, the Fascists would forsake terror, pursue moderate aims, and act within the constitution. But the liberals were wrong; they had completely misjudged the antidemocratic character of Fascism.

The Fascist State in Italy

Consolidation of Power

In October 1922, when the liberal regime in Italy capitulated, the Fascists by no means held total power. Anti-Fascists still sat in parliament and only four of fourteen ministers in Mussolini's cabinet were Fascists. Cautious and shrewd, Mussolini resisted the extremists in his party who demanded a second revolution—the immediate and preferably violent destruction of the old order. In this early stage of Fascist rule, when his position was still tenuous, Mussolini sought to maintain an image of respectability and moderation. He tried to convince the power structure that he intended to operate within the constitution, that he did not seek dictatorial power. At the same time he gradually secured his position and turned Italy into a one-party state. In 1923, an electoral law, approved by both chambers of the parliament, decreed that the party with the most votes in a national election (provided that the figure was not less than 25 percent of the total votes cast) would be granted two-thirds of the seats in the Chamber of Deputies. In the elections of 1924, which were marred by Fascist terrorism, Mussolini's supporters received 65 percent of the vote. Even without the implementation of the new electoral law, the opponents of Fascism had been enfeebled; Mussolini had consolidated his power.

When socialist leader Giacomo Matteotti protested Fascist terror tactics, Fascist thugs killed him (in 1924). Although Mussolini had not ordered Matteotti's murder, his vicious attacks against his socialist opponent inspired the assassins. Repelled by the murder, some sincere democrats withdrew from the Chamber of Deputies in protest and some influential Italians called for Mussolini's dismissal. But the majority of liberals, including the leadership, continued to support Mussolini. And the king, the papacy, the army, large landowners, and industrialists, still regarding Mussolini as the best defense against internal disorder and socialism, did not lend their support to an anti-Fascist movement.

Pressed by the radicals within the Fascist party, Mussolini moved to establish a dictatorship. In 1925–26, he eliminated non-Fascists from his cabinet, dissolved opposition parties, smashed the independent trade unions, suppressed opposition newspapers, replaced local mayors with Fascist officials, and organized a secret police to round up troublemakers. Many anti-Fascists fled the country or were deported.

Mussolini then turned on the extremist Fascists, the local chieftains (*ras*) who had led squadristi in the early days of the movement. Lauding violence, daring deeds, and the dangerous life, the ras were indispensable during the party's formative stage. But Mussolini feared that the radical adventurism of the ras posed a threat to his per-

sonal rule. And their desire to replace the traditional power structure with people drawn from their own ranks could block his efforts to cooperate with the established elite—industrialists, aristocratic landowners, and army leaders. Mussolini therefore expelled some squadristi leaders from the party and gave others positions in the bureaucracy to tame them.

Mussolini was less successful than Hitler and Stalin in fashioning a totalitarian state. The industrialists, the large landowners, the church, and to some extent even the army, never fell under the complete domination of the party. Nor did the regime possess the mind of its subjects with the same thoroughness as the Nazis did in Germany. Life in Italy was less regimented and the individual less fearful than in Nazi Germany or Communist Russia. The Italian people might cheer Mussolini, but few were willing to die for him.

Control of the Masses

Like Communist Russia and Nazi Germany, Fascist Italy used mass organizations and mass media to control minds and regulate behavior. As in the Soviet Union and the Third Reich, the Fascist regime created a cult of the leader. "Mussolini goes forward with confidence, in a halo of myth, almost chosen by God, indefatigable and infallible, the instrument employed by Providence for the creation of a new civilization," wrote the philosopher Giovanni Gentile.[4] To convey the image of a virile leader, Mussolini had himself photographed barechested or in a uniform with a steel helmet. Other photographs showed him riding horses, driving fast cars, flying planes, and playing with lion cubs. Mussolini frequently addressed huge throngs of admirers from his balcony. His tenor voice, grandiloquent phrases, and posturing—jaw thrust out, hands on hips—captivated audiences; idolatry from the masses, in turn, intensified Mussolini's feelings of grandeur. Elementary school textbooks depicted Mussolini as the savior of the nation, a modern-day Julius Caesar.

Fascist propaganda inculcated habits of discipline and obedience: "Mussolini is always right." "Believe! Obey! Fight!" Propaganda also glorified war: "A minute on the battlefield is worth a lifetime of peace." The press, radio, and cinema idealized life under Fascism, implying that Fascism had eradicated crime, poverty, and social tensions. Schoolteachers and university professors were compelled to swear allegiance to the Fascist government and to propagate Fascist ideals, while students were urged to criticize instructors who harbored liberal attitudes. Millions of youths belonged to Fascist organizations in which they participated in patriotic ceremonies and social functions, sang Fascist hymns, and wore Fascist uniforms. They submerged their own identities into the group.

Economic Policies

Fascists denounced economic liberalism for promoting individual self-interest, and socialism for instigating conflicts between workers and capitalists that divided and weakened the nation. The Fascist way of resolving tensions between workers and employers was to abolish independent labor unions, prohibit strikes, and establish associations or corporations that included both the workers and employers within a given industry. In theory, representatives of labor and capital would cooperatively solve labor problems in a particular industry. In practice the representatives of labor turned out to be Fascists who protected the interests of the industrialists. Although the Fascists lauded the corporative system as a creative approach to modern economic problems, in reality it played a minor role in Italian economic life. Big business continued to make its own decisions, paying scant attention to the corporations.

Nor did the Fascist government solve Italy's long-standing economic problems. To curtail the export of capital and to reduce the nation's dependency on imports in case of war, Mussolini sought to make Italy self-sufficient. To win the "battle of grain," the Fascist regime brought marginal lands under cultivation and urged farmers to concentrate on wheat rather than other crops. Although wheat production thus increased substantially, total agricultural output declined because wheat was planted on land more suited to animal husbandry and fruit cultivation. To make Italy industrially self-sufficient, the regime limited imports of foreign goods, with the result that Italian consumers paid higher prices for Italian-manufactured goods. Mussolini posed as the protector of the little people, but under his regime the power and profits of big business grew and the standard of living of small farmers and urban workers declined. Government attempts to grapple with the depression were halfhearted. Aside from providing family allowances—an increase in income with the birth of each child—the Fascist regime did little in the way of social welfare.

The Church and the Fascist Regime

Although anticlerical since his youth, Mussolini was also expedient. He recognized that coming to terms with the church would improve his image with Catholic public opinion. The Vatican regarded Mussolini's regime as a barrier against communism and as less hostile to church interests and more amenable to church direction than a liberal government. Pope Pius XI (1922–1939) was an ultraconservative whose hatred of liberalism and secularism led him to believe that the Fascists would increase the influence of the church in the nation.

In 1929, the Lateran Accords recognized the independence of Vatican City, repealed many of the anticlerical laws passed under the liberal government, and made religious instruction compulsory in all secondary schools. The papal state, Vatican City, became a small enclave within Rome over which the Italian government had no authority. Relations between the Vatican and the Fascist government remained fairly good throughout the decade of the 1930s. One crisis arose in 1931 when Mussolini, pushed by militant anticlericals within his party, dissolved certain Catholic youth groups as rivals to Fascist youth associations, but a compromise that permitted the Catholic organizations to function within certain limits eased tensions. When Mussolini invaded Ethiopia and intervened in the Spanish Civil War, the church supported him. Although the papacy criticized Mussolini for drawing closer to Hitler and introducing anti-Jewish legislation, it never broke with the Fascist regime.

The New German Republic

In the last days of World War I, a revolution brought down the German imperial government and led to the creation of a democratic republic. In October 1918, the German admirals had ordered the German navy to engage the British in the English Channel, but the sailors, anticipating peace and resentful of their officers (who commonly resorted to cruel discipline), refused to obey. Joined by sympathetic soldiers, the mutineers raised the Red Flag of revolution. The revolt soon spread, as military men and workers demonstrated for peace and reform and in some regions seized authority. Reluctant to fire on their comrades and also fed up with the war, German troops did not move to crush the revolutionaries. On November 9, 1918, the leaders of the government announced the end of the monarchy, and Kaiser William II fled to Holland. Two days later, the new German republic, headed by Chancellor Friedrich Ebert (1871–1925), a Social Democrat, signed an armistice agreement ending the war. Many Germans blamed the new democratic republic for the defeat—a baseless accusation, for the German generals, knowing that the war was lost, had sought an armistice.

In February 1919, the recently elected National Assembly met at Weimar and proceeded to draw up a constitution for the new state. The Weimar Republic—born in revolution, which most Germans detested, and military defeat, which many attributed to the new government—faced an uncertain future.

Threats from Left and Right

The infant republic, dominated by moderate socialists, faced internal threats from both the radical left and the radical right. In January 1919, the newly established German Communist party, or Spartacists, disregarding the advice of their leaders Rosa Luxemburg and Karl Liebknecht, took to the streets of Berlin and declared the government

of Ebert deposed. To crush the revolution, Ebert turned to the Free Corps—volunteer brigades of ex-soldiers and adventurers, led by officers loyal to the emperor, who had been fighting to protect the eastern borders from encroachments by the new states of Poland, Estonia, and Latvia. The men of the Free Corps relished action and despised Bolshevism. They suppressed the revolution and murdered Luxemburg and Liebknecht on January 15. In May 1919, the Free Corps also marched into Munich to overthrow the soviet republic set up there by communists a few weeks earlier.

The Spartacist revolt and the short-lived soviet republic in Munich (and others in Baden and Brunswick) had profound effects on the German psyche. The communists had been easily subdued, but fear of a communist insurrection remained deeply embedded in the middle and upper classes, a fear that drove many of them into the ranks of the Weimar Republic's right-wing opponents.

The Spartacist revolt was an attempt by the radical left to overthrow the republic; in March 1920, the republic was threatened by the radical right. Refusing to disband as the government ordered, detachments of the right-wing Free Corps marched into Berlin and declared a new government headed by Wolfgang Kapp, a staunch nationalist. President Ebert and most members of the cabinet and National Assembly fled to Stuttgart. Insisting that it could not fire on fellow soldiers, the German army, the *Reichswehr,* made no move to defend the republic. A general strike called by the labor unions prevented Kapp from governing and the coup collapsed. However, the Kapp Putsch demonstrated that the loyalty of the army to the republic was doubtful.

Economic Crisis

In addition to uprisings by the left and right, the republic was burdened by economic crisis. During the war, Germany financed its military expenditures not by increasing taxation but through short-term loans, thereby accumulating a huge debt that now had to be paid. A trade deficit and enormous reparation payments worsened the nation's economic plight. Unable to meet the deficit in the national budget, the government simply printed more money, causing the value of the German mark to decline precipitously. In 1914, the mark stood at 4.2 to the dollar; in 1919, 8.9 to the dollar; in early 1923, 18,000 to the dollar. In August 1923, a dollar could be exchanged for 4.6 million marks, and in November for 4 billion marks! Bank savings, war bonds, and pensions, representing years of toil and thrift, became worthless. Blaming the government for this disaster, the ruined middle class became more receptive to rightist movements that aimed to bring down the republic.

With the economy in shambles, the republic defaulted on reparation payments. Premier Raymond Poincaré (1860–1934) of France took a hard line and in January 1923 ordered French troops into the Ruhr—the nerve center of German industry. Responding to the republic's call for passive resistance, factory workers, miners, and railroad workers in the Ruhr refused to work for the French. To provide strike benefits for the Ruhr workers, the government printed yet more money, making inflation even worse.

In August 1923, Gustav Stresemann became chancellor. The new government lasted only until November 1923, but during those one hundred days Stresemann skillfully placed the republic on the path to recovery. Warned by German industrialists that the economy was at the breaking point, Stresemann abandoned the policy of passive resistance in the Ruhr and declared Germany's willingness to make reparation payments. Stresemann issued a new currency backed by a mortgage on German real estate. To reduce public expenditures that contributed to inflation, the government fired some civil-service workers and lowered salaries; to get additional funds, it raised taxes; to protect the value of the new currency, it did not print another issue. Inflation receded and confidence was restored.

A new arrangement regarding reparations also contributed to the economic recovery. Recognizing that in its present economic straits Germany could not meet its obligations to the Allies or secure the investment of foreign capitalists, Britain and the United States pressured France to allow a reparation commission to make new proposals. In 1924, the parties accepted the Dawes Plan, which reduced reparations and based them on Germany's economic capacity. During the negotiations, France agreed to withdraw its troops from the Ruhr, another step toward easing tensions for the republic.

From 1924 to 1929, economic conditions improved. Foreign capitalists, particularly Americans, were attracted by high interest rates and the low cost of labor. Their investments in German businesses stimulated the economy. By 1929, iron, steel, coal, and chemical production exceeded prewar levels. The value of German exports also surpassed that of 1913. This spectacular boom was due in part to more effective methods of production and management and the concentration of related industries in giant trusts. Real wages were higher than before the war, and improved unemployment benefits also made life better for the workers. It appeared that Germany had also achieved political stability, as threats from the extremist parties of the left and the right subsided. Given time and economic stability, democracy might have taken firmer root in Germany. But then came the Great Depression. The global economic crisis that began in October 1929 starkly revealed how weak the Weimar Republic was.

Fundamental Weaknesses of the Weimar Republic

German political experience provided poor soil for transplanting an Anglo-Saxon democratic parliamentary system. Before World War I, Germany had been a semiautocratic state ruled by an emperor who commanded the armed forces, controlled foreign policy, appointed the chancellor, and called and dismissed parliament. This authoritarian system blocked the German people from acquiring democratic habits and attitudes; still accustomed to rule from above, still adoring the power state, many Germans sought the destruction of the Weimar Republic.

Traditional conservatives—the upper echelons of the civil service, judges, industrialists, large landowners, army leaders—were contemptuous of democracy and were avowed enemies of the republic. They wanted to restore a pre-1914 Prussian-type government that would fight liberal ideals and protect the fatherland from Bolshevism. Nor did the middle class feel a commitment to the liberal-democratic principles on which the republic rested. The traditionally nationalistic middle class identified the republic with defeat in war and the humiliation of the Versailles treaty; rabidly antisocialist, this class saw the leaders of the republic as Marxists who would impose on Germany a working-class state. Right-wing intellectuals often attacked democracy as a barrier to the true unity of the German nation. In the tradition of nineteenth-century Volkish thinkers, they had contempt for reason and political freedom and glorified instincts, blood, and action. In doing so, they turned many Germans against the republic, thereby eroding the popular support on which democracy depends. German historian Kurt Sontheimer concludes:

> Nothing is more dangerous in political life than the abandonment of reason. The intellect must remain the controlling, regulating force in human affairs. The anti-democratic intellectuals of the Weimar period betrayed the intellect to "Life." They despised reason and found more truth in myth or in the blood surging in their veins. . . . Had they a little more reason and enlightenment, these intellectuals might have seen better where their zeal was leading them and their country.[5]

The Weimar Republic also showed the weaknesses of the multiparty system. With the vote spread over a number of parties, no one party held a majority of seats in the parliament (Reichstag), so the republic was governed by a coalition of several parties. But because of ideological differences, the coalition was always unstable and in danger of failing to function. This is precisely what happened during the Great Depression. When effective leadership was imperative, the government could not act. Political deadlock caused Germans to lose what little confidence they had in the democratic system. Support for the parties that wanted to preserve democracy dwindled, and extremist parties that aimed to topple the republic gained strength.

Supporting the republic were Social Democrats, Catholic Centrists, and German Democrats; a coalition of these parties governed the republic during the 1920s.* Seeking to bring down the republic were the Communists, on the left, and two rightist parties—the Nationalists and the National Socialist German Workers' party, led by Adolf Hitler.

The Rise of Hitler

The Early Years

Adolf Hitler (1889–1945) was born in the town of Braunau am Inn, Austria, on April 20, 1889, the fourth child of a minor civil servant. Much of his youth was spent in Linz, a major city in Upper Austria. A poor student at secondary school, although by no means unintelligent, Hitler left high school and lived idly for more than two years. In 1907, the Vienna Academy of Arts rejected his application for admission. With the death of his mother in December 1907, the nineteen-year-old orphan (his father had died in 1903) drifted around Vienna viewing himself as an art student. Contrary to his later description of these years, Hitler did not suffer great poverty, for he received an orphan's allowance from the state and an inheritance from his mother and an aunt. When the Vienna Academy again refused him admission in 1908, he did not seek to learn a trade or to work steadily, but earned some money by painting picture postcards.

Hitler was a loner, often given to brooding and self-pity. He found some solace by regularly attending Wagnerian operas (much admired by Ger-

*The Social Democrats hoped one day to transform Germany into a Marxist society, but they had abandoned revolutionary means and pursued a policy of moderate social reform. The largest party until the closing months of the Weimar Republic, the Social Democrats were committed to democratic principles and parliamentary government. The Catholic Center party opposed socialism and protected Catholic interests, but like the Social Democrats supported the republic. The German Democratic party consisted of middle-class liberals who also opposed socialism and supported the republic. Although the right-wing German People's party was more monarchist than republican, on occasion it joined the coalition of parties that sought to preserve the republic.

man nationalists for their glorification of German folk traditions), by fantasizing about great architectural projects that he would someday initiate, and by reading. He read a lot, especially in art, history, and military affairs. He also read the racial, nationalist, anti-Semitic, and Pan-German literature that abounded in multinational Vienna. This literature introduced Hitler to a bizarre racial mythology: a heroic race of blond, blue-eyed Aryans battling for survival against inferior races. The racist treatises preached the danger posed by mixing races, called for the liquidation of racial inferiors, and marked the Jew as the embodiment of evil and the source of all misfortune.

In Vienna, Hitler came into contact with Georg von Schönerer's Pan-German movement. For Schönerer, the Jews were evil not because of their religion, not because they rejected Christ, but because they possessed evil racial qualities. Schönerer's followers wore watch chains etched with pictures of hanged Jews. Hitler was particularly impressed with Karl Lueger, the mayor of Vienna, a clever demagogue who skillfully manipulated the anti-Semitic feelings of the Viennese for his own political advantage. In Vienna, Hitler also acquired a hatred for Marxism and democracy and the conviction that the struggle for existence and the survival of the fittest are the essential facts of the social world. His years in Vienna emptied Hitler of all compassion and scruples and filled him with a fierce resentment of the social order that he felt had ignored him, cheated him, and condemned him to a wretched existence.

When World War I began, Hitler was in Munich. He welcomed the war as a relief from his daily life, which had been devoid of purpose and excitement. Volunteering for the German army, Hitler found battle exhilarating and he fought bravely, twice receiving the Iron Cross.

The experience of battle taught Hitler to value discipline, regimentation, leadership, authority, struggle, ruthlessness—values that he carried with him into the politics of the postwar world. The shock of Germany's defeat and revolution intensified his commitment to racial nationalism. To lead Germany to total victory over its racial enemies became his obsession. Like many returning soldiers, he required vindicating explanations for lost victories. His own explanation was simple and demagogic: Germany's shame was due to the creators of the republic—the "November criminals"; and behind them was a Jewish-Bolshevik world conspiracy.

The Nazi Party

In 1919, Hitler joined the German Workers' Party, a small right-wing group and one of the more than seventy extremist military-political-Volkish organizations that sprang up in postwar Germany. Displaying fantastic energy and extraordinary ability as a demagogic orator, propagandist, and organizer, Hitler quickly became the leader of the party, whose name was changed to National Socialist German Workers' party (commonly called *Nazi*). As leader, Hitler insisted on absolute authority and total allegiance—a demand that coincided with the postwar longing for a strong leader who would set right a shattered nation. Without Hitler, the National Socialist German Workers' party would have remained an insignificant group of discontents and outcasts. Demonstrating a Machiavellian cunning for politics, Hitler tightened the party organization and perfected the techniques of mass propaganda.

Like Mussolini, Hitler incorporated military attitudes and techniques into politics. Uniforms, salutes, emblems, flags, and other symbols infused party members with a sense of solidarity and camaraderie. At mass meetings, Hitler was a spellbinder who gave stunning performances. His pounding fists, throbbing body, wild gesticulations, hypnotic eyes, rage-swollen face, and repeated, frenzied denunciations of the Versailles treaty, Marxism, the republic, and Jews inflamed and mesmerized the audience. Many listeners—and his speeches generally attracted people already hostile to the Weimar Republic—were swayed by Hitler's earnestness, conviction, and self-confidence. They believed that Hitler and his movement could restore Germany's strength and pride. Hitler instinctively grasped the innermost feelings of his audience—its resentments and its longings. "The intense will of the man, the passion of his sincerity seemed to flow from him into me. I experienced an exaltation that could be likened only to religious conversion," said one early admirer.[6]

In November 1923, Hitler attempted to seize

power (the Munich or "Beer Hall" putsch) in the state of Bavaria as a prelude to toppling the republic. The putsch failed and the Nazis made a poor showing—they quickly scattered when the Bavarian police opened fire. Ironically, however, Hitler's prestige increased, for when he was put on trial, he used it as an opportunity to denounce the republic and the Versailles treaty and to proclaim his philosophy of racial nationalism. His impassioned speeches, publicized by the press, earned Hitler a nationwide reputation and a light sentence—five years' imprisonment with the promise of quick parole. While in prison, Hitler dictated *Mein Kampf,* a rambling and turgid work that contained the essence of his world-view.

The unsuccessful Munich putsch taught Hitler a valuable lesson: armed insurrection against superior might fails. He would gain power not by force but by exploiting the instruments of democracy—elections and party politics. He would use apparently legal means to destroy the Weimar Republic and impose a dictatorship. As Nazi propaganda expert Joseph Goebbels would later express it: "We have openly declared that we use democratic methods only to gain power and that once we had it we would ruthlessly deny our opponents all those chances we had been granted when we were in the opposition."[7]

Hitler's World-View

Some historians view Hitler as an unprincipled opportunist and a brilliant tactician who believed in nothing, but cleverly manufactured and manipulated ideas that were politically useful in his drive for power. To be sure, Hitler was not concerned with the objective truth of an idea but with its potential political usefulness. He was not a systematic thinker like Marx. Whereas communism claimed the certainty of science and held that it would reform the world in accordance with rational principles, Hitler proclaimed the higher validity of blood, instinct, and will and regarded the intellect as an enemy of the soul. Hitler nevertheless possessed a remarkably consistent ideology, as Hajo Holborn concludes:

> Hitler was a great opportunist and tactician, but it would be quite wrong to think that ideology was for him a mere instrumentality for gaining power. On the contrary, Hitler was a doctrinaire of the first order. Throughout his political career he was guided by an ideology . . . which from 1926 onward [did] not show any change whatsoever.[8]

Hitler's thought comprised a patchwork of nineteenth-century anti-Semitic, Volkish (see page 561), Social Darwinist (see page 533), antidemocratic, and anti-Marxist ideas. From these ideas, many of which enjoyed wide popularity, Hitler constructed a world-view rooted in myth and ritual. Given to excessive daydreaming and never managing to "overcome his youth with its dreams, injuries, and resentments,"[9] Hitler sought to make the world accord with his fantasies—struggles to the death between races, a vast empire ruled by a master race, a thousand-year Reich.

Racial Nationalism Nazism rejected both the Judeo-Christian and the Enlightenment traditions and sought to found a new world order based on racial nationalism. For Hitler, race was the key to understanding world history. He believed that Western civilization was at a critical juncture. Liberalism was dying, and Marxism, that "Jewish invention," as he called it, would inherit the future unless it was opposed by an even more powerful world-view. "With the conception of race National Socialism will carry its revolution and recast the world," said Hitler.[10] As the German barbarians had overwhelmed a disintegrating Roman Empire, a reawakened, racially united Germany, led by men of iron will, would carve out a vast European empire and deal a decadent liberal civilization its deathblow. It would conquer Russia, eradicate communism, and reduce to serfdom the subhuman Slavs, "a mass of born slaves who feel the need of a master."[11]

In the tradition of crude Volkish nationalists and Social Darwinists, Hitler divided the world into superior and inferior races and pitted them against each other in a struggle for survival. This fight for life was a law of nature and of history. The Germans, descendants of ancient Aryans, possessed superior racial characteristics; a nation degenerates and perishes if it allows its blood to be contaminated by intermingling with lower races. Conflict between races was desirable, for it strengthened and hardened racial superiors; it made them ruthless—a necessary quality in this Darwinian world. As a higher race, the Germans were entitled to conquer and subjugate other races. Germany must acquire *Lebensraum* (living space) by expanding eastward at the expense of the racially inferior Slavs.

The Jew as Devil An obsessive and virulent anti-Semitism dominated Hitler's mental outlook. (See pages 563–567 on anti-Semitism.) In waging war against the Jews, Hitler believed that he was defending Germany from its worst enemy. In Hitler's mythical interpretation of the world, the Aryan was the originator and carrier of civilization. As descendants of the Aryans, the Germans embodied creativity, bravery, and loyalty. As the counterpart of the Aryan, the Jew personified the vilest qualities. "Two worlds face one another," said Hitler in a statement that clearly reveals the mythical character of his thought, "the men of God and the men of Satan! The Jew is the anti-man, the creature of another god. He must have come from another root of the human race. I set the Aryan and the Jew over and against each other."[12] Everything Hitler despised—liberalism, intellectualism, pacifism, parliamentarism, internationalism, communism, modern art, individualism—he attributed to the Jew.

For Hitler, the Jew was the mortal enemy of racial nationalism. The moral outlook of the ancient Hebrew prophets, which affirmed individual worth and made individuals morally responsible for their actions, was totally in opposition to Hitler's morality, which subordinated the individual to the national community. He once called conscience a Jewish invention. The prophetic vision of the unity of humanity under God, equality, justice, and peace were also in opposition to Hitler's belief that all history is a pitiless struggle between races and that only the strongest and most ruthless deserve to survive.

Hitler's anti-Semitism also served a functional purpose. By concentrating all evil in one enemy, "the conspirator and demonic" Jew, Hitler provided the masses with a simple, consistent, and emotionally satisfying explanation for all their misery. By defining themselves as the racial and spiritual opposites of Jews, Germans of all classes felt joined together in a Volkish union. By seeing themselves engaged in a heroic battle against a single enemy who embodied evil, their will was strengthened. Even failures and misfits gained self-respect. Anti-Semitism provided insecure and hostile people with powerless but recognizable targets on whom to focus their antisocial feelings.

The surrender to myth served to disorient the intellect and to unify the nation. When the mind accepts an image such as Hitler's image of Jews as vermin, germs, and satanic conspirators, it has lost all sense of balance and objectivity. Such a disoriented mind is ready to believe and to obey, to be manipulated and to be led, to brutalize and to tolerate brutality; it is ready to be absorbed into the collective will of the community.

The Importance of Propaganda Hitler understood that in an age of political parties, universal suffrage, and a popular press—the legacies of the French and Industrial revolutions—the successful leader must win the support of the masses. To do this, Hitler consciously applied and perfected elements of circus showmanship, church pageantry, American advertising, and the techniques of propaganda that the Allies had effectively used to stir their civilian populations during the war. To be effective, said Hitler, propaganda must be aimed principally at the emotions. The masses are not moved by scientific ideas or by objective and abstract knowledge, but by primitive feelings, terror, force, discipline. Propaganda must reduce everything to simple slogans incessantly repeated and must concentrate on one enemy. The masses are aroused by the spoken, not the written word—by a storm of hot passion erupting from the speaker "which like hammer blows can open the gates to the heart of the people."[13]

The most effective means of stirring the masses and strengthening them for the struggle ahead, said Hitler in *Mein Kampf,* is the mass meeting. Surrounded by tens of thousands of people, individuals lose their sense of individuality and no longer see themselves as isolated. They become members of a community bound together by an esprit de corps reminiscent of the trenches during the Great War. Bombarded by the cheers of thousands of voices, by marching units, by banners, by explosive oratory, individuals become convinced of the truth of the party's message and the irresistibility of the movement. Their intellects over-

FrauenWarte
die einzige parteiamtliche frauenzeitschrift

HEFT 19 · 8. JAHRGANG
1. APRILHEFT 1940

Nazi Magazine Cover of Mother and Son. Nazi propaganda proclaimed the strength of the German Aryans through symbols easily grasped and guaranteed to strike proud nationalistic chords. (*Institut für Zeitgeschichte, München*)

his genius for propaganda and organization to strengthen the loyalty of his cadres and to instill in them a sense of mission. In 1925, the Nazi party counted about 27,000 members; in 1929, it had grown to 178,000 with units throughout Germany. But its prospects seemed dim, for since 1925, economic conditions had improved and the republic seemed politically stable. In 1928, the National Socialists (NSDAP) received only 2.6 percent of the vote. Nevertheless, Hitler never lost faith in his own capacities or his destiny; he continued to build his party and waited for a crisis that would rock the republic and make his movement a force in national politics.

The Great Depression, which began in the United States at the end of 1929, provided that crisis. As Germany's economic plight worsened, the German people became more amenable to Hitler's radicalism. The Nazis tirelessly expanded their efforts. Everywhere they staged mass rallies, plastered walls with posters, distributed leaflets, and engaged in street battles with their opponents of the left. Hitler promised all things to all groups, avoided debates, provided simple explanations for Germany's misfortunes, and insisted that only the Nazis could rescue Germany. Nazi propaganda attacked the communists, the "November criminals," the democratic system, the Versailles treaty, reparations, and, above all, the Jews. It depicted Hitler as a savior. Hitler would rescue Germany from chaos; he understood the real needs of the Volk; he was sent by destiny to lead Germany in its hour of greatest need. These propaganda techniques worked. The Nazi party went from 810,000 votes in 1928 to 6,400,000 in 1930, and its representation in the Reichstag soared from 12 to 107.

The Social Democrats (SPD), the principal defenders of democracy, could draw support only from the working class; to the middle class, the SPD were hated Marxists. Moreover, in the eyes of many Germans the SPD were identified with the status quo, that is, with economic misery and national humiliation. The SPD simply had no program that could attract the middle class or arouse its hope for a better future.

To the lower middle class the Nazis promised effective leadership and a solution to the economic crisis. To them the Great Depression was the last straw, final evidence that the republic had failed

whelmed, their resistance lowered, they lose their previous beliefs and are carried along on a wave of enthusiasm. "The man who enters such a meeting doubting and wavering leaves it inwardly reinforced; he has become a link to the community."[14]

Hitler Gains Power

When Hitler left prison in December 1924, after serving nine months, he proceeded to tighten his hold over the Nazi party. He relentlessly used

and should be supplanted by a different kind of regime. They craved order, authority, and leadership and abhorred the disputes of political parties that provided neither. They wanted Hitler to protect Germany from the communists and organized labor. The traumatic experience of the Great Depression caused many bourgeois—hitherto apathetic about voting, politically immature, impatient, and easily excitable—to cast ballots. The depression was also severe in England and the United States, but the liberal foundations of these countries were strong; in Germany they were not, because the middle class had not committed itself to democracy, nor indeed did it have any liking for it. Democracy endured in Britain and the United States; in Germany it collapsed.

But Nazism was more than a class movement. It appealed to the discontented and disillusioned from all segments of the population—embittered veterans, romantic nationalists, idealistic intellectuals, industrialists and large landowners frightened by communism and social democracy, rootless and resentful people who felt they had no place in the existing society, the unemployed, lovers of violence, and newly enfranchised youth yearning for a cause. The Social Democrats spoke the rational language of European democracy. The Communists addressed themselves to only a part of the nation, the proletariat, and were linked to a foreign country, the Soviet Union. The Nazis reached a wider spectrum of the population and touched deeper feelings.

And always there was the immense attraction of Hitler. Many Germans were won over by his fanatic sincerity, his iron will, and his conviction that he was chosen by fate to rescue Germany. What a new party member wrote after hearing Hitler speak expressed the mood of many Germans: "There was only one thing for me, either to win with Adolf Hitler or to die for him. The personality of the Fuehrer had me totally in its spell."[15] Many others, no doubt, voted for Hitler not because they approved of him or his ideas but because he was a strong opponent of the Weimar Republic. What these people wanted, above all, was the end of the republic they hated.

Meanwhile, the parliamentary regime failed to function effectively. According to Article 48 of the constitution, during times of emergency the president was empowered to govern by decree, that is, without parliament. When President Paul von Hindenburg (1847–1934), the aging field marshal, exercised this emergency power, in effect the responsibility for governing Germany was transferred from the political parties and parliament to the president and chancellor. Rule by the president, instead of by parliament, meant for one thing that Germany had already taken a giant step away from parliamentary government in the direction of authoritarianism.

In the election of July 31, 1932, the Nazis received 37.3 percent of the vote and won 230 seats, far more than any other party but still not a majority. Determined to become chancellor, Hitler refused to take a subordinate position in a coalition government. Meanwhile, the recently resigned chancellor, Franz von Papen, persuaded Hindenburg, whose judgment was distorted by old age, to appoint Hitler chancellor. In this decision Papen had the support of German industrialists, aristocratic landowners, and the Nationalist party.

As in Italy, the members of the ruling elite were frightened by internal violence, unrest, and the specter of communism. They thought Hitler a vulgar man and abhorred his demagogic incitement of the masses. But they regarded him as a useful instrument to fight communism, block social reform, break the back of organized labor, and rebuild the armament industry. Hitler had cleverly reassured these traditional conservatives that the Nazis would protect private property and business and go slow with social reform. Like the Italian upper class, which had assisted Mussolini in his rise to power, the old conservative ruling elite intrigued to put Hitler in power. Ironically, this decision was made when Nazi strength at the polls was beginning to ebb. Expecting to control Hitler, conservatives calculated badly, for Hitler could not be tamed. They had underestimated his skill as a politician, his ruthlessness, and his obsession with racial nationalism. Hitler had not sought power to restore the old order but to fashion a new one. The new leadership would be drawn not from the traditional ruling segments but from the most dedicated Nazis, regardless of their social background.

Never intending to rule within the spirit of the constitution, Hitler quickly moved to assume dictatorial powers. In February 1933, a Dutch drifter with communist leanings set a fire in the Reichstag. Hitler persuaded Hindenburg to sign an emergency decree suspending civil rights on the pretext that the state was threatened by internal subversion. The chancellor then used these emergency powers to arrest, without due process, Communist and Social Democratic deputies.

In the elections of March 1933, Nazi thugs broke up Communist party meetings and Hitler called for a Nazi victory at the polls to save Europe from Bolshevism. Intimidated by street violence and captivated by Nazi mass demonstrations and relentless propaganda, the German people elected 288 Nazi deputies in a Reichstag of 647 seats. With the support of 52 deputies of the Nationalist party and in the absence of Communist deputies who were under arrest, the Nazis now had a secure majority. Hitler then bullied the Reichstag into passing the Enabling Act (in March 1933), which permitted the chancellor to enact legislation independently of the Reichstag. With astonishing passivity, the political parties had allowed the Nazis to dismantle the government and make Hitler a dictator with unlimited power. Hitler had used the instruments of democracy to destroy the republic and create a dictatorship. And he did it far more thoroughly and quickly than Mussolini had.

Nazi Germany

Mussolini's Fascism exhibited much bluster and bragging, but Fascist Italy did not have the industrial and military strength or the total commitment of the people necessary to threaten the peace of Europe. Nazism, on the other hand, demonstrated a demonic quality that nearly destroyed Western civilization. The impact of Hitler's sinister, fanatic, and obsessive personality was far greater on the German movement than was Mussolini's character on Italian Fascism. Also contributing to the demonic radicalism of Nazism were certain deeply rooted German traditions that were absent in Italy—Prussian militarism, adoration of the power-state, and belief in the special destiny of the German Volk. These traditions

made the German people's attachment to Hitler and Nazi ideology much stronger than the Italian people's devotion to Mussolini and his party.

The Leader-State

The Nazis moved to subjugate all political and economic institutions and all culture to the will of the party. There could be no separation between the private life and politics; ideology must pervade every phase of daily life; all organizations must come under party control; there could be no rights of the individual that must be respected by the state. The party became the state, its teachings the soul of the German nation.

Unlike absolute monarchies of the past, a totalitarian regime requires more than outward obedience to its commands; it seeks to control the inner person, to shape thoughts, feelings, and attitudes in accordance with the party ideology. It demands total allegiance and submission. An anonymous Nazi poet succinctly expressed the totalitarian goal:

> We have captured all the positions
> And on the heights we have planted
> The banners of our revolution.
> You had imagined that that was all that we
>   wanted
> We want more
> We want all
> Your hearts are our goal,
> It is your souls we want.[16]

The Third Reich was organized as a leader-state in which Hitler, the *Fuehrer* (leader), embodied and expressed the real will of the German people, commanded the supreme loyalty of the nation, and held omnipotent power. As a Nazi political theorist stated: "The authority of the Fuehrer is total and all-embracing . . . it embraces all members of the German community. . . . The Fuehrer's authority is subject to no checks or controls; it is circumscribed by no . . . individual rights; it is . . . overriding and unfettered."[17] To the Fuehrer the German people owed complete loyalty. In practice, however, the Nazi state was not a coherent and monolithic political system held together by commands issuing from one source. Rather, the nation was composed of organizations and individuals competing with one another for influence, power, and plunder.

To strengthen the power of the central government and coordinate the nation under Nazism, the regime abolished legislatures in the various German states and appointed governors who made certain that Nazi directives were carried out throughout the country. The Nazis took over the civil service and used its machinery to enforce Nazi decrees. In this process of *Gleichschaltung* (coordination), the Nazis encountered little opposition. The political parties and the trade unions collapsed without a struggle.

In June 1933, the Social Democratic party was outlawed, and within a few weeks the other political parties simply disbanded on their own. In May 1933, the Nazis seized the property of the trade unions, arrested the leaders, and ended collective bargaining and strikes. The newly established German Labor Front, an instrument of the party, became the official organization of the working class. Although there is evidence that the working class in 1933 would have resisted the Nazis, the leadership never mobilized proletarian organizations. With surprising ease the Nazis had imposed their will over the nation.

Hitler made strategic but temporary concessions to the traditional ruling elite. On June 30, 1934, Nazi executioners swiftly murdered the leaders of the SA (the storm troopers who had battled political opponents) to eliminate any potential opposition to Hitler from within the party. With this move, Hitler also relieved the anxieties of industrialists and landowners, who feared that Ernst Röhm, the leader of the SA, would persuade Hitler to remove them from positions of power and to implement a program of radical social reform that would threaten their property.

The execution of the SA leaders (including Röhm) was also approved by the generals, for they regarded the SA as a rival to the army. In August, all German soldiers swore an oath of unconditional allegiance to the Fuehrer, cementing the alliance between the army and National Socialism. The army tied itself to the Nazi regime because it valued the resurgence of militaristic values and applauded the death of the Weimar Republic. German historian Karl Dietrich Bracher concludes: "Without the assistance of the Army,

at first through its toleration and later through its active cooperation, the country's rapid and final restructuring into the total leader state could not have come about."[18]

Economic Life

Hitler had not sought power to improve the living standards of the masses but to convert Germany into a powerful war machine. Economic problems held little interest for this dreamer in whose mind danced images of a vast German empire. For him the "socialism" in National Socialism meant not a comprehensive program of social welfare but the elimination of the class antagonisms that divided and weakened the fatherland. Radicals within the party wanted to deprive the industrialists and landowners of power and social prestige and expropriate their property. The more pragmatic Hitler wanted only to deprive them of freedom of action; they were to serve, not control, the state. Germany remained capitalist, but the state had unlimited power to intervene in the economy. Unlike the Bolsheviks, the Nazis did not destroy the upper classes of the Old Regime. Hitler made no war against the industrialists. From them he wanted loyalty, obedience, and a war machine. German businessmen prospered but exercised no influence on political decisions. The profits of industry rose, but the real wages of German workers did not improve. Nevertheless, workers lauded the regime for ending the unemployment crisis.

Nazism and the Churches

Nazism conflicted with the core values of Christianity. "The heaviest blow that ever struck humanity was the coming of Christianity," said Hitler to intimates during World War II.[19] Had Germany won World War II, the Nazis would no doubt have tried to root Christianity out of German life. In 1937, the bishop of Berlin defined the essential conflict between Christianity and Nazism:

> *The question at stake is whether there is an authority that stands above all earthly power, the authority of God, Whose commandments*

are valid independent of space and time, country and race. The question at stake is whether individual man possesses personal rights that no community and no state may take from him; whether the free exercise of his conscience may be prevented and forbidden by the state.[20]

Nazism could tolerate no other faith alongside itself. Recognizing that Christianity was a rival claimant for the German soul, the Nazis moved to repress the Protestant and Catholic churches. In the public schools, religious instruction was cut back and the syllabus changed to omit the Jewish origins of Christianity. Christ was depicted not as a Jew, heir to the prophetic tradition of Hebrew monotheism, but as an Aryan hero. The *Gestapo* (secret state police) censored church newspapers, scrutinized sermons and church activities, forbade some clergymen to preach, dismissed the opponents of Nazism from theological schools, and arrested some clerical critics of the regime.

The clergy are well represented among those Germans who resisted Nazism; some were sent to concentration camps or were executed. But these courageous clergy were not representatives of the German churches which, as organized institutions, capitulated to and cooperated with the Nazi regime. Both the German Evangelical and German Catholic churches demanded that their faithful render loyalty to Hitler; both turned a blind eye to Nazi persecution of Jews; both condemned resistance and found much in the Third Reich to admire; both supported Hitler's war. When Germany attacked Poland, starting World War II, the Catholic bishops declared: "In this decisive hour we encourage and admonish our Catholic soldiers, in obedience to the Fuehrer, to do their duty and to be ready to sacrifice their whole existence."[21] Both churches urged their faithful to fight for fatherland and Fuehrer, pressured conscientious objectors to serve, and celebrated Nazi victories.

Varied reasons explain why the German churches, which preached Christ's message of humanity, failed to take a stand against Nazi inhumanity. Many German church leaders feared that resistance would lead to even more severe measures against their churches. Traditionally the German churches had bowed to state authority and

detested revolution. Church leaders also found some Nazi ideas appealing. Intensely nationalistic, antiliberal, antirepublican, and anti-Semitic, many members of the clergy were filled with hope when Hitler came to power. The prominent Lutheran theologian who "welcomed that change that came to Germany in 1933 as a divine gift and miracle"[22] voiced the sentiments of many members of the clergy. Such feelings encouraged prolonged moral nearsightedness, not a revolt of Christian conscience. When the war ended the German Evangelical church leaders lamented:

. . . we know ourselves to be one with our people in a great company of suffering and in a great solidarity of guilt. With great pain do we say: Through us endless suffering has been brought to many people and countries. . . . We accuse ourselves for not witnessing more courageously, for not praying more faithfully, for not loving more ardently.[23]

Shaping the "New Man"

Propaganda had helped the Nazis come to power. Now it would be used to consolidate their hold on the German nation and to shape a "new man" committed to Hitler, race, and Volk. Hitler was a radical revolutionary who desired not only the outward form of power but also control over the inner person—over the individual's thoughts and feelings. The purpose of Nazi propaganda was to condition the mind to revere the Fuehrer and to obey the new regime. It intended to deprive individuals of their capacity for independent thought. By concentrating on the myth of the race and the infallibility of the Fuehrer, Nazi propaganda sought to disorient the rational mind and to give the individual new standards to believe in and obey. Propaganda aimed to mold the entire nation to think and respond as the leader-state directed. Even science had to conform to Nazi racial ideology. Thus Johannes Stark, a Nobel Prize winner, held that scientific thought is a function of race:

. . . natural science is overwhelmingly a creation of the Nordic-Germanic blood component of the Aryan peoples. . . . The Jewish spirit is wholly different in its orientation. . . .

True, Heinrich Hertz made the great discovery of electromagnetic waves, but he was not a full-blooded Jew. He had a German mother, from whose side his spiritual endowment may well have been conditioned.[24]

The Ministry of Popular Enlightenment, headed by Dr. Joseph Goebbels (1897–1945), controlled the press, book publishing, the radio, the theater, and the cinema. Goebbels, holder of a doctoral degree in the humanities, was intelligent and a master in the art of propaganda; he was also vain, cynical, and contemptuous of the very masses he manipulated. But the German people were not merely passive victims of clever and ruthless leaders. "The effective spread of propaganda and the rapid regimentation of cultural life," says Bracher, "would not have been possible without the invaluable help eagerly tendered by writers and artists, professors and churchmen." And the manipulation of the minds of the German people "would not have been effective had it not been for profound historically conditioned relations based . . . on a pseudoreligious exaggerated nationalism and on the idea of the German mission."[25] Although some intellectuals showed their abhorrence of the Nazi regime by emigrating, the great majority gave their support, often with overt enthusiasm. Some individuals rejected Nazi propaganda, but the masses of German people came to regard Nazism as the fulfillment of their nationalist longings.

The Nazis tried to keep the emotions in a state of permanent mobilization, for Hitler understood that the emotionally aroused are most amenable to manipulation. Goose-stepping SA and SS (elite military and police) battalions paraded in the streets; martial music quickened the pulse; Nazi flags decorated public buildings; loudspeakers installed in offices and factories blared the Nazi message, and all work stopped for important broadcasts. Citizens were ordered to greet each other with "Heil Hitler," a potent sign of reverence and submission. The regime made a special effort to reach young people. All youths between the ages of ten and eighteen were urged to join the Hitler Youth, and all other youth organizations were dissolved. At camps and rallies, young people paraded, sang, saluted, and chanted: "We were slaves; we were outsiders in our own coun-

try. So were we before Hitler united us. Now we would fight against Hell itself for our leader."[26]

Nazification of Education The schools, long breeding grounds of nationalism, militarism, antiliberalism, and anti-Semitism, now indoctrinated the young in Nazi ideology. The Nazis instructed teachers how certain subjects were to be taught; and to ensure obedience, members of the Hitler Youth were asked to report suspicious teachers. Portraits of Hitler and Nazi banners were displayed in classrooms. War stories, adventures of the Hitler Youth, and ancient Nordic legends replaced fairy tales and animal stories in reading material for the young. The curriculum upgraded physical training and sports, curtailed religious instruction, and introduced many courses in "racial science." Decidedly anti-intellectual, the Nazis stressed character building over book learning. They intended to train young people to serve the leader and the racial community, to imbue them with a sense of fellowship for their Volkish kin, that sense of camaraderie found on the battlefield. Expressions of individualism and independence were suppressed.

The universities quickly abandoned freedom of the mind, scientific objectivity, and humanist values. "We repudiate international science, we repudiate the international community of scholars, we repudiate research for the sake of research. Sieg Heil!"[27] declared one historian. Even before the Nazi takeover, many university students and professors had embraced Volkish nationalism and right-wing radicalism. Two years before Hitler came to power, for example, 60 percent of all undergraduates supported the Nazi student organization, and anti-Semitic riots broke out at several universities.

For seventy years or more, the professors had preached aggressive nationalism, the German destiny of power, hero worship, irrational political Romanticism, and so forth, and had increasingly deemphasized, if not eliminated, the teachings of ethical and humanist principles. . . . Essentially neither [professors nor students] wanted to have anything to do with democracy. In the Weimar Republic . . . both groups, on the whole, seemed equally determined to tear down that Republic. The profes-

sors did their part by fiery lectures, speeches, and writings; the students did theirs in noisy demonstrations, torch-light parades, vandalism, and physical violence. . . . When Hitler came to power, both professors and students fell all over themselves to demonstrate their allegiance.[28]

In May 1933, professors and students proudly burned books considered a threat to Nazi ideology. Many academics praised Hitler and the new regime. Some 10 percent of the university faculty, principally Jews, Social Democrats, and liberals, were dismissed, and their colleagues often approved. "From now on it will not be your job to determine whether something is true but whether it is in the spirit of the National Socialist revolution," the new minister of culture told university professors.[29] Numerous courses on Nazi ideology were introduced into the curriculum.

Giant Rallies Symbolic of the Nazi regime were the monster rallies staged at Nuremberg. Scores of thousands roared, marched, and worshiped at their leader's feet. These true believers, the end product of Nazi indoctrination, celebrated Hitler's achievements and demonstrated their loyalty to their savior. Everything was brilliantly orchestrated to impress Germans and the world with the irresistible power, determination, and unity of the Nazi movement and the greatness of the Fuehrer. Armies of youths waving flags, storm troopers bearing weapons, and workers shouldering long-handled spades paraded past Hitler, who stood at attention, his arm extended in the Nazi salute. The endless columns of marchers, the stirring martial music played by huge bands, the forest of flags, the chanting and cheering of spectators, and the burning torches and beaming spotlights united the participants into a racial community. "Wherever Hitler leads we follow," thundered thousands of Germans in a giant chorus. The Nuremberg rallies were among the greatest theatrical performances of the twentieth century.

Terror Terror was another means of ensuring compliance and obedience. The instrument of terror was the SS, which was organized in 1925 to protect Hitler and other party leaders and to stand guard at party meetings. Under the leadership of Heinrich Himmler (1900–1945), a fanatic believer in Hitler's racial theories, the SS was molded into an elite force of disciplined, dedicated, and utterly ruthless men. Myopic, narrow-chested, and sexually prudish, Himmler contrived a cult of manliness. He envisioned the SS, who were specially selected for their racial purity and physical fitness, as a new breed of knights—Nietzschean supermen who would lead the new Germany.

The SS staffed the concentration camps established to deal with political prisoners. Through systematic terror and torture, the SS sought to deprive the inmates of their human dignity and to harden themselves for the struggles that lay ahead. Knowledge that these camps existed and that some prisoners were never heard from again was a strong inducement for Germans to remain obedient.

Anti-Semitic Legislation

The Nazis deprived Jews of their German citizenship and instituted many anti-Jewish measures designed to make them outcasts. Thousands of Jewish doctors, lawyers, musicians, artists, and professors were barred from practicing their professions, and Jewish members of the civil service were dismissed. A series of laws tightened the screws of humiliation and persecution. Marriage or sexual encounters between Germans and Jews were forbidden. Universities, schools, restaurants, pharmacies, hospitals, theaters, museums, and athletic fields were gradually closed to Jews.

In November 1938, using the assassination of a German diplomat by a Jewish youth as a pretext, the Nazis organized an extensive pogrom. Nazi gangs murdered scores of Jews and burned and looted thousands of Jewish homes and synagogues all over Germany; 20,000 Jews were thrown into concentration camps. The Reich then imposed on the Jewish community a fine of 1 billion marks. These measures were a mere prelude, however; the physical extermination of European Jewry became a cardinal Nazi objective during World War II (see Chapter 34).

Mass Support

The Nazi regime became a police state symbolized by mass arrests, the persecution of Jews, and concentration camps that institutionalized terror. Yet

Jews Being Rounded Up to Enter Concentration Camps. Hitler broadened his campaign against the Jews in a prelude to the full-scale persecution during World War II, when he sought the "final solution of the Jewish problem" through genocide. (*Collection Viollet*)

fewer heads rolled than people expected, and in many ways life seemed normal. The Nazis skillfully established the totalitarian state without upsetting the daily life of the great majority of the population. Moreover Hitler, like Mussolini, was careful to maintain the appearance of legality. By not abolishing parliament or repealing the constitution, he could claim that his was a legitimate government. By consolidating power in stages and retaining the institutions of the republic, the Nazis lulled both Germans and people in other countries into believing that legitimate statesmen governed Germany.

To people concerned with little but family, job, and friends—and this includes most people in any country—life in the first few years of the Third Reich seemed quite satisfying. People believed that the new government was trying to solve Ger-

many's problems in a vigorous and sensible manner, in contrast to the ineffective Weimar leadership. By 1936, the reinvigoration of the economy, stimulated in part by rearmament, had virtually eliminated unemployment, which had reached 6 million people jobless when Hitler took power. An equally astounding achievement in German eyes was the rebuilding of the war machine and the restoration of power in international affairs. It seemed to most Germans that Hitler had awakened a sense of self-sacrifice and national dedication among a people dispirited by defeat and depression. He had united a country torn by class antagonisms and social distinctions and given the little people a sense of pride. Workers had jobs, businessmen profits, and generals troops—what could be wrong?

Many intellectuals, viewing Hitlerism as the

victory of idealism over materialism and of community over selfish individualism, lent their talents to the regime and endorsed the burning of books and the suppression of freedom. To them, Hitler was a visionary who had shown Germany and the world a new way of life—a new creed.

Hitler's spectacular foreign policy successes made the world take notice of the new Germany. Having regained confidence in themselves and their nation, Germans rejoiced in Hitler's leadership, regretted not at all the loss of political freedom, and remained indifferent to the plight of the persecuted, particularly Jews. Hitler's popularity and mass support rested on something far stronger than propaganda and terror. The simple truth is that he had won the hearts of a sizable proportion of the German people. To many Germans, Hitler was exactly as Nazi propaganda had depicted him: "He stands like a statue grown beyond the measure of earthly man."[30]

There was some opposition and resistance to the Hitler regime. Social Democrats and communists organized small cells. Some conservatives who considered Hitler to be a threat to traditional German values and some clergy who saw Nazism as a pagan religion in conflict with Christian morality also formed small opposition groups. But only resistance from the army could have toppled Hitler. Some generals, even before World War II, urged such resistance, but the overwhelming majority of German officers either preferred the new regime, were too concerned about their careers to do anything, or considered it dishonorable to break their oath of loyalty to Hitler. These officers would remain loyal until the bitter end. Very few Germans realized that their country was passing through a long night of barbarism, and still fewer considered resistance.

Liberalism and Authoritarianism in Other Lands

The Spread of Authoritarianism

After World War I, in country after country, parliamentary democracy collapsed and authoritarian leaders came to power. In most of these countries, liberal ideals had not penetrated deeply; liberalism met resistance from conservative elites.

Spain and Portugal In both Spain and Portugal, parliamentary regimes faced strong opposition from the church, the army, and large landowners. In 1926, army officers overthrew the Portuguese republic that had been created in 1910, and gradually Antonio de Oliveira Salazar (1889–1970), a professor of economics, emerged as dictator. In Spain, after antimonarchist forces won the election of 1931, King Alfonso XIII (1902–1931) left the country and Spain was proclaimed a republic. But the new government, led by socialists and liberals, faced the determined opposition of the ruling elite. The reforms introduced by the republic—expropriation of large estates, reduction of the number of army officers, dissolution of the Jesuit order, and closing of church schools—only intensified the old order's hatred.

The difficulties of the new Spanish republic mounted: workers, near starvation, rioted and engaged in violent strikes; the military attempted a coup; Catalonia, with its long tradition of separatism, tried to establish its autonomy. Imitating the example of France (see page 740), the parties of the left, including the communists, united in the Popular Front, which came to power in February 1936. In July 1936, General Francisco Franco (1892–1975), stationed in Spanish Morocco, led a revolt against the republic. He was supported by army leaders, the church, monarchists, landlords, industrialists, and the Falange, a newly formed fascist party. Spain was torn by a bloody civil war. Aided by Fascist Italy and Nazi Germany (see page 768), Franco won in 1939 and established a dictatorship.

Eastern and Central Europe Parliamentary government in eastern Europe rested on weak foundations. Predominantly rural, these countries lacked the sizable professional and commercial classes that had promoted liberalism in western Europe. Only Czechoslovakia had a substantial native middle class with a strong liberal tradition. The rural masses of eastern Europe, traditionally subjected to monarchical and aristocratic authority, were not used to political thinking or civic responsibility. Students and intellectuals, often gripped by a romantic nationalism, were drawn to antidemocratic movements. Right-wing leaders also played on the fear of communism. When parliamentary government failed to solve internal problems, the opponents of the liberal state seized the helm. Fascist movements, however, had little success in eastern Europe. It was authoritarian regimes headed by traditional ruling elites—army leaders or kings—that put an end to democracy there.

With the dissolution of the Hapsburg Empire at the end of World War I, Austria became a democratic republic. From the start, it suffered from severe economic problems. The Hapsburg Empire had been a huge free-trade area, permitting food and raw materials to circulate unimpeded throughout the empire. The new Austria lacked sufficient food to feed the population of Vienna and needed raw materials for its industries. Worsening its plight was the erection of tariff barriers by each of the states that had formerly been part of the Hapsburg Empire. Between 1922 and 1926, the League of Nations had to rescue Austria from bankruptcy. The Great Depression aggravated Austria's economic position. Many Austrians believed that only an *Anschluss* (union) with Germany could solve Austria's problems.

Austria was also burdened by a conflict between the industrial region, including Vienna, and the agricultural provinces. Factory workers were generally socialist and anticlerical; the peasants were strongly Catholic and antisocialist. The Social Democrats controlled Vienna, but the rural population gave its support to the Christian Socialist party. Each party had its own private army: the workers had the *Schutzbund* and the provincials the *Heimwehr*. During the Great Depression, Chancellor Engelbert Dollfuss (1892–1934) sought to turn the country into a one-party state. In February 1934, police and Heimwehr contingents raided Social Democratic headquarters. When the Social Democrats called a general strike, Dollfuss bombarded a workers' housing project, killing 193 civilians, and suppressed the Social Democratic party. Austria had joined the ranks of authoritarian states.

When Hitler came to power in Germany, Austrian Nazis pressed for Anschluss. In July 1934, a band of them assassinated Dollfuss, but a Nazi plot to capture the government failed. Four years later, however, Hitler would march into Austria,

bringing about the Anschluss desired by many Austrians.

The new Hungary that emerged at the end of World War I faced an uprising by communists inspired by the success of the Bolsheviks in Russia. Béla Kun (1885–1937), supported by Russian money, established a soviet regime in Budapest in March 1919. But Kun could not win the support of the peasants and was opposed by the Allies, who helped Rumania crush the revolutionary government. In 1920, power passed to Admiral Miklós Horthy (1868–1957), who instituted a brief white terror that exceeded the red terror of the Kun regime. During the Great Depression, the Horthy government, which favored the large landholders, was challenged by the radical right, which preached extreme nationalism, anti-Semitism, and anticapitalism and sought to win mass support through land reform. Its leader, Gyula Gömbös (1886–1936), who served as prime minister from 1932 to 1936, sought to align Hungary with Nazi Germany. Seeking to regain territories lost in World War I and aware of Hitler's growing might, Hungary drew closer to Germany in the late 1930s.

Poland, Greece, Bulgaria, and Rumania became either royal or military dictatorships. The new state of Czechoslovakia, guided by President Tomáš Masaryk (1850–1937) and Foreign Minister Eduard Beneš (1884–1948), who were both committed to the liberal-humanist tradition of the West, preserved parliamentary democracy. Its most serious problem came from the 3.1 million Germans living within its borders, primarily in the Sudetenland (see page 560). The German minority founded the Sudetenland German party, which modeled itself after Hitler's Nazi party. Hitler later exploited the issue of the Sudetenland Germans to dismember Czechoslovakia.

The Western Democracies

While liberal governments were everywhere failing, the great Western democracies—the United States, Britain, and France—continued to preserve democratic institutions. In Britain and the United States, fascist movements were no more than a nuisance. In France, fascism was more of a threat, because it exploited a deeply ingrained hostility in some quarters to the liberal ideals of the French Revolution.

The United States The central problem faced by the Western democracies was the Great Depression, which started in the United States. In the 1920s, hundred of thousands of Americans had bought stock on credit; this buying spree sent stock prices soaring well beyond what the stocks were actually worth. In late October 1929, the stock market was hit by a wave of panic selling; prices plummeted. Within a few weeks, the value of stocks listed on the New York Stock Exchange fell by some 26 billion dollars. A terrible chain reaction followed over the next few years. Businesses cut production and unemployment soared; farmers unable to meet mortgage payments lost their land; banks that had made poor investments closed down. American investors withdrew the capital they had invested in Europe, causing European banks and businesses to fail. Throughout the world, trade declined and unemployment rose.

When President Franklin Delano Roosevelt (1882–1945) took office in 1933, over 13 million Americans—one-quarter of the labor force—were out of work. Hunger and despair showed on the faces of the American people. Moving away from laissez faire, Roosevelt instituted a comprehensive program of national planning, economic experimentation, and reform known as the New Deal. Although the U.S. political and economic system faced a severe test, few Americans turned to fascism or communism, and the government, although engaging in national planning, did not break with democratic values and procedures.

Britain Even before the Great Depression, Britain faced severe economic problems. Loss of markets to foreign competitors hurt British manufacturing, mining, and shipbuilding; rapid development of water and oil power reduced the demand for British coal, and outdated mining equipment put Britain in a poor competitive position. To reduce costs, mine owners in 1926 called for salary cuts; the coal miners countered with a strike and were joined by workers in other industries. To many Britons, the workers were leftist radicals trying to overthrow the government. Many wanted the state to break the strike. After nine days, industrial workers called it off, but the

miners held out for another six months; they returned to work with longer hours and lower pay. Although the General Strike had failed, it did improve relations between the classes, for the workers had not called for revolution and they refrained from violence. The fear that British workers would follow the Bolshevik path abated.

The Great Depression cast a pall of gloom over Britain. The Conservative party leadership tried to stimulate exports by devaluing the pound and to encourage industry by providing loans at lower interest rates, but in the main, it left the task of recovery to industry itself. Not until Britain began to rearm did unemployment decline significantly. Despite the economic slump of the 1920s and the Great Depression, Britain remained politically stable, a testament to the strength of its parliamentary tradition. Neither the communists nor the newly formed British Fascist party gained mass support.

France In the early 1920s, France was concerned with restoring villages, railroads, mines, and forests that had been ruined by the war. From 1926 to 1929, France was relatively prosperous; industrial and agricultural production expanded, tourism increased, and the currency was stable. Although France did not feel the Great Depression as painfully as did the United States and Germany, the nation was hurt by the decline in trade and production and the rise in unemployment.

The political instability that had beset the Third Republic virtually since its inception continued, and hostility to the republic mounted. As the leading parties failed to solve the nation's problems, a number of fascist-type groups gained strength. On February 6, 1934, right-wing gangs threatened to invade the Chamber of Deputies. What brought on the crisis was the exposure of the shady dealings of Alexander Stavisky, a financial manipulator with high government connections. The resultant violence left hundreds wounded and several dead. The whole affair was too poorly organized to constitute a serious threat to the government. But to the parties of the left—socialists, communists, and radicals—the events of February 6–7 constituted a rightist attempt to establish a fascist regime.

Fear of growing fascist strength at home and in Italy and Germany led the parties of the left to form the Popular Front. In 1936, Léon Blum (1872–1950), a socialist and a Jew, became premier. Blum's Popular Front government instituted more reforms than any other ministry in the history of the Third Republic. To end a wave of strikes that tied up production, Blum gave workers a forty-hour week and holidays with pay and guaranteed them the right to collective bargaining. He took steps to nationalize the armaments and aircraft industries. To reduce the influence of the wealthiest families, he put the Bank of France under government control. By raising prices and buying wheat, he aided farmers. Conservatives and fascists denounced Blum as a Jewish socialist who was converting the fatherland into a communist state. "Better Hitler than Blum," grumbled French rightists.

Despite significant reforms, the Popular Front could not revitalize the economy. In 1937, the Blum ministry was overthrown and the Popular Front, always a tenuous alliance, fell apart. Through democratic means the Blum government had tried to give France its own New Deal, but the social reforms passed by the Popular Front only intensified hatred between the working classes and the rest of the nation. France had preserved democracy against the onslaught of domestic fascists, but it was a demoralized and divided nation that confronted a united and dynamic Nazi Germany.

Notes

1. Quoted in Zeev Sternhill, "Fascist Ideology," in Walter Laqueur, *Fascism: A Reader's Guide* (Berkeley: University of California Press, 1976), p. 338.

2. Quoted in John Weiss, *The Fascist Tradition* (New York: Harper & Row, 1967), p. 9.

3. F. L. Carsten, *The Rise of Fascism* (Berkeley: University of California Press, 1969), p. 53.

4. Quoted in Max Gallo, *Mussolini's Italy* (New York: Macmillan, 1973), p. 218.

5. Kurt Sontheimer, "Anti-Democratic Thought in the Weimar Republic," in *The Path to Dictatorship, 1918–1933*, trans. by John Conway with an introduction by Fritz Stern (Garden City, N.Y.: Doubleday Anchor Books, 1966), pp. 48–49.

6. Quoted in Joachim C. Fest, *Hitler,* trans. by Richard and Clara Winston (New York: Harcourt Brace Jovanovich, 1974), p. 162.

7. Quoted in Karl J. Newman, *European Democracy between the Wars* (Notre Dame, Ind.: University of Notre Dame Press, 1971), p. 276.

8. Hajo Holborn, *Germany and Europe* (Garden City, N.Y.: Doubleday, Anchor Books, 1971), p. 215.

9. Fest, *Hitler,* p. 548.

10. Quoted in Alan Bullock, *Hitler: A Study in Tyranny* (New York: Harper Torchbooks, 1964), p. 400.

11. *Hitler's Secret Conversations, 1941–1944,* with an introductory essay by H. R. Trevor Roper (New York: Farrar, Straus & Young, 1953), p. 28.

12. Quoted in Lucy S. Dawidowicz, *The War Against the Jews, 1933–1945* (New York: Holt, Rinehart and Winston, 1975), p. 21.

13. Adolf Hitler, *Mein Kampf* (Boston: Houghton Mifflin, 1962), p. 107.

14. Ibid., p. 479.

15. Cited in Ian Kershaw, "Hitler and the Germans," in Richard Bessel, ed., *Life in the Third Reich* (New York: Oxford University Press, 1987), pp. 43–44.

16. Quoted in J. S. Conway, *The Nazi Persecution of the Churches* (New York: Basic Books, 1968), p. 202.

17. Quoted in Helmut Krausnick, Hans Buchheim, Martin Broszart, and Hans-Adolf Jacobsen, *Anatomy of the SS State* (London: Collins, 1968), p. 128.

18. Karl Dietrich Bracher, *The German Dictatorship,* trans. by Jean Steinberg (New York: Praeger, 1970), p. 243.

19. *Hitler's Secret Conversations,* p. 6.

20. Quoted in Hans Rothfels, "Resistance Begins," in *The Path to Dictatorship*, pp. 160–161.

21. Quoted in Guenter Lewy, *The Catholic Church and Nazi Germany* (New York: McGraw-Hill, 1965), p. 226.

22. Quoted in Hermann Graml, et al., *The German Resistance to Hitler* (Berkeley: University of California Press, 1970), p. 206.

23. Quoted in Conway, *The Nazi Persecution of the Churches*, p. 332.

24. Excerpted in George L. Mosse, ed., *Nazi Culture* (New York: Grosset & Dunlap, 1966), pp. 206–207.

25. Bracher, *The German Dictatorship*, pp. 248, 251.

26. Quoted in T. L. Jarman, *The Rise and Fall of Nazi Germany* (New York: New York University Press, 1956), p. 182.

27. Quoted in Horst von Maltitz, *The Evolution of Hitler's Germany* (New York: McGraw-Hill, 1973), pp. 433–434.

28. Ibid., pp. 438–439.

29. Quoted in Bracher, *The German Dictatorship*, p. 268.

30. Quoted in Fest, *Hitler*, p. 532.

Suggested Reading

Allen, William Sheridan, *The Nazi Seizure of Power* (1965). An illuminating study of how the people of a small German town reacted to Nazism during the years 1930–1935.

Bissel, Richard, ed., *Life in the Third Reich* (1987). Essays dealing with various aspects of life in Hitler's Germany; good overviews.

Bracher, Karl Dietrich, *The German Dictatorship* (1970). A highly regarded analysis of all phases of the Nazi state.

Broszat, Martin, *The Hitler State* (1981). A detailed anatomy of the internal structure of the Third Reich.

Bucheim, Heim, *Totalitarian Rule* (1968). Nature and characteristics of totalitarianism, by a German scholar.

Bullock, Alan, *Hitler: A Study in Tyranny* (1964). An excellent biography.

Cassels, Alan, *Fascist Italy* (1968). A clearly written introduction.

Conway, J. S., *The Nazi Persecution of the Churches* (1968). Nazi persecution of the churches and the capitulation of the clergy.

Fest, Joachim C., *Hitler* (1974). An excellent biography.

Haffner, Sebastian, *The Meaning of Hitler* (1979). A German journalist's inquiry into Hitler's successes and failures.

Jackel, Eberhard, *Hitler's Weltanschauung* (1972). An analysis of Hitler's world-view.

Kirkpatrick, Ivone, *Mussolini: A Study in Power* (1964). A solid biography.

Laqueur, Walter, ed., *Fascism: A Reader's Guide* (1976). A superb collection of essays.

Mack Smith, Denis, *Mussolini* (1982). By a leading historian of modern Italy.

Maltitz, Horst von, *The Evolution of Hitler's Germany* (1973). In trying to explain how it was possible, the author discusses the German roots of Nazism.

Mayer, Milton, *They Thought They Were Free* (1955). The lives of ordinary citizens who became Nazis.

Mosse, George L., *Nazi Culture* (1966). A representative collection of Nazi writings with a fine introduction.

Paxton, Robert O., *Europe in the Twentieth Century* (1975). A first-rate text with an excellent bibliography.

Rogger, Hans, and Eugen Weber, eds., *The European Right* (1966). A valuable collection of essays on right-wing movements in various European countries.

Spielvogel, Jackson J., *Hitler and Nazi Germany* (1988). Clearly written, up-to-date survey.

Turner, Henry A., ed., *Reappraisals of Fascism*. A collection of useful essays.

Review Questions

1. How did fascist principles "stand for the sheer, categorical, definitive antithesis to the world of democracy . . . to the world which still abides by the fundamental principles laid down in 1789"?

2. Why did some Italians support Mussolini?

3. How did Mussolini bluff his way to power?

4. How did Mussolini try to extend his control over Italy?

5. What were Mussolini's policies toward the church? The economy?

6. In what ways was Mussolini less effective than Hitler in establishing a totalitarian state?

7. How was Hitler's outlook shaped by his experiences in Vienna?

8. What was the significance of the Munich Putsch of 1923?

9. What were Hitler's attitudes toward democracy, the masses, war, the Jews, propaganda?

10. Why did Hitler's views prove attractive to Germans?

11. How was Hitler able to gain power?

12. How did the Nazis extend their control over Germany?

13. How did Nazism conflict with the core values of Christianity? What was the general policy of the Nazis toward the churches? Why did the German churches generally fail to take a stand against the Nazi regime?

14. What was the purpose of the giant rallies?

15. By 1939, most Germans were enthusiastic about the Nazi regime. Explain this statement.

16. What lessons might democratic societies draw from the experience of fascist totalitarianism?

17. After World War I, in country after country, parliamentary democracy collapsed and authoritarian leaders came to power. Explain.

18. How did the United States, Britain, and France try to cope with the Great Depression?

33

Thought and Culture in an Era of World Wars: Disorientation, Doubt, and Commitment

T he presuppositions of the Enlightenment, already eroding in the decades prior to the Great War, seemed near collapse after 1918—another casualty of trench warfare. Westerners no longer possessed a frame of reference, a common outlook for understanding nature, themselves, their times, or the past. The triumph of Bolshevism in Russia, the emergence of fascism—both directly linked to the Great War—and the depression also profoundly disoriented the European mind.

There were a variety of responses to this crisis of consciousness. Some intellectuals succumbed to despair or found escape in their art. Others sought a new hope in the Soviet experiment or in fascism; still others reaffirmed the rational-humanist tradition of the Enlightenment. Christian thinkers, repelled by the secularism, materialism, and rootlessness of the modern age, urged Westerners to find renewed meaning and purpose in their ancestral religion. A philosophical movement, called existentialism, aspired to make life authentic in a world stripped of universal values.

Intellectuals and Artists in Troubled Times

Postwar Pessimism

After the Great War, Europeans looked at themselves and their civilization differently. It seemed that in science and technology Europeans had unleashed powers they could not control and that belief in the stability and security of European civilization was an illusion. Also illusory was the expectation that reason would banish surviving signs of darkness, ignorance, and injustice and usher in an age of continual progress. European

Salvador Dali (1904–1989): *Apparition of Face and Fruit-dish on a Beach.* (*Wadsworth Atheneum, Hartford. The Ella Gallup Sumner and Mary Catlin Sumner Collection*)

745

intellectuals felt they were living in a "broken world." In an age of heightened brutality and mobilized irrationality, the values of old Europe seemed beyond recovery. "All the great words," wrote D. H. Lawrence, "were cancelled out for that generation."[1] The fissures discernible in European civilization prior to 1914 had grown wider and deeper. To be sure, Europe also had its optimists—those who found reason for hope in the League of Nations and in the easing of international tensions and improved economic conditions in the mid-1920s. However, the Great Depression and the triumph of totalitarianism intensified feelings of doubt and disillusionment.

The somber mood that gripped European intellectuals in the immediate postwar period had been anticipated by Freud in 1915, when he wrote:

> We cannot but feel that no event has ever destroyed so much that is precious in the common possessions of humanity, confused so many of the clearest intelligences or so thoroughly debased what is highest. . . . the war in which we had refused to believe broke out, and it brought—disillusionment. . . . It tramples in blind fury on all that comes in its way, as though there were to be no future and no peace among men after it is over. It cuts all the common bonds between the contending peoples, and threatens to leave a legacy of embitterment that will make any renewal of these bonds impossible for a long time to come.[2]

A pessimistic outlook also pervaded Freud's *Civilization and Its Discontents* (1930), in which he held that civilized life was forever threatened by the antisocial and irrational elements of human nature. Other expressions of pessimism abounded. In 1919, Paul Valéry stated: "We modern civilizations have learned to recognize that we are mortal like the others. We feel that a civilization is as fragile as life."[3] "We are living today under the sign of the collapse of civilization,"[4] declared humanitarian Albert Schweitzer in 1923. "There is a growing awareness of imminent ruin tantamount to a dread of the approaching end of all that makes life worthwhile,"[5] said German philosopher Karl Jaspers in 1932. The novels of Aldous Huxley rejected belief in progress and expressed a disenchantment with the modern

world. Ernest Hemingway's *The Sun Also Rises* (1926) described a lost postwar generation. In Erich Maria Remarque's *All Quiet on the Western Front* (1929), a German soldier ponders the war's impact on youth.

> I am twenty years old; yet I know nothing of life but despair, death, fear, and fatuous superficiality cast over an abyss of sorrow. I see how peoples are set against one another, and in silence, unknowingly, foolishly, obediently, innocently slay one another. I see that the keenest brains of the world invent weapons and words to make it yet more refined and enduring. . . . all my generation is experiencing these things with me. . . . What do they expect of us if a time ever comes when the war is over? Through the years our business has been killing. . . . Our knowledge of life is limited to death. What will happen afterwards?[6]

In "The Second Coming" (1919), William Butler Yeats conveyed this sense of dark times:

> Mere anarchy is loosed upon the world,
> The blood-dimmed tide is loosed, and everywhere
> The Ceremony of innocence is drowned;
> The best lack all conviction, while the worst
> Are full of passionate intensity.
> Surely some revelation is at hand
> Surely the Second Coming is at hand.[7]

T. S. Eliot's "The Waste Land" (1922) is pervaded by the image of a collapsing European civilization. Eliot creates a macabre scenario. Hooded hordes, modern-day barbarians, swarm over plains and lay waste cities. Jerusalem, Athens, Alexandria, Vienna, and London—each once a great spiritual or cultural center—are now "falling towers." Amid this destruction, one hears "high in the air / Murmur of maternal lamentation."[8]

Carl Gustav Jung, a Swiss psychologist who broke with Freud, said in *Modern Man in Search of a Soul* (1933):

> I believe I am not exaggerating when I say that modern man has suffered an almost fatal

shock, psychologically speaking, and as a result has fallen into profound uncertainty. . . . The revolution in our conscious outlook, brought about by the catastrophic results of the World War, shows itself in our inner life by the shattering of our faith in ourselves and our own worth. . . . I realize only too well that I am losing my faith in the possibility of a rational organization of the world, the old dream of the millennium, in which peace and harmony should rule, has grown pale.[9]

In 1936, Dutch historian Johan Huizinga wrote in a chapter entitled "Apprehension of Doom":

We are living in a demented world. And we know it. . . . Everywhere there are doubts as to the solidity of our social structure, vague fears of the imminent future, a feeling that our civilization is on the way to ruin. . . . almost all things which once seemed sacred and immutable have now become unsettled, truth and humanity, justice and reason. . . . The sense of living in the midst of a violent crisis of civilization, threatening complete collapse, has spread far and wide.[10]

The most influential expression of pessimism was Oswald Spengler's *The Decline of the West*. The first volume was published in July 1918 as the Great War was drawing to a close, and the second volume in 1922. The work achieved instant notoriety, particularly in Spengler's native Germany, which was shattered by defeat. Spengler viewed history as an assemblage of many different cultures that, like living organisms, experience birth, youth, maturity, and death. What contemporaries pondered most was Spengler's insistence that Western civilization had entered its final stage and that its death could not be averted.

Spengler defined a culture as a spiritual orientation that pervades a people's literature, art, religion, philosophy, politics, and economics; each culture has a distinctive style that distinguishes it from another culture. The ancient Greeks, said Spengler, viewed themselves as living in a clearly defined and finite world. Hence classical sculpture was characterized by the life-sized nude statue, architecture by the temple with small columns,

and political life by the small city-state rather than by a kingdom or an empire. Modern Westerners have a different cultural orientation, said Spengler; they exude a Faustian urge to expand, to reach out. Thus Europeans developed perspectival art that permits distance to be depicted on a canvas; they sailed the oceans, conquered vast regions of the globe, and communicated over great distances by telephone and telegraph.

Spengler maintained that cultures, like biological organisms, pass through necessary stages—a heroic youth, a creative maturity, and a decadent old age. In its youth, during the Renaissance, said Spengler, Western culture experienced the triumphs of Michelangelo, Shakespeare, and Galileo; in its maturity, during the eighteenth century, Western culture reached its creative height in the music of Mozart, the poetry of Goethe, and the philosophy of Kant. But now, Faustian culture, entering old age, shows signs of decay—a growing materialism and skepticism, a disenchanted proletariat, rampant warfare and competition for empire, decadent art forms. "Of great painting or great music there can no longer be, for Western people, any question,"[11] concluded Spengler.

To an already troubled Western world, Spengler offered no solace. The West, like other cultures and like any living organism, is destined to die; its decline is irreversible, its death inevitable, and the symptoms of degeneration are already evident. Spengler's gloomy prognostication buttressed the fascists, who claimed that they were creating a new civilization on the ruins of a dying European civilization.

Literature and Art: Innovation, Disillusionment, and Social Commentary

Postwar pessimism did not prevent writers and artists from perpetuating the cultural innovations initiated before the war. In the works of D. H. Lawrence, Marcel Proust, André Gide, James Joyce, Franz Kafka, T. S. Eliot, and Thomas Mann, the modernist movement achieved a brilliant flowering. Often these writers gave expression to the troubles and uncertainties of the postwar period.

Franz Kafka (1883–1924), whose major novels, *The Trial* and *The Castle,* were published after his death, did not receive recognition until after World War II. Yet perhaps better than any other novelist of his generation, Kafka grasped the dilemma of the modern age. In Kafka's world, human beings strive to make sense out of life, but everywhere ordinary occurrences thwart them. They are caught in a bureaucratic web that they cannot control; they live in a nightmare society dominated by oppressive, cruel, and corrupt officials and amoral torturers—a world where power is exercised without limits and traditional values and ordinary logic do not operate. In *The Trial,* for example, the hero is arrested and eventually executed without knowing why. In these observations, Kafka proved a prophet of the emerging totalitarian state. (Kafka's three sisters perished in the Holocaust.)

Kafka, a German-speaking Jew in the alien Slav environment of Czechoslovakia, was intimidated by a tyrannical father. At a young age he contracted tuberculosis, from which he died. In giving expression to his own deep anxieties, he expressed the feelings of alienation and isolation that characterize the modern individual; he explored life's dreads and absurdities, offering no solutions or consolation. In Kafka's works people are defeated and unable to comprehend the irrational forces that contribute to their destruction. The mind yearns for coherence but, Kafka tells us, uncertainty, if not chaos, governs human relationships. We can neither be certain of our own identities or of the world we encounter, for human beings are the playthings of forces too unfathomable to comprehend, too irrational to master.

Before World War I, the German writer Thomas Mann (1875–1955) had earned a reputation for his short stories and novels, particularly *Buddenbrooks* (1901), which portrayed the decline of a prosperous bourgeois family. At the outbreak of the war, Mann was a staunch conservative who disliked democracy; after the war he drew closer to the values of the Western liberal-humanist tradition, supporting the Weimar Republic and attacking the Nazi cult of irrationalism. After Hitler's seizure of power, Mann went to Switzerland and eventually to the United States, where he remained a resolute foe of totalitarianism.

In the *Magic Mountain* (1924), Mann reflected on the decomposition of bourgeois European civilization. The setting for the story is a Swiss sanitarium, whose patients, drawn from several European lands, suffer from tuberculosis. The sanitarium symbolizes Europe, and it is the European psyche that is diseased.

One patient, the Italian Ludovico Settembrini, stands for the humanist ideals of the Enlightenment—reason, individual liberty, and progress. Although Mann is sympathetic to these ideals, he also indicts Settembrini for his naive faith in progress, his shallow view of human nature, which gives little significance to the will, and his lofty rhetoric. Seeing the human being as purely rational, Settembrini foolishly believes that people will mend their ways once they are enlightened by reason's sweet voice. Thus, he even claims that merely by looking at a sick person "rationally," he cured him.

Pitted against Settembrini is Leo Naphta, a Spanish-trained Jesuit of Jewish-Polish descent who rejects completely the Italian's liberal-humanist values. He is an authoritarian who insists that people do not need freedom but authority, whether it be the state or God; he is a fanatic who subscribes to torture and terror. Believing that the dictatorship of the proletariat is the means of salvation demanded by the age, Naphta embraces Marxism. Borrowing from medieval mysticism, Nietzschean irrationalism, and Marxist militancy, he attacks every facet of the existing order.

Mynheer Peeperkorn, a wealthy Dutch planter from Java, is nonintellectual, illogical, and inarticulate, but he radiates pure vitality and emotional intensity. This charismatic personality dwarfs the humanist and the authoritarian and dominates the patients, who find him irresistible.

The *Magic Mountain* raised, but did not resolve, crucial questions. Was the epoch of rational-humanist culture drawing to a close? Did Europeans welcome their spiritual illness in the same way that some of the patients in the sanitarium had a will-to-illness? How could Europe rescue itself from decadence?

D. H. Lawrence (1885–1930), the son of an illiterate British coal miner, was saddened and angered by the consequences of industrial society—the deterioration of nature, tedious work divorced from personal satisfaction, a life-denying quest for wealth and possessions. He looked back longingly on preindustrial England and wanted people to reorient their thinking away from moneymaking and suppression of the instincts. In *Lady Chatterley's Lover* (1928) and other works he dealt with the clash between industrial civilization and the needs of human nature, between regimentation and passion.

Like nineteenth-century romantics, Lawrence found a higher truth in deep-seated passion than in reason; this led him to rail against Christianity for stifling human sexuality. Like Nietzsche, he believed that excessive intellectualizing destroyed the life-affirming, instinctual part of human nature. In 1913 he wrote:

> My great religion is a belief in the blood, the flesh, as being wiser than the intellect. We can go wrong in our minds. But what our blood feels and believes and says is always true. The intellect is only a bit and a bridle. What do I care about knowledge. All I want is to answer to my blood without fribbling intervention of mind, or moral, or what not. . . . We have got so ridiculously mindful, that we never know that we ourselves are anything.[12]

Many writers, shattered by World War I, disgusted by fascism's growing strength, and moved by the terrible suffering of the depression, became committed to social and political causes. Erich Maria Remarque's *All Quiet on the Western Front* (1929) was one of many antiwar novels. In *The Grapes of Wrath* (1939), John Steinbeck captured the suffering of American farmers driven from their land by the Dust Bowl and foreclosure during the depression. George Orwell's *The Road to Wigan Pier* (1937) recorded the bleak lives of English coal miners. Few issues stirred the conscience of intellectuals as did the Spanish Civil War, and many of them volunteered to fight with the Spanish republicans against the fascists. Ernest Hemingway's *For Whom the Bell Tolls* (1940) expressed the sentiments of these thinkers. In *Mario and the Magician* (1930), Thomas Mann explicitly attacked fascism and implied that it would have to be resisted by arms.

The new directions taken in art before World War I—abstractionism and expression—con-

Thomas Mann (1875–1955) at the Danubian Congress, New York, 1938. In his novel *Buddenbrooks* (1901), Mann chronicled the decay of a prosperous commercial family. In *The Magic Mountain* (1924), he probed the minds of patients in a tuberculosis sanatorium. These people were symbols of an equally diseased Europe. (*AP/Wide World Photos*)

tinued in the postwar decades. Picasso, Mondrian, Kandinsky, Matisse, Rouault, Braque, Modigliani, and other masters continued to refine their styles. In addition, new art trends emerged that mirrored the trauma of a generation that had experienced the war and lost its faith in Europe's moral and intellectual values. (See color insert "The Emergence of Modern Art.")

In 1915 in Zurich, artists and writers founded a movement called Dada to express their revulsion against the war and the civilization that spawned it. From neutral Switzerland, the movement spread to Germany and Paris. Dada shared in the postwar mood of disorientation and despair.

Marcel Duchamp (1887–1968): Bicycle Wheel, 1951. Dadaist Marcel Duchamp turned his back on a world that had gone insane in World War I. The irrational subject in art became the norm; the artist's intention was to shock and scandalize. Art began an exploration of a world of chaos. *(Third version, after lost original of 1913. Assemblage: metal wheel and painted wood stool, overall height 50½". Collection, The Museum of Modern Art, New York. The Sidney and Harriet Janis Collection)*

Dadaists viewed life as essentially absurd (*Dada* is a nonsense term) and cultivated indifference. "The acts of life have no beginning or end. Everything happens in a completely idiotic way,"[13] declared the poet Tristan Tzara, one of Dada's founders and its chief spokesman. Dadaists expressed contempt for artistic and literary standards and rejected both God and reason. "Through reason man becomes a tragic and ugly figure,"

said one Dadaist; "beauty is dead," said another. Tzara declared:

> What good did the theories of the philosophers do us? Did they help us to take a single step forward or backward? . . . We have had enough of the intelligent movements that have stretched beyond measure our credulity in the benefits of science. What we want now is spontaneity because everything that issues freely from ourselves, without the intervention of speculative ideas, . . . represents us.[14]

For Dadaists the world was nonsensical and reality disordered; hence they offered no solutions to anything. "Like everything in life, Dada is useless,"[15] said Tzara.

Dadaists showed their contempt for art (one art historian calls Dada "the first anti-art movement on record"[16]) by deliberately producing works devoid of artistic value. Marcel Duchamp's *Bicycle Wheel* is an example, as is his Mona Lisa with a mustache. Despite the Dadaists' nihilistic aims and "calculated irrationality," says art historian H. W. Janson, "there was also liberation, a voyage into unknown provinces of the creative mind." Thus Duchamp's painting with the nonsense title *Tu m'* was "dazzlingly inventive [and] far ahead of its time."[17]

Dada ended as a formal movement in 1924 and was succeeded by surrealism. Surrealists inherited from Dada a contempt for reason; they stressed fantasy and made use of Freudian insights and symbols in their art to reproduce the raw state of the unconscious and to arrive at truths beyond reason's grasp. To penetrate the interior of the mind, said André Breton, a French surrealist poet, the writer should "write quickly without any previously chosen subject, quickly enough not to dwell on and not to be tempted to read over what you have written."[18] Writing should not be dictated by the intellect but should flow automatically from the unconscious. Surrealists tried to portray the world of fantasy and hallucination, the marvelous and the spontaneous. Breton urged artists to live their dreams, even if it meant seeing "a horse galloping on a tomato." In their attempt to break through the constraints of rationality in order to reach a higher reality—that is, a "Surreality"—leading surrealists like Max Ernst (1891–

1976), Salvador Dali (1904–1989)—see page 744—and Joan Miró (1893–1983) produced works of undeniable artistic merit.

Artists, like writers, expressed a social conscience. George Grosz combined a Dadaist sense of life's meaninglessness with a new realism to depict the moral degeneration of middle-class German society. In *After the Questioning* (1935), Grosz, then living in the United States, dramatized Nazi brutality; in *The End of the World* (1936) he expressed his fear of another impending world war. Still another German artist, Käthe Kollwitz, showed a deep compassion for the sufferer—the unemployed, the hungry, the ill, the politically oppressed (see page 687).

In a series of paintings, *The Passion of Sacco and Vanzetti* (1931–32), American artist Ben Shahn showed his outrage at the execution of two radicals. William Gropper's *Migration* (1932) dramatized the suffering of the same dispossessed farmers described in Steinbeck's novel *The Grapes of Wrath*. Philip Evergood, in *Don't Cry Mother* (1938–1944), portrayed the apathy of starving children and their mother's terrible helplessness.

In his etchings of maimed, dying, and dead soldiers, German artist Otto Dix produced a powerful visual indictment of the Great War's cruelty and suffering. In *Guernica* (1937), Picasso memorialized the Spanish village decimated by saturation bombing during the Spanish Civil War. In the *White Crucifixion* (1938), Marc Chagall, a Russian-born Jew who had settled in Paris, depicted the terror and flight of Jews in Nazi Germany.

Communism: "The God That Failed"

The economic misery of the depression and the rise of fascist barbarism led many intellectuals to find a new hope, even a secular faith, in communism. They praised the Soviet Union for supplanting capitalist greed with socialist cooperation, for replacing a haphazard economic system marred by repeated depressions with one based on planned production, and for providing employment for everyone when joblessness was endemic in capitalist lands. American literary critic Edmund Wilson said that in the Soviet Union, one felt at the "moral top of the world where the light never really goes out."[19] British political theorists Sidney and Beatrice Webb declared that there was no other country "in which there is actually so much widespread public criticism and such incessant reevaluation of its shortcomings as in the USSR."[20] To these intellectuals, it seemed that in the Soviet Union a vigorous and healthy civilization was emerging and that only communism could stem the tide of fascism. For many, however, the attraction was short-lived. Sickened by Stalin's purges and terror, the denial of individual freedom, and the suppression of truth, they came to view the Soviet Union as another totalitarian state and communism as another "god that failed."

One such intellectual was Arthur Koestler. Born in Budapest of Jewish ancestry and educated in Vienna, Koestler worked as a correspondent for a leading Berlin newspaper chain. He joined the Communist party at the very end of 1931 because he "lived in a disintegrating society thirsting for faith," was moved by the depression, and saw communism as the "only force capable of resisting the onrush of the primitive [Nazi] horde."[21] Koestler visited the Soviet Union in 1933, experiencing firsthand both the starvation brought on by forced collectivization and the propaganda that grotesquely misrepresented life in Western lands. Although his faith was shaken, he did not break with the party until 1938 in response to Stalin's liquidations.

In *Darkness at Noon* (1941), Koestler explored the attitudes of the Old Bolsheviks who were imprisoned, tortured, and executed by Stalin. These dedicated communists had served the party faithfully, but Stalin, fearful of opposition, hateful of intellectuals, and driven by megalomania, denounced them as enemies of the people. In *Darkness at Noon*, the leading character, the imprisoned Rubashov, is a composite of the Old Bolsheviks. Although innocent, and without being tortured, Rubashov publicly confesses to political crimes that he never committed.

Rubashov is aware of the suffering that the party has brought to the Russian people:

> . . . *in the interests of a just distribution of land we deliberately let die of starvation about five million farmers and their families in one*

year. . . . [to liberate] human beings from the shackles of industrial exploitation . . . we sent about ten million people to do forced labour in the Arctic regions and the jungles of the East, under conditions similar to those of antique galley slaves. . . . to settle a difference of opinion, we know only one argument: death. . . . Our poets settle discussions on questions of style by denunciations to the secret police. . . . The people's standard of life is lower than it was before the Revolution, the labour conditions are harder, the discipline is more inhuman. . . . Our Press and our schools cultivate Chauvinism, militarism, dogmatism, conformism and ignorance. The arbitrary power of the Government is unlimited, and unexampled in history. Freedom of the Press, of opinion and of movement are as thoroughly exterminated as though the proclamation of the Rights of Man had never been. We have built up the most gigantic police apparatus, with informers made a national institution, and with the most refined scientific system of physical and mental torture. We whip the groaning masses of the country towards a theoretical future happiness, which only we can see.[22]

Nevertheless, Rubashov remains the party's faithful servant; true believers do not easily break with their faith. By confessing, Rubashov performs his last service for the Revolution: for the true believer, everything—truth, justice, and the sanctity of the individual—are properly sacrificed to the party.

Reaffirming the Christian Philosophy of History

By calling into question core liberal beliefs—the essential goodness of human nature, the primacy of reason, the efficacy of science, and the inevitability of progress—the Great War led thinkers to find in Christianity an alternative view of the human experience and the crisis of the twentieth century. Christian thinkers, including Karl Barth, Paul Tillich, Reinhold Niebuhr, and T. S. Eliot, asserted the reality of evil in human nature and assailed liberals and Marxists for postulating a

purely rational and secular philosophy of history and for anticipating an ideal society within the realm of historical time. In the Christian conception of history as a clash between human will and God's commands, these thinkers found an intelligible explanation for the tragedies of the twentieth century. In 1933, Christopher Dawson, an English Catholic thinker, wrote:

> *If our civilization is to recover its vitality, or even to survive, it must cease to neglect its spiritual roots and must realize that religion is not a matter of personal sentiment which has nothing to do with the objective realities of society, but is, on the contrary, the very heart of social life and the root of every living culture.[23]*

In 1934, the British historian Arnold Toynbee published the first three volumes of his monumental *A Study of History*, in which he tried to account for the rise, growth, breakdown, and disintegration of civilization. Underlying Toynbee's philosophy of history was a religious orientation, for he saw religious prophets as humanity's greatest figures and higher religions as humanity's greatest achievement. Toynbee attributed the problems of Western civilization to its breaking away from Christianity and embracing of "false idols," particularly the national state which, he said, had become the object of Westerners' highest reverence.

Toynbee regarded nationalism as a primitive religion that induces people to revere the national community rather than God. This deification of the parochial—tribal or local—community intensifies the brutal side of human nature and provokes wars among people sharing a common civilization. To Toynbee, Nazism was the culmination of the worst elements in modern European nationalism, "the consummation . . . of a politico-religious movement, the pagan deification and worship of parochial human communities which had been gradually gaining ground for more than four centuries in the Western world at large."[24] The moral catastrophe of Nazism, he said, demonstrates the inadequacy of liberal humanism, for the Enlightenment tradition proved a feeble barrier to Nazism's rise and spread. The secular values of the Enlightenment, divorced from Christianity, are insufficient to restrain human nature's basest impulses. For the West to save itself, said Toynbee, it must abide by the spiritual values of its religious prophets.

Reaffirming the Ideals of Reason and Freedom

Several thinkers tried to reaffirm the ideals of rationality and freedom that had been trampled on by totalitarian movements. In *The Treason of the Intellectuals* (1927), Julien Benda, a French cultural critic of Jewish background, castigated intellectuals for intensifying hatred between nations, classes, and political factions. "Our age is indeed the age of the *intellectual organization of political hatreds*,"[25] he wrote. These intellectuals, said Benda, do not pursue justice or truth, but proclaim that "even if our country is wrong, we must think of it in the right."[26] They scorn outsiders, extol harshness and action, and proclaim the superiority of instinct and will to intelligence; or they "assert that the intelligence to be venerated is that which limits its activities within the bounds of national interest."[27] The logical end of this xenophobia, said Benda, "is the organized slaughter of nations and classes."[28]

José Ortega y Gasset, descendant of a noble Spanish family and a professor of philosophy, gained international recognition with the publication of *The Revolt of the Masses* (1930). Ortega held that European civilization, the product of a creative elite, was degenerating into barbarism because of the growing power of the masses, who lack the mental discipline and commitment to reason to preserve Europe's intellectual and cultural traditions. Ortega did not equate the masses with the working class and the elite with the nobility; it was an attitude of mind, not a class affiliation, that distinguished the "mass-man" from the elite. The mass-man, said Ortega, has a commonplace mind and does not set high standards for himself. He is inert until driven by an external compulsion. Faced with a problem, he "is satisfied with thinking the first thing he finds in his head" and "crushes . . . everything that is different, everything that is excellent, individual, qualified, and select. Anybody who is not like everybody, who does not think like everybody, runs the risk of

being eliminated."[29] Such intellectually vulgar people, declared Ortega, cannot understand or preserve the processes of civilization. The fascists exemplify this revolt of the masses:

Under fascism there appears for the first time in Europe a type of man who does not want to give reasons or to be right, but simply shows himself resolved to impose his opinions. This is the new thing: the right not to be reasonable, the "reason of unreason." Hence I see the most palpable manifestation of the new mentality of the masses, due to their having decided to rule society without the capacity for doing so.[30]

The mass-man, said Ortega, does not respect the tradition of reason; he does not enter into rational dialogue with others or defend his opinions logically.

[Because his thoughts are] nothing more than appetites in words. . . . the mass-man would feel himself lost if he accepted discussion. . . . Hence the "new thing" in Europe is to have done with discussions, and detestation is expressed for all forms of intercommunion which implies acceptance of objective standards, ranging from conversation to Parliament, and taking in science. This means that there is a renunciation of the common life based on culture which is subject to standards, and a return to the common life of barbarism.[31]

The mass-man rejects reason and glorifies violence—the ultimate expression of barbarism. If European civilization is to be rescued from fascism and communism, said Ortega, the elite must sustain civilized values and provide leadership for the masses.

Ernst Cassirer, a German philosopher of Jewish lineage, emigrated after Hitler came to power, eventually settling in the United States. A staunch defender of the Enlightenment tradition, Cassirer wrote in 1932, just prior to Hitler's triumph:

More than ever before, it seems to me, the time is again ripe for applying . . . self-criticism to the present age, for holding up to it

Marcel Gromaire: The War, 1925. The shapes of art in the 1920s and 1930s often found inspiration in machines. Some would celebrate a world of mechanized efficiency. Gromaire saw that man had turned into a frighteningly efficient killing machine. (*Cliché: Musée de la Ville de Paris/© ARS N.Y./SPADEM 1988*)

that bright clear mirror fashioned by the Enlightenment. . . . The age which venerated reason and science as man's highest faculty cannot and must not be lost even for us. We must find a way not only to see that age in its own shape but to release again those original forces which brought forth and molded this shape.[32]

In his last work, *The Myth of the State* (1946), Cassirer described Nazism as the triumph of mythical thinking over reason. The Nazis, said Cassirer, cleverly manufactured myths—of the race, the leader, the party, the state—that disoriented the intellect. Germans who embraced these myths surrendered their capacity for independent judgment, leaving themselves vulnerable to manipulation by the Nazi leadership. Cassirer warned:

In politics we are always living on volcanic soil. We must be prepared for convulsions and eruptions. In all critical moments of man's social life, the rational forces that resist the rise of old mythical conceptions are no longer sure of themselves. In these moments the time of myth has come again. For myth has not been really vanquished and subjugated. It is always there, lurking in the dark and waiting for its hour and opportunity. This hour comes as soon as the other binding forces of man's social life . . . lose their strength and are no longer able to combat the demonic mythical powers.[33]

To contain the destructive powers of political myths, Cassirer urged strengthening the rational-humanist tradition and called for the critical study of political myths, for "in order to fight an enemy you must know him. . . . We should carefully study the origin, the structure, the methods, and the technique of the political myths. We should see the adversary face to face in order to know how to combat him."[34]

Like Cassirer, and many other German-Jewish intellectuals, Erich Fromm, a social theorist and psychoanalyst, settled in the United States after the Nazi seizure of power. In *Escape from Freedom* (1941), Fromm sought to explain the triumph of Nazism within the larger context of European history. With the end of the Middle Ages, he said, the individual grew increasingly independent of external authority and experienced new possibilities for personal development. The individual's role in the social order was no longer rigorously determined by birth; increasingly the world was explained in natural terms, freeing people from magic, mystery, and authority; and the possibility for the full development of human potential here on earth was proclaimed. In the political sphere, this new orientation culminated in the democratic state. However, while Westerners were becoming more "independent, self-reliant, and critical," they also became "more isolated, alone, and afraid."[35]

During the Middle Ages, said Fromm, the individual derived a sense of security from a structured social system that clearly defined the role of clergy, lords, serfs, and guildsmen and from a Christian world-view that made life and death purposeful. Modern Westerners have lost this sense of security. Dwelling in vast cities, threatened by economic crises, no longer comforted by the medieval conception of life's purpose, they often are tormented by doubts and overwhelmed by feelings of aloneness and insignificance. People try to overcome this "burden of freedom" by surrendering themselves to a person or power that they view "as being overwhelmingly strong"; they trade freedom for security by entering into "a symbiotic relationship that overcomes . . . aloneness."[36]

Because modern industrial society has made the individual feel powerless and insignificant, concluded Fromm, fascism is a constant threat. Fromm would meet the challenge of fascism by creating social conditions that lead the individual to be free and yet not alone, to be critical and yet not filled with doubts, to be independent and yet feel an integral part of humankind.

Existentialism

Intellectual Background

The philosophic movement that best exemplified the anxiety and uncertainty of Europe in an era of world wars was existentialism. Like writers and artists, existentialist philosophers were responding to a European civilization that seemed to be in the throes of dissolution.

What route should people take in a world where old values and certainties had dissolved, where universal truth was rejected and God's existence was denied? How could people cope in a society where they were menaced by technology, manipulated by impersonal bureaucracies, and overwhelmed by feelings of anxiety? If the universe is devoid of any overarching meaning, what meaning could one give to one's own life? These questions were at the crux of existentialist philosophy.

Basic Principles

Existentialism does not lend itself to a single definition, for its principal theorists did not adhere to a common body of doctrines. For example, some existentialists were atheists, like Jean Paul Sartre, or omitted God from their thought, like Martin Heidegger; others, like Karl Jaspers, believed in God but not in Christian doctrines; still others, like Gabriel Marcel and Nikolai Berdyaev, were Christians, and Martin Buber was a believing Jew. Perhaps the essence of existentialism appears in the following principles, although not all existentialists would subscribe to each point or agree with the way it is expressed.

1. Reality defies ultimate comprehension; there are no timeless truths that exist independently of and prior to the individual human being.

2. Reason alone is an inadequate guide to living, for people are more than thinking subjects who approach the world through critical analysis. They are also feeling and willing beings who must participate fully in life, who must experience existence directly, actively, passionately. Only in this way does one live wholly and authentically.

3. Thought must not merely be abstract speculation but must have a bearing on life; it must be translated into deeds.

4. Human nature is problematic and paradoxical, not fixed or constant; each person is like no other. Self-realization comes when one affirms one's own uniqueness; one becomes less than human when one permits one's life to be determined by a mental outlook—a set of rules and values—imposed by others.

5. We are alone. The universe is indifferent to our expectations and needs, and death is ever stalking us.

6. We are free. It is in the act of choosing freely from among different possibilities that the individual shapes an authentic existence. There is a dynamic quality to human existence; the individual has the potential to become more than he or she is.

Nineteenth-Century Forerunners

Three nineteenth-century thinkers—Sören Kierkegaard (1813–1855), Fëdor Dostoevski (see Chapter 28) and Friedrich Nietzsche (see Chapter 28)—were the principal forerunners of existentialism. Their views of reason, will, truth, and existence greatly influenced twentieth-century existentialists.

Kierkegaard Sören Kierkegaard, a Danish religious philosopher and Lutheran pastor, held that self-realization as a human being comes when the individual takes full responsibility for his or her life; the individual does this by choosing one way of life over another. In making choices, said Kierkegaard, the individual overcomes the agonizing feeling that life in its deepest sense is nothingness.

For Kierkegaard, the highest truth is that human beings are God's creatures. However, God's existence cannot be demonstrated by reason; the crucial questions of human existence can never be resolved in a logical and systematic way. For Kierkegaard, the individual does not know God through disinterested reflection but by making a passionate commitment to him. In contrast to Christian apologists who sought to demonstrate that Christian teachings did not conflict with reason, Kierkegaard denied that Christian doctrines were objectively valid; for him, Christian beliefs were absurd and irrational and could not be harmonized with reason. The true Christian, said Kierkegaard, commits himself to beliefs that are unintelligible; with confidence, he plunges into the absurd.

Twentieth-century existentialists took from Kierkegaard the idea that an all-consuming dread is the price of existence. Dread can cause us to flee from life and to find comfort in delusions, but it can also spark courage, for it is an opportunity to make a commitment. For both Kierkegaard and twentieth-century existentialists, the true philosophical quest is a subjective experience—the isolated individual, alone and without help, choosing a way of life, struggling with his or her own being to make a commitment. Only in this way does the individual become a whole person. Kierkegaard's dictum that "it is impossible to exist without passion"—that our actions matter to us—is at the heart of existentialism.

Dostoevski Although existentialist themes pervade several of Dostoevski's works, it is in *Notes from the Underground* (1864) that he treats explicitly the individual's quest for personal freedom, self-identity, and meaning and the individual's revolt against established norms—themes that are crucial to the outlook of twentieth-century existentialists.

Nietzsche For several reasons Friedrich Nietzsche was an important forerunner of existentialism. Nietzsche said that philosophical systems are merely expressions of an individual's own being and do not constitute an objective representation of reality; there is no realm of being that is the source of values. Nor does religion provide truth, for God is dead. And, asked Nietzsche, is not this godless world absurd? Nietzsche held that modern Westerners had lost all their traditional supports.

To overcome nothingness, said Nietzsche, individuals must define life for themselves and celebrate it fully, instinctively, heroically. Nietzsche's insistence that the individual confront existence squarely, without hypocrisy, and give meaning to it—his own meaning—was vital to the shaping of existentialism.

Twentieth-Century Existentialists*

Heidegger The German philosopher Martin Heidegger (1889–1976), generally regarded as the central figure in the development of twentieth-century existentialist thought, presents a problem to students of philosophy. First, Heidegger rejected being classified as an existentialist. Second, he wrote in a nearly incomprehensible style that obscured his intent. Third, in 1933, Heidegger, recently appointed as rector of the University of Freiburg by Hitler's government, joined the National Socialist party and publicly praised Hitler and the Nazi regime. The following year he resigned as rector and gave no further support to the Third Reich, although he did continue to sympathize with some Nazi ideals. Heidegger's dal-

---

*The following discussions are based on works written before 1946.

liance with Nazism caused some thinkers either to dismiss him or to minimize his importance as a philosopher.

Heidegger's principal book, *Being and Time* (1927), is a path-breaking work in twentieth-century philosophy. In it Heidegger asked: what does it mean to be, to say I am? Most people shun this question, said Heidegger; consequently they live inauthentically, merely accepting a way of life set by others. Such people, he said, have "fallen from being"; they do not reflect on their existence or recognize the various possibilities and choices that life offers. Rather, they flee from their own selves and accept without reflection society's values. Neither their actions nor their goals are their own; they have forfeited a human being's most distinctive qualities—freedom and creativity.

To live authentically, declared Heidegger, the individual has to face explicitly the problem of Being; that is, one has to determine one's own existence, create one's own possibilities, and make choices and commitments. Choosing, said Heidegger, is not just a matter of disengaged thought, for the human creature is more than a conscious knower. The authentic life encompasses the feelings as well as the intellect; it is a genuine expression of a person's whole being.

Coming to grips with death, said Heidegger, provides us with the opportunity for an authentic life. The trauma of our mortality and finiteness, the image of the endless void in which Being passes into non-Being, overwhelms us with dread; we come face to face with the insignificance of human existence, with the directionless lives that we pursue. To escape this dread, said Heidegger, some people simply immerse themselves in life's petty details or adopt the values prescribed by others. But dread of death is also an opportunity. It can put us in touch with our own uniqueness, our own Being, permitting us to take hold of our own existence and to make life truly our own.

The authentic life requires, said Heidegger, that we see ourselves within the context of historical time, for we cannot escape that our lives are bound by conditions and outlooks inherited from the past. Human beings are thrown into a world that is not of their own making; they dwell in a particular society that carries with it the weight of the past and the tensions and conflicts of the present. Without knowledge of these conditions,

Heidegger declared, events and things will always impose themselves on us, and we will not have the courage to reject conventions that are not of our own making.

Jaspers Karl Jaspers (1883–1969), a German psychiatrist turned philosopher, was a leading figure in the existentialist movement. Jaspers came into disfavor with the Nazi regime (he advocated liberal-humanist values and his wife was Jewish) and lost his position as professor of philosophy at Heidelberg University. Like Kierkegaard, Jaspers held that philosophy and science cannot provide certainty. Also like Kierkegaard, he sought to discover the genuine self through an encounter with life. Like Heidegger, he held that while death makes us aware of our finitude, thereby promoting anxiety, it also goads us to focus on what is truly important and to do so immediately. Jaspers insisted that the individual has the power to choose; to be aware of this freedom and to use it is the essence of being human. He declared in 1930:

> *Man is always something more than what he knows of himself. He is not what he is simply once for all, but is a process; he is . . . endowed with possibilities through the freedom he possesses to make of himself what he will by the activities on which he decides.*[37]

Feelings of guilt and anxiety inevitably accompany free will, said Jaspers; nevertheless, we must have the courage to make a choice, for it is in the act of choosing that the individual shapes his or her true self.

Jaspers rejected revealed religion, dogma, and the authority of churches, but he did postulate what he called "philosophical faith." He thought of human existence as an encounter with Transcendence—"the eternal, indestructible, the immutable, the source [that] . . . can be neither visualized nor grasped in thought."[38] Jaspers did not equate Transcendence with God in the conventional sense, but the concept is laden with theistic qualities. Although not a traditional Christian, Jaspers was no atheist.

Sartre The outlook of several French existentialists—Jean Paul Sartre (1905–1980), Maurice Merleau-Ponty (1908–1961), Albert Camus (1913–1960), and Simone de Beauvoir (1908–

Jean Paul Sartre and Simone de Beauvoir, 1956. The major philosophical movement in the twentieth century is existentialism. Sartre and de Beauvoir were two of its first exponents. (*AP/Wide World Photos*)

1987)—was shaped by their involvement in the resistance to Nazi occupation during World War II. Sartre, the leading French existentialist, said their confrontation with terror and torture taught them "to take evil seriously." Evil is not the effect of ignorance that might be remedied by knowledge or of passions that might be controlled, said Sartre; rather, it is a central fact of human existence and is unredeemable. Facing capture and death, the members of the Resistance understood what it is to be a solitary individual in a hostile universe. Living on the cutting edge of life, they rediscovered the essence of human freedom: they could make authentic choices. By saying no to the Nazis and resisting them, they confronted existence squarely.

Sartre served in the French army at the outbreak of World War II and was captured by the Germans. Released after the French surrender, he taught philosophy while serving in the Resistance.

In addition to his philosophic writings, Sartre, after World War II, gained international acclaim for his novels and plays, many of them written from an existentialist point of view.

The individual is self-defined said Sartre. "Not only is man what he conceives himself to be, but he is also only what he wills himself to be. . . . Man is nothing else but what he makes of himself. . . . existentialism's first move is to make every man aware of what he is and to make full responsibility of his existence rest on him."[39]

In contrast to Kierkegaard and Jaspers, Sartre defined himself as an atheist and saw existentialism as a means of facing the consequences of a godless universe. Atheistic existentialism, he said, begins with the person and not with God, a pre-established ethic, or a uniform conception of human nature. The individual has nothing to cling to but is thrown into the world "with no support and no aid."[40] It is the first principle of existentialism, said Sartre, that we must each choose our own ethics, define ourselves, and create ourselves through involvement with others and the world. In this way the individual gives life meaning. We are what we do, said Sartre; each individual is "nothing else than the ensemble of his acts, nothing else than his life. . . . man's destiny is within himself."[41]

Religious Existentialism Several thinkers are classified as religious existentialists, among them Nikolai Berdyaev (1874–1948), an exile from communist Russia; Martin Buber (1878–1965), a Jew who fled Nazi Germany; and Gabriel Marcel (1889–1973). During World War I, Marcel served with the French Red Cross accounting for soldiers missing in battle. This shattering experience brought the sensitive thinker face to face with the tragedy of human existence. A growing concern with the spiritual life led him to convert to Catholicism in 1929.

The modern individual, said Marcel in 1933, "tends to appear to himself and to others as an agglomeration of functions." A person is viewed as an entrepreneur, a laborer, a consumer, a citizen. The hospital serves as a repair shop, and death "becomes, objectively and functionally, the scrapping of what has ceased to be of use and must be written off as a total loss."[42] In such a functional world, maintained Marcel, people are valued for what they produce and possess. If they do not succeed as merchants, bookkeepers, or ticket-takers, people judge them and they judge themselves as personal failures. Such an outlook suffocates spirituality and deprives the individual of the joy of existence. It produces an "intolerable unease" in the individual "who is reduced to living as though he were in fact submerged by his function. . . . Life in a world centered on function is liable to despair because in reality this world is *empty,* it rings hollow."[43]

Marcel wanted people to surpass a functional and mechanical view of life and to explore the mystery of existence—to penetrate to a higher level of reality. Marcel held that one penetrates ultimate reality when one overcomes egocentricity and exists for others, when one loves and is loved by others. When we exist through and for others, when we treat another person not as an object performing a function but as a "thou" who matters to us, we soar to a higher level of existence. When we are actively engaged with others in concrete human situations, we fulfill ourselves as human beings; when we actively express love and fidelity toward others, life attains a higher meaning. Such involvement with others, said Marcel, provides us with a glimpse of a transcendent reality and is a testimony to God's existence. Marcel maintained that faith in God overcomes anxiety and despair, which characterize the modern predicament. It also improves the quality of human relationships, for if we believe that all people matter to God, they are more likely to matter to us.

The Modern Predicament

The process of fragmentation that had begun in European thought and the arts at the end of the nineteenth century accelerated after World War I. Increasingly, philosophers, writers, and artists expressed their disillusionment with the rational-humanist tradition of the Enlightenment; they no longer shared the Enlightenment confidence in either reason's capabilities or human goodness, and they viewed perpetual progress as an illusion.

For some thinkers the crucial problem was the great change in the European understanding of truth. Since the rise of philosophy in ancient Greece, Western thinkers had believed in the existence of objective, universal truth—truths that were inherent in nature and applied to all peoples at all times. (Christianity, of course, also taught the reality of truth as revealed by God.)

It was held that such truths—the natural rights of the individual, for example—could be apprehended by the intellect and could serve as a standard for individual aspirations and social life. The recognition of these universal principles, it was believed, compels people to measure the world of the here and now in the light of rational and universal norms and to institute appropriate reforms. It was the task of philosophy to reconcile human existence with the objective order.

During the nineteenth century, the existence of universal truth came into doubt. A growing historical consciousness led some thinkers to maintain that what people considered truth was merely a reflection of their culture at a given stage in history, their perception of things at a specific point in the evolution of human consciousness. These thinkers, called historicists, held that universal truths were not woven into the fabric of nature. There are no natural rights of life, liberty, and property that constitute the individual's birthright; there are no standards of justice or equality that are inherent in nature and ascertainable by reason. It was people, said historicists, who elevated the beliefs and values of an age to the status of objective truth. This radical break with the traditional attitude toward truth contributed substantially to the crisis of European consciousness that marked the first half of the twentieth century. Traditional values and beliefs, either those inherited from the Enlightenment or those taught by Christianity, no longer gave Europeans a sense of certainty and security; people were left without a normative order to serve as a guide to living.

By the early twentieth century, the attitude of Westerners toward reason had undergone a radical transformation. Some thinkers who placed their hopes in the rational tradition of the Enlightenment were distressed by reason's inability to resolve the tensions and conflicts of modern industrial society. Moreover, the growing recognition of the nonrational—of human actions determined by hidden impulses—led people to doubt that reason plays the dominant role in human behavior. Other thinkers viewed the problem of reason differently. They reviled an attitude of mind that found no room for Christianity because its teachings did not pass the test of reason and science. Or they attacked reason for fashioning a technological and bureaucratic society that devalued and crushed human emotions and stifled individuality; these thinkers insisted that human beings cannot fulfill their potential, cannot live wholly, if their feelings are denied. They agreed with D. H. Lawrence's critique of rationalism: "The attribution of rationality to human nature, instead of enriching it, now seems to me to have impoverished it. It ignored certain powerful and valuable springs of feeling. Some of the spontaneous, irrational outbursts of human nature can have a sort of value from which our schematism was cut off."[44]

While many thinkers focused on the limitations of reason, others, particularly existentialists, pointed out that reason was a double-edged sword; it could demean as well as ennoble the individual. These thinkers attacked all theories that subordinated the individual to a rigid system. They denounced positivism for reducing human personality to psychological laws, and Marxism for making social class a higher reality than the individual. They rebelled against political collectivization that regulated individual existence to the needs of the corporate state, and they assailed modern technology and bureaucracy, creations of the rational mind, for fashioning a social order that devalued and depersonalized the individual, denying people an opportunity for independent growth and a richer existence. These thinkers held that modern industrial society, in its drive for efficiency and uniformity, deprived people of their uniqueness and reduced flesh and blood human beings to cogs in a mechanical system.

Responding to these critics of reason, other philosophers maintained that it was necessary to reaffirm respect for the rational tradition first proclaimed by the ancient Greeks and given its modern expression by the Enlightenment philosophes. Reason, said these thinkers, was indispensable to civilization. What they advocated was broadening the scope of reason to accommodate the insights into human nature advanced by romantics, Nietzsche, Freud, modernist writers and artists, and others who explored the world of feelings, will, and the subconscious.

In the decades shaped by world wars and totalitarianism, intellectuals raised questions that went to the heart of the dilemma of modern life. How can civilized life be safeguarded against human irrationality, particularly when it is channeled into political ideologies that idolize the state, the leader, the party, or the race? How can individual human personality be rescued from a relentless rationalism that reduces human nature and society to mechanical systems and seeks to regulate and organize the individual as it would any material object? Do the values associated with the Enlightenment provide a sound basis on which to integrate society? Can the individual find meaning in what many now regarded as a meaningless universe? World War II gave these questions a special poignancy.

Notes

1. Quoted in Barbara Tuchman, *The Guns of August* (New York: Macmillan, 1962), p. 440.

2. Sigmund Freud, "Thought for the Times on War and Death," in the *Standard Edition of the Complete Psychological Works of Freud,* James Strachey, ed. (London: Hogarth Press, 1957), pp. 275, 278.

3. Quoted in Hans Kohn, "The Crisis in European Thought and Culture," in Jack J. Roth, ed., *World War I: A Turning Point in Modern History* (New York: Knopf, 1967), p. 28.

4. Quoted in Franklin L. Baumer, "Twentieth-Century Version of the Apocalypse," *Cahiers d'Histoire Mondiale (Journal of World History),* 1, no. 3 (January 1954), 624.

5. Ibid.

6. Erich Maria Remarque, *All Quiet on the Western Front,* trans. by A. W. Wheen (Boston: Little, Brown, 1929), p. 224.

7. W. B. Yeats, "The Second Coming," *Collected Poems of W. B. Yeats* (New York: Macmillan, 1956), pp. 184–185.

8. T. S. Eliot, "The Waste Land," *Collected Poems, 1909–1962* (New York: Harcourt, Brace, 1970), p. 67.

9. Carl Gustav Jung, *Modern Man in Search of a Soul,* trans. by W. S. Dell and Cary F. Baynes (New York: Harcourt, Brace, 1933), pp. 231, 234–235.

10. Johan Huizinga, *In the Shadow of Tomorrow* (London: Heinemann, 1936), pp. 1–3.

11. Oswald Spengler, *The Decline of the West,* trans. by Charles F. Atkinson (London: Allen & Unwin, 1926), p. 40.

12. Harry T. Moore, ed., *The Collected Letters of D. H. Lawrence* (New York: Viking, 1962), I, p. 180.

13. Tristan Tzara, "Lecture on Dada (1922)," trans. by Ralph Mannheim, in Robert Motherwell, ed., *The Dada Painters and Poets* (New York: Witterborn, Schultz, 1951), p. 250.

14. Ibid., p. 248.

15. Ibid., p. 251.

16. Edward Lucie-Smith, in Donald Carrol and Edward Lucie-Smith, *Movements in Modern Art* (New York: Horizon Press, 1973), p. 49.

17. H. W. Janson, *History of Art,* 2nd ed. (Englewood Cliffs, N.J.: Prentice-Hall, 1977), p. 661.

18. André Breton, *What Is Surrealism?* trans. by David Gascoyne (London: Faber & Faber, 1936), p. 62.

19. Quoted in David Caute, *The Fellow Travellers* (New York: Macmillan, 1973), p. 64.

20. Ibid., p. 92.

21. Richard Crossman, ed., *The God That Failed* (New York: Bantam Books, 1951), pp. 15, 21.

22. Arthur Koestler, *Darkness at Noon* (New York: Macmillan, 1941), pp. 158–159.

23. Quoted in C. T. McIntire, ed., *God, History, and Historians* (New York: Oxford University Press, 1977), p. 9.

24. Arnold J. Toynbee, *Survey of International Af-*

fairs, 1933 (London: Oxford University Press, 1934), p. 111.

25. Julien Benda, *The Betrayal of the Intellectuals,* trans. by Richard Aldington (Boston: Beacon Press, 1955), p. 21.

26. Ibid., p. 38.

27. Ibid., p. 122.

28. Ibid., p. 162.

29. José Ortega y Gasset, *The Revolt of the Masses* (New York: W. W. Norton, 1957), pp. 63, 18.

30. Ibid., p. 73.

31. Ibid., pp. 73–74.

32. Ernst Cassirer, *The Philosophy of the Enlightenment,* trans. by Fritz C. A. Koelln and James P. Pettegrove (Boston: Beacon Press, 1955), pp. xi–xii.

33. Ernst Cassirer, *The Myth of the State* (New Haven: Yale University Press, 1946), p. 280.

34. Ibid., p. 296.

35. Erich Fromm, *Escape from Freedom* (New York: Avon Books, 1965), p. 124.

36. Ibid., pp. 173, 246.

37. Karl Jaspers, *Man in the Modern Age,* trans. by Eden and Cedar Paul (Garden City, N.Y.: Doubleday Anchor Books, 1951), p. 159.

38. Quoted in John Macquarrie, *Existentialism* (Baltimore: Penguin Books, 1973), p. 246.

39. Jean Paul Sartre, *Existentialism,* trans. by Bernard Frechtman (New York: Philosophical Library, 1947), pp. 18–19.

40. Ibid., p. 28.

41. Ibid., pp. 38, 42.

42. Gabriel Marcel, "On the Ontological Mystery," in *The Philosophy of Existentialism,* trans. by Manya Harari (Secaucus, N.J.: Citadel Press, 1980), p. 10.

43. Ibid., p. 12.

44. Cited in Anthony Arblaster, *The Rise and Decline of Western Liberalism* (Oxford: Basil Blackwell, 1984), p. 81.

Suggested Reading

See also the books suggested for reading at the end of Chapter 28.

Barrett, William, *Irrational Man* (1958). Especially good on the intellectual and cultural roots of existentialism.

Blackham, H. J., *Six Existentialist Thinkers* (1952). Useful analyses of Kierkegaard, Nietzsche, Jaspers, Marcel, Heidegger, and Jean Paul Sartre.

———, ed., *Reality, Man and Existence* (1965). Essential works of existentialism.

Cain, Seymour, *Gabriel Marcel* (1963). A brief, informative survey.

Cruickshank, John, ed., *Aspects of the Modern European Mind* (1969). A useful collection of sources in modern intellectual history.

Jaspers, Karl, *Man in the Modern Age* (1930). A discussion of modern problems, particularly the impact of technology as seen from a half-century ago.

Kaufmann, Walter, ed., *Existentialism from Dostoevsky to Sartre* (1956). The basic writings of existentialist thinkers.

McIntire, C. T., ed., *God, History, and Historians* (1977). Selections from Christian thinkers; many deal with the crises of the twentieth century.

Macquarrie, John, *Existentialism* (1972). A lucid discussion of existentialism.

Pawel, Ernst, *The Nightmare of Reason* (1984). A recent biography of Kafka.

Perry, Marvin, *Arnold Toynbee and the Crisis of the West* (1982). Toynbee's understanding of the nature, meaning, and destiny of Western civilization.

Wagar, W. Warren, ed., *European Thought Since 1914* (1968). A valuable collection of sources.

Review Questions

1. What factors contributed to a mood of pessimism in the period after World War I?

2. What signs of decay did Spengler see in Western civilization?

3. Better than any other novelist of his time, Kafka grasped the dilemma of the modern age. Discuss this statement. Do his insights still apply today?

4. In *The Magic Mountain,* Mann reflected on the decomposition of bourgeois European civilization. Discuss this statement.

5. What was D. H. Lawrence's attitude toward industrial society? Do you agree with him?

6. In what ways were both Dada and surrealism an expression of the times?

7. How did art and literature express a social conscience during the 1920s and 1930s?

8. Why were many intellectuals attracted to communism in the 1930s?

9. What is the theme of *Darkness at Noon*?

10. How did Toynbee interpret nationalism and Nazism?

11. What did Ortega mean by the "mass-man"? What dangers were presented by the mass-man?

12. Why did Benda entitle his book *The Treason of the Intellectuals*?

13. What was Cassirer's attitude toward the Enlightenment? How did he interpret Nazism?

14. How did Fromm explain the rise of Nazism?

15. What were some of the conditions that gave rise to existentialism? What are the basic principles of existentialism?

16. Why are each of the following considered forerunners of existentialism: Dostoevski, Kierkegaard, and Nietzsche?

17. Why are each of the following considered to be existentialists: Heidegger, Jaspers, Sartre, and Marcel?

18. What do you like, or dislike, about existentialism?

34

World War II: Western Civilization in the Balance

From the early days of his political career, Hitler dreamed of forging a vast German empire in central and eastern Europe. He believed that only by waging a war of conquest against Russia could the German nation gain the living space and security it required and, as a superior race, deserved. War was an essential component of National Socialist ideology, and it accorded with Hitler's temperament. For the former corporal from the trenches, the Great War had never ended. Hitler aspired to political power because he wanted to mobilize the material and human resources of the German nation for war and conquest. Although historians may debate the question of responsibility for World War I, few would deny that World War II was Hitler's war:

> It appears to be an almost incontrovertible fact that the Second World War was brought on by the actions of the Hitler government, that these actions were the expression of a policy laid down well in advance in Mein Kampf, *and that this war could have been averted up until the last moment if the German government had so wished.*[1]

Western statesmen had sufficient warnings that Hitler was a threat to peace and the essential values of Western civilization, but they failed to rally their people and take a stand until Germany had greatly increased its capacity to wage aggressive war.

The Aftermath of World War I

World War I had shown that Germany was the strongest power on the Continent. In the east, the German army had triumphed over Russia; in the west, Britain and France could have hoped

St. Paul's Cathedral During the London Blitz. (*Associated Newspapers/Pictorial Parade*)

765

for no more than a deadlock without the aid of the United States. The Treaty of Versailles had weakened Germany but had not permanently crippled it.

In the decade after the war, responsibility for preserving the peace settlement rested essentially with France. The United States had rejected the treaty and withdrawn from European affairs; Soviet Russia was consolidating its revolution; Britain, burdened with severe economic problems, disarmed, and traditionally hostile to Continental alliances, did not want to join with France in holding Germany down. France sought to contain Germany by forging alliances with the new states of eastern Europe, which the French hoped would serve as a substitute for alliance with a now untrustworthy communist Russia. France thus entered into alliances with Poland, Czechoslovakia, Rumania, and Yugoslavia during the 1920s. But no combination of small eastern European states could replace Russia as a counterweight to Germany. Against Hitler's Germany, the French alliance system would prove useless.

A feeling of general hope prevailed during the 1920s. The newly created League of Nations provided a supranational authority to which nations could submit their quarrels. At the Washington Naval Conference (1921–22), the leading naval powers—the United States, Britain, France, Italy, and Japan—agreed not to construct new battleships or heavy cruisers for a ten-year period and established a ratio of capital ships between them. It was hoped that avoiding a naval arms race would promote international peace.

In the Locarno Pact (1925), Germany, France, and Belgium agreed not to change their existing borders, which meant, in effect, that Germany had accepted both the loss of Alsace and Lorraine to France and the demilitarization of the Rhineland—two provisions of the Versailles treaty. The Locarno Pact held the promise of a détente between France and Germany. But it was only an illusion of peace, for Germany gave no such assurances for its eastern border with Czechoslovakia and Poland, France's allies.

Other gestures that promoted reconciliation followed. In 1926, Germany was admitted to the League of Nations, and in 1928, the Kellogg-Briand Pact renouncing war was signed by most nations. The signatories condemned war as a solution for international disputes and agreed to settle quarrels through peaceful means. Ordinary people welcomed the Kellogg-Briand Pact as the dawning of a new era of peace, but because the pact contained no clauses for its enforcement, the agreement only fostered the illusion of peace.

Nevertheless, between 1925 and 1930, hopes for reconciliation and peace were high. Recovery from the war and increased prosperity coincided with the easing of international tensions. As evidence of the new spirit of conciliation, France and Britain withdrew their forces from the Rhineland in 1930, four years ahead of the time prescribed by the Versailles treaty.

The Road to War

Hitler's Foreign Policy Aims

After consolidating his power and mobilizing the nation's will, Hitler moved to implement his foreign policy objectives—the destruction of the Versailles treaty, the conquest and colonization of eastern Europe, and the domination and exploitation of racial inferiors. In some respects, Hitler's foreign policy aims accorded with the goals of Germany's traditional rulers. Like them, Hitler sought to make Germany the pre-eminent power in Europe. During World War I, German statesmen and generals had sought to conquer extensive regions of eastern Europe, and in the Treaty of Brest-Litovsk, Germany took Poland, the Ukraine, and the Baltic states from Russia. But Hitler's racial nationalism—the subjugation and annihilation of inferior races by a master German race—marked a break with the outlook of the old governing class. Germany's traditional conservative leaders had never restricted the civil rights of German Jews and had sought to Germanize, not enslave, the Poles living under the German flag.

In foreign affairs, Hitler demonstrated that same blend of opportunism and singleness of purpose that had brought him to power. He behaved like a man possessed, driven by a fanatical belief that his personal destiny was tied to Germany's future. Here, too, he made use of propaganda to undermine his opponents' will to resist. The Nazi propaganda machine, which had effectively won the minds of the German people, became an instrument of foreign policy. Nazi propaganda tried to win the support of the 27 million Germans living in Europe and the Americas, outside the borders of the Reich proper; to promote social and political disorientation in other lands, the Nazis propagated anti-Semitism on a worldwide basis; Nazi propagandists tried to draw international support for Hitler as Europe's best defense against the Soviet Union and Bolshevism. The Nazi anticommunist campaign "convinced many Europeans that Hitler's dictatorship was more acceptable than Stalin's and that Germany—'the bulwark against Bolshevism'—should be allowed to grow from strength to strength."[2]

As Hitler anticipated, the British and the French backed down when faced with his violations of the Versailles treaty and threats of war. Haunted by the memory of World War I, Britain and France went to great lengths to avoid another catastrophe—a policy that had the overwhelming support of public opinion. Moreover, Britain suffered from a bad conscience regarding the Versailles treaty. Believing that Germany had been treated too severely, and woefully unprepared for war from 1933 to 1939, Britain was amenable to making concessions to Hitler. Although France had the strongest army on the Continent, it was prepared to fight only a defensive war—the reverse of its World War I strategy. France built immense fortifications, called the Maginot Line, to protect its borders from a German invasion, but it lacked a mobile striking force that could punish an aggressive Germany. The United States, concerned with the problems of the Great Depression and standing aloof from Europe's troubles, did nothing to strengthen the resolve of France and Britain. Since both France and Britain feared and mistrusted the Soviet Union, the grand alliance of World War I was not renewed. There was an added factor: suffering from a failure of leadership and political and economic unrest that eroded national unity, France was experiencing a decline in morale and a loss of nerve. It consistently turned to Britain for direction.

British statesmen championed a policy of appeasement—giving in to Germany in the hope that a satisfied Hitler would not drag Europe through another world war. British policy rested on the disastrous illusion that Hitler, like his Weimar predecessors, sought peaceful revision of the Versailles treaty and that he could be contained through concessions. This perception was as misguided as the expectation of Weimar conservatives that the responsibility of power would compel Hitler to abandon his National Socialist radicalism. Some British appeasers, accepting the view that Nazi propaganda cleverly propagated and exploited, also regarded Hitler as a defender of European civilization and the capitalist economic order against Soviet communism.

In *Mein Kampf*, Hitler had explicitly laid out his philosophy of racial nationalism and *Lebensraum* (living space), and as dictator, he had established a one-party state, confined political opponents to concentration camps, and persecuted Jews. But the proponents of appeasement did not properly assess these signs. They still believed that Hitler could be reasoned with. Appeasement, which in the end was capitulation to blackmail, failed. Germany grew stronger and the German people more devoted to the Fuehrer. Hitler did not moderate his ambitions, and the appeasers did not avert war.

Breakdown of Peace

To realize his foreign-policy aims, Hitler required a formidable military machine; Germany had to rearm. The Treaty of Versailles had limited the size of the German army to 100,000 volunteers; restricted the navy's size; forbidden the production of military aircraft, heavy artillery, and tanks; and disbanded the general staff. Throughout the 1920s, Germany had evaded these provisions, even entering into a secret arrangement with the Soviet Union to establish training schools for German pilots and tank corpsmen on Russian soil.

In March 1935, Hitler declared that Germany was no longer bound by the Versailles treaty. Germany would restore conscription, build an air force (which it had been doing secretly), and strengthen its navy. The German people were ecstatic over Hitler's boldness. France protested but offered no resistance; and Britain negotiated a naval agreement with Germany, thus tacitly accepting Hitler's rearmament.

A decisive event in the breakdown of peace was Italy's invasion of Ethiopia in October 1935.

Mussolini sought colonial expansion and revenge for a defeat the African kingdom had inflicted on Italian troops in 1896. The League of Nations called for economic sanctions against Italy, and most League members restricted trade with the aggressor. But Italy continued to receive oil, particularly from American suppliers. Believing that the conquest of Ethiopia did not affect their vital interests and hoping to keep the Italians friendly in the event of a clash with Germany, neither Britain nor France sought to restrain Italy, despite its act of aggression against another member of the League of Nations.

Mussolini's subjugation of Ethiopia discredited the League of Nations, which had already been weakened by its failure to deal effectively with Japan's invasion of the mineral-rich Chinese province of Manchuria in 1931. At that time the League formed a commission of inquiry and urged nonrecognition of the puppet state of Manchukuo created by the Japanese, but the member states did not restrain Japan. Ethiopia, like Manchuria, showed that the League was reluctant to use force to resist aggression.

On March 7, 1936, Hitler marched troops into the Rhineland, violating both the Versailles treaty and the Locarno Pact. German generals had cautioned Hitler that such a move would provoke a French invasion of Germany and reoccupation of the Rhineland, which the German army, still in the first stages of rearmament, could not repulse. But Hitler gambled that France and Britain, lacking the will to fight, would take no action.

Hitler had correctly assessed the Anglo-French mood. Britain was not greatly alarmed by the remilitarization of the Rhineland. Hitler, after all, was not expanding the borders of Germany but was only sending soldiers to Germany's frontier. Such a move, reasoned British officials, did not warrant risking a war. France regarded the remilitarization of the Rhineland as a grave threat. It deprived France of the one tangible advantage that it had obtained from the Treaty of Versailles—a buffer area. Now German forces could concentrate in strength on the French frontier, either to invade France or to discourage a French assault if Germany attacked Czechoslovakia or Poland, France's eastern allies. France lost the advantage of being able to retaliate by invading a demilitarized zone.

Three factors explain why France did not try to expel the 22,000 German troops that occupied the zone. First, France would not act alone, and Britain could not be persuaded to use force. Second, the French general staff overestimated German military strength and thought only of defending French soil from a German attack, not of initiating a strike against Germany. Third, French public opinion showed no enthusiasm for a confrontation with Hitler.

The Spanish Civil War of 1936–1939 was another victory for fascism. Nazi Germany and Fascist Italy aided Franco; the Soviet Union supplied the Spanish republic. The republic appealed to France for help, but the French government feared that the civil war would expand into a European war. With Britain's approval, France proposed the Nonintervention Agreement. Italy, Germany, and the Soviet Union signed the agreement but continued to supply the warring parties. By October 1937, some 60,000 Italian "volunteers" were fighting in Spain. Hitler sent from 5,000 to 6,000 men and hundreds of planes, which proved decisive. By comparison, the Soviet Union's aid was meager.

Without considerable help from France, the Spanish republic was doomed, but Prime Minister Léon Blum continued to support nonintervention. He feared that French intervention would cause Germany and Italy to escalate their involvement, bringing Europe to the edge of a general war. Moreover, supplying the republic would have dangerous consequences at home, because French rightists were sympathetic to Franco's conservative-clerical authoritarianism.

In 1939, the republic fell, and Franco established a dictatorship. The Spanish Civil War provided Germany with an opportunity to test weapons and pilots and demonstrated again that France and Britain lacked the determination to fight fascism. It also widened the breach between Italy and Britain and France that had opened when Italy invaded Ethiopia and drew Mussolini and Hitler closer together. In October 1936, Mussolini sent his foreign minister to visit with Hitler in Berlin. The discussions bore fruit, and on November 1, Mussolini proclaimed that a Rome-Berlin "Axis" had been created.

Map 34.1 German and Italian Aggressions, 1935–1939 ▶

World Wars and Totalitarianism: The West in Crisis

Figure 1 Le Corbusier: Notre-Dame-du-Haut, 1950–1955, at Ronchamp, France. (© *Mangin 1978/Photo Researchers, Inc.*)

The Emergence of Modern Art

Figure 2 Paul Gauguin: *Ia Orana Maria*, 1891. Oil on canvas. H. 44¾ in. W. 34½ in. (*The Metropolitan Museum of Art, Bequest of Samuel A. Lewisohn, 1951. 51.112.2*)

Figure 3 Paul Cézanne: *Madame Cézanne in a Red Chair*, 1877. (*Museum of Fine Arts, Boston. Bequest of Robert Treat Paine, II*)

Figure 4 Pablo Picasso: *Les Demoiselles d'Avignon*, 1907. Oil on canvas. 8 ft. by 7 ft. 8 in. (*Collection, The Museum of Modern Art, New York. Acquired through the Lillie P. Bliss Bequest*)

Toward the end of the nineteenth century, obscure groups of artists working in France and Germany began to re-evaluate the meaning and function of art. By the 1890s the tumultuous changes of the preceding century had profoundly altered the world-view of many intellectuals. To some artists the cool, orderly figure style and calm compositions of the Renaissance, based on Greco-Roman models, and the more elaborate baroque and neoclassical styles of the seventeenth and eighteenth centuries no longer seemed appropriate forms of artistic expression.

Freed from the grip of classical values, artists began to recognize the power and eloquence of non-Western art. Like many others of his time, France's Paul Gauguin (1848–1903) was attracted to the art of "primitive" people because they seemed uncorrupted by industrial society, closer to the earth, and more in tune with nature. The elemental force of nature, respect for non-European traditions, and the simple, "primitive" style of painting (using little modeling and strong outline) all appear in Gauguin's *Ia Orana Maria* or *Hail Mary* (Figure 2).

During the 1880s, the Dutch painter Vincent van Gogh (1853–1890) and Gauguin recognized that color, like other formal elements, could act as a language in and of itself. The local or "real" color of an object does not necessarily express the artist's experience. Artists, according to van Gogh and Gauguin, should seek to paint things not as they appear to the eye, but as they are felt. (See van Gogh's painting opening Chapter 28.)

In pre–World War I Germany, the group of artists known as Expressionists developed some of these ideas, often using bold, flat color to convey psychological forces that Sigmund Freud had explored. For example, *The Street, Berlin* by Ernst Ludwig Kirchner (1880–1938) (Figure 5) is depicted not with "realistic" colors but with colors that convey the tension, stress and isolation of modern urban life.

Alongside the revolution in color, another revolution was occurring in the use of space. From about 1880 on, Paul Cézanne (1839–1906) developed a new way of expressing the experience of seeing. He sought to create paintings with perfectly designed compositions, true both to the subject matter and to his own perceptions. He also wanted to subsume and build upon the Western artistic tradition.

Madame Cézanne in a Red Chair (Figure 3) has the monumentality of a majestic baroque portrait. The space of the painting, however, is not treated as a block viewed from a stationary position. Instead, the space is compressed, and a variety of viewpoints appear. The figure looks solid because brushstrokes of various colors create the illusion of volume. These multicolored brushstrokes also produce a kind of mosaic pattern lying on the painting's surface. The work is striking for its breadth and order, revealing the deep concentration inherent in Cézanne's vision.

Between 1909 and 1914 in Paris, Pablo Picasso (1881–1973) and Georges Braque (1882–1963) worked together to develop a new style, which is called cubism. Cubist space is even more shallow and compressed than the space of Cézanne. The idea of multiple views is extended so that the shifts of viewpoint are more numerous and more extreme.

This variety of viewpoints appears in Picasso's *Les Demoiselles d'Avignon* (Figure 4). This complex and powerful painting continues a

Figure 5 Ernst Ludwig Kirchner: *Street, Berlin*, 1913. Oil on canvas. 47½ in. by 35⅞ in. (*Collection, The Museum of Modern Art, New York. Purchase*)

long tradition in Western art of representing nude female figures. In fact, in the decade preceding the creation of *Demoiselles*, Cézanne had painted an important series of bathers. Traditionally, Western European nudes had been idyllic, subtly erotic images portraying ideal feminine beauty. Picasso saw a different potential for the female nude, perceiving that it could also express the energies and forces of nature in the same way that the female fertility images in the art of Africa or the Pacific islands do. To tap this energy required a new, simple, forceful style, one that built on some of the conventions developed in preindustrial non-Western art.

Throughout the period from 1890 to 1914, avant-garde artists were de-emphasizing subject

Figure 6 Henry Moore: *Family Group*, 1948–1949. Bronze, cast 1950. 59¼ in. by 46½ in., at base 45 by 29⅞ in. (*Collection, The Museum of Modern Art, New York, A. Conger Goodyear Fund*)

matter and stressing the expressive power of such formal qualities as line, color, and space. It is not surprising that some artists finally began to create work that did not refer to anything seen in the real world. Piet Mondrian (1872–1944), a Dutch artist, saw the cubist art of Picasso and Braque just before World War I. The cubists had compressed the space of their paintings and reduced subject matter to insignificance. For Mondrian the next step was to eliminate illusionistic space and subject matter. His *Broadway Boogie-Woogie,* for example, seems entirely flat (Figure 8). Its effect is

musical. Moving from colored rectangles to black bands, from tiny squares to broad, syncopated blocks of color, one feels the visual rhythm of the painting.

Many postwar artists continued to develop geometric abstraction, among them Frank Stella (b. 1936). Unlike Mondrian's painting, which has a kind of rhythm that appears as one looks at the work over a period of time, Stella's *Hiraqla* (Figure 9) delivers its entire message at one stroke. Its huge size (ten by twenty feet) and vibrant, unexpected colors make the painting's impact even greater.

Figure 7 *Above:* Walter Gropius: Bauhaus, 1925–1926, at Dessau, Germany. (*Leonard/Bauhaus-Archiv, Berlin*)

Figure 8 *Right:* Piet Mondrian: *Broadway Boogie Woogie*, 1942–1943. Oil on canvas. H. 50 in. W. 50 in. (*Collection, The Museum of Modern Art, New York. Given anonymously.*)

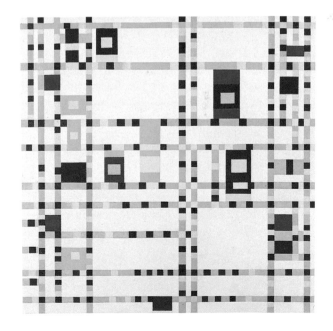

Geometric abstraction has been a major theme in many fields of twentieth-century art. Mondrian's work was a great inspiration, not only for painters, but for architects and graphics designers as well, because he envisioned the complete integration of art and the human environment. The Bauhaus, an institute established in Germany in 1919, fostered the creation of high quality art, design, and architecture that could be made available to people of all socioeconomic levels. The building designed by Walter Gropius (1883–1970) (Figure 7) exemplifies the Bauhaus ideal in its simplicity and directness. Gropius avoids monotony and sterility by arranging rectangular voids and solids in a rhythmic, dynamic way, very much akin to Mondrian's painting.

Figure 9 Frank Stella: *Hiraqla,* 1968. (© *Frank Stella/Collection of Mr. and Mrs. Graham Gund*)

Notre-Dame-du-Haut (Figure 1), a chapel designed by Swiss architect Le Corbusier (1887–1965), represents another trend in modern architecture, one that might be called "primitivist." For this sanctuary on a mountaintop, Le Corbusier used reinforced concrete to create great walls and overhangs; these and the concealed doors to the sacred interior evoke prehistoric and ancient religious constructions.

Twentieth-century artists have devised new definitions for art, invented new ways of treating color, space, and drawing, explored new media, and developed abstract, nonreferential styles. At the same time, however, some very gifted artists, such as Henry Moore (b. 1898), have used traditional media (bronze) to continue the Western tradition of monumental figure sculpture. Within that tradition, Moore treats universal human concerns, such as the dangers of war and the bonds of family and children (Figure 6). His figure style expresses the timelessness of the theme of family love by recalling associations with Neolithic fertility images.

—KATHERINE CRUM

Franco's Troops in Guernica, Spain. In 1937, Hitler welcomed Francisco Franco's call for military aid. He was eager to test the might of Germany's air force in a trial blitzkrieg. Guernica was leveled quickly and ruthlessly. Picasso's *Guernica* captured the barbarism of the event; this mural went beyond memorializing the individual town to condemn inhumanity in general. (*UPI/Bettmann Newsphotos*)

One of Hitler's aims was incorporation of Austria into the Third Reich. The Treaty of Versailles had expressly prohibited the union of the two countries. But in *Mein Kampf*, Hitler had insisted that an Anschluss was necessary for German Lebensraum. In February 1938, under intense pressure from Hitler, Austrian Chancellor Kurt von Schuschnigg promised to accept Austrian Nazis in his cabinet and agreed to closer relations with Germany. Austrian independence was slipping away, and increasingly, Austrian Nazis undermined Schuschnigg's authority. Seeking to gain the support of his people, Schuschnigg made plans for a plebiscite on the issue of preserving Austrian independence. An enraged Hitler ordered his generals to draw up plans for an invasion of Austria. Hitler then demanded Schuschnigg's resignation and the formation of a new government headed by Arthur Seyss-Inquart, an Austrian Nazi.

Believing that Austria was not worth a war, Britain and France informed the embattled chancellor that they would not help in the event of a German invasion. Schuschnigg then resigned, and Austrian Nazis began to take control of the government. Under the pretext of preventing violence, Hitler ordered his troops to cross into Austria, and on March 13, 1938, Austrian leaders declared that Austria was a province of the German Reich. The Austrians celebrated by ringing church bells, waving swastika banners, and attacking Jews and looting their property.

Czechoslovakia: The Apex of Appeasement

Hitler had obtained Austria merely by threatening force. Another threat would give him the Sudetenland of Czechoslovakia. Of the 3.5 million people living in the Sudetenland, some 2.8 million were ethnic Germans. The Sudetenland contained key industries and strong fortifications; since it bordered Germany, it was also vital to Czech security. Deprived of the Sudetenland, Czechoslovakia could not defend itself against a German attack. Encouraged and instructed by Germany, the Sudeten Germans, led by Konrad Henlein, shrilly denounced the Czech government for "persecuting" its German minority and depriving it of its right to self-determination. The Sudeten Germans agitated for local autonomy and the right to profess the National Socialist ideology. Behind this demand was the goal of German annexation of the Sudetenland.

While negotiations between the Sudeten Germans and the Czech government proceeded, Hitler's propaganda machine accused the Czechs of hideous crimes against the German minority and warned of retribution. Hitler also ordered his generals to prepare for an invasion of Czechoslovakia and to complete the fortifications of the French border. Fighting between Czechs and Sudeten Germans heightened the tensions. Seeking to preserve peace, Prime Minister Neville Chamberlain (1869–1940) of Britain offered to confer with Hitler, who then extended an invitation.

Britain and France held somewhat different positions toward Czechoslovakia—the only democracy in eastern Europe. In 1924, France and Czechoslovakia had concluded an agreement of mutual assistance in the event either was attacked by Germany. Czechoslovakia had a similar agreement with Russia, but with the provision that Russian assistance depended on France's first fulfilling the terms of its agreement. Britain had no commitment to Czechoslovakia. Some of the British officials, swallowing Hitler's propaganda, believed that the Sudeten Germans were indeed a suppressed minority entitled to self-determination, and that the Sudetenland, like Austria, was not worth a war that could destroy Western civilization. Hitler, they said, only wanted to incorporate Germans living outside of Germany; he was only carrying the principle of self-determination to its logical conclusion. Once these Germans lived under the German flag, argued these British officials, Hitler would be satisfied. In any case, Britain's failure to rearm between 1933 and 1938 weakened its position. The British chiefs of staff believed that the nation was not prepared to fight, that it was necessary to sacrifice Czechoslovakia to buy time.

Czechoslovakia's fate was decided at the Munich Conference (September 1938) attended by Chamberlain, Hitler, Mussolini, and Prime Minister Édouard Daladier (1884–1970) of France. The Munich Agreement called for the immediate evacuation of Czech troops from the Sudetenland and its occupation by German forces. Britain and France then promised to guarantee the territorial integrity of the truncated Czechoslovakia. Both Chamberlain and Daladier were showered with praise by the people of Britain and France for keeping the peace.

Critics of Chamberlain have insisted that the Munich Agreement was an enormous blunder and tragedy. Chamberlain, they say, was a fool to believe that Hitler, who sought domination over Europe, could be bought off with the Sudetenland. Hitler regarded concessions by Britain and France as signs of weakness; they only increased his appetite for more territory. Second, argue the critics, it would have been better to fight Hitler in 1938 than a year later, when war actually did break out. To be sure, in the year following the Munich Agreement, Britain increased its military arsenal, but so did Germany, which built submarines and heavy tanks, strengthened western border defenses, and trained more pilots.

Munich Conference, 1938. England's Prime Minister Neville Chamberlain (left) was lauded as a keeper of the peace after the Munich Conference; the praise was short-lived. Adolf Hitler (middle) used the following months to undermine the territorial integrity of Czechoslovakia. With the end of Czech independence, Hitler's plans for European domination could not be denied. (*Imperial War Museum, London*)

Had Britain and France resisted Hitler at Munich, it is likely that the Fuehrer would have attacked Czechoslovakia. But Czechoslovakia would not have lain down and died. The Czech border defenses, which had been built on the model of the French Maginot Line, were formidable. The Czechs had a sizable number of good tanks, and the Czech people were willing to fight to preserve their nation's territorial integrity. By itself the Czech army could not have defeated Germany. But while the main elements of the German army were battling the Czechs, the French, who could mobilize a hundred divisions, could have broken through the German West Wall, which was defended by only five regular and four reserve divisions, invaded the Rhineland, and devastated German industrial centers in the Ruhr. (Such a scenario, of course, depended on the French overcoming their psychological reluctance to take the offensive.) And there was always the possibility that the Soviet Union would have come to Czechoslovakia's aid in fulfillment of its agreement.

After the annexation of the Sudetenland, the Fuehrer plotted to extinguish Czechoslovakia's existence. He encouraged the Slovak minority in Czechoslovakia, led by a fascist priest, Josef Tiso, to demand complete separation. On the pretext of protecting the Slovak people's right of self-determination, Hitler ordered his troops to enter Prague. In March 1939, Czech independence came to an end.

The destruction of Czechoslovakia was of a different character from the remilitarization of the Rhineland, the Anschluss with Austria, and the annexation of the Sudetenland. In all these previous cases, Hitler could claim the right of self-determination, Woodrow Wilson's grand principle. The occupation of Prague and the end of Czech independence, though, showed that Hit-

Chronology 34.1 Road to World War II

1931	Japan invades Manchuria
March 1935	Hitler announces German rearmament
October 1935	Italy invades Ethiopia
1936–1939	The Spanish Civil War
March 7, 1936	Germany remilitarizes the Rhineland
October 1936	The Berlin-Rome Axis is formed
November 1936	German-Japanese anticommunist pact
July 1937	Japan invades China
March 13, 1938	Anschluss with Austria, which becomes a German province
September 1938	The Munich Agreement—Germany's annexation of Sudetenland is approved by Britain and France
1939	Franco establishes a dictatorship in Spain
March 1939	Germany invades Czechoslovakia
April 1939	Italy invades Albania
May 22, 1939	The Pact of Steel between Hitler and Mussolini
August 23, 1939	Nonagression pact between Germany and Russia
September 1 & 3, 1939	Germany invades Poland; Britain and France declare war

ler really sought European hegemony. Outraged statesmen now demanded that the Fuehrer be deterred from further aggression.

Poland: The Final Crisis

After Czechoslovakia, Hitler turned to Poland, demanding that the free city of Danzig be returned to Germany and that railways and roads, over which Germans would enjoy extraterritorial rights, be built across the Polish Corridor, linking East Prussia with the rest of Germany. Poland refused to restore the port of Danzig, which was vital to its economy. The Poles would allow a German highway through the Polish Corridor but would not permit German extraterritorial rights. France informed the German government that it would fulfill its treaty obligations to aid Poland. Chamberlain also warned that Britain would assist Poland.

On May 22, 1939, Hitler and Mussolini entered into the Pact of Steel, promising mutual aid in the event of war. The following day, Hitler told his officers that Germany's real goal was the destruction of Poland. "Danzig is not the objective. It is a matter of expanding our living space in the east, of making our food supplies secure. . . . There is therefore no question of sparing Poland, and the decision remains to attack Poland at the first suitable opportunity."[3] In the middle of June, the army presented Hitler with battle plans for an invasion of Poland.

Britain, France, and the Soviet Union had been engaged in negotiations since April. The Soviet Union wanted a mutual-assistance pact including joint military planning, and demanded bases in Poland and Rumania in preparation for a German attack. Britain was reluctant to endorse these demands, fearing that a mutual-assistance pact with Russia might cause Hitler to embark on a mad adventure that would drag Britain into war. Moreover, Poland would not allow Russian troops on its soil, fearing Russian expansion.

At the same time, Russia was conducting secret talks with Nazi Germany. Unlike the Allies, Hitler could tempt Stalin with territory that would serve as a buffer between Germany and Russia. Moreover, a treaty with Germany would give Russia time to strengthen its armed forces. On August 23, 1939, the two totalitarian states signed a nonaggression pact that stunned the world. A secret section of the pact called for the partition of Poland between the two parties and Russian control over Latvia and Estonia. By signing such an agreement with his enemy, Hitler had pulled off an extraordinary diplomatic coup: he blocked the Soviet Union, Britain, and France from duplicating their World War I grand alliance against Germany. The Nazi-Soviet Pact was the green light for an invasion of Poland, and at dawn on September 1, 1939, German troops crossed the frontier. When Germany did not respond to their demand for a halt to the invasion, Britain and France declared war.

The Nazi Blitzkrieg

Germany struck at Poland with speed and power. The German air force, the *Luftwaffe*, destroyed Polish planes on the ground, attacked tanks, pounded defense networks, and bombed Warsaw, terrorizing the population. Tanks opened up breaches in the Polish defenses, and mechanized columns overran the foot-marching Polish army, trapping large numbers of soldiers. The Polish high command could not cope with the incredible speed and coordination of German air and ground attacks. By September 8, the Germans had advanced to the outskirts of Warsaw. On September 17, Soviet troops invaded Poland from the east. On September 27, Poland surrendered. In less than a month the Nazi *blitzkrieg* (lightning war) had vanquished Poland.

The Fall of France

For Hitler the conquest of Poland was only the prelude to a German empire stretching from the Atlantic to the Urals. When weather conditions were right, he would unleash a great offensive in the west. Meanwhile, the six-month period following the defeat of Poland was nicknamed the "phony war," for the fighting on land consisted only of a few skirmishes on the French-German border. Then, in early April 1940, the Germans struck at Denmark and Norway. Hitler wanted to ensure that Swedish iron ore would continue to reach Germany through Norwegian territorial waters. He knew that Britain and France had plans to occupy the mining region and the key Swedish and Norwegian ports. In addition, Hitler expected to establish naval bases on the Norwegian coast from which to wage submarine warfare against Britain.

Denmark surrendered within hours. A British-French force tried to assist the Norwegians, but the landings, badly coordinated and lacking in air support, failed. The Germans won the battle of Norway. But the Norwegian campaign produced two positive results for the Allies: Norwegian merchant ships escaped to Britain to be put into service; and Winston Churchill (1874–1965), who had opposed appeasement, replaced Chamberlain as British prime minister. (The German victory in Norway eroded Chamberlain's support in the House of Commons, and he was forced to give up the helm.) Dynamic, courageous, and eloquent, Churchill had the capacity to stir and lead his people in the struggle against Nazism.

On May 10, 1940, Hitler launched his offensive in the west with an invasion of neutral Belgium, Holland, and Luxembourg. While armored forces penetrated Dutch frontier defenses, airborne units seized strategic airfields and bridges. On May 14, after the Luftwaffe bombed Rotterdam, destroying the center of the city and killing many people, the Dutch surrendered.

A daring attack by glider-borne troops gave Germany possession of two crucial Belgian bridges, opening the plains of Belgium to German *Panzer* (tank) divisions. Believing that this was the main German attack, French troops rushed to Belgium to prevent a German breakthrough, but the greater menace lay to the south on the French frontier. Meeting almost no resistance, German Panzer divisions had moved through the narrow mountain passes of Luxembourg and the dense Forest of Ardennes in southern Belgium. On May 12, German units were on French soil near Sedan. Thinking that the Forest of Ardennes could not be penetrated by a major German force, the French had only lightly fortified the western extension of the Maginot Line; the failure to counterattack swiftly was a second mistake. The best elements of the Anglo-French forces were in Belgium, but the Germans were racing across northern France to the sea, which they reached on May 20, cutting the Anglo-French forces in two.

The Germans now sought to surround and annihilate the Allied forces converging on the French seaport of Dunkirk, the last port of escape. Inexplicably, Hitler called off his tanks just as they prepared to take Dunkirk; instead he ordered the Luftwaffe to finish off the Allied troops, but fog and rain prevented German planes from operating at full strength. Taking advantage of this breathing space, the Allies tightened their defenses and prepared for a massive evacuation. While the Luftwaffe bombed the beaches, some 338,000 British and French troops were ferried across the English Channel by destroyers, merchant ships, motorboats, fishing boats, tugboats, and private yachts. The British left all their equipment on the beaches but saved their armies to fight another day. Hitler's personal decision to hold back his tanks made the miracle of Dunkirk possible.

Meanwhile the battle for France was turning into an even worse disaster for the French. Whole divisions were cut off or in retreat, and millions of refugees in cars and carts and on motorcycles and bicycles fled south to escape the advancing Germans. On June 10, Mussolini also declared war on France. With authority breaking down, demoralization spreading, and resistance dying, the French cabinet appealed for an armistice, which was signed on June 22 in the same railway car in which Germany had agreed to the armistice ending World War I.

How can the collapse of France be explained? Neither French military leaders, who experienced

Hitler and His Aides in Front of the Eiffel Tower. In 1940, after military successes in Belgium and Holland, the German forces overcame France. Hitler (center, right) saw the fall of France as a proof of the invincibility of the Reich and a predestined reversal of the humiliation felt by Germans at their defeat in World War I. (*UPI/Bettmann Newsphotos*)

the debacle, nor historians are in agreement as to the relative strength of the French and German air forces. It is likely that the Germans and the French (including the British planes based in France) had some 3,000 planes each. But many French planes—in what still remains a mystery—stayed on the airfields; the planes were there, but the high command either did not use them or did not deploy them properly. Unlike the Germans, the French did not comprehend or appreciate the use of aviation in modern warfare. The French had as many tanks as the Germans, and some were superior in quality. Nor was German manpower overwhelming. France met disaster largely because its military leaders, unlike the German command, had not mastered the psychology and technology of motorized warfare. "The French commanders, trained in the slow-motion methods of 1918, were mentally unfitted to cope with panzer pace, and it produced a spreading paralysis among them," says British military expert Sir Basil Liddell Hart.[4] One senses also a loss of will among the French people—a product of internal political disputes that divided the nation, poor leadership, the years of appeasement and lost opportunities, and German propaganda, which depicted Nazism as irresistible and the Fuehrer as a man of destiny. It was France's darkest hour. According to the terms of the armistice, Germany occupied northern France and the coast. The French military was demobilized, and the French government, now located at Vichy in the south and headed by Marshal Pétain, the hero of World War I, would collaborate with the German authorities in occupied France. Refusing to recognize defeat, General Charles de Gaulle (1890–1970) escaped to London and organized the Free French forces. The Germans gloried in their revenge; the French wept in their humiliation; the British gathered their courage, for they now stood alone.

The Battle of Britain

Hitler expected that after his stunning victories in the west, Britain would make peace. The British, however, continued to reject Hitler's peace overtures, for they envisioned only a bleak future if Hitler dominated the Continent. "The Battle of Britain is about to begin," Churchill told the people of Britain. "Upon this battle depends the survival of Christian civilization. . . . if we fail, then . . . all we have known and cared for will sink into the abyss of a new Dark Age."[5]

With Britain unwilling to come to terms, Hitler proceeded in earnest with invasion plans. A successful crossing of the English Channel and the establishment of beachheads on the English coast depended on control of the skies. Marshal Hermann Goering assured Hitler that his Luftwaffe

could destroy the British Royal Air Force (RAF), and in early August 1940, the Luftwaffe began massive attacks on British air and naval installations. Virtually every day during the "Battle of Britain," weather permitting, hundreds of planes battled in the sky above Britain. "Never in the field of human conflict was so much owed by so many to so few," said Churchill of the British pilots, who rose to the challenge. On September 15 the RAF shot down sixty aircraft, convincing Hitler that Goering could not fulfill his promise to destroy British air defenses, and on September 17 the Fuehrer postponed the invasion of Britain "until further notice." The development of radar by British scientists, the skill and courage of British fighter pilots, and the inability of Germany to make up its losses in planes saved Britain in its struggle for survival. With the invasion of Britain called off, the Luftwaffe concentrated on bombing English cities, industrial centers, and ports. Every night for months, the inhabitants of London sought shelter in subways and cellars to escape German bombs, while British planes rose time after time to make the Luftwaffe pay the price. British morale never broke during the "Blitz."

Invasion of Russia

The obliteration of Bolshevism and the conquest, exploitation, and colonization of Russia were cardinal elements of Hitler's ideology. In Russia the Nazi empire would take control of wheat, oil, manganese, and other raw materials, and the fertile Russian plains would be settled by the master race. German expansion in the east could not wait for the final defeat of Britain. In July 1940, Hitler instructed his generals to formulate plans for an invasion of Russia. On December 18, Hitler set May 15, 1941, for the beginning of Operation Barbarossa, the code name assigned for the blitzkrieg against the Soviet Union. Events in the Balkans, however, forced Hitler to postpone the date to the latter part of June.

Seeking to make Italy a Mediterranean power and to win glory for himself, Mussolini had ordered an invasion of Greece. In late October 1940, Italian troops stationed in Albania—which Italy had occupied in 1939—crossed into Greece. The poorly planned operation was an instant failure;

within a week, the counterattacking Greeks advanced into Albania. Hitler feared that Britain, which was encouraging and aiding the Greeks, would use Greece to attack the oil fields of Rumania, which were vital to the German war effort, and to interfere with the forthcoming invasion of Russia. Another problem emerged when a military coup overthrew the government of Prince Paul in Yugoslavia, which two days earlier had signed a pact with Germany and Italy. Hitler feared that the new Yugoslav government might gravitate toward Britain. To prevent any interference with Operation Barbarossa, the Balkan flank had to be secured. On April 6, 1941, the Germans struck at both Greece and Yugoslavia. Yugoslavia was quickly overrun and Greece, although aided by 50,000 British, New Zealand, and Australian troops, fell at the end of April.

For the war against Russia, Hitler assembled a massive force—some 4 million men, 3,300 tanks, and 5,000 planes. In the early hours of June 22, 1941, the Germans launched their offensive over a wide front. Raiding Russian airfields, the Luftwaffe destroyed 1,200 aircraft on the first day. The Germans drove deeply into Russia, cutting up and surrounding the disorganized and unprepared Russian forces. The Russians suffered terrible losses. In a little more than three months, 2.5 million Russian soldiers were killed, wounded, or captured and 14,000 tanks destroyed. Describing the war as a crusade to save Europe from "Jewish Bolshevism," German propaganda claimed that victory had been assured.

But there were also disquieting signs for the Nazi invaders. The Russians, who had a proven capacity to endure hardships, fought doggedly and courageously, and the government would not consider capitulation. Russian reserve strength was far greater than the Germans had estimated. The Wehrmacht (German army), far from its supply lines, was running short of fuel, and trucks and cars had to contend with primitive roads that turned into seas of mud when the autumn rains came. One German general described the ordeal: "The infantryman slithers in the mud, while many teams of horses are needed to drag each gun forward. All wheeled vehicles sink up to their axles in the slime. Even tractors can only move with great difficulty. A large portion of our heavy artillery was soon stuck fast. . . . The strain that all this

caused our already exhausted troops can perhaps be imagined."[6] Conditions no longer favored the blitzkrieg.

Early and bitter cold weather hampered the German attempt to capture Moscow. Without warm uniforms, tens of thousands of Germans suffered from frostbite; without antifreeze, guns did not fire. The Germans advanced to within twenty miles of Moscow, but on December 6, a Red Army counterattack forced them to postpone the assault on the Russian capital. The Germans were also denied Leningrad, which since September had been almost completely surrounded and under constant bombardment. During this epic siege, the citizens of Leningrad displayed extraordinary courage in the face of famine, disease, and shelling that cost nearly 1 million lives.

By the end of 1941, Germany had conquered vast regions of Russia but had failed to bring the country to its knees. There would be no repetition of the collapse of France. The Russian campaign demonstrated that the Russian people would make incredible sacrifices for their land and that the Nazis were not invincible.

The New Order

By 1942, Germany ruled virtually all of Europe from the Atlantic to deep into Russia. Some conquered territory was annexed outright; other lands were administered by German officials; in still other countries, the Germans ruled through local officials sympathetic to Nazism or willing to collaborate with the Germans. Over this vast empire, Hitler and his henchmen imposed a New Order.

Exploitation and Terror

"The real profiteers of this war are ourselves, and out of it we shall come bursting with fat," said Hitler. "We will give back nothing and will take everything we can make use of."[7] The Germans systematically looted the lands they conquered, taking gold, art treasures, machinery, and food supplies back to Germany and exploiting the industrial and agricultural potential of non-German lands to aid the German war economy. Some foreign businesses and factories were confiscated by the German Reich; others produced what the Germans demanded. Germany also requisitioned food from the conquered regions, significantly reducing the quantity available for local civilian consumption. German soldiers were fed with food harvested in occupied France and Russia; they fought with weapons produced in Czech factories. German tanks ran on oil delivered by Rumania, Germany's satellite. The Nazis also made slave laborers of conquered peoples. Some 7 million people from all over Europe were wrested from their homes and transported to Germany. These forced laborers, particularly the Russians and Poles, whom Nazi ideology classified as subhumans, lived in wretched, unheated barracks and were poorly fed and overworked; many died of disease, hunger, and exhaustion.

The Nazis ruled by force and terror. The prison cell, the torture chamber, the firing squad, and the concentration camp symbolized the New Order. In the Polish province annexed to Germany, the Nazis jailed and executed intellectuals and priests, closed all schools and most churches, and forbade Poles from holding professional positions. In the region of Poland administered by German officials, most schools above the fourth grade were shut down. Himmler insisted that it was sufficient for Polish children to learn "simple arithmetic up to five hundred at the most; writing of one's name; a doctrine that it is a divine law to obey the Germans and to be honest, industrious, and good."[8] The Germans were particularly ruthless toward the Russians, whom they regarded as an especially low form of humanity. Soviet political officials were immediately executed; many prisoners of war were herded into camps and deliberately starved to death. In all, the Germans took some 5.5 million Russian prisoners, of whom more than 3.5 million perished.

Extermination

Against the Jews of Europe, the Germans waged a war of extermination. The task of imposing the "Final Solution of the Jewish Problem" was given to Himmler's SS, and they fulfilled these grisly duties with fanaticism and bureaucratic efficiency. In exterminating the Jewish people the Nazis were symbolically destroying essential values of the Western tradition—reason, freedom, equality, toleration, compassion, and individualism—which they despised and with which the Jews, because of their unique historical experience, were identified.

Regarding themselves as idealists who were writing a glorious chapter in the history of Germany, the SS tortured and murdered with immense dedication. The mind of the SS was dominated by the mythical world-view of Nazism, as the following tract issued by SS headquarters reveals:

> *Just as night rises up against the day, just as light and darkness are eternal enemies, so the greatest enemy of world-dominating man is man himself. The sub-man—that creature which looks as though biologically it were of absolutely the same kind, endowed by Nature with hands, feet and a sort of brain, with eyes and mouth—is nevertheless a totally different, a fearful creature, is only an attempt at a human being, with a quasi-human face, yet in mind and spirit lower than any animal. Inside this being a cruel chaos of wild, unchecked passions: a nameless will to destruction, the most primitive lusts, the most undisguised vileness. A sub-man—nothing else! . . . Never has the sub-man granted peace, never has he permitted rest. . . . To preserve himself he needed mud, he needed hell, but not the sun. And this underworld of sub-men found its leader: the eternal Jew!*[9]

Special squads of SS—the *Einsatzgruppen*, trained for mass murder—followed on the heels of the German army into Russia. Entering captured villages and cities, they rounded up Jewish men, women, and children, herded them to execution grounds, and slaughtered them with machine-gun and rifle fire. Aided by Ukrainian, Lithuanian, and Latvian auxiliaries, along with contingents from the Rumanian army, the Einsatzgruppen massacred some 1.5 million Jews. Units of the regular German army, the Wehrmacht, actively

Map 34.2 World War II: The European Theater ▶

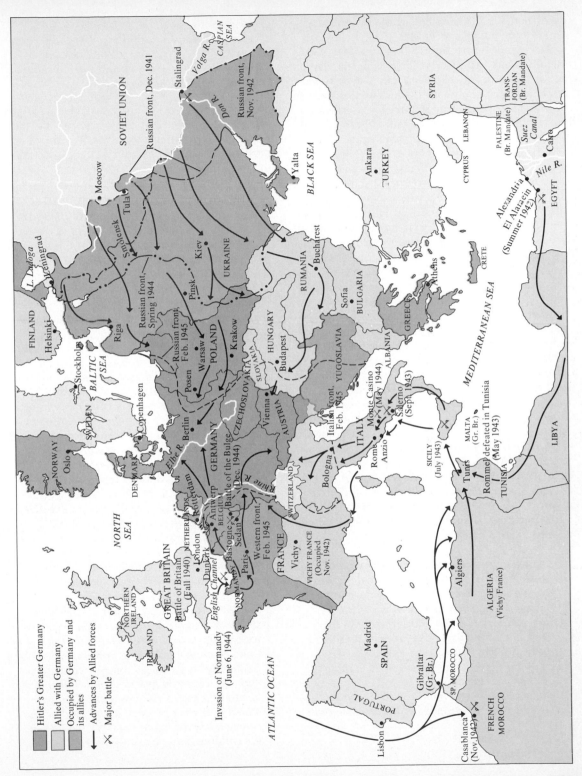

CASPIAN SEA

Volga R.

Stalingrad

Russian front, Dec. 1941

Russian front, Nov. 1942

Don R.

SOVIET UNION

Moscow

Yalta

BLACK SEA

Tula

Ankara

TURKEY

SYRIA

TRANS-JORDAN (Br. Mandate)

PALESTINE (Br. Mandate)

LEBANON

Suez Canal

CYPRUS

Cairo

Nile R.

EGYPT

Alexandria

El Alamein (Summer 1942)

Smolensk

Kiev

UKRAINE

Pinsk

Russian front, Spring 1944

L. Ladoga

Leningrad

FINLAND

Helsinki

Bucharest

RUMANIA

Sofia

BULGARIA

Riga

Russian front, Feb. 1945

Warsaw

POLAND

Krakow

Posen

SLOVAKIA

Hungary

Budapest

GREECE

Athens

CRETE

MEDITERRANEAN SEA

Stockholm

BALTIC SEA

SWEDEN

Copenhagen

DENMARK

Berlin

Elbe R.

CZECHOSLOVAKIA

Vienna

AUSTRIA

YUGOSLAVIA

Italian front, Feb. 1945

ALBANIA

Monte Casino (May 1944)

Salerno (Sept. 1943)

MALTA (Gr. Br.)

LIBYA

NORWAY

Oslo

NORTH SEA

Rhine R.

GERMANY

Battle of the Bulge (Dec. 1944)

SWITZERLAND

Bologna

ITALY

Rome

Anzio

SICILY (July 1943)

Tunis

Romme defeated in Tunisia (May 1943)

TUNISIA

GREAT BRITAIN

Battle of Britain (Fall 1940)

London

Amsterdam

Rotterdam

NETHERLANDS

BELGIUM

Antwerp

Bastogne

Dunkirk

Sedan

Paris

Western front, Feb. 1945

FRANCE

Vichy

VICHY FRANCE (Occupied Nov. 1942)

English Channel

NORMANDY

NORTHERN IRELAND

IRELAND

Invasion of Normandy (June 6, 1944)

ATLANTIC OCEAN

Madrid

SPAIN

Gibraltar (Gr. Br.)

PORTUGAL

Lisbon

SP. MOROCCO

Algiers

ALGERIA (Vichy France)

FRENCH MOROCCO

Casablanca (Nov. 1942)

Hitler's Greater Germany

Allied with Germany

Occupied by Germany and its allies

Advances by Allied forces

Major battle

participated in the rounding up of Jews and sometimes in the actual shootings.

In Poland, where some 3.3 million Jews lived, the Germans established ghettos in the larger cities. Jews from all over the country were crammed into these ghettos, which were sealed off from the rest of the population. The German administration deliberately curtailed the food supply, and many Jews died of malnutrition, disease, and beatings. In the ghettos, the Polish Jews struggled to maintain community life and to preserve their spirit. They established schools (forbidden by the German authorities), prayed together (also forbidden), organized social services, and kept hidden archives so that future ages would have a historical record of their ordeal.

To speed up the Final Solution, concentration camps, originally established for political prisoners, were transformed into killing centers and new ones were built for that purpose. Jews from all over Europe were rounded up—for "resettlement," they were told. The victims dismissed rumors that the Germans were engaged in genocide. They simply could not believe that any nation in the twentieth century was capable of such evil. "Why did we not fight back?* . . . I know why. Because we had faith in humanity. Because we did not really think that human beings were capable of committing such crimes," declared one survivor.[10] Jammed into sealed cattle cars, eighty or ninety to a car, the victims traveled sometimes for days, without food or water, choking from the stench of vomit and excrement, and shattered by the crying of children. Disgorged at the concentration camps, they entered another planet.

> *Corpses were strewn all over the road; bodies were hanging from the barbed-wire fence; the sound of shots rang in the air continuously. Blazing flames shot into the sky; a giant smoke cloud ascended about them. Starving, emaciated human skeletons stumbled forward toward us, uttering incoherent sounds. They fell down right in front of our eyes gasping out their last breath.*
>
> *Here and there a hand tried to reach up, but when this happened an SS man came right*

*On Jewish resistance, see page 781.

> *away and stepped on it. Those who were merely exhausted were simply thrown on the dead pile. . . . Every night a truck came by, and all of them, dead or not, were thrown on it and taken to the crematory.[11]*

SS doctors quickly inspected the new arrivals, "the freight," as they referred to them. Rudolf Hoess, commandant of Auschwitz—the most notorious of the murder factories—described the procedure:

> [I] estimate that at least 2,500,000 victims were executed and exterminated [at Auschwitz] by gassing and burning, and at least another half million succumbed to starvation and disease, making a total dead of about 3,000,000. This figure represents about 70 per cent or 80 per cent of all persons sent to Auschwitz as prisoners, the remainder having been selected and used for slave labor in the concentration camp industries. . . .
>
> The "final solution" of the Jewish question meant the complete extermination of all Jews in Europe. I was ordered to establish extermination facilities at Auschwitz in June, 1941. . . . It took from three to fifteen minutes to kill people in the death chamber, depending upon climatic conditions. We knew when the people were dead because their screaming stopped. We usually waited about one-half hour before we opened the doors and removed the bodies. After the bodies were removed our special commandos took off the rings and extracted the gold from the teeth of the corpses. . . .
>
> The way we selected our victims was as follows. . . . Those who were fit to work were sent into the camp. Others were sent immediately to the extermination plants. Children of tender years were invariably exterminated since by reason of their youth they were unable to work. . . . We endeavored to fool the victims into thinking that they were to go through a delousing process. Of course, frequently they realized our true intentions, and we sometimes had riots and difficulties due to that fact. Very frequently women would hide their children under clothes, but of course when we found them we would send the children in to be exterminated.[12]

The naked bodies, covered with blood and excrement and intertwined with each other, were piled high to the ceiling. To make way for the next group, a squad of Jewish prisoners emptied the gas chambers of the corpses and removed the gold teeth, which along with the victims' hair, eyeglasses, and clothing, were carefully collected and catalogued for the war effort. Later, the bodies were burned in crematoria specially constructed by I. A. Topf and Sons, of Erfurt. The chimneys vomited black smoke and the stench of burning flesh permeated the entire region. Jewish leaders in the United States and Britain, who got word of the killings, pleaded with the Allies to bomb the rail lines to Auschwitz and the gas chambers, but the Allies did nothing. The killing process went on relentlessly.

Auschwitz was more than a murder factory. It also provided the German industrial giant, I. G. Farben, which operated a factory adjoining the camp, with slave laborers, both Jews and non-Jews. The working pace at the factory and the ill treatment by guards was so brutal, reported a physician and inmate, that "while working many prisoners suddenly stretched out flat, turned blue, gasped for breath, and died like beasts."[13]

Auschwitz also allowed the SS, the elite of the master race, to shape and harden themselves according to the National Socialist creed. A survivor recalls seeing SS men and women amuse themselves with pregnant inmates. The unfortunate women were "beaten with clubs and whips, torn by dogs, dragged by the hair, and kicked in the stomach with heavy German boots. Then, when they collapsed, they were thrown into the crematory—alive."[14] By systematically overworking, starving, beating, terrorizing, and degrading the inmates, by making them live in filth and sleep sprawled all over each other in tiny cubicles, the SS deliberately sought to strip prisoners of all human dignity, to make them appear, behave, and believe that they were indeed "sub-man," as National Socialist ideology viewed them. When prisoners, exhausted, starved, diseased, and beaten, became unfit for work, generally within a few months, they were sent to the gas chambers. Many went mad or committed suicide; some struggled desperately, defiantly, and heroically to maintain their humanity. Nazi extermination camps, perhaps the vilest assault on human dignity ever conceived, were the true legacy of National Socialism, and the SS, the true end product of National Socialist indoctrination and idealism.

There have been many massacres during the course of world history. And the Nazis murdered many non-Jews in concentration camps and in reprisal for acts of resistance. What is unique about the Holocaust—the systematic extermination of European Jewry—was the Nazis' determination to murder without exception every single Jew who came within their grasp, and the fanaticism, ingenuity, and cruelty with which they pursued this goal. Despite the protests of the army, the SS murdered Jews whose labor was needed for the war effort, and when Germany's military position was desperate, the SS still diverted military personnel and railway cars to deport Jews to the death camps.

The Holocaust was the terrible fulfillment of Nazi racial theories. Believing that they were cleansing Europe of worthless life and a dangerous race that threatened Germany, Nazi executioners performed their evil work with dedication, assembly-line precision, and moral indifference—a terrible testament to human irrationality and wickedness. Using the technology and bureaucracy of a modern state, the Germans killed approximately 6 million Jews—*two-thirds* of the Jewish population of Europe. Some 1.5 million of the murdered were children. Tens of thousands of entire families were wiped out without a trace. Centuries-old Jewish community life vanished, never to be restored. Burned into the soul of the Jewish people was a wound that could never entirely heal. Written into the history of Western civilization was an episode that would forever cast doubt on the Enlightenment conception of human goodness, rationality, and the progress of civilization.

Resistance

Each occupied country had its collaborators who welcomed the demise of democracy, saw Hitler as Europe's best defense against communism, and profited from the sale of war material. Each country also produced a resistance movement that grew stronger as Nazi barbarism became more visible and prospects of a German defeat more likely. The Nazis retaliated by torturing and executing captured resistance fighters and killing hostages—generally fifty for every German killed.

In western Europe the resistance rescued downed Allied airmen, radioed military intelligence to Britain, and sabotaged German installations. Norwegians blew up the German stock of heavy water needed for atomic research. The Danish underground sabotaged railways and smuggled into neutral Sweden almost all of Denmark's 8,000 Jews just before they were to be deported to the death camps. The Greek resistance blew up a vital viaduct, interrupting the movement of supplies to German troops in North Africa. After the Allies landed on the coast of France in June 1944, the French resistance delayed the movement of German reinforcements and liberated sections of the country. Belgian resistance fighters captured the vital port of Antwerp.

The Polish resistance, numbering some 300,000 at its height, reported on German troop movements and interfered with supplies destined for the eastern front. In August 1944, with Soviet forces approaching Warsaw, the Poles staged a full-scale revolt against the German occupiers. The Poles appealed to the Soviets, camped ten miles away, for help. Thinking about a future Russian-dominated Poland, the Soviets did not move. After sixty-three days of street fighting, remnants of the Polish underground surrendered and the Germans destroyed what was left of Warsaw.

Russian partisans numbered several hundred thousand men and women. Operating behind the German lines, they sabotaged railways, destroyed trucks, and killed scores of thousands of German soldiers in hit-and-run attacks.

The mountains and forests of Yugoslavia provided excellent terrain for guerrilla warfare. The leading Yugoslav resistance army was headed by Josip Broz (1892–1980), better known as Tito. Moscow-trained, intelligent, and courageous, Tito organized the partisans into a disciplined fighting force that tied down a huge German army and ultimately liberated the country from German rule.

Jews participated in the resistance movements in all countries and were particularly prominent in the French resistance. Specifically Jewish resistance organizations emerged in eastern Europe, but they suffered from shattering hardships. They had virtually no access to weapons. Poles, Ukrainians, Lithuanians, and other East European peoples with a long history of anti-Semitism gave little or no support to Jewish resisters—at times, even denounced them to the Nazis, or killed them. For centuries, European Jews had dealt with persecution by complying with their oppressors, and they had unlearned the habit of armed resistance that their ancestors had demonstrated against the Romans. The Germans responded to acts of resistance with savage reprisals against other Jews, creating a moral dilemma for any Jew who considered taking up arms. Nevertheless, revolts did take place in the ghettos and concentration camps. In the spring of 1943, the surviving Jews of the Warsaw ghetto, armed only with a few guns and homemade bombs, fought the Germans for several weeks.

Italy and Germany also had resistance movements. After the Allies landed in Italy in 1943, bands of Italian partisans helped to liberate Italy from fascism and the German occupation. In Germany, army officers plotted to assassinate the Fuehrer. On July 20, 1944, Colonel Claus von Stauffenberg planted a bomb at a staff conference attended by Hitler, but the Fuehrer escaped serious injury. In retaliation, some 5,000 suspected anti-Nazis were tortured and executed in exceptionally barbarous fashion.

The Turn of the Tide

The Japanese Offensive

At the same time that Germany was subduing Europe, its ally, Japan, was extending its dominion over areas of Asia. Seeking raw materials and secure markets for Japanese goods, and driven by a xenophobic nationalism, Japan in 1931 had attacked Manchuria in northern China. Quickly overrunning the province, the Japanese established the puppet state of Manchukuo in 1932. After a period of truce, the war against China was renewed in July 1937. Japan captured leading cities, including China's principal seaports, and

Map 34.3 World War II: The Pacific Theater ▶

Japanese Empire, 1931
Japanese Empire, 1942
Extent of Japanese expansion
Allied advances

SOVIET UNION

ASIA

MONGOLIA

MANCHURIA

Peiping
(Peking)

KOREA

Hiroshima

JAPAN

Tokyo

Nagasaki

CHINA

Shanghai

PACIFIC OCEAN

TAIWAN

OKINAWA
1945

IWO JIMA
1945

MIDWAY 1942

Hong
Kong

MARIANA IS.

WAKE

HAWAIIAN IS.
Pearl Harbor

THAILAND

BURMA

FRENCH
INDOCHINA

Manila

PHILIPPINE IS.
LEYTE 1944

SAIPAN

GUAM
1944

MARSHALL
IS.

MALAYA

BORNEO

Singapore

CAROLINE IS.

SUMATRA

DUTCH EAST INDIES

JAVA

NEW
GUINEA

SOLOMON IS.

TARAWA
1943

GILBERT IS.

GUADALCANAL
1942

ATTU

KISKA
1943

ALEUTIAN IS.

INDIAN OCEAN

AUSTRALIA

Brisbane

34 *World War II: Western Civilization in the Balance*   **783**

Kamikaze Attack on the *Hornet*, Painted from Combat Experience by Lt. Dwight C. Chepler, U.S.N.R. With the bombing of Pearl Harbor, Japan had destroyed much of the American fleet and ex-pected a quick, easy victory. The U.S. triumph at the Battle of Midway on June 4, 1942, however, broke Japan's initiative. (*Popperfoto*)

inflicted heavy casualties on the poorly organized Chinese forces, forcing the government of Jiang Jieshi (Chiang Kai-shek) to withdraw to Chungking in the interior.

In 1940, after the defeat of France and with Britain standing alone against Nazi Germany, Japan eyed Southeast Asia—French Indochina, British Burma and Malaya, and the Dutch East Indies. From these lands Japan planned to obtain the oil, rubber, and tin vitally needed by Japanese industry and enough rice to feed the nation. Japan hoped that a quick strike against the American fleet in the Pacific would give it time to enlarge and consolidate its empire. On December 7, 1941, the Japanese struck with carrier-based planes at Pearl Harbor in Hawaii. Taken by surprise, the

Americans suffered a total defeat: the attackers sank seventeen ships, including seven of eight battleships; destroyed 188 airplanes and damaged 159 others; and killed 2,403 men. The Japanese lost only 29 planes. After the attack on Pearl Harbor, Germany declared war on the United States. Now the immense American industrial capacity could be put to work against the Axis powers—Germany, Italy, and Japan.

By the spring of 1942, the Axis powers held the upper hand. The Japanese empire included the coast of China, Indochina, Thailand, Burma, Malaya, the Dutch East Indies, the Philippines, and other islands in the Pacific. Germany controlled Europe almost to Moscow. When the year ended, however, the Allies seemed assured of victory. Three decisive battles—Midway, Stalingrad, and El Alamein—reversed the tide of war.

At Pearl Harbor the Japanese had destroyed much of the American fleet. Assembling a mighty flotilla (8 aircraft carriers, 11 battleships, 22 cruisers, and 65 destroyers), Japan now sought to annihilate the rest of the United States Pacific fleet. In June 1942, the main body of the Japanese fleet headed for Midway, 1,100 miles northwest of Pearl Harbor; another section sailed toward the Aleutian Islands in an attempt to divide the American fleet. But the Americans had broken the Japanese naval code and were aware of the Japanese plan. On June 4, 1942, the two navies fought a strange naval battle; it was waged entirely by carrier-based planes, for the two fleets were too far from each other to use their big guns. Demonstrating marked superiority over their opponents and extraordinary courage, American pilots destroyed 4 aircraft carriers and downed 322 Japanese planes. The battle of Midway cost Japan the initiative. With American industrial production accelerating, the opportunity for a Japanese victory had passed.

Defeat of the Axis Powers

After being stymied at the outskirts of Moscow in December 1941, the Germans renewed their offensive in the spring and summer of 1942. Hitler's goal was Stalingrad, the great industrial center located on the Volga River; control of Stalingrad would give Germany command of vital rail transportation. The battle of Stalingrad was an epic struggle in which Russian soldiers and civilians contested for every building and street of the city. So brutal was the fighting that at night half-crazed dogs sought to escape the city by swimming across the river. A Russian counterattack in November caught the Germans in a trap. Exhausted and short of food, medical supplies, weapons, and ammunition, Friedrich Paulus, commander of the Sixth Army, urged Hitler to order a withdrawal before the Russians closed the ring. The Fuehrer refused. After suffering tens of thousands of additional casualties, their position hopeless, the remnants of the Sixth Army surrendered on February 2, 1943. Some 260,000 German soldiers had perished in the battle of Stalingrad and another 110,000 were taken prisoner.

In January 1941, the British were routing the Italians in northern Africa. Hitler assigned General Erwin Rommel (1891–1944) to halt the British advance. Rommel drove the British out of Libya and with strong reinforcements might have taken Egypt and the Suez Canal. But Hitler's concern was with seizing Yugoslavia and Greece and preparing for the invasion of Russia. In the beginning of 1942, Rommel resumed his advance, intending to conquer Egypt. The British Eighth Army, commanded by General Bernard L. Montgomery, stopped him at the battle of El Alamein in October 1942. The victory of El Alamein was followed by an Anglo-American invasion of northwest Africa in November 1942. By May 1943, the Germans and Italians were defeated in North Africa.

After securing North Africa, the Allies, seeking complete control of the Mediterranean, invaded Sicily in July 1943 and quickly conquered the island. Mussolini's fellow fascist leaders turned against him, and the king dismissed him as prime minister. In September, the new government surrendered to the Allies, and in the following month Italy declared war on Germany.

Italian partisans, whose number would grow to 300,000, resisted the Germans, who were determined to hold on to central and northern Italy. At the same time, the Allies fought their way up the peninsula. The fighting in Italy would last until the very end of the war. Captured by partisans, Mussolini was executed (April 28, 1945) and his dead body, hanging upside-down, was publicly displayed.

On June 6, 1944—D-Day—the Allies landed on the beaches of Normandy in France. They had assembled a massive force for the invasion—2 million men and 5,000 vessels. Although they suspected an imminent landing, the Germans did not think that it would occur in Normandy and they dismissed June 6 because weather conditions were unfavorable. The success of D-Day depended on securing the beaches and marching inland, which the Allies did despite stubborn German resistance on some beaches. By the end of July, the Allies had built up their strength in France to a million and a half. In the middle of August, Paris rose up against the German occupiers and was soon liberated.

As winter approached, the situation looked

Two Inmates of Changi Prison Camp After Release, 1945. World War II in the Pacific theater continued three months after the Allied victory in Europe on May 7, 1945. After the United States dropped a second atomic bomb on Japan at Nagasaki on August 9, Japan surrendered, and the prisoners who survived their ordeal in Japanese camps like Changi were released. (*Popperfoto*)

hopeless for Germany. Brussels and Antwerp fell to the Allies; Allied bombers were striking German factories and mass-bombing German cities in terror raids that took a terrible toll of life. The desperate Hitler made one last gamble. In mid-December 1944, he launched an offensive to split the Allied forces and regain the vital port of Antwerp. The Allies were taken by surprise in the

Battle of the Bulge, but a heroic defense by the Americans at Bastogne helped stop the German offensive.

While their allies were advancing in the west, the Russians were continuing their drive in the east, advancing into the Baltic states, Poland, and Hungary. By February 1945, they stood within one hundred miles of Berlin.

Also in February the Allies in the west were battling the Germans in the Rhineland, and on March 7, 1945, American soldiers, seizing a bridge that the Germans had failed to destroy, crossed the Rhine into the interior of Germany. By April 1945, British, American, and Russian troops were penetrating into Germany from east and west. From his underground bunker near the chancellery in Berlin, a physically exhausted and emotionally unhinged Hitler engaged in wild fantasies about new German victories. On April 30, 1945, with the Russians only blocks away, the Fuehrer took his own life. In his last will and testament, Hitler again resorted to the vile lie: "It is not true that I or anybody else in Germany wanted war in 1939. It was wanted and provoked exclusively by those international statesmen who either were of Jewish origin or worked for Jewish interests."[15] On May 7, 1945, a demoralized and devastated Germany surrendered unconditionally.

After the victory at Midway in June 1942, American forces attacked strategic islands held by Japan. American troops had to battle their way up beaches and through jungles tenaciously defended by Japanese soldiers, who believed that death was preferable to the disgrace of surrender. In March 1945, 21,000 Japanese perished on Iwo Jima; another 100,000 died on Okinawa in April 1945 as they contested for every inch of the island. On August 6, 1945, the United States dropped an atomic bomb on Hiroshima, killing more than 78,000 people and demolishing 60 percent of the city. President Truman said that he ordered the atomic attack to avoid an American invasion of the Japanese homeland that would have cost hundreds of thousands of lives. Truman's decision has aroused considerable debate. Some analysts say that dropping the bomb was unnecessary, that Japan, deprived of oil, rice, and other essentials by an American naval blockade and defenseless against unrelenting aerial bombardments, was close to surrender and had indicated as such. It has been suggested that with the Soviet Union about to enter the conflict against Japan, Truman wanted to end the war immediately, thereby depriving the U.S.S.R. of an opportunity to extend its influence in East Asia. On August 8, Russia did enter the war against Japan, invading Manchuria. After a second atomic bomb was dropped on Nagasaki on August 9, the Japanese asked for peace.

The Legacy of World War II

World War II was the most destructive war in history. Estimates of the number of dead range as high as 50 million, including 20 million Russians, who sacrificed more than the other participants in both population and material resources. The war produced a vast migration of peoples unparalleled in modern European history. The Soviet Union annexed the Baltic lands of Latvia, Lithuania, and Estonia, forcibly deporting many of the native inhabitants into central Russia. The bulk of East Prussia was taken over by Poland, and Russia annexed the northeastern portion. Millions of Germans fled or were forced out of Prussia and regions of Czechoslovakia, Rumania, Yugoslavia, and Hungary, places where their ancestors had lived for centuries. Material costs were staggering. Everywhere cities were in rubble; bridges, railway systems, waterways, and harbors destroyed; farmlands laid waste; livestock killed; coal mines wrecked. Homeless and hungry people wandered the streets and roads. Europe faced the gigantic task of rebuilding. Yet Europe did recover from this material blight, and with astonishing speed.

World War II produced a shift in power arrangements. The United States and the Soviet Union emerged as the two most powerful states in the world; the traditional Great Powers—Britain, France, Germany—were now dwarfed by these *superpowers*. The United States had the atomic bomb and immense industrial might; the Soviet Union had the largest army in the world and was extending its dominion over eastern Europe. With Germany prostrate and occupied, the principal incentive for Soviet-American cooperation had evaporated.

Whereas World War I was followed by an intensification of nationalist passions, after World War II, western Europeans progressed toward cooperation and unity. The Hitler years had convinced many Europeans of the dangers inherent in extreme nationalism, and fear of the Soviet Union fortified the need for greater cooperation.

World War II accelerated the disintegration of Europe's overseas empires. The European states could hardly justify ruling over Africans and Asians after they had fought to liberate European lands from German imperialism. Nor could they ask their peoples, exhausted by the Hitler years and concentrating all their energies on reconstruction, to fight new wars against Africans and Asians pressing for independence. In the years just after the war, Great Britain surrendered India, France lost Lebanon and Syria, and the Dutch departed from Indonesia. In the 1950s and 1960s, virtually every colonial territory gained independence. In those instances where the colonial power resisted independence for the colony, the price was bloodshed.

The consciousness of Europe, already profoundly damaged by World War I, was again grievously wounded. Nazi racial theories showed that in an age of sophisticated science, the mind remains attracted to irrational beliefs and mythical imagery; Nazi atrocities demonstrated that people will torture and kill with religious zeal and machinelike indifference. The Nazi assault on reason and freedom demonstrated anew the precariousness of Western civilization. Both the Christian and Enlightenment traditions had failed the West. Some intellectuals, shocked by the irrationality and horrors of the Hitler era, drifted into despair. To these thinkers, life was absurd, without meaning; human beings could neither comprehend nor control it. In 1945, only the naive could have faith in continuous progress or believe in the essential goodness of the individual. The future envisioned by the philosophes seemed further away than ever.

World War II ushered in the atomic age. At the end of the war, only the United States had the atomic bomb, but soon the Soviet Union and other states acquired an arsenal of atomic weapons. That people now possess the weapons to destroy themselves and their planet is the ever-present, ever-terrifying, and ultimately most significant legacy of World War II.

Chronology 34.2 World War II

September 27, 1939	Poland surrenders
November 1939	Russia invades Finland
April 1940	Germany attacks Denmark and Norway
May 10, 1940	Germany invades Belgium, Holland, and Luxembourg
May 14, 1940	The Dutch surrender
May 27–June 4, 1940	British forces are evacuated from Dunkirk
June 22, 1940	France surrenders
August–September 1940	The battle of Britain
September 1940	Japan begins conquest of Southeast Asia
October 1940	Italian troops cross into Greece
April 6, 1941	Germany attacks Greece and Yugoslavia
June 22, 1941	Germany launches offensive against Russia
December 7, 1941	Japan attacks Pearl Harbor; United States enters the war against Japan and Germany
1942	The tide of battle turns in the Allies' favor: Midway (Pacific Ocean), Stalingrad (Soviet Union), and El Alamein (North Africa)
April–May 1943	Uprising of Jews in Warsaw ghetto
September 1943	Italy surrenders to Allies, following invasion
June 6, 1944	D-Day—Allies land in Normandy, France
August 1944	Paris is liberated; Poles revolt against German occupiers
January 1945	Soviet troops invade Germany
March–April 1945	Allies penetrate Germany
May 7, 1945	Germany surrenders unconditionally
August 1945	United States drops atomic bombs on Hiroshima and Nagasaki; Soviet Union invades Manchuria; Japan surrenders

Notes

1. Pierre Renouvin, *World War II and Its Origins* (New York: Harper & Row, 1969), p. 167.

2. Z. A. B. Zeman, *Nazi Propaganda* (New York: Oxford University Press, 1973), p. 109.

3. *Documents on German Foreign Policy, 1918–1945,* vol. VI (London: Her Majesty's Stationery Office, 1956), series D, no. 433.

4. Basil H. Liddell Hart, *History of the Second World War* (New York: G. P. Putnam's Sons, 1970), pp. 73–74.

5. Winston S. Churchill, *The Second World War: Their Finest Hour* (Boston: Houghton Mifflin, 1949), 2:225–226.

6. Quoted in William L. Shirer, *The Rise and Fall of the Third Reich* (New York: Simon & Schuster, 1960), p. 860.

7. *Hitler's Secret Conversations, 1941–1944,* with an introductory essay by H. R. Trevor Roper (New York: Farrar, Straus & Young, 1953), p. 508.

8. Quoted in Gordon Wright, *The Ordeal of Total War* (New York: Harper Torchbooks, 1968), p. 124.

9. Quoted in Norman Cohn, *Warrant for Genocide* (New York: Harper Torchbooks, 1967), p. 188.

10. Gerda Weissman Klein, *All But My Life* (New York: Hill & Wang, 1957), p. 89.

11. Judith Sternberg Newman, *In the Hell of Auschwitz* (New York: Exposition, 1964), p. 18.

12. *Nazi Conspiracy and Aggression,* vol. 6 (Washington, D.C.: United States Government Printing Office, 1946), pp. 787–789.

13. Quoted in Joseph Borkin, *The Crime and Punishment of I. G. Farben* (New York: The Free Press, 1978), p. 143.

14. Gisella Perl, *I Was a Doctor in Auschwitz* (New York: International Universities Press, 1948), p. 80.

15. Excerpted in George H. Stein, ed., *Hitler* (Englewood Cliffs, N.J.: Prentice-Hall, 1968), p. 84.

Suggested Reading

Bauer, Yehuda, *A History of the Holocaust* (1982). An authoritative study.

Baumont, Maurice, *The Origins of the Second World War* (1978). A brief work by a distinguished French scholar.

Calvocoressi, Peter, and Guy Wint, *Total War* (1972). A good account of World War II.

Cohn, Norman, *Warrant for Genocide* (1967). An astute analysis of the mythical components of modern anti-Semitism.

Des Pres, Terrence, *The Survivors* (1976). A sensitive analysis of life in the death camp.

Eubank, Keith, *The Origins of World War II* (1969). A brief introduction, with a good bibliographical essay.

Gilbert, Martin, and Martin Gott, *The Appeasers* (1963). A study of British weakness in the face of Hitler's threats.

Hilberg, Raul, *The Destruction of the European Jews* (1967). A monumental study of the Holocaust.

Hildebrand, Klaus, *The Foreign Policy of the Third Reich* (1973). A brief assessment of Nazi foreign policy.

Marks, Sally, *The Illusion of Peace* (1976). The failure to establish peace in the period 1918–1933.

Marrus, Michael R., *The Holocaust in History* (1987). An excellent summary of key issues and problems.

Michel, Henri, *The Shadow War* (1972). An analysis of the European resistance movement, 1939–1945.

————, *The Second World War,* 2 vols. (1975). Translation of an important study by a prominent French historian.

Remak, Joachim, *The Origins of the Second World War* (1976). A useful essay, followed by documents.

Wiesel, Elie, *Night* (1960). A moving personal record of the Holocaust.

Review Questions

1. What efforts promoted international reconciliation during the 1920s? How did these efforts only foster the illusion of peace?

2. What were Hitler's foreign-policy aims?

3. Why did Britain and France practice a policy of appeasement?

4. Discuss the significance of each of the following: Italy's invasion of Ethiopia (1935), Germany's re-militarization of the Rhineland (1936), the Spanish Civil War (1936–1939), Germany's union with Austria (1938), the occupation of Prague (1939), and the Nazi-Soviet Pact (1939).

5. What factors made possible the quick fall of France?

6. What problems did the German army face in Russia?

7. Describe the New Order the Nazis established in Europe.

8. In your opinion, what is the meaning of the Holocaust for Western civilization? For Jews? For Christians? For Germans?

9. Discuss the significance of each of the following battles: Midway (1942), Stalingrad (1942–1943), El Alamein (1942), and D-Day (1944).

10. What was the legacy of World War II?

VII

The Contemporary World:
The Global Age

Since 1945

35

Europe After 1945:
Recovery, Realignment, Division

At the end of World War II, Winston Churchill lamented: "What is Europe now? A rubble heap, a charnel house, a breeding ground for pestilence and hate."[1] Everywhere the survivors counted their dead. War casualties were relatively light in Western Europe. Britain and the Commonwealth suffered 460,000 casualties; France, 570,000; and Italy, 450,000. War casualties were heavier in the east—5 million people in Germany, one in every five persons in the total population of Poland (largely because of the extermination of 3 million Polish Jews), one in every ten in Yugoslavia, and over 20 million in the Soviet Union. The material destruction had been unprecedentedly heavy in the battle zones of northwestern Europe, northern Italy, and Germany, growing worse farther east, where Hitler's and Stalin's armies had fought without mercy to people, animals, or the environment. Industry, transportation, and communication had come to a virtual standstill; bridges, canals, dikes, and farmlands were ruined. Ragged, worn people picked among the rubble and bartered their valuables for food, while strangers straggled by. Members of families searched for each other; prisoners of war made their way home; Jews from extermination camps or from hiding places returned to open life; displaced persons by the millions sought refuge.

Added to the human miseries was the historic fact that Europe had been dethroned from the central position in world affairs it had occupied in recent centuries. It was politically cut in half. The division arose because in pursuing Hitler's armies, the Soviet troops had overrun Eastern Europe and penetrated into the heart of Germany. The Yalta agreement of February 1945, signed by Roosevelt, Churchill, and Stalin on Stalin's home ground in the Crimean peninsula, turned the prevailing military balance of power into a political settlement, with Soviet promises (not kept) for free elections

The Big Three at Yalta: Churchill, Roosevelt, and Stalin. (*National Archives*)

Marshall Plan Aid. Since much of Europe lay in rubble at the conclusion of World War II, the U.S. Congress approved the European Recovery Program (the official name of the Marshall Plan) in 1948. The funds were to be used to buy U.S. goods. The earliest aid, however, went toward agricultural assistance and housing construction to alleviate malnutrition and homelessness. (*UPI/Bettmann Newsphotos*)

in Soviet-dominated Eastern Europe. The American bargaining position at Yalta was weakened by the expectation that Soviet help would be needed for victory over Japan.

Europe's future now depended on two countries, the United States and the Soviet Union, which soon became embroiled in an embittered cold war. Both nations were outsiders in Europe; both had risen from their combined victory over Hitler as superpowers, towering far above the great European empires of the past. The superpowers divided Europe between themselves. The Soviet Union, exhausted by the war and fearful for its security, imposed its grim tradition of dictatorship, while the United States, virtually unharmed by the war, brought the boons of its wealth and power to help rebuild Western Europe. Henceforth, the United States stood out as the heir to

and guardian of the Western tradition, a political giant come into its own.

Western Europe

U.S. military power had liberated Western Europe from Hitler's tyranny. Thereafter, U.S. military presence and superiority in nuclear weapons protected Western Europe against the widely dreaded westward expansion of Soviet communism. Against that threat, the United States and the countries of Western Europe established the North Atlantic Treaty Organization (NATO) in 1949. NATO combined the armed forces of

Map 35.1 Western Europe After 1945

the United States, Canada, Portugal, Norway, Iceland, Denmark, Italy, Britain, France, and the Benelux countries (Belgium, Holland, and Luxemburg). Greece and Turkey soon joined; West Germany was included in 1955, and Spain in 1982. The postwar rebuilding of Western Europe proceeded under the protection of U.S. military power. The American influence also provided the foundations for political stability under democratic constitutions, as well as for material prosperity based on free enterprise in a market economy.

Even before committing itself to a military presence, the United States had begun an extensive program of financial assistance for the economic recovery of Western Europe. In June 1947, Secretary of State George C. Marshall announced an impressive scheme of economic aid formally called the European Recovery Program, but widely known as the Marshall Plan. By December 1959, the Marshall Plan had supplied Europe with a total of over $74 billion in aid, a modest pump-priming for the subsequent record upswing in U.S., Western European, and even global prosperity. Western Europe recovered, and the United States gained economically strong allies and trading partners.

U.S. military and economic pre-eminence after the war also prepared the way for the influx of American ways of life and culture abroad. The languages of Western Europe became permeated with American words and phrases. Young people especially favored American popular music as well as fashions. More generally, Western Europeans adopted the casual American lifestyle. Cultural Americanization perhaps progressed furthest in West Germany, which was especially receptive after the collapse of Nazi rule. There, as a prominent film director put it, the Americans had colonized the German subconscious.

European Unity

Although Europeans share a common cultural heritage, the diversity of their history and national temperaments has burdened them in the past with incessant warfare. After two ruinous world wars, many people at last began to feel that the price of violent conflict had become excessive; war no longer served any national interest. The extension of Soviet power made some form of Western European unity attractive. The first call for a united Europe was sounded by Winston Churchill who, reviving a project first launched in the seventeenth century, declared in 1946: "We must build a kind of United States of Europe."[2]

Despite such hopes, the major governments of Western Europe and their peoples were not prepared suddenly to submerge their separate national traditions under a common government empowered to regulate their internal affairs. Political unity was not forthcoming, but in the field of economics the movement for unity made headway.

Western European economic cooperation began rather modestly with the creation of the European Coal and Steel Community (ECSC) in 1951. It drew together the chief Continental consumers and producers of coal and steel, the two items most essential for the rebuilding of Western Europe. Its members were France, West Germany, the three Benelux countries, and Italy; these six countries thus became the core countries of Western European unity. Their design was to put the Ruhr industrial complex, the heart of German industrial power, under international control, thereby promoting cooperation and reconciliation as well as economic strength. Their project was endorsed by the West German Chancellor Konrad Adenauer, who expected it to restore confidence in his country. West Germany has stood in the forefront of European integration since then.

Emboldened by the success of the ECSC, the Six soon pressed forward. "In order to maintain Europe's place in the world, to restore her influence and prestige, and to ensure a continuous rise in the living standards of her people," their foreign ministers, led by Belgium's Paul-Henri Spaak, prepared two treaties, signed in Rome in March 1957. One treaty created a European Atomic Energy Community (called Euratom) for joint research on nuclear energy, and the other established the European Economic Community, also known as the Common Market. The EEC, which eventually absorbed Euratom, became the focus of the European search for unity, prosperity, and power.

Minimally, the EEC was to be a customs union, creating a free market among the Six, with a common external tariff for protection from the rest of the world, yet pledged to participate in the worldwide reduction of trade barriers. At the same time the EEC aimed higher: it was to improve living conditions among the people, help reduce the differences between the various regions and countries, and mitigate "the backwardness of the less favored" among member countries. It also promised to confirm "the solidarity which binds together Europe and overseas countries" in the spirit of the United Nations. Finally, it called on the other states of Europe to join the Six "in an ever closer union."[3] Toward the outside world the EEC was empowered to act as agent for its members in all commercial transactions. It has negotiated a great variety of special agreements with an ever-widening circle of Western European states and Third World countries.

It was clear from the outset that free trade within the EEC called for increasing uniformity among all the factors affecting the marketplace. The free movement of goods and people encouraged standardization and cooperation in every aspect of the economy. For that reason, the "Eurocrats" in Brussels, the headquarters of the European Economic Community, were forever eager to extend their authority. They and the governments of the Six also worked hard to make the Common Market more inclusive. In 1973, the original Six were joined by three new members— Great Britain, Ireland, and Denmark.

The Nine, now calling themselves simply the European Community (EC), began to work for greater integration in foreign affairs. The foreign ministers of the EC met for regular consultation, trying to head off any conflicts among themselves or with outside powers. They presented a common front for effective negotiations with the Soviet Union in 1973–1975 at the Helsinki Conference on Security and Cooperation in Europe— the larger Europe that includes the Soviet Union and its Eastern European satellites as well. Favoring a relaxation of tension between the superpowers, they joined the United States in signing the Helsinki Agreements, thereby accepting as permanent the division of Europe produced by World War II.

Political integration among the Nine also made some progress. In June 1979, direct elections were held for delegates to the European Parliament sitting at Strasbourg. Although possessing only advisory power, the Strasbourg Assembly provides the first transnational representative forum for the discussion of common concerns. Thereafter, efforts at political integration began to flag, beset by differences in economic conditions and national policy, disillusioned public opinion, and hostility between the superpowers.

Progress in economic integration, however, continued. By 1979, three more states had applied for membership in the EC: Spain, Portugal, and Greece. The inclusion of less well-off states presented the EC with difficult challenges; it had to adjust to the influx of cheap labor and competing farm products under conditions of high unemployment and agricultural overproduction. After long preparation, the three applicants became full members in 1986.

Forever at odds with each other, especially over agricultural subsidies, the key members realize that there is no effective alternative to working together. In 1992, they hope to abolish all remaining barriers, creating a truly "common market" for the EC's 320 million customers. All told, the EC carries much weight in the world. It constitutes the largest single trading entity, conducting over one-fifth of the world's commerce.

Economic Developments

The most striking fact of recent history in the West, as in the world generally, is the unprecedented economic advance. Between the early 1950s and the late 1970s, production in Western Europe and the United States, as elsewhere, surpassed all previous records. By the time the economic advance came to an end, it had created a new world economic order requiring adjustments in Western Europe, the United States, and around the world.

In the immediate aftermath of the war the necessities of reconstruction demanded the fullest use of state authority. Following long-standing tradition, most European governments extended their control over essential economic functions. Nearly everywhere, the biggest banks were nationalized, together with key industries and public utilities; nationwide economic planning was harnessed to the same purpose. Social welfare programs were also extended. As a result, the standard of living improved dramatically. Health services, housing, and educational opportunities were provided for almost everyone.

With the arrival of the Marshall Plan and under U.S. prodding, the trend swung back from state control to private enterprise working together with public authority. All national economies in Western Europe thus became "mixed economies," combining public and private enterprises in complex interlocking arrangements.

The rapid postwar economic advance was not, however, destined to last. It had been fed by abundant and exceptionally cheap supplies of oil, but after 1973 the Organization of Petroleum Exporting Countries (OPEC) drastically raised the price of that essential source of energy. OPEC's action aggravated adverse worldwide economic trends that had been evident since the late 1960s (and were caused in part by the U.S. war in Vietnam). Inflation, unemployment, falling productivity, competition (from Japan especially) in automobiles and electronics, and a worldwide economic recession plagued all the governments of Western Europe. After another oil crisis in 1979, the economy recovered, and prosperity continued through the middle 1980s. Unemployment in Western Europe, however, remained high, even in West Germany, the strongest country economically.

The increase in the public sector everywhere has been offset in recent years in the private sector. Private-sector influence has been enhanced by mergers, consolidations, and the rise of large holding corporations, often with monopoly or near-monopoly status. Stimulated by the expansion of U.S. multinational corporations into Western Europe and by the opportunities offered by the European Community, many European companies have become multinational and grown bigger than any nationalized industry. The Western European economy is now dominated by gigantic private and public enterprises that are tied to other parts of the world and subject to a growing volume of transnational regulation and guidance. Western Europe is also participating in the immense technological upsurge of the age. In science and technology, in research and development, Western Europeans are determined to stand up to American and Japanese competition for leadership.

Political Developments

Boosted by rising standards of living and by U.S. power, the overall trend of political life in the West since World War II has been toward constitutional democracy. Although Spain and Portugal retained their prewar dictatorships until the mid-1970s and Greece for a time wavered between democracy and dictatorship, by the late 1970s even these countries had conformed to the common pattern. Membership in the European Community requires democratic government; the expansion of its membership has confirmed the liberal-democratic tradition.

In most countries the political parties covered the spectrum of political creeds. Communists and various factions of socialists, dedicated to state control of the economy, constituted the left. On the right the conservatives generally adhered to nineteenth-century liberalism and to laissez-faire economics. Authoritarian or protofascist right-wing movements periodically rose and waned, but they never had a serious chance; nor did the terrorists, who came to the fore in the early 1970s. Depending on local circumstances, terrorism stood to the left of communism or to the extreme right; militant regionalism also spawned terrorism.

Political power essentially lay with the center parties, which claimed the largest support. These parties proceeded pragmatically, steering a cautious course between state control and free enterprise. Depending on circumstances, they allied themselves with the moderate left or the moderate right, with socialists or conservatives. They reconstituted their political platforms around the established traditions of Western Europe: Christianity and liberal democracy. In continental Western Europe the political and economic reconstruction after the war was largely the work of Christian Democratic parties, known in France as Mouvement Républicain Populaire (MRP)—rather short-lived under the conditions of French politics; in West Germany as the Christian-Democratic Union (CDU); and in Italy as the Christian Democrats, lasting to the present. Great Britain, whose constitution remained intact throughout the great wars, retained its traditional two-party system. But here, too, the winning majorities for both parties came from center votes shifting toward either the Conservative or the Labour party.

It was a sign of the times that ideologically oriented moderate socialist parties did poorly at the polls. Strong immediately after the war, they lost support the longer they adhered to their doctrines. The new social awareness in private enterprise, the rise of the welfare state, and the complexity of modern life reduced their appeal. Dogmatic socialists quarreled, splintered, and declined in power, or else they turned pragmatist, creating reformist mass parties slightly left of center. For example, both the West German Social Democratic party (SPD) and the British Labour party supported a number of mildly socialist policies but avoided a socialist program.

The major communist parties of Western

Europe, especially those of Italy and France, also could not escape the temper of the times. Dropped in 1947, in response to U.S. pressure, from the government coalitions in their countries, communists steadily held their own in the next three decades; in France they polled between one-fifth and one-fourth of the total vote, and in Italy up to one-third. Recently, however, their success at the polls has declined. Whatever their strength, communists have been condemned to play the role of frustrated, ineffectual opposition, even in Italy. Barred from national leadership, communists have been effective in local government, especially in Italy, where they run the administration of most communities, including large cities.

But gradually patriotism, prosperity, the shortcomings of the Soviet system, and the complexity of all things modern eroded the dogmatism of Western European communists. By the mid-1970s a new variety of communism called Eurocommunism emerged. It was determined to prove itself under the established democratic ground rules as a mass movement dedicated to better government. In the increasingly conservative politics of the 1980s, however, Eurocommunism faded into insignificance.

Problems and Tensions

Western Europe did not escape serious problems and tensions. With the rise of the public sector and the increase in social services, government and bureaucracy grew huge and more impersonal. Individuals felt dwarfed by the state and lost in a complex, interdependent society. The massive spurt of affluence had unsettling effects on European culture. Although prosperity provided more people with more material goods, it also encouraged a hedonistic self-indulgence that ran contrary to the puritan strain in Western tradition. Material security and abundance undermined the bourgeois work ethic; life became too easy.

Young people, especially, were in ferment, tending to repudiate the new affluence and the complexity on which it was based. They also emphasized its drawbacks: stark inequality in the world, social callousness at home, the breakdown of human intimacy and community, and the

mounting strain on human energy and integrity. In their protest, some of the young sided with a romantic counterculture, disdaining traditional middle-class restraints, above all in sex, and proclaiming their solidarity with all oppressed peoples around the world. On the whole, the protest was nonpolitical, a part of the new "youth culture" that had split off from the dominant culture of adult society.

In 1968, youthful frustration broke into politics—angrily and sometimes destructively—foremost in France and slightly less drastically throughout Western Europe (as it did, more mildly, in the anti–Vietnam War agitation in the United States). During May 1968, a spontaneous and embittered demonstration of students and workers in Paris set off a massive general strike such as France had not seen since 1936. Yet no revolution followed, no sudden social change, only a conservative backlash at the next national election. The majority of the French people, like their contemporaries elsewhere, realized that they could not escape the vast size and complexity that burdens contemporary state and society. The events of 1968, however, made them more aware of the need for the human touch in all official business.

Some impatient young protesters, meanwhile, turned to outright terrorism, especially in West Germany and Italy. In their eyes, the entire system of state and society was inhumane and deserved destruction by any means available. The targets of their attacks were leading representatives of "the system": politicians, industrialists, judges, and the police. After a few spectacular assassinations, public opinion began to favor more effective countermeasures, thus curtailing terrorist violence.

Meanwhile, youthful protest had turned to environmental issues, most notably in West Germany through the rise of the Green party. The Greens, as they called themselves, directed attention to the adverse effects of modern industry on human beings and the ecology. They agitated against the pollution of water and air, dramatized the plight of dying forests, and opposed nuclear power plants. Volatile, erratic, and unsuited for political organization, the Greens nevertheless succeeded in alerting public opinion to the damaged natural environment.

Tensions in the body politic were also reflected in the rise of separatist and nationalist movements within well-established nation-states. Great Britain was troubled by nationalist movements in Wales and Scotland, and especially in Northern Ireland, where Catholics and Protestants, driven by long-standing political and religious differences, continued their murderous confrontations; the violence occasionally spilled over into England. France suffered from separatist movements in the northwest and southwest. In Belgium, Walloons and Flemings strained their country's unity. In Spain, the restoration of constitutional government after the death of General Franco in 1975 was marred by the terrorism of Basque extremists hoping to create a Basque state. Terrorists of all kinds established links with their counterparts in other troubled areas of the world, creating a sort of international terrorist movement. Raw violence offered to young idealists the opportunity for politically aware and self-denying heroism, but it provided no answer to the intricate problems of modern society.

Another source of tension flowed from the influx of a particular group of newcomers, called guest workers. Attracted to Western Europe and Scandinavia by economic opportunity, they came from southern Europe, the countries of North Africa, Greece, Turkey, and elsewhere. Even after the onset of economic recession, many of them remained, raising families and claiming citizenship while retaining their culture or religion. They have been the object of discrimination and a source of political tension and occasional violence.

Agitation over the nuclear arms race also stirred tensions. Throughout Western Europe, men and women gathered in mass demonstrations calling attention to the threat of nuclear war. The demonstrations reached a peak in the fall of 1983 when the United States began a program of placing intermediate-range nuclear missiles close to the Soviet Union. These protests proved ineffectual because of the widespread fear of Soviet expansionism. Yet the threat of nuclear bombs destroying Western Europe keeps the movement for ending the arms race alive as a political force.

Confronted with the new cultural diversity, the corruption of traditional morals by the new affluence, and the vehemence of political agitation, the guardians of traditional religion faced troubling questions. The Roman Catholic church passed through much collective soul-searching during the great council of Vatican II (1962–1965), asking how traditional dogma and pastoral care could be reconciled with modern conditions. Earnestly searching for answers, the council infused new vitality into the worldwide church. Among Protestants, whether in the established state churches (as in West Germany, the Scandinavian countries, and Great Britain) or in free churches, confusion also reigned. Church membership generally declined, especially in established churches; fundamentalist churches and sects like Jehovah's Witnesses gained members, as did non-Western world religions like Bahai.

Underneath their outward conformity and ready acceptance of the material boons of contemporary society, many Western Europeans live in spiritual doubt, their inner lives out of tune with their outward existence. Tied to global interdependence, suspended among troubled national economies and halfhearted economic integration under the European Community, and caught in the tensions between the two superpowers, the peoples of Western Europe face an uncertain future—in their material conditions and in all aspects of their lives.

The Leading Western European States

France

After 1945, France, reorganized under its fourth republican constitution, quickly laid the foundation for its subsequent rapid economic advance. Under the leadership of Jean Monnet, an able group of economists and planners mapped out strategies and institutions that have become models of state guidance in a mixed economy of public and private enterprise. During the 1950s, the French economy grew at a very respectable rate.

In national politics the sense of common purpose was less evident. In 1946, the new constitution creating the Fourth Republic followed the pattern of the Third. The twenty-six short-lived governments of the Fourth Republic valiantly coped with a number of grave problems, putting down communist-led strikes in 1947 and 1948, assisting in the organization of Western European defense, laying the groundwork for the European Economic Community, and promoting political reconciliation with Germany.

A major problem that France faced in these years was decolonization. In two areas, the French army fought colonial liberation movements to the bitter end. In Indochina the French army suffered a resounding defeat in 1954. In Algeria, administratively a part of France proper, French settlers and soldiers were determined to thwart demands for independence.

The long and bloody Algerian conflict had serious repercussions for French political life. In 1958, the insubordination of army leaders brought down the Fourth Republic with a resounding call for the return of General Charles de Gaulle, the leader of the Free French forces in World War II. De Gaulle then wrote the constitution of the Fifth Republic, largely to suit his own style as president. Elections were held regularly, reinforced by referendums, but they were manipulated to give support to the president; in emergencies the president could even claim dictatorial powers. Although De Gaulle thought that he embodied France's greatness and therefore stood above all political parties, his political instincts remained moderate.

De Gaulle's grand design was simple enough: to restore France to its rightful place in Europe and the world. At home this meant that France had to modernize its economy, encourage science and technology, and regain a common will. Abroad it had to assert its presence by all means available—cultural, economic, political, and even military. De Gaulle insisted that France have its own nuclear force, and he pulled France out of the NATO high command. He increased French prestige among Third World countries, consenting to Algerian independence over the protest of the army and retaining the good will of the new African states formerly under French rule. But his France, a mere middle-size state in the global world, was too small for De Gaulle's ambition; his grand style in foreign policy did not survive him. His successors, Georges Pompidou (1969–1974), and Valéry Giscard D'Estaing (1974–1981), did emphasize, however, that France was "the third

nuclear power" after the United States and the Soviet Union and was determined to assert its independence.

After De Gaulle's death, France produced no leader of equal stature. President Pompidou avoided his precedessor's flamboyant style but was unable to mend the country's political disunity. Giscard D'Estaing—aristocratic, increasingly aloof, and tainted with scandal—was even more troubled by lack of mass support. His attempt to make France "an advanced liberal society" led to endless friction in the center-right coalition on which he depended for legislative action.

On the left, meanwhile, communists and socialists (the latter led by François Mitterrand) competed for working-class and peasant votes. Their feuds prevented the emergence of a left-of-center government until 1981, when the communists reluctantly agreed to a coalition dominated by Mitterrand. As a result of that year's election Mitterrand, an experienced politician and noted intellectual, replaced Giscard D'Estaing. The new president shifted course to the left with a program to nationalize industries and banks and increase government jobs. But even more than his predecessor, he was plagued by the adversities besetting the country's economy.

The socialist remedies applied by Mitterrand failed, forcing the government into a course of unpopular austerity. Not surprisingly, the socialists lost to the conservatives in the parliamentary elections of March 1986, forcing President Mitterrand to appoint a conservative prime minister, Jacques Chirac. Despite the political differences between the president and the prime minister, despite terrorist violence, government has proceeded effectively. On the left, the communists have lost much of their constituency. On the extreme right, hard-liners court popularity by attacking North Africans trying to establish themselves in the country. Yet public opinion has held to a conciliatory middle course, with a slight socialist bent. In 1988, Mitterrand was re-elected for a second seven-year term.

Whether governed under a center-right or socialist-left course, the Fifth Republic has been held back by the forces of tradition. The French distrust their government as well as impersonal large-scale industrial or commercial organizations. Many French peasants have failed to become efficient farmers, and still more have left the land altogether. Society is localized and divided by social status. The political parties on which the government relies are unstable and shifting, often centered more on personalities than on issues. Deeply patriotic and determined to uphold their country's military strength in Europe, the French wonder whether becoming more modern means becoming less French.

West Germany

In 1945, its cities in ruins, Germany had been defeated, occupied, and branded as a moral outcast for the horrors that Nazi rule had brought to Europe. Divided among four occupying powers, the German nation was politically extinct. Prussia, considered to be the source of German militarism, was dissolved; extensive eastern lands were handed to Poland and the Soviet Union; and some territory also was returned to France. The dream of national glory that had provided the chief momentum in German life for more than a century was over.

By 1949, two new and chastened Germanys had emerged. The Federal Republic of Germany, formed from the three western zones of occupation, faced a hostile, Soviet-dominated German Democratic Republic in the east. The partition of Germany signified not only the destruction of Germany's traditional political identity but also a personal tragedy for almost all Germans: families were split as the division interrupted communication between the two Germanys. The national trauma reached a peak in August 1961 when the East German government suddenly threw up a wall dividing the city of Berlin and for years tightly sealing off East from West Germany.

The cold war proved a boon to West Germany; feared and despised though they were, the West Germans were needed. Located next door to the Red Army, they were in a strategic position for the defense of Western Europe. Even more important, German industry and expertise were indispensable for the success of the Marshall Plan. Finally, a democratic West Germany would aid the course of Western European unity.

The Adenauer Era On this basis, the Federal Republic of Germany (far larger than its communist counterpart to the east and the most populous of all Western European countries) began to build a political identity of its own. The new West Germany was a demilitarized and decentralized federal state consisting of ten member states (plus West Berlin, which continued to exist under a special status). The executive power was held by the chancellor, who was checked by both a democratically elected parliament and the representatives of the member states.

Because of constitutional precautions against the proliferation of parties, only three emerged: two dominant parties, the Christian-Democratic Union (CDU) and the Social-Democratic party of Germany (SPD), and a minor one, the Free Democratic party (FPD). The latter enjoyed the advantage of being indispensable to either of the major parties for a parliamentary majority. The CDU was the dominant party under the long chancellorship of Konrad Adenauer (1949–1963).

Adenauer was the founding hero of the Federal Republic of Germany. A vigorous old-timer (he was seventy-five when appointed chancellor), known as a courageous anti-Nazi in the Hitler years, he represented the pro-Western, liberal-democratic tradition of the Weimar Republic. His aim was simple: restore respect for Germany in cooperation with the United States and the leading states of Western Europe. Never giving up hope for the reunification of Germany, he worked foremost for the integration of West Germany into the emerging Western European community. Yet while boycotting all relations with the communist German Democratic Republic, Adenauer also promoted normal relations with Moscow. As a patriot, he rebuilt a cautious continuity with the German past, shouldering responsibility for the crimes of the Nazi regime.

Adenauer's chancellorship proved popular, for it provided the stability and order required for West Germany's spectacular economic advance. Adenauer's economic policy was conducted by Minister of Finance Ludwig Erhard, who preferred private enterprise in a liberal market economy safeguarded from monopolies and made socially responsible through the extensive participation of labor unions. Given the opportunity,

West Germans threw themselves into rebuilding their economy and their country, quickly creating a citadel of economic strength. Their exports grew famous throughout the world, and their currency became the soundest in Western Europe. The whole world admired the West German "economic miracle."

Adenauer's policy paid off within a few years; West Germany regained its sovereignty. In 1955, a cautiously remilitarized West Germany became a member of NATO, and in 1957 the country was a founding member of the European Economic Community, of which it soon became the linchpin. Subsequent West German governments have generally followed the course set by Adenauer, completing Germany's rehabilitation when, in 1972, both West and East Germany were admitted to the United Nations.

After Adenauer After the Adenauer era, German voters gradually shifted from center-right to center-left; in 1969, the SPD emerged as the leading party. Under Chancellors Willy Brandt (1969–1974) and his more pragmatic successor, Helmut Schmidt (1974–1982), it ruled in coalition with the small FDP, guiding German politics with remarkable stability. Willy Brandt expanded Adenauer's foreign policy (as well as opportunities for the West German economy) through better cooperation with the German Democratic Republic and countries of the Soviet bloc. His initiative for the "opening toward the East" contributed to a temporary relaxation of tension—the brief era of *détente* in the early 1970s—in relations between the superpowers. During these years neither political extremists nor terrorists managed to shake public confidence in the constitution.

German minds, however, were hardly at peace. The Nazi era remained a moral embarrassment. After the war, the Nuremberg trials of the major war criminals had been followed by de-Nazification under West German courts. Members of Nazi elite organizations were barred from public office and higher education. Many people guilty of atrocities were prosecuted; others went into hiding in Germany or abroad; Jews themselves tracked down some notable fugitives, like Adolf Eichmann, and brought them to justice. (Eichmann was tried in Jerusalem in 1961.) The search

and the trials still continue, the West German Parliament having consistently refused to enact a statute of limitations on crimes committed under the Nazis. In an effort at restitution, the government also has paid damages to Israel and to survivors among Nazi victims and their kin.

Although older Germans are still troubled by the Nazi years, the generation now growing up feels less burdened by the catastrophes of a rapidly receding past. The major aspects of Nazi rule have been openly aired; Nazi anti-Semitism has even been dramatized by the showing on German television of the American program "Holocaust." "We are all responsible for the unspeakable sorrow that occurred in the name of Germany," said Richard von Weizsäcker, president of West Germany in 1985, in attempting to make Germans face up to their past.

Meanwhile, public attention has been drawn to the physical environment, threatened by industrial pollution and nuclear power, as well as by war. The loosely organized Greens express a romantic alienation from contemporary society and politics. All the same, they have carried their agitation into parliamentary elections, at the expense largely of the Social Democrats, a party increasingly splintered under the impact of economic recession. The young people have also frightened the uneasy elders, who in the face of recession and rising hostility to the Soviet Union, have turned more conservative. In 1982, Helmut Schmidt was replaced by Helmut Kohl, the leader of the CDU, who continues to govern with the help of the indispensable FDP and with public support.

Even under a right-center government Germans are uneasy, confronted with major challenges testing the unity of the country. Party organizations weaken; consensus turns brittle in the uneasy search for a persuasive political identity that will give West Germany a respectable place in a divided Europe and a tension-ridden world. The economy, although strong, must adjust to greater worldwide competitiveness; there will be continued unemployment amid remarkable prosperity. Although caught in the vying forces of the United States and the Soviet Union, West Germany is determined, even under a conservative government, to advance the unity of West and East Germany, to maintain its economic ties to the members of the Soviet bloc, and to reduce the intensity of Soviet–U.S. confrontation.

Great Britain

In 1945, Britain was a member of the victorious alliance. It had escaped foreign occupation and suffered less physical damage than any other European belligerent; its political institutions were intact, its prestige and democratic convictions riding high. Yet after this moment of glory it passed through a steady decline, requiring of its people a drastic reassessment of their place in the world.

World War II compounded Britain's long-standing economic woes, leaving the country impoverished and highly vulnerable in its dependence on imported food and raw materials. The British Empire was gradually and peaceably dismantled. Unlike the French, the English fought no last-ditch wars for retaining colonial control. British sea power waned, replaced by the U.S. navy and air force. Confronted with the choice between maintaining a global military presence and building a welfare state at home, the British people clearly preferred the latter. Although still enjoying a special relationship with the United States, the British were thrown back on their own resources. Among themselves they quarreled over autonomy for Scotland and Wales. In the late 1960s the ever-simmering conflict in Northern Ireland between Protestants and the large Catholic minority broke into unending and often vicious violence.

In their association with Western Europe, the British also fared poorly. Their first application for membership to the EEC, made in 1961, was vetoed by De Gaulle; they were not admitted until twelve years later in 1973. But it soon became apparent that Britain not only constituted an economic liability rather than an asset to the other members, it also gained no immediate benefit for itself. Comparatively poor, insular, and hesitant about merging its fortune with Western Europe, the United Kingdom still glories in the traditions of empire, although by current standards of power and productivity it has become a second-rate state.

Under these circumstances, successive British governments have done well in holding the ship of state together. A Labour government under Clement Attlee (1883–1967), elected immediately after the war, carried out the wartime promises of increased social services. Health care for the British people, traditionally deficient by Western European standards, was particularly improved. For better control over the national economy, the Labour government also nationalized the Bank of England, public transport, and the coal mines; eventually even the iron and steel industries came under government ownership.

The Labour government, which lost the 1951 election largely because it seemed to have prolonged the postwar austerity unnecessarily, was succeeded by the Conservatives. With Winston Churchill as prime minister, they rode the postwar tide of prosperity. In 1959, under Harold Macmillan, the Conservatives successfully campaigned for reelection under the slogan "You've never had it so good." They favored private enterprise but continued the extension of the welfare state, most notably by an ambitious public construction program that greatly improved British housing.

Economic setbacks, scandal, failure in foreign policy, and indifferent leadership among the Conservatives brought the Labour party back into power from 1964 to 1970; their promise was to boost the ailing economy. That, however, proved a difficult task. British industry had not modernized itself as rapidly as its chief competitors. It was hampered by poor management and frequent strikes, many of them caused by disputes among rival labor unions. British exports were lagging while imports soared; the value of the pound continued to decline. Costly imports and pressures for higher wages and welfare benefits contributed to high inflation.

Behind the economic ills lay a political problem: how to restrain the demands of British labor unions for a higher income and how to counter the strikes by which the workers backed up their demands. On this ground, the Labour party was weak, since it depended on union support. Under the strain its leader, Harold Wilson, could hardly keep peace between the pragmatic majority and the socialist left wing. Yet when the Conservatives returned to power in 1970, they were equally helpless to restrain the unions. In 1974, Prime Minister Edward Heath called a general election over the question: Who rules Britain, the government or the unions? The voters preferred the Labour party, by a small margin. Reversing themselves in 1979, the voters elected a Conservative government under Margaret Thatcher, the first woman prime minister in British history.

"Maggie" Thatcher soon proved herself an "Iron Lady." A vigorous partisan of private enterprise, she favored the return of nationalized industries to private hands. Aided by high unemployment she succeeded in breaking the power of the labor unions. She also fought inflation with rigorous austerity (although she never tried to eliminate unemployment benefits and other essentials of the welfare state); she has preferred to let adversity bestir British employers and workers into efficiency and innovation. She also electrified the raw nerve of patriotism, long dulled by a decline of imperial fortune, when British forces drove an Argentine occupying force out of the distant Falkland Islands; located off the coast of Argentina in the South Atlantic Ocean, they are one of Britain's remaining possessions. In her domestic and foreign policies, Thatcher has stressed her close ties to the U.S. government under President Reagan.

Against Thatcher's popularity the opposition has been powerless. The Labour party, torn by factionalism and deserted by many workers, is in decline. Some of its former supporters have moved toward the old Liberal party, now allied with a new Social Democratic party. However, this loose coalition has not proved itself to be a viable political force. In the mid-1980s, Margaret Thatcher's popularity has increased. In the election of 1987, she led the Conservatives to victory for the third time, becoming the longest-serving prime minister in modern English history.

During the 1980s, the British economy has improved; London has regained some of its former glory as a powerful financial center. The south of England has prospered, while the old, outmoded industrial areas of the Midlands and the north have declined, causing widespread unemployment, poverty, and occasional violence. Everywhere in the country the influx of people from the former colonies in Asia, Africa, and the West Indies has provoked racial friction. British society has lost its homogeneity—and some of its tolerance.

Italy

A country half the size of France yet with a population larger by several million, Italy has always occupied an ambiguous position in Europe. It has been respected, even revered, for its illustrious Roman past. It has also been condemned or even ridiculed for its backwardness in modern times, for its shaky or dubious liberal democracy, for its penchant for living beyond its means, and for its me-too desire for power culminating in Mussolini's theatrical bid for empire. The victory of the Anglo-American countries allied with the Soviet Union had a sobering effect. Fascism was refuted, its chief henchman punished. In 1946, even the monarchy, discredited by its subservience to Mussolini, was rejected. Italy was humbled and ravaged by the war.

After the war, Italy became a democratic republic that even the communists were pledged to uphold. The constitution, approved in 1947, resembled that of the French Fourth Republic, which meant that Italy would suffer from weak and unstable government. The average span of Italian cabinets to the present has been less than a year.

Hopeful for the future, the new republic could not escape the past. Italy has always been divided by internal rifts, the chief of which is the contrast between north and south, each worlds apart from the other. A lively localism impeded national unity; so did an anarchical individualism. Far from forming an organic whole, the state and the individual were in continuous tension and conflict. The political parties, scattered over a wide spectrum of opinion from communism to neofascism, likewise enjoyed little internal cohesion, except for the communists. The socialists were ceaselessly in agitation among themselves, without, however, losing their following. The Christian Democrats were the leading party, closely associated with the Catholic church. Despite continuing corruption they have contributed continuity to Italian politics, supplying the prime ministers and forming and reforming coalitions with lesser parties. From 1976 to 1978, they even enjoyed the tacit support of the communists. But the Christian Democrats were only a loose alliance of Catholics split into right, center, and left; in 1983, their support shrank to about a third of the popular vote. As a result, a socialist (Bettino Craxi) became the prime minister, heading an unstable coalition for nearly four years, the longest tenure in postwar Italian politics. In the summer of 1987, Craxi resigned amid a growing awareness that the country needed strong leadership at the center. No such leadership has emerged among his successors.

Spurred by the new postwar opportunities, Italian enterprise produced a striking economic advance. Its rate of growth, culminating in the years 1958–1962, propelled it into the ranks of the ten leading industrial nations of the world. Private corporations (like Fiat) and industries under large government holding companies led the way in introducing an efficiency that unfortunately had no parallel in the civil service or the government. The boom was aided by cheap and abundant labor, by high profits reinvested in innovation, and by the timely discovery of natural gas and some oil in the Po Valley. As a result, personal incomes, particularly in northern Italy, came to resemble those of the richer European countries. Italy seemed to have caught up.

The sudden spurt of industrialization inevitably aggravated the traditional weaknesses in Italian society. The economic advance remained incomplete, merely superimposing a layer of progressive prosperity on a backward and divided country. In their eagerness to catch up, most Italians preferred to live well for the moment rather than save for the future. The contradiction led to a deterioration in Italy's position in the European Community and to widespread apathy in the face of mounting corruption in the government and terrorist violence. Terrorists (not counting the criminal elements) have come from the extremes at both ends of the political spectrum. The neofascists, however, have been less active than the left-wing Red Brigades. Trying to create conditions favoring the overthrow of the ineffectual democratic constitution, the terrorists have resorted to bombings, kidnapings, maimings, and political murders, including that in 1978 of the much-respected Aldo Moro, leader of the Christian Democratic party.

What form of government can provide better leadership? Some have suggested a presidential republic like De Gaulle's. A "historic compromise" between the communists and the Christian Democrats was once advocated by Enrico Berlinguer, the secretary of the Italian Communist party and a leading Euro-communist. A neofascist regime supported by the army is the solution proposed by some. Given the strong democratic pull exerted by the European Community and NATO, extreme solutions are unlikely. The decline of communist strength and the marked economic upswing of recent years have not provided stability for the coalitions running the government, but they have calmed Italian life and politics.

The instability of Italian politics reflects the problems of Western Europe as a whole. Can that powerful and prosperous part of the world, the cradle of Western civilization, restrain national sovereignty and economic localism in its separate countries in order to play a constructive role in world affairs? Western Europe now is a vital but complex and divided center in a polycentric, interdependent world. It struggles, however halfheartedly, to achieve greater economic and political cohesion, aware that only unity can enhance its role in world affairs. The area is knitted into the world economy separately, by countries, and jointly through the Economic Community, and it participates in all agencies of the United Nations. Considered fully developed, Western Europe plays a significant part in assisting the developing countries. It also furnishes the headquarters for the Organization for Economic Cooperation and Development (OECD), which serves the most highly industrialized countries in Europe, North America, and the Far East. In the struggle between the superpowers, Western Europe tries to follow a middle course. Aiming to gain greater independence from the United States in the future, it fears far more the Soviet Union, the Eurasian giant to the east, caught up like Western Europe in inexorable change.

Eastern Europe

Four trends dominated the evolution of the Soviet Union after 1945: the continuing increase in Soviet military power, matched by caution in foreign policy; the gradual relaxation of the extreme measures of national mobilization designed by Stalin; the marked improvement in the material condition of the people; and the routinization of party rule—government action became more predictable. With these trends the Soviet Union further adapted to essential aspects of the Western style of achievement.

Stalin's Last Years

In Soviet experience, World War II was another cruel landmark in the long succession of wars, revolutions, and crises that had started in 1914; nothing basically changed even after its end. The liberation from terror and dictatorship, which many soldiers had hoped for as a reward for their heroism, never occurred. Stalin viewed the postwar scene in the light of his life's lessons. He had helped Lenin seize power and fight the cruel civil war in fear and hatred of the capitalist world. As Lenin's successor, he had demanded unprecedentedly brutal efforts from his people to strengthen Soviet Russia against its enemies. The epic struggle against the Nazi invaders had further hardened the man of steel. Sixty-six years old in 1945, corrupted by unlimited power and unrestrained adulation, Stalin displayed in his last years an unrelenting ruthlessness and a suspiciousness raised to the pitch of paranoia.

Stalin's assessment of Soviet Russia's condition at the end of the war was consistent with his previous thinking. He saw no ground for relaxing control. The country still had immense problems: the large anti-Soviet populations in Eastern Europe; the lack of atomic weapons; the traditional poverty; the destruction wrought by the war; the political unreliability of returning soldiers and prisoners of war; and the overwhelming strength of the United States. Wherever he looked, Stalin saw cause for concern. The government, the party, communist ideology, the economy—all were in disarray. The generals were riding high, threatening his own supremacy and that of the party. Ideological control had slackened during the war. The exhausted people were in danger of falling into a postwar slump, yearning for greater freedom in their personal lives. Tired and hungry as they

were, how could they be goaded to work for the speedy reconstruction of their country? How could the party be reinvigorated? Communist parties in other lands not directly under his thumb were to be trusted even less. Against these threats, Stalin had to exercise full Bolshevik vigilance. His indomitable ambition, undiminished by age, was to build up Soviet power in his lifetime, whatever the human cost. More Five-Year Plans, more terror were needed.

On this familiar note the Soviet Union slid from war into peace, staggering through the hardships and hunger of the war's aftermath, mourning its dead soldiers, desperately short of men. As before, the peasants were squeezed to the utmost to furnish the state with food without receiving more than the barest minimum in return. The urban-industrial population fared slightly better. With planning, much selfless hard work, manpower released from the army, and resources requisitioned from all occupied territories, industrial production was back to prewar levels within three years—no mean achievement.

With the return to Five-Year Plans came a deliberate tightening of ideological control. The party boss of Leningrad, Andrei Zhdanov (1896–1948), lashed out against well-known literary figures for their "escapist, unorthodox, and unSoviet" thinking. His target was any form of Western influence and personal withdrawal from the tasks set by the party. Thus thousands of returning soldiers and prisoners of war, who had seen too much in the West, were sent to forced-labor camps; the Soviet intelligentsia was again terrorized into compliance with the party line.

A shrill, dogmatic superpatriotism became mandatory for all Soviet citizens. This patriotism extolled Russia's achievements, past and present, over those of the West. Even scientists had to submit, at a fearful cost to research (except in nuclear physics). Zhdanov singled out the most famous composers, Dmitri Shostakovich and Sergei Prokofiev, whom he accused of "bourgeois formalism," a derogatory term for refined artistic standards. Zhdanovism, as the anti-intellectual campaign was called, was accompanied by renewed political terror, again centered on Leningrad. In 1948, the chief leaders of the heroic struggle against the Nazi siege were arrested and shot.

The cold war drove Stalin to further exertions, some of them ill-considered. Eastern Europe had to be brought under a tight rein. In 1948, he foisted Stalinist regimes on Eastern Europe, except for Yugoslavia. There Marshal Tito thwarted his plans, breaking the unity of world communism under Soviet leadership.

The next year, Stalin had to accept, although he did not welcome, the victory of the Chinese communists under Mao Zedong. Mao's triumph established a potentially threatening China along the Soviet Union's open borders in southeastern Asia; it also created a competing variant of communism. For these reasons, relations between the Russian and Chinese Communist parties were not as friendly as Americans feared. In 1950, the North Korean communists, possibly with Stalin's approval, attacked South Korea, which further intensified the cold war.

In his last years Stalin withdrew into virtual isolation, surrounded by a few fawning and fearful subordinates, and his sickly suspicion worsened. Before he died, he "recognized" a plot among the doctors who treated him and personally issued orders for their torture (which killed one of them). When on March 5, 1953, the failing dictator died of a stroke, his advisers sighed with relief, but many people wept: to them Stalin was the godlike leader and savior of the nation.

One of the most remarkable people of the twentieth century, Stalin was a towering figure in the Russian mold of Ivan the Terrible or Peter the Great. The human costs of his labor were immense, but of his achievements in raising Soviet power there can be no doubt. By 1949, sooner than expected, Soviet Russia possessed the atomic bomb. By 1953, at the same time as the United States, it had the hydrogen bomb as well. Stalin also helped lay the foundation for *Sputnik I* (meaning "fellow traveler"—of the Earth), the first artificial satellite to orbit the earth.

More important perhaps, Stalin also bequeathed to his successors a tamed and even cowed population, more malleable and cooperative than any previous generation. Stalin himself was the last of the self-willed, self-centered revolutionaries. His successors were masterful organization men ruling over obedient and hard-driven subjects; the party could now count on a growing number of people with a personal stake in the regime and its institutions.

Khrushchev: A New Course Stalled

The chief question after Stalin's death was: who would succeed him and in what manner? The succession struggles of the 1920s and their bloody aftermath in the terror purges were still on everybody's mind. How would the issues be settled this time? Would the new leadership be able to cope with Russia's difficult problems? Above all, how were the new leaders to deal with Stalin?

The most hated among Stalin's potential heirs was Lavrenti Beria, the head of the secret police and the vast empire of forced-labor camps. In December 1953, he was suddenly executed, together with his chief henchmen, for having been a "foreign spy." These cynical accusations and violent deaths were the last gasp of Stalinism; ever since, the rivals for supreme leadership have died of natural causes.

Gradually leadership was assumed by a team headed by Nikita Khrushchev (1894–1971), who breathed fresh air into Soviet life. Khrushchev was the driving force behind the "thaw" that emptied the forced-labor camps and allowed the return to their native regions of most nationalities that had been forcibly resettled during the war. He even dared to attack Stalin himself.

After 1953, Stalin had been cautiously downgraded and even denounced under the cover of charges against the cult of personality. In a speech at the Twentieth Party Congress in February 1956, Khrushchev brought the issue to a sudden head. His audience gasped with horror as he recited the facts: "Of the 139 members and candidates of the Party Central Committee who were elected at the 17th congress, 98 persons, i.e., 70%, were arrested . . . and shot. . . ." In this vein, Khrushchev cited example after example of Stalin's terror, summing up with the charge that "the accusations were wild, absurd, and contrary to common sense" and that the tortures used to extract confessions were "barbaric, cruel, and inhuman." He also enumerated Stalin's mistakes, as for instance in not sufficiently preparing for Hitler's attack in 1941. Throughout, he revealed, Stalin had "discarded the Leninist methods of convincing and educating" and "abandoned the

Map 35.2 Eastern Europe After 1945 ▶

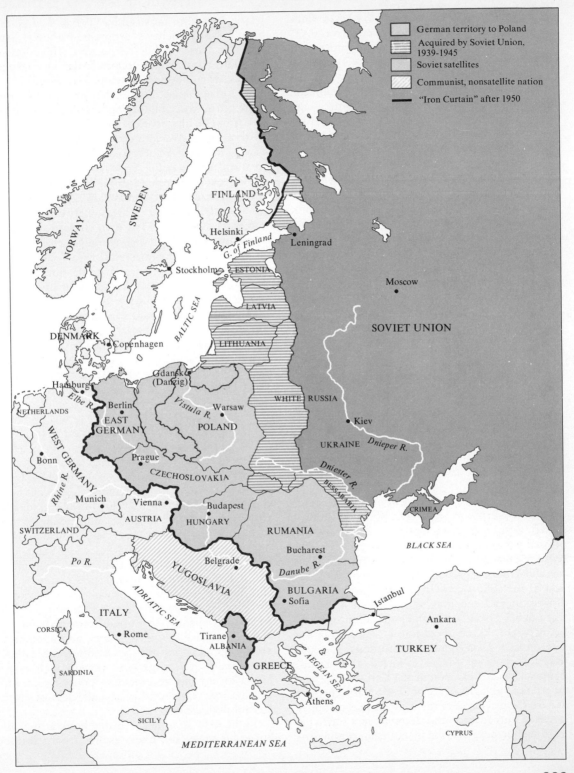

Legend

- German territory to Poland
- Acquired by Soviet Union, 1939–1945
- Soviet satellites
- Communist, nonsatellite nation
- "Iron Curtain" after 1950

NORWAY

SWEDEN

FINLAND

Helsinki

G. of Finland

Leningrad

Stockholm

ESTONIA

Moscow

LATVIA

SOVIET UNION

DENMARK

Copenhagen

BALTIC SEA

LITHUANIA

Gdansk
(Danzig)

Hamburg

Elbe R.

NETHERLANDS

Berlin

EAST
GERMANY

Vistula R.

Warsaw

POLAND

WHITE RUSSIA

Kiev

Bonn

WEST GERMANY

Rhine R.

Prague

CZECHOSLOVAKIA

UKRAINE

Dnieper R.

Munich

Vienna

AUSTRIA

Budapest

HUNGARY

Dniester R.

BESSARABIA

CRIMEA

SWITZERLAND

Po R.

YUGOSLAVIA

Belgrade

RUMANIA

Bucharest

Danube R.

BLACK SEA

ITALY

ADRIATIC SEA

BULGARIA

Sofia

Istanbul

Ankara

TURKEY

CORSICA

Rome

Tirane

ALBANIA

GREECE

AEGEAN SEA

SARDINIA

SICILY

Athens

CYPRUS

MEDITERRANEAN SEA

35 Europe After 1945: Recovery, Realignment, Division

method of ideological struggle for that of administrative violence, mass repression, and terror. . . ."[4] Three years after Stalin's death, these were potent and unsettling revelations; yet they were needed. Without criticizing the Soviet system, they acknowledged and rejected the excesses of Stalinism. In so doing, they lifted from Soviet politics—and from people's consciences—an intolerable burden of crime and complicity, restoring a modicum of honesty and humaneness.

Khrushchev's revelations created a profound stir around the world and promoted defection from communist ranks everywhere. Among the Soviet satellite countries, Poland was on the brink of rebellion by 1956; a workers' uprising forced a change of leadership. In Hungary in 1956, the entire communist regime was overthrown before the Red Army reoccupied the country. Only Mao objected to the downgrading of Stalinism.

Personable and approachable, ever admonishing officials high and low and pushing his rapidly changing projects, Khrushchev talked to all and sundry in a folksy, unceremonious manner that occasionally bordered on bad taste. He was excitable and carried away by visions of Soviet superiority, particularly after the launching of Sputnik I in early October 1957. Sputnik I boosted Khrushchev's pride beyond bounds. In 1957, he boasted to visiting Americans, "We will bury you," meaning that the Soviet Union would soon outproduce the United States in all essentials of life and would take its place as the model for the world.

Eager to prod his country toward a higher level of Marxist-Leninist ideology, Khrushchev presented a new party program and impatiently pressed for reforms in industry, agriculture, and party organization. An idealist of sorts, he called for wider public participation in the administration of the country, extending freedom of public discussion and encouraging individual initiative. Khrushchev also allowed the publication of Aleksandr Solzhenitsyn's short novel, *One Day in the Life of Ivan Denisovich,* which offered the first public glimpse of life at a forced-labor camp. Against his better judgment, Khrushchev permitted the public showing of abstract art. He tried to curb the privileges of the well-entrenched upper layers of bureaucracy and declared, in a move toward democracy, that the dictatorship of the proletariat had been replaced by "the state of all the people." Khrushchev's program, however, provoked increased public restlessness. There lurked too many repressed tensions in Soviet life, ready to surface when political controls were eased.

In foreign policy Khrushchev professed to promote peace. But while trying to reduce the role of the army, he also made some provocative moves by threatening Western access to West Berlin and placing missiles in Cuba; U.S. pressure forced him to withdraw in both cases. Not wishing to help communist China build atomic weapons, he recalled, after mutual recrimination, all Soviet advisers in 1960, causing a break between the two communist nations. Mao then charged him with "revisionism" as well as imperialism.

In whatever he undertook, Khrushchev could not escape his Stalinist training; arbitrariness and impetuosity counteracted his good intentions. His ceaseless reorganizations and impatient manner antagonized wide sections of state and party administration. In October 1964, while he was on vacation, his comrades on the politburo unceremoniously ousted him for "ill health" or, as they later added, his "hare-brained schemes." He was retired and allowed to live out his years in peace.

Brezhnev: Confidence and Stagnation

Khrushchev was succeeded, as was Stalin, by a group of leaders acting in common. Among these men, Leonid Brezhnev (1906–1982) gradually rose to the fore. He was a versatile administrator who with prodigious energy and dedication had advanced to key responsibilities under Stalin and Khrushchev. Under his leadership the government of the U.S.S.R. turned from a personal dictatorship into an oligarchy—the collective rule of a privileged minority. Brezhnev's style stressed reasoned agreement rather than command; he respected security of office, status, and autonomy among the rank and file. Soviet officials breathed more easily, feeling grateful toward their boss. Soviet society in turn grew less authoritarian; life became less regimented. The harshness of party control diminished.

In the early to mid-1970s, the brighter tone of Soviet life under Brezhnev resulted from a fortuitous change in global politics. Up to the mid-1970s, the United States was embroiled in the Vietnam War; hostility toward the Soviet Union in the United States and Western Europe receded. International relations entered a limited phase of peaceful cooperation called *détente*. (For a discussion of détente and Soviet foreign policy at that time, see Chapter 36.) Under the Helsinki Agreements of 1975, the political boundaries established in central Europe at the end of World War II were at last sanctioned. At the same time the Soviet Union achieved a rough parity in nuclear weapons with the United States; henceforth, it was protected by deterrence just like the United States. Never before in Soviet history had the country enjoyed such external security. As a result, the rigors of authoritarian rule could be relaxed and the country be opened, cautiously, to the outside world.

Young people, for instance, were allowed access to Western styles of music and dress. More issues of state policy were opened to public debate and more latitude granted to artistic expression. The lifeless stereotypes of socialist realism gave way to more candid treatment of human reality and even of tragedy; art moved closer to actual experience, although still in a running battle with censorship. Interest in religion revived. More significantly, Russian nationalism, anti-Western and even anti-Marxist, reappeared from the pre-Soviet past. In part, it responded to the marked increase in the non-Russian population of the Soviet Union; in part, it replaced Marxist-Leninist ideology, which as one communist admitted, had turned into "stale bread." Even the party seemed sympathetic to the new nationalism.

Dissent, furthermore, was treated with greater circumspection. Dissenters distributed a variety of protest writings, known by their mode of production as *samizdat* (self-published), which sometimes exhibited high artistic and scholarly qualities. The fate of dissenters, however, remained uncertain. For example, Andrei Sakharov, who had helped to develop the Soviet H-bomb but subsequently defended human rights, was exiled from Moscow and placed under house arrest. The most adamant critics, like Aleksandr Solzhenitsyn or Andrei Amalrik, were expelled (or allowed to emigrate). Other critics who stayed were declared insane and confined in mental hospitals, following a practice

begun under Nicholas I. The secret police (KGB) remained as powerful as ever.

Eager to match the rhetoric of Western political ideals, the Brezhnev government issued in 1977 a new constitution. Under that document, "the Soviet people . . . establish the rights, liberties and duties of citizens as well as the principles of organization and aims of the socialist state of all the people. . . ."[5] Democracy was an intrinsic part of the Soviet political vision. It required, however, that the people work hard in prescribed socialist fashion.

Under Brezhnev, the life of the hard-working Soviet elite, at least, became more abundant and secure; Soviet power was also more visible and respected in the world. Technicians, scientists, and managers—the country's most crucial assets —felt committed out of self-interest to order and continuity. Their housing improved, and they could now obtain household appliances and television sets. The greatest concession to consumerism was the production of automobiles for private use, at least among the privileged, although services and road facilities remained limited. Living conditions did not match those of Western Europe, but unemployment was rare. Job security became both a boon to the population and a source of economic inefficiency.

Brezhnev continued to give top priority to heavy industry and capital construction. Roads, bridges, railways, pipelines for gas and oil, mines and oil wells, steel mills and power plants were necessary to give the huge country an adequate infrastructure. The U.S.S.R. forged ahead of the smaller and better-equipped United States in the production of iron, steel, coal, and cement; it took advantage of its ample reserves of fossil fuels. The center of industrial activity began to shift gradually eastward, into western Siberia, with careful planning of newly integrated industrial regions. Soviet planners continued to pay special attention to the defense and space industries, both crucial to the country's prestige in the world.

Despite intensive government attention, Soviet agriculture remained the least productive sector of the economy. The motivation of collective farmers continued to be poor. They preferred raising their own produce on their small private plots to working in the collective work brigades. The young people drifted to the cities, which offered more amenities. Bad harvests through the 1970s forced the government to import large quantities of grain (mostly from the United States), thereby increasing Soviet dependence on capitalist countries.

All economic activity remained subject to vigorous central planning (apart from the thriving black market, called "underground capitalism"). Planning grew to an unimagined complexity that belied the claim of rational control. Problems piled up for the future. To combat inefficiency and to increase productivity, Brezhnev did not hesitate to search for closer economic ties with capitalist countries around the world. He was aware that the Soviet Union needed access to advanced technology to keep up with Western Europe, the United States, and emerging Japan.

Brezhnev's foreign policy proceeded in the spirit of détente. The calmer political climate allowed the Soviet government to relax its emigration controls; more Jews were permitted to leave the country. At the same time, the Soviet grip on the Eastern European peoples smarting under Soviet rule was eased, casting Soviet policy in a more favorable light. Détente also allowed cautious initiatives in making Soviet influence felt more vigorously around the world.

But détente did not solve all Brezhnev's problems. The continued tensions within the Soviet bloc prevented the government from implementing its paper promise for open contact with Western countries, given as part of the Helsinki Agreements. The Soviet leader still had reason to fear the subversive attractiveness of Western, and above all, American, society. He was also afraid of communist China, at that time courted by the United States. The pressure of the huge Chinese population on their long southeastern border kept all Soviet leaders nervous about their eastern territories. Brezhnev felt even more apprehensive about the rise of an anti-Soviet fundamentalist Islamic government in Afghanistan. The Soviet invasion of that country in 1979 proved to be his costliest mistake (see Chapter 36).

By 1980, the era of confidence was fading. Grateful for quieter times after their strenuous exertions in past decades, the Soviet people had too readily lapsed back into traditional ways; corruption crept into Brezhnev's own family. The rest of the world forged ahead at a rapid clip; the optimism of the mid-1970s about Soviet

achievements had been premature. Frequently ill after 1975, Brezhnev lost his former vigor. He died in 1982, bequeathing a heavy burden to his successors.

Gorbachev's Challenge

Brezhnev's immediate successors, chosen by agreement among top party officials, were old men who survived in office only for a short time. Former KGB chief Yuri Andropov (age 68), in poor health from the start, died in early 1984. He was replaced by Konstantin Chernenko, a man of Brezhnev's generation likewise in poor health, who lasted until early 1985. In that year, Mikhail Gorbachev (b. 1931) took over, representing at last a younger and more sophisticated age group that had grown up in the calmer times after Stalin's death.

Self-confident, energetic, and articulate—a leader who talked freely to people in all stations of life—Gorbachev stood out as a polished version of Khrushchev. Keenly aware of his country's problems and eager to confront them, he did not hesitate to state them bluntly. "The practical actions of the Party and state agencies," he announced to the Twenty-seventh Congress of the Communist party in February 1986, "lag behind the demands of the times and of life itself. . . . Problems grow faster than they are solved. Sluggishness, ossification in the forms and methods of management decrease the dynamism of work. . . . Stagnation begins to show up in the life of society. . . ."[6]

Gorbachev certainly knew the demands of the times. The Soviet Union had to update its industrial and agricultural productivity to compete with Japan, South Korea, Taiwan, the countries of Western Europe, and the United States. In particular, the Soviet Union lagged in the design and production of computers for educational institutions and public use; apart from space exploration, it was woefully behind in high technology. A sobering demonstration of inefficiency and mismanagement occurred in late April 1986 when, because of staff misjudgment, a reactor at the nuclear power plant at Chernobyl exploded, spewing dangerous radiation high into the atmosphere; poisonous fallout covered much of Europe. Wherever

Gorbachev looked, the mismanagement caused by rigid, centralized planning stifled innovation. Such planning thwarted individual initiative throughout the Soviet economy at a time when even communist China was reintroducing private enterprise.

As a result, the Soviet standard of living declined even more compared to that of other major countries. The comparison, unavoidable in the age of instant global communications, discredited Marxism-Leninism as well as the entire Soviet system. In the global race for material progress, the Soviet Union fell visibly behind. Under these conditions, the escalating arms race of the 1980s put the country under a special strain. How could there be any improvement in the standard of living—or in the country's overall position—when more and more resources had to be fed into armaments? Gorbachev certainly inherited a major downturn in his country's fortunes when he assumed leadership of the Communist party. How was he to cope with it?

Gorbachev had his responses ready when he addressed the party congress. He demanded no less than a fundamental reorganization—a *perestroika*—of the Soviet system, with the party in charge but responding more readily to the plans and hopes of Soviet citizens. Even more than his predecessors, he advocated "the democratization of society," hoping to stimulate participation by ordinary citizens, especially at their place of work and in local administration. He called for multiple candidates for elected posts, a novel experience for Soviet voters. To loosen up administrative rigidity, he also granted greater freedom to local entrepreneurs in agriculture, industry, and consumer services, demanding that supply and demand be closely coordinated as in a free market.

Even more significantly, Gorbachev tried to overcome the widespread indifference and lassitude with a new policy of openness (*glasnost*) in the discussion of public affairs. Let all the problems of Soviet society, hitherto kept under cover, be openly discussed: corruption, abuse of power, disregard for legality, and stifling of criticism. Domestic news began to depict Soviet reality more accurately. There was also a novel candor about the Soviet past. During the seventieth anniversary of the Bolshevik Revolution, Gorbachev asserted that "the guilt of Stalin . . . for the wholesale

repressive measures and acts of lawlessness is enormous and unforgivable." For Soviet readers the first Soviet edition of Pasternak's *Doctor Zhivago* was published.

The new openness was accompanied by an appeal to conscience and moral values. Under glasnost, honesty and initiative for the common good became public virtues; "spirituality" now was a communist ideal. Gorbachev also assured Soviet citizens that they should not hesitate to speak out freely. "We are for the diversity of public opinion, a richness of spiritual life. We need not fear openly raising and solving difficult problems of social development, criticizing and arguing. It is in such circumstances that the truth is born and that correct decisions take shape."[7]

"New Thinking" in Foreign Policy

Gorbachev also recognized the need for reducing the traditional isolationism of Soviet life and for winning good will abroad. He called for a new mode of thinking and for a fresh look at the Soviet Union's position in the world, continually emphasizing that nuclear weapons and global interdependence forced a basic change in international relations as well as in Soviet ideology. Abandoning traditional Leninist pretensions, he conceded that "we do not claim to be able to teach others."[8] He also stressed common human interests over class confrontation. National security in the nuclear age, he urged, called for superpower cooperation for the sake of common survival. In the spirit of glasnost, he frankly admitted that the adverse prospects of his country's economy forced him to advocate not only "normal international relations" but also an end to the arms race.

Setting an example, with a touch of Western sartorial elegance, he traveled abroad and cautiously lifted the restrictions barring access to the outside world. Jewish emigration was eased; foreign firms were invited to help stimulate the Soviet economy; high-level discussions between Russians and Americans became commonplace. Compelled to give priority to domestic improvement, Gorbachev worked toward reducing the tensions with his country's neighbors along the U.S.S.R.'s long, open boundaries. He promised to withdraw the

Reagan and Gorbachev in Geneva, 1985. After alternating periods of cold war and détente, the United States and the Soviet Union have attempted to curb the staggering costs of military expenditures by seeking more peaceful coexistence. In spite of the show of friendship, distrust still continues. (*AP/Wide World Photos*)

mit, an agreement was signed to dismantle intermediate-range nuclear missiles in Western and Eastern Europe, a cautious beginning to a process that, according to Gorbachev, might eventually end the nuclear threat. The Washington summit certainly produced a more favorable climate for future U.S.–U.S.S.R. cooperation. Yet the overall prospects remained dim because of the widespread American distrust of the Soviet Union.

What Chances for Gorbachev?

Gorbachev's pleas regarding domestic and foreign policy have fallen on responsive ears among the intellectuals in his country and thoughtful people around the world. But can he transform the masses of his country (numbering about 270 million) into enterprising and cooperative citizens? Can he create an international climate helpful for domestic reconstruction?

The obstacles in his own country are numerous. The entrenched bureaucracy resists loss of control. Public lethargy proves deep-seated; drunkenness (much attacked by Gorbachev) remains common; antipathy to uncomprehended modern ways has not diminished. Petty specialization and intense localism produce a narrowness of outlook hostile to the larger perspectives demanded by Gorbachev's reforms. People are not inclined to work harder when there is no immediate prospect of a higher standard of living. The revival of the Russian Orthodox Church, celebrating in 1988 the coming of Christianity to Russia one thousand years ago, introduces further resistance to modernization.

More threateningly, the call for openness encourages the innate tensions of Soviet society to surface, causing disorientation and disunity. Demonstrators under the Kremlin walls call for the reassertion of traditional Russian nationalism (including anti-Semitism); others protest on behalf of suppressed minorities, including Jews. Common people are still afraid of contact with foreigners. Patriots distrust Gorbachev's plea for nuclear disarmament; recalling Hitler's attack in 1941, they advocate a stronger Soviet Union. Among the divided peoples of the Soviet Union, Gorbachev's glasnost threatens to reassert the traditional distrust and discord; Azerbaijani Mus-

Soviet army from Afghanistan by the end of 1988, admitting that the invasion of Afghanistan had been a mistake. Stepping forward as an eloquent advocate of peace and disarmament, he pleaded for international cooperation in solving the human problems on earth, especially among countries of the Third World.

His initiatives bore fruit in much-publicized summit meetings with President Reagan in Reykjavik (1986) and most successfully in Washington, D.C., in December 1987. At the Washington sum-

lims and Armenian Christians have come to blows. The stability of the country is endangered.

To counter these critics, Gorbachev has praised the past and present accomplishments of the Soviet regime. He has pressed for Soviet leadership in space technology. He has predicted the eventual decay of capitalism and the ultimate triumph of socialism, rallying support for his cause. Yet how can he channel, by command from the top (however considerately worded), into the economic mainstream the private initiative that provides goods and services to the black market? How can he create the capacity for spontaneous social cooperation now missing among a people compelled for centuries to obey orders from above; how can he overcome the instinctive fear of taking risks in innovation; how can he cope with all the other ingrained remnants of backwardness? The economic prospects for perestroika are discouraging indeed.

In foreign relations, the prospects hardly look better. Anti-Soviet hostility is deeply rooted in the United States and is combined with fear of Soviet military power. What lasting guarantees can Gorbachev offer for his policy of peace and disarmament? Has he not said that he will maintain adequate defenses for his country? The peoples surrounding the Soviet Union, from the Far East to central Asia and Western Europe, likewise retain their suspicions, often abetted by dissidents within the Soviet Union. The tensions around the world and the common penchant for violence do not bode well for the relaxed international relations envisaged by Gorbachev as necessary for success in recasting Soviet society.

The Soviet Satellites

Soviet Russia's power is closely tied to the fate of the countries located to the west and southwest. When the Red Armies poured into the lands of eastern and central Europe in 1944–45 on their way to Berlin, Stalin was faced with a historically unique opportunity—Soviet Russia controlled the entire area up to the Elbe River in the heart of Germany, a huge territorial buffer against future invasions from the West. Conditions there were hardly favorable to continued Soviet rule. Admittedly, many inhabitants of the lands under Soviet occupation were fellow Slavs (excepting the Germans, Baltic peoples, Hungarians, and Rumanians), and some Eastern Europeans belonged to the Orthodox church, another tie—at least to traditional Russia. Yet most of the occupied peoples (except perhaps the Bulgarians) shared a common suspicion of, or even hostility toward, the giant to the east. Some of them—Poles, Czechs, and certainly Germans—saw themselves as representatives of the superior culture of the West; they looked westward for a better future. All remembered centuries of foreign domination and were passionately nationalist. The Germans, of course, wanted to rejoin their compatriots in the West. Under any regime, these countries (now containing about 100 million people) would have been difficult to govern: for most of them the years of national independence between the world wars had not been peaceful. By extending his country's territorial sway westward, Stalin had added to the region's political instability as well as to Soviet insecurity.

The Stalinization of Eastern Europe

Whatever the prospects, Stalin seized the opportunity. As the Red Armies fought their way west, Eastern European communists, trained in the Soviet Union, followed behind them. The Baltic States (Lithuania, Latvia, Estonia), seized after the Nazi-Soviet Pact of 1939 and then lost to Hitler, were reincorporated into the Soviet Union as "soviet socialist republics." Elsewhere Stalin respected, outwardly at least, the national sovereignty of the occupied countries by ruling through returning native communists and whatever sympathizers he could find.

By the end of 1948, however, the countries of eastern and southeastern Europe had emerged as "people's democracies." The Soviet Union continued to claim the right, based on conquest, of intervening at will in the internal affairs of its satellites. Thus the pall of Stalinism hung over war-torn and impoverished Eastern Europe. The puppet regimes leveled the formerly privileged classes, curtailing or abolishing private enterprise. The economy was socialized and rigid, and hasty plans were implemented for industrialization and the collectivization of agriculture. Religion and the churches were repressed and political liberty and free speech stamped out. Even the "proletarian masses" derived few benefits from the artificial revolution engineered from Moscow, because Stalin drained Eastern Europe of its resources for the sake of rebuilding the Soviet Union. Contact with Western Europe or the United States was banned. Each satellite existed in isolation, surrounded by borders fortified with barbed wire and watch towers set along mined corridors cut through the landscape. Fear and terror reached deep into every house and individual soul as little Stalins copied their mentor's style in East Berlin, Warsaw, Prague, Budapest, Sofia, and Bucharest.

Two exceptions to this trend emerged: Albania and Yugoslavia, located on the flanks of the Soviet westward surge. During the war, indigenous communist parties had conducted successful guerrilla war in these countries; the parties rose to power when the Germans withdrew, each under the leadership of a strong man: Enver Hoxha in Albania and Josip Broz, known as Marshal Tito, in Yugoslavia. A Stalinist even after Stalin's death, Hoxha turned against Moscow in 1961, making Albania a satellite of Mao's China. Tito (1892–1980), in contrast, became a symbol of defiance to Stalin. During World War II, he had led the Yugoslav resistance movement against Nazi occupation. A convinced and hardened communist, Tito was also a Yugoslav patriot committed to rebuilding and unifying his country.

Yugoslavia escaped Soviet occupation, but Stalin did not ignore it. In June 1948, he tried to get rid of Tito. His words, recalled by Khrushchev, were: "I will shake my little finger and there will be no more Tito; he will fall." To Stalin's dismay, Tito did not fall. On the contrary, backed by his party and his people, Tito pioneered, with increasing confidence, his own brand of communism. His prescription of socialist ownership of production combined with workers' control and popular participation in government guided his country on an independent course. A federation uniting peoples of different cultures and religions, Marxist Yugoslavia took a prominent role in creating a bloc of nonaligned Third World countries trying to stay clear of superpower conflict. Next door, the communist regime in tiny Albania also pursued an independent course, preferring China's Mao Zedong to Stalin and his successors, allowing little contact with the outside world until very recently.

Elsewhere in Eastern Europe, Soviet control continued. All communist parties (by whatever name) were guided by Moscow; Soviet troops remained strategically stationed in the area. Economic life was regulated by the Council of Mutual Economic Assistance (sometimes called COMECON), planned in 1949 as a move to counter the Marshall Plan. In 1955, a further bond was created in the Warsaw Pact, or Warsaw Treaty Organization. It coordinated the armies of the satellite countries with the Red Army as a military instrument for preserving the ideological and political unity of the bloc and for counterbalancing NATO.

A New Era: Permissiveness and Reprisals

Stalin's successors, realizing that continued repression among the satellites would provoke trouble, began to relax their controls. A new era began for eastern and southeastern Europe. The Soviet satellites began to move toward greater national self-determination, searching for their own forms of industrialization, collectivization of agriculture, and communist dictatorship. The history of the region since 1953 was thus a series of experiments to determine what deviations from Soviet practice in domestic politics and what measure of self-assertion in foreign policy the Kremlin would tolerate.

No event proved more crucial than Khrushchev's attack on Stalin in 1956. It set off a political earthquake throughout the bloc, discrediting Stalinists and encouraging moderates in the parties, reviving cautious discussion among intellectuals, and even arousing visions of national self-determination.

The first tremors of protest rumbled in June 1956 in Poland—the largest and most troublesome of the satellite countries. The crisis came to a head in October: would Poland revolt, inviting invasion by the Red Army, or would Khrushchev ease Soviet control? The Soviet boss yielded in return for a Polish pledge of continued loyalty to the Soviet Union. Thereafter, Poland breathed more freely, clinging to its Catholic faith as a cornerstone of its national identity.

Although the "Polish October" ended peacefully, events moved to a brutal showdown in Hungary. The Stalinists had suppressed national pride in Hungary for too long. On October 20, 1956, an uprising in Budapest raised anti-Soviet feeling to a fever pitch and forced Soviet troops to withdraw from the country. Next, a moderate communist government, eager to capture popular sentiment, called for Western-style political democracy and Hungary's withdrawal from the Warsaw Pact. Thoroughly alarmed, and with the backing of Mao and even Tito, the Soviet leaders struck back. On November 4, 1956, Soviet troops re-entered the country and crushed all opposition. Yet the bold uprising had left its mark.

The new communist leader of Hungary, János Kádar (b. 1912), was a moderate, who with Khrushchev's approval built a pragmatic regime of consumer-oriented "goulash communism" that granted considerable opportunity to private enterprise. Kádar's regime also allowed noncommunists to participate extensively in public affairs. Relaxation and decentralization of planning made possible in the 1970s a remarkable increase in popular prosperity and individual freedom; the Hungarian experiment became the envy of all other Soviet-bloc countries and invited imitation even in the Soviet Union itself. In return for this moderate self-determination, the Hungarians resumed their membership in the Warsaw Pact and demonstrated loyalty to the Soviet leadership. In its essentials the Kádar regime has lasted even beyond Kádar's retirement in 1988.

After 1956, Soviet leaders grew more circumspect in their approach to the satellite countries' internal affairs, allowing increasing diversity of political development. No country went further in asserting its identity than Rumania, which was given special leeway by the Kremlin because it was surrounded on all sides by other Soviet-bloc countries and preserved a Stalinist dictatorship under Nicolae Ceausescu (in power since 1967).

The post-Stalin permissiveness was never without risks, however, even under the milder regime of Brezhnev, as was shown in Czechoslovakia in 1968. A new group of Czech communists led by Alexander Dubček sought to liberalize their regime to include noncommunists, allow greater freedom of speech, and rid the economy of the rigidities that for so long had prevented prosperity. Their goal was a "humanist democratic socialism," or "socialism with a human face"—a communist party supported by public good will rather than by the secret police.

This program panicked the governments of East Germany, Poland, and the Soviet Union. On August 21, East German, Polish, Hungarian, and Soviet troops, under the provisions of the Warsaw Pact, carried out a swift and well-prepared occupation of Czechoslovakia but failed to break the rebellious will of its communists. While Soviet tanks rumbled through Prague, an extraordinary Czechoslovak party congress secretly met in choked fury. Never had the Soviet leaders encountered such united resistance by a communist party! Nonetheless, the revolt ended in failure. The party was purged; all reforms were cancelled; and the country was reduced to abject hopelessness. But the Soviet Union paid a high price: a cry of moral outrage resounded around the world; protests were heard even in Moscow.

In the Brezhnev years, on the whole, caution and moderation prevailed. Soviet leaders could point to the positive results of their control over eastern and southeastern Europe. They had promoted industrialization in predominantly agrarian and comparatively backward countries; they had reduced the gap between rich and poor, substantially advancing education and cultural opportunity. They had also muted the instability and violence so evident in the region in the past.

Yet Moscow's efforts to integrate its satellites' economies into its own even less advanced economy never succeeded. One by one, the satellite governments resumed ties with capitalist states, incurring considerable indebtedness in the process. Soviet control loosened even further in the Gorbachev era, causing new problems. How could the Soviet government retain control over its satellites while allowing them greater independence? Soviet control, in fact, has still not won popular acceptance, as is most obvious in the case of Poland.

Solidarity Flag at a Papal Mass in Poland, 1983. The unevenness of economic advance and the deep-rooted nationalism in the Soviet satellite countries continue to breed dissent. In Poland the independent labor union called Solidarity erupted in 1980. Its advocacy of free elections led to the imposition of martial law in 1981. Although suppressed, Solidarity persists as a political force. (*Fabian/Sygma*)

Poland Since 1970 Even after 1956, Poland has not been quiet. Industrial workers, presumably the real masters in communist regimes, have embarrassed their government by taking the lead in pressing for freedom. In 1970, Polish troops shot some workers who were protesting a sharp increase in consumer prices; yet the protesters' martyrdom forced a change in communist leadership. Agitation continued when the economy declined

(in part because of low morale in industry and the regime's opposition to private farming). Soviet assistance and massive loans from Western European countries brought no relief. The slightest relaxation of Soviet control only encouraged Polish nationalism, which, for lack of other outlets, had long found expression in the Roman Catholic church.

When a Polish cardinal became Pope John Paul II in 1978, patriotism surged. In 1980, workers under the leadership of an electrician named Lech Walesa succeeded, with the blessing of the church, in forming an independent labor union called Solidarity. Pressured by relentless strikes, the government, just reorganized under a new leader, recognized the union despite threats of Soviet intervention. In 1981, matters came to a head: some of Solidarity's more radical members spoke of bringing free elections to Poland. In December, a military dictatorship, suddenly formed under General Wojciech Jaruzelski, imposed martial law. Walesa and other leaders of Solidarity were arrested, and protesting workers were dispersed by force. Nonetheless, subsequent visits by the pope in 1983 and 1987 showed that the Catholic church survived as a political factor, as did Solidarity. Jaruzelski's rule proved to be by no means monolithic. As the Polish economy deteriorated and the standard of living declined, he faced mounting difficulties. When in November 1987 he asked in a public referendum for support of economic and political reforms (including "a profound democratization of political life"), a majority of the voters abstained or voted against him. Committed to glasnost, Jaruzelski openly admitted defeat, unable to offer more attractive solutions.

The Polish people are aware that they cannot liberate themselves from Soviet rule. Yet a durable pattern of Soviet domination that lets Poles find their own way economically and politically will be difficult to evolve. Meanwhile, popular cynicism toward the regime and its ideology increases.

East Germany The Poles receive little sympathy in their troubles from their western neighbor, the German Democratic Republic (East Germany), Moscow's most reliable satellite. Established simultaneously with the Federal Republic of Germany (West Germany), it controls the parts of the old Germany assigned at the end of the war to Soviet occupation, minus the territories ceded to Poland. The Soviet Union's westernmost outpost and indispensable for its contribution to the economy of the entire Soviet bloc, East Germany is closely watched by the politburo.

Under the leadership of German communists who had spent the Nazi years in the Soviet Union and therefore felt no responsibility for Nazi atrocities, the German Democratic Republic at first shared the fate of all Soviet satellites. Industry was nationalized, agriculture collectivized, and the people were regimented under the Communist party (here called the Socialist Unity party). Because of its close historical association with West Germany, however, it soon developed its own distinctive character.

Protests against Stalinism appeared earlier than elsewhere. In June 1953, the workers of Berlin staged an uprising, gaining some concessions. Then followed a steady exodus of skilled manpower to West Germany, mostly via West Berlin. More than 3 million people escaped before the East German government, in August 1961, suddenly threw up a wall—the famous "Berlin Wall"—and built equally deadly barriers along the entire border with West Germany. For a time, all contact between the two Germanys ceased.

With increased control over their people, the communist leaders—first Walter Ulbricht and, since the early 1970s, Erich Honecker—concentrated on advancing the economy, with marked success. Their people, numbering less than a quarter of the West German population, enjoy the highest standard of living in the entire Soviet bloc.

In 1972, détente led to the establishment of diplomatic relations between the two Germanys and to closer economic ties, which made East Germany virtually a beneficiary of the European Community. Welcoming close economic relations with West Germany for their own good, the Soviet masters raised no objections. They are opposed, however, to any speculation about German reunification. The leaders of the Democratic Republic consider their country a separate "socialist" Germany, drawing on the best elements in the German past, including Martin Luther's Reformation and Prussian efficiency. They can rely on their subjects' resigned acceptance of their rule. East Germans are aware of their privileged position within the Soviet bloc; they recognize the futility of revolt and work hard at their jobs. Secretly they may hope to escape someday to the West, to which they have daily access through West German television.

Their leaders meanwhile pursue a difficult course. Dependent on the Soviet Union and aware of their subjects' secret desires, they need good relations with West Germany. The Bonn government contributes in many ways to East Germany's high standard of living. It is also a partner with East Germany in the attempt to reduce the hostility between the superpowers and thus to assure peace for the peoples of central Europe. The state visit in 1987 of Erich Honecker to West Germany was applauded as a step in the right direction.

Currently, the relaxation of tension in international relations is a chief concern of the Kremlin, and it applies to the Soviet satellites as well. Gorbachev would like to lift the heavy hand of Soviet domination, introducing more open discussion and popular participation in government and the economy. Yet everywhere he runs into major obstacles. The local economies stagnate; material incentives are in short supply. In every satellite country except Hungary the local communist regimes are rigidly controlled by men afraid of disorder and loss of productivity in the wake of perestroika. The problems faced by Gorbachev in the Soviet Union apply here, too, under the added burden of a much-resented foreign rule that cannot be overthrown. Nuclear deterrence protects the Soviet hold over its satellites.

The Soviet Union in an Age of Globalism

In the seventy-odd years between the collapse of the Russian state at the end of World War I and Gorbachev's era, communist Russia has changed from a backward country of tradition-bound peasants to a modern superpower claiming equality with the United States. Soviet Russia has suc-

Chronology 35.1 Europe after 1945

1945	Eastern Europe occupied by Red Army
1947	The Marshall Plan inaugurated; Zhdanovism in U.S.S.R.
1948	Czech coup; Stalinization of Eastern Europe; Tito's Yugoslavia breaks with the Soviet Union
1949	People's Republic of China established under Mao Zedong; NATO formed
1953	Stalin dies
1956	Khrushchev's secret speech on Stalin's crimes; the Polish October; the Hungarian uprising crushed
1957	Sputnik launched—the space age begins; the EEC established
1961	Berlin Wall built, dividing the city of Berlin
1964	Khrushchev ousted; Brezhnev and Kosygin installed as leaders in U.S.S.R.
1968	Czechoslovakia's "Prague Spring"—Dubček's "Socialism with a human face"
1971	Détente in East-West relations
1972	Diplomatic relations between East and West Germany established
1975	Helsinki Agreements
1979	Soviet Union invades Afghanistan
1980	Solidarity trade union in Poland
1982	Brezhnev dies, succeeded by Andropov (died 1984) and Chernenko (died 1985)
1985	Gorbachev becomes U.S.S.R. leader
1987	Gorbachev-Reagan summit in Washington; INF Treaty agreed
1988	Soviet Union withdraws from Afghanistan

ceeded partly because of the exertions and sacrifices exacted by the Stalin revolution and World War II, and partly because of two additional factors. First, at the end of World War II, Soviet Russia moved into the political vacuum created in eastern and central Europe by the German defeat; its landlocked empire held together while the overseas empires of Western Europe fell apart. Second, thanks to the strenuous efforts made by its postwar leaders, the Soviet Union now possesses nuclear weapons roughly equal to those of the United States. As long as the balance of terror prevents a nuclear war, the country is more secure militarily than ever before in its history.

In its seven decades, the Soviet Union has tried to make its presence felt over the entire world— strengthening its borders, holding tightly onto its territorial gains, and advertising with imposing moral righteousness its achievements as an example for all peoples. The U.S.S.R. has been inspired by its long-range goal, hoping like the United States to reshape the world in its own image. National liberation movements directed against Western nations have found a willing ally in Moscow. Always feeling humiliated by Western superiority, Moscow has endeavored to outdo the West on its own terms, whether in spectacular technological feats like space exploration, or in its military bases set up around the world, or in the ultimate promise of providing the best society.

Yet the Leninist dream of world revolution has vanished. The Kremlin now conducts its foreign affairs pragmatically, guided by a sober sense of self-interest. Cautiously trying to assert its power in competition with the United States, Soviet Russia has become dependent on the developed industrial countries in the widening network of global interdependence. More than ever, the U.S.S.R. needs to draw on Western know-how (along with Japan's) to satisfy the material wishes of its subjects, whom it can no longer insulate from the outside world.

At home, too, Soviet leaders have reason to worry. Revolutionary zeal has faded among their peoples, who crave freedom and prosperity but lack the knowledge and the self-discipline necessary for managing an innovative industrial economy. The peoples also lack a firm sense of unity. The ethnic and religious diversity of the Soviet Union continues to provide a source of disloyalty. More ominously, the rapid population growth of non-Russian nationalities in Soviet central Asia threatens the traditional preponderance of the Russian population in the Soviet Union.

All along, the Soviet people have been united and made powerful and modern by a deliberate system of national control. Even Gorbachev's improvements, reminiscent of Peter the Great's reforms, are imposed from above by the Communist party with due emphasis on discipline. Discipline is needed to suppress the discord and disorder always ready to erupt. Although Gorbachev prefers peaceful persuasion with the help of open discussion, repression is kept in reserve to be used when needed. The Leninist dream of transforming backward Russia into a communist paradise remains an inconclusive experiment in a profoundly divided and violent world.

Notes

1. Quoted in Walter Laqueur, *Europe Since Hitler* (Baltimore: Penguin Books, 1970), p. 118.

2. Quoted in Roger Morgan, *West European Politics Since 1945* (London: Batsford, 1972), p. 91.

3. Preamble to Treaty of Rome, 1958, in ibid., pp. 132–133.

4. Nikita S. Khrushchev's speech (in translation) in *The Crimes of the Stalin Era: Special Report to the 20th Congress of the Communist Party of the Soviet Union,* annotated by Boris I. Nicolaevsky, *The New Leader* (New York), 1956.

5. "The New USSR Constitution," *The Current Digest of the Soviet Press,* 40 (November 9, 1977), p. 2.

6. Mikhail Gorbachev, "Report to the 27th Party Congress," February 25, 1986. *Current Soviet Policies,* 9 (1986): 10.

7. Gorbachev's Speech at the 70th Anniversary of the Bolshevik Revolution, quoted in the *New York Times,* November 3, 1987, section A, p. 3.

8. Mikhail Gorbachev, *Perestroika: New Thinking for Our Country and the World* (New York: Harper & Row, 1987), p. 144.

Suggested Reading

Amalrik, Andrei, *Notes of a Revolutionary* (1982). A noted dissident on the fate of dissidents under Brezhnev.

Ascherson, Neal, *The Polish August: The Self-Limiting Revolution* (1982). A good insight into the rise and fall of Solidarity.

Barzini, Luigi, *The Italians* (1977). A superb, far-ranging introduction to contemporary Italy.

Becker, Jillian, *Hitler's Children: The Story of the Baader-Meinhof Terrorist Gang* (1977). Good insights into the terrorist state of mind.

Childs, David, ed., *Honecker's Germany* (1985). Current developments in East Germany's economy, culture, and foreign relations.

Cohen, Stephen F., *Sovieticus: American Perceptions and Soviet Realities* (1985). A lively collection of articles on current Soviet affairs, first published in *The Nation*, 1982–1984.

Craig, Gordon, *The Germans* (1982). Key aspects of postwar 1945 Germany in historical perspective.

Davies, Norman, *God's Playground: A History of Poland* (1982). A much-praised survey, introducing the reader to Poland's history.

De Gaulle, Charles, *Memoirs of Hope, Renewal and Endeavor* (1971). An autobiographical account of his work after 1958, reflecting the grandeur of the man.

Dornberg, John, *The New Germans, Thirty Years After* (1975). A German-born American journalist looks at the many faces of contemporary Germany.

Fetjo, François, *A History of the People's Democracies: Eastern Europe Since Stalin* (1971). A good survey of Eastern Europe immediately after World War II.

Goldman, Marshall I., *Gorbachev's Challenge: Economic Reform in the Age of High Technology* (1987). Problems facing the Soviet economy and obstacles to reform. A sequel to the author's *U.S.S.R. in Crisis* (1985).

Gorbachev, Mikhail, *Perestroika: New Thinking for Our Country and the World* (1987). The authoritative account by the Soviet leader, covering both domestic and foreign affairs.

Havel, Vaclav, et al., *The Power of the Powerless: Citizens Against the State in Central-Eastern Europe* (1985). Czech writers discuss the crisis of human identity brought about by "living within a lie" under totalitarian control in the Eastern satellite countries.

LaPalombara, Joseph, *Democracy Italian Style* (1987). A guide to the modern Italian state and a portrayal of how the convoluted Italian political system works.

Medvedev, Roy, and Zhores A. Medvedev, *Khrushchev: The Years in Power* (1983). A sympathetic biography by two prominent Soviet dissidents.

Nay, Catherine, *The Black and the Red: François Mitterrand—the Story of an Ambition* (1987). A popular biography of the left-wing French president and his life in French politics.

Pond, Elizabeth, *From the Yaroslavsky Station: Russia Perceived* (1981). A sensitive American correspondent takes the train from Moscow to Vladivostok and describes her experiences.

Sampson, Anthony, *The Changing Anatomy of Britain* (1983). A perceptive and well-informed British journalist analyzes contemporary Britain; an excellent survey.

Smith, Hedrick, *The Russians* (1976). The best account by an American journalist in recent years of everyday life in the Soviet Union.

Solzhenitsyn, Aleksandr, *Cancer Ward* (1968). A novel in which a cancer ward in a Tashkent hospital is used as a metaphor for Stalin's Russia. Based on the author's own experiences.

Wylie, Lawrence, *Village in the Vaucluse* (1974). A well-written glimpse of French peasant life through the eyes of an American anthropologist.

Periodicals

Current Digest of the Soviet Press (Columbus, Ohio). Provides weekly translations of the most significant items in the Soviet press.

Current History (Philadelphia). Current analyses of European and Soviet affairs.

Europe: The Magazine of the European Community (Washington, D.C.). Articles on Western European affairs.

Foreign Affairs (New York). The foremost American periodical on foreign relations.

Problems of Communism (Washington, D.C.). Coverage of Soviet-related subjects.

Review Questions

1. What do you consider the biggest changes to have taken place in Western Europe after World War II?

2. Trace the evolution of the European Community. What information about its current activities do you find in the current news?

3. Which of the major peoples of Western Europe faced the greatest adjustments after World War II? What reasons do you give for your choice?

4. France and Italy are often compared because of their common Latin heritage. Do you see any similarities in their histories after 1945?

5. What have been the major problems of govern-

ment in Great Britain since 1945? What has been the recent news about Britain?

6. How, after the partition of Germany in 1945, did West Germany rise to its present pre-eminence in the European Community and in world affairs?

7. How do you account for the rise of terrorism in postwar Europe? What about European terrorists in the recent news?

8. What was the postwar role of the United States in Western Europe? In which country, would you say, did the United States play the largest role?

9. What do you consider to be the major problems confronting Western European society? If you lived in Western Europe, what programs and what policies would you support?

10. What problems in the Soviet Union did Stalin face after the end of World War II? How did he try to cope with them?

11. What happened to Stalinism after Stalin's death? Under Khrushchev? Under Gorbachev?

12. Imagine that you are a member of the politburo. What would be your major anxieties? What would be your sources of pride?

13. What are the objectives of Gorbachev's policies? What are the obstacles? How would you rank Gorbachev among Stalin's successors?

14. How do Soviet leaders view their Eastern European satellites? How do these satellite countries view the Soviet Union?

15. What are the aims of Soviet foreign policy? How do Soviet foreign-policy aims compare with those of the United States?

36

International Relations
in an Age of Superpowers

W orld War II propelled the Earth's inhabitants from their traditional ways within the loosely meshed network of commerce, finance, and power politics that had grown out of the expansion of Europe, into an inescapable, tight, global interdependence. Whatever the differences between them, close neighbors as well as people in distant lands were thrust together in intense interaction, whether for cooperation or conflict, for peace or war. As the colonial empires of the Western European states dissolved, the liberated peoples in Asia and Africa formed sovereign countries, initially patterned after the Western European democracies. These new countries, too, plunged into the universal competition for wealth and power. They became involved in the rivalry between the superpowers, while also often bitterly feuding among themselves.

In the late 1980s, the global community has become an unruly association of some 160 sovereign states. They include China, the largest, with over 1 billion inhabitants. Next in population are India with 785 million people; the Soviet Union (which has the largest territory) with 270 million; and the United States with 240 million. Among the smallest states is the Republic of Seychelles (islands in the Indian Ocean), with 65,000 inhabitants. The global community also runs the gamut of economic levels, from the "advanced industrial" to the "least developed" countries; from the rich, with an average annual per capita income of $11,388 in the United States, to the poor, with an average annual per capita income of barely $150 in Mali (West Africa)—according to the most recent figures available. Never before in human history have so many diverse peoples—5 billion in 1987, and many more expected in the future—been crowded onto the planet, all prevented from understanding each other by differing languages, religions, and cultures. Never before has there ex-

The United Nations Building in New York. (*UN Photo*)

isted such sharp disagreement about the realities that human beings face in the present and the future. Political competition, which provokes many local wars and heats the cold war rivalry between the superpowers, clashes continually with the need and desire for peaceful coexistence and cooperation.

The United Nations

Goals

The new globalism, with its attendant hopes of peace and progress, began to take shape at the end of World War II. In April 1945, the victorious wartime coalition led by the United States established the United Nations (UN). Its charter pledged

> . . . to save succeeding generations from the scourge of war, which twice in our lifetime has brought untold sorrow to mankind, and to reaffirm faith in fundamental human rights, in the dignity and worth of the human person, in the equal rights of men and women and of nations large and small . . . to promote social progress and better standards of life in larger freedom.

The founding members promised "to maintain international peace and security," as well as "to employ international machinery for the promotion of the economic and social advancement of all peoples."

The United Nations considered itself to be a peace-keeping organization, designed to "achieve international co-operation in solving international problems of an economic, social, cultural, or humanitarian character, and in promoting and encouraging respect for human rights and for fundamental human freedom for all without distinction of race, language, or religion." It aimed at "harmonizing the action of nations in the attainment of these common ends."[1] For work on these goals, the charter set up an Economic and Social Coun-

cil. In addition, the colonial powers were urged to prepare their subjects for eventual independence with the help of a UN Trusteeship Council.

Three years later, in 1948, the members of the United Nations (with the exceptions of the Soviet Union and the Union of South Africa) underscored the charter's purpose in a Universal Declaration of Human Rights. The declaration announced that "the recognition of the inherent dignity and of the equal and inalienable rights of all members of the human family is the foundation of freedom, justice and peace in the world." These ringing phrases, often restated in subsequent UN documents, extended to all humanity the ideals by which modern Western societies had guided their political practice.

Structure

The task of implementing the UN's ambitious and idealistic goals was entrusted foremost to the UN Security Council. Its permanent members represented the five most powerful countries: the United States, the Soviet Union, Britain, France, and Nationalist China (doomed to be overthrown by communists led by Mao Zedong in 1949). These five were joined by six members (later increased to ten) from the General Assembly. Each of the permanent members was given the right to veto any resolution before the council. This provision meant that disagreement between key members could not be overcome by majority rule; the UN was not meant to be a world government. The fatal flaw was that both the United States and the Soviet Union could veto each other's proposals, thus leading to a stalemate in the Security Council. The General Assembly of the UN, however, was composed of all members on an equal footing, and entitled to discuss any relevant business and take action by majority vote. The UN staff work was entrusted to the secretary-general, who worked at the UN headquarters in New York City. He headed an international civil service recruited from member countries.

With the help of interested governments, a host of world-spanning specialized agencies has evolved under UN auspices. Among them are the International Atomic Energy Agency, the Food and Agriculture Organization, the UN Educational,

Scientific and Cultural Organization (UNESCO), the World Health Organization (WHO), and the UN Children's Fund (UNICEF). Closely allied with the UN are the autonomous economic organizations, such as the General Agreement on Tariffs and Trade (GATT), the International Monetary Fund (IMF), and the International Bank for Reconstruction and Development (known as the World Bank). The last two organizations provide crucial aid to developing countries. The United Nations has also organized innumerable conferences on urgent issues of common concern, including population, food, and environmental control. In conflicts between some countries, it has provided peace-keeping forces drawn from neutral member states. All these activities have promoted the new globalism, carrying out the UN mandate according to the dictates of changing political circumstances.

Effectiveness

During its early years, the UN was largely an instrument of U.S. foreign policy, most prominently so during the Korean War, which was waged primarily by the United States with UN endorsement. (The Soviet Union was not able to veto the UN approval of the war because at that time it was boycotting the Security Council for its refusal to replace Nationalist China with communist China.) In the 1960s, however, with the increasing admission of members from newly decolonized countries, the balance of voting power within the UN membership swung away from the United States and its allies. As a result, the UN's popularity in the United States suffered and support lagged, putting the UN in financial crisis.

In any case, because of the disunity among its members, the UN has been able neither to prevent the many small wars that have flared up in Asia, the Mideast, Africa, or Central America nor to reduce, let alone stop, the nuclear arms race. Although the UN can claim to have kept alive the vision of a just and peaceful world order with which it started in 1945, it still operates at the mercy of traditional power politics—especially the cold war between the United States and the Soviet Union.

The Origins of the Cold War

The cold war (the phrase was coined in 1947 by the American financier Bernard Baruch) stemmed from the divergent historical experiences and the incompatible political ambitions of the United States and the Soviet Union, which clashed head-on as the new global order began to take shape. How would the superpowers handle the postwar reconstruction? As the overseas empires of Britain, France, and other Western European nations were dissolving, which superpower would become the predominant influence in the world? Around these questions, the relentless and often brutal political competition that had always been an intrinsic part of Western civilization intensified. The states of Europe had traditionally fought for supremacy, escalating their contests into world wars in the twentieth century. Now the two superpowers, both tied to the European tradition, vied for universal domination, extending the European framework of power politics over the entire world.

During the war, the basic differences between the West and the U.S.S.R. had been glossed over. Western self-interest had dictated giving the utmost support to the Red Army—the more powerful it was, the easier the Western onslaught against Hitler would be. Stalin, however, had never shed his Bolshevik fear of capitalist superiority; nor had Western leaders, Churchill foremost, given up their anticommunism. Once the common danger receded, the differences between political institutions and ideologies pushed again to the fore, aggravated by the flush of victory and postwar opportunity.

American leaders were determined not to lose the initiative in world affairs, having tried during the war to extend U.S. influence around the world. Stalin, too, was unwilling to forgo the advantages derived from Germany's defeat. Like his American rivals, he sought to increase his country's power and prestige. Thus, hostility escalated between the superpowers, propelled by mutual fear, aggressive self-protection, raised ambitions, and collective pride.

Starting in 1945, the grim logic of irreconcilable political rivalry took its course, despite the pledge for the peaceful settlement of disputes written into the charter of the United Nations. Since both countries could veto any resolution of the Security Council, the United Nations proved useless for promoting reconciliation—it turned instead into a minor stage for confrontation.

The Cold War in Eastern Europe

The incompatibility of objectives had become clear even before the end of hostilities. As the Red Army moved through Eastern Europe, the fate of the East European peoples hung in the balance. Would the promise of self-determination and democratic freedom espoused by the Western allies be applied to them? Or would Stalin treat them as conquered peoples, knowing that left to their own devices they would return to their traditional anti-Soviet orientation?

Attention first focused on Poland. The Western allies, advancing from the Atlantic against Hitler's armies, were in no position to stop Stalin from doing as he wished. As the Red Army occupied Poland, Stalin installed a pro-Soviet governing regime. Other countries in Eastern Europe suffered the same fate. Ever worried about the security of his country's western boundaries, Stalin incorporated the East European countries into a buffer zone for protection against Western attack. The Soviet occupation of Eastern Europe was considered a dire calamity by the local populations and their sympathizers in Western European nations and the United States. But short of starting another war, the latter countries were powerless to intervene.

Germany's fate became an even more crucial bone of contention. The division of Germany into zones of occupation had been agreed to in 1944, but a permanent partition of the country was ruled out at the Potsdam Conference in August 1945. Yet from the start the Soviets proceeded on their own. They removed from their zone all portable resources, taking them to their own ravaged territories. They brought in planeloads of docile German communists under Walter Ulbricht (1893–1973) to take charge of political reconstruction. The Soviets also barred observers from other occupying powers—the United States, Britain, and later France—which meanwhile had put their political imprint on their own zones.

The foreign ministers of the four occupying powers kept trying—in Paris, Moscow, and London—to arrive at common conditions for a peace treaty with Germany, but each time they drifted further apart. In 1947, Britain, France, and the United States began to combine their zones, and in 1949, the West German Federal Republic was established and Berlin divided. Stalin matched every step of the Western powers by formally consolidating communist rule in his zone, even blocking overland access from the west to Berlin in 1948–49, thereby adding anguish over the partition of Germany to the oppression in Eastern Europe.

The Cold War Intensifies

The United States and the Soviet Union collided also in Western Europe as its peoples tried to recover from the war. Communists had been prominent in the anti-Nazi resistance movements of Italy and France; they now claimed their share in the postwar reconstruction of their countries. Fearing that they were Stalin's agents, Americans by overt and covert means drove them from all positions of influence; the new democratic governments were solidly anticommunist.

Further afield, in the eastern Mediterranean, Stalin was suspected of aiding communist guerrillas in the Greek civil war of 1946–47. The guerrillas were supported by the neighboring Soviet-dominated countries of Albania, Bulgaria, and Yugoslavia; Stalin's influence on the course of the war was, in fact, minimal. He did, however, lay claim not only to the Straits of Constantinople but also to the former Italian colony of Libya, and he unduly prolonged the wartime Soviet occupation of northern Iran.

To the Russians, the territorial extension of Soviet rule seemed limited compared to the worldwide expansion of the American presence. After 1945, the United States dominated the

Map 36.1 The Cold War: U.S. and Soviet Alliances in the 1940s and 1950s ▶

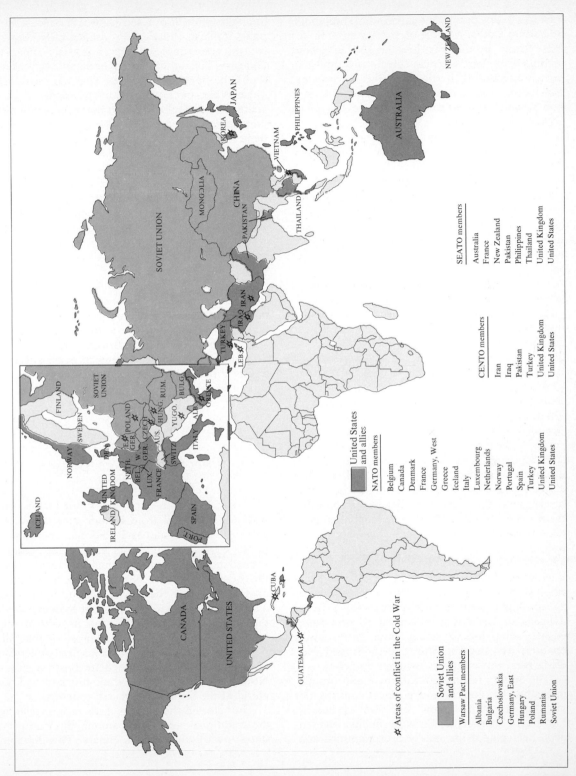

Areas of conflict in the Cold War

United States and allies

NATO members
Belgium
Canada
Denmark
France
Germany, West
Greece
Iceland
Italy
Luxembourg
Netherlands
Norway
Portugal
Spain
Turkey
United Kingdom
United States

Soviet Union and allies

Warsaw Pact members
Albania
Bulgaria
Czechoslovakia
Germany, East
Hungary
Poland
Rumania
Soviet Union

SEATO members
Australia
France
New Zealand
Pakistan
Philippines
Thailand
United Kingdom
United States

CENTO members
Iran
Iraq
Pakistan
Turkey
United Kingdom
United States

Pacific Ocean, occupying Japan, the Philippines, and South Korea. A string of military bases linked U.S. forces in the Far East with U.S. troops stationed in West Germany, with an outpost in Soviet-surrounded Berlin. For the time being, Americans also held a monopoly on the atomic bomb, which proved to be a subtle threat against Soviet expansionism.

In March 1947, alarmed by the threat of Soviet penetration into the eastern Mediterranean and by British weakness in that area, President Harry S Truman proclaimed the Truman Doctrine: "It must be the policy of the United States to support free peoples who are resisting attempted subjugation by armed minorities or by outside pressures."[2] The Truman Doctrine was the centerpiece of the new policy of *containment*, of holding Soviet power within its then-current boundaries. U.S. military and economic support soon went to Greece and Turkey. Thus, a sharp reversal took place in American foreign policy; prewar isolation gave way to worldwide vigilance against any Soviet effort at expansion. In June 1947, the United States took a further step toward strengthening the West. Secretary of State George C. Marshall announced an impressive scheme of economic aid to Europe (the European Recovery Program) for rebuilding prosperity and stability (see page 795).

These measures were accompanied by a massive ideological mobilization of American opinion against communism and a new apprehension about national security. As a result, the armed forces and the defense industries supporting them—the "military-industrial complex," in President Eisenhower's words—gained unprecedented political power in U.S. politics. Allied with them, after their establishment in 1947, were the Central Intelligence Agency (CIA) and the National Security Council (NSC). The purpose of the latter agency was to alert the president to any external dangers to the country. American intelligence agents soon locked horns with their Soviet counterparts, copying Soviet methods and even using Nazi war criminals for their purposes.

The Soviets responded quickly. Stalin brutally intensified ideological and political controls not only in his own country but also in Eastern Europe. In February 1948, with couplike suddenness, he replaced the mildly procommunist coalition government of Czechoslovakia with an outright Stalinist clique. Less dramatically, Soviet control was completed over Bulgaria, Romania, Hungary, Poland, and East Germany. Only Marshal Tito, the wartime hero of Yugoslav resistance to Nazi rule, and now the country's leader, eluded Stalin's reach. Stalin also promoted a Communist Information Bureau (COMINFORM) to enforce tighter obedience among communist parties in Eastern and Western Europe. By these and similar actions he profoundly alarmed Western Europeans who, three years after the end of the war, redoubled their search for military security.

The most spectacular test between the two superpowers took place from June 1948 to May 1949, after the Soviet authorities severed all overland access to the western sectors of Berlin. The Soviets aimed to starve into submission a half-city of about 2 million inhabitants who, because of their freedom, were "a bone in the communist throat" (as Khrushchev later put it). West Berlin was saved by an impressive airlift in which, under U.S. direction, the French, British, and Americans flew in supplies around the clock in all kinds of weather. In response to these conditions NATO was formed.

The Arms Race Begins

The year 1949 was a turning point in the cold war, which spread from Europe into the world at large, intensifying as it did so. The victory of the Chinese communists under Mao Zedong seemed more threatening to the United States than the Berlin blockade. Now another communist giant had joined the Soviet Union. Even more alarming was the fact that, sooner than expected, the Soviet Union had exploded its first atomic bomb, breaking the U.S. monopoly of that all-powerful weapon, which had inspired American self-confidence in the immediate postwar years. Now Americans felt that they also had to keep ahead of the Soviets in nuclear weapons.

Thus started the nuclear arms race, escalating the traditional arms race among the European states toward an ominous climax. This development was indeed cause for alarm. If nuclear weapons were to be used in a future war, war would become suicide; there would be no winners, only losers. It is no wonder that scientists from the start turned pessimistic. Said Albert Einstein: "The unleashed power of the atom has changed everything save our modes of thinking, and thus we drift toward unparalleled catastrophes."[3] But were people prepared to give up the age-old mode of settling international conflicts by war? In any case, if one side possessed nuclear weapons, the other side had to develop them too. The only safeguard lay in mutual deterrence, in assuring the opposition that if it launched its nuclear weapons, it too would suffer unacceptable loss. Thus, after the Americans took the initiative in building more deadly hydrogen bombs, the Soviet Union quickly followed suit.

Peace and national security henceforth required a balance of deadly terror. Yet how, in the incessant technological improvements of nuclear weapons, could a balance be achieved? Under the circumstances, it was natural that each side wished to gain an edge of superiority over the other. Facing the threat of nuclear war, political leaders in all countries, and especially in the superpowers, became more apprehensive in their foreign policies. Vigilance was needed everywhere in the world.

The Growth of Military Alliances

In June 1950, war broke out in Korea, a country divided in 1945 between a pro-Soviet communist regime in the north and a pro-American regime in the south. Eager to restore Korean national unity and mistakenly assuming U.S. nonintervention, the North Korean army invaded South Korea, possibly with Stalin's approval. Immediately the Americans took countermeasures, gaining UN backing for their war against North Korea. Under the command of General Douglas MacArthur, South Korean and U.S. troops, assisted by a token force from other UN members, fought their way north toward the Chinese border. Fearing for his own security, Mao Zedong thereupon dispatched Chinese "volunteers" to drive back the approach-

ing enemy in a surprise attack. Forced to retreat, General MacArthur's troops eventually withdrew from North Korea. Peace was restored in 1953, with the division of Korea reaffirmed; South Korea became an outpost of U.S. power.

East Asia in these years seemed an area especially threatened by Soviet expansionism. In 1954, Vietnamese communist liberation forces led by Ho Chi Minh defeated the French colonial army at Dien Bien Phu; their victory was followed by the division of Vietnam into a northern half under communist rule and a southern half, which now became a problematical U.S. client state. Tension also arose over the Chinese offshore islands of Quemoy and Matsu. These islands were considered potential communist jumping-off points for the invasion of Taiwan, where the Chinese anticommunists ejected from Mao Zedong's China in 1949 had found a safe shelter with support from the United States and its allies in the Pacific area. Other places considered likely for Soviet takeovers included Malaysia and Indonesia, both troubled by political unrest in the early years of decolonization. After Stalin's death his successor, Khrushchev, while proclaiming the need for peaceful coexistence, revived Lenin's policy of recruiting Soviet allies among the victims of colonialism; in 1960, he visited Indonesia.

The evidence of revived Soviet global ambition redoubled Washington's resolve to contain Soviet power. Under President Dwight D. Eisenhower, the United States extended its military alliances into central and East Asia for reasons stated when he assumed office: "The freedom we cherish and defend in Europe and in the Americas is no different from the freedom that is imperiled in Asia." As a result, two more alliance systems were added to NATO. The Central Treaty Organization (CENTO) united Turkey, Iraq, Iran, and Pakistan with Britain and the United States. Iran was at that time a loyal ally of the United States (and remained so until the overthrow of the shah in 1979). It was strategically important because a pro-Western Iran could prevent Soviet access to the crucial oil reserves of the Persian Gulf. The purpose of CENTO was to protect the southern neighbors of the Soviet Union from Soviet penetration.

The anti-Soviet alliance of lands further east was called the Southeast Asia Treaty Organiza-

The First Man on the Moon. After the Soviet Union launched the world's first artificial satellite in October 1957, U.S. scientific prestige sank to a low point. The moon landing by two U.S. as- tronauts—Armstrong and Aldrin—in 1969 restored faith in American science and technology. In the 1970s, rivalry in space was combined with a race for missile superiority. (*NASA*)

tion (SEATO). It contained, besides the United States, Britain, and France, the Asian countries of Pakistan and Thailand, and, in the Pacific Ocean, the Philippines, Australia, and New Zealand. In the Mideast, Israel constituted an additional reliable U.S. ally. Still closer to home, in the Western Hemisphere, the United States made sure, by economic pressure, subversion, or military intervention if necessary, that no pro-Soviet or even Marxist regime established itself.

By 1956, the United States was allied with 42 other states in strategic locations around the world, meddling if necessary in their internal affairs to assure their loyalty. The United States has maintained a massive global military presence ever since, its fleets roaming the oceans, its soldiers guarding its hundreds of military bases, and its intelligence satellites circling the skies. The Soviet government took its countermeasures, building up its fleet, placing its military advisers where possible in Asian or African countries, and trying to match U.S. intelligence operations. The military build-up led to an unending sophisticated secret war of espionage, counterespionage, and probing the enemy's defenses, all carefully hidden from public awareness.

The Dawn of the Space Age

The U.S.–Soviet rivalry assumed a still more intensive form in 1957. The Soviet government sent the first space satellite, Sputnik I, into orbit around the earth, shocking complacent Americans into a keen awareness of their vulnerability. Sputnik opened up a new dimension of competition; power politics henceforth extended into outer space. For a number of years, the Soviets remained ahead in the prestigious field of space exploration, sending the first astronaut into orbit in 1961. The Americans triumphantly caught up in 1969, when they landed a man on the moon. Eventually, other countries joined the American and Soviet ventures into space, for military or commercial gain. In this manner, Western science and technology introduced human beings to the infinity of the cosmos.

As Sputnik opened up the space age, the arms race entered an even more ominous phase. The intercontinental ballistic missile (ICBM), a space rocket tipped with a nuclear warhead, was born, a weapon that fundamentally changed the destiny of the United States. Protected by oceans east and west and by friendly neighbors north and south, it had hitherto been invulnerable to hostile attack. Now the country lay open to nuclear destruction from Soviet missiles streaking across the North Pole. To the Soviet Union, however, the ICBM merely added another threat to its traditional insecurity. To guard themselves better with the help of new technology, both countries began to station satellites in space for spying on each others' weapon developments and military activities. In 1960, panicky over falling behind in the missile race, the United States also started building submarines able to launch ICBMs from underwater, subsequently making them a major part of its nuclear strike force.

The city of Berlin remained a source of contention. In 1958, Khrushchev tried to stop the westward escape of East Germans through Berlin by threatening to end its status as an open city. The threat was subsequently withdrawn, but trouble continued. In 1960, a conciliatory meeting between Eisenhower and Khrushchev regarding Berlin turned sour because a U.S. spy plane (the *U-2*) was shot down deep inside the Soviet Union, its pilot surviving to confess the purpose of his mission. The CIA had for some time been carrying out aerial reconnaissance over Soviet territory. In the following year, the trouble over Berlin came to a head. Unexpectedly and overnight, the East German government threw up a wall that cut the city in half, sealing off Soviet-held East Berlin from the West. West Berlin, however, remained free, guarded to this day by American, English, and French troops.

The Berlin Wall. Although an open city since the end of World War II, Berlin was physically divided overnight in 1961 when the East German government erected the wall that still separates the city. The Berlin Wall and the Cuban missile crisis of 1962 brought the U.S. and Soviet superpowers to two of the most dangerous crises in the long history of the cold war. (*UPI/Bettmann Newsphotos*)

The Cuban Missile Crisis

Confrontation between the superpowers rose to a terrifying climax in 1962 during the Cuban missile crisis. In 1959, the infamous dictatorship of Fulgencio Batista had been toppled by Fidel Castro (b. 1927), a left-wing revolutionary. Refused American aid because the economic interests of U.S. landowners in Cuba were threatened by his agrarian reform law, Castro turned to the Soviet Union. Agrarian reform was enforced by a strong, centralized government, making Cuba into a totalitarian state. After an American attempt to overthrow him—the bungled Bay of Pigs operation—Castro was ready to turn his country into an outpost of Soviet power. Khrushchev planned to exploit this foothold within the Western Hemisphere by installing Soviet nuclear missiles in Cuba. The United States, admittedly, had for some time stationed nuclear weapons in Turkey within easy reach of Soviet targets. But the reverse situation—allowing a major Soviet threat close to home—was alarming. President John F. Kennedy demanded that Khrushchev withdraw the Soviet missiles from Cuba. For an awesome moment, the cold war confrontation threatened to turn into a very hot nuclear war. In the end, however, Khrushchev backed down, a move that contributed to his fall from power two years later. No Soviet missiles were stationed in Cuba.

The shock of the Cuban missile crisis temporarily reduced the high pitch of Soviet–U.S. hostility. The imminence of a nuclear exchange had a sobering effect, leading to halfhearted attempts to control the ever more costly arms race. The first step was the establishment of a hotline between Washington and Moscow in 1963 to provide effective communication in case of crisis. Soon thereafter, both countries, joined by many others, banned nuclear tests (with their poisonous radioactive fallout) in the atmosphere, in outer space, and under water. Five years later (1968), the Non-Proliferation Treaty was signed by virtually all governments around the world; in theory, it banned the transfer of nuclear weapons or weapons technology to states not yet producing such weapons. By that time, the "nuclear club" included, besides the United States and the Soviet Union, Britain, France, and China. In practice, however, the treaty had little effect. India joined the nuclear club in 1974; other nations—including Israel, Pakistan, and South Africa—were suspected of constructing bombs in secret.

The Vietnam War

Tensions continued in various parts of the world throughout this period. The new countries in Asia and Africa, emerging from colonial rule and trying to build up their power as fast as possible, were tempted to copy the Soviet methods of polit-ical mobilization; they offered seductive opportunities for Soviet global ambitions. From the U.S. perspective, the biggest challenge arose in Vietnam, where the communist regime in the north threatened to take over South Vietnam as well.

The threat had started with the partition of the country in 1954. From the north, the authoritarian regime of Ho Chi Minh, backed by indigenous nationalism and Soviet aid, cast its shadow over a disorganized south. In the south, American sponsors, with the help of Ngo Dinh Diem, a Catholic anticommunist patriot long resident in the United States, tried to create a democratic nation. Providing South Vietnam with the stability and strength needed to resist communist infiltration required increasing U.S. aid, including troops to fight off the communist guerrillas, called the Vietcong.

Building democracy in that disorderly country soon became a patriotic concern, tempting U.S. presidents from Eisenhower to Nixon into ever deeper involvement in South Vietnamese affairs. In response to confused reports of a North Vietnamese attack on U.S. gunboats in the Gulf of Tonkin, President Lyndon B. Johnson in 1964 obtained congressional support for taking "all necessary measures" to protect U.S. forces in the area and to keep South Vietnam pro-American. If the communists prevailed there, so the argument ran, all the other countries in East and Southeast Asia emerging from colonial rule would fall like dominoes under communist influence. Under President Johnson, U.S. intervention in South Vietnam became the (undeclared) Vietnam War.

Under cover of extensive secrecy, the U.S. government shipped to Vietnam nearly half a million soldiers, equipped with the most advanced chemical weapons and electronic equipment available. Yet victory eluded the American forces. The North Vietnamese government and its people withstood the cruelest punishment of bombs and chemical weapons ever inflicted on human beings. Nor was South Vietnam spared; virtually every South Vietnamese family saw relatives killed or maimed, and their farms and livelihoods were ruined for generations to come. In early 1968, the Vietcong forces launched a well-planned counterattack, the Tet offensive, which, despite its mili-

Map 36.2 Southeast Asia and the Vietnam War ▶

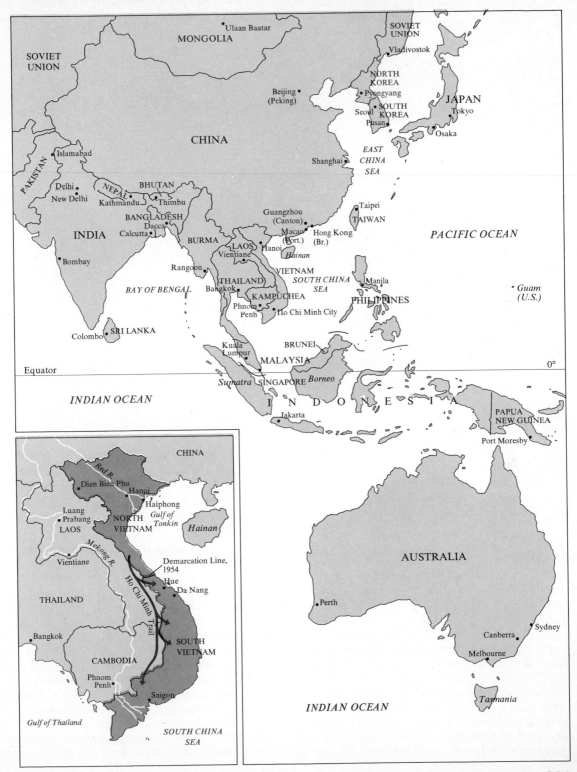

Bogged Down in Vietnam. The domino theory, which predicted the fall of East Asian countries to communist rule, led to American defense of South Vietnam against a threatened takeover by communist North Vietnam. Between 1964 and 1973, U.S. involvement in the unsuccessful Vietnam War cost tens of thousands of American and Vietnamese lives, ruined South Vietnam, and polarized U.S. public opinion over the morality of the war. (*AP/Wide World Photos*)

tary failure and huge Vietcong losses, proved their continued vigor. The Tet offensive was a turning point in American public opinion, which became increasingly critical of the conduct of the war. The mounting brutality did not lead to the desired results.

In the face of rising domestic opposition and unbroken Vietcong resistance, it was clear to President Richard M. Nixon, elected in 1968, that the war had to be ended by "peace with honor." While he initiated negotiations with North Vietnam, U.S. forces put pressure on the enemy by attacking communist bases and supply routes in neighboring Cambodia and Laos. Civilians were bombed more fiercely than had been the case in

World War II (even the use of atomic weapons was considered). In 1973, by agreement with North Vietnam, the United States withdrew its forces from the area. In 1975, Vietnam was reunited under communist rule; Ho Chi Minh had triumphed against the mightiest nation in the world.

As the Vietnam War proved, U.S. power was limited. The United States could not by brute force establish a democratic regime under conditions utterly alien to the American experience. Furthermore, the extension of the war into Cambodia and Laos had the unintended effect of leading to increased strength among communist insurgents and to the establishment of communist regimes in both countries by 1975. Yet, contrary to earlier fears, the other dominoes in the area did not fall. Soviet influence in East Asia declined as Mao's China broke away from its Soviet ally. Under President Nixon, U.S.–Communist Chinese relations were resumed; the People's Republic of China was seated on the UN Security Council. Meanwhile, Indonesia had come under U.S. influence, and the new countries of Southeast Asia stayed safely away from communism. In the Mideast, too, the United States scored an advantage. In 1972, the Egyptian government expelled the Soviet military mission on which it had staked its strength for some years.

Détente—and More Cold War

Improvements to the nuclear arsenal continued throughout the 1960s and 1970s. After 1966, U.S. missiles carried three warheads, each sixteen times more powerful than the Hiroshima bomb. In 1968, the Soviets responded in kind, only to find their weapons outmoded in 1970 by American ICBMs, each equipped with a multiple independently targeted re-entry vehicle (MIRV) capable of hitting up to ten widely scattered targets. By 1975, the Soviets too had MIRVed their ICBMs. Meanwhile, in 1968, the Soviet Union had taken the lead with antiballistic missiles (ABMs) designed to destroy incoming missiles; the United States followed suit in 1972. In that year, however, both countries consented to limit antiballistic missile systems to a minimum; neither side considered them effective, which made agreement easier. Research on this project, however, as on all other weapons, never ceased.

The ABM treaty in 1972 reflected a new phase in U.S.–Soviet relations, soon known by the term *détente*. There were good reasons for a relaxation of tensions. U.S. concentration politically and militarily on Vietnam had diverted attention from the Soviet Union; as a result of their humiliation in the war, Americans had become more realistic. Feeling more secure, the Soviet leaders in turn softened the aggressive tone of their foreign policy. In addition, West Germany's chancellor,

Willy Brandt, was eager to reduce the strain between West and East Germany. He concluded treaties with the Soviet Union, Poland, and East Germany, formally accepting the division of Germany and assuring continued Western contact with West Berlin. Calmer times returned at last to central Europe. Tension was also eased by the admission of both West and East Germany to the United Nations.

Of broader significance were the Helsinki Agreements of 1975, signed in neutral Finland, amid considerable pomp, by all European governments plus Canada and the United States. The first of these agreements legitimized all borders drawn in central Europe at the end of the war; they took the place of the peace that had never been officially concluded. Another agreement, especially important to the Soviet Union, stipulated the free exchange of technical and scientific data. The final agreement, and subsequently the most troublesome, called for the free movement of peoples and ideas across what Churchill had called the "iron curtain." Could all those who wished to escape from oppression now leave the Soviet Union or its satellite countries? The Soviet government could hardly afford free contact with the outside world.

Meanwhile, détente, combined with the fact that the Soviet Union had achieved parity in ICBMs and therefore felt more secure, favored further agreements for slowing down the arms race. Together with the ABM treaty, the first Strategic Arms Limitation Treaty (SALT I) was negotiated. It froze the number of strategic missile launchers at existing levels and stipulated that the construction of more ballistic missiles be offset by the dismantling of older equipment of the same type. Hopes ran high that even more stringent reductions of nuclear delivery systems and warheads might be negotiated. Yet SALT II, which spelled out these hopes in specific detail, fell victim to the collapse of détente in 1979. That treaty was not ratified by the United States, although its terms were voluntarily adhered to by both sides even after détente had faded.

In fact, détente had never been deeply rooted. There were the continuous violations of civil and human rights by the Soviet government. Additional friction arose subsequently over a pro-Soviet regime in Ethiopia, followed by the dispatch of Cuban soldiers and experts to Angola.

Soviet Tanks in Afghanistan. With the invasion of Afghanistan in 1979 to restore a pro-communist regime, the Soviet Union embarked on a war often called the Soviet Vietnam. The cold war resumed in earnest between the superpowers. U.S. President Ronald Reagan characterized the Soviet Union as "the evil empire." (*AP/Wide World Photos*)

Obviously, by U.S. judgment, the Soviet Union had not given up its expansionist ambitions. The traditional harassment of Jews in the Soviet Union especially soured U.S.–Soviet relations, leading on the eve of the Helsinki Agreements to discrimination against Soviet trade. American suspicion of Soviet motives never abated, breaking into full force again in 1979 when, after the overthrow of the pro-American shah of Iran by Islamic fundamentalists, the Soviet Union invaded Afghanistan to forestall a similar Islamic takeover.

In Afghanistan a long-established moderate pro-Soviet government (that received American as well as Soviet development aid) had collapsed under pressure from rebellious Islamic fundamentalists opposed to modernization. Worried about the fundamentalists' appeal to the 50 million Islamic peoples in the Soviet Union, the Soviet government under Brezhnev sent troops into Af-

ghanistan to restore a strong pro-Soviet regime, thereby setting off a bitter civil war. For Americans, the Soviet invasion of Afghanistan constituted dramatic proof of Soviet expansionism. Stepping up its hostility against what President Ronald Reagan called "the evil empire," the U.S. government sent military aid to the Afghan insurgents, making it difficult for the Soviet government to extricate itself with honor from this Vietnam-like venture. Now the U.S.–Soviet confrontation was extended to a highly sensitive area on the Soviet southern border.

The resumption of the cold war also revived the arms race. All along, nuclear weapons had become more diversified, allowing greater selectivity in their use. Long-range missiles were joined by intermediate-range missiles. Less powerful missiles were adapted to battlefield use, obscuring the distinction between nuclear and conventional warfare. In 1981, the United States introduced the neutron bomb, a weapon capable of killing people by massive doses of fatal radiation without destroying their cities. The following year, it started production of the nuclear-tipped cruise missile, a small, rather inexpensive, and highly accurate weapon that flies fast at low altitudes and is difficult to detect. The United States thereby gained another temporary advantage over the Soviet Union.

In 1983, President Reagan announced an even more ambitious project, the Strategic Defense Initiative (SDI), nicknamed "Star Wars," designed to build a space shield of electronic equipment over the United States capable of destroying incoming weapons. Critics pointed to its technological complexity and exorbitant cost, as well as to its ineffectiveness. Deadly Soviet missiles could still hit American targets. In any case, SDI propelled the arms race further into space, promoting in turn space-based antisatellite weapons in a burst of scientific and technological research by the arms industries of the United States and NATO countries.

After 1985, the new Soviet leader, Mikhail Gorbachev, undertook a major initiative for arms limitation, hoping to abolish nuclear weapons by the year 2000. The high costs of the arms race seriously impeded the reforms in the Soviet economy that he was so urgently promoting. After lengthy negotiations involving the NATO members as well, the United States and the Soviet Union agreed at the Washington summit conference in late 1987 to a treaty to eliminate intermediate-range nuclear weapons (the INF treaty), which raised hopes for reducing long-range missiles as well. Since the Washington summit, the arms race has become subject to reconsideration. How many nuclear weapons are really needed for deterrence? Certainly, many more nuclear warheads exist than are necessary for assured mutual destruction. And what is the benefit of such suicidal annihilation? As Gorbachev asked, should the antagonists rather be concerned with mutual security?

These questions point to a reduction of nuclear overkill capacity and to more rational management of deterrence in the future. Considering Soviet Russia's need for concentrating on internal reform and U.S. concern over the darkening prospects for its prosperity, there are signs at the end of the 1980s for a more lasting era of détente.

Yet fear persists, especially in Western Europe. If intermediate-range nuclear weapons are to be abolished, will the existing conventional military forces be sufficient to repel Soviet aggression? The Soviet government in turn is afraid of Western military, economic, and political superiority; it wants to preserve its freedom from external pressure. The basic causes of the arms race remain in place: the incompatibility of the Soviet system with Western democracy and the mutual incomprehension of the considerations motivating the rivals. The long-range ambitions of both superpowers remain unchanged—the United States still perceives itself as the leader of a global mission for democracy, while the U.S.S.R. still believes in a communist course for humanity's future.

Under these conditions it is not surprising that the overwhelming majority of UN members never cease to protest the economic and humanitarian consequences of the arms race. They have strong arguments. By a 1985 estimate, the development, building, and maintenance of nuclear weapons cost $1.7 million every minute, thus draining resources from essential social services and depriving the illiterate, sick, and hungry multitudes everywhere of aid and comfort. The United Nations still endorses its resolution of 1978, which states:

> *Mankind today is confronted with an unprecedented threat of self-extinction arising from the massive and competitive accumulation of the most destructive weapons ever produced. Existing arsenals of nuclear weapons alone are more than sufficient to destroy all life on earth. . . .*
>
> *In a world of finite resources there is a close relationship between expenditure on armaments and economic and social development. . . The hundred of billions of dollars spent annually on the manufacture or improvement of weapons are in sombre and dramatic contrast to the want and poverty in which two thirds of the world's population live.*[4]

The UN, however, has been unable over the years to save humanity from the specter of nuclear war. U.S. security analysts still argue that nuclear deterrence remains the best guarantee of peace between the superpowers. After all, there has been no global war since World War II.

Chronology 36.1 International Relations in an Age of Superpowers

1944–1945	Stalin imposes Soviet rule in Eastern Europe
April 1945	United Nations established
1946–1947	Greek Civil War
1947	Cold War starts; Truman Doctrine; Marshall Plan inaugurated
1948	UN's Universal Declaration of Human Rights
1948–1949	Stalinization of Eastern Europe; Berlin airlift
1949	Federal Republic of Germany (West Germany) established; NATO formed; first Soviet atomic bomb exploded; People's Republic of China established under Mao Zedong
1950–1953	Korean War
1953	American and Soviet hydrogen bombs developed
1954	Siege of Dien Bien Phu
1957	Sputnik launched—the space age begins
1959	Castro overthrows Batista regime in Cuba
1960	American Inter-Continental Ballistic Missile developed
1961	Berlin Wall built, dividing the city of Berlin
1962	Cuban missile crisis
1963–1973	Vietnam War
1964	Gulf of Tonkin incident
1969	Non-Proliferation Treaty
1972	Détente; Anti-Ballistic Missile Treaty
1975	Helsinki Agreements
1979	Shah of Persia ousted; Soviet Union invades Afghanistan
1983	Strategic Defense Initiative announced
1987	Gorbachev-Reagan summit in Washington; INF Treaty agreed

Notes

1. All the foregoing quotations are from the Preamble and Article I of "The Charter of the United Nations," *Yearbook of the United Nations*, 37 (New York: Department of Public Information, United Nations, 1983), p. 1325.

2. "The Truman Doctrine," *Major Problems in American Foreign Policy: Documents and Essays*, vol. 2, ed. by Thomas G. Paterson (Lexington, Mass.: D. C. Heath, 1978), p. 290.

3. Ralph E. Lapp, "The Einstein Letter That Started It All," *New York Times Magazine*, August 2, 1964.

4. "Universal Declaration of Human Rights," *Yearbook of the United Nations, 1948–49* (New York: Columbia University Press, 1950), p. 535.

Suggested Reading

Garrison, Mark, and Abbot Gleason, eds., *Shared Destiny: Fifty Years of Soviet-American Relations* (1985). Distinguished experts reflect on the blunders, misperceptions, and lost opportunities that have created the gulf between the two countries.

Gelb, Norman, *The Berlin Wall* (1987). An on-the-spot account of the building of the wall. Implications for the city, for the two Germanys, and for East-West relations are considered.

Schell, Jonathan, *The Fate of the Earth* (1982). The book everybody should read about the prospects for and the results of a nuclear war.

Ulam, Adam B., *Dangerous Relations: The Soviet Union in World Politics, 1970–1982* (1983). Soviet foreign relations under Brezhnev.

UN Yearbook. Annual report on the work of the United Nations and agencies.

Van Dusen, Henry P., *Dag Hammarskjöld: The Statesman and His Faith* (1967). An introduction to the work of the United Nations as reflected in the life of its most prominent official.

Weisberger, Bernard A., *Cold War, Cold Peace: The United States and Russia Since 1945* (1984). A history of four decades of tension, conflict, détente, and living with the nuclear threat.

Yergin, Daniel, *Shattered Peace: The Origins of the Cold War and the National Security State* (1977). The best book on the subject, written with verve and insight.

Periodicals

Bulletin of the Atomic Scientists (Chicago) was founded by concerned scientists in 1945 to examine the connections between global politics and nuclear weapons.

Current History (Philadelphia) and *Foreign Affairs* (New York) analyze foreign policy and the arms race.

Review Questions

1. What are the aims of the United Nations? Do you consider the UN to be a useful organization? If so, in what respects is it useful?

2. What do you consider to be the origins of the cold war? Is there any evidence that, with better understanding on both sides, it might have been avoided?

3. How did the cold war affect the organization of Europe from 1947 to 1958?

4. What do you consider to be the driving force behind the arms race? How do you personally assess the arms race?

5. How is space exploration related to the arms race?

6. What were the causes of détente? Was détente a temporary phenomenon growing out of the particular circumstances of the early 1970s, or does it have a lasting basis?

7. What were the effects of the Cuban missile crisis? Are crises like that needed to slow down the arms race?

8. What were the consequences of the Vietnam War for the United States?

37

The New Globalism

Below the surface of worldwide trade and global politics, a profound and still unfinished process of cultural transformation is at work. No other civilization in history has managed to universalize itself to the extent of imposing its achievements and its spirit on all others the way Western civilization has. For better or worse, Europeans and people of European descent have taken the initiative in creating the irreversibly interdependent world with which the present and all future generations must cope. Penetrating all lands, the West has revamped a fragmented world of villages, loosely structured political communities, and a few effective nation-states into a quarrelsome global community.

Non-Western peoples everywhere must adjust, in the name of modernization, to the institutions, machines, and human attitudes evolved by Western civilization. The pressure of global power politics and of international trade and finance, as well as their own ambition to be counted in the world, leaves non-Westerners no choice. In trying to adjust, they often find themselves in permanent conflict with their indigenous traditions. The agonizing task of fusing Western and non-Western ways in order to build a modern state and a modern economy started with the process of decolonization after the end of World War II.

Decolonization and Worldwide Westernization

After World War II, a new phase in the relationship between the West and non-Western peoples began. It gave vent to the accumulated resentment of previous generations. The rising militancy of nationalist movements bloomed amid the declining resources of the colonial empires. The political

Hong Kong Street Scene with McDonald's. (*Robert Harding Picture Library*)

843

agitation of the war, in which many colonial soldiers loyally fought, fired the desire for political independence; after all, freedom and self-determination had been prominent Allied war slogans. France and Holland had been overrun by Nazi Germany, their Asian colonies by the Japanese; they had no strength left for colonial rule. Great Britain, exhausted by the war, also was ready to let its colonies go as soon as it could responsibly do so. Equally important, the United States, in its new superpower role, took a decidedly anti-imperialist stand. The Soviet Union, although it tightened control over its Asian subject nationalities and reacted to its geographic insecurity in Eurasia, also affirmed its customary moral support for all oppressed peoples. Too weak to provide aid, the Soviet Union nevertheless furnished a heroic model of rapid mobilization for ambitious leaders in non-Western countries (see Chapter 31).

In this setting, a mighty groundswell of decolonization after 1946 abolished all overseas empires and propelled their former subjects into independent statehood. At best, the colonial powers, under the threat of violence, relinquished their control quietly. At worst, they were driven out by bitter wars of liberation. Sometimes independence was followed by civil war. Whatever the course of events, decolonization profoundly altered the political landscape of the world, giving the non-Western states a worldwide numerical superiority over their former masters and ending for good the unquestioned ascendancy of the West. Great was the jubilation in Asia and Africa.

Decolonization began when in 1946 the United States granted independence to the Philippines. In 1947, India and Pakistan attained sovereign statehood. In 1948, Burma and Ceylon (later renamed Sri Lanka) emerged. In 1949, it was the turn of the Dutch possessions in Indonesia. In 1954, the French quit Laos, Cambodia, and Vietnam (leaving the Americans to defend South Vietnam against the communist revolutionaries of North Vietnam until 1973). In 1956, France freed its northern African colonies, Morocco and Tunisia (but not Algeria, which attained independence in 1962 after a cruel revolutionary war).

To the cheers of black people everywhere, Ghana in 1957 declared its independence, the first sub-Saharan African country to do so. After 1959, virtually all French and English posses-

sions in Africa were decolonized. In 1960, the Belgians reluctantly left the Congo (now called Zaire), which started independence amid a civil war. By 1975, even the Portuguese, determined to the last to keep their African colonies, were driven out. In 1980, white-ruled Rhodesia became the African state of Zimbabwe. Only in South Africa and Southwest Africa (renamed Namibia) did white settlers, including the long-established Afrikaners, continue to defy black majority rule.

In the Mideast, Egypt and Saudi Arabia, which had become independent before World War II, were joined between 1951 and 1971 by other free Arab states. By the mid-1970s, Western colonialism had formally come to an end. But the accumulated resentments of colonial rule and the struggle for independence remained a potent political legacy.

For a time, expectations ran high that the days of humiliation had ended and that non-Western peoples could build societies free of exploitation and inhumanity, yet still follow the pattern of the European nation-state. Although often fiercely anti-Western, the new states kept the boundaries drawn by their colonial masters and adopted both the ambitions and the trappings of European rule. National anthems, flags, armies, navies, and air forces all proclaimed national power. Putting forth the most advanced ideals of democracy, socialism, and the welfare state, the new constitutions were paper models of enlightened government. Moreover, they put the most Westernized and cosmopolitan elements in the population into the seats of power, where they had so long yearned to be. But disillusionment arrived swiftly. After independence, the new masters discovered that their countries were unprepared for achieving the global respectability that they craved. Often excruciatingly poor, composed of quarreling ethnic groups that felt no attachment to the new nation, and crowded with illiterate, disease-ridden, stubborn peasants, the new countries entered the race for power and prestige with severe handicaps.

These countries quickly learned that the competition for status is exceedingly keen; under the new globalism, the world is perceived as a pyramid of prestige and power. At the top—the "First World"—stand the advanced countries, repre-

Map 37.1 New States in Africa and Asia ▶

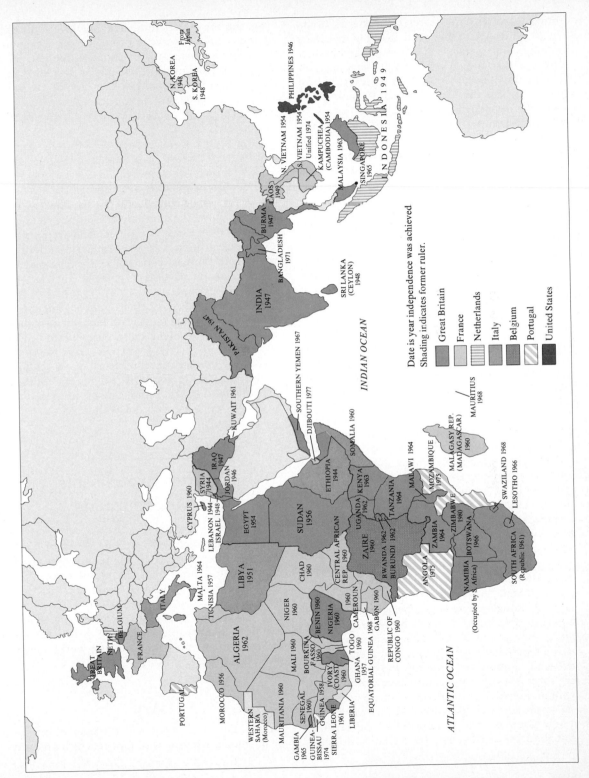

Date is year independence was achieved
Shading indicates former ruler.

Great Britain
France
Netherlands
Italy
Belgium
Portugal
United States

N. KOREA 1948
S. KOREA 1948
From Japan
PHILIPPINES 1946
N. VIETNAM 1954
S. VIETNAM 1954
Unified 1974
KAMPUCHEA (CAMBODIA) 1954
MALAYSIA 1963
SINGAPORE 1965
LAOS 1949
INDONESIA 1949
BURMA 1947
BANGLADESH 1971
SRI LANKA (CEYLON) 1948
INDIA 1947
PAKISTAN 1947
SOUTHERN YEMEN 1967

INDIAN OCEAN

DJIBOUTI 1977
KUWAIT 1961
IRAQ 1944
SYRIA 1944
JORDAN 1946
CYPRUS 1960
LEBANON 1944
ISRAEL 1948
EGYPT 1954
SUDAN 1956
ETHIOPIA 1944
SOMALIA 1960
KENYA 1963
UGANDA 1962
MALAWI 1964
MOZAMBIQUE 1975
MALAGASY REP. (MADAGASCAR) 1960
MAURITIUS 1968
SWAZILAND 1968
LESOTHO 1966

MALTA 1964
TUNISIA 1957
ITALY
BELGIUM
NETH.
FRANCE
GREAT BRITAIN
PORTUGAL
MOROCCO 1956
LIBYA 1951
CHAD 1960
CENTRAL AFRICAN REP. 1960
ZAIRE 1960
RWANDA 1962
BURUNDI 1962
TANZANIA 1964
ZAMBIA 1964
ZIMBABWE 1980
BOTSWANA 1966
ANGOLA 1975
NAMIBIA (Occupied by S. Africa)
SOUTH AFRICA (Republic 1961)

ALGERIA 1962
NIGER 1960
MALI 1960
BOURKINA FASSO 1960
NIGERIA 1960
CAMEROUN 1960
GABON 1960
EQUATORIAL GUINEA 1968
REPUBLIC OF CONGO 1960
BENIN 1960
TOGO 1960
GHANA 1957
IVORY COAST 1960
GUINEA 1958
LIBERIA
SIERRA LEONE 1961
GUINEA-BISSAU 1974
SENEGAL 1960
GAMBIA 1965
MAURITANIA 1960
WESTERN SAHARA (Morocco)

ATLANTIC OCEAN

37 The New Globalism   845

senting essentially the states of Western Europe and North America; they were joined in the 1960s by Japan. The Soviet Union and its satellites occupy the "Second World," while the majority of humanity occupies the lower-level "Third World," where the "less developed" rank above the "least developed" countries.

"Backwardness," in any form and by any name, represents humiliation to be escaped as fast as possible by "development"—by catching up to the "advanced" countries. "Development" aims at raising the standard of living, at industrialization, at participation in scientific and technological progress, and foremost, at prestige in the world. In this sense, the struggle for development among non-Western peoples represents the culmination of westernization. All humanity strives to "modernize"—to master institutions and technologies originally developed by the West. But how?

Unfortunately, the newcomers to modern statehood were entirely unprepared for managing the large-scale organizations required for statehood and global competition. Although anti-Western by political instinct and determined to preserve their inherited cultural identity, they were compelled to abide by the rules of power laid down by the West and enforced by the new globalism. Trying to assert their independence, the new countries nevertheless had to copy the Western nation-state and its style of economic competition and achievement. To do so requires institutions and attitudes that parallel those in the West. These states need not only the visible aspects of Western accomplishment like statehood or industrialism but also the invisible collective social discipline built up over many centuries in Western history.

People generally do not realize how Western civilization has created among its peoples a tradition of peaceful, voluntary cooperation on a large scale. Although professing liberty and individualism, people in the Western democracies maintain a society that provides the essentials of life with almost clocklike regularity. In their politics too, ready compliance with law and order is present, together with willing submission to majority opinion. Freedom and individualism obviously do not negate social cooperation and teamwork; they even encourage civic responsibility and creative contributions to the common welfare. Although

asserting themselves to be free individuals, people conform to the ever more complex social regulations and sophisticated machines of modern life. Their unconscious discipline makes possible democratic government, patriotic loyalty, and a productive economy. By these accomplishments the West has gained ascendancy over the non-Western peoples.

The West has not been able to transfer to the non-Western world the hidden discipline that makes its own governments and societies work. If the Western peoples are not aware of the invisible dynamics behind their achievements, how can the others follow their example? Lacking the unstated prerequisites, the others fall prey, under the Western impact, to disorientation and alienation. The Western concepts of freedom and individualism, in particular, provoke anarchy and antisocial selfishness.

Thus, compelled by their own self-interest to follow the Western model but hampered by their inability to transplant these deep-rooted values successfully, non-Western peoples have been saddled with burdensome problems. So an endless round of political, social, economic, and cultural experimentation has begun among them as they search for equality with the Westerners.

Perilous Experiments in Modernization

Determined to mobilize people by the use of Western or Western-derived cultural skills, each non-Western country has conducted its own experiments in modernization, limited by its own history and resources, and all too often has been drawn into war with its neighbors. Ranging from remarkable success to brutal failure, these efforts offer a panorama of a world in agonized transition.

Asia

Japan The most spectacular model of triumphant modernization was Japan, which enjoyed the benefit of a headstart. Starting in 1867 under the Meiji emperor (see page 615), the Japanese government, with the full support of leading elements of Japanese society, deliberately copied those aspects of Western civilization that lay behind superior military power, including Western forms of government, law, education, science, and technology. At the same time Japan kept its own spiritual traditions. A unique case, the Japanese contributed from their own history the essentials of modern power: a high level of technical competence, a strict self-discipline needed for civic cooperation, and a tradition of readily absorbing foreign cultures into their own without giving up their own identity.

The fusion of Western and Japanese culture was not complete, however. In the 1930s, the Japanese warrior heritage gained the upper hand; it encouraged an anti-Western orientation that led to war—and disaster. Defeated and utterly exhausted, Japan had to make a new start, laboring for seven years under U.S. occupation. The Americans imposed a Western democratic constitution and, while preserving the role of the emperor, abolished the traditional strongholds of power. Thus began Japan's miraculous rise to the position of economic superpower, rivaling and, in some respects, even outpacing the United States.

This miracle was possible, first of all, because the country started with a clean slate. Its own industrial capacity destroyed, it began reconstruction by humbly taking the best and the latest advances in technology and industrial science from the United States and Western Europe, gradually learning to improve the imported techniques and concentrating on long-range goals. Second, undaunted by their misery after the war, the Japanese people were willing to work hard and live austerely, putting the welfare of the country ahead of their individual gain. Third, the tradition of selfless civic cooperation, unbroken by defeat and foreign occupation, permeated the political, economic, and social life of the country; little time was lost in social conflict, strikes, or work stoppages. Finally, national pride ran high, spurred by the desire to escape the humiliation of 1945, by the marked successes in industrial technology, and by the world's respect for the superior quality of Japanese products. In the 1970s, Japanese steel, ships, cameras, automobiles, and computers were rated among the best—if not *the* best—in the world; Japanese firms dominated world trade, entering into partnership with firms in the United States and other countries. By the 1980s, Japan's industrial and financial strength began to threaten the United States' economy. The Japanese standard of living rose, although not to the American level.

Admittedly, Japan was aided by the fact that, under American military protection, it could concentrate entirely on peacefully advancing its economy in the expanding world market. It manifested no political ambition except to maintain the worldwide stability necessary for its economic security; more than any other country it depended for its prosperity on the secure flow of imports and exports. By necessity, therefore, Japan became the most globally minded country, leading the way, some observers suggest, into the twenty-first century. Yet questions remain: In the global competition can an economic superpower survive over the long haul without wielding corresponding political clout? Can the fusion of Western and Japanese ways withstand the strains of increased participation in world politics? Can the Japanese maintain their unique civic-mindedness despite their involvement with other countries and cultures? In any case, at the end of the twentieth century, Japan is the envy of non-Western countries in which indigenous tradition and Western ways forever refuse to mesh.

China While Japan rose from ashes to economic glory, events next door in China took a different and infinitely more tragic course. The Chinese experiment in modernization after World War II is known as Maoism, from the name of its leader, Mao Zedong (Mao Tse-tung, 1898–1976), chairman of the Chinese Communist party. Coming from a peasant family somewhat better off than most, Mao became a student of Western learning; he went into politics with the Chinese Communist party, risking his life and living under extreme hardships as he was pursued by the forces of Chiang Kai-shek. He tried to win the peasants over to the demanding routines of guerrilla warfare, political agitation, and more efficient agriculture. His success came because he stayed close to the people and, unlike other rulers of China, showed genuine concern for their needs.

Chairman Mao with Teachers and Schoolchildren in 1959. Mao overestimated the creativity of the masses to conquer all obstacles, but he united China under his rule. With nuclear capability and a quarter of the world's population, China is a potential world force. (*UPI/Bettmann Newsphotos*)

Throughout World War II, the Chinese communists fought the Japanese invaders more vigorously than did Chiang's forces. In the civil war following World War II, the communists defeated Chiang's Kuomintang (Guomindong), and in 1949, with superior organization and purpose, as well as with peasant support, they became masters of a New China, reunited and liberated at last from foreign domination.

The communist victory was dearly bought. The Chinese people had suffered terribly in the conflict with Japan and the civil war. Nor was the communist victory the end of their trials. Although poor, internally disorganized and externally weak,

communist China was ambitious—by virtue of both its Maoist Marxism and the splendid heritage of Old China—to be a leader in human progress. Chairman Mao thought of his work as a continuing cultural revolution that would carry China to the glory of full communism. It proved to be an endless and discouraging ascent.

To motivate the huge population in his vast country, Mao had to develop his own approach. He rejected the Stalinist approach to modernization, which would create a bureaucracy of administrators and condemn the Chinese masses to the sullen passivity that had ruined the former Chinese empire. Mao preferred to take a slower road, hoping to stimulate the ingenuity of the peasants—at the price of letting China fall further behind in acquiring the latest methods of economic productivity. He trusted that the creativity of the masses would conquer all obstacles, although many of his ablest comrades remained unconvinced.

Mao also oversimplified the complexities of industrial society. This trait showed up disastrously when in 1958 he staked his leadership on a campaign to create giant communes engaged in agriculture, industry, education, defense, and administration. As his Soviet critics had predicted, this Great Leap Forward into communism proved a catastrophe; 25 to 30 million Chinese died of starvation. Mao for a while retired from the limelight. At the same time the Chinese communists, angered by Soviet arrogance and traditionally suspicious of Russian territorial ambition at China's expense, broke away from Moscow's leadership. The Sino-Soviet rift inflicted a serious blow to the unity of world communism. For the next two decades, until a lessening of hostilities in the 1980s, the two huge countries held each other in mutual distrust. The Chinese dreaded the Soviet troops and their missiles near their country's long boundaries. The Soviet government feared invasion by the Chinese masses.

China's isolation was greatest in 1966, when Mao, with the help of the army, staged the Great Proletarian Cultural Revolution. It was directed at entrenched and autocratic bureaucrats and experts, and at any lingering veneration of the Chinese past or foreign models. The agents of this new revolution were young zealots carrying a little red book called *Quotations from Chairman Mao.*

In these years Chairman Mao was God; never was the cult of personality and revolutionary zeal carried to greater extremes. The revolution closed universities and institutes of scientific research for many years and carried the country to the verge of economic and civic chaos; it unleashed a wave of violence as brutal as Stalin's terror, discrediting in its aftermath the integrity of revolutionary idealism. The only experts spared were the scientists working on nuclear weapons, the most prestigious instruments of national security. Four years later, Mao, having purged potential rivals, returned to a calmer course. Yet he laid down no firm guidelines for governing the country with continuity. At his death in 1976, at the age of eighty-three, it was clear that China was still unstable.

Nonetheless, Mao stands out as one of the greatest political leaders of the twentieth century. He had, at a heroic personal risk and a high price for his people, restored unity and a common purpose to China.

Mao left to his successors a troubled country. Admitting that he had made mistakes, they cautiously reversed his policies, reinstating the victims of the Great Proletarian Cultural Revolution and setting a new course toward the "Four Modernizations"—in science and technology, in industry, in agriculture, and in national defense. Under the leadership of Deng Xiaoping (b. 1904), they allowed a measure of private enterprise and, more important, opened the country to the outside world. Though fearing the subversion of their Chinese ways and communist dedication, they still were eager to attract foreign enterprise from Europe, the United States, Japan, and even Taiwan and Hong Kong, to help them accomplish their goals. "The purpose of socialism," declared Deng, "is to make the country rich and strong." In a short time they have made their country more self-assured and prosperous.

Yet the pressure of a huge and growing population on the country's limited resources remains a baffling problem. China has attempted during the 1980s to curb its population growth, at first by coercive methods that attracted worldwide criticism and achieved only partial success. Official attempts to limit families to one child have been resisted. China's population, now 1.2 billion, is expected to rise to at least 1.5 billion early in the next century.

Transforming the teeming masses of China, characterized early in the century as "a sheet of sand," into a national team as disciplined as their Japanese neighbors remains another unresolved challenge. Deng, having opened his country to Western ways, handed over leadership to younger men in 1987. His successors waver between loosening party controls and reaffirming them, between inviting foreign enterprise and containing disruptive foreign influences. They are forced to cope also with rebellion in fundamentalist Buddhist Tibet.

In contrast with the experiment on the mainland, the Chinese offshore island of Taiwan, where the survivors of the Kuomintang fled, proved a remarkable success under far more favorable circumstances. Firmly ruled by a dictatorial regime under U.S. military protection, working with a small population open to the outside world, and benefiting from heavy American investment, prosperous Taiwan has been held up by Western traditionalists as proof that free enterprise is superior to Marxist collectivism as practiced on mainland China. Smallness combined with easy access to the world market and American help obviously facilitated economic modernization.

India Yet another experiment was started in India which, with its 785 million people, is the most populous nation in the world after China. British political tradition and the diversity of people helped to preserve a pluralist democratic order, protected by a federal constitution. Under the leadership of Jawaharlal Nehru (1889–1964), the country started its independence in 1947 with high hopes and Five-Year plans; industrialization was considered essential for overcoming poverty and unemployment. Still, as Nehru observed, "We are not only industrializing the country through democratic processes, but also, at the same time, trying to maintain the unique features in Indian philosophy and way of life and the individuality of India. Thus we believe we shall serve the Indian people best and perhaps the rest of the world also."[1] India too wanted to be a global model.

Reality took a less promising course. Admittedly, the country's industry and agriculture made remarkable progress, with assistance from Western countries and the Soviet Union; India did

India's Political Heroes: Nehru and Gandhi.
Mohandas Gandhi led India to independence
through his heroic pacifism. As the first prime
minister of independent India, Pandit Nehru made
his nation the most prominent nonaligned Third
World country. He tried to alleviate the poverty
and overcome the traditionalism of the Indian people. (*AP/Wide World Photos*)

manage to feed itself. But modernization created
two Indias existing side by side in stark contrast.
Westernized India is capable even of exporting industrial equipment; it lives in reasonable comfort.
Yet the other India persists—poor, traditional,
caste-ridden, violent, and with little hope for improvement. Ancient customs long suppressed by
the British, like widow-burning or banditry, have
stealthily re-emerged. Tensions run high between
the Westernized and traditional Indias. Nehru's
hope for an organic combination of the best in
Indian tradition with industrial modernism has
not materialized.

The country is burdened also by fear of its
neighbor, Islamic Pakistan, with whom it quarreled over Kashmir, waging a brief, undeclared
war in 1965. The neighbors went to war again in
1971 when East Pakistan became independent
Bangladesh, pouring 10 million refugees into India. India and Pakistan have continued their uneasy relations to the present. India, a nuclear
power since 1974, incites Pakistan to match that
feat, with powerful neighbors taking sides (China
with Pakistan, the Soviet Union with India), while
an American fleet dominates the Indian Ocean.

Two disasters wracked India in 1984. An uprising by Sikh extremists demanding more autonomy was dealt with harshly by the government. A few months later, Prime Minister Indira Gandhi was assassinated by Sikh members of her own security force; her son Rajiv was swiftly sworn in as prime minister. Widespread violence erupted against Sikhs throughout the country. Later in the year, poisonous gas leaking from an insecticide plant in Bhopal killed over two thousand people and injured thousands more in the worst industrial accident in the world to date. All in all, the Indian experiment has not fulfilled Nehru's hope. It has been inconclusive at best and beset by tragedies.

Southeast Asia Further east, meanwhile, the greatest catastrophes in the collision between traditional cultures and the realities of modern life took place in French Indochina, now called Vietnam, Cambodia (Kampuchea), and Laos. Little touched by Western ways until the 1940s, these countries thereafter were plunged into the vortex of world politics. In Vietnam a liberation movement under Ho Chi Minh (1890–1969) ousted the French colonialists in 1954; following the Chinese model, it set up a communist regime in North Vietnam and began fighting to reunite the country.

South Vietnam, meanwhile, had come under American protection and was defended against North Vietnam in a murderous war (see Chapter 36).

The Americans withdrew in 1973 as the communists swept aside the inept South Vietnamese army. Yet a unified communist Vietnam made no progress subsequently in living up to its Marxist promise of peace and well-being; it embarked instead on expansion into strife-torn neighboring Cambodia (Kampuchea).

In the wake of the American withdrawal, Cambodian communists, called the Khmer Rouge, seized power under their leader Pol Pot, an enraged patriot radicalized in Paris and fanatically determined to avenge the brutalities committed in his country by both Vietnamese and Americans. He drove over 2 million people from the capital city of Phnom Penh and tried to establish a new order based on ideologically regimented rural communes. Hundreds of thousands of people died in the evacuation and more died later in the coun-

tryside. In 1979, the blood-stained and starving country, together with Laos, was occupied by Vietnamese troops, visiting further catastrophe on its people.

Meanwhile, Chinese soldiers made an inroad into Vietnam in 1980 as punishment for the Vietnamese occupation of Cambodia and neighboring Laos. Clashes continued along the China-Vietnam border. Chinese residents of Vietnam were forcibly ejected from the country by the Vietnamese government, which put them out to sea without a place to land—a shocking reminder that nationalist passion outweighs communist solidarity and human decency. Vietnam has kept Southeast Asia up to the border of Thailand in a state of near-war ever since. By 1988, however, the utter exhaustion of all combatants improved the prospects for peace.

The Middle East

Islamic Lands Another bloody experiment in modernization took place in Iran. The shah of Iran, Mohammed Riza Pahlavi (1919–1980), pressed a precipitous revolution of Westernization from above. With the help of his country's oil riches, Western investments, and American weapons, the shah attempted to build a modern state and economy, disregarding his country's religious leaders and savagely repressing all resistance. But the forces of tradition, threatened with extinction, struck back. Deeply stirred, Shiite Muslim fundamentalists, basing their creed on the Koran and moving the mass of people to acts of bravery and martyrdom, staged a revolution that drove out the shah in early 1979.

Then began a new experiment, as extreme as that of the shah, under Ayatollah (the highest rank of religious leader) Ruholla Khomeini (b. 1902). An aged, unbending, and puritanical Muslim, he decries all Western influences, trying to make his Iran—half modern and half traditional—conform to the simple teachings of the prophet Muhammad. Yet Khomeini and his supporters cannot escape modernity. They have proclaimed a constitution and held elections. They must collect taxes to run the government and buy weapons to fight secessionist Kurds. They must satisfy the expectations of their people for a better life, give jobs to the unemployed, conduct foreign relations, import food, and sell oil. Although they denounce the materialist immorality of the West and rage against the United States, they must come to terms with the complex Western instruments of power if their revolution is to survive.

In September 1980, President Saddam Hussein of Iraq sent his armies against Khomeini's Iran. The turmoil in Iran may have led him to expect an easy victory, but the Iran-Iraq war has continued inconclusively ever since, claiming over a million casualties. In 1987, it brought the United States fleet into the Persian Gulf to protect the oil shipments of its allies. In 1988, the weary belligerents at last began to prepare for peace.

No experiment in modernization, or in protest against it, has proved conclusive in the Middle East. Experimentation continues in the Arab states near the Persian Gulf where immense oil wealth, suddenly descending on ancient desert kingdoms, calls for equally immense adjustments. Here, too, the Koran is the guide to life. Yet is the spiritual ascendance and the social and political order built under the inspiration of the Koran compatible with oil money? Can the Koran bring peace to the Middle East?

Egypt, having made a tenuous peace with Israel in 1979, tries to be a source of peace, like Saudi Arabia, with little success. Palestinians, craving a homeland, live scattered throughout the area, unwilling to recognize the existence of Israel. And Lebanon, splintered into many warring factions, is caught in apparently endless civil war. Behind the regional tensions looms the conflict between the superpowers, each furnishing military and political support to its local allies. Modernization has come to the Middle East mostly through war.

Israel Both superpowers are involved in the most protracted conflict in the Middle East, the wars between Arabs and the new state of Israel. War started in 1948–49, when, over the bitter opposition of the Palestinians and their Arab allies, the State of Israel was founded in Palestine, which had been a British mandate since 1920. Israel, which brought together Jews from many lands, faced an uncertain future amid relentless terror and counterterror.

In 1956, Egypt under Colonel Gamal Abdel Nasser (1918–1970), who had just started his own experiment in leading Egypt to glory, took over the Suez Canal (hitherto under British control), while warring with Israel. Israel victoriously struck back. Military mobilization for further wars continued, on Israel's side with generous U.S. help, on the Arab side with Soviet support. War broke out again in 1967, leading within six days to a resounding Israeli victory: Israel's warplanes destroyed the airpower of the surrounding Arab states of Egypt, Syria, Iraq, and Jordan in a surprise attack. Drastic Arab defeat, however, did not prevent a further attack by Egypt and Syria on an unprepared Israel in 1973, on Yom Kippur. Both Egypt attacking from the south and Syria from the Golan Heights in the north made impressive gains in the early days of the war until a hurried mobilization by the Israeli army held and repulsed Arab attacks. Israel broke through on the Egyptian front and crossed to the west bank of the Suez Canal. In the north the Syrian lines were pushed back, although the war with Syria dragged on into 1974.

Neighboring Lebanon, which was being torn apart by civil war, was invaded by Israel in 1982. Israel was determined to drive the displaced Palestinians, organized as a political and military force by the Palestine Liberation Organization (PLO), from that country. The PLO had built up a network of strongholds in Lebanon, subjecting northern Israel to shelling and terrorist infiltration. Meanwhile, the Lebanese conflict had attracted U.S. military intervention as part of a multinational peace-keeping force. Marines landed in Beirut in 1983 but were swiftly withdrawn after a suicide truck bomb destroyed the marine headquarters, leaving 239 dead. The attack was thought to be the work of a fundamentalist Shiite Moslem group with ties to Iran. Despite the Israeli invasion and Lebanon's internal disintegration, Palestinian patriots continued to raid Israel, unrestrained by the presence of a UN peace-keeping force. Humiliating Arab defeats drove embittered Palestinians to increasing acts of terror against Israel and its allies, exporting

Map 37.2 The Middle East. (Other OPEC members include the African nations of Algeria, Gabon, Libya, and Nigeria; Ecuador and Venezuela in South America; and Indonesia.) ▶

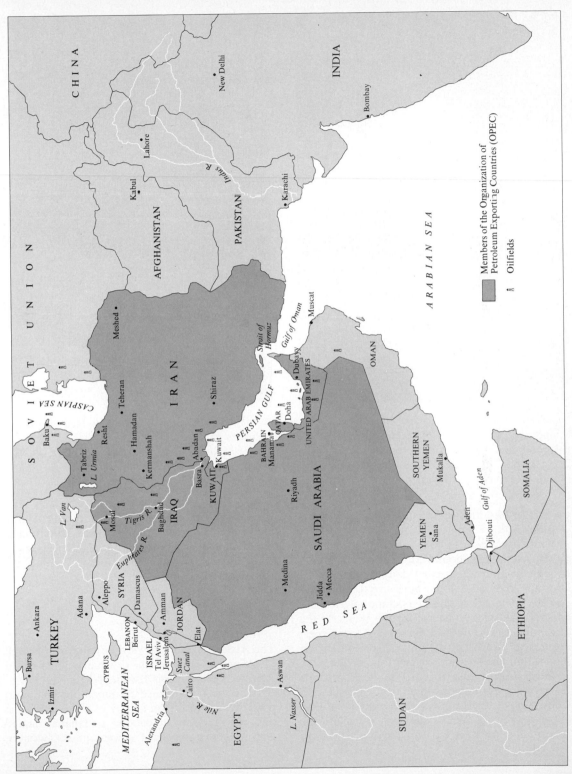

 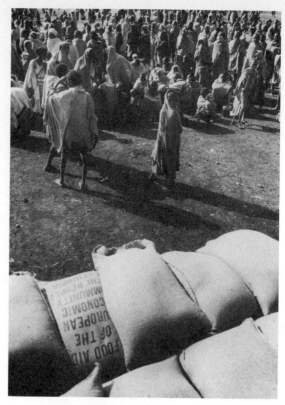

Supermarket in Oman (left) and Food Relief in Ethiopia. Western nations, benefiting from their agricultural efficiency, try to help raise standards of living around the world. They export their products to relatively prosperous countries like Oman on the Persian Gulf. They also help feed people in countries haunted by famine like Ethiopia. (*Left photo: © Rene Burri/Magnum Photos, Inc. Right photo: © Sebastiao Salgado/Magnum Photos, Inc.*)

the fury of Middle Eastern politics into other parts of the world.

Israel has great assets. It can count on the loyalty of its citizens, bound together by a common religion and life threatened daily by war. Israel also has free access to American capital and power; in its desire for democratic government and civil liberties, it is part of the West. At the same time, Israel is a hazardous, long-range experiment. Can it prevent the bitter disputes between secular and ultra-orthodox Jews from dividing the country? Can it fuse together its heterogeneous Jewish peoples, many of them from non-Western lands? Above all, can it evolve a constructive relationship with its Arab neighbors, especially the Palestinians, many of whom were displaced from their homeland? Bitterness has escalated into bloodshed between Israelis and Palestinians, threatening to spill over into neighboring states and causing division and dismay among the American friends of Israel.

Africa

The African experience of decolonization is well illustrated by the example of Ghana. The hero of African liberation was Kwame Nkrumah (1909–1972), who transformed the small but comparatively advanced British colony of the Gold Coast into the independent country of Ghana, named after a fabled medieval empire in the western

Sahel region of central Africa. From Ghana, Nkrumah hoped to advance the ideal of a powerful united Africa. He symbolized the promise of liberated Africa, preaching Pan-Africanism.

Democratic at the outset, Nkrumah's regime soon turned into a personal dictatorship; his one-party state became an instrument for the personal enrichment of his lieutenants, despite its increasingly socialist ideology. Nkrumah took Ghana out of the British Commonwealth, spent the financial reserves left from British rule on hasty and overambitious ventures of economic development, and antagonized the leaders of other newly independent African states. He soon lost the confidence of even his own people. Exiled in 1966 by a military coup, he died a spokesman for a Soviet-oriented scientific socialism that allowed little room for the glorification of African tradition. His successors—military, civilian, and military again—have failed to restore the promise or even the prosperity with which Ghanaian independence began.

The tribulations of Ghana were shared by most of the other newly created African states. Starting with democratic constitutions, they changed into one-party states, military dictatorships, or personal regimes. Some of them were benevolent, like those of Jomo Kenyatta of Kenya or Julius Nyerere of Tanzania. All had to try desperately to hold their multiethnic states together, while also paying lip service to African unity. Throughout sub-Saharan Africa, loyalty still centers on family, lineage, and ethnic groups. Only the most uprooted, foreign-educated Africans put their country first.

Unity often was preserved by compulsion and repression, sometimes degenerating into genocidal violence. In a few lands, time-honored African forms of government were perverted by the demands of statehood into unbridled personal rule, rendered murderous by imported Western techniques, as in the case of Idi Amin Dada of Uganda. Some lands, like the formerly French colonies of Senegal and the Ivory Coast, remained closely associated with their ex-masters; there economic conditions improved and governments remained stable. Among the former English colonies, Nigeria was rent by a destructive civil war and barely prevented secession of a large section of the country. By 1979, the most powerful of the sub-Saharan states, its economy buoyed by large exports of oil, Nigeria changed from a military to a civilian regime, beginning a short-lived experiment of democratic rule. Immediately after the first election in early 1984, the army again took over under conditions of serious economic distress precipitated by the sudden decline in oil exports. It promised return to civilian rule in 1992.

As for economic conditions, the testimony (in 1988) of the executive secretary of the United Nations Economic Commission for Africa, a Nigerian, speaks for itself.

> The drought and famine which almost completely ravaged and battered the continent only a few years ago is back again in force. . . . There can be no doubt that, more than ever before, Africa is facing one of its most intractable development dilemmas! The economic and social crisis which has engulfed our continent for so long has become severely aggravated. . . . Indeed, the situation seems to have gone from bad to worse for many of our economies, with one economic crisis succeeding the other.[2]

How are Africans going to help themselves when the markets for African goods and the sources of capital, knowledge, and technology continue to lie in the developed industrial countries?

There are other severe problems: high birthrates (highest in Kenya) and adverse climate. In 1984–85, sub-Saharan Africa suffered a prolonged drought in which over a million people died. Trapped in their poverty, decimated by disease (including AIDS), and deeply in debt to the leading industrial countries, most African states face a grim future.

At the southern tip of the continent, in the Republic of South Africa, the Africans' desire for self-determination is thwarted by a small minority of European settlers, who date their hold on the country back to the seventeenth century (see Chapter 27). Clinging to their cultural heritage, the Afrikaners (as they call themselves) also want to continue their advanced industrial economy, which benefits their nonwhite subjects and their African neighbors as well. They bitterly, and often brutally, resist all pressure to end their policy, called *apartheid,* of favoring whites and oppressing the black population. There looms endless conflict, agitating the African continent, the superpowers, and world opinion. How, under the circumstances, is it possible to give reality to the promise of equality and freedom written into the Universal Declaration of Human Rights?

Latin America

Africa's problems are familiar to the countries of Latin America. After their independence in the early nineteenth century, they have failed to duplicate the progress of North America or Europe. These Latin American nations have been beset by many ills: poverty, rapid population increase, unemployment (or underemployment), malnutrition, ethnic diversity, political instability, and a deep sense of frustration. In the 1980s, after the worldwide economic upswing of the 1960s and 1970s, their fortunes sagged. In 1987, Latin America's foreign debt, a telling index of its economic crisis, exceeded $400 billion. Declining standards of living put a heavy burden on the new democratic regimes that replaced the military juntas previously in power.

In Argentina, the brutal rule of the generals, which began in 1976, collapsed in 1983 after their humiliation by Britain in the contest over the Falkland Islands (see Chapter 36), but the military continues to threaten the civilian government of President Raúl Alfonsín. In neighboring Chile, by contrast, military rule, instituted in 1973 with help from Washington, still reigns under General Augusto Pinochet, whose rule proceeds under a constitution sanctioning his election (and reelection) by plebiscite. In Brazil, the largest South American country, industrialization has advanced rapidly, following the example of Asian countries like South Korea, but its large, heterogeneous population (140 million) is not easily governed. In 1985, after 21 years of military rule, Brazil adopted a democratic constitution, although governmental inefficiency and corruption persist. Further north, Venezuela has enjoyed the most stable democratic government in Latin America, benefiting from its rich oil deposits, although suffering from the sharp decline in oil prices after 1979. Neighboring Colombia, meanwhile, struggles with drug producers and their agents, who ter-

rorize both government and society. In Latin America, drug exports have proved to be the only reliable source of foreign exchange for countries with a chronic imbalance of trade and heavy foreign indebtedness, mostly to U.S. banks.

The Latin American country most significant to the United States is Mexico, its southern neighbor. A federal republic under its constitution of 1917, it has been ruled in recent years by the Institutional Revolutionary party (PRI), which follows a middle course between conservatives and Marxists, the latter eager to mobilize (without apparent success) the discontent of the poor. The election of 1988, however, has revived party pluralism. Political stability has been ensured, in part, by U.S. and foreign investments, but these also contribute to the country's heavy foreign debt, which reduces indigenous economic initiative. Even more alarming is the high birthrate among the 90 million Mexicans; it outpaces any foreseeable capacity for feeding and gainfully employing the spiraling multitudes. The traditional safety valve of illegal migration to the U.S. labor market is not likely to operate indefinitely.

The small Central American countries south of Mexico, lacking (except for Costa Rica) the preconditions for democratic government, are a battleground between Marxist revolutionaries siding with the poor and conservative dictatorships allied to the rich as well as to the United States. The Marxists look toward Cuba, where Fidel Castro follows the Soviet pattern of modernization while also extending his influence among anti-Western regimes, especially in Africa. Yet his experiment fares no better than its Soviet model.

More than developing countries elsewhere, Latin America—and especially Central America—manages its affairs under the shadow of the United States. Washington protects the interests of American firms operating in the area, and, above all, tries to keep Soviet influence out of this politically volatile part of the world. For both these reasons, all U.S. presidents since World War II have dispatched armed forces to squash, in President Johnson's words, "the specter of communism." In the 1980s, President Reagan supported the training and arming of the contra forces in his effort to overthrow the socialist Sandinista government in Nicaragua. In 1983, he ordered the invasion of the tiny island-state of Grenada to save it from a purported Cuban takeover.

The assumption by the United States government that left-wing governments will inevitably ally themselves with the Soviet Union has become a self-fulfilling prophecy because of U.S. military intervention. Both Fidel Castro in Cuba and President Daniel Ortega in Nicaragua received long-term Soviet aid and military assistance, thus extending Soviet influence into the Western Hemisphere—a result that U.S. policy had been expressly designed to avert. Cold war politics continue to be played out in small, poor Third-World countries.

Development: Which Way?

As the foregoing cases show, the experiments of Westernization and modernization, of adjustment to an interdependent, competitive world, have exacted an excruciating human toll from societies culturally unprepared for drastic changes. Unwilling and unable to break with their cultural heritage yet eager to reap the benefits of modernity, people still wonder: which way should they go, the Western, or "capitalist," way, or the socialist way?

As the case histories show, Western democracy has little or no chance. Sooner or later the disunity resulting from rapid change amid incompatible Western and non-Western ways produces authoritarian governments. But regimes that recognize free enterprise allow their subjects considerable leeway for their own experiments in adjustment; amid appalling inequality and corruption, some people do learn to sharpen their wits to cope with innovation. Under socialist systems, in contrast, people are compelled to conform to the official experiment, also amid appalling inequality and corruption. Neither the democratic nor the socialist model has helped to advance equality, peace, or human rights in the world.

Nor have the efforts of the United Nations brought about the desired results. The General Assembly, dominated by developing countries, has passed resolutions and issued an elaborate blueprint for a New International Economic Order. But the dialogue between the advanced and the developing countries has made no headway. The rich tell the poor to help themselves by changing their ways; the poor protest that without help from the rich they do not have even the tools for learning how to change. Meanwhile the elite among the poor countries splurge scarce money on luxuries in order to imitate the splendor of the global leaders. The hard fact is that cultural adjustment to the competition of global coexistence is a challenge still beyond the comprehension of the bulk of humanity.

The basic question is this: Can the socially responsible self-discipline built into Western civilization—and indispensable for all large-scale human organization—be transferred to people in other cultures lacking this tradition? Can that social responsiveness be expanded everywhere to make the peaceful management of global interdependence possible?

Concluding Reflections: Optimism or Pessimism?

The world is inhabited by over 5 billion human beings; the figure is expected to be around 6 billion by the year 2000, and higher thereafter. Helping to sustain them are a vast array of originally Western achievements: the nation-state, industrialism, science and technology, and world-spanning organizations for business and international cooperation. Some non-Western peoples are now matching Western accomplishments; keeping up with the latest innovations has become an ardent desire—or even an outright necessity—among all people, no matter how attached to their past they feel. Survival depends on mastery of the skills of modernity—originally Western skills—in economic productivity, in scientific and technological progress, and in the development of the most advanced weapons; these capabilities are the keys that command power and prestige in the world. Thus, through Westernization and economic interdependence, the new globalism has become an irresistible worldwide reality; it has ominously accelerated the pace of change. Has the transformation been for the better or worse?

Cause for Optimism

Westerners naturally dwell on the positive aspects. Global interdependence, they argue, has vastly increased worldwide cooperation. For the first time in all human experience, people from the entire world have a chance to work together for the common good. Look at the impressive results. The volume of world trade has tripled, providing new material security for human life—and resulting in a rapid increase in the world's population. People hitherto isolated have been brought into worldwide circulation, with new opportunities for personal development; they have become mobile in their search to improve their lot.

Global interdependence, furthermore, has stimulated minds over the entire world, recruiting talent from many countries. The advances in all fields of learning have been astounding. Science and technology, more closely linked than ever, have increased human control over nature beyond the wildest dreams of earlier ages. Physicists have explored the atom down to the smallest components of matter; biologists have laid bare the genetic structures of animate matter. At the opposite end of the scale, human beings have set foot on the moon. Rockets with sophisticated equipment have been sent deep into the solar system. Advances in electronics have brought the whole world to remote villages in Asia and Africa through radio and television. Computers, indispensable to scientists and engineers, have invaded everyday life in finance and business, even in ordinary households.

In the arts and literature the interaction of cultural influences from all parts of the world has been a creative stimulus. Even more significantly, concern for human dignity has spread. However spurned in practice, the United Nations Universal Declaration of Human Rights sets a worldwide standard as a guide for the future. Agencies like Amnesty International keep track of human rights violations; others send relief in case of famine, epidemic, or natural catastrophe. These developments have created a mood of optimism for some people, who perceive a chance for enlightened control of human destiny over the entire world. Postwar prosperity encouraged an international effort at cooperation to bring natural resources and world population into a steady equilibrium, to provide greater equality around the world, and to avoid devastating world wars. That mood is still alive in some quarters.

Cause for Concern

At the same time, however, there is a contrary mood of pessimism. Despite all the progress, the bulk of humanity is still miserable; more people means more poverty. Inadequate supplies of food, clean water, and medical help diminish the opportunities of about half the world's population. Underfed, diseased, and untrained people perpetuate or even increase the already widespread poverty. Also, the postwar rise in living standards experienced by some peoples is receding in many countries.

The richest and the poorest in the world now live virtually side by side, thanks to modern means of communication. It is no wonder that the anger of the poor is rising. Since World War II, all well-meant efforts to bridge the gap between rich and poor have failed; in fact the gap has widened. And more, the good life among the well-to-do in the metropolitan centers of the world constantly raises the expectations of the poor. Yet the resources of their own societies cannot possibly meet those expectations. The poor can hardly improve themselves when they have no money for even the most basic necessities. Meanwhile, global military expenditures exceed the combined gross national product of China, India, and sub-Saharan Africa. Third-World military outlays grow even faster, as a percentage of their GNP, than those of the developed countries. More money is spent on trading weapons on the international market than on trading grains.

Added to this dismal picture is the rising scarcity of the basic resources—arable land, water, clean air, and fuel—needed to support ever-larger populations. The new globalism has raised, for the first time in human existence, alarm over the limited physical resources of Planet Earth. Anxiety also has risen over the migration of the poor from villages to the ever-expanding cities, and from

Map 37.3 World Population Densities ▶

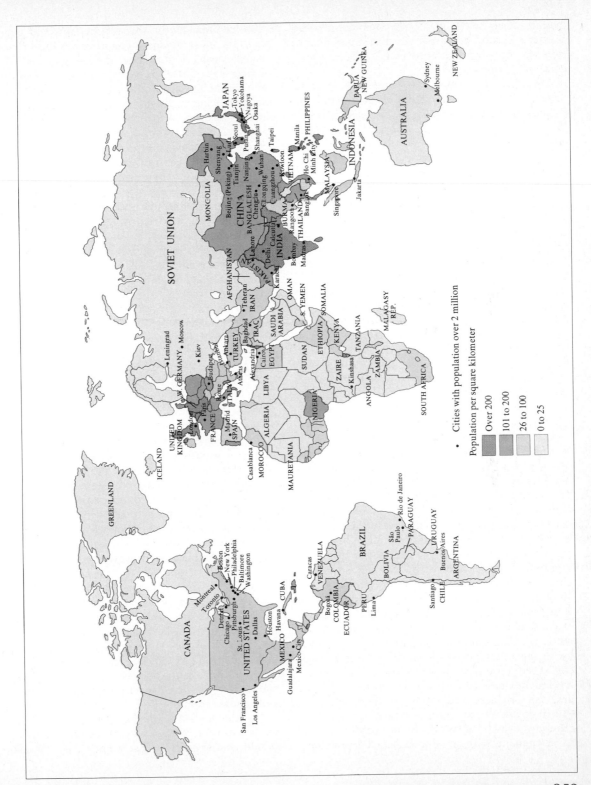

Cities with population over 2 million

• Population per square kilometer

Over 200
101 to 200
26 to 100
0 to 25

overcrowded lands to richer opportunities in Western Europe or North America. Such migration has already heightened racial, religious, and cultural tensions.

Disabled by poverty, non-Western lands also have to struggle with cultural disorientation. In most non-Western parts of the world, traditional cultures have been subverted by Western influence. A generally Western-educated elite follows a Western lifestyle—sometimes with irresponsible extravagance—while still tied to native tradition. The bulk of the population is caught between tradition and Western ways, far closer to the parochial past than to the global present. The old ways, with their moral obligations justified by tradition and religion, are discredited by the influx of modernity from the West which, however, teaches no effective alternative morality. The moral vacuum encourages corruption, violence, and, all too often, utter inhumanity. Under these conditions, stable governments have little chance to emerge, and without stable governments, effective self-help seems impossible. The historical record of the past thirty years shows a rising level of violence within the new states created after World War II and in the rest of the world as well. The faster the population increases, it seems, the greater the human toll of anger and violence. The brutal communist and fascist regimes before World War II have their imitators in many parts of today's world. Terrorism born of desperation and fanaticism is rising around the world; the suppression of terrorism requires further violence.

In other ways, too, the countries of the West themselves are no longer immune to the troubles they have created around the world. They are caught in headlong change. They suffer from the economic competition of newly industrialized countries, Japan foremost. The prosperity of the West rests on shaky foundations. The developing countries are deeply in debt to the leading industrial countries. Yet the latter are unable to coordinate their own national economies. In the 1980s, for instance, the people of the United States have consumed more than they produced. Their growing indebtedness to their closest partners and allies, the Japanese and the West Germans, is a source of additional strain and threatens a world economy, which the World Bank in 1987 judged to be stagnant, with an unprecedented depression.

More importantly, the self-confidence of people in the most advanced countries has been challenged, raising doubts about the universal benefits of their way of life. The widespread preoccupation with technology, for instance, has not refined human sensibilities; the improvement of human relations has not kept pace with technological innovation. As a result, the quality of life has suffered. The former sense of common purpose, moreover, has been undermined also by the free influx of foreign ways, which threatens the cultural security of Western countries, as does military belligerence around the world.

Pushed to the defensive, Western countries have become alarmed about their security. Together with their Soviet adversary, they have created weapons that can wipe out the human race altogether. Given the rising tide of hostility around the world, is it possible to prevent these weapons from being used? Will the nuclear holocaust, which will kill non-Westerners as well, be the culmination of Western civilization?

Coping with the Future

Optimists and pessimists, as well as pro-Western and anti-Western voices, clash furiously in the contemporary world. In the growing confusion, powerful groups of fundamentalists want to go back to the preglobal past, to the old creeds, and not only in the West. Many Western-trained intellectuals in non-Western countries cultivate ancient traditions. Others want to reorder the world according to universal prescriptions such as socialism or communism, which hold the past in contempt. Americans advertise their own experience as a prescription for global peace and happiness. Meanwhile, many people, confused by the diverse views and data that impinge upon them, tend to shrink into themselves, concentrating on the work before them and seeking their own pleasures. They thereby aggravate the fragmentation and promote violence in a world that can serve its inhabitants only by raising their sights and improving their capacity for peaceful worldwide cooperation.

Looking back over the long evolution of Western civilization to its present culmination, we should take to heart, in case we grow too complacent about the accomplishments of Western civilization, the warning of the English statesman Walter Bagehot. He pointed out that the decline of the Roman and English nations lay in their failure to understand the institutions that they had created. Can the present generation of Western peoples, above all Americans, understand our greatest institution—the newly created global community—and shape its development according to the moral and intellectual qualities that have given the West its pre-eminence?

That is where the future begins.

Notes

1. Jawaharlal Nehru, "Foreword" to Jean Filliozat, *India, the Country and Its Traditions* (Englewood Cliffs, N.J.: Prentice-Hall, 1962), p. 1.

2. "Extracts from the Speech by Adebayo Adedeji at the Opening of the ECA Council of Ministers in Niamey," *West Africa*, May 2, 1988, p. 789.

Suggested Reading

Achebe, Chinua, *Man of the People* (1966). A great Nigerian novelist describes the ways of Nigerian politics after independence.

———, *No Longer at Ease* (1960). A novel describing the trials of a Nigerian returning home after being educated in England.

Barnet, Richard J., *The Lean Years: Politics in the Age of Scarcity* (1980). A useful survey of the relationship between population and world resources, with an eye to the politics involved.

Butterfield, Fox, *China: Alive in the Bitter Sea* (1982). An illuminating account of life in China by a *New York Times* correspondent.

LaFeber, Walter, *Inevitable Revolutions: The United States in Central America* (1983). The collision of U.S. national security and commercial interests with revolutionary aspirations and reform.

Liang Heng and Judith Shapiro, *Son of the Revolution* (1983). A personal account of life in Mao's China during the Cultural Revolution.

Mansfield, Peter, ed., *The Arabs* (1985). A basic guide to the Arab world.

Naipaul, V. S., *A Bend in the River* (1977). Insights into culture conflict in central Africa.

———, *India: A Wounded Civilization* (1978). An account of India in the clash of cultures by one of the world's foremost contemporary writers, himself the product of several cultures.

Nkrumah, Kwame, *Ghana: The Autobiography of Kwame Nkrumah* (1957). An excellent insight into the man who took the lead in bringing independence to Africa.

North-South: A Program for Survival. The Report of the Independent Commission on International Development Issues under the Chairmanship of Willy Brandt (1980). A significant document on the needs for peace, justice, and jobs in the Third World.

Oz, Amos, *In the Land of Israel* (1983). An invaluable background book on the people and politics of Israel.

Sick, Gary, *All Fall Down: America's Tragic Encounter with Iran* (1985). An insider's account of the fall of the shah and the subsequent hostage crisis.

Vogel, Ezra, *Japan Number One* (1980). A challenging view of Japan's rapid advance.

Review Questions

1. How does the present world order differ from the world in which Western civilization originated and evolved?

2. How do the conditions of the developed countries differ from those in the developing countries?

3. Outline the effects of decolonization. What benefits were expected, and what were the actual consequences?

4. In what respect does the modern development of

Japan differ from that of China, India, or the African countries?

5. What were the conditions and the problems facing Mao Zedong in his effort to modernize China? In what respects did he succeed? In what respects did he fail?

6. What would you say were the chief developments in the Indian subcontinent after World War II? What is the current news from that part of the world?

7. Which area of the world do you consider the most troublesome and dangerous from the point of view of U.S. national security?

8. Do you consider yourself an optimist or a pessimist? What do you see as the major problems confronting your generation?

Index

French Revolution, 422(map); chronology of, 438; agriculture and, 464
Freud, Sigmund, 637–639, 746
"Friendly societies," 475
Fromm, Erich, 754–755
Fronde, 350

Gaelic League, 582
Galen, 380
Galilei, Galileo, 304, 378–379, 384
Gallipoli campaign, 678
Gama, Vasco da, 314
Gandhi, Indira, 851
Gandhi, Mohandas K., 608, 612, 706, 850(illus.)
Gandhi, Rajiv, 851
Gargantua and Pantagruel (Rabelais), 278
Garibaldi, Giuseppe, 550–551
Gaskell, Elizabeth, 529
Gaugin, Paul, 642
General Assembly, of United nations, 826
Geneva, Reformation in, 296–297
Gentile, Giovanni, 722
German Confederation, 554
German Democratic party, 726
German Democratic Republic, 818–819
German Labor Front, 733
German People's party, 726n
German Workers' Association, 588
German Workers' Party, *see* Nazi party
Germany: spread of Renaissance to, 275–276; Lutheran revolt in, 288–294; failure to unify, 360–362; Reformation in, 360–362; war of liberation against Napoleon, 453–454; nationalism in, 497; Revolution of 1848, 515–516, 518; unification of, 552(map), 552–557; unification of, chronology of, 557; nationality problems in, 558–560; Volkish thought and, 561–563; anti-Semitism in, 563–567; Bismarckian constitution for, 588; *Kulturkampf* in, 588; socialism in, 588–589; industrialization of, 588–591; on eve of World War I, 589–591; imperialism of, 603–604; unification of, 659; alliance system of, 659–660; Bismarck's goals and, 660; Triple Entente and, 660, 662–663; ethnic groups in, before World War I, 661(map); Austria encouraged by, 666–667; start of World War

I and, 672–674, 676; last World War I offensive of, 679–680; Treaty of Versailles and, 683–684; Weimar Republic of, 724–726; Nazi, 732–738; aftermath of World War I, 765–766; antecedents of World War II and, 766–774; Treaty of Versailles and, 767; in World War II, 769(map), 774–777; annexation of Sudetenland, 771–773; invasion of Poland, 773–774; in Battle of Britain, 776; invasion of Russia, 776–777; under Nazi rule, 777–782; resistance in, 782; Federal Republic of, 802–803, German Democratic Republic, 818–819; division of, 828
Germany and the Next War (von Bernhardi), 533
Geyl, Pieter, 456
Ghana, 854–855; independence of, 844
Ghettos, 780
Gide, André, 747
Gioconda, La, see Mona Lisa
Giorgione, 275
Giotto, 263(illus.), 272
Girondins, 431, 432, 434
Giscard D'Estaing, Valéry, 801
Gladstone, William E., 579, 580, 581, 622–623
Glanvill, Joseph, 333
Glasnost, 813
Global interdependence, 858
Glorious Revolution, *see* English Revolution
Gnosis, 377
Goebbels, Joseph, 728, 735
Goering, Hermann, 776
Goethe, Johann, 483
Gogh, Vincent van, 642
Gold, in Mexico, 314, 315
Gömbös, Gyula, 739
Gombrich, E. H., 275
"Good neighbor" policy, 627
Gorbachev, Mikhail, 712, 812–815, 814(illus.), 819, 821, 839
Gordon, Charles "Chinese," 622–623
Gothic architecture, *see* Art Essay: Medieval and Renaissance Art (Contents)
Government, provisional, following Russian Revolution of 1917, 695–696
Goya, Francisco, 483(illus.)
Granada, 340, 341
Grand Duchy of Warsaw, 448, 450, 454
Grande Armée de la Russie, 455

Grand Empire, 448, 450–451
Grand Lodge, 391
Grand National Consolidated Trade Union, 475
Grapes of Wrath, The (Steinbeck), 749, 751
Gravitation, universal, 380
Great Britain, *see* Britain
Great Depression: in Japan, 616; in Latin America, 627; Weimar Republic and, 725; in Austria, 739; in Britain, 740; in United States, 740
Great Fear, 427–428
Great Rebellion, 610
Great Schism, 285
Great Trek, 620
Greece, revolution in, 506
Green, Thomas Hill, 542
Green party (Germany), 799, 803
Grey, Edward, 669
Gropper, William, 751
Grosz, George, 751
Guernica (Picasso), 751
Guilds, 473
Guise, House of, 297, 343, 348
Guizot, François, 511, 512
Gulag Archipelago, The (Solzhenitsyn), 712
"Gunboat diplomacy," 627
Guomindong (Kuomintang) party, 614, 848, 849
Gustavus Adolphus, king of Sweden, 362
Gutenberg, Johann, 276
Guzmán, Gaspar de, count of Olivares, 344–345

Habeas corpus, 355
Haggard, H. Rider, 606
Hale, Matthew, 333
Halley, Edmund, 379–380
Hals, Frans, 360
Hamlet (Shakespeare), 279
Hapsburg Empire: in New World, 343; Austrian, 361–362; peoples of, 504(map), 518; nationality problems in, 558–560
Hardenberg, Karl von, 502
Hardie, Kier, 580
Hard Times (Dickens), 529
Hargreaves, James, 465
Hart, Basil Liddell, 776
Harvey, William, 381
Heath, Edward, 804–805
Hegemony, 369
Heidegger, Martin, 755, 756–757
Heimwehr, 739
Heisenberg, Werner, 648–649
Helmholtz, Hermann von, 531
Helsinki Agreements, 797, 837